SECOND EDITION

Marriages and Families

Changes, Choices, and Constraints

Nijole V. Benokraitis
University of Baltimore

PRENTICE HALL, Upper Saddle River, New Jersey 07458

This book is dedicated to my husband, Vitalius;
to our children, Andrius and Gema;
to my mother, Ona Radavicius Vaicaitis;
and to my brothers, Casimir and John Vaicaitis

Library of Congress Cataloging-in-Publication Data

Benokraitis, Nijole V. (Nijole Vaicaitis)
    Marriages and families : changes, choices, and constraints /
Nijole V. Benokraitis.—2nd ed.
      p.   cm.
    Includes bibliographical references and index.
    ISBN 0-13-199548-0
    1. Family—United States. 2. Marriage—United States. I. Title
HQ536.B45 1996
306.8'0973—dc20
                                      95–639
                                        CIP

Acquisitions editor: Nancy Roberts
Development editor: Virginia Otis Locke
Editorial/production editor: Serena Hoffman
Interior design: Jeannette Jacobs
Design supervisor: Anne Bonanno Nieglos
Buyer: Mary Ann Gloriande
Editorial assistant: Pat Naturale
Copy editor: Mary Louise Byrd
Illustrations: Moore Electronic Design
Photo researchers: Joelle Burrows, Barbara Salz
Photo supervision: Lorinda Morris-Nantz
Cover art: Legacy by Synthia Saint James. Oil on canvas. Collection of the artist. *Legacy* expresses the unity of the family and of all peoples of the world and the importance, to all cultures, of learning.

© 1996, 1993 by Prentice-Hall, Inc.
Simon & Schuster/A Viacom Company
Upper Saddle River, New Jersey 07458

Printed in the United States of America
10 9 8 7 6 5 4 3 2 1

ISBN: 0-13-199548-0

Prentice-Hall International (UK) Limited, *London*
Prentice-Hall of Australia Pty. Limited, *Sydney*
Prentice-Hall Canada Inc., *Toronto*
Prentice-Hall Hispanoamericana, S.A., *Mexico*
Prentice-Hall of India Private Limited, *New Delhi*
Prentice-Hall of Japan, Inc., Tokyo
Simon & Schuster Asia Pte. Ltd., *Singapore*
Editora Prentice-Hall do Brasil, Ltda., *Rio de Janeiro*

BRIEF CONTENTS

CONTENTS

iv

BOXED FEATURES

CRITICAL ISSUES

ASK YOURSELF

PREFACE

Polls and surveys show that Americans still believe in marriage and the family, and the issue of family values stimulates vigorous debate, from the campus to Congress. As the second edition of this book goes to press, however, our society faces some very serious family-related issues. Some, like the continuation of such programs as Aid to Families with Dependent Children (AFDC), have become politicized. Others, such as the increase in domestic violence, have been highlighted by media attention. Still others, ignored by the media, raise troubling concerns: for example, the rising number of children born out of wedlock, especially to mothers who are poor and teenage mothers, the inability of many working families to rise above the poverty level, and the obstacles that divorced, remarried, and stepfamilies face.

Marriages and Families: Changes, Choices, and Constraints offers students a comprehensive introduction to these and other issues surrounding marriage and the family today. Although written from a sociological perspective, the book incorporates material from such other disciplines as history, economics, social work, psychology, law, and anthropology. Moreover, the research that supports this new edition—most of it from the 1990s—encompasses both quantitative and qualitative studies. Nationally representative and longitudinal data are supplemented with insights from clinical, case, and observational studies.

MAJOR THEMES AND ISSUES

Marriages and Families continues to be distinguished from other textbooks in several important ways. It offers comprehensive coverage of the field, allowing instructors to choose from a wide array of chapters that best suit their particular needs. It balances theoretical and empirical discussions with practical examples and guidelines. It highlights important contemporary changes in society and the family. It explores the choices that are available to family members, as well as the constraints that many of us do not recognize. It examines the diversity of American families today, using cross-cultural and multicultural comparisons to encourage creative thinking about the many critical issues that confront the family of the twenty-first century.

Changes in the Contemporary Family

Changes that are affecting the structure and functioning of today's family inform the pages of every chapter of this book. In addition, several chapters focus on some major transformations in American society. Chapter 13 examines the growing cultural diversity of the United States, focusing on African American, Native American, Latino, and Asian American marriages and families. Chapters 6 and 7 look at Americans' changing attitudes toward sexuality and sexual behavior as evidenced, for example, in the results published in the 1994 survey by the University of Chicago's National Opinion Research Center. Chapter 18 discusses the ways in which the rapid "graying of America" has affected the lifestyles of grandparents, family members' roles as caregivers, and family relations in general. And Chapter 19 analyzes some of the changes in social policies that affect the family and speculates on the future of American marriages and families.

A Wider Array of Choices

On the individual level, family members have many more choices today than ever before. People feel freer to postpone marriage, to cohabit, or to raise children as single parents. As a result, household forms vary greatly, ranging from commuter marriages to those in which several generations live together under the same roof.

More and Often Tougher Constraints

Although family members' choices are more varied today, people also face greater macro-level constraints. Their options are increasingly limited by the policies of formal organizations like the government. They are influenced by demographic changes, such as the rising number of recent immigrants and an increasingly diverse racial-ethnic population. And they are affected by medical, political, economic, religious, and military institutions. It is because modern families will continue to encounter dramatic changes that I have framed many discussions of individual choice within the larger picture of institutional changes and constraints.

Cross-Cultural and Multicultural Diversity

Because contemporary American marriages and families vary greatly in terms of structure, dynamics, and cultural heritage, discussions of gender roles, class, race, ethnicity, and sexual orientation are integrated throughout this book. To further strengthen students' understanding of the growing diversity among today's families, I have also included a series of boxes that focus on families from many cultures. Both text and boxed materials are intended to broaden students' cultural knowledge and to encourage them to think about the many forms families may take and the ways in which family members may interact.

NEW FEATURES IN THIS EDITION

The first change many readers may notice is the new four-color format of this textbook. This change has not only enhanced the attractiveness of the overall design but has given more life and visual appeal to illustrations and photographs.

At least 70 percent of *Marriages and Families* has been revised to incorporate new research, recent surveys, and current examples and illustrations from the media. And largely in response to students' comments, I've created several entirely new features: the *Data Digest* that begins each chapter, the author's files quotations, and the Taking Action sections at the end of each chapter.

Data Digest

Complaints by students (both mine and others') that they are sometimes overwhelmed by "all those numbers" made me think about how to make Census Bureau data, the findings of empir-

ical studies, and demographic trends more interesting and digestible. The *Data Digest* that introduces each chapter not only provides students with a thought-provoking overview of current statistics and trends but makes this material more accessible.

Material from the Author's Files

Many instructors who reviewed the first edition of *Marriages and Families*, and many students as well, liked the anecdotes and personal experiences with which I illustrated sometimes "dry" theories and abstract concepts. In this new edition I weave more of this sort of material into the text. Thus, many examples from discussions in my own classes are included (cited as "from author's files") to help bring theoretical perspectives and concepts to life.

Taking Action

A common question from my own students has been, "Can't we *do* something about [issue X]?" And sometimes students have asked me for practical information: for example, "How can I find a good child care center?" or "Can anyone help my sister get out of an abusive marriage?" In response to these needs, I've created a new end-of-chapter section called *Taking Action*. It tells students how to get information (usually free) on particular topics; how to get personal assistance—such as counseling or therapy—for themselves or others; how to contact organizations that deal with specific problems; and how to find campus speakers who can address many of the issues discussed in the book.

In most of my courses I require students to undertake applied projects, such as becoming politically involved on a family-related issue or volunteering research services to nonprofit family agencies. Thus the *Taking Action* sections also suggest ideas for course projects that my students have enjoyed working on, either individually and collectively.

Finally, because electronic mail subscriptions for contemporary discussion lists are becoming so widely available at reasonable or no cost to students, I've also included E-mail addresses for new and established lists that discuss the workplace, family research, aging, sex, gender, sexual orientation, and many other family-related topics.

PEDAGOGICAL FEATURES

The pedagogical features in *Marriages and Families* have been designed specifically to capture students' attention and to facilitate their understanding and recall of the material. Some of these features are familiar from the first edition, but many are new. Each has been carefully crafted to ensure that it ties in clearly to the text material, enhancing its meaning and applicability.

Original and Lively Illustration Program

A picture, they say, is worth a thousand words. So are a good diagram, an eye-catching figure, and an appealing graphic. Every chapter of this book contains entirely new figures that, in bold and original artistic designs, present such concepts as the exchange theory of dating, romantic versus lasting love, and theories of mating and that present simple statistics in innovative and visually appealing ways.

More than half the photographs are new. Again we have taken great care to select informative photographs that illustrate the text. A number of boxes now contain photographs, and scattered throughout the book are large silhouetted photographs that enliven images of the family.

Topical Box Series

Of the 102 boxes in *Marriages and Families,* almost half are entirely new to this edition. Reflecting and reinforcing the book's primary themes, three categories of boxes focus on the changes, choices, and constraints that confront today's families. A fourth category discusses cultural differences, and a fifth explores critical issues in family life. Self-assessment quizzes that help students evaluate their own knowledge and acquire insights make up the sixth type of box.

- **Changes boxes**—some historical, some anecdotal, and some empirically-based—show how marriages and families have been changing or are expected to change in the future. For example, a box in Chapter 14 shows how the role of the working mother has evolved over the years.

- **Choices boxes** illustrate the kinds of decisions families can make to improve their well-being, often highlighting options that family members may be unaware of. In Chapter 11, for instance, a box shows how to increase the probability of having healthy babies.

- **Constraints boxes** illustrate some of the obstacles that limit our options. They highlight the fact that although most of us are raised to believe that we can do whatever we want, we are often constrained by macro-level socioeconomic, demographic, and cultural factors. For example, a box on the ten biggest myths about the African American family reveals some of the stereotypes that African American families confront on a daily basis.

- **Cross-Cultural/Multicultural boxes** illustrate the richness of varying family structures and dynamics, both within the United States and in other countries. For example, one box contrasts the American style of dating with arranged courtship and marriage in Muslim societies.

- **Critical Issues boxes** focus on emerging or unsolved problems that many families are facing now or will probably encounter in the near future. For example, one box shows how our tax structure imposes a "marriage penalty."

- **Ask Yourself** New to this edition, this series of self-assessment quizzes not only encourages students to think about and to evaluate their knowledge about marriage and the family but helps them develop guidelines for action, both on their own and others' behalf. For example, "If This Is Love, Why Do I Feel So Bad?" helps the reader evaluate and make the decision to leave an abusive relationship.

Key Terms and Glossary

Important terms and concepts are boldfaced and defined in the text and listed at the end of each chapter. All key terms and their definitions are repeated in the glossary at the end of the book.

Additional Reading

For faculty and students who seek additional information on particular topics, each chapter ends with a list of books in the area of marriage and the family, including some classics and many scholarly journals. Each list usually also includes a few entries from the popular press, such as self-help titles, contributions by well-known journalists and policy makers, or books that have generated public debate on marriage and family issues. To reflect the diversity of thought about marriages and families today, these bibliographies include material by and about members of both sexes and many racial-ethnic groups.

NEW AND EXPANDED TOPICS

In *Part I, "Marriage and the Family in Perspective,"* three chapters deal with defining and studying marriages and families as well as the evolution of American families from colonial days to the present. I discuss a number of new topics: the effect of politics on family-related research, as exemplified by the National Institutes of Health's 1994 recommendation that women and minority members be included in medical research (Chapter 2); and the impact of the Great Depression and World War II on the family (Chapter 3). These chapters also expand and update material on family research by women and people of color and changes in the male provider role.

The development of gender roles and the ways in which women and men learn to love and to express love and sexuality are the focus of *Part II, "The Individual and the Developing Relationship."* New topics include gender schema theory (Chapter 4), stalking behavior and biological theories of love (Chapter 5), the role of popular culture in shaping our images of sex and sexuality (Chapter 6), celibate spouses and sexuality and the elderly (Chapter 7). In these four chapters expanded and updated materials include changes in men's social roles (Chapter 4), love and intimacy in Asia and the Middle East (Chapter 5), sexual scripts, homosexuality, bisexuality, and sex education (Chapter 6), sexual behavior in adolescents and in young adults, and STDs and HIV/AIDS (Chapter 7).

In *Part III, "Individual and Marital Commitments,"* I focus on the micro-level and macro-level variables that influence when, whom, and whether we will marry. New topics include the filter theory of mate selection, so-called serious casual dating, and Latina rites of passage (Chapter 8); the "marriage penalty" and older never-marrieds (Chapter 9); and "married singles," interracial marriages, gay and lesbian "marriage," and marital rituals and customs (Chapter 10).

I've updated and expanded materials on cross-cultural dating (Chapter 8); cohabitation, Latino and African American singles, and gay and lesbian couples (Chapter 9); and social-class differences and families of color (Chapter 10).

The decision to have or not to have children and the broad range of parent-child relationships are the subjects of *Part IV, "Parents and Children."* I introduce new material on genetic engineering and on the reasons for male infertility (Chapter 11); on the pros and cons of bonding with one's infant, spanking as a form of discipline, and absentee fathers (Chapter 12); recent immigration and undocumented workers, backlash against immigrants, and California's Proposition 187 (Chapter 13). Expanded and updated are discussions of abortion, international adoptions, and foster homes (Chapter 11); the father's role in child rearing (Chapter 12); and Native American cultures and their recent entrepreneurial efforts (Chapter 13).

Part V, "Conflicts and Crises," deals with some of the major economic and interpersonal problems that families confront today. New topics include moonlighting; part time and overtime work; unemployment; violence in the workplace; the daddy penalty; pregnancy discrimination laws, and the benefits and limitations of the Family and Medical Leave Act, as well as an entire new section on the family and the workplace (Chapter 14); the consequences of family violence, violence against "out-of-town" brides in immigrant families, violence against women in many cultures, a comparison of the battered woman and the incarcerated prisoner, and an explanation of family violence based on conflict theory (Chapter 15). I have updated and expanded material on homelessness and sexual harassment in the workplace (Chapter 14); battered husbands, why battered women do not leave their husbands, the abuse of steroids, and anorexia (Chapter 15); phases of separation, child custody arrangements, and divorce mediation.

Finally, *Part VI, "Changes and Transitions,"* examines some of the recent changes in family life and social policy and speculates on how the family will fare in the future. I introduce new discussions of the stability of remarriages, the intricacies of intergenerational relationships in merged households, the characteristics of successful remarried families and stepfamilies (Chapter 17); depression, helping a child grieve the death of a family member, and housing options for the elderly (Chapter 18); and the issue of family values (Chapter 19). I have expanded and updated the material on the distribution of resources (e.g., prenuptial agreements) when two families merge; remarriage and stepparenting among racial-ethnic families (Chapter 17); minority children living with grandparents (Chapter 18); and the dying process and controversies over welfare (Chapter 19).

SUPPLEMENTS

The supplements package for this textbook is of exceptional quality. From the *Instructor's Manual* to the *Themes of the Times*, each component has been meticulously crafted to amplify and illuminate materials in the text itself.

Instructor's Resource Manual This manual offers learning objectives, chapter outlines, teaching tips, suggestions for classroom activities, topics for class discussion, written assignments, lists of audiovisual and software resources, and *Study Tips*. The manual includes suggestions for relating specific clips from the *Video Library* to particular chapters and topics in *Marriages and Families*.

Test Item File This test bank contains 1900 multiple-choice, true-false, and essay questions that are page-referenced to the text.

Prentice Hall Custom Test Prentice Hall's new testing software program permits instructors to edit any or all items in the *Test Item File* and add their own questions. Other special features of this program, which is available for Dos, Windows, and Macintosh, include random generation of an item set, creation of alternate versions of the same test, scrambling question sequence, and test preview before printing.

 ABC News/Prentice Hall Video Library for Marriage and the Family Video is the most dynamic supplement you can use to enhance a class, but the quality of the video material and how well it relates to your course still make all the difference. Prentice Hall and ABC News are now working together to bring you the best and most comprehensive video ancillaries available in the college market.

Through its wide variety of award-winning programs—"Nightline," "Business World," "On Business," "This Week with David Brinkley," "World News Tonight," and "The Health Show"—ABC offers a resource for feature and documentary-style videos related to the chapters in *Marriages and Families: Changes, Choices, and Constraints*. The programs have extremely high production quality, present substantial content, and are hosted by well-versed, well-known anchors.

Prentice Hall and its authors and editors provide the benefit of having selected videos and topics that will work well with this course and text and include notes on how to use them in the classroom.

 **The New York Times Supplement** *The New York Times* and Prentice Hall are sponsoring *Themes of the Times*, a program designed to enhance student access to current information relevant to the classroom. Through this program, the core subject matter provided in the text is supplemented by a collection of timely articles from one of the world's most distinguished newspapers, *The New York Times*. These articles demonstrate the vital, ongoing connection between what is learned in the classroom and what is happening in the world around us. To enjoy the wealth of information of *The New York Times* daily, a reduced subscription rate is available. For information, call toll-free: 1–800–631–1222.

Prentice Hall and *The New York Times* are proud to co-sponsor *Themes of the Times*. We hope it will make the reading of both textbooks and newspapers a more dynamic, involving process.

Transparency Acetates Taken from graphs, diagrams, and tables in this text and other sources, over 50 full-color transparencies offer an effective means of amplifying lecture topics.

Study Guide This supplement for students offers chapter outlines and summaries, definitions of key concepts, self tests, applied exercises for each chapter of the book, and *Study Tips*.

Study Tips Appearing in both the *Study Guide* and the *Instructor's Manual*, this useful essay offers students a guide to effective studying. Topics include how to prioritize study materials, how to take good class notes, and how to test yourself and review as you read a textbook.

ACKNOWLEDGMENTS

A number of people have made researching and writing *Marriages and Families: Changes, Choices, and Constraints* an enjoyable experience. First, I would like to thank my students. Their lively exchanges during and outside of class shaped my thinking about the joy and pain of marital, family, and other interpersonal relationships. In addition, their insightful comments and questions helped me refocus much of my research and writing. Tanvir Ahmed, Christine Howard, Natasha Bias, Marcy Plimack, Renita Richardson, and Judy Shaw also provided valuable research assistance, and I am especially grateful to Deborah Dougherty for volunteering to do some of my time-consuming computerized searches and data entry.

The generous exchanges of information by colleagues on two electronic mail lists were especially valuable. Many thanks to the subscribers of FAMLYSCI, Family Science Network (Gregory W. Brock, moderator/list owner) and to WMST-L, Women's Studies List (Joan Korenman, moderator/list owner).

I am grateful to the reference and circulation staff at the University of Baltimore's Langsdale Library for their continuous assistance. Carole Mason, Mary Mohr, and Tami Taylor kept track of several hundred inter-library loan requests. Jim Foster was most effective in running interference when these requests ran into snags. Ann Kirby and Gerrie Myers were always helpful in processing and helping me locate materials. Carol Vaeth was extraordinary in accessing materials from a variety of academic and public libraries when I had only partial references. Both Carol and Susan Wheeler went out of their way to track down materials and to help me sharpen my research skills on E-mail. In addition to providing reference help, Mary Schwartz spent many hours teaching my students how to collect data on family trees using a variety of computerized and archival sources. I am also grateful to Steve LaBash for responding to my innumerable questions and requests for information quickly and efficiently. Finally, I thank Robert Pool, Law Library, for his technical support and continuous E-mail messages and articles in my mailbox with a "Have you seen this?" note.

Throughout this project, the researchers at the U.S. Bureau of the Census have been very helpful in answering questions and providing recent data. I am especially grateful to Arlene Saluter, demographic statistician in the marriage and family branch.

I owe many thanks to the reviewers of both the first and second editions of this book. The contributions of the following people were critical in developing this book: Virginia Anderson, Lamar University; Grace Auyang, University of Cincinnati RWC; Gerald Barman, University of Alaska, Fairbanks; Diane Beeson, California State University, Hayward; Marion Bihm, McNeese State University; Sally Bould, University of Delaware; Dudley Campbell, Los Angeles Pierce College; Cynthia Chan-Imanaka, Seattle Central Community College; Jerry Clavner, Cuyahoga Community College; John Crowley, Manchester Community Technical College; Mark Eckel, McHenry County College; Michael P. Farrell, University of Buffalo, State University of New York; Joe R. Feagin, University of Florida, Gainesville; Juanita Firestone, University of Texas, San Antonio; Joseph Garza, Georgia State University; Michael Goslin, Tallahassee Community College; Gary Hodge, Collin County Community College; Marilyn Howell, Trinity College; Terry E. Huffman, Northern State University; John P. Hutchinson, Essex Community College; Leslie B. Inniss, Florida State University; Ross Klein, Memorial University, Newfoundland; Shirley Klein, Brigham Young University; Larry Lance, University of North Carolina, Charlotte; Joseph J. Leon, California State Polytechnic University; Jerry Michel, Memphis State University; Purna C. Mohanty, Paine College; Charles Petranek, University of Southern Indiana; Phil Piket, Joliet Junior College; Robert Pinder, Texas Tech University; Dolores Pitman, Mesa State College; Mark Rank, Washington University; Karen Seccombe, University of Florida, Gainesville; Ronald L. Taylor, University of Connecticut; Verta Taylor, Ohio State University; Kenrick Thompson, Northern Michigan University; LurlineWhittaker, Morgan State University; Faith Willis, Brunswick College.

At Prentice Hall, Nancy Roberts, editor-in-chief for social sciences, has been a wonderful "boss," colleague, and friend. She has been patient, encouraging, and understanding, and has provided both emotional and technical support throughout the revision of this second edition. Despite the demands of her position, she has always been quick to respond to questions and requests and has always made me feel as if I'm Prentice Hall's only author. Virginia Otis Locke, my development editor, must surely be one of the best editors in the publishing industry. She has suggested interesting graphics, inundated me with newspaper and book clippings, and provided me with comments that have made this textbook much more readable. She's helped me balance my feminist perspective and "tell it like it is" style with my respect both for objectivity and for the diversity of my audience. She has facilitated the work on appendixes and has supervised the artwork and photo selections. I am indebted to Ginny for her probing questions, intelligent suggestions, and insightful comments throughout this project. Even when I felt grumpy and stressed out over deadlines, Ginny was always patient and tactful and maintained her sense of humor.

Serena Hoffman, my production editor, has been the most benevolent of taskmasters. In addition to making sure that deadlines were met, she has orchestrated and supervised the innumerable tasks required to produce the complex product that is a textbook, including the manuscript's copy editing, the coordination of design, illustrations, and text for final composition, and permissions for materials quoted or adapted. Mary Louise Byrd did a great job of copy editing, and Mary Helen Fitzgerald meticulously acquired our permissions. Joelle Burrows researched the art on the cover and the chapter opening pages, and Barbara Salz moved mountains to acquire the particular photographs we wanted in the text. I wish to extend my sincere gratitude to Kris Kleinsmith and her marketing staff. I am also grateful to the sales representatives at Prentice Hall who have provided feedback from faculty.

Gary Moore, Associate Professor of Public Health at the University of Massachusetts, turned my rough sketches and ideas into wonderful, original artwork that students will truly enjoy. Gary has managed to illustrate concepts and statistics so innovatively that students who are usually tempted to avoid figures will find themselves studying the graphs and charts with interest.

Last, but not least, I thank my family for their unfaltering support, understanding, and encouragement. Among other things, my husband, Vitalius, and our son, Andrius, have given me innumerable hours of assistance with hardware and software problems. Gema, our daughter, has helped me choose some of the photographs for this edition and enabled me to keep my work in perspective by insisting that I hike with her and play racquetball with Vitalius as well. A word of thanks, too, to my brother, Casimir, for providing long-distance technical advice.

The reactions of faculty and students to the first edition of this book have helped me enormously in preparing this second edition. I hope instructors and students will be equally responsive to this new edition.

Nijole V. Benokraitis
University of Baltimore
Department of Sociology
1420 N. Charles Street
Baltimore, MD 21201
Voicemail: 410-837-5294
Fax: 410-592-6006
E-mail: BENOKRAITIS@UBMAIL.UBALT.EDU

ABOUT THE AUTHOR

Nijole V. Benokraitis, professor of sociology at the University of Baltimore, has taught the Marriage and Family course for 15 years and says it's her favorite class, although her courses in Racial and Ethnic Relations, Gender Roles, and Introductory Sociology run a very close second. Professor Benokraitis, who received her doctorate in sociology from the University of Texas at Austin, is a strong proponent of applied sociology and requires her students to enhance their study of course topics through interviews, direct observation, and other hands-on methods of learning. She also enlists her students in community-service activities, such as tutoring and mentoring inner-city high school students, writing to government officials and other decision makers about specific social problems, and volunteering research services to nonprofit organizations.

Professor Benokraitis, who immigrated to the United States from Lithuania with her family when she was six years old, is bilingual and bicultural. She is coauthor of *Modern Sexism: Blatant, Subtle, and Covert Sex Discrimination* (which has been translated into Japanese) and *Affirmative Action and Equal Opportunity: Action, Inaction, and Reaction,* and is coeditor of *Seeing Ourselves: Classical, Contemporary, and Cross-Cultural Readings in Sociology.* She is currently working on a reader on subtle sex discrimination as well as on a reader to accompany *Marriages and Families: Changes, Choices, and Constraints.* Professor Benokraitis has published numerous articles and book chapters on such topics as institutional racism, discrimination against women in government, fathers in two-earner families, displaced homemakers, and family policy. Her current research interests include domestic violence and intergenerational conflicts in stepfamilies.

Professor Benokraitis has served as both chair and graduate program director of the University of Baltimore's Department of Sociology and has chaired numerous university committees. She has also been a faculty advisor to Alpha Kappa Delta, the sociological honor society, and the Sociology Club. The recipient of grants and fellowships from many institutions, including the National Institutes of Mental Health, the Ford Foundation, the American Educational Research Association, the Administration on Aging, and the National Endowment for the Humanities, Professor Benokraitis has also received several faculty research awards at the University of Baltimore. She has for some time served as a consultant in the areas of sex and race discrimination to women's commissions, business groups, colleges and universities, and programs of the federal government, and she has made several appearances on radio and television, most recently as a panel member on a PBS program on gender communication differences.

Professor Benokraitis lives in Maryland with her husband, Dr. Vitalius Benokraitis, a computer scientist, and their two children, Gema and Andrius. Gema, a communications graduate of Towson State University, is a talented amateur photographer and an avid competitive cyclist. Andrius is a computer science major at Virginia Polytechnic Institute.

1
The Changing Family

Betty Patterson, Navajo Rug

Data Digest

- In 1991, only half of the 65.7 million children under age 18 in the United States lived in **a traditional nuclear family**.
- The percentage of **people who never marry has doubled,** from 5 percent in the 1950s to 10 percent in 1992.
- The **marriage rate fell** by almost 30 percent between 1970 and 1990, and the **divorce rate increased** by nearly 40 percent. In 1990, half of all first marriages were expected to end in divorce, and the divorce rates after remarriage were even higher.
- The **average age at which people marry** for the first time was higher in the mid-1990s than at any time during the past century: 26.5 years for men, 24.5 years for women.
- In 1993, one of every four babies was born to an **unmarried mother,** compared with one of every ten babies in 1970.
- In the mid-1990s, about half of all children could expect to spend some part of their childhood in a **single-parent home;** there were nearly 10 million single parents, an increase of more than 40 percent since 1980. More than 8 million of these parents were single mothers, and nearly 2 million were single fathers.
- More than half of all **mothers with preschool-age children were in the labor force** in 1992, compared with only one in five in 1960.
- In 1993, more than 20 percent of U.S. **children were living in poverty,** and 10,000 children died of poverty-related causes.

SOURCES: Bacher, 1993; Rawlings, 1994; Saluter, 1994; U.S. Bureau of the Census, 1993, 1994.

In a 12-year study of 6,500 family units, researchers described a wide range of household arrangements. Consider the following descriptions:

- Bill, a 48-year-old Caucasian American man, lived with his wife, Marjorie, in 1968. No children or other relatives lived with the couple. In 1977, Bill's wife died, and Bill lived by himself for two years. Then, at the age of 59, he married again and established a home with his new wife.
- Lidia, a 32-year-old Hispanic American woman, was separated from her husband and maintained a home for herself and her seven children. In 1977, her mother, Blanca, moved in and stayed for two years. In 1979, Blanca and three of her grandchildren left to form another household together. Lidia stayed in her own household with her other four children, of whom the youngest was her 17-year-old son.
- Harry, a 71-year-old African American man, headed a household that included his wife and a 6-year-old grandson. In 1974, Harry was widowed and continued living with his grandson. In 1979, his daughter Althea moved in with him, and the following year a second grandchild was added to the household (Richards et al., 1987).

Two generations ago, the typical American family consisted of a father, a mother, and three or four children. Clearly, contemporary family arrangements are more fluid and more transitory. Does this shift reflect changes in individual preferences, as people often assume, or are other forces at work here? As this chapter will show, although individual choice has brought about some alterations in family structure, many of these changes have been adjustments to larger societal transformations. We will also see that, despite historical and recent evidence to the contrary, we continue to cling to a number of other myths about the family. Before we examine these issues, however, we need to define what we mean by marriage and family.

WHAT IS MARRIAGE?

Although the concept of **marriage** has become more complex, the currently accepted definition—a socially approved mating relationship—is very broad. Because this definition invokes the concept of the social **norm**—a culturally defined rule for behavior—it includes variations on marriage that we find in many different societal and cultural groups. Among the norms that help define marriage are formal laws and religious doctrines or rituals. For example, in order to be legally married, U.S. citizens must meet specified requirements (e.g., minimum age) in any state. And because the Catholic Church prohibits the dissolution of what it considers the holy sacrament of marriage, in the eyes of their church, devout Catholics cannot be divorced.

Despite such societal and cultural variations, however, marriages in most Western industrialized countries have some common characteristics. In general, married couples are expected to share economic responsibilities, to engage in sexual activity only with their spouses, and to bear and raise children.

In the United States, laws governing marriage have changed more rapidly than have social customs or regional practices. For example, although miscegenation laws, which prohibit interracial marriages, were declared unconstitutional by the U.S. Supreme Court in 1967, customs, attitudes, and practices among many groups in American society continue to discourage such unions. Furthermore, as violent outbursts in white neighborhoods in Massachusetts, New York, and New Jersey in recent years have shown, intolerance of interracial dating is not limited to the South or to rural areas. In 1991, actor-director Spike Lee released a movie called *Jungle Fever* that brought this controversial topic into the public arena.

Marriages in the United States are legally defined as either ceremonial or nonceremonial. A *ceremonial* marriage is one in which the couple must follow procedures specified by the state or other jurisdiction, such as buying a license, getting blood tests, and being married by an authorized official. Some states also recognize the *nonceremonial*, or **common-law marriage**, which is established by *cohabitation* (living together) and/or evidence of *consummation* (sexual intercourse). Common-law marriages are recognized as legal in 13 states and the District of Columbia. In both kinds of marriage, the parties must meet minimal age requirements, and they cannot engage in **bigamy**; that is, they cannot be married to a second person while a first marriage is still legal.

When common-law relationships are dissolved, unless there is a written contract, the legal repercussions can be complex, as the famous case described in "Our Love Doesn't Need a Piece of Paper" indicates: Michelle Marvin received nothing when she split up with actor Lee Marvin, although they had lived together for six years. Had they signed an agreement or been legally married, Michelle Marvin would have been entitled to some of the $3.6 million Lee Marvin earned over the period of their relationship. Thus, even when common-law marriage is considered legal, marriage provides more rights. Interestingly, however, in a number of states children born to common-law partners, although considered illegitimate, have the same legal rights as children born to partners in a ceremonial marriage.

WHAT IS A FAMILY?

Although it may seem unnecessary to define familiar terms like *family*, meanings vary among groups of people and change over time. Moreover, such definitions have important consequences for policy decisions, often determining what rights and obligations of family members are recognized by legal and other social institutions. For example, not until 1977 did federal regulations allow unmarried, low-income couples to qualify as families and apply for public housing. As another example, in most cases of adoption, the child is not legally a member of the adopting family until the adoption has been approved by both social service agencies and the courts. Thus, definitions of *family* affect people's lives and the choices they make and that are made for them.

Traditionally, the family has been defined as a unit made up of two or more people who are related by blood, marriage, or adoption and who live together, form an economic unit, and bear and raise children. But because this description excludes a multitude of diverse groups who also consider themselves families, the traditional definition has been challenged in recent years. Social scientists have asked: Are childless couples families? What about cohabiting couples? Foster parents and their charges? Three elderly sisters living together? Gay and lesbian couples, with or without children? Communes in which child rearing is assumed by people other than the child's parents?

As yet, social scientists have been unable to come up with answers to these questions; the complexity of contemporary family arrangements is very great (Cowan et al., 1993). Because we need a working definition, here we define **family** as "any sexually expressive or parent–child relationship in which: (1) people live together with a commitment, in an intimate, interpersonal rela-

Our Love Doesn't Need a Piece of Paper

Marvin v. Marvin (1976, 1979, 1981) was not the first legal case that examined the rights and obligations of nonmarital cohabitants, but it is the most famous. The case coined the term **palimony**, meaning the cash settlement made to an unmarried live-in partner by the partner who wants to split up. Although it is not a legal concept, and although Michelle Marvin never succeeded in collecting palimony, the term has become widely accepted.

Michelle Triola and Lee Marvin met while Marvin was starring in the movie *Ship of Fools* and Triola was employed as a singer at a Los Angeles nightclub but also working as a stand-in on the same film. In 1970, Lee Marvin told Triola to leave their Malibu beach house; when he withdrew financial support from her, she went to court.

According to her testimony, Triola had given up her lucrative career as an entertainer and singer to devote herself full time to Lee Marvin as a companion, homemaker, housekeeper, and cook. In return, she claimed, Marvin had agreed to provide financially for her for the rest of her life. Triola testified that Marvin said, "When two people love each other, there is no need for a license." In court, Lee Marvin denied having ever said this.

During the six years of their relationship, Triola and Marvin often traveled to such places as England for the filming of *The Dirty Dozen* and Micronesia for *Hell in the Pacific*. Among other benefits, the defense pointed out, Triola received a Mercedes-Benz, several fur coats, and enjoyed "the pleasures of life on the California beach in frequent contact with many film and stage notables."

In 1979, the Los Angeles Superior Court awarded Triola $104,000 "for rehabilitation pur-poses so that she may have the economic means to reeducate herself and to learn new, employable skills or to refurbish those utilized." Two years later, however, the California Court of Appeals ruled that no award was necessary because Triola had benefited both economically and socially from the relationship and had sustained no damages (Swisher et al., 1990).

Even when a partner receives palimony, the amount may be negligible. In a recent case, for example, when a couple split up after living together for eight years, a Wisconsin jury awarded the woman $7,900 for her cooking, cleaning, and food shopping. However, her ex-boyfriend was awarded $1,289 on a counterclaim in which he contended that she had benefited by the housing he provided to her and her children and by repairs he made to her car (Presser, 1993).

---

tionship; (2) the members see their identity as importantly attached to the group; and (3) the group has an identity of its own" (Chilman et al., 1988: 18). Be warned that not all social scientists will agree with this definition, for it does not explicitly include legalized marriage, procreation, or child rearing. However, definitions may become even more complicated—and more controversial—in the future. For instance, medical technology has made it possible for a child at birth to have more than two parents:

A sperm donor, an egg donor, the woman providing the womb for gestation, the man expecting to raise the child, and the woman expecting to raise the child. When one considers the added parental possibilities that emerge through divorce, remarriage, stepparenting, foster care, and other guardianship arrangements, we discover that family trees increasingly resemble inextricably intertwined vines of ivy (Spanier, 1989: 5).

It is only recently that definitions of the family have begun to recognize the heterogeneity of ethnic minority families. Particularly in African American and Latino communities, ties with **fictive kin**, or nonrelatives who are accepted as part of the family, may be stronger and more lasting than the ties established by blood or marriage (Dilsworth-Anderson et al., 1993). Because the U.S. Census Bureau's definition of a family does not include people who live with nonrelatives, many children who are cared for by fictive kin are not registered as family members (Hill, 1993).

FUNCTIONS OF THE FAMILY

Although family structures differ, most contemporary families fulfill similar functions. In this section we explore the four major tasks today's family is expected to perform: legitimizing sex-

Reprinted by permission of Tribune Media Services.

ual activity, bearing and raising children, providing emotional support to family members, and establishing members' place in society.

Families in preindustrial societies continue to fulfill other traditional functions, such as educating their children, serving as an important economic unit, taking care of their elderly, and providing religious instruction to family members. It is worth noting that some families in technologically advanced societies—for example, Native Americans, Hispanic Americans, Asian Americans, the Amish—continue to perform the latter two functions.

Legitimizing Sexual Activity

Every society has norms regarding who may engage in sexual relations with whom and under what circumstances. One of the oldest rules is the **incest taboo**, which forbids sexual intercourse between close blood relatives, such as brother and sister, father and daughter, or mother and son. Many people believe that incest taboos were created to avoid the birth of physically and/or mentally deficient individuals as a result of inbreeding.

Although sexual relations between close relatives can increase the incidence of inherited genetic diseases and abnormalities, incest taboos have primarily *social bases*. They were probably designed to maintain the family in several ways. First, they minimize sexual competition within families by limiting sexual activity to spouses. Second, by forcing people to marry outside their immediate family, incest taboos forge political

and economic ties with other families. Third, these taboos maintain kinship boundaries that determine relatives' rights and obligations toward each other (Macionis, 1993).

Two other rules define the "right" marriage partner: The principle of **endogamy** requires that people marry and/or have sexual relations within a certain group, such as Jews marrying Jews or African Americans marrying African Americans. **Exogamy** requires marriage outside the group, such as not marrying one's relatives. (We explore endogamy and exogamy further in Chapter 8.) Although we Americans like to think that we have free choice in dating and marriage patterns, intensely felt societal, religious, subcultural, and familial rules, however implicit, usually govern our choice of dates and life partners.

Exogamy and endogamy can also be very explicit. Quebec, for example, which contains 25 percent of the Canadian population, has been threatening secession since the early 1990s because its people are afraid of losing their French language, customs, and heritage through intermarriage and assimilation into the non-French Canadian population (Craig, 1994).

Procreation and Socialization of Children

Procreation is an essential function of the family. Although some married couples choose to remain childless, most want to raise families, and some go to great lengths to have the children they want. Today couples who are unable to conceive naturally for various reasons (e.g., a

CHAPTER 1 *The Changing Family* **5**

woman's fallopian tubes may be blocked; a man's sperm count may be too low) have increasing numbers of options (see Chapter 11).

Once a couple become parents, the family embarks on another critical function, that of socialization. Through **socialization**, the child acquires the language, accumulated knowledge, attitudes, beliefs, and values of its society and culture and learns the social and interpersonal skills needed to function effectively in society.

Some argue that the family is less powerful today in socializing its young than it was in the past because of changes in other institutions and practices. With more mothers of young children in the work force, child-care centers and preschool programs are playing an increasing role in socialization. Moreover, in states that have extended the length of the academic year, school-age children are spending even less time with their parents. And whether at home or in child-care centers, significant numbers of children are spending more time watching television than interacting with family and friends. Most preschoolers can sing dozens of commercial jingles years before they learn nursery rhymes, recite the ABCs, or memorize prayers. According to Ishwaran (1989), however, the modern family has acquired the important function of coordinating the specialized agencies (e.g., schools, game or sports organizations, religious groups) that influence and have a considerable amount of control over their children.

Emotional Support

Despite the changes we've just discussed, the family remains a critical primary group that provides its members with love, understanding, security, acceptance, and companionship through intimate, long-term, face-to-face interaction. The family is also expected to support its members in times of psychological crises and emotional stress.

The importance of primary-group emotional support for healthy development has been well documented (Goslin, 1969; Walters and Stinnett, 1971). For example, in the early 1990s, several U.S. television news programs spotlighted desolate Romanian orphanages where infants and toddlers, given minimal attention by overworked caretakers, rocked incessantly, did not speak, and showed few signs of being human. These children had been abandoned by parents

Providing love, comfort, and emotional support in times of distress is one of the most important things family members do for one another.

who had been forced by the Romanian dictator Nicolae Ceausescu to bear and raise children they could not afford to feed and care for. (Ceausescu allegedly denied contraceptives to his people so that they would produce the large population of laborers he wanted. He and his wife were executed in 1989.) Hundreds of U.S. families responded by trying to adopt these children, hoping to undo the damage done by the cruel conditions under which they were being raised.

Social Placement and Social Roles

To a great extent, our position in society is acquired through our family. We are born into a certain social class, ethnic or racial group, and religious affiliation. Although we can later change some of these memberships, our family shapes our initial definition of who we are (and are not) and our place in society. The family also teaches us social roles. As we discuss later in this book, although the roles associated with gender and marital and parental status have not undergone a dramatic transformation during the past 200 years, they have certainly changed in numerous ways (see Chapters 3, 4, 11, and 12).

Diversity in Marriages, Families, and Kinship Systems

Although the basic family functions we have described are common to most cultures, each society has specific norms that specify acceptable marriage and family forms. Thus, there is considerable diversity among families both across and within cultures.

Social scientists often differentiate between **family of orientation**—the family into which a person is born—and **family of procreation**—the family a person forms later by marrying and having or adopting children. Each type of family is part of a larger **kinship system**, or network of people who are related by blood, marriage, or adoption. Although the **nuclear family**, made up of a husband, a wife, and their children, has decreased considerably in number in the United States (see the Data Digest), it is still predominant in North America and most other Western countries. Social scientists also refer to this family form as the **conjugal family,** which, although it includes the children of a marriage, puts the emphasis on the marital relationship.

In much of the preindustrial world, which contains most of the world's population, the most common family form is the **extended family,** in which two or more generations (such as the family of orientation and the family of procreation) live together or in adjacent dwellings. Although the term **consanguine family**, which gives primary emphasis to blood relationships, refers to parents, children, and grandparents, it is also sometimes used in place of extended family.

Some social scientists are predicting that in industrialized societies where single-parent families are on the increase, extended families may become more common. Such families can make it much easier for a single parent to work outside the home, raise children, and perform needed but time-consuming household tasks. Because remarriage rates are high, however, it remains to be seen whether extended families will become widespread.

No matter what family form is dominant in a society, the overall kinship system is defined by a variety of formal laws or informal norms that determine such important things as inheritance rights and the way in which children are named. Four of the most common sets of norms that define and regulate kinship are forms of marriage, patterns of authority, residential patterns, and patterns of descent.

Forms of Marriage

There are several forms of marriage that may be sanctioned by a society. In **monogamy**, one man is married to one woman. **Polygamy**, in which a man or woman has two or more spouses, is subdivided into *polygyny*—one man married to two or more women—and *polyandry*—one woman with two or more husbands. In group marriage, two or more men and two or more women live together and have sexual relations with each other.

Although industrial societies forbid polygamy, small pockets of societies sometimes ignore both state and religious laws. The Mormon Church banned polygamy in the late 1800s, but as late as 1987, men in the small town of Pinesdale, Montana, still had more than one wife. Receiving no complaints about this situation, state officials simply left these Mormon fundamentalists alone (*New York Times*, 1987).

Because divorce and remarriage are common in the United States and in many European countries, residents of these countries are said to practice **serial monogamy**; that is, they marry several people, but one at a time—they marry, divorce, remarry, redivorce, and so on. Anthropologist George Murdock found that only about 20 percent of societies are strictly monogamous. Others permit either polygamy or mixtures of polygamy and monogamy.

Polygyny is common in many non-Western countries, especially among monarchs and other wealthy men. For example, King Sobhuza of Swaziland, who died in 1972 at the age of 83, had 100 wives. Although in Africa very few men can afford more than one wife, many African tribes have long considered it a man's right to marry as many wives as he can support (Okie, 1993).

Polygynous marriages can be either formal or informal. In a study of marriage forms in Nigeria, Karanja (1987) differentiates between an inside wife and an outside wife. An "inside wife," who marries a Nigerian man in a church or civil ceremony, typically subscribes to the Christian ideal of monogamy in marriage. However, under native law and custom, her husband may also "marry" (no official ceremony is performed) an "outside wife." The outside wife has regular sexual relations with her "husband," is financially maintained by him, establishes an autonomous residence, and has children whose paternity is acknowledged by the man. Outside wives, however, have limited social recognition and status and considerably less political and legal recognition than do inside wives. As the box "The Outside Wife" indicates, outside wives and their mates are often professional people.

The very rare practice of polyandry is illustrated by the Todas, a small pastoral tribe that flourished in south India until the late nineteenth century. The Toda woman who married one man became the wife of his brothers—including brothers born subsequent to the marriage—and all lived in the same household. When one of the brothers was with the wife, "he placed his cloak and staff outside the hut as a warning to the rest not to disturb him" (Queen et al., 1985: 19). Marital privileges rotated among the brothers, there was no evidence of sexual jealousy, and one of the brothers, usually the oldest, was the "legal" father of the first two or three children. Another brother could become the legal father of children born later. Polyandry exists in societies that are characterized by a limited amount of land and harsh environmental conditions in which the men have the primary food-producing role (Cassidy and Lee, 1989).

Group marriage is also rare, although there are documented cases among the Reindeer Chukchee of Siberia and the Siriono, wandering hunters of the Bolivian jungles (Stephens, 1963). Some groups in the United States like the Oneida, formed in the mid-1800s, and the countercultural communes formed between 1965 and 1975 in opposition to the prevailing culture, experimented with group marriage, but these communities were short-lived (Kephart, 1987).

Patterns of Authority

No matter what form the marriage takes, patterns of authority determine who has the power in the family. Three common patterns exist: patriarchal, matriarchal, and egalitarian. In a **patriarchy** the authority is held by the eldest male, who is usually the father. In a **matriarchy** the authority is held by the eldest female, usually the mother. In the third, **egalitarian pattern**, authority is shared equally by both husband and wife.

Most societies are patriarchal. Males are considered heads of the household and dominate the economic, social, and domestic spheres of the family. In a patriarchy the young must submit to and obey the old, especially the older men (Hutter, 1988). As women increase their economic power, egalitarian patterns are emerging in industrial societies, but the changes are very slow, as we will discuss in later chapters.

CROSS CULTURAL

The Outside Wife

Temi, 38 years old, is a British-trained doctor in private practice in Lagos, Nigeria. Her father (now retired) was a university professor and her mother was a high school teacher. Temi's first church marriage, in which she had two children, ended in divorce. She is now an outside wife of an eminent businessman, with whom she has a child. She lives in a flat rented by her "husband" on Victoria Island, said to be where the who's-who of Nigeria live.

Temi sees no contradiction in her way of life:

Look, I lived in England for years and I know there you are expected to be monogamously married. Well, I am not in England now, am I? (She laughs.) My first husband was a fine gentleman, but, let's face it, he had no money. Most of our spare time was spent bickering over who was going to pay the bills. It was intolerable. In the end I decided to quit. Financial straits for me are history. My children are in school abroad. My husband recently bought me a Mercedes Benz, and I am building a house here in Lagos with his help. We also plan to buy a home in the U.S.

Temi's "husband" has two other wives. The church, or inside wife, is a doctor like herself; the other outside wife is an attorney who practices and lives in Lagos (Karanja, 1987: 255–56).

Residential Patterns

Families also vary in terms of where family members live. The three most common ways in which families establish a residence are patrilocal, matrilocal, and neolocal. In the *patrilocal* residential pattern, newly married couples live with the husband's consanguineous family. In a *matrilocal* pattern, newly married couples live with the wife's consanguineous family. A *neolocal* residence is one in which the newly married couple sets up its own residence. Because around the world families tend to be consanguineal rather than nuclear, the most common pattern is residence with the husband's family.

In industrial societies, married couples typically have established their own residences. In the early 1990s, however, there has been an increasing tendency for young married adults to live with the parents of either the wife or husband or sometimes with the grandparents of one of the partners. About half of all families starting out cannot afford a medium-priced house because they haven't the cash for a down payment and the costs of closing (Savage and Fronczek, 1993). As we will show in later chapters, divorced mothers and their children also frequently live with parents or grandparents.

Patterns of Descent

In tracing kinship and determining who has what name, property rights, obligations, and duties, three common patterns are employed: *patrilineal*, in which kinship is traced through the father's line; *matrilineal*, in which kinship is traced through the mother's line; and *bilineal* (or bilateral), in which kinship is traced through both lines.

In preindustrial societies, patrilineal descent generally dominates (O'Kelly and Carney, 1986). For example, in many African countries property and leadership rights are inherited by males (Hill, 1993). In industrial societies, kinship is usually traced bilaterally; property may be handed down through both the mother's and the father's sides of the family, and children may take the name of either side. Use of both family names has long been common in Asian and Latino families, and since the early 1980s, a number of U.S.-born couples use hyphenated family names to reflect both sides of the family. Also, increasing numbers of women are deciding to keep their own names when they marry.

MYTHS ABOUT MARRIAGE AND THE FAMILY

Despite evidence that contradicts some of our beliefs about marriages and families, a variety of myths continues to affect the way we think about these institutions. Five of the most common are: (1) families were happier in the past; (2) marrying and having children are the "natural" things to do; (3) "good" families are self-sufficient; (4) every family is always a bastion of love and support; and (5) it is possible, and we should all strive, to be a "perfect" family.

Myths can be *dysfunctional* when they result in negative (although often unintended) consequences that disrupt a family. For example, the myth of the perfect family can make us miserable because we feel there is something wrong with us if we do not live up to that ideal scenario. We may put off really living while we wait for the perfect mate, or for our children to become what we want them to be, or for our in-laws to accept us as we are. We may become very critical of family members or withdraw emotionally because we don't fit into a mythical mold.

Myths can also divert our attention from widespread social problems that may underlie to crises in individual families. If people blame themselves for the gap they perceive between image and reality, they may be unable to recognize or challenge the external forces, such as social policies, that create problems on the individual level. For example, if we believe that only bad, sick, or maladjusted people beat their children, we will recommend solutions at the individual level, such as counseling, support groups, and therapy. As you will see in later chapters, however, many family problems result from large-scale problems such as racism, poverty, and unemployment.

When myths help to maintain the social system, as they sometimes do, they can be *functional*, promoting efficiency in social functioning (Guest, 1988). For example, myths give us hope that we can have a good marriage and family life, and as a result we don't give up at the first sign of problems. Myths thus help us maintain our emotional balance during crises. And myths can free us from guilt or shame. For instance, "We just fell out of love" is a more acceptable explanation for getting a divorce than "I used bad judgment" or "I realized that I prefer to live alone."

The same myth may be both functional and dysfunctional. A belief in the decline of the family has been functional, for example, because it provides a livelihood for countless scholars, journalists, social workers, and government employees (Caplow et al., 1982). But this same myth is also dysfunctional when people become unrealistically preoccupied with finding self-fulfillment and happiness.

Myths About the Past

We often hear that in "the good old days" there were fewer problems, people were happier, and families were stronger. Because of the widespread influence of movies and television, many of us cherish romantic notions of the frontier days as portrayed in John Wayne films, of the antebellum South of *Gone with the Wind*, and the strong, poor, but loving rural family presented in the 1970s television series "The Waltons" and "Little House on the Prairie."

Many historians argue, however, that such golden ages never in fact existed, and we glorify them only because we know so little about the past (Coontz, 1992). Even in the 1800s, many families experienced desertion by a parent or the births of illegitimate children (Demos, 1986). Family life in the "good old days" was filled with deprivation, loneliness, and physical dangers, as the box "Diary of a Pioneer" illustrates. Families worked very hard and were often decimated by accidents, illness, and disease. Even in the mid-1940s, average life expectancy meant that parental death often led to stepfamilies and to child placements in extended families, foster care, or orphanages. Thus, the chances of not growing up in an intact family were actually greater in the past than they are now (Walsh, 1993).

Myths About What Is Natural

Many people have strong opinions about what is natural or unnatural in marriages and families. For example, although remaining single is more acceptable in the 1990s than in earlier times, there is still a lingering suspicion that something is wrong with a person who does not marry. We sometimes also have misgivings about childless marriages or other committed relationships:

"It's only natural to want to get married and have children."

"Do you suppose they're infertile?"

"Maybe they're too selfish to have children."

"Gays are violating human nature."

"It's unnatural for a 25-year-old man to marry a 55-year-old woman."

"Women are natural mothers."

Like these Nebraska homesteaders, many families in the so-called "good old days" lived in dugouts like this one, made from sod cut from the prairies.

Diary of a Pioneer

Many historians point out that life on the old frontier was anything but romantic. Malaria and cholera were widespread. Pioneer cabins, because of their darkness, humidity, and warmth, as well as their gaping windows and doors, made ideal environments for mosquitoes. Women and children have been described as doing household tasks with "their hands and arms flailing the air" against the hordes of attacking mosquitoes (Faragher, 1986: 90).

Historian Joanna Stratton examined the letters, diaries, and other documents of pioneer women living on the Kansas prairie between 1854 and 1890. The following selection is from a diary of a 15-year-old girl:

A man by the name of Johnson had filed on a claim just west of us and had built a sod house. He and his wife lived there 2 years, when he went to Salina to secure work. He was gone 2 or 3 months and wrote home once or twice, but his wife grew very homesick for her folks in the east and would come over to our house to visit mother.

Mother tried to cheer her up, but she continued to worry until she got bedfast with the fever. At night she was frightened because the wolves would scratch on the door, on the sod, and on the windows, so my mother and I started to sit up nights with her. I would bring my revolver and ammunition and ax and some good-sized clubs.

The odor from the sick woman seemed to attract the wolves, and they grew bolder and bolder. I would step out, fire off the revolver, and they would settle back for a while when they would start a new attack. I shot one through the window and I found him lying dead in the morning.

Finally the woman died and mother laid her out. Father took some wide boards that we had in our loft and made a coffin for her. Mother made a pillow and trimmed it with black cloth, and we also painted the coffin black.

After that the wolves were more determined than ever to get in. One got his head in between the door casing, and as he was trying to wriggle through, mother struck him in the head with an ax and killed him. I shot one coming through the

window. After that they quieted down for about half an hour, when they came back again. I stepped out and fired at two of them but I only wounded one. Their howling was awful. We fought these wolves five nights in succession, during which time we killed and wounded four gray wolves and two coyotes.

When Mr. Johnson arrived home and found his wife dead and his house badly torn down by wolves he fainted away. After the funeral he sold out and moved away (Stratton 1981: 81).

Rebecca Bryan Boone, wife of the legendary American pioneer Daniel Boone, endured months and sometimes even years of solitude when Boone hunted in the woods or went on trading trips. Besides household chores, she chopped wood, cultivated the fields, harvested the crops, and hunted for small game in the woods near her cabin. Although Rebecca was a strong and resourceful woman, she told a traveling preacher that she felt "frequent distress and fear in her heart" (Peavy and Smith, 1994: xi).

Other beliefs, also surviving from so-called simpler times, are that we grow up naturally knowing how to have a successful marriage and that love is enough to guarantee a happy marriage. "All that people have to do," the popular belief goes, "is follow their instincts."

In reality, if motherhood is natural, why do many women choose not to have children? If homosexuality is unnatural, how do we explain its existence since time immemorial? If getting married and creating a family are natural, why do millions of men refuse to marry their pregnant partners and then abandon their children?

Myths About the Self-Sufficient Family

Some of Americans' most cherished values include individual achievement, self-reliance, and self-sufficiency. The great number of best-selling books on such topics as parenting, combining work and marriage, and having "good sex" attest to our belief that we can improve ourselves, we can pull ourselves up by our bootstraps.

Although we do have many choices in our personal lives, few families, past or present, have been entirely self-sufficient. Most of us need some kind of help at one time or another. For example, because of unemployment, underemployment, and recession, the poverty rate has increased by 40 percent since 1970; in the mid-1990s, about one in six families lives in poverty. As we will see in Chapter 14, many of the "working poor" are two-parent families. Even though the United States is one of the wealthiest countries in the world, its child poverty rate is two to three times higher than that in Sweden, Switzerland, Norway, West Germany, Canada, Australia, and the United Kingdom (Children's Defense Fund, 1990).

The United States also has a higher infant mortality rate than many other countries. As you can see from Figure 1.1, among a large group of industrialized countries, the United States ranks only twentieth in terms of infant well being (United Nations Children's Fund, 1994). The plight of U.S. black children is even worse; here the United States ranks fortieth, lower even than such developing countries as Costa Rica, Poland, Malaysia, Chile, Sri Lanka, Bulgaria, and Colombia (Children's Defense Fund, 1994). Thus, millions of families are far from being self-sufficient in maintaining their own or their children's well-being. (We discuss the effects of poverty further in Chapters 11 and 14.)

The middle class is not self-sufficient either. Historian Stephanie Coontz (1995) points out that during the 1950s and 1960s many middle-class families were able to prosper not because of family savings or individual enterprise but as a result of federal housing loans, education payments, and publicly financed roads. In fact, very few areas of family life are free of the influence of government, business, or politics. Consider a function we all take for granted—owning and driving a car. The typical car owner has to deal with car dealers, banks, insurance companies, state motor vehicle departments, auto mechanics, and, sometimes, police and the courts. On the other hand, a family that doesn't own a car has even less autonomy. The need to rely on public transportation restricts employment choices and the family's access to the best bargains in housing, food, and clothing, adequate medical care, and recreational facilities.

According to some authorities, it is the most affluent families who benefit most from public assistance. Taxpayers subsidize private schools, bankrupt companies, savings and loan bailouts, and generous tax loopholes enjoyed by the largest corporations (see, e.g., Barlett and Steele, 1992).

The Myth of the Family as a Loving Refuge

The family has been described as providing a "haven in a heartless world" (Lasch, 1977: 8). Although one of the major functions of the family is to provide love, nurturance, and emotional support, the home can also be one of the most

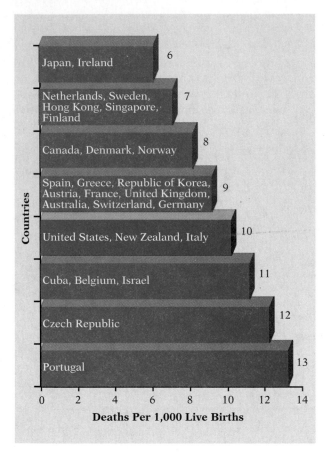

Figure 1.1 **Rates at Which Children Under Age 5 Die: Selected Countries, 1992.** *UNICEF's single most important indicator of the welfare of a nation's children is the under-5 mortality rate, or USMR. Defined as the probability that a child will die between birth and 5 years of age, the USMR is calculated as the number of deaths of children under 5 per 1,000 live births in a given country. This statistic reflects a wide variety of factors, including mother's nutritional health and health knowledge, the availability of prenatal, maternal, and child health services, family income and food intake, and the quality of water and general sanitation* (United Nations Children's Fund, 1994).

physically and psychologically brutal settings in society. As you will see in Chapter 15, an alarming number of children suffer from physical and sexual abuse from family members, and there is a high rate of violence between marital partners.

Many parents find it stressful to try to balance work and family responsibilities. Moreover, concern about crime, drugs, and unemployment has made many parents less than optimistic about their children's future. In a recent national poll, 37 percent of those surveyed said they expect their children to have a lower quality of life and to be worse off financially than they, the parents, are (*U.S. News & World Report*, 1993). The worry that underlies such responses is bound to affect family dynamics. If family members are unrealistic about the daily pressures they confront, the level of tension may rise. And especially for families who suffer from health or economic problems—roughly 15 percent of the U.S. population that lives below or barely above the poverty level, according to the U.S. Bureau of the Census, (1993)—the home may be loving, but it is hardly a haven.

Myths About the Perfect Family

Myths about the perfect family are even more harmful. Many of our images of family life come from television shows (Spigel and Mann, 1992). Since the 1950s, most programs about families have reflected stereotypes, misinformation, or filmmakers' fantasies. In the 1950s, shows like "Father Knows Best," "My Little Margie," "The Adventures of Ozzie and Harriet," and "Leave It to Beaver" provided an escape from reality. A little later, fantasies were also spun by such shows as "The Partridge Family," "The Brady Bunch," "The Waltons," and "Little House on the Prairie." In all of these programs, families solve their problems in half an hour or an hour and live happily ever after.

"Roseanne" was one of the first family sitcoms to attempt more realism than earlier television shows, portraying not only a blue-collar family but one whose members bickered and fought with each other constantly.

In the 1970s, when television producers suddenly realized that viewers were not all white but people of all racial and ethnic backgrounds, a number of shows focusing on stereotypical African American families were introduced: "Good Times" portrayed a poor, black family trying to survive in a housing project; "Sanford and Son" featured a black junk collector who was always manipulating his son; "The Jeffersons" presented a wealthy, black owner of a dry-cleaning business who was married to an intelligent (and often wiser) woman and who spent most of his time trying to be accepted by the white business community.

In the mid-1980s, "The Cosby Show" garnered widespread popularity when it presented yet another fantasy—wealthy, African American, professional parents who wore designer clothes and whose children all attended college. Even Theo, the son whose grades in school were consistently low and who seemed to have little motivation to do well in school, was accepted at a prestigious private university. There were never any serious conflicts in this family. The lawyer-mother and obstetrician-father, who seemed almost always to be at home, were consistently understanding and maintained a sense of humor. And in general, the children were well behaved and obedient. The show was a phenomenal success. Many applauded it for providing positive role models and challenging the stereotype that all African Americans are on welfare or in blue-collar jobs, but others criticized the program as unrealistic (Taylor, 1989; Frazer and Frazer, 1993).

In the mid-1990s, the commercial television networks were hailed by some observers for airing a number of more realistic shows about families of color. For example, in "Roc," the close-knit, extended family had disagreements but handled problems with dignity and intelligence. In "South Central," a single mother struggled to raise her children in a community rife with crime, violence, and drugs. Both shows were canceled, however, because of low ratings. According to some researchers, many African Americans do not want to see TV shows that feature working-class characters (Zurawik, 1994). A number of other shows that cast people of color in a negative light continue to flourish, however (see the box "African American Families on Television—Realistic or Stereotypical?").

THREE PERSPECTIVES ON THE CHANGING FAMILY

We introduced this chapter with several definitions of the family, and we discussed the functions of the family, the ways families vary, and various myths about family life. Now we are ready to look at the major theme of this chapter—how the family is changing.

A number of writers have suggested that the family is falling apart (e.g., Footlick, 1990). Quite commonly, journalists and scholars refer to the "vanishing" family, "troubled" marriages, and "appalling" divorce statistics as sure signs that the family is disintegrating. Moreover, it is not unusual to find textbooks with collections of articles such as "The Trouble with Parents," "When You Doubt Your Parents Love You," "My Shattered American Family," and "When Parents Fight" (Lewis and Stafford, 1986). And if you watch talk shows, you probably wonder whether there are *any* normal families or marriages left in America.

Although many parents worry about the future of their children, several surveys suggest that the general population is optimistic about the family. For example, in a recent study of high school seniors, 76 percent said that having a good marriage and family life was "extremely important," up from 73 percent in 1976 (*The Public Perspective*, 1994). A national survey of people between the ages of 26 and 45 found that 93 percent felt that their family life was very important (Gallup and Newport, 1991a). As you will see in Chapter 2, however, people's attitudes and beliefs are not always synonymous with their behavior. Some of the most passionate advocates of family life may be unwilling to make the personal and job sacrifices that family cohesion sometimes requires. Nevertheless, most Americans are much more upbeat about the family than are many social scientists, politicians, and journalists.

During the 1970s and 1980s, the debate over the state of the family became increasingly heated and hit a peak during the 1992 presidential campaign when Vice President Dan Quayle threw down the gauntlet with his speech about family values. Although many derided Quayle, the topic pervaded the debates between President George Bush and presidential candidate Bill Clinton. Two years later, President Clinton and some others

African American Families on Television— Realistic or Stereotypical?

In 1994 ABC launched "All-American Girl" with a great deal of fanfare; this was the first time that an Asian American actress played the lead in a prime-time network program. Critics, however, were quick to assert that Margaret Cho appeared to be more "Valley Girl" than daughter of an immigrant Korean family, that the show was "more sitcom than Seoul," and that the program tried too hard to make the family's lifestyle white and middle class (Marin and Lee, 1994; Southgate, 1994). In addition, these critics pointed out, the insensitive casting—all Cho's family members are played by actors of Chinese, Japanese, and other Asian origins—may send a message that "Asian Americans are all alike."

Families of varying racial and ethnic backgrounds are even less visible on television, however. For example, according to a study by the Center for Media and Public Affairs, Latinos are less visible in prime time in the 1990s than they were in the 1950s (Gerbner, 1993). Not only do they comprise only 1 percent of all characters portrayed on television, but they are more likely than any other group to be depicted as poor or criminal (Mittelstadt, 1994). There are, however, an increasing number of television series dominated by African American characters. Some see this as progress; others have blasted the shows as continuing to caricature black households.

At his induction into the Academy of Television Arts and Sciences Hall of Fame, Bill Cosby denounced the networks for reinforcing shallow stereotypes of African Americans: "How many times has the punch line been, 'We're going to kick butt'? How many times has the punch line been about genitalia or big breasts?" Tim Reid, who starred in "Frank's Place" during the 1980s has described many of the comedies depicting African American culture as "more of a tragedy" (Hammer, 1992).

Some observers feel that most TV producers, who are white and who still control most shows about blacks, have "fallen back on tired, overused motifs" and negative characterizations (Hammer, 1992; Harris, 1992; Waters, 1993), for example:

❑ *The Lech* According to these writers, TV shows overflow with black males consumed by their own testosterone. On "Martin," Martin Lawrence has been described as sex-obsessed, "hoisting his crotch, spewing black jive stereospeak–'Girl, gimme some wet mouth!'" In "The Sinbad Show," the comic plays what has been described as a "babe-hounding doofus." In "Out All Night," the ever sex-hungry Vidal Thomas drools over a sexy neighbor: "Right now I'm delivering pizza [for a living]. And in my personal life . . . I deliver hot and on top!"

❑ *The Buffoon* In "Living Single," the two male neighbors are usually presented as klutzy, not too bright, and sexist. They drop in by announcing, "We hungry," and make numerous jokes about big butts and nappy hair. In "Hangin' with Mr. Cooper," substitute teacher Mark Cooper engages in juvenile antics like gluing a student to his chair.

❑ *The Dumb, Sexy Woman* In "Living Single," four young African American women share a New York apartment. Critics assert that although all four characters have college degrees and upscale jobs, "they behave like man-crazed Fly Girls." In "The Fresh Prince of Bel Air," the daughter is presented as man-crazy as well as shallow and superficial.

Others feel that these critical remarks are unjustified. They argue, for example, that Martin's relationship with his girlfriend is complex and sensitive. Some point out that the fact that Sinbad, a bachelor, is raising two foster children says something positive about the importance of male authority figures in many so-called fractured African American families. Similarly, "On Our Own" features a black man attempting to take care of his six brothers and sisters. "Me and the Boys" is also about a widower raising his three sons with the help of his stepmother. And in "Fresh Prince," the main character, although apparently raised in the slums, is intelligent, insightful, and mature.

Do you think that these and other programs cast African Americans in a negative light? Or do you think they present realistic images? Note, also, how many programs focus on black fathers as the single parent when, in fact, only about 2 percent of all black children live with their fathers only (U.S. Bureau of the Census, 1994). How would you explain this contradiction?

seem to have concluded that perhaps Quayle had been right after all.

The status of the American family continues to spark debate among three schools of thought. One group contends that the family is deteriorating; a second argues that the family is changing but not deteriorating; and a third, smaller group maintains that the family is stronger than ever.

The Family Is Deteriorating

More than 100 years ago, the *Boston Quarterly Review* issued a dire warning: "The family, in its old sense, is disappearing from our land, and not only our institutions are threatened, but the very existence of our society is endangered" (cited in Rosen, 1982: 299). In the late 1920s, E. R. Groves (1928), a well-known social scientist, stated that marriages were in "extreme collapse." Some of his explanations for what he called the "marriage crisis" and high divorce rates have a surprisingly modern ring: hedonism, too much luxury, independence, financial strain, and incompatible personalities.

Even those who were optimistic a decade ago have become more pessimistic in recent years because recent data on family "decay" are more compelling. Some of these data include an increase in divorces and desertions, high rates of children born out of wedlock, millions of "latchkey children" (see Chapter 12), an increase in the number of people deciding not to get married, unprecedented numbers of single-parent families, and a decline of parental authority in the home

Why have these changes occurred? Echoing Groves, those who feel the family is in trouble cite such reasons as lack of individual responsibility, lack of commitment to the family, and just plain selfishness. Many men and women, it is claimed, are unwilling to invest their psychological and financial resources when they do have children or give up on marriages too quickly when there are problems (Popenoe, 1988, 1992). Especially during the 1992 family-values exchanges, many politicians argued that the family is deteriorating because most people put their own individual needs over family duties.

Some journalists in mainstream newsmagazines claim that many people in the United States have ignored their moral obligation to the family:

For many, marriage is more like a hobby than a commitment, a phase instead of a trust. We are

becoming a country of deadbeat dads who don't pay their bills and dead-tired moms who work two jobs to pick up the slack. Even many parents who pay for their children don't pay attention to their children (Roberts, 1994: 11).

Others feel that educators and scholars play a crucial role in generating distorted information about the family. For instance, contemporary philosophers are accused of emphasizing friendship, compatibility, and interpersonal love and being indifferent to the children who are traumatized by divorce (Sommers, 1989). Many social scientists propose that divorce can serve as a foundation for individual renewal and new beginnings (e.g., Skolnick, 1991). Others point out that divorce, in general, makes people worse off: women become poorer, children become distressed; a single parent is likely to be overwhelmed with economic and emotional responsibilities; and children born out of wedlock are generally also born into poverty (Wilson, 1993).

Some observers blame many of the family's problems on mothers who work outside the home. If mothers stayed at home and took care of their children, these writers maintain, we would have less delinquency, fewer high school dropouts, and more children who are disciplined (Hamburg, 1993).

The Family Is Changing, Not Deteriorating

Other writers argue that the family has not changed as much as we think. Although more mothers have entered the labor force since 1970, the mother who works outside the home is not a new phenomenon (Stacey, 1990). Mothers sold dairy products and woven goods during colonial times, took in boarders around the turn of the century, and held industrial jobs during World War II (Chafe, 1972). The number of married women in the labor force doubled between 1930 and 1980 but *quadrupled* between 1900 and 1904 (Stannard, 1979). Furthermore, family problems such as desertion, illegitimacy, and child abuse have always existed. In an examination of the family literature published during the 1930s, Broderick (1988) found that a number of early studies dealt with such issues as divorce, desertion, and family crises due to discord, delinquency, and depression.

Even the rise in the number of single-parent families is not a wholly new trend. Although the percentage of single-person households has doubled during the past three decades, this number *tripled* between 1900 and 1950 (Stannard, 1979). Furthermore, divorce is not a modern problem. Divorce began to be more common in the eighteenth century, when parents no longer could control their adult married children, the importance of romantic love began to rise, and women began to have greater access to divorce (Cott, 1976). There is no question, however, that a greater proportion of people divorce today than ever before, and that more early marriages are ending in divorce. As a result, the decision of many singles to postpone marriage until they are older, more mature, and have stable careers may often be a sound one. We'll have more to say about the issue of whether divorce is functional or dysfunctional in Chapter 16.

Finally, many social scientists point out that the major problems families face are not the result of individual defects but reflect the difficulties of maintaining a family during periods of rapid change and economic recessions. These kinds of changes have confronted families for years, in most Western countries as well as the rest of the world (Schoettler, 1994).

The Family Is Stronger than Ever

Could it be that our nostalgic myths based on half-truths about the past make us see the contemporary family as weak and on the decline? Some writers think so and assert that family life today is much more loving than in the past. Consider the treatment of women and children in colonial days. If they disobeyed strict patriarchal authority, they were often severely punished. And, in contrast to some of our sentimental notions, only a small number of white, middle-class families enjoyed a life that was both gentle and genteel:

For every nineteenth-century middle-class family that protected its wife and child within the family circle . . . there was an Irish or a German girl scrubbing floors in that middle-class home, a Welsh boy mining coal to keep the home-baked goodies warm, a black girl doing the family laundry, a black mother and child picking cotton to be made into clothes for the family, and a Jewish or an Italian daughter in a sweatshop making "ladies'" *dresses or artificial flowers for the family to purchase (Coontz, 1992: 11–12).*

Moreover, as we will discuss in Chapter 3, the 1950s, the so-called "Golden Fifties" era, brought only a flicker of contentment to a minuscule number of white, middle-class, suburban U.S. families. And contrary to what many people think they remember, the fifties were not a time of innocent, traditional dating and the postponement of sexual gratification. Kinsey and his associates (1953) reported that 20 percent of women and 71 percent of men age 16 to 20 had had premarital coitus (see Chapter 7).

About 43 percent of the current adult U.S. population can be classified as **baby boomers**, people born to the post–World War II generation, between 1946 and 1964. Now largely in their 30s and 40s, many boomers want a strong family unit (Gallup and Newport, 1991a). As they age, some are beginning to question the sacrifices they made in choosing work over family life. One national survey, for example, found that 78 percent of adults said they would prefer to work flexible hours, even if it meant slower career advancement, so that they have more time to enjoy life with their families (Aburdene and Naisbitt, 1992).

Another possible reason for greater family strength today is that many people have living grandparents, feel closer to them, and often receive both emotional and economic support from these family members. The current growth of the older segment of the population will produce four-generation families early in the twenty-first century. On the one hand, more adults in their 60s will be caring for 80- to 90-year-old parents. On the other hand, more children and grandchildren will grow up knowing and enjoying their older relatives. Three-quarters of people age 65 to 74 who are still living independently say they're in good health, and even among people 75 and older, two-thirds consider themselves healthy (Vobejda, 1992). Thus, extended families may be the norm in the future, and family ties may thus be strengthened.

Each of the three schools of thought on the status of the family makes a reasonable argument for its position. How, then, can we decide which perspective is the correct one? Is the family weak, or is it strong? The answer will depend in large part on how we define, measure, and interpret family "weakness" and family "strength"—issues we address in Chapter 2.

HOW ARE FAMILIES CHANGING?

We've discussed some changes in the way the family carries out its basic functions and how familial relationships are formed. Now let us look at some major changes that have occurred in the 1980s and 1990s: in the racial and ethnic composition of families, their demographic boundaries, their forms, and their economic status.

Racial-Ethnic Changes

There are more than 130 distinct ethnic or racial groups among the almost 250 million people living in the United States. As Table 1.1 shows, by 2020 almost a third of the U.S. population will be multiracial (U.S. Department of Commerce, 1991). More than 16 million Americans speak a language other than English at home. As you can see from Table 1.2, some of the fastest growing groups of non-English-speaking people are those from the Middle East and Southeast Asia.

African Americans are the largest racial-ethnic group, followed by the Spanish-speaking population. We don't have exact numbers for the total Hispanic American population, for many individuals are undocumented aliens—people who have entered the United States illegally. Although in 1990 the Chinese, Filipinos, and Japanese still ranked as the largest Asian American groups, during the 1980s, Southeast Asians, Indians, Koreans, Pakistanis, and Bangladeshis registered much faster growth. Mexicans, Puerto Ricans, and Cubans were the dominant groups among Latinos, but their growth rate, too, was outpaced by people from mostly Central and South American countries, such as El Salvador, Guatemala, Colombia, and Honduras.

Table 1.1
U.S. Racial and Ethnic Composition 1950–2020

	1950	1990	2020
White	86%	76%	70%
African American	10	12	14
Hispanic American	3	9	11
Asian American and other	1	3	5

SOURCES: Population Reference Bureau, 1988; U.S. Department of Commerce, 1991.

Table 1.2
The Top 20 Languages Spoken in the United States

LANGUAGE USED AT HOME	TOTAL SPEAKERS OVER 5 YEARS OLD		PERCENTAGE CHANGE
	1990	1980	
Spanish	17,339,000	11,549,000	50.1
French	1,703,000	1,572,000	8.3
German	1,547,000	1,607,000	−3.7
Italian	1,309,000	1,633,000	−19.9
Chinese	1,249,000	632,000	97.7
Tagalog	843,000	452,000	86.6
Polish	723,000	826,000	−12.4
Korean	626,000	276,000	127.2
Vietnamese	507,000	203,000	149.5
Portuguese	430,000	361,000	19.0
Japanese	428,000	342,000	25.0
Greek	388,000	410,000	−5.4
Arabic	355,000	227,000	57.4
Hindi, Urdu	331,000	130,000	155.1
Russian	242,000	175,000	38.5
Yiddish	213,000	320,000	−33.5
Thai	206,000	89,000	131.6
Persian	202,000	109,000	84.7
French Creole	188,000	25,000	654.1
Armenian	150,000	102,000	46.3

Note: *In 1990, the total number of U.S. residents 5 years old and over speaking a language other than English at home was 38 percent higher than it was in 1980.*
SOURCE: U.S. Bureau of the Census, 1993, p.51.

Demographic Changes

Demographic fluctuations in such areas as the distribution of the population, population mobility, and birth and death rates have affected the family. Two demographic changes have had especially far-reaching consequences for family life. First, fertility rates have declined. Since the end of the eighteenth century, American women have been bearing fewer children, having them closer together, and finishing child rearing at an earlier age. Second, the median age of the population has risen from 17 in the mid-1800s to nearly 30 in the 1980s. Both these shifts mean that a growing proportion of the U.S. population now experiences the so-called "empty-nest syndrome"—the departure from the home of grown children—at an earlier age, as well as earlier grandparenthood and prolonged widowhood. Other changes can be seen in the nature of households, the numbers of singles and cohabitants, the rates of marriage and divorce, the rise of one-parent families, the increasing number of working mothers, and the rapid increase in the number of stepfamilies.

Family and Nonfamily Households A **household** is composed of a group of related and/or unrelated people living together in the same dwelling. The Census Bureau divides households into two major categories: family and nonfamily (see Figure 1.2). A *family household* consists of the householder and at least one additional person related to the householder through marriage, birth, or adoption. A *nonfamily household* is composed of a householder who lives either alone or exclusively with people unrelated to her or him. An estimated 67 percent of households in 1993 were either nonfamily households or families with no children, a substantial increase from 55 percent in 1970.

Singles and Cohabitants Singles make up one of the fastest-growing groups, accounting for 13 percent of all households in 1960 but more than 25 percent in 1993 (Saluter, 1994). The decrease in household size shown in Figure 1.2 was due, among other reasons, to fewer children per family, more one-parent families, increasing age at first marriage, and greater age segregation—the tendency of young and old people to live separately.

Marriage-Divorce-Remarriage As the Data Digest points out, one out of every two first marriages is expected to end in divorce. And, as we will see in Chapter 17, divorce rates after a second marriage are even higher. What types of marriages are the most likely to end in divorce? Teen marriages and marriages entered into because the woman became pregnant. And which marriages are the most stable? First marriages of women over the age of 30.

Whether or not a couple has children seems to have little effect on either divorce or remarriage. The finding that women with lower educational levels are more likely to divorce and/or remarry than are those with college degrees suggests the importance of age and maturation in lasting marriages. We examine marriage, divorce, and remarriage in Chapters 10, 16, and 17.

One-Parent Families As more adults remain single and as divorce rates increase, the number of children living with one parent also increases. The proportion of one-parent families has almost tripled—from 9 percent in 1960 to nearly 25 percent in 1990. As Figure 1.3 shows, the proportion of children living with a divorced parent decreased slightly between 1980 and 1990, but those living with a never-married parent have increased considerably—from around 4 percent in 1960 to nearly 31 percent in 1990. Of all one-parent families, almost 90 percent are mother–child families (U.S. Bureau of the Census, 1994). One-parent households are discussed in Chapters 11, 12, and 16.

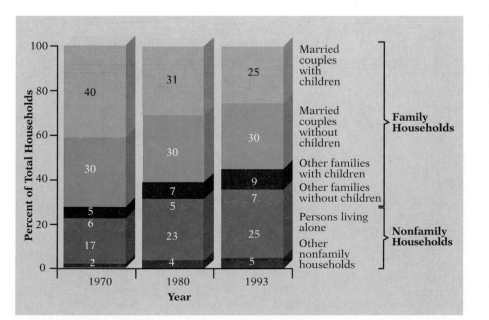

Figure 1.2 Changes in U.S. Household Composition, 1970–1993. Due to rounding, figure totals may vary between 99 and 101 (Based on Rawlings, 1994).

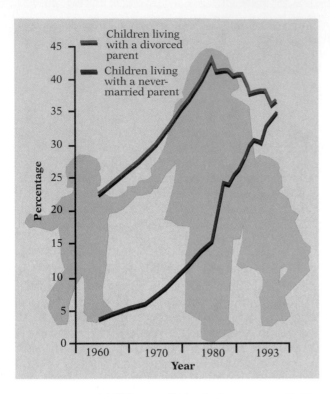

Figure 1.3 **Children of Single Parents, 1960– 1993** (Saluter, 1994, p. xiii).

Working Mothers The increased participation of mothers in the labor force has been one of the most important changes in family roles. Two-earner couples with children rose from 33 percent in 1976 to 55 percent in 1990 (U.S. Bureau of the Census, 1991a). Half of all mothers with children under 1 year of age are in the labor force. We explore the problems of working mothers and two-earner couples in Chapter 14.

Stepfamilies Stepfamilies are becoming much more common. An estimated 25 percent of children live with a stepparent by the time they are 16 years old. Compared with mothers in biological and adoptive families, mothers in stepfamily situations tend to be younger; both mothers and stepfathers generally have less formal education; and stepfamilies have lower median family incomes (Miller and Moorman, 1989). Besides dealing with economic problems, family members must also cope with a number of complex relationships involving step-, half-, and full siblings as well as ex-spouses and past and current in-laws. (See Chapter 17 for more detail on these issues.)

Many of these changes in family life are not

unique to the United States. Almost all developed countries have seen such changes as a decline in fertility rate, an aging population, a high divorce rate, and an increase in out-of-wedlock childbirths. Some of these trends are even more pronounced in other countries. In the late 1980s, for example, the percentage of unmarried couples who were living together was twice as high in Canada and France as in the United States and almost five times as high in Sweden and Holland. The percentage of births to unmarried women was about twice as high in Sweden and Denmark (Rich, 1990).

Poverty and Homelessness

The gap between the haves and the have-nots is increasing, and the poor are getting poorer. Of all racial-ethnic groups in the United States, African Americans are the most likely to be poor. In 1992, almost 12 percent of whites, 33 percent of African Americans, 29 percent of Latinos, and 13 percent of Asian Americans and Pacific Islanders were living below the poverty level (annual income of $14,335 or less). Forty percent of

Although we generally think of the homeless as people who are drug abusers or who have psychiatric problems, many young families are victims of economic recessions, job loss, and other misfortunes.

those in poverty were children (U.S. Bureau of the Census, 1993).

The increases in poverty and homelessness are explained, in large part, by economic recessions, unemployment, low-paying jobs, and the increase of one-parent families. Unfortunately, a willingness to work hard does not protect families and their children from poverty. In the mid-1990s, nearly one in two low-income householders worked, an increase of 40 percent over 1979. Even a full-time job, however, could not keep almost one-third of this group out of poverty (U.S. Bureau of the Census, 1993).

Estimates of the number of homeless range from 250,000 to almost 5 million (Eitzen and Zinn, 1994). The numbers are so large that in the 1990 census, the Census Bureau tried for the first time to count the homeless. The Urban Institute interviewed more than 1,700 homeless users of soup kitchens or shelters and found that 15 percent were children (Rich, 1988); however, the percentage of U.S. homeless who are children may be as high as 38 percent. According to a report by the National Academy of Sciences (1988), on any given night 100,000 children have no homes. Note that these figures from the Urban Institute and the National Academy of Sciences do not include runaways or children kicked out by their parents.

WHY FAMILIES ARE CHANGING

Clearly, we are seeing *changes* in the family, and these changes reflect both the *choices* people make and the *constraints* that limit those choices. To study people's choices, social scientists take a **micro-level perspective,** focusing on small-scale patterns of social interaction in specific settings. In contrast, to study the constraints that limit individuals' options, social scientists take a **macro-level perspective**, focusing on large-scale patterns that characterize society as a whole. Both perspectives and the ways in which they interface are crucial to an understanding of the family (Cowan et al., 1993).

Micro-level Explanations

Picture the following scenario: Two students meet in college, fall in love, marry after graduation, find well-paying jobs, and live the good life—feasting on brie and lobster, driving a Corvette, and the like. Then they have an un-

planned child. The wife quits her job to take care of the baby, the husband loses his job, and the wife goes to work part time. She has difficulty balancing her multiple roles of mother, wife, and employee. The stress and arguments between the partners increase, and the marriage ends.

When asked what went wrong here, most students take a micro viewpoint and blame the individuals: "They should have saved some money." "They didn't really need a Corvette." "She should have got her old job back after he got fired." "Their contraceptive practices were ineffective," and so on.

On the one hand, there's much to be said for micro-level perspectives. Many marriage and family textbooks stress the importance of individual choices, and some give short shrift to the importance of macro-level variables. As you will see throughout this book, some of the biggest societal changes that have had a major impact on families began with the efforts of one person who took a stand on an issue. For example, Mary Beth Whitehead's refusal to give up her right to see the baby she bore as a surrogate mother and the ensuing court battles created national debates about the ethics of the new reproductive technologies. As a result, many states have instituted surrogacy legislation.

Moreover, countless numbers of people have overcome enormous personal obstacles and have risen above family problems that to many of us would seem insurmountable. As the box "Bertice Berry Challenges Racial and Gender Stereotypes" shows, Bertice Berry's humble origins didn't stop her from obtaining a Ph.D. or landing a successful talk show that reached millions of people.

On the other hand, micro explanations should be kept in perspective. They are limited, and they cannot explain some of the things over which families have very little control. For these broader analyses, we must turn to macro explanations.

Macro-level Explanations

Many macro-level constraints limit or shape our choices. Such constraints include economic forces, technological innovations, social movements, and family policies.

Economic Forces The Industrial Revolution brought about widespread changes that affected the family. By the late eighteenth century, the domestic industries that had employed large

Bertice Berry Challenges Racial and Gender Stereotypes

Bertice Berry, the sixth of seven children, was raised by her single mother in a run-down section of Wilmington, Delaware. With a scholarship from an anonymous benefactor, Berry attended Jacksonville University in Florida. During college she worked part time as a social worker and interned at a shelter for battered women and rape victims. After her graduation cum laude in 1982, she worked as a researcher for the Victims' Assistance Agency in Florida and designed an intake format for rape crisis centers.

At Kent State University, Berry completed her master's degree in one year, with a 4.0 grade point average, and then taught sociology and statistics at the university, where she earned a Ph.D. in sociology in 1988. Her doctoral dissertation, "Colorism: The Impact of Black on Black Discrimination," was on the tendency of African Americans to ascribe higher status to lighter-skinned blacks than to those with darker skin.

In a nationally syndicated television talk show, "The Bertice Berry Show," Berry often focused discussions on violence against women, child abuse, and the misuse of drugs (Lyons, 1992; Alesci, 1993; personal correspondence, 1994). Berry says she enjoys challenging stereotypes about race, gender, and physical beauty and raising the general public's awareness of important social issues.

Getting her message across with humor proved especially effective with Berry's students at Kent,

who praised her for her comedic teaching style. She has moonlighted as a stand-up comic at night clubs, and she continues to make about 200 appearances annually as a comedian and as a lecturer on serious topics like sexual discrimination and harassment and racism. The National Association for Campus Activities, a student services organization of 1500 colleges and universities, voted her the 1991 and 1992 "Comedian of the Year."

In 1993 Berry's mother telephoned to say that one of Berry's sisters had become addicted to cocaine and that unless a family member could help, the sister's three children (an 8-year-old, 1-year-old, and a newborn) would be handed over to child protective services. Although initially Berry had doubts about her ability to raise children, she rose to the task and a year later she wrote, "I finally have mastered diapers (now I am baffled by potty training). But I have changed tremendously. I am more patient, and much more responsible. I have to be" (Berry, 1994: 8).

numbers of women and children were replaced by factories. As family members became less self-sufficient and worked outside the home, parents' control over their children diminished. In the latter half of the twentieth century, many manufacturers moved their companies to third-world countries to increase their profits. Such moves resulted in relocations and unemployment for many U.S. workers. Job dissatisfaction, unemployment, and financial distress disrupted many marital relationships and families.

Many African Americans have been concerned that immigration, another external economic factor, is diminishing their job opportunities. As we've noted, Latinos and people from

Asian countries will constitute the fastest-growing groups in the United States as we move into the twenty-first century. Because a large proportion of African Americans are still employed in skilled and semiskilled blue collar jobs, the influx of new immigrants, who are also competing for such jobs, constitutes a serious economic threat to many working-class African American communities (Hill, 1993). And in some areas, concern among whites is rising; for example, in 1994 California voters approved Proposition 187, which would deny schooling, medical care, and other benefits to illegal immigrants, all of whom have heretofore been cared for by the state's welfare agencies.

As the U.S. economy has shifted from an emphasis on manufacturing to a more service-oriented economy, millions of low-paying jobs have replaced higher-paying manufacturing jobs. This has wrought havoc with many families' finances. At the other end of the continuum, the increasing use of high-tech equipment like computers means that people must spend more time learning the new technologies, and this often means postponing marriage, family, and independence from the family of orientation. Recessions also affect family roles and structures. For example, although household incomes increased significantly during the mid-1980s, they have not regained the ground they lost in the recessions of the mid-1970s because of inflation. Those under age 25 saw the most dramatic losses in median income—a drop of 18 percent between 1979 and 1984 (Russell and Exter, 1986). In large part, this income erosion explains why so many people age 18 to 24 have moved back with their parents or never moved out in the first place.

Technological Innovations Advances in medical and other health-related technologies have led both to a decline in birth rates and to a prolongation of life. On the one hand, the invention of the birth-control pill in the early 1960s meant that women could prevent unwanted pregnancies, pursue a higher education, and seek long-term jobs. Improved methods of pre- and postnatal care have released women from the need to bear six or seven children just so that one or two will survive. On the other hand, because the average man or woman can now expect to live into his or her 70s and beyond, poverty after retirement is more likely, medical services can eat up savings, and the middle-aged—sometimes called the "sandwich generation"—must deal with both their own children and their aged parents (see Chapters 12 and 18).

Televisions, videocassette recorders (VCRs), microwave ovens, and personal computers have also affected families. Instead of watching shows together, people record what they want and watch the shows individually at a later time. The computer has made it possible for increasing numbers of people to work at home, with the result that they may go long periods without interacting with colleagues and coworkers or with family members. Families less often eat meals together because of the convenient fast-food franchises, the variety of frozen, microwavable meals, and because many parents work different shifts. Finally, if friends and relatives have electronic mail (E-mail) communication systems (such as America Online, Prodigy, and CompuServe) on their personal computers, they can go long periods without talking with each other.

Social Movements A number of social movements have contributed over the years to changes in the family. The civil rights movement of the 1960s had considerable impact on many African American families. Using affirmative action, some African Americans were able to take advantage of educational and economic opportunities that improved their families' economic status.

The women's movements, in the late 1800s and especially during the 1960s, transformed women's roles. As women gained more rights in law, education, and employment, many became less financially dependent on men and started questioning traditional assumptions about gender roles. The up side of this is that women have made great advances in their ability to make personal choices and have significantly more professional options. The down side is expressed by a number of observers who, as we will see in Chapter 6, believe that the so-called "sexual revolution" did many women more harm than good. According to this view, when women began to seek their own sexual fulfillment, they became more willing to enter into nonmarital sexual relationships. The result was more out-of-wedlock children who are not supported by their biological fathers.

The gay rights movements that began in the 1970s challenged discriminatory laws in such areas as housing, adoption, and employment. Although many lesbian women and gay men (as well as sympathetic heterosexual people) feel that the challenges have so far resulted in only very minimal changes, some clearly defined changes have in fact occurred. As we discuss in later chapters, some companies are providing benefits to the gay or lesbian partners of employees, a number of colleges and universities offer courses in gay and lesbian studies, and some adoption agencies offer assistance to lesbians and gays who want to become parents.

Family Policies Government policy affects practically every aspect of family life. Thousands of rules and regulations, both civil and criminal, at the local, state, and federal levels, govern domestic matters: laws about when and whom we can marry, how to dissolve a marriage, how children's rights are to be protected in a divorce, how we treat one another within the home, and even how we dispose of our dead. Families do not just passively accept policy changes, however. Parents themselves have played critical roles in such major social policy changes as the education of handicapped children and joint custody of children after divorce. In Chapter 19 we will consider the effects of government policy on families in more detail.

A CROSS-CULTURAL PERSPECTIVE

This text includes material both on American subcultures (Native Americans, African Americans, Asian Americans, and Latinos) and on other cultures for a number of reasons. First, unless you are a full-blooded Native American, your kin were immigrants to this country who contributed their particular cultural beliefs and practices to the shaping of current North American family institutions. American families today are a mosaic of many cultural, religious, ethnic, and racial groups and social classes. Because this diversity is increasing, a traditional white, middle-class model is no longer adequate to understand American marriages and families.

A second reason for this cross-cultural approach is that the world is shrinking. Compared to even 10 years ago, more Americans are traveling outside the United States, more international students attend American colleges and universities, and more exchange programs for students and scholars are offered at all educational levels. Furthermore, the dramatic events of the 1990s in Eastern Europe, South Africa, and Central America have enabled oppressed countries that had been closed to the rest of the world since 1940 to become independent and open up to trade, travel, and education. We need to understand the practices and customs associated with family life in other cultures.

A third reason for the text's perspective is that U.S. businesses are beginning to recognize the importance of understanding cross-cultural differences. Since the late 1980s, more companies have been requiring their employees to take crash courses about other cultures before they are sent abroad. For example, one of my students who won a job with a Fortune 500 company felt she had gained an edge over some very tough competition with her knowledge of Portuguese and of Brazil's cultural institutions.

Business is not the only sector to recognize the importance of understanding diversity. Many educators believe that a multicultural perspective is becoming essential to the professional preparation of researchers, faculty, counselors, and therapists who will study and interact with people from many different social, economic, and national backgrounds (Smith and Ingoldsby, 1992).

Finally, understanding other countries challenges our notion that American marriage forms are "natural" or inevitable. According to Hutter (1988), "Americans have been notorious for their lack of understanding and ignorance of other cultures. This is compounded by their gullible ethnocentric belief in the superiority of all things American and not only has made them unaware of how others live and think but also has given them a distorted picture of their own life." Hutter's perspective—and that of this book—is that understanding other people helps us understand ourselves.

CONCLUSION

Many of us are ambivalent about *change*. Since 1992 both Democrats (for example, President Bill Clinton) and Republicans (for example, Dan Quayle) have endorsed traditional family values. In many surveys Americans have said that such traditional family values as having a happy marriage and providing emotional support to their family are more important than having a rewarding job or being free from obligations to do whatever they want (Glenn, 1992).

We often make *choices* that are contrary to traditional family values, however. For example, many people divorce because they are personally unhappy, and some even use their children as pawns in protracted divorce battles (see Chapter 16). Thus, some parents place their highest priority on their own happiness and ignore their children's emotional needs.

As most of the chapters in this textbook show, some of the discrepancies between what we say and what we do reflect economic and political *constraints* at the macro level. With appropriate information, the family can be more effective in dealing with some of these constraints. In the next chapter we discuss how social scientists define, measure, and collect information about marriages and families.

Taking Action

SUMMARY

1. Although the traditional family composed of husband, wife, and children is still predominant in U.S. society, the definition of family has been challenged to include such nontraditional arrangements as single parents, childless couples, foster parents, and siblings sharing a home. Advances in reproductive technology have opened up the possibility of still more varied redefinitions of the family.

2. The family continues to fulfill such basic functions as producing and socializing children, providing family members with emotional support, legitimizing and regulating sexual activity, and placing family members in society.

3. Marriages, families, and kinship systems vary in terms of whether marriages are monogamous or polygamous; whether familial authority is vested in the man or in the woman or both share power; whether a new family resides with the family of the man or of the woman or creates its own home; and how the kinship system determines the naming of children and inheritance rights.

4. The many deep-rooted myths about the family include erroneous beliefs about how the family was in "the good old days"; about the "naturalness" of marriage and family as human interpersonal and social arrangements; the self-sufficiency of the family; the family as a refuge from outside pressures; and the "perfect family."

5. Social scientists generally agree that the family is changing, but they disagree as to whether it is changing in drastic and essentially unhealthy ways, whether it is simply continuing to adapt and adjust to changing circumstances, or whether it is changing in ways that will ultimately make it stronger.

6. A number of specific changes are occurring in U.S. families: there is more racial and ethnic diversity; membership is more varied than that of the traditional nuclear family; and there are more single-parent families, stepfamilies, and families in which the mother works outside the home.

7. The reasons for changes in the family can

be analyzed on two levels: Micro-level explanations emphasize individual behavior—the choices that people make and the personal and interpersonal factors that influence the choices they make. Macro-level explanations focus on large-scale patterns that characterize society as a whole and that may serve as constraints on individual options. Some constraints are economic factors, technological advance, social movements, and government policies that affect families.

8. Understanding the family requires an appreciation of racial, ethnic, religious, and cultural diversity, both at home and around the world.

KEY TERMS

marriage 2
norm 2
common-law marriage 3
bigamy 3
family 3
palimony 4
fictive kin 4
incest taboo 5
endogamy 5
exogamy 5

socialization 6
family of orientation 7
family of procreation 7
kinship system 7
nuclear family 7
conjugal family 7
extended family 7
consanguine family 7
monogamy 7

polygamy 7
serial monogamy 7
patriarchy 8
matriarchy 8
egalitarian pattern 8
baby boomers 17
household 19
micro-level perspective 21
macro-level perspective 21

ADDITIONAL READING

The following anthologies present information on marriage and family research and on racially and ethnically diverse American families.

MARK HUTTER, ed., *The Family Experience: A Reader in Cultural Diversity* (New York: Macmillan Publishing Company, 1991).

LORNE TEPPERMAN and SUSANNAH J. WILSON, eds., *Next of Kin: An International Reader on Changing Families* (Englewood Cliffs, NJ: Prentice Hall, 1993).

These books address the issue of whether the family is weakening or becoming stronger:

JOYCE BLOCK, *Family Myths: Living Our Roles, Betraying Ourselves* (New York: Simon & Schuster, 1994).

STEPHANIE COONTZ, *The Way We Never Were: American Families and the Nostalgia Trap* (New York: Basic Books, 1992).

EDWARD L. KAIN, *The Myth of Family Decline* (New York: Lexington Books, 1990).

ARLENE SKOLNICK, *Embattled Paradise: The American Family in an Age of Uncertainty* (New York: Basic Books, 1991).

JUDITH STACEY, *Brave New Families: Stories of Domestic Upheaval in Late Twentieth-Century America* (New York: Basic Books, 1990).

BARRIE THORNE with MARILYN YALOM, eds. *Rethinking the Family: Some Feminist Questions* (Boston: Northeastern University Press, 1992).

2

Studying Marriage and the Family

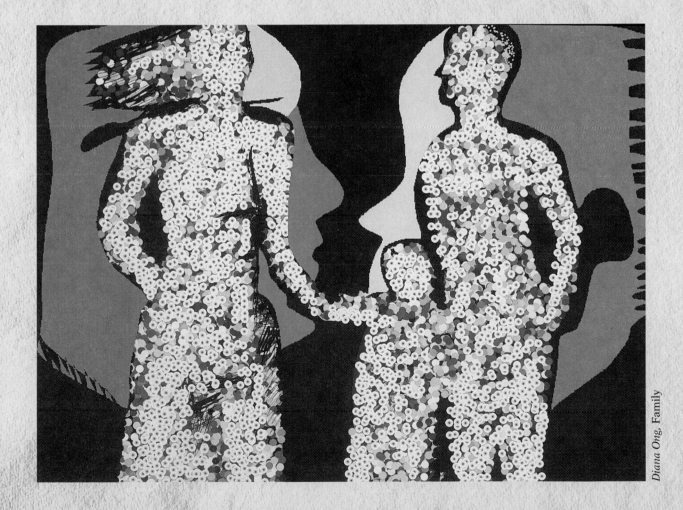

Diana Ong. Family

Data Digest

- Of all marriage and family research studies, **more than 65 percent rely on surveys;** fewer than 5 percent use the observation method.

- **Focus groups can cost more than $3,000** when they involve a group of three to six people working five to six days, but when volunteers participate, these groups can cost next to nothing.

- Face-to-face interviews have a high response rate (up to 99 percent), but they are also expensive. A **typical interview can cost about $50 an hour,** including training, pretesting, transportation, wages, and follow-up interviews.

- U.S. newspapers and magazines initiated the readership poll in 1824. Elmo Roper founded one of the oldest independent public opinion polls in 1933, and three years later, in the presidential election, **opinion polls established a national reputation for scientific sampling** when Roper, George Gallup, and Archibald Crossley correctly predicted a Roosevelt landslide.

- **People are less trusting of some types of surveys** than of others. In a recent study, 81 percent of respondents were willing to rely on scientific studies that describe the causes of disease, 63 percent said they believed consumer survey reports of how many people like a particular product, but only 54 percent said they trusted the results of general public opinion polls.

SOURCES: Nye, 1988; Crossen, 1994; Krueger, 1994.

The *New York Times* and CBS News conducted a national telephone poll of 1,055 teenagers aged 13 to 17 about gender roles. Describing the results as a "battle of the sexes," the reporter commented that a majority of the boys surveyed said that most of the boys they knew considered themselves better than girls, whereas most of the girls surveyed said the girls they knew saw boys as equals. Here are the questions that elicited these responses (Lewin, 1994, emphasis added):

Do most girls you know think of boys as:

    [ ] Equals
    [ ] *Better than themselves*
    [ ] Don't know

Do most boys you know think of girls as

    [ ] Equals
    [ ] *Lesser than themselves*
    [ ] Don't know

Do you see any problem with these questions? Did you notice, for example, that asking girls if boys are *better* than girls and asking boys if girls are *lesser* than boys biases the answers that will be given? In effect, although perhaps unintentionally, this phrasing enhanced the likelihood that the respondents would give the answers they did.

Research is never flawless, but scholarly publications are usually "refereed"—that is, peers review the research before it is published. In contrast, the mass media are relatively immune to criticism, even when their reports are biased, simplistic, or wrong (Gans, 1979). As a result, many people who rely only on the media for information often get a very skewed picture of marriages and families, as well as of other aspects of life.

This chapter, written as nontechnically as possible, will help you evaluate the enormous amount of information you encounter on a daily basis. We begin with a discussion of why a basic understanding of family theory and research is important.

WHY ARE THEORIES AND RESEARCH IMPORTANT IN OUR EVERYDAY LIVES?

Many students shudder at the thought of reading about theory and research, especially in elective courses. This is not surprising because the very words *theory* and *research* often intimidate people. First of all, many people distrust numbers; statistics challenge comfortable beliefs. Moreover, because of the amounts of data that we are expected to absorb every day—data that are sometimes contradictory—we are not sure whom or what to believe. Nevertheless, there are two very practical reasons why theory and research are important to us: they can help us understand ourselves and our families, and they can make us better informed "consumers" as we make changes in our own marriages and families or in our beliefs about these social institutions.

Understanding Our Family Life

Many aspects of our everyday family lives can be explained by theoretical perspectives or research. For example, does spanking correct bad behavior? Suppose at a family barbecue a 2-year-old throws a temper tantrum. An adult comments, "What that kid needs is a good smack on the behind." Another person immediately disagrees: "All kids go through this stage. Just ignore it." Who's right? In fact, empirical data show that neither ignoring a problem nor inflicting physical punishment stops misbehavior (see Chapter 12).

Being an Informed Consumer

In *Overcoming Math Anxiety*, Tobias (1978: 25) states that many people are afraid not only of numbers but of "all manner of data." Yet our world is becoming more quantitative; it is rare to pick up a magazine or newspaper and not see numbers that affect some aspect of our lives. Medical researchers numb us with the probabilities of dying earlier than expected because of our genetic inheritance, lifestyle, or environment. We are inundated with information on the importance of exercising, lowering cholesterol levels, and not smoking. We hear terrifying statistics about the likelihood of our being mugged, robbed, raped, becoming divorced, or having our children abused by a caretaker, relative, or family member.

Some of the information we get is sound, but some is biased or generated by unlicensed, self-proclaimed "experts" who know less about family life than you do. As the box "Popular Magazines and Self-Help Books: Let the Reader Beware" shows, one of the best ways to protect yourself from quacks, charlatans, and con artists is to be informed. This chapter will not transform you into a social scientist on the spot, but it will help you ask some of the right questions. In order to learn how not to construct questionnaires like the one with which we opened this chapter and how reputable and useful social research is performed, you need to understand something about the most influential theories of marriage and the family that guide social science investigation.

FRAMEWORKS FOR STUDYING FAMILIES

A **theory** is a set of logically related statements that try to explain why a phenomenon occurs. A theory enables us to propose specific topics for study, and it also helps us to analyze the findings of our research. As you saw in Chapter 1, however, analyses of a particular phenomenon or series of events may address different aspects of a problem. For example, micro analysts, who examine everyday social interaction in specific settings, might explain teenage runaways as victims of interpersonal family problems; macro analysts might consider how the economy creates family problems that encourage adolescents to leave home.

In this chapter we look briefly at six of the most influential theoretical approaches to the study of marriage and the family: two macro-level theories (structural-functional and conflict theories) and four micro-level theories (symbolic interaction, social exchange, developmental, and general systems theories) (see Figure 2.1). Although in examining any marriage and family topic, researchers typically use more than one theory to explain a given phenomenon or set of events, and although, as you will see, the theories do overlap, for the sake of clarity we'll look at each perspective separately.

Structural-Functional Theory

Structural-functional theory examines the relationship between the family and the larger society, as well as the internal relationships among family members. When sociologists study how the family is structured, they examine how the parts work together in fulfilling the functions or tasks necessary for the family's survival.

As we discussed in Chapter 1, two of the major functions of the family are to socialize children and to place family members into acceptable adult social roles. From the functionalist perspective, these tasks are best accomplished when spouses or partners carry out distinct and specialized roles—one called *instrumental*, the other *expressive* (Parsons and Bales, 1955). According to this view, the **instrumental role** is held by the husband and/or father, the "breadwinner." Playing the instrumental role means providing food and shelter for the family and, at least theoretically, being hardworking, tough, and competitive. Assuming the **expressive role**,

Popular Magazines and Self-Help Books: Let the Reader Beware

People who write self-help books are extremely well-adjusted folks, on a first-name basis with all their feelings, free of phobias and anxieties, and bursting with self-esteem. Right? Wrong, says an editor of a company that specializes in publishing self-help psychology books. For example, two authors of a volume on stress are on the verge of suing each other, a best-selling book on phobias lacks the author's photo because the author has a phobia about having his picture taken, and many manuscripts come from people claiming that the words were dictated to them by God (Quick, 1992).

A major weakness of many self-help books and articles in popular magazines is that they are based on personal opinion and experience rather than scholarly research. Rosenblatt and Phillips (1975) argue that although the single best thing about these magazine articles is that most of them encourage people to believe that they can change their lives, they also "violate commonly accepted standards of scholarship." This can lead to four serious problems:

1. *Threats to relationships*. Many articles encourage the reader to make new demands on a spouse or on children. Although this kind of assertiveness may be important in improving an individual's life, making such changes unilaterally may increase conflict in the family.

2. *Feelings of inadequacy*. Many popular writers tie a person's feelings of adequacy to his or her relationships with family members. This ignores the satisfaction and self-confidence that can be acquired from work, friendships, participation in organizations, and solitary pursuits.

3. *Oversimplification of problems*. Many popular writers gloss over complex factors in family relationships. For example, in pointing out that a reduction in sexual activity can lead to depression, they may ignore the fact that depression can be caused by many other factors, such as menopause and "the change of life" (Chapter 7); the birth of a new baby (Chapter 11); poverty, unemployment, and broken homes (Chapters 14 and 15); or bereavement (Chapter 18).

4. *Irresponsible recommendation of professional help*. Many Americans not only find the idea of seeking professional help frightening but are ill-equipped to evaluate the qualifications of potential counselors or therapists. Writers who simply recommend that people seek help without providing guidelines for distinguishing between high-quality and low-quality professionals do the public a great disservice.

Readers of popular articles and books about the family should ask themselves the following basic questions:

❏ Does the writer document assertions?

❏ Does the writer cite research and/or clinical experience or only anecdotal material as sources? If the writer cites himself or herself, are the references scholarly or anecdotal?

❏ Does the book or article describe only a few families with problems but then generalize the findings to all families?

❏ Does the writer make it sound as though the world is exceedingly simple and easy to understand?

---

the wife and/or mother is the homemaker. Theoretically, playing the expressive role means providing the emotional support and nurturing qualities that sustain the family unit and support the husband/father. The homemaker does the housework, cares for the children, and bolsters the husband's/father's ego by listening, encouraging, and supporting his efforts whenever possible. Not surprisingly, these family roles characterize what social scientists refer to as the *traditional family*.

These and other roles that family members may play are functional; that is, they are created to promote the smooth functioning of the family—to preserve order, stability, and equilibrium and to provide the physical shelter and emotional support that can ensure the health and survival of family members. Anything that interferes with these tasks of the family is seen as dysfunctional because it jeopardizes this smooth functioning of the group. For example, the physical abuse of one member by another is dysfunc-

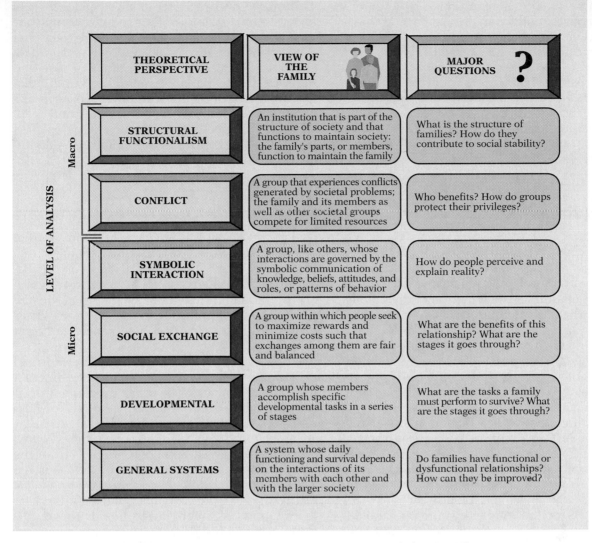

THEORETICAL PERSPECTIVE	VIEW OF THE FAMILY	MAJOR QUESTIONS
STRUCTURAL FUNCTIONALISM *(Macro)*	An institution that is part of the structure of society and that functions to maintain society: the family's parts, or members, function to maintain the family	What is the structure of families? How do they contribute to social stability?
CONFLICT *(Macro)*	A group that experiences conflicts generated by societal problems; the family and its members as well as other societal groups compete for limited resources	Who benefits? How do groups protect their privileges?
SYMBOLIC INTERACTION *(Micro)*	A group, like others, whose interactions are governed by the symbolic communication of knowledge, beliefs, attitudes, and roles, or patterns of behavior	How do people perceive and explain reality?
SOCIAL EXCHANGE *(Micro)*	A group within which people seek to maximize rewards and minimize costs such that exchanges among them are fair and balanced	What are the benefits of this relationship? What are the stages it goes through?
DEVELOPMENTAL *(Micro)*	A group whose members accomplish specific developmental tasks in a series of stages	What are the tasks a family must perform to survive? What are the stages it goes through?
GENERAL SYSTEMS *(Micro)*	A system whose daily functioning and survival depends on the interactions of its members with each other and with the larger society	Do families have functional or dysfunctional relationships? How can they be improved?

LEVEL OF ANALYSIS

Figure 2.1   Major Theoretical Perspectives on Marriage and the Family

tional because the negative physical and emotional consequences threaten the family's survival and its ability to function.

There are two kinds of functions. **Manifest functions** are intended and recognized; that is, they are present in a clearly evident way. **Latent functions** are unintended and unrecognized; they are present but are not immediately obvious. Consider the marriage ceremony. The primary manifest function of the marriage ceremony is to publicize the formation of a new family unit and to legitimize sexual intercourse. Its latent functions include the implicit communication of a "hands-off" message to past or future suitors, the outfitting of the new couple with household goods and products, and the re-

definition of family boundaries to include in-laws or stepfamily members.

Finally, structural functionalists note that the family is just one institution among others that functions to maintain society. The family affects and is affected by such other major institutions as religion, government, and the economy. As you saw in Chapter 1, for example, most families depend on the government for financial assistance or education payments.

Critique Structural functionalism has come under attack for being so conservative in its emphasis on order and stability that it ignores social change. For example, this perspective typically sees high divorce rates as dysfunctional and as signaling the disintegration of the family rather than as indicators of change (perhaps people leaving an unhappy situation). Nor does this perspective show how families interact on a daily basis, "up close and personal." Structural functionalism has also been criticized for seeing the family narrowly, through white, male, middle-class lenses (Andersen, 1993). And some feel that structural-functionalist terms like "equilibrium" are unclear and difficult to measure (McIntyre, 1981).

Conflict Theory

Although the conflict perspective has a long history, it became popular during the late 1960s when African Americans and feminists started to challenge structural functionalism as the dominant explanation of marriage and the family. **Conflict theory** examines the ways in which groups disagree and struggle over power and compete for scarce resources (such as wealth and prestige). In contrast to structural functionalists, conflict theorists see conflict and the resulting changes in traditional roles as natural, inevitable, and often desirable.

According to conflict theory, many family difficulties are the result of widespread societal problems. For example, shifts in the U.S. economy that led to a decline in manufacturing and an increase in the service professions have resulted in the loss of many blue-collar jobs. This has had a profound influence on many families, sending some into a spiral of downward mobility. Racial discrimination has a negative impact on many families, affecting such crucial factors as access to health services, education, and employment. And, as you will see in Chapter 15, many researchers argue that it is society's acceptance of male dominance over women and children that has made the family one of the major settings for violence in our culture.

Conflict theorists see society not as cooperative and stable but as a system of inequality in which groups compete for scarce goods and services. Thus, these theorists see a continuous tension between the "haves" and the "have-nots," the latter mainly children, women, people of color, the elderly, and the poor. Much research based on conflict theory focuses on how those in power—typically white, middle-aged, wealthy, Protestant, Anglo-Saxon males—dominate political and economic decision making in American society.

Critique Conflict theorists have been criticized for overemphasizing conflict and coercion at the expense of order and stability. Some feel that conflict theory presents a harsh view of human nature and neglects the importance of love and self-sacrifice, which are essential to family relationships. Because it examines institutional rather than personal opportunities and constraints, this perspective is sometimes seen as less useful than others in explaining everyday individual behavior.

Symbolic Interaction Theory

Unlike the structural-functionalist and conflict theories, **symbolic interaction theory** is a micro-level theory that looks at the everyday behavior of individuals. It can be defined as a theory of human interaction as governed by the symbolic communication of knowledge, ideas, beliefs, and attitudes and how people interpret situations.

This theory looks at subjective, interpersonal meanings and at the ways in which we interact with and influence each other by communicating through *symbols*—words, gestures, or pictures that stand for something. If we are to interact effectively, our symbols must have *shared meanings*, or agreed-upon definitions. One of the most important of these shared meanings is the *definition of the situation*, or the way we perceive reality and react to it. We learn our definitions of the situation through interaction with **significant others**—people who play an important emotional role in our socialization, such as parents, friends, relatives, and teachers.

According to symbolic interaction theory, each family member has one or more **roles**—patterns of behavior attached to a particular *status*, or position, in society. For example, a man may be a husband, father, grandfather, brother, son, uncle, and so on. Roles call for different behaviors both within and outside the family, and people modify and adjust their roles as they interact with other role players. For example, a woman's interactions with her husband will be different from her interactions with her children. And she will interact still differently when she is teaching a class of students, talking to a colleague in the hall, or addressing a professional conference.

Dating is an example of symbolic interaction. Typically, in the 1960s, everyone "knew" what dating was; in other words, family members, friends, and relatives all shared the same definition of the situation. The boy called the girl at least a week in advance, he had suggestions for the date (a movie, usually), he arrived on time, he chatted with the girl's parents while waiting for his date to appear, she was fashionably late, both were dressed in their best clothes, he had a car, he paid for the date, she repaid him by being attentive, he got her home by curfew, she invited him in for a soft drink, they chatted and/or flirted for a while, and he left. This traditional dating pattern was sometimes violated, but not too often—at least not among the working and middle classes.

Dating and the role behaviors it encompasses have changed since the 1960s, and parents and teenagers no longer share the same definition of the situation. As you will see in Chapter 6, many parents today complain that they do not understand their children's casual dating behavior and informal dress codes; many adolescents accuse their parents of being unreasonable or old-fashioned in expecting to meet their dates or being given an outline of the evening's agenda.

Critique One of the most common criticisms of symbolic interaction theory is that because it emphasizes micro relationships, it ignores the impact on family relationships of larger social factors such as economic forces and racial discrimination. For example, many macro-level rules limit dating choices to particular racial, religious, age, or social-class groups (see Chapter 1).

Although there has been more research on father–child bonds in recent years (see Chapter 12), some authors feel that symbolic interactionists focus on only a few family relationships, particularly husband–wife or mother–child interactions (Schvaneveldt, 1981). And finally, because symbolic interactionists often study only white, middle-class families—the most likely to cooperate in research—the findings of their studies are rarely representative of racial-ethnic and other socioeconomic groups (Winton, 1995).

Social Exchange Theory

The fundamental premise of **social exchange theory** is that any social interaction between two people is based on the efforts of each person to maximize rewards and minimize costs. As a result, individuals will continue in a relationship only as long as it is perceived as more rewarding than costly (see Figure 2.2). People bring to the relationships certain resources—some tangible, some intangible—such as energy, money, material goods, status, intelligence, good looks, youth, power, talent, fame, or affection. According to this theory, these resources can be "traded" for more, better, or different resources that another person possesses. And as long as costs are equal to or lower than benefits, these exchanges will be seen as fair or balanced.

From the social exchange perspective, it is when the costs outweigh the rewards that most marriages lead to separation or divorce. One or both partners feel that they're not getting anything out of the relationship. On the other hand, many people stay in unhappy marriages because the rewards seem equal to the costs: "It's better

Figure 2.2   Dating Trade-offs

According to the children of J. Seward Johnson, the Johnson & Johnson heir who died in 1979, their father's December-May marriage was clearly an exchange of money for beauty, and they contested the will that left his entire $500 million fortune to his young wife, Barbara.

than being alone"; "I don't want to hurt the kids"; "It could be worse." Although some of our cost–reward decisions are conscious, others are not. For example, some people stay in abusive situations because they feel they have nothing to gain by leaving. This is especially true of those (often women) who have been socialized to believe that they have no bartering chips ("You'll be lucky if anyone marries you," "You're dumb," "You're ugly," and so on).

Think about all the people you talked to yesterday. How many interactions can you recall that were not based on cost–reward considerations? Probably very few. What about the last date you had? Do you plan to see her or him again? Why or why not?

Critique Exchange theorists have been accused of giving too much weight to rational behavior. People do not always logically and carefully calculate the potential cost and reward of every decision. For example, Linda, one of my

students, spent every Saturday, the only day she wasn't working or in class, driving from Baltimore to Philadelphia to visit a grandmother who was showing early symptoms of Alzheimer's disease. Linda's mother and several nurse's aides were giving the grandmother, who often didn't recognize Linda, good care. Nonetheless, Linda gave up her "dating evening" because "I just want to make sure Grandma is OK."

Exchange theory also implies that each exchange is evaluated and made on a fairly short-term basis. Many groups, however, share cultural values that sanction continuous, long-term costs in the interest of achieving long-term goals such as social advancement. The Chinese mothers in the film *The Joy Luck Club* had endured a lifetime of sacrifices in unhappy and unfulfilling relationships in the hope that their daughters would have better lives. Even when some of the daughters disappointed their parents, the mothers continued to love and support them.

Developmental Theories

In a third micro-level perspective, **developmental theories** examine the many ways in which families journey through time in the **family life cycle**—a series of stages, each of which focuses on different sets of events that a family goes through from the early days of marriage to the death of one or both partners. As family members progress through the life cycle, they accomplish **developmental tasks**; that is, they learn to fulfill role expectations and responsibilities such as showing affection and support for family members and socializing with others outside the family.

"The better equipped a family is for each of its members to meet developmental tasks and the more closely the family accomplishes its group tasks, the more successful is the development of the family" (Rowe, 1981: 199). For example, in the film *What's Eating Gilbert Grape*, an obese mother is unable to perform such parental tasks as preparing birthday parties for her children, cooking, cleaning, and shopping because she can barely move around the house. As a result, Gilbert and his two sisters take on these and other responsibilities. Instead of dating and socializing, which are normal developmental tasks during adolescence, Gilbert parents his younger brother, and all three older children run the household. Only after the mother dies are the children "freed" to live their own lives.

Among the several variations of the family life cycle that have been proposed, one of the earliest and best known is Duvall's (1957). According to classic developmental theory like Duvall's, the family life cycle begins with marriage and continues through having and raising children, seeing the children leave home, retirement, to the death of one or both spouses (see Table 2.1). According to such classic developmental theories, the nuclear family is a semi-closed social system. In the earliest stages, individuals learn reciprocal roles within the family; as children grow and begin to interact with outsiders, they learn reciprocal roles that are external to the family unit, as in school, church, or play groups. Thus, they acquire the developmental tasks that enable them to survive (and thrive) in a society. For example, most preschool programs teach young children to share their toys, take turns in playing games, and deal with anger. These skills of cooperation, waiting, and self-control will be critical in getting along with people in the future.

Over time, developmental theories have become more sophisticated. Theorists acknowledge, for example, that developmental stages and tasks vary in different kinds of families, such as single-parent families, childless couples, and grandparent–child families. Also, the complex situations and problems that confront families in an aging society are multigenerational and interactive rather than one-generational and linear (Jerrome, 1994). For example, if an elderly parent becomes ill, adult family members may have to learn new developmental tasks such as caregiving, at the same time that they struggle to meet competing needs of spouses or children. As

we will see in Chapter 18, a "sandwich generation" is typically made up of middle-aged women who expend enormous energy and resources in providing for both younger and older generations (McCaslin, 1993).

Finally, the nature of the family life cycle may differ greatly among poor, racial-ethnic, and white, middle-class families. As the box "Kinscripts: Ensuring Family Survival in Tough Situations" shows, to keep their members together throughout the life cycle, poor families must be more creative than most.

Critique Developmental theories have generated a great deal of research, especially on the internal dynamics of marital and family communication and interaction. Critics, however, point out several limitations. First, some feel that the stages are artificial because "the processes of life are not always so neatly and cleanly segmented" (Winton, 1995: 39). Second, despite the recent work on kinscripts, there is still some validity in earlier criticisms (e.g., Hohn, 1987) that because developmental theories are generally restricted to nuclear and stable families, they neglect families that take other forms. Third, there is increasing concern about the exclusion of gay and lesbian families from family life cycle theory (Laird, 1993). Accomplishing developmental tasks may be especially difficult in gay and lesbian families because the viability of such families is continually challenged. If the relationship is secret or if it is ignored or denied by other family members, there may be persistent stress. And, unlike many heterosexual couples, homosexual partners seldom enjoy the rootedness of a multigenerational family (Slater and Mencher, 1991). Fourth, some question why life cycle theories ignore sibling relationships, which are among the most important emotional resources we have throughout life and especially after the last parent dies (McGoldrick, 1993). Finally, developmental theories are not very useful in comparing family life cycles across historical periods or different cultures (White, 1991).

General Systems Theory

General systems theory views the family as a system, a functioning unit whose daily operations and survival depend on the interactions of its members with each other and with larger social groups. Whereas a symbolic interactionist would examine how interactions crisscross a

Table 2.1 _____

The Classic Portrayal of the Family Life Cycle

Does this model illustrate your family of orientation? What about your family of procreation? If not, how have the stages been different?

Stage 1	Couple without children
Stage 2	Oldest child less than 30 months old
Stage 3	Oldest child between $2\frac{1}{2}$ and 6 years old
Stage 4	Oldest child between 6 and 13 years old
Stage 5	Oldest child between 13 and 20 years old
Stage 6	Period starting when first child leaves family until the youngest leaves
Stage 7	Empty nest to retirement
Stage 8	Retirement to death of one or both spouses

Rebecca Anderson, 54 years old and battling lupus, became a mother again when she took in five nieces and nephews whose three different sets of parents could not care for them. Anderson's husband, Alton, who does not live with her, helps with the children occasionally but provides no financial support.

Kinscripts: Ensuring Family Survival in Tough Situations

Family life cycle patterns differ markedly in terms of needs, resources, gender roles, migration patterns, education, and attitudes toward family and aging (McGoldrick et al., 1993). Studying low-income African American families, Burton and Stack (1993) have proposed the concept of the *kinscript* to explain the life courses of many multigenerational families. The kinscript arises in response to both extreme economic need and intense commitment by family members to the survival of future generations, and it requires family interaction in three domains: kin-work, kin-time, and kin-scription.

Kin-work is the collective labor that families must accomplish to endure over time. It includes family help during childbirth, intergenerational care for children or dependents, and support for other relatives. For example, a 76-year-old widower parented three preschool children after their mother started "running the streets":

There ain't no other way. I have to raise these babies, else the service people will take 'em away. This is my family. Family has to take care of family else we won't be no more (Burton and Stack, 1993: 105).

Kin-time is the shared understanding among family members of when and in what sequence kin-work should be performed. Kin-time provides for learning developmental tasks during such transitions as marriage, childbearing, and grandparenthood and includes temporal guides for assuming family leadership roles and caregiving responsibilities. A woman receiving assistance from her mother and other female kin describes the complex but cooperative pattern that characterizes the care of her child:

Well, on the days Damen has school, my mother picks him up at night and keeps him at her home. And then when she goes to work in the morning, she takes him to my grandmother's house. And when my little sister gets out of school, she picks him up and takes him back to my mother's house. And then I go and pick him up (Jarrett, 1994: 41–42).

Kin-scription is the process by which kin-work is assigned to specific family members, most often women and children. Women often find it difficult to refuse kin demands. One woman, who had lost her first love 14 years earlier at the age of 21, provides an example of the interplay of family power, kin-scription, and the role of women:

When Charlie died, it seemed like everyone said, since she's not getting married, we have to keep her busy. Before I knew it, I was raising kids, giving home to long-lost kin, and even helping the friends of my mother. Between doing all of this, I didn't have time to find another man (Burton and Stack, 1993: 107).

Many people believe that poor families or those on welfare are doomed to pass this dependency down from generation to generation (Hill, 1993). As the kinscript framework suggests, however, many low-income, multi-generational families have well-defined family scripts that enable family members to survive by depending on kin rather than on public assistance.

family (who talks to whom during dinner), a general systems theorist would focus on subsystems within the family (husband–wife, parent–child, or sibling relationships). As the boundaries of the family change—through birth, death, or entry into the labor force, for example—the focus of the analysis may shift from individuals to groups, organizations, even to entire societies. The diversity of the systems approach can be seen in the subject areas it explores, which include the way family patterns evolve, how individual dispositions affect family members, and the interplay of needs, feelings, and thoughts (Rosenblatt, 1994).

You may have noticed that the systems approach is compatible with symbolic interaction theory. In fact, those who rely on symbolic interaction—clinicians, counselors, and social workers—often use systems theory in examining patterns of interaction among family members. They study the way spouses and children relate to each other, and they consider which interaction patterns are most destructive in interpersonal relations and how family members can be taught to change everyday behavior. Systems theory posits that family units have particular boundaries that must be maintained. The family may become dysfunctional if boundaries are blurred as, for example, if a wife receives no affection from her husband and looks for it in her son. The family's goal is to remain intact and stable so that it can adapt and maintain itself over the life course.

Critique Some critics have argued that general systems theory has generated a lot of terminology but little insight into how the family functions (Holman and Burr, 1980; Nye and Berardo 1981). Because the theory originated in the study of dysfunctional families in clinical settings, some question whether its ideas can be applied to healthy families.

Although we've discussed the six major theories of marriage and the family separately, in interpreting data or deciding on intervention strategies, researchers and clinicians often combine several of these perspectives with each other or with one or more of a variety of other theoretical approaches. For example, a counselor attempting to help a couple having marital problems might draw on social exchange, symbolic interaction, and systems theories.

You've now had an introduction to some of the most influential theoretical perspectives that guide researchers and practitioners in their work. We turn next to a consideration of the ways people collect information about marriages and families.

METHODS AND TECHNIQUES IN SOCIAL SCIENCE RESEARCH

Probably the first systematic collection of data about the family was compiled by the French social scientist Frederick LePlay. LePlay's detailed analyses of the family budgets of 36 working-class families, published in 1855, led eventually to the "minimum standard of living" concept that welfare agencies still use to determine a family's economic needs (Broderick, 1988). Since LePlay's time, data on marriages and families have come from five major sources: survey research and focus groups; clinical research and case studies; observation; secondary analysis; and evaluation research. To understand these different strategies for gathering data, you should first become familiar with the notions of concept, variable, reliability, validity, and time frames.

Concepts and Variables

A **concept** is a word or set of words that expresses an abstract idea about some aspect of the world. All of us use hundreds of concepts everyday—family, love, responsibility, and so on. A **variable** is something that varies that we may wish to measure or evaluate—a quality or quantity that changes over situations or time. Consider the concept of race, an important variable in the social sciences. As the box "'Race and Ethnicity'—Don't Box Me In" shows, although people who fill out forms of one kind or another are often distressed by having to check boxes that don't fit them, there are some practical economic and political advantages in racial-ethnic categorizations.

Reliability and Validity

Besides deciding which variables will measure a concept best, researchers are always concerned about increasing reliability and validity. **Reliability** is the consistency with which a research instrument produces the same results repeatedly, whether it is administered to different individuals at one time or to the same individuals over a period of time. For example suppose you

"Race and Ethnicity"– Don't Box Me In

Are you ever offended by a questionnaire that asks you to check a box indicating your race or ethnicity? Your college or university has probably asked you to identify yourself in terms of race more than once. And it has probably offered you multiple-choice categories to choose from. Unfortunately, the standard categories today—African American, Asian, Hispanic, Native American, white, and "other" don't suit a lot of people. And there are a number of reasons for the growing discomfort:

❑ *"I don't fit anywhere"* Students with roots in Caribbean nations such as Haiti or Santo Domingo are not African American and are reluctant to call themselves black because they identify with their national and ethnic heritage, not race. A student from Portugal will not want to check Hispanic; a student born and raised in Texas will look

for a Mexican American rather than a Hispanic category.

❑ *"I'm not sure"* Students from countries such as Armenia and India often fluctuate between checking white or "other" because they don't feel they belong in either group. And what box would you check if you were a native of the Bahamas? Or if you were a black Canadian?

❑ *"What if I fit into several categories?"* If you're biracial (African American and white, for example), should you check African American, white, or "other"? And what if you're multiracial? Should you check "other" or all the relevant categories provided as well as "other"?

Nearly 2 million children, or more than 4 percent of all U.S. children, are multiracial, yet during the 1990 census their families were forced to describe them as "white," "black," or "other" instead of claiming inheritance from all branches of their families.

Why should colleges and towns or cities care whether people in their communities identify themselves by race or ethnic group and in what way? Because government grants to educational institutions often depend on having a specified proportion of students in a certain racial or ethnic group. Because funding for such intercollegiate organizations as the Hispanic Student Association depends on the same kind of data. And because, among the general public on both state and local levels, ethnic information is used to enforce fair voting, housing, and credit laws and to monitor school desegregation, support minority-owned businesses, and compile health statistics. Thus, if a census undercounts, say, African Americans or Latinos, these groups could lose political representatives in their districts (*Baltimore Sun*, 1994a; Shea, 1994; Worthington, 1994).

---

ask couples "How long have you been married?" If a wife says 15 years and a husband says 13 years, the question you are asking is not producing a reliable, or consistent, response. You might find that asking couples "When did you get married?" will yield more reliable answers.

Validity is the accuracy of a research instrument; it is an assessment of whether the instrument actually measures what it is supposed to measure. Suppose you ask people, "How many children do you have?" You may assume that the respondent is giving you the number of children in the family now. However, the respondent may be including children who were stillborn or who died at a young age. Your results will not be valid because you are asking about the number of living children, whereas the respondent is including children who are dead but who are still considered part of the family.

Time Frames

Most empirical studies of the family are either cross sectional or longitudinal. **Cross-sectional research** collects data on different individuals or groups at a single point in time. In contrast, **longitudinal research** collects data at different points in time. Suppose you want to find out if your fellow students believe that date rape is a problem on your campus. If you were conducting a cross-sectional study, you might survey 10 percent of all the students during, say, the month of October 1996. In contrast, if you were interested in finding out whether students' beliefs on this issue were changing, you would survey groups of students more than once, say, in October 1996, 1997, and 1998. This would be a longitudinal study. (Longitudinal studies also differentiate between sampling the same or dif-

© Benita Epstein, 1994.

ferent students. You can learn more about this complex issue in a research methods course.)

Because they provide data on social change, longitudinal studies are generally considered more informative than cross-sectional studies. However, longitudinal studies also present a number of problems: they are expensive and time-consuming; researchers sometimes lose interest in a project, move to different institutions, or die; and the strategies for longitudinal data analysis are fairly complex. As a result, in marriage and family research and in most other research, cross-sectional studies are more common than longitudinal studies.

Survey Research and Focus Groups

In **survey research,** researchers systematically collect data from respondents either by questionnaire or in some form of interactive interview. Ideally, they would like to study all the units or elements of the population in which they are interested—say, all college students who abstain from sexual intercourse. A **population** is any well-defined group of people about whom we want to know something specific. For several reasons, however, obtaining information from populations is problematic. Privacy acts may prevent us from identifying the population, for example, or the population may be so large that it would be too expensive and time consuming to conduct the research.

Researchers, therefore, typically draw a **sample**, a group of people (or things) that are repre-

sentative of the population they wish to study. In drawing a sample, researchers must decide whether to use probability or nonprobability sampling. In a *probability* sample, each person (or thing) has an equal chance of being selected because the selection is random. In a *nonprobability* sample, researchers use other criteria such as convenience or the availability of respondents. Nonprobability samples are easier to compile, but because the units are not drawn randomly, they may not be representative of the larger population and thus the findings of the study cannot be generalized to a larger population.

Questionnaires and Interviews Survey data are collected using questionnaires, face-to-face or telephone interviews, or a combination of these techniques. Questionnaires can be mailed, used during an interview, or self-administered. Student course evaluations are good examples of self-administered questionnaires. In interviews, the researcher and the respondent interact directly, either face to face or by telephone. The latter approach is becoming increasingly popular because it is a relatively inexpensive way to collect data. Representative samples can be obtained through *random-digit dialing*, which involves selecting area codes and exchanges followed by four random digits. In the procedure called *computer assisted telephone interviewing (CATI)*, the interviewer uses a computer to select random telephone numbers and then types the respondents' replies into the computer.

Focus Groups In recent years, researchers have been using focus groups to explore issues before they engage in a large survey project (Morgan, 1993; Krueger, 1994). Usually 6 to 12 members of a **focus group** participate in a guided discussion of a particular topic. For example, "Do you feel that the child-care facilities at this college/university are adequate or inadequate?" Although a focus group can become a relatively unstructured bull session, it often provides important information. For example, a focus group may help to establish or change institutional regulations, such as rules for prosecuting date rape on campus, or it may facilitate interaction among people who are working together on a project, such as company supervisors who are considering implementing flex-time policies for parents.

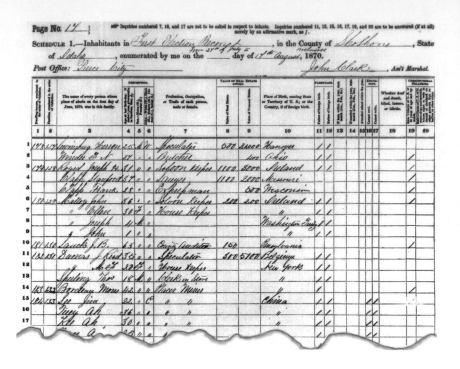

Modern census taking is often difficult and time consuming, but in 1870, when this Pierce City, Idaho, census was recorded, it may have been even more difficult to count heads. Miners, ranchers and their cooks, and even farmers were often out on the land or in the mountains for days and weeks at a time.

Strengths   Surveys are usually inexpensive, simple to administer, and have a fast turn-around rate. With assurance that their answers will remain anonymous, respondents are generally willing to answer questions on such sensitive topics as income, sexual behavior, and the use of drugs.

Face-to-face interviews have high response rates compared to other data-collection techniques (see Data Digest). Interviewers can also record the respondent's body language, facial expressions, and intonations, which can sometimes be as useful as the verbal response. Moreover, if a respondent does not understand a question or is reluctant to answer, the interviewer can clarify, probe, or keep the respondent from digressing. An astute interviewer can also gather information on such variables as social class by observing the respondent's home and neighborhood.

Like questionnaires, telephone surveys are relatively inexpensive, and they provide a quick means of gathering information. Telephone interviews provide a nearly unlimited pool of respondents (more than 98 percent of all homes have at least one telephone), and they often elicit more honest responses on sensitive issues than could be obtained in a face-to-face interview. Respondents are less likely to be affected by interviewer bias in this type of survey, and researchers have more control over interviewer procedures.

Weaknesses   One of the main weaknesses of surveys that use mailed questionnaires is a low response rate, often under 50 percent. If the questions are unclear or complicated, a respondent may simply throw the questionnaire away. Moreover, those who do respond may be very different from those who do not. Some of the least representative surveys are those that tap self-selected respondents, such as readers of particular magazines. Norman Bradburn, of the National Opinion Research Center, has called these surveys SLOPS, for "Self-Selected Opinion Polls" (cited in Tanur, 1994).

Unlike questionnaires and telephone surveys, face-to-face interviewing can be very expensive (see Data Digest). Even trained interviewers sometimes misinterpret answers because of their own prejudices, or they elicit biased responses by their own body language. Men may be less candid with female interviewers than with male interviewers (Herod, 1993; Kane and Macaulay, 1993). And the interview environment itself can affect responses. For example, women may be less willing to admit they have been raped if questioned by interviewers of different racial or ethnic backgrounds or in the presence of family members (Marcus, 1990).

Because people have become oversaturated with marketing research, many use answering machines to screen or avoid all telephone surveys. And if a researcher does succeed in getting through to a respondent, there is great pressure to keep the interview brief; bored or tired respondents may simply hang up before the interview is completed.

Because the survey is the research approach you will encounter most often, it is important that you be an informed consumer. Table 2.2 lists some questions you should ask before believing or citing the results.

Clinical Research and Case Studies

Unlike survey research, which explores large-scale social processes and changes, **clinical research** studies individuals or small groups of people who seek help for both physical and social problems from mental health professionals (Miller and Crabtree, 1994). Many clinical researchers focus on problems in family relationships, intervene in traumatic situations such as marital rape and incest, and try to change dysfunctional system networks such as hostile communication patterns between spouses or suicidal teenagers.

Clinical research is based on the *case-study method*, which is the traditional approach used by social workers, psychologists, clinical sociologists, and marriage counselors. These clinical practitioners work with families on a one-to-one basis using several techniques, including interviews, analysis of records, and direct observation. The written report of this research, the case study itself, provides in-depth information and can generate detailed and vivid descriptions of family life.

Strengths A major strength of clinical research and case studies is that they are typically linked with long-term counseling, which is useful for many individuals or families. Useful intervention strategies can be disseminated fairly quickly to thousands of other practitioners. Also, clinicians often offer insights about family dynamics that can enrich theories such as symbolic interaction or general systems and that can be examined in larger populations through surveys or focus groups.

Weaknesses Clinical and case studies are usually time-consuming and expensive. Because they are based on individuals or small groups of people, the findings are not generalizable to larger populations. Clinicians typically see only people with severe problems or people who are willing and financially able to seek help. Thus, the results are not necessarily applicable to the average person or even to other troubled families.

Observation

In **observation**, researchers collect data by systematically observing people in their natural surroundings. In *participant observation*, researchers interact normally with the people they are studying but do not reveal their identities as researchers. For example, if you quietly examined interaction patterns between the "stars" and the "black sheep" during a family reunion, you would be engaging in participant observation. In *nonparticipant observation*, researchers study phenomena without being part of the situation. For example, child psychologists or sociologists often study how young children play together or how they form play groups through one-way mirrors. (For a discussion of other variations in observation research, see Adler and Adler, 1994.)

In many studies, researchers combine both participant and nonparticipant observation. For example, anthropologist Glenda Roberts (1994) spent two years studying blue-collar women at a large Japanese manufacturing plant that made lingerie and leisure wear. Roberts was interested in exploring the tensions that arose between women who wanted to work until retirement

---

Table 2.2

Can I Trust This Survey?

Surveys are often used in the public opinion polls reported on television and in newspapers. Asking a few basic questions about the survey will help you evaluate its credibility:

Who sponsored the survey? A government agency, a nonprofit partisan organization, a nonprofit nonpartisan organization, or a group that's lobbying for change?

What is the purpose of the survey? To provide objective information, to promote an idea or a political candidate, or to get attention through sensationalism?

How was the sample drawn? Randomly? Or was it a SLOP (see text)?

What was the sample size?

How were the questions worded? Were they clear, objective, loaded, or biased? If the survey questions are not given, why not?

How did the researchers report their findings? Were they objective or did they make value judgments?

Researchers often study child development by observing children in natural settings.

and those who held to the predominant cultural belief that women should work only a few years and spend most of their time raising children and promoting their husbands' careers. Roberts worked on the shop floor with the women, interviewed her co-workers formally and informally, and sent questionnaires to the women asking about their child-care strategies. Placing her own 20-month-old daughter in a child-care center, Roberts learned that the center was critical of professional Japanese women who left their children in child-care centers. Working-class women had no problems, but highly educated women encountered disapproval for placing their careers above their children's welfare because their jobs were not seen as critical for the family's economic survival.

Strengths Studies that use observation often provide a deeper understanding of behavior than "one-shot" data-collection methods because the phenomena are studied over time. Observation is also more flexible than some other methods be-

cause the researcher can modify the research design even after data collection has begun. For example, the researcher can decide to interview (rather than just observe) key people after the research has started. Although costs vary, observation can be done fairly inexpensively. For example, University of Pennsylvania sociologist Elijah Anderson (1990) has been able to study socialization patterns in the poor neighborhoods of Philadelphia for a number of years (Coughlin, 1994). Most important, observation does not disrupt a "natural" situation; thus, the respondents are not influenced by the researcher's presence.

Weaknesses If a researcher needs elaborate recording equipment or must travel far or extensively or live in a different society or community for an extended period of time, observation research can be very expensive. Researchers who study other cultures must often learn a new language, relocate, and adjust to different cultural norms (Freedman, 1986). For example, anthropologist Jean Briggs (1970) spent months living with an isolated Eskimo band in the Arctic before she even learned to communicate with her subjects. It may also be very difficult to balance the role of participant and observer. In a study of black men in a Chicago community, sociologist Mitchell Duneier (1992) found that the men sometimes turned to him for advice or involved him in political discussions about the neighborhood.

It may be very difficult to quantify the observations of such variables as relationships, informal rules, and linguistic nuances. In addition, the researcher may have little control over selecting samples or may face constraints on the kinds of data that can be collected. And if the group being observed is large, the researcher may have to hire and train assistants, whose work must then be supervised and checked. Although sophisticated technology now permits faster, more complete, and more complex coding and recording of information, researchers continue to confront reliability problems. For example, it is difficult to train coders to assess and record information in a consistent manner.

Secondary Analysis

Besides using surveys, clinical/case studies, and observation, researchers rely heavily on secondary analysis. **Secondary analysis** is the analysis of data that have been collected by someone else. Such data may be historical materials (e.g., court proceedings), personal documents (e.g., letters and diaries), public records (e.g., federal information on immigration, state or county archives on births, marriages, and deaths), and official statistics (e.g., Census Bureau publications). As you will see, many of the statistics throughout this textbook rely on such official sources of information as the U.S. Bureau of the Census.

Strengths   In most cases, secondary analysis is accessible, convenient, and inexpensive. Census Bureau information on such topics as marriage, number of children in single-parent families, and divorce is readily available at public and college/university libraries. Also, many academic institutions buy the tapes containing national data, which can then be used for faculty/student research or for class-related projects. Because *secondary data* are often longitudinal, there is the added advantage of examining trends (such as age at first marriage) over time.

Weaknesses   Because secondary data have been collected by someone else, the information may be inadequate to a researcher's purpose. For example, some of the data on remarriages and redivorces have been collected only since the early 1990s. Thus, it is impossible for a researcher to make comparisons over time. Further, as the box "The 1990 Census" illustrates, it is not easy to gather information on individuals who do not want to be counted or who are suspicious of census enumerators. Because historical documents may be fragile, housed in only a few libraries in the country, or part of private collections, it is not always possible to get access to them. Also, if the materials do not reflect exactly what the researcher is looking for, the researcher may have to make concessions and change the direction of the research or ignore variables that she or he wanted to analyze. In addition, materials may be incomplete, or it may be difficult to determine their validity and reliability.

Evaluation Research

An important source of information about marriage and family issues is the growing body of **evaluation research** that assesses the effectiveness of a wide variety of social programs in both the public and private sectors. Many government and nonprofit agencies provide services that affect the family both directly and indirectly; housing programs, programs to prevent or deal with teenage pregnancy, work-training programs, care for infants with AIDS, and drug-rehabilitation programs are examples. Because local and state government budgets have been cut since the early 1980s, service-delivery groups have become increasingly concerned about the effectiveness and efficiency of their programs.

Like clinical research, evaluation research is *applied*; it assesses the efficiency and effectiveness of a specific social program for a specific agency or organization, evaluating that program's achievements in terms of its original goals (Weiss, 1972). The findings of the research are generally used to make decisions that are intended to improve the operations of the program, decisions that affect both the sponsoring agency and the people the program helps.

Strengths and Weaknesses   Evaluation research, which relies on all of the standard methodological techniques described in this section, is both one of the most exciting and frustrating areas of study. It is exciting because it examines actual efforts to deal with problems that confront families. Because no new data need to be collected, the costs are usually low. And the research can be very valuable to those who must manage the program under study. It helps managers keep a program on course because it highlights discrepancies between the original objectives and how the program is actually working (Peterson et al., 1994).

Evaluation research can be frustrating, however, because politics plays an important role. Even though the research is solicited by supervisors, they are not happy if the results show that the program is excluding the most needy group, that the administrators are wasting money, or that caseworkers are making serious mistakes. Also, if staff members have to be trained to change their behavior to meet the program's objectives, the costs may escalate and be outside the agency's budget.

In summary, researchers have to weigh the benefits and limitations of each research approach in designing their studies (see Table 2.3). Often, they use a combination of several strategies in achieving their research objectives.

CONSTRAINTS

The 1990 Census

As the U.S. Census Bureau geared up for its 1990 head count, the utter impossibility of counting everyone in the country became evident. New York City neighborhoods that are notorious for crime and drug dealing were expected to put the bureau to the ultimate test: "It'll be hard to get people to go into partially occupied buildings, into known drug buildings," conceded Earl McGiver, who oversaw the bureau's work in the South Bronx.

The U.S. Census has never been completely accurate. The Census Bureau acknowledges particular difficulty in locating African Americans, who are on average poorer than other people and who thus often live in unconventional families and in unsafe neighborhoods. According to the bureau, census takers in 1960 missed nearly one of every ten children under 5 years of age and nearly two of every ten black men in their 40s. In 1980, the census undercounted by 1.4 percent as a result of double-counting some people and missing far more.

Such omissions have important consequences because census num-bers control the distribution not only of political power—by determining how many congresspersons will be sent to the House of Representatives—but of money. "It costs less than $10 for the Census Bureau to count a person, but that person is worth $150 (in federal funds) to New York," said Peter Coleman, who supervised the city's census activities.

In 1990, it cost about $4 to count a person by mail, but about $30 for each person reached in a face-to-face interview. The homeless, of course, aren't easily reached by mail or any other way, but until a census dress rehearsal was held in St. Louis in 1988, it hadn't occurred to anyone to count people who sleep on the streets or in abandoned buildings. After a canvass of parks and street corners between 2 A.M. and 4 A.M. one day in March, enumerators spent the next two and a half hours standing outside derelict buildings to count squatters as they emerged. After this experiment, the bureau instructed enumerators not to wake up sleeping people. "We were scaring people half to death—both the homeless person and the enumerator," said Cynthia Taueber, a census official in charge of counting the homeless. Thus, enumerators had to guess the age, sex, and race of those they saw asleep.

Census Bureau policy is to hire enumerators to work near their homes. In the South Bronx, therefore, most enumerators were African American or Latino. "If you send a white person into the South Bronx," said Kenny Mitchell, who supervised a team of enumerators, "they'll think he's a cop."

In the end, the success of the census depended on the integrity and ingenuity of individual enumerators. To encourage honesty and limit "curb-stoning"—standing on the curb and faking responses—the Census Bureau reinterviewed randomly selected households and checked out some enumerators' counts that exceeded an area's averages. Despite all these efforts, the 1990 Census missed nearly 10 million people and counted over 4 million people twice. The percentage of blacks missed was six times greater than the percentage of whites, the largest difference since 1940 (Wessel, 1989; *Baltimore Sun*, 1994).

RESEARCH ON AND BY WOMEN AND MINORITIES

The inclusion of women, gay men and lesbians, the elderly, people of color, and other racial-ethnic and often powerless minority groups in sociological research, including marriage and family studies, is a relatively recent phenomenon. In a classic and prize-winning study, *The Negro Family in the United States*, E. Franklin Frazier (1939) identified specific urban social structures that presumably brought about family deterioration among African American families. It was not until the late 1960s that two other prominent African American sociologists, Andrew Billingsley (1968) and Charles Willie (1970), published further analyses of black family life. And in 1971, in an elite and traditionally male-dominated sociological journal, Pauline Bart (1971) argued that women are "metaphorically and literally invisible" in sociological research.

By the late 1970s, a number of research findings were published in articles and books not just about women and minorities but more important, by women, African American, and gay and lesbian scholars. For example, some white women scholars have infused traditional research methods approaches with feminist perspectives that include a broad range of materials by and about women (see, e.g., Reinharz, 1992; Sollie and Leslie, 1994). Others are challenging definitions of poverty that

At the Eliza Shirley House in Philadelphia, a 1990 census taker helped homeless women complete the census forms.

ignore the working mother who pays high costs for child care (Renwick and Bergmann, 1993). Female African American scholars have pushed theories to include the intersections of class, race, and gender (see, e.g., Collins, 1990; Dill, 1994).

Native American, Asian, and Hispanic American scholars are also revising history in "their own words and stories as told in their oral histories, conversations, speeches, soliloquies, and songs, as well as in their own writings—diaries, letters, newspapers, magazines, pamphlets, placards, posters, flyers, court petitions, autobiographies, short stories, novels, and poems" (Takaki, 1989: 7–8). These and other examples of the burgeoning literature on and by women and

minorities inform the rest of this book, helping to challenge and dispel many stereotypes.

What factors have encouraged both the greater participation of women and minorities in research and the inclusion of these groups in more and more studies? Some writers attribute these changes purely to demographic trends. Elder (1984), for example, cites higher divorce rates, the rising number of working mothers, the increased incidence of teenage pregnancy, and the growth in the population of older women. Others have argued that women scholars have made such an impact because they have been able to fill large gaps in our knowledge. For example, historians have pointed out that a study of women's documents has given us a more accurate picture of the American family from the past (Jones, 1985; Fox-Genovese, 1990; Chafe, 1992).

Despite these advances, research on women, children, and people of color is still not a high-priority area. As we saw in Chapter 1, although the United States is one of the richest countries in the world, it ranks below many other industrial countries in child mortality rates, and this high death rate reflects primarily black infant mortality. And despite the fact that taxes paid by women pay for half of all U.S. medical research, the National Institutes of Health (NIH), a major source of funding for health-care research, devotes less than 10 percent of its research funds to women's health problems (see Chapter 4).

The NIH recently issued guidelines requiring scientists to include women and people of color as research subjects in clinical trials. A number of prestigious (white male) scientists argued that

Table 2.3

Five Data-Collection Methods in Family Research

METHOD	STRENGTHS	WEAKNESSES
Survey research/focus groups	Questionnaires are fairly inexpensive and simple to administer; interviews have high response rates; findings are often generalizable	Mailed questionnaires may have low response rates; respondents may be self-selected; interviews may be expensive
Clinical research/case studies	Help subjects with family problems; offer insights for theory development	Usually time-consuming and expensive; not generalizable
Observation	Flexible; offer deeper understanding of family behavior; usually inexpensive	Difficult to quantify and to maintain observer/subject boundaries; reliability problems
Secondary analysis	Usually accessible, convenient, and inexpensive; often longitudinal and historical	Information may be incomplete; some documents may be inaccessible; data may lack validity or reliability
Evaluation research	Usually inexpensive; valuable in real-life applications	Often political; may require training staff members

such guidelines are "ridiculous" because, biologically, women and people of color are "fundamentally" the same as white males (Burd, 1994). If that is true, why, then, have women and people of color typically been excluded as research subjects?

ETHICAL AND POLITICAL ISSUES IN SOCIAL RESEARCH

Social science researchers work in a social context in which they interact daily with individuals and groups of different backgrounds and interests. It is not surprising that they often confront ethical and political dilemmas.

Ethical Concerns

For the most part, research errors are unintentional. They result from ignorance of statistical procedures, simple arithmetic mistakes, or inadequate supervision. These kinds of honest errors are often caught by referees who review academic articles and books before publication or by scholars who evaluate funding requests.

Because so much research relies on human subjects, the federal government and many professional organizations have devised codes of ethics. Common to most of these codes, regardless of the discipline or type of research method used, are several minimal rules for professional conduct; these rules are summarized in the box "The Basic Principles of Ethical Social Research."

As you might imagine, some data-collection methods are more susceptible to ethical violations than others. Surveys are less vulnerable than observation, for example, because in many surveys researchers do not interact directly with subjects, interpret their behavior, or become personally involved with the respondents.

Political Issues

Politicians are particularly distrustful of social science research. Senator William Proxmire became famous for his "Golden Fleece" awards to social research projects, including studies on stress and tension, that he ridiculed as wasting taxpayer money (Neuman, 1994). The legitimacy of social science research becomes especially suspect to political and religious groups when research focuses on sensitive social, moral, and political issues (Stanfield, 1993).

One of the most sensitive research areas is human sexuality. The first widely publicized research on sexuality was carried out by Alfred Kinsey and his colleagues in the late 1940s and

CRITICAL ISSUES

The Basic Principles of Ethical Social Research

❑ All researchers are responsible for the ethical behavior of everyone involved in performing the research they conduct, including themselves.

❑ Researchers must obtain all subjects' consent to participate in the research and their permission to quote from their responses and comments, particularly if the research concerns sensitive issues or if subjects' comments will be quoted extensively.

❑ Researchers may not exploit subjects or research assistants involved in the research for personal gain.

❑ Researchers must never harm, humiliate, abuse, or coerce the participants in their studies, either physically or psychologically. This proscription includes the withholding of medications or other services or programs that might benefit subjects.

❑ Researchers must honor all guarantees to participants of privacy, anonymity, and confidentiality.

❑ Researchers must use the highest methodological standards and be as accurate as possible.

❑ They must describe the known limitations and shortcomings of the research in their published reports.

❑ They must identify the sponsors who funded the research.

❑ Researchers must acknowledge the contributions of research assistants (usually underpaid and overworked graduate students) who participate in the research project.

❑ Researchers must make the details of their studies and the findings available to people who request them.

CONSTRAINTS

The Politics of Sex Research

Research on sexual behavior is important because it "lifts the pluralistic ignorance [about sex] and tells us what people are doing" (Udry, 1993: 105). Some groups prefer not to know about sexual behavior, however, and accuse researchers of legitimating "nontraditional" sexual behavior.

In 1991, both the U.S. secretary for health and human services and the Congress got involved in the politics of sex research by blocking $40 million research projects on adolescent and adult sexual behavior that had already been peer-reviewed, approved, and funded by the National Institutes of Health (NIH). Why and how did this happen? The following is a brief account of how social, political, and religious factors interacted to bring about the demise of these projects:

❑ In early 1988, the National Institute of Child Health and Human Development and the National Institute of Mental Health approved two studies of human sexual behavior. One study focused on adult behavior; the other, referred to as the American Teenage Study, examined adolescent behavior.

❑ As these studies were gearing up in 1991, Louis Sullivan, secretary for health and human services, appeared on a Christian Action Net-

work talk show and was asked why he was funding the American Teenage Study. He said he knew nothing about it.

❑ A few days later, the front page of the *Washington Times* carried both a story about the secretary's talk-show appearance and an article quoting the head of the (conservative) Family Research Council as opposing the American Teenage Study.

❑ Shortly thereafter, both Pat Robertson of the Christian Coalition and the Concerned Women of America, a conservative group, encouraged "outraged" Christians to write their congressional representatives.

❑ The Christian Action Network then circulated petitions to NIH to cancel the study. Viewers also inundated local school boards with letters demanding that the study not be carried out in local communities and enclosed a letter in which then-Congressman William Dannemeyer (R–California) condemned the study.

❑ C-SPAN and every major newspaper in the country carried the story.

❑ In Congress, opposition to the two studies was led by Congressman Dannemeyer and Senator Jesse Helms. According to Helms, "These

sex surveys . . . have not been concerned with legitimate scientific inquiry as much as they have been concerned with a blatant attempt to sway public attitudes in order to liberalize opinions and laws regarding homosexuality, pedophilia, anal and oral sex, sex education, teenage pregnancy and all down the line."

❑ In 1992, Congress withdrew the funds for both studies.

Local jurisdictions have also refused to let social scientists conduct research on adolescent sexual behavior. For example, the Centers for Disease Control and Prevention developed a questionnaire to measure major health problems of adolescents, including drug and alcohol abuse, unsafe sexual practices, physical inactivity, poor eating habits, and smoking. Although Maryland school officials initially approved the survey and planned to send it to 3,000 randomly selected ninth- and eleventh-grade students at 30 public high schools, the survey was scrapped because parents in several counties felt that the survey might make the school systems look bad (if a high incidence of drug use or pregnancy were reported) and because they felt that the research invaded student privacy (Fiester, 1993; Udry, 1993).

---

early 1950s. Although the studies challenged many common stereotypes of male and female sexual behavior—and shocked many people in the process (see Chapters 6 and 7)—Kinsey's work was generally regarded as scholarly and pioneering. Recently, however, Kinsey has been accused of such things as exaggerating the prevalence of some kinds of "forbidden" sexual acts (such as sodomy) and being more interested in becoming the world's foremost sex researcher

than in conducting scientifically rigorous research (see Reisman and Eichel, 1990).

Despite such charges, many social scientists consider Kinsey's research to be a major springboard that launched scientific investigations of human sexuality in the following decades. Many people are still suspicious of research on sex, however. As "The Politics of Sex Research" box shows, research authorizations may be rescinded and funding may be withdrawn because studies on sex—especially studies of adolescent sexual behavior—are opposed by conservative religious groups, school administrators, or politicians who feel that such research undermines traditional family values.

Research guidelines are particularly difficult to follow when there are both ethical and political conflicts, as is often the case in cross-cultural studies. In a study of the social and emotional development of black South African children, Ivy Goduka, a black South African who was pursuing a Ph.D. at Michigan State University, describes some of the problems that arise when ethical codes designed in one cultural and political context are applied in a quite different culture. For example, because Goduka expected problems in gaining access to research sites, she practiced deception which she now readily admits to (but feels guilty about):

My research was designed to study black children under apartheid and originally was titled "Behavioral Development of Black South African Children Under Apartheid." After I alerted my guidance committee to problems I would encounter with this title, the committee allowed me to change it. The committee also was afraid that the government of South Africa would view this title as challenging the status quo, and would not allow me access to areas where blacks live. Consequently, I changed the title to "Behavioral Development of Black South African Children: An Ecological Approach." This was a less threatening yet all-inclusive title that would save me from the possibility of refused access or even possibly going to jail. The human ecological framework used in this study also helped in phrasing a title acceptable to the government of South Africa. It was acceptable because it sounded like social science jargon and thus apolitical (Goduka, 1990: 335).

This and similar studies raise the (still) unresolved issue of whether deception can be used if it is "for the greater good" and uncovers social or personal injustice.

CONCLUSION

As this chapter shows, understanding marriage and the family is not an armchair activity engaged in by ivory tower philosophers. Like the family itself, the study of the family reflects *changes* and *constraints*—in this context, in theories and research methods. There has been considerable progress in the family field, and researchers have more *choices* as to methodology. At the same time, "there is plenty of reason for marriage and family scholars to be modest about what they know and humble about what they do not" (Miller, 1986: 110). According to one critic, research explanations are sometimes inadequate because social scientists ignore the historical context that has shaped the contemporary family (Adams, 1988). In the next chapter we will look at some of these historical processes.

Taking Action_____

Get On Line!

Colleges and universities are providing students with greater access to **electronic mail (E-mail).**
• Through Bitnet (one of the linkages to Internet), you can join **academic subscription lists,** or forums, that include both students and faculty. Some of the lists that are most germane to this chapter are the following:

POR@GIBBS.OIT.UNC.EDU (Public Opinion Research Discussion List)

ASUE@ALPHA.AUGUSTANA.EDU (Applied Sociology in Undergraduate Education)

METHODS%UNMVA.BITNET@ARIZVM1.CCIT.ARIZONA.EDU (Social Science Research Methods Instructors)

WMST-L@UMDD.BITNET (Women's Studies List)

FAMLYSCI@UKCC.UKY.EDU (Family Science Network)

FEMISA@CSF.COLORADO.EDU (Discusses gender issues, especially from international and cross-cultural perspectives)

AFROAM-L@HARVARDA.BITNET (Critical Issues in African American Life and Culture)

• Although several hundred books on the **Internet** were published in 1994 alone, here are a few sources that might be useful for the novice:

Daniel P. Dern, *The Internet Guide for New Users* (New York: McGraw-Hill, 1994).

Edward T. L. Hardie, ed., *Internet: Mailing Lists* (Englewood Cliffs, NJ: Prentice Hall, 1994).

Ed Krol, *The Whole Internet: User's Guide &* *Catalog* (Sebastopol, CA: O'Reilly & Associates, 1994).

Tracy LaQuey, *The Internet Companion*, 2nd ed. (Reading, MA: Addison-Wesley, 1994).

Javed Mostafa, Thomas Newell, and Richard Trenthem, *The Easy Internet Handbook* (Castle Rock, CO: Hi Willow Research & Publishing, 1994).

SUMMARY

1. Although many people are suspicious of statistics, data of all kinds are becoming increasingly important in our daily lives. Information derived from social science research affects much of our everyday behavior, shapes family policy, and provides explanations for social change.

2. The most influential theories of marriage and the family are the two macro-level perspectives of structural functionalism and conflict theory and four micro-level theories: symbolic interaction, social exchange, developmental, and general systems. Researchers and clinicians often use several theoretical perspectives in interpreting data or in choosing intervention strategies.

3. Longitudinal research studies provide more useful information about social change, but cross-sectional studies are more common because they are less expensive and less time-consuming.

4. The survey is one of the most common data-collection methods used in social science research. Surveys rely on questionnaires, interviews, or a combination of the two. Both questionnaires and interviews have advantages and limitations that researchers consider in designing their studies. Focus groups are often used to explore ideas before a survey is launched.

5. Clinical research and case studies provide a deeper understanding of behavior because phenomena can be studied intensively and over time. However, such research is also time-consuming and limited to small groups of people.

6. Observation also offers a deeper understanding of behavior and is usually inexpensive. The results of this type of research are difficult to quantify, however, and the researcher may experience difficulty in maintaining a balance between observation and participation.

7. Secondary analysis uses data collected by other researchers (such as historical documents and official government statistics). It is usually an accessible, convenient, and inexpensive source of data. One primary limitation of this method is that existing data may not provide information on the variables a particular researcher may want to examine.

8. Evaluation research, an applied research technique, is often used to assess the effectiveness and efficiency of social programs that offer services to families.

9. In recent years, studies of marriage and the family have been enriched because research on and by women and minority group members has filled large gaps in our knowledge.

10. All social scientists are expected to adhere to professional ethical standards both in conducting research and in reporting the results. Because political issues often affect research, however, conducting research is not as simple as it seems.

KEY TERMS

ADDITIONAL READING

The following books examine theoretical approaches to the study of the family:

IVAN F. NYE and FELIX M. BERARDO, eds., *Emerging Conceptual Frameworks in Family Analysis* (New York: Praeger, 1981).

JETSE SPREY, ed., *Fashioning Family Theory* (Newbury Park, CA: Sage, 1990).

A number of textbooks provide an overall view of social science research procedures. All deal with such standard topics as theory construction, research design, data-collection methods, data analysis, and ethical issues, and several focus on the family or on race relations research:

EARL BABBIE, *The Practice of Social Research,* 6th ed. (Belmont, CA: Wadsworth, 1992).

THERESE L. BAKER, *Doing Social Research*, 2nd ed. (New York: McGraw-Hill, 1994).

ANNE P. COPELAND and KATHLEEN M. WHITE, *Studying Families* (Newbury Park, CA: Sage, 1991).

JANE F. GILGUN, KERRY DALY, and GERALD HANDEL, eds., *Qualitative Methods in Family Research* (Newbury Park, CA: Sage, 1992).

W. LAWRENCE NEUMAN, *Social Research Methods: Qualitative and Quantitative Approaches* (Englewood Cliffs, NJ: Prentice Hall, 1994).

JOHN M. STANFIELD II, ed., *A History of Race Relations Research: First-Generation Recollections* (Newbury Park, CA: Sage, 1993).

Several books examine research techniques from a feminist perspective. Here are two:

MARY MAYNARD and JUNE PURVIS, eds., *Researching Women's Lives from a Feminist Perspective* (Bristol, PA: Taylor & Francis, 1994).

SHULAMIT REINHARZ, *Feminist Methods in Social Research* (New York: Oxford University Press, 1992).

A number of journals publish theoretical essays and research findings. Some of the most important in the marriage and family literature are *Journal of Family Psychology*, *Journal of Marriage and the Family*, *Family Process*, *Journal of Family Issues*, *Family Relations*, *Journal of Family History*, and *Family Perspective*. For studies using clinical and case study approaches, see, for example, the *Archives of Family Practice*, *Family Practice*, *Journal of Family Practice*, and the *Family Practice Research Journal* (the latter is especially easy for undergraduates to use).

One of the most informative publications about the family is *Statistical Abstract of the United States*. It is published annually by the U.S. Bureau of the Census and has hundreds of tables of data that are useful in studying family-related issues.

To keep abreast of public opinion research, look at *The Gallup Monthly* and *The Public Perspective*. Both periodicals publish information on a variety of family-related topics.

3
The Family in Historical Perspective

Data Digest

- During the **Great Depression,** hundreds of thousands moved to other towns and cities in the hope of getting jobs. The Southern Pacific Railroad threw **more than half a million transients** off its boxcars in a single year. At least 200,000 of these transients were adolescents, most of them male.

- During **World War II, 15 million men and women served** in the armed forces.

- Of the 1.3 million married couples whose male partners were in the armed forces, more than 20 percent had **children under age 10.**

- **Nearly a half million U.S. citizens were killed** in World War II, and about 183,000 children lost their fathers.

- **Almost 7 million women worked outside their homes** during the war, and 75 percent of them were married. The number of women employed in defense industries shot up 460 percent between 1939 and 1943: in ship construction, women employees rose from 36 to more than 160,000; in electrical work, from 100,000 to 374,000; and in the operation of heavy equipment, from 340,000 to more than 2 million. Some of the greatest **employment gains were made by African American women.** Those employed as servants fell from 72 to 48 percent, while the proportion employed in factories grew from 7 to almost 20 percent.

- **Divorce rates surged** from 321,000 in 1942 to 610,000 in 1946, after the end of the war. By 1950, a million veterans had been divorced.

SOURCES: Chafe, 1972; Tuttle, 1993.

Spencer Tracy, Academy Award–winning actor who died in 1967, once remarked: "There were times my pants were so thin I could sit on a dime and tell if it was heads or tails." Tracy wasn't the only one. Social scientists are showing that "the good old days" never existed for most people. This raises some interesting questions: Were the colonists as virtuous as we learned in grade school? Did communities really pull together to help each other during the Depression? Were the fifties as fabulous as many people say? Penetrating the stereotypes about the past helps us understand family life today. American families in the 1990s reflect many of the changes and constraints of earlier eras. Furthermore, such macro variables as economics, social class, race, and ethnicity have played a significant role in shaping the modern family.

Much of this chapter focuses on Native Americans, African Americans, Mexican Americans, and European immigrants—four groups that were especially exploited from the seventeenth through the nineteenth centuries. This chapter also shows how the American family was affected by the Great Depression, World War II, and the decade of the 1950s, the so-called Golden Fifties. In Chapter 13 we will examine the contemporary experiences of the groups we discuss here as well as those of others.

THE COLONIAL FAMILY

The diversity that characterizes families today also existed in colonial times. Although colonial families differed from modern families in terms of social class, religious practices, and geographic dispersion, such factors as family roles and family structure were very similar.

Family Structure

The nuclear family was the most prevalent family form both in England and in the first settlements of New England. An elderly grandparent or an apprentice sometimes lived for a while with or near the family, but few households were made up of extended families for long periods of time (Goode, 1963; Laslett, 1971). Although families typically raised six or seven children, high infant mortality rates made household sizes small, with large age differences between children. The Puritans—Protestant colonists who adhered to strict moral and religious values—believed that the community had a right to intervene in families that did not perform their duties properly. In the 1670s, for example, the Massachusetts General Court directed towns to appoint "tithingmen" to oversee every 10 or 12 households. They were to ensure that marital relations were harmonious and that parents disciplined unruly children (Mintz and Kellogg, 1988).

Unlike later times, the colonial period saw few individuals surviving outside the family structure. Most of the colonial settlements were small—fewer than 100 families—and each family was considered a "little commonwealth" that performed a variety of functions. The family was a self-sufficient *business* that produced and exchanged commodities; all family members worked together to meet the family's material needs. At the same time, the family was a *school* that taught children to read. It was a *vocational institute* that taught children specific skills and prepared them for jobs through apprenticeships. The family also served as a miniature *church* that taught its members daily prayers, personal meditation, and formal family worship in the community. It was a *house of correction*; the courts sentenced idle or criminal people to live as servants in the families of more reputable citizens. Finally, the family also served as a *welfare institution* because each family was expected not only to give its members medical and other care but to provide a home and care for other relatives who were orphaned, aging, infirm, or homeless (Demos, 1970). As we shall see, all of these functions changed considerably with the onset of industrialization.

Sexual Relations

The Puritans tried to prevent premarital intercourse in several ways. One was **bundling,** a New England custom in which a young man and woman, both fully dressed, spent the night in a bed together, separated by a wooden board. The custom was adopted because it was difficult for the young suitor, who had traveled many miles, to return home the same night, especially during harsh winters. Because the rest of the family shared the room, it was considered quite proper for the bundled young man and woman to continue their conversations after the fire was out (McPharlin, 1946).

According to historians, premarital and extramarital sex were not uncommon. According to some authorities, between 20 and 33 percent of colonial women were pregnant at the time of marriage (Hawke, 1988; Demos, 1970). Keep in mind, however, that sexual activity was generally confined to engaged couples; the idea of a casual meeting that included sexual intercourse would have been utterly foreign to the Puritans. On the other hand, among young women who immigrated to the South as indentured (contracted) servants, out-of-wedlock births were not uncommon. Female indentured servants typically came to the United States alone because they were from families whose lower socioeconomic status meant they could not all migrate together. Because these often very young (under 15) women were alone and vastly outnumbered by men in the colonies, there was ample opportunity for premarital sex (Harari and Vinovskis, 1993).

What do you suppose might have happened to the "centerboard" shown in this sketch of early Pennsylvania bundling after the young woman's parents went to bed? The couple could hope that the family—who often slept in the same room—were good sleepers.

In the Puritan community, the primary offenses of adultery and illegitimacy were condemned because they threatened the family structure. Sometimes a straying spouse was denounced publicly:

CATHERINE TREEN, the wife of the subscriber, having, in violation of her solem vow, behaved herself in the most disgraceful manner, by leaving her own place of abode, and living in a criminal state with a certain William Collins, a plaisterer, under whose bed she was last night, discovered, endeavoring to conceal herself, her much injured husband, therefore, in justice of himself, thinks it absolutely necessary to forewarn all persons from trusting her on his account, being determined, after such flagrant proof of her prostitution, to pay no debts of her contracting (cited in Lantz, 1976: 14).

Few records document men's extramarital affairs because a husband's infidelity was considered "normal." Moreover, because the courts did not enforce a father's economic obligation to a child born out of wedlock, it was women, and not men, who paid the costs of bearing and raising illegitimate children (Ryan, 1983). As you can see, the so-called double standard (which we discuss later) is not a modern invention.

Husbands and Wives

Husband and wives worked together to make sure that the family survived. Colonial America, like modern society, expected spouses to have strong personal as well as economic relationships. Inequalities, however, were very much a part of early American family life.

Personal Relationships
In general, women were subordinate to men, and the wife's chief duty was obedience to her husband. New England clergymen often referred to male authority as a "government" that the female must accept as "law," and in the South, husbands often denounced assertive wives as "impertinent" (Ryan, 1983). A woman's social status as well as her power and prestige in the community came from the patriarchal head of the household—either her husband or her father.

At the same time, according to a writer in 1712, the "well-ordered" family was based on a number of mutual spousal responsibilities (Benjamin Wadsworth, cited in Scott and Wishy, 1982). Husbands and wives were expected to love each other and to show "a very great affection." They should be chaste and faithful to each other, and they were encouraged to be patient and to help each other: "If the one is sick, pained, troubled, distressed, the other should manifest care, tenderness, pity, compassion, & [sic] afford all possible relief and succour" (p. 86).

In Plymouth, women had the right to transfer land. In 1646, for example, when one man wanted to sell his family's land, the court called in his wife to make sure that she approved. The courts also sometimes granted liquor and other business licenses to women (Demos, 1970). And they sometimes offered a woman protection from a violent husband. The Plymouth court ordered a whipping for a man for "abusing his wife by kiking her of from a stoole into the fier" (Mintz and Kellogg, 1988: 10). Such protections were not typical in the colonies outside of Plymouth, however.

In a few cases, the local courts would permit divorce. The acceptable grounds were limited to desertion, adultery, bigamy, and impotence. Incompatibility was recognized as a problem, but not serious enough to warrant divorce. It was not until about 1765, when romantic love emerged as a basis for marriage, that "loss of affection" was mentioned as a reason for divorce (Cott and Pleck, 1979).

Work and the Economy
Although men were expected to be industrious, hardworking, and ambitious and were held responsible for the family's economic survival, husbands and wives were not segregated into rigid work roles. Men, women, and children all produced, cultivated, and processed goods for the family's consumption. When necessary, men would care for and discipline the children while women worked in the fields. On the other hand, much of women's work was directed toward meeting the needs of others. In his 1793 *Female Guide*, a New Hampshire pastor defined a woman's role as "piety to God—reverence to parents—love and obedience to their husbands—tenderness and watchfulness over their children—justice and humanity to their dependents" (quoted in Cott, 1977: 22–23).

Moreover, although prosperity and industry were praised in both sexes in colonial times, men were expected to initiate economic activity, and women were expected to support men and to be frugal. In 1692, Cotton Mather, an influential minister and author, described women's economic role as being only "to spend (or save) what others get" (Cott, 1977).

In some cases, unmarried women, especially widows and those who had been deserted by their husbands, turned their homemaking activities into self-supporting businesses. Some used their homes as inns, restaurants, or schools. Others sold homemade foods or performed domestic tasks for others. Women living outside of town could make a living by washing, mending, nursing, midwifery, or producing cure-all and beauty potions. One woman's advertisement for her "Beautifying Wash" resembles modern marketing communications about cosmetic products:

It makes the Skin soft, smooth and plump, it likewise takes away Redness, Frechkles, Sun-burnings, or Pimples, and cures Postures, Itchings, Ring-Worms, Tetters, Scurf, Morphew, and other like Deformities of the Face and Skin, (Intirely free from any Corroding Qualities) and brings to it an exquisite Beauty (quoted in Matthaei, 1982: 66).

Some widows continued their husband's businesses in such "masculine" areas as chocolate and mustard production, soap making, cutlery, coach making, rope making, publishing, printing, horse shoeing, net making, whaling, and running grocery stores, bookstores, drugstores, and hardware stores. And some of these businesswomen placed ads, on a regular basis, in the local newspapers (see Matthaei, 1982).

Generally, however, women's, especially wives', economic roles were severely limited. Women had little access to credit, could not sue to collect debts, were restricted from owning property, and were less likely to be chosen as executors of wills, especially if their husbands had complicated estates (Ryan, 1983).

Children's Lives

Colonial America was characterized by poor sanitation, crude housing, limited hygiene, and dangerous physical environments. Infant and child mortality rates were high. Between 10 and 30 percent of all children died before their first birthday, and fewer than two out of three children lived to see their tenth birthday. Cotton Mather fathered fourteen children, but only one outlived his father; seven died shortly after birth, one died at age 2, and five died in their early twenties (Stannard, 1979).

Children in colonial times were dominated by the concepts of repression, religion, and respect (B. Adams, 1980). The Puritans believed that children were born with original sin and were inherently stubborn, willful, selfish, and corrupt. The Reverend John Robinson, a leading preacher among the Pilgrims, wrote: "Surely there is in all children . . . a stubbernes and stoutnes of minde arising from naturall pride which must in the first place be broken and beaten down, that so the foundation of their education being layd in humilitie and tractableness, other virtues may in their time be built thereon" (quoted in Earle, 1899: 192).

The entire community—parents, school, church, and neighbors—worked together to keep children "in their place." As you can see from Figure 3.1, compared to contemporary standards, colonial children, at least in New England, were expected to be extraordinarily well disciplined, obedient, and docile. Within 40

years of their arrival in Plymouth, however, many colonists worried that their families were disintegrating, that parents were becoming less responsible, and that children were losing respect for authority. Ministers repeatedly warned parents that their children were frequenting taverns, keeping "vicious company," and "tending to dissoluteness (unrestrained and immoral behavior)" (Mintz and Kellogg, 1988: 17).

Wealthy families in the South were more indulgent with their children than were well-to-do families in the northern colonies, but child labor was nearly universal throughout the colonies at other levels of society. Even very young children worked hard in their own homes or as indentured servants or slaves. Virginia, for example, received several shiploads of "friendless boys and girles," evidently kidnapped in England and sent to the colony to provide cheap and docile labor for the American planters (Queen et al., 1985).

Because girls were expected to be homemakers, their formal education was meager. The New England colonies educated boys, but girls were banned from higher education. They were commonly admitted to the public schoolhouse only during those hours and seasons when boys were occupied with other affairs or were needed in the fields. As one farmer stated, "In winter it's too far for girls to walk; in summer they ought to stay at home to help in the kitchen" (quoted in Earle, 1899: 96). Women who succeeded in getting an education were often ridiculed:

One woman who dared to write a theological treatise was rudely rebuffed by her brother: "Your printing of a book is beyond your sex and doth rankly smell." John Winthrop—the first governor of the Massachusetts Bay Colony—maintained that such intellectual exertion could even rot the female mind. He attributed the madness of Ann Hopkins, wife of the Connecticut governor, to her intellectual curiosity: "If she had attended her household affairs and such things as belong to women and not gone out of her way to meddle in the affairs of men whose minds are stronger, she'd have kept her wits and might have improved them usefully" (Ryan, 1983: 57).

Social Class and Regional Differences

The colonial family's experiences were not the same across all groups; there were a number of regional and social-class variations. In a study of

OF CHILDREN'S BEHAVIOR WHEN AT HOME

1. Make a Bow always when you come Home, and be immediately uncovered [take off your hat].

2. Be never covered at Home, especially before thy Parents or Strangers.

3. Never Sit in the Presence of thy Parents without bidding, tho' no Stranger be present.

4. If thou passest by thy Parents, at any Place where thou seest them, when either by themselves or with Company, Bow towards them.

5. If thou art going to speak to thy Parents, and see them engaged in discourse with Company, draw back and leave thy piece until afterwards; but if thou must speak, be sure to whisper.

6. Never speak to thy Parents without some Title of Respect, viz. Sir, Madam, & c., according to their Quality.

7. Approach near thy Parents at no time without a Bow.

8. Dispute not, nor delay to Obey thy Parents' Commands.

9. Go not out of Doors without thy Parents leave, and return within the Time by them limited.

10. Come not into the Room where thy Parents are with Strangers, unless thou art called, and then decently; and at bidding go out; or if Strangers come in while thou art with them it is Manners, with a Bow, to withdraw.

11. Use respectful and courteous, but not insulting or domineering, Carriage or Language towards the Servants.

12. Quarrel not nor contend with thy Brethren or sisters, but live in love, peace, & unity.

13. Grumble not nor be discontented at any thing thy Parents appoint, speak, or do.

14. Bear with Meekness and Patience, and without Murmuring or Sullenness thy Parents' Reproofs or Corrections: Nay tho' it should so happen that they be causeless or undeserved.

Figure 3.1   Rules for Colonial Children (Wadsworth, 1712, in Scott and Wishy, 1982).

Salem families between 1790 and 1810, for example, Farber (1972) found three social classes with very different socialization patterns that supported the economic structure. In the *merchant class*, or the upper class, the patriarchs typically were shipping and commercial entrepreneurs. The oldest son continued the commercial enterprises and invested the family's profits in other high-paying ventures. There was no need to inculcate strong motives for upward social mobility because the family businesses were inherited and partnerships were expanded through first-cousin marriages. The *artisan class*, or the middle class, was characterized by highly skilled occupations, apprenticeship systems, and cooperation among relatives. Children were encouraged to be upwardly mobile and to achieve security in a livelihood. The *laboring class*, or the working class, was made up mainly of migrants in the community. These people, who had no voting privileges and little education, provided much of the necessary unskilled labor for the merchant class.

Colonial families also differed across regions. Whereas in the North, people settled in villages, in the South, people settled on isolated plantations and farms. There was also a rigid stratification system between wealthy families, poor whites, indentured servants, and black slaves in the South.

COLONIZATION AND SLAVERY

European explorers and settlers who invaded the North American continent in the sixteenth and seventeenth centuries pushed the Native Americans, the original inhabitants, out of their territories, and large numbers of these peoples succumbed to starvation and illnesses and epidemics foreign to them. Except for people who arrived in the colonies as servants—and in general they *chose* to indenture themselves—African Americans are the only people who did not come to America voluntarily. Rather, they came enslaved and helped to build the new country of "freedom." A third group of people who were instrumental in the economic growth of the United States were the Mexican Americans, who, as we shall see, were treated as outsiders even though they were an important source of labor in an expanding economy. The experiences of these three peoples were quite different. Some families and/or tribes fared better than others, and there was considerable diversity within each group.

Native Americans

Native Americans migrated from northeastern Asia to North America over a period of 30,000 years. By the time European settlers arrived, it is estimated that there were almost 18 million Indians living in North America, speaking approximately 300 languages (John, 1988). About 160 distinct languages are still spoken in the United States and Canada (Price, 1981). Native Americans were enormously diverse racially, culturally, and linguistically. This variation was reflected in kinship and family systems, as well as in interpersonal relations.

Kinship and Family Systems The Indian societies in North America included bands (Arctic, Subarctic, Great Basin, and Plateau), tribes (Northeast, Plains, Southwest, and U.S. west coast), and chiefdoms (Southeast and Canadian west coast). *Bands* were characterized by equality between men and women, little polygyny and small residential households. *Tribes,* which had some egalitarian characteristics and more polygyny, often built large residential structures, like the pueblos in the Southwest. *Chiefdoms* had class structures that often included slaves at the bottom; they were polygynous, and lived in elaborate houses (Price, 1981).

Family structures and practices varied across regions. For example, polygyny was practiced in more than 20 percent of marriages among Indians of the Great Plains and the northwest coast, whereas monogamy was practiced almost exclusively among such agricultural groups as the Hopi, Iroquois, and Huron. Among the agricultural tribes in eastern and southwestern America, where women played a major role in food production, inheritance through the mother's side was common, and young couples lived more often with the woman's family. Among most Native American groups, the most important stages of the life cycle were birth, puberty, marriage, and death. Again, however, there were many variations—some intricate and some more casual—that governed marriage, relations with in-laws, and religious rituals.

Some historians tell us that Indian women were better off than their white counterparts in many instances. In contrast to filmmakers' stereotypes of the passive Indian woman and docile squaw, Indian women actually wielded considerable power and commanded respect in many bands and tribes. The box "Native American Women: Chiefs, Physicians, Politicians, and Warriors" describes some of the societal roles that Indian women of colonial times played. Approximately 25 percent of North American Indian tribes were matrilineal. Indian women in these tribes owned all the houses, the household furnishings, the fields and gardens, the work tools, and the livestock—and all of this property was passed on to their female heirs (Mathes, 1981).

Marriage and Divorce In most cases, Native Americans married at a young age. Women typically married between the ages of 12 and 15, after reaching puberty. Men married at slightly older ages, between 15 and 20, usually after they had shown an ability to hunt or to provide for a family. Some families arranged their children's marriages; others allowed young men and women to choose their own spouses.

Family forms also varied. Among the Shoshone there were no formal marriage ceremonies; the families simply exchanged gifts. Also, there were no formal rules of residence. The newly married couple could live and move along with the family of either the groom or the bride or establish its own independent unit.

Native American Women: Chiefs, Physicians, Politicians, and Warriors

Before they were forced onto reservations, where they adopted many customs and practices of the larger society, many Native American women and men had egalitarian relationships. Besides being wives and mothers, many Indian women were also chiefs, physicians, politicians, and warriors.

Chiefs: In some cases, women became chiefs because of their achievements on the battlefield. In other cases, they replaced husbands who died. Like men, female chiefs could declare war, resolve disputes in the community, and punish offenders.

Physicians: Women could be medicine women, or shamans, the Indian equivalent of doctors. Among the Zuni and other Pueblo cultures, for example, women were members of the Rain Priesthood, the most important religious group. Women also played crucial spiritual leadership roles among the An-

Delaware Nation council chief and educator Linda Poolaw was asked to choose works for an exhibition for the Smithsonian's National Museum of the American Indian. Poolaw's ancestors once lived on Manhattan island.

ishinaabe, Blackfoot, Chilula, and Dine tribes.

Politicians: Because many tribes were matrilineal and matrilocal, many women were powerful politically. Among the Lakota, for ex-

ample, a man owned nothing but his clothing, a horse for hunting, weapons, and spiritual items. Homes, furnishings, and other property belonged to wives. In many tribes, women were influential decision makers in the community.

Warriors: Among the Apache, some women warriors were as courageous, daring, and skillful as the men, and Cheyenne women fighters distinguished themselves in war. Lakota women maintained four known warrior societies of their own, and among the Cherokee, one of the toughest warriors was a woman who also headed a women's military society. Women could stop—and they did stop—war parties by refusing to supply the necessary food for the journey. And among the Iroquois, a woman could initiate a war party because she was entitled to demand that any murdered member of her clan be replaced by a captive (Mathes, 1981; Stockel, 1991; Jaimes and Halsey, 1992).

Mohave marriages were similarly casual— there was no dowry, gift exchange, or wedding ceremony. The only rules were designed to prevent incest. A man could not marry a woman to whom direct blood relationship could be traced either through his mother or father or who was a member of his own clan. The married couple took up residence with the husband's parents. Divorce was simple—either partner could initiate the separation—and fairly common among young adults, who remarried easily.

Among the Zuni of the Southwest, marriages were arranged casually, and the groom moved into the bride's household. The Zuni and other groups made divorce easy. If a wife was fed up with a demanding husband, all she had to do was put his belongings outside their home, and they were no longer married. The man, though he might be unhappy, accepted the dismissal

and returned to his mother's household. If it were a husband seeking a divorce, he would tell his wife he was going hunting and then never return (Stockel, 1991).

In the Great Plains, most Teton marriages were arranged by parents, but some were based on romantic love. Marriages were often lifetime associations, but divorce was easy and not uncommon. A man could divorce a wife for adultery, laziness, or even excessive nagging. Divorce was usually agreed to by both parties, but a man could humiliate a wife by casting her off publicly at a dance or other ceremony. A truly generous husband who had evidence of adultery would— instead of cutting off his wife's nose (literally) and demanding a payment from her lover—force the couple to leave the band and even provide them with a horse and other property to show his magnanimous nature.

Children Most Indian families were small because of high infant and child death rates and because mothers nursed their children for several years, often abstaining from sexual relations until the child was weaned. Throughout most Native American groups, childhood was considered to be a happy time, and parents were generally kind and loving. Mohave parents, for example, were indulgent; childhood was a carefree time, and disciplinary methods, only rarely invoked, were mild. Similarly, the Zuni treated children with kindness and little physical restraint. Children were taught to be polite, gentle, and unaggressive, and unruly children were frightened into conformity by stories of religious bogeymen rather than by physical punishment. The grandparents on both sides of the family took an active part in the education of the children and told stories that inculcated the lore and the values of the tribe.

In general, children were greatly desired and welcomed. Adults fussed over the babies; they were gentle and permissive in terms of weaning and toilet training and imposed few responsibilities.

Puberty In most Indian societies, puberty rites were more elaborate for girls than for boys. Among the most intricate rituals were those of the Arctic and Subarctic groups. Among the Alaskan Nabesna, for example, the menstruating girl was secluded, observed strict food taboos, was forbidden to touch her own body with her hands (lest sores break out), and was forbidden to travel with the tribe. Among the Navajo, girls underwent impressive rites with an all-night "sing" on the fourth ceremonial night. In contrast, among the Mohave, the observance of a girl's puberty was a private family matter that did not include any rituals.

The Zuni marked rites of passage for boys twice—between 5 and 9 and again between 11 and 14. Each time the ceremony included purification and exorcism rites. Among the Teton, a boy's puberty was marked by a series of events, such as his first successful bison hunt, his first war party, his first capture of enemy horses, and other deeds, all of which were marked by his father with feasts and gifts to others.

Also of great importance in some tribes was the *vision quest*—a supernatural experience in which a "familiar spirit" indicated the course the boy's adult life would take and which involved

fasting, isolation, and self-torture. The young boy fasted for four days before leaving the tribe's camp and took ritual purifying sweat baths in a small dome-shaped sweat lodge. On leaving the camp, the boy found an isolated place—frequently a butte top or other elevated spot—where he waited for four days and nights or until he received a supernatural vision. The boy fasted and frequently gashed his arms and legs. The vision came to the boy when a supernatural being took pity on the boy and instructed him (Spencer and Jennings, 1977).

The Impact of European Cultures The French, Spanish, Portuguese, and British played a major role in destroying much Native American culture. Missionaries, determined to convert the "savages" to Christianity, were responsible for some of this destruction. With no understanding of the crucial importance in the normal functioning and survival of the native societies of many practices unfamiliar to them, missionaries tried to eliminate religious ceremonies and such practices as polygyny and matrilineal inheritance (Price, 1981). Most exploitation was economic, however. Europeans saw the opportunities for exploiting the abundant North American resources of gold, land, and fur.

Indian tribes coped with numerous methods of destruction, including military slaughter, enslavement, forced labor, land confiscation, coerced mass migration, and involuntary religious conversions (Collier, 1947). In addition, by the end of the seventeenth century, staggering numbers of Native Americans in the East had died from such Old World diseases as influenza, measles, smallpox, and typhus. The Plymouth colony was actually located in a deserted Indian village whose inhabitants had been devastated by epidemic diseases brought by Europeans. By the 1670s, only 10 percent of the original Native American population of New England had survived. At least 50 tribes became extinct as a result of disease and massacre. During the eighteenth and nineteenth centuries, the diversity of Native American family practices was reduced even further in the tribes of both the east and the west through missionary activities, intrusive federal land policies, poverty on reservations, marriage with outside groups, and federal government inducements to relocate Native Americans to urban areas (John, 1988).

African Americans

John Rolfe reported in his journal that on August 20, 1619, at the Jamestown settlement in Virginia, "there came . . . a Dutch man-of-warre that sold us 20 negars." These first African Americans in the English North American colonies were brought over as indentured servants. After their terms of service, they were free to buy land, marry, and hire their own labor. These rights were short-lived, however. By the mid-1660s, the southern colonies had passed laws prohibiting blacks from testifying in court, owning property, making contracts, traveling without permission, congregating in public places, and contracting marriages. As Table 3.1 shows, the slave trade grew in both the northern and the southern colonies over several decades. Note, also, that European and African American indentured servants were treated differently.

Some early statesmen, like Thomas Jefferson, publicly decried the institution of slavery but supported it privately. As you can see from Table 3.1, while drafting the Declaration of Independence, Jefferson denounced the king of England for allowing the importation of slaves. In 1809, however, Jefferson argued that "the Negro slave in America must be removed beyond the reach of mixture" for the preservation of the "dignity" and "beauty" of the white race (Bergman, 1969). At the same time, Jefferson had a slave mistress and fathered children with her. Inconsistent to the end, he freed five of his slaves in his will but left the rest to his heirs.

Marriage Throughout the colonies, it was difficult for a slave to find a spouse. In northern cities, most slaves lived with their masters and were restricted from associating with other slaves. In the southern colonies, most slaves lived on plantations that had fewer than 10 slaves. Because the plantations were far apart and the sex and age ratios were skewed, it was difficult for slave men and women to find a spouse of roughly the same age. In addition, overwork and high death rates due to widespread disease meant that marriages did not last very long (Mintz and Kellogg, 1988).

After the importation of slaves into the United States was prohibited in 1807, breeding increased in importance. To ensure that slaves would remain on the plantations, many owners recognized familial relationships among slaves, encouraged them to have large families, and provided living

Table 3.1

More Than Two Hundred Years of African-American Slavery

1619—The Dutch sold 20 Africans to the colonists at Jamestown, Virginia.

1624—The Dutch in New York imported black workers from Angola and Brazil to work on Hudson Valley farms.

1629–1636—Slavery was introduced in the Connecticut, Maryland, and Delaware colonies.

1638—New England became involved in the slave trade: Captain William Pierce of Salem, Massachusetts, sailed the *Desire* to the West Indies and exchanged Pequod Indian slaves for goods and black slaves.

1640—In Virginia, three fugitive indentured servants were captured and tried. The Dutchman and Scotsman were sentenced to serve four extra years; the African American was given a life sentence of servitude.

1640—In Virginia, a white man who had associated with a black woman had to do penance in church; the woman was whipped.

1641—The Massachusetts Body of Liberties recognized slavery as legal.

1688—The administrators of Canada begged Louis XIV to allow black slavery because of the acute labor shortage. The king finally gave his approval to Governor Denonville.

1692—Maryland law required seven years of service of any white man who married or had a child by a black woman. There were penalties for white women "allowing themselves to be with child by colored persons" and for free or enslaved blacks guilty of sexual intercourse with white women.

1776—Thomas Jefferson's original draft of the Declaration of Independence denounced George III for allowing the importation of slaves.

1777—Slavery was abolished in Vermont.

1792–1836—Kentucky, Tennessee, Louisiana, Mississippi, Missouri, and Arkansas were admitted to the Union as slave states.

1807—Although slavery was still legal, the importation of slaves was prohibited by law.

1833—The American Anti-Slavery Society was founded.

1852—Harriet Beecher Stowe published the now-classic *Uncle Tom's Cabin*.

1860–Abraham Lincoln was elected president.

1860–1861—Seven Deep South states seceded from the Union.

1863—The Emancipation Proclamation was issued.

1865—The Thirteenth Amendment to the U.S. Constitution became law; Lincoln was assassinated.

1866—Congress approved the Fourteenth Amendment; the Ku Klux Klan was founded.

SOURCES: Bergman, 1969; Faragher et al., 1994.

quarters. Yet slave marriages were fragile institutions. As the box "A Slave Auction" shows, owners often separated slave families for economic reasons. Studies of slave families in Mississippi, Tennessee, and Louisiana show that between 35 to 40 percent of marriages were terminated by such actions (Gutman, 1976; Matthaei, 1982).

Family Structure   Until the 1970s, sociologists and historians argued that slavery had emasculated black fathers, forced black mothers to be family matriarchs, and destroyed the African American family. Historian Herbert Gutman dispelled many of these beliefs with his study (1983) of 21 urban and rural communities in the South between 1855 and 1880. Gutman found that 70 to 90 percent of African American households were made up of a husband and wife or a single father. Thus, he said, most families were intact and not matriarchal. Furthermore, most women who were heads of households were alone because their husbands had died, not because they had never married, and they usually had only one or two children. Thus, according to Gutman, African American families were surprisingly stable and intact.

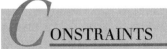

CONSTRAINTS

A Slave Auction

In the mid-1970s, Alex Haley, a journalist who had taught himself to read and write during a 20-year career in the U.S. Coast Guard, was catapulted to fame when his book *Roots: The Saga of an American Family* (1976) became a best-seller and was made into one of the first mini-series on television. In the book, Haley traced the six generations of his ancestors, the first of whom was abducted at the age of 16 from Gambia, West Africa, in 1767. The following excerpt is an equally powerful description of how African families were destroyed by slavery:

During the day a number of sales were made. David and Caroline were purchased together by a Natchez planter. They left us, grinning broadly, and in a most happy state of mind, caused by the fact of their not being separated. Sethe was sold to a planter of Baton Rouge, her eyes flashing with anger as she was led away.

The same man also purchased Randall. The little fellow was made to jump, and run across the floor, and perform many other feats, exhibiting his activity and condition. All
the time the trade was going on, Eliza was crying aloud and wringing her hands. She besought the man not to buy him, unless he also bought herself and Emily. She promised, in that case, to be the most faithful slave that ever lived. The man answered that he could not afford it, and then Eliza burst into a paroxysm of grief, weeping plaintively. Freeman turned round to her, savagely, with his whip in his uplifted hand, ordering her to stop her noise, or he would flog her. He could not have such work–such snivelling; and unless she ceased that minute, he would take her to the yard and give her a hundred lashes. Yes, he would take the non-sense out of her pretty quick. . . . Eliza shrunk before him and tried to wipe away her tears, but it was all in vain. She wanted to be with her children, she said, the little time she had to live.

All the frowns and threats of Freeman could not wholly silence the afflicted mother. She kept on begging and beseeching them, most piteously, not to separate the three. Over and over again she told them how she loved her boy. A great many times she repeated her former promises–how very faithful and obedient she would be, how hard
she would labor day and night, to the last moment of her life, if he would only buy them all together. But it was of no avail; the man could not afford it. The bargain was agreed upon, and Randall must go alone. Then Eliza ran to him, embraced him passionately, kissed him again and again, told him to remember her–all the while her tears falling in the boy's face like rain.

Freeman damned her, calling her a blubbering, bawling wench, and ordered her to go to her place, and behave herself, and be somebody. He swore he wouldn't stand such stuff [but] a little longer. He would soon give her something to cry about, if she was not mighty careful, and that she might depend on.

The planter from Baton Rouge, with his new purchase, was ready to depart.

"Don't cry, mama. I will be a good boy. Don't cry," said Randall, looking back, as they passed out of the door.

What has become of the lad, God knows. It was a mournful scene indeed. I would have cried myself if I had dared (Solomon Northrup, cited in Meltzer, 1964: 87–89).

Several African American scholars have also argued that the slave family structure has been misrepresented by white middle-class historians and sociologists who described black family life as pathological simply because it did not conform to white middle-class norms (McAdoo, 1986; Staples, 1988). The analyses of some pioneering African American scholars were sometimes equally misleading, however. For example, E. Franklin Frazier (1939), a respected authority on the African American family, popularized the theme of family disorganization as a legacy of slavery. He also blamed black matriarchy for many family problems and encouraged African Americans to assimilate into the white world. W. E. B. DuBois (1903), another prominent African American scholar, had challenged such views earlier but was not taken seriously until the 1980s.

Husbands and Fathers One example of the historical misrepresentation of African American families is the portrayal of slave husbands and fathers. In contrast to popular conceptions of the African American male as emasculated and powerless, Genovese (1981) argued that adult male slaves were important role models for boys:

Trapping wild turkeys required considerable skill; not everyone could construct a "rabbit gum" equal to the guile of the rabbits; and running down the quick, battling raccoon took pluck. For a boy growing up, the moment when his father thought him ready to join in the hunting and to learn to trap was a much-sought recognition of his own manhood (pp. 239–40).

Hunting, trapping animals, and fishing were functional, not recreational. These activities reduced families' nutritional deficiencies and supplemented monotonous and inadequate diets.

Many African American men served as surrogate fathers to many children, blood relatives and others. Black preachers, whose eloquence and moral force commanded the respect of the entire community, were also influential role models. Men made shoes, wove baskets, constructed furniture, and cultivated the tiny household garden plots allotted to families by the master (Jones, 1985). Some male slaves were also apprenticed in skilled jobs, promoted to better jobs, and granted cash bonuses for loyal service (Ryan, 1983). They were excluded, however, from political, economic, and educational institutions.

It is interesting to note that for centuries, male European serfs and peasants could not protect their wives or children from lords and warlords, yet no one questioned their masculinity, whereas the masculinity of African American men has been impugned. Even though this kind of intervention was often fatal, there are numerous slave narratives documenting men's attempts to save their daughters, mothers, and wives from sexual exploitation by their masters (Genovese, 1981; Staples, 1988).

Wives and Mothers Images of strong slave mothers and wives have dominated portrayals of African American families both in films and in print. Many historical documents describe African American women as survivors who resisted the slave system. For example, one proud daughter recalls, "My mother was the smartest black woman in Edes . . . she would do anything. She made as good a field hand as she did a cook. She was a demon, loud and boisterous, high-spirited and independent. I tell you she was a captain" (quoted in Ryan, 1983: 162–63).

Mothers reared the children, cooked the food, maintained the slave cabin, and worked in the fields. Because the African American woman was often both a "mammy" to the plantation owner's children and a mother to her own, she experienced the exhausting *double day*—a full day of domestic chores plus a full day of work outside the home—at least a century before middle-class white women coined the term. Black women got little recognition for this grueling schedule and were often subjected to physical punishment; even pregnant and nursing mothers did not escape such abuse. According to Jones (1985), pregnant slaves were sometimes forced to lie facedown in a specially dug depression in the ground, which protected the fetus while the mother was whipped, and some nursing mothers were whipped until "blood and milk flew mingled from their breasts" (p. 20).

In the South, only a few female slaves worked in the master's house, known as "the big house." Most female slaves over 10 years of age worked in the field, sunup to sundown, six days a week, and had to work hard to piece together a semblance of family life:

A female field hand might be granted a month off for childbirth or be allowed to return from the fields three or four times a day to nurse a newborn infant. Occasionally, women were permitted to leave the fields early on Saturday to perform some chores around the slave quarters. Their homes were small cabins of one or two rooms, which they usually shared with their mate and their children, and perhaps another family secluded behind a crude partition. . . . Slave women were often responsible for manufacturing soap, candles, and clothes for their families, as well as cooking crude meals (Ryan, 1983: 159).

Popular films like *Gone with the Wind* have often portrayed house slaves as doing little more than adjusting Miss Scarlett's petticoats and announcing male suitors. In reality, domestic work was as hard as field work. Fetching wood and water, preparing three full meals a day over a smoky fireplace, and pressing clothes for an entire family was backbreaking labor. Female servants sometimes had to sleep on the floor at the foot of the mistress's bed. They were also often forced into sexual relations with the master. Injuries were common, minor infractions met with swift and severe punishment, and servants suffered abuse ranging from jabs with pins to beatings that left them disfigured for life (Jones, 1985).

After Emancipation After slavery was abolished, many slaves legitimized their marriages, even though the one-dollar fee for the marriage license cost about two weeks' pay for most. In Hinds County, Mississippi, 15 years after emancipation, African Americans bought 75 percent of the marriage licenses issued, even though they constituted less than 75 percent of the population between 15 and 44 years of age. A legal marriage was an impressive status symbol, and a wedding was a festive event (Degler, 1981; Staples, 1988).

Even where slavery had destroyed particular families, kinship networks survived. After slavery's end, African American families began naming children after blood relatives—uncles, aunts, siblings, and grandparents—thus preserving these kinship ties.

Some writers have claimed that the African American family, already disrupted by slavery, was further weakened by urban migration to the North in the late 1800s (Frazier, 1939; Moynihan, 1970). However, many black migrants made extensive efforts to maintain contact with their kin and families in the South. When black men migrated alone, "A constant flow of letters containing cash and advice between North and South facilitated the gradual migration of whole clans and even villages" (Jones, 1985: 159). Others returned home frequently to join in community celebrations, or to help with planting and harvesting on the family farm. Thus, many African American families remained resilient despite difficult conditions.

Mexican Americans

Mexican American families compose a very heterogeneous population. Some trace their roots to the Spanish and Mexican settlers in the Southwest before the arrival of European immigrants; others migrated from Central and South America to North America at the beginning of the twentieth century.

Territory that was originally Mexican was annexed by the United States in 1848 after 30 years of war and conflict. Despite the provisions of the Treaty of Guadalupe Hidalgo, which guaranteed security of their property, Mexican landowners had their lands confiscated or were defrauded by land speculators. By the mid-nineteenth century, Mexican families lost most of their land to the U.S. government. In spite of treaty promises, old land grants were ignored, and the lands were treated as property of the U.S. government (Feagin and Feagin, 1993). Most of the Mexicans and their descendants became landless laborers. The dispossession of land and depletion of their economic base have had long-term negative effects on Mexican American families (see Chapter 13).

Work and Gender Whether they lived and grew up in the United States or migrated from Mexico, Mexican laborers were essential to the prosperity of southwestern businesses. Mexican migrants were assigned to particular jobs by gender, and even though many had done skilled work in Mexico, employers purposely refrained from hiring them to do such work because "they are available in such [great] numbers and . . . they [would] do the most disagreeable work at the lowest wages" (Feldman, 1931: 115).

During the 1800s, women and children worked as almond pickers and shellers. Men typically worked on the railroads and in mining or in agricultural, ranching, or low-level urban occupations (such as dishwasher). Women worked as domestics, cooks, live-in house servants, and laundresses, in canning and packing houses, and in agriculture (Camarillo, 1979). By the 1930s, Mexican women made up a major portion of the labor pool of the garment manufacturing sweatshops in the Southwest. Even though American labor codes stipulated a pay rate of $15 a week, Mexican women were paid less than $5, and some earned as little as 50 cents a week. If the women protested, they lost their jobs. Illegal migrants were especially vulnerable because they were intimidated by threats of deportation (Acuna, 1988). Despite the economic exploitation, however, many Mexican families preserved traditional family structure, child rearing, and family roles.

Family Structure Mexican society was characterized by what is called **familism**; that is, family relationships took precedence over individual well-being. (As we will see in Chapter 13, familism still characterizes the Mexican American culture.) Moreover, the nuclear family grew to embrace an extended family of several generations, including cousins, within which the relationships were both emotionally and financially supportive (Moore and Pachon, 1985).

A key factor in conserving Mexican culture was the concept and practice of **compadrazgo,** in which close relationships were established and maintained among parents, children, and the children's godparents. The *compadres,* or co-parents, were godparents who enlarged family ties, rather like the fictive kin described in Chapter 1. Godparents were close family friends who had strong ties with their godchildren throughout life and participated in such rites of passage as baptism, confirmation, first communion, and marriage. The godparents in the *compadrazgo* network provided both discipline and support. They expected obedience, respect, and love from their godchildren, but they were warm and affectionate with the children and helped them financially when they could. Among poor or rural families, godparents also provided trips away from home. For girls, who led cloistered and protected lives, visiting among godparents' families was a major form of recreation (Williams, 1990).

Children The handful of diaries, letters, and other writings that are available suggests that, at least in middle- and upper-class families, children were socialized according to gender. Although boys did some chores that might have been labeled "women's work," they also had considerably more freedom than girls. Young girls were severely restricted in their social relationships outside the home. The overwhelming concern was that a girl should learn how to be a good mother and wife—a refuge for the husband, a virtuous example for her children, and the "soul of society" (del Castillo, 1984: 81).

A diary kept from 1889 to 1892 by a teenage girl who lived on the outskirts of San Antonio indicates that her brother was responsible for helping with such family tasks as laundry and chopping wood and that he was allowed to go into town on errands and to travel around the countryside on his horse. In contrast, she was not allowed to go into town with her father and brother or to attend chaperoned dances in the town. She could not visit neighbors, and in a six-month period, she attended only one social event when, at Christmastime, her family traveled into town to visit her aunt (del Castillo, 1984).

Many middle-class Mexican American children who were born in the United States had a prolonged adolescence, living with their parents until young adulthood. This was because, in general, Mexican American families believed in protecting children as long as possible. The practice was more common among affluent families, where children stayed at home to learn to take care of inherited land and wealth. In contrast, working-class children left home earlier to seek wage-paying jobs.

Much socialization of children was based on religious teachings and parental role models. It was not uncommon for children to memorize long passages from the religious catechism. Although the upper classes were more permissive, all children were taught respect for their parents and elders. In California, parents even took their children to public executions (until the 1870s, when such executions were banned) to teach them the fatal consequences of evil acts.

Family Roles Even though many mothers were forced by economic necessity to work outside the home, women were the cultural guardians of family traditions. In spite of the disruptions caused by migratory work, women nurtured Mexican culture through folklore, songs, baptisms, weddings, and celebrations of birthdays and saints' days (Garcia, 1980). In the traditional family, women defined their roles primarily as homemakers and mothers.

In the Mexican American family, the male head of the family had all the authority. Masculinity was expressed in the concept of *machismo*, which stresses such male attributes as dominance, assertiveness, pride, and sexual prowess. (The considerable controversy surrounding the interpretation of *machismo* is discussed in Chapter 13.) This notion of male preeminence carried with it the clear implication of a double standard; men could engage in premarital and extramarital sex, for example, but women were expected to remain virgins or faithful to their husbands and to limit their social relationships, even after marriage, to family and female friends (Mirande, 1985; Moore and Pachon, 1985).

The European Influence Although they suffered less physical and cultural destruction than Native Americans, Mexican Americans endured a great deal at the hands of European frontiersmen, land speculators, and politicians. Anglos (a term originally used by many Mexicans to mean whites of non-Mexican descent; now sometimes used to mean people of Anglo-Saxon descent) justified taking over Mexican land by describing Mexicans as having a "distinctly low mental caliber," being incapable of self-government, and working cheaply (Carlson and Colburn, 1972). By the mid-1800s, when most Mexican Americans were beginning to experience widespread exploitation, new waves of European immigrant families were also put under the yoke of industrialization.

INDUSTRIALIZATION AND EUROPEAN IMMIGRATION

The lives of many people in the United States were changed considerably during the period from about 1820 to 1920. Two massive waves of immigration occurred between 1830 and 1930. More than 10 million immigrants—mostly English, Irish, Scandinavian, and German—arrived during the first wave, from 1830 to 1882. During the second wave, 1882 to 1930, immigrants were predominantly Russian, Greek, Polish, Italian, Austrian, Hungarian, and Slavic.

The Industrial Revolution brought about extensive mechanization, which shifted home manufacturing to large-scale factory production. As the economic structure changed, a small group of white, Anglo-Saxon, Protestant (often referred to as WASP), upper-class families prospered from the backbreaking labor of Hispanic Americans, Asians, European immigrants, and many American-born whites. For millions of other families, the changes in work style brought poverty, family dislocations, and enormous hardships. European immigrants sustained some of the most severe pressures on family life.

Family Life

As farming became large scale and commercial and as factories developed, families lost many of their production functions. Most family members had to work outside the home to purchase goods and services. Although it is not clear exactly how it happened, family life changed.

In the middle classes, husbands and wives developed separate spheres of activity. The husband went out to work (the "breadwinner") and the wife stayed home to care for the children (the "housewife"). Couples had more freedom in choosing partners on the basis of compatibility and personal attraction because romantic love became the basis for marriage. As households became more private, ties with the larger community became more tenuous, and spouses now turned to each other for affection and happiness. New attitudes about the "true woman" became paramount in redefining the role of the wife as nurturer and caregiver rather than workmate. In the lower socioeconomic classes, many mothers worked outside the home and in low-paying jobs. Children dropped out of school to work and help support their families, and spouses had little time to display love and affection.

The Debut of "True Womanhood" By the late eighteenth century, a small group of northern merchants had monopolized the import business and wealthy southern planters had greatly expanded their land holdings and crop production. The wives and daughters of these elite business leaders devoted much of their energy to "a conspicuous display of personal adornment and social graces." The women spent much of their time socializing, throwing lavish parties, and adorning their homes and themselves: "The upkeep of her appearance . . . might involve preparation of the cosmetic base, aqua vitae, a potion requiring 30 ingredients, 2 months' cultivation, and an impossible final step: 'shake the bottle incessantly for 10 to 12 hours'" (quoted in Ryan, 1983: 85–86).

By the early 1800s, most men's work was totally separated from the household, and family life became oriented around the man's struggle in the economy at large. The "good" wife made the home a comfortable retreat from the pressures that the man faced in the workplace. Between 1820 and 1860, women's magazines and religious literature defined the attributes of **true womanhood.** Women were judged as "good" if they had four cardinal virtues: piety, purity, submissiveness, and domesticity (Welter, 1966). As the box "Characteristics of True Womanhood" suggests, working-class women were not considered capable of being "true women" because, like men, most worked outside the home.

Children and Adolescents Fathers' control over children began to erode even before the onset of the Industrial Revolution. By the end of the seventeenth century, fathers had less land to divide among sons. This meant that fathers had less authority over their children's (especially sons') sexual behavior and choice of a marriage partner. The fact that the percentage of women who were pregnant at the time of marriage shot up to more than 40 percent by the middle of the eighteenth century (Mintz and Kellogg, 1988) suggests that parents had become less effective in preventing premarital intercourse.

Because a marriage had become less likely to involve agreements about the distribution of family land and property, children were less dependent on their fathers for economic support. Moreover, new opportunities for nonagricultural work and a shortage of labor allowed many children to leave home and escape strict fathers.

Perhaps the biggest change was that, largely in the middle class, children began to be perceived and treated as not just small adults but as

_C_HANGES

Characteristics of "True Womanhood"

One author describes nineteenth-century working-class women as "without corsets, matrons with their breasts unrestrained, their armpits damp with sweat, with their hair all over the place, blouses dirty or torn, and stained skirts" (Barret-Ducrocq, 1991: 11). According to Barbara Welter (1966), the rules for the "true woman" of the upper classes (and these rules trickled down to middle-class, but not working-class, women) were quite different.

The loss of purity was worse than death. Mrs. Eliza Farrar, in _The Young Lady's Friend_ (1837), gave practical advice about staying out of trouble: "Sit not with another in a place that is too narrow; read not out of the same book; let not your eagerness to see anything induce you to place your head close to another person's."

Men were the movers, the doers, the actors. Women should be pure, gentle, passive, submissive, childlike, weak, dependent, and pro-

tected. They should work silently, unseen, and only for affection, not for money or ambition. Women should marry, but not for money. They should choose "only the high road of true love and not truckle to the values of a materialistic society" (Welter, 1966). A woman should submerge her own talents and devote herself "to sustain her husband's genius and aid him in his arduous career." Domesticity was a woman's most prized virtue. Nevertheless, one of the most important functions of woman as comforter was her role as nurse. The sickroom needed her "higher qualities" of patience, mercy, gentleness, and housewifely arts (Welter, 1966).

Home was supposed to be a cheerful place, so that brothers, husbands, and sons would not go elsewhere in search of a good time. Women were not only the "highest adornment of civilization" but were supposed to keep busy at "morally uplifting tasks." Fortunately, housework was seen as uplifting. For example, making beds was good exercise, the repetitive-

ness of routine tasks inculcated patience and perseverance, and proper management of the home was a surprisingly complex art: "There is more to be learned about pouring out tea and coffee than most young ladies are willing to believe" (Welter, 1966).

The true woman was expected to have a special affinity for flowers: "A woman never appears more truly in her sphere than when she divides her time between domestic avocations and the culture of flowers." She could write letters, "an activity particularly feminine since it had to do with the outpourings of the heart," practice singing and playing an instrument, or even read. Because women were dangerously addicted to novels, however, they should avoid them because they interfered with "serious piety." If a woman simply had to read, she should choose spiritually uplifting books from a list of "morally acceptable authors." On the whole, religious biographies were preferred (Welter, 1966).

individuals in a particular stage of life. Around 1800, the concept of original sin—which decrees that children are inherently bad—gave way to the notion that children were innocent creatures with the capacity for either good or bad. Children began to spend more time playing than working, and adolescence gained recognition as an additional stage of life that had no adult responsibilities. More books for and about children were published, and people began to recognize children's individuality by giving them names that were different from their father's or mother's. In the nineteenth century, people began for the first time to celebrate birthdays, especially those of children. There was also a marked decline in the use of corporal punishment, and physicians and others now recognized the early onset of sexual feelings in children (Aries, 1962; Degler, 1981; Demos, 1986).

Among the working classes and the poor in the nineteenth century, however, child labor was widespread, and children made a critical contribution to their families' income. In a Massachusetts survey of working-class families in 1875, for example, children under age 15 contributed nearly 20 percent of their families' income (Mintz and Kellogg, 1988).

The Impact of Immigration

Immigration played a key role in the Industrial Revolution in the United States. Immigrants provided a large pool of unskilled and skilled labor that fueled emerging industries and gave investors huge profits. In the first large waves of immigration during the late 1800s, paid middlemen arranged for the shipment of immigrants to waiting industries. For example, Asians were channeled into the western railroads, Italians were funneled into public works projects and used as strike breakers, and Hungarians were directed toward the Pennsylvania mines. Later immigrants followed these established ties into industrial America (Bodnar, 1985).

Work Very few immigrant families escaped dire poverty. Because men's wages were low, most married women also worked. Many were not counted by the census because they worked outside of organized industries. For example, many women worked at home at such tasks as flower making, threading wires through tags, or crocheting over curtain rings. Some worked as cleaning women or seamstresses or took in laun-

These Pennsylvania miners and "breaker boys"—youngsters who sorted the mined coal into graded categories—worked long hours for very low pay. Like most miners of the period, they were immigrants or the sons of immigrants, and they made the U.S. Industrial Revolution possible.

dry or sold cakes (Weatherford, 1986). Others took in boarders and lodgers, especially after their children had left home (Hareven, 1984). And, like the men, women of different ethnic groups tended to move into specific jobs. For example, Italian women were more likely than Polish or Greek women to reject domestic labor, which would take them out of the Italian community and into other people's homes. Consequently, they were more likely to work as seasonal laborers for fruit-and-vegetable processing companies. In this way, they also avoided competing for work with their frequently unemployed husbands (Squier and Quadagno, 1988). By the turn of the century, as Figure 3.2 shows, a woman's occupation seemed to be associated with her race and ethnicity.

By 1890, all but 9 of the 369 industries listed by the U.S. Census Bureau employed women. Many of these industries were especially eager to hire "greenhorns" and women "just off the boat" who would work for low wages. Greenhorns were often underpaid or not paid at all. In some cases, employers delayed wage payments for several months and then closed up the shops, disap-

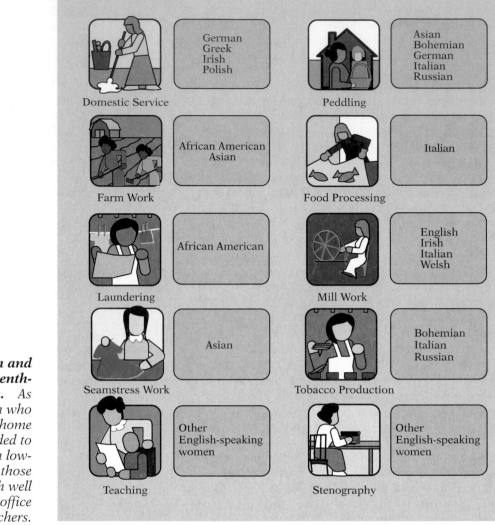

Figure 3.2 Women and Work in Nineteenth-Century America. *As you can see, women who worked outside the home in the 1800s tended to cluster in certain low-paying jobs. Only those who spoke English well were hired as office workers or teachers.*

Domestic Service — German, Greek, Irish, Polish

Peddling — Asian, Bohemian, German, Italian, Russian

Farm Work — African American, Asian

Food Processing — Italian

Laundering — African American

Mill Work — English, Irish, Italian, Welsh

Seamstress Work — Asian

Tobacco Production — Bohemian, Italian, Russian

Teaching — Other English-speaking women

Stenography — Other English-speaking women

pearing overnight (Manning, 1970). By the turn of the century, some Irish girls as young as 11 began leaving home to work as servants; 75 percent of all Irish teenage girls became domestic servants (Ryan, 1983). Many had to perform child-care tasks even though they were hired only to do housekeeping, were sexually assaulted by the male employers, and were not paid their full wages.

Many manufacturing jobs were segregated by sex. For example, in the tobacco industry, even though cigar rolling had traditionally been a woman's task in Slavic countries, men filled this well-paying job. Immigrant women were relegated to damp and putrid basement rooms where they stripped the tobacco used by the

men. In the metal trades, men who had gone through apprenticeships worked with lighter and more intricate sand cores (devices used in molding steel) and had high-paying jobs. In contrast, immigrant women hauled heavy sand cores through dusty shops to fuming ovens (Ryan, 1983).

Housing One of the biggest problems for immigrant families was the lack of decent housing. In a review of some of the historical literature, Weatherford (1986) describes some families' homes; one Philadelphia tenement house held 30 families in 34 rooms. A Lithuanian woman lived with her husband and five children in a tiny closet of a home that contained only slightly more air space than the law required for one adult. New York City police, enforcing health department orders, found many immigrants' rooms that, less than 13 square feet in all, slept 12 men and women, most of them on the floor. The buildings themselves were jammed together so that the population of an immigrant city block was equal to that of an entire town; women increased their kitchen wall space by reaching out the window and hanging utensils on the outside of the house next door.

Epidemics and disease were common to immigrant families. A cholera epidemic that barely touched the rest of New York City killed nearly a fifth of the residents of a crowded immigrant neighborhood. Because a third of tenement rooms had no windows or ventilation, many immigrants contracted tuberculosis. A 1912 study done in Lawrence, Massachusetts, where the population was 90 percent immigrant, found that a third of the spinners in the textile mills died of respiratory diseases, such as pneumonia and tuberculosis, before they had worked 10 years. These diseases were promoted by the lint, dust, and machine fumes of the unventilated mills. Further, the excruciating noise of the mills often resulted in deafness, and many workers were injured by faulty machines (Weatherford, 1986).

Dilapidated housing and epidemics were not the only problems the immigrant family faced. In a pioneering study of Polish immigrants, Thomas and Znaniecki (1927) found that people suffered many of the ills that come with poverty and isolation in a strange and often hostile new environment—a breakdown of marital and family relations, crime, delinquency among their children, and general demoralization. Living quarters shared with relatives put additional pressures on already-strained conjugal ties.

Prejudice and Discrimination Like Native Americans and African Americans before them, white immigrants, no matter what their country of origin, met with enormous prejudice, discrimination, and economic exploitation. What is especially interesting is that prejudice and discrimination were fostered by high-ranking, highly respected, and influential people who had been educated in the most prestigious institutions of higher learning in America (see the box "Attitudes Toward European Immigrants"). Despite the prejudice and discrimination, however, most white immigrant and racial-ethnic families over-

came enormous obstacles. Rarely complaining, they worked at low-status jobs with low-paying wages and encouraged their children to achieve and move up.

THE EMERGENCE OF THE "MODERN" FAMILY

The economic depression of the 1930s, World War II of the 1940s, the baby boom of the 1950s, and the increasing economic and political unrest of the years since the 1960s have all influenced the American family—sometimes for better, sometimes for worse. By the beginning of the twentieth century, what came to be called the companionate family was on the rise (Burgess et al., 1963).

Rise of the Companionate Family (1900–1930)

The turn of the century saw married couples increasingly stressing the importance of sexual attraction and compatibility in their relationships. Particularly in the middle classes, the notion of companionship, or the *companionate family*, encompassed a couple's children. Affection between parents and children was more intimate and more openly demonstrated, and adolescents were given greater freedom from direct parental supervision. This new independence generated public criticism, however. Many of the popular magazines, such as *The Atlantic Monthly*, *The Ladies' Home Journal*, and the *New Republic*, worried about "young people's rejection of genteel manners, their defiant clothing and hairstyles, their slang-filled language, and their 'lewd' pastimes . . . (such as smoking, attending petting parties, and going out on school nights). Public condemnation and moral outrage were widespread" (Mintz and Kellogg, 1988: 119). Do any of these complaints about young people sound familiar?

The Great Depression (1929–1939)

Many of us have heard stories about families that coped and families that collapsed during the widespread unemployment and poverty that characterized the Great Depression. In fact, families had a great variety of experiences, influenced largely by such factors as residence, social class, gender, and race.

Attitudes Toward European Immigrants

On October 28, 1886, President Grover Cleveland dedicated the Statue of Liberty in New York Harbor on whose pedestal are inscribed Emma Lazarus's famous welcoming words: "Give me your tired, your poor, your huddled masses yearning to breathe free. . . ." As the following selections show, however, Lazarus's poem did not reflect the reality:

1886—The U.S. consul in Budapest advised that Hungarian immigrants were not "a desirable acquisition" because, he claimed, they loved whiskey as much as the Chinese loved opium, they lacked ambition, and they would work as cheaply as the Chinese, which would interfere "with a civilized laborer's earning a 'white' laborer's wages."

1891—Congressman Henry Cabot Lodge called for the restriction of immigration because [referring especially to Jews and Poles] the immigrants represented the "lowest and most illiterate classes," which were "alien to the body of the American people."

1910—The eugenics movement was devoted to improving the human species by controlling hereditary factors in mating. Its members believed that immigration, through intermarriage, would contaminate the "old stock" with feeblemindedness, criminality, and pauperism. Many eugenicists were located in prominent eastern universities. It was Robert DeCourcey War, for example, a Boston-born Harvard graduate and professor, who helped form the Immigration Restriction League in 1894.

1914—Edward A. Ross, a prominent sociologist at the University of Wisconsin, considered himself one of the nation's immigration watchdogs. He wrote: "That the Mediterranean people are morally below the races of northern Europe is as certain as any social fact."

1922—Kenneth L. Roberts, a Cornell graduate, served as a correspondent for the *Saturday Evening Post* in Washington, D. C., and in Europe, turning out numerous articles on the immigration question. He warned that "if a few more million members of the Alpine, Mediterranean, and Semitic races are poured among us, the result must inevitably be a hybrid race of people as worthless and futile as the good-for-nothing mongrels of Central America and Southeastern Europe."

1946—After World War II, the immigration of displaced persons revived old fears. Influential senators, like Pat McCurran, James Eastland, and Richard Russell, argued that political immigrants should not be permitted to enter the United States because of their "alien philosophies" and "biological incompatibility with Americans' parent stocks."

1963—Harvard sociologists Nathan Glazer and Patrick Moynihan described Puerto Rican Americans as weak, disorganized, and "sadly defective" in their culture and family system (Glazer and Moynihan, 1963: 88–90; Carlson and Colburn, 1972: 311–50; for other stereotypes about immigrants, see Feagin and Feagin, 1993).

Urban-Rural Residence Our most common images of the Depression are photographs of long lines at employment agencies in large cities, but many farm families were equally devastated. Among tenant families, husbands sometimes left their families to search for jobs. Some women who could not cope with such desertion took drastic steps to end their misery. In 1938, for example, a Nebraska farm mother of 13 children committed suicide by walking into the side of a train because "she had had enough" (Fink, 1992: 172). Even when husbands stayed at home, some families lost their land and personal property. Mothers and fathers made enormous sacrifices to feed their children. As one jobless Oregonian father stated: "We do not dare to use even a little soap when it will pay for an extra egg or a few more carrots for our children" (cited in McElvaine, 1993: 172).

To help support their families, many young men and women raised on farms moved to cities to find work. Young women were more likely to find jobs because there was a demand for low-paying domestic help. Although the wages were low, many young women tried to help their families:

Alice [from a farm in Nebraska] got a domestic job in Chicago through family friends. She sent some of her ten-dollar weekly paycheck to her parents' farm home: "I didn't send much, but I would buy clothes for my sisters—sweaters and skirts and things like that. . . . [My brother] was in high school. I sent him money. I know he bought his suit for graduation and he was real pleased because of that" (Fink, 1992: 180).

In some cases, fathers wore a son's suits for job interviews because they could not afford to buy their own clothes: "They're all we've got now. We take turns wearing 'em" (McElvaine, 1993: 181).

Social Class The Depression had the most devastating effect on working-class and poor families. Women who worked did so because of poverty rather than to earn "pin money," or extra spending money. More than half of all women were employed in low-paying jobs, such as domestic and personal service and apparel and canning factories. The poorest states—South Carolina, Mississippi, Louisiana, Georgia, and Alabama—had the highest proportion of married working women (Cavan and Ranck, 1938; Chafe, 1972).

In contrast to the middle classes, children from working classes did not have carefree teenage years during the 1930s. Boys, especially, were expected to work after school or to leave school entirely to supplement their family's meager income. When mothers found jobs, older children, especially girls, looked after their younger brothers and sisters and often had to drop out of school to do so (McElvaine, 1993).

Some children who became part of the "transient army" that drifted from town to town looking for work were injured or maimed in the process. For example, one of the children who traveled from train to train was a Pennsylvania Dutch boy nicknamed Blink:

He had lost an eye when a live cinder blew into his face while he was riding an open car on the Santa Fe railroad. A bloody socket forms a small and ever-weeping cave on the left side of his face. . . . Tears streak his cheek, furrowing the dirt and coal soot, leaving a strange moist scar alongside his nose (Watkins, 1993: 60).

Most of the transients slept in lice-ridden and rat-infested housing when they could afford to pay the 10 or 15 cents for a urine-stained mattress on the floor. Others slept on park benches, under park shrubbery and bridges, in doorways, in packing crates, on construction sites, or in abandoned automobiles (Watkins, 1993).

As blue-collar unemployment in the male-dominated industrial sectors increased, white-collar clerical and government jobs expanded, and women took many of these jobs. It was the wages of white middle-class women that enabled their families to maintain, even during the Depression, the standard of living and consumer habits that had been established during the affluent 1920s (Ryan, 1983).

Families in the upper middle classes fared even better. Although many incomes decreased, the sacrifices of fairly affluent families were minor. Some families cut down on entertainment, did not renew club memberships, and decreased such outside family services as domestic help. Few women reported problems in food budgets, and many of these families continued to take summer vacations. In fact, there was even an increase in the number of families that owned radios, musical instruments, and new cars (Morgan, 1939).

Race Although the Depression was an economic disaster for many Americans, African Americans suffered even more greatly. Unemployment was much higher among blacks than whites, for as layoffs began in late 1929 and accelerated in the following years, blacks were often the first to be fired. By 1932, unemployment among African Americans had reached approximately 50 percent nationwide. As the economic situation deteriorated, many whites demanded that blacks be replaced by white workers in such occupations as garbage collector, elevator operator, waiter, bellhop, and street cleaner. In some government jobs, an unofficial quota of 10 percent black enrollment was set, on the theory that this represented, roughly, the percentage of blacks in the general population. In fact, though, only about 6 percent were employed by the government. Even those who were able to keep their jobs faced great hardship; a 1935 study in Harlem found that from the onset of the Depression, skilled black workers experienced a drop of nearly 50 percent in their wages (McElvaine, 1993; Watkins, 1993).

Gender Roles In many families, unemployment played havoc with gender roles. Because the position of the husband and father was based on his occupation and his role as provider, if he lost his job he often suffered a decline in status within the family. Men, understandably, were despondent: "Sometimes the father did not go to bed but moved from chair to chair all night long" (Cavan and Ranck, cited in Griswold, 1993: 148). And with the ability to provide often went authority and the respect of a man's children. Adolescents became more independent and more rebellious (Griswold, 1993).

In 1932, a federal executive order decreed that only one spouse could work for the federal government. The widespread unemployment of men thus put pressure on women, especially married women, to resign from some occupations. School boards fired married female teachers, and some companies dismissed married women. More than 77 percent of the school districts in the United States would not hire married women, and 50 percent had a policy of firing women who married (Milkman, 1976; McElvaine, 1993). When women did work, the federal government not only permitted lower pay rates for women than men but promoted sex discrimination as well. For example, men on Works Progress Administration (WPA) projects were paid $5 per day; women received only $3.

World War II (1939–1945)

World War II wrought even greater changes in the lives of American families. These changes, which began to be felt in 1941, after the United States entered the war, affected both work roles and family life.

Work Roles When the United States entered World War II, there was a scarcity of workers, especially in the defense and manufacturing industries, because many able-bodied men were drafted. Initially, employers were not enthusiastic about recruiting women for traditionally male jobs, and many women (especially white middle-class women) were unwilling to violate traditional gender roles. In 1942, employers— prompted by both the Women's Bureau of the U.S. Department of Labor and organized women's groups—attempted to fill many jobs, especially those in nontraditional positions, with women. The government, supported by the mass media, was enormously successful in convincing both men and women that "woman's place is in the workplace" and not the home:

They created "Rosie the Riveter," who became the lauded symbol of the woman temporarily at work. In all the media, women at work were pictured and praised, and the woman who did not at least raise a "victory garden" or work as a volunteer for

the Red Cross was made to feel guilty. . . . Even the movies joined in. The wife or sweetheart who stayed behind and went to work . . . became as familiar a figure as the valiant soldier-lover for whom she waited (Banner, 1984: 219).

As the Data Digest shows, millions of women, including middle-aged mothers (and even grandmothers), now worked in shipyards, steel mills, and ammunition factories. They welded, dug ditches, and operated forklifts. Some of the greatest gains were made by African American women, who, for the first time, were recruited into high-paying jobs. Hundreds of thousands of domestic servants and farm workers left their jobs for much better paying positions in the defense and other industries. In the superb documentary film entitled *The Life and Times of Rosie the Riveter*, African American women describe the pride and exhilaration they felt in having not only well-paying jobs but jobs they genuinely enjoyed doing.

Because of the labor shortages, this was the only time when even working-class women were praised for working outside the home. Examining two of the best-selling magazines—the *Saturday Evening Post* and *True Story*, Honey (1984) found that both periodicals supported the government's propaganda efforts before, during,

Many women who worked in American factories, steel mills, and shipyards while their men fought World War II found it hard to give up their new-found competence and independence when the war was over.

and shortly after World War II by casting working-class women in very positive roles:

Stories and advertisements glorified factory work as psychologically rewarding, as emotionally exciting, and as leading to success in love. Both magazines combated class prejudice against factory work by portraying working-class men and women as diligent, patriotic, wholesome people. The Post fostered positive images of blue-collar work by describing the intellectual challenges of problem solving and praising American ingenuity involved in war production. Working-class women were resourceful, respectable, warmhearted, and resilient. In True Story, *characters experienced pride in their working-class origins and were glad to be an important part of the nation (Honey, 1984: 186–87).*

Family Life Although divorce rates had been increasing slowly since the turn of the century, they hit a new high in 1946, a year after the end of World War II. The war had a direct, negative effect on many families. Some wives and mothers who had worked during the war enjoyed their newfound economic independence and decided to end problematic marriages. In other cases, families disintegrated because of the strains brought about by the return of a partially or completely incapacitated husband. But it was alcoholism, which was rampant among veterans, that was believed to be the major cause of the upward spiral of postwar divorces (Tuttle, 1993).

For some people, the war deferred, rather than caused, divorce. Some couples, caught up in war hysteria, courted for a very short time and married impulsively before the man was shipped out. Other couples who might have been on the brink of divorce did not make the break "under the rationalizing aegis of patriotism" (Mowrer, 1972). In still other cases, when the husband was away for a prolonged period of time, both the bride and the young soldier matured, changed, and found they had little in common when they were reunited.

Perhaps one of the most difficult problems faced by families with returning war veterans was the reaction of children to fathers they barely knew or had never even seen. As the box "Daddy's Coming Home!" suggests, despite widespread rejoicing about the end of the war, a father's return was unsettling for many children in a variety of ways.

The "Golden" Fifties

After World War II, when women were no longer needed in the workplace and returning veterans needed jobs, the propaganda about family roles changed almost overnight. "Rosie the Riveter" advertisements were replaced by ads depicting happy housewives totally engrossed in vacuum cleaners and the latest home products. Heroines in short stories and women's magazines were no longer the nurses dying at the front, but mothers who devoted themselves exclusively to cooking, caring for their children, and pleasing their husbands. Movies and television shows celebrated two stereotyped portrayals of women—sweet, innocent virgins, like Doris Day and Debbie Reynolds, or sexy bombshells like Marilyn Monroe and Jayne Mansfield. Television applauded domesticity on such popular shows as "I Love Lucy," "Ozzie and Harriet," "Leave It to Beaver," and "Father Knows Best." The mannish, work-oriented clothes worn by women during the war

Reprinted with special permission of King Features Syndicate.

"Daddy's Coming Home!"

Soldiers returning from World War II encountered numerous problems, including unemployment and high divorce rates (Mowrer, 1972; Tuttle, 1993). Some of the difficulties returning dads and their children experienced were especially problematic.

Historian William M. Tuttle, Jr., (1993) solicited 2,500 letters from men and women, now in their 50s and 60s, who were children during World War II. What most of these people had in common were the difficulties they and their families experienced in adjusting to the return of their fathers from military service.

Some individuals recalled being afraid that their fathers would not stay and thus trying not to become too attached. Some were bitter that their fathers had left in the first place. Others, especially those who were preschoolers at the time, were frightened of the strange men who

The "G.I. Bill," enabled many World War II veterans to go to school and improve their job opportunities, but daily life for vets with families, like William Oskay, Jr., and his wife and daughter, was not luxurious.

suddenly moved into their homes. One woman remembered watching "the stranger with the big white teeth" come toward her; as he did, the four-year-old ran upstairs in terror and hid under a bed.

Some people recalled resenting their fathers for disrupting their lives. Grandparents had often pampered children they helped to raise. On the other hand, the returning father, fresh from military experience, was often a strict disciplinarian and saw the child as "a brat." In many cases, the children were very close to their mothers and protective of their siblings; they became jealous and resentful of fathers for displacing them. Other children were disappointed when the idealized images they had constructed of "Daddy" did not match reality. Or fathers who had been described as kind, sensitive, and gentle returned troubled or violent.

Readjustment was difficult for both the children and their fathers. Although some families slowly adjusted to the changes, in many families the returning fathers and their children never developed a close relationship.

---

were replaced by full skirts, defined bosoms, tiny waists, and very high heels. The average age at which women married decreased from 21.5 years in 1940 to 20.1 years in 1956. Countless marriage manuals and child-care experts, like Dr. Benjamin Spock, told women to be submissive and stay at home to raise their children. By the mid-1950s, 60 percent of female undergraduates were dropping out of college to marry (Banner, 1984).

As we noted in Chapter 1, during the generation right after World War II the nation experienced a baby boom. Family plans that had been disrupted by the war were renewed. Although women continued to enter the job market, many middle-class families, spurred by the mass media, sought a traditional family life in which the husband worked and the wife played the domestic role. The editor of *Mademoiselle* declared that women in their teens and twenties had decided to avoid careers and instead chose to raise

as many youngsters as the "good Lord" gave them. As households increased in size, "togetherness" became a watchword. "A family is like a corporation," one writer observed. "We all have to work for it." Many articles touted the value of families engaging in "creative" activities together, and the outdoor barbecue and cross-country camping trip became the vogue in family recreation (Chafe, 1972).

Suburbs mushroomed, accounting for nearly two-thirds of the population increase in the decade of the fifties. The interest in moving to the suburbs reflected structural and attitudinal changes. According to Rothman (1978), the federal government, fearful of a return to depression conditions, underwrote the construction of homes in the suburbs. Low-interest mortgages were made available to the general public, and veterans were offered the added inducement of being able to purchase a home with a $1 down payment. Massive highway construction programs enabled people to commute from the city to the suburbs. Families wanted more roominess, seclusion, and an escape from city noise, crime, dirt, and crowding. Finally, the larger space offered more privacy for both children and parents: "The spacious master bedroom, generally set apart from the rooms of the children, was well-suited to a highly sexual relationship. And wives anticipated spending many evenings alone with their husbands, not with family or friends" (Rothman, 1978: 225–26).

The suburban way of life added a new dimension to the traditional role of women:

The duties of child-rearing also underwent expansion. Suburban mothers volunteered for library work in the school, took part in PTA activities, and chauffeured their children from music lessons to scout meetings. Perhaps most important, the suburban wife was expected to make the home an oasis of comfort and serenity for her harried husband. "Modern man needs an old-fashioned woman around the house," the novelist Sloan Wilson declared. Newsweek stressed the importance of a woman understanding the tensions of her husband's job, and . . . emphasized how crucial it was for her to be a "model of efficiency, patience, and charm" (Chafe, 1972: 217–18).

Were such changes desirable? And did they really take place in most families? Some writers have proposed that many of these presumed shifts in people's beliefs and behavior are actually myths, not reality. Table 3.2 explores the downside of the 1950s.

The Family Since the 1960s

In this chapter we have laid the groundwork for the remaining chapters of the book. Beginning with Chapter 4, we shall be examining marriage and the family in recent decades. In the 1970s, for example, families had lower birth rates and higher divorce rates, and larger numbers of women entered colleges and graduate programs. In the 1980s, more people over 25 years of age postponed marriage, and many of those who were already married delayed having children. Out-of-wedlock births, especially among teenage girls, and one-parent households increased precipitously (see Chapter 9). There was also a burgeoning of two-income families and adult children

---

Table 3.2 _____

The Not-So-Golden Fifties

"Contrary to popular opinion," writes historian Stephanie Coontz, "'Leave It to Beaver' was not a documentary." In fact, the 1950s were riddled with many family problems, and people had fewer choices than they do now. Here are some examples:

Consumerism was limited; 25 percent of families were poor in the mid-1950s.

There was *little choice in many products.* For example, in 1950, a supermarket stocked an average of 3,750 items; in the 1990s, most markets carry more than 16,500 items. In the '50s, many prepared foods were loaded with lard, salt, sugar, and harmful preservatives. By the 1980s, the medical community were blaming such products for obesity and heart disease.

African Americans and other people of color faced *severe discrimination* in employment, housing, and access to recreational activities.

Both men and women were pressured into *rigid, socially acceptable family roles.* Bachelors, for example, were sometimes described as "immature," "infantile," "deviant," or even "pathological."

Domestic violence and child abuse were not discussed. Marilyn Van Derbur, crowned Miss America in 1958, has only recently admitted publicly that her wealthy, respectable father abused her sexually from the time she was five until she left home for college at eighteen.

Some writers believe that the 1950s were *sterile, conformist, and materialistic,* but these suggestions got little media attention.

Suburban living was not as widespread as we are led to believe, nor was it accessible to many families. In fact, the United States is much more suburban now than it was in the fifties. In addition, families of color could not buy homes in the suburbs because of widespread housing discrimination.

Many young people were forced into *"shotgun" marriages* because of premarital conception; young women were pressured to give up their babies for adoption.

About one-fifth of mothers had *paying jobs.* Although childcare services are still minimal, they were practically nonexistent during the 1950s.

Many people tried to escape from their unhappy lives through *alcohol or drugs.* The consumption of tranquilizers was virtually unheard of in 1955, but by 1958 had reached 462,000 pounds per year and in 1959 soared to almost 1.2 million pounds annually.

SOURCES: Coontz, 1992; Crispell, 1992; Reid, 1993.

---

who continued to live at home with their parents because of financial difficulties (see Chapter 12).

Economic problems have become more severe in the 1990s. Many young married couples cannot afford to buy a house, the number of families below the poverty level has been increasing steadily, and even middle-class families depend on two incomes to keep up with the cost of living (see Chapter 14). Racial and ethnic diversity has been increasing. On the one hand, this promises a culturally richer society. On the other hand, many white Americans feel threatened by the growth of nonwhite families, and some have responded with violence and racist attacks (see Chapter 13).

CONCLUSION

If we examine the family in a historical context, we see that *change*, and not stability, has been the norm. Furthermore, the family differed by region and social class even during colonial times. We also see that the experiences and *choices* open to Native Americans, African Americans, Mexican Americans, and many European immigrants were very different from those of "middle America," experiences that were romanticized by many television programs during the 1950s. Families were also affected by such macro-level *constraints* as wars and shifting demographic characteristics. Many families survived despite enormous hardships, disruptions, and dislocations. They are still coping with such macro-level constraints as an unpredictable economy and such micro-level variables as greater choices in family roles, however. The next chapter, on gender roles, examines some of these choices and constraints.

Taking Action

Roots, Trees, and Other Historical Data

History is fun, especially when you can explore it through your own family.

• If your professor assigns a "do-something-you-like" project, you might consider researching **your family tree.** There are many ways to do this: comb your relatives' attics for letters or diaries; interview your elderly family members about their experiences during the Great Depression and World War II, and trace your roots by examining court records, tombstones, and newspaper obituaries. Many Mormon churches provide remarkable genealogical resources and services. Some references to get you started include:

> Charles L. Blockson, *Black Genealogy* (Englewood Cliffs, NJ: Prentice Hall, 1977)
> Laverne Galeener-Moore, *Collecting Dead Relatives: An Irreverent Romp Through the Field of Genealogy* (Baltimore: Genealogical Publishing Co., 1987)
> Val D. Greenwood, *The Researcher's Guide to American Genealogy* (Baltimore: Genealogical Publishing Co., 1990).
> Ralph J. Crandall, *Shaking Your Family Tree: A Basic Guide to Tracing Your Family's Genealogy* (Dublin, NH: Yankee Publishers, 1986).

> Gilbert Doane and James Bell, *Searching for Your Ancestors*, 6th ed. (Minneapolis: University of Minnesota Press, 1992).
> Arthur Kurzweil, *From Generation to Generation: How to Trace Your Jewish Genealogy and Personal History* (New York: Schocken Books, 1982).

You can also get a computer disk for tracing family trees from Reasonable Solutions (800–876–3475).

• If you're a history buff (or major), you might consider joining H-NET, which deals with women's history, history of the American South, urban history, and other historical issues. The address is LISTSERV@UICVM.UIC.EDU.

• For some general historical information, you might subscribe to STUMPERS. According to the moderator/owner, this is a networking resource for reference questions that have most people, in essence, stumped: "After failing to find a satisfactory answer to your question in the usual library reference sources, turn to the people on STUMPERS. You could get an answer and, possibly, learn about a new reference source." Most of the questions on STUMPERS are historical. Also, be prepared for a lot of mail. To join STUMPERS, address your message to MAILSERV@CRF.CUIS.EDU.

SUMMARY

1. Historical factors have played an important role in shaping the contemporary family. The early exploitation of Native American, African American, and Mexican American families has had long-term economic effects on these groups in American society.

2. The colonial family was a self-sufficient unit that performed a wide variety of functions. Children were part of the family work force and were expected to be docile and well behaved. Premarital sex was not uncommon, wives' work was subordinate to husbands', and family practices varied across social classes and geographic regions.

3. Native American families were extremely diverse in function, structure, sexual relations, puberty rites, and child-rearing patterns. European armies, adventurers, and missionaries played major roles in destroying many tribes and much of the Native American culture.

4. Contrary to popular belief, many African American households had two parents, men played important roles as fathers or surrogate fathers, and most slave women worked as hard as the men did in the fields and not the "big house."

5. Mexican American families were dispossessed of their lands, which were taken over by European American settlers. Despite severe economic exploitation, many families survived through cohesive family networks and strong family bonds.

6. By the nineteenth century, industrialization had changed some aspects of the family. Marriages were based more on love and choice rather than on economic considerations, parental roles within the family became more sex-segregated, and in the middle class the "true woman," who devoted most of her time to looking beautiful and pleasing her husband, emerged.

7. Millions of European immigrants who worked in labor-intensive jobs at very low wages made it possible for industrialization to progress rapidly. Many immigrants, including women and children, faced severe social and economic discrimination and had to put up with dilapidated housing conditions and chronic health problems.

8. The most devastating effects of the Great Depression were felt by working-class families. While middle-class families cut back on luxuries, working-class men experienced widespread unemployment and their wives took jobs in the most menial and low-paying jobs.

9. World War II had a mixed effect on families. For the first time, many women, especially African American mothers, found jobs that paid a decent salary. However, many families were also disrupted by death, divorce, and incompatibility.

10. After the war, suburbs boomed and birth rates surged. The family roles of white middle-class women were expanded to include full-time nurturance of children and husbands. Husbands' roles were largely limited to work. The "golden fifties" was largely a mythical portrayal of the American family of that decade.

KEY TERMS

bundling   53
familism   64

compadrazgo   64
machismo   65

true womanhood   66

ADDITIONAL READING

TANIA BAYARD, *A Medieval Home Companion: Housekeeping in the Fourteenth Century* (New York: HarperCollins, 1991). This is a "fun" little book that reads like some of the literature on "true womanhood." It was written around 1393 by an elderly citizen of Paris to his 15-year-old bride, instructing her on moral and domestic duties. Some of the topics include the wife's chastity, love, caring for a husband (including ridding their bed of fleas), and managing a household.

RUTH B. MOYNIHAN, SUSAN ARMITAGE, and CHRISTINE FISCHER DICHAMP, eds., *So Much to Be Done: Women Settlers on the Mining and Ranching Farms* (Lincoln: University of Nebraska Press, 1990). Nineteen narratives by women settlers from diverse backgrounds. The narratives—culled from diaries, letters, memoirs, and autobiographies—describe the attitudes and day-to-day lives of people in the frontier West.

WILLIAM M. TUTTLE, JR., *Daddy's Gone to War: The Second World War in the Lives of America's Children* (New York: Oxford University Press, 1993). The author uses a mix of anecdotal material and statistics in describing how mothers and their children coped during World War II. Some of the topics include Pearl Harbor, fears and nightmares, working mothers and latchkey children, racial and cultural hostility, Daddy's coming home, and the homefront children at middle age.

In the last few years, a number of scholars have focused on the immigration experiences of Europeans, Asians, and Spanish-speaking peoples. Some current analyses include the following:

RICHARD D. ALBA, *Ethnic Identity: The Transformation of White America* (New Haven, CT: Yale University Press, 1990).

ROGER DANIELS, *Coming to America: A History of Immigration and Ethnicity in American Life* (New York: Harper Perennial, 1990).

THOMAS SOWELL, *Race and Culture: A World View* (New York: Basic Books, 1994).

RONALD TAKAKI, *A Different Mirror: A History of Multicultural America* (Boston: Little, Brown, 1993).

DAVID HURST THOMAS, JAY MILLER, RICHARD WHITE, PETER NABOKOV, and PHILIP J. DELORIA, *The Native Americans: An Illustrated History* (Atlanta, GA: Turner Publishing Co., 1993).

4

Gender Roles:
More Choices,
More Constraints

Archibald J. Motley, Jr., Cocktails

Data Digest

National polls have found striking **gender gaps** on some recent issues:

• During the Persian Gulf conflict, men tended to favor the **use of force**, whereas women endorsed economic sanctions. On the first night of bombing, an ABC-*Washington Post* survey found that 84 percent of men but only 68 percent of women approved of going to war.

• Fifty-seven percent of women but only 31 percent of men agreed with the **not-guilty verdict for Lorena Bobbitt** (who cut off her husband's penis).

• The Portland *Oregonian* found that 60 percent of women and 34 percent of men in the state wanted **Senator Bob Packwood** to resign for allegedly making unwanted sexual advances to women.

• Before **Tonya Harding** was actually charged with the attack on fellow figure skater Nancy Kerrigan, 58 percent of the men polled and 45 percent of the women thought Harding should remain on the U.S. Olympic team.

• When an American teenager in Singapore confessed to **acts of vandalism**, 61 percent of U.S. men and 39 percent of women approved of caning him as a punishment.

SOURCES: Colburn, 1991; Pertman, 1994; *The Public Perspective*, 1994.

In 1993, the evening before a football game in Boston, Houston Oilers tackle David Williams decided to stay at the hospital with his wife after their son was born. The Oilers managers were miffed. They said that Williams had plenty of time to be with his family and make the football game. So they docked him a week's pay: $125,000. The incident stimulated some controversy for a few weeks. Was Williams really letting his teammates down? Is a football game more important than being with one's wife and child in the first hours of the infant's life?

We keep hearing that the 1990s are "really different" because both men and women have a lot of options. Do they? This chapter examines gender roles: how they are learned and how they affect our everyday relations in marriage and the family.

THE DIFFERENCE BETWEEN SEX AND GENDER

Sex, *gender*, and *gender role* are not synonymous. **Sex** is the group of biological characteristics with which we are born—chromosomal, anatomical, hormonal, and other physical and physiological attributes—that determine whether we are male or female. **Gender**, on the other hand, refers to learned attitudes and behaviors that characterize people of one sex or the other; gender is based on social and cultural expectations rather than on physical qualities. Thus, whereas we are *born* either male or female, we *learn* either the masculine or the feminine gender. Sociologist Judith Lorber (1994) calls gender a social institution, an invention by human beings. Like the concept of family itself, the concept of gender helps us organize social life in culturally patterned ways.

As we saw in Chapter 1, one of the functions of the family is to teach its members appropriate social roles. Among the most important of these are **gender roles**—distinctive patterns of attitudes, behaviors, and activities that society prescribes for females and males. We learn to become masculine or feminine through interaction with family members and the larger society. Thus, for example, in most societies traditionally men are expected to provide physical shelter, food, and clothing for their family members, and women are expected to nurture and teach their children interpersonal skills and to tend to the everyday needs of their family members. Our notions of what is appropriate behavior for each sex are so deeply embedded in our culture that most of us conform to the expected gender roles without thinking about it.

Gender roles shape our lives at work, at home, and in social groups. At home, men are more likely to change the oil in the car, and women are more likely to change the baby's diaper. In the workplace, women more often operate the fax machine, but men more often give orders about what to fax. As we will see in the next section, gender roles vary, depending on situational factors as well as race or ethnicity and social class, and they also vary over time and across cultures.

THE NATURE-NURTURE DEBATE: IS ANATOMY DESTINY?

For some social scientists, differentiating between sex and gender, or gender role, is extremely important. If gender roles are learned, these scientists argue, they can also be unlearned. Other social scientists and biologists, though, believe that observed differences in the ways women and men behave are attributable to their innate, biological characteristics, and not to social and cultural expectations. This difference of opinion is often called the "nature-nurture" debate (see Table 4.1).

Sigmund Freud (1856–1939), the founder of modern psychoanalysis, was one of the first writers to propose that "anatomy is destiny." Freud believed that female and male infants acquired gender roles differently because of anatomical differences. According to Freud, girls realize they have no penis, experience penis envy, blame the mother for their lack of a penis, and focus their affections on the father. In time, they realize their own similarity to the mother and identify with her, replacing their wish for a penis with a desire to have a child. Despite the fact that the Freudian notion of gender-role acquisition has been rejected by many scholars, some theorists still maintain that, to a great extent, anatomy determines behavior.

The question of whether male and female differences are due to heredity (nature) or environment (nurture) has been hotly debated since the 1970s (see, for example, O'Kelly, 1986; Mirowsky and Ross, 1987; Andersen, 1993; Lindsey, 1994). Those who believe that masculine and feminine traits are innate argue that men are born with the drive to be ambitious and successful, that women are happiest when they are making a home for their family and caring for their children, that women are "naturally" better parents, and that men are "naturally" more aggressive. Those who believe that nurture is more important than nature argue that there are more similarities than differences between women and men, that gender roles are learned differently in various societies, and that there are no scientific data showing that biology *causes* men and women to act differently.

How Important Is Nature?

There are some established biological differences between men and women. For instance, infant mortality rates are higher for boys, and boys are afflicted with more genetic disorders, such as night blindness, myopia (nearsightedness), hemophilia, progressive deafness, and juvenile glaucoma (Montagu, 1974). The senses of smell and taste are more acute in females than in males, females' hearing is better and lasts longer than men's, and, on average, women live seven years longer than men do.

Scientists believe that many of these differences between men and women are due to hormonal action. All males and females share three sex **hormones**—chemical substances secreted into the bloodstream by glands of the endocrine system. They are *estrogen* (dominant in females and produced by the ovaries), *progesterone* (present in high levels during pregnancy and also secreted in the ovaries), and *testosterone* (dominant in males, where it is produced by the testes). All of these hormones are produced in very small quantities in both sexes before puberty. After puberty, different levels of these hormones in males and females result in different changes. For example, testosterone, the dominant male sex hormone, strengthens muscles but threatens the heart. It triggers production of low-density lipoprotein, which clogs blood vessels. Thus, males are at twice the risk of coronary heart disease as are females. The dominant female sex hormones, especially estrogen, make blood vessels more elastic and strengthen the immune system, giving females more resistance to infection (Boston Women's Health Book Collective, 1992).

Table 4.1

The Nature-Nurture Debate

NATURE	NURTURE
DIFFERENCES IN MALE AND FEMALE BELIEFS, ATTITUDES, AND BEHAVIOR ARE:	DIFFERENCES IN MALE AND FEMALE BELIEFS, ATTITUDES, AND BEHAVIOR ARE:
Innate	Learned
Biological, physiological	Psychological, social, cultural
Due to heredity	Due to environment
Fairly fixed	Very changeable

Do Hormones Affect Gender Roles? Yes, sometimes. Major hormonal differences between men and women are responsible for **premenstrual syndrome**, or **PMS**, from which many women suffer to one degree or another. PMS, which occurs a few days before menstruation, results from a malfunction in the production of hormones during the menstrual cycle. Affecting about 80 percent of women, PMS causes physical symptoms including cramps, headache, bloating, mood change, dizziness, constipation, backache, and sluggishness. Emotional symptoms may include depression, physical aggression, guilt feelings, and anxiety. The symptoms, which can be severe or mild, can often be treated by exercise, dietary changes, or nutrition supplements (Palmer et al., 1991).

So far as we know, men do not undergo similar cyclical changes in hormonal levels. Journalists sometimes state or imply that male hormones lead to violent behavior. Although there is some evidence that high aggression may elevate testosterone levels, there are no scientific data that high testosterone levels cause aggression (Jacklin and Baker, 1993). This suggests that if males are more violent than females or behave in aggressive ways at an early age, the differences are probably due to gender-role expectations rather than hormones.

Does Biology Correspond with Gender Identity? Usually, but not always. **Gender identity** is a person's emotional and intellectual awareness of being either male or female. Gender identity, which typically does correspond to a person's biological sex characteristics, is learned in early childhood and is very resistant to change. On rare occasions, however, gender identity may be inconsistent with a person's physical sex. Such inconsistencies are illustrated by the research on hermaphrodites and transsexuals.

Hermaphrodites are people born with both male and female sex organs (internal and/or external). Typically, parents choose a sex for the child and pursue surgical and hormonal treatment to change the ambiguous genital organs. The parents typically raise the child in the selected gender role: the name is male or female, the clothes are masculine or feminine, and the child is taught to behave in gender-appropriate ways. Once again, therefore, socialization is important in determining a child's gender identity.

Transsexuals are people who feel that their gender identity is out of sync with their anatomical sex. Transsexuals often describe themselves as feeling "trapped in the wrong body." In one of the most publicized cases, Richard Raskind, a married man with two children who was a top-notch tennis player and a respected ophthalmologist, not only underwent surgery and became Renee Richards but also argued, although unsuccessfully, that he should be allowed to play tennis tournaments as a woman.

No one knows the reasons for transsexualism. The exact number of transsexuals is unknown, but Pauly (1974) estimated that there are 1 in 100,000 male transsexuals and 1 in 130,000 female transsexuals. Some undergo surgery (which costs about $60,000), but others opt for only hormonal treatments. Although there is little research in this area, some studies have found that between 60 and 80 percent of the patients have no problems in sexual adjustment after they undergo a sex-change operation and do not regret their decision (Sorenson, 1981; Mate-Kole et al., 1990).

All of this research challenges the notion that anatomy is destiny. What about the effect of nurture on gender roles?

How Important Is Nurture?

How many times have you heard people say that "men are naturally more aggressive" or that "women are naturally better parents"? In fact, research, especially cross-cultural research, shows that both of these beliefs are false.

"Men Are Naturally More Aggressive" In the 1930s, anthropologist Margaret Mead (1935) studied three tribes that lived within short distances of each other in New Guinea. She found three combinations of gender roles. Among the Arapesh, both men and women were nurturant with their children. The men were cooperative and sensitive, and they rarely engaged in warfare. The Mundugumors were just the opposite. Both the men and women were competitive and aggressive. Neither parent showed much tenderness, and both often used physical punishment to discipline the children. The Tchumbuli demonstrated the reverse of Western gender roles. The women were the economic providers, and the men took care of children, sat around gossiping, and spent a lot of time decorating themselves for tribal festivities. Mead concluded that attributes long considered either masculine or feminine (such as aggression) were culturally, not biologically, determined.

Mead's findings were supported by research on the Tasaday of the Philippines. Tasaday men are rarely angry or hostile, and they do not punish their children physically or fight with neighboring tribes. Indeed, the Tasaday's language does not even include words for "enemy," "fight," "weapon," "murder," or "war" (Nance, 1975).

If men were naturally more aggressive than women, we would find that men are frequent perpetrators of violent acts like homicide across all societies. This is not the case, however. As you can see from Figure 4.1, the rates of homicide in which the assailant is male vary considerably among a number of countries, and the rate

Figure 4.1 Incidence of Deadly Assault by Males in Selected Industrialized Countries. Although the incidence of male violence varies considerably worldwide, one of the highest rates may be found in Colombia, South America, where of every 100,000 men, 79 have committed murder. Among industrialized countries, however, the highest rate is in the United States (Newsweek, 1990, p. 7; Brooke, 1994, p. A6).

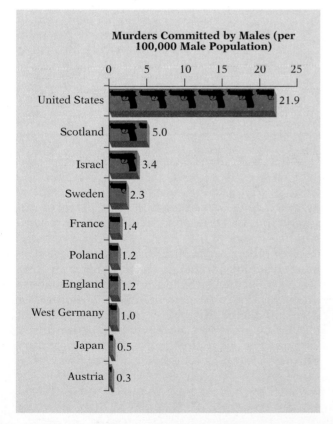

for the United States is by far the highest in the Western world. Is it possible that American men are genetically more aggressive than men in other countries? Inasmuch as the United States is a nation made up of people from many nations, races, and cultures, that seems unlikely. Instead, the United States has a high incidence of male aggression because Americans condone male violence.

According to Miedzian (1991), U.S. society encourages and rewards male aggression socially, culturally, legally, and politically. That is, American political leaders typically use war and force in countries around the world, sports and violence often go hand in hand, films and videos often glorify murder and brutality, and the boys' sections of toy stores look like a military arsenal. In addition, as we discuss in Chapter 15, wife abuse and murder still go largely unpunished. Male violence is deeply embedded in many major institutions of American life; evidently in many other countries it is not.

Even though the United States has one of the highest rates of male violence in the world, a recent United Nations report noted that women in many countries are often brutalized and persecuted by men. As the box "The Worldwide War Against Women" shows, discrimination and violence against women vary across countries as a function of differing cultural and religious values, customs, and laws.

"Women Are Naturally Better Parents" According to a Gallup poll (Table 4.2), many Americans see men and women as having quite

Table 4.2

The Top Ten Personality Characteristics Ascribed to Men and Women

TERMS MOST OFTEN USED BY MEN AND WOMEN TO DESCRIBE MEN		TERMS MOST OFTEN USED BY WOMEN AND MEN TO DESCRIBE WOMEN	
Aggressive	64%*	Emotional	81%*
Strong	61	Talkative	73
Proud	59	Sensitive	72
Disorganized	56	Affectionate	66
Courageous	54	Patient	64
Confident	54	Romantic	60
Independent	50	Moody	58
Ambitous	48	Cautious	57
Selfish	47	Creative	54
Logical	45	Thrifty	52

*Percentage of those surveyed.
SOURCE: Adapted from DeStefano and Colasanto, 1990, p. 29.

The Worldwide War Against Women

According to a United Nations report, women make up half the world's population, do two-thirds of the world's work, earn one tenth of the world's income, and own one-hundredth of the world's property. Despite women's contributions to the welfare and advancement of their societies and cultures, they are widely mistreated in many countries around the world.

❏ *China:* A culture that values boys more than girls, China has used advances in sonogram technology to help prospective parents identify—and abort—female fetuses. Despite official government condemnation of the practice, the gap between the number of male and female births is widening.

❏ *India and Pakistan:* If a groom and his family decide a bride's dowry is too small, she may be persecuted or be burned to death. In 1992, for example, India had more than 4,700 "dowry deaths." Aborting female fetuses is also widespread in India.

❏ *Kuwait:* Although Kuwaiti women are now allowed to drive and no longer have rigid dress codes, they still cannot vote. Household maids, many from the Philippines, are often victims of "unintentional" abuses and murders.

❏ *Latin America:* A macho culture pervades most countries in Latin America, unofficially condoning wife abuse, rape, and other forms of violence against women.

❏ *Morocco:* If a woman commits adultery, the law permits the husband to maim or kill her as punishment. Adulterous husbands, on the other hand, are not punished at all.

❏ *Norway:* Even though women dominate the political scene, they are still hired last, fired first, paid less than men, and held back from the top jobs.

❏ *Russia:* Women have been laid off in many sectors in disproportionate numbers and channeled into second-rate jobs. Women applying for office jobs are often told that their duties include sleeping with the boss.

❏ *Saudi Arabia:* A divorced woman may keep her children until they are 7. Although she may visit them, the children are then raised by the father's relatives. (The box later in this chapter on the life of women in Saudi Arabia illustrates some of the other problems faced by women in this country.)

❏ *South Africa:* A woman is raped every 83 seconds. Domestic work is the primary occupation for black women, and the average salary is about $80 a month.

❏ *Thailand:* Young rural women are kidnapped or bought from their parents for prostitution. An estimated 1 million women work in Thai brothels.

❏ *United States:* On average, women earn 71 percent of what men in the same jobs earn, and a woman with a college degree earns about the same as a man who has completed one year of high school. Among single mothers, about 60 percent live in or near poverty (Eddings, 1994; MacFarquhar et al., 1994; Guttman et al., 1994; Seter, 1994).

---

different personality characteristics. Men are often seen as aggressive, strong, and independent, whereas women are described as emotional, sensitive, and affectionate. Such different gender-role expectations help explain why we often hear that "parenting comes more naturally to mothers than to fathers." There are two principal reasons why mothers have generally been awarded custody of the children in divorce cases. First, until recently, most fathers have not sought custody. They believed that mothers are naturally better parents; they thought they couldn't provide the necessary nurturance; or they didn't want the children because their jobs often required them to be at work anywhere

from 8 to 14 hours per day. Second, many judges, social workers, and even fathers assumed that mothers and children have a natural bond.

If mothers are natural parents, why are hospitals teaching mothers how to bond with their infants? Further, why do some mothers abuse their children, place them in foster homes, or even kill them? Historical research shows that mothering does *not* come naturally for many women. For example, many eighteenth-century European mothers sent their children away to be cared for by wet nurses: "The child would be whisked away over long roads to some peasant cottage where, if it survived the trip, it would spend the next two years" (Shorter, 1975: 175). Wives of small storekeepers and artisans also sent their infants to wet nurses so that they could help their husbands in the shop. Poor women in rural areas often put their own children out at very low rates to take nursing jobs in other households.

Today, most social scientists agree that nature and nurture interact to explain gender roles. Biological processes are often mediated through cultural influences. Emphasizing only biological differences, however, limits the chances for gender equality both at home and in the workplace (Bem, 1994).

TRADITIONAL GENDER ROLES AND STEREOTYPES

Former president George Bush and his wife, Barbara, are models of traditional gender roles. According to Hackett and McDaniel (1989), Barbara met George at a prep-school dance when she was 16 ("He was the first boy I ever kissed"). Three years later she dropped out of Smith College to marry him. After George graduated from Yale in 1948, he and his bride moved to Texas, where he entered the oil business and she settled down to raise their five children. In 1966, George Bush was elected to Congress and in 1988 to the presidency of the United States. Through it all, Barbara Bush played the role of the politician's wife and loyal helpmate. Although she has always been more liberal than her husband on issues such as the equal rights amendment and only recently has come out strongly in favor of abortion rights, during her husband's presidency Barbara was careful to keep her political opinions to herself in order not to contradict his political authority (Bush, 1994).

Instrumental and Expressive Roles

As you saw in Chapter 2, traditional gender roles are instrumental or expressive. *Instrumental role players* (husbands and fathers) must be "real men." A "real man" is a procreator, a protector, and a provider. He must produce children because this will prove his virility, and having boys is especially important to carry on his family name. The procreator must also be a protector. He must be strong, powerful, and courageous in maintaining his family's physical safety. The provider is sometimes overwhelmed by the requirements of multiple roles, such as "the breadwinner," "the dutiful husband," and "the dutiful son" (Gaylin, 1992; Betcher and Pollack, 1993).

If the traditional male is a "superman," the traditional female is an only slightly more modern version of the "true woman" you met in Chapter 3. In the best-selling *The Total Woman* (1973: 87–88), for example, Morgan gave her readers "assignments" to help them achieve "total womanhood":

1. Accept your husband just as he is. Write out two lists—one of his faults and one of his virtues. Take a long, hard look at his faults and then throw the list away; don't ever dwell on them again. Only think about his virtues. Carry that list with you and refer to it when you are mad, sad, or glad.

2. Admire your husband every day. Refer to his virtue list if you need a place to start. Say something nice about his body today. Put his tattered ego back together with compliments.

3. Adapt to his way of life. Accept his way of life. Accept his friends, food, and lifestyle as your own. Ask him to write the six most important changes he'd like to see take place at your house, then set out to accomplish these changes with a smile. Be a "Yes, let's!" woman some time of every day.

In another best-seller, *Fascinating Womanhood*, Andelin (1974: 114–15) advised women not to pursue a career because this was "one of the greatest threats to a man's position of No. 1." Her advice included pretending to be frail and fearful, never doing such masculine things as handling financial problems, obeying the man's rules, and never competing with him. The 1992 film *Fried Green Tomatoes* portrayed the traditional woman very vividly. The main character had spent much of her time trying to please everyone except herself, even though she was frustrated and unhappy doing so. She was able to break out of that mold only when she met a woman who told her fascinating tales about women who had become "liberated" years earlier.

If you think that Andelin's and Morgan's advice to women is dated, think again. In a recent book on how to catch a man, for example, Allen and Harmon (1994) instruct women to flirt, to listen to men even when they're bored to death, and to wait for the man to call because wooing is "his role, not yours." In addition, almost every issue of *Cosmopolitan* magazine encourages women to play dumb, use sex, and manipulate men in other sex-stereotypical ways.

Many women have internalized these gender expectations and live up to them. For example, in a study of two coeducational middle schools in northern California, Orenstein (1994) found that female students, no matter how bright and no matter whether they were middle class and white or from minority groups in low-income neighborhoods, lived up to the traditional definition of girls: pretty and polite but not too aggressive, not too outspoken, and not too smart. If young women want to be popular with both male and female peers they often "dumb down" to them and to teachers as well.

Expressive role players (wives and mothers) provide the emotional support and nurturing qualities that sustain the family unit and support the father/husband. They must be warm, sensitive, and sympathetic. For example, the expressive role player consoles a teenage daughter when she breaks up with her boyfriend, encourages her son to try out for the Little League baseball team, and is always ready to comfort a husband who has had a bad day at work.

One of the best examples of women's expressive roles is that of *kinkeeper*. The role is often passed down from mother to daughter. Kinkeepers are important communication links between family members. They spend a lot of time writing to family members, visiting friends and families, and organizing or holding family gatherings during the holidays or for special events like birthdays and anniversaries. They also often act as the family helper, problem solver, or mediator (C. Rosenthal, 1985).

The Benefits and Costs of Traditional Gender Roles

Traditional gender roles have both benefits and costs. These roles may be chosen consciously, or they may be a product of habit, custom, or socialization. Remember, too, that traditional relationships vary. In some, partners feel loving and committed; in others, people feel as though they are trapped or sleepwalking.

Benefits Traditional gender roles promote stability, continuity, and predictability. Because every person knows what is expected of him or her, rights and responsibilities are clear. Men and women do not have to argue over who does what: If the house is clean, *she* is a "good wife"; if the bills are paid, *he* is a "good provider." Using the exchange model, if the costs and benefits of the relationship are fairly balanced and each partner is happy, traditional gender roles can work very well. As long as both partners live up to their role expectations, they are safe in assuming that they will be taken care of financially and emotionally/sexually by one another.

Because images of traditional gender roles are "valued by our families, honored by our culture, and immortalized by our mythologies," women win love and approval for following the rules (Harris, 1994:x). And some women stay in traditional relationships because as long as they live up to the idealized role, they don't have to make autonomous decisions or assume responsibility when things go wrong.

An accommodating wife or mother can enjoy power and prestige both through her husband's accomplishments and through her own control of the household. As a selfless wife, she can enjoy the benefits of her husband's success in politics or the corporate world. She can meet powerful people and maintain relationships with them, and as a good mother, she not only controls and dominates her children but can also be proud of guiding and enriching their lives (Harris, 1994).

Costs Traditional gender roles have their drawbacks. If a husband cannot or does not want to be the sole breadwinner, or if a wife does not want to do all the housework, there will be conflict.

Some of this conflict can be lessened if families change employment roles while maintaining traditional gender-role values and responsibilities. For example, in a study of middle-class families in several Mexican cities, anthropologist Linda Hubbell (1993) found that the husbands permitted their wives to work outside the home to avoid slipping out of the middle class. They readjusted and rationalized their traditional family values in several ways. Even women who ran their own businesses left family decision making to the husband; the women often hired servants instead of asking their husbands to help with the housework; and they were very careful not to be accused of any on-the-job sexual liaisons because this would cast doubt on the husband's virility. Thus, this group managed to protect traditional values even as gender roles were changing.

Learning from her dad how to cook can be a lesson with double value for a little girl: not only does she gain competence, but she learns that cooking is an acceptable activity for a man.

Another cost of traditional gender roles is loneliness. A strong but unemotional male may be hard to live with if he does not communicate. Sometimes the seemingly unemotional male is quiet because he feels enormous pressure (Kaufman, 1993). The dutiful worker, husband, and father may feel overwhelmed by his responsibilities and may be very unhappy with his life. A traditional male may believe that he never quite lives up to the standard of manhood. Although he has not failed completely, he has not succeeded, either: "I fell just short" or "Something went astray" (Gaylin, 1992: 241).

On the female side, the responsibilities suddenly thrust on a woman in her role as wife or mother can create problems if she is truly dependent and helpless. Moreover, such traditional values as being nurturant, dependent, and submissive can discourage some women from leaving abusive relationships.

Another problem is that traditional roles often invoke the double standard. When President Bill Clinton nominated Zoe Baird as attorney general, she withdrew her name after admitting she had hired an illegal alien couple as her baby sitter and chauffeur and had not paid Social Security taxes and other employee benefits. The next candidate, Judge Kimbe Wood, withdrew her name from consideration not because she had broken any laws, but because she was concerned about merciless scrutiny of her life. In contrast, Secretary of Commerce Ronald H. Brown was never asked by members of Congress about his child-care arrangements, and he passed the nominating process easily. Later, however, he admitted that he had failed to pay legally required Social Security taxes for a part-time domestic employee.

Just as alive and well as the double standard is the **gender-role stereotype**—the belief and expectation that both women and men display rigid, traditional gender-role characteristics. The box "College Seminars for (Male and Female) Sexists" offers a tongue-in-cheek look at such stereotypes. Traditional roles have been idealized for so long that many of us think they are normal. A young executive described her expectations of the male provider role, even though she recognized that this was "crazy":

If Roger can't get his act together our marriage is in jeopardy. It's not the money; I can support us all well enough. But—and I know you'll think this is crazy or something given all the things I believe in about men and women being equal and all that—but . . . boy, this is hard to say . . . well, here goes. I just don't think I can respect him if he isn't capable of taking care of his own family, even if he doesn't have to because I can (Rubin, 1983: 26).

People may take stereotypes seriously and act on them. In the airline industry, for example, more than 90 percent of all flight attendants are women, many of whom are older and juggling careers and motherhood. Although some airlines have eliminated the height and weight standards that were originally industry-wide, many still maintain these requirements despite a clear shift in the life circumstances of their employees. In 1990, American Airlines was sued for demanding that its flight attendants meet 1959 weight requirements. Such requirements are discriminatory because they are not related to job conditions. For example, weighing 135 pounds versus 125 pounds has nothing to do with being bi-

CHOICES

College Seminars for (Male and Female) Sexists

During the last few years, a number of messages have appeared on electronic mail (E-mail) either challenging or reinforcing gender-role stereotypes. Although the original sender(s) could not be traced, some subscribers have suggested that colleges establish as a requirement for graduation the completion of specific and parallel seminars for men and women. Here are some of the suggested courses:

SEMINARS FOR MEN

1. You Can Do Housework, Too

2. How Not to Act Like an Ass When You Are Obviously Wrong

3. Get a Life–Learn to Cook

4. Spelling–Even You Can Get It Right

5. How to Stay Awake After Sex

6. Garbage–Getting It to the Curb

7. How to Put the Toilet Seat Down

8. Combating Stupidity

SEMINARS FOR WOMEN

1. You Can Change the Oil, Too

2. How Not to Sob Like a Sponge When Your Husband Is Right

3. Get a Life–Learn to Kill Spiders Yourself

4. Balancing a Checkbook–Even You Can Get It Right

5. How to Stay Awake During Sex

6. Shopping–Doing It in Less Than 16 Hours

7. How to Close the Garage Door

8. Combating the Impulse to Nag

---

lingual (which is especially important in international flights), providing necessary medical assistance, or evacuating passengers during emergencies.

Gender-role stereotyping persists, in part, because it is profitable for business. The unpaid work that women do inside the home (such as domestic labor, child rearing, and emotional work) means that companies don't have to pay for child-care services or counseling for stressed-out male employees. And if there is only one breadwinner, many men may work extra hours without pay to keep their jobs. Thus, companies increase their profits. If women are convinced that their place is in the home, they will take part-time jobs that have no benefits, will work for less pay, and will not complain. This increases the corporate world's pool of exploitable and expendable low-paid workers (Eitzen and Baca Zinn, 1994). Finally, traditional roles can maintain male privilege and power. If women are seen as not having leadership qualities (see Table 4.2), men can dominate political and legal institutions and shape the laws and policies that maintain their vested interests.

These costs and benefits usually overlap. Most people balance the advantages and disadvantages of taking on or continuing in traditional gender roles. As the box "Japan's Next Empress—Walking a Step Behind?" illustrates, such decisions are not limited to the ordinary citizen.

The Persistence of Traditional Gender Roles

A recent issue of a newsmagazine ran a special section entitled "Men, Women and Computers." The cover showed a young man and woman holding their computer monitors. Both were

Japan's Next Empress—Walking a Step Behind?

On June 9, 1993, Masako Owada married Japan's Crown Prince Naruhito, Emperor Akihito's elder son. Crown Princess Masako will be Japan's next empress. The event was highly publicized by the Western media because the princess's background was inconsistent with her future role. She had attended two elite universities, Harvard and Oxford, and was a magna cum laude graduate. She speaks five languages and, until her marriage, had held a prestigious but grueling job in which she was the lone woman—working for the Japanese Ministry of Foreign Affairs on economic relations between the United States and Japan. In her new life, Masako is surrounded by ladies-in-waiting and conservative bureaucrats who will "orchestrate her every move for the rest of her life."

While most of the Japanese people were delighted with Masako's decision to marry the Crown Prince (even though she deliberated for a number of weeks before giving her consent to his proposal), many young Japanese women were dismayed. They felt that it was a waste of her education and her talents and that she would become a political puppet. They feared that as Crown Princess she would become passive, devoured by tradition, and would always walk a step behind the Crown Prince (Helm, 1993; Powell, 1993).

sweating and had desperate expressions on their faces. Balloons displayed the inner thoughts of each: the woman, "Is he as cute as his E-mail?"; the man, "Bet she'll love my war games" (*Newsweek*, 1994).

SOCIALIZATION THEORIES: HOW WE LEARN GENDER ROLES

A common misconception is that the gender roles we learn at an early age are carved in stone and do not change after about age 4. In fact, gender roles can—and do—change throughout the life cycle. Before we can understand how such change occurs, however, we need to examine, briefly, some of the major perspectives on gender-role learning: social learning theory, cognitive development theory, and gender-schema theory.

Social Learning Theory

The central notion in **social learning theory** is that people learn new attitudes, beliefs, and behaviors through social interaction, either by reinforcement of their behavior or by watching others. Thus, we learn some gender-role behaviors by direct reward or punishment. A little girl who puts on her mother's makeup may be told she is cute, but her brother will be scolded ("boys don't wear makeup"). We learn gender roles also through indirect reinforcement. For example, if a little boy's male friends are punished for crying, he will learn that "boys don't cry."

We also learn gender roles through imitation or role modeling of same-sex significant others. In principle, because parents are available and emotionally important to children, they are the most powerful role models, but other role models include caregivers, friends, and even television characters. Behavior and attitudes change as the situations and expectations in the environment change. Thus, books and television programs play an important role in expanding or constricting gender-role expectations. Social learning theories see behavior not as fixed at an early age but as changing throughout the life cycle (Bandura and Walters, 1963; Lynn, 1969).

Cognitive Development Theory

Cognitive development theory, based on the work of Jean Piaget (1950, 1954), sees learning as an active process in which children interact with their environment and then, using the mental processes of thinking, understanding, and reasoning, interpret and apply the information they have gathered. According to Lawrence Kohlberg (1969), children learn gender-role identity by understanding and accepting perceived reality rather than by being reinforced for certain behaviors or modeling them. Thus, for example, in contrast to a social learning sequence ("the boy wants rewards, the boy is rewarded by boy things, therefore, he wants to be a boy"), cognitive theory assumes a different sequence: "The boy asserts he is a boy. He then wants to do boy things; therefore, the opportunity to do boy things and the presence of masculine models is rewarding" (Kohlberg, 1969: 432).

Thus, in contrast to social learning theories, the cognitive development perspective argues that the child acquires basic male or female values on her or his own. According to this theory, children pass through developmental stages in learning gender-appropriate attitudes and behavior. By the age of 3 to 4, the girl knows she is a girl and prefers "girl things" to "boy things" simply because she likes herself and that which is familiar or similar to herself. After masculine/feminine values are acquired, the child tends to identify with same-sex figures. The age at which a child moves through the developmental stages posited by this theory varies by the child's cognitive, intellectual, and maturity level (Kohlberg, 1969; Maccoby, 1990). By age 5, however, most children anticipate disapproval from their peers for playing with opposite-sex toys and don't do so (Bussey and Bandura, 1992).

Gender Schema Theory

Elements of cognitive development theory have been incorporated into a newer perspective, known as gender schema theory. **Gender schema theory** focuses on how male and female newborns become conventionally masculine and feminine adults. *Schema* are cognitive (or mental) information-processing categories that organize and guide a person's perceptions of a vast array of cultural stimuli (Bem, 1983). For example, when girls realize that cultural expectations of being feminine include being affectionate, understanding, and emotional, they incorporate these perceptions into their emerging gender schema and adjust their behavior accordingly. The same is true of boys, who incorporate such male gender schema as being brave, forceful, and tough.

Children use gender schema to evaluate the behavior of others as gender appropriate ("good") or gender inappropriate ("bad"). Because most cultures polarize gender characteristics into rigid categories, children become gender schematic themselves, without even realizing it. Eventually, children become conventionally sex-typed because they evaluate different ways of behaving in terms of the cultural definitions of gender appropriateness and reject any way of behaving that

does not match their sex (Bem, 1993). Gender schema may become more rigid during adolescence, when young people often feel compelled to conform to peers' gender-role stereotypes, but may become more flexible again during adulthood (Stoddart and Turiel, 1985). Generally, however, people who have internalized sex-typed standards tend to expect stereotypical behavior from others or to ignore nonstereotypical behavior that is incongruent with their gender schemas (Hudak, 1993; Renn and Calvert, 1993).

These three perspectives—social learning theory, cognitive development theory, and gender schema theory—are often used together. One perspective is not better than another, just different.

SOCIALIZATION AGENTS: WHO TEACHES GENDER ROLES?

As we have discussed, theorists try to explain how we learn gender roles. The next question is who does the teaching. The most important teachers are parents (and other adult caregivers), peers, teachers, and the media.

Parents

Parents are usually the first and most influential source of learning about gender roles. Many children are raised in sex-stereotyped physical surroundings:

[Our] results showed that boys were provided with more sports equipment, tools, and large and small vehicles. Girls had more dolls, fictional characters, child's furniture, and other toys for manipulation. They wore pink and multicolored clothes more often, had more pink pacifiers and jewelry. Boys wore more blue, red, and white clothing. They had more blue pacifiers. Yellow bedding was more frequently observed in the girls' rooms, while blue bedding and curtains were more prevalent in the boys' rooms (Pomerleau et al., 1990: 339).

Parents begin to treat infants differently right after birth. Girls are held more gently and cuddled more, whereas boys are jostled more and played with more roughly. Parents are more likely to put females in a nearby high chair and male infants on the floor or in a playpen. Thus, girls are kept closer to a parent and in a more confined area. Boys are frequently given toys that demand more space (such as trains and car sets), whereas girls receive dolls or dollhouses, which require less space. Also, toys that boys receive (such as footballs and basketballs) encourage leaving the home; girls' toys (such as vacuums, play ovens) are designed to be used within the home (Knapp and Hall, 1992). Even when children in kindergarten and elementary school request gender-atypical toys (as sports equipment for girls or arts and crafts for boys), parents give gender-typical toys, such as cars and trucks for boys and dolls or miniature kitchen sets for girls (Etaugh and Liss, 1992). Thus, both toys and the usage of space encourage traditionally gender-appropriate behavior, activities, and interests.

Despite parental sex stereotyping, very young children play just as enthusiastically with either "masculine" or "feminine" toys. In a study of families in a child-care center in Ontario, Canada, Idle and associates (1993) recorded the way parents and children—a father and his child, a mother and her child—played with 15 randomly arranged toys. The children ranged in age from 27 to 64 months. "Feminine" toys included a baby doll, a kitchen set, a dollhouse with furniture, and a telephone. "Masculine" toys included a truck, a ball, a train, a Fisher-Price gas station with cars, and a tool set. The gender-neutral toys included a puzzle, a book, a stuffed animal, Play-Doh with accessories, and blocks. Interestingly, the researchers found that both parents were less likely to use "feminine" toys because they were the least entertaining. Regardless of which toys the parents chose, however, the child was just as interested in playing. This suggests that parents can play a key role in introducing their children to toys that are not gender typed.

Parents communicate differently with boys and girls, starting at a very early age. Both mothers and fathers use more words about feelings and emotions when speaking with girls than when speaking with boys. Fathers tend to use more directives ("Bring that over here") and more threatening language ("If you do that again, you'll be sorry") with their sons than with their daughters. Mothers ask for compliance rather than demand it—"Could you bring that to me, please?" By the time they start school, boys use threatening, commanding, and dominating language ("If you do that one more time, I'll sock you"). In contrast, girls emphasize agreement and cooperation ("Maybe we can play together tomorrow") (Shapiro, 1990).

Differing gender-role expectations continue throughout childhood. As early as the first, second, and third grades, boys are expected to do better in mathematics than are girls. For example, in a longitudinal study of approximately 2,100 families in 14 school districts in suburban Michigan, researchers found that parents had stereotypical (and accurate) perceptions of their children's competencies in math, English, and sports. The researchers speculated that parents *expected* their daughters to be better in English and their sons to excel in math and sports, so they provided the support and advice to enable them to do so. The researchers concluded that this encouragement built up the children's confidence in their abilities and thus helped to enable them to master the various skills (Eccles et al., 1990).

In a study of fifth graders and their families in Vermont, Bronstein (1988) found that whereas mothers spent equal amounts of time working on projects with both sons and daughters, only fathers of sons worked on projects with their children. Also, fathers were four times more likely to work on a computer with sons than with daughters. Fathers engaged in more *social* interaction with daughters than with sons; they were more interested in the *cognitive* achievements of sons. Bronstein suggested that fathers' behavior may be limiting boys' social and emotional development. In their greater restrictiveness with sons and gentleness with daughters, fathers may be communicating the expectation that boys, if not handled firmly, are more likely to be out of control, whereas girls can be trusted to behave more reasonably and responsibly. These are messages that may shape children's self-concepts along traditional gender-based lines. They may reinforce aggressive behaviors in boys and provide them with fewer opportunities to learn cooperation, empathy, and interpersonal skills. They may also limit girls' curiosity about the outside world by confining their activities to the home.

Sex-differentiated expectations continue throughout adolescence. In a classic study conducted in the 1950s, undergraduate women reported three major sources of differences between themselves and their brothers when they were younger (Komarovsky, 1950). First, the sons were given *earlier and more frequent opportunities for independence.* The boys were freer to play away from home, to return later, and to pick their own activities, movies, and books. They were younger than their sisters when they walked to school, a movie, or a baseball game without an adult. The pattern continued when, later, they took their first trip alone or a job away from home.

Second, the sons enjoyed a *higher degree of privacy in personal affairs*. One woman's recollection illustrates this:

My brother is 15, 3 years younger than I am. When he goes out after supper mother calls out: "Where are you going, Jimmy?" "Oh, out." Could I get away with this? Not on your life. I would have to tell in detail where to, with whom, and if I am half an hour late mother sits on the edge of the living-room sofa watching the door (Komarovsky, 1950: 510).

Third, the daughters were held to a *more exacting code of filial and kinship obligations*. When Grandma or Aunt Jane needed somebody to run an errand, the daughter was more likely to be called upon. In what may be seen as preparation for the kinkeeper role we discussed earlier, more pressure to attend and observe birthdays, anniversaries, and other family festivals was brought to bear on girls than on boys.

For the most part, Komarovsky's findings continue to be relevant. Throughout the years, many college students have reported similar experiences. For example, college women, but not college men, often say that being away at college is the first time that they enjoy privacy, greater independence, and a sense of relief in not having to worry about baby-sitting cousins or doing the weekly grocery shopping for an aging relative.

Toys, Play, and Peer Interaction

Play is generally sex-typed. Boys are still more likely than girls to play with warlike toys, to participate in warlike games and sports, and to react aggressively to (real or imagined) verbal, personal, or physical threats (Colburn, 1991). Toys for boys encourage exploring spatial dimensions and use step-by-step instructional styles that encourage the use of logic and provide some understanding of concepts that children will use in science and mathematics (Cargan, 1991).

In both catalogues and toy stores, girls' sections contain cosmetics, dolls and accessories, arts-and-crafts kits, and housekeeping and cooking toys. In contrast, boys' sections feature sports equipment, building toys, workbenches, and construction equipment. Thus, boys' toys emphasize activity, mobility, and problem solving, whereas girls' toys develop passivity, domestic skills, and imaginative play.

Both journalists and scholars have noted an "electronic gender gap" in the $15-billion-a-year video game industry, concluding that children's software and video games are overwhelmingly male oriented:

Of the 82 full- or double-page ads for the newest and hottest games in a recent issue of Electronic Gaming Monthly, *61 brimmed with macho appeal, hyping classic sports titles to search-and-destroy missions and to kick-and-punch competitions. Eighteen seemed to be more gender-inclusive, for*

When an avid toy train collector who was a new grandfather was asked at Christmas time why he gave one of his prized trains to his daughter's baby boy but none to his son's new daughter, he replied, "Why would I give her a train?" Giving children gender-stereotyped toys is a habit that's not easy to break.

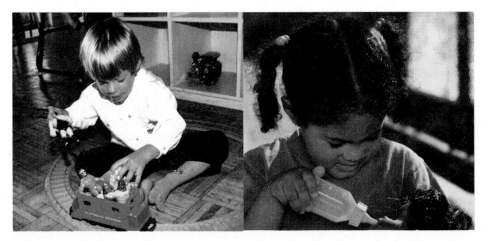

games such as Aladdin and The Lord of the Rings. Only three made pitches specifically aimed at girls— including ads for an updated Ms. PacMan and . . . [the] fast-action basketball competition Jammit showing an athletic woman slam-dunking over a man (Oldenburg, 1994: D5).

War, violence, aggression, and sexism have been the hallmarks of many computer games geared to young boys (Jacobs, 1994). A video game called Night Trap required players to save scantily clad sorority sisters from a gang of hooded killers. The game was removed from Toys-R-Us stores after parents complained about its emphasis on sex and violence. Thus, consumer protests can have an impact on toy production and sales.

Even educational games tend to be male oriented. According to one high school teacher of computer literacy, "There's baseball math, all-star baseball, monster madness, where you have to kill the monsters to spell words. It's all dominance games where you have to trample someone" (quoted in Morse, 1995: 17). Because computer games are often seen as a gateway to computer technology, teachers are concerned about girls' exclusion from commercial and educational video games. Children who are familiar with video games are often more confident in using other software in school.

Whereas boys' toys are more likely to encourage competition and follow strict rules, girls' toys usually foster nurturance and emotional expressiveness. Since the early 1990s, and before "political correctness" was a buzzword, one of the steady sellers among girls age 3 to 7 was the "Mommy Doll." She was available in both African American and white versions. There were Mommies "off to work," dressed in red suits and black pumps, Mommies "out for fun," wearing sweatsuits and designer running shoes, and Mommies "on the go," outfitted in polka-dot dresses (Corey, 1990b). Because most mommies are not in professional jobs (even when they are, they don't wear red suits and little black pumps) and don't have time to jog or go out just for fun, some people thought that the "Mommy Doll" was especially offensive. It not only stereotyped women who are wives and mothers, but it promoted stereotypes of middle-class working mothers as "having it all"—beautiful, young, well dressed, well built, and worst of all, having the time and the outfits to be "out for fun" and "on the go." In reality, working mothers, regardless

of socioeconomic status, are often happiest when they can get out of their pantyhose and heels, spend a few quiet hours by themselves, and aren't trying to be supermoms.

Although behavior varies across situations, boys and girls often play differently. Girls tend to play alone or one-on-one, whereas boys are more likely to play in teams and to interact more. Girls are more cooperative and play repetitive games with simple rules, such as jump rope. In contrast, boys are more competitive and play more complicated and elaborate games, such as football (Lever, 1978). Some efforts are being made to encourage more team sports among girls, and there are certainly more women's teams in college today than in the past. However, women's athletics, except for some of the Olympic competitions, are still not taken very seriously. For example, girls' teams may not have uniforms or travel budgets, and they frequently get inferior athletic equipment (see Benokraitis and Feagin, 1995, for a discussion of the research on gender and sports).

Teachers and Schools

Teachers often treat boys and girls differently in the classroom. Even when their behavior is disruptive, "problem girls" often receive less attention than do either "problem boys" or "nonproblem boys." Moreover, teachers tend to emphasize "motherwork" skills for girls, such as nurturance and emotional support. Although both girls and boys are evaluated on academic criteria, such as work habits and knowledge, girls are also more likely than boys to be evaluated on such nonacademic criteria as grooming, personal qualities, and appearance (American Association of University Women, 1992).

In their research on classroom interaction, Sadker and Sadker (1994) found that boys are given more time to talk in class, are called on more often, and are given more positive feedback. Teachers are more likely to give answers to girls or to do the problems for them, but to expect boys to find the answers themselves. Researchers videotaped 20 teachers who taught male and female students two different lessons. One was stereotypically masculine (mechanics), and the other was stereotypically feminine (vocabulary). The researchers found that although female teachers were less stereotypical than male teachers, both sexes were less positive toward students for whom the material being taught was considered gender inappropriate. Thus, teachers were more supportive and encouraging when girls did well in vocabulary and when boys did well in mechanics (Hechtman and Rosenthal, 1991).

This sex stereotyping often continues in high school. Indeed, guidance counselors, who play an important role in helping students make career choices, are particularly guilty of such behavior. Even well-intentioned counselors often steer girls into vocational training, such as secretarial work or data processing, rather than college preparatory programs. Girls who are in college preparatory programs are often encouraged to take courses in the social sciences and humanities rather than mathematics or the sciences (Renzetti and Curran, 1995).

Since the late 1980s, various groups have criticized the Scholastic Aptitude Test (SAT)—the exam required for many college admissions—as being sex-biased. Some of the critics maintain that males are more familiar with subjects like math and science, which make up a large part of the basic test. Interestingly, until about age 12, girls often outperform boys in mathematics. A few years later, however, boys' scores tend to be much higher. The most distressing finding is that the gap in scores between men and women is highest for women with A+ grades (Evangelauf, 1989). This implies that women study hard and get good grades but often are not advised to take coursework that the SAT emphasizes.

Books and Textbooks For years, studies of children's books and textbooks have reported two primary findings: (1) Women are much less visible than men, and (2) when women are depicted, they are not as important as men. A classic study of children's books that was awarded the Caldecott Medal (given by the Children's Service Committee of the American Library Association for excellence in books published for children in the third through sixth grades) and of the best-selling books in the Little Golden Book series found that females were inconspicuous, often nameless, and generally underrepresented in the titles, pictures, stories, and central roles (Weitzman et al., 1972). When the study was replicated a decade later, the findings were similar. Girls were still portrayed as passive, submissive, and nurturing, whereas boys were independent, adventurous, and active (Williams et al., 1987). For example, boys build treehouses, compete in sports, and sail off to adventures; girls watch, cheer them on, or have cookies ready when the boys return.

In several more recent replications, Kortenhaus and Demarest (1993) found that females were more likely to be represented in books but in roles that do not reflect the actual behavior of females or males in our society. For example, girls "are still busy creating problems that require masculine solutions" rather than solving problems themselves. And Crabb and Bielawski (1994) found that female characters were still overwhelmingly portrayed as using household objects (cooking utensils, brooms, sewing needles), whereas male characters used objects for work outside the home (pitchforks, plows, construction tools).

In another much-cited study, researchers analyzed 134 elementary school readers and found, again, that boys were shown as active, creative and involved in interesting adventures whereas girls usually played passive or domestic roles (Women on Words and Images, 1975). When Purcell and Stewart (1990) replicated the study, they found some progress. Girls appeared just as often as boys, and women's biographies outnumbered those of men. There were still some striking differences, however:

Even though girls are now shown in active roles, they are still shown as needing rescue in many more instances than are boys. Girls are shown as being very brave while waiting for rescue, but they still cannot help themselves out of trouble. Although stories do show boys babysitting and crying over a bruise, boys are still portrayed many times as being forced to deny their feelings to show their manhood (Purcell and Stewart, 1990: 184).

Today, nonstereotypical books are more readily available, especially for preschoolers, than ever before. And some research shows that very young children are generally open to stories that describe nontraditional male roles, such as boys playing with dolls (Taylor et al., 1993). If parents or teachers tend to stereotype gender roles, however, children will not be exposed to these resources. Moreover, as the box "Textbooks Are Still Male!" indicates, gender stereotyping is still widespread in high school and college textbooks.

The Popular Culture

It is impossible not to be influenced by the media's myths and unrealistic images of everyday life. The research in this area has boomed during the last

Textbooks Are Still Male!

Although publishers of high school textbooks have made an effort to eliminate gender stereotyping, women are still largely invisible (see Renzetti and Curran, 1995). In history textbooks, for example, much of the material still focuses on wars and on men's rather than women's technological inventions (see Benokraitis and Feagin, 1995).

In 1994 I was asked by a teacher in an affluent and progressive suburban high school to speak on gender issues to an advanced class of juniors. Not wanting to be repetitious, I looked at their history text-book to see what issues had received the least coverage. Much to my surprise, the textbook offered only two paragraphs on women since the 1950s: one discussed the women's rights movement in the 1960s; the other described the Equal Rights Amendment.

Many textbooks in colleges and professional schools also ignore women or present them in stereotypical ways. For example, Kathleen Mendelsohn and her associates (1994) analyzed more than 4,000 illustrations in 12 anatomy and physical diagnosis textbooks used in medical schools. The anatomy textbooks used illustrations of male bodies more than twice as often as female bodies. In the texts on physical diagnosis, the illustrations of women were largely confined to chapters on reproduction, falsely implying that female and male physiology differ only in respect to their reproductive organs. The researchers conclude that "women are dramatically underrepresented in illustrations of normal, nonreproductive anatomy" and that "males continue to be depicted as the norm or the standard. As a result, students may develop an incomplete knowledge of normal female anatomy" (p. 1269).

decade and is too extensive to discuss fully here. Nonetheless, a few examples from advertising, magazines, television, and the movies will illustrate how the media reinforce sex stereotyping.

Advertising Much of the advertising aimed at children is stereotypical. Although girls are sometimes included in advertisements for educational toys, typically they are featured in doll and domestic toy ads. Most of the advertising aimed at children uses blond, blue-eyed, freckled children. Children of color are most likely to be a face in a crowd, or they are used to promote a product as "cool" or trendy. For example, African American children routinely appear in commercials that plug sports shoes (even Nikes for infants) or in music commercials (such as Apple Jacks cereal and Pocket Rockers cassettes) (Seiter, 1993).

Channeling African American children into sports and music commercials reinforces the stereotype that they are "natural" in sports and music—and, by default, "not natural" in educational or other pursuits. The few exceptions include some makers of preschool-age toys. They are more likely than other manufacturers to use African American, Asian American, and Caucasian children together in their ads. McDonald's, also, has cast a variety of kids (including Latinos, African Americans, and Asian Americans) for its commercials (Seiter, 1993).

Advertising, in both magazines and television, has recently changed its implicit message about adult roles. A few years ago, women were told that their kitchen floors should be spotless and that "ring-around-the-collar" was one of life's worst sins. Today, however, the ring-around-the-collar commercials are usually limited to daytime television. In contrast, commercials during evening prime-time broadcasting (8:00 P.M. to 11:00 P.M.) are targeted at working women and are more likely to portray women in positions of authority and in settings away from home.

In one tear-jerker commercial for United Airlines, a woman leaves her daughter at a child-care center, flies off to another city for a business meeting, makes a great presentation, dashes to the plane, arrives at the center, and throws her arms open to her daughter, who runs, smiling, to meet her. Some of the ad executives patted themselves on the back for producing a "message that rings true" because "there's no room for fairy tales or cartoons" (Browning, 1991). The problem is that many viewers may believe that such commercials and ads are not cartoons or fairy tales. How many women have jobs where they make presentations at executive-level meetings hundreds of miles away and then pick up their children at a child-care center, every hair still in place?

Weekend television, which presents male-dominated and male-oriented sports programs, is still filled with big-bosomed, scantily-clad young women cavorting in beer commercials, ex-athletes plugging car sales, and a variety of other commercials that feature men involved in insurance, computer, stock investment, or other business activities (Craig, 1992). Because many men and women now work night shifts and on weekends, however, advertisers are missing much of their target audience. Many men are not watching weekend sports, and many working mothers are not watching prime-time shows.

Stereotypical advertising is not limited to television commercials. In a study of medical advertisements in three prominent medical journals (*Journal of the American Medical Association*, *The New England Journal of Medicine*, and *Annals of Internal Medicine*), Leppard and colleagues (1993) found that although heart disease is the leading cause of death in women, males vastly outnumbered females in cardiovascular drug ads. In addition, the facial expressions of men were more likely to be serious, whereas those of women were often pleasant. The researchers suggest that such depictions may contribute to physicians' perceptions of male medical problems as being more serious and those of women as more emotionally based—that is, smiling people are probably healthier than those who are serious or scowling.

Magazines Most magazines present graphic images of gender stereotypes. For example, magazines aimed at male adolescents emphasize improving their mechanical skills and success in sports, but those for adolescent girls are full of articles and ads on being more popular, thin, and beautiful. Celebrities are often used as role models to promote these messages.

Men's magazines assume that most men spend all of their time thinking only about sex. Since the early 1970s, however, *Playboy*'s circulation has plummeted from almost 7 million to about 3 million, and *Penthouse*'s has shrunk from 3 million to 1.7 million. Some writers believe that the circulations of these longtime leaders have dropped because they do not reflect many men's growing interest in other issues, such as health, children, and work (Henry and Whitaker, 1990). On the other hand, the male audience for violent pornographic materials has been increasing (Russell, 1993). Some feel that men's increased interest in pornographic movies is healthy because it enhances marital sex. They say that watching pornographic films leads to more intense and frequent sex and to more open communication about sex (Nobile and Nadler, 1994). On the other hand, some observers note that the violence depicted against women in pornographic films desensitizes men to rape, domestic violence, and other assaults against women (Dworkin, 1989; Dobson, 1994).

Television and MTV Children spend considerably more time in front of the television set than they do interacting with parents, family members, teachers, or friends. The average child will have watched 5,000 hours of television by the time he or she enters first grade and 19,000 hours by the end of high school—more time than he or she will spend in class (Zoglin, 1990). Some child experts tout the positive effects of television, claiming that young children acquire a large repertoire of skills, speech patterns, and points of view (Brazelton, 1991). Nevertheless, there is evidence that children who watch a lot of television perform more poorly on writing tests and that they may develop sedentary patterns that can lead to obesity (Zoglin, 1990).

Television molds children's views of how the sexes should behave (Richmond-Abbott, 1992), and some studies have found that the more television children watch, the more they subscribe to male-female stereotypes (Lips, 1993). Indeed, some writers feel that gender and race stereotypes are probably at their worst in children's television programming (Andersen, 1993). For example, Seiter (1993: 185) found that the images aimed at boys in Ghostbusters and at girls in My Little Pony, two of the most popular children's programs over time, were highly sex-stereotypical. Table 4.3 lists some of the images Seiter describes. Do you agree or disagree that these images stereotype people by their gender? Do the two programs have redeeming qualities and, if so, what are they?

Even on the highly acclaimed "Sesame Street," the best-known characters are male: Big Bird, Kermit, Bert, Ernie, Snuffalupugus, Grover, and Cookie Monster. Two female puppets, Betty Lou and Prairie Dawn, are less interesting and do not appear regularly, and Miss Piggy, who is presumably intelligent and assertive, spends most of her time on looking good (not easy for a pig) and trying to "bag" Kermit. It's also important to note that middle-class white boys are often at the center of children's programming, whereas children of color and girls of all races are "dispersed to the

Table 4.3

Gender-Stereotyped Messages in Two Children's Television Programs

GHOSTBUSTERS	MY LITTLE PONY
Main characters as adult men	Main characters as girls
The hero as viewer's equal	The heroine as better than viewer
Hierarchical group	Democracy of peers
Emotions masked	Emotions valued
Playful attitude toward work	Putting play aside to help others
Boastfulness	Insecurity and modesty
Fear as an enjoyable thrill	Overcoming fear
Blasting the enemy away	Persuading the enemy to change
Technology	Nature
Contemporary urban setting	Idyllic pastoral setting
Comedy and horror film	Music and romance

SOURCE: Adapted from Seiter, 1993, p. 185.

sidelines as mascots, companions, victims" (Seiter, 1993: 37).

The portrayals of women on television are rarely representative of women in the general population. Few programs feature black or Latino women. Most programs depict women in high-paid, professional careers, such as doctors or lawyers, even though in real life many women are poor or working class and most work in clerical and service occupations. Even when women are presented in nontraditional roles, they are unrealistic. In "Evening Shade," for example, the coach's wife, who is a successful attorney at a major firm, is rarely shown practicing law. Even more amazingly, she is never impatient, stressed out, or burnt out. At the other end of the continuum is Murphy Brown, a successful journalist who is always impatient, rude, and aggressive. Both characters have been popular probably because they reflect fantasies. In real life, professional women who are always at home, bulldoze their way into men's clubs, or snap at bosses do not last very long (Alcock and Robson, 1990).

Some media analysts feel that much of television programming is not representative of the experiences of women, middle-class families, the elderly, and people of varying ethnic and racial backgrounds because it reflects the experience and values of its creative leaders—network presidents, vice presidents, producers, and writers. These people are almost exclusively white, middle-aged, and male. More than 80 percent grew up in large metropolitan areas and live in California or the Boston-Washington corridor, and almost two-thirds earn more than $200,000 a year (Lichter et al., 1991). Thus, they are often out of touch with the experiences of most Americans. As a result, people who are heavy television viewers may have more stereotypical perceptions of gender than do light viewers.

Some of the most disturbingly gender-stereotypical programming is found in Music Television (MTV) videos. Over the years, a number of researchers have found MTV a powerful transmitter of gender stereotypes, and recent research continues to support this observation. For example, Sommers-Flanagan and colleagues (1993) found that most of the 313 music videos they examined reinforced sex-role stereotyping and presented negative attitudes toward women. These researchers found that men appeared nearly twice as often as women; men engaged in significantly more aggressive and dominant behavior; women engaged in significantly more sexual and subservient behavior; and women were more frequently the object of explicit, implicit, and aggressive sexual advances. Signorielli and associates (1994) found that the characters in 119 MTV commercials, like those in the music videos, are stereotyped: For example, female characters appeared less frequently, and when they did, they were permitted to do little more than wear skimpy clothing, look sexy, and receive men's sexual attention. The researchers concluded that MTV commercials preserve and perpetuate stereotypes about women: "If adolescents, as is likely, utilize MTV as a source of social learning about gender roles, then they receive warped views of the roles and responsibilities of women in society" (pp. 99–100).

A major problem, according to Gerbner's (1993) study of 1,371 television programs, is that "the world of television seems to be frozen in a time-warp of obsolete and damaging representations." For example, in prime-time television the female ratio is only 1:3, in children's programs it is 1:4, and in national news coverage it is 1:5. Seniors of both genders are greatly underrepresented; indeed, they seem to be vanishing instead of increasing in numbers, as they are in real life. When older women are presented, they are most likely to play villains, witches, or mentally ill characters. In a survey of 867 Hollywood executives, directors, writers, and actors, 28 to

30 percent said that gender and racial stereotypes, respectively, were "very serious" problems on television (Walsh, 1994).

Movies Films rarely portray women and men in nonstereotypical gender roles. Consider some of the recent portrayals of men in movies. In *True Lies*, the hero is a macho, aggressive, and tough male, whereas his wife is helpless and passive. In *Forrest Gump*, the hero is a simpleton, and the love of his life has been abused by her father, heckled by sleazy strip-joint customers, and slugged by at least one man. In *Regarding Henry*, the domineering father and employer and adulterous husband had to be shot in the head to become a good husband and father. In *Wolf*, the hero is a monster. And in *Mrs. Doubtfire*, the doting father becomes a transvestite in order to visit his children. As syndicated columnist Ellen Goodman noted, "OK, OK, a good man is hard to find. But it's a whole lot harder to find him at the movies" (1994: 11a).

Little boys get more movie roles than little girls. As the box "No Girls Allowed in Hollywood" shows, most recent films have featured boys. Although there are many female movie stars, there are few notable women's roles and even fewer women's films (where the movie deals with women's issues from a female perspective). In the early 1990s, there were a few exceptions, such as *Fried Green Tomatoes*, *A League of Their Own*, and *Thelma and Louise*, which were commercial hits.

Somewhat controversial, *Thelma and Louise* was labeled a "women's film" because the two main characters shot a rapist, took revenge on a trucker who made offensive advances to them, and eluded law enforcement officers. Thus, women, not the men around them, took control of their lives and made their own decisions. Many women cheered as Thelma and Louise played out their audience's fantasies of revenge on hostile, cruel, or abusive men. Nonetheless, many films still portray violent or demeaning behavior toward women. In reviewing *Falling Down*, for example, a movie critic stated that "the most applause came when Duvall's character stands up to his obviously troubled wife by telling her to shut up and cook supper" (Sterritt, 1993: 13).

CONTEMPORARY GENDER ROLES IN ADULTHOOD

Childhood and adolescent gender-role experiences are greatly influenced by parents, friends, teachers, and the media. As we've seen, young people are still frequently getting the message that the traditional gender roles are the "ideal." Are our adult experiences different?

CONSTRAINTS

No Girls Allowed in Hollywood

Major roles for girls in Hollywood films are few and far between, but boys star in a wide variety of films. Here are some examples of recent popular films that featured boys:

❑ *Lean on Me*: Young boys experience bonding and "rites of passage."

❑ *Free Willy*: A boy tames, trains, and then frees a killer whale.

❑ *Home Alone* and *Home Alone II*: A young boy outwits adults.

❑ *Searching for Bobby Fischer*: A boy becomes a chess champion.

❑ *Mighty Ducks*: Boys become hockey champions.

❑ *Rookie of the Year*: A boy be-comes a major-league baseball champion.

❑ *Last Action Hero*: A boy is a sidekick to Arnold Schwarzenegger's supercop.

❑ *The Man Without a Face*: A boy becomes best pal to his tutor.

❑ *Forever Young*: Two boys rescue the hero from a deep freeze.

❑ *The Sandlot*: Boys find an ally in a big-leaguer.

❑ *Lost in Yonkers:* Two brothers change a mean grandma.

❑ *Sleepless in Seattle*: The determined matchmaker is a boy.

❑ *The Lion King*: The orphaned male cub becomes a king of animals.

❑ *Angels in the Outfield*: A boy who manages a baseball team is aided by angels.

❑ *The War*: About heroism and father and son relationships.

❑ *Silent Fall:* An 8-year-old autistic boy has the answers to a murder.

Katharine Hepburn, the well-known actress, is reported to have said, "Sometimes I wonder if men and women really suit each other. Perhaps they should live next door and just visit now and then." This statement may seem jaundiced, but it contains a germ of truth.

Although white males make up just 39 percent of the population, they have most of the power:

[Males] account for 82.5 percent of the Forbes 400 (folks worth at least $265 million), 77 percent of Congress, 92 percent of state governors, 70 percent of tenured college faculty, almost 90 percent of daily-newspaper editors, 77 percent of TV news directors. They dominate just about everything but NOW and [the] NAACP; even in the NBA, most of the head coaches and general managers are white guys (Gates et al., 1993, 49).

Nevertheless, men—especially working class and middle-class white men—feel that they're being attacked from all sides. As Figure 4.2 shows, about half the white men who responded to a recent study in *Newsweek* said they felt they were losing influence, jobs, and income to women and people of color and that they were paying, unfairly, for the "sins of the fathers" (Gates, 1993). Some white men point out that more women than

men are now enrolled in colleges and that by the year 2000, two out of every three new workers will be women or people of color.

Many Americans believe that adults have more options than ever before to "do gender" any way they want. Although there are more choices than in the past, there are still constraints. These constraints frame our behavior in the home, the workplace, and the consumer market.

The Home: Who Does the Work?

Because many mothers work outside the home today, there is more pressure on fathers to share in child rearing. Some fathers have reported that it took them some time to become concerned about child safety or to be more "tuned in" to their children: "I don't always hear the kids calling right away. It'll maybe take one or two times—two or three times—before I actually notice what's going on. But more and more, I think that's changed" (Coltrane, 1989). Others have become more understanding of the drudgery involved in housework and are more willing to buy expensive appliances (such as self-cleaning ovens) to make the work easier.

A recent *Good Housekeeping*/Roper survey of

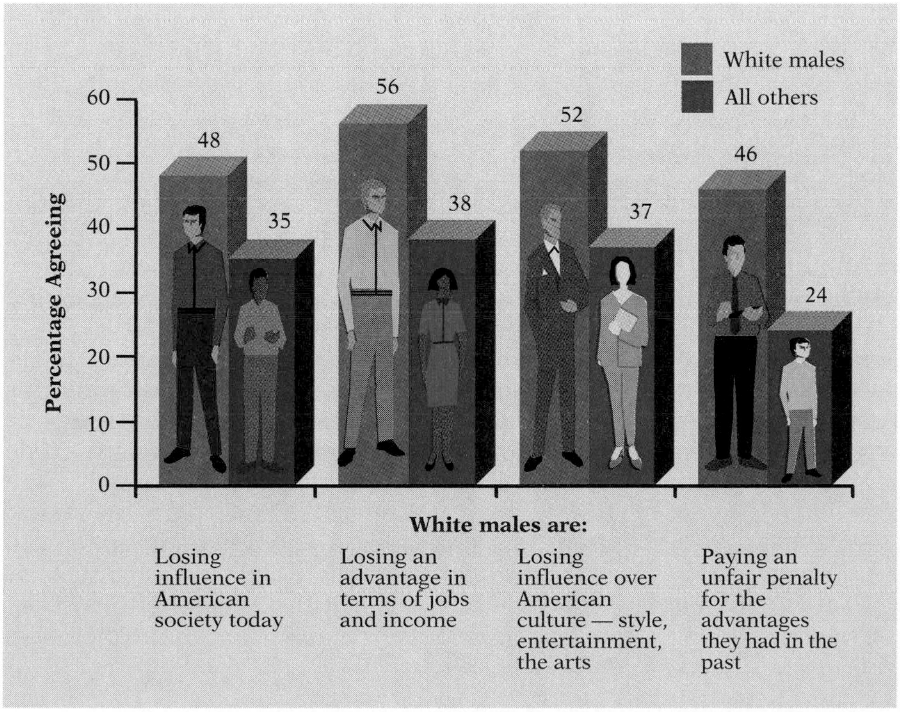

Figure 4.2 Are White Males Being Clobbered?
In a recent Gallup poll, 62 percent of respondents said that men have a better life than women in the United States, up from 32 percent in 1975. Moreover, more than 60 percent (women, 71 percent, men 52 percent) said that society favors men over women (Newport, 1993). As the Newsweek *poll reported here shows, however, many white men feel they are losing power and influence. Which set of data do you think is right?*
(Gates, 1993, pp. 50, 52.)

Like this Bentley College student, increasing numbers of women are attending college part time while working and raising their children.

check in by phone with the babysitter (Hochschild and Machung, 1989: 24).

Some men feel they are exemplary husbands or partners because they help with some of the typical household chores, such as washing dishes, doing the grocery shopping, or sorting the laundry. Women sometimes complain, however, that such participation is peripheral and superficial:

I'm always amused when my husband says that he'll "help" me make our bed. I guess he "helps" because he feels making the bed is my responsibility, not his, even though we both sleep in it. When I mow the lawn, it's no big deal. But when he occasionally helps make the bed or does the dishes, he expects a litany of thank-you's and hugs (author's files).

Women sometimes experience greater stress than men. Because they have either more responsibility or a greater share of the work, they are often doing two things at once, such as writing checks while returning phone calls. In addition, women do more of the tedious household chores, such as scrubbing the toilet, whereas men prefer to tend to their children and do "fun" things with them, like going to the movies or the zoo.

Fathers may feel very close to their children and be affectionate with them, but they are still less involved in child care. For example, in a study of single fathers, Risman (1986) reported that less than half stay home with a sick child, 12 percent could not name at least three of the youngest child's friends, and 5 percent did not know any of their children's friends. Some men believe child care is simply not their job. Chapter 10 will examine the division of labor in the home more closely.

Friends and relatives also reinforce traditional gender roles. It is not uncommon for friends, peers, and relatives to be suspicious of any man who does "women's work." Male friends often pressure fathers to spend more time with the peer group than with their children. In some cases, to avoid being ostracized, men who attend their children's functions at school or stay home with a sick child lie about getting out of work early or coming in late (Coltrane, 1989).

American families (Dortch, 1994) found that husbands may do less around the house than they think they do; for example, 70 percent of fathers of children aged 8 to 17 said they prepare dinner for the family, but fewer than half of the children agreed. In most cases, one of the major sources of tension is that many fathers do not participate in the "second shift"—household work and child care after returning from work. In a study of 52 professional couples, Hochschild and Machung (1989) found that women work roughly 15 more hours each week than men do in housework and child care. Even when men share the work, women feel more responsible for caring for the home and children:

More women than men kept track of doctor's appointments and arranged for kids' playmates to come over. More mothers than fathers worried about a child's Halloween costume or a birthday present for a school friend. They were more likely to think about their children while at work and to

The Workplace and Sexual Harassment

The way men and women are treated in the workplace affects how they feel about themselves when they are among family and friends. Most women are in low-paying, low-status occupations that have little autonomy or power (see Chapter 14). Often even women in managerial or professional jobs are denied the opportunities and benefits offered to men in comparable jobs. In 1983, for example, a woman sued Price Waterhouse, a prestigious accounting firm, when the company refused her a partnership. Of the 900 partners in 90 Price Waterhouse offices in the United States, only 27 were women. The district court awarded the complainant a partnership in 1990, which she subsequently turned down for a better offer. Price Waterhouse's reasons for denying her a partnership highlight some gender-stereotypical notions of how women should behave at work:

As a management consultant, Ms. Hopkins brought in more business than any of the other 87 candidates for partnership in 1983, all men. But she irritated staff members, including some women. They regarded her as harsh, impatient, excessively demanding. There were complaints that she behaved too much like a man, cursing, smoking, drinking beer at lunch, wearing no makeup, and carrying a briefcase instead of a purse. One Price Waterhouse partner said she needed a "course at charm school," according to testimony. A partner who supported her candidacy advised her to "walk more femininely, talk more femininely, dress more femininely." He suggested that she wear makeup and jewelry and get her wavy brown hair styled (Epstein, 1990: 1A, 12A).

Sexual harassment in the workplace had a generally low profile until the Senate confirmation hearings of Clarence Thomas, a candidate for the U.S. Supreme Court. In October 1991, the issue of sexual harassment got national coverage when Anita Hill, a law professor at the University of Oklahoma, testified that in the early 1980s Thomas had sexually harassed her while he was her supervisor and the director of the Equal Employment Opportunity Commission.

Sexual harassment is any unwelcome sexual advance, request for sexual favors, or other conduct of a sexual nature that makes a person uncomfortable and interferes with her or his work. Harassment includes touching, staring at, or making jokes about a person's body, nonreciprocated requests for sexual intercourse, and rape. Although a landmark Supreme Court decision in 1986, *Meritor Savings Bank v. Vinson*, ruled that sexual harassment violates federal laws against discrimination and is unlawful, sexual harassment continues to be a common problem in the workplace and in schools. Men in particular often say that they are confused about what is sexual harassment and what is not, claiming that they don't see the difference between flirting or complimenting someone and what is being called sexual harassment. Actually, the difference is quite clear: If someone says "stop it" and you don't, it's sexual harassment. We discuss the prevalence, consequences, and legal ramifications of sexual harassment in more detail in Chapter 14.

The Consumer Marketplace

Both women and men face marketplace perils as consumers. Perhaps you have had the unpleasant experience of having your car insurance not renewed if you filed claims totaling as little as $2,000. After Hurricane Andrew devastated the Miami area in 1992 and the Midwest was flooded in 1993, many families were unable to renew their homeowner insurance policies because insurers claimed that they suffered high losses.

Consumer problems like this are more serious for women than for men. Women are often overcharged for car and home repairs, even when they have some expertise in these areas. Even more disturbing is the fact that women routinely pay more and get less as consumers in many everyday transactions. For example, women are charged, on average, over 27 percent more than men to dry-clean a basic white cotton shirt and 25 percent more than men for a basic shampoo, cut, and blow-dry. Moreover, women rarely get free alterations when they purchase expensive clothing in the same stores that do not charge men for alterations on their clothing purchases (Whittelsey, 1993). Millions of women invest in stocks or bonds and, again, experience unequal treatment. Stockbrokers are four to six times more likely to tell men about a wide range of investments (such as corporate bond funds, money market funds, and IRAs); twice as likely to explain investments to men and to urge men to open accounts (because they assume women will be confused by explanations and have less money to invest); and they ask men more probing questions about their finances (Wang, 1993).

LANGUAGE AND COMMUNICATION

Language enables us to communicate, to interpret and organize our environment, and to give meaning to our everyday experiences. On the other hand, language can also limit our ideas and thought processes.

In *You Just Don't Understand*, sociolinguist Deborah Tannen (1990) proposes that women and men have distinctive communication styles that include different purposes, different rules, and different ways of interpreting communications. For example, Tannen says, women are most likely to use "rapport-talk": a way of establishing connections and negotiating relationships. They are most concerned with how people feel and with making people feel at home. In contrast, men are more likely to use "report-talk," a way of exhibiting knowledge and skill, and holding center stage through verbal performance such as storytelling, joking, or giving information. For example, if a man comes home and his (female) partner asks, "How was your day?" she probably expects rapport-talk in response (such as office gossip). Often, however, she will get report-talk: "Fine. Had some problems with my new software but got 'em straightened out before I left." Not hearing what she expects, the woman may be miffed, and her partner will probably not understand why she's upset.

Julia Wood (1994: 141–45) has suggested some other differences between women's and men's communication patterns. We discuss these differences in the next two sections.

Women's Speech

Because women tend to use communication to develop and maintain relationships, talk for them is often an end in itself. It is a way to foster closeness and understanding. A second important characteristic of women's speech is the effort to establish equality between people. Thus, women often encourage a speaker to continue by showing interest or concern ("Oh, really?" "I feel the same way sometimes"). A related characteristic is showing support for others ("You must have felt terrible"). Women often ask questions that probe for a greater understanding of feelings and perceptions ("Do you think it was deliberate?" "Were you glad it happened?"). A fifth characteristic is conversational "maintenance work." Women often ask a number of questions that encourage conversation ("Tell me what happened at the meeting"). A sixth quality is a personal, concrete style: Women often use details, personal disclosures, and anecdotes. By using concrete rather than vague language, women's talk clarifies issues and feelings so that people are able to understand and identify with each other.

A final feature of women's speech is tentativeness. This may be expressed in a number of ways. *Verbal hedges* ("I kind of feel you may be wrong") and qualifiers ("I may not be right, but . . .") modify, soften, or weaken other words or phrases. Men often give direct commands (such as "Let's go"), whereas women appear to show uncertainty by hedging ("I guess it's time to go"). *Disclaimers* weaken the message because they may suggest to the listener that the speaker is not serious, sincere, or very interested in the exchange. Women are more likely to use such disclaimers as "If you don't mind, could we . . . " or "Of course I don't know anything about politics, but I think. . . . " Women also use more *verbal fillers*—words or phrases such as "okay," "well," "you know," and "like" to fill silences. *Verbal fluencies*—sounds like "mmh," "ahh," and "unhuh"—serve the same purpose. Women use fillers and fluencies much more frequently when they are talking to men than to other women (Lakoff, 1990; Pearson, 1985: 185–86).

Men's Speech

A prominent feature of men's speech is *instrumentality*; men tend to use speech to accomplish specific purposes. They often focus on problem solving: getting information, discovering facts, and suggesting courses of action or solutions. Thus, for men, speech is more often a means to an end than the end itself. Masculine speech is also characterized by *exerting control*—to establish, enhance, or defend their personal status and their ideas by asserting themselves and, often, challenging others. Men are much less likely than women to offer what women consider empathic remarks (such as "That must have been very difficult for you"), and they are less likely to express sympathy or to divulge personal information about themselves.

Another feature of men's communication is *conversational dominance*. In most contexts, men usually dominate the conversation, speaking more frequently and for longer periods of time. They also show dominance by interrupting others, reinterpreting the speaker's meaning, or rerouting the conversation. Men tend to express themselves in assertive, often absolutist, ways. Compared with women, their language is typically more forceful, direct, and authoritative; tentativeness is rare. Finally, men are apt to communicate more often in abstract terms, a reflection of their more impersonal, public style.

AMBIVALENCE ABOUT CHANGE

Since the 1950s, women's roles have changed more dramatically than men's. Yet many Americans remain ambivalent about women's role in politics and the workplace. For example, in 1977 when people were asked whether "it is better for everyone involved if the man is the achiever outside the home and the woman takes care of the home and family," 65 percent said "yes." In 1991, even though increasing numbers of women were working outside the home, 41 percent still said "yes" (Grigsby, 1992).

Perhaps there is ambivalence because breaking out of traditional gender roles can be unsettling. Many young men and women still expect to participate in basically the same categories of activity (work, family, education), but they differ in their assumptions about the nature and extent of that participation. Men more commonly define their future almost exclusively in terms of career accomplishments and rarely consider family-related obstacles. In contrast, women who want families assume that their career may be deflected, suspended, or halted contingent on child rearing, and most accept such contingencies as the problems of "being a woman" (Kahne, 1992; Moen, 1992; Tavris, 1992).

The implications are unsettling. A number of social scientists are predicting that such contradictions and inconsistencies are bound to result in serious **role conflict**—the frustration and uncertainties experienced by a person who is confronted with the requirements of two or more roles that are incompatible with each other. Role conflict can result in tension, stress, hostility, aggression, and even physical problems.

Changing Gender Roles: Controversial Issues

The late 1980s and early 1990s spawned a number of heated debates about the roles of men and women in society. For example, many churches had to review their policies when women began to press to serve as ministers and priests. In 1988, the Massachusetts Episcopal diocese elected the Reverend Barbara C. Harris, a 58-year-old African American, as the first female bishop in the 460 years of the Anglican community. The choice triggered threats of schism and derogatory charges. Among other things, Reverend Harris was accused of being "vitriolic, abrasive, and confrontational." When she was challenged for having no college or seminary degrees, she pointed out that many male bishops in the church did not have these educational credentials, either (Hyer, 1988). More recently, the Christian Men's Movement, an evangelical group, has sponsored numerous male bonding rallies at stadiums. Although the movement hopes to restore male leadership in the home by preventing divorce and encouraging men to take more responsibility for their children, there is also concern that churches are becoming more "feminized" because of the increase in the number of female pastors (Woodward and Keene-Osborn, 1994).

Another controversial issue is the role of

Changing gender roles and ambivalence about these changes are highlighted in the issue of whether women like Lieutenant Tanya Brinkley, shown here near Kuwait City during the Gulf War, should serve in combat.

women in military combat. The federal laws that prohibit women from serving in combat also limit women's advancement and promotions, which are typically earned on the battleground. Traditionally, women's participation has been restricted to the service force, which includes the military police. In 1989, a young female captain who happened to be in the combat area successfully led a military police platoon into battle during the U.S. invasion of Panama. The incident triggered public debates about the appropriateness of women serving in combat.

One year later, the United States waged the Persian Gulf War. More than 30,000 women—making up about 6 percent of the U.S. troops in the Gulf area—were involved in Operation Desert Storm, and the lines became blurred between combat and noncombat jobs. Women flew cargo-carrying helicopters, serviced tanks and trucks, operated Patriot antimissile systems, policed military installations, guarded prisoners of war, and resupplied troops at the front lines. At least seven died and two were taken prisoner. In 1993, Congress repealed the statutory ban on assigning women to fly combat planes in the navy and air force. But the marines and the army continue to keep women out of infantry, armor, and field artillery units. Because these are the three main routes for rising to the top ranks, this effectively blocks women's advancement to senior leadership positions.

Is Androgyny the Answer?

Women have become angrier about stereotypical gender roles and expect men today to be more egalitarian. In 1990, a nationwide, longitudinal survey of 3,000 women indicated that women had become more critical of men than they had been a generation before (Roper Organization, 1990). Based on the data in Table 4.4, do you think men are changing? Or are women?

Some social scientists feel that androgyny may be the solution to sexist attitudes about love, sex, and marriage. In **androgyny**, both culturally defined masculine and feminine characteristics are blended within the same person. According to Bem (1975), who did much of the pioneering work on androgyny, our complex society requires that people have both these kinds of abilities. Adults must be assertive, independent, and self-reliant, but they must also relate to other people, be sensitive to their needs, and provide them with emotional support. Theoretically, androgyny allows

Table 4.4 _____
Are Women More Critical of Men Today?

	PERCENTAGE OF WOMEN AGREEING	
	1970	1990
Beliefs About Male Attitudes and Behavior		
Most men think only their own opinions about the world are important.	50%	58%
Most men find it necessary for their egos to keep women down.	49	55
Most men look at a woman and immediately think how it would be to go to bed with her.	41	54
Most men are interested in their work and life outside the home and don't pay much attention to things going on at home.	39	53
Most men are basically kind, gentle, and thoughtful.	67	51
Things That Particularly Annoy Women		
A woman being looked on as a sex symbol instead of having sense in her head	66	80
Women being left home while men go out for a good time	70	76
Pictures of nude women in men's magazines	43	61
Jokes about women drivers, mothers-in-law, or dumb blondes	32	53
A man talking about women as girls and not as women	31	53

SOURCE: Adapted from Roper Organization, 1990, pp. 54–55.

people to play both roles. The box "Are There More Than Two Gender Roles?" illustrates androgynous roles in several cultures.

One writer (Martin, 1990) has suggested that androgyny might be especially beneficial for men. Many men might stop being workaholics, relax on weekends, refrain from engaging in risky sexual behavior (to demonstrate their sexual prowess), live longer, and stop worrying about being "real men." If we were more comfortable when children display nontraditional traits, this writer suggests, assertive girls and nonaggressive boys would be accepted. And because society frowns more deeply when boys reject traditional roles than when girls do so, androgyny might take some of the pressure off men, giving them more freedom to be and do whatever they want. What do you think?

Are There More Than Two Gender Roles?

In some cultures, gender roles are not always in sync with biological sex. Some people, including homosexuals, are treated almost like a "third sex." Although they differ from the majority, they are neither stigmatized nor ostracized.

In Arabic cultures, the *xanith* is seen as "intermediate"—a cross between a man and a woman. He wears the ankle-length tunic of the male but the tight waist of the female dress. He keeps his hair at medium length; men cut their hair short, women wear their hair long. The *xanith* is permitted to move freely among women (no man is given this freedom) and to share their social life, intimate gossip, and activities. Unlike women, however, the *xanith* is not ruled by men. He has the right to go about in public unaccompanied and to live alone (Money, 1988).

Among many American Indian tribes, from Alaska to Mexico's Yucatan, the *berdache* is often a shaman, or medicine man, and a healer. He dresses as a woman, does women's work, and may engage in sex with a male. Among the Crow, a warrior who takes a *berdache* for a wife is neither scorned nor ridiculed by the males of the tribe (Callender and Kochems, 1987).

The counterpart of the *berdache* in the Navajo community is the *nadle*. Highly respected by the Navajo, *nadles* are seen as very compassionate people who care for their families and help others. Parents are pleased if a *nadle* takes an interest in their child because *nadles* are seen as very good with children. No one would ever try to change a *nadle* because "that is just their character, the way they are" (Money, 1988: 100). The *nadle* can choose either a male or female sexual partner.

Among the Mojave Indians, a male who chooses to live as a woman is called an *alyha*. After an initiation ceremony, the *alyha* is treated as a woman. The *alyha* dresses as a woman, works with women, and even mimics a woman's menstrual flow by cutting his upper thigh. If the *alyha* marries a man, there is a ceremonial "birth" and "death" of a child. In contrast, a female who wishes to become a male is known as a *hwame*. She dresses and acts like a man, marries a female, and sets up a residence like other Mohave males (Doyle, 1985).

In India, the *hijra* include elements of both male and female roles. As part of a religious ceremony, a man has his external genitals removed and practices sexual abstinence. This is believed to make him sacred and a source of blessings for health, fertility, and prosperity. It is also believed that he has the power to cause infertility through curses on others. The *hijra* often perform at weddings and religious ceremonies as dancers or musicians (Nanda, 1990).

CROSS-CULTURAL VARIATIONS IN GENDER ROLES

Each culture has its own gender-role norms and values, and the degree of equality between men and women differs widely across societies. As we discussed earlier, cross-cultural variations constitute some of the best evidence that gender roles are learned and not inherited.

At one end of the continuum are many societies, primarily in the Middle East and in third-world countries, where women are almost totally dominated by men. As the box "To Be a Woman in Saudi Arabia" shows, although Saudi women are gaining more independence, they are still held back in many areas. Even in Egypt, one of the Arab world's most tolerant societies, women have been experiencing highly repressive measures. Some women's associations have been shut down, domestic violence in rural areas is common, and although female circumcision is illegal, virtually all the women in poor communities have been circumcised during childhood by midwives or by doctors who say they are doing it to prevent homosexuality or to "beautify" women (Lief, 1994).

In India, most women are under the authority of fathers, brothers, husbands, or husbands' families and are often considered property (epitomized by the *dowry* that the bride's family pays to the groom's). In China's traditional family, a new wife spends most of her time in the service of her mother-in-law. A wife can be divorced if she fails to bear children, and she has no property rights after a divorce. Confucian values dictate that a woman is always under male authority—first her father's, then her husband's, then her sons'. In much of China that outlook has not changed very much. A recent study found that

CHANGES

To Be a Woman in Saudi Arabia

In 1991, during the Persian Gulf War, both U.S. troops and Saudi Arabian soldiers experienced considerable culture shock, much of it revolving around the very different roles of women in Saudi Arabia and the United States. Saudi Arabia is an Islamic fundamentalist country where women wear veils and walk behind their husbands. They may not work in a setting where men are present, travel on their own, or officially drive a car. To "shelter them from men" and "protect their honor," separate shopping areas, theaters, restaurant seating sections, and beaches are provided for women, and there are even separate universities and medical schools for them.

Saudi soldiers reacted angrily when they saw American women doing "man's work," like giving other soldiers orders, repairing planes, or driving trucks. Although female U.S. troops continued to perform their assigned duties, in order to minimize Saudi distress, orders were issued to American women not to wear T-shirts, shorts, or other "revealing" clothing. Women had to keep long sleeves rolled down, despite the heat of the desert climate.

In 1990, about 40 Saudi women, including a number of professors and

Many western women believe in the value of sex-segregated educational institutions, but in Islamic countries it is men who impose, not women who choose, separate facilities.

physicians, protested Islamic tradition by driving their own cars. The women were immediately arrested and suspended from their jobs. Leaflets were passed out at mosques during Friday prayers, accusing the women of undermining Saudi morality and showing signs of "American secularism." The women's names, telephone numbers, and addressees were printed and distributed, and predictably, menacing telephone calls followed (Dowell, 1990).

At King Saud University, where several of the women protesters taught, the *mutawain*, or religious police, forced administrators to disband part of the women's graduate program because male teachers were supervising female students. All lectures by men in the women's part of the university were canceled, as were science courses in which men supervised women in lab work. Finally, the entire women's graduate school was forcibly closed for five days (Ruby, 1990).

Some observers feel that whether or not women should drive cars was not the real issue. According to these authorities, many Saudis simply feared that any change in women's roles would lead to further demands. "Women driving could lead to social disorder, and any conflict in the country does not help the leadership and the people," a male university professor said. "The social fabric in this country cannot tolerate this" (Ruby, 1990: 3A). By the early 1990s, some 60,000 Saudis had attended U.S. universities and might be expected to escalate demands for change at home. This group, how-ever, accounts for only 1 percent of the population (Dowell, 1990).

---

one of the highest causes of death in China was suicide, and the peak was among females age 15 to 25 who lived in rural areas. The researchers suggested that marriage problems and poverty may be the major causes of suicide in this group (Li and Baker, 1991).

Some observers feel that since *glasnost*, the position of Eastern European women has eroded. They have been hit the hardest by crime and unemployment. Even though women account for nearly half of all the scientists, 40 percent are only assistants. Moreover, the government is run almost exclusively by elderly and

middle-aged men who are not interested in women's issues (Watson, 1993). In Russia, because of widespread male alcoholism, fathers' authority in the home has diminished, and women and mothers have most of the responsibility of child care and housekeeping (Drakulic, 1993).

At the other end of the continuum are those societies, like France and Sweden, that are considered more progressive than the United States. Sweden has very generous maternity and paternity leave policies, for example. All families with newborn babies are given an 18-month leave from work at 90 percent compensation and a government subsidy of $1,667 per child every year for child care (Herrstrom, 1990).

Many other societies, such as Japan, are in the middle of the continuum. Japan is often described as a father-absent, achievement-oriented society where men devote most of their lives to the company and work-related activities. Working wives do double duty, spending more than three hours a day on housework when the average man puts in only eight minutes, and spend most of their "free" time checking on homework and escorting their children to extracurricular activities. Some changes are taking place, however. According to one writer, the Japanese woman today "is equally likely to be single, married, living with a partner, or divorced; to have children or be childless; and to be working part- or full-time" (Iwao, 1993). Increasing numbers of women are challenging their traditionally submissive roles. They are pursuing higher education, entering the labor force, and moving into fields that were once considered exclusively male, such as engineering. Finally, although entrusting child care to strangers was once unthinkable, today child-care centers are experiencing a booming business in Japan (Shimomura, 1990; Takayama, 1990).

CONCLUSION

There is no doubt that the last 20 years have seen *changes* in some aspects of gender roles. More people today say they believe in gender equality, and unprecedented numbers of women have entered the labor force. Do most people really have more *choices*, though? Having taken on more responsibility, women are becoming increasingly resentful of the burden of both domestic and economic jobs, especially in a society that devalues them and their labor. Men, although often freed from the sole-breadwinner role, feel that their range of choices is narrowing as women compete with them in more sectors of society.

Significant change in gender roles confronts *constraints* at every level: personal, group, and institutional. Those who benefit from gender-role inequality will resist giving up their privileges and economic resources, although, as conditions in some other countries show, changes in ideology, socialization practices, work, and family structures are possible. In the next chapter we will see some of the effects of the changes that have already taken place in gender attitudes and behavior as we look at loving and intimate relationships.

Taking Action

Lobbying for Gender Equality

Were you bothered by anything you learned from this chapter? Then read on, and get involved!

• About four to six weeks before Christmas every year, local newspapers, newsmagazines, parents' magazines, and television stations feature the hottest toys or books as presents. You can organize a modest letter-writing campaign (or just write letters yourself) requesting that information on **nonsexist toys and reading materials** be included in the reviews.

The trend for toys to be more representative of society is underscored by the appearance of more male dolls and more multicultural dolls on the shelves of major stores. Two companies founded by African American entrepreneurs are Olmec Toys, based in New York City, and Cul-

tural Toys, based in Minneapolis. The latter makes Dinkytown Daycare Kids from Native American, African American, and Latino backgrounds, as well as a doll that uses a wheelchair. If the big retailers in your area don't carry these lines, ask them to do so.

• Several groups document and protest **media exploitation of women and people of color** and encourage subscriber participation. Two of these are Challenging Media Images of Women, P.O. Box 902, Framingham, MA 01701, and Mediawatch, P.O. Box 618, Santa Cruz, CA 95061. Mediawatch reports comments from subscribers about sexist media materials and tells subscribers where to file complaints. In its Fall 1994 newsletter, for example, Mediawatch noted that an educational publishing company, Scholastic, Inc., teamed up with Revlon cosmetic company to create a teaching guide titled, "Hot Looks, Cool Style." The guide, which was sent to 29,000 home economics teachers, included activities like the following: "Good Hair Day/Bad Hair Day: Ask students to bring in pictures of themselves from days they consider 'good' and 'bad' hair days. Mount the pictures on a bulletin board and have students describe what a good or bad hair day means to them." To respond to such "educational" materials, Mediawatch suggests that you contact Scholastic, Inc., 730 Broadway, 9th Floor, New York, NY 10003, and Revlon Group, Inc., 21 East 63rd Street, New York, NY 10021.

According to Mediawatch, Hi Tech Entertainment, maker of Nintendo, is targeting the female pre-teen market with a range of Barbie video games such as "Super Model" that highlight "such feats as Barbie navigating a mall maze to meet Ken for a date." If you think that Barbie, a role model for millions of little girls, could use her time more productively, contact Nintendo of America, Inc., 4820-150th Ave. NE, Redmond, WA 98052.

• A good source of suggestions for taking action on **women's issues** is Donna Jackson's *How to Make the World a Better Place for Women in Five Minutes a Day* (New York: Hyperion, 1992). For example, Jackson suggests ordering "This Insults Women" stickers and putting them on demeaning advertisements, posters, or movie ads throughout the campus.

• A number of E-mail lists address gender-role issues. Some of these are WMST-L%UMDD. BITNET@ UBE.UB.UMD.EDU (Women's Studies list); FEMISA @CSF.COLORADO.EDU (discusses gender issues, especially from cross-cultural perspectives); FEMINISM-DIGEST%NCAR.UCAR.EDU@NCARIO (a sociology list that discusses a variety of gender-role issues); and SASH-L%ASUACAD.BITNET@UBE.UB.UMD (Sociologists Against Sexual Harassment list).

Faculty members at a growing number of colleges and universities are setting up computer bulletin boards (CBB) through which they can engage students in expanded discussions of course materials, outside of the classroom setting. O'Hare and Kahn (1994) provide an excellent discussion of how to establish and operate such a bulletin board, using the CBB they set up for their own Women's Studies course as an example.

SUMMARY

1. Sex and gender are not interchangeable terms. Sex refers to the biological characteristics we are born with. Gender refers to the attitudes and behaviors society expects of each sex.

2. Scholars continue to debate how much of our behavior is a reflection of nature (biology) and how much of nurture (environment). Although biology is important, there is little evidence that women are naturally better parents, that men are naturally more aggressive, or that men and women are inherently different in other than anatomy and physiology.

3. Traditional gender roles are based on the beliefs that women should fulfill expressive functions and that men should play instrumental roles.

4. Playing traditional roles has both positive and negative consequences. On the positive side, men and women know what is expected of them. On the negative side, traditional roles often create stress and anxiety.

5. Many theoretical perspectives try to explain how we learn gender roles. Social learning theory argues that gender roles are learned by reward and punishment and by imitation and role modeling. Cognitive development theory assumes that children learn gender identity through interacting with and interpreting the behavior of others. Gender schema theory proposes that children organize their experience by developing information-processing categories, or schema, that they use to develop a gender identity.

6. We learn gender expectations from many sources—parents, peers, teachers, and the media. Many of these socializing influences continue to reinforce traditional male and female gender roles.

7. During much of our adult life, our activities are sex-segregated. Typically, men and women play different roles in the home, the workplace, and as consumers.

8. Men and women communicate differently. These differences are often unintentional, but they may create misunderstandings between women and men.

9. Although many people, especially women, are unhappy about their "double shifts," there is a great deal of ambivalence about changing gender roles.

10. There is considerable variation across cultures in terms of equality between men and women. Many societies are male-dominated, but others are considerably more progressive than the United States.

KEY TERMS

sex 80
gender 80
gender roles 80
hormones 81
premenstrual syndrome (PMS) 82

gender identity 82
gender-role stereotype 87
social learning theory 89
cognitive development theory 89
gender schema theory 90

sexual harrassment 101
role conflict 103
androgyny 104

ADDITIONAL READING

There are hundreds of excellent books and articles on gender roles. Some of the best sources for current research are the journals *Signs*, *Sage: A Scholarly Journal on Black Women*, *Sex Roles*, and *Gender and Society*.

Although some publications in the following list focus on women, others on men, and still others on gender-role issues overall, every work cited discusses and expands on ideas we have covered in this chapter:

LEONORE LOEB ADLER, ed., *International Handbook on Gender Roles* (Westport, CT: Greenwood Press, 1993). Authors who have lived and worked in each of the 31 countries covered in this reader discuss gender roles from infancy through old age.

MAXINE BACA ZINN and BONNIE THORNTON DILL, eds., *Women of Color in U.S. Society* (Philadelphia: Temple University Press, 1994). Over a dozen articles on employment, education, and family life as well as a reaction on "rethinking gender."

NIJOLE V. BENOKRAITIS and JOE R. FEAGIN, *Modern Sexism: Blatant, Subtle, and Covert Discrimination*, 2nd ed. (Englewood Cliffs, NJ: Prentice Hall, 1995). The authors describe a number of types of blatant, subtle, and covert sex discrimination and suggest some remedies.

ELISABETH BUMILLER, *May You Be the Mother of a Hundred Sons: A Journey Among the Women of India* (New York: Random House, 1990). An insightful analysis of the everyday lives of men and women in India.

VICTORIA KATHERINE BURBANK, *Fighting Women, Anger and Aggression in Aboriginal Australia* (Berkeley, CA: University of California Press, 1994). An anthropologist shows that fighting is common among contemporary aboriginal women in Mangrove, Australia; women fight with men and with other women. The book focuses on women as aggressors and shows how Western theories stereotype female aggression and victimization.

BETTINA FLORES, *Chiquita's Cocoon* (New York: Villard, 1990). The author encourages Latinas to fight traditional cultural oppression while holding on to their rich cultural heritage.

SCOTT HELLER, "Scholars Debunk the Marlboro Man: Examining Stereotypes of Masculinity," *Chronicle of Higher Education*, February 3, 1993, pp. A6, A7, A10. Discusses some 28 recent books on masculinity and male roles.

MICHAEL S. KIMMEL and MICHAEL A. MESSNER, eds., *Men's Lives*, 3rd ed. (New York: Allyn & Bacon, 1995). An anthology of readings that define masculinity and the issues that men confront during their lifetimes.

RICHARD G. MAJORS and JACOB U. GORDON, eds., *The American Black Male: His Present Status and His Future* (Chicago: Nelson-Hall, 1994). Twenty-one articles examine the history and present status of the African American male, his psychosocial development, his search for empowerment, and his future.

PEGGY ORENSTEIN, *Schoolgirls: Young Women, Self-Esteem, and the Confidence Gap* (New York: Doubleday, 1994). This book examines why, despite their high grades and other achievements, many girls' self-esteem plummets during the middle school years. An earlier book on gender and self-esteem is Lyn Mikel Brown and Carol Gilligan's *Meeting at the Crossroads* (New York: Ballantine Books, 1992).

DEBORAH TANNEN, *Talking from 9 to 5* (New York: Morrow, 1994). As the title suggests, Tannen examines gender communication patterns in the workplace.

JULIA T. WOOD, *Gendered Lives: Communication, Gender, and Culture* (Belmont, CA: Wadsworth, 1994). This book discusses how gender, culture, and communication intersect, and examines gendered communication in close relationships, school settings, the media, and other situations.

5
Love Is a Many-Splendored Thing— Or Is It?

Data Digest

Stevie Wonder "just called to say I love you"; the Beatles told us that "all you need is love"; Kenny Rogers felt "life is good but love is better." On the other hand, Tina Turner called love "a second-hand emotion," and Paul Simon described "fifty ways to leave your lover." The Supremes "can't hurry love," and Yaz advised "don't walk away from love." Janet Jackson will do it "anytime, anyplace." "All I want is you," sing U2; All 4 One are "so much in love"; Bob Marley needs only "one love"; and Peter Gabriel sees love "in your eyes." As these lyrics suggest, love can be both euphoric and painful. But just what is love? And why is it so important?

THE IMPORTANCE OF LOVE

Love—as both a feeling and a behavior—is essential for human survival. The family is typically our earliest and perhaps most important source of love and emotional support (see Chapter 1). Babies and children deprived of love have been known to develop a wide variety of problems—for example, depression, headaches, physiological impairments, and neurotic and psychosomatic difficulties—that sometimes last a lifetime. In contrast, infants who are loved and cuddled typically gain more weight, cry less, and smile more (Bowlby, 1969). By 5 years of age, they have been found to have significantly higher IQs and to score higher on language tests (Klaus and Kennell, 1976).

Unlike most mammals, human beings are physically helpless for a long period. At the same time, the human being's potential for learning during the first year of life is enormous. At birth, the human brain weighs about 350 grams, but by the end of the first year it has more than doubled in size; at 825 grams, it has reached nearly 60 percent of the weight of the adult brain. Oxygen, warmth, and food are the infant's most basic necessities, but to thrive and grow emotionally and intellectually, the child needs constant care by loving people (Gaylin, 1986).

Love for oneself, or self-love, is also essential to the growing individual. Actress Mae West once said, "I never loved another person the way I loved myself." Although such a statement may seem self-centered, it is actually quite insightful. Social scientists describe self-love as an important basis for self-esteem. Among other things, people who love themselves are more open to criticism and less demanding of others. Fromm (1956) saw self-love as a necessary prerequisite for loving others. People who do not love themselves may not be able to return love but may constantly seek love relationships to bolster their own poor self-images (Casler, 1974). Before we discuss some of these issues, let us define the concept of love.

What Is Love?

Love is an elusive concept. On the one hand, we have all experienced love and feel we know what it is. On the other hand, when asked what love is, people will give a variety of answers. What we mean by love depends on whether we are talking about love for family members, friends, or lovers. As the box "The Breadth and Depth and Height of Love" illustrates, love has been a source of inspiration, wry witticisms, and even political action.

Love has many dimensions. It can be romantic, exciting, obsessive, and irrational. It can also be platonic, calming, altruistic, and sensible. "Love is ecstasy and torment, freedom and slavery. Poets and songwriters would be in a fine mess without it. Plus, it makes the world go round" (Gray, 1993: 47). Many researchers feel that love defies a single definition because it varies in degree and intensity and across social contexts. At the very least, three elements are necessary for a love relationship: (1) a willingness to please and accommodate the other, even if this involves compromise and sacrifice; (2) an acceptance of the other person's faults and shortcomings; and (3) as much concern about the loved one's welfare as one's own (Safilios-Rothschild, 1977). And, as you will see shortly, people who say they are "in love" emphasize intimacy, disclosure, and commitment.

In any type of love, caring about the other person is essential. Although love may involve passionate yearning, respect is a more important quality. Respect is inherent in all love: "I want the loved person to grow and unfold for his own sake, and in his own ways, and not for the purpose of serving me" (Fromm, 1956: 23–24). If respect and caring are missing, the relationship is not based on love. Instead, it is an unhealthy or possessive dependency that limits the lovers' social, emotional, and intellectual growth (Peele and Brodsky, 1976).

Love, especially long-term love, has nothing in common with the images of love or frenzied sex that we get from Hollywood, television, and most novels. Because of these images, people believe

CHANGES

The Breadth and Depth and Height of Love

Throughout the centuries many writers have commented on the varieties, purposes, pleasures, and pain of love. Love is universal; it is a focus of concern in all societies.

❏ *Jesus (4 B.C.–A.D. 29):* "A new commandment I give unto you, that ye love one another."

❏ *I Corinthians 13:4–7:* "Love is patient and kind; love is not jealous or boastful; it is not arrogant or rude. Love does not insist on its own way; it is not irritable or resentful; it does not rejoice at wrong, but rejoices in the right. Love bears all things, believes all things, hopes all things, endures all things."

❏ *William Shakespeare (1564–1616)* "To say the truth, reason and love keep little company together nowadays" (from *A Midsummer Night's Dream*).

❏ *Hindustani proverb:* "Life is no longer one's own when the heart is fixed on another."

❏ *Duc Francois de La Rochefoucauld (1613–1680):* "True love is like ghosts, which everyone talks about but few have seen."

❏ *Ninon de Lenclos (1620–1705):* "Much more genius is needed to make love than to command armies."

❏ *Irish saying:* "If you live in my heart, you live rent-free."

❏ *Elizabeth Barrett Browning (1806–1861):* "How do I love thee? Let me count the ways. I love thee to the depth and breadth and height my soul can reach."

❏ *Henry Wadsworth Longfellow (1807–1882):* "Love gives itself; it is not bought."

❏ *Japanese saying:* "Who travels for love finds a thousand miles only one mile."

❏ *William Thackeray (1811–1863):* "It is best to love wisely, no doubt; but to love foolishly is better than not to be able to love at all."

❏ *Robert Browning (1812–1889):* "Take away love and our earth is a tomb."

❏ *Benjamin Disraeli (1804–1881):* "The magic of first love is our ignorance that it can ever end."

❏ *Marlene Dietrich (1901–1992):* "Grumbling is the death of love."

❏ *Turkish proverb:* When two hearts are one, even the king cannot separate them.

❏ *Che Guevara (1928–1967):* "The true revolutionary is guided by a great feeling of love."

❏ *Woody Allen (1935–):* "Sex alleviates tension and love causes it."

❏ *Cher (1946–):* "The trouble with some women is that they get all excited about nothing—and then marry him."

a variety of myths about love. These misconceptions often lead to unrealistic expectations, stereotypes, and disillusionment. (To test your general knowledge about love, see the box "How Much Do You Know about Love?"). In fact, "real" love is closer to what one author called "stirring-the-oatmeal" love (Johnson, 1985). This type of love is neither exciting nor thrilling but is relatively mundane and unromantic. It means paying bills, putting out the garbage, scrubbing toilet bowls, being up all night with a sick baby, and performing myriad other "oatmeal" tasks that are not very sexy.

Some partners take turns stirring the oatmeal. Others leave the relationship in search of a candlelit gourmet meal in a romantic setting. Why do some lovers stay while others leave? Some psychologists suggest that the answer can be found in attachment theories.

ATTACHMENT, COMMITMENT, AND INTIMACY

Attachment theory states that "our primary motivation in life is to be connected with other people—because it is the only security we ever have. Maintaining closeness is a bona fide survival need" (Johnson and Marano, 1994: 34; see also Bowlby, 1969; Weiss, 1976). A number of psychologists believe that both physical and emotional attachment are critical in the evolution of love in children as well as adults.

Attachment and Children

The classic studies on attachment behavior were conducted by Harry and Margaret Harlow (1962). In their experiments, the Harlows studied the behavior of infant monkeys that were raised by two kinds of "mothers." The "wire mother" was a simple construction of wire, whereas the frame of the "cloth mother" was covered by foam rubber and terry cloth; both "mothers" had simulated monkey faces. In one cage the wire mother dispensed milk to a group of monkeys; in the other cage the cloth mother fed the infants. Regardless of which mother provided them milk, when both groups of monkeys were frightened, they invariably ran and clung to the cloth mother. The Harlows concluded that warmth and comfort were even more important to the infant monkeys than was the nourishment necessary for survival.

Studies of infants have supported the Harlow results. As you saw in Chapter 1, a number of researchers have found that children who are raised in impersonal environments (orphanages, some foster homes, or unloving families) show emotional and social underdevelopment, language and motor skills retardation, and mental health problems.

First developed by the British psychiatrist John Bowlby in the 1960s and later elaborated by the U.S. psychologist Mary Ainsworth (1978), attachment theory has found growing support by developmental theorists. Ainsworth, who observed mothers and infants separating and reuniting in both natural and experimental situations, noticed that the infants differed in their attachment styles. About two-thirds were characterized as *secure* in their attachment, with sensitive and responsive mothers. They showed some distress when left with a stranger, but when the mother returned, the child clung to her for just a short time and then went back to exploring and playing.

When mothers were inconsistent—sometimes

Although Margaret and Harry Harlow's work on attachment in infant monkeys is among the most famous in the psychological literature, some critics claim that the monkeys were so devastated by confinement with "wire mothers" and by isolation from other monkeys that they could not ever function normally. Do you think the Harlows' work was justified?

How Much Do You Know about Love?

The following statements are based on the material in this chapter. Eight or more correct answers show that you know a myth when you hear one.

	Fact	Fiction
1. There is an ideal mate for every person; just keep looking.	☐	☐
2. Women are more romantic than men.	☐	☐
3. Love conquers all.	☐	☐
4. Men's and women's love needs are different.	☐	☐
5. Real love lasts forever.	☐	☐
6. Everybody falls in love sooner or later.	☐	☐
7. Love brings happiness and security.	☐	☐
8. Love endures and overcomes all problems.	☐	☐
9. Men are more interested in sex than in love.	☐	☐
10. Love and marriage go together like a horse and carriage.	☐	☐

Answers

All ten statements are myths!

1. We can love many people, and we can love many times. This is why some people marry more than once. We typically marry someone we grew up with, lived close to, or met in college or on the job.

2. Men fall in love more quickly, are more romantic, and suffer more intensely when their love is not returned.

3. Because one out of two marriages ends in divorce, love is not enough to overcome all problems and obstacles. Differences in race, ethnicity, religion, economic status, education, and age can often stifle romantic interest.

4. Both men and women want trust, honesty, understanding, and respect.

5. A love can be real but not last eternally; good marriages do not always last a lifetime. People today live much longer, the world is more complex, and partners change as they mature and grow older.

6. Some people have deep-seated emotional scars that make them suspicious and unloving; others are too self-centered to give love.

7. Love guarantees neither love nor security. In a study of college students and adults who said they were in love, only 56 percent described themselves as secure. The others reported feeling generally insecure or anxious.

8. People who love each other make sacrifices, but emotional or physical abuse should not be tolerated. Eventually, even "martyrs" become unhappy, angry, depressed, and resentful.

9. During the romantic stage, both women and men may be more interested in sex than in love. As love matures, both value such attributes as faithfulness, patience, and making the other person feel wanted.

10. As many arranged marriages in countries around the world show, love is not an indispensable ingredient in a happy marriage. Other factors, such as similar values, complementary life goals, comparable attitudes toward money, and parallel child-rearing philosophies are equally (if not more) important. In general, love should be one criterion, but not the only one, in deciding whom and when to marry.

Infants denied nurturance and the opportunity to form emotional attachments may develop into adults who cannot love others and who have limited social skills.

affectionate, sometimes aloof—about 19 percent of the infants displayed *anxious/ambivalent* attachment styles. They showed distress at separation but rejected their mothers when they returned. The remaining 21 percent of the infants, most of whom had been reared by caregivers who ignored their physical and emotional needs, displayed *avoidant* behavior when their caregivers returned from an absence. Researchers later proposed that adult love reflects these three attachment styles.

Attachment and Adults

Why are some people afraid of emotional intimacy and of making long-term commitments? Cindy Hazan and her associates (1987; Shaver et al., 1988) tested attachment theory on adults. They devised a "love quiz" based on the three attachment styles identified by Ainsworth and then administered the quiz to 108 college students and 620 adults in the surrounding community who said they were in love. The three attachment styles reflected the relationships they reported having had with their parents.

Secure adults (about 56 percent of the sample), who generally described their parents as having been warm and supportive, were more trusting of their romantic partners and more confident of a partner's love. They could be intimate in their relationships and reported trusting and happy relationships that lasted, on average, about ten years. *Anxious/ambivalent adults* (about 20 percent) had a tendency to fall in love easily and wanted a commitment almost immediately. *Avoidant adults* (24 percent of the sample) reported little trust for other people, had the most cynical beliefs about love, and were not very good at either intimacy or making a commitment.

The studies by Hazan and her colleagues were based on small, nonrandom samples. And because they were not longitudinal, there is no direct evidence that the parent-child attachments of the respondents really influenced their experiences in adult love. Nevertheless, many life-cycle researchers feel that attachment is a useful concept in explaining love relationships across the life span (Norris and Tindale, 1993). Several studies have found that people with a secure attachment style report higher levels of satisfaction, intimacy, trust, and commitment in their relationships than do people with anxious or avoidant attachment characteristics (Collins and Read, 1990; Feeney and Noller, 1990; Feeney et al., 1993).

Somewhat surprisingly, the relationships of people with anxious or avoidant attachment styles often last four to five years (Bartholomew, 1993). Apparently this is not because the partners are happy but because avoidant men have low expectations of their partners to begin with, and anxious women work hard to maintain a relationship (Kirkpatrick and Davis, 1994). Even in the case of a bitter divorce, the partners often experience a sense of connection. They feel emotionally bound to each other, even when they can't stand to be with each other (Ambert, 1992).

THEORIES OF LOVE AND LOVING

A number of theoretical explanations have been proposed for why and how people love. Biological theories tend to focus more on the *why* of love, but psychological, sociological, and anthropological approaches try to deal with the *how* as well. As you will see, the line between why and how is a fine one. Take, for example, the notion of commitment. We can talk about the desire and need for commitment as part of the reason for loving, but we can also talk about commitment as a way or style of loving.

Biological, Psychological, and Sociological Theories

You might say that biologists, psychobiologists, and biological anthropologists look at love under the microscope, while social scientists use a wide-angle lens. These distinctions parallel the nature-nurture debate we discussed in Chapter 4.

Biological perspectives maintain that love is founded in evolution, biology, and chemistry. Biologists and others see romance as serving the evolutionary purpose of drawing males and females into long-term partnerships, which, as we've seen, are essential to child rearing. On open and often dangerous grasslands, one parent could care for offspring while the other foraged for food.

When lovers claim that they feel "high" and as if they are being swept away, it's probably because they are literally flooded by chemicals. A meeting of eyes, a touch of hands, or a whiff of scent sets off a flood that starts in the brain and races along the nerves and through the bloodstream. The results are familiar: flushed skin, sweaty palms, and heavy breathing (Ackerman, 1994). Natural amphetamines like dopamine, norepinephrine, and phenylethylamine (PEA) are responsible for these symptoms. PEA is especially effective; it revs up the brain, causing feelings of elation, exhilaration, and euphoria:

No wonder lovers can stay awake all night talking and caressing. No wonder they become so absent-minded, so giddy, so optimistic, so gregarious, so full of life. Naturally occurring amphetamines have pooled in the emotional centers of their brains; they are high on natural "speed" (Fisher, 1992: 53).

PEA highs don't last long, though, which may explain why passionate or romantic love is short-lived.

What about love that endures beyond the first few years? According to the biological perspective, another set of chemicals helps maintain relationships. As infatuation wanes and attachment grows, a new group called endorphins, chemically similar to morphine, that reside in the brain takes over. Unlike PEA, endorphins calm the mind, eliminate pain, and reduce anxiety. This, biologists say, explains why people in long-lasting relationships report feeling comfortable and secure (Walsh, 1991; Fisher, 1992).

Remember that there is no hard evidence for biological theories. One observer has noted, for example, that these evolutionary perspectives are "exceeding the limits of knowledge, scientific method, and credulity" (Swedlund, 1993: 1053). Nonetheless, they provide food for thought.

Psychological and sociological perspectives claim that culture, not PEA, is Cupid. The social scientific theories that we discuss here and that are listed in Table 5.1 can help us understand the components and processes of love.

Table 5.1

Theories of Love

THEORY	CHARACTERISTICS
Attachment theory	Suggests that both physical and emotional attachment are critical in the evolution of love.
Fromm's theory of love	Popularized the idea of the existence of several types of love, including brotherly love; maternal and paternal love; infantile, immature, and mature love; and erotic love.
Maslow's theory of love	Differentiates between deficiency-love—a selfish, one-sided love—and being-love—a giving and unselfish love.
Reiss's wheel theory of love	Describes four stages of love—rapport, self-revelation, mutual dependency, and personality need fulfillment—that turn like a wheel to produce a relationship.
Clockspring alternative theory	Examines love relationships as clock-springs that can end if they are wound too tightly; associations can wind and unwind many times.
Sternberg's triangular theory of love	Emphasizes three components of love that comprise a triangle: intimacy, passion, and decision/commitment.

Fromm's Theory of Love

In his best-seller, *The Art of Loving*, Fromm described love as "the only satisfactory answer to the problem of human existence." He differentiated among several types of love, including brotherly love; maternal and paternal love; infantile, immature, and mature love; and erotic love. Fromm's perspective was important because it popularized the idea that there are several types of love, only one of which is erotic.

Brotherly love encompasses a sense of responsibility, care, and respect for all human beings. For Fromm, a mother's love was innate and unconditional, whereas a father's love was task oriented. Fathers, he proposed, taught their children about law and order, discipline, travel, and adventure. Sociologists now challenge these different views of mother's and father's love, however. Loving the infant is seen as just as important for fathers as it is for mothers; and single parents, regardless of gender, have been found to exhibit both types of love (see Chapter 12).

As children grow up, Fromm said, their love becomes less self-centered. Infantile love says, "I love because I am loved"; immature love says, "I love you because I need you"; and mature love says, "I need you because I love you." Finally, erotic love is the most deceptive kind of love because it is based on physical intimacy and "is soon explored and soon exhausted" (Fromm, 1956: 35–45).

Maslow's Theory of Love

In 1968, Abraham Maslow, a psychologist, described two types of love: deficiency-love and being-love. **Deficiency-love** is a selfish type of love that fulfills one partner's needs only. Men who love women who take care of their emotional and sexual needs, who look up to them, and who are subordinate to them may be exhibiting deficiency-love. Similarly, women who love men who provide for them financially and who are powerful and successful are often experiencing this selfish type of love. In such relationships, the lovers depend on each other to satisfy their own needs rather than accommodate their partners. In terms of exchange theory (see Chapter 2), each partner is expecting high benefits and few, if any, costs.

In contrast, **being-love** is giving and unselfish. Instead of loving someone because he or she fulfills a partner's needs, the person exhibiting being-love appreciates the other's good qualities regardless of weaknesses and limitations. Because being-love is not possessive, both partners can grow and mature.

Reiss's Wheel Theory of Love

Sociologist Ira Reiss (1960, Reiss and Lee, 1988) has proposed a "wheel theory" of love (see Figure 5.1) that generated much research for several decades. Reiss describes four stages of love: rapport, self-revelation, mutual dependency, and personality need fulfillment. In stage one, the partners establish *rapport* based on similar cultural backgrounds, such as upbringing, social class, and education. (As you saw in Chapter 1, families and kin groups typically have strong endogamous rules that discourage relationships with people from different ethnic, racial, religious, and socioeconomic groups.) Without this rapport, according to Reiss, the would-be lovers would not have enough in common to establish an initial interest.

In stage two, *self-revelation* brings the couple closer together. Because each person feels more at ease in the relationship, he or she is more likely to discuss hopes, desires, fears, and ambitions and to engage in sexual activities. As the couple becomes more intimate, the partners' *mutual dependency* increases in stage three, and they exchange ideas, jokes, and sexual desires. In the fourth and final stage, the couple experiences *personality need fulfillment*. The partners confide in each other, make mutual decisions, support each other's ambition, and bolster each other's self-confidence.

Like spokes on a wheel, these stages can turn many times—that is, they can repeat themselves over and over. For example, partners build some rapport; then they reveal bits of themselves; then they build more rapport; then begin to exchange ideas, and so on. And the spokes may keep turning indefinitely to produce a deep and lasting relationship. Or the wheel may stop after a few turns during a fleeting romance. The romantic wheel may "unwind"—even in one evening—if the relationship is weakened by arguments, reluctance to reveal oneself, or competing interests.

The Clockspring Alternative Theory

Sociologist Dolores Borland (1975) modified the wheel theory, proposing that love relationships be viewed as "clocksprings," like those in a watch. Like clocksprings, associations can wind and unwind several times as love swells or ebbs. Ten-

Figure 5.1 The Wheel Theory of Love. Reiss likened his four stages of love to the spokes of a wheel. As the text describes, a love relationship begins with the stage of rapport and, in a lasting relationship, continues to build as the wheel turns, deepening rapport, fulfillment, and mutual dependence and increasing the honesty of self revelation (Based on Reiss, 1960: 139–45).

sions, caused by events like pregnancy and the birth of a child, may wind the spring tightly, but if the partners communicate and work toward a common goal, such tensions may solidify rather than weaken a relationship. On the other hand, relationships can end abruptly if they are so tightly overwound that they cannot grow or if one partner feels threatened by increasing intimacy:

An argument, a new relationship, the birth of a child, or prolonged intermittent stress are examples of incidents that can "wind up" a relationship and lead to a tighter bond and increased understanding through communication and working together toward a common goal. Those same incidents can unwind a relationship to a lessened degree of rapport, self-revelation, mutual dependencies, and personality needs met, if, for example, the argument is destructive rather than constructive (Borland, 1975: 291–92).

Albas and Albas (1987) note that both the wheel theory and the clockspring theory ignore the variations in intensity among the stages of a relationship. People may love each other, but the intensity of their feelings may be high on one dimension and low on another. For example, where a couple stays together for the sake of their children, the intensity of personality need fulfillment might increase while the intensity of the couple's rapport might decrease significantly.

Sternberg's Triangular Theory of Love

Instead of focusing on stages of love, psychologist Robert Sternberg and his associates (1986, 1988) have posited that there are three important components of love—intimacy, passion, and commitment. *Intimacy* encompasses feelings of closeness, connectedness, and bonding. *Passion* leads to romance, physical attraction, and sexual consummation. *Decision/commitment* has a short- and a long-term dimension: in the short term, partners make a decision to love each other; in the long term, they make a commitment to maintain that love for one another.

According to Sternberg, love can vary in its mix of intimacy, passion, and commitment. Relationships thus range from nonlove, in which all three components are absent, to consummate

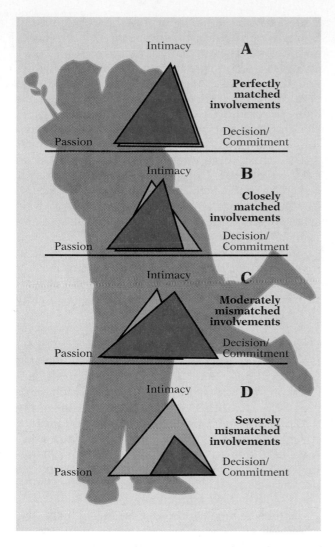

Figure 5.2 Sternberg's Triangular Theory of Love. *This theory of love allows us to see how people can be very close on some dimensions but very far apart on others* (Adapted from Sternberg, 1988).

love, in which all the components are present. Even when all components are present, they may vary in intensity and over time for each partner. In his triangular theory of love, Sternberg presents these three components as forming a triangle (see Figure 5.2). In general, the greater the mismatching, the greater the dissatisfaction in a relationship. Let's use Jack and Jill to illustrate this model. If Jack and Jill are "perfectly matched" (Figure 5.2A), they will be equally passionate, intimate, and committed, and their love will be "perfect." Even if the degree to which they want intimacy and commitment varies a little, they may still be

closely matched (Figure 5.2B). However, if both are about equally passionate, but Jack wants more intimacy than Jill does, and Jill is unwilling to make the long-term commitment that Jack wants, this couple will be "moderately mismatched" (Figure 5.2C). And if they want to marry each other (make a commitment), but Jill is neither as intimate nor as passionate as Jack, they will be severely mismatched (Figure 5.2D).

Like the other perspectives we've discussed, the triangular theory of love has limitations. For example, "perfectly matched" love can be found only in Disney movies. Also, Sternberg calls a relationship that is committed but neither intimate nor passionate (see Figure 5.2D) "empty." How do you think people who care for severely ill spouses or partners over many years would respond to this description?

Lee's Styles of Loving

One of the most widely cited and studied approaches to love was developed by the Canadian sociologist John A. Lee (1973, 1974). Although not a full-fledged theory, Lee's approach was built on his collection of more than 4,000 statements about love from hundreds of works of fiction and nonfiction, ranging from the literature of ancient Greece and the Bible through the work of medieval, Victorian, and modern writers. Administering a 30-item questionnaire based on this research to people in Great Britain and Canada, Lee derived from their responses six basic styles of loving: eros, mania, ludus, storge, agape, and pragma (see Table 5.2), all of which both overlap and vary in intensity in real life.

Table 5.2

Lee's Six Styles of Love

	MEANING	CHIEF CHARACTERISTICS
Eros	Love of beauty	Powerful physical attraction
Mania	Obsessive love	Jealousy, possessiveness, and intense love dependency
Ludus	Playful love	Carefree quality, casualness; fun-and-game approach
Storge	Companionate love	Peaceful and affectionate love based on mutual trust and respect
Agape	Altruistic love	Self-sacrificing, kind, and patient love
Pragma	Practical love	Sensible, realistic

SOURCES: Adapted from Lee, 1973; and Lee, 1974, pp. 46–51.

Eros Eros (root of the word *erotic*) is the love of beauty. Because it is also characterized by powerful physical attraction, eros epitomizes "love at first sight." This is the kind of love often described in romance novels, where the lovers are immediately lovestruck and experience palpitating hearts, lightheadedness, and intense emotional desire.

Erotic lovers want to know everything about the loved one—what she or he dreamed about last night and what happened on the way to work today. Erotic lovers often like to wear matching T-shirts, identical bracelets, and matching colors, to order the same foods when dining out, and to be identified with each other as totally as possible (Lasswell and Lasswell, 1976).

Mania Characterized by obsessiveness, jealousy, possessiveness, and intense dependency, **mania** may also find expression in anxiety, sleeplessness, loss of appetite, and headaches. Manic lovers are consumed by thoughts of their beloved and have an insatiable need for attention and signs of affection (Lee, 1974).

Often irrational, manic lovers may even consider suicide because of real or imagined rejection. Because of their high level of anxiety, manic lovers frequently have sexual problems. Mania is probably associated with low self-esteem and a poor self-concept, and as a result, manic people are typically not attractive to those who have a strong self-concept and high self-esteem (Lasswell and Lasswell, 1976).

Ludus Ludus is carefree and casual love that is considered "fun and games." Its pleasure comes more from playing the game than from winning the prize. Physical appearance is less important to ludic lovers than self-sufficiency and a nondemanding partner (Lasswell and Lasswell, 1976). They try to control their feelings and may have several lovers at one time. They are not possessive or jealous, largely because they don't want lovers to become dependent on them (Lee, 1974). Ludic lovers have sex for fun, not emotional rapport. Indeed, in their sexual encounters they are typically self-centered and may be exploitative because they do not want commitment, which they consider "scary."

Storge Storge (pronounced "stor-gay") is a slow-burning, peaceful, and affectionate love that "just comes naturally" with the passage of time and the enjoyment of shared activities. Storge-type relationships lack the ecstatic highs and lows of despair that characterize some other styles; sex occurs late in this type of relationship, and the goals are usually marriage, home, and children. Even if they break up, storgic lovers are likely to remain good friends (Lee, 1974).

The storgic lover finds routine home activities relaxing and comfortable. Because there is mutual trust, temporary separations are not seen as a problem. Occasions like anniversaries, birthdays, and Valentine's Day are not important to storgic lovers and may be forgotten or overshadowed by other matters (Lasswell and Lasswell, 1976). Storgic love may also be called *conjugal love;* affection develops over the years, as in many lasting marriages. Passion may be replaced by spirituality, respect, and contentment in the enjoyment of each other's company (Murstein, 1974).

Agape The classical Christian type of love, **agape** (pronounced "ah-gah-pay") is altruistic, self-sacrificing, and directed toward all humankind. It is a self-giving love in which partners help each other develop their maximum potential without considering the advantages or costs to themselves (Murstein, 1974). Agape is always kind and patient, never jealous or demanding, and it does not seek reciprocity. Lee points out, however, that he has never yet interviewed an unqualified example of agape.

Intense agape can border on masochism. For example, an agapic person might wait indefinitely for a lover to be released from prison or from a mental hospital, might tolerate an alcoholic or drug-addicted spouse, or might be willing to live with a partner who engages in illegal or immoral activities (Lasswell and Lasswell, 1976).

Pragma According to Lee, **pragma** is rational and based on practical considerations, such as compatibility and perceived benefits. Indeed, it can be described as "love with a shopping list." A pragmatic person seeks compatibility in such things as background, education, religious views, and vocational and professional interests. If one love does not work out, the pragmatic person moves on, quite rationally, to search for someone else. Computer-matching services typically are based on pragmatic views (Lee, 1974).

Pragmatic lovers are realistic about their own assets, decide on their "market value," and set off to get the best possible "deal." If the assets of either partner change, a pragmatic lover may feel that his or her contract has been violated and may search for another partner. Pragmatic lovers look out for their partners, encouraging them, for example, to ask for a promotion or to finish college. They are also practical in divorce; for example, a couple might stay together until the youngest child finishes high school or until both partners find better jobs (Lasswell and Lasswell, 1976).

Researchers have developed dozens of scales to measure the constructs of love and intimate relations that Lee proposed (see Tzeng, 1993). Table 5.3 presents some items from the Love Attitudes Scale that was originally developed by the Lasswells and modified by later researchers.

Love in Long-term Relationships

It's easier to fall in love than to stay in love. Unfortunately, there is no one formula for sustaining a long-term relationship; many variables play a role in maintaining love. Consider, for example, socioeconomic status. The Beatles told us that "money can't buy you love," but researcher Tom Smith (1994) says they were wrong. Analyzing the findings of two national polls that asked people whether they were in love, Smith found an association between money and love: "The pattern suggests that having enough income to be out of poverty may alleviate financial problems enough to reduce stress and thereby facilitate feelings of love" (p. 34). So, although money may not buy love, its absence may encourage falling out of love.

And consider style of loving: There's some evidence that storgic, or companionate, love may be the most productive of long-term love relationships. Hecht et al. (1994) interviewed 144 women and men who said they were in love with each other. Those who were the happiest described their love as companionate (feeling of togetherness, of connectedness, sharing, and supporting each other) or committed. Committed lovers, ruled by the head as much as the heart, were faithful to each other and were planning their future together. For more guidelines on how to achieve a satisfying, lasting relationship, see the box "Helping Love Flourish."

All of these perspectives—biological, psycho-

Table 5.3
Some Items from the Love Attitudes Scale

If you're dating, you can use this scale to examine your own and your partner's feelings. If you've never been in love or have no partner now, answer in terms of what you think your responses might be. Keep in mind that there are no wrong answers to these statements; they're designed simply to improve your understanding. For each item, mark a "1" for "strongly agree," "2" for "moderately agree," "3" for "neutral," "4" for "moderately disagree," and "5" for "strongly disagree."

Eros

_____ 1. My partner and I were attracted to each other immediately after we first met.

_____ 2. Our lovemaking is very intense and satisfying.

_____ 3. My partner fits my standards of physical beauty/handsomeness.

Ludus

_____ 4. What my partner doesn't know about me won't hurt him/her.

_____ 5. I sometimes have to keep my partner from finding out about other partners.

_____ 6. I could get over my partner pretty easily and quickly.

Pragma

_____ 7. In choosing my partner, I believed it was best to love someone with a similar background.

_____ 8. An important factor in choosing my partner was whether or not he/she would be a good parent.

_____ 9. One consideration in choosing my partner was how he/she would reflect on my career.

Agape

_____ 10. I would rather suffer myself than let my partner suffer.

_____ 11. My partner can use whatever I own as she/he chooses.

_____ 12. I would endure all things for the sake of my partner.

Storge

_____ 13. I expect to always be friends with the people I date.

_____ 14. The best kind of love grows out of a long friendship.

_____ 15. Love is a deep friendship, not a mysterious, passionate emotion.

SOURCES: Lasswell and Lasswell, 1970, pp. 211–24; Hendrick and Hendrick, 1992; and Levesque, 1993, pp. 219–50.

logical, and sociological—try to explain the nature of love and some of the characteristics that promote or hinder the development and continuation of love. There are many other theories of love that we cannot present here, but you can explore the topic further in the Additional Readings list at the end of the chapter.

Helping Love Flourish

Although they do not guarantee everlasting love, several practitioners (Cowan and Kinder, 1987; Hendrix, 1988; Osherson, 1992) have suggested some "rules" for creating a loving environment:

Rule 1: Relationships do not just happen; we create them. Good relationships are the result of conscious effort and work.

Rule 2: One partner should be pleased, rather than threatened, by the other partner's successes or triumphs.

Rule 3: A lover is not a solution to a problem. Love may be one of life's greatest experiences, but it is not life itself.

Rule 4: Love is about acceptance— being sympathetic to another's flaws and cherishing the person's other characteristics that are special and lovable.

Rule 5: Lovers are not mind readers. Open communication is critical.

Rule 6: It is not what you say; it is what you do. Quite often, communication is used to manipulate, induce guilt, or place blame, even though it is presented as positive and loving. Communication can be, and very often is, a weapon.

Rule 7: Stable relationships are always changing. We must learn to deal with both our own changes as

individuals and the changes we see in our mates.

Rule 8: Love is poisoned by infidelity. If a loved one is deceived, it may be impossible to reestablish trust and respect.

Rule 9: Blame is irresponsible. It discourages communication, makes people feel angry, and damages self-esteem.

Rule 10: Giving is contagious. People who feel loved, accepted, and valued are more likely to treat others in a similar manner.

Rule 11: Love does not punish; it forgives. It may be difficult to forget cruel words or acts, but forgiveness is essential in continuing a healthy relationship.

Rule 12: Even though partners are very close, they must respect the other person's independence and his or her right to develop personal interests and other friendships.

THE JOYS AND PERILS OF ROMANTIC LOVE

Because romantic love permeates literature, the theater, films, and television, as well as the other arts, it is worthwhile examining this often fleeting form of love. As you will see, romantic love, a combination of Lee's manic and ludic styles, can be both exhilarating and disappointing.

Some Characteristics of Romantic Love

Tennov (cited in Hatfield, 1983: 114) described romantic love as follows:

1. Lovers find it impossible to work, to study, or to do anything but think about the beloved.

2. They long to be loved in return, but they are shy in the presence of their beloved.

3. Their moods fluctuate wildly; they are ecstatic when they hope they might be loved, despairing when they feel they're not.

4. They find it impossible to believe that they could ever love again.

5. They fantasize about how their partners will declare their love.

6. When everything seems lost, romantic lovers' feelings are even more intense than usual;

their hearts ache at the thought that they might lose the other.

7. They search for signs (a squeeze of the hand, a knee that doesn't move away, a gaze that lingers) that signify their beloved's desire.

8. They feel like walking on air when the other seems to care.

9. They care so desperately about the other that nothing else matters; they are willing to sacrifice anything for love.

10. Their love is "blind," and they idealize each other.

Thus, romantic love is idealized, emotional, passionate, and melodramatic. People from other cultures may see it as bizarre and frivolous, but Western countries take romantic love very seriously. It is considered the most legitimate reason for living together, getting married, or getting a divorce ("the spark is gone"). Romantic love thrives on two beliefs—love at first sight and fate.

Love at First Sight Romantic love was more likely in the 1800s for three reasons: life expectancy was short; living in isolated towns and homes made it difficult to meet a variety of people; and most people did not live long enough to fall in love more than once. Today, with increased life spans, geographic mobility, and high divorce rates, however, we may fall in love with many people during our lifetime. Yet love at first sight that lasts forever is a popular American image of love.

According to Douglas and Atwell (1988), it's not surprising that people fall in love at first sight. Unlike most of our everyday feelings, such love has an air of mystery; it's novel, it's unusual. In addition, love at first sight typically overtakes people who not only are very lonely and starved for physical affection but who have had little experience with love and sex. Finally, people fall in love with love itself through romantic stories in movies, television, novels, and magazines. Listen to Angelina, who steeped herself in romantic love stories starting in her early teens:

I . . . [drooled] over True Confessions. . . . The only type of love I thought there should be was an idealized romantic love. By the summer after seventh grade I had my honeymoon all figured out, right down to the pink ostrich feathers that I would do my stripper dance in to seduce my captivated and thoroughly charmed husband (Douglas and Atwell, 1988: 190).

Angelina was in love at least three times, and each time the relationship failed.

Fate Fate is often seen as an important component of romantic love. Songs tell us that "you were meant for me" and "that old black magic has me in its spell." In reality, fate has little to do with romantic love. In several studies of college students, romantic love was ignited not by fate but by such factors as similar socioeconomic background, physical attractiveness, and a need for intimacy (Shea and Adams, 1984; Benassi, 1985).

Romantic Love and Long-Term Love

Many characteristics of romantic love overlap those of long-term love (some combination of eros, ludus, storge, agape, and pragma). In a review of the literature on love and romantic love, Fehr (1993) found a common core of feelings in both types of love. As Figure 5.3 shows, there is considerably more overlap than one might expect; both value such characteristics as trust, understanding, and honesty. There are also some striking differences, however. First, romantic love is simple, whereas lasting love is more complicated. For example, it takes much less effort to plan a romantic evening than to be patient with a partner day after day, year after year. Second, romantic love is self-centered, whereas long-term love is altruistic. For example, romantic lovers are often swept away by their own fantasies and obsessions, but lasting love requires putting the other before self and making the partner feel wanted.

Cross-Cultural Comparisons

If we look at love cross-culturally, we find many variations. In societies like India, love is not necessarily a prerequisite for marriage. Even highly educated Indian men and women who date non-Indians while living in Western countries often consent to arranged marriages. Re-

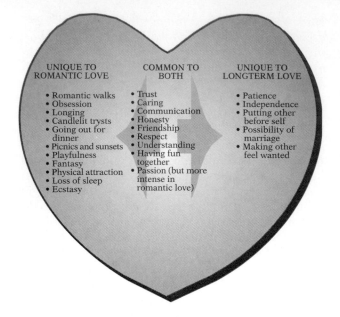

UNIQUE TO ROMANTIC LOVE
- Romantic walks
- Obsession
- Longing
- Candlelit trysts
- Going out for dinner
- Picnics and sunsets
- Playfulness
- Fantasy
- Physical attraction
- Loss of sleep
- Ecstasy

COMMON TO BOTH
- Trust
- Caring
- Communication
- Honesty
- Friendship
- Respect
- Understanding
- Having fun together
- Passion (but more intense in romantic love)

UNIQUE TO LONGTERM LOVE
- Patience
- Independence
- Putting other before self
- Possibility of marriage
- Making other feel wanted

Figure 5.3 *Romantic Love and Longterm Love: Similar But Different. Try to rate your own relationship, if you are currently involved with someone, according to the characteristics shown here. Is your relationship one of romantic love? Or longterm love? Try to rate other relationships between people you know as well* (Based on Fehr, 1993, pp. 87–120).

spect for parents' wishes, family traditions, and duty to the kin group are more important than love. According to an economics student at Delhi University:

This whole concept of love is very alien to us. We're more practical. I don't see stars, I don't hear little bells. But he's a very nice guy, I get along with him fine, and I think I'm going to enjoy spending my life with him (Bumiller, 1989: 93).

Anthropologists William Jankowiak and Edward Fischer (1992) found evidence of romantic love in 89 percent of the 166 cultures they studied and concluded that romantic love is not a product of Western culture but constitutes "a human, universal, or at the least a near-universal" phenomenon. A number of studies suggest that romance is least important in societies where kin relationships take precedence over conjugal relationships. In this research, which largely studied college students, students in Burma and India were found to be the least romantic. In another traditional society, college students in one Mexican university said that storgic, agapic, and pragmatic

love were more desirable than manic, erotic, and ludic love styles (Leon et al., 1994).

American and German students were more likely to say that romance is very important in love than were Japanese students, although the latter were more likely to believe that true love lasts forever. Japanese students, however, were also more likely to state that marriage may result in disillusionment (Simmons et al., 1986). Despite images of French men as being flirtatious and romantic, Murstein and his associates (1991) found that American college students were more likely to endorse manic, emotional love while French students emphasized agapic, or compassionate and self-sacrificing love. The researchers suggested that the predominance of Catholics in the French sample may have accounted for their higher scores on agape.

Attitudes toward love may also vary by gender. In a study of university students and nonstudents in Sydney, Australia, Hong and Faedda (1994) found that whereas women ranked the most important romantic act as "hearing or saying I love you," men gave the highest rank to "making love." This sounds as if women want affection, and men want sex, but for another view, see the "Critical Issues" box later in the chapter. In a study of 223 Korean students at a Seoul college, Brown (1994) found that the men were more romantic than women. For example, they were more likely to believe in love at first sight and to say that common interests are not important in marriage. In contrast, most of the female students said that "love is just an emotion, but marriage is reality" (p. 188).

Unrequited Love

In unrequited love, one person's romantic feelings are not reciprocated by another person. Why does this happen? There are several reasons. First, a person may "fall upward" in love. That is, someone who is less physically attractive may fall in love with someone who's gorgeous. As you will see in Chapter 8, there is a tendency for people of similar degrees of attractiveness to date and marry. Thus, love for someone who is much more attractive may go unrequited. The rebuff is even more painful if the person being rejected senses that simple physical appearance is the reason (Baumeister and Wotman, 1992). We often hear both women and men complain that the object of their affections "never took the time to get to know me," implying that such things as personality, intelligence, and common interests should be more important than looks.

Unrequited love may also be the outcome when only one of two people who have been seeing each other wants to move from casual dating to a serious romance. Realizing that the person one is dating, and perhaps having sexual relations with, is in it "just for the fun of it" and does not want to escalate the relationship to something more serious or exclusive can be very distressing.

People who are rejected after entering into a sexual relationship are especially likely to feel that they were led on and then dumped. Although the rejected tend to see rejecters as aloof, "teases," or even sadistic heartbreakers, in fact, they usually are "ordinary, well-meaning people who find themselves caught up in another person's emotional whirlwind and who themselves often suffer acutely as a result" (Baumeister and Wotman, 1992: 203). Rejecters often agonize over how to disengage themselves from their admirers without hurting them.

The End of Romance

Almost all of the research on romantic love shows that it is short-lived because love changes over time, and flaws that seemed "cute" during a whirlwind courtship may become unbearable a year after marriage. For example, his dumpy furniture may have seemed quaint until she realized that he refused to spend any money on home furnishings. And values, especially religious values, become increasingly important after the birth of the first child (Trotter, 1986: 54). Although she at first seemed quite willing to raise children in both the Catholic and Jewish faiths, when their son Kevin was born, her Judaism, which she had not practiced for ten years, became more important to her than his Catholicism.

THE FUNCTIONS OF LOVE

Love fulfills many purposes. Some are functional because they help to maintain societies; others are dysfunctional because they threaten a species' existence and its peaceful relations on an individual, group, or societal level. Some see a lack of love as pathological because it produces detached individuals who are not governed by societal rules about morality, justice, and order (Fine, 1985). This section discusses demographic variables and such positive functions of love as survival, improving longevity and the quality of life, control, inspiration, fun, and lust. Dysfunctional aspects of love are examined in the last section of the chapter.

Demographic Factors

Something as unromantic as demography plays a role in love. In one study, students who perceived that members of the opposite sex were relatively scarce expressed more desire for commitment than did students who thought that members of the opposite sex were plentiful. The researchers concluded: "In the face of scant opportunities for new relationships, people seem to learn to love the one they are with: They invest more in their romantic relationship, like it more, and are more committed to it" (Jemmott and Ashley, 1989: 1209).

Such demographic variables as age, income, and occupation also play an important role in romantic relationships. For example, in one study, 40 percent of the men but only 9 percent of the women over age 54 were involved in romantic relationships. Why? There is a shortage of older males, the researchers pointed out, and a superabundance of young females. In the same study, almost 90 percent of the African American women aged 55 and older said that they were not married or romantically involved. This is an age group in which relationships may simply be more costly for women than they are for men. An elderly man may expect housekeeping from his partner as well as caretaking if he becomes ill. An elderly woman, especially if she is financially secure, may be unwilling to be burdened with more housework because she is looking forward to a more relaxed lifestyle (Tucker and Taylor, 1989).

Survival

As we discussed earlier, some scholars argue that love is necessary to ensure human survival. In a tongue-in-cheek article, one psychologist suggested that romantic love is a "nuisance," "an evolutionary device," and "a nasty trick played upon us by nature to keep our species going," especially during the childbearing years (Chance,

1988: 23). In fact, love does keep our species going. Because children can be conceived outside of love and marriage, there is no guarantee that those engaging in sexual intercourse will feel an obligation to care for their offspring. Unlike sex, love implies a commitment. Thus, by promoting interest in caring for helpless infants, love ensures the survival of the species.

Longevity

Love prolongs life. As discussed earlier, studies have shown that infants who do not receive love may grow up seriously handicapped emotionally. Perhaps the most dramatic example of love's impact is suicide. People who commit suicide often feel socially isolated, unloved, or unworthy of love (Hendin, 1982; Osgood, 1985). Suicide is far more prevalent among the divorced than it is among married people. Divorced people also tend to suffer more serious illnesses and more chronic disabling conditions than do married couples (Kiecolt-Glaser et al., 1987). Although these studies do not suggest a causal relationship between marriage and health, it appears that those who are in loving relationships may experience fewer health problems.

Quality of Life

Love affects the quality of our lives as well as how long we live. At least half of all teenage runaways are escaping violence, abuse, or incest. Battered wives and rape victims become suspicious, fearful, and bitter, sometimes for the rest of their lives. In contrast, terminally ill patients, AIDS victims, and paraplegics report that they can accept death or cope with their handicaps when they are surrounded by supportive, caring, and loving family members and friends.

Control

Adolescents and young adults in Western society usually have little control over their lives. Unlike earlier generations, in which children started working outside the home early in life (see Chapter 3), today's adolescents who go to college are usually not saddled with adult responsibilities, such as taxes, mortgages, and full-time jobs, until their early 20s. Because of this prolonged adolescence, adults, especially parents, try to teach their children responsibility by imposing a variety of restrictions through setting curfews,

screening friends, and requiring high academic achievement and work on weekends. Adolescents may rebel. They may take drugs, be truant, hang out with the "wrong crowd," become sexually promiscuous, or violate curfews. Mate selection, justified by love, is one of the few areas in which adolescents and young adults can exert some control over their lives (Beigel, 1951).

Inspiration

Some of the all-time most popular love stories—*Romeo and Juliet*, *West Side Story*, *Camelot*, and *Love Story*, for example—are tragedies. Nevertheless, "they inspire a soaring hope within us that we will find the same magic power of love that has transformed the lives of our tragic heroes and heroines" (Douglas and Atwell, 1988: 274).

The same messages are reflected in popular music. In the blues, someone has "done me wrong." In country music, Lucille leaves her hardworking husband and kids, and Ruby "takes her love to town." In rock and roll, lovers are stood up, ignored, used, manipulated, or left. In religious music, Jesus consoles those who have been abandoned, exploited, or have led sinful lives. In all of these music genres, the one underlying theme is the idea that "real" love will help us overcome our problems. Thus, love inspires us not to give up because life can get better.

Fun

Without love, life is "a burden and a bore" (Safilios-Rothschild, 1977: 9). Even though love can be extremely painful, it can also be fun. Regardless of age, love can be pleasurable and exciting. It is both comforting and fun to plan to see a loved one, to travel together, to get ready for a date, to write and receive letters, cards, and presents, to talk about personal activities, to attend your child's first piano recital, to have someone care for you when you are sick or grumpy, and to know that someone will pick you up at the airport in the middle of the night. Love is reassuring and comfortable, a diversion from mundane, day-to-day activities.

We sometimes feel pressured to fall in love because of our friends' or our family's expectations that it's "fun" or "the right thing to do." For example, in a study of student life at a residential college, Holland and Eisenhart (1990: 120) found that there was constant pressure on women by their peers to become involved with romance:

"They were continually being invited to or asked to help organize parties, mixers, and dances . . . to make arrangements to visit bars, attend sports events, join clubs, take certain courses, go away for the weekend, and even go to the library in order to meet men." Some resisted such pressure, but most did not.

Lust

One psychologist sees love as a "cultural invention" to justify lust. According to this view, although people crave sex, they feel guilty, so they use love as an excuse for sex (Chance, 1988). Love is thus a license for unconventional and irresponsible behavior that is generally considered socially unacceptable. Adolescents rationalize having sex because "we are in love." In recent years, some movie stars have referred to their illegitimate births as "love children."

GENDER AND SEXUAL ORIENTATION DIFFERENCES

For most people, men and women alike, caring, trust, respect, and honesty are central to love. There are some differences, however, in the ways men and women conceive the nature of love and in the ways they express it. In addition, although both heterosexuals and homosexuals share many of the same feelings and behaviors, there are also some differences in their experiences of love.

Differences in Expressing Love

When they fall in love, women and men are equally passionate. Over the long run, however, women appear to be more pragmatic and to spend more effort maintaining a relationship. Also, men and women tend to view sexual relations differently.

Are Men or Women More Romantic? Contrary to popular perceptions, men seem to fall in love faster and are more romantic than women. In one of the earliest studies in this area, Hobart (1958) administered a romanticism scale to college students and found that, in general, men scored as more romantic than women. Agreement with such statements as "To be truly in love is to be in love forever" and "A person should marry whomever he loves regardless of social position" was scored as "romantic." Being

"nonromantic" meant agreeing with such statements as "Lovers ought to expect a certain amount of disillusionment after marriage" and "Most of us could sincerely love any one of several people equally well." As some writers have pointed out, however, a researcher's definition of "romantic" is crucial. In another well-known study, the researchers found that although men tended to fall in love more quickly, women were more intense, more euphoric, and more likely to idealize the love object (Kanin et al., 1970).

Nevertheless, replications of Hobart's research have yielded very similar results. Knox and Sporakowski (1968) concluded that women were more practical because they had more at stake in the relationship: (1) women were more pressured by parents and relatives to marry "wisely"; (2) women were more dependent on men for economic security; and (3) women were more family oriented and thus concerned about having a successful marriage. In their research on loving styles, Hendrick and Hendrick (1992) found that, in general, men are more ludic, or game playing, whereas women tend to be more storgic and pragmatic. One of women's biggest complaints today is that the men who profess to love them are reluctant to marry. Women often belittle men for being "commitment dodgers," "commitment phobics," "paranoid about commitment," and "afraid of the M word." Given the tremendous costs of unprotected sex, pregnancy, and childbirth, it is not surprising that many women are angry when their lovers refuse to marry (Buss, 1994).

In a review of the literature on love and romance, Hatfield (1983) concluded that women love more than they are loved in return and are willing to sacrifice more for love than men are. Women also seem to work harder on love than men do, spending more time on trying to understand, express, and manage their feelings. On the other hand, women are usually the ones who decide when to break off a relationship. And after the breakup, men are more likely than women to be sad, lonely, depressed, and unwilling to accept the situation; they are also more violent and possessive than women are when a relationship ends (Lester, 1985; Herman, 1989).

Women often feel they have more to lose if they are not rational and practical. Because they themselves are often discriminated against in the workplace, women are more concerned about a potential mate's social, occupational, and economic status; a woman's own economic status frequently still depends on the man's (see also

Chapter 14). In contrast, because they are rarely dependent on a woman's economic status, men are generally freer to be more spontaneous and romantic. They often complain about the women they date: "The first thing she wants to know is where I work, what I do, what kind of car I drive, and how much money I make," implying that women are only concerned about what they can get out of a relationship.

Are Women or Men More Intimate? We often hear that men are less intimate than women. There are many possible definitions of intimacy, including the intensity of a relationship and sexual expression (Brehm, 1992). When women complain about a lack of intimacy, they usually mean that the man doesn't express his thoughts or feelings. Many men believe that such expectations are unfair because they show their intimacy through sex.

A few years ago advice columnist Ann Landers sparked a nationwide controversy when she reported that many women prefer being touched, hugged, cuddled, and kissed over having sexual intercourse. In general, men and women in loving relationships may see intimacy differently and engage in sexual activity for different reasons. A wife complains: "I think being close means sharing. He thinks being close means screwing! When he's anxious or insecure, he wants sex; it reassures him." The husband, however, feels that his wife should accept sex as a substitute for intimacy:

I think women have this need to analyze everything, talk it through down to every little detail, no matter how private it might be. Just because I come home and don't immediately start spilling my guts about everything that happened at work doesn't mean I don't love her. She gets all over me for not being "feeling," whatever that means. Women need all this feeling, emotion stuff from relationships. Men don't. It just means that men are different from women and need different things (McGill, 1985: 190–91).

Gifts are a powerful means of communication because they are concrete expressions of love, affection, or intimacy (Cheal, 1987). Men sometimes give gifts because they find it easier than talking, but many wives complain that presents are not adequate substitutes for the husband's or father's active participation in the family. Women sometimes also accuse men of limiting gift giving to the holidays and birthdays

and avoiding showing affection the rest of the year (McGill, 1985). For another view of male expressions of intimacy in families, see the box "Do I Love You? I Changed Your Oil, Didn't I?"

Gender-Role Orientation

Showing love also depends on attitudes about gender roles. Couples who have traditional, breadwinner/homemaker attitudes about the roles of men and women emphasize dependency and compatibility, whereas those couples with less traditional gender-role orientations tend to emphasize communication and intimacy (Critelli et al., 1988). Both traditional and less traditional couples feel that passion changes to companionate love if each partner perceives equity in the relationship—a balance between giving and getting (Hatfield and Walster, 1981).

Same-Sex Love

During the nineteenth century, friendships were almost exclusively same sex because women's and men's social spheres were rigidly defined

Both homosexual love and heterosexual love include passion, intimacy, togetherness, as well as mutual respect and admiration.

"Do I Love You? I Changed Your Oil, Didn't I?"

We often hear that men are less loving than women because they equate love with sex and never talk about their feelings. Several social scientists disagree. According to Francesca Cancian (1990: 171), the fault lies not in our men but in our definitions of loving, which ignore masculine styles of showing affection:

We identify love with emotional expression and talking about feelings, aspects of love that women prefer and in which women tend to be more skilled than men. At the same time we often ignore the instrumental and physical aspects of love that men prefer, such as providing help, sharing activities, and sex.

Cancian calls excluding men's ways of showing affection as the "feminization of love." Because of this bias, men rarely get credit for the kinds of loving actions that are more typical of them. According to Carol Tavris (1992: 255):

What about all the men . . . who reliably support their families, who put the wishes of other family members ahead of their own preferences, or who act in a moral and considerate way when conflicts arise? Such individuals are surely being mature and loving, even if they are not articulate or do not value "communication."

Thus, a man who is a good provider or who changes the oil in his wife's car or fixes his child's bike is showing just as much love as the wife who tells her husband she loves him and shares her innermost thoughts and feelings with him. Actions may not "speak louder than words," but perhaps they can have an equal impact.

There are several negative consequences of the "feminization of love." First, it assumes that women need love more than men and are more dependent on men for emotional satisfaction. Second, emphasizing only the expressive side of love ignores or diminishes the importance of women's *instrumental* activities, such as working inside and outside the home. Finally, the feminization of love intensifies the conflicts over intimacy between women and men. As the woman demands more verbal contact, the man feels increased pressure and withdraws. The woman may then intensify her efforts to get closer. This leads to a vicious cycle where neither partner gets what she or he wants. As the definition of love becomes more feminized, men and women move farther apart rather than closer together (Tucker, 1992). One way to break this vicious cycle is to give both men and women credit for the things they *do* to show their love for each other and for their families.

(Swain, 1992). Although most of these friendships were not sexual, some were. They were referred to as "romantic friendships" until the twentieth century, when medical circles began to use such terms as "homosexual" or "lesbian." Today, many gay men openly admit they are lovers and talk about loving each other (in contrast to having loveless one-night stands). Lesbians are more likely to describe a variety of relationships ranging from romantic but asexual relationships to passionate, sexual love (see, for example, Rothblum and Brehony, 1993).

Heterosexual and same-sex love are very similar. Regardless of sexual orientation, most partners want to be emotionally close, expect faithfulness, and often plan to grow old together. Breakups are as painful for most same-sex partners as they are for most heterosexual couples. A few years ago, for example, one of my straight A students was devastated when his partner left. The student's grades suddenly plummeted be-cause he was unable to concentrate on his courses; he became depressed and wanted to drop out of college. With some counseling and enormous fortitude, he finished his senior year and graduated with honors.

One of the biggest differences between heterosexual and same-sex love is that lesbians and gay men cannot show their affection in public. As you will see in Chapters 6 and 7, there are more differences between men and women in expressing sexual love than there are differences between heterosexual and same-sex love.

BARRIERS TO EXPERIENCING LOVE

Any number of obstacles can bar our way to love. Some barriers are *macro-level*—for example, the impersonality of mass society, our culture's double standard for men and women, its emphasis on individualism, its influence on fam-

ily expectations, and its negative view of homosexual love, often called *homophobia*. Other barriers are *micro-level*—for example, certain kinds of personality characteristics and family experiences. An understanding of some of these obstacles can give us more choices and more control, and it can also help us accept some constraints that we can't change.

Mass Society

Mass society's bureaucratic systems, along with burgeoning technologies like answering machines, fax machines, electronic mail, and telemarketing services decrease the opportunities for face-to-face interaction among people and tend to dehumanize interpersonal communication. In response, as you will see in Chapter 8, a "love industry" has mushroomed. Computerized matchmaking, personal ads, singles bars, dinner clubs, and dozens of books on how to find love promise to counteract the isolation and impersonality of our society. In major cities like New York, bookstores have begun to provide quiet areas where customers can read, drink coffee, and meet other customers, and there are even "singles laundromats" equipped with bars and restaurants.

The Double Standard

As you saw in Chapter 4, there is still a great deal of social inequality between men and women. The double standard is one of the most damaging forms of inequality because it often impedes the development of love. The fact that our society still implicitly condones men's having sex without love but condemns women who "sleep around" as "sluts," "whores," and "tramps"

makes many women angry and resentful of men. This creates a lack of mutual trust and often leads to playing intricate power games in which men often perceive women as sneaky, scheming, and gold-digging, and women often see men as sex-hungry, irresponsible, and domineering.

"Me-First" Individualism

Our cultural values encourage individualism and competition rather than community and cooperation. This emphasis on the individual leads to a preoccupation with self. In the 1980s we heard statements like "Look out for Number One," "If it feels good, do it," and "I come first." We have been steeped in narcissistic messages that preach self-improvement, self-actualization, self-aggrandizement, and self-serving behavior, often at the expense of the couple or the family (Lasch, 1978). Measuring love purely in terms of feeling good leaves us unequipped to handle its hard, painful, or demanding aspects (such as supporting a partner during unemployment or caring for a loved one who has a long-term illness).

Family Expectations

Most societies exert control over love through the norms and values that are internalized in the family. Recall from Chapter 1 that one important function of the family is status placement. Because courtship, mate selection, and marriage merge kinship lines, they have the potential to change not only individuals' but families' positions in the social structure. These processes may be considered "too important to be left to children," and families (especially the upper classes) may invest considerable energy and resources to control love before it blossoms. We examine this issue in greater detail in Chapter 8.

Homophobia

In general, society not only disapproves of homosexual behavior and unions but sees homosexual couples as less in love and less satisfied with their relationships than heterosexual couples (Testa et al., 1987). Heterosexual and homosexual love, however, are very similar. Individuals confide experiences and feelings, enjoy each other's company, accept and respect each other, and provide mutual assistance (Davis, 1985). Lesbian and gay relationships are no more and no less loving than those of heterosexuals. Homophobic attitudes on the part of the general public, as well as discrimination in the workplace and even physical assaults, have made it difficult for many gays and lesbians to establish secure and loving relationships and have discouraged many homosexual couples from "coming out of the closet," or admitting their homosexuality in public.

Individual Personality Characteristics

Sometimes personality traits or family history get in the way of finding love. For example, such childhood and adolescent experiences as being treated like outcasts, having nonsupportive relationships with peers, or being victimized by bullies have led some men literally to fear love—to fear participation in courtship, marriage, and family roles (Gilmartin, 1987). Many children, especially girls, whose parents have undergone hostile divorces report that they are cynical about love or are afraid to fall in love (Wallerstein and Blakeslee, 1989).

As you saw earlier, some psychiatrists and psychologists also believe that attachment problems during childhood are replayed in adulthood. Some of these problems include a fear of commitment and doubts about one's ability to inspire love in another. For example, a child who has grown up in a cold and unloving family may be suspicious of potential partners in adulthood who are warm and loving ("I wonder what she's after"). Or a child who was molested by a family member or relative may be distrustful of future relationships (see Chapter 15).

WHEN LOVE GOES WRONG

The topic of a recent talk show was something like "Do You Use Jealousy to Keep Your Lover?" The panelists were women in their 20s and 30s who regaled the audience with stories of how they used jealousy to jolt their inattentive husbands or to get even with a boyfriend's "wandering eye." The implication was that making someone jealous or using other forms of manipulation not only is acceptable behavior but may be a particularly desirable way to spark or maintain a relationship. Such tactics often backfire, however. They are usually unhealthy and even hazardous to emotional and physical well-being.

Jealousy: Trying to Control Love

Typically, people experience the feeling of *jealousy* when they believe a love relationship is being threatened, usually by a rival, for the affections of their lover. The jealous person is usually suspicious of his or her partner, often obsessive, and frequently angry and resentful. Some people are also jealous of their partner's spending time with family members, relatives, or hobbies (Brehm, 1992). Although some researchers (e.g., Salovey and Rodin, 1989) have suggested that jealousy has a positive function in helping people identify those relationships that are truly important to them, writer Ayala Pines observes, "Jealousy is like a hot pepper. Use it mildly, and you add spice to the relationship. Use too much of it and it can burn" (quoted in Maggio, 1992: 175).

Love flourishes when it is based on trust and respect for the other's individuality. According to a number of researchers, jealousy is usually an unhealthy manifestation of insecurity, low self-esteem, and possessiveness (see Greenberg and Pyszczynski, 1985; De Moja, 1986; Douglas and Atwell, 1988). Both males and females who report high jealousy tend to depend heavily on their partners for self-esteem, consider themselves inadequate as mates, and feel that they are more deeply involved in their relationship than their partners are. In addition, often people who are jealous either have been or are still unfaithful (White and Mullen, 1989). All these findings strongly suggest that jealousy is a serious threat to love.

Some jealous lovers become obsessed. They constantly daydream, make numerous phone calls, send flowers, cards, gifts, and love letters, or continuously check up on their partner's whereabouts. Males tend to act out violently by hurting or killing their lovers; women are more likely to damage or destroy property, like scratching a lover's car or spraying it with paint (Tuller, 1994).

Jealousy and Stalking   In recent years, *stalking* by a jealous lover has been recognized as a serious problem. California passed the first anti-stalking law in 1990. Many people believe the legislation was the result of the shooting death of television actress Rebecca Schaeffer. Schaeffer had received numerous love letters and death threats from a male fan, but she ignored both. The fan eventually tracked down her address and shot her in front of her home. By the mid-1990s, all 50 states had adopted anti-stalking laws.

Unfortunately, these laws rarely discourage suitors (almost always men) from threatening, harassing, or even killing those who reject them. Although those who stalk celebrities—like the man who scaled the 8-foot wall around pop star Madonna's property—make the headlines, as many as 80 percent of stalking cases involve ordinary people who either were once married to each other or had dated one another (Ingrassia et al., 1993).

A more recent variation is stalking on electronic mail, known as e-mail. As this book goes to press, only Michigan has expanded its stalking legislation into the electronic realm. The laws will be tested when a man goes to trial for pursuing a woman by electronic mail and on her answering machine after she told him to stop bothering her. The accused stalker said he was looking forward to the trial because "it would give him a chance to see the woman face to face and to explain once again that his attraction to her was romantic, not sinister" (Lewis, 1994: B18).

Is Jealousy Universal?   Although it is apparently widespread, jealousy is not universal. Surveying two centuries of anthropological reports, Hupka (cited in Adams, 1980: 105) was able to characterize two types of cultures, one in which jealousy was uncommon—for example, the Todas of southern India—and one in which jealousy was commonplace—for example, the Apache Indians of North America.

How were these societies different? Toda culture, Hupka found, did not encourage possessiveness of either material objects or people. It placed few restrictions on sexual gratification, and it did not make marriage a condition for women's social recognition. In contrast, Apache society prized virginity, paternity, and fidelity. While an Apache

man was away from home, he had a close relative keep secret watch over his wife and report on her behavior when he returned.

Based on the variations he found across cultures, Hupka concluded that jealousy is not innate but learned. In addition, jealousy is common in many modern-day societies. Surveying students in Hungary, Ireland, Mexico, the Netherlands, the former Yugoslavia and Soviet Union, and the United States, he discovered clear evidence of jealousy in all seven nations (Hupka et al., 1985).

Other Types of Controlling Behavior

Jealousy is not the only type of unhealthy, controlling behavior in love relationships. Threatening the withdrawal of love or inducing feelings of guilt can be deeply distressing to a partner; inflicting severe emotional and physical abuse can be devastating.

"If You Loved Me . . . "   One of the most common appeals for sex (especially by men) is based on the threat of the loss of a love relationship: "If you really loved me, you'd show it." People use the loss or withdrawal of love to manipulate other behavior as well. Faculty tell many stories about students who choose majors they hate because their parents insist that they become a doctor, a lawyer, an accountant, and so on. Many women drop out of college because their husbands or boyfriends accuse them of placing more importance on earning their degrees than on maintaining their homes, preparing dinner, and being free on weekends to spend time with them.

Essentially, controlling people want power over others. They use "love" to manipulate and exploit those who care about them. With pressure and ultimatums, they force partners to sacrifice their own interests. Whether such control is well intentioned or malicious, it is designed to ensure the controller's happiness, not the happiness of the person being manipulated.

Controllers are not all alike: "A wealthy executive may use money and influence, while an attractive person may use physical allure and sex" to manipulate another (Jones and Schecter, 1992: 11). Moreover, as the box "If This Is Love, Why Do I Feel So Bad?" shows, controllers use a variety of strategies in dominating a relationship. And they may switch strategies from time to time to keep the controlled person off balance or because the con-

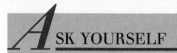
If This Is Love, Why Do I Feel So Bad?

If you feel bad, what you're experiencing may be control, not love (see Clarke, 1990). Controllers use whatever tactics are necessary to maintain power over another person: some of these are nagging, cajoling, coaxing, flattery, charm, threats, self-pity, blame, insults, and humiliation. In the worst cases, controllers may physically injure and even murder people who refuse to be controlled. As you read this brief list (based on Jones and Schecter, 1992: 16–22), check any items that seem familiar to you. Individually, the items may seem unimportant, but if you check off more than two or three, you may be dealing with a serious controller.

_____ My partner calls me names: dummy, jackass, whore, creep, bitch, moron.

_____ My partner always criticizes me and makes even a compliment sound like a criticism: "This is the first good dinner you've cooked in months"; "Can't you ever fix anything right?"

_____ Always right, my partner con-tinually corrects things I say or do.

_____ If I'm five minutes late, I'm scared my partner will be mad.

_____ My partner withdraws into silence, and I have to figure out what I've done wrong and apologize for it.

_____ My partner is jealous when I talk to new people.

_____ My partner often phones or unexpectedly comes by the place I work to see if I'm "okay."

_____ My partner acts very cruelly and then says I'm too sensitive and can't take a joke.

_____ When I try to express my opin-ion about something, my partner doesn't respond, walks away, or makes fun of me.

_____ I have to account for every dime I spend, but my partner keeps me in the dark about our bank accounts.

_____ My partner says that if I ever leave he or she will commit suicide and I'll be responsible.

_____ When my partner has a temper tantrum, he or she says it's my fault or the children's.

_____ My partner makes fun of my body.

_____ Whether my partner is with us or not, he or she is jealous of every minute I spend with my family or other relatives or friends.

_____ My partner grills me about what happened whenever I go out.

_____ My partner makes sexual jokes about me in front of the children and other people.

_____ My partner throws things at me, hits, shoves, or pushes me.

---

troller sometimes has momentary regrets about being manipulative.

The Guilt Trip People use guilt to justify actions that really have nothing to do with love. Guilt can be used to increase social status, to make people more like us, or to get something we want. It is not uncommon for parents, in particular, to invoke the love/guilt complex to influence children's behavior: "If you loved me, you'd go to college. I've made a lot of sacrifices to save up for your education"; or "If you marry that Catholic [or Jew or Protestant], how can I face Rabbi Katz [or Mr. Beirne or Father Mulcahey] again!" Objectively, the parents might be right because a college education is a good investment, and marriage outside of one's religious group often presents problems. The danger, however, is that the parents may be more concerned about their *own* needs than their children's.

The guilt trip can be used by many family members and does not end at adulthood. Older parents and relatives sometimes use guilt to manipulate middle-aged children. One of the most disabling guilt trips is the "affection myth," where children are taught that love is synonymous with caregiving. Thus, children and grandchildren may feel that, no matter what their own circumstances are, they must care for the older family members at home. As a result, younger family members sometimes endure enormous stress, when often their elderly relatives might actually get much better medical care at a skilled nursing facility (Jarrett, 1985).

Emotional and Physical Abuse   Love is sometimes used to justify severe emotional or physical neglect and abuse, but violence is *never* a manifestation of love. Unfortunately, newspapers and television talk shows often imply that battered women and children love their abusers, rarely probing—as we will in Chapter 15—the many and varied reasons why those who are abused often remain in violent and destructive relationships. Why do you suppose no one asks the victims what they mean by "love"? Do they mean the relief they feel during the intervals when they are *not* beaten? And if they have always been battered, do they really know what love is?

A partner who is sarcastic or controlling, a parent who severely spanks or verbally humiliates a child—such people are not doing what they do out of love for those who love them or for their "own good," as they often insist. They are simply expressing anger and brutality. According to Gelles and Cornell (1990: 20), "the most insidious aspect of family violence" is that children grow up unable to distinguish between love and violence and believe "that it is accept-

able to hit the people you love." The film *What's Love Got to Do with It?*, based on singer Tina Turner's biography, dramatically portrayed the effects on Turner of enduring violence for years because she believed that doing so proved her love and commitment to her husband, Ike.

CONCLUSION

Love can be a many-splendored thing. When it is healthy, love *changes* how we feel about ourselves and others. It can inspire us and motivate us to care for friends, lovers, and family members. Love also creates *choices* in finding happiness during dating, marriage, and old age. There are *constraints*, however, because we sometimes confuse love with jealousy or controlling behavior.

Love is essential to human growth and development, but it is often shrouded in myths and surrounded by formidable barriers. For those who are willing to learn and to work at it, love is attainable and can be long-lasting. Do love and sex go together? Not always. We examine this and other matters related to sexuality in the next two chapters.

Taking Action

Help Others, Help Yourself

Once you start doing things for others, you'll find it easier to do things for yourself, which makes doing things for other people even more pleasurable, and the cycle continues. Try it!

• **Many people in your community will thrive on a little affection** from you a few hours a week: AIDS victims and babies at hospitals, the elderly in nursing homes, and children of single parents in Big Brother and Big Sister programs. Also, many older people can take care of themselves at home but can't perform such tasks as shopping, mowing the lawn, and paying bills. Thus, many would be grateful for help from volunteers organized by a campus fraternity or sorority or other community group.

• Whether you are dating, cohabiting, or mar-

ried, be smart about **your present and future love relationships.** This chapter has two "Ask Yourself" boxes and lists several self-help books in the Additional Readings section. Use these materials to think about whether your relationships are healthy or unhealthy. Trite though it may sound, there are many fish in the ocean. Keep fishing until you catch the one that's healthy, and dump the ones that are sick.

• **If you are being stalked, don't delay action** for a moment. Contact your local police department or state district attorney's office immediately to find out what you can do. And for the benefit of others, talk with instructors (especially in social science courses) about inviting speakers who can address this issue in class or during a college-wide lecture series. Most faculty would welcome your help in setting up such a program.

SUMMARY

1. Love is critical for human survival. It nourishes us physically, emotionally, and socially.

2. Loving oneself is a prerequisite for loving others.

3. Love is an elusive and complex phenomenon. Because it varies in degree and intensity among people and across social contexts, love is difficult to define. Minimally necessary for a loving relationship are the willingness to please and accommodate the other, acceptance of the other's shortcomings, and as much concern about the other's well-being as about one's own.

4. Attachment theory holds that warm, secure, loving relationships in infancy are essential to emotional health and to the formation of loving relationships in adulthood.

5. There are many approaches to understanding love and loving. Fromm differentiated among immature and mature love, maternal and paternal love, love for all humankind, and erotic love. Maslow contrasted selfish (deficiency) and unselfish (being) love. Reiss described four stages of love: rapport, self-revelation, mutual dependency, and personality need fulfillment. Borland suggested that love winds and unwinds as tensions build and are resolved. Sternberg focused on the interrelationships among passion, intimacy, and decision/commitment. And Lee described six styles of loving in relationships.

6. In our society, romantic love is generally the basis for cohabitation, marriage, and divorce. Although romantic love can be exhilarating, it is often short-lived and can be very disappointing.

7. In contrast to popular beliefs, men are typically more romantic than women and suffer more when a relationship ends. Women are more prone to express their love verbally and to work at a relationship, but they are also more pragmatic about moving on when love goes awry.

8. Love serves many functions, and people fall in love for a variety of reasons. Simple availability of partners is one determining factor; others include age, occupation, income, a wish to have children, survival, quality of life, independence and control, inspiration, and just plain fun.

9. There are many barriers to love. Macro-level barriers include the depersonalization of mass society, the double standard for men and women, our society's emphasis on individual achievement and advancement, its negative view of homosexual love, and family expectations and pressures. Micro-level obstacles include personality characteristics and childhood experiences.

10. Several kinds of negative and controlling behavior can kill love. Contrary to popular thought, jealousy is not a healthy sign of love but is usually destructive and sometimes even dangerous. Other harmful forms of love include threatening loved ones with the withdrawal of love, using guilt trips, and hurting them physically and emotionally.

KEY TERMS

ADDITIONAL READING

There are hundreds of books about love on the market. The following list includes classic writings (C), scholarly works (S), and popular self-help books (P).

LAURIE ABRAHAM, LAURA GREEN, MAGDA KRANCE, JANICE ROSENBERG, JANICE SOMERVILLE, and CARROLL STONER, eds., *Reinventing Love: Six Women Talk about Lust, Sex, and Romance* (New York: Plume, 1993).

Personal experiences of love, including first love, the old boyfriend, bad sex, romance and being love struck, letting go, and relationship complications. (P)

DIANE ACKERMAN, *A Natural History of Love* (New York: Random House, 1994). A history of love in ancient Egypt, Greece, and Rome, during the Middle Ages and today. There is also a chapter on the physiological chemistry of love. (S)

JOHN F. CROSBY, *Illusion and Disillusion: The Self in Love and Marriage*, 5th ed. (Belmont, CA: Wadsworth, 1991). Scholarly research and counseling experience are combined in an analysis of the processes and problems in love. (S)

LILLIAN FADERMAN, *Odd Girls and Twilight Lovers: A History of Lesbian Life in Twentieth-Century America* (New York: Columbia University Press, 1991). An examination of how the definitions of "intimate friendship" have changed. (S)

HELEN FISHER, *Anatomy of Love: The Natural History of Monogamy, Adultery, and Divorce* (New York: Norton, 1992). Examination of the evolutionary and biological development of love, intimacy, and courting. (S)

ERICH FROMM, *The Art of Loving* (New York: Harper & Row, 1956). The varieties of spiritual, familial, and interpersonal love. (C)

SUSAN S. HENDRICK and CLYDE HENDRICK, *Romantic Love* (Newbury Park, CA: Sage, 1992). Overview of history and theories of love and some contemporary research findings, including the authors'. (S)

STEPHEN KERN, *The Culture of Love: Victorians to Moderns* (Cambridge, MA: Harvard University Press, 1992). Examination of love in novels and works of art. (S)

ASHLEY MONTAGU, ed., *The Meaning of Love* (New York: Julian Press, 1953). Writers from several disciplines and backgrounds examine the many meanings of love. (C)

SAMUEL OSHERSON, *Wrestling with Love: How Men Struggle with Intimacy with Women, Children, Parents and Each Other* (New York: Fawcett Columbine, 1992). Discusses the differences in how men and women perceive love. (P)

CAROL TAVRIS, *The Mismeasure of Woman* (New York: Simon & Schuster, 1992). Challenges some popular ideas about love, sex, marriage, and intimacy. (S)

OLIVER C. S. TZENG, *Measurement of Love and Intimate Relations: Theories, Scales, and Applications for Love Development, Maintenance, and Dissolution* (Westport, CT: Praeger, 1993). An excellent resource on theories about and scales measuring love and intimacy. (S)

ANTHONY WALSH, *The Science of Love: Understanding Love and Its Effects on Mind and Body.* (Buffalo, NY: Prometheus Books, 1991). Examination of the physical chemistry of love. (S)

JACK YORK and BRIAN KRUEGER, *Beyond Putting the Toilet Seat Down: 423 Real Comments from Men and Women about Their Relationships* (Cincinnati, OH: Armchair Press, 1993). This lighthearted little book presents complaints and other comments gathered by the authors as they traveled to 26 cities in their "Gripemobile" van. (P)

6

Understanding Human Sexuality

Miriam Shapiro, The Garden of Eden

Data Digest

• The percentage of **men who say it is easy to talk about sex with a partner** increased from 59 percent in 1984 to 71 percent in 1994. The proportion of women feeling this way remained the same: 86 percent.

• **People have a vast sexual repertoire.** In a recent national study of women and men aged 18 to 65, sexual activities included kissing (93 percent), cunnilingus (45 percent), fellatio (32 percent), anal sex (8 percent), and bondage (5 percent).

• Men are nearly twice as likely to **masturbate** during the course of their lifetime than women are (92 percent and 58 percent, respectively).

• According to a recent national survey, on average, **people in the United States have sex about once a week,** and about 27 percent of men and 30 percent of women have sex only a few times a year or not at all. A little over 1 percent of married men reported having no sex at all, and 13 percent reported having sex a few times a year. The comparable rates for married women were 3 percent and 12 percent, respectively.

• In the same survey, 2.8 percent of men and 1.4 percent of women identified themselves as **homosexual or bisexual.** Within these groups, 3 percent of white men, 1.5 percent of African American men, and 3.7 percent of Latino men identified themselves as homosexual or bisexual. Comparable figures for women were 1.7 percent for whites, 0.6 percent for African Americans, and 1.1 percent for Latinas.

• People in the United States have **mixed feelings about homosexuality.** Although 65 percent say they want to ensure equal rights for gays, 50 percent oppose extending civil rights laws to homosexuals (in housing and employment, for example), and 70 percent oppose allowing gays and lesbians to adopt children. Some differences in opinion are associated with gender; a recent Gallup poll found that a majority of women (56 percent) favored extending civil rights protection to homosexuals, compared with just 35 percent of men.

SOURCES: Moore, 1993; Oliver and Hyde, 1993; Shapiro et al., 1993; Clements, 1994; Ingrassia and Rossi, 1994; Laumann et al., 1994.

A few years ago, basketball star Wilt Chamberlain announced that he had slept with about 20,000 women. According to Chamberlain, that "equaled out" to having sex with 1.2 women a day, every day since he was 15 years old. Sex includes more than sleeping with 1.2 people a day, however. Both physical pleasure and intimacy must accompany the sexual act to promote the social bonding of kinship and family ties in a society. This chapter examines some of the constraints and options that are part of this bonding process.

LEARNING TO BE SEXUAL

John Barrymore, the noted American actor, once said: "The thing that takes up the least amount of time and causes the most amount of trouble is sex." If sex causes a lot of trouble, it is probably because most of us know very little about it. In a recent national survey, the Kinsey Institute found that 55 percent of U.S. adults failed a sex

knowledge test (similar to the one in the box "How Much Do You Know about Sex?" Reinisch, 1990). The researchers concluded that the American public is not getting accurate information about sex. John Money, an authoritative sex researcher, said the survey showed "how much of what people do know is pure bunk and mythology" (*Baltimore Sun*, 1990d: 5A).

A little girl asked her mother the age-old question, "Where did I come from?"

"The stork brought you," her mother nervously replied.

But the little girl persisted. "Where did Daddy come from?" she asked.

"I think the doctor brought him in his little black bag," Mom said anxiously.

Undaunted, the little girl asked again, "Well, where did Grandma and Grandpa come from?"

"They were found in a cabbage patch. Now, that's enough questions," Mom scolded.

The next day, the little girl went to school and reported to her second-grade class, "For

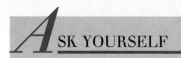

How Much Do You Know about Sex?

The items that follow are based on material presented in Chapters 6 and 7. As you study each chapter, you'll find the answers to any questions you couldn't answer. After reading each question carefully, circle just one answer.

1. What do you think is the age at which the average, or typical, American first has sexual intercourse?
   a. 11 or younger   e. 18–19
   b. 12-13   f. 20
   c. 14-15   g. 21 or older
   d. 16-17

2. Out of every ten married American men, how many would you estimate have ever had an extramarital affair–that is, have been sexually unfaithful to their wives?
   a. Fewer than one out of ten
   b. One out of ten (10%)
   c. About two out of ten (20%)
   d. About three out of ten (30%)
   e. About four out of ten (40%)
   f. About five out of ten (50%)
   g. About six out of ten (60%)
   h. About seven out of ten (70%)
   i. About eight out of ten (80%)
   j. More than eight out of ten

3. A person can get AIDS by having anal (rectal) intercourse even if neither partner is infected with the AIDS virus.
   True   False

4. Petroleum jelly, Vaseline Intensive Care Lotion, baby oil, and Nivea are good lubricants to use with a condom or diaphragm.
   True   False

5. About 10 percent of the U.S. population is exclusively homosexual.
   True   False

6. A woman or teenage girl can get pregnant during her menstrual flow (her period).
   True   False

7. A woman or teenage girl cannot get pregnant if the man withdraws his penis before he ejaculates.
   True   False

8. Unless she is having sex, a woman does not need to have regular gynecological examinations.
   True   False

9. Problems with erection are most often due to psychological or emotional problems.
   True   False

10. Menopause, or change of life, causes most women to lose interest in having sex.
    True   False

11. What do you think is the length of the average man's erect penis?
    a. 2-4 inches
    b. 5-7 inches
    c. 8-9 inches
    d. 10-11 inches
    e. 12 inches or longer

12. Most women prefer a sexual partner with a larger-than-average penis.
    True   False

Scoring the test: Each question is worth 1 point. Score each item and add up your total number of points.

CORRECT ANSWERS:

1. d	5. false	9. false
2. d	6. true	10. false
3. false	7. false	11. b
4. true	8. false	12. false

A score of 11 or 12 is an "A"; 9 or 10 a "B"; 8 a "C"; 7 a "D"; and fewer than 7 points an "F."

---

over three generations, there has not been a normal birth in my family!"

As this anecdote illustrates, our sexual behavior is not "natural" or "instinctive" but is learned in a societal context. In at least eight known societies, for example, kissing is seen as repulsive:

When the Thonga first saw Europeans kissing they laughed, expressing this sentiment: "Look at them—they eat each other's saliva and dirt." The Siriono never kiss, although they have no regulation against such behavior. The Tinguian, instead of kissing, place the lips near the partner's face and suddenly inhale (Ford and Beach, 1972: 49).

Sexual development takes place over a period of time. In the *normative* stage, children learn gender roles and related values and norms about both appropriate and inappropriate sexual expression. Parents (or parent substitutes) have considerable control over the types of influences to which the child is exposed. In the *informational* stage in early adolescence, young people learn about sexual anatomy and physiology, primarily from peers. In the *behavioral* stage in late adolescence and young adulthood, people engage in sexual activity and learn the behavioral aspects of sexuality from a partner (DeLamater and McCorquodale, 1979; Turner and Rubinson, 1993).

How Do We Learn to Be Sexual?

Ideally, we learn about sex and sexuality from parents or guardians, who are experienced, have children's interests at heart, and are presumably good sources of information. Some of the conservative movements in the late 1980s sought to censor sex-education courses, library books, and certain college courses because they were believed to dilute parental influence in sex education. In reality, this is not the case.

Parents Research shows that children actually get very little information from their parents. In a 12-year study of more than 8,000 students at Syracuse University who had college-educated parents, less than 15 percent said they received a meaningful sex education from their parents:

Usually girls were told about menstruation. The rest of the teaching could be summed up in one word: Don't. The boys were on their own, except for an occasional single prepuberty talk with Dad, who made vague analogies involving the birds and bees and ended the talk with "If worse comes to worst, be sure to use a rubber" (Gordon, 1986: 22).

Many parents are uncomfortable talking with their children even about the birds and bees, much less sex.

Peers Because, in many cases, preadolescents reach puberty or start experimenting with sex before any instruction is available at home or school, peers often become authoritative voices. Sanders and Mullis (1988) found that although nearly all the college students they studied felt that sex education should come from parents, peers were the most common sources of information about sex.

Unfortunately, because peers are typically misinformed about sex, the instruction is akin to the blind leading the blind. Peers do provide positive socialization, however. For example, they are often more open about discussing sexuality issues, provide support when a friend feels insecure about visible signs of maturing (such as the growth of breasts or face hair), or encourage friends to seek information about birth control if parents are unwilling to talk about contraception. Also, adolescents often learn from each other about developing intimate relationships within peer groups (Gecas and Seff, 1991).

Religious Influences Religion has less impact in shaping adolescents' attitudes and behavior today than it did for previous generations:

I come from a strict Italian Catholic family that does not believe in premarital sex. They believe that sex should only be shared among married couples and also only used for conception. They also feel that children should not learn about sex until they're adults. I have discovered through an aunt that traditionally in our family, you're not given "the talk" until the wedding day. This talk is usually given by the mother saying that sex is a duty that should be done for your husband. I feel that by that time I will probably be able to teach my mother a few things about sex (20-year-old college student; quotation from author's files).

Studer and Thornton (1987) found that the religious commitment of churchgoing adolescents diminished their likelihood of having sexual intercourse. Those who did engage in sex were less likely to use contraceptives because visiting a clinic would mean that they had "sinned." As a result, they were more likely to become pregnant.

Being religious does not preclude having premarital sexual intercourse. A Gallup survey of college undergraduates found that although 43 percent of students said that religion was very important in their lives, many had been treated for a sexually transmitted disease. Furthermore, 37 percent of the women who had had abortions said that religion was very important to them. The senior editor for the Christian Broadcasting Network (for whom the survey was done) said, "On the one hand, most college students do believe in God, but on the other hand, their beliefs don't seem to have much effect on their lifestyles" (Leatherman, 1989: A23). As we will see later in this chapter, religious affiliation seems less important in sexual behavior today than other variables such as marital status and education (Laumann et al., 1994; Michael et al., 1994).

Adolescents' attitudes may be a reflection of some of the recent changes in religious institutions themselves. In the mid-1980s, for instance, a survey of religious teachers and pastors representing mainline Christian and Jewish groups found that 60 percent said that fornication is morally permissible; 90 percent said that there should not be legal sanctions against extramarital sex; and 25 percent said that adultery is morally permissible (cited in Meer, 1985a). Although religious values may be changing in some groups, change is not universal. For example, during the 1991 annual assembly of Presbyterian Church-USA, the nation's fourth largest Protestant body, a task force report recommended that the denomination endorse responsible premarital or extramarital sexual relationships between adults and ordain homosexuals. Both recommendations were rejected (Stepp, 1991).

Popular Culture   Because parents rarely talk about sex and peers rarely have the facts, young people often get their information from the popular culture. Television, movies, music, magazines, romance novels, and sometimes pornographic materials have become powerful sources of information—or misinformation—about sex.

MOVIES   During the 1950s and 1960s, most films presented teenagers as nice kids who spent most of their time surfing, attending beach parties, and playing adolescent cat-and-mouse courtship games. Such portrayals were flattering compared to those in more recent films. In the typical teenage film of the 1970s and 1980s (such as *American Graffiti, Tuff Turf, Sixteen Candles, Heavenly Bodies, Mischief, Revenge of the Nerds,* and the *Porky's* films), teenage viewers were taught that crude and vulgar behavior is hilarious, that sex is the only thing that is important in life, and that violent and manipulative sex is fun.

In the late 1980s, the Motion Picture Association of America realized that most filmgoers were not adolescents and that including graphic sex scenes would make more money. There was an explosion of films portraying oral sex, such as *The Big Easy, Fatal Attraction, An Officer and a Gentleman,* and *Bull Durham*. Thus, "the last decade's inescapable vision of kids groping toward their first fumbling encounter is finally giving way to images of consenting adults on the screen" (Dowell, 1988). Because rating systems are not strictly enforced (few moviegoers are stopped from seeing R-rated films) and videos are accessible to most age groups, it is not unusual for adolescents or even younger children to get their sex education from middle-aged directors and producers who put their sexual fantasies on film.

Examining 17 films aimed at adolescents, Whatley (1994) found that almost all deemphasized the dangers of sexuality: "Pregnancy is rarely a fear; contraceptives are almost never mentioned; and disease transmission, even in the age of AIDS, is nearly absent as a concern" (p. 191). In fact, there is more focus on not getting caught giving parties when parents are absent or breaking curfews than with sexual experimentation (as in *Cooley High, Risky Business, Weird Science,* and *Bill and Ted's Bogus Journey*).

TELEVISION   Television has a significant impact on our attitudes about sex. Unfortunately, many of the images are misleading and even dangerous. In a study of sexual behavior in soap operas in 1979 and 1987, Lowry and Towles (1989) found that the 1987 soaps gave the following messages:

- Sex between unmarried and/or promiscuous people is the norm.

- There are no consequences for jumping into bed with anyone and everyone.

- Pregnancy and sexually transmitted diseases (STDs) are not a problem.

- Spur-of-the-moment sex (especially between unmarried partners) is very romantic.

Many of the most popular evening programs also offer an unattractive picture of sex. For example, in "Cheers," Sam Malone, the self-centered and not-too-bright hero, seduces intelligent, career-oriented women, Diane and Rebecca, as well as a deluge of other attractive women. In shows like "Married . . . with Children" and "Roseanne," the wives are constantly ridiculing or manipulating their husband's sexuality. "Dallas," "Falcon Crest," and "Dynasty" probably contained as many extramarital bedroom scenes as they did commercials. Even in more substantive shows, such as "L.A. Law" and "Hill Street Blues," many of the segments ended with the main characters between the sheets.

Some observers point out that many television shows promote teen sex or ridicule teen virginity. For example, in "Blossom," the 14-year-old title character debated "going to second base" with her boyfriend and engaged in some heated "action"; in "True Colors," an 18-year-old was ridiculed by his entire family because he was still a virgin; in "Roseanne," Becky became sexually active at 16; and in "Doogie Howser, M.D.," Doogie celebrated his eighteenth birthday by going to bed with his girlfriend for the first time (Medved, 1992). One reason teenage sex is encouraged may be that the top writers for television differ from their audience on moral and

In a study of two time periods—1954–64 (early rock) and 1965–75 (later rock)—Moore et al. (1979) found that the later period reflected an openness and permissiveness about sex for both males and females. More recently, popular rock groups, such as NWA (Niggers with Attitude), Geto Boys, 2 Live Crew, and especially Snoop "Doggy" Dog, describe rape and the mutilation of the genitals of their female partners and glorify sodomizing women. A monitor of rock lyrics analyzed the contents of As Nasty as They Wanna Be, a popular album that sold almost 2 million copies, and found more than 300 uses of two increasingly heard four-letter words, as well as 163 uses of the term "bitch," 87 descriptions of oral sex, and 117 explicit terms for male or female genitals (reported in Medved, 1992). Music videos rarely portray sex accompanied by love, sacrifice, and respect.

In summary, the media project particular images about sex because it is profitable. These images rarely depict reality, however, so many adolescents are receiving distorted ideas about sex and sexuality.

A FEW WORDS OF CAUTION ABOUT SEX RESEARCH

At the turn of the century, the noted German philosopher and poet Friedrich Nietzsche wrote that "when a woman becomes a scholar, there is usually something wrong with her sexual organs." In 1878, the prestigious British Medical Journal printed a series of letters in which physicians argued that the touch of a menstruating woman would spoil hams (Masters et al., 1986). As Table 6.1 shows, our approach to sexuality has changed quite a bit since the turn of the century. Not everyone will agree that the studies on sex described in this table are "scientific" or "landmarks," but they do represent some of the most influential work on sexual behavior in the twentieth century and have provided springboards for later research.

As we discussed in Chapter 2, all research has limitations and weaknesses. The study of sexuality is especially vulnerable, largely because it is extremely difficult to ensure that samples are truly representative. As you read the rest of this chapter and Chapter 7, keep in mind the following points:

First, many people simply do not want out-

Brenda and Dylan are teen-age lovers in "Beverly Hills 90210."

religious questions: among these writers, 45 percent said they had no religious affiliation, but in polls of the general population, only 4 percent give the same response (Woodward, 1992).

MUSIC Some rock music and many rock videos reinforce the idea that sex and female victimization go together. The typical rock video portrays women as seductresses or murder victims. Women are shown locked in cages, dressed in fishnet and leather, and enjoying sadistic sexual intercourse. More than half of the videos shown on the Music Television Network (MTV) feature or suggest violence, present hostile sexual relations between men and women as commonplace and acceptable, and show male heroes torturing and murdering women for fun (National Coalition on Television Violence, 1984). In a study of rock videos, Shorr (1985) concluded that, through their music, teenagers and young adults "continue to live in a society in which males perceive females to be little more than sex objects."

Table 6.1 _____

Some Landmark Studies on Sex

RESEARCHERS	MAJOR STUDIES	SCIENTIFIC CONTRIBUTIONS
Sigmund Freud (1856–1939)	*Three Essays on Sexuality* (1905), plus numerous essays and papers contained in 20 volumes of psychoanalytic thought on sexual development and other topics	Theory of psychosexual stages. Demonstrated the importance of sexuality to human existence. Although controversial, psychoanalysis (the study of unconscious motives) remains a widely used method of treatment today.
Havelock Ellis (1859–1939)	*Studies in the Psychology of Sex* (1897–1910)	Research based on hundreds of case studies. "Modern" views on issues such as masturbation. Refuted notion that only "bad" women had sexual desire. Emphasized psychological rather than physical causes of many sexual problems.
Alfred C. Kinsey (1894–1956)	*Sexual Behavior in the Human Male* (1948); *Sexual Behavior in the Human Female* (1953)*	Ground-breaking work using large-scale surveys. Presented unparalleled body of information about sexuality on such topics as oral sex, multiple orgasm in women, and homosexuality.
William Masters (1915–) and Virginia Johnson (1925–)	*Human Sexual Response* (1966)	Twelve years of laboratory research examined almost 10,000 physiological sexual responses of 312 men and 382 women. Major contributions on physical changes during masturbation and orgasm. This intial study followed by years of further research on human sexuality.
Morton Hunt (1920–)	*Sexual Behavior in the 1970s* (1974)	Study of 2,026 people in 24 surveys and in-depth interviews that examined changes between the 1940s and 1970s in such areas as premarital intercourse, sexual fantasies, and oral sex.
John Money (1921–)	A number of studies published since the mid-1950s.	Classic works on hermaphrodites, sex-role changes, and genetic/environmental contributions to sex.
Ira Reiss (1925–)	*Journey into Sexuality* (1986)	Has been working for almost three decades on such topics as premarital sex, homosexuality, and sex in the family.

Kinsey's book on male sexuality was published with Wardell Pomeroy and Clyde Martin; the co-authors on the female sexuality book were Wardell Pomeroy, Clyde Martin, and Paul Gebhard.

siders probing into such intimate matters as their sexual behavior. As a result, people who volunteer to participate in this kind of research may be quite different from the average person, and that can skew research results. As a matter of fact, that was one of the major criticisms directed at the Kinsey studies described in Table 6.1. Although the samples were large and Kinsey and his associates tried to correct the problem of nonrandom sampling by interviewing a variety of groups, the groups studied still overrepresented white, college-educated people and un- derrepresented poorly educated groups and people of color.

Second, even if it were possible to assemble a representative group of respondents, it is extremely expensive to do so, and, as you saw in the box "The Politics of Sex Research" in Chapter 2, politicians have vetoed many of the funding proposals for nationwide studies of sexual behavior. So, again, most researchers are forced to rely on captive audiences such as college students, especially those enrolled in introductory courses on marriage and the family, sociology, and psychology. Efforts to survey large audiences at low cost, like the survey questionnaires some magazines ask readers to fill out and return, often backfire. Although periodicals with large circulations—100,000 and more—offer researchers big samples, only a fraction of the readers participate in the surveys. Thus, respondents do not represent a cross section either of the general population or of the magazine's readers. For example, 33 percent of the respondents in a 1982 *Playboy* magazine survey said that they had engaged in group sex (King et al., 1991). Do you think that such high numbers are representative of the entire country?

Third, certain populations, such as working classes and inner-city adolescents, are overstudied because they are less likely to realize that they can refuse to participate. *Fourth*, sampling techniques are sometimes flawed. For example, randomly selected numbers from telephone books (or computer-generated telephone numbers) are not really random because some people (about 4 percent) do not have telephones or have unlisted numbers. None of these millions of people has an equal chance of participating in a study.

Finally, our changing cultural views concerning what is "normal" and "abnormal" influence scientific views. For example, as you will see later in this chapter, explanations of homosexuality have changed in the last few years. Thus, research on sexuality and sexual behavior continues to change, and what you read today may be different tomorrow.

Figure 6.1 1994 Sex Survey Findings: Sex is Largely Monogamous and Very Satisfying. *These findings from the 1994 nationwide U.S. survey of sexual behavior surprised some observers. Nearly three-quarters of respondents said they had had only one sexual partner in the preceding year (A); more than 85 percent said they were both physically and emotionally satisfied with their partners (B); and two-thirds of men had had no more than 10 partners since the age of 18 (the comparable figure for women was 90 percent)* (Based on Laumann et al., 1994: 177–180; 369).

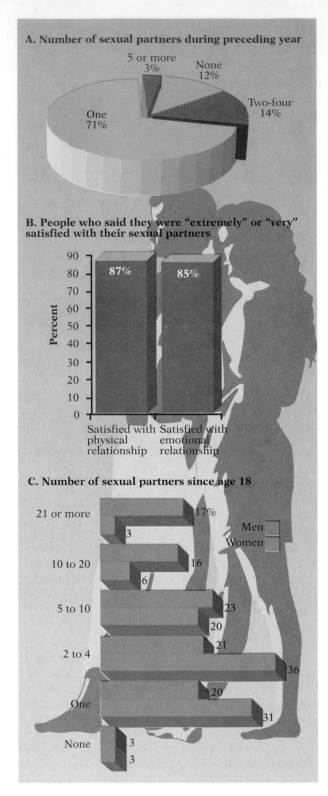

A. Number of sexual partners during preceding year

- 5 or more 3%
- None 12%
- Two-four 14%
- One 71%

B. People who said they were "extremely" or "very" satisfied with their sexual partners

Satisfied with physical relationship: 87%
Satisfied with emotional relationship: 85%

C. Number of sexual partners since age 18

Men / Women

Category	Men	Women
21 or more	17%	3
10 to 20	16	6
5 to 10	23	20
2 to 4	21	36
One	20	31
None	3	3

SEXUAL ACTIVITY

As the Data Digest indicates, people engage in a wide spectrum of sexual behaviors. Nevertheless, according to a recent national survey conducted by four social scientists through the National Opinion Research Center at the University of Chicago (the "Sex Survey"), most Americans have fairly conventional sex lives. A large percentage had one or no sex partners over the year of the study, more than 85 percent said they were happy with their sexual relationships, and the median number of partners the respondents had had since age 18 was relatively "average" (see Figure 6.1). It's important to keep in mind, too, that sex is not just sexual intercourse; the expression of sexuality encompasses many other behaviors, including masturbation, petting, and oral sex.

Masturbation

In his film *Annie Hall,* Woody Allen described masturbation as "having sex with someone I love." When asked about sex in the future, Robin Williams responded: "What's sex going to be in the 1990s? It's going to be you—and you." **Masturbation** refers to sexual self-pleasuring that involves some form of direct physical stimulation. It may or may not result in orgasm. Masturbation typically involves rubbing, stroking, fondling, squeezing, or otherwise stimulating the genitals, but it can also be self-stimulation of other body parts, such as the breasts, the inner thighs, or the anus.

Early in this century masturbation was branded as a source of damage to the brain and nervous system. It was believed to cause a variety of problems, such as bad breath, blindness, deafness, acne, and heart murmurs. In 1918, for example, Marie Carmichael Stopes, the author of the best-seller *Married Love,* was reportedly deluged with letters from female readers who expressed anxieties about masturbation. One woman wrote that masturbation had "worn out [her] sexual organs . . . before they were put to their proper use." In their *Handbook for Girl Guides,* Sir Robert Baden-Powell (the founder of the Boy Scout movement) and his sister, Agnes, told their readers that "secret bad habits" (masturbation) could cause madness (Holtzman, 1982).

Some physicians treated masturbation with recommendations for prayer or exercise. Others went much farther:

"Treatment" for boys included piercing the foreskin of the penis with wire, applying leeches to the base of the penis, or cutting the foreskin with a jagged scissors. "Treatment" for girls included applying a hot iron to the thighs or clitoris or removing the clitoris in an operation called a clitoridectomy. Adults could buy various commercial devices, such as metal mittens, an alarm that went off when the bed moved, rings with metal teeth or spikes to wear on the penis at night, or guards worn against the female's vulva. Some of these horrors were so popular that they were advertised in the Sears-Roebuck catalog (Wade and Cirese, 1991: 46).

Although today it is known that masturbation causes no physical harm, Victorian attitudes still linger among the general public. Parents rarely discuss masturbation with their children. Even teenagers who are masturbating feel guilty or uncomfortable talking about it (Coles and Stokes, 1985). In her advice column, Ann Landers recommended self-gratification or mutual masturbation as "a sane and safe alternative to intercourse, not only for teenagers, but for older men and women who have lost their partners." Sex educators were delighted by her advice, but some religious groups were "shocked and disappointed." Despite the controversy, Landers stated that "this could be the most useful column I have written since I started" (Friedman, 1993). In 1994, however, President Clinton fired Surgeon General Joycelyn Elders, his own appointee, when she added to her growing list of controversial positions a proposal to include teaching about masturbation in sex-education programs in schools (Suro, 1994). As some researchers have noted, "Masturbation remains in the shadows, a practice that few discuss" (Michael et al., 1994: 158).

Discovering Masturbation Masturbation often begins in childhood and occurs commonly throughout the life cycle. Prepubertal children may stimulate themselves without realizing that what they are doing is sexual. For example, one girl learned when she was 8 years old that she could produce an "absolutely terrific feeling" by squeezing her thighs together (Nass et al., 1981: 77). And many teenagers discover masturbation accidentally:

15-year-old boy: "Ever since I can remember I have known that people do it but never under-

stood how enjoyable it was until I was about 11. I was in a Jacuzzi sitting right next to a water jet. Quite by accident I found myself stimulated and really enjoyed it."

16-year old boy: *"I was asleep and woke up with an erection. I rubbed it against the bed and kept it up because it felt so good."*

15-year-old girl: *"I discovered masturbation when I was drying myself with a towel."*

16-year-old girl: *"I discovered on the uneven parallel bars in gymnastics that if I leaned against the bar in a specific way in which my vagina was pressured, it would feel pleasant" (Hass, 1979: 88–89).*

Social and Demographic Variations Many variables affect the frequency with which people engage in masturbation. Some of these are gender, marital status, education, and ethnicity. Most research shows a clear gender gap in masturbation rates, beginning in puberty, but over time this gap has narrowed somewhat. In the mid-1950s, a Kinsey survey showed that 45 percent of male respondents but only 15 percent of female respondents reported having masturbated to orgasm by the age of 13 (Kinsey et al., 1953). By 1974, these figures had risen to 63 percent and 33 percent, respectively (Hunt, 1974).

The 1994 Sex Survey (Laumann et al., 1994), based on the responses of 3,432 adults aged 18 to 59, found that more than a third of male respondents and over half of female respondents said they had never masturbated. Respondents in this study who reported masturbating once a week were characterized as follows:

■ The largest group within this category was composed of people aged 30 to 34; 35 percent were men and 9 percent were women.

■ Of those who were married, men were more likely to masturbate than women (17 percent and 5 percent, respectively), but the highest rates of masturbation were reported by those who had never been married and were not cohabiting (41 percent for men, 12 percent for women).

■ Within this group some of the most striking differences reflected educational level: 34 percent of men with graduate degrees masturbated regularly, compared to only 19 percent of men with less than a high school education; the comparable rates for women were 14 per-

cent and 8 percent. The researchers suggested that "it is likely that the better educated have more secular views in general, have more liberal views of sexual activity in particular regardless of their religious affiliation, and are more likely to consider pleasure a major goal of sexual activity" (p. 84).

■ For both men and women, the primary reasons for masturbation were to relieve sexual tension and for sheer physical pleasure (pp. 80–87).

The Sex Survey researchers also found large differences by race and ethnicity. Black men (60 percent) were twice as likely as whites, Latinos, and Asians to say they never masturbated. The differences between women who said they had never masturbated were less striking: 56 percent for white women, 68 percent for black women, and 66 percent for Latinas (Laumann et al., 1994). One researcher has suggested that masturbation rates among black men may be lower than among other ethnic groups of men because African American men have traditionally viewed masturbation as an admission of inability to seduce a woman (Belcastro, 1985).

Frequency of masturbation, like that of other sexual activities, declines with age. One third of women and 43 percent of men in their 70s reported masturbating about three times a month (Brecher, 1984). Note, however, that these estimates may be low; many older adults are reluctant to discuss their sexual behaviors (King et al., 1991). Questions such as "How often do you masturbate?" may be intimidating and even guilt-inducing to people now in their 60s and 70s who grew up when masturbation was surrounded by the myths we discussed earlier (see Laumann et al., 1994).

Myths and Morality As we've already seen, there are many misconceptions about masturbation. Adolescents often feel guilty because they believe that masturbation is not a "normal" expression of sexuality, even though authorities on sexual behavior now find it perfectly normal. Women in particular tend to feel guilty because they are trained to please men rather than themselves (see Chapter 4). In fact, masturbation fulfills several needs: it can relieve sexual tension, control sexual impulses, provide a safe means of sexual experimentation (avoiding disease and unwanted pregnancy), increase sexual self-confidence, combat loneliness, and may ultimately transfer valuable learning to two-person love-making. Masturbation can be as sexually satisfying as intercourse, and it does not hinder the development of social relationships during young adulthood or create problems in a marriage (Leitenberg et al., 1993; Kelly, 1994). Although masturbation is not essential in people's sexual lives, it does not lead to mental illness, homosexuality, or a decrease in the production of semen (*The Economist*, 1993).

Each person must decide whether or not to masturbate based on her or his religion and values. Long-term guilt and worry about masturbation can cause negative feelings and low self-esteem. If such feelings are intense, talking with a health provider or other professional counselor might be advisable.

Petting

Kinsey and associates defined petting as physical contact between people to produce erotic arousal but without engaging in sexual intercourse. **Petting,** which includes touching, stroking, and fondling various parts of the body, especially the breasts and genitalia, is generally more acceptable than intercourse because it is less intimate and does not result in pregnancy. Although they may deny it now, our grandparents apparently had remarkable petting skills:

Petting is an indigenous form of amusement that has more devotees than the combined practitioners of all other sports. Accomplished petters are able to remain in a love-death clinch while their car speeds along at 70 miles an hour; others continue the mysterious contortions of the rite straight through hamburgers and coffee; still others simultaneously kiss and chew gum at 90 revolutions per minute; while outdoor petters throw peanuts to zoo monkeys with one hand and pet with the other (Cohn, 1943: 156).

In the past, researchers sometimes differentiated between petting and necking. They defined petting as sexual touching below the waist and necking as any other sexual touching, including kissing. More recently some researchers are including oral sex in some definitions of petting.

By the early 1950s (when, theoretically, at least, no one had sex until after marriage), 81 percent of boys and 84 percent of girls had had experience with petting by the age of 18. Approximately 23 percent of the men and 32 percent of the women between the ages of 16 and 20 had petted to orgasm (Kinsey et al., 1953). More recently, interviews with first-year college students about their high school sexual experiences showed that 40 percent of the women and 50 percent of the men reported having experienced orgasm during petting (Masters et al., 1986).

Oral Sex

Oral sex includes several types of stimulation. **Fellatio** (from the Latin word for "suck") refers to oral stimulation of a man's penis. **Cunnilingus** (from the Latin words for "vulva" and "tongue") refers to oral stimulation of a woman's genital organs. Fellatio and cunnilingus can be performed singly or simultaneously. Simultaneous oral sex is sometimes referred to as "69," indicating the physical positions of the partners.

Although many adolescent couples stop at petting, there may also be oral-genital contact either preceding intercourse or instead of it. One survey of 17- to 18-year-olds found that 41 percent of the women and 33 percent of the men had performed oral sex on a member of the opposite sex (Haffner, 1993). A national study of men between 20 and 39 years of age reported that almost 80 percent of those who were currently married had either performed or received oral sex (presumably with their spouses). The same study found substantial overall differences by race. Among white men, 79 percent had performed oral sex, compared with 73 percent among Latino men and 43 percent among black men (Billy et al., 1993).

Similarly, in a study of undergraduates, Belcastro (1985) found that black females were significantly less likely to have performed fellatio than white females (48 percent and 82 percent, respectively). Belcastro suggested that the infrequent reporting of fellatio among black women is probably largely due to their perception of fellatio as an unclean and demeaning act. In contrast, white females often reported using fellatio as a method of birth control.

Oral sex is often reflected in films, although the depictions are more often of cunnilingus than of fellatio (*Murder in the First, Basic Instinct, Natural Born Killers, Pulp Fiction*, and *Fatal Attraction*, for example). In movies, the woman usually experiences a frenzied orgasm.

She hyperventilates, groans, moans, and practically faints from the presumed sexual ecstasy. Reactions in real life tend to be considerably less dramatic. Some people find oral sex pleasurable or engage in it (probably without the moans and groans) to please their partner. Others complain about the odors (although bathing solves the problem for both sexes), do not enjoy it, or find it revolting. When Wade and Cirese (1991: 334) asked their students what bothers them about oral sex, they got the following responses:

One woman wrote, "I can't swallow his semen! Choke! Choke!" Another wrote, "I always want to say 'Well, would you like me to blow my nose in your mouth?' That's how I feel about it; I'm not trying to be rude."

Engaging in oral sex, as in many other sexual behaviors, depends on personal preference.

Sexual Intercourse and Human Sexual Response

Most people understand sexual intercourse to mean heterosexual, vaginal-penile penetration, but the term actually refers to any sort of sexual coupling, including oral and anal. The word "coitus" specifically means penile-vaginal intercourse, and unless noted otherwise, we will use sexual intercourse to refer to coitus.

Sexual Intercourse Among both men and women, the first heterosexual intercourse takes place, on average, between ages 16 and 17. As Chapter 7 shows, however, some adolescents, especially boys, begin to be sexually active in their early teens. By age 65, men report that they've had sex with an average of 15 women; women have had sex with an average of 8 men (Clements, 1994). Thus, men have almost twice as many sexual partners as do women by the time they reach their "golden years." As Figure 6.2 shows, average monthly sexual intercourse peaks between ages 25 and 34 and then declines over the years. This pattern suggests that, with time, people develop other interests besides sex that become a high priority in maintaining a family or a relationship.

How often people have sex varies by marital status and closeness of the relationship. As Figure 6.3 shows, married couples and cohabitants

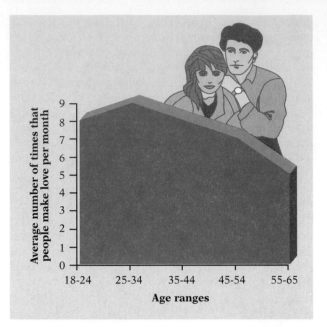

*Figure 6.2 **How Often Do I Love Thee? Frequency of Lovemaking Over the Life Cycle*** (Clements, 1994:5).

have considerably higher rates of sexual intercourse than single persons do. Such figures challenge popular perceptions of "swinging singles." Several studies also report that married people are happier with their sex lives than either single people or cohabitants (Billy et al., 1993; Clements, 1994; Laumann et al., 1994). These findings lend support to the notion, discussed in Chapter 5, that sexual intercourse is more than just the sexual act—that it also involves intimacy, commitment, and love.

The 1994 Sex Survey researchers commented that "contrary to the historically popular stereotype of group differences in rates of sexual contact, we found only minor variations in frequency of partnered sex across race and ethnicity, religious affiliation, and level of education" (Laumann et al., 1994: 89). Overall, these researchers found that African Americans have sex with a partner about as often as whites, although Hispanics had slightly higher rates. About a third of all male respondents—whites, blacks, and Latinos—said they had sex two or three times a week. Interestingly, however, about a third each of black and white women reported having sex with a partner a few times a year or not at all.

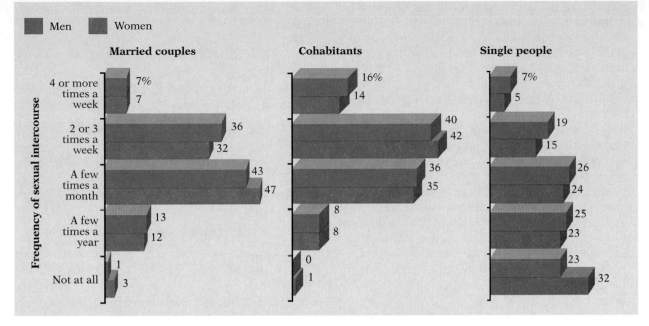

Figure 6.3 *Cohabitants and Married Couples Have More Fun Than Singles.*
As the text points out, married couples and people who live together have sexual intercourse considerably more often than single people (Based on Laumann et al., 1994:88–89).

Level of education did not affect the frequency with which women had sex with a partner, although the more education men had, the less likely they were to have had little or no sex. Similarly, religion was not a highly significant factor in frequency of sex: Protestants, Catholics, and nonreligious people were rated about the same. Thus, Americans of the same age and marital status are remarkably similar in the frequency with which they have sex (see also Billy et al., 1993).

Why are these groups so similar in sexual experience? Michael et al. (1994) propose that it is our many myths about racial and religious groups that lead us to expect otherwise. In reality, there is nothing about being a member of a particular racial or religious group or at a particular educational level that translates into more or less sexual desire or sexual opportunity. As you saw earlier, having an easily accessible partner, such as in marriage or cohabitation, seems to have the largest impact on the frequency of sexual activity.

Four Stages of Human Sexual Response In 1954, William Masters began an intensive ten-year investigation into the anatomy and physiology of human sexual responses. (See Appendix A for a discussion of male and female sexual anatomy.) Masters and his longtime partner, Virginia Johnson (1966), with the aid of more than 700 married and single women and men who volunteered to participate in the studies, scrutinized intercourse and masturbation in the laboratory by watching, recording, and measuring both the internal and external physiological details of intercourse and orgasm. Determining that human sexual response involves a four-stage cycle—excitement, plateau, orgasm, and resolution—these researchers documented each stage in terms of changes in body parts, blood pressure, pulse, and breathing.

EXCITEMENT In the first, **excitement phase,** both men and women experience an increase in blood pressure, pulse rate, and breathing. In the male, the first responses to sexual stimulation are the swelling and erection of the penis and partial elevation of the testes. Female excitement results in vaginal lubrication, accompanied by clitoral swelling. The clitoris elongates, and the vagina increases in width and length.

PLATEAU   Additional physical changes occur in the **plateau phase,** the second stage of sexual response. In the female, with continued sexual stimulation, the lips of the vulva undergo extreme swelling. The clitoris begins to withdraw into its hood, and there is a further increase in the width and depth of the vagina. In the male, the circumference of the head of the penis (called the coronal ridge) increases, and the testes become 50 percent larger. Heart rate and blood pressure in both men and women continue to rise. During this phase, the penis may emit several drops of fluid that are not semen but may contain sperm cells. If this fluid is discharged while the penis is in the vagina, a woman can be impregnated. Thus, withdrawal before ejaculation, commonly used as a means of contraception, is often totally ineffective in preventing conception.

ORGASM   Sexual tension reaches its peak, or climax, during **orgasm** and is suddenly discharged. This third stage of sexual response lasts only a few seconds. In the male, it is characterized by three or four major contractions of the entire length of the urethra, also at 0.8-second intervals, which accounts for the spurting of semen during ejaculation. This is followed by several seconds of minor contractions, which are lower in frequency. The female experiences three to six intense contractions of the outer third of the vagina, at 0.8-second intervals, followed by several seconds of minor contractions that also are lower in frequency and intensity. Orgasm is normally a very intense physiological response for both males and females. Heart rate, which has steadily increased during the plateau phase, can reach a high of as much as 180 beats per minute (normal is 70–80). Blood pressure and respiratory rates may increase dramatically. Many people experience a sense of loss of oxygen and respond by breathing heavily.

What many people don't realize is that ejaculation and orgasm are not the same phenomenon. They can be experienced independently of each other because they are affected by different neurological and vascular systems. Few men are aware that during the course of one night they probably have as many as five erections, each lasting approximately 30 minutes. This is true even of men with impotence problems (Coote, 1991). Although we often hear that a penile erection, ejaculation, and orgasm occur at the same time, there are actually nine possibilities (Stoltenberg, 1993):

- Penile erection without ejaculation and orgasm
- Penile erection and ejaculation without orgasm
- Penile erection and orgasm without ejaculation
- Orgasm without penile erection and ejaculation
- Orgasm and ejaculation without penile erection
- Orgasm and penile erection without ejaculation
- Ejaculation without penile erection and orgasm
- Ejaculation and penile erection without orgasm
- Ejaculation and orgasm without penile erection
- Penile erection, ejaculation, and orgasm pretty much all at the same time

Because penile erections, ejaculations, and orgasms do not occur simultaneously, men who argue that a penile erection *must* be followed by ejaculation during sexual intercourse lest they suffer dire consequences are, quite simply, wrong. There is no scientific evidence that any man has ever died of a "terminal erection"!

Do you believe that women and men experience orgasm differently? Read the box "How Do Orgasms Differ by Gender?" before continuing with this paragraph. Actually, the major difference between male and female orgasms is that women can have multiple orgasms within a very short space of time, whereas most men cannot. As you will see shortly, although some men can become erect again almost immediately after ejaculation and orgasm, most need at least 20 minutes if not more to recover erectile capacity (Coote, 1991).

Recent research suggests that there are individual variations in reaching orgasm. Some people may skip stages, experiencing orgasm, for example, in the excitement stage. And women may experience different kinds of orgasms: clitoral, uterine (which is characterized by involuntary breath holding due to a contraction in the mus-

How Do Orgasms Differ by Gender?

Read each of the following descriptions of orgasm. Is the speaker a man or a woman?

	Man	Woman
1. For me, orgasm feels like a building wave of emotion. First I notice a pulsing sensation that is quite localized, then it spreads through my whole body. Afterwards, I feel tired but also superrelaxed.	☐	☐
2. My anxiety about sex definitely inhibits my orgasm. There are times that I feel some intense sensations, but usually I am too inhibited to really let myself go. If I am not very comfortable with my partner, it is very difficult to come. I have orgasms most easily when I masturbate.	☐	☐
3. Basically, I feel a glow which starts in my genitals and then spreads through my whole body. Sometimes one orgasm is enough, and other times it is not completely satisfying.	☐	☐
4. I think orgasm is overrated. I sometimes spend over an hour getting turned on, and then the orgasm takes only a few seconds. I'd like to learn how to make the feeling of orgasm last longer.	☐	☐
5. I concentrate all my attention on the sensations in the genitals [then] I completely lose contact with everything around me. My body feels incredibly alive and seems to vibrate. Afterwards, I just want to hold my lover and be very still.	☐	☐

Answers: All of the descriptions of orgasm are by men.

SOURCE: Based on Vance and Wagner, 1976: 87–98.

---

cle at the back of the throat), and a combination of clitoral and uterine. Many women prefer or require clitoral stimulation to reach orgasm. Response patterns are the same regardless of the source of sexual stimulation. That is, an orgasm that comes from rubbing the clitoris can't be distinguished physiologically from one that results from breast stimulation alone or from intercourse.

In the past decade claims have been made that a region of the front wall of the vagina has a high degree of erotic sensitivity. Called the *G spot* (or *Grafenberg spot,* for the German physician who first suggested its presence in 1950), this area has been described as a mass of tissue about the size of a small bean, which swells to the size of a dime or larger when stimulated. The existence of a G spot that contributes to pleasure and orgasm is controversial, however, because some studies have found no evidence of its existence (Masters et al., 1992).

RESOLUTION After orgasm, in the **resolution phase,** the fourth and last stage of the sexual response cycle, the male's penis begins a rapid loss of swelling and erection. This is followed by a slower shrinking of the penis until it returns to its normal state. In the female, the clitoris returns to its normal position, followed by a slower reduction in the size and level of swelling. Breathing, heart rate, and blood pressure return to normal in both partners. During this stage, most men experience a **refractory period**—a time during which they can't become sexually aroused. This period usually lasts at least 20 minutes and may be considerably longer as a man grows older.

Myths about Sexual Response One of the biggest concerns expressed by men is that their penises are not big enough to stimulate women during intercourse (Reinisch and Beasley, 1990). There is no evidence of a correlation between clitoris, breast, or penis size and orgasm. Similarly, there is no evidence for the belief that, compared to white men, black men have larger penises, a greater sexual capacity, or an insatiable sexual appetite. Nonetheless, myths about penis size and orgasms persist:

Penis size is a hot topic with [my] female coworkers. One woman made a comment about how you can tell the size of a man's penis by how large his hands are. This is the same rumor I used to hear in high school which was about five years ago. I thought my generation was smarter. Also, I heard that the larger the penis size the more intense an orgasm you could achieve. I tried to tell them that this is not fact but fiction but they said that I didn't know what I was talking about (author's files; female college student).

A second misconception about sexual response is that the male can always tell if his female partner had an orgasm. To appease or please their partners, women sometimes fake orgasms and in general they are successful (Hite, 1987). Except in the movies, women's orgasms are rarely accompanied by dramatic moans and groans, asthmatic breathing, and clutching of the bedposts. Response can be explosive or mild, depending on a woman's emotional or physical state, stress, tension, alcohol consumption, and a variety of other factors.

Finally, the idea that simultaneous orgasm (both partners experiencing orgasm at the same time) is the ultimate peak in sexual pleasure became popular in the 1950s and was advocated enthusiastically in numerous marriage manuals. Many people tried to "fine-tune" the timing of their responses, but working so hard at sex usually resulted in a loss of spontaneity (Masters et al., 1986). Although simultaneous orgasm can be exhilarating, so are independent orgasms.

THE SEXUAL REVOLUTION AND MODERN SEXUAL SCRIPTS

No one has been able to pinpoint when or why people in the United States became more sexually "progressive." There is some agreement, however, that the so-called "sexual revolution" of the late 1960s fostered long-term changes from the 1970s through the present.

The Sexual Revolution

The late 1960s are often blamed (or praised, depending on your point of view) for the "sexual revolution." Some point to the increases in the rates of premarital intercourse, cohabitation, and illegitimate births as indicators of sexual promiscuity (see Chapter 1). There certainly has been a shift in our sexual attitudes and behavior, but the changes are probably not as revolutionary as we are often led to believe.

In the late 1940s, social norms emphasized that love, sex, and marriage were deeply and permanently intertwined. By the early 1960s, however, questions about sexual morality were less clear-cut and more personal rather than family-oriented. For example, the Masters and Johnson study in 1966 challenged traditional notions of women as passive recipients of men's presumed unbridled interest in sex. Also, women's growing economic independence gave them more power to assert themselves in interpersonal relationships (Ehrenreich et al., 1986). Greater openness about sexuality made sex less shameful and mysterious. Reproductive sex was replaced by a growing acceptance of recreational sex largely because the birth-control pill ("the Pill") meant that, for women, sex and childbearing could be separated. Finally, the sanctions against premarital sex were greatly reduced. By the mid-1970s, the fear of pregnancy, the concepts of sin and guilt, and the value of virginity had changed considerably, especially for teenagers (Bell and Coughey, 1980).

The sexual revolution was instrumental in promoting sex education for teenagers and in encouraging more open communication about sex between men and women. There were also costs, however, especially for women. Women "were pressured more than ever [by men] to be sexually liberated . . . and then were accused of being uptight and puritanical if [they] didn't want sex or wanted more than sex" (Elshtain, 1988: 41). Giving women more sexual freedom without increasing their economic freedom also resulted in greater vulnerability. As women became "free sexual agents," men were released from any responsibility regarding marriage or parenthood (Ehrenreich et al., 1986).

Sexual Scripts

Whereas physiological responses are automatic, our intimate relationships and our behavior are products of our culture. Although we like to think that our sexual behavior is spontaneous, even our erotic feelings are conditioned by the society we live in (see Chapter 4). Sexual activity occurs within the framework of sexual scripts that tell people how to behave and think in particular situations. A **sexual script** specifies the formal or informal norms for legitimate or unacceptable sexual activity, the eligibility of sexual partners, and the boundaries of sexual behavior in terms of time and place. For example, U.S. culture prohibits sexual intercourse with children, discourages relationships with same-sex partners, and frowns upon sexual activities in public places. As we will discuss in Chapter 8, these expectations also govern dating and mate-selection processes.

Traditional Sexual Scripts

Men and women have different sexual scripts. In traditional sexual scripts, men were expected to take the initiative in sexual encounters, and women were expected to give pleasure. Furthermore, men and women were said to experience sex differently. Men were supposed to be assertive, confident, and aggressive. Sex was for orgasm, not intimacy, and the man was always in charge, always ready for sex, and always able to have an erection. Any physical contact was a sign for sex, which always equaled intercourse. And, for men, the more often the orgasms, the better the sex. In contrast, women were expected to be compliant and responsive and to make the man happy. Engaging in sex without being in love was wrong. Sex was for men, love was for women, and therefore women must be romanced to get them to comply (see Chapter 5).

Contemporary Sexual Scripts

Despite the sexual revolution, modern sexual scripts are not very different from the more traditional scripts. For example, a girl may wear tight jeans because they are in style, but a boy may think she is trying to be seductive. A girl may go to a boy's house just to talk, but the boy may assume she is consenting to sex (Tavris, 1992).

Some authors feel that male scripts still reflect dominance rather than intimacy with female sex partners. According to Franklin (1988), men learn objectification, fixation, and conquest during their early years. They *objectify* women (woman as object: any woman will do). They *fixate* on parts of females' bodies—their legs, hips, breasts. They *conquer* women, both to affirm their heterosexuality and to prove their sexual prowess to other men. Franklin points to the increasing rates of rape, sexual assaults on children, and women's complaints about men's lack of intimacy as evidence of men's sexual-dominance scripts.

For young girls, sex still occurs most often in the context of close, romantic relationships, whereas many boys see sex as an end. Girls are more likely to have fewer partners and to engage in sex to "keep boyfriends" (Sprecher and McKinney, 1993). In one study, Hite (1981: 594–95) found that some men complained that women are "just too passive" and frequently do not want to learn how to "turn men on" through fellatio, caressing their genitals, and foreplay. At the same time, however, "many men jealously guarded their prerogative of being 'in charge' and dominant in the male-female relationships and resented any attempts by women to become more assertive or active sexually."

The male emphasis on dominance and control is changing very slowly. For example, some men admit that they are searching for emotional inti-

In dressing to "look sexy," women are following the latest styles—which are created largely by men—not inviting sexual intercourse—which is what some men often assume.

macy and not just sex. When there are sexual problems, more men are willing to attend therapy sessions with their partners and to acknowledge that they may be the reason for the difficulties (Osherson, 1992). Furthermore, some men encourage women to be more aggressive and are interested in following women's directives about how to give greater sexual pleasure.

The Double Standard Revisited The double standard—the traditional social norm that permits greater freedom in one or more important spheres of life to men than to women—emerged during the nineteenth century and still shapes much of the behavior of women and men today (see Chapters 3, 4, and 5). Although today more women are having premarital intercourse and are expressing their erotic needs more clearly and more often, gender-related scripts continue to reflect a double standard. For example, virginity is still a highly prized commodity for women but not for men. In a study of college students, Robinson and colleagues (1991) found that women who engage in premarital sex are considered "immoral" by many men and women even though both groups accepted male premarital sex. Most recently, Oliver and Hyde (1993) found that males were more permissive and less anxious than women were about having sex with other partners when they were engaged or in a committed relationship.

The most serious (some would say frighten-ing) indicator of the double standard is the increasing rate at which rape and other sexual assaults are made on women. Consider the "Spur Posse" case in California. In 1993 eight members of a suburban high school, many of them top athletes at the school, created a clique called the "Spur Posse." Their primary goal was to "score" with as many girls as possible. They kept track of the girls with whom they had intercourse, and some bragged that their individual tallies ran into the 60s. In at least seven cases, girls from 10 to 16 years old said they had been raped. The district attorney's office pressed charges against only one minor on charges of having sex with a 10-year-old girl, but even this case was not prosecuted.

Although most people in the community and the United States were shocked by the charges, a number of students at the high school came to the "Spur Posse's" defense because "sex is simply a fact of adolescent life." Some of the parents condoned their sons' behavior. One father boasted to reporters about his son's virility, and others maintained that what the athletes did was no different from the behavior of such heroes as Wilt Chamberlain, whom we discussed at the beginning of the chapter (Seligmann et al., 1993). Thus, some of the parents were proud of their sons' "scoring," and they saw the behavior as "masculine" rather than as rape.

Finally, the double standard is not limited to the Western world. For example, foot-binding

Do you think the activities of the Spur Posse, some of whom are shown here, were acceptable or unacceptable? Should these boys have been prosecuted for rape, or were the California courts right to drop the case?

was practiced widely among the upper classes in China for at least a thousand years. At about age 5, girls' feet were bound so that they wouldn't grow. All toes except the big toe were bent under and into the sole of the foot and bound with cloth as tightly as possible. Sometimes one or more toes rotted and dropped off. Foot-binding was justified as a standard of feminine beauty; tiny feet were deemed beautiful and thus an asset that made a woman more marriageable. Contemporary researchers maintain, however, that the custom simply ensured male erotic pleasure because their wives could barely walk, could not run away, and were readily accessible as sexual objects. Custom and tradition limited women's sexuality but allowed men to engage in marital (and extramarital) sexual activity whenever they wanted to do so (Dworkin, 1974; Herbert, 1989).

Many observers believe that female circumcision, still practiced extensively in Africa, Southeast Asia, and the Middle East, reflects a double standard that allows men to mutilate women under the guise of making them more marriageable. Men have no comparable restrictions. With increased emigration from Africa and the Mideast, female mutilation is now also practiced in the United States (Kaplan et al., 1993).

Female circumcision generally involves extensive damage to the sexual organs and has long-term effects on the women's health. In 1979, the World Health Organization denounced female circumcision as indefensible on medical and humane grounds. The Kenyan government banned female mutilation in 1990, but the procedure is still widely performed in Kenya and many other countries. As the box on pp. 158 and 159, "Tradition or Torture? Female Genital Mutilation," shows, millions of girls are still subjected to these procedures.

Sexual Fantasies: Healthy or Unhealthy?

Most of us have sexual fantasies, no matter what our age or marital status. We fantasize differently, though, depending on whether we're male or female. Males' and females' different sexual scripts lead young girls, for example, to have elaborate fantasies that often focus more on activities leading up to intercourse, whereas boys tend to envision very specific sexual acts:

17-year-old girl: "It is always my boyfriend and it is very romantic. We are sitting in front of the fireplace with champagne, and I'm wearing this sexy dress, and he's just relaxed with his shirt open, and he's dressed nice. And we kiss and pretty soon we're on the floor in front of the fire caressing each other and taking off each other's clothes. Then we have sexual intercourse."

17-year-old boy: "I usually think of the most erotic pleasure conceivable. For example, placing my penis in between a girl's breasts and rubbing her breasts together. Licking her pubic hair. Having an ejaculation of sperm outside of the vagina and rubbing my sperm all over her legs and stomach and breasts" (Hass, 1979: 113–21).

Although the actual content of sexual fantasies differs between males and females, most fantasies have very similar themes. The most common include the following:

- *Experimentation*: Trying something the person has never done before (such as sex with a prostitute or an animal, or incest).
- *Conquest*: Forcing or being forced or seduced by someone else.
- *Switching partners* : Having sex with a former partner (an old boyfriend or girlfriend) or with a celebrity.
- *Group sex*: Group orgies that may also be bisexual.
- *Watching*: Watching and then joining in, or watching one's spouse have sex with someone else.
- *Rape*: Either as the rapist or the victim; some heterosexual men occasionally have fantasies about being raped homosexually.
- *Sadomasochism*: Inflicting or receiving pain; fantasies with sadomasochistic themes such as images of being beaten, tied, chained, handcuffed, or spanked.

Gender differences in sexual fantasies often mirror differences in gender roles (see Table 6.2). Women's fantasies are typically more romantic, passive, and submissive than are men's. Even when women fantasize about "unusual" sex practices, they are less likely to act them out. For example, in a survey of 2,000 adults, twice as many men as women said that they had actually realized such fantasies as incest, sex with defeca-

Table 6.2

The 20 Most Common Sexual Fantasies among Americans

	PERCENTAGE REPORTING	
	MEN	WOMEN
Oral sex	75	43
Sex with a famous person	59	39
Multiple partners	57	24
Sex with someone of another race	52	25
Swapping partners	42	15
Sex with a teenager	42	8
Sex in a public place	39	26
Sex with a much younger person	39	15
Anal sex	39	14
Using sexual devices	38	29
Sex with a much older person	34	15
Being a porno star	30	10
Sex with a fictional TV character	30	20
Sex with dominance or submission	27	19
Calling a telephone sex line	20	7
Sex with a physical object	15	11
Sex mixed with violence	13	4
Incest	13	3
Sadomasochistic sex	12	7
Sex with an animal	8	3

SOURCE: Patterson and Kim, © 1991. Used by permission of Prentice-Hall Press, A Division of Simon & Schuster.

tion, sadomasochism, or sex with an animal (Patterson and Kim, 1991).

Some clinical psychologists and psychoanalysts argue that erotic fantasies are harmful because they lessen intimacy in a relationship, indicate sexual alienation, and reduce personal involvement (see Masters et al., 1986: 271-73, for a review of these criticisms). Most experts feel that sexual fantasies are emotionally and psychologically healthy, however. Some people use fantasies to reach orgasm. Fantasies can provide a safety valve for pent-up feelings or a harmless escape from boring, everyday routines: "To be covered in whipped cream and wrestle my lover, then the loser has to lick it off," or "Having sex on the 50-yard line at a sold-out football game" (Patterson and Kim, 1991: 79). Fantasies can also boost our self-image because we need not worry about penis size, breast size, or weight. Because we have total control in producing and directing the fantasy, we can change or stop it anytime we want. In some cases, fantasies are mental rehearsals for future sexual experiences (Masters et al., 1992).

Fantasy and reality are seldom the same, of course. Clark Gable was one of the most popular, dashing, and handsome movie-screen lovers. His role as Rhett Butler in *Gone with the Wind* is still a source of fantasy for many women. When Carole Lombard, one of his wives, was asked about his prowess as a lover, however, she reportedly said, "Gable's no Gable." Similarly, a female groupie who had sexual intercourse with band members on a regular basis spun an elaborate fantasy about Mick Jagger of the Rolling Stones. When she finally had sex with Jagger, she had to resort to her fantasy because, she said, the real Mick Jagger was disappointing in bed (Singer, 1980). Thus, people who actualize their fantasies may be very disillusioned.

SEX AND SEXUAL ORIENTATION

No one knows why people are heterosexual, homosexual, or bisexual. Some researchers think that we are born with a sexual orientation—a preference for partners of the opposite sex (het-

Reprinted with special permission of King Features Syndicate.

Homosexuality in Non-Western Cultures

In their classic studies, Ford and Beach (1972) examined data on 190 societies in Oceania, Eurasia, Africa, North America, and South America. They suggested three generalizations about homosexual behavior: (1) There is a wide divergence of social attitudes toward homosexuality; (2) homosexuality occurs in all societies regardless of societal reactions; and (3) males seem more likely to engage in homosexual activity than females.

In several non-Western societies, homosexual behavior during boyhood and adolescence is a rite of passage before the male switches to heterosexuality in adulthood. Among the Sambia of Papua New Guinea, from birth until somewhere between ages 7 and 10, boys interact frequently with females and live in heterosexual households. At about age 10, boys engage in specific homosexual rituals in order to attain the status of man-

hood and, ultimately, heterosexuality. The Sambia believe that fellatio is essential for the boys to grow big and live a long life. The young initiates are told to ingest semen as if it were food. In time, a boy's taking semen supposedly causes puberty and makes him manly enough to inseminate women.

Beginning around puberty, the second phase of adolescent socialization involves a role reversal: Boys cease being the fellator and become the recipients of fellatio. Although these activities are seen as pleasurable and may lead to sexual excitement and orgasm, the boys are also being introduced, slowly, to females. In their late teens or early 20s, young men are expected to find a wife and turn to heterosexuality. They are expected to be close, sensitive, and sexually proficient partners for their wives and to have children (Herdt, 1984; Baldwin and Baldwin, 1989).

Bisexual behavior among a non-homosexual population has been documented in other cultures as well. For example, Hirsch (1990)

argues that both homosexuality and bisexuality in China date back to at least the Bronze Age. Because marriage was seen as the bonding of two family groups rather than the romantic union of two individuals, both upper-class and peasant men sometimes maintained a heterosexual marriage and a homosexual liaison. Heterosexual marriages were important for both groups because children played a vital role: For the rich, they ensured progeny to continue the family line; for the poor, they provided agricultural labor and caretaking during old age.

Today, most Chinese see homosexuality as rare or even nonexistent in China. The reasons for Chinese and Western intolerance of homosexuality are different, however. Whereas Westerners reject homosexuality largely on religious or moral grounds, homosexuality in China is seen as potentially undermining the family structure, which forms the foundation of Chinese society.

---

erosexual), the same sex (homosexual), or both sexes (bisexual). Although heterosexuality is the predominant adult sexual orientation, homosexuality occurs in nearly all known societies (see the box "Homosexuality in Non-Western Cultures"). Many gay men and lesbians deny or try to suppress their sexual preference, however, because our society is still suspicious and disapproving of homosexuals.

Homosexuality

A **homosexual** (from the Greek root *homo*, meaning "same") is a person who is sexually attracted to people of the same sex. In contrast, **heterosexuals** are attracted to partners of the opposite sex. Male homosexuals prefer to be called *gays*; female homosexuals are called *lesbians*.

For years termed a mental disorder by the

American Psychiatric Association (APA), homosexuality finally "came out of the closet" in 1974, when the APA officially announced that it was not, after all, an illness. Since then gay men and lesbians have fought discriminatory behaviors and laws. By the early 1980s, homosexuals were organizing "Gay is beautiful" parades; influential men and women were revealing their sexual preferences; and gays and lesbians had gained greater political power.

Prevalence of Homosexuality How many gay men and lesbians are there? No one knows for sure, largely because measuring homosexuality is not an easy task. For example, should we measure homosexuality by asking people whether they identify themselves as gay or lesbian? Or are people to be considered homosexual if they have ever engaged in same-sex sexual behavior?

Tradition or Torture?
Female Genital Mutilation

Alice Walker, the Pulitzer Prize–winning novelist and author of *The Color Purple*, has joined with others in launching a campaign to end the genital mutilation of young girls. Walker argues that women should no longer be enslaved to the "barbaric" traditions of men. Countries that practice female circumcision, however, believe that the West ought to mind its own business and tolerate customs different from its own.

Several types of female circumcision are practiced in Africa and the Middle East. The two most common, which remove all or parts of the female's external genitalia, or vulva (see Appendix A), are excision and infibulation. In *excision*, part or all of the clitoris is removed in a procedure called a clitoridectomy, and part or all of the labia minora (see Appendix A) is removed as well. This operation often results in scar tissue that blocks the vaginal opening. *Infibulation* combines removal of the clitoris and labia minora with excision of the in-

ner layers of the labia majora. The raw edges of these inner layers are then sewn together with cat gut or acacia thorn. Three or four of these thorns pierce what remains of the vaginal lips, holding them together. A sliver of wood or straw is inserted into the tiny opening that remains, allowing for the slow, and often painful, passage of urine and the menstrual flow. When the female marries, her husband manually and with his penis enlarges the opening for intercourse, and the opening must be further enlarged for childbirth. In many cases, the opening is then closed in another excision or infibulation, and the cycle begins again.

The age at which the mutilations are carried out varies from area to area. Among the Jewish Falashas in Ethiopia and the nomads of the Sudan, the girl may be only a few days old; in Egypt and many countries of central Africa, she may be anywhere from 3 to 9 years old. The younger the girl, the less likely she is to know what's going to happen to her and, therefore, the less likely she is to resist. The circumci-

sion usually involves immobilizing the little girl by tying her arms behind her back and the women participants (sometimes including her mother) holding the child's thighs apart. The "operator," an old village woman, cuts off the clitoris and then scrapes the flesh from the labia lips even though "the little girl howls and writhes in pain." The operation lasts from 15 to 20 minutes, depending on the ability of the woman performing the circumcision and the resistance of the child.

Female mutilation is still carried out at all levels of society—from members of the elite and professional classes to the simplest villagers. In rural areas, the instruments include razor blades, scissors, kitchen knives, or pieces of glass. Antiseptic techniques and anesthesia are generally unknown.

Why are girls mutilated? The most common answer is that the practice is based on custom, religion, or "medical facts":

❑ The clitoris is poisonous and will kill a man or make him impotent.

What about people who, although they have other-sex partners, desire same-sex partners and see themselves as homosexual but are afraid to come out? Furthermore, what about men and women who identify themselves as heterosexuals but can be sexually aroused only when they fantasize about same-sex intercourse? Because of these complicating issues, in most research the prevalence of homosexuality is generally measured by simply asking people whether they identify themselves as heterosexual, homosexual, or bisexual.

Homosexuality is more visible today than in the past, but no one knows whether the percentage of homosexuals has increased or decreased. In one of the most comprehensive surveys at the time, Kinsey et al. (1948) estimated that 10 percent of white American males were more or less

exclusively homosexual for at least three years of their lives between the ages of 16 and 55, and 4 percent were exclusively homosexual on a lifelong basis. The statistics for women were much lower. Kinsey et al. (1953) estimated that 12 to 13 percent of all women and 8 to 9 percent of all married women had had sex with another woman. Only 2 to 3 percent of women were mostly or exclusively homosexual on a lifelong basis, however.

Several recent national surveys have produced data on lifelong homosexual behavior that are quite similar to Kinsey's figures. In the 1994 Sex Survey, 1.4 percent of women said they thought of themselves as homosexual or bisexual, and about 2.8 percent of the men identified themselves in this way. (Similar ranges have been reported in Billy et al., 1993, and Clements, 1994.)

- The clitoris is unpleasant to both sight and touch; the removal of such ugly genitalia will make women more attractive to men.

- Circumcision enhances fertility.

- Circumcision, and especially the enlargement of the vaginal orifice by tearing it downward, enlarges the vagina and makes childbearing easier.

- Circumcision prevents women from masturbating.

- Circumcision increases male sexual pleasure.

The first four of these statements are wholly untrue. And it is in the truth of the last two that some, at least, of the real intent is revealed: enforcement of the double standard that has allowed men complete sexual fulfillment and denied it to women.

A number of immediate and long-term complications are associated with female circumcision: the girl can hemorrhage and die; the bad eyesight of the operator or the resistance of the child can cause cuts in other organs (such as the urethra or bladder); a rupture of the internal division between the vagina and the bladder or the vagina and the rectum may cause a continual dribbling of urine or feces for the rest of the woman's life; women feel severe pain during intercourse (we discuss this issue in Chapter 7); women sometimes become sterile due to infections that ascend into the reproductive organs; their husbands may use razors, knives, or other instruments to enable them to penetrate the vagina; and during childbirth, even if the opening is made wider for the baby's birth, the woman may experience perineal tears or may even die because the baby cannot push through the mutilated vulva.

In cultures that practice female circumcision, it is generally believed that women are highly sexed and by nature promiscuous. Circumcision curbs their wild sexual desires and a constricted vagina ensures virginity. Because of social pressure, even mothers who disapprove of their daughters' circumcision participate in the practice because if they refuse, their daughter(s) would be ostracized, remain unmarried, and consequently become financially destitute. Thus, disabling women makes them more marriageable, more dependent on their husbands for economic survival, and, consequently, available for any sexual, emotional, or domestic demands made upon them. As a reward, the young girls who undergo circumcision receive special clothes and good food associated with the event and often feel proud of being like everyone else (Herbert, 1989; Lightfoot-Klein, 1989: Dorkenoo and Elworthy, 1992; Kaplan et al., 1993).

Female genital mutilation seems barbaric to most Americans. But what about comparable practices in the United States and other Western countries? Even though they are voluntary, are silicone breast implants, collagen injections, and liposuction any more "civilized" in making women's bodies more acceptable to men?

Social and Demographic Characteristics

About twice as many white and Latino men and women identify themselves as gay as do African American men and women (see the Data Digest). Gays and lesbians are not distributed evenly across the country or across educational levels. As Figure 6.4 shows, they tend to live in large cities and, as a group, to be more highly educated than the general population.

As we will discuss shortly, gays and lesbians for years have faced considerable prejudice and discrimination, a fact that has certainly affected their tendency to cluster in major metropolitan centers. Interestingly, lesbians are less likely than gays to live in big cities, for a number of reasons. First, few large cities have substantial lesbian communities, possibly because there appear to be fewer lesbians than gay men. Second, because lesbians are relatively monogamous, as we will discuss, they may not be as attracted as gays often are to cities, where one can expect to find a great number of potential sexual partners (see also Chapters 5, 7, and 11). Third, there is evidence that our society is generally more accepting of (or at least less suspicious of and less prejudiced toward) women who live together than of men who live together. If lesbian couples can successfully live more closeted lives than can gay male couples, they may not need the anonymity of a large city to pursue their lifestyles (Michael et al., 1994).

Why do the data suggest that gays and lesbians are better educated than the average person? One reason may be that middle-class and college-educated gays and lesbians are simply more willing to report their sexual preferences

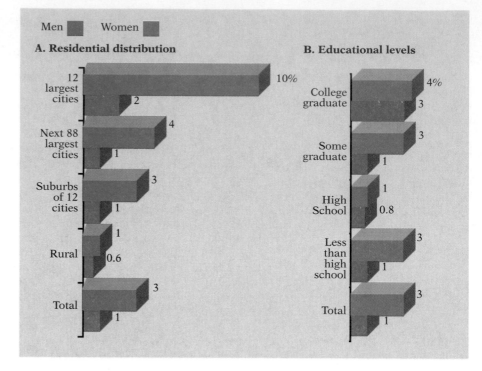

Figure 6.4 Gays and Lesbians: Educational and Residential Characteristics. *Among respondents in the Sex Survey, men who said they'd had same-sex sexual partners during the preceding year tended to live in large cities, but women were more widely dispersed among urban and rural areas (A). Higher levels of education tended to set lesbians apart from the general population, but gays were less clearly distinguished by educational level (B)* (Based on Laumann et al., 1994:303–304).

than are other homosexuals (Michael et al., 1994). In addition, the college-educated may be more willing to admit their homosexuality because some colleges and universities have taken a supportive stance toward same-sex relationships—for example, by extending the same housing and health benefits to them as to heterosexual couples (see Chapter 9). College-educated gays may thus feel less rejection due to their sexual orientation.

Formation of a Gay/Lesbian Identity Although many children experiment with same-sex acts, this does not necessarily mean that they are gay or lesbian. Homosexual identity generally develops over many years. This process of developing a lesbian or gay identity, of recognizing oneself as homosexual, is referred to as "coming out" and often begins in childhood or adolescence, although it may begin at any stage in the life cycle. (Note that "coming out" is also used to refer to the act or process of revealing oneself publicly as a gay male or lesbian.)

Coming out usually involves a number of stages. At first, the person senses that she or he is "different": there may be an attraction to a childhood playmate; a heavy crush on an older person (often a teacher); teenage dreams of romantic scenes with the "wrong" sex partner; or

feelings of boredom and reluctance in dating heterosexual peers (Wolf, 1979). Some gay adults recall feeling alienated because, unlike their peers, they felt no opposite-sex interest (Herdt and Boxer, 1992).

Puberty ushers in a second phase of coming out. All adolescents experience dramatic biological, emotional, and social changes, and one of the most important changes is a growing awareness of their sexuality. Gay and lesbian adolescents often experience their first same-sex attrac-

For both lesbians and gays, attending a gay pride rally is often an important part of accepting and affirming their identity as a homosexual.

tion at this time. They often feel confused, guilty, or afraid and may deny their emerging feelings. In extreme cases, the guilt or self-hatred may even result in suicide (Gibson, 1989).

The third phase involves the person's self-definition and self-acceptance as gay or lesbian. She or he may begin to talk about same-sex relationships fairly openly (at least among family and friends), join gay rights organizations, lobby for politicians who are supportive of legalizing gay marriage, and so on. Behavior during this stage varies widely. One of my students, for example, felt that a major sign of coming out was not hiding his lover's photographs when a plumber or electrician arrived at his apartment. In another case, a student who was too embarrassed as an undergraduate to participate in discussions of lesbianism during one of my courses on gender roles not only organized a lesbian rights student club in law school but is now actively defending gay and lesbian litigants in court.

Even when they have accepted their own sexual preference, some people never reveal this to others or they do so only selectively. In a study of African American, Latino, Asian, and Caucasian male adolescents, for example, the researchers found that one of the greatest impediments to self-disclosure was traditional family values. Those whose families emphasized religion, marriage, and having children, and who spoke a language other than English at home, tended to have stronger feelings of self-rejection (Newman and Muzzonigro, 1993). Even in the most loving and accepting homes, disclosure may not be easy. The family may be rebuffed by friends, feel that it was somehow their fault, or lament the grandchildren they may now never have (Dew, 1994).

Gender and Sexual Orientation
Many researchers assert that gender is a more powerful distinguishing factor among people than sexual orientation is—that is, there are more similarities between heterosexual and homosexual men than between lesbians and gays. First, lesbians and heterosexual women usually have monogamous relationships; gays and heterosexual men are more likely to have more than one lover at a time. A second difference is that for lesbians and heterosexual women, love and sex usually go hand in hand; many gays and heterosexual men often separate emotional intimacy and sex. Third, lesbians and heterosexual women are much less likely to be aroused by visual stimuli than are gays and heterosexual men. The size of the pornography market, which caters to the latter, supports the notion that gay and heterosexual men typically see sex as a commodity. Fourth, both lesbians and heterosexual women are considerably less interested in sex with strangers (or in public places) than are many gays and heterosexual men. Both groups of men cruise for sexual partners; women do not. Fifth, whereas many gays and heterosexual men want as much sexual variety as possible, most women seek long-term partners and less exotic experimentation. Finally, it is heterosexual and homosexual men who are the mainstay of such industries as prostitution, pornography, topless or gay bars, escort services, and adult bookstores (Brehm, 1985; Goode, 1990).

Don't be misled into thinking that analyses of this type are "male bashing." These researchers are simply pointing out that our sexual preferences may be considerably less important in shaping our everyday behavior than our gender-role expectations (see also Chapter 4).

What Causes Homosexuality?
A number of theories have been proposed to explain homosexual preference and behavior. Three of the most influential of these approaches include the psychoanalytic, learning, and biological theories.

Stated very briefly, *psychoanalytic theories* suggest that homosexuals come from families made up of domineering mothers and weak fathers or cold, rejecting mothers and absent fathers (see Bieber et al., 1962; Wolff, 1971). There are two problems with psychoanalytic theories, however. First, many are based on case histories of unhappy, maladjusted people who are not representative of the larger population. Second, these theories do not explain why individuals from families with absent fathers or rejecting mothers do not become homosexual (and, conversely, why those raised in families like those portrayed in shows like "Father Knows Best" and "The Cosby Show" do become homosexual). Furthermore, controlled studies have failed to support the proposition that early family relationships explain homosexuality (Bell et al., 1981).

Learning theories argue that homosexuality, like any other behavior, is learned through a process of rewards and punishments. Experiences with same-sex partners will be reinforcing and thus continued. Another explanation is that behavior is learned through imitation and role modeling. Learning theories, however, do not explain why homosexuality continues despite punishment. Nor do they explain why heterosexual parents produce homosexual children and homosexual parents produce heterosexual children. Learning theories are most useful in explaining why there are such large cultural differences in attitudes about homosexuality (Baldwin and Baldwin, 1989).

Biological theories state that either genes or sex hormones determine sexual preference. Genetic theorists believe that homosexuality is an inherited trait, possibly the result of a recessive gene. For example, Cooper (1978) reviewed a series of studies on homosexuality and found significantly higher rates of homosexuality among identical twins than among fraternal twins. In 1993, Bailey and Pillard interviewed homosexual men and their brothers and found that 52 percent of the identical twins of homosexual men were also homosexual, compared to only 22 percent of fraternal twins and 11 percent of adopted brothers.

Continuing the twin-study format, Bailey and Pillard (1993) examined the incidence of lesbianism in 108 lesbian women with identical or nonidentical twin sisters, and 32 additional lesbians who had adoptive sisters. Among the identical twins of the lesbians, 48 percent were also lesbian, but only 16 percent of the lesbian nonidentical pairs and 6 percent of the genetically unrelated sisters were lesbians. Because the occurrence of homosexuality in those who share identical genes—twins—was so much more likely than in the other sets of siblings, the researchers concluded that biology plays a role in female homosexuality.

A number of studies have focused on physical or physiological differences between homosexual and heterosexual people. Ellis and Ames (1987) conducted an extensive review of both human and animal research on sex hormones and concluded that sexual orientation must be determined before birth. And in one of the most controversial studies on homosexuality, neuroscientist Simon LeVay (1993) examined thin slices of autopsied brain tissue from 19 homosexual men, 16 presumed heterosexual men, and 6 presumed heterosexual women. Isolating tissue from the hypothalamus, an organ deep in the center of the brain that helps to regulate the sex drive and many other basic body functions, LeVay found that a small segment of the anterior (forward) hypothalamus differed significantly in size between heterosexual and homosexual men.

Other studies continue to stir up the debate over a biological basis for homosexuality. In one study, scientists took blood samples from gay men and their families and searched the family DNA for genes that might pass on sexual preferences. Among their sample of male subjects, men's maternal uncles and cousins on the mothers' side seemed most likely to be gay. According to the researchers, 33 out of the 40 pairs of brothers had in common a particular region of the X chromosome (which boys inherit only from their mothers) and where the gene favoring homosexuality was thought to lie (Hamer et al., 1993).

None of the studies of twin comparisons or physiological characteristics have been conclusive. At this point many researchers speculate that sexual orientation is determined by a combination of factors that are both genetic and cultural (see King et al., 1991).

Bisexuality

A **bisexual** is a man or woman who is sexually attracted to people of both sexes. In the popular vernacular, bisexuals are often referred to as "AC/DC," referring to the two opposite electric currents; "switch hitters," borrowed from baseball jargon for a person who bats from either the right or left side of home plate; and "swingers," a term from the 1970s connoting sexual sophistication and open-mindedness (Masters et al., 1992). According to some authorities, bisexuals are more likely than heterosexuals to transmit the AIDS virus to sexual partners (we discuss this further in Chapter 7). Kinsey and associates (1953) found that 9 percent of single women and 16 percent of single men in their 30s could be classified as bisexual. In contrast, a recent national survey reported that only about 1 percent of women and 3 percent of men said they were bisexual (Clements, 1994). These figures are also close to those found by the Sex Survey, as you saw earlier. Kinsey's figures may have been inflated because his samples were volunteers who were not representative of the larger population.

Kinsey proposed that a person's sexuality could range, along a seven-point continuum, from exclusive heterosexuality to exclusive homosexuality. Bisexuality, a blend of both heterosexuality and homosexuality, falls in the middle of the continuum. Adapting Kinsey's scale to a study of 100 bisexuals in the San Francisco area, Martin Weinberg and associates (1994) concluded that bisexuality is a "mingling of sexual feelings, behaviors, and romantic inclinations that does not easily gel with society's categories of typical sexuality" (p. 49). Moreover, they found clear gender differences in the nature of the sexual experience as well as the nature of relationships and the choices people make within their relationships.

Both women and men said that in sexual acts women were more affectionate, personal, tender, caring, nurturing, comforting, and loving. As one woman noted, "Women care about satisfying you sexually and emotionally." And, again, the clearest male-female difference in the nature of a relationship was seen in the ability to express emotions. Both women and men thought it was more difficult for men to reveal their feelings:

Men seem to have a compulsion to [ignore] their own feelings, whereas women are more open and honest about their feelings (male respondent).

Women like to talk about their feelings much more. Men talk about impersonal things—cameras, sports; women talk about their families and their children (female respondent) (Weinberg et al., 1994: 53).

Finally, these researchers found that the choices both women and men reported making in sexual activity and intimate relationships often reflected institutionalized gender scripts (see Chapter 4) rather than behavior that seemed unique to bisexuality. Men preferred attractive partners rather than unattractive ones, for example, and both men and women turned to women when they wanted an emotional involvement and to men when they sought "intellectual sharing."

What causes bisexuality? No one knows. In one of the most extensive studies on this subject, Blumstein and Schwartz (1977) interviewed 156 men and women in a number of cities across the United States who had a history of bisexuality. The respondents ranged in age from 19 to 62 and reflected a broad spectrum of occupations, educational levels, and sexual histories.

Blumstein and Schwartz found "no such thing as a prototypical bisexual career." The majority of men and women had had no same-sex experiences prior to adulthood, and only very rarely reported the problematic family patterns—such as weak, distant fathers and over-bearing mothers—that have been suggested as causal factors in homosexuality. Moreover, many respondents reported taking different routes in identifying themselves as bisexual:

A number of men who had decided they were homosexual at an early age and lived in almost exclusively homosexual networks later met women with whom they had sexual relationships for the first time in their lives. A very large number of both male and female respondents had made at least one full circle—an affair with a man, then one with a woman, and finally back to a man, or vice versa (Blumstein and Schwartz, 1977: 36).

Like the causes of homosexuality, the roots of bisexuality are still in question. Future research may determine whether the causes are cultural, genetic, or both.

Societal Reactions to Homosexuality

Societies vary greatly in their responses to homosexuality. As you saw earlier, some societies are punitive, some tolerate and/or even encourage homosexuality either in adulthood or in childhood, and some require limited homosexual activities during puberty ceremonials. In the United States, societal reactions include both homophobia and a greater acceptance of gays and lesbians.

Homophobia The fear and hatred of homosexuality, **homophobia,** has many sources. Many social scientists consider homophobia an expression of a deeply rooted insecurity about a person's own sexuality and gender identity. Homophobic people often have a strong fundamentalist religious orientation and typically are poorly informed about the nature of homosexuality and its possible causes.

Many people still believe that homosexuality is a conscious choice or a contagious disease that can be "caught" through seduction, infection, or role modeling. For example, a small town in Mississippi became the focus of attention when two lesbian women wanted to transform a 120-acre pig farm into a feminist spiritual retreat and a shelter for homeless women and children. The women received death threats; they found a dead dog draped over their mailbox, and their house was shot at. Many of the town's residents, including clergymen, expressed the belief that the women were recruiting young girls into a lesbian lifestyle (Lynch, 1994).

Conflicting societal views of homosexuality can be seen in some contradictory Colorado legislation in 1992. The state passed a referendum overturning local laws that prohibited discrimination against gays and lesbians. Then, on the grounds that the referendum was unconstitutional because of existing laws, the Colorado Supreme Court placed an injunction on the enforcement of the laws it authorized. Nevertheless, many groups in about a dozen states were preparing similar antigay ordinances a year later (Stumbo, 1993).

Increasing Acceptance Since the late 1980s, there has been an increase in the general acceptance of homosexuality. Although, as the Data Digest shows, many people oppose adoption and civil rights laws for gays and lesbians, homosexuals have achieved equal rights in at least some areas. For example, more than 60 colleges and universities now offer health and other benefits to gay and lesbian couples. Most of these institutions require that to apply for domestic-partner status, an employee must be of legal age to marry and must have been sharing a household on a continuing basis for six to twelve months (Collison, 1993).

Since 1989, the City College of San Francisco has had a department of gay and lesbian studies. Allegheny College, the University of California at Berkeley, and the University of Iowa are among several institutions that are trying to establish minor programs in gay studies, and the City University of New York is developing a Ph.D. program in this field. Such programs, however, have not enjoyed enthusiastic support from all quarters. When Kent State University offered "The Sociology of Gays and Lesbians," and the course was filled quickly by 75 students, a Republican Ohio legislator complained to Kent State's president that neither he nor his constituents wanted their tax dollars spent for a course on homosexuality: "A course like this tends to legitimize an abnormal lifestyle that, in my opinion, is contributing to the disintegration of the moral fiber of our society" (Cage, 1994: A19).

In the last few years, a number of films and television shows have focused on homosexuals or incorporated them as ongoing characters. Even though some gay men charged that the movie *Philadelphia* presented an unrealistic portrayal of gays' struggle with AIDS, it was a commercial success. Many film critics (both straight and gay) praised the movie for addressing the rejection gay men endure in their everyday lives. Nonetheless, *Philadelphia* has been the only commercial movie so far to examine gay life and AIDS.

In comparison, some observers feel that commercial television has come a long way in its portrayal of gays and lesbians. For example, in the 1970s' popular show "Marcus Welby, M.D.," one episode revolved around a male teacher who molested a teenage boy. The implication was that gay men are also pedophiles. In another episode, Dr. Welby advised his patient to suppress his homosexual tendencies and he'd be a good husband and father. In 1977, actor Billy Crystal played the first continuing gay character, Jodie, on ABC's "Soap," a spoof of soap operas. The National Gay Task Force denounced Jodie's portrayal as a stereotype because he was "a limp-wristed, simpering boy who wears his mother's clothes, wants a sex change operation, and allows everyone to insult him without a word of response" (Zurawik, 1994: 10H). Nonetheless, some observers were heartened that a major network would even introduce a gay character as a regular in a popular series.

In the 1990s, gays and lesbians began to appear on many television networks. In 1994, for example, two gay men—bed-and-breakfast owners Eric and Ron—were married with great ceremony on the popular "Northern Exposure." In "Sisters," a lesbian character, Norma Lear, came out of the closet to her parents. In "Roseanne," actress Sandra Bernhard (who has described herself as bisexual in real life) not only came out of the closet but also played a role in the highly publicized episode in which Roseanne was kissed by a lesbian. And, a gay character in "Melrose Place" has been one of the main roles in the series.

Some observers see such programming as progress, but others are offended. For example, 56 percent of the people in a recent poll felt that media portrayals of gays have had a negative influence on society, 33 percent felt the images have a positive influence, and 11 percent weren't sure (Shapiro et al., 1993). It's worth noting that Fox decided not to air the last season's episode of "Melrose Place" in 1994, which involved a gay kiss (Zurawik, 1994). Nevertheless, some critics feel that television doesn't go far enough, pointing out that, for example, in "The Kiss" episode, Roseanne was back in bed with her husband in the final scene to reassure viewers that heterosexuality was better then homosexuality. In

1995, a New York–based group called the Family Defense Council protested NBC's TV movie about the dismissal of a lesbian military officer, called "Serving in Silence." The film contains a scene in which Colonel Margarethe Cammermeyers (played by Glenn Close), who was discharged from the U.S. army in 1992 after acknowledging that she was a lesbian, kisses another woman. The Family Defense Council spokeswoman said that showing lesbians kissing on TV is "immoral and promotes homosexuality" and that "the great majority of people in the country don't want to see this kind of stuff on TV" (Robb, 1995: 7D).

SEX EDUCATION: WHERE IS IT?

According to one author, our knowledge about sex "has been corrupted by any number of absurd or destructive ideas, almost all of them put forward by people whose main interest is not sex but making money or names for themselves" (Marin, 1983: 54). As you saw at the beginning of this chapter, most American adults are ignorant about sex. Is it any wonder that adolescents know even less? Most have little information about reproductive anatomy and functioning or about contraception (contraceptive methods are discussed in Appendix B). Some of the most common misconceptions about sex and contraceptive methods are illustrated by the following remarks made by male and female adolescents (Scott et al., 1988: 675–82):

The pill: "It kills the egg." "It stops girls permanently from having kids." "The babies are born early." "[It makes] you paralyzed." "The pill kills the sperm in the vagina."

The IUD (intrauterine device:) "It lasts 5 years, then it may sink in and be hard to take out." "It causes strokes and headaches." "It can catch on the baby's foot if you get pregnant." "The girl might forget to change it every month."

The diaphragm: "It can get stuck." "It may burst." "The girl has to replace it once a month."

Cream/foam/jelly: "It can cause an infection." "Jelly kills the sperm and may affect the man's penis."

Douche: "It washes the baby out."

Condom: "The rubber stops circulation in the penis." "If you use them more than one time, they get stuck in the vagina." "Most girls are afraid of it—that it will come off and stay inside them." "It may explode."

In a study of urban, low-income, African American and Hispanic youth ages 15 and 24, Norris and Ford (1994) found that young men, especially, were unwilling to use condoms because they claimed that sex didn't feel right when condoms were used, that it was embarrassing to buy or put on condoms, and that using condoms would make the partner think they were having sex with other people. Thus, these youths were more likely both to become infected with STDs or HIV and to impregnate their partners.

Despite the lack of sexual knowledge among most young people, the American public has mixed feelings about sex education. Some counties refuse to fund any program in the schools that counsels unmarried people about contraceptives. Others have barred all sex-education courses, arguing that sex should be taught only in the home. Many parents are often unable or unwilling to provide their children with the information they need. Further, many elementary and high school teachers are no better prepared than are parents to teach children and adolescents about human sexuality.

The Content of Sex Education

In states and local school districts that permit sex education in the schools, courses still focus largely on puberty, the reproductive system, dating, and the responsibilities of parenthood. Asked to rate sex-education classes, many high school students have criticized their courses as repetitive and superficial and as failing to provide practical information (such as access to birth-control methods) or to address the social and psychological aspects of sexuality (such as whether or when to have sex) (Minton, 1993).

Parents and Teachers In towns and cities across the United States a very vocal minority of parents has been effective in opposing sex education in schools. This group argues that sex education in the schools will put ideas into young children's heads and increase promiscuity.

There are two problems with these arguments. The first is that most parents do *not* teach

At King Junior High School in Berkeley, California, the 9th-grade "social-living" class includes instruction in sexual anatomy. Do you think teachers should provide this information, or should parents be responsible for educating their children about sexuality?

their children about sex. Rather than engage in an open dialogue with adolescents (admittedly, this is not always easy to do because many adolescents think their parents are old-fashioned), parents often lapse into "adultspeak": They tend to tell adolescents what to do without discussing the reasons for or implications of various behaviors, such as everything that's required to care for a child after it is born (Fullilove et al., 1994). Moreover, many parents have an unrealistic image of the role they actually play in their children's sex education. Rozema (1986) conducted a literature review of studies that compared parents' and children's answers about sex education. Although 75 percent of fathers and nearly 66 percent of mothers said they were their children's major sources of sex information, only 7 percent of the young men and 29 percent of the young women saw their parents in the same light. Most said they got their information from peers.

The second problem is that parents sometimes provide inaccurate, incomplete, or misleading information. For example, Tucker (1989) found that although mothers said that they were their daughters' primary source of information about the menstrual cycle, intercourse, and contraception, most of the daughters felt that their

mothers' talks were "cursory and in the form of clichés." The mothers gave little information on such topics as male and female anatomy and the availability or correct use of contraceptives.

Finally, a number of educators feel that sex education is taught too late. Most schools do not start teaching about sex until the ninth or tenth grade, but many students start experimenting with sex by the end of the seventh grade (Minton, 1993).

Gender Stereotypes Gender stereotypes and the double standard are apparently common among some immigrants who hold very traditional views of sexual behavior. Haitian, Portuguese, and several groups of Latino high school students reported that sexual activity for adolescent males is generally accepted by both adults and their peers as part of normal male adolescence, but that girls who have more than one boyfriend may be labeled "loose" in their communities. Educators face several problems here. One dilemma is how to encourage female assertiveness in the face of cultural norms that disapprove of it (Ward and Taylor, 1994). Another problem is how to encourage such assertiveness without at the same time encouraging sexual freedom that may harm the young women.

In another example of the double standard, many sexually active adolescents still believe that the responsibility for contraception lies with the female. Among one group, many of whom had had sex by age 13 (nearly 56 percent of the boys and 19 percent of the girls), nearly 50 percent of the boys and 27 percent of the girls said that birth control was the girl's responsibility (Wilson, 1989). In a similar study of ninth-grade, inner-city adolescents, Reis and Herz (1989) found that the majority of 13-year-old boys felt no responsibility whatsoever to use birth control.

What Have We Learned So Far?

Placing sex education in the context of a values framework may be more successful than value-free education. A values framework focuses on moral and ethical issues that guide a person's actions and decisions. It differentiates between right and wrong and emphasizes the worth of each individual and the individual's responsibility to the group and society. At the same time, a values framework encourages students to voice and listen to varying opinions, to consider different values, and to examine the consequences of different choices with respect to sexual matters. For example, in a study of adolescents between the ages of 14 and 18 who were members of a large Protestant church in a Dallas suburb, Powell and Jorgensen (1985) found that 77 percent of the adolescents in a program that stressed values said that the program made them feel more confident, more knowledgeable, and less confused about sexual choices.

Another example comes from the Emory University School of Medicine, which implemented an innovative outreach program to help eighth graders postpone sexual involvement (Howard and McCabe, 1990). The program used teenage role models to present information, identify pressure areas, role-play responses to pressures, teach assertiveness skills, and discuss problem situations. By the end of the eighth grade, students who had not participated in the program were as much as five times more likely to have begun having sex than were those who had been in the program. The program students were also more likely to continue to postpone sexual involvement through the ninth grade, to have less sexual activity after the ninth grade, and to have fewer pregnancies.

Which sex-education programs are the most effective? Probably those that endorse more than one approach in communicating with young people. In a review of numerous school-based programs, Kirby and associates (1994) found that the most effective curricula had six common characteristics. First, they were grounded in social learning theories that recognized the importance of societal pressure and taught youths how to resist peer pressure to engage in sex. Second, they focused on specific issues such as delaying the initiation of intercourse or using protection.

Third, through experiential activities they conveyed information on the risks of unprotected sex and how to avoid those risks. The most effective programs were active and personalized: Students participated in small group discussions, games or simulations, role playing, and brainstorming and in real-world exercises such as locating contraceptives in local drugstores and visiting family-planning clinics. Fourth, effective programs included activities that addressed the problem of social and media pressure to have sex (such as the use of sex in advertising designed to sell products, or the "lines" that people typically use to persuade someone to have sex). Fifth, they reinforced age- and experience-appropriate individual values and group norms against unprotected sex. For example, instruction about postponing sexual intercourse was aimed at middle school–age students; information about how to use condoms was directed at older students. Finally, through role playing and other techniques, the best programs developed skills in communication, negotiation, and refusal to bow to pressure.

CONCLUSION

One of the biggest *changes* since the turn of the century is that we are better informed about human sexuality. Today we have more *choices* in sexual activity because our society is generally more accepting of sex outside of marriage and of same-sex partners. But there are also a number of *constraints*. One constraint shared by people of all ages is the lack of accurate information about human sexual anatomy and physiology. Another that is particularly important for the young is the absence of a framework of values to support them in making responsible decisions. Sexual decision making continues to be important throughout the life cycle, as we will see in the next chapter.

Taking Action

Help a Teenager Say Yes to Responsible Sexual Behavior

In many marriage and family courses, college students are required to undertake a practical or applied project. Here are some ideas for getting involved in programs that are designed to educate young people about sexuality and the risks of unprotected sexual activity.

• Most educators welcome college students as **volunteers or assistants in sex-education classes.** Find out what the middle school and high school in your area are or are not doing in sex education, and volunteer a few hours a week. You might review and suggest videos, prepare instructional materials, or help implement an existing sex-education curriculum. For example, one of my students, working with teachers and the principal, prepared a brochure to discourage teenage sex that was distributed widely among middle schoolers and their parents.

• The Adolescent Pregnancy Prevention Clearinghouse at the Children's Defense Fund (25 E Street N.W., Washington, DC 20001; 202–628–8787) has a $1 brochure entitled "Preventing Children Having Children: What You Can Do" (suggested in Jackson, 1992). Order the brochure and ask about materials on successful **programs to prevent pregnancy.** Then write letters to the editor, to school principals, and to school boards endorsing some of these materials. Be sure always to identify yourself as a college student because many adults still perceive college students as irresponsible, self-centered people who don't care about the important issues that confront our society.

• Find out how to get copies of national and local **posters that discourage early sex or teach older teenagers to use condoms.** One source is Campaign for Our Children, 120 West Fayette Street, Suite 1200, Baltimore, MD 21201 (410–576–9015). Student clubs could devote part of their proceeds from fund-raising to purchase these posters. Then ask junior high or high school principals and educators for permission to hang the posters in the schools. Be sure that your club's or college's affiliation is very visible on the posters. This shows middle schoolers and high school students that many college students support abstinence and/or use of safer methods during sexual intercourse.

SUMMARY

1. Sex involves more than physical pleasure. Emotional intimacy and communication must accompany the sexual act to ensure long-term, committed, and happy relationships.

2. Sexual activity encompasses many behaviors other than sexual intercourse, for example, masturbation, petting, and oral sex.

3. All people experience the four stages of physiological sexual response—excitement, plateau, orgasm, and resolution—but our sexual behaviors and intimate relationships are shaped by our cultural expectations and often differ between the genders.

4. There has probably been more of an evolution, rather than a revolution, in our sexual attitudes and behavior since the turn of the century. Most Americans today report fairly conventional and satisfying sexual relationships.

5. Sexual scripts specify what is legitimate or unacceptable sexual activity and delineate the boundaries of sexual behavior. Although sexual scripts are less traditional today than they were in the past, the double standard is still widespread.

6. Sexual fantasies are healthy in providing a safety valve for pent-up feelings, boosting our self-image, and anticipating sexual activity with others.

7. People differ in their sexual orientation—that is, their preference for partners of the opposite sex (heterosexual), the same sex (homosexual), or both sexes (bisexual). No one knows why sexual orientation varies. Competing explanations include psychoanalytic, learning, and biological theories.

8. Although homosexuals have made some progress in achieving civil rights, homophobia is still a common reaction to gay men and lesbians. Homophobia is often a reflection of ignorance about homosexuality, insecurity about a person's own sexuality, and authoritarian perspectives toward life in general.

9. Most of us do not learn about sex in the home. Much of our information, and misinformation, come from peers and the media.

10. Despite the lack of knowledge about sex, there is a great deal of resistance to sex education in the schools. When sex education is taught, the most effective programs are those that are targeted at appropriate age groups and that emphasize values and involve students in specific, risk-reducing activities.

KEY TERMS

ADDITIONAL READING

Journals devoted to human sexuality topics include *Archives of Sexual Behavior, Family Planning Perspectives, Journal of Homosexuality, Journal of Sex and Marital Therapy, SIECUS Report,* and *Journal of Sex Research.*

BRUCE BAWER, *A Place at the Table: The Gay Individual in American Society* (New York: Poseidon Press, 1993). Criticizing the most radical groups of the gay subculture for focusing only on sexuality, the author examines contemporary attitudes toward homosexuality in marriage, family politics, education, religion, and literature.

KAREN BOURIS, *The First Time: Women Speak Out about "Losing Their Virginity"* (Berkeley, CA: Conari Press, 1993). Interviews with 150 women about their first experience of sexual intercourse, which range from romantic love to "just get it over with" to incest.

JANICE M. IRVINE, ed., *Sexual Cultures and the Construction of Adolescent Identities* (Philadelphia: Temple University Press, 1994). Readings showing how adolescent sexuality is shaped by ethnic and racial identity.

EDWARD O. LAUMANN, JOHN H. GAGNON, ROBERT T. MICHAEL, and STUART MICHAELS, *The Social Organization of Sexuality: Sexual Practices in the United States* (Chicago: University of Chicago Press, 1994). A comprehensive book on sexual behavior in the United States based on a national probability sample. Topics include heterosexual and homosexual activities, cohabitation, sexually transmitted infections, and fertility. The findings have also been published in a "general interest" version by Robert T. Michael, John H. Gagnon, Edward O. Laumann, and Gina Kolata, *Sex in America: a Definitive Survey* (Boston: Little, Brown, 1994).

SIMON LEVAY, *The Sexual Brain* (La Jolla, CA: MIP Press, 1993). The major theme of this book deals with the many variations in human sexual behavior. Some of the topics include why human beings are sexual beings, how and why we become sexual, and the role of nature and nurture in producing sexual behaviors and sexual feelings.

WILLIAM H. MASTERS, VIRGINIA E. JOHNSON, and ROBERT C. KOLODNY, *Heterosexuality* (New York: HarperCollins, 1994). Topics include sex and sexuality; sexual dysfunctions; HIV infection, AIDS, and other sexually transmitted diseases; and sex and aging.

ROBERT WAYNE PELTON, *Loony Sex Laws That You Never Knew You Were Breaking* (New York: Walker, 1992). Unusual or unenforced sex laws in the United States and many other countries. For fun.

MARTIN S. WEINBERG, COLIN J. WILLIAMS, and DOUGLAS W. PRYOR, *Dual Attraction: Understanding Bisexuality* (New York: Oxford University Press, 1994). Based on a study of bisexuals in San Francisco, examines such topics as becoming bisexual, marriage, jealousy, being "out," homosexuality, and facing AIDS.

FRANCES YOUNGER, *Five Hundred Questions Kids Ask about Sex (and Some of the Answers)* (Springfield, IL: Charles C. Thomas, 1992). Written by a longtime public school sex education counselor, this book provides a breakdown of some of the most commonly asked questions by (and the author's answers to) children, ranging from elementary school through high school. It also includes questions of children in special education classes.

7

Sexual Expression Throughout the Life Course

Data Digest

- In general, 70 percent of teenagers claim that they were still **virgins at age 16.**

- At the same time, in a survey of high school students, **almost 50 percent of females and 61 percent of males reported having had sexual intercourse.** Among African Americans, the figures were 60 percent for females and 88 percent for males; among whites, they were 47 percent for females and 57 percent for males; and among Latinos, 45 percent for females and 63 percent for males.

- Among sexually experienced high school seniors, **almost a third report having had four or more partners.**

- According to a Centers for Disease Control survey of high school students, only **49 percent of males and 40 percent of females reported using some method of contraception** at last intercourse.

- Among college students who report premarital sexual activity, **the gender gap has narrowed.** In 1965, 29 percent of the women and 65 percent of the men said they were having sex; by the early 1990s, 62 percent of freshmen women and 66 percent of the men said they were sexually active.

- **Disapproval of extramarital sex increased** from 70 percent in 1973 to over 77 percent in 1991. About 17 percent admit having had sex outside of marriage

- Although they make up only 12 percent of the U.S. population, **African Americans represent almost 32 percent of persons with AIDS.** Similarly, although less than 10 percent of the population, **Latinos make up almost 17 percent** of AIDS-infected people.

SOURCES: Robinson et al., 1991; Pepe et al., 1993; Centers for Disease Control, 1992, 1994; Morin, 1994; *Siecus*, 1994; Smith, 1994.

Melanie (a fictitious name), one of my students, describes a recent experience:

My sister and I were on a cruise in the Bahamas over Christmas break. The director of activities addressed the passengers about all the wonderful events taking place on the ship. He began by telling a joke, but no one knew it was a joke until the punch line. He said, "I was on my way down to greet all of you, and in closing my cabin door, I accidentally brushed a woman's breast with my elbow. When I apologized, she said, "That's all right, young man. If the rest of you is nearly as hard as your elbow, I'm in room 345." My sister and I were completely appalled and walked out of the room.

Melanie said that she wasn't a prude, but she thought such a remark was highly unprofessional in that situation. Then she added, "I guess you just can't get away from sex nowadays."

Some people on the cruise probably enjoyed the joke. Others, like Melanie and her sister, were offended. In either case, it is probably true that "you can't get away from sex nowadays." Our sexual lives affect us as individuals and fam-

ily members, from birth to death. In Chapter 6 we examined the ways in which people learn to be sexual. This chapter focuses on sexual behavior throughout the life cycle.

REASONS FOR ENGAGING IN SEXUAL ACTIVITY

Sex, especially the first experience of intercourse, doesn't "just happen." As you saw in the last chapter, we learn sexual scripts in society. Sex is usually not spontaneous but progresses through such stages as approaching each other, flirting, touching, or asking directly for sex. Though usually a passionate act, sex for the first time in a particular relationship typically occurs after some planning and thought (Sprecher and McKinney, 1993).

Christopher and Cate (1984) found several general reasons underlying the decision to have sex for the first time:

Affection/communication: Partners love each other, feel they can talk to each other, or expect to marry.

Arousal/receptivity: Partners experience physical arousal or receptivity to sexual advances.

Obligation and pressure: One partner may feel an obligation to have intercourse for fear of hurting the other's feelings or losing the other's interest. Partners may also be pressured to have sex by peers who engage in intercourse.

Curiosity: Inexperienced partners may be curious about sex itself; some people may be curious about how it would be to make love to a particular person.

Circumstantial: One or both partners may lose control because they've consumed alcohol or other drugs, or one partner might plan a seduction.

Once people have committed to a close and ongoing relationship, they also have a number of reasons to continue to have sexual relations. Reviewing some of the literature on sex in close relationships, Sprecher and McKinney (1993) concluded that sex serves many functions (see Figure 7.1 for a summary of the reasons for first sexual intimacy and the functions served by a continuing sexual relationship). Sex can be an expression of *love* and *affection*. It can increase *intimacy*, a feeling of closeness that is emotional (allowing the expression of feelings), social (encouraging the sharing of friends), intellectual (promoting the sharing of ideas), and recreational (leading to a sharing of interests and hobbies). Sex can encourage *self-disclosure*: Learning how to tell a partner what feels good in sexual activity can promote disclosure of oneself in other ways. Sex also helps promote *interdependence* because the partners depend on each other for sexual satisfaction.

Once a close relationship develops, partners must engage in maintenance strategies to keep the relationship going. Sexual and other physical expressions of intimacy are one such strategy, although there are many other ways (and perhaps even more important ones) of *maintaining a relationship,* such as communicating clearly with one another, respecting each other, and making sacrifices for a partner. Finally, both love and sex pro-

Figure 7.1
Why We Have Sex.

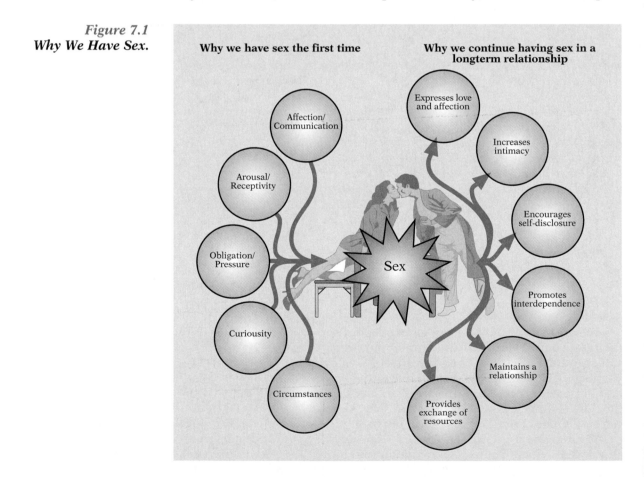

vide an *exchange of resources* in an intimate relationship (see discussion of social exchange theory in Chapter 2). Such an exchange may be sincere; for example, a shy person may like a partner who is assertive during lovemaking. In other cases, however, an exchange may be manipulative; for example, a sexually desirable person may use sex as a weapon or a tool for acquiring power, status, or money (Flores, 1994).

PREMARITAL SEX

The first sexual experience can be happy and satisfying. It can also be a source of worry, disappointment, or guilt:

My first time was very unpleasant. The boy I was with rushed and fumbled around and then came so fast it was over before it started. I thought, "What's so great about this?" For weeks afterward, I was afraid I had V.D. and had bad dreams about it (Masters et al., 1992: 226).

Whether the first experience is euphoric or disastrous, premarital sex has become more socially acceptable for adults over the years. For example, the proportion of women who feel that premarital sexual intercourse is immoral decreased from 65 percent in 1970 to 45 percent in 1990 (Roper Organization, 1990). But approximately 86 percent of adults in a national survey said that premarital intercourse for teenagers ages 14 to 16 is always or almost always wrong (Smith, 1990). Despite this disapproval, many adolescents are having premarital sex.

Sex and Adolescence

For many adolescents in the United States, becoming a sexual being is not an easy process. Unlike some nonindustrialized societies, Western countries do not have rites of passage to mark the onset of adulthood or clearly agreed-upon rules of sexual behavior after puberty. Instead, adolescents often seek and get information about sex from unreliable sources. It has been estimated that the average teenager sees between 1,900 and 2,400 sex-related messages per year on television alone (Brown et al., 1990). As we discussed in Chapter 6, many of these messages may not only be inappropriate for young people but also dangerous (as when they fail to emphasize the importance of using contraceptives, especially condoms).

The tasks adolescents face as they navigate through unknown sexual waters are formidable: They must forge an identity that includes culturally dictated gender-role expectations. They must learn about sexual and romantic relationships. They must develop a personal set of sexual values (Masters et al., 1994). Many adolescents have sexual intercourse before accomplishing these tasks. For example, by age 13, 20 percent of African American, 3 percent of white, and 4 percent of Latino boys said they had had sexual intercourse (Sonenstein et al., 1991). By the ninth grade, 37 percent of female and almost 50 percent of male high school students surveyed reported having had sexual intercourse (Centers for Disease Control, 1992). Even though all these rates are high, African American high school students report the highest rates of early sexual activity and Latinos and whites the lowest (see the Data Digest).

Some adolescents say they regret having become sexually active so early. A random telephone survey of 503 teenagers in grades nine through twelve, for example, found that 62 percent of the sexually active girls and 48 percent of the boys said they "should have waited until they were older." In addition, although 81 percent of the boys said that "sex is a pleasurable experience," only 59 percent of the girls agreed (*Siecus*, 1994). Although the study did not ask why sex was or was not pleasurable, the results could indicate that adolescents are not mature enough to deal with some of the emotional issues (such as commitment) or practical problems (such as pregnancy) that can result from sexual intercourse.

Adolescent sex sometimes results in unwanted pregnancy, which can be highly traumatic for a teenage girl and for her teenage partner as well.

Reasons for Adolescent Sex "Raging hormones," the old explanation for adolescent sex, is more fiction than fact. Although adolescents who mature early are more likely to become sexually active at a younger age, the degree of interest in sex varies among young people. Some feel a need for frequent sexual gratification, but many do not (Kelly, 1994).

One reason for early premarital sex, especially for boys, is *peer pressure*. Boys as young as 13 brag about their sexual prowess (though often they are lying) and ridicule friends who have not "scored." Boys may even challenge a friend to "prove his manhood" (Besharov, 1993). Girls, still taught to be accommodating and supportive (see Chapters 4 and 6), may have sex because they want to please a boyfriend. Interestingly, when an obstetrics and gynecology professor at Emory University asked 1,000 girls in Atlanta what subject they most wanted to learn about in sex education classes, 82 percent answered, "How to say no without hurting the other person's feelings" (reported in Besharov, 1993: 57).

Environmental factors also play an important role in early premarital sex. There is no one reason for early sexual experience; rather, various risk factors (see in Table 7.1) produce a cumulative effect. The more of these factors that are present in an adolescent's (or even a preadolescent's) life, the more likely it is that he or she will become sexually active at an early age.

The opportunity for adolescent sex is greater today than in the past. Getting a temporary driving license at the age of 15, which many states permit, makes it easier to meet prospective sexual partners. In households where a single parent or both parents work outside the home, teens can have sex at home without being caught. Moreover, many parents feel helpless against the rising tide of teenage sexual behavior and don't even try to discuss abstinence or contraception with their adolescent children (Besharov, 1993).

Early sexual experiences are also influenced by cultural attitudes and expectations. For example, finding that among Miami teenagers Latino women knew the least about human anatomy and contraceptive methods, Scott et al. (1988) underlined the importance of two concepts among Latin American women: *verguenza* ("shame"), which particularly connotes shame and embarrassment about body parts and the notion that "good" girls should not know about sexuality; and *marianismo* (from the name of the

Table 7.1 _____

What Factors Are Most Likely to Lead to Early Sexual Intercourse among Adolescents?

Use of alcohol or other drugs, such as marijuana, hashish, cocaine, crack, heroin, angel dust, tranquilizers, barbiturates, or amphetamines

Delinquent behavior, such as stealing, hitting an adult at school, getting into physical fights with peers, or selling drugs

Smoking

Dating before age 16

Having a low grade point average

Dropping out of school

Frequent geographic moves, which decrease parental supervision while parents are involved in the mechanics of the move or in finding new jobs; children sometimes use sex to establish new friendships or combat loneliness

Lack of parental support; an adolescent may feel that a parent doesn't care about him or her, is not available, or does not include the children in important decision making

Experiencing parental divorce during adolescence

Poverty

Sexual abuse

Minimal parental monitoring of the adolescent's activities and friends

Permissive parental values toward sex (more commonly reported by males than females)

A lack of neighborhood monitoring, such as "keeping an eye on what teens are up to" or reporting unacceptable behavior to parents

Involvement in a committed relationship

Virgin Mary), which comprises a set of values relating to chastity, purity, and virtue.

Despite these traditional expectations, however, sexual behavior among Latino girls is changing. As you saw in the Data Digest, over 40 percent of Latino high school girls report that they have had sexual intercourse. Although these self-reports, like others, may or may not be reliable, there is evidence that as immigrants assimilate into U.S. culture, their children often internalize peer values and behaviors. A study of Cuban families in New Jersey highlighted this generation gap in attitudes about daughters' virginity. Although mothers still taught their daughters that virginity was a highly regarded virtue, one teenager said, "If you are a virgin, you are a nerd, . . . an oddity." Based on a "silent agreement," younger Cubans had premarital sex and parents pretended not to know (Prieto, 1992).

Finally, some premarital sexual experiences

Abstinence
makes the heart
grow fonder.

It's not easy to sell young people on abstinence. Can you think of other messages that would be equally or more effective?

15-year-old boy: *"When I tried to talk with them, they gave 'old' opinions and then they changed the subject. They tried to impress on me the importance of virginity. They seemed very uptight and after that experience I did not try again."*

17-year-old girl: *"I can't be open with my parents about sex because they don't want me doing anything more than 'necking' and they would be angry if they knew I did more"* (Hass, 1979: 166–68).

Another reason adolescents are reluctant to discuss sex with their parents is that they do not want to disappoint, hurt, or shock them. Many teenagers feel that parents see them in an unrealistically innocent light, and they do not want to tarnish this idealized image

16-year-old boy: *"They probably think I've done stuff but not as much as I have. They think I'm just a good basketball player and a goody-two-shoes."*

16-year-old girl: *"They have so much faith and trust in me. It would just kill them if they found out I had made love before. There's a lot of pressure on me to be good since I'm the most successful of my brothers and sisters. They feel I'm a reflection of all their efforts and their ideal child"* (Hass, 1979: 168).

Interestingly enough, even though the Hass research was published almost two decades ago, the reasons for not talking to parents about sex have remained fairly constant.

Children's sexual attitudes and behavior are affected by gender and family stability. Adolescent girls raised in homes without fathers or in divorced or stepfamilies are much more likely than others to become sexually active at an early age. The likelihood that boys will be sexually active early on is affected more by disruption in family structure than by structure, per se. Thus, for example, boys who changed from a two-parent household to a single-mother household were more likely to be sexually active at an early age than were boys who had been raised in single-mother or other types of households from birth (Kinnaird and Gerrard, 1986; Newcomer and Udry, 1987; Dorius et al., 1993). This may be due to a lack of parental supervision during the divorce process or to the entertainment, by either parent, of overnight guests, sending the message that sex outside of marriage is acceptable.

are nonvoluntary. In a recent study of female adolescents in the seventh, ninth, and eleventh grades, Small and Kerns (1993) found that 10 percent of the eleventh graders reported forced intercourse and 11 percent reported unwanted touching. The most common factors associated with a young girl's being forced to have sex include her mother's having an abusive boyfriend, illicit drug use (by the parent, victim, or the nonparental abuser), lack of parental monitoring in the home, a history of sexual abuse in the victim's family, and the victim's living apart from parents before the age of 16.

How Influential Are Parents? One reason children and parents rarely discuss sex is that, except for issues directly related to pregnancy and childbirth, many parents feel uncomfortable talking about sex (Brock and Jennings, 1993). Moreover, if teenagers feel that they and their parents have different attitudes, they, too, will be reluctant to discuss sex:

Sex and Young Adults

Like their younger counterparts, more college-aged students are also engaging in sex. Premarital intercourse has increased considerably since the mid-1960s, especially among women (see the Data Digest). The post–high school years represent a transitional phase for most young adults. High school graduates who take jobs, enroll in vocational training programs, or join the military services have more opportunity and money for recreational pursuits that may include sex. Many young adults who go on to college—especially in a residential setting—find themselves free for the first time from parental supervision. This first experience of independence among people of the same age and social class provides a fertile environment for courting and mating.

Who Initiates Sexual Contact? Traditional sexual scripts dictate that the man should initiate sexual contact because "nice girls don't." Some young women are becoming much more assertive, however. For example, instead of sitting by the phone, they frequent singles bars, call men they're interested in, and in other ways put themselves in situations that invite sexual contact, such as going to a man's apartment or dorm room. In steady dating relationships, women may touch or stroke a partner and compliment his sexuality or make other positive comments about his appearance to arouse him (O'Sullivan and Byers, 1993).

Men and women may define initial sexual contact differently, however. Anderson and Aymami (1993) found that male college students reported female encouragement of sexual contact more often than female students reported initiating such contact. Attributing this discrepancy to traditional gender roles, the researchers suggested that if women see men as "always ready and interested in sex," they may view their own behavior as simply giving the man what he already wants, not as initiating something that *they* want. It's also possible that the notion of a woman initiating sexual contact is so contrary to many men's expectations that they exaggerate such behavior when they recall and report it.

Do Women and Men Have Different Reasons? College-aged males and females often engage in sex for different reasons. Women typically describe their first sexual experience as being with someone they love or within the confines of a serious relationship, either going

Although women still are more likely than men to have sex only in a committed relationship, many young women today admit to enjoying casual sex, and they are also more likely than in the past to initiate sexual activity.

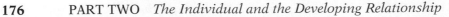

steady or engaged. Today's young women may rationalize intercourse in the same way that earlier generations justified petting ("It's O.K. if I love him"). In contrast, men are more likely to have had their first sexual experience with someone they consider "just a friend" or with someone they just met (Christopher and Cate, 1988). Across racial and ethnic groups, parents appear to be more tolerant of premarital sex in sons than in daughters (Padilla and O'Grady, 1987; Prieto, 1992). The growing numbers of women who are having intercourse when "just dating," however, suggest that these traditional views may be changing.

There is also some evidence that the notion that sex is acceptable only in a committed relationship may be false. A study of racially diverse college students found women inconsistent in their attitudes toward traditional gender-role expectations and sexual behavior: Although 92 percent of females and 65 percent of males said that an emotional involvement was always or generally necessary for them to participate in sexual intercourse, 44 percent of the females and 65 percent of the males reported they had had sex without such involvement (Lottes, 1993).

But Will You Respect Me Tomorrow? Not if we're having casual sex, according to recent research. Several studies report that many men still have a double standard about sex and commitment. They often judge sexually permissive women as acceptable or even desirable for casual dates or as regular sexual partners but unacceptable for long-term commitments or as marriage partners. In contrast, the women in these studies viewed sexually permissive men as less desirable as either casual dates or long-term partners (Sprecher et al., 1991; Oliver and Sedikides, 1992). As more women have premarital sex, it's not clear where people are going to find virgins or partners with little sexual experience.

Is Virginity Making a Comeback?

We live in a society that is full of contradictions about sex (see the box "Looking for a Virgin?"). We look down on poor women who have children out of wedlock, but feature the illegitimate children of rock stars and other celebrities in mainstream magazines. Extramarital affairs and *intermarital* sexual relationships (having sex between marriages) are becoming commonplace,

CONSTRAINTS

Looking for a Virgin?

"Minneapolis" wrote a "Dear Ann Landers" letter that illustrates the difficulty of finding a virgin in a sexually permissive society:

I am a single male in my mid-twenties. I've had a great deal of sexual experience, but now I am ready to settle down and get married. I want to marry a virgin. Although I've been around a lot, I insist on having an untouched woman for a wife. I will not get married unless I can find one. I realize that as I get older, most virgins will be a lot younger than I am. In fact, a friend told me most virgins today are 12 or younger. I'm not the kind of man who could date anyone under 18.

How can I find what I'm looking for?

Ann Landers replied, "Dear Minneapolis: Men like you make me tired. You and your horny brothers would have better luck if you left some virgins alone in your younger years" (*Washington Post*, December 15 1993, D12).

Although Landers was not very sympathetic, "Minneapolis" is not alone in wanting a virgin for a spouse. For example, in the study of a racially diverse college campus cited earlier, Lottes (1993) found that 12 percent of the men and 7 percent of the women said it was "very important" or "important" to marry a virgin.

The quest for virgins may be-

come increasingly difficult because some religious groups are beginning to accept nonmarital sex. The Rabbinical Assembly Commission on Human Sexuality, which sets official policy for Conservative rabbis, has encouraged acceptance of nonmarital sexual practices. The commission focused its report on "mature people," condemned adultery, and said that marriage is still the appropriate place for sexual relations, but nevertheless offered guidelines for sex outside of marriage. In response, some Orthodox rabbis rejected the proposals as being "against every and any Jewish principle of human behavior" (Somerville, 1994).

but we tell children that sex outside of marriage is wrong.

Despite these contradictions, virginity and sexual abstinence are not cultural dinosaurs, and, in fact, several factors encourage both. The first is physical health. As you will see later in this chapter, some sexually transmitted diseases have devastating results, such as sterility, deformities in infants, and death. Early sexual activity can cause long-term problems (such as an unwanted pregnancy or a baby raised in poverty), especially because about half of all adolescents do not use condoms or any other form of disease prevention or birth control.

A second basis for sexual abstinence is one's set of moral or religious values. For example, during the 137th Southern Baptist Convention, over 100,000 adolescents and young adults pledged chastity before marriage. The movement called True Love Waits began in 1993, when 59 teens took vows of chastity. Since then, it has spread to 26 other Christian groups, including the Roman Catholic Church.

A third factor encouraging abstinence is situational necessity. Someone whose energy is consumed by work, family, or other obligations may not even notice the loss of sexual activity. Unlike food, sleep, and shelter, sex is not a prerequisite for physical survival. Sexual relationships can certainly be satisfying and rewarding, but neither virginity nor abstinence is fatal.

A final reason for abstinence is that many young people are uninformed about sex. As we discussed in Chapter 6, there is a great deal of misinformation about the use of contraceptive methods to prevent pregnancy and condoms to prevent infection from sexually transmitted diseases and HIV. Even adolescents who are informed about sex may not use condoms (Kraft, 1993). Because so many people are ill-informed, and because, as you will see later, increasing numbers of heterosexual women are becoming HIV-infected, women should be much more adamant about protecting themselves (see the box "No Rubbers? No Romping!").

MARITAL SEX

Compared to premarital and especially extramarital sex, marital sex has elicited very little attention from scholars. Despite an avalanche of how-to books on making marriages sexier and more orgasmic, several recent studies report that most married couples are happy with their sex lives.

Frequency of Sex

As we discussed in Chapter 6, a recent national study found that about 40 percent of married people have sex with their partner two or more times a week and about half of all married people have sex with their spouses a few times a month (Laumann et al., 1994). This rate is much higher, as Figure 6.3 showed, than the rate for noncohabiting single people.

Marital sexual activity typically decreases with both partners' age and longevity of the marriage. As a marriage matures, concerns about earning a living, making a home, and raising a family become more pressing than lovemaking.

CHOICES

"No Rubbers? No Romping!"

One of my students, a young woman in her mid-20s who had been seeing the same man for several years, said she had one rule that she never broke: "No rubbers? No romping."

The following dialogue, which has been modified, is based on an anonymous handout that was circulating several years ago:

He: "I won't feel as much if I have a condom on."

She: "You won't feel anything if you don't have a condom on."

He: "I don't have any condoms and we don't want to go out and get some."

She: "I happen to have some with me. What's your favorite color?"

He: "I know I'm clean; I haven't had sex with anyone in months."

She: "I'm clean, too, but either of us could have an infection and not know about it."

He: "It will interrupt sex."

She: "I'll put it on for you. You'll love it."

Couples who report a decline in sexual activity often attribute the change to such things as familiarity and fatigue:

When you're married, there's no pressure to do it when you don't want to or are tired. We have great fun when we do. When I go out, sure, I look but it's great not having to chase girls anymore (cited in Montefiore, 1993: 69).

Changes in leisure time can also reduce sexual activity. As we will see in later chapters, recessions and unemployment have forced many families into the two-paycheck mold, adding the stress of double days to many women's lives. Thus, the revelation, in Figure 7.2, that sex is a much lesser concern for both men and women than managing finances, spending time together, communicating, and sharing household duties should come as no surprise.

Although the frequency of sex decreases, the longer people are married the more likely they are to report that they are very satisfied with their current sex life (Mattox, 1994). And remember that there is a broad range of individual variation. Among some couples, the frequency of sexual intercourse may remain constant or even increase over the years. Among others, sexual expression may change: Intercourse may decrease, but fondling and genital stimulation that lead to orgasm may increase.

Sex and Marital Happiness

There is an old anecdote that one day President and Mrs. Calvin Coolidge (known as "Silent Cal," Coolidge was U.S. president from 1923 to 1928) were visiting a government farm. When Mrs. Coolidge passed the chicken pens, she asked how often the rooster copulated each day and was told "Dozens of times." "Please tell that to the President," Mrs. Coolidge said. The president passed the pens and was told about the rooster. "Same hen every time?" the president asked. "Oh, no, Mr. President, a different one each time." The president said, "Tell that to Mrs. Coolidge."

Does the novelty in lasting marriages wear off? Not at all. Based on a literature review of the relationship between sex and marital happiness, Brehm (1985) concluded that the general quality of a marital relationship is more important than the sex. The studies Brehm examined, the earliest of which was undertaken in 1938, suggested that frequency of sexual intercourse did not correlate with marital happiness. Moreover, the studies conducted in the late 1970s showed that even couples who argue a lot can be very happy if they share common leisure-time activities and enjoy doing some things together.

Social class, however, may affect marital happiness. Greeley (1991) found that college-educated married couples were more likely than non-college-educated couples to say that their spouses respected them and were good lovers and to report such erotic activities as swimming together in the nude. In contrast, in-depth interviews with working-class couples revealed a great deal of dissatisfaction in the sexual relationships, especially among women. The wives complained that their husbands saw sex as a "wife's duty" and resented

Figure 7.2 What People Would Most Like to Change in Their Relationships. *In this Roper survey of married couples, both men and women rated sex only sixth among aspects of their relationships they would like to change. Interestingly, the only parameter on which they disagreed widely was the performance of household chores* (Roper Organization, 1990).

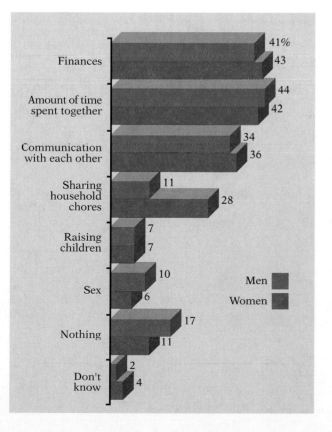

husbands who would not communicate during the day but would expect sex at bedtime. These women submitted to oral sex, even though they did not enjoy it, for various reasons. Some were afraid of losing their husbands. Others used oral sex as a bribe: "He gets different treats at different times, depending on what he deserves. Sometimes I let him do that oral stuff you're talking about to me. Sometimes when he's very good, I do it to him" (Rubin, 1976).

Although such social-class differences should not be generalized, they can be partly explained in terms of exchange theories. Middle-class couples report having more egalitarian relationships than do working-class couples. Middle-class couples have more resources to recharge their sexual relationships by taking romantic trips, having intimate dinners in expensive restaurants, or hiring baby-sitters so they can spend more time together. And because college-educated women have more resources—such as income—they are less likely to remain in marriages in which costs outweigh benefits. Thus, middle-class women can leave a marriage if their husbands' demands—sexual or other—become offensive.

Is the Importance of Sex Exaggerated?

The false notion that most Americans have unhappy sex lives has become big business. Magazines, books, movies, television programs, psychiatrists, counselors, sex clinics, and massage parlors—all benefit financially by convincing us that we need more or better sex. Society has become so obsessed with this subject that sex manuals are constantly on best-seller lists. Yet many of the advice books actually take the joy out of sex. Lewis and Brissett's (1967) analysis of sex manuals concluded that such manuals transform coitus into work, teaching readers to study "techniques," evaluate the "product," and keep to "production schedules."

When sexual intercourse decreases later in marriage, some couples worry that they have "lost that lovin' feelin'." As we have seen, however, less frequent sex is neither unusual nor abnormal. Even young married couples report that companionship is often more important than sexual passion. As one man stated:

I think it's very important, but I don't think it's number one or even number three on the list. On my list it would come fourth. Marriage, as far as

I'm concerned, is friendship and companionship; that ranks first. Then there's consideration for one another, and then trust, and then fourth I'd say your physical relationship. And those three that come before hopefully enhance what you experience in your physical relationship (Greenblatt, 1983: 298).

Finally, the apparent decline in sexual intercourse over time may reflect artificially high rates of first-year intercourse; that is, the latter may not represent what people would "normally" do if they didn't feel pressured to have frequent sex.

EXTRAMARITAL SEX

HUSBAND: *Honey, if I died, would you get remarried?*
WIFE: *Well, I suppose so.*
HUSBAND: *Would you and he sleep in the same bed?*
WIFE: *I guess we would.*
HUSBAND: *Would you make love to him?*
WIFE: *He would be my husband, dear.*
HUSBAND: *Would you give him my golf clubs?*
WIFE: *No. He's left-handed.*

What Is Extramarital Sex?

Hunt (1969) asked 91 people whether the following situation constituted an extramarital affair: "A married person has sexual relations with someone he or she picked up in a bar." Those who had been unfaithful in their own marriages were less likely to see the situation as an affair than were those who had been faithful to their partners. Men typically saw the example as an affair. Women, however, said this was not an affair but "cheating," "running around," or "stepping out."

Hunt observed that "even the seemingly unambiguous term 'infidelity' is not uniformly defined." A number of men said that having sexual relations with a call girl while away from home on business was not "real infidelity" because it did not include caring for the woman or seeing her on a regular basis. In contrast, a *People* magazine survey found that 70 percent of respondents believed that a sexual act is not necessary for a person to be unfaithful; lust was enough to qualify (cited in Frenkiel, 1990).

People use the terms *affair, infidelity, adultery,* and *extramarital sex* interchangeably. For our purposes, *extramarital sex* is sexual contact with someone other than a person's spouse. Pittman (1989: 20) put it more succinctly by defining its opposite, *sexual exclusivity*: "the genitals stay out of the hands or whatever of outsiders."

Rates of Extramarital Sex

Therapists who appear on talk shows often cite rates of extramarital sex as being in the area of 70 percent for men and 50 percent for women. Although such sensationalism is great fodder for talk shows, national surveys have shown that most Americans are faithful, and that extramarital sex rates have even decreased slightly since 1991 (see Table 7.2).

Interestingly, however, when researchers asked people who were either married or had been married at one time whether they had ever committed adultery, 16 percent said yes (21 percent of men, nearly 13 percent of women).

Reasons for Extramarital Sex

Popular magazines routinely publish articles that imply it is a woman's fault if her husband is unfaithful. The articles offer advice on how to please a husband, like refraining from nagging, having cosmetic surgery, losing weight, buying sexy lingerie, and preparing romantic dinners. Interestingly, magazines very rarely advise a husband to please his wife so that she will not be tempted to have an affair.

The complex reasons for adultery include both macro and micro explanations. Although they overlap and are often cumulative, we present them separately for the sake of clarity.

Table 7.2 _____

Married People Who Admitted Having Extramarital Sex During the Preceding Year, 1988–93

	ALL RESPONDENTS	MEN	WOMEN
1988	3.9%	5.0%	2.8%
1989	3.6	5.8	1.7
1990	3.8	5.3	2.3
1991	4.4	5.4	3.4
1993	2.9	4.1	1.9

SOURCES: Cited in Morin, 1994.

Macro Reasons Among the many macro explanations for extramarital sex, five are especially significant:

1. *Economic recessions and depressions* place strains on families. Underemployment (employment below a person's level of training and education), layoffs, and unemployment can create pressures that may increase the incidence of extramarital affairs, family violence, and even lead to suicide. Husbands and wives who are forced to work different shifts or to live in different cities may develop intimate relationships with others.

2. The *purpose of marriage* has changed for many people. Although procreation is still important, many couples today marry primarily for companionship and intimacy. When these needs are not met, outside relationships may become more appealing.

3. In the *anonymity of urban life,* one may meet many people every day and yet be lonely. Unlike small-town residents, people in large cities often get married without knowing each other well, and, as a result, incompatible values may surface only later. Moreover, socially disapproved behaviors like adultery can be concealed more easily in the city.

4. Because today people have greater *longevity,* marriages can last as long as 50 to 60 years, increasing the chances for conflict, dissatisfaction, and infidelity.

5. Beginning in the 1960s, *social movements* have been challenging the status quo in many areas, advocating rights for such groups as women, homosexuals, senior citizens, victims, and children. According to McGinnis (1981), the rise of extramarital affairs has grown out of a similar urge to change past restrictions.

Micro Reasons There are also a number of micro explanations for extramarital sex:

1. *Attitudes about sex* in general are changing. As we have seen, premarital sex is becoming common. Thompson (1983), based on a review of the literature on extramarital sex, has proposed that premarital sexual permissiveness is the best predictor of extramarital sex.

2. *Social roles*, especially women's roles, are changing. Even happily married women may

have sex outside of marriage in response to more liberal sexual attitudes. Some continue an adulterous relationship even when they recognize that it may wreck their marriage:

Dear Ann Landers: I have been married to a wonderful man for 20 years. . . . Everyone says I am lucky to have him. We get along beautifully and have no major problems. Will you please tell me why I am having an affair behind his back? I cannot figure out what on earth is wrong with me. I realize that what I am doing is cheap and tacky (also dangerous), but I don't want to stop. . . . I think I love the other man, Ann, but in a different way. There is a certain excitement to sneaking around. . . . Deep down I know I am playing with dynamite. Counseling has not provided me with any answers. Please help me before I wreck several lives. P.S. The other man is also married and has a family. Signed, Bananas in Rochester (Baltimore Sun, September 13, 1989e: B10).

Landers told "Bananas" to find another counselor.

3. The *need for emotional satisfaction* or, conversely, the *need to escape emotional isolation* may propel a married partner into extramarital sex. An extramarital relationship can make someone feel more desirable, more attractive, and more loved. Women who engage in extramarital sex often do so because they feel that their husbands do not communicate and have no time for them except in bed:

A 28-year-old from Kansas, who has been having an affair for two years, wrote, "My sex life with my husband was good, very good. But . . . . we shared nothing but sex. He never wanted to talk to me about his work, or about mine, or go anywhere, or do anything. It . . . was like going to bed with a stranger" (Wolfe, 1981).

What is ironic is that husbands and wives often appear to be having affairs for complementary reasons: While women complain that their husbands will not talk with them, men often say that they are looking for someone to talk to and someone who will listen to them (Bass, 1988).

Sometimes people become involved in extramarital relationships to counteract sexual deprivation caused by a spouse's long-term illness. And when people are separated from their spouses because of military duty or con-

stant business trips, they may have "flings" to decrease loneliness. Finally, a "midlife crisis" (discussed later) may lead some people to try to prove to themselves that they are still physically and socially desirable.

4. People have greater *expectations of the quality of life* and may be tempted to try *different sexual experiences.* Searching for something new and better has become a way of life in the United States, and sometimes this search is for new and better sex partners. An extramarital affair may offer an opportunity for sexual experimentation (such as oral sex); the lover may be more physically appealing or may provide feedback that supports a positive sexual self-image for the partner (Weil, 1993). Walsh (1991) posits that even happily married men may seek "novelty" through extramarital sex. Some people have extramarital affairs for fun; even women admit being unfaithful "just for the sport of it" (Krance et al., 1993). And sometimes status, prestige, and power are powerful aphrodisiacs (see the box "All the Presidents' Women").

5. People sometimes have extramarital sex as a form of *revenge or retaliation* against a spouse for involvement in a similar activity or "for some sort of nonsexual mistreatment, real or imagined, by the other spouse" (Kinsey et al., 1953: 432).

6. An extramarital relationship may provide *a way out of marriage.* Women, especially, can find the courage to leave an unsatisfying marriage if they realize they have better options. Some people might even deliberately initiate an affair as an excuse to dissolve an unhappy marriage (Walsh, 1991).

7. Finally, there is *greater opportunity for extramarital sex* today, especially for women. Present in increasing numbers in the workplace, women have more contact with men. If their marital relationships are not satisfying, they may become closer to and emotionally involved with a coworker (Hall, 1987).

Signs of Possible Infidelity

Pop psychologists suggest that there are usually signs that an extramarital affair is going on. Some of these signs include dramatic changes in sexual behavior (both positive and negative), a sudden interest in personal appearance, telephone calls at unexpected times, and suspicious

CONSTRAINTS

All the Presidents' Women

Extramarital sex and politics have been frequent bedfellows in the White House. As you saw in Chapter 3, Thomas Jefferson had an African-American mistress and several illegitimate children. Franklin Roosevelt had a 30-year relationship with his wife's social secretary, Lucy Mercer Rutherford. Grover Cleveland was elected to office even after a story was published about his illegitimate son. Warren G. Harding's mistress, Nan Britton, wrote about their affair and posed with their illegitimate daughter. Kay Summersby, Dwight D. Eisenhower's mistress and World War II driver, published a book about their affair after his death. Asked about Lyndon Baines Johnson's philandering, his wife, Lady Bird, said, "My husband loved all people, and half the world's people are women." John Kennedy's womanizing was known to the press for years, but it was not written about during his lifetime (Dubrow et

General "Ike" Eisenhower, Supreme Commander of the Allied Forces in World War II, attending a London musical with his lover, Lieutenant Kay Summersby (on his left); his wife, Mamie, was at home in the states.

al., 1987; Sullivan, 1991). Although he has denied it, Bill Clinton has been accused of having extramarital affairs with Gennifer Flowers and of propositioning Paula Jones in a hotel room while he was governor of Arkansas.

During the past few years the ex-

tramarital sexual escapades of other highly visible men like Senator Gary Hart, Donald Trump, Jim Bakker, and Jimmy Swaggart have made headlines. Not even the respected civil rights leader Martin Luther King, Jr. has escaped such allegations. In 1994, Prince Charles of England admitted that he had been unfaithful to his wife, Diana, with Camilla Parker Bowles, an old flame. In the mid-1990s, several high-ranking British male politicians (who were known for preaching "family values") admitted having extramarital affairs with both men and women, as well as having children out of wedlock (Harris, 1994). Power is a sexual magnet. Like other kinds of resources, sex can be traded for benefits that powerful people control (Lips, 1991). Because most of the power in the United States and other Western countries still resides with men, they can often use sex to their personal advantage.

---

credit-card bills. Because many people go through changes in midlife, losing weight or getting a hairpiece does not mean a spouse should reach for the telephone number of the nearest detective agency. Recognizing signs of possible infidelity, however, might help bring issues into the open and help the couple deal with problems. The quiz in the box "Is Your Spouse Having an Affair?" should help clarify some possible signs of infidelity.

When Affairs End

Men involved in extramarital affairs are generally older and have much higher incomes than their female partners. Often they have been a woman's boss or mentor. Women are usually less powerful and more dependent in an affair; and the more dependent a woman is, the more likely that the man will end the relationship and

that she will suffer pain and humiliation when it ends. Only about 10 percent of adulterous relationships end in marriage (Lawson, 1988), and the average length of an affair is a year (Patterson and Kim, 1991). Thus, most people have to deal with ending an extramarital affair sooner or later. In her study of "the other woman," Richardson (1985) found three types of endings to affairs: shock-out, drag-out, and wind-down.

In the *shock-out* ending (most often brought about by men), the affair ends abruptly and often heartlessly:

I was going into the hospital to have my tubes tied so I wouldn't get pregnant and confuse things between us. He was supposed to come into town to bring me. He didn't show up, so I drove myself. I didn't ever hear from him again. Later I learned that he had fallen in love with someone else and had left his wife for her (p. 131).

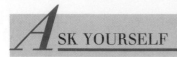
Is Your Spouse Having an Affair?

No one of the following observations is proof that your spouse is having an extramarital affair, and there may be other explanations for any one or several of the attitudes or behaviors described. If you answer yes to a number of these statements, however, you may want to investigate further (McGinnis, 1981; Weil, 1993).

For both spouses

☐ Do you receive frequent phone calls in which the caller hangs up?

☐ Are there strange charges on phone bills or credit cards?

☐ When your partner is at home, is he or she restless?

☐ Does the name of a particular colleague, friend, or neighbor come up regularly in conversations with your partner?

☐ Has your partner become more belligerent or does he or she provoke more fights?

For wives

☐ Is your husband suddenly having difficulty achieving or sustaining an erection or experiencing frequent impotence? When you seek possible explanations, such as extreme fatigue, preoccupation with financial or other problems, concern about work, depression, or physical illness, does none seem to apply?

☐ Has your husband suddenly started to act like a sex-starved, hot-blooded sexual athlete?

☐ Does your husband often seem moody, irritable, and withdrawn for no visible reason?

☐ Have there been recent sharp shifts in your husband's personality and tastes: Is he less stingy and more generous; less conservative and more liberal; less rigid and more experimental? Has he bought new underwear (bikini style)? Is he dressing a little more youthfully?

☐ Is your spouse spending more time away from you, giving such reasons as business trips, conferences, overtime work, night school, evening meetings, client entertainment, or parties at the homes of business associates? Despite his reasonable explanations, is he increasingly touchy if you ask such questions as "Where are you going tonight?" or "What time do you expect to be home?" Has he been coming home after you've already gone to bed and fallen asleep, as if he doesn't want to face you at that hour?

For husbands

☐ Has your wife's sexual passion suddenly diminished? Or does she put on a passionate act that doesn't quite convince you? Or is she actually more passionate? Is she having multiple orgasms that she never had before? If she's having an affair, it may have aroused her sexually so that she's more erotic and wants to make love frequently in new and more exciting ways.

☐ Does she have a new air of self-confidence?

☐ Is your wife more socially outgoing and assertive?

☐ Is she dressing in a more modern style? Is she using more (or less) makeup and paying more attention to her hairdo?

☐ Does your wife spend more time away from home, shopping (and taking longer to do it), eating out, going to evening meetings, visiting with friends, and so on?

☐ Is she spending more time with a woman friend who's known to have had several extramarital affairs?

Another woman, who had twice changed jobs and twice moved across the country to be near her married lover, simply received a postcard:

I am moving to Korea. Due to a lack of propinquity, I shall be removed without a chance to totally resolve our relationship. Have a good life (p. 132).

The *drag-out* ending is characterized by a long, drawn-out, on-again–off-again process. Here, the woman is convinced that her lover will leave his wife. When he does not live up to this promise, she ends the relationship. He persuades her to get back together and promises, again, that this time he will really leave his wife—after Christmas, when his wife finds a job, and so on, and the affair continues. It may be many years before the "other" woman realizes that her lover will never leave his wife and at last leaves *him.*

In the *wind-down* ending, the affair just peters out. Even assertive women are sometimes reluctant to end an affair. Ultimately, some problems can't be resolved, or the clash between expectation and reality is too disappointing to ignore:

When my father died, I was so alone. He [the married lover] had to go to a picnic—a picnic. Hers. He said he couldn't get out of it. Her picnic versus me. I hated him then. Nothing was ever right after that (p. 131).

Consequences of Extramarital Sex

One clinician describes the discovery of a spouse's affair as the "emotional equivalent of having a limb amputated without an anesthetic" (McGinnis, 1981: 154). The injured spouse typically feels deceived, betrayed, even devastated, at the discovery of a partner's infidelity. The aggrieved person may suffer from doubts about his or her own desirability, adequacy, or worth: "I obviously failed in some way . . . I guess nobody wants me" (Beck, 1988: 285)

There is some evidence that men and women respond differently to the discovery of an extramarital affair. Women are generally more disapproving and perceive more destructive consequences than do men (Thompson, 1984). Whereas men tend to focus their jealousy and anger on the rival male ("I'll *kill* him"), women experience a more generalized sense that they have lost their partner's attention, caring, and concern (Scarf, 1987). Women are thus more likely to distrust the adulterous spouse in general. Both men and women, however, may be justifiably concerned about pregnancy, sexually transmitted diseases, and AIDS.

Although the cheating partner may also experience negative reactions—for example, guilt can result in impotence during marital sex—it is clearly the injured partner who suffers the most. Even if the spouses no longer love each other, the agony can be great and the person is likely to go through any or all of the stages described in Table 7.3.

Clinicians point out that most extramarital affairs devastate the entire family. They can have an especially negative impact on children, who often feel insecure and confused, particularly if the marriage collapses because of the affair. Very young children are self-centered, so they may feel that they are somehow to blame for what has happened (Pittman, 1989).

Extramarital sex also has broad structural implications for society as a whole. Group solidarity is necessary for a society's survival. As we

---

Table 7.3

A Spouse's Extramarital Affair: Discovery and Recovery

Stage 1: Amazement, disbelief, confusion, disorientation. Sometimes an injured spouse feels he or she "knew it all along."

Stage 2: Raging emotions, such as anger, fear, anxiety, hatred, resentment, sorrow, despair, and guilt. Wounded pride, feelings of betrayal and rejection, a sense of irreparable loss. The injured person may feel unattractive, abandoned, or worthless because his or her spouse has turned away.

Stage 3: An aching sense of disillusionment, alienation, loneliness, and self-pity or a smoldering desire to punish and retaliate.

Stage 4: Either a compulsion to learn all the facts of the affair or a wish not to know anything about it at all. The injured partner may press for details in order to feel the pain, to store up ammuniton to use against the spouse, or to gain insight into what the affair offered that the marriage did not.

Stage 5: Exploration of alternatives. The injured partner tries to decide whether to terminate the marriage, accept the affair, try to build a closer and more rewarding relationship with the spouse, or have an affair of her or his own in order to retaliate, and tries to weigh the effects these choices would have on all members of the family.

Stage 6: Learning to live with what has happened. The cheated partner tries to maintain or rebuild damaged self-esteem and participate actively in life, with or without the spouse, and to put the experience in the past.

SOURCE: Based on McGinnis, 1981.

---

saw in Chapter 1, family members depend on one another for emotional support, and the unity and cohesiveness of the family can be threatened by intruding outsiders. Even though families now take many different forms, a considerable number of Americans still view those who engage in extramarital sex as being morally bankrupt (see Data Digest).

SEXUALITY AND LATER LIFE

We are sexual until we die. As we mature, however, our sexual interests, abilities, and responses change.

Biological Changes

For most women, changes in the internal and external reproductive organs begin in their early 40s. Women's ovaries gradually stop producing estrogen and progesterone, and the menstrual cycle becomes irregular and eventually ceases. After menopause some women experience vaginal changes, which may include a thinning of the vaginal walls, decreased elasticity, and dryness. None of these changes impairs a woman's capacity for sexual enjoyment, however, and because the clitoris does not undergo noticeable change, sexual stimulation remains pleasurable.

Physiological changes occur in men as well. Achieving an erection can take minutes instead of seconds, and manual stimulation may be necessary to achieve erection. Erections also become less firm and full. During sexual excitement, the testicles do not lift toward the body as markedly, sperm production is reduced, and the secretion of male sex hormones dwindles. An older man's ejaculations are less forceful, less seminal fluid is ejaculated; and the penis more quickly returns to a flaccid state. Repeated ejaculations are less frequent; it may take a day or more before men in their 60s or 70s can have another erection.

For both sexes, the physiological changes that come with aging by no means preclude sexual activity or lessen its pleasure. Contrary to what many teenagers and young adults think, people over 40 are not on their sexual deathbeds and can have extremely satisfying sexual relationships. The physical changes simply make things happen a little more slowly, a little less frequently, and with a little less intensity.

The Middle Years

In the middle years women undergo menopause, a physiological change in the reproductive system that has a number of common signs and clearly definable consequences. Men may experience an analogous change, the so-called climacteric, but the phenomena associated with this presumed change may be more psychological than physiological.

Menopause and Climacteric It is only in recent years that **menopause**—the cessation of the menstrual cycle and the loss of reproductive capacity—has been studied seriously. One reason for this is that early in this century many women died, often in childbirth, long before they could experience "the change of life," as it was once called. Now gynecologists study not only all the stages of the menstrual cycle but *perimenopause* as well, a phenomenon that precedes menopause itself and has many of the same symptoms. Whereas menopause typically begins in a woman's mid-40s to early 50s, perimenopause can

occur as early as the late 30s. The symptoms of both perimenopause and menopause include "hot flashes" (sudden experience of overall bodily heat, sometimes accompanied by sweating), irregular menstrual cycles with uncharacteristically heavy or light bleeding, mood changes, vaginal dryness, fatigue, migraine headaches, backaches, insomnia, loss or increase of appetite, diarrhea or constipation, urinary incontinence, and more frequent urinary tract infections (Smith, 1993).

Not all women experience all these phenomena, and some hardly notice that they are going through menopause. Hot flashes affect only about 10 percent of all women, and in any case they usually last only a minute or so. Rarely, a woman will experience a "drenching sweat" or be awakened from sleep. Most women do not consider menopause a time of crisis, and many enjoy sex more because they are no longer bothered by menstruation, the need for contraception, or the fear of pregnancy (Fausto-Sterling, 1985).

According to some social scientists, the subjective experience of menopause may reflect cultural as well as biological influences. For example, studying menopausal women in Massachusetts, Canada, and Japan, Lock (1993) found that compared to North American women, Japanese women reported a considerably lower incidence of such problems as hot flashes, fatigue, irritability, feelings of depression, and stiffness in the joints. Lock proposes that because most Japanese women have extensive family responsibilities, which often include caring for elderly parents or relatives as well as young children, they may regard complaining about menopause as "pure self-indulgence" and thus report fewer physiological problems. This does not mean that they do not experience the same physiological changes, only that they endure them quietly.

Many physicians prescribe hormone replacement therapy for menopausal women. Because it is believed that most menopausal symptoms are caused by lowered estrogen levels, hormone replacement therapy compensates for the lesser amounts of this primary female hormone. However, there has been some concern that estrogen treatments might produce side effects like gallbladder stones, elevated blood pressure, and uterine cancer. Some of the most recent research suggests that a mixture of two hormones, estrogen and progestin, is better than estrogen alone, protecting women not only against the risk of uterine cancer but against heart attacks as well (Brody, 1994). Because physicians still know so little about menopause, and in the light of social science findings like those we've described, some writers have suggested substituting natural "treatments" like eating a more healthy diet, quitting smoking, stopping the consumption of alcohol and other drugs, and starting a daily exercise program (Greer, 1992; Sheehy, 1992).

Whether there is a **male climacteric,** or change of life analogous to female menopause, is controversial. Although testosterone production does decline with age, unlike women, men do not lose their reproductive capacity. Some men have fathered children in their late 70s. Only a small percentage of men complain of nervousness, depression, decreased sexual desire, inability to concentrate, irritability, and other emotional reactions in middle age, and research on the male mood cycle has been only suggestive. It may be that the male "change of life" is a more general "midlife crisis," in which men look back over their lives and, sometimes, feel distress at not having achieved all that they might have.

Midlife Crisis Both men and women may experience sexual burnout in the middle years. More than simply boredom, which can certainly be one of its precursors, *sexual burnout* is typically marked by a sense of physical depletion, emotional emptiness, and a negative self-concept. Caught in the throes of sexual burnout, the middle-aged adult develops feelings of sexual helplessness and hopelessness, as though nothing can be done to rekindle erotic passion or pleasure. Sexual burnout occurs not only in married couples but also in singles who have been very active sexually (Masters et al., 1992).

Some people cope with sexual burnout by ignoring it. Others simply accept it. Still others try to recapture their youthful passion by having sex with numerous, or younger, partners. Many people, especially women, work desperately to combat the effects of aging and the loss of their physical attractiveness through such cosmetic surgery procedures as liposuction (fat removal), eyelid surgery, and face-lifts.

Other people in their middle years experience a resurgence of sexual passion. Couples who have no children living at home and need not care for elderly parents are freed from time-consuming responsibilities. They have more time and energy for talking, intimacy, and sex. Thus, "the empty nest may actually be a love nest" (Woodward and Springen, 1992: 71).

Sexuality and the Aged

An elderly gentleman was walking through the woods when he heard a voice. "Down here, look down here," said the voice. The man looked down and saw a frog. "Pick me up, pick me up," insisted the frog. The man picked up the frog. The frog said, "I'm really a beautiful princess under a spell. Kiss me on the lips. I'll turn into a beautiful woman and fulfill all your sexual fantasies." The man looked at the frog and dropped it in his pocket. "Hey," yelled the frog, "Didn't you hear me? I said I'll turn into a beautiful woman and fulfill all your sexual fantasies." The man replied, "Look, I'm 83 years old and I'm much more impressed with a talking frog."

As this anecdote illustrates, sexuality among the aged is still viewed by the general public in a negative way. We are a youth-oriented society and sometimes find it difficult to imagine that the elderly can fall in love and feel physical attractions. It doesn't help that the expression of

GEECH © 1994 Universal Press Syndicate. Reprinted with permission. All rights reserved.

sexuality among aging people is rarely portrayed in popular culture. Films that feature the elderly—*Trip to Bountiful* and *Driving Miss Daisy*, for example—generally deal with themes that are nonsexual and that fit our image of the aged, such as frailty, illness, and reminiscence about "the good old days." One reason the film *Cocoon* was so popular may have been that it presented the elderly as rediscovering their sexuality.

When sexuality among older people is presented on television, the portrayal often borders on caricature and generally focuses on women. For example, in "Who's the Boss," Mona, one of the main characters and a grandmother, was also the neighborhood slut. In "The Golden Girls," Blanche was the stereotypical promiscuous southern belle, and in "Dear John," one of the back-row characters was an elderly woman whose lines were limited to lecherous comments about sex. The few television shows that feature older people as intelligent, productive, and interesting include "Murder She Wrote," "Matlock," "In the Heat of the Night," and "The Bill Cosby Mysteries." Now that the "baby boomers" are aging, perhaps there will be more programs featuring older actors.

In the later years, sexuality encompasses a wide range of acts and feelings, from hugging and holding hands to sexual intercourse. In a survey of over 4,000 readers of *Consumer Reports*, 66 percent of the women and 80 percent of the men 70 and older were still sexually active: At least 50 percent reported having had sex once a week, 43 percent of the women practiced fellatio, 56 percent of the men engaged in cunnilingus, and both sexes were still experimenting with anal sex and vibrators (Brecher, 1984). In a study of the sexual practices of 202 men and women aged 80 to 102 (that's right, 102!), 47 percent of the respondents were having sexual intercourse and 34 percent engaged in oral sex. Also, 88 percent of the men and 71 percent of the women still fantasized or daydreamed about the opposite sex (Bretschneider and McCoy, 1988). Another study of 60- to 80-year-old women and men in Sweden found that 61 percent of the 509 respondents were engaging in intercourse, mutual sexual stimulation, and masturbation (Bergstrom-Walan and Nielsen, 1990).

As people age, the biggest impediment to sex is usually not lack of desire or ability but a lack of available sexual partners. This is especially true for women. For every 100 females over age 65, there are only 69 males. Because our culture frowns on liaisons and marriages between older women and younger men but smiles on matches between older men and younger women, older women are less likely to have a large pool of eligible sexual partners.

It's not until about the age of 75 that the frequency of sexual activity, in both men and women, begins to decline significantly, and this is generally because of health problems. Heart disease, diabetes, prostate trouble, and vascular illnesses can interfere with sexual desire and activity. And some illnesses, like diabetes and arteriosclerosis, as well as some medications for hypertension (high blood pressure), can cause impotence in older men (Butler and Lewis, 1986). But despite these physiological problems, older men and women both engage in and enjoy sex. When a 90-year-old woman who married an 18-year-old man was asked by a reporter, "Aren't you afraid of what could happen on the honeymoon? Vigorous lovemaking might bring on injury or even a fatal heart attack!" she smiled and replied, "If he dies, he dies!"

The Double Standard of Aging

The double standard persists throughout old age. Whereas gray-haired men in their 60s are considered "distinguished," their female counterparts are just "old." Men are not under the same pressure to remain young, trim, and attractive. Moreover, if a 73-year-old man marries a 23-year old woman, we call it a "May–December wedding," but if a 45-year-old woman dates a 25-year-old man, she is accused of "robbing the cradle."

One of the most visible examples of the differential treatment of older women is found among television news anchors. Both local and national stations are bulging with aging male anchors. Mike Wallace, for example, now in his late 70s, still hosts CBS's "60 Minutes." Harry Reasoner chose to retire at age 68 but was still a contributing correspondent to the show until his death later that year. With a few exceptions, such as Barbara Walters, few women over age 50 are in comparable positions.

Furthermore, most of us are accustomed to seeing male movie stars in their 60s and 70s playing romantic lead roles with actresses in their 20s. In the movie *Blaze*, 64-year-old Paul Newman cavorted with a stripper played by 28-year-old Lolita Davidovitch; in *Wolf*, 57-year-old Jack Nicholson co-starred with 37-year-old Michelle Pfeiffer; in *I Love Trouble*, Nick Nolte, age 53, had an amorous relationship with 29-year-old Joely Richardson;

and in *Greedy*, 75-year-old Kirk Douglas chased and caught his 23-year-old star Olivia D'Abo (*Mediawatch*, 1994). In contrast, aging female movie stars rarely play romantic roles, much less opposite men in their 20s. Listen to actress Joanne Woodward compare her own public image to that of her husband, actor Paul Newman: "He gets prettier; I get older" (Allgeier, 1983: 149).

HOMOSEXUAL RELATIONSHIPS

As we discussed in Chapter 6, there are more similarities between heterosexual and homosexual women and between heterosexual and homosexual men than there are between heterosexuals and homosexuals. Nonetheless, there are several important similarities between homosexual and heterosexual couples: All couples feel conflict between attachment and autonomy. They experience positive feelings about relationships and make future plans together. Furthermore, just as heterosexual couples differ, homosexual couples are diverse as well.

Diversity in Homosexual Relationships

A study of approximately 1,000 homosexual couples living in the San Francisco area found great diversity in the relationships (Bell and Weinberg, 1978). Although this study did not represent a cross section of the homosexual population, it illustrates a range of relationships, sexual behavior, and lifestyles that is not unlike the range found among heterosexual relationships. Bell and Weinberg found five primary types of relationships: close, open, functional, dysfunctional, and asexual.

- *Close-coupled* homosexuals (10 percent of men, 28 percent of women) live in one-to-one, same-sex relationships. They have relatively few sexual problems, good communication, and few sexual partners. They often lead a "happy-couple" life, spending evenings at home and leisure time together.
- *Open-coupled* homosexuals (18 percent of men, 17 percent of women) live in one-to-one, same-sex relationships but also have many outside sexual partners and spend a relatively large amount of time "cruising" (deliberately searching for a casual sex partner). They are more likely to have sexual problems and to regret their homosexuality than are close-coupled homosexuals.

- *Functional* homosexuals (15 percent of men, 10 percent of women) are not "coupled" and have a high number of sexual partners and few sexual problems. They tend to be younger and to have few regrets about their homosexuality and high levels of sexual interest.
- *Dysfunctional* homosexuals (12 percent of men, 5 percent of women) are not coupled either. Although they have many sexual partners and a great deal of sexual activity, they experience substantial numbers of sexual problems. They cruise a great deal, have many regrets about being homosexual, worry about maintaining a partner's affection, suffer from feelings of sexual inadequacy, and are very conflict-ridden.
- *Asexual* homosexuals (16 percent of men, 11 percent of women) are low in sexual interest and activity and are not coupled. They are also more secretive about their homosexuality.

Homosexual couples do many of the same sexual things as do heterosexuals, with the exception of penile-vaginal intercourse. All other feelings and activities are basically the same, including kissing, caressing, hugging, nipple stimulation, and other nongenital touching or foreplay, as well as oral and anal sex. Many homosexuals regard arousal as more important than ejaculation. Lesbian sexual activities include cunnilingus, manual masturbation, body-to-body rubbing of breasts or clitorises, and slow, sensual body caressing and kissing (Bell and Weinberg, 1978). Like heterosexuals, homosexuals use a variety of positions to achieve sexual satisfaction, and not all couples participate in or enjoy all sexual activities (Reinisch and Beasley, 1990).

The Costs and Benefits of Homosexuality

Like all intimate and loving relationships, homosexual relationships can have many benefits for the partners. Unlike heterosexual relationships, however, those between gays and lesbians often confront some pretty high costs. According to several researchers (Blumstein and Schwartz, 1977; Strommen, 1990), four major problems contribute to the fragility of these relationships:

1. Many adolescents and young adults become isolated from family and heterosexual friends out of fear of disclosure; they are afraid that if

they reveal their sexual orientation, they may lose the support of their families or be subjected to emotional or even physical abuse.

2. Many homosexuals whose partners formerly led heterosexual or bisexual lives live with the fear that incentives like economic support from a spouse, acceptance from family members, or loss of stigma will persuade their partners to return to a "straight" (heterosexual) life.

3. Gays and lesbians sometimes experience increased role stress because their expectations of one another with respect to such things as household duties are ambiguous. Particularly if both partners are employed, the couples have to work out egalitarian domestic responsibilities.

4. Becoming parents may be a problem. For example, if lesbian mothers have children from previous marriages, they may fear that they will lose their children if they disclose their sexual orientation. Or if a lesbian couple want to have a child, they face the high costs of assisted reproduction techniques like artificial inseminaton or the emotional and even legal complications of natural conception.

One of the most serious problems faced by homosexual couples is the fact that they do not enjoy the same legal rights and protections as do heterosexual couples. Because homosexual marriage is illegal in the United States, not even long-term relationships are protected by law and in fact, current laws encourage people to have "illicit" affairs and then punish them for doing so. Some states still prohibit all sexual intercourse except between husband and wife, but the laws against homosexual acts are enforced more widely and vigorously than are those against unmarried heterosexual partners. For example, in 1990 the Maryland Court of Appeals ruled that oral sex between consenting heterosexual adults is no longer illegal in that state as long as the activity occurs in private and does not involve prostitution. In ruling that a statute barring "unnatural and perverted sexual practices" does not apply to "consensual, noncommercial heterosexual activity" performed privately by adults, however, the court allowed for the continued enforcement of the law in cases involving homosexuals (Leff, 1990).

There are also advantages to homosexual relationships. First, same-sex relationships are more egalitarian because neither person is assigned a superior gender role. Second, these relationships are less role bound. Most people perform roles because of preference, not duty. Either or both partners may nurture the children, fix the car, wash the dishes, or shingle the roof, depending on their abilities and talents rather than socially determined gender norms. Third, the partners are more knowledgeable about each other's emotional and physical needs. Because they both come from the same sex culture, they understand the needs and problems of their gender. Finally, because women are not socialized to seek sexual conquests, lesbians can have long-term relationships that are not threatened by competition (Blumstein and Schwartz, 1977).

SEXUAL DYSFUNCTIONS

Sexual expression is not always a smooth and carefree process. In the national sex survey cited earlier, one in five women and one in ten men reported that sex is not pleasurable for them (Laumann et al., 1994). There are many reasons for dissatisfaction with sex—poor general health, unhappiness with available sex partners, and not feeling loved by a partner. Most couples, at some time or other, may experience **sexual dysfunctions,** or conditions in which the ordinary physical responses of sexual function are impaired. As we will discuss, sometimes these problems are physiological, sometimes they are interpersonal, and sometimes they reflect a combination of both physiological and interpersonal factors. Inhibited sexual desire, or the lack of interest in sex, may affect almost a third of women, and premature ejaculation, or a man's inability to postpone ejaculation and orgasm, may trouble almost 30 percent of men (see Figure 7.3). In general, however, serious sexual dysfunctions affect relatively small numbers of people.

Male Sexual Dysfunctions

Erectile dysfunction, or **impotence,** is the inability to attain or maintain an erection. It is a rare man who does not experience this problem at least once in his lifetime. Impotence can occur at any age and can assume many different forms. Typically, the male with erectile dysfunction has partial erections that are too weak to permit insertion in the vagina. Sometimes firm erections quickly disappear when intercourse is attempted. In other instances, a man may be able to have normal erections under some circumstances but not

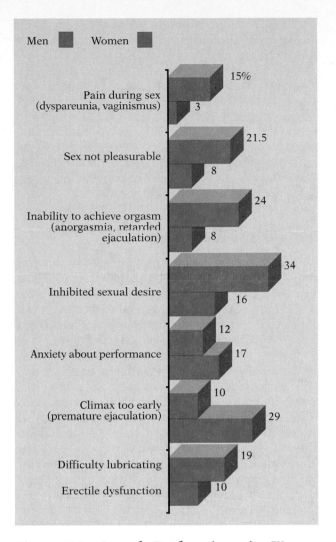

Pain during sex (dyspareunia, vaginismus) — 15% / 3

Sex not pleasurable — 21.5 / 8

Inability to achieve orgasm (anorgasmia, retarded ejaculation) — 24 / 8

Inhibited sexual desire — 34 / 16

Anxiety about performance — 12 / 17

Climax too early (premature ejaculation) — 10 / 29

Difficulty lubricating — 19

Erectile dysfunction — 10

Figure 7.3 **Sexual Dysfunctions in Women and Men.** *Although both men and women may be anxious about their sexual performance and both may experience a lack of desire, their principal difference appears to be that women are often insufficiently aroused or ready for sex, whereas men may be overeager. How might this problem be resolved?* (Laumann et al., 1994: 369).

others. For example, there may be no problem during masturbation, but the man may experience difficulty during sexual intercourse.

Impotence can have a negative effect on the female partner's self-esteem if she feels that she is not sexually desirable or is doing something wrong. Most continuing erectile dysfunctions—some estimates are as high as 86 percent—have an organic basis, such as circulatory problems, neurological disorders (due to multiple sclerosis or spinal-cord injury, for example), hormone im-

balances, and infections or injuries of the penis, testes, urethra, or prostate gland. Diabetes, alcoholism, prescription medications (such as drugs for high blood pressure), and amphetamines, barbiturates, and narcotics can also cause erectile dysfunction.

Several other male dysfunctions are related to ejaculation. The most common of these dysfunctions is **premature ejaculation**—unintentional ejaculation before or while the male tries to enter his partner or soon after intercourse begins. An estimated 15 to 20 percent of all American men ejaculate prematurely on a regular basis. Whereas many female partners are understanding and accepting of the problem, others may feel angry, avoid sex, or seek another lover. Some men are not bothered, but others may question their masculinity or suffer from low self-esteem. Some may experience heightened anxiety about performance, which, in turn, exacerbates the condition.

Premature ejaculation is believed to be caused by psychological factors. For example, many therapists believe that the early sexual experiences of many males—which involve hurrying through intercourse for fear of being caught (such as in a car, a parent's house, or a public place)—teach many men to rush through sex. Others suggest that men who view women as sex objects are more likely to ejaculate prematurely, regardless of the woman's readiness. Other ejaculatory problems, such as the backward spurting of the semen into the bladder during orgasm, known as *retrograde ejaculation*, and ejaculation in the vagina only after a lengthy period and strenuous efforts (*retarded ejaculation*), or failure to ejaculate or achieve orgasm at all, may be caused by drug use, alcoholism, neurological disorders, and prescription medicines.

Female Sexual Dysfunctions

Approximately 2 to 3 percent of adult women are affected by **vaginismus,** or pain during penetration because of involuntary spasms of the muscles surrounding the outer third of the vagina. Vaginismus can be so severe that it prevents not only intercourse but even insertion of a finger or tampon. A woman's partner may deliberately avoid intercourse because vaginismus can be painful. Some men may become passive about sex, whereas others become impatient or openly hostile and may seek other sexual partners.

Vaginismus may have organic causes, such as poor vaginal lubrication, drugs that have a drying effect on the vagina (such as antihistamines, tran-

"I sense a little anxiety when we approach the subject of sex."

Scott Arthur Masear.

quilizers, or marijuana), diabetes, vaginal infections, or pelvic disorders. It can also reflect psychological difficulties, such as anxieties about intercourse, a fear of injury or harm to the internal organs, trauma (due to rape or abortion, for example), a strict religious upbringing in which sex was equated with sin, or fear of or hostility toward men. Such psychological problems are often treated by relaxation exercises followed by a gradual dilation of the vagina.

Another female sexual dysfunction is **anorgasmia**—the inability to reach orgasm. Anorgasmia, which used to be called frigidity, has several variations. In *primary anorgasmia*, a woman has never had an orgasm. In *secondary anorgasmia*, a woman who was regularly orgasmic at one time is no longer. And in *situational anorgasmia*, a woman is able to achieve orgasm only under certain circumstances, such as through masturbation.

Some anorgasmic women find that sex is satisfying and stimulating even though they have never experienced an orgasm. For others, the condition can lead to lowered self-esteem, a sense of futility, and depression. About 5 percent of cases of anorgasmia are attributed to organic causes. Orgasm can be blocked by severe chronic illness, diabetes, alcoholism, neurological problems, hormone deficiencies, pelvic disorders (due to infections, trauma, or scarring from surgery), or drugs (including narcotics, tranquilizers, and blood pressure medications). Other reasons for anorgasmia have an interpersonal basis. For example, women's most common sexual complaints include not getting enough sex because the partner gets tired too fast; intercourse does not last long enough; the partner is unskilled; the woman cannot readily lubricate because there is not enough foreplay; sex is boring ("same place, same time, same channel," according to one woman); and the timing is bad ("He wants to have sex only when he wants. It's rarely, if ever, at my convenience") (Patterson and Kim, 1991: 73–74).

Finally, approximately 15 percent of adult women experience **dyspareunia**, or painful intercourse, several times a year. Another 1 to 2 percent are believed to have painful intercourse on a regular basis. Men, too, can experience dyspareunia (it is sometimes associated with problems of the prostate gland), but this disorder is believed to be much more common in women than in men. Like anorgasmia, female dyspareunia may be caused by any of a number of physical conditions, including poor vaginal lubrication, drugs, infections, diseases, and pelvic disorders.

Inhibited Sexual Desire

Both men and women can experience another common sexual problem, **inhibited sexual desire (ISD),** or a low interest in sex. Although the exact incidence of ISD is unknown, approximately 33 percent of the people who consult sex therapists do so because of ISD problems. It is important to remember that a low level of interest in sex is not uncommon. It creates a problem only when it becomes a source of personal distress. An extreme example of ISD is **sexual aversion,** in which people experience persistent or intense feelings of anxiety or panic in sexual situations and avoid sexual contact altogether. The causes of ISD are both organic and nonorganic. Organic factors include hormone deficiencies, alcoholism, kidney failure, drug abuse, and severe chronic illness. Nonorganic factors include fatigue, overwork, depression, and poor lovemaking skills (Turner and Rubinson, 1993).

Relationship Factors and Sexual Dysfunction

Personal and cultural factors play an important role in sexual expression. Many people do not realize that sex is not just a physiological response. Good or bad sex reflects the quality of our interpersonal relationships, especially in long-term situations. According to Wade and Cirese (1991), therapists typically encounter four interpersonal problems that are destructive to sexual relationships. The first is *anger and hostility*. Dissension and conflict are inevitable in any close relationship, but long-term resentments can sour erotic feelings and behavior. Resentments arising from serious disputes about money, child rearing, friends, and leisure time can result in conflicts in bed:

My husband and I were always arguing over his participation in the care of our home and in family activities. I'd nag, and he'd agree to help more around the house or to take the kids off my hands for a few hours, but then he wouldn't do it. He'd come home, wolf down his dinner, and disappear into the den for 3 hours, with hardly a word to me. Yet at bedtime he was ready to screw. I was so angry I'd just go limp and passive. There was no way I was going to have an orgasm, or even show arousal. My lack of enthusiasm was a way of hurting him back (Wade and Cirese, 1991: 390).

Even when anger and hostility are justified, they often have a negative effect on the relationship. In some situations, partners may withdraw from sex altogether or sabotage the sexual relationship either consciously or unconsciously. For example, people may pick fights just as sex is about to begin, find excuses for not having sex ("I forgot to call my mother"), initiate sex when the partner is clearly not interested, or become slovenly and unattractive to keep the partner at a distance.

A second destructive problem in interpersonal relationships is *boredom*. Boredom may be related specifically to sexual activity—it always takes place at the same time and in the same way—or it may reflect a general disinterest in the partner. Some people like sexual relations that are predictable; others, though, become bored with predictability.

Third, *conflicting sexual expectations* can also be harmful to the relationship. One partner may demand oral sex, for example, but the other may find this activity repulsive. This kind of incompatibility may be especially problematic if one of the partners becomes more eager to experiment with different sexual activities after comfortable expectations have been established.

Finally, *poor communication* is a constant problem in interpersonal relationships. Instead of saying what they want in sex, most people are reluctant to say anything, fearing to seem critical of the partner or to demand something they think the partner may not want to give. Suppressing their own needs may lead them to become angry and to strike out verbally at the partner ("You don't love me anymore"). Because many people find communicating about sex so difficult, they often deny the problem and allow it to fester.

As we discussed in Chapter 4, many problems with interpersonal relationships reflect larger cultural values. Even though many women now work outside the home and more men are taking on domestic tasks, there is still a widespread belief that there are proper roles for men and women when it comes to sex. For example, many people still feel that the man should be the initiator in sex, that women should be seductive but not openly sexual, and that "really good" women have sex to have children rather than for pleasure. Such cultural ideas still play a major role in creating a distance between men and women and can lead to resentment and sexual problems.

Treating Sexual Problems

Because many sexual dysfunctions are caused by *organic* (physical or physiological) problems, a person experiencing such a dysfunction should first see a physician. If a thorough examination reveals no organic abnormalities, the physician may recommend that the person consult a psychiatrist or therapist. Be careful, however. Because sex therapy is largely an unregulated profession, people can offer their services with little more preparation than having attended a few workshops or reading a book. Even "sex therapists" who are well intentioned may be insufficiently qualified. Thus, people seeking help in this area should contact sex-therapy centers that are affiliated with universities, medical schools, or hospitals. They can also seek advice about qualified therapists from local medical societies, psychological associations, or family physicians. Finally, even when a clinician is qualified, trained, and competent, people should feel free to change to a therapist who may be better suited to their temperament and personality.

SEXUALLY TRANSMITTED DISEASES, HIV, AND AIDS

Infections and illnesses that are transmitted almost solely through sexual intercourse are referred to as sexually transmitted diseases. We will discuss a number of these before turning to an examination of the human immunodeficiency virus (HIV) and the acquired immunodeficiency syndrome (AIDS). HIV and AIDS are also transmitted through sexual contact but they may also be spread by contaminated intravenous drug needles and by blood transfusions.

Sexually transmitted diseases (STDs) are infections that are spread by contact, sexual or nonsexual, with body parts or fluids that harbor specific microorganisms (generally bacterial or viral). The term *sexually transmitted* indicates that sexual contact is the most common means of transmission. Both of the oldest known STDs—syphilis and gonorrhea—have now been joined by more than 20 other diseases (see Appendix D for more information on some of these diseases and their treatment). Today *syphilis* is the least common STD; the most common is *chlamydia,* a bacterial infection. When present, the symptoms of chlamydia are often similar to those of *gonorrhea.* Chlamydia is especially dangerous. Even if there are no symptoms, if untreated, chlamydia can cause permanent damage to the reproductive organs, such as infertility in women and sterility in men.

An estimated 13 million people acquire a sexually transmitted infection each year in the United States. Two thirds of STD cases occur in persons under 25 years of age, and 3 million teenagers are infected with STDs annually (Centers for Disease Control, 1993). Table 7.4 presents the incidence of some of the most common STD infections for 1992, the most recent year for which such data are available.

One survey of women found that 84 percent thought "it won't happen to me," even though many were in high-risk categories and two-thirds admitted they knew almost nothing about STDs. Women contract sexual diseases more easily than men (we will discuss why shortly) and generally experience more severe complications. Many women go undiagnosed until permanent damage is done, in large part because most federal funding for the treatment of sexual diseases goes to 4,000 special clinics where two-thirds of the patients are men (*Baltimore Sun,* 1994i). As a

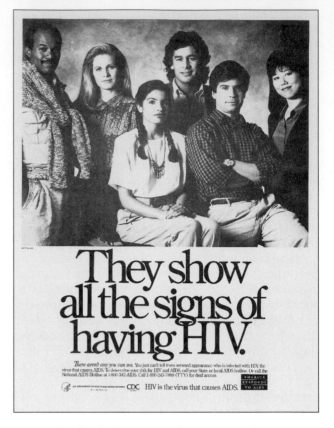

You can't tell who has HIV infection or AIDS, so protect yourself and others by responsible sexual behavior.

result, more than a million women a year get pelvic inflammatory disease, become infertile, or develop life-threatening pregnancies. As one professor of medicine summed it up, "Doctors can't fix most of the things you can catch out there. There's no cure for herpes or genital warts. Gonorrhea and chlamydial infection can ruin your chances of ever getting pregnant and can harm your baby if you do" (Noble, 1991: 8).

One of the most serious (and still fatal) STDs is the **human immunodeficiency virus (HIV)** that causes **acquired immunodeficiency syndrome,** or **AIDS,** a degenerative condition that attacks the body's immune system and renders it unable to fight a number of diseases, including some forms of pneumonia and cancer. First reported on June 5, 1981, by early 1994, AIDS had taken the lives of 220,000 Americans (Centers for Disease Control, mimeographed data, 1994). In fact, new AIDS cases increased by 111 percent between 1992 and 1993.

Table 7.4 _____
***Estimated Incidence of Selected STDs
in the United States, 1992***

STD	INCIDENCE
Chlamydia	4,000,000
Trichomoniasis	3,000,000
Urethritis	1,200,000
Gonorrhea	1,100,000
Human papilloma virus (HPV) (genital warts)	500,000–1,000,000
Genital herpes	200,000–500,000
Syphilis	123,500

SOURCE: Centers for Disease Control, 1993: 29

Although first discovered in gay men, AIDS is now spreading fastest among heterosexuals and especially among heterosexual women, who have no reported contact with the two groups at highest risk—gay or bisexual men and intravenous drug users. According to a recent study, women are more than twice as likely as men to become infected with the virus that causes AIDS for a number of reasons. First, the genital surface exposed to the virus in women is much more extensive than in men. Second, it is believed that vaginal secretions from an HIV-infected woman are less potent than an infected man's semen, which is capable of packing high concentrations of the virus. Third, a man's exposure to the virus is limited to the duration of sex, but semen remains in a woman's body after intercourse (Nicolosi, 1994).

Heterosexuals with the highest risk for HIV infection are teenagers, adults with multiple sex partners, people who suffer from other sexually transmitted diseases, and people who live in areas where AIDS is prevalent, particularly the South and the Northeast. "Multiple partners" does not mean having relationships with several partners at once, by the way, but with several partners, one at a time, over a longer period. Thus, the more partners you have, and the more partners your partners have had, the greater the danger of your becoming infected.

One widespread misperception is that midlife women are relatively immune to HIV infection. In fact, 11 percent of all AIDS victims over 45 are women. More than 2,400 new cases of AIDS in women 45 and over were reported to the U.S. Centers for Disease Control in 1993, and approximately half of the women over 50 with AIDS are women of color (Tichy and Talashek, 1992). According to the Center for Women Policy Studies (1994), the life situations of midlife and older women are important factors relating to their possible risk for infection. For example, because more older women than men are unmarried, they may be sexually involved with men who may not tell them that they are using drugs or are having sexual relations with other women or men. In addition, married women who are older may be less assertive than younger women and may feel they cannot insist on condoms or refuse their husbands' sexual demands.

Belgian researchers have identified as many as 30 strains of the AIDS virus that often elude conventional tests used to detect their presence in blood (*Washington Post,* 1994). Figure 7.4

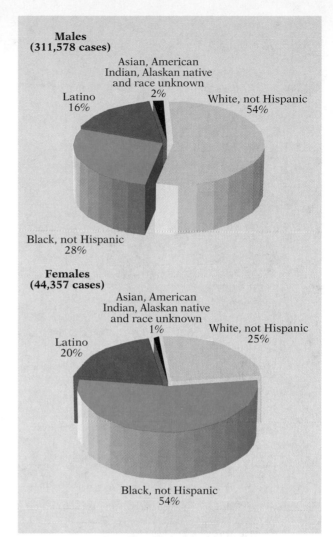

Figure 7.4 Men and Women Diagnosed with AIDS as of December 31, 1993. *More than half of the men with AIDS in this sample were white, whereas more than half of the women were black. Among men in all racial-ethnic groups, the primary source of infection was reportedly either homosexual or bisexual contact; the next most important source was intravenous (IV) drug use. Among women the primary source of infection was reported to be IV drug use; the next most important source was heterosexual contact with an infected man* (Centers for Disease Control and Prevention, 1994:9–10).

shows how AIDS cases are distributed by gender and by racial-ethnic group; Figure 7.5 contrasts the frequency of several different modes of transmission of this disease between adults and adolescents, on the one hand, and children on the other.

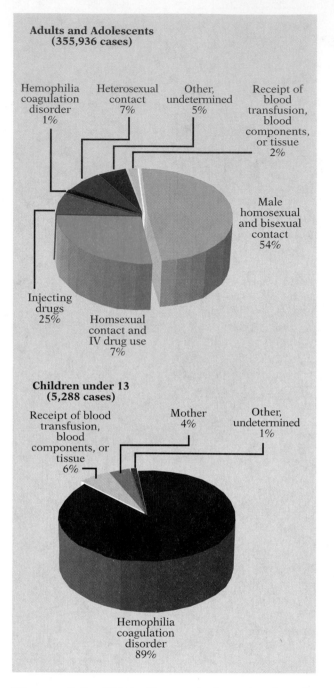

**Adults and Adolescents
(355,936 cases)**

Hemophilia coagulation disorder 1%

Heterosexual contact 7%

Other, undetermined 5%

Receipt of blood transfusion, blood components, or tissue 2%

Male homosexual and bisexual contact 54%

Injecting drugs 25%

Homsexual contact and IV drug use 7%

**Children under 13
(5,288 cases)**

Receipt of blood transfusion, blood components, or tissue 6%

Mother 4%

Other, undetermined 1%

Hemophilia coagulation disorder 89%

Figure 7.5 **AIDS Transmission Modes in Adults and Children, December 31, 1993.** *More than half of the adults infected with AIDS in this sample were male and were found to have contracted the disease through sexual activity with other men. A quarter of cases were attributed to the use of intravenous drugs. Among children, the primary source of infection was the use of infected blood in medical treatments for such disorders as hemophilia* (Centers for Disease Control, 1994:9–10).

Although AIDS cannot be cured (see Appendix D), it can be prevented (see the box "AIDS—Know the Facts and Act Responsibly"). Nevertheless, many people, even those who know how AIDS is transmitted, continue to take risks. One national probability sample found that only 17 percent of those with multiple sexual partners, 13 percent of those with risky sexual partners (people who are infected with HIV, have injected drugs in the past five years, are nonmonogamous, the recipients of blood transfusions, or hemophiliacs), and 11 percent of untested blood-transfusion recipients used condoms all the time (Catania et al., 1992). Supporting these findings is a report of a study of the patrons of ten bars in four cities in southern Ontario, Canada (Herold and Mewhinney, 1993). The researchers found that 32 percent of those surveyed had never used a condom and 44 percent had not used a condom the last time they had casual sex with someone they had just met.

AIDS is disproportionately high among people of color (see the Data Digest), in part because of educational, socioeconomic, and cultural factors. For example, in states where sex education is allowed but not required, schools with predominantly minority enrollments are less likely to devote time to HIV/AIDS education (Denson et al., 1993). If budgets are low and schools are understaffed, resources are generally funneled into academic areas rather than such "luxuries" as health or sex-education classes. According to several national studies, people with low incomes and those who do not complete high school are less likely to use condoms and more likely to have sexual intercourse with high-risk partners (Catania et al., 1992; Mosher and Pratt, 1993).

Cultural factors in the incidence of AIDS are many and varied. A study of Latino men in California, for example, found that many were very vulnerable to contracting AIDS because they had a poor understanding of how HIV infection is transmitted. Some of the men believed that people who are physically strong and healthy can avoid becoming infected or can fight off HIV once they become infected. Others said that they could readily recognize a woman who posed an AIDS risk by her appearance or social circumstances (such as whether she is known to their friends or family, or whether she is respectful of her parents). Although a few men insisted that they were capable of self-control, others said they could not control the "devil" inside, especially when they had been drinking (Forrest et al., 1993). In addition, many said that they used condoms only spo-

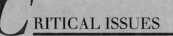
AIDS—Know the Facts and Act Responsibly

Although most people know what AIDS is, there are still many misperceptions about how HIV is transmitted and the risk of infection. Despite much evidence to the contrary, many people still believe that AIDS can be contracted through casual contact. For example, one political science professor refused to handle papers submitted by a student with AIDS (*Chronicle of Higher Education*, 1991). Many others believe that AIDS can be contracted through sharing utensils with someone who has the disease or by being coughed on or sneezed on. On the other hand, some believe that AIDS can't be transmitted by people infected with HIV (McNally and Mosher, 1991; Wilson, 1993). Such misperceptions account, in part, for the continuous increase in AIDS cases.

According to a variety of brochures distributed by the Centers for Disease Control, using condoms correctly is critical in preventing the transmission of STDs and HIV:

❏ *Use only condoms made of latex rubber.* Look for the word *latex* on the package. Don't be fooled by advertising or sales talk into buying lambskin or natural membrane condoms. They are ineffective because they contain tiny holes from the pores in the original material. Only latex rubber creates an effective barrier against HIV.

❏ Condoms should always be *stored in a cool, dry place,* away from heat and sun. Don't keep condoms in an automobile glove compartment, for example.

❏ When you open a condom package, *don't use teeth, fingernails, or other sharp objects*; you may damage the condom inside.

❏ Never use a condom more than once. Use a *new latex condom for each act of intercourse*—whether vaginal, anal, or oral.

❏ Put the condom on *after the penis is erect but before any sexual contact.* When putting on a condom, make sure there is a little space at the tip—enough to hold the ejaculate (semen).

❏ *Don't go to sleep* while the penis is still within the vagina; semen could leak out of the condom into the vagina. *Withdraw the penis very carefully* to avoid dislodging the condom and spilling semen.

❏ Wrap in a tissue and *throw away the used condom immediately*.

❏ *For added protection*, use a lubricant—birth-control foam, jelly, or cream—along with the condom; choose one that contains the *chemical barrier nonoxynol-9*, a spermicidal agent that also protects against disease. Never use water-based lubricants like hand lotion, cold cream, baby oil, petroleum jelly, or shortening. These provide no protection *and* they can cause a condom to weaken and tear.

❏ Place a small amount of the foam, cream, or jelly *on the inside tip* of the condom before unrolling it.

❏ After unrolling the condom over the erect penis, place some of the foam, cream, or jelly on the *outside of the condom*. For vaginal sex, insert an applicator full of spermicide inside the vagina for extra protection.

---

radically because "a man should be willing and able to perform sexually whenever the opportunity arises." Another study found that the Latino men who were most likely to understand how HIV is spread and to use condoms were those who were English-speaking, better educated, and more "Americanized" (Marin et al., 1993).

Although AIDS among heterosexuals is spreading faster than among homosexuals, many gay men continue to have unprotected intercourse. The most commonly cited excuse for risky sexual conduct is the influence of drugs or alcohol, followed by sexual passion, as an expression of love ("I don't want my lover to feel I reject him just because he has HIV"), and because partners pressure them not to use condoms (Levine and Siegel, 1992). Gary Remafedi, a researcher who surveyed gay teenagers in Minnesota, found that 63 percent were at "extreme risk" of having been exposed to HIV because they had had unsafe sex or had shared needles even though they were knowledgeable about the causes of AIDS (reported in Coleman, 1994).

One might expect that college students would be more likely than adolescents to practice safe sex because they are more mature and more informed about STDs and AIDS, but this is not necessarily the case. In one study, 25 percent of college students surveyed reported no change in their sexual activities in response to the AIDS epidemic. Over 75 percent said they had had up to four sexual partners within the 12 months preceding the study but did not see themselves as being at high or even average risk for contracting AIDS. The researchers speculated that many of the students were under the mistaken impression we referred to earlier in this section, that "multiple partners" means two or more partners *at the same time* (Gray and Saracino, 1991). In another study, 44 percent of students reported using condoms less than half the time for vaginal intercourse; 90 percent of those who engaged in anal sex did not use condoms (Oswalt and Matsen, 1993). The researchers suggested that even though most students are aware of AIDS and its mode of transmission, many see the condom as a birth-control device rather than a method of disease prevention. Thus, many college students have a high likelihood of being exposed to AIDS.

CONCLUSION

Although today we have more *choices* in our sexual expression, particularly in respect to sex outside of marriage, we also face some serious *constraints*. The double standard still defines appropriate behavior for men and for women differently. Gay men and lesbians still face discrimination and harassment because of their sexual practices. And our health and lives and the lives of our children are threatened by the rising incidence of STDs, HIV infection, and AIDS. These *changes* have significant effects on both men and women in their search for suitable partners for marriage and other long-term relationships. We will look at some of these issues in the next several chapters.

Taking Action

Protecting Yourself And Others

Because in the mid-1990s sex is often literally a matter of life or death, you can help protect yourself and others by not becoming infected with STDs or HIV. We've given you some advice on the use of condoms (see the box "AIDS—Know the Facts and Act Responsibly"). For more detailed information about sexually transmitted diseases, consult one or more of the following resources:
• The CDC National **STD Hotline** (800-227-8922) answers questions and will send you a variety of brochures on STDs in a plain envelope.
• The CDC National **AIDS Clearinghouse** (800-458-5231) will send you brochures on the use of condoms and on early HIV infection, as well as information on women and HIV/AIDS. Again, the materials come in a plain envelope.

The CDC also offers an AIDS hotline in Spanish (800-344-7432) and one for the hearing impaired (800-243-7889).
• ETR Associates (800-321-4407) provides a variety of materials on such topics as **abstinence, reproductive health, STDs, HIV/AIDS, and drug abuse.** Some of their eye-catching and thought-provoking brochures include "101 Ways to Get High Without Drugs," "101 Ways to Stay Alive," "101 Ways to Stress the Best," and "101 Ways to Make Love Without Doin' It."
• If you or someone you know is experiencing sexual difficulties and want to call a reputable **sex therapist,** contact the American Academy of Clinical Sexologists (202-462-2122), the Society for Sex Therapy and Research (212-241-6758), or the American Association of Sex Educators, Counselors, and Therapists (312-644-0828).

SUMMARY

1. Our sexual lives affect our families and marriages from birth to death. Regardless of age or marital status, sexual expression plays an important role throughout the course of life.

2. Premarital sex, especially among teenagers, has increased considerably since the 1950s. The biggest increases have occurred for white teenage women.

3. There are many reasons for this increase,

including early maturation, peer pressure, lack of parental influence, and the use of force by one person.

4. Like their younger counterparts, more college students are also engaging in sex. Since the 1960s, the gap between the frequency of sexual activity reported by men and by women has narrowed considerably.

5. Marital sex typically decreases over the

course of a marriage, but married couples report enjoying a variety of sexual activities besides sexual intercourse.

6. Extramarital sex may seem romantic, but few extramarital affairs last beyond a year or two, only 10 percent result in marriage, and many have devastating effects on a family.

7. Despite the stereotypes about sexuality and aging, people who are 70 years old and over continue to engage in sexual activities, including intercourse, oral sex, masturbation, and sexual fantasy.

8. Homosexual partners experience many of the same feelings as do heterosexuals and face some of the same problems in their relationships with each other. Major factors that differentiate gay and lesbian couples from heterosexual cou-

ples are society's disapproval of the former's sexual practices and their consequent lack of legal rights in many areas.

9. Almost all couples experience sexual dysfunctions at least once in their lifetime. Many sexual dysfunctions are physiological; others are psychological or interpersonal. Treatment resources for both types of dysfunction are readily available.

10. Although today more people are informed about STDs, HIV infection, and AIDS, many are still engaging in high-risk sexual behavior, such as having sex with many partners and not using condoms. The rates for AIDS are especially high among people of color and they are increasing among heterosexual women.

KEY TERMS

menopause   186
male climacteric   187
sexual dysfunction   190
erectile dysfunction (impotence)   190
premature ejaculation   191
vaginismus   191
anorgasmia   192

dyspareunia   192
inhibited sexual desire (ISD)   192
sexual aversion   192
sexually transmitted diseases (STDs)   194
human immunodeficiency virus (HIV)   194
acquired immunodeficiency syndrome (AIDS)   194

ADDITIONAL READING

HENRY ABELOVE, MICHELE AINA BARALE, and DAVID M. HALPERIN, eds., *The Lesbian and Gay Studies Reader* (New York: Routledge, 1993). A number of the 42 essays in this anthology deal with lesbian and gay sexuality.

ROBERT N. BUTLER and MYRNA I. LEWIS, *Love and Sex after 60* (New York: Harper & Row, 1986). An easy-to-read book that examines such topics as normal physical changes in sexuality, the effects of drugs on sexual functioning, common emotional problems related to sex, and learning new patterns of lovemaking.

CAROL CASSELL, *Straight from the Heart: How to Talk to Your Teenagers about Love and Sex* (New York: Simon and Schuster, 1987). A useful guidebook for parents on what to say (and not to say), when to say it, and how to respect teenagers' privacy.

GERMAINE GREER, *The Change: Women, Aging and the Menopause* (New York: Knopf, 1992). Another very readable book on this topic is Gail Sheehy, *The Silent Passage: Menopause* (New York: Random House, 1992).

DALMA HEYN, *The Erotic Silence of the American Wife* (New York: Turtle Bay Books, 1992). This book describes the discontents of many women who are expected to live up to sexual stereotypes.

JOAN HUBER and BETH E. SCHNEIDER, eds., *The Social Context of AIDS* (Newbury Park, CA: Sage, 1992). This reader offers a variety of articles on AIDS and class, gender, and race, on risky behavior, and on policies that affect people with AIDS.

ALICE S. ROSSI, ed., *Sexuality across the Life Course* (Chicago: University of Chicago Press, 1994). As the title suggests, this book examines sexuality throughout the life cycle, including premarital, marital, and extramarital sex.

SUSAN SPRECHER and KATHLEEN MCKINNEY, *Sexuality* (Newbury Park, CA: Sage, 1993). The authors cover a variety of topics, including the beginning of a sexual relationship, sexual behavior and satisfaction in close relationships, and sexual coercion in relationships.

8
Becoming a Couple: Dating, Rating, and Mating

Data Digest

- In a recent magazine poll, about **80 percent of teenage girls,** age 12 to 17, said they would ask a boy to the prom if no one asked them.

- In 1993, **almost 73 million U.S. adults were single**—divorced, widowed, or never married—an increase of nearly 18 percent over the preceding ten years.

- Some nations had a **shortage of marriageable women** in the mid-1990s. For example, in India there were nearly 133 single men for every 100 single women, and in China there were nearly three single men for every two single women.

- In a study of 272 never-married people between 18 and 30 years of age, **women used minor aggression** (throwing something, pushing, slapping) almost twice as often as men (38 percent versus 22 percent) and **severe aggression** (especially kicking, biting, and hitting) six times as often as men (19 percent versus 3 percent). However, in dating relationships, **women sustained more injuries than men,** and they were two to three times more likely to experience unwanted sexual intercourse.

- According to a study by the Harvard School of Public Health, about 16 percent of college students (male and female) are nondrinkers; however, 28 percent of the men and 19 percent of the women students reported being drunk three or more times in the past month. **About 95 percent of violent crime on campus is alcohol- or drug-related**: Seventy-three percent of the assailants and 55 percent of the victims of rape had used alcohol or other drugs.

SOURCES: Roberts, 1991; Stets and Henderson, 1991; Ward et al., 1991; Adler and Rosenberg, 1994; Cowherd, 1994; Saluter, 1994; Shenon, 1994; *U.S. News & World Report,* 1994.

Queen Elizabeth I of England once commented, "I would rather be a beggar and single than a queen and married." In contrast, some Americans invest small fortunes in the search for a spouse; others, though, are quite innovative. A 76-year-old widower in a wealthy Baltimore neighborhood paid $400 for a professionally made 6-foot-by-6-foot sign for his front lawn that read "Wanted: a Wife!" This oversized advertisement proclaimed that the widower wanted someone between age 40 and 60 who was smart and could cook and drive. He also required a photo and résumé and a month-long tryout. When asked what he had to offer a prospective wife, he replied, "I'm good-looking." Although some of the neighbors were appalled by such a "tacky" approach, the widower had 12 applicants shortly after the sign was erected (Leung, 1994).

Courtship can be fun and exhilarating, but it can also be disappointing and even painful. In this chapter you will see that although we have more choices today than in the past (see the box "Courting Throughout History"), various constraints shape contemporary mate-selection behavior.

WHY DO WE DATE?

The reasons for **dating**—the process of meeting people socially for possible mate selection—seem evident, but dating is considerably more complicated than just meeting new people or having fun. Some sociologists describe the courtship process as a **marriage market,** in which prospective spouses compare the assets and liabilities of eligible partners and choose the best available mate. In this sense, even though dating is romantic and enjoyable, it is also a serious enterprise.

Dating also fulfills a number of specific functions that enhance people's sociopsychological development and, ultimately, promote a society's continuity. These functions vary according to a person's age, gender, motivation, and life-cycle stage. Dating functions can be either *manifest*—the purposes are visible, recognized, and intended—or *latent*—the purposes are unintended or not immediately recognized. Keep in mind that these functions often overlap.

Courting Throughout History

Historians have found a remarkable continuity in some courtship patterns (Kimmel, 1984). Contrary to what we might think, young people in colonial America were often given a surprising degree of freedom in sexual expression. For example, a young suitor in Towanda, Pennsylvania, wrote in his diary that, after the family members went to bed, "my beloved and I went down, made a fire, and sat down to talk and kiss and embrace and bathe in love" (Rothman, 1983: 396). And a young woman wrote passionately to her lover:

O! I do really want to kiss you. How I should like to be in that old parlor with you. I hope there will be a carpet on the floor for it seems you intend to act worse than you ever did before by your letter. But I shall humbly submit to my fate and willingly too, to speak candidly (Rothman, 1983: 401).

But there were also practical considerations. In colonial New England, parents would conduct economic negotiations, and most young men could not even think about courtship until they owned land. They were advised to "choose by Ears, as well as Eyes" and to select women who were industrious, hardworking, and sensible. Affection was expected to blossom into love *after* marriage.

Some women were very down-to-earth about courtship. A New York woman wrote: "I am sick of all this choosing. If a man is healthy and does not drink and has a good little handful of stock and a good temper and is a good Christian, what difference can it make to a woman which man she takes?" (Ryan, 1983: 40-41).

Before the Industrial Revolution, most courtship activities took place within the hustle and bustle of community life. Young people could meet after church services, during picnics, or at gatherings like barn raisings, corn huskings, and dances. The buggy ride was especially popular: There was no room for a chaperone, and "the horse might run away or lose a shoe so that one could be stranded on a lonely country road" (McPharlin, 1946: 10).

With the advent of bicycles and telephones, parlor sofas and front-porch swings were quickly abandoned. At the turn of the century people began to use the term *dating*, which referred to couples setting a specific date, time, and place to meet. When the automobile came into widespread use in the early 1920s, dating took a giant step: "The car provided more privacy and excitement than either the dance hall or the movie theater, and the result was the spread of petting" (Rothman, 1984: 295). Young people had the mobility to meet more frequently, informally, and casually.

Manifest Functions of Dating

One of the most important functions of dating is *recreation*. Dating should be fun. Waller (1937) saw dating as "pure thrill seeking." Although recent studies suggest that dating has become more serious and marriage oriented, it is still fun (Gordon, 1981). And as more people postpone marriage, dating has become an important recreational activity in its own right.

Another important manifest function is *companionship*. Especially as people age, dating may be important for developing and maintaining long-term friendships rather than just for recreation or "thrills" (McCabe, 1984). Dating can be a valuable source of companionship, especially after retirement, when leisure hours increase.

Finally, whether people admit it or not, dating is usually a step in *mate selection*. Adolescents often become angry if their parents criticize their dates with such remarks as, "We don't want you to marry this guy" or "She's not good enough for you." The teenager's impatient rebuttal is usually, "I'm not going to *marry* him (her). We're just dating!" Parents are often critical, however, because they recognize that dating *can* lead to marriage. Young people are engaging in "comparison shopping," acquiring knowledge of what sorts of people they are attracted to and may want to marry (Whyte, 1990). In contrast, there is little need for dating in cultures where parents control their children's mate selection, where values focus on the needs of the family rather than those of the individual, or where love is not the basis for marriage (see later sections of this chapter).

Latent Functions of Dating

The manifest purpose of "meeting new people" tends to obscure a function of dating that is less visible but especially important—that of *socializa-*

tion, in which people learn to adjust and adapt their own behavior to that of others. Through dating, people learn about expected gender roles; they learn about family structures that are different from their own; and they learn about unfamiliar attitudes, beliefs, and values. This kind of learning may be especially important for high school students, who can test and hone their self-confidence and their communication skills in a one-on-one setting (Ramu, 1989; Berk, 1993).

Gaining social status is another important latent function of dating. In the mid-1930s Waller found that college students tried to date the "most desirable" people on campus. Dating a very attractive coed or the son of wealthy parents enhanced one's status and prestige. This function has not changed. It is not unusual, for example, to hear someone brag about dating the captain of the football or cheerleading team, a vice president of a prestigious company, or a successful attorney.

A related function of dating is *fulfilling ego needs*. Being asked out on a date or having one's invitation accepted boosts a person's self-esteem and self-image. If the date goes well, or if the partner is understanding, flattering, or attentive, self-confidence will be enhanced.

Finally, dating provides *opportunities for sexual experimentation and intimacy*. As we discussed in Chapter 6, many teenagers learn about sex during dating.

Manifest and latent functions of dating may change over time. Roscoe et al. (1987) examined dating patterns at three developmental stages: early adolescence (sixth grade), middle adolescence (eleventh grade), and late adolescence (college). These researchers found that, whereas early and middle adolescents were most interested in recreation, romantic intimacy, and status, late adolescents cited sexual intimacy, companionship, and learning socialization skills as the most important aspects of dating. Furthermore, whereas early adolescents emphasized such things as fashionable dress and peer approval, late adolescents were more interested in the dating partner's future goals and job prospects. Thus, as people mature, their expectations about dating change.

FORMS OF DATING

Dating is changing for people of all ages. Although traditional dating is still widespread, there are a number of new forms of dating as well as some combinations of traditional and contemporary dating. In this section we discuss the categories listed in Table 8.1.

Traditional Dating

In traditional dating, males and females follow clearly defined expectations in meeting and spending time with each other. The one-on-one traditional date is the foundation of other formal dating, such as coming-out parties and going steady.

Traditional Dates The *traditional date*, which at least among the middle classes dominated up through the 1970s, is a fairly formal way of meeting potential spouses. The girl waits to be asked out, the boy picks her up at her home, and she is almost always late, giving Mom and Dad a chance to chat with the boy. The boy has specific plans for the evening, the couple have a good time, and he brings her home by curfew. Some 1950s television series like "Father Knows Best," "The Patty Duke Show," "Bachelor Father," and "My Three Sons," although idealized, often portrayed this type of date.

The downside of the traditional date is the expectation that because the boy pays for the date, the girl must show her gratitude in some way, usually through a good-night kiss, petting, or intercourse. The TV show "Happy Days" suggested that in the 1950s dating implied "making out." And in the popular "Mary Tyler Moore Show" during the 1970s, career women Mary and Rhoda often were pushing amorous dates out of their apartments.

Table 8.1 _____
The Many Varieties of Dating

Traditional
Traditional dates
Coming-out, *quinceañeras*
Going steady

Contemporary
Hanging out
Getting together
"Goin' with"
Serious casual dating and serious dating

Traditional-Contemporary Combinations
Cruising
Proms, homecomings
Mixers
Dinner dates

Dating in the middle of the twentieth century was more structured than it is today. Although casual dates weren't unheard of, formal dates ruled by codes of dress and behavior were very common.

Coming-Out and the Quinceañera The continuing popularity of traditional dating is particularly noticeable in such formal events as *coming-out parties*, where young women—usually of the upper classes—are "introduced to society." In some Latino communities, for example, the *quinceañera* (translated loosely as "fifteen years") is a coming-out party that celebrates a girl's entrance into adulthood. The *quinceañera* is an elaborate and dignified religious and social affair given by the girl's parents that begins with a Catholic mass, followed by a reception at which 14 couples (each couple represents one year in the girl's life before the *quinceañera*) serve as her attendants. The event includes a traditional waltz in which the young woman dances with her father, a champagne toast, and the tossing of a bouquet to the boys to determine who wins the first dance with the young woman. The Latino girl may be allowed to date boys after her *quinceañera*. There is no comparable rite of passage for Latino boys (Leff, 1994).

Going Steady Going steady and "getting pinned" became popular after World War II. *Going steady,* which often meant that the partners were seeing only each other, usually came after a couple had had a number of dates, and it preceded engagement (Tuttle, 1993). Going steady was not necessarily expected to result in marriage. It eliminated many of the anxieties associated with traditional dating but allowed emotional and sexual intimacy without a long-term commitment. It did, however, give a "hands-off" message to possible competitors. It is not clear how widespread going steady is today; it may be more common in high schools in rural areas (Gordon and Miller, 1984).

Going steady reportedly increases self-esteem for both sexes. This effect is likely to be greater in boys, for whom having a steady date is considered an achievement, especially if the girl is popular. In contrast, girls usually see steady dating as an opportunity to develop meaningful interpersonal relations (Samet and Kelly, 1987).

Contemporary Dating

Contemporary dating falls into two general categories: *casual dating,* which includes hanging out, getting together, and "goin' with," and *serious dating,* which includes serious casual dating and the serious dating that can lead to cohabitation, engagement, and marriage.

Hanging Out Parents and adolescents in many American homes engage in a familiar dialogue:

PARENT: *Where are you going?*
TEENAGER: *Out.*
PARENT: *What will you do?*
TEENAGER: *Nothing.*
PARENT: *Who will be there?*
TEENAGER: *I don't know.*
PARENT: *When will you be back?*
TEENAGER: *I'm not sure.*
PARENT: *Leave a phone number, please.*
TEENAGER: *We'll probably be moving around a lot.*

The exasperated parent sometimes explodes: "What do you *mean* you don't know? Moving around a lot? *Where?*" The adolescent, equally frustrated, replies, "I won't know 'til I get there."

Whether *hanging out* occurs on a neighborhood street corner, at a diner or pizza parlor, or in a mall, it is a time-honored adolescent pastime. A customary meeting time and place may be set, with people coming and going; or once a group gets together and the members decide what they want to do, the information is spread (at amazing speed) by telephone. Hanging out is possible both because many parents respect their teenagers' privacy and independence and because most 16- and 17-year-olds have access to cars.

Getting Together *Getting together* is a combination of hanging out and cruising. A group of friends meet at a friend's house, a club, or a

In one ritual of the Latino "quince," as it's familiarly known, the young woman's father slips on her first pair of high heels. In the Miami Cuban community, some families spend as much as $50,000 on a daughter's quinceañera.

party. Because most people do not come with dates, there can be a lot of mixing. The initial effort can be organized by either males or females, and the group often pools its resources, for the use of alcohol or other drugs may be part of the activities. Because participants are not formally dating, there is a lot of flexibility in meeting new people and initiating relationships.

The significant characteristic of getting together is "floating." The group may meet at someone's pool for a few hours, decide to go to a party later, spend a few hours at a pizza place, and wind up at another party. Young adults see getting together as normal and rational—"You get to meet a lot of people" or "We can go someplace else if the party is dead"—but it concerns parents. Even if the teenagers call from the various locations to tell parents where they are (although it is easy not to do so), parents worry that the gatherings can become unpredictable or dangerous.

Getting together is a popular form of dating for many reasons. Because the activities are spontaneous, there is little anxiety about preparing for a formal date or initiating or rejecting sexual advances. It is also a less threatening emotional experience because the participants do not have to worry about finding a date or getting "stuck" with someone (like a blind date) for the whole evening. It also relieves females of sexual pressure. Because the women may help organize the get-together, share in the expenses, and come alone or with friends (not as part of a couple), there is a greater opportunity for them to

develop relationships that are based not only on physical attraction but also on shared interests. People may pair off, participate in the group as a couple, or gradually withdraw to spend more time together, but there is less pressure to have a date as a sign of popularity. Finally, getting together decreases parental control over the choice of one's friends. Parents usually do not know many of the adolescents and are less likely to disapprove of the friendships or to compare notes with other parents.

"Goin' With" *"Goin' with,"* or going together, lies somewhere between getting together and going steady. Although the couples are not planning to get engaged, they are also not seeing other partners. "Goin' with" sometimes starts before puberty, even though the relationships of fourth-, fifth-, and sixth-graders usually last only a few weeks (Thorne, 1993). For older children, "goin' with" may last months or even years. The advantage of "goin' with" is having a stable relationship when many other things around the young person are changing and unpredictable (physiological changes, divorcing parents, preparation for college or a job). The disadvantage is that such a relationship discourages meeting new people during a developmental stage when adolescents experience many changes in their attitudes and interests within relatively short periods of time.

Serious Casual Dating and Serious Dating
There is often an intermediate step between casual dating like hanging out and getting together and serious dating like cohabitation and becoming engaged. One author calls this step *serious casual dating*: You recognize that a woman or man "might actually fit your romantic vision of a relationship and decide that you want to get closer" (Sterling, 1992: 165). Sex is probably the least important factor in this relationship. Instead, partners may compare expectations and habits, look for compatibility or complementarity in their personality traits, search for similarities in their beliefs and values, develop trust, and express loyalty, acceptance, admiration, and support for each other (Sterling, 1992).

Traditional-Contemporary Combinations

Several dating patterns incorporate both traditional customs and contemporary innovations. Today it is more acceptable for either sex to initiate dates or to invite a partner to a prom or dinner, but many of the *gender scripts* (behaviors expected of people because of their sex) remain remarkably traditional.

Cruising Cruising was common during the 1940s and 1950s. Several teenagers (usually boys) would pack into a car and drive around the neighborhood to see "what's going on." Whistling at girls, hollering to friends, and racing against other cars were considered part of the fun. Cruising has made a comeback in many towns and suburbs. Both girls and boys cruise, and teenagers claim the practice is just flirtation. Nonetheless, some communities have tried to ban cruising because teenagers are accused of clogging traffic, littering the streets with beer cans, and playing their music too loudly (*Newsweek*, 1990b).

Proms and Homecoming Parties *Proms and homecoming parties* continue to be among the most popular dating events. As in the past, they are formal or semiformal. Women get corsages, men are typically responsible for transportation and other expenses, and both sexes invest quite a bit of time and money in preparing for these events. Contemporary changes include occasional invitations to these events by women to men instead of the reverse; attending these events in small groups of friends rather than with partners; and extending an event by holding sleepovers (presumably chaperoned by parents), staying out all night and returning after breakfast, or continuing the festivities into the weekend at a nearby beach or other recreational place.

Mixers *Mixers*, particularly popular social functions in colleges and universities during the 1960s and 1970s, are informal dances where students, especially freshmen, can get acquainted. Although some students describe mixers as a "meat market," it is still one of the ways—besides parties and dances—to meet people of the opposite sex (Holland and Eisenhart, 1990), especially in sex-segregated colleges. Mixers have also appeared at the lower educational levels. For example, middle schools often use heavily chaperoned mixers as a regular part of the schools' social activities.

Dinner Dates One of the most traditional forms of dating, the *dinner date*, is still popular today, especially among adults. One observer has

"Mixers" have long served as a respectable way for young adults to meet one another.

noted that there is no more widespread courtship ploy than offering food in the hope of gaining sexual favors: "Around the world men give women presents prior to lovemaking. A fish, a piece of meat, sweets, and beer are among the delicacies men have invented as offerings" (Fisher, 1993: 43).

Dinner dates, and especially first dates of any kind, are still highly scripted. For example, in a study of college students, Rose and Frieze (1993) found considerable gender typing on the first date. Men typically initiated the date, drove the car, opened doors, and started sexual interaction (such as kissing good night or making out). Women spent a good deal of time on their appearance, depended on the men to make the plans, and often responded to men's sexual overtures. The researchers concluded that making a "good impression" early in the dating relationship is still largely synonymous with playing traditional gender roles.

In contrast to the past, the dinner date or the first date does not always signal "paying off" with sex. The rise of the women's movement in the 1970s led to the custom of *going dutch*, in which men and women split the costs of a date. Sharing dating expenses both frees women to initiate dates and relieves them from feeling they are expected to reciprocate a man's generosity with sexual favors.

Perhaps the least gender-typed dating, at least on first dates, is between same-sex partners. In a study of lesbians and gay men, Klinkenberg and Rose (1994) found little gender typing compared to heterosexual dating: Both partners participated more equally in orchestrating the date, maintaining the conversation, and initiating physical contact. There was also less concern about appearance.

CONTEMPORARY MATE-SELECTION METHODS

The variety of mate-selection methods has burgeoned in recent years. Advances in computer technology have added to the methods available today, all of which promise (but do not necessarily provide) options for meeting a prospective spouse.

Personal Classified Advertisements

Personal classified advertisements used to be published in the back pages of "smutty" magazines. Increasingly, however, mainstream newspapers include "personals" in their daily or weekend issues. For example, *The Globe and Mail*, Canada's national newspaper, regularly features a personal classified ads section in its Saturday edition. Similarly, many suburban, religious, and local newspapers now carry personal ads.

There has been no systematic research on the success rate of personals, but one study found that men are twice as likely as women to place these ads. In addition, the ads examined sought companions with stereotypical gender-role characteristics: male advertisers tended to emphasize such traits as appearance and attractiveness in the women they hoped to meet; women advertisers looked for intelligence, a college degree, and financial status in the male companions they sought (Davis, 1990).

The advantages of classified ads include anonymity, low cost and time savings, and a choice of applicants. A major disadvantage is that advertisers often exaggerate their desirable attributes (such as attractiveness). In addition, "selective truth telling" is commonplace. For example, single women often omit mentioning having children in the ads (Ahuvia and Adelman, 1992).

A recent variation is the "voice personal," which promises to "put you together with someone who shares similar interests, dreams, and goals." For example, a person can place a 20-word classified ad in the newspaper and record a personal voice greeting as well. People responding to the ad can browse through the voice greet-ings, make selections, and leave advertisers a message. Both typically pay about two dollars per minute to place or retrieve messages.

Mail-Order Brides

Some American men seeking wives patronize mail-order services that publish photographs and descriptions of women, usually from developing countries. The typical subscriber lives in a metropolitan area, is about 41 years old, divorced, earns more than $20,000 a year, and has completed two or more years of college (Krich, 1989). Men who seek mail-order brides have been described by women's rights activists as "losers" who want sock-sorters or live-in nurses. Although the men do not deny that they want housekeepers, they complain that American women are self-centered or promiscuous:

American girls left me really disappointed. . . . They're pushy, spoiled rotten, and they talk like sailors. They're not cooperative, but combative— and they never appreciate what you do for them. In the morning, you wonder how many guys before me? Was it the football team? . . . They're not psychologically together. They just don't seem to know what they want (Krich, 1989: 385, 387).

Mail-order brides are usually 20 years younger than their prospective husbands. They often live in poverty, are unwed or abandoned mothers, and are unacceptable to the men in their own countries. Frequently, they see marriage as the fastest way to enter the United States legally (Belkin, 1986). Unfortunately, some are subjected to mental or physical abuse by the men they marry, yet fear to seek help lest they be deported.

After the death of Soviet communism in the early 1990s, some American entrepreneurs became wealthy by matching U.S. men with Russian women. Because alcoholism and wars had led to a scarcity of eligible men in Russia, there was an oversupply of single, attractive women who dreamed of having American husbands who, they assumed, would treat them as equals (Sullivan, 1994). Typically, however, the men seeking these matches are looking for women who are not only attractive but "unliberated"— someone who would cook, clean, "follow the man's lead," and take care of the man rather than pursue a career or her own interests. Some

Russian women are disappointed by such traditional expectations and back out of the match. Many, however, are enthusiastic about bride-seeking Americans. According to one journalist, an attractive 21-year-old accountant stated:

I heard that American men don't like to marry American women because they're very emancipated. We are more domestic, I think. I don't know American women, so maybe I am wrong, but I think maybe they are crazy. Because, first of all for me is to have children and a good husband, and second of all is maybe to have a good business (Schillinger, 1994: 16–17).

Marriage Bureaus

In some countries, classified ads and especially marriage bureaus have replaced the old-fashioned, community-based matchmaker (see the box "Modern Arranged Marriages in India"). In the United States, prices, services, and personal attention vary according to the needs of the client. For example, in one case a rabbi and his wife are subsidized by the United Jewish Foundation and rely on intuition and "God's direct intervention" to help Jewish singles find each other. In another case, the retired director of a nonprofit health agency charges $65 for two introductions and another $40 for additional matches (based on "an old lady's gut feeling"). At the more expensive "Meet the Elite" dating service in New York City, clients pay at least $10,000 for a more rigorous selection process in which all subscribers are investigated by detectives, undergo medical examinations and handwriting analysis, and are analyzed by the company's psychologist (Hirsh, 1988; Polk, 1988). One-on-one services where a matchmaker searches for someone who is "just right for you" can cost up to $25,000 (Tennesen, 1993).

Computer Cupids

Computer-dating brochures promise love, romance, and marriage:

Compatibility Unlimited. A deeply fulfilling relationship is something that just about everyone wants, yet very few people achieve. . . . Fill out the personality test below [50 items] and return it to us today. 15,000 people have already become members. Don't you think one of them is right for you?

Singles Choice, a members-only organization, is composed of people just like you: successful, single, and goal-oriented. The Singles Choice program brings you together with successful singles like yourself on a regular referral basis. In almost no time at all you'll be with people who complement and enhance your lifestyle.

CROSS CULTURAL

Modern Arranged Marriages in India

In India, the loyalty of the individual to the family is a cherished ideal. To preserve this ideal, marriages are carefully arranged to avoid selecting inappropriate mates; brides and grooms rarely choose their own spouses. In some cities, people are combining traditional aspects of arranged marriages with very nontraditional methods of finding prospective spouses.

Among the literate classes, newspaper advertisements and computer services are replacing traditional matchmakers. Every Sunday the newspapers are filled with classified ads inviting inquiries about "smart, well-educated, professional boys" and "really beautiful, homely, university graduate girls." ("Homely" in India does not mean unattractive but that a woman would make a good homemaker—that is, wife, mother, and housekeeper.)

This style of mate selection is not confined to Indians living in India. For example, Sanjit, a 34-year-old engineer, has lived in the United States since he was 12. Sanjit's family received 103 responses when they placed the following ad in *The Times of India*: "Alliance invited for smart, Bengali Hindu engineer, 34, 185 cms (6 feet), settled in the United States, music addict, no encumbrances." Sanjit's family narrowed the list down to seven women and then started negotiations, writing or calling the women's families. Sanjit said he hoped his family would find the right woman so he could get married on his next trip to India (*Baltimore Sun,* 1989).

Many people find computer-dating services appealing because they are busy at work, have less time to date or look for eligible partners, or are disenchanted with singles bars. Nevertheless, many are disappointed by the results. Although they pay between $2,000 and $4,000 for a one- to three-year membership, only about 3 percent of matches lead to long-term relationships or marriage. For example, one man spent $2,600 to join a matchmaking service and met ten women, none of whom were even remotely interested in him (Corey, 1993).

Many computer-dating services use 5- to 10-minute videotapes, where the candidates talk about themselves and their interests. This method is not very effective because data on too many prospective partners can create an information overload and result in poor decision making (Woll and Young, 1989). And even when clients find attractive possibilities, a match is not guaranteed because videotapes and written summaries are simply not accurate predictors of personality traits, values, and long-term behavior (see Ahuvia and Adelman, 1992, for a review of some of this research). Many people believe that finding dates through computer services is safer than picking them up in bars, but all dating involves the risk of such serious problems as sexual pressure, aggression, and violence.

The most recent computer cupids are electronic networks. If people have a computer, a modem, and a telephone, they can subscribe to computer networks (see the "Taking Action" section) that have "rooms" where subscribers "meet" hundreds of other people and discuss anything from radishes to romance. One of the advantages of electronic liaisons is that people use code names and remain anonymous for as long as they choose. In addition, conversing through the computer allows people to get to know each other without worrying about physical appearance. People can ignore messages or they can get involved and develop romantic relationships. In fact, some networks have even had weddings on-line: In one case, the happy couple typed their vows on one computer terminal while the minister typed his lines on another, and more than and 75 subscribers "witnessed" the wedding (Catalfo, 1994).

Electronic romances can also become offensive or intimidating. Rejected suitors may start stalking or harassing their love interests (Plotnikoff, 1994). Lovers who quarrel or break up

are quite capable of sending hundreds of vindictive and hostile messages to the person who has spurned them before the network management bounces the offender by closing the account or otherwise blocking access to the network (Catalfo, 1994).

CHOICES AND CONSTRAINTS IN DATING AND MATE SELECTION

Many people believe that "This is America. I can date anyone I want." Compared to even ten years ago, people do have more dating and mate-selection options today. As the discussion in this section shows, however, there are also many constraints.

The Permanent Availability Model

In the early 1960s, sociologist Bernard Farber challenged traditional explanations of mate selection and marriage with his *permanent availability model*. In essence, Farber (1964) argued that adults are "permanently available" for marriage with anyone and at any time. Noting that the family was changing from a closed to an open system, Farber proposed that because individuals' needs and desires also change over time, they "may not suffice to maintain the marriage." Because divorce and remarriage rates were increasing, and youth and glamour were becoming more important, Farber felt "playing the field" would prepare people for change better than would settling on a spouse at an early age.

The permanent-availability model is probably more applicable today than it was three decades ago. As we will see, although still bound by norms of exogamy and endogamy, mate-selection options are increasing for many people, and they are increasing throughout the life cycle rather than just during early adulthood.

Exogamy and Endogamy

As we saw in Chapter 1, much of our mating behavior is shaped by rules of exogamy, which require that we marry outside of certain groups, and of endogamy, which require us to marry within certain social groups or categories. Exogamy generally requires that we marry outside of nuclear and extended families. Most societies prohibit dating or marriage between siblings and between parents and children, aunts and uncles, or first cousins. Many states in the United States also prohibit marriage between half-siblings. About half the states forbid marriage between in-laws and between stepchildren and stepparents. In some societies, such as India, exogamy rules may prohibit marriage between individuals of similarly named clans, even though the families have never met and live several hundred miles apart (Gupta, 1979).

Endogamy requires people to date and marry within their racial, ethnic, social, religious, and age groups. Many Jews encourage their children to marry Jews, many Latino parents are dismayed if their children marry Anglos, and very few of the rich and powerful marry outside their social class. Despite the popularity of the film *Pretty Woman*, men—even pimps—rarely marry prostitutes. In fact, films like this and the Harlequin romantic novels are probably popular because they reflect many people's fantasies about breaking out of the boundaries imposed by our rigid mate-selection rules and expectations.

Ethnicity and Race Although there are data on interracial marriage (see Chapter 10), research on interracial and interethnic dating is practically nonexistent. Films like *Jungle Fever*, *Bodyguard*, and *Mississippi Masala* romanticize interracial relationships and sex, but in real life, interracial dating is still highly controversial. For example, a high school principal in Alabama threatened to cancel the senior prom if interracial couples planned to attend. Although he later withdrew the threat, the principal's initial action led to lawsuits, angry exchanges between white and black parents in the community, and, ultimately, the torching of the high school (Gross and Smothers, 1994).

Within the African American community, skin hue and features can also be a political issue: "Blacks often judge each other on the basis of the skin color of those with whom they date and mate. The Black man who goes out exclusively with light-skinned women may be accused of having a color complex" (Russell et al., 1992: 107). According to researcher Robert L. Douglas, the more strongly a man identifies with

Although endogamy continues to be a strong force in choosing a mate, interracial and interethnic marriages are more and more common today.

his African heritage, the less likely he is to be attracted to light-skinned black women (cited in Russell et al., 1992). Thus, endogamy shapes behavior within as well as across racial lines.

Religion Religion can play a major role in dating and mate selection. All three of the major religions in the United States—Catholicism, Protestantism, and Judaism—have traditionally opposed interfaith marriages. Nonetheless, interreligious dating (and marriage) has been steadily increasing.

Jews have the lowest interreligious marriage rates. In Canada, for example, 74 percent of Jews marry within their religious group, compared to only 23 percent for some Protestant groups (Larson and Munro, 1990). In the United States, however, Jewish intermarriage has increased from about 6 percent in the early 1960s to nearly 40 percent in the 1980s (Mindel et al., 1988).

Jews, who constitute about 3 percent of the total U.S. population, have one of the lowest birth rates and one of the "oldest" populations (Farber et al., 1988). About 40 percent of Jews are over the age of 45, compared to 30 percent of the general population. Thus they consider intermarriage to be a serious threat to Jewish identity and culture. Some Jews actively discourage intermarriage, and some parents arrange marriage for their children (Hartman, 1988). Dozens of synagogues have started Jewish dating services and singles programs, and even Reformed Jews are encouraging non-Jewish spouses to convert (Gruson, 1985).

Most religions oppose interreligious marriage because of the belief that it weakens individual commitment to the faith. For example, Markstrom-Adams (1991) found that church leaders told Mormon adolescents to date only within their own religion. One reason was that only Mormons are allowed to participate in the highly valued ceremony of marrying in a Mormon temple. In the Roman Catholic Church, interfaith couples must sign a premarital agreement promising to raise the children as Catholics.

There has been a general decline in the percentage of people who attend religious services. For example, those reporting "never" attending religious services increased from 6 percent in 1967 to 16 percent in 1993 (Roper Center, 1994). There is little evidence, however, that the declines are due to interfaith marriage. Many offspring of marriages between Catholics and non-Catholics still identify themselves as Catholics and often participate in church-related activities (Petersen, 1986). This may reflect the determination of the more devout partner in an interfaith marriage to raise the children in his or her religion, especially if the other spouse is apathetic or neutral about the importance of religion.

Age Americans tend to marry within the same age group; the man is typically two to three years older than the woman. If there are large age differences, and especially if the woman is the older dating partner, families and friends will be more likely to disapprove. Large age differences may also lead to generation gaps in attitudes about lifestyle, such as music preferences, recreation, and family activities. Furthermore, a much older man may be unwilling to have children, especially if he has a family by a previous marriage or is expected to share in the child-rearing responsibilities (see Chapter 18). Even if he wants to raise a second family, he may not have the energy or patience to deal with high-spirited or rambunctious progeny.

Social Class Most people marry within their social class because they share similar attitudes, values, and lifestyles. Even when people from different ethnic groups intermarry, they usually belong to the same social class (Mindel et al., 1988). Physical distance also limits the field of eligibles. Parents may not feel the need to exert pressure on their children to marry someone of their "own kind" because communities already reflect social-class segregation. Finally, even workplaces and educational systems often reflect social-class endogamy. For example, blue-collar and white-collar workers rarely interact in the workplace. Eckland (1968) referred to colleges and universities as "matrimonial agencies" that are arranged hierarchically; students at Ivy League, private, state-supported, and community colleges have few chances to meet one another.

Hypergamy, or marriage with someone who is from a higher socioeconomic background, is more characteristic of women than men. In Singapore, for example, women had been staying single longer because they wanted husbands who were better educated, wealthier, and even taller than they were (Mydans, 1988). Alarmed that college-graduate women were not getting married and that men with university degrees were rejecting intelligent women in favor of more docile and physically attractive, uneducated women, Singapore's government set up a social development unit to help foster romance. Although highly criticized, the agency's services included arranging dates and sponsoring reduced-rate "love-boat" cruises for the educated elite singles. The government also advertised abroad for eligible bachelors, promising citizenship in return for marriage to the "right" women (Crossette, 1985).

Japan has run marriage bureaus since 1933. When applicants fill out the forms, hypergamy is very evident: "The women ask for university graduates, making at least $40,000 to $50,000, not previously married, working as a bureaucrat. The men ask for high school graduates who are young. Period" (Tanaka, 1994: 2A).

Increasing numbers of college-educated men and women in the United States expect that their partners will be similar to themselves in intelligence, ability, success, education, and income. Nevertheless, a sizable percentage still expects that the husband will make significantly more money, have a higher educational level, and be more intelligent and more successful than the wife (Ganong and Coleman, 1992).

WHY WE CHOOSE EACH OTHER: MATE-SELECTION THEORIES

Sociologists have suggested several theoretical perspectives to explain mate selection. None is perfect, but each perspective offers insights about the dating process. Three that are used most often are filter theory, exchange theory, and equity theory.

Dating as a Sifting Process: Filter Theory

Theoretically, we have a large pool of eligible dating partners. In reality, as you have seen, our field of potential partners is limited by our culture. **Filter theory** suggests that people searching for partners tend to go through a process of filtering out eligible people according to certain specific criteria and thus narrow the pool of potential partners to a relatively small number of candidates (Kerckhoff and Davis, 1962). Some of the most important filtering criteria are geographic proximity, age and social networks, values, sexual orientation, length of courtship, and physical attractiveness. Most recently, the pres-

ence of HIV infection and AIDS has been added to the selection process. Figure 8.1 depicts the filter theory of mate selection.

Propinquity Geographic closeness, or **propinquity,** plays a major role in mate selection. Communities are typically organized by social class; schools, churches, and recreational facilities re-

Figure 8.1 The Filter Theory of Mate Selection. *According to filter theory, most of us narrow our pool of prospective partners by selecting people we see on a regular basis who are most similar to us in terms of such variables as age, race, values, social class, sexual orientation, and physical attractiveness.*

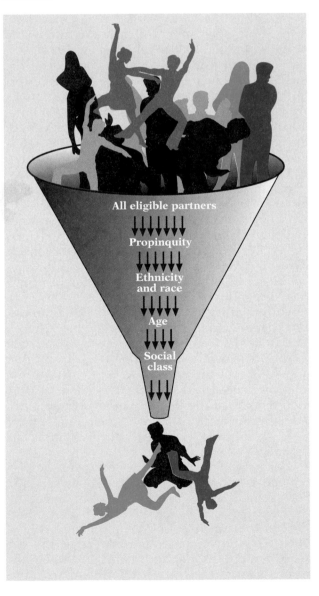

flect the socioeconomic levels of neighborhoods. It is highly unlikely that children living in upper-class neighborhoods will even meet those in middle-class, much less working-class, families. In one of the earliest studies of physical proximity and marriage, Bossard (1932) found that 50 percent of the Philadelphia couples surveyed had lived within 20 blocks of each other prior to marriage. Twenty years later, Clarke (1952) recorded almost the same findings in Columbus, Ohio, where more than half of married adults had lived within 16 blocks of each other at the time of their first date.

Although families are more geographically mobile today, interacting with people we see on a regular basis is still an important factor in dating and mating (Morgan, 1981). Many people report having met their spouses in high school, college, at work, or in the community through religious and other organizations. With a few exceptions (such as publications targeted at specific religious or ethnic groups), the most successful publishers of singles magazines are usually those that emphasize geographic proximity (Enrico, 1993). Most people do not have the time and resources to maintain long-distance romances.

Social Networks   The vast majority of singles meet their dating partners through such social networks as mutual friends (92 percent) or parties (90 percent) (Austrom and Hanel, 1985). Friends function as informal marriage market intermediaries who introduce people with similar backgrounds and interests to each other (Ahuvia and Adelman, 1992). Besides providing introductions and being a source of blind dates, friends may either support or discourage a dating relationship.

Some studies suggest that parents play a minimal role in direct courtship (Leslie et al., 1986), but it must be remembered that parents have already influenced the field of eligibles by choosing where to live. Moreover, by helping young people select a college or university, parents further narrow dating choices in terms of social class.

Values   Mate-selection methods may have changed, but has there been a corresponding change in the values that underlie our choices? Comparing college students' responses as to what they wanted in a future mate, Hudson and Henze (1969) found that over three widely spaced studies—1939, 1956, and 1967—desirable traits didn't change much. Students wanted partners who were dependable, emotionally stable, intelligent, sociable, and good-looking. They sought pleasing dispositions, good health, and similar religious background and social status, as well as evidence of mutual attraction. The researchers concluded that "social change in the area of mate selection has not been as great as indicated by the press, feared by the parent, and perhaps hoped by . . . youth" (p. 775).

The characteristics of the "ideal partner" had not changed very much by the late 1980s, either. In one study, the most important traits cited by undergraduates were honesty, trust, communication, sharing, thoughtfulness, intelligence, understanding, wit, openness, patience, gentleness, kindness, and a sense of humor (Laner, 1989). As Table 8.2 indicates, after marriage, qualities related to compatibility, such as being considerate and good company, become more important than having an exciting personality or being physically attractive.

Sexual Orientation   One rule of exogamy is that we must marry someone of the opposite sex. Denmark, Norway, and Sweden, however, extend legal recognition to same-sex marriages. In the United States, in 1990, two gay lovers filed a lawsuit against the city government of Washington, D.C., for denying them a marriage license (Gaines-Carter, 1990). By the mid-1990s, many large U.S. cities and about a dozen states permitted homosexual couples to file "domestic-partners" documents that recognized an ongoing relationship without granting the partners any

Table 8.2 _____
The Most Important Qualities in a Mate

ORDER OF PRIORITY	MARRIED COUPLES	UNMARRIED STUDENTS
1	Good company	Kind and understanding
2	Considerate	Exciting personality
3	Honest	Intelligent
4	Affectionate	Physically attractive
5	Dependable	Healthy
6	Intelligent	Easygoing
7	Kind	Creative
8	Understanding	Wants children
9	Interesting to talk to	College graduate
10	Loyal	Good earning capacity

SOURCE: Buss and Barnes, 1986.

legal rights. Also, some Protestant denominations are allowing religious marriage ceremonies for homosexuals (Richardson, 1990b).

Length of Courtship   There is a strong correlation between the length of time spent dating and marital satisfaction (Grover et al., 1985; see also Chapter 10). In general, marriage between people who know each other well before marrying is less likely to end in divorce. Longer periods of acquaintance screen out incompatible partners and reveal potential problems. Further, if both partners have similar educational-occupational levels, the couple will typically not be separated while one member pursues advanced schooling or a better job.

Physical Attractiveness   Physical attractiveness has been found to be more important for men than it is for women in choosing a date (Woll and Young, 1989). For example, sampling 111 personal profiles provided to *Living Single* magazine by both men and women, Bolig et al. (1984) found that women included more infor-

Men assign more importance to physical attractiveness than women do, but both sexes tend to choose partners whose degree of attractiveness closely matches their own.

mation about their education, career, and family interests, whereas men emphasized their interests and activities as well as their own degree of physical attractiveness. Clearly, women respondents did not endorse the traditional exchange of a woman's youth and beauty for a man's wealth or status. However, although men cited personality traits as important, the next most important characteristic for them was attractiveness, and they were much more likely than the women to require photos of potential dates.

A number of studies show that men and women choose partners whose level of physical attractiveness is similar to their own (see Berscheid et al., 1982). Physically attractive people benefit from a "halo effect"; they are assumed to possess other desirable social characteristics as well, such as warmth, sexual responsiveness, kindness, strength, modesty, sensitivity, poise, sociability, and good character. They are also seen as likely to have more prestige, happier marriages, more social and professional success, and more fulfilling lives in the future (Dion et al., 1972). Despite these perceptions, it appears that life satisfaction is much the same for very attractive and not so attractive people (Brehm, 1992).

HIV/AIDS   AIDS has narrowed the pool of eligible dating partners. In a study of dating behavior in 1983 and 1988, Roche and Ramsbey (1993) found that both males and females had become more conservative in their attitudes and behavior since learning about AIDS. The biggest problem is that some people either don't know that they are HIV-infected or don't tell their partners. Partners who are aware of the infection may have very ambivalent feelings. For example, a 27-year-old woman told her boyfriend about her physical status before they became intimate. He didn't leave her. However, besides using condoms, he also insisted on wearing rubber gloves during intercourse, and immediately afterward he would jump out of bed and into the shower (Seligmann et al., 1992). Fearing such reactions, a number of HIV-infected singles have limited their dating to people who are also infected, and some people have organized dating clubs for singles with AIDS.

In general, you should be cautious if a relationship is moving faster than you want. The box titled "Is This a Jewel or a Worthless Stone?" offers some practical tips for filtering out undesirable candidates as you look for a long-term partner.

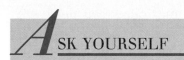
Is This a Jewel or a Worthless Stone?

Our habits, personalities, attitudes, and values don't usually change dramatically after marriage, but because often "love is blind," many people overlook serious flaws and marry Mr. or Ms. Wrong. Here are some red flags that should alert you to possible problems.

✖ **Don Juans and other sexual predators.** Decent men and women don't make a career of getting others into bed or of bragging about sexual conquests. Men, who are more likely than women to expect sex in casual dating, admit using a variety of lines to persuade women to have sex. These Don Juans will declare their love for you ("I love you," "I don't want to have sex with you—I want to make love to you"); attempt to gain your sympathy or flatter you ("You're one of the most beautiful women I've ever seen, and I would be honored to spend the night with you," "I never met anyone like you before"); make meaningless promises ("Our relationship will grow stronger," "I'll respect you even more," "I swear I'll get a divorce"); threaten you with rejection ("If you don't have sex, I'll find someone who will," "Our relationship really needs to move on," "If you loved me, you would"); put you down if you refuse ("You're really old-fashioned"); or challenge you to prove you're normal ("Are you frigid?" "Are you gay?").

✖ **Incompatibility of basic values.** Initially, it may be exciting to be with someone who's very different. In the long run, however, serious differences in values may jeopardize a relationship. If your partner spends a lot of time at the office and attends an endless round of meetings and receptions, whereas you look forward to gatherings of family or friends or to quiet times at home, you may have difficulty making a relationship work. If your partner wants you to be a full-time homemaker and raise children, but you want a career, it's not going to work. If your partner likes to curl up with a mystery novel, but you want to entertain friends or go out every weekend, you may be in for trouble.

✖ **Carrying around emotional baggage.** You're in trouble if you can't have a conversation without a partner's complaining about his ex-wife, comparing you to her "saintly" dead husband, or talking about past lovers.

✖ **Extreme jealousy and violent tendencies.** Run as fast as you can from a partner who is possessive, jealous, or violent. Such characteristics as a bad temper, frequent angry outbursts, constant criticism, and excessive argumentativeness will not decrease in the future.

✖ **Substance abuse.** The person addicted to alcohol or other drugs is the wrong choice for a mate. Watch for such things as slowed responses, slurred speech, glassy eyes, extreme mood swings, unexplained absences, or failure to keep dates. If any of these occur, you may have a problem.

✖ **Excessive time spent with others.** Does your partner spend several nights a week with other friends or with family members while you spend time alone? If your partner is always on the phone with family members or friends, or if family "emergencies" frequently come before your needs, there will probably be similar conflicts in the future.

✖ **Mr. Flirt and Ms. Tease.** If you are a woman whose partner constantly flirts with your sister and girlfriends, or a man whose girlfriend is a big tease, you are headed for trouble. Flirting might seem cute at first, but you will tire of it very quickly.

✖ **Lack of communication.** Good communication is critical for a good relationship. Talking about one's feelings, needs, desires, aspirations, and fears increases intimacy. Watch out for feelings of boredom or evidence of your partner's disinterest, finding that you have little to talk about, and frequent long silences.

✖ **Control freaks.** Does your partner always try to control you or the relationship? Do you constantly feel criticized, judged, scrutinized, and corrected, especially in public? Stay away from partners who are determined to change you.

✖ **Trouble holding a job.** In a bad economy, people get laid off or have to find new jobs, but if your partner never seems able to keep a decent job, blames someone or something else for this failure, and expects you to pay the bills, think twice about continuing the relationship. You may end up supporting a ne'er-do-well for the rest of your life.

Sources: Powell, 1991; Collison, 1993; Kenrick et al., 1993; Anonymous, 1994.

Dating as a Trade-Off: Social Exchange Theory

Recall from Chapter 2 that, according to *social exchange theory*, people are attracted to prospective partners who they believe will provide them with the best possible "deal" in a relationship. This may not sound very romantic, but social exchange theorists argue that it is the basis of most relationships.

Arguing that every relationship carries both rewards and costs, social exchange theory posits that people will begin (and remain in) a relationship if the rewards are high and the costs are low. Rewards may be intrinsic characteristics (intelligence, a sense of humor), directly rewarding behavior (sex, companionship), or access to desired resources (money, power). Costs, the "price" paid, may be unpleasant or destructive behavior (inattentiveness, insults, violence) or literal losses (money, time).

Historically, because women were expected to bear children and be homemakers, physical attractiveness was one of the few assets they could offer in an exchange. Men, on the other hand, had a variety of resources to offer, including money, education, and power, and thus had more dating options. Today, as more women earn college degrees and establish careers, they are increasing their assets and thus can be more selective in dating relationships. As this happens, however, the pool of eligible partners for both sides is reduced.

As more women compete for jobs and as the economy worsens, women's values about desirable traits in men are changing. Although they are interested in men who are competent workers and who are high earners, women today are more concerned about sharing housework and child-rearing responsibilities (see Chapters 10 and 14). Thus, economic security may be less important than companionship and expressiveness. Men who do not think such characteristics are important will be seen as less desirable partners.

Dating as a Search for Egalitarian Relationships: Equity Theory

Equity theory, first formulated by Walster et al. (1973), tries to predict when individuals will perceive injustice and how they will react when they find themselves enmeshed in inequitable relationships. An extension of social exchange theory, equity theory advances some basic propositions:

- Individuals try to maximize their *outcomes,* which are defined as rewards minus costs.

- When people find themselves in an inequitable relationship, they become distressed. The greater the inequity, the greater the distress.

- People in an inequitable relationship will attempt to eliminate their distress by restoring equity. The greater the inequity, the harder they will try to restore equity.

Equity theory reflects the American sense of "fair play," the notion that one has a right to expect a reasonable balance between costs and benefits in life. When costs exceed benefits, people try to regain some of their benefits. Consider Tim and Tammy, who were initially happy with their dating relationship. Among other cost-benefit outcomes, she helped him with his calculus and he helped her write a paper on contemporary American novelists. Tim and Tammy began having sexual intercourse, spent as much time as possible together, and shared similar extracurricular interests. Their relationship at this point appeared egalitarian. By the end of the semester, however, Tammy was still helping Tim with his calculus assignments, but Tim was no longer available to help Tammy with her English papers because he had joined the swim team. According to equity theory, Tim and Tammy will have to "renegotiate" their costs and benefits if the relationship is to continue.

CROSS-CULTURAL VARIATIONS IN MATE SELECTION

Most countries do not have the "open" courtship systems common in Western nations. Many factors promote traditional mate-selection arrangements, including religion, a country's rate of industrialization, the economic status of women, and family structure.

Traditional Societies

In some Mediterranean and East Asian societies, the **dowry**—the money, goods, or property a woman brings to a marriage—is still an important basis for mate selection. Women with large dowries have a competitive edge in attracting suitors (Gaulin and Boster, 1990).

As in India (see the earlier box on arranged

marriages), in many countries parents still arrange marriages for their children. Although arranged marriages are more common in the villages of Egypt than in its cities, they occur among all social classes and account for between 50 and 75 percent of all marriages (Cowell, 1988). In Saudi Arabia, Islamic (Muslim) society regulates the lives of its women strictly. During the Persian Gulf War in 1991, Saudis had little concern that American and European soldiers would father children or bring home Saudi brides, as was so common in World War II and the Korean and Vietnam wars, because in Saudi Arabia, the groom must be Muslim. Most Saudi women cover themselves in black, are forbidden to drive or drink, accept arranged marriages, and live with their parents, who act as chaperones. If a foreigner wanted to marry a Saudi woman, he would need permission from both her parents and the government, but most Saudi women would not pursue such a liaison because it would bring shame to their families (*Baltimore Sun*, 1990e). The box "Matchmaking in Muslim Societies" provides a closer look at the criteria that many Muslim parents use in selecting partners for their children.

Although, as we saw in Chapter 4, small groups of Saudi and other Middle East women are challenging some strict Muslim dating restrictions, many Muslim women, including those living in the United States, believe in arranged marriages. Listen to a Muslim mother from Sierra Leone describe the arranged marriages of her sons and daughter:

We are saved from the evils of teen-age pregnancy that you see nowadays. We are saved from AIDS. We are saved from all sorts of different diseases, all

---

CROSS CULTURAL

Matchmaking in Muslim Societies

No matter where they live—North America, South Asia, or the Mideast—many Muslim families preserve family consistency and continuity through arranged marriages. Marriage in Islamic society is basically a family rather than an individual affair, and both sons and daughters are raised to expect arranged marriages. Although children do have veto power, the norm is to let the parents and other kin initiate and decide the matter. Thus, even college-educated youth in countries like Pakistan do not think it is necessary for them to meet their future spouses before they are married (Ba-Yunus, 1991).

What criteria do parents use in choosing a son- or daughter-in-law? Although priorities vary among families, two of the most important criteria for a future son-in-law are competence and education or training that will provide his wife with economic and social assets equal to or better than those of her parents, and close ties between the son-in-law and the daughter's family, whether or not they live near the latter's family. In addition, according to one mother, "We look for wisdom, patience, good sense, not qualities that may be more exciting, but which soon disappear" (Alibhai-Brown, 1993: 29).

For a prospective daughter-in-law, the major criterion is her ability to be integrated into the son's existing family, including, if possible, patrilocal residence for the young couple. Because in Muslim society the man is expected to be the provider, his wife's education is more a social enhancement than an essential socioeconomic asset (Qureshi, 1991).

Islamic societies forbid dating and "other illicit meetings of the sexes" but allow polygyny. To reduce the number of unmarried middle-aged women, matchmakers in Saudi Arabia have set up services that provide wives for husbands who seek more than one wife. These services have apparently been flooded with telephone calls and faxes from devout Muslims in Sweden, the United States, and countries in the Middle East. One matchmaker, who has a half-dozen computer-terminal assistants to store data and keep up with the demand, is helped by his own four wives in assessing possible matches. Despite the protests of some Saudi housewives, who do not want their husbands to acquire additional wives, the matchmaking business is thriving (Boustany, 1994).

As in the semiarranged matches in India, most women are practical and religious: "I am a Saudi woman, 36, finished elementary school and have never been married. I wish to marry a man who fears God and heeds him and who will treat me to God's satisfaction, and who will also help me memorize the Koran and attend religion lessons, not younger than 40" (Boustany, 1994: A14).

---

sorts of evil vices being practiced, especially by the teenagers of America (Somerville, 1994: 4B).

Many young Asian Muslims who live in the United States agree with their parents about the benefits of arranged marriages. When a journalist interviewed nine teenage Muslim girls at a school in Birmingham, three were envious of girls who had the freedom to go out and fall in love. But the other six were either ambivalent or very critical of the way this freedom was used against the girls by boys who picked them up and discarded them without any concern for their self-respect. One of the girls described her best friend, who is "always tortured about whether her boyfriend likes her or not, if she is fat, attractive, how many silly Valentine's cards she gets. I couldn't go through all of that. It's crazy" (Alibhai-Brown, 1993: 29).

Changing Societies

Some countries in Asia are also experiencing dramatic changes in the way people meet and select mates. In some cases, these changes are the result of a shortage of women; in others, the rising number of women who pursue higher education and careers has led to the postponement of marriage for many.

Both India and China have recently experienced a glut of single men and a scarcity of single women (see Data Digest). In both countries the preference for boys has led to the killing of millions of female infants and to the deaths of many others as a result of neglect—poor nutrition, inadequate medical care, or desertion. An unmarried woman has thus become a scarcity. China has responded by implementing some Western-style mate-selection methods. In Beijing, for example, computer-dating services began operating in 1989, and some television shows feature men who are searching for wives (Shenon, 1994).

In China, finding a mate has become a community affair in which both public and private sectors participate. In some factories and offices, formal Youth Leagues have organized cultural activities through which young people can meet one another. Marriage-introduction institutes, sponsored by local governments, have sprung up in Shanghai, Beijing, Tianjin, and smaller cities. Newspapers and magazines run columns about finding the ideal mate on a regular basis (Hershatter, 1984).

Finding partners through personal advertisements is also popular in China. The desirable attributes differ quite a bit from those in the United States, however. Linlin (1993) compared previous studies of Chinese and American researchers in this area and found some striking cultural differences:

- All the Chinese advertisers were marriage-minded and family-oriented, whereas many of their counterparts in the United States wanted someone to have fun with.

- Chinese advertisers emphasized health, both because health of both spouses is very important in a lasting marriage and because physical health implies good mental health.

- Because most male advertisers expect their future spouses to be virgins, marital status got close attention.

- Chinese women expect the husband to be the major decision maker. Thus, signs of being resolute and career-minded were important.

- Chinese advertisers rarely asked about humor or communication because these qualities are seen as important in public life rather than in marriage and family life.

- Because few people are overweight in China, weight was not an important issue.

- Because there is a housing shortage in China, male suitors with apartments were seen as particularly attractive.

In Beijing, one of the most popular television programs, called "We Meet Tonight," was first televised in 1990. Initially, many Chinese were unwilling to appear publicly to search for mates because they expected to be ridiculed by family and friends. Shortly after the program aired, however, parents were selecting mates for their children, adult children were seeking companions for their parents, and friends urged their office colleagues to participate. The producers estimate that 30 percent of the people who have appeared on the show have gotten married. Computer matchmaking is also very popular in Beijing. A 39-year-old computer engineer founded a computer network in 1992 and has expanded the system to some provincial cities and even as far as the United States and

Canada to help mainland Chinese studying abroad find companions (Ji, 1993).

In Japan and Korea the mating game has begun to suffer, in part because more women are acquiring a college education, finding jobs, postponing marriage, or preferring to remain single. Japan has one of the highest average ages of marriage—28.4 years for males and 25.8 years for females. It also has one of the most severe labor shortages. To retain the loyalty of unmarried employees in the under-40 age bracket, several companies are including marriage in their benefit packages and have engaged matrimony brokerage firms to act as matchmakers. Men are less successful than women in finding a mate because the pool of single women has been diminishing; 60 percent of all Japanese between the ages of 20 and 39 are single men. Matchmaking companies are thriving because they teach men how to date, court, and select a wife (Shearer, 1990). A recent innovation includes a bank of videophones where singles can talk one-on-one with every online member of the opposite sex for $100 to $150 per session (Thornton, 1994).

In Korea, in the 25- to 29-age bracket, the ratio of eligible men to women is almost four to one.

Moreover, as Korea has become more industrialized and urbanized, many women have moved to cities. Women who are used to the urban lifestyle refuse to accept the monotony of rural life, physical labor, sharing a home with aged or aging in-laws, and husbands who are reluctant to help wives do home chores such as cooking and babysitting (Hoon, 1993). As a result, villagers and farmers have difficulty finding wives. Marriage bureaus such as Seoul's Committee to Help Find Brides for Farm Bachelors report only modest rates of success; the committee matched only 44 couples in almost three years.

COURTSHIPS IN CRISIS

So far we have focused on the positive side of dating—how people meet each other and what qualities they look for in marital partners. Courtship also has a dark side. It can be disappointing and even dangerous. This section examines some major problems in dating, suggests how to recognize risk factors for sexual aggression and date rape, and proposes some solutions for avoiding and eliminating courtship violence.

"No question I've had to rein in my natural playfulness in dealing with today's woman."

Drawing by D. Reilly; © 1994 The New Yorker Magazine, Inc.

Power, Control, and Aggression

Sociologist Willard Waller's (1937) *principle of least interest* is useful in explaining the balance of power in the traditional male-female dating and courtship relationship. Why do so many women still sit "waiting for the telephone to ring" even when they are in steady dating relationships? According to Waller, the male continues to have more power than the female because he is usually the partner with the least interest. The person with more power is less dependent on others, less interested in maintaining the relationship, and, as a result, has more control (Lloyd, 1991). Conversely, the person with less power, usually the female, is more likely to be dependent, to try to maintain the relationship, and, often, to be exploited as a result (Sarch, 1993).

It is important to recognize, however, that women can also dominate a relationship. When the control is nonviolent and nonsexual, women may be more likely than men to try to control a relationship. For example, in a national study of single, never-married people between the ages of 18 and 30, Stets (1993) found that women were more likely than men to report keeping tabs on their partners, making their partners do what they themselves wanted rather than what the partners wanted, and generally setting the rules in the relationship. How might you explain this finding? Are women more aggressive than men, and is that why men try to control them with violence? Or, following the least interest principle, do women feel a greater need to manage or control a relationship because they have less power and are more dependent on their partners?

In both men and women, control often increases as a relationship progresses from casual to more serious dating (Stets, 1993). Men are much more likely to use physical force and sexual aggression as a means of getting their own way or of intimidating a partner and "striking fear" into her (Stets and Pirog-Good, 1990). Women are also physically and emotionally abusive, however. The box "How Abusers Control Dating Relationships" examines some of these methods of control.

Courtship Violence

Courtship violence, the physical abuse of a steady dating partner, can start at a very early age:

Dear Ann Landers:

I know you've written a lot about battered women, but most people aren't aware that teenage girls can be battered too.

I began dating a terrific-looking guy when I was 16. . . . A year later I was scared to death of him. I didn't dare tell my family. . . . If I broke one of his rules, he would beat me up. Once, when I wore my jeans too tight (according to him), he locked me in the trunk of his car. I thought I would suffocate. It was a horrible experience.

My family knew nothing of the hell he put me through. He made an effort to put the bruises where no one would see them. On the rare occasion when they were visible (like a black eye), I would tell people I had had an accident.

I was the ideal child—I had straight A's, got home on time, did all my household chores and never gave my parents any trouble. It wasn't until I attempted suicide at the age of 18 and then got some great counseling that I began to understand how he had taken control of my life.

Lucky to Be Out of It

Dear Lucky:

*This is not the first letter I've printed from a teenager who was battered by her boyfriend. My advice has been to get out at once. No guy is worth it (*Washington Post, *February 4, 1991: B11).*

Prevalence Courtship violence is widespread, and because this problem is underreported by both men and women, it is much more serious than the figures indicate (Ward et al., 1991). A recent study has estimated that 30 percent of high school students have experienced physical or sexual violence in dating relationships (Gardner, 1994). A national sample of more than 2,600 women and 2,100 men found that 37 percent of the men and 35 percent of the women had inflicted some form of physical aggression on their dating partners (White and Koss, 1991).

Although both women and men can be victims of courtship violence (see Data Digest), women usually resort to violence in retaliation or self-defense. According to Cate and Lloyd (1992), women also sustain more physical injuries than men.

Length of Relationships Courtship violence is rarely a one-time event. Only about 50 percent of couples end relationships after the first violent act; others go on seeing one another despite con-

How Abusers Control Dating Relationships

Both men and women try to control relationships. Although the following categories are based on the experiences of women who have been victims, men are also subject to abusive dating relationships.

❑ *Blaming*: Blaming is often based on jealousy; almost anything the partner does is considered provocative. For example, a man may criticize his partner for not being at home when he calls or for talking to another man. He may say he loves her so much that he can't stand for her to be with others, especially other men.

❑ *Emotional Abuse*: Coming from a person the victim thinks she or he loves, emotional abuse is very powerful. Insults, which attack a person's feelings of independence and self-worth, are generally intended to get a partner to accede to an abuser's demands ("Don't wear your skirt so short—it makes you look like a hooker" or "No one else will ever want you"), denigrate the victim, and imply she had better do what the partner wants or be left without anyone.

❑ *Coercion, Intimidation, and Threats:* Abusers may coerce compliance with their wishes by threatening to expose embarrassing secrets, often about the partner's sexual behavior, to family or friends. Coercion may also be used to get partners to engage in illegal acts, such as shoplifting, drug dealing, or prostitution, usually to get money for the abuser. A controller may intimidate a partner, just to show "who's boss": "We'd be lying in bed and he'd just decide to kick me out of the house and make me leave, no matter what time it was—three A.M., whatever—and I'd have to get out." Threatening to commit suicide or to attack a partner's family is not uncommon among abusers.

❑ *Isolation:* Typically, abusers spend a lot of time and energy watching their victims. For example, one man got his friends to find out what his girlfriend's daily activities were; then he forced her to stay at home or punished her if she wasn't home when he called. In another case, a student elected the same major as his girlfriend's, home economics, just to monitor her behavior. If these isolating techniques work, they break the partner's ties with other friends and increase the victim's dependence on the abuser.

❑ *Physical Abuse*: Violent acts range from slaps and shoves to beatings, rape, and attacks with weapons. Many abusers manage to convince a partner, on each occasion of abuse, that "I really love you" and "This will never happen again"—but it does. And in some cases, the last time the abuser strikes, he or she kills.

❑ *Sexual Abuse:* Conflicts about sex often lead to violence. Often a male abuser decides whether to have sex, which sex acts are acceptable, and whether or not the couple should use condoms or other contraceptive devices to prevent AIDS and other STDs.

SOURCES: Gamache, 1990: Ingrassia et al., 1993; Rosen and Stith, 1993.

---

tinuing occurrences of violence (Henton et al., 1983). Apparently, many victims interpret the violence as evidence of love (Lloyd, 1991).

In a study of more than 600 college students, Muehlenhard and Linton (1987) found that, on average, students had known the person who abused them for almost a year before the violent incident occurred. The incidence of violence may be higher in long and serious relationships because issues of control and power become more central. Moreover, in a committed relationship, unmet expectations may erupt in more intense, negative reactions (Stets, 1993). In some cases, couples who stay in abusive relationships seem to have accepted violence as a legitimate means of resolving conflict. It is almost as if they are testing the strength of their relationship, as if they are saying, "If we can survive this, we can survive anything" (Lloyd, 1991).

Acquaintance and Date Rape

Acquaintance rape refers to rape of a person who knows or is familiar with the rapist. Acquaintance rapists may include neighbors, friends of the family, coworkers, or people the victim meets at a party or get-together. **Date rape** is unwanted, forced sexual intercourse in the context of a dating situation; the victim and the perpetrator may be on a first date or in a steady dating relationship. In a study at a southern university, Johnson and colleagues (1992) found that 20 percent of the women had been raped in a dating situation. One of the reasons date rape is so common, and one of the reasons it comes as a great shock to the victim, is that, typically, the rapist seems to be "a nice guy"—polite, clean-cut, and even a leader in the community or on campus (Benokraitis and Feagin, 1995).

Generally speaking, men who commit date rape hold traditional views of the relations between men and women, seeing themselves as in charge and women as submissive. According to Shotland (1989), there are three basic types of date rape: early date rape, beginning date rape, and relational date rape. In *early date rape,* a man rapes a woman while the partners are still getting to know each other. The rape is most likely to occur if the woman's protests come late (after foreplay has begun) or are not forceful. Even though it is the man who doesn't control himself, there is a double standard at work because women are expected to be "sexual gatekeepers."

The *beginning date rapist* has had many sexual partners and a history of aggressive incidents and antisocial acts. He assumes that his date is promiscuous, and he expects consensual sex. When she refuses his sexual advances, he feels he has been treated inequitably and rapes her. The *relational date rapist* has conservative sexual values. He has had few prior sexual partners and believes that rape is part of a romantic script in which the woman protests at first but then willingly complies. When protest does not turn to compliance, he rapes her.

Reasons for Courtship Violence and Date Rape

There are many reasons for courtship violence and date rape. Some of the most important explanations include misogyny, gender-role expectations, media messages, and peer pressure.

Misogyny Misogyny, the hatred of women, can be fatal. In December 1989, for example, a gunman who called women "a bunch of feminists" massacred 14 female students at the University of Montreal and then killed himself. The murders spurred campus officials across the United States and Canada to provide more workshops and seminars on sexism and on date rape, but many students have not gotten the message that courtship violence and date rape are ways of

striking out against women (especially independent and self-confident women) who are challenging men's right to control them (Stets and Pirog-Good, 1987). At Queens College in New York City, male students reacted to a "No Means No" informational campaign by hanging signs from their windows that read "No Means Tie Her Up" and "No Means More Beer," and, during homecoming, by selling boxer shorts with the words "No Non" that, in the dark, changed to read "Yes Oui" (Motherwell, 1990).

Women who date traditional men (see Chapter 4) may find themselves in a catch-22 situation:

If she allows him to pay for the date then he may infer sexual interest. Alternatively, if she contributes to the cost of the date, he may feel threatened and may be more likely to be sexually aggressive as a means of regaining control of the situation. . . . If she accepts an invitation from him for a date, [he may] arrange the circumstances of the date in a manner that could be conducive to sexual overtures. On the other hand, if she asks him out on the date, then she may be perceived as liberated, assertive and hence, wanting to have sex (Szymanski et al., 1993: 33).

Traditional men can be sexually aggressive and not feel guilty because "She deserved it," or "Women enjoy sexual violence." Such men may also feel that aggression against weaker people, especially women, is condoned by our society (Walker et al., 1993).

Gender-Role Expectations and Media Images

As we discussed in Chapter 4, the media often create and reinforce gender-stereotypical images of both women and men. According to Gardner (1994), in such television programs as "Melrose Place" and "Beverly Hills 90210," men believe they must be in charge and have many partners, whereas a woman thinks she must be beautiful and compliant and have a boyfriend in order to have status among her friends.

Women are more likely than men to take the blame for courtship violence. For example, in a study of college students, LaJeune and Follette (1994: 137) concluded that women were more likely than men to blame themselves for dating violence because "females are socialized to accept more responsibility for relationship conflict than males are." In addition, acquaintance rape is often seen as less serious than stranger rape. Both male and female college students in one study saw the woman as encouraging or being responsible for acquaintance rape (Szymanski et al., 1993).

Peer Pressure   Peer pressure is one of the major reasons why people are violent and why they don't leave abusive dating relationships. Peer groups that condone male sexual aggression are likely to include females who have been sexually abused by boyfriends or other men and to see violence as "no big deal" (Gwartney-Gibbs and Stockard, 1989). Furthermore, because "the pressure to date is fierce" and having any boyfriend is better than having none, young girls often stay in abusive relationships (Ingrassia et al., 1993). Having a boyfriend is often seen as "one of the ways you are successful as a girl" (Gardner, 1994: 12).

Peer pressure may be even more important in college. For example, in a study of fraternity members, Sanday found that many of the men saw sexual behavior as a "hunt" in which the most successful hunter is the one who traps the largest number of prey:

[According to one fraternity man], when a man has many partners, he is not only admired by other men, but he believes that women will think he is an incredible lover. Many men get bothered if they are having sex with only one woman because it makes them question their attractiveness and masculinity in the eyes of other women. This man was so worried . . . that he set quotas. . . . Once he decided to have intercourse with 13 new and different girls before the end of the semester. . . . He explained that the joy of sex was "not just the pleasure derived from the act, but the feeling of acceptance and approval of my masculinity which goes along with having sex with a new person" (Sanday, 1990: 114).

According to Martin and Hummer (1993), some fraternities work very hard to create a macho image. Some, for example, use women as bait to recruit new pledges: Brochures and videotapes display shapely and attractive female students, implying that access to women for sexual gratification is a norm and a benefit of fraternity membership. A similar message is given in fraternity brothers' conversations with new recruits: "We always tell the guys that you get sex all the time, there's always new girls." In other cases, men admit that their strategies include getting women drunk to get them into bed.

Consequences of Courtship Violence and Date Rape

Violence and rape violate both body and spirit; they can affect every aspect of the victim's life. Women who are raped may not only lose their ability to trust others but may also lose confidence in their ability to judge people's characters. Even though they are not responsible for the attack, they may feel ashamed and blame themselves for the rape. Fear of men, of going out alone, and of being alone becomes part of their lives, as do anger, depression, and sometimes inability to relate to a caring sexual partner. Table 8.3 lists other specific consequences of courtship violence and date rape.

Recognizing the Risk Factors for Courtship Violence and Date Rape

Most courtship violence and date rapes occur in situations that seem safe and familiar. This is why these behaviors often come as a great shock to victims, who often cannot believe what is happening. Two of the greatest factors for sexual aggression include the use of alcohol or other drugs and high-risk activities and locations.

Table 8.3
Emotional and Behavioral Difficulties Often Experienced by Female Victims of Courtship Violence or Date Rape

General depression: Some signs are changes in eating and sleeping patterns and unexplained aches and pains. Depressive symptoms may prevent women from attending classes, completing course assignments, or functioning effectively on the job.

Dissatisfaction with a particular course, a major, or college in general or with the victim's job.

A sense of powerlessness, helplessness, and vulnerability.

Loss of self-confidence and self-esteem.

Changes in the victim's attitudes toward sexual relationships in general and in her behavior within an intimate relationship.

Irritability with family, friends, or coworkers.

Generalized anger, fear, or anxiety.

Inability to concentrate, even on routine tasks.

Development of dependency on alcohol or drugs.

Source: Benokraitis and Feagin, 1995.

In urban centers, the cocktail party provides a favorite meeting ground for singles, but drinking too much may pave the way for trouble later in the evening.

Use of Alcohol or Other Drugs   The use of alcohol and other drugs often accompanies aggression and date rape (see Data Digest). Alcohol lowers inhibitions against violence and it also reduces a woman's ability to resist. Among fraternity men who want to coerce women into having sex, the use of alcohol or other drugs is common. A group of men may encourage a woman to down drink after drink, or they may spike her drinks. If the situation escalates into sexual activity, fraternity men may watch one another perform various sexual acts with the drugged woman and then brag about it afterward (Boeringer et al., 1991).

Some fraternity members restrict the term *rape* to situations that involve physical force. Anything else they call *seduction,* and they see nothing wrong with using drugs or verbal persuasion to, as they phrase it, "work a yes out." Distinguishing between rape and seduction, the men studied commented, "With rape she never gives in. With seduction, she might say no for a while, but then she gives up and decides that she wants sex too. Physical force is the difference" (Sanday, 1990: 118).

Dating Location and Activity   One of the riskiest locations for date violence is a parked car. Parking provides privacy, and men generally assume that a woman willing to engage in some sexual activity when parked in a remote spot will "go all the way." Date rape is also common in men's apartments, where the aggressors are on their own "turf" and can be assured of not being interrupted.

Men report that they are often sexually aggressive after movie dates. It is possible that a film's content can prompt sexual aggression. Many mainstream, nonpornographic movies have portrayed women as reacting positively to sexual aggression, thus promoting the notion, among both men and women, that violent sex is okay or even desirable.

Some Solutions

Because violent behavior and rape are learned behavior, they can be unlearned. We need solutions on three levels: individual, organizational, and societal.

To begin with, on the *individual* level, women, as the primary victims, must become more "savvy" and avoid risky dating situations. One of these situations, drinking, can be prevented by both sexes.

Much can be done on the *organizational* level, but few colleges or universities have taken concerted action against sexual aggression on campus. Most institutions suspend or dismiss students who are caught cheating, yet they rarely punish date rape or even define it as rape:

Reproach is often reserved only for the woman: "She shouldn't have gotten drunk, she shouldn't have gone to the fraternity party, she shouldn't have danced provocatively, she shouldn't have done this, she shouldn't have done that" (McMillen, 1990; A3).

If colleges and law enforcement agencies prosecuted sexual violence, it would probably decrease.

Finally, to make a serious dent in the incidence of courtship violence and date rape, we must change *societal* attitudes and beliefs about male and female roles in courtship and dating, about sexual behavior, and about violence. The traditional notion that it is the woman's job to maintain relationships often leads women to blame themselves when things go wrong and to overlook, forgive, or excuse sexual aggression (Lloyd, 1991).

There has been some movement toward legal remedies. The Student Right-to-Know and Campus Security Act of 1990 requires colleges to report crimes, and the Higher Education Reauthorization Act of 1992 requires reporting of both forcible and nonforcible rape. Students can have assaults investigated by local police, not just college security, and victims of sexual assault have many new rights, such as the right to have someone of their choosing present at a hearing, to learn the outcome of judicial hearings, and to be offered options for changing academic and living situations.

BREAKING UP

Nearly half of all dating relationships break up before marriage (for a good summary of the literature on the dissolution of relationships, see Cate and Lloyd, 1992). The reasons for breakups include unequal commitment on the part of each partner, arguments, pressure from parents, geographic separation, deception, avoidance of open communication, and boredom.

Gender Differences in Breaking Up

When men initiate a breakup, they are more likely to cite such logistic reasons as "living too far apart" than personal problems. Women, on the other hand, are likely to cite personal reasons such as "differences in interests," "differences in intelligence," "conflicting ideas about marriage," "my desire to be independent," or "my interest in someone else" (Hill et al., 1976).

How can we explain these differences? For one thing, men have better-paying jobs, are typi-cally more independent, and thus can perhaps "afford the luxury of being romantic" or of taking a more global view of a relationship. Largely because of economic reasons, women have to be more practical; in our youth-oriented society, women's peak years of marriageability are shorter than men's. Thus they may tend to take dating more seriously, seeing it as a screening device for marriage. In contrast, men are more likely to see dating as an outlet for romance and recreation (Margolin, 1989). Also, because many women tend to distinguish between "liking" and "loving," their criteria for falling in love may be more demanding than men's, and they may reevaluate their relationships more carefully.

Classic songs warn us that "breaking up is hard to do." It is. And it's not surprising that those with the greatest investments in a relationship—for example, people who feel they have few desirable alternatives—suffer the most (Simpson, 1987). Having the support of friends and family may go a long way toward easing the pain. This explains, in large part, why breaking up may sometimes be more traumatic for gay men and lesbians, who often feel that they cannot discuss their romantic breakups with anyone (Martin, 1993). However, breaking up a dating or cohabiting relationship is much less complicated than breaking up a marriage (see Chapter 16). You'll recall that Farber's permanent-availability model suggests that we have no predestined partners. Instead, one of the important functions of dating and courtship is to filter out unsuitable prospective mates. Thus, breaking up is a normal process. If anything, it should probably occur more often than it does.

Dating Contracts and Detective Agencies

Because in recent years some dissatisfied lovers have sued each other for such things as failure to disclose HIV infection and the costs of cross-country travel to meet a long-distance lover, it has been suggested that people draw up dating contracts. Such contracts could address issues like preliminary medical examinations to detect STDs or other serious illness, responsibility for an unwanted pregnancy or birth, ownership of property bought jointly during the relationship, the disposition of partners' gifts to each other at the time of breakup, and entitlement to a partner's future earnings (Cornish, 1987). Contracts might take some of the romance out of dating, but because many people are postponing mar-

riage and staying in uncommitted relationships for a longer time, dating contracts may become a "normal" feature of the courtship process.

Detective agencies have become a booming industry. Fears about AIDS and concerns about economic rip-offs have sent many single women to private detectives to check out a suitor's employment history, credit record, and sexual habits. These services can cost anywhere from $500 to $10,000; it costs more to follow someone around to nightclubs for several weeks than simply to obtain financial data or marital histories (Johnson, 1989). The growing use of detective agencies suggests that some people, especially women, are trying to be less vulnerable in a society that is more anonymous, impersonal, and sometimes even physically dangerous.

CONCLUSION

We have more *choices* in mate selection today than ever before. There are also many *constraints*, however. Besides the pressure to date and mate with people who are most similar to us in race, religion, ethnicity, and socioeconomic status, some partners must also deal with aggression and violence. More choice can sometimes make choosing more difficult, and more constraints may discourage our moving from casual to serious dating and from there to permanent commitments. One response to today's array of choices and constraints in mate selection is to postpone marriage. In fact, a significant *change* today is the decision of many people to stay single longer, which is the subject of the next chapter.

Taking Action

Meeting People OnLine and Avoiding Date Violence on Campus

Meeting new people has both its bright and dark sides, particularly with the rising incidence of rape in many areas.

• On the bright side are the numerous commercial **computer networks where people "meet" each other** to discuss common inter-

ests. Two of these include America Online (800–827-6364) and CompuServe (800-848-8199). The services are not cheap, however. America Online, which is cheaper than CompuServe, costs $9.95 a month, plus $3.50 an hour, with five free hours per month.

• On the darker side, dating partners must sometimes deal with **violence and aggression on campus.** A good source of recent crime statistics on many campuses with enrollments over 5,000 is Douglas Lederman's "Colleges Report Rise in Violent Crime," *The Chronicle of Higher Education,* February 3, 1995, pp. A31, A42; and the related "Fact File: Crime Data from 796 Colleges and Universities," pp. A32–A41.

• College students can do several things to **increase campus safety.** For example, every college or university that receives even a small amount of federal funding is required to collect and release information on rape statistics, campus crime, and security measures (such as patrolling and lighting). Publishing such information in the campus paper would provide a valuable service to students and would remind college officials that student safety should be a high priority.

• Many organizations present **seminars and workshops on rape awareness and date rape.** You might get a group of students together, get campus officials' permission to hold such an event, and contact the nearest office of an organization that can provide this service. Start by contacting one of the following: Men's Anti-Rape Resource Center (301-386-2737); Security on Campus (215-768-9330); or Campus Violence Prevention Center at Towson State University (410-830-2178).

SUMMARY

1. Courtship is rarely as smooth and romantic as novels and films suggest. Although we have more choices today than in the past, there are also a variety of constraints that shape our mate-selection behavior.

2. Dating fulfills both manifest and latent functions. Manifest functions include recreation, companionship, fun, and mate selection. Latent functions include socialization, social status, sexual experimentation, and meeting intimacy and ego needs.

3. Dating forms have changed over the years. Although people still engage in traditional dating, many adolescents and young adults, especially, have forsaken traditional dating for more informal methods like hanging out and getting together.

4. Adults use a variety of mate-selection methods to meet a potential spouse, including personal classified ads, marriage bureaus, and computerized services.

5. Much of our dating and mate-selection behavior is shaped by exogamous and endogamous rules that define appropriate mates in terms of race, ethnicity, religion, age, and social class.

6. Our field of eligibles is further limited by such factors as geography, social networks, values, sexual orientation, length of courtship, physical attractiveness, and sexually transmitted diseases.

7. The theoretical perspectives most commonly cited to explain mate selection today are filter theory, exchange theory, and equity theory.

8. Unlike the United States and some other Western nations, most countries around the world do not have "open" courtship systems. Rather, marriages are arranged by families and restricted to members of the same culture, religion, or race.

9. Although dating is often fun, there are also many risks and problems. Women, especially, are often victims of sexual pressure and aggression, courtship violence, and date rape. The many reasons for this victimization of women include misogyny, power differentials between men and women, a lack of concern by many college officials, and insufficient legal sanctions.

10. Both dating violence and the rising incidence of **AIDS** have motivated some partners, especially women, to become more careful in selecting dates and having sexual intercourse. Some experts have encouraged the use of dating contracts and detective agencies before getting involved in long-term relationships.

KEY TERMS

The best sources for current research on dating and mate selection include such academic periodicals as *Sex Roles, Adolescence, Journal of Applied Social Psychology, Family Relations,* and *Journal of Social and Personal Relationships.* For articles on courtship violence and date rape, consult *Violence & Victims, Victimology: An International Journal, Journal of Interpersonal Violence,* and *Deviant Behavior: An Interdisciplinary Journal.*

SHARON S. BREHM, *Intimate Relationships,* 2nd edition (New York: McGraw Hill, 1992). Both classic and recent findings on such topics as getting together, love and romance, sexuality, relationship development, conflict, and relationship breakup.

DAVID M. BUSS, *The Evolution of Desire: Strategies of Human Mating* (New York: Basic Books, 1994). Topics include the origins of mating, what men and women want, casual sex, attracting a partner, staying together, and breaking up.

RODNEY M. CATE and SALLY A. LLOYD, *Courtship* (Newbury Park, CA: Sage, 1992). This book traces the history of courtship, presents some of the most influential theories, and discusses sexual aggression and violence.

BARRY DYM and MICHAEL L. GLENN, *Couples: Exploring and Understanding the Cycles of Intimate Relationships* (New York: HarperCollins, 1993). An exploration of the way dating and relationships change over the life course and how they vary for lesbian, gay, and heterosexual couples.

JANET Z. GILER and KATHLEEN NEUMEYER, *Redefining Mr. Right: a Career Woman's Guide to Choosing a Mate* (Oakland, CA: New Harbinger Publications and Marin Publications, 1992). Practical tips "for finding a compatible man for the 90s career woman."

CAROLE MARKIN, *Bad Dates: Celebrities (and Other Talented Types) Reveal Their Worst Nights Out* (New York: Citadel Press, 1990). A lighthearted look at some of the worst dates that celebrities—Kareem Abdul-Jabbar, Johnny Bench, Alice Cooper, Ted Danson, Whoopi Goldberg, Waylon Jennings, Bubba Smith, and Gloria Steinem are included—have experienced.

MARK METHABANE and GAIL METHABANE, *Love in Black and White: The Triumph of Love over Prejudice and Taboo* (New York: HarperCollins, 1992). A personal account of an interracial couple who met, married, and are raising a family. The authors chronicle their experiences in dealing with stereotypes and living in a racist society. Another useful source on this topic is Walter R. Johnson and D. Michael Warren, eds. *Inside the Mixed Marriage: Accounts of Changing Attitudes, Patterns, and Perceptions of Cross Cultural and Interracial Marriages* (Lanham, MD: University Press of America, 1994).

9
To Marry or to Tarry? Singlehood and Other Options

Diego Rivera, Two Women

Data Digest

- **People 30 to 34 years old who have never married have tripled in number** since 1970. By 1993, among women this group had grown from 6 to 19 percent and among men from 9 to 30 percent.

- The **number of unmarried adults increased** from 37.5 million in 1970 to 72.6 million in 1993.

- In 1993, there were 6 **unmarried couples** for every 100 married couples, compared with only 1 for every 100 in 1970.

- Despite the often-cited shortage of eligible men, in some age groups there are **more unmarried men than women.** Unmarried in 1993 were 53 percent of men and 41 percent of women age 25 to 29, 38 percent of men and 30 percent of women age 30 to 34, and 31 percent of men and 26 percent of women age 35 to 39.

- Among some groups the **numbers of never-married people have been increasing.** In 1993, among African Americans in their early 30s (age 30 to 34), over 43 percent of women and 48 percent of men had never married, compared with 11 and 9 percent, respectively, in 1970. The corresponding percentages among whites and Latinos were 16 percent for white women and 27 percent for white men and 18 percent for Latino women and 29 percent for Latino men.

- In 1993 **more than 1 in every 8 people age 15 and over lived alone.**

SOURCES: Russell, 1994; Saluter, 1994; U.S. Bureau of the Census, 1994.

A couple who had been dating for several years went out to a Chinese restaurant for dinner one evening. After studying the menu, the man turned to the woman and asked, "How would you like your rice—fried or boiled?" She looked him straight in the eye and replied, "Thrown." Sound corny? Maybe not. Television programs like "The Dating Game," "The Love Connection," and "Studs" continue to thrive and, according to talk-show host Oprah Winfrey, one of the most popular programs she ever produced involved matchmaking between single women and Alaskan bachelors. Almost all talk shows devote several programs a year to reuniting people with their "first loves," with the intention of rekindling old flames that may blaze with passion and result in marriage. In general, most people eventually make that "love connection" and marry but until then—or if the relationship fizzles—there is more freedom today than ever before to pursue other options.

Since the 1970s, nontraditional family forms have increased. Today, many people view marriage as just one possible selection from a smorgasbord of relationship choices. Because nearly 95 percent of all Americans eventually marry, marriage remains the norm, but a growing number of people maintain unmarried living arrangements. This chapter examines four nontraditional lifestyles: singlehood, cohabitation, homosexual households, and communes.

BEING SINGLE

Household size has been shrinking since the 1940s. The average number of people per household was 2.6 in 1993, down from 3.7 in 1940. A major reason for the decrease is the growing number of people living alone (see Figure 9.1). Nevertheless, marriage rates have increased since the 1970s. By 1993, the percentage of never-married males age 65 and over had decreased from 8 to 4 percent, and the comparable figures for females were 8 and 5 percent (Saluter, 1994). Thus, more people today try marriage at least once.

How, then, do we explain the rise in singlehood? The major reason is that people are *delaying* marriage. As Figure 9.2 illustrates, the median age at first marriage has increased for both men and women. The median ages of nearly 27 and 25 for men and women, respectively, are the oldest at first marriage ever recorded by the Census Bureau. (Remember that the *median* represents the midpoint. Thus, half of all men were almost 27 or older and half of all women were almost 25 or older the first time they got married.) Women are especially likely to postpone marriage. Between 1980 and 1993, their median age at first marriage rose by almost three years. From a historical perspective, our current tendency to delay marriage is more the norm than the exception, at least for men. As Figure 9.2

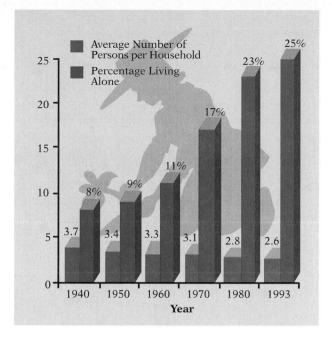

Figure 9.1 The Shrinking Household. *Both the decline in the average number of people per household and the rapidly rising numbers of people living alone have contributed to the smaller contemporary household* (Rawlings, 1994, A1, A2).

shows, men's median age at first marriage in 1890 was only slightly lower than in 1993. The median for women, however, has increased, especially since 1960. For both sexes, age at first marriage was lowest during the 1950s and 1960s than at any other time.

The unmarried population in the United States has almost doubled since 1970 (see Data Digest). In 1993, unmarried adults—defined by the Census Bureau as those who have never married or who are currently divorced or widowed—represented 39 percent of the population 18 years and over (Saluter, 1994). Why has the number of unmarried people become so large? In the first place, because cohabitation is more widely accepted, people feel less pressure to get married by their early twenties. Second, mothers with children born out of wedlock and even of different fathers face much less ostracism today than in the past. Third, divorce is more acceptable now than in the past. Thus, larger numbers of people are single for a greater portion of their lives. And because widowed men are more likely to remarry than are widowed women, there are eligible single women across all age groups (see Chapters 16, 17, and 18).

The Diversity of Singles

Singles constitute an extremely diverse group: They may be widowed, divorced, separated, or never married. In his typology of marriage and singlehood, Stein (1981) differentiates between voluntary and involuntary singlehood:

- *Voluntary temporary singles* are open to marriage but place a lower priority on searching for mates than on other activities, such as education, career, politics, and self-development. This group includes men and women who cohabit.

- *Voluntary stable singles* include people who have never married and are satisfied with that choice, those who have been married but do not want to remarry, those who are living together but do not intend to marry, and those whose lifestyles preclude the possibility of marriage, such as priests and nuns. Also included are single parents—both never married and formerly married—who are not seeking mates and who are raising

Figure 9.2 At What Age Do Men and Women First Marry? *As the text points out, the median age of first marriage for men is almost the same in 1993 as it was in 1890, but the median for women shows a generally rising trend* (Based on data from Saluter, 1994, Table B).

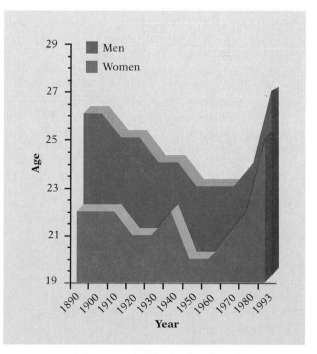

their children alone or with the help of relatives or friends.

- *Involuntary temporary singles* are those who would like to be married and are actively seeking mates. This group includes those who are widowed or divorced and single parents who would like to get married.

- *Involuntary stable singles* are primarily older divorced, widowed, and never-married people who wanted to marry or remarry but did not find a mate and now accept their single status. This group also includes singles who suffer from some physical or psychological impairment that prevents them from being successful in the marriage market.

A person's position in these categories can change over time. For example, voluntary temporary singles may marry, divorce, and then become involuntary stable singles because they are unable to find another suitable mate.

Staples (1981) developed a typology that challenged the stereotypes of single African American men as promiscuous and as avoiding stable relationships. Staples's *free-floating single* is unattached and dates randomly. The *single in an open-couple relationship* has a steady partner but also dates others. The *single in a closed-couple relationship* expects his partner to be faithful. *Committed singles* often live with their partners, may be engaged, and consider their relationship permanent. The *accommodationist*, who is generally in an older age group, lives a solitary life and does not date or have heterosexual contacts. As you've probably concluded, single men of all racial-ethnic groups probably fit these categories, not just African Americans. Thus, there are many types of African American singles, not just one stereotypical model, and single men of all racial-ethnic groups are more similar than different.

Why People Are Remaining Single Longer

There are many reasons why the numbers of singles have increased since the 1970s. In general, being single is no longer considered deviant. More people are recognizing that there are positive aspects of singlehood (see Table 9.1). Still, there are other important factors in deciding whether to marry or to remarry.

Many singles are disillusioned by marriage. In

Table 9.1

Marry? Tarry? Which Shall I Choose?

PUSHES TO GET MARRIED	PULLS TO REMAIN SINGLE OR RETURN TO SINGLEHOOD
Companionship, partnership	Privacy, few constraints
Faithful sexual partner	Varied sexual experiences
Dependability, love	Exciting, changing lifestyle
Sharing mutual interests	Meeting new friends with different interests
Pooling economic resources	Economic autonomy
Social approval for "settling down" and producing grandchildren	Freedom from responsibility to care for spouse or children
Becoming a part of something larger than self	Basic need for independence

SOURCES: Based on Stein, 1981; Carter and Sokol, 1993.

one national poll, for example, 56 percent of single women and 59 percent of single men agreed with the statement "I'm happier than most of my married friends" (Roper, 1990). In another national survey, Patterson and Kim (1991) reported that many singles are reluctant to marry because some of their friends have unhappy marriages. Marriage typically occurs later for children from one-parent families than for those from intact families (Goldscheider and Goldscheider, 1993). Disruptive family relationships, in particular, such as divorce or prolonged years of conflict between parents, can have a negative effect on young adults' perceptions of marriage.

One of the biggest advantages of remaining single is independence. Singlehood provides privacy and autonomy for both men and women. As one man stated:

I can yell as loud as I want and no one can hear me. I can fart and no one will hold their nose. I can be stupid and no one will laugh. I can have pets and no one will complain (Simenauer and Carroll, 1982: 246).

Single women may feel liberated from housework and domestic chores:

I feel like a person set free from prison. Not having to prepare dinner every night. Not having to sweep and sew on buttons. Staying away from the vacuum cleaner unless I feel like approaching it. . . . and not having to worry so much about appearances. I am very joyful about all this (Simenauer and Carroll, 1982: 245).

The *Quality Time* cartoon by Gail Machlis is reprinted by permission of Chronicle Features, San Francisco, California.

Being single is also alluring because of seemingly unlimited opportunities for dating or sex. Unlike married couples, singles can engage in sex with more than one partner without the fear of getting caught or feeling guilty. The AIDS epidemic, however, has dampened some people's enthusiasm for casual sex and sexual relations with multiple partners.

Ethnicity and family values also influence singlehood. For example, because they place great value on a college education, many Asian American families discourage early marriage. Young men and women who consider themselves very religious, who frequently attend religious services, and who have studied in Catholic schools are more likely to marry at younger ages because they don't see cohabitation as an acceptable alternative to marriage (Goldscheider and Goldscheider, 1993).

Macro-level changes also affect the likelihood of delaying marriage. Employment difficulties explain, in part, the growing percentage of younger men who are postponing marriage. For example, in 1973, the typical male high school dropout found a regular job at about age 22. Today, it can take until age 26 for a dropout to find a full-time job that can support a family. Even then, supporting a family may be difficult because the average annual earnings of dropouts

have been cut in half since 1973 (Amott, 1993). The economic situation for many college-educated men is also worsening rather than improving (see Chapter 14).

Comparing Women and Men

As you saw earlier, women are more likely than men to delay marriage. In their later years, women are also more likely to live alone (see Figure 9.3). There are several reasons for differ-

Figure 9.3 Living Alone: 1970 to 1993. As these data show, older men and women are the most likely to live alone. Men age 25 to 44 are somewhat more likely to live alone than women (Adapted from Saluter, 1994, x).

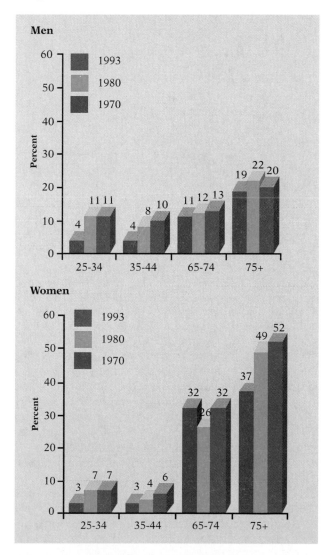

ences in marital status and living arrangements between the sexes.

Some cite the marriage squeeze as the principal contributor to women's postponement of marriage. The **marriage squeeze** is the term originally given to the situation resulting from the baby boom of the late 1940s and early 1960s (see Chapter 1), wherein large numbers of women reached marriageable status only to find a scarcity of suitable partners. This shortage of men may have had a number of reasons, including higher mortality rates among male infants, lower life expectancy rates, and absence or death caused by war. In the case of baby boomers, it has also been suggested that the large numbers of women born in that generation found few partners because women tend to marry men a few years older than themselves. The marriage squeeze reversed itself during the mid-1990s, however, and there are now many more never-married men than women in most age groups (see Data Digest).

Why, then, do so many women complain that "there's nothing out there"? One reason is that some men simply don't want to get married:

Ed . . . is a charming, handsome, 48-year-old Washington, D.C., lobbyist who plans evenings that most women just fantasize about. His dates may involve box seats at a performance of Tosca, *champagne served during the intermission, dinner at the best Italian restaurant. . . . What Ed is not planning is a long-term relationship: "I have had four very important relationships," he says. "Each one lasted about three years, but at a certain point the woman wanted marriage and I didn't"* (Szegedy-Maszak, 1993: 88).

Many single men view marriage as a major economic responsibility that they don't want to undertake. Moreover, some men don't want to participate in child care and other activities that women now expect them to share. Because of the increase in premarital sex, most men can have sex without getting married (see Chapter 7). Some men fear that a marriage may end in divorce. And, according to Evatt (1993: 86), some may suffer from the "Grass is Greener Syndrome and fear making a choice they'll later regret."

Women aren't rushing into marriage either. Some women feel that they can't have both a career and a family at the same time and choose to advance their professional lives before marrying and starting a family. Because some men are unsympathetic to a woman's need to combine ca-

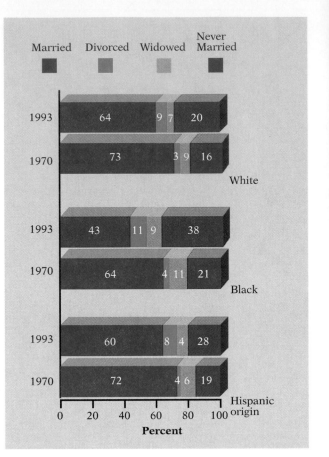

Figure 9.4 Changes in Marital Status, by Race and Hispanic Origin, 1970 and 1993. *The percentage of people who are married has decreased, but the percentage of divorced and never married has increased. Note that persons of Hispanic origin may be of any race* (Saluter, 1994, vi).

reer and family, many educated and professional women have little incentive to marry or stay married (Bennett et al., 1988; Collette, 1993). Older women are also more likely than older men to remain single because they have caretaker responsibilities for relatives, primarily aging parents (see Chapter 18).

Latino and African American Singles

As indicated in the Data Digest, the unmarried population has increased among many groups. Figure 9.4 compares data on whites, blacks, and persons of Hispanic origin since 1970 (there are no similar data on Asian Americans). The biggest changes characterize African Americans and those of Hispanic origin. For example, in 1993, 38 percent of black adults over the age of 18 had never been married, up from 21 percent in 1970. The proportion of Hispanic-origin adults over 18 who had never married rose from 19 to 28 percent during the same period.

Latinos Because there has been less research on Latino singles than on African American singles we have less information about long-term changes. There are several possible explanations for the increasing rates of singlehood, however. For example, the Latino population is much younger than the non-Latino population. Moreover, large numbers of young people who are migrating for economic reasons may be postponing marriage until they can support a family (Becerra, 1988). The Cuban community, which has always emphasized the importance of marriage and children, has been assimilating Americanized values and behaviors, and second-generation Cuban Americans are more likely to postpone marriage for the same reasons as whites (Szapocznik and Hernandez, 1988). Finally, Puerto Rican women tend to have more children out of wedlock than do either Mexican American or Cuban American women. Because they also have extensive kinship networks both in the United States and in Puerto Rico, Puerto Rican women may be less dependent on having a husband to help raise the children (Sanchez-Ayendez, 1988).

Researchers point out, however, that Latino men expect to marry even if they don't do so. Using Census Bureau data, for example, South (1993) found that more than either white or black men, Hispanic men *wanted* to marry. South suggests that, for Hispanic men, "marriage and parenthood may be important signals of achievement, visible to the family of origin and the wider community" (p. 368).

African Americans Large numbers of African Americans are postponing marriage, but an even higher proportion may never marry (Saluter, 1994). There are several reasons for this change that reflect both structural factors and personal attitudes. A major reason is the shortage of marriageable men among African Americans. Some estimate that there are eight black men for every ten black women (Amott, 1993; Anders, 1994). This makes a marital commitment unnecessary in the eyes of some men. In regions where unemployment rates for African American men are the highest, marriage rates are the lowest (Wilson, 1987). During the 1980s, as U.S. corporations started closing factories and moving their facili-

ties to developing countries, many women were absorbed into low-paying jobs in both the private and public sectors. Many men who lost their jobs became reluctant to commit themselves to marriage and the support of children.

African American men also have a lower life expectancy than their white counterparts. Occupational hazards in dangerous jobs have claimed many men's lives. At least in part because of a lack of preventive medical care, mortality rates for heart disease are almost three times higher for blue-collar workers—many of whom are African American—than for managerial and professional groups. Urban African American males face a 10 percent chance of being killed in street crimes, compared to a 2 percent chance for white males. The "war on drugs" has led to the incarceration of increasing numbers of men who are disproportionately men of color. The number of people incarcerated almost tripled between 1970 and 1990. In 1990, nearly 25 percent of African American men between the ages of 20 and 29 were in prison, on probation, or on parole (Amott, 1993).

Unfavorable social and economic conditions have exacerbated the eligibility problem for educated, middle-class, African American women as well. Many middle-class men are already married, and women are reluctant to "marry down." They are also unwilling to give up their financial independence. As one 37-year-old, successful professional African American woman stated, "I don't think I could handle asking somebody for money for toiletries" (Vobejda, 1991a: A12). Personal preferences also play a role in being single. One national study concluded that although never-married women see marriage as a preferable state, they delay marriage because they have high expectations of a male family head who has economic resources to support a family (Bulcroft and Bulcroft, 1993). Because of their advantage in numbers, some middle-class African American men simply screen out assertive, independent, or physically unattractive women. According to some, many successful black men have internalized the white middle-class values of success, leadership, and sexual performance, and many black women feel they can't find mates who are sensitive, supportive, and affectionate (Chapman, 1994). And, like many whites, blacks from divorced families tend to shun marriage (Bulcroft and Bulcroft, 1993).

Social mobility also affects singlehood. Many parents of girls from lower-middle-class and middle-class black families tend to emphasize educational attainment over early marriage. As a result, African American women pursuing higher education may place a higher priority on academic achievement than on developing personal relationships (Holland and Eisenhart, 1990). Others have tight social schedules because they devote most of their time to successful businesses they have started and to community activities (C. Jones, 1994).

There are parallel trends among African Americans and the larger society. In both groups more babies are being born to unmarried women, there is a rise in the number of female-headed families, and fewer children are living in two-parent families (see Chapters 11 and 12).

Myths and Realities About Being Single

Being single has many advantages, but some of the benefits have been exaggerated or romanticized. Here are some of the most popular myths about singlehood (Cargan and Melko, 1982):

1. *Singles are tied to their mother's apron strings.* In reality, there are few differences between singles and marrieds in their perceptions of and relationships with parents or other relatives.

2. *Singles are selfish and self-centered.* In reality, singles often value friends more than married people do, and they tend to be more active in community service.

3. *Singles are well-off financially.* A number of single professionals are affluent, but more singles than marrieds live at or below the poverty level. In general, married couples are better off financially because both partners

work. In fact, our taxes support singles rather than married couples (see the box "The Marriage Penalty").

4. *Singles are happier.* Although singles spend more time in leisure activities such as attending movies, restaurants, and clubs, they are also more likely to be lonely, to be depressed when they are alone, and to feel anxious and stressed.

5. *There is something wrong with people who do not marry.* There is nothing wrong with being or staying single. Many singles feel that the disadvantages of marriage outweigh the benefits.

Singlehood is not a rose garden; it has some thorns and prickles. For example, Cargan and Melko found that singles feel that they do not fit into married society. Many singles become quite involved in family life, however (see the box "Do Singles Have More Fun?").

Problems of Being Single

Consider some of the ups and downs of singlehood. Some problem areas include physical and emotional well-being, aging, and accessibility to housing.

Physical and Emotional Well-Being   In terms of personal well-being, single men have the most problems, married men the fewest. Compared to married men, single men have higher mortality rates and a higher incidence of alcoholism, suicide, schizophrenia, and other mental health problems (Coombs, 1991). This may be due to the fact that married men have less time and money to engage in high-risk behavior (such as using al-

CRITICAL ISSUES

The Marriage Penalty

Politicians, both Democrats and Republicans, routinely applaud nuclear families and criticize nontraditional family households. In practice, however, they have passed laws that benefit singles and penalize most married couples (see Freifeld, 1994). Using the logic that

two can live more cheaply than one, the federal government has historically taxed married couples at a higher rate than single people (Gage, 1994; Crenshaw, 1994).

Suppose each partner had a taxable income of $30,000 in 1993. If they were married, their tax would be $12,010. If they were unmarried, their tax would be $5,534 each, or

$11,068. The difference, or what is commonly known as "the marriage penalty," is $942.

If this $942 were invested every year at an interest rate of 6 percent for 30 years and compounded annually, it would grow to a retirement nest egg of $74,473 (Whitlock, 1994).

CONSTRAINTS

Do Singles Have More Fun?

One indicator of fun is how people spend their money on recreational activities. Because women's earnings are still only 68 percent of men's, women have less income for both necessities and recreation. There are several interesting (but probably not surprising) differences between men and women in terms of spending patterns. First, single women spend more on food consumed at home, housing, apparel, health care, personal care services, and reading material. In contrast, single men spend more on eating out, alcohol, transportation, entertainment, tobacco, and retirement, pension, and contributions to Social Security.

Second, women who live alone spend only half of what bachelors spend on entertainment but more than men do on pets and home-centered entertainment products. When single men "play," they are likely to spend money on fees and admissions to events and on sporting goods and electronic equipment (such as stereos and computers).

A third difference is that women spend more on others than on themselves. For example, single women spend 20 percent of their entertainment money on toys for family members' children, whereas only 10 percent of the single man's entertainment dollar is spent on children's toys (Exter, 1990).

It appears that single women devote much of their time and money to pleasing others rather than themselves. They take care of aging parents and relatives, and they provide numerous supportive services to the extended family:

I believe I was born for a certain purpose here on earth. My purpose has been to take care of all these kids that have come along. Of course, they call me their second mother. I'm not as close as they would have been to their real mother, but I take care of those kids. If my sister wanted to go out someplace, she just called me and I'd usually stay with them (Allen and Pickett, 1987: 524).

Caring for sick family members, serving as surrogate mothers, and ensuring that the family is cohesive and functioning are often full-time responsibilities. Thus, many single women have less leisure time for recreation than do single men.

cohol or other drugs) because of greater family responsibilities. In addition, married men often have wives who urge their spouses to have annual physical checkups, who prepare healthier meals, and who may generally be more concerned about preventing illness.

On a day-to-day basis, however, single women encounter more problems than do single men: "Fear is the problem. I carry mace and have a shotgun (loaded). I have eight phones in my house so I can cover myself and call the police. This is because of an actual threat I once got" (Simenauer and Carroll, 1982: 237, 241). Because of the rising incidence in recent years of rape and other violent crimes against women, single women, who often live alone, are more likely than their married counterparts to be mugged, burglarized, or raped. Professional women who travel have encountered problems in hotel accommodations and have been advised by media articles to take such precautions as getting a room next to the elevator, using an initial instead of a first name when checking into hotels, and not opening the door even to people who identify themselves as hotel employees.

Unmarried people of both sexes face a number of prejudices. They are often accused of being "immature" or "flighty" ("When are you going to put down roots?" "Are you ever going to settle down?"). In addition, they may be given more responsibilities at work because they are viewed as having more free time. For example, some single professional women complain that they are often expected to do the "little extras" at work: "To serve on more committees, volunteer for more overtime, or to give up more holidays and weekends—because they are perceived as having nothing better to do" (Cejka, 1993: 10).

Aging For singles who date and want to marry, the double standard still favors men. Aging women are typically seen as "over the hill," whereas aging men are often described as "mature" and "distinguished." Because more women are becoming financially independent, however, they are less likely to depend on successful, "mature" men for their economic stability. There is also a greater tendency, as one grows older, to become choosier. At the same time, there are fewer choices because the most desirable people are already married to other most desirable people (Hendrick and Hendrick, 1992b).

Single women and men often work long hours at their jobs, sometimes because they want to advance their careers, but sometimes because they're perceived as being less burdened with home and family responsibilities.

Housing Have you ever driven past a plush condominium that's for "adults only"? Such residences often advertise amenities like pools, saunas, jacuzzis, and elaborate athletic facilities. In reality, however, few singles can afford such luxurious housing. Many can't find adequate employment and are forced to live in modest housing or to share rental units. Because of increasing housing costs and decreasing incomes, more young singles are living with their parents. For example, the proportion of young adults age 18 to 24 living with their parents increased from 47 percent in 1970 to nearly 53 percent in 1993 (U.S. Bureau of the Census, 1994). Students who used to go away to college are now more likely to attend a nearby community college or university and to live at home because they or their families can't afford the rising costs of tuition and board (Schrof, 1994).

Older Never-Marrieds

There is little literature on elderly people who have never married, probably because fewer than 5 percent of men and women age 65 and over fall into this category (Saluter, 1994). Some professionals see the never-married elderly as lonely and as enduring many problems. For ex-

ample, older never-married men who lose their jobs may suffer more damage to their self-esteem if, as is often the case, they have no close family members to give them emotional or other kinds of support. Never-married women—especially those who gave up jobs to care for their aging parents—may not have an adequate income or retirement benefits in their own old age. And women with college or professional degrees not only have to struggle with actual discrimination on the job but also must often deal with the societal stigma of being "career women."

On the other hand, some older people are delighted that they have remained single. A commitment to another person may be satisfying, but it also means making compromises and limiting one's own freedom:

When I was a little girl and, later on, an adolescent, it never occurred to me that I would not meet the man of my dreams, get married, and live happily ever after. Now, at fifty-four, it seems unlikely, though not impossible, that this will happen. Not only do I live alone but I actually like it. I value my space, my solitude, and my independence enormously and cannot [imagine] the circumstances that would lead me to want to change it (Cassidy, 1993: 35).

Never-marrieds do not have to deal with the desolation of widowhood or divorce. Many develop extensive social networks among friends and relatives. They work, date, and engage in a variety of hobbies, volunteer work, church activities, and lasting relationships (see the box "Long Live Spinsterhood!"). Never-married people also appear more likely to develop the self-reliance that is helpful in coping with aging (Hooyman and Kiyak, 1991).

As you can see, singlehood has both advantages and disadvantages for adults of all ages. There are many reasons for remaining single, and this choice will probably be made more often in the future as singlehood becomes an increasingly acceptable way of life.

COHABITATION

Cohabitation is a living arrangement in which two people who are not related and not married live together and usually have a sexual relationship. Cohabitants are sometimes called **POSSLQs** (pronounced "possel-kews"), meaning "persons of the opposite sex sharing living quarters." The Cen-

Long Live Spinsterhood!

Rather than revile being single, some never-married older women have revived the practice, and even made it an art! In 1993, for example, one of the best-selling books was *Having Our Say: The Delany Sisters' First 100 Years* (Delany et al., 1993). In their book, Sarah (Sadie) Delany, born in 1889, and Annie Elizabeth (Bessie) Delany, born in 1891, discuss their experiences over more than 100 years of life. Neither Bessie nor Sadie is apologetic about having remained single (and, according to Giles and Sawhill, 1993, they prefer to be called "maiden ladies" rather than the odious "old maids"). On the contrary, they have enjoyed living together all their lives. They still do their own cooking, they do daily exercises, and they have an 87-year-old housekeeper who comes in twice a month (Henneberger, 1993).

Bessie and Sadie are daughters of a slave who became the country's first African American bishop of the Episcopal Church. Bessie was the second black female dentist in New York State, and Sadie became the first black home economics teacher in a New York City high school. The sisters never married because they were busy in their careers and because "in those days it never occurred to most people that a women could have a career AND get married." Bessie says that "We were popular, good-looking gals, but I think we were too smart, too

Sadie and Bessie Delany chat in their New York home. In March of 1995, a play based on their book, Having Our Say, *opened on Broadway to considerable critical acclaim.*

independent for most men" (Delany et al., 1993:85).

Some never-married older women resent being grouped with young singles because they feel it jeopardizes their economic reputations. Although Florence King (1993) writes with a bit of tongue-in-cheek, she argues that the term *spinster* should be resurrected under "marital status" categories because

Spinsters give females a good name. . . . We come to work on time with no visions of babysitters and day-care

centers dancing . . . in our heads; we can work overtime on a moment's notice, and there is never any spit-up on our paperwork (King, 1993: 72).

According to King, it is because self-supporting spinsters are lumped into a category of "single women" that includes divorcees with children and young unmarried women who have bill-paying problems that spinsters have problems getting credit and increasing their credit lines.

sus Bureau, which does not ask about emotional involvement or sexual relationships, identifies cohabiting couples by counting unmarried-couple households. An *unmarried-couple household* is "composed of two unrelated adults of the opposite sex (one of whom is the householder) who share a housing unit with or without the presence of children under 15 years old" (Saluter, 1994: vii).

Arrangements in which there is no romantic involvement—for example, a landlady and a college tenant or platonic roommates—are included under the Census Bureau's cohabitation umbrella, but these households represent a minuscule number of unmarried-couple households.

Since 1970, the number of unmarried-couple households in the United States has increased al-

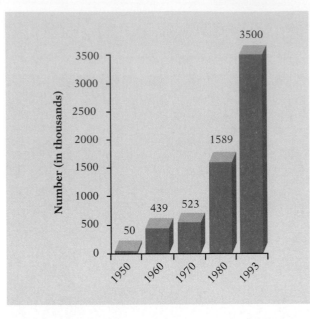

Figure 9.5 Rising Numbers of Cohabitant Households, 1960–1993. As you can see, the first big increase in the numbers of unmarried couples living together was roughly eightfold, from about 50,000 in 1950 to 439,000 in 1960. Leveling off for a decade, the numbers shot up again after 1970 (Saluter, 1994, vii).

most sevenfold (see Figure 9.5). Keep in mind, however, that only 4 percent of the population is cohabiting at any point in time (Bumpass and Sweet, 1989). Cohabitation usually postpones marriage (or remarriage); it rarely replaces marriage permanently.

Types of Cohabitation

There are several types of cohabitation. The most common are part-time/limited cohabitation, premarital cohabitation, and cohabitation that is a substitute for a legal marriage.

A form of cohabitation that people "drift" into gradually is called **part-time/limited cohabitation** (Macklin, 1974). A couple that spends a great deal of time together may eventually decide to move in together. The decision may be based on a combination of reasons, such as convenience, sharing expenses, and sexual accessibility. There is no long-term commitment in this type of arrangement, and most often, marriage is not the couple's goal. Cohabitants may feel that living together provides more intimacy than singlehood but less of a commitment than marriage (Rindfuss and VandenHeuvel, 1990). Sometimes

one or both partners use cohabitation to gain independence from parental values and influence.

In **premarital cohabitation,** the couple is testing the relationship before making a final commitment. In this sense cohabitation may be a *trial marriage.* If a trial marriage does not lead to formal marriage the couple will usually end the relationship. Trial marriages may be especially attractive to partners who doubt that they can deal successfully with problems that arise from differences in personalities, interests, age, race, or previous marital status. For many people, premarital cohabitation is "a new step between dating and marriage" (Gwartney-Gibbs, 1986).

A **substitute marriage** is a long-term commitment between two people without a legal marriage. Motives for substitute marriages vary widely. For example, one or both partners may still be legally married to someone else or may be divorced and reluctant to remarry. In some cases, one partner may be highly dependent or insecure and thus prefer any kind of relationship to being alone. In other cases, partners may feel that a legal ceremony is irrelevant to their commitment to each other (see the box "Our Love Doesn't Need a Piece of Paper" in Chapter 1). In recent years, a number of entertainment celebrities have made their nonmarital living arrangements (as well as their out-of-wedlock children) public—for example, Sam Shepard and Jessica Lange, Farrah Fawcett and Ryan O'Neal, Goldie Hawn and Kurt Russell—and have made it clear that they have no intention of marrying. Or, like Mick Jagger and Jerri Hall, they have married after many years of cohabitation. For better or worse, the public has accepted these "lifestyles of the rich and famous" as alternatives to traditional marriage.

There is also some evidence that partner choices differ depending on the kind of cohabitation relationship that people seek. That is, partners who expect a long-term relationship (a trial marriage) are much more likely than those who expect a short-term relationship to choose partners who are similar in age, race, and religion. Thus, "A different kind of relationship calls for a different kind of partner" (Schoen and Weinick, 1993: 413).

Characteristics of Cohabitants

Cohabitants share some general characteristics. They are mostly young adults (68 percent are under age 35) and never-marrieds (53 percent), although a sizable proportion (34 percent) have been divorced (Thornton, 1988). Cohabitation rates are higher for women than for men and most common for those with low socioeconomic status who grew up in broken homes or in families that depended on welfare (Bumpass et al., 1991).

Most cohabiting relationships are relatively short-lived, with a median duration of 15 to 18 months. When these relationships end, about 60 percent result in marriage and 40 percent in a breakup. Cohabitation is more likely to result in marriage for white and Latino women than for African American women. For example, by age 44, nearly 94 percent of white women had married, compared to only 64 percent of black women (London, 1991).

Living together is more common in large cities, in the U.S. Northeast and West, and among people who are more politically liberal and less actively religious (Thornton, 1991). The finding that young people whose mothers approve of cohabitation marry at significantly later ages than young people whose mothers disapprove of cohabitation suggests that family values may be an important factor in the decision to cohabit (Axinn and Thornton, 1993).

Although cohabitation first gained notoriety among college campuses, most cohabitants are not college students. About 40 percent of cohabiting couples have children in the household and a quarter of these have children age 10 or older (Bumpass et al., 1991). This represents a substantial increase over the 27 percent of cohabiting couples with children recorded by the Census Bureau in 1980 (U.S. Bureau of the Census, 1991a). One reason for this increase may be that women in lower socioeconomic levels postpone divorce because of the financial expenses but continue to build their families by having children with cohabitants (see Loomis and Lansdale, 1994).

Cohabitants like this California couple tend to have a more contemporary approach to the roles men and women play within marriage.

contribute to marital stability because a later age is one of the best predictors of a stable marriage (see Chapter 16).

Cohabitation can enable people to establish a meaningful relationship instead of participating in superficial dating games. Long periods of intimate contact afford an opportunity for self-disclosure and may foster growth and maturity. Living with someone can be annoying at times, but partners may gain a deeper understanding of their partners' needs, expectations, and weaknesses. They may gain self-confidence as they learn to deal with each other on a daily basis. Cohabitation may avert bad marriages and subsequent divorces if it gives partners a more realistic view of each other and forces them to recognize and deal with opposing values, opinions, and ideas (Bumpass and Sweet, 1989). And it can help people find out how much they really care about each other when they have to cope with such unpleasant realities as a partner who doesn't pay overdue bills.

The Pluses and Minuses of Cohabitation

Cohabitants generally recommend cohabitation. Like other living arrangements, however, cohabitation has both advantages and disadvantages.

Advantages Cohabitation can provide couples with the emotional security of an intimate relationship but at the same time allow them to maintain their independence in many areas. They can dissolve the relationship without legal problems, or they may marry with a feeling that they have established a sound foundation (J. Crosby, 1991). Simply postponing marriage can

Disadvantages Cohabitants often face the same kinds of problems as married couples (see Chapters 10–12). Some partners experience a loss of identity or a feeling of being trapped. They may feel restricted from participating in activities with friends. And one or both partners may dislike being overdependent on the other. If, like most cohabiting couples, cohabitants are sexually intimate, they can experience the same kinds of sexual problems that married couples encounter, including a lack of sexual interest, failure to achieve orgasm, fear of pregnancy, and susceptibility to infections. Most important, if people are not honest about their sexual histories, partners can contract sexually transmitted diseases, HIV infection, or AIDS (see Chapter 7).

Unmarried couples also have problems that married couples are less likely to confront. They may be ambivalent about not dating other people, for example. If one or both sets of parents of the couple disapprove of or reject the relationship, the couples may experience tension. If one or both partners are keeping their living arrangement secret, they may fear discovery by friends and relatives and feel guilty about lying. Some cohabiting partners often concoct elaborate schemes for mail and telephone service to avoid being found out.

The partners may also differ in their intentions. Women typically see cohabitation as a trial marriage, whereas men may be more interested in convenient sex (see Chapters 5 and 6). In addition, and as you saw in Chapter 1, the lack of legal bonds can create problems when the relationship is dissolved. Because partners can abandon the relationship at the first sign of trouble, there is less motivation for growth and for learning how to deal with problems and conflict.

Does Cohabitation Exploit Women?

Although some women think that cohabitation will promote egalitarian gender roles, this is rarely the case. Women in cohabiting relationships still do more of the cooking and other household tasks traditionally assigned to women. Several studies suggest that cohabiting arrangements exploit women economically. When both partners are working, some cohabiting men insist that women pay half of all expenses, even though women earn much less than men. In addition, cohabiting men are much less likely to be employed than are married men, but cohabiting women are much more likely to be employed than married women (Khoo, 1987). It would seem that many women should be wary of developing long-term cohabiting relationships. The costs might be higher than the benefits.

Does Cohabitation Lead to Better Marriages?

Despite the contention of many couples who live together that cohabitation leads to better marriages, most research suggests that marriages that follow cohabitation have a higher dissolution rate than do marriages that begin without cohabitation. Those who live together may argue less, but they tend to have more problems with alcohol and drug use and sexual infidelity (Bumpass and Sweet, 1989; Teachman et al., 1991).

Why does living together not lead to better marriages? There are several possible explanations. For young people especially, cohabitation may be a way of avoiding the responsibilities of marriage. As a result, they may make less effort to communicate with one another and to work out problems. There is also a difference between cohabitants who intend to marry their partners and those who do not. The latter put less effort into the relationship, are less likely to compromise, and tend to have poorer communication skills for solving interpersonal problems. Thus, "those who cohabit with no intention of marrying are ill equipped for a lasting relationship" (Stets, 1993b: 256).

Couples who cohabit usually expect more from marriage than others and are less likely to adapt to traditional marital role expectations. Most cohabitants believe that any relationship should be ended if either partner is dissatisfied. In contrast, adults who do not cohabit may bring the more traditional view of the marriage bond as sacred to their marriages (Cherlin, 1992). Or the experience of cohabitation itself may lead to instability: Cohabitants used to more autonomy may be quick to leave a marriage (DeMaris and MacDonald, 1993). In addition, former cohabitants may be less able to weather the storms that some complex family structures (such as those involving stepchildren) present (Teachman and Polonko, 1990).

Cohabitation and the Law

Unmarried couples have very little legal protection (see, for example, Stone, 1993). In a recent case in Sacramento, California, a state appeals court ruled that a landlord had the right to refuse to rent an apartment to an unmarried heterosexual couple because the owner considered sex outside of marriage sinful. Thus, renting the apartment would violate the religious freedom of the apartment owner. The opinion of the presiding judge noted that because the California legislature had not passed laws giving cohabitants the same housing rights as those of married couples, there was no basis for extending the same housing-rights protection to unmarried couples as to married couples (*New York Times*, 1994).

According to many legal experts, in financial matters, cohabitants' best protection on a daily basis is to maintain separate ownership of possessions. Partners should not have joint bank accounts or credit cards. They should prepare a written agreement about debts and how bills are to be paid. Shared leases should also be negotiated before moving in together. If partners buy real estate together they should spell out carefully, in writing, each person's share of any profit. Homeowners' and renters' insurance policies should carry both partners' names so that the possessions of both are clearly covered. Cars should not be registered in a woman's name just to escape the high insurance premiums commonly charged men under 25. If there is an accident, the woman will be liable even if the man was driving.

Health insurance plans that cover a spouse almost never extend to an unmarried partner. If either partner is not covered by a group health plan at work, unmarried couples should buy their own protection against catastrophic medical costs. A medical power of attorney will permit an unrelated person not only to visit a critically ill partner but to make medical decisions for him or her.

If a partner dies and leaves no will, relatives, no matter how distant, can claim all of his or her possessions. The cohabiting partner has no claim at all. Cohabiting couples' best course is to put everything possible in writing. If a couple has children, both unmarried parents must acknowledge biological parenthood in writing in order to protect the children's future claim to financial support and inheritance (see Chapter 17). Partners can name each other as beneficiaries in life insurance policies. To make sure their wishes are carried out in probate (the process by which a will is certified as genuine) and that no kin inherit undeserved assets, an unmarried couple should prepare wills. Few pension plans allow unmarried partners to receive survivor retirement benefits, something elderly unmarried couples must consider carefully (see Chapter 18).

It may seem unromantic to discuss legal matters when we are talking about people who love each other. If or when a cohabiting relationship ends, however, the legal problems can be overwhelming. Many attorneys recommend that cohabitants draw up a contract similar to a premarital document. The document in Appendix E describes some of the complex issues that must be dealt with.

Cohabitation in Other Countries

Unlike the United States, some countries encourage rather than impede cohabitation. In Sweden, for example, 99 percent of married couples live together before marriage; in Denmark, 80 percent cohabit. Why these high rates? In large part, because these countries' governments offer single women economic security. In Sweden, birth-control information and some contraceptive devices are free. Moreover, since 1976, Swedish women have been able to obtain an abortion on request up to the eighteenth week of pregnancy. All parents, married or unmarried, receive a children's allowance from the state, and divorced and single mothers are entitled to cash advances on child-support payments if a child's father fails to pay. Norway's social policies are similar (Blanc, 1987; Haas, 1992).

Nevertheless, cohabitation does not decrease divorce rates in these countries. This is probably because, as in the United States, cohabitants may have a weaker commitment to the institution of marriage. A nationwide Swedish survey found that among women who cohabited before marriage, divorce rates were almost 80 percent higher than among those who had not cohabited. The longer women cohabited, the higher their chances of having a stable marriage. However, and among all women whose marriages remained intact for eight years, divorce rates for previous cohabitants and noncohabitants were the same (Bennett et al., 1988). All of these data suggest that both women's economic security and long cohabitation periods may decrease divorce after the cohabitants marry.

HOMOSEXUAL HOUSEHOLDS

Just as there is no typical lifestyle for unmarried heterosexual couples, there is no one lifestyle typical of committed homosexual couples. And just as countries vary in the degree to which they accept or reject cohabitation, they vary in their attitudes toward homosexual households. In 1990, the Danish legislature voted by a two to one margin to legalize homosexual marriage. Gays and lesbians were thereby enabled to enter a "registered partnership" that gives them the same rights as heterosexual couples in such matters as housing and retirement pensions. Among the few rights still withheld from Danish homosexuals are the right to adopt children and the right to hold a wedding in the dominant Lutheran Church. (It is already common, however, for clerics to bless homosexual partnerships.)

As we will see, the U.S. attitude toward homosexual unions is less favorable. On the one hand, increasing numbers of universities offer courses on lesbian and gay studies and fund conferences on homosexual issues (Evans and Wall, 1991). On the other hand, open hostility and violence against homosexuals appear to be increasing. For this reason, the U.S. Justice Department's Community Relations Service hotline, originally set up for reporting hate crimes based on race, color, or national origin, has now been expanded to include antigay and religious violence (see the "Taking Action" section in this chapter).

Gay and Lesbian Couples

Two of the most widespread misconceptions about homosexuals are that they are mentally ill and that they seduce children. In fact, homosexuals are psychologically as normal as heterosexuals and lead ordinary lives that are not very different from anybody else's (see the box "One Day of Lavender Lesbians").

Both homosexual and heterosexual couples want close and loving relationships. A major difference, however, is that homosexual partners rarely assume the traditional breadwinner/homemaker roles. They are more likely to share domestic and housework chores, and they don't get into the power struggle that often results from the fact that men earn more than women. Partners are usually financially independent, there are no legal formalities to negotiate, there may be no children involved, and—a mixed blessing, some would say—family and friends rarely discourage the end of the relationship.

Gay and lesbian relationships, like those of their heterosexual counterparts, are not always harmonious. For example, in a study of 75 gay, 51 lesbian, and 108 heterosexual couples who did not reside with children, Kurdek (1994) found that all cohabitants, whether heterosexual or homosexual, experienced similar degrees of conflict in four areas—power, personal flaws, intimacy, and personal distance. In terms of *power*, all subjects were equally likely to report arguments about finances, lack of equality in the relationship, and possessiveness. They were also equally likely to complain about such *personal flaws* as smoking or drinking, driving style, and personal grooming. There was no significant difference in the numbers of reports from both groups of dissatisfaction in *intimacy*, especially in sex and not showing enough affection. Finally, both groups were equally likely to complain that their partners were *physically distant*, usually because of job or school commitments.

Gay and heterosexual groups did differ in two areas, however. According to Kurdek, the heterosexual couples were more likely to argue over personal values, social and political issues, and relationships with the partner's parents, whereas the gay and lesbian couples reported greater distrust, especially over previous lovers. Kurdek suggests that suspicion may be a more common phenomenon among gay and lesbian cohabitants because their previous lovers are likely to remain in their social support networks, increasing the likelihood of jealousy and resentment.

As we discussed in Chapter 6, there are probably more differences between men and women than there are between homosexuals and heterosexuals. Gay men, like heterosexual men, tend to separate love and sex and to have more brief relationships, whereas both lesbian and heterosexual women are more interested in integrating sex with emotional intimacy in a lasting relationship (Kurdek and Schmitt, 1986).

An important similarity between gay and heterosexual couples is that, in both cases, successful relationships are characterized by more open communication and supportive families (Meyer, 1990). Both gay and lesbian couples, however, perceive less social support from family members than do married or cohabiting couples. The greatest rejection often comes from racial-ethnic families, whose attitudes tend to be more traditional and conservative. For one thing, traditional values about marriage and the family are often reinforced by religious beliefs. In some faiths homosexual behavior is considered aberrant or a sin. Family members are expected to marry and to continue the traditional family structure. A related reason is that racial-ethnic families have strong extended family systems. A homosexual family member may be seen as jeopardizing not only the intrafamily relationships but also the extended family's continued strong

One Day of Lavender Lesbians

The modern gay and lesbian rights movement was launched in 1969 when New York City police entered the Stonewall Inn to harass gay patrons of this popular Greenwich Village bar (Carabillo et al., 1993). Gay bars had been similarly harassed for years, without resistance, but this time the patrons fought back, and the incident received national coverage. Although many gays and lesbians have "come out" since "Stonewall," many more have not because they fear physical violence and job discrimination.

According to Barrett (1989), if all lesbians became visible for one day (say, by turning lavender), we would see many gay women making important contributions to society, including raising children who will also be productive members of society. This same argument can be made for gay men and gay fathers.

One day of lavender lesbians would convince Americans that gay women are everywhere. A secretary who once said to her female supervisor, "I'd never be around those gay/lesbian people. They're sick!" would suddenly look up and see that the woman whom she has liked and respected for years is "one of them." In Brooklyn a 20-year-old competitor for the Miss USA title dropping in at her mother's apartment would realize with a shock that both her mother's skin and that of her mother's best friend was lavender. A nurse walking into a hospital room would instantly know that her very ill patient and the woman who sat by her side were lovers. In California, a father who "would like to put all queers on an island and blow them up" would be confronted with two lavender daughters. Parishioners in a Methodist Church would see their minister's lavender hands holding the Bible. A Mexican American computer expert, a WASP producer of television commercials, a University of New Hampshire student, a Cherokee poet, an Asian American social worker, a high school gym teacher, a Detroit manufacturing executive, an accountant in Frederick, Maryland, would all walk from their homes and onto the streets as lavender women. And in Ann Arbor, Michigan, Nancy and Sherry would wheel their child in his stroller down the street.

Lesbians are everywhere, and their lives are as varied as are the lives of women whose erotic attention is focused on men. As one woman stated, "The only thing true about all lesbians is they are all women" (Barrett, 1989: 24).

---

association with the ethnic community (Morales, 1990).

Lesbian and Gay Families

Legal marriage between homosexual partners is banned by every state in the United States. However, some homosexual couples have religious or public ceremonies in which they exchange vows and rings to show their commitment to one another. (We discuss this topic in more detail in Chapter 10.)

Approximately 20 percent of gay men and 33 percent of lesbians are or have been married to heterosexual partners in the past. About 50 percent of gay men have children from these marriages, and some 56 percent of lesbians have children from former marriages living with them (Harry, 1983). Lesbian families may be *nuclear*, in which all children are either born to or adopted by the couple; *blended*, in which the children come from one or both women's prior relationships (usually with a man); and *extrablended*, which includes children from both sources (Clunis and Green, 1988).

Almost a third of lesbians have become mothers through some form of assisted reproduction (Salholz et al., 1990; see also Chapter 11), and the trend is growing. In 1988, for example, nearly 40 percent of the women inseminated at the Sperm Bank of Northern California, a service run by feminists in Oakland, were lesbians. The numbers of prospective lesbian mothers had doubled since the sperm bank opened in 1982 (Kolata, 1989).

Studies to date show no adverse effects on children raised in homosexual households. Indeed, some studies have reported typical gender stereotyping; daughters of lesbians tend to have strong female identities, and sons "hang out with the guys" and play sports (Salholz et al., 1990). Researchers also suggest that gay parents can be effective role models. For example, respected gay men can help decrease the delinquent behavior

Gay parents who work outside the home often have to struggle, just as heterosexual parents do, for quality time with their children.

of gay-bashing, help children focus on the quality of a relationship rather than on the sex of the partner, and provide children with a broader spectrum of role models that encourage making personal choices independent of societal pressures to conform (Bozett and Sussman, 1990).

Despite these benefits, some psychiatrists, psychologists, and other clinicians foresee difficulties for children raised in homosexual families. They speculate that when girls grow up they may have difficulty in intimate relationships with men, and that boys may be uncomfortable with their role as males. If lesbian parents are openly hostile toward men, or gay parents toward women, these difficulties could be worsened. Moreover, children born through artificial insemination into a lesbian family might have to deal with multiple issues, including being raised by a lesbian couple and not knowing their biological father (Kolata, 1989b).

Some homosexual parents dismiss these concerns, and others fear that "coming out" will mean losing the children in a divorce battle. Even when child custody is not an issue, many women fear that their children will reject them

or be upset or harmed by the knowledge that their mother is a lesbian. There is also evidence that children of gay parents are harassed by the children of heterosexual parents. Consequently, many gay parents and their children practice a variety of "impression-management" techniques, such as referring to the live-in lover as "uncle" or "aunt" and being discreet in talking about gay parents to outsiders (Harry, 1988).

Although there is somewhat greater acceptance of homosexual relationships today than in the past, widespread discrimination and prejudice still exist. If gay and lesbian parents internalize this hostility, they may experience self-hatred that can manifest itself in such self-destructive behavior as substance abuse or violent behavior toward a partner (Renzetti and Curran, 1989).

Economic Issues

One of the major problems for homosexual couples is job discrimination. Traditionally, male homosexuals have clustered in "feminine" positions like that of teacher, librarian, and social worker because they felt they would be safe against discrimination. For many people, however, this tactic simply underlined the popular stereotype of gay males as effeminate.

The American public is very ambivalent about homosexuality. On the one hand, a *Newsweek* poll found that 67 percent of those surveyed approved of health insurance for gay partners and 70 percent approved of inheritance rights (Turque et al., 1992). On the other hand, the same poll found that 61 percent disapproved of adoption rights for gay partners. The percentage of people who think that homosexual relationships should be legalized has increased slightly, from 43 percent in 1977 to 58 percent in 1992 (Colasanto, 1989; Turque et al., 1992). In addition, a dozen states around the country have been organizing to repeal existing gay rights laws or to prevent the enactment of any such laws at either the state or local level (Knickerbocker, 1993).

In 1994, when Ikea, a Swedish company with 12 stores in the United States, launched a 30-second commercial showing a gay couple shopping for a dining room table, the commercial drew both praise and protests. Some people applauded the commercial. Others, including some conservative religious groups, urged their members not to shop at Ikea and to call or write the company with their complaints. Shortly after the ad began airing, an Ikea store in Hicksville, New York, had to be evacuated after an anonymous caller claimed a bomb was planted there in protest of the commercial, but none was found (Marbella, 1994).

Gays and lesbians report many cases of dismissal or lack of promotions on the job (Squirrel, 1989; Benokraitis and Feagin, 1995). Many people, however, feel that homosexuals should have equal rights, especially in jobs. It is difficult to explain this seeming contradiction. Perhaps it is in the younger generations that attitudes are changing; people under 30 are typically more accepting of homosexuality. When basketball superstar Magic Johnson, an avowed heterosexual, announced in 1991 that he tested positive for the HIV virus, many people stopped blaming homosexuals for the AIDS epidemic.

Public ambivalence about legalizing homosexuality may also reflect tightening state and local budgets. For example, when the Minneapolis city council considered legalizing "domestic partnerships," many residents protested, claiming it was more important to increase police salaries than to implement health benefits for either homosexual or heterosexual cohabitants (Larson and Edmondson, 1991).

Legal Issues

Homosexual parents face a variety of legal problems. Most state laws recognize only the biological mother as the child's parent and do not allow her lesbian partner to adopt the child. If the biological mother dies, the partner can lose custody (Thompson, 1990). Lesbian partners may also be denied the right to be with and to care for lovers who are ill or incapacitated. In one case, the father of an adult woman who had suffered brain damage in a car accident won legal guardianship and barred his daughter's lesbian lover from seeing her (Findlen, 1987).

Some feel that recognizing same-sex marriage would be only a symbolic act that might even have deleterious economic or legal effects. For example, lesbian mothers now have the same tax benefits for children as do other couples or single mothers. Social Security benefits are usually irrelevant because both partners in most gay and lesbian couples work and have ac-

crued their own retirement benefits. If same-sex marriage were legalized, tax withholding forms might reveal information that could result in even greater discrimination for a gay or lesbian in the workplace.

Many issues, however, are not just symbolic. If gay marriages were legal, for example, inheritance could not be contested by family members and relatives. Current rent-control regulations that define "family" in traditional terms can prevent access by gay families to housing. Furthermore, like heterosexual cohabitants, homosexual families are not entitled to the hospitalization or bereavement leaves that married couples enjoy. Family courts are sometimes reluctant to give custody of children or even visiting rights to lesbian mothers or gay fathers because of the fear that the children might become homosexual (Dean, 1991).

It may take a long time for attitudes and laws to change. In the late 1980s, gay activists began to engage in *outing*, or publicizing the names of alleged homosexuals who had chosen not to divulge their sexual preference. For example, in 1992 the children of two influential conservative Republicans were "outed." One was John Schlafly, the son of Phyllis Schlafly, who has spent much of her life campaigning against homosexuality and who has denounced proposals for AIDS education as "the teaching of safe sodomy." The other was Diane Mosbacher, daughter of George Bush's friend and campaign aide, Bob Mosbacher (Cohen, 1992). Proponents of outing argued that if gays in respected and powerful positions were forced to come out of the closet, they could be pressured into public commitments and political action to improve the situation for homosexuals. The tactic was very controversial but short-lived.

COMMUNAL HOUSEHOLDS

Communes are collective households in which children and adults live together. The adults may be married or unmarried. Some communes permit individual ownership of private property; others do not. There is a great deal of variation in the amount of sharing of economic, sexual, and decision-making rights.

Communes are not a contemporary phenomenon. They are believed to have existed since 100 B.C. Today there are an estimated

1000 communes in the world. The popularity of communal living has fluctuated in the United States, but its membership has never exceeded more than a tenth of a percent of the entire population. Commune members are distinctive but not "deviant." They tend to be younger than the national average. Married people, Protestants, and blacks are underrepresented, whereas college graduates and Jews are overrepresented (Zablocki, 1980).

Both nineteenth-century and contemporary communes have differed widely in their respective time periods in terms of structure, values, and ideology (Kantor, 1970). In the nineteenth century many such communities wrestled with the issue of monogamy and had very different solutions. One group, the Icarians, made marriage mandatory for all adult members. Others, such as the Shakers and Rappites, required everyone, including husbands and wives, to live celibate lives. The Mormons, in emphasizing group rather than individual well-being, adopted polygyny. Others practiced free love, where sexual intercourse was permissible to all members and was not regulated by norms about marriage or monogamy (Muncy, 1988).

The Oneida community practiced "complex marriage," in which every adult was theoretically married to every other member. Oneida girls were initiated into sexual intercourse by much older men shortly after their first menses (menstruation). Communal child care presumably freed mothers to pursue their highest calling— serving God. According to some sources, mothers had the greatest difficulty with the idea that community adults, not biological parents, were responsible for raising children (Dalsimer, 1981).

Contemporary communes also vary in terms of parent-child arrangements. On an Israeli kibbutz, for instance, parents often see their children during meals and in the evenings. There are strong emotional parent-child ties, and parents are very involved in the decision making concerning their child's future (O'Kelly and Carney, 1986). Today, however, many kibbutz-raised children are opting to raise their own children in a nuclear family structure (Kaffman, 1993).

Heiss (1986) charges that both the historical communes and the rural, "hippie" communes of the 1960s were "notorious for the burdens carried by women." Women typically did their traditional tasks and participated in men's work as well. Contemporary urban communes have come the closest to an equitable division of labor. The purpose of urban communes is to create a collective household and a shared home rather than a countercultural attack on the current system. Both men and women often work in traditional 9-to-5 jobs, make about equal financial contributions, and share the routine household functions. Most of the child care, however, still rests with the mother.

Most communes have been short-lived. Often, the members are unwilling to give up their autonomy or private property. In a society that emphasizes individuality and competition, it is difficult to subordinate individual rights and privileges "for the greater good." There may be conflict and jealousy regarding sexual relationships (Zablocki, 1980). Furthermore, communes that practiced polygamy or free love "drew the wrath" of a culture that believed that sexual relations outside of marriage and monogamy are evil (Muncy, 1988). Other groups are dwindling because of a lack of new membership. For example, the Shakers have nine members left in one "family" in Maine. The members are quite elderly, and most of the buildings and grounds have now been turned into tourist attractions (Kephart and Zellner, 1991).

Communal living has attracted little recent interest from researchers. In their book on unconventional lifestyles, for example, Kephart and Zellner (1991: ix) have eliminated the chapter on modern communes "because the modern communal movement is dead, or at least dormant." Other social scientists feel that communal living has changed but not disappeared. For example, Shostak (1987) points out that middle-class singles participate in communal living arrangements in which people share the household work and expenses. Especially in the anonymity of many urban areas, communal living provides companionship and social interaction.

Communal living is also common on many college campuses. For example, fraternities, sororities, and houses that are rented and shared by five or six students fulfill many of the social and economic functions that characterize all communes. At the other end of the continuum, a growing proportion of older people are experimenting with communal living as an alternative to moving in with children or living in a nursing home. As the box "Senior Communes" illustrates, the communal movement is not only providing emotional and financial support for some elderly but is also changing the traditional definition of the family.

Senior Communes

Some communities provide care for the elderly and their families in communal settings (see Chapter 18). For instance, adult day-care programs provide meals and activities in which elderly clients share jointly. Geriatric foster-care programs place nonrelated elderly people in private residences where they usually receive assistance with the tasks of daily living but may also join in tasks and activities of the family whose home they share (Conner, 1992).

In some states, the elderly play an active role in communal residential life. For example, in the private residences maintained in Florida by the Share-A-Home Association, elderly residents hold the power and make all the important decisions. Their authority ranges from hiring and firing staff and voting on new members to choosing menus and organizing entertainment. Started in 1960 as a nonprofit organization, Share-A-Home enables older people to live together as a family, sharing expenses and functioning as a single household unit. In this environment the members not only fulfill their basic needs but also provide one another with companionship and emotional support.

A case involving a Share-A-Home group in Winter Park, Florida, gave a new legal definition to the concept of family. In 1971, the Orange County Board of Commissioners filed a suit against a Share-A-Home facility, claiming that it was a boardinghouse and as such was in violation of the single-family zoning ordinance in its neighborhood. The Share-A-Home group in question consisted of 12 older people, age 61 to 94, who had formed a communal type of family and were living in an old 27-room

Sharing tiresome household tasks can be a bonus of particular value to older people.

house. The Orange County code defined a family as "one or more persons occupying a dwelling and living as a single housekeeping unit." Although this definition did not stipulate that the persons living as a unit must be related, the plaintiff's main argument for not recognizing the elderly group as a family was the fact that they were not related. The court ruled, however, that the group met the legal definition of a family: "any group that pools its resources with the intention of sharing the joys and sorrows of family life is a family." Because these seniors were living in the same household, sharing the same

kitchen, splitting living costs, and giving one another support and understanding, they were a bona fide family.

The Share-A-Home Association is set up so that a home is truly a home and not an institution. By pooling their financial resources, elderly people can enjoy a higher standard of living than they could afford alone. For those elderly who have limited incomes, are lonely, and are no longer totally independent, the Share-A-Home Association appears to offer a viable solution (Harris, 1990).

CONCLUSION

There have been a number of *changes* in relationships outside of, before, and after marriage. Some of our *choices* include staying single longer, not marrying at all, cohabiting, forming same-sex households, or participating in communal living arrangements. These choices are not without *constraints*, however. For example, many of our policies do not encourage or protect most of these relationships under the law. Although there is less pressure to marry, most of us will do so at least once in our lifetime. In the next chapter we examine the institution of marriage.

Taking Action

Learn More About Different Lifestyles

The variety in contemporary lifestyles may seem overwhelming at times, but it offers the chance to learn about others.

• Many people "drift" into **cohabitation** without much planning or forethought. This may result in unexpected problems and hostility in resolving disagreements about property, paying debts, and other legal issues when the partners split up. Ask your professor to invite a lawyer who prepares nonmarital or prenuptial agreements to visit your class. What are the greatest sources of conflict when a relationship breaks up? Use the lawyer's advice to compare your expectations with those of someone you are considering living with, are already living with, or plan to marry.

• You can report **antigay violence** by calling 1-800-347-HATE. The call may seem inconsequential to you, but if everyone reported such behavior, we would have better estimates of the prevalence of hate crimes and of the scope of the problem our society must deal with. To join an e-mail list that discusses gay and lesbian issues in college, you can subscribe to GAYNET-REQUEST@ATHENA.MIT.EDU. Another list, QSTUDY-L is a forum for academic discussions pertaining to "queer theory," an umbrella term that encompasses lesbian, gay, bisexual, and transsexual/transgender studies (LISTSERV @UBVM.BITNET or LISTSERV@UBVM.CC. BUFFALO.EDU).

• Most **senior day-care centers,** which are typically understaffed and underfunded, welcome even an hour of volunteer work per week by college students. For example, one of my students (with limited desktop publishing skills) prepared a small book of the most popular recipes submitted by the center's members. The recipes had been lying around for several years because there was no one on the staff who had the time to work on the project. With modest funding from local merchants, the center will use the recipe book to raise money to purchase exercise equipment. During this project, the student learned a great deal about the issues that concern older, single people.

SUMMARY

1. Diverse lifestyles have always existed, but in the past 20 years, many new family forms have increased, including singlehood, cohabitation, homosexual households, and senior communes.

2. Household size has been shrinking since the 1940s. A major reason for the decrease is the growing number of people who are postponing marriage and living alone.

3. People are postponing marriage more often because there is a greater acceptance of cohabitation and of children born out of wedlock.

4. Singles constitute an extremely diverse group. Some have been widowed, divorced, or separated; others have never been married. Some singles choose their status, whereas others are single involuntarily.

5. There are many reasons why the numbers of singles have increased since the 1970s. Some of the reasons are demographic, such as the marriage squeeze, whereas others reflect personal choices. African Americans, especially educated African American women, are the most likely to postpone marriage or never marry.

6. Cohabitation has boomed since the 1970s. Although most cohabitation is short-lived, in some cases it is a long-term substitute for legal marriage. Cohabitation is not restricted to the young. Most cohabitants have been divorced or have children in the home. As with other lifestyles, cohabitation has both advantages and disadvantages.

7. Homosexual households reflect another alternative lifestyle. Just as there is no "typical" lifestyle for heterosexual singles, there is no one lifestyle typical of homosexuals. There are also some differences between the households of gay men and lesbians.

8. Homosexual relationships have become more visible, and they are more likely to be accepted than they once were. Nonetheless, homosexual households still face problems that do not characterize nonmarried heterosexual relationships.

9. Communal living arrangements have changed since the turn of the century and even since the 1970s. They are less numerous and less popular today, but they still fulfill the economic and social needs of many adults.

10. A growing number of elderly people are choosing to live in communal residences rather than move in with their children or live in retirement or nursing homes.

KEY TERMS

marriage squeeze   234
cohabitation   238
POSSLQ   238

part-time/limited cohabitation   240
premarital cohabitation   240
substitute marriage   240

ADDITIONAL READING

PHILIP BLUMSTEIN and PEPPER SCHWARTZ, *American Couples: Money, Work, Sex* (New York: Morrow, 1983). The most extensive study of homosexual, married, and cohabiting couples to date. Provides numerous, in-depth examples of everyday interaction and decision making.

FREDERICK W. BOZETT and MARVIN B. SUSSMAN, eds., *Homosexuality and Family Relations* (New York: Harrington Park Press, 1990). Examines some of the daily problems faced by gay men, lesbians, and their families. Some topics include homosexuals married to heterosexuals, adoptions, gay and lesbian adolescents, and the impact of AIDS.

AUDREY B. CHAPMAN, *Entitled to Good Loving: Black Men and Women and the Battle for Love and Power* (New York: Holt, 1994). A family therapist suggests why black singles are more reluctant to marry than other racial-ethnic groups.

SARAH DELANY, A. ELIZABETH DELANY, with AMY HILL HEARTH, *Having Our Say: The Delany Sisters' First 100 Years* (New York: Kodansha International, 1993). Two educated, never-married African American women over 100 years old describe their experiences of childhood, schooling, work, and dating, as well as the joys of being single.

TUULA GORDON, *Single Women: On the Margins?* (New York: New York University Press, 1994). Emphasizing the diversity of single women, this book presents qualitative data gathered in interviews with single women in the United States and Europe.

WILLIAM M. KEPHART and WILLIAM W. ZELLNER, *Extraordinary Groups: An Examination of Unconventional Lifestyles*, 4th ed. (New York: St. Martin's Press, 1991). An informative book for students who are interested in examining communal living arrangements (such as Gypsy life) that are typically not covered in textbooks on marriage and the family.

10
Marriage and Marital Communication

Data Digest

- In a national study of high school seniors, **76 percent said it was "extremely important"** to have a good marriage and family life.

- In 1994, the average American spent **almost $18,000 for a formal wedding.** In the same year, 4 percent of Americans got married in Las Vegas, where the ceremony can take as little as 7 minutes and cost $30. Most couples marrying in Las Vegas are over 35 and marrying for the second (or third, or fourth) time.

- Honeymooners account for 25 percent of U.S. pleasure-travel business; the **average honeymoon couple spends about $3000.** Of the honeymooners who travel outside the United States, about a third spend as much as $5000.

- In 1993, **over 6 percent of all marriages were between teenagers** 15 through 19 years of age.

- On the average, wives who work outside the home still do **over 80 percent of the household work.**

- Although still relatively rare, **interracial marriages accounted for 1.2 million, or about 2.2 percent,** of all married couples in 1993; this was a considerable increase over the 0.7 percent recorded for 1970.

SOURCES: Smolowe, 1993; John, 1994; Munk, 1994; *Public Perspective*, 1994; Rawlings, 1994; Saluter, 1994; *U.S. News & World Report*, 1994

One of actress Mae West's best-known quips was "Marriage is a great institution, but I'm not ready for an institution yet." West was clearly in the minority in her thinking. Despite the increases in cohabitation, divorce, and out-of-wedlock births, nearly 95 percent of the U.S. population believe in marriage enough to marry at least once (see Chapter 9). High marriage and remarriage rates are strong indicators of the value Americans place on the institution of marriage.

Some people become disillusioned with the idea of marriage because of the many misconceptions about marriage and unrealistic expectations that are deeply ingrained in our culture. A marriage will indeed be short-lived if the relationship is based on myths and misinformation. Before reading the rest of this chapter, take "A Marriage Quiz" (see the box "Ask Yourself"). It should encourage you to think more critically about some of our assumptions about marriage.

WHY WE MARRY

In the United States, most couples get married because they are "in love." For example, in a cross-cultural study of college students, Levine (1993) found that although in India, where arranged marriages are common, only 24 percent of students said that love was an important reason for getting married, in the United States 86 percent of students said they would not marry if they were not in love. As we saw in Chapter 9, many Americans are single because they have not found "the right person," which strongly suggests that they're looking for love. The reasons for marrying are more complex than this, however. Despite what people *say* are their reasons for marrying (see Figure 10.1), marriage reflects a complex interplay between micro-level and macro-level variables.

Individual Choices and Constraints

On the individual level, there are many factors in the decision to marry. An important reason for marrying is *to have children.* A couple may marry because they plan to raise a family and want their children to be legitimate. Or they may decide to marry because the woman becomes pregnant. Among white women in their 20s involved in cohabitation, cohabiting often leads to marriage if pregnancy ensues (Manning, 1993).

Another goal in getting married is *companionship*, or its opposite, *to avoiding being alone.* Young adults may feel left out when their married friends start excluding them from social functions. Living with someone not only may prevent loneliness but, in traditional relationships, may provide a man with a housekeeper or a woman with economic resources. Older people sometimes look for caretakers. An elderly man may want a wife who will cook, clean, and care for him if he becomes frail or sick (see Chapter 18).

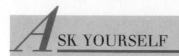

A Marriage Quiz

To respond to each statement, circle either True or False.

1. A husband's marital satisfaction is usually lower if his wife is employed full time than if she is a full-time homemaker.	True	False
2. Marriages that last many years almost always have a higher level of satisfaction than marriages that last only a few years.	True	False
3. In most marriages, having a child improves marital satisfaction for both spouses.	True	False
4. The best single predictor of overall marital satisfaction is the quality of the couple's sex life.	True	False
5. Overall, married women are physically healthier than married men.	True	False
6. African American women are happier in marriage than are African American men.	True	False
7. Marital satisfaction for a wife is usually lower if she is employed full time than if she is a full-time homemaker.	True	False
8. "If my spouse loves me, he/she should instinctively know what I want and need to be happy."	True	False
9. In a marriage in which the wife is employed full time, the husband usually shares equally in housekeeping tasks.	True	False
10. "No matter how I behave, my partner should love me because he/she is my spouse."	True	False
11. Anglo husbands spend more time on household work than do Latino husbands.	True	False
12. Husbands usually make more lifestyle adjustments in marriage than do wives.	True	False
13. "I can change my spouse by pointing out his/her inadequacies and bad habits."	True	False
14. "Either my spouse loves me or does not love me; nothing I do will affect how my spouse feels about me."	True	False
15. The more a spouse discloses positive and negative information to his/her partner, the greater the marital satisfaction of both partners.	True	False
16. For most couples, maintaining romantic love is the key to marital happiness over the life span.	True	False

Scoring the Marriage Quiz

All of the items are false. The more "true" responses you gave, the greater your belief in marital myths. The quiz is based on research presented in this chapter and on Larson (1988: 8–9).

Many people marry *to satisfy emotional needs.* Singles in their early 30s often talk about "missing something" in their lives and expect marriage and children to fill the gap. For men, who may be reluctant to confide in friends or colleagues, wives may be important "sounding boards" (Tannen, 1990). And as we discussed in Chapter 9, women often cite companionship and having someone to talk to as the main reasons for getting married. For both women and men, marriage can create kin "out of strangers"; marriage ensures that there will be more relatives around to help out or to consult when things go wrong (Murray, 1994).

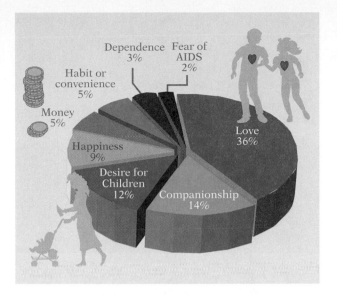

Figure 10.1 The 1990s: Why We Say We Marry. *Well over a third of the people sampled in this study said they married for love. As the text shows, however, there are many other reasons for getting married* (Based on Patterson and Kim, 1991).

Marriage is sometimes an *escape* from a bad situation. As one woman stated: "I came from an abusive family . . . he offered stability and comfort and that's all I wanted" (Barreca, 1993: 139). Marriage is an attractive alternative to living at home for some young adults, especially for those whose parents or stepparents are seen as rejecting or authoritarian. Women particularly may feel that marriage will provide them with greater freedom and autonomy and an escape from parental supervision.

Social pressure is often an important factor in marriage. Although being single is becoming more acceptable, many people still get married because it is expected of them:

"I got married because my family thought I should," explains a divorced journalist in her late forties. *"I was finished with school and I wasn't sure what to do next. Getting married seemed to be a step in the right direction."*

"I got married because we were living together for so many years—four in all—that it became increasingly annoying and intrusive to have to explain why we weren't married," declared . . . *an accountant in her late twenties* (Barreca, 1993: 139–140).

American culture prescribes marriage as the norm and the foundation of family life. Unmar-

ried women, especially, often dread family get-togethers because they will be asked over and over again whether they are dating "someone special." The older they are, the more often friends and relatives ask about marriage plans.

Finally, *physical attractiveness* may play an important role in the decision to marry. As we've seen in earlier chapters, physical appearance strongly affects dating and mating. It is often assumed that people who are physically attractive are also sexually responsive, warm, interesting, kind, and outgoing (see Chapters 5 and 8). This *halo effect*—the tendency for one's overall judgment of a person to be affected by a single characteristic—results in more instances of "love at first sight" and early proposals of marriage.

Macro-Level Variables

Decisions about marriage are often shaped by macro-level phenomena and events like war, technology, and social movements. For example, marriage rates tend to drop slightly during wartime and to increase after a war (Rodgers and Thornton, 1985). Although out-of-wedlock children are more acceptable now than in the past, advances in contraceptive technology have led to a decrease in unplanned pregnancies and "shotgun marriages." The women's movement opened new educational, occupational, and legal opportunities for women, giving them other options besides marriage. The gay rights movement encouraged homosexuals to be more open about their sexual preferences and relieved the pressure some felt to marry.

Economic factors also play an important role in delaying or encouraging marriage. Economic depressions and unemployment tend to postpone marriage for men (Ogburn, 1927; Rodgers and Thornton, 1985). In contrast, economic opportunities, as well as a belief that a person has access to those opportunities, encourage men to marry (Landale, 1989; Landale and Tolnay, 1991).

The effects of employment on women's tendency to marry are somewhat contradictory. On the one hand, being employed increases a woman's chances of meeting eligible men and may enhance her attractiveness as a potential contributor to a household's financial resources (see Chapter 9). In a national study of women under age 29 who decided to marry, Oropesa et al. (1994) found that white and black women who were successful in the labor market (being employed and having high incomes) were more likely to marry than their nonemployed counterparts, despite the shortage of eligible men. On the other hand, greater economic independence decreases a woman's interest in early marriage (Bianchi and Spain, 1986; see also Chapter 9). Parental resources also affect men and women differently. Inherited income gives men a more stable economic base for marriage, but women are more likely to use inheritances to delay marriage (Goldscheider and Waite, 1986).

Living at home with parents encourages marriage, whereas moving out of the parental home delays marriage. In general, those who move out very early in young adulthood are the most likely to postpone marriage. This is especially true for women, who gain more from independence than men do and also typically lose more independence than men do when they marry. In addition, women are more integrated into social networks, so that loneliness is not as much of a problem for them as it is for men (Goldscheider and Waite, 1987). Living independently encourages marriage only when people—usually men—both leave home early and accumulate resources, usually through full-time work (Goldscheider and DaVanzo, 1989; McLaughlin et al., 1993).

Race is another macro-level influence that affects a person's decision to marry. When there are plenty of jobs available, African American men and women are likely to marry and have children (Fossett and Kiecolt, 1993). Deteriorating employment conditions often discourage young African American men from getting married, however; this is especially true when over 50 percent of black men in a given area are jobless, employed only part time, or working at poverty-level wages (Lichter et al., 1991). Discrimination in employment contributes to this problem, making many African American males poor economic providers, as we shall discuss in Chapter 13. And at all age levels, an unemployed or underemployed man may be a liability rather than an attractive marital partner (Horton and Burgess, 1992; Blake and Darling, 1994). For example, a study of African American women age 55 and over found that many of the women were not interested in marrying or remarrying because they perceived many of the eligible but unemployed men as a potential "drain on their own finances" (Tucker et al., 1993).

Thus, factors at the societal level complicate and often shape our decisions about whether or not to marry. Marriages are often influenced by

Elizabeth Taylor's economic independence and celebrity status enabled her to do something many older woman still hesitate to do—marry Larry Fortensky, a man several years her junior.

demographic and legal factors that are beyond the control of the average person. For example, as we saw in Chapter 9, marriage is forbidden to homosexual members of society. The box "Should Gay Rites Be Legalized?" explores some of the issues that surround the legalization of homosexual unions.

OUR MARRIAGE RITUALS

Marriage is a critical rite of passage in almost every culture. The major events that mark the beginning of a marriage are engagement, shower and bachelor parties, and the wedding itself.

Engagement

According to the *Guinness Book of Records*, the longest engagement was between Octavio Guillen and Adriana Martinez of Mexico, who took 67 years to make sure they were right for each other. Most engagements are at least 65 years shorter than this.

Traditionally, an **engagement** formalized a couple's decision to marry and usually was signaled by an *engagement ring* given by the man to the woman. Engagement was the last step in the courtship process leading to marriage. Before "popping the question," the man typically asked the woman's parents for their approval (or blessing), and the couple generally refrained from sexual intercourse until the wedding night. The

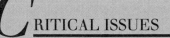

Should Gay Rites Be Legalized?

At this time, no U.S. state permits two persons of the same sex to marry legally. In 1993 Hawaii's supreme court ruled that refusing to license the marriage of gay and lesbian couples violated the state constitution's laws against gender discrimination. In response, however, Hawaii's legislators passed a bill reiterating that marriage is meant for "one man and one woman." Because all states recognize marriages performed in any other state, the decision by any one state to legalize same-sex marriage would have widespread implications.

Yale University historian John Boswell fanned this controversy in 1994 by citing ancient documents that sanctioned and celebrated homosexual marriage. Among other rituals Boswell claimed to find described such marriage ceremonies as the joining of right hands while a priest read a prayer of blessing and the exchange of kisses. Some historians have argued, however, that the rituals celebrated "brotherhood" or "fraternity" rather than same-sex marriage (McMillen, 1994; Selby, 1994).

Should same-sex marriage be legal? Some observers think the pressure to legalize homosexual marriage has just begun. More than 70 major companies now offer *domestic partner benefits*, such as health benefits, for gay partners (see Glaser and Wolf, 1994; Mackey, 1994; and Myles, 1994, for a discussion of domestic partner issues). Nevertheless, many gay couples argue that they don't have the same protections that married couples take for granted, such as bereavement leaves, inheritance rights, tax breaks, and Social Security benefits (see Wisensale and Heckart, 1993).

During a gay rights march in Washington, D.C., in 1993, 1500 homosexual couples participated in a "wedding," complete with ministers and rice. The idea of gay marriage, however, still arouses strong social and religious opposition. Although attitudes toward gay rights have generally become more liberal, a recent poll found that 70 percent of Americans oppose same-sex marriage. Conservative Christians argue that because marriage exists for the purpose of procreation, it follows that homosexual unions are "unnatural" (Salholz et al., 1993). Do you think gays and lesbians should be allowed to marry legally? Why or why not?

bride's parents usually covered the wedding expenses, and the couple often planned a romantic, expensive honeymoon for which the groom's parents sometimes paid.

Today many couples cohabit before they get married, and as a result engagements are often casual and informal. If couples are older when they marry, and if both partners work, they may purchase engagement and wedding rings jointly. They may also dispense with formal wedding announcements in the local newspapers and forgo the honeymoon. Despite the changing attitudes toward premarital sex and the rise of cohabitation, a national study reported not long ago that 29 percent of respondents said they were virgins on their wedding night (Patterson and Kim, 1991).

Whether or not the couple follows traditional customs, an engagement serves several functions. First, it sends a message to other possible suitors to "keep their hands off" the future bride and bridegroom. Second, it gives both partners a chance to become better acquainted with their future in-laws and to strengthen themselves as a couple. Third, it provides each partner with information about a prospective spouse's potential or current medical problems (through blood tests, for example). Fourth, it legitimates premarital counseling, either secular or religious (such as Catholic engagement-encounter weekends), especially if the partners are of different races, religions, or ethnicities. Finally, if the couple has been living together (and/or has had a child out of wedlock), the engagement makes the union legal.

In the traditional view, women enter marriage enthusiastically, but men are unsuspecting victims who have been "caught" or "trapped" into marrying. These mythic notions have been institutionalized in the bridal shower and bachelor party that for years have been part of most young couples' prewedding activities. Today, however, there is a growing tendency in middle-class America for both women and men to attend *engagement parties* to celebrate the coming marriage of a couple together. These parties often supplant the two more traditional events: the *bridal shower*, at which female friends and relatives "shower" a bride with both personal and household gifts and celebrate the beginning of a new partnership and home, and the *bachelor party*, at which the groom's friends typically lament their friend's imminent loss of freedom and celebrate one "last fling."

The Wedding

Recent years have seen some atypical weddings. In 1992, for example, in a single ceremony in Seoul's Olympic Stadium, the Reverend Sun Myung Moon, founder of the Unification Church, married 20,000 couples from 131 nations and another 10,000 couples by simultaneous satellite hookups between Korea and five other countries—Brazil, the Philippines, Zaire, Kenya, and Nigeria. The couples, all of whom were total strangers, were matched two years earlier by the Reverend Moon during a meeting held in a New York City hotel ballroom:

*He said all participants wore badges giving their name, education and age. Men sat on the floor on one side of the ballroom and women on the other while Mr. Moon talked about love and marriage and paced the floor sizing people up (*Baltimore Sun, *1992: 2A).*

And, in 1994, the first wedding by video conference hookup took place in New York City at PC Expo, a computer convention and exhibition. The bride and bridegroom were attending the convention, and the judge officiated from California.

Most weddings are more traditional. Even when the partners are very young—as is still common in some countries, like India—a wedding marks the end of childhood and the acceptance of the responsibilities of adulthood. Often the ceremony is performed in a religious setting, like a church or synagogue, where a cleric such as a minister or rabbi officiates. Although most ceremonies follow prescribed language, many modern couples write their own vows and recite them at the ceremony. The ceremony generally reinforces the idea that the marriage commitment is a sacred and eternal bond that continues even after death—"till death us do part." The presence of family, friends, and witnesses affirms the acceptance and legitimacy of the union by both immediate relatives and the larger community.

In Western society a number of ritual acts and activities have come to be associated with the celebration of a marriage. The box "Some Cherished Wedding Rituals" illustrates the historical origins of some of our current marriage rituals.

At the August 1992 satellite-hookup marriage ceremony performed by the Reverend Sun Myung Moon of the Unification Church, brides and grooms who could not be present were represented by photographs held by their spouses-to-be. For these couples, who were separated for logistic reasons, the Church's required 40-day wait for consummation may not have been such a burden.

CHANGES

Some Cherished Wedding Rituals

Most of our time-honored customs associated with engagement and marriage, like rings and honeymoons, originally symbolized love and romance (Ackerman, 1994). Many were designed to ensure the fertility of the couple and the prosperity of their household. Some, however, also reflected the subordinate position of the woman in the union:

❏ The *best man* was a warrior friend who helped a man capture and kidnap a woman he desired (usually from another tribe).

❏ The Anglo-Saxon word *wedd*, from which our "wedding" is derived, meant the groom's payment for the bride to her father. Thus a wedding was literally the purchase of a woman.

❏ Carrying the bride *over the threshold* is not simply a romantic gesture. Originally, it symbolized the abduction of the daughter who would not willingly leave her father's house.

❏ After a man captured or bought a bride, he disappeared with her for a while in a *honeymoon*, so that her family couldn't rescue her. By the time they found the couple, the bride would already be pregnant. In America, around 1850, the honeymoon was usually a wedding trip to visit relatives. A better economy, safety, and comfort of railroad and ocean travel popularized more distant and independent honeymoon trips (Kern, 1992).

❏ The *engagement ring* was given to symbolize eternity. The medieval Italians favored a diamond ring because of their superstition that diamonds were created from the flames of love.

❏ It was the soldiers of ancient Sparta who first staged *stag parties:* "The groom feasted with his male friends on the night before the wedding, pledging his continued loyalty, friendship, or love. . . . The function of this rite of passage was to say good-bye to the frivolities of bachelorhood, while swearing continued allegiance to one's comrades. It was important for the groom to reassure his friends that they wouldn't be excluded from his life now that it included a family" (Ackerman, 1994: 270).

❏ Some time in the 1890s, the friend of a newly engaged woman held a party at which a Japanese parasol filled with little gifts was turned upside down over the bride-to-be's head, producing a shower of presents. Readers of fashion pages, learning of this event, then wanted bridal *showers* of their own.

❏ In medieval times the wedding party's *flower girl* carried wheat to symbolize fertility. Perhaps for symmetry, the *ring bearer* also appeared in the Middle Ages.

❏ Although in biblical times it was the color blue that symbolized purity, in 1499 Anne of Brittany set the pattern for generations to come by wearing a *white wedding gown* for her marriage to Louis XII of France. The white bridal gown came to symbolize virginity and is still worn by most first-time brides, even though many are not virgins. Today, even women who remarry sometimes wear white, but they are advised by etiquette experts to forgo pure white as well as other symbols of virginity such as a veil, a train, and orange blossoms.

❏ The first *wedding ring* was probably made of iron, so it wouldn't break. The Romans believed that a small artery or "vein of love" ran from the third finger to the heart and that wearing a ring on that finger joined the couple's hearts and destiny.

❏ The ancient Romans baked a special wheat or barley cake that they broke over the bride's head as a symbol of her hoped-for fertility. The English piled up small cakes as high as they could, and bride and groom tried to kiss over the cakes without knocking the tower over; success meant a lifetime of prosperity. The cakes evolved into a *wedding cake* during the reign of England's King Charles II, whose French chefs decided to turn the cakes into an edible "palace" iced with white sugar. Today, many European-born couples are met at the door before the reception with bread and salt. The salt is thrown behind the couple to ward off evil spirits, and the bread symbolizes an offering to the gods to ensure that the new household has plentiful harvests.

❏ *Tying shoes to the car bumper* probably came from ancient cultures. For example, the Egyptians exchanged sandals at a wedding ceremony to symbolize an exchange of property or authority. A father would give the groom his daughter's sandal to show that she was now in his care. In Anglo-Saxon marriage, the groom tapped the bride lightly on the head with the shoe to show his authority. Later, people began throwing shoes at the couple and somehow (perhaps a bride or groom was knocked out and protested this rather hostile activity) this evolved into the current practice.

TYPES OF MARRIAGES

When a happily married couple was asked to what they owed their successful marriage of 40 years, the husband replied, "We dine out twice a week—candlelight, violins, champagne, the works! Her night is Tuesday; mine is Friday."

As this anecdote suggests, happily married couples are not joined at the hip. And those who are may not necessarily be happy. Of the many types of marriages that exist, we will explore two in this section: enduring marriages, in which the partners may or may not be happy, and "married singles," in which the partners may or may not be good friends.

Enduring Marriages

Until the mid-1960s, social scientists proposed fairly simple descriptions of marriage. A happy marriage was one that did not end in divorce and in which the husband and wife fulfilled the traditional instrumental and expressive roles (see Chapters 2 and 4). Challenging these superficial portrayals of married life, Cuber and Haroff (1965) studied 400 "normal," upper-middle-class marriages in which the partners ranged in age from 35 to 55 and identified five types of marriage: conflict-habituated, devitalized, passive-congenial, vital, and total. Some were happy and some were not, but all endured.

In a **conflict-habituated marriage,** the partners fight, both verbally and physically, but do not believe that fighting is a reason for divorce. They feel that fighting is an acceptable way to try to solve problems, and they thrive on the incompatibility. Usually the reason for the conflict is insignificant, and the partners seldom resolve their disputes.

The partners in a **devitalized marriage** are deeply in love when they marry, spend much of their time together, and have a strong, satisfying sex life. As time goes on, they continue to spend time together—raising the children, entertaining, or meeting community responsibilities—but begin to do so out of obligation, not joy. They get along and see no alternatives to the marriage and, as a result, do not consider a divorce. Although one or both partners may be unhappy about the situation, they are both resigned to it.

A **passive-congenial marriage** is established by partners who marry with low emotional investment and minimal expectations that do not change. Fairly independent, the partners achieve satisfaction from other relationships, such as those with their children, friends, and colleagues, and they maintain separate spheres of activities and interests. Passive-congenial couples emphasize the practicality of the marriage over emotional intensity.

In the **vital marriage,** partners' lives are closely intertwined. They spend a great deal of time together, resolve conflict through compromise, and often make sacrifices for each other. They consider sex important and pleasurable. When a disagreement occurs, it is over a specific issue and is quickly resolved.

Finally, in the **total marriage,** which is similar to the vital marriage, the partners participate in each other's lives at all levels and have few areas of tension or unresolved hostility. Spouses share even more facets of their lives with each other and may work together or share projects, friends, and outside interests. This type of marriage is more all-encompassing than the vital marriage.

Finding that approximately 80 percent of the marriages they studied fell into the first three categories, Cuber and Haroff characterized these as **utilitarian marriages** because they appeared to be based on convenience. The researchers called the last two types **intrinsic marriages** because the relationships seemed to be inherently rewarding. In their sample, vital marriages made up 15 percent of the population, and total marriages accounted for only 5 percent.

Although the Cuber-Haroff typology has been widely cited, it has several limitations. Note, for example, that couples who report minimal conflict are classified as "vital" and "total," whereas the more typical couples who admit having problems are given such negative labels as "devitalized" and "conflict-habituated." These labels may reinforce the idea that couples who argue or who have separate activities have inferior marriages.

In a more recent study, Lavee and Olson (1993) collected data on nine dimensions of marriage from 8385 couples who participated in either marital therapy or marital enrichment programs. The dimensions and the seven types of marital couples that the researchers identified are presented in Figure 10.2. Although some of the types are similar to Cuber and Haroff's typology, Lavee and Olson reported more complexity and variety in marital relationship patterns.

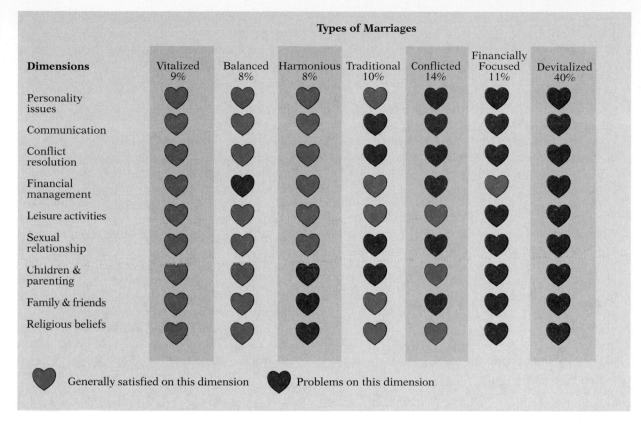

Figure 10.2 **How Marriages Differ.** *Note that although the typologies offered by Lavee and Olson (shown here) and by Cuber and Haroff (see text) differ both in category content and in number of categories, their overall percentages paint a similar picture. That is, 75 to 80 percent of marriages are essentially based on convenience. Partners must also deal with such issues as personality differences, relationships with family and friends, and conflict resolution* (Based on data in Lavee and Olson, 1993, Figure 1, p. 332).

Married Singles

Another type of marriage might be characterized by what I call married singles. **Married singles** are married partners who, by choice or necessity, live under the same roof, may be good friends, and may or may not have sexual intercourse but who have in many ways drifted apart because of conflicting work schedules, interests, personality differences, or other reasons.

Although there has been no research on this concept, several writers have found a number of characteristics that may well describe such marriages. As Avna and Waltz (1992) have pointed out, some marriages are companionable even though the partners no longer engage in sexual intercourse. Both partners may have low sex drives, and over time they may engage in sex less

and less or lose all interest in it. They may see other aspects of family life (such as raising children) as more important and time-consuming, and they may enjoy each other's company on a day-to-day basis.

In other cases, marital partners' jobs may force them to live in different cities (as we discuss in Chapter 14). Such commuter marriages require men and women to establish separate residences and often prevent them from getting together more than once a week or even once a month. Commuter partners often develop separate friendships and live as singles most of the time.

Barreca (1992) suggests that some people purposely marry partners who will be absent: "I married him for better or worse, but not for lunch." In these marriages, an absent husband frees up his wife for other "adventures," both sexual and nonsexual. The wife has the advantage of a husband who legitimizes the couple's children and who is responsible for taking care of his family while the wife is generally free to do as she pleases. In many cases, however, it may be the husband rather than the wife who leads a "married single" life. If he is often on the road or at the office, the husband is free to live his life as he pleases while the wife may be at home (or both home and work) and caring for the children.

Finally, partners who live with alcoholics or other drug abusers often must function as singles. They have no spouse to talk to, they may not want to discuss their problems with family members, and they may feel isolated if the spouse refuses to change his or her behavior or seek help. Or the onset of a serious physical illness in one partner may plunge the other into solitude:

Ellen and Roy had been married for ten years when he was diagnosed with multiple sclerosis. The disease took its slow and predictable course, transforming Roy from a vital and handsome artist into a sullen and degenerating invalid. . . . While his courage helped them to adjust, his fatigue and limitations proved to be most difficult for Ellen. It was not merely that she sorely missed the healthy Roy, but she was overwhelmed by the huge amounts of time she was without him. When he slept, rested, or was in the hospital, Ellen found

herself both lonesome for Roy and feeling very much alone in the world. She would wander the foyers of their apartment and haunt the hallways of the hospital beleaguered by a desperate sense of solitude (Rosenzweig, 1992: 229–30).

TEENAGE MARRIAGES

Teenage marriages constitute a large proportion of all marriages (see Data Digest). In most states, the minimum ages for legal marriage are 18 for the boy and 16 for the girl. There are many variations across states, however. For example, in New York both boys and girls can marry legally at 14.

The wisdom of these liberal laws may be questioned, however. A considerable amount of research shows that many teenage marriages are overwhelmed by a variety of constraints (see the box "Problems of Teenage Marriages"). Males who marry as adolescents complete fewer years of education, earn less income, and work in lower-status occupations than do those who first marry as adults. Such factors as dropping out of high school, having children at an early age, and experiencing marital disruption can have negative rippling effects over periods of 30 to 40 years (Teti et al., 1987; see also Chapter 16).

Marriage because of pregnancy, especially among teenagers, often ends in divorce. Teenage parents who have or expect a child are very likely to drop out of school because they need full-time

This teenage couple in Brooklyn, New York, face tremendous odds. Even though they love their baby, balancing the many demands a child places on young parents can overtax even older and better-established couples.

CONSTRAINTS

Problems of Teenage Marriages

The biggest problem with teenage marriages is not that the partners are young but that U.S. society does not prepare teenagers for marriage. Instead, adolescents typically are expected to go through a long period of social and emotional growth between puberty and the late teen years, a period that is usually free of adult responsibilities (Zabin and Hayward, 1993). As a result, most teenagers are unprepared for marriage and parenthood.

The letter that follows, written to a popular advice columnist, describes some of the problems that many married teenage couples encounter. Their romanticized ideas of marriage are shattered very quickly, and they find that their sexual passion does not guarantee marital happiness.

Let me tell you what it is like to be married at 17. It is like living in this dump on the third floor. Your only window looks out on somebody else's third-floor dump. It is like coming home so tired you feel nearly dead from standing all day at your checker's job in the supermarket. But you don't dare sit down because you might never get up. And there are so many things you have to do—cooking, and washing, and ironing. But you go through the motions, and you hate your job.

You ask yourself, "Why don't you quit?" And you know why. Because there are grocery bills and drug bills and the rent to pay. And Jimmy's crummy little check from the lumberyard won't cover them. That's why.

Then you tell the sitter good-bye and you try to play with the baby until Jimmy comes home. Only sometimes you don't feel like it. But you do it anyway because you feel guilty about being away from her all day. Then you mix the formula and wash diapers, and you hate doing it. You wonder how long it will be before she can tell that you hate it. And wouldn't it be awful if she knew already?

Then Jimmy doesn't come home, and you know he decided to go out with the boys again and do the things he should have gotten done before he married you.

So finally you eat the lousy meal by yourself and go to bed and cry your eyes out. When he does come home, you can tell he's been drinking, but you don't say a word because he hates to be told anything. So you try to go to sleep and dream about your parents and your brothers and the kids you knew at school. You think about the great meals your mother used to cook and how nice your room was at home. Then you remember how she tried to talk you out of marrying so young, and you got mad at her and called her a dried-up old woman and accused her of having forgotten what it was like to be in love. . . .

You wonder how different your life would have been if you had gone to college. You have the feeling that Jimmy and the baby are all part of a bad dream. But you know it's no dream. It's for real. So you reach over to touch Jimmy, and he pushes you away and says something mean. So you cry yourself to sleep and wake up with a splitting headache. What a way to start another day of hard work! (Baltimore Sun, June 6, 1989: C8).

jobs so they can care for the baby. Because teenage wives shoulder most of the household responsibilities, they are less likely than their husbands to finish high school. Employment opportunities are very limited for people without high school degrees. In the current economic climate even college graduates have difficulty finding suitable employment. Even if married teens finish high school and take college courses, they rarely obtain advanced degrees (Teachman and Polonko, 1988). With minimal education, teens tend to earn very low incomes and, as a result, often sink into poverty. This can lead to other strains that may lead to desertion or divorce (Edelman, 1987). There are always exceptions—sometimes marriages because of pregnancy become happy, fulfilling relationships—but they are not typical.

Even if a teenage married couple have no children, such marriages suffer from four serious problems: (1) sexual disappointment that results from the realization that everyday problems like paying bills have the highest priority; (2) difficulty in gaining emotional freedom from parents who want to control the marriage; (3) coping with the very common perception that one has lost one's independence; and (4) handling anger (Lobsenz, 1985).

There is some evidence that in rural areas, where they are more common, teenage marriages have fewer problems. Early marriages may be more acceptable—even encouraged—in rural communities, where there are fewer educational and employment opportunities. The greater community support and the perception that early marriage and parenthood are normative seem to result in fewer detrimental consequences (Heaton et al., 1989).

INTERRACIAL MARRIAGE

Some sociologists and anthropologists have estimated that 75 to 90 percent of African Americans have white ancestors and about 1 percent of white Americans—millions of people—have black ancestors without knowing it (Davis, 1991). Most of this mixed ancestry is largely the result of slaveowners' and other white men's raping black women during slavery (see Chapter 3). Laws against miscegenation existed in America as early as 1661. It wasn't until 1967, in the U.S. Supreme Court's *Loving* v. *Virginia* decision, that antimiscegenation laws were overturned nationally.

The majority of marriage partners in the United States are of the same race, but 1 out of 50 marriages crosses racial boundaries (see Data Digest). What many people don't realize is that only about 20 percent of interracial marriages are between African Americans and whites; in 77 percent of interracial marriages, the wife is white and the husband is a race other than white or black (U.S. Bureau of the Census, 1994).

Why have interracial marriage rates increased? There are probably a number of reasons. Among Japanese Americans, for example, intermarriage may be due to a shrinking number of eligible partners of Japanese origin or descent and to greater assimilation into American culture. The rate at which Japanese have been immigrating to the United States in recent years has declined. Many families who have been in the country for four or five generations may be more accepting of intermarriage (Leon and Weinstein, 1991).

Some of the increase in interracial marriage may reflect changing attitudes: American approval of interracial marriage rose from 20 percent in 1968 to 48 percent in 1991 (Gallup and Newport, 1991b). In a study of black-white marriages in the Los Angeles area, Kouri and Lasswell (1993) found that the increased socioeconomic mobility of African Americans has provided greater opportunity for interracial contact through housing, schools, work, and leisure activities. There is also some evidence that interracial marriage is, at least for some white women, a means of upward mobility. Studying marriages between black men and white women in 33 states, Kalmijn (1993) found that in most of these unions the men were of higher status than the women.

Although a growing number of people are deciding to intermarry, there is much evidence that such marriages, especially between whites and blacks, are often met with hostility, discrimination, and racist slurs. In 1993, for example, African American talk show host Montel Williams reportedly blasted the media for criticizing his white wife, a former actress and exotic topless dancer, and their interracial marriage (*Jet*, 1993a). In the same year, a white assistant cook sued his supervisors at the White House alleging that he was passed over for promotion and subjected to threats of physical harm because he married a black woman (*Jet*, 1993b). Biracial author Lise Funderberg (1994: 25) notes that "few interracial couples escape all the land mines that are historically placed in their paths: from being disowned by both sides of the family to the occasional stare or muttered comment on the street."

White Americans who reject racial intermarriage are not alone. Washington (1993: 335) notes that although, in principle, racial intermarriage is "good, right, moral, democratic, valuable, laudable, Christian, human, and honorable," he also notes that many African Americans at all social ranks disapprove of intermarriage and especially black-white marriages. With a significant shortage of marriageable black men, many black women feel betrayed or deserted when a black man marries a white woman. Some black activists feel mixed marriages weaken African American solidarity (Myra, 1994). Others worry that biracial children will be rejected by both white and black communities. Despite such concerns, Funderberg (1994: 378) found that many of the 65 biracial adults she interviewed took on "the challenges of race and identity with determination and humor."

HOW MARRIAGES CHANGE THROUGHOUT THE LIFE CYCLE

Most marriages change as the partners grow older. This section briefly describes five types of marriages across the life cycle: the first-year marriage, the family with young children, the family with adolescent children, the middle-aged family, and the family in later life. At each stage, partners must work together to attain specific goals and to deal with conflict.

First-Year Marriages

Many newlyweds keep romance alive by making love frequently, talking openly, and spending as much time as possible together. They also have to deal with several realities of married life, however. First, they need to put their mutual relationship before ties with others. In particular, they must strike a balance between their relationships with their in-laws and their marital bond as a couple (Sarnoff and Sarnoff, 1989). Parents who fear losing contact with their married children sometimes create conflict by making frequent telephone calls and visits and "meddling" in the couple's life.

Most couples face numerous decisions, such as how to budget and how to divide up household tasks, and they may realize, for the first time, that they have different perspectives on many issues (Arnold and Pauker, 1987). On the other hand, the new couple also enjoys many benefits. They no longer have to play the dating game and can now relax with someone they love. If they want to conceive a child, preparing for parenthood can be an exhilarating experience (see Chapter 11). Finally, being married enhances a person's social standing as a mature adult.

The Family with Young Children

As you saw in Chapter 1, one of the most important functions of the family is to socialize children to become responsible and contributing members of society. Families with small children spend much of their time teaching rules, showing children how to live up to cultural expectations, and inculcating such values as doing well at school, following the rules, being kind, controlling one's temper, doing what one is asked, being responsible, getting along with others, and trying new things (Acock and Demo, 1994). However much parents love their children, teaching values, rules, and expectations takes enormous time and energy.

This may explain why marital satisfaction tends to decrease once a couple has children. As we discuss in Chapter 14, working parents may have to deal with heavy workloads, employment insecurity, career mobility, and geographic moves, with the result that they have neither the time nor the resources to perform either work or family functions adequately. Working-class mothers who work for low pay and have preschool children often have little time to discuss daily matters with their husbands, regardless of how caring and understanding their husbands are (Schumm and Bugaighis, 1986). Middle-class parents may be torn between competing demands at home, at work, and the community (coaching children's sports during the weekends, attending neighborhood meetings or school functions during the evenings).

Although upper-class parents have the wealth and power to assure their children excellent schooling as well as varied extracurricular activities, they are likely to see their children only rarely because of their many responsibilities:

Rose Kennedy, writing about her experience rearing her children, points out that her husband was absent the vast bulk of the time when the children were young. Joseph Kennedy was deeply involved in financial affairs that eventually created the family fortune, and he could spare very little time for his children (LeMasters and DeFrain, 1989: 113–14).

The Family with Adolescent Children

Family values that are held by most Americans, such as support, mutual respect, and communication, face their greatest test in families with adolescent children (Larson and Richards, 1994). Besides all the usual "developmental tasks" associated with the physical changes of puberty and emotional maturation, adolescents today face more complicated lives than ever before. They must cope with such distressing and often dangerous phenomena as divorce, parental unemployment, and violence and drugs in their schools and their neighborhoods.

The potential for conflict within the family often increases as adolescents begin to press for autonomy and independence. But conflict sometimes is brought on not by the children but by a dip in the parents' marital happiness as a result of the midlife crises we discussed in Chapter 7 (Steinberg and Silverberg, 1987). For example, parents may feel frustrated because the children appear unappreciative of parental sacrifices made for them over the years. We return to the adolescent years in Chapter 12.

The Middle-Aged Family

Although social scientists used to characterize middle-aged parents, particularly mothers, as experiencing the *empty-nest syndrome*—depression and a lessened sense of well-being—when children left home, more recently researchers have suggested that marital happiness and well-being follow a U-shaped curve. That is, couples report considerable happiness before the birth of children; marital satisfaction plummets while children are in the home; then happiness increases again after the children move out (Glenn, 1991).

The departure of children gives some married couples a chance to relax and enjoy each other's company:

Now that our . . . son is away [at college] we can talk about subjects that interest only us without having to consider whether he feels left out. We can talk about people he doesn't know without explaining who they are. . . . [Or we can] simply eat in companionable silence without the pressure to use mealtime for interacting with our kids (Rosenberg, 1993: 306–307).

A new phenomenon is that because of a bad economy, low income, divorce, or the high cost of housing, many young adults either don't leave their parents' home in the first place or move back. Two popular television shows, "The Boys Are Back" and "Empty Nest," have taken a lighthearted look at what some observers have referred to as the "boomerang generation": The parents try to launch their children but, like boomerangs, they keep coming back.

The Family in Later Life

In retirement, some of the most difficult adjustments for older partners are the loss of an occupation and the necessity to be at home with a spouse all day long. Most people look forward to showering attention and affection on their grandchildren, but, as we shall see in Chapters 16 and 17, if children divorce, grandparents may be caught in the middle of the conflict. If one partner's health is poor, the couple must deal with wills and other estate management concerns. And if one spouse is widowed, she or he may have to forge new relationships. We look at these and other issues on the family in later life in Chapter 18.

DOMESTIC WORK

In discussing gender roles in the home (Chapter 4), we introduced the topic of how household work is apportioned between women and men. We now look at the issue of who is responsible for homemaking in greater depth, first as it applies to housework, then in relation to child care, and finally as it is affected by traditional gender-role expectations.

Housework: A Shared Responsibility?

Men are doing slightly more and women slightly less housework than 30 years ago. Nevertheless, there are still significant differences. According to a 1993 study conducted by the Families and Work Institute, women are almost six times more likely to cook for the family, five times more likely to do the shopping, and eleven times more likely to clean the house than their husbands (cited in Pennebaker, 1994). In a national study of dual-earner couples, wives reported spending over 32 hours per week on housework compared to 7 hours reported by their husbands (Blair, 1993).

Overall, women are still doing 80 percent of the traditional female jobs, such as cooking, cleaning, and laundry, as well as 37 percent of the traditionally male jobs (such as minor home repairs and yardwork). Although women have begun to do less housework because they have taken on paying jobs and have fewer children than in the past, this decrease in the amount of housework they perform has not been affected significantly by men's greater contribution. In fact, men's participation in traditionally female tasks increased by only 2 hours a week between 1965 and 1985 (Robinson, 1988).

Effect of Employment Status It might be expected that husbands of women who are employed outside the home would share in household chores to a greater extent, but this is not necessarily the case. Most husbands, whether they're employed and work long hours or are unemployed, still share little of the housework (Shamir, 1986; Moen, 1992). Some studies have found that even when women are employed, they tend to do about two thirds of all household tasks and three fourths of the most time-consuming tasks, such as cooking and cleaning (Coltrane and Ishii-Kuntz, 1992; Demo and Acock, 1993). Although husbands in remarried families do more of such household tasks as cooking, meal cleanup, shopping, laundry, and housecleaning than husbands in first marriages, their wives still do 80 percent of the housework (Ishii-Kuntz and Coltrane, 1992).

Effect of Race and Ethnicity Men's housework roles often vary by race and ethnicity. For example, a recent national survey of families found that employed Latino and African American men spend more time doing household tasks than white men, including such typically female tasks as meal preparation, washing dishes, and cleaning house (Shelton and John, 1993). Even so, men and women do not share equally in household work. Moreover, although African American and Latino women have a long history of full-time work outside the home, they still bear a disproportionate share of housework and child care (Billingsley, 1992).

Effect of Social Class The division of household labor also varies by social class. Although 14 percent of all Americans pay for outside help with household chores, working women are no more likely than nonworking women to have cleaning help; it is a matter of who can afford it. Thirty percent of people who earn $50,000 or more a year have domestic help or employ a cleaning person, whether or not the wife works outside the home (DeStefano and Colasanto, 1990).

The higher a wife's socioeconomic status, the more likely it is that her husband will help with family tasks. Several studies have shown that wives who have achieved high levels of education and who earn high incomes get more help from their husbands than do wives who work at the lower end of the occupational scale (Moen, 1992; Perry-Jenkins and Folk, 1994). One or more of a number of factors may be at work here: Educated, professional women may have more power in the home; women with high-powered jobs may be required to spend longer hours at work; and/or independently successful women may feel more comfortable asking for help from their spouses.

Child Care

In some racial-ethnic groups, many women can count on their kin to help raise and nurture their children. For example, whether married or single, African American mothers are much more likely than their white counterparts to receive help with child care from supportive kin networks (Jayakody et al., 1993; see also Chapter 2, on kinwork). And although Latino wives have the major share of child-care tasks, some Latino husbands report being much more involved in child rearing than their own fathers were (Coltrane and Valdez, 1993).

Although the number of young children at home and the average age of the couple typically have no effect on the relative proportion of housework each spouse does, in families with young children, employed wives spend longer hours in child care than do either their husbands or nonemployed wives. In particular, employed mothers with very young children spend 24 hours more a week in child-care activities than do their husbands. Because the husband's job typically takes priority over his wife's, she is the one who usually rearranges her work schedule when a child is sick. Nearly nine out of ten working mothers care for their children when they are sick, compared to only one out of ten working fathers (DeStefano and Colasanto, 1990).

Gender-Role Expectations

Is men's lower participation in household tasks the result of long-accepted cultural views of men's and women's proper roles? Usually, but not always. Some studies have found that women's own attitudes may contribute to the imbalance between men's and women's sharing in domestic work. For example, one national poll found that a majority (66 percent) of men and women agreed that women are more capable of managing a household than are men (DeStefano and Colasanto, 1990). Moreover, an even more recent poll found that 40 percent of men and 47 percent of women still agreed that men should be the breadwinners and women the homemakers (Newport, 1993; see also Figure 10.3). If women believe that work will not be done or that it will not be done competently unless *they* do it, other family members may shy away from helping out. Indeed, Fader (1985: 91) argues that women sometimes make themselves miserable because "we insist on the privileges of house power, then feel angry and overburdened when our husbands treat the responsibilities as 'our work.'"

According to Fader, some women actively discourage their husbands' help by criticizing their

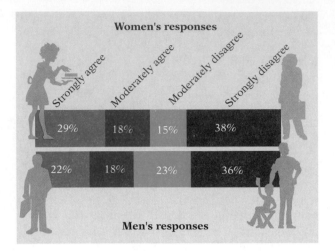

Women's responses

Strongly agree | Moderately agree | Moderately disagree | Strongly disagree

| 29% | 18% | 15% | 38% |

| 22% | 18% | 23% | 36% |

Men's responses

Figure 10.3   Man = $$$, Woman = Housework?
A recent Gallup poll asked Americans, "Do you agree or disagree with this statement: It is generally better for society if the man is the achiever outside the home and the woman takes care of the home and family"? Are you surprised at how many women and men still think that woman's place is in the home, and that the man should be the achiever outside the home? (Based on data in Newport, 1993, p. 12).

work: "He uses too many pots when he cooks" or "He doesn't load the dishwasher right." Or, as Tannen (1990) suggests, women sometimes fail to request help directly because they expect their husbands to *know* that they can't do it all alone. For instance, a woman whose outside work responsibilities have grown may simply expect her husband to know that he must pick up the children from ballet practice; if she does not specifically tell him that she needs to share this task, can he be blamed for not taking it over?

Responsibility and control are sometimes hard to give up. A woman asked to relinquish authority in the one area that she has dominated may be reluctant to give up her role as home-maker. And some employed mothers enjoy the challenge of being both a great wife and mother and a successful professional (Haas, 1980). Moreover, because American society is still generally suspicious of women who are not full-time home-makers (again, see Figure 10.3), and because these attitudes are often projected in magazines, books, textbooks, and media images, it is not entirely surprising that many mothers keep trying to be "supermoms."

In most cases, however, a woman struggling to meet the challenges of work and family is responding to the generalized expectation that it is she and not her husband who must somehow manage to handle both work and family duties (Swiss and Walker, 1993). In a study of women engineers, for example, McIlwee and Robinson (1992) found that women, their employers, and women's husbands usually agreed that, once a child was born, it was the wife's and not the husband's responsibility to interrupt, scale back, or abandon a career. Even many men who consider themselves feminists are willing to share child care but still see housework as "women's work" (Deutsch et al., 1993). As a result, professional wives are often both self-critical and frustrated in trying to meet cultural expectations of doing well both at work and at home (Biernat and Wortman, 1991). In time, the frustration may result in the wife's dissatisfaction with the marriage (Piña and Bengston, 1993). In at least one case it resulted in an essay that has become a classic in its own time; see the box "Why I Want a Wife."

MARITAL SUCCESS AND HAPPINESS

Satisfaction with one's marital role is an important factor in the success of a marriage. The concept of marital success, however, is difficult to define. Researchers have defined and studied "marital success," "marital satisfaction," "marital quality," and "marital happiness" differently, but often use these terms interchangeably (see Fincham and Bradbury, 1987; Glenn, 1991). Because there is no generally agreed-upon definition, researchers describe the success or happiness of marriages which are based on the marital partners' own evaluations.

What's Important in a Successful Marriage?

National polls show that since the 1970s, what people consider to be "very important" in marriage hasn't changed much (see Table 10.1). In both 1974 and 1990, for example, both men and women considered love, sexual fidelity, and the ability to talk about feelings with each other the most important elements of a good marriage. As you can see from Table 10.1, fewer men and women believe that having children is important; indeed, having children is now seen as one

Why I Want a Wife

The essay excerpted here has been reprinted over 200 times in at least ten different countries (Brady, 1990). Written by Judy Brady [then Judy Seiters] in 1972, the article satirizes the traditional view of woman as wife and mother:

I am A Wife. . . . Why do I want a wife? . . . I want a wife who will work and send me to school . . . and take care of my children. I want a wife to keep track of the children's doctor and dentist appointments [and] . . . mine, too. I want a wife to make sure my children eat properly and are kept clean. . . . I want a wife who takes care of the children when they are sick, a wife who arranges to be around when the children need special care because . . . I cannot miss classes at school. . . .

I want a wife who will take care of my physical needs. I want a wife who will keep my house clean . . . pick up after me . . . keep my clothes clean, ironed, mended, replaced when need be, and who will see to it that my personal things are kept in their proper place so that I can find what I need the minute I need it. I want a wife who cooks the meals, a wife who is a good cook. I want a wife who will plan the menus, do the necessary grocery shopping, prepare the meals, serve them pleasantly, and then do the cleaning up while I do my studying. I want a wife who will care for me when I am sick and sympathize with my pain. . . .

I want a wife who . . . makes love passionately and eagerly when I feel like it, a wife who makes sure that I am satisfied. And, of course, I want a wife who will not demand sexual attention when I am not in the mood. . . . I want a wife who assumes the complete responsibility for birth control, because I do not want more children. . . . And I want a wife who understands that my sexual needs may entail more than strict adherence to monogamy. . . .

When I am through with school and have a job, I want my wife to quit working and remain at home so that my wife can more fully and com-pletely take care of a wife's duties.

My God, who wouldn't want a wife?

---

of the least important aspects of a good marriage. The fact that financial security has become more important than any other characteristic for a good marriage probably reflects many people's concern about recessions and unemployment (see Chapter 14).

"His and Her Marriage"

More than 20 years ago Jessie Bernard (1973) coined the phrase "his and her marriage" to show that many men and women experience marriage differently. Much recent research sup-

---

Table 10–1

What Makes a Good Marriage?

1974			1990	
WOMEN	MEN	THINGS CONSIDERED "VERY IMPORTANT"	WOMEN	MEN
90%	86%	Being in love	87%	84%
79	70	Spouse's sexual fidelity	85	78
88	83	Being able to talk together about feelings	84	78
71	66	Keeping romance alive	78	76
78	70	Being able to see the humorous side of things	76	69
74	64	Having similar ideas on how to raise children	72	63
77	73	Having a good sexual relationship	72	74
68	61	Having similar ideas on how to handle money	71	65
62	52	Spouse understanding what you do every day	67	57
68	64	Liking the same kind of lifestyle, activities, and friends	64	62
49	49	Financial security	63	61
51	51	Having children	48	41
28	23	Having similar backgrounds	34	29

SOURCE: Roper Organization, 1990.

ports Bernard's observation that there are still many gender differences in adjusting to married life as well as in the pursuit of health and happiness.

Consider the process of **identity bargaining,** in which newly married partners readjust their idealized expectations to the realities of their life together (Blumstein, 1976). In identity bargaining, partners negotiate adjustments to their new roles as husband and wife. In *foreclosure,* a type of adjustment in which one partner gives in to the new demands of the relationship by narrowing his or her own options, wives often accommodate their husbands' needs:

He wanted me home and a meal on the table when he came through the door, and he wanted everything in its place. He wanted to be out partying and with his friends. The first few years of marriage it was me trying to keep up with him. Of course, when I didn't have any children it was not a problem. But I'm not the cocktaily type person. I enjoy them, but I don't like doing it night after night. I don't drink. I like more educational, broadening type experiences (Marks, 1986: 226).

Married life also increases the number of social roles each partner plays, thereby increasing the potential for role conflict. At least at the present time women play more roles in marriage than men. Most men and many women today play provider roles but, as we've discussed, women are generally responsible for such additional roles as housekeeper, cook, and nanny, as well as for planning and coordinating a family's social activities and keeping in touch with extended family members. And some women must take on the most demanding role of all—that of mother—very quickly, for today as many as 20 percent of women are pregnant at the time they marry.

Marriage and Health

A number of social scientists have found that married people are generally healthier and happier than are those who are single, divorced, or widowed (see Ross et al., 1991, for a summary of some of this literature and Mastekaasa, 1994, for a 19-country study). Married people have lower rates of heart disease, cancer, stroke, pneumonia, tuberculosis, cirrhosis of the liver, and syphilis, and they less frequently attempt suicide and have fewer automobile accidents than singles. Married partners report less incidence of depression, anxiety, and other forms of psychological distress, and they are less likely to say they are sick, to be disabled, to visit the doctor, or to be hospitalized than unmarried people. Furthermore, married people have substantially lower mortality rates for almost all causes of death than do unmarried people of the same age and sex (Bowling, 1987; Kaprio et al., 1987; Litwack and Messeri, 1989).

Being married does not automatically guarantee better health, however. Several studies have found that married women are *less* healthy than married men. One factor that may contribute to the difference is the multiplicity of women's role responsibilities. Working women with young children in families in which both spouses' earnings are low are much more likely to report depression than married men, full-time homemakers, or employed married women who have no child-care or economic problems (Verbrugge, 1979; Gove, 1984; Anson, 1989).

If a marriage is unhappy and the partners try to "stick it out for the sake of the children," depression may result—especially if one of the partners is unsupportive, experiences role conflict, or has low self-esteem. Thus quality wins out: It is more important to be happily married than just to be married. In fact, studies have shown that people who have divorced and remarried successfully are less susceptible to health problems than are those who remain in unhappy marriages (see Ross et al., 1991).

Why the general positive relationship between marriage and physical and psychological well-being? On the one hand, it may be that good health and happiness make people more desirable. That is, fit and healthy people may be more likely to find and keep mates than those who have higher illness rates (see Booth and Johnson, 1994). On the other hand, it may be that enjoying emotional, social, and physical support from a spouse improves one's general health and longevity. The feeling of security that such support brings may lower anxiety and prevent or lessen depression. It may also reduce risky activities and encourage healthy behavior. For example, married people are more likely to quit smoking and to maintain diets low in cholesterol, and they are less likely to drink heavily, get into fights, drive too fast, or take other risks that increase the likelihood of accidents and injuries. In addition, wives tend to encourage behaviors that prolong life, such as getting regular medical checkups. And when one partner does become ill, the physical and emotional support spouses provide during recuperation after surgery or other medical treatment can help speed recovery. Finally, higher household incomes are correlated with good physical and mental health (Ross et al., 1991).

In a national study, Hahn (1993) found that married women rated their health higher than divorced, separated, widowed, and never-married women. According to Hahn, married women, whether or not they work outside the home, have a sense of security that their well-being is not entirely dependent on their own earnings. They have access to better housing and better food and services, and they are more likely to own their homes. Whether they are full time homemakers or work part time, married women are also more likely to have health coverage through their husbands' job benefits. All these economic factors provide access to health services and thus reduce the psychological worry over possible illness.

Happiness in Marriage

Although more women than men report being very happy in their marriages, the rates at which both sexes report marital happiness have been declining since the early 1970s (Glenn and Weaver, 1988; Greeley, 1991). Greeley (1991) has attributed men's decreases of marital happiness to age. That is, younger men appear to be less satisfied with many things—their family life, their income, and their jobs. As they grow older and their jobs and income improve, they become more satisfied with family life and are thus happier personally.

According to Greeley, women's emotional satisfaction in marriage is a bit more complex. In his study, the least happy women were working mothers who were born in the 1950s. These women reported high levels of pressure and many concerns about health and finances. Greeley concluded that women's declining satisfaction is due not to a global unhappiness with marriage but to discontentment brought on by the changes in role expectations for women.

Is there a recipe for an enduring and happy marriage? Couples who say they are happy in their marriages have described three main ingredients. First, each spouse must have a positive attitude toward the other and like the other "as a person" and a good friend. Second, both part-

ners see marriage as a long-term commitment and a sacred institution in which the vow of "till death us do part" is taken seriously and conflict is avoided. For example, a salesperson who has been married 36 years advises, "Discuss your problems in a normal voice. If a voice is raised, stop. Return after a short period of time. Start again. After a period of time both parties will be able to deal with their problems and not say things that they will be sorry about later" (Lauer and Lauer, 1985). In fact, partners who stay together are much less likely to insult or put a partner down from the very beginning of marriage (Notarius and Markman, cited in Schrof, 1994).

Finally, happily married couples often say that providing emotional support is more important than love (see Erickson, 1993). A few years ago, the *Washington Post* conducted a survey of people who were happily married. Although the sample was highly self-selective, some of the comments about trust, privacy, and respect are instructive:

There are times when each of us needs to be alone, we need to have our space. It is very important in our marriage, to know that if he buries himself in a book or I in an old movie, we respect each other's privacy. (Married 9 years)

We like the personhood of the one each married, and we respect the capabilities of each other. . . . The undergirding strength of our marriage has been the trust that we have in each other. (Married 38 years)

He makes me feel smart, pretty, capable and cherished. (Married 21 years)

I asked my husband why he thought our marriage was a success, and he said it was because we don't "compete with each other" and because we "respect each other's independence." I agree. (Married 33 years) (Mathias, 1992: B5).

In contrast, partners in unhappy marriages keep trying to change one another to fulfill their own needs. They often become frustrated and angry when their efforts fail. Instead of cooling off and thinking a problem through, as the salesperson quoted earlier advises, the partners react when they are angry. Hostile, sarcastic criticisms may lead to verbal or physical abuse. And, because people in unhappy marriages often spend minimal time together, there is little chance that their problems can be resolved through discus-

When married couples work together on projects, they often learn better ways of communicating and of resolving difficulties. The seven years this couple spent building their California home may have helped them build their marriage as well.

sion or by sharing common activities or day-to-day interaction.

Marital Burnout

Contrary to what one might expect, people who are unhappy in their marriages don't always end up in divorce court. **Marital burnout,** the gradual deterioration of love and ultimate loss of an emotional attachment between marital partners, can go on for many years (Kayser, 1993). The American journalist Helen Rowland once commented that, before marriage, a man will lie awake thinking about something his lover said, but that after marriage he'll fall asleep before his wife finishes saying it. In a third scenario of marital burnout, the wife doesn't even notice that her husband falls asleep in the middle of her sentence.

In marital burnout, even if spouses share housework and child care, one spouse may fail to provide the other with emotional support. A partner may complain that his or her partner is not confiding innermost thoughts and feelings, doesn't stick by the partner during bad times, or

doesn't initiate talks about problems (Erickson, 1993). Marital burnout can develop so slowly and quietly that couples are often not aware of it. According to Kayser (1993), marital burnout does not occur overnight. The death of marital love includes several phases. All emotional bonds finally evaporate in the last phase (see Table 10.2).

Sometimes one partner in a marriage will hide dissatisfaction for many years. At other times both partners try to ignore the warning signs (see the box "Am I Heading Toward Marital Burnout?"). Social exchange theory (Chapter 2) would suggest that when the costs in the relationship become much greater than the benefits, the couple will probably seek a divorce.

POWER, CONFLICT, AND COMMUNICATION

Power and conflict are normal and inevitable in close relationships. Although it is unrealistic to expect communication to cure all marital problems, effective communication can decrease power struggles and conflict that might lead to marital dissolution.

Table 10.2
The Death of Marital Love

Phase I: Disillusionment. Partners feel disappointed and disenchanted with the marriage. They are aware that the relationship is not going well and have doubts about their spouses and the marriage itself.

Phase II: Hurt. Partners feel treated unfairly and abused or lonely. They feel that the costs of keeping the relationship going are higher than the rewards. They are aware that their emotional and social needs are not being met or that their partners think they are not important.

Phase III: Anger. Partners feel resentment, hostility, indignation, or bitterness. Hurts accumulate over time, they blame or distrust their partners, and negative thoughts about their partners begin to outnumber positive thoughts.

Phase IV: Ambivalence. Partners alternate between despair and hope but are indecisive about what to do. They try to make the marriage work for the children's sake, for economic reasons, or because of religious convictions that marriage is forever, but they also think about giving up.

Phase V: Disaffection. Partners now feel indifferent about the marriage, detached, alienated, and apathetic. They have little desire to be emotionally close to their partners, they feel that their partners cannot satisfy their needs, and they believe that any changes their partners may make in their attitudes and behavior are too late (Kayser, 1993:20–21).

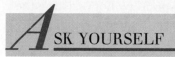
Am I Heading Toward Marital Burnout?

All marriages have ups and downs, and checking off even as many as seven of the following items doesn't necessarily mean your marriage is in trouble. However, the more items you check, the wiser you may be to look further into these symptoms of burnout. And the earlier you recognize symptoms, the better your chances of saving your marriage (Based on Stinnett and DeFrain, 1985; Kayser, 1993).

- ☐ You've lost interest in each other
- ☐ You feel bored with each other
- ☐ There's a lack of communication; neither of you listens to the other
- ☐ You seem to have nothing in common
- ☐ You don't do things together, don't want to do things together, or can't find the time to do things together
- ☐ Marriage is no longer your top priority; such things as careers, relatives, religion, friends, hobbies, and/or lovers are more important
- ☐ Deep down, you want a divorce
- ☐ Inflexibility: you can no longer compromise with each other
- ☐ Minor irritations become major issues
- ☐ You no longer try to deal honestly with important issues
- ☐ You find yourself making family decisions alone
- ☐ You have no desire for physical touching of any kind
- ☐ Your relationships with other people are more intimate than your relationship with your spouse
- ☐ The children have begun to act up; they have frequent trouble at school, get into fights with friends, or withdraw
- ☐ "Small talk" dominates your conversations with your spouse
- ☐ One of you controls the other through tantrums, violence, or threats of suicide or violence
- ☐ You are both putting your own individual interests before the good of the marriage
- ☐ You can't talk about money, politics, religion, sex, or other touchy subjects
- ☐ You avoid each other
- ☐ One or both of you subject the other to public humiliation
- ☐ You are no longer concerned about how either you or your partner look
- ☐ You have increasing health problems, such as headaches, back pain, sleeplessness, high blood pressure, recurring colds, or emotional ups and downs
- ☐ One or both of you is abusing alcohol or other drugs
- ☐ Family functions, such as doing things together, decrease
- ☐ One or both of you is irritable and sarcastic
- ☐ You are staying in the relationship because it is easier than being on your own
- ☐ You no longer have disagreements or arguments; it doesn't seem to matter

Theories and Types of Power

As we have seen, many of the dynamics in marriage have to do with who has the power to make decisions in family-related matters. Sociologists define **power** as the ability to impose one's will on others. That is, a person or group has power when it can get others to do what it wants. Whether we are talking about a dating relationship, a family, or a nation, some individuals and some groups have more power than others. Marital partners must make many decisions, starting with wedding arrangements and including housework, parenthood, and each partner's roles within the marriage. They must also resolve communication problems and the problems faced by working wives/mothers. Where do people get power in a marriage?

Resource and Exchange Theories
Some scholars use resource theories to explain family structures and marital power. Typically, the spouse with more resources has more power in decision making. Thus, a husband who earns more money than his wife or has more control over household finances has more power (Vogler and Pahl, 1994). One kind of resource often accompanies another. For example, people with high incomes often also have more education and/or high occupational status. As you saw earlier in this chapter, as women increase their resources through paid work, they become less dependent on their husbands and more powerful in demanding that household chores and child care be shared.

Resource theory can combine with exchange theory to explain the trade-offs husbands and wives often negotiate. Spouses develop an explicit or implicit agreement to exchange such resources as time and money. The control of economic resources is a major, but not the only, determinant of who has the greatest power in the family. Lips (1991) points out, for example, that even in families in which the wives are doctors, professors, lawyers, or other professionals, the couple's mode of decision making may be strongly traditional rather than based on "simple, rational economics." In addition, men who are not occupationally successful may be especially unlikely to see their wives' employment as a resource because it crushes their ego and identity as a provider. In response, women may give up their power even though they are the breadwinners: "Sensitive to their husbands' feelings of failure, some wives respond by not resisting their husband's dominance to 'balance' his low self-esteem" (Pyke, 1994: 89).

Types of Power
Power is not limited to tangible things such as money. Love, for example, is an important source of power. As you saw in Chapter 8, the *principle of least interest* explains why, in a dating relationship, the person who is less interested is more powerful than the committed partner. In marriage, similarly, if you are more committed to your marriage than your spouse is, you have less power. As a result, you may refrain from expressing negative feelings, defer to your partner's wishes, or do things you don't want to do.

Other nonmaterial sources of power include access to information or having particular abilities or talents. For example, husbands often have more decision-making power about how to spend money on expensive things (such as houses or cars) because they are usually more knowledgeable about financial matters, investments, and negotiating contracts. In traditional households, wives may have more power than their husbands in the furnishing of a home or raising children because they devote more time to shopping, have good organizing skills, or are more familiar with neighborhood professionals, such as pediatricians, who provide important services.

Conflict: Reasons and Remedies

Because we tend to see the family as a retreat from the problems of the outside world (Chapter 1), we may often suppress conflict: It seems inconsistent with an idealized picture of the family as a haven. All families, however, and no matter how supportive and caring they are, experience conflict (Roberts and Krokoff, 1990). Comedian Phyllis Diller's quip, "Don't go to bed mad. Stay up and fight!" is actually insightful. Conflict is not in and of itself a bad thing. If families recognize conflict and actively attempt to resolve it, conflict can serve as a catalyst in deepening relationships (Rosenzweig, 1992). In this section we look first at some of the most common sources of conflict and then consider coping techniques and family counseling alternatives.

What Do Couples Fight About?
Married couples fight about a variety of things. The most common disagreements are over gender roles,

loyalty, money, power, sex, privacy, and children (Betcher and Macaulay, 1990).

Gender roles and how they are filled can often cause disagreements; as we have seen, spouses often have different attitudes and beliefs about who should do what in a family. If they cannot come to an agreement, tension may rise and quarrels can become more frequent. Today, when traditional husbands fail to meet their working wives' expectations that there should be greater equity in the division of household work, serious conflict can ensue (Lye and Biblarz, 1993).

Loyalty is often defined quite differently by men and women. Although many women today share stereotypically male values about competition and success in the workplace, they still tend to put loyalty to the immediate family over work relationships. Many men have strong family and friendship ties, but they may construe loyalty differently. Because they are focused more on career, profession, company, organization, or job, they tend to put these aspects of their lives first and to see themselves as loyal to their families if they are good providers and faithful to their wives. Many women, on the other hand, define loyalty as emotional closeness and interpersonal understanding. As a result, they tend to interpret husbands' preference for going out with their buddies over going to the movies with their wives as disloyalty.

Money is a very common source of conflict. Arguments over money generally focus on how—or how not—to spend it. Conflicts over how money is spent may become particularly intense if a working wife has no input and feels that her husband's decisions are "unfair" (Blair, 1993).

Although arguments typically erupt over specific expenditures, they are really based on different, sometimes opposing, value systems. For example, because Mary's family of orientation is emotionally important to her, she spends a lot of money on long-distance telephone calls to them, which infuriates John because he thinks he and the children should be enough emotional support for her. John, on the other hand, spends a lot of money on stereo equipment because listening to music helps him to relax. But Mary thinks turning on the radio can produce the same effect and thus sees this as a waste of money.

Power struggles can engender marital conflict on many dimensions. Some contentions may be over economic power. Even when wives work, husbands may feel that the man should be the one to decide how the money should be spent. Related to this, there may be conflict about who sets the household rules. Whether they are explicit or implicit, rules about dealing with in-laws, making large purchases, disciplining the children, or entertaining friends may be sources of marital conflict. There are also differences in the ways partners exercise power. The person with less power may use manipulation (such as flattery), supplication (crying or acting helpless), or disengagement (sulking, playing the martyr, or not speaking). The more powerful person is more likely to be autocratic (for example, by claiming to be better informed) or to bully (through threats, insults, ridicule, or violence).

Sex can also be a source of marital conflict. As we have discussed, women are more likely to equate sex with emotional intimacy and to resent it if their husbands express affection only when they want to make love (Oggins et al., 1993). Partners may also feel embarrassed or uncomfortable about communicating what they want, both in terms of physical stimulation and emotional expressiveness. Some couples experience *performance anxiety*. That is, they may worry about their physical appearance or about whether they are satisfying their partners. They may agree to sex (even when they are too tired to enjoy it) because they worry about being seen as frigid or unmasculine. The most serious problem may be unwanted sex. In a recent national survey, 9 percent of the wives reported being forced to have sex against their will at least once during the marriage (Schrof and Wagner, 1994).

Privacy in terms of space, time, emotion, and property is a crucial need of many marital partners. No matter how close a couple is, partners can run into problems if they do not respect each other's needs for privacy, including having space and time to be alone. A wife, for example, may resent her husband's barging into the bathroom because it may be one of the few times during the day when she can be alone. Similarly, many men have workshops, not because they produce great furniture, but because it gives them a chance for solitude. Many couples fight about privacy because they equate it with secrecy, but privacy and secrecy are not synonymous. For example, some couples never open each other's mail, not because they are afraid a partner may get a letter from a lover but because they respect each other's privacy.

Children may strengthen a marriage, but they

are also a common source of conflict. Spouses may have different philosophies about such issues as discipline, the importance of teaching young children self-control, and the kinds of responsibilities a child should be given. Because more mothers work today, more parents are splitting child care, especially if the spouses have shiftwork (see Chapter 14). As more spouses collaborate in child rearing, there is more opportunity for clashes between different approaches to raising children. For example, although a wife may expect her husband to take on more child-care tasks, she may also resent his insistence on making decisions about playmates, bedtimes, or curfews. As we shall discuss in Chapter 17, children are especially likely to be a source of conflict in remarriages.

Common Ways of Coping with Conflict

Conflicts are normal. What may not be normal or healthy is the way a family handles the conflict. Taping family interactions, Vuchinich (1987) found that families typically used four techniques to end conflict: submission, compromise, standoff, and withdrawal.

1. *Submission.* One person submits to another; the conflict ends when the first person agrees with or goes along with the other.
2. *Compromise.* Partners find a middle ground between their opposing positions; each must give a little in order to accept this compromise. The compromise can be suggested by a partner or by a third party.
3. *Standoff.* The disputants drop the argument without resolving it; they agree to disagree and move on to other activities. No one wins or loses, and the conflict ends in a draw.
4. *Withdrawal.* When a disputant withdraws, he or she refuses to continue the argument, either by "clamming up" or by leaving the room. Among the four techniques, withdrawal is the most disruptive of family interaction because there is no resolution.

Although many family therapists teach compromise as the best way to settle marital quarrels, Vuchinich found that family fights ended in compromise only 14 percent of the time. In 61 percent of the cases he studied, fights ended in a standoff: Conflicts were allowed to "run their course," and family members moved on to other issues. This suggests that there are several peaceful methods, besides compromise, of resolving conflict.

Someone once noted that the difference between a good marriage and a not-so-good marriage is that in the latter a couple leaves about three or four things unsaid every day. That is, say what's on your mind, tell it like it is, and so on. According to the well-known psychotherapist Arnold Lazarus, however, one of the biggest myths about marriage is that it is okay to "let it all hang out." Some spouses unleash "emotional napalm" at their partners on the grounds that "if a man can't let down his hair at home and blow off some steam, he's likely to end up with stomach ulcers or have a heart attack." Displaced rage, unbridled attacks, and physical aggression are not normal ways of handling conflict, however (Lazarus, 1985).

Despite Lazarus's caution, some counselors instruct partners to confront each other openly and even bluntly. Such ventilation is helpful only if partners are willing to listen. If both are spilling their feelings at the same time, neither can listen to the other, and the hostility escalates. Increasing rage can lead to physical abuse. On the other hand, denying conflict can destroy a marriage. Avoiding conflict may work in the short term, but in the long run, if wives are too compliant and fail to express disagreement or anger, and if husbands refuse to engage in discussions because they are stubborn, defensive, or withdrawn, the marriage will deteriorate (Gottman and Krokoff, 1989; Betcher and Macauley, 1990).

Family Therapy and Counseling

Because conflict is inevitable and failing to deal with it can be disastrous, family therapy and counseling has become a booming industry. Although there are no precise figures, it has been estimated that 40 percent of American households seek counseling (*Better Homes and Gardens,* 1988). One of the fastest-growing nonprofessional groups is Worldwide Marriage Encounter, begun by a Catholic priest in Barcelona in 1962. During weekend retreats, married couples are taught communication and conflict resolution skills (Collins, 1986).

Therapy and counseling may not always be successful. (Jacobson and Addis, 1993, provide a review and critique of marriage and family therapy techniques.) Many counselors have internalized cultural stereotypes about gender roles and may not be effective in diagnosing and treating

A competent marriage counselor may help a couple find effective ways of resolving conflicts and develop greater satisfaction in their daily interactions.

particular problems. During the 1980s, for example, feminists challenged traditional family therapy models that tended to blame women for marital and family problems (Avis, 1985; Luepnitz, 1988). Furthermore, many people are not comfortable in seeking advice. They may be embarrassed, can't afford the costs, deny they have a problem, want to find their own solutions, or do not trust "shrinks."

Offering alternatives to formal counseling, both researchers and practitioners have published books and articles of advice, including guidelines for "fair fighting" (see the box "Ground Rules for Fair Fighting"). Fights that humiliate, embarrass, browbeat, or demoralize the other person will not clear the air. Rules for fair fighting do not guarantee a resolution of conflict, but because they are based on negotiation and compromise, they offer partners a better chance of developing more constructive ways of dealing with conflict.

Creating Better Communication

Because our most intimate relationships are in the family, communication is a critical component of family life. Whether the interaction is between wives and husbands or parents and children, communication can be either constructive or destructive. An important first step in effective communication is self-disclosure.

Self-Disclosure **Self-disclosure** is telling another about oneself, honestly offering one's thoughts and feelings, and hoping that truly open communication will follow (Hendrick and Hendrick, 1992b). A consistent finding in the literature on self-disclosure is that *reciprocity* is important if self-disclosure is to be effective in communication and conflict resolution. Many social scientists see self-disclosure as integral to exchange theory's model of family interaction. That is, reciprocal self-disclosure may increase partners' liking for and trust in each other, eliminate a lot of guesswork in the communication, and provide a balance of costs and benefits.

Women tend to disclose more than men but to hold back disclosure when they anticipate an uncaring, unemotional, or otherwise negative response. Men tend to disclose more to women than to men but to withhold disclosure when they feel they will get an emotional (rather than an objective and dispassionate) response. In nonmarital relationships, males disclose more fully to females than to other males, probably because they see women as nonthreatening in both work and social relationships (Arliss, 1991).

Disclosure can be either beneficial or harm-

CHOICES

Ground Rules for Fair Fighting

As the text has suggested, therapists, counselors, and researchers themselves hold conflicting views as to whether and how marital partners and families should handle conflict. In general, however, many agree that arguing the issues is healthier than suffering in silence. According to Hendrickson (1994), "a good fight is an essential ingredient" in building a good marriage. Keeping silent or sidestepping conflict diminishes love and respect. And Brehm (1992) maintains that avoiding fights can create superficial marital relationships.

The following suggestions may be helpful in changing some of our most destructive behavior patterns, however unconscious or unintentional:

1. Don't attack your partner. He or she will only become defensive and will be too busy preparing a good rebuttal to hear what you have to say.

2. Avoid ultimatums; no one likes to be backed into a corner.

3. Say what you really mean, and don't apologize. Lies are harmful, and apologetic people are rarely taken seriously.

4. Avoid accusations and attacks; do not belittle or threaten.

5. Start with your own feelings. "I feel" is better than "You said . . ." Focus on the problem, not the other person.

6. State your wishes and requests clearly and directly; do not be manipulative, defensive, or sexually seductive.

7. Limit what you say to the present or near present. Avoid long lists of complaints from the past.

8. Refuse to fight dirty:
   ❑ No *gunnysacking*, or keeping one's complaints secret and tossing them into an imaginary gunnysack that gets heavier and heavier over time

   ❑ No *passive-aggressive behavior*, or expressing anger indirectly as in criticism, sarcasm, nagging, or nitpicking
   ❑ No *silent treatment*; keep the lines of communication open.
   ❑ No *name calling*.

9. Use humor and comic relief. Laugh at yourself and the situation—but not at your partner. Learning to take ourselves less seriously and to recognize our flaws without becoming so self-critical that we wallow in shame or self-pity can have a healing effect during fights.

10. Strive for closure as soon as possible after a misunderstanding or disagreement by resolving the issue. This prevents dirty fighting and, more important, it holds the partners to their commitment to negotiate until the issue is either resolved or defused (Crosby, 1991; Rosenzweig, 1992).

ful, depending on whether the reaction is supportive or worsens already negative feelings. Disclosure is beneficial under four conditions (Derlega et al., 1993):

1. *Esteem support* can reduce a person's anxiety about troubling events. If the listener is attentive, sympathetic, and uncritical, disclosure can motivate people to change significant aspects of their lives.

2. A listener may be able to offer *information support* through advice and guidance. For example, people under stress may benefit by knowing that their problems are not due to personal deficiencies.

3. Disclosure can provide *instrumental support* if the listener offers concrete help, such as shopping for food or caring for the speaker's children if she or he is ill.

4. Even if a problem is not easily solved, listeners can provide *motivational support*. For example, if a husband is distressed about losing a job, a wife can encourage him to keep "pounding the pavement" and assuring him that "we can get through this."

When, on the other hand, is self-disclosure detrimental? If the feedback is negative, disclosure may intensify a person's already low self-esteem. (Disclosure: "I'm so mad at myself for not sticking to my diet." Response: "Yeah, if you had, you'd have something to wear to the party tonight.") Where self-esteem is strong, however, even negative feedback to self-disclosure may fail to shoot the person down. One of my students, in her mid-40s, said she was anxious about attending the honors banquet for students with outstanding GPAs because "I'll look like everyone's grandmother." Expecting support, she asked her husband to attend the ceremony because she felt "out of place." He replied, "Well, just don't go. Everyone will wonder what an old lady is doing there and no one will hire you, anyway." (She attended alone, by the way, had a wonderful time and got a job offer by the end of the summer.)

Finally, self-disclosure does not work miracles overnight. In the short run, it may feel awkward and embarrassing. Over time, however, self-disclosure—if it is practiced by both partners and by parents and children—can decrease our tension and guilt feelings, increase our self-esteem and enhance our ability to cope in stressful situations (Derlega et al., 1993).

Do We Want to Communicate? People may be poor communicators, but they may also fear to speak openly and clearly for a variety of reasons. Rubin (1983) describes the lack of communication in marriage as "the approach-avoidance dance": Women, especially, she claims, want their husbands not only to communicate but to *want* to communicate—to want to know how their wives feel, what they think, and what they worry about. On the other hand, Rubin says, women are also sometimes relieved by a lack of communication because they can choose what is and is not said (see also Barreca, 1993).

Goldberg (1987) argues that communication is little more than an illusion. Because we are defensive, Goldberg claims, we send contradictory messages to each other. For example, women want men to open up, but they don't want them to expose anything that is weak or needy or that will threaten women's sense of security. They tell men to share their feelings, but they don't want to hear anything that will make them feel anxious or attacked. According to Goldberg, although women want to be independent and assertive, they retreat to the "feminine-manipulative" approach because this will not scare off a man. Men, however, are also defensive. They want to be left alone emotionally, but they also want a woman to be there for them physically. They want a woman to be independent but, at the same time, they fear she may leave them or not need them, or that they may feel unmasculine.

Barriers to Marital Communication Even when people really do want to communicate, they are not sure how to do so. Despite our best intentions, many of us communicate in ways that do not result in meaningful interaction. Some of the most common communication problems include the following:

1. *Not listening.* Both partners may be so intent on making their point that they are simply waiting for their turn to speak rather than listening to the other person. One of the most important components in communication is really listening to the other person instead of rehearsing what we plan to say when he or she pauses for a breath (Noller, 1984).

2. *Not responding to the issue at hand.* If partners are not listening to each other, they will not address the problem. There are three common miscommunication patterns in unhappy couples. In *cross-complaining*, partners present their own complaints without addressing the other person's point. In *counterproposals*, a spouse ignores a partner's proposal for a solution and presents his or her own ideas (Krokoff, 1987). In *stonewalling*, one of the partners turns into a stone wall: He or she may "Hmmmm" or "Uh, huh," but the partner neither really hears nor responds to the message, and there is a stony silence (Gottman, 1994a).

3. *Blaming, criticizing, nagging, and arguing.* Instead of listening and being understanding, partners may feel they are neglected or unappreciated. They feel their spouse magnifies their faults, belittles them, accuses them unjustly, and makes them feel worthless and stupid. The blamer is a fault-finder who criticizes relentlessly and speaks in generalizations: "You never do anything right," "You're just like your mother/father" (Gordon, 1993: 82).

4. *Using scapegoats.* Scapegoating is an ineffective way of avoiding communication about a problem by blaming others for everything that goes wrong. It is often a way of trying to change our partners and not ourselves. We may be uncomfortable about being expressive because we had cold and aloof parents, or we might be suspicious about trusting people because we were taken advantage of by a best friend. However, blaming parents, teachers, relatives, siblings, or friends for our communication problems is debilitating and counterproductive (Noller, 1984).

5. *Using coercion or contempt.* Related to scapegoating, partners may be punitive and force acceptance of their point of view. If this works, coercive behavior can continue. Contempt can also be devastating in marriage. The most visible signs of contempt include

insults and name-calling, hostile humor, mockery, and body language such as rolling your eyes, sneering, and curling your upper lip (Gottman, 1994a).

6. *Using the silent treatment.* Not talking to your spouse is one of the best ways to build up anger and hostility. Initially, the "offender" may work very hard to make the silent partner feel loved and to talk about a problem. Eventually, however, the partner who is being subjected to the silent treatment may get fed up and look for someone else (Rosenberg, 1993).

Effective Communication Patterns It is important that marital partners overcome communication problems, for over time they can lead to an erosion of the marital relationship. But it takes time to forge good communication networks. Psychologist John Gottman interviewed and studied more than 200 couples over 20 years and found that the difference between marriages that lasted and those that split up was a "magic ratio" of 5 to 1; that is, five positive reactions for every one negative interaction:

As long as there was five times as much positive feeling and interaction between husband and wife as there is negative, the marriage was likely to be stable over time. In contrast, those couples who were heading for divorce were doing far too little on the positive side to compensate for the growing negativity between them (Gottman, 1994a: 41).

According to researchers and practitioners, there are a number of ways to increase positive communication and decrease negative interaction patterns in marriage:

- *Ask for information.* If your spouse has a complaint ("I never get a chance to talk to you because you're always dealing with the kids"), address the issue. Find out more about why your spouse is upset; don't be defensive ("Well, if you were around more often, we could talk").

- *Get inside the other person's world.* See things from the other person's point of view. When we disagree on an issue, it is not always because "I'm right and you're wrong." It is more likely due to the fact that we have different perspectives.

- *Create a caring communion.* Strong family members value each other, and they let that appreciation shine through. As a result at least two good things happen: Positive self-concepts are reinforced, and a climate for continued effective communication is facilitated.

- *Keep the monsters in late-night movies.* Do not engage in "monster" behavior—do not criticize, evaluate, or act superior.

- *Keep it honest.* Honesty not only means not lying, it means not manipulating others. Do not resort to bullying, outwitting, blaming, dominating, or controlling. Do not play on dependency or become a long-suffering martyr. All of these methods of manipulating others lead to false and shallow relationships.

- *Make it kind.* Some people use "brutal honesty" as an excuse for cruelty. Maintain a balance of honesty and kindness.

- *Be specific.* A specific complaint is easier to deal with. "You never talk to me" is harder to manage than "I wish we could have 30 minutes each evening without television, the paper, or the kids."

- *Become allies.* Attack the problem rather than each other. If you treat each other as best friends and not as enemies, you have a better chance of resolving the problem.

- *Express appreciation.* Thanking your spouse for something he or she has done will enhance the relationship.

- *Share your hopes.* Sharing hopes is integral to a strong relationship. Hopes can range from the mundane ("I hope you don't have to work this weekend") to ambitious goals ("What if we invest our money to buy a condo near the mountains for our retirement?").

- *Use nonverbal communication to express your feelings.* Nonverbal acts, such as hugging your spouse, smiling, and holding his or her hand can sometimes be more supportive than anything you might say (Stinnett and DeFrain, 1985; Gold, 1992; Knapp and Hall, 1992; Gordon, 1993).

Should People Sign Marriage Contracts?

Some couples write marriage contracts to avoid conflict and power struggles, especially over financial issues. Although marriage contracts are not uncommon among the very rich (such as Donald Trump and Marla Maples), most people do not draw up marriage contracts because it seems unromantic and because little property is involved. It was a common practice during the seventeenth and eighteenth centuries, however. For example, in 1683 John French and Eleanor Veazie signed a marriage contract in which John agreed "not to meddle with or take into his hand" any part of the estate that Eleanor had inherited from her former husband and to leave her 4 pounds a year (which could also be paid in pork, beef, malt, or corn) and "the new end of the dwelling house" after his death. He also promised to let her sell their apples and to give her a place for her garden plot (Scott and Wishy, 1982: 70–72). And in 1855 Lucy Stone and Henry Blackwell signed a marriage contract that protested such accepted practices as the husband's control and guardianship of their children and the woman's taking the husband's name (McElroy, 1991).

Some of the arguments for and against marriage contracts are similar to those for cohabitation contracts (discussed in Chapter 9). Those who oppose marriage contracts feel that they set a pessimistic tone for the marriage and that disagreements about the contents might even derail wedding plans. Marriage contracts are not always binding in court, and if the contract is executed in a state other than where it was drawn up, the couple will still have problems. Further, because people change over time, their initial viewpoints may no longer be reflected in the contract (Sloane, 1987).

Attorneys recommend making a list of issues that could be potential problems, including each partner's financial condition, medical status, and prior marital involvements. The contract should also include a section on home life that discusses the allocation of household chores and expenses incurred in maintaining the home and automobiles as well as property rights. Couples are even cautioned to spell out what kind of birth control they will use, what the responsibilities of each partner are regarding children of either's previous marriage, who will pay for any career costs, and how a child's name will be selected (Swisher et al., 1990).

Despite drawbacks, marriage contracts are drawn up for roughly 5 percent of all first marriages and 20 percent of remarriages (Stark, 1993). If there are children from a first marriage or if one partner has considerable resources, the contract makes ending a bad marriage less complex and expensive. Even people entering their first marriage see contracts as useful if they have come from broken homes and have unpleasant memories of their parents "slugging it out in court" (Deutsch, 1986). Because women—especially those who have not worked outside the home or have done so only on a part-time basis—are the ones who usually suffer financially after a divorce (see Chapter 16), a contract gives them some legal protection. Contracts may also help prospective partners clarify their expectations about their rights and responsibilities. A contract can force couples to deal with issues they might be unwilling to discuss, such as having or not having children, sharing previously acquired property,

It has nothing to do with how much I love or trust you; we need a prenuptial agreement because I earn so much more than you.

© CHRONICLE FEATURES 1994

The *Quality Time* cartoon by Gail Machlis is reprinted by permission of Chronicle Features, San Francisco, California.

raising the children in interfaith marriages, and disposing of prior debts. As Appendix E shows, a marriage contract can cover a long list of topics.

Also, the AIDS epidemic may make marriage contracts more attractive. Large numbers of bisexual men do not disclose their bisexual activities to their wives (see Chapter 7), and an estimated 20 percent of the male homosexual population marry at least once (Dullea, 1987). There may be equal numbers of heterosexual men and women and IV drug users who have lied to their prospective spouses about having practiced safe sex. They may even be carrying the AIDS virus although it has not yet shown up in blood tests. In all these cases, marriage contracts might make some people more honest about their sexual preferences and experiences and provide some legal protection to the innocent partner if the marriage breaks up because of deception.

CONCLUSION

Someone once said that marriages are made in heaven, but the details have to be worked out here on earth. Working out those details is an ongoing process throughout a marriage. The biggest sources of conflict and *change* are disagreements over household work and communication. Many working women are feeling burnt out by double shifts and expect more *choices* in the distribution of homemaking and child-care chores. One *constraint* that could result from this increasingly problematic situation would be a decision in the future by increasing numbers of women not to marry (or remarry). At the moment, however, marriage is one of the most important rites of passage for almost all of us. Another is parenthood, on which we focus in the next two chapters.

Taking Action

Starting Out Right

Some common problems in marriage can be prevented or minimized by starting out with a real effort to communicate and negotiate.

• **Weddings can cost $25,000 and more** these days. Although marriage rituals are important, many couples go into debt to celebrate their weddings, spending money they could use in setting up their new homes and for other purposes on elaborate gowns, flowers, and receptions. If you are planning to marry (or remarry), consult some books that offer practical tips on decreasing the costs. (See, for example, Diane Warner's *How to Have a Big Wedding on a Small Budget,* Cincinnati, Ohio: Writer's Digest Books, 1992).

• Since one of the major sources of dissatisfaction in marriage is housework, one way to lessen conflict is for a family to **make a chart** of domestic duties and rotate duties among family members each week. Everyone will do such unpleasant household tasks as scrubbing the toilet bowl, cleaning the oven, and mopping the kitchen, but no one will have to do these chores every week. Such a system can help men appreciate how much time is spent on seemingly "simple" tasks, and it can help children learn to be responsible and reliable.

• Communication problems begin well before marriage. Using the section on "Barriers to Effective Marital Communication" in this chapter, **make an inventory of how you and your partner communicate** now and ask your partner to do the same. Then discuss, openly, how you might resolve problems caused by different styles of communicating. Each of you might also draw up your own marital contract and then compare and discuss your marital expectations.

SUMMARY

1. The most common micro-level reason for marrying is love, but many couples' decisions to marry are affected by such macro-level variables as war, changes in technology, and social movements.

2. Marriage, an important rite of passage into adulthood, is associated with many traditions, rituals, and rules. Many of these rituals reflect historical customs.

3. There are several types of marriage. Most endure despite conflict over such issues as parenting, communication, finances, sex, and religious attitudes.

4. Teenage marriages are typically overwhelmed by problems. Most end in divorce.

5. Interracial marriage, although still fairly infrequent, has become considerably more common since the late 1960s. Despite the verbal acceptance of interracial marriage by many Americans, interracial couples still encounter hostility, prejudice, and discrimination.

6. Marriages change throughout the life cycle. In general, having children decreases marital satisfaction, but satisfaction rises again when grown children leave the home. Throughout the life cycle, families adjust in raising young children, communicating with adolescents, and enjoying the empty-nest and grandparenting stages.

7. Despite the increasing frequency with which both married partners work outside the home, women still bear the major burden of household chores and child care.

8. Men and women often experience marriage differently. Some of these differences reflect the differential status of men and women in society and the way household and child-care tasks are organized.

9. Marriage generally increases a person's chances for good health. Married women, however, are less likely to enjoy good health than are married men.

10. Resource theories are commonly used to explain how power is apportioned and used within a family. Power resides not only in such tangible things as money and property but also in love, in having access to information, and in having particular abilities or talents.

11. Most marriages break down not because of conflict but because couples fail to cope adequately with conflict. Marital counseling may be useful in teaching some partners conflict resolution skills and better communication methods. Self-disclosure is important to effective communication, but couples should recognize that disclosing all their innermost thoughts may be detrimental rather than helpful.

12. Some couples write marriage contracts to avoid unnecessary power struggles and conflict in their marriages.

KEY TERMS

engagement 256
conflict-habituated marriage 260
devitalized marriage 260
passive-congenial marriage 260
vital marriage 260

total marriage 260
utilitarian marriage 260
intrinsic marriage 260
married singles 261
identity bargaining 270

marital burnout 272
power 274
self-disclosure 277

ADDITIONAL READING

LISE FUNDERBURG, *Black, White, Other* (New York: Morrow, 1994). Presents interviews of 65 biracial adults from a variety of professions and socioeconomic classes and discusses how they deal with being biracial.

JOHN GOTTMAN, *Why Marriages Succeed or Fail* (New York: Simon & Schuster, 1994). Based on a study of 2000 couples over 20 years, Gottman offers insights into how partners who fight and disagree can have enduring marriages.

CATHERINE JOHNSON, *Lucky in Love: The Secrets of Happy Couples and How Their Marriages Thrive* (New York: Penguin, 1992) Examines such issues as love, work, marital fighting, and sexual problems.

WALTON R. JOHNSON and D. MICHAEL WARREN, eds., *Inside the Mixed Marriages: Accounts of Changing Attitudes, Patterns, and Perceptions of Cross-Cultural and Interracial Marriages* (Lanham, MD: University Press of America, 1993). Articles written by mixed-marriage (interethnic, interracial) couples.

LAURIE LEVIN and LAURA GOLDEN BELLOTTI, *You Can't Hurry Love: An Intimate Look at First Marriages After 40* (New York: Penguin, 1993). Examines such topics as why some people postpone marriage until their 40s, balancing careers, and becoming parents.

PEPPER SCHWARTZ, *Peer Marriage: How Love Between Equals Really Works* (New York: Free Press, 1994). Argues that couples can develop and maintain egalitarian relationships through close companionship and a collaboration of love and labor.

DEBORAH J. SWISS and JUDITH P. WALKER, *Woman and the Work/Family Dilemma: How Today's Profes-*

sional Women are Finding Solutions (New York: Wiley, 1993). Considers such issues as combining careers and raising children, being superwoman, choosing the right partner, and the myths and realities of merging family and work roles.

RUBIE S. WATSON and PATRICIA BUCKLEY EMBREY, eds., *Marriage and Inequality in Chinese Society* (Berkeley: University of California Press, 1991). The articles in this anthology explore Chinese marriage from 1000 B.C. to the present.

11
To Be or Not to Be a Parent: More Choices, More Constraints

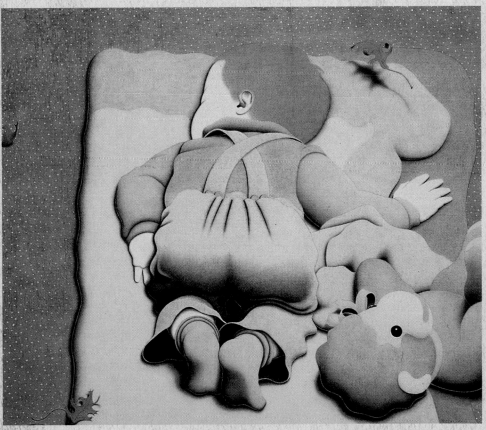

Data Digest

- A husband-wife family in the United States may spend as much as **a third of their annual income** on a child.

- Among U.S. women in 1992, those 25 to 29 years old had the **highest fertility rates.** They had 30 percent of all births, although they represented only 17 percent of all women of childbearing age. Women in their 30s, who represented 37 percent of childbearing women, had 34 percent of all births, and women under 20 or over 40 had the fewest births—8 and 2 percent, respectively.

- Of women with babies at home, **54 percent are in the labor force.**

- Between 1982 and 1992, out-of-wedlock births increased dramatically. Among college graduates and high school students, **out-of-wedlock births approximately doubled,** rising from 3 to 7 percent and from 17 to 33 percent, respectively. Among never-married women 18 to 44 years old, the rate rose from 15 to 24 percent; among women with less than a high school education it increased from 35 to almost 50 percent.

- The **birth rate among U.S. females** age 15 to 19 was 61 per 1000 in 1992. This was considerably higher than in other industrial nations such as the United Kingdom (33), Canada (26), Australia (22), Italy (10), France (9), the Netherlands (8), and Japan (4).

SOURCES: Bachu, 1993; U.S. Department of Agriculture, 1994; Moore, 1995.

A successful and prestigious psychiatrist in his 50s took his 80-year-old mother to a performance of the Metropolitan Opera in New York City. They were making their way out the lobby doors to the physician's Mercedes when his mother turned to him and checked: "Do you have to go to the bathroom, dear?"

As this anecdote suggests, a parent is forever. We may change colleges, buy and sell houses and cars, switch careers, and even marry more than once, but when we become parents we form a lifelong, irreversible relationship. Although today we are freer to decide whether or not we want to have children, these choices are more complicated than ever before.

PARENTHOOD: THE PLUSES AND THE MINUSES

Today we have an array of choices about parenting. Most people can decide whether and when to have children. We can postpone parenthood longer than was ever possible before. We can have children despite physiological barriers that prevent normal conception or birth. And we can decide to remain childless altogether. We cover all these possibilities in this chapter and begin with the choices facing the married-couple family.

Married-Couple Families: Reactions to the First Pregnancy

Most couples have children because they really want them. A couple may discuss family size before getting married, set up a savings account for their children's college education, enroll in a health plan that will cover pregnancy costs, and even buy a house to accommodate the family they plan. Almost 57 percent of all pregnancies in the United States are unintended, however (Herman, 1994).

Whether planned or not, a couple's first pregnancy is an important milestone. The reactions of both partners to the news of pregnancy can vary depending on a number of factors. Cowan and Cowan (1992: 35–48) have found four distinct reaction patterns:

- *Planners* are couples who actively discuss the issue and who make a joint decision to conceive a child. They anticipate an intimate relationship with their children, and they look forward to watching their children grow up. They are typically jubilant about becoming pregnant. As one wife said, "When the doctor called with the news that I was pregnant, I was so excited I wanted to run out in the street and tell everybody I met."

- *Acceptance-of-fate couples* are pleasantly surprised and quietly welcoming of a child even though they have not specifically planned a pregnancy. Often, these couples have engaged "in a partly unconscious or unspoken game of Russian roulette" by using contraceptive methods only sporadically or not at all.

- *Ambivalent couples* have mixed feelings before and after conception and even well into the pregnancy. As one wife noted, "I felt confused, a mixture of up and down, stunned, in a daze." Ambivalent couples decide to have the baby because one partner feels strongly about having a child and the other partner (usually the husband) goes along reluctantly.

- *Yes-no couples* are ambivalent about having children, even late in the pregnancy. For these couples, having a baby is just one of many unresolved issues. Typically, the wife decides to go ahead with the pregnancy regardless of what her husband thinks, and the pregnancy sometimes causes a separation or divorce.

Watching their child learn and grow, loving the child and receiving the child's love and affection are among the pleasures of raising a family that couples most often cite.

The Benefits and Costs of Having Children

Parenthood has both benefits and costs. Some people weigh these issues before deciding to have a baby, but many do not.

Benefits In a seven-nation study, some of the advantages of having children cited by both men and women were affection, close family ties, a feeling of immortality, and a sense of accomplishment. Being cared for during old age was an especially important reason for having children in nonindustrialized countries (Berelson, 1983). When a nationwide U.S. survey (Gallup and Newport, 1990b) asked parents about the "greatest plus, or the thing you gain most, from having children," the most common responses were: Children bring love and affection; it is a pleasure to watch them grow; they bring joy, happiness, and fun; they create a sense of family; and they bring fulfillment and a sense of satisfaction.

Most couples place a high priority on raising healthy and happy children. Even new parents who are still struggling with a colicky infant (whose abdominal distress causes it to cry frequently) delight in the baby's social and physical growth. It is not unusual for parents to say that having children brings a new dimension to their lives that is even more fulfilling than their jobs, their relationships with friends, or their leisure activities. Men, and especially men in higher socioeconomic positions, are often viewed as "stable" and "reliable" when they become "family men." And because many men spend little time in household chores and child rearing (see Chapter 10), they have more to gain economically and socially by having a child (Seccombe, 1991).

Costs Clarence Darrow, the famous attorney, once said that "the first half of our lives is ruined by our parents and the second half by our children." Parenthood is not paradise. To begin with, raising children is expensive. According to the Family Economics Research Group of the U.S. Department of Agriculture, middle-income ($32,000 to $54,100 per year) families spend between 16 and 20 percent of their earnings on a child every year from the child's birth to age 17. Figure 11.1 shows a typical year's expenditures of $6870 for a child one or two years old.

As the costs of having children rise, many people restrict the size of their families. If they

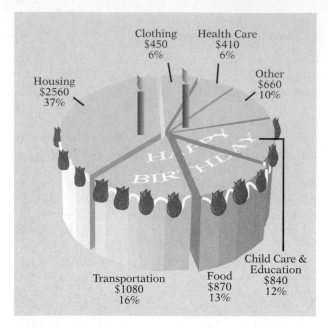

Figure 11.1 *What a Middle-Income Family Spends During the First Two Years of a Child's Life. The Family Economics Research Group of the USDA estimated, in 1993, that families with an average annual income of $42,600 spent a total of $6870 per year on each child under 2, or 16 percent of their earnings. These figures do not include the costs of prenatal care or delivery* (Based on U.S. Department of Agriculture, 1994, p. 16).

do not, the family may experience increased economic stress (Folbre, 1994). Contrary to what many think, it is *not* selfish to consider economic costs before having a child. In fact, it is selfish not to do so because a child raised in a poverty-stricken home may suffer lifelong disadvantages. One problem may be finding suitable housing. Large houses are expensive, and some rental units exclude children or limit their number. Families in the low-income range often have fewer housing options.

Children also carry emotional costs. As you saw in Chapter 10, in several studies couples reported that their happiest time was before the arrival of the first child and after the departure of the last child. As the husband and wife become more focused on the child, interpersonal relationships may deteriorate. Fathers may feel more pressure to succeed on the job and to participate in child care; mothers may report burnout in trying to balance work and home responsibilities (Ventura, 1987).

Pregnancy: Its Joys and Tribulations

Pregnancy can be exciting and a time of joy, particularly when it is planned or welcomed wholeheartedly. For both prospective parents it can deepen feelings of love and intimacy, and it can draw them closer in planning for the child's future. (For a lighthearted but sympathetic look at being the "perfect pregnant father," see Pennebaker, 1994.) At the same time, pregnancy—especially the first pregnancy—can arouse fears, such as having a healthy baby, knowing how to care for the baby properly, and providing for it economically.

The expectant mother may face numerous discomforts. In her first *trimester* (three-month period), she will probably experience frequent nausea, heartburn, insomnia, shortness of breath, painful swelling of the breasts, and fatigue. She may also be constantly concerned over the health of her *fetus* (the term for the unborn child from eight weeks until birth), especially if either she or the baby's father has engaged in any of the high-risk behaviors described in the box "Having Healthy Babies."

Feeling and "hearing" a fetus move can be exciting for all members of a family.

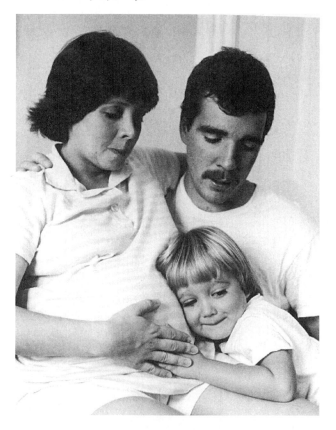

CHOICES

Having Healthy Babies

Most babies are born healthy. If high-risk behaviors are not controlled or eliminated, however, the baby can be unhealthy. Both *smoking* and *poor nutrition* have been linked with the risk of spontaneous abortion, premature birth, low birth weight, and illness in childhood. Low birth rate (which affects 7 percent of all newborns) increases the infant's chances of sickness, retarded growth, respiratory problems, infections, lower intelligence, learning problems, poor hearing and vision, and even death. Even when the mother is a nonsmoker, men who smoke are 60 percent more likely than nonsmokers to have children who develop leukemia and 60 percent more likely to father children with tumors or brain cancer (Alvarado, 1991).

Chronic drinking during pregnancy may lead to **fetal alcohol syndrome (FAS)**, a condition characterized by such physical abnormalities as congenital heart defects and defective joints and, often,

mental retardation. Between one and three of every 1000 newborns suffers from FAS, which can also result in retarded physical and mental growth and lagging motor development. As one report put it: "A pregnant woman . . . can hide her bottles, but in the delivery room she can't hold back the seriously underdeveloped child who often arrives steeped in pungent amniotic fluid that's really an 80-proof marinade" (Leerhsen and Schaefer, 1989: 57).

Mothers who use *illicit drugs* (heroin, cocaine, morphine, and opium) are likely to have infants who are addicted at birth. An estimated 222,000 newborns a year face possible health damage from their mothers' drug abuse (*Baltimore Sun*, 1994g). The baby may experience problems that include prenatal strokes, lasting brain damage, seizures, premature birth, retarded fetal growth, and malformations. Even common prescription drugs or drugs bought off the shelves can affect the fetus. Some of these include antihistamines, some antibiotics, tranquilizers, bar-

biturates, and excessive amounts of vitamins A, D, B_6, and K (Boston Women's Health Collective, 1992).

Problems from *infectious diseases* are numerous. A woman who contracts German measles during the first three months of pregnancy may give birth to a deformed or retarded child. And some research suggests that men exposed to substances such as lead, alcohol, and some anticancer medications, as well as nuclear radiation and poisonous herbicides, could conceive children with serious physical and mental abnormalities (Purvis, 1990).

Sexually transmitted diseases are also dangerous to the unborn child. A woman with gonorrhea may have a child who becomes blind after passing through the infected vagina. Herpes or syphilis can result in a spontaneous abortion, a stillborn birth, or a baby born brain-damaged, deformed, blind, or deaf. Finally, and perhaps most serious of all, a parent with AIDS can pass the deadly disease on to the fetus.

The second trimester can be very exciting because the mother begins to feel daily (and later continuous) movement as the fetus becomes more active. *Sonograms* (pictures taken by means of sound waves) can reveal an image of the baby and even, sometimes, indicate its sex. On the down side, backaches may become a problem, and fatigue tends to set in more quickly. In her third trimester, a woman may start losing interest in sexual activity, which becomes awkward and difficult because of her growing abdomen. The pregnant woman begins to retain water during this period and may feel physically unattractive and clumsy. Once-simple automatic tasks, like getting up from a sofa, turning over in bed, or picking something up from the floor, may now require planning and sometimes even assistance.

Vaginal births may be quick or they may be long and exhausting. A *cesarean section* (surgical removal of the baby from the womb through the abdominal wall) usually results in a lot of pain, gas, and bloody discharge for several weeks after delivery, and infections and fevers are also common.

Parents have more birthing choices than in the past that make delivery more pleasant and family-oriented. For example, many hospitals have established *birthing rooms,* special areas in the hospital that are brightly decorated and hospitable compared to the standard antiseptic hospital decor. The woman usually remains in the same room during both labor and delivery, and family and friends have greater privacy and intimacy in visiting the mother and baby.

Effects of Parenthood on Both Mother and Father

Parenthood may be disappointing at first because it is steeped in romantic misconceptions. And often we expect too much of mothers and ignore fathers.

Mothers and Their Newborns A widespread myth is that there is instant bonding between mother and newborn baby. In reality, some mothers are negative about the appearance of their new babies and may not even be very interested in them initially (Entwisle and Doering, 1981). Even proud fathers have described their newborns as resembling an old, wrinkled football.

Many women experience **postpartum depression**—"the blues" that appear after the birth of the baby. Some of this depression may be chemically caused: The sudden drop in the levels of estrogen and progesterone as the concentrations of these hormones in the placenta are expelled with other afterbirth tissue may have a depressive effect. And the high levels of the body's natural painkillers, called *beta-endorphins,* that the mother's body produces during labor also drop after birth. As a result the mother may "crash," contributing to the postpartum depression.

In addition, some physicians and health practitioners suggest that our society is unrealistic in expecting women to recover six weeks after childbirth. Half of all women experience one or more of a number of physical problems for some 12 months after childbirth: sinus problems, acne, hemorrhoids, vaginal discomfort, pain during intercourse, and difficulty reaching orgasm (Gjerdingen et al., 1993). Finally, newborn infants require frequent feeding and almost constant care, which may contribute to a feeling of fatigue and depression (King et al., 1991).

A major source of anxiety for women is whether they will be good mothers. As we have seen, although marital roles change for both parents, responsibility for caring for the baby tends to fall more heavily on new mothers. As a result, some mothers feel frustrated or stressed out at first, not realizing that such reactions are normal during the early months of parenting (Richardson, 1993).

A New World for Fathers Becoming a father is not something men generally think about years before the event. According to Osherson (1992: 209), "Unlike career achievement or working, which we rehearse and practice for even as children, fatherhood is not a crucial part of our identities until we actually become fathers." Shapiro (1987) interviewed both expectant and recent fathers, ranging in age from 18 to 60, and concluded that men tend to experience several fears and concerns, which they usually keep to themselves. (Those who do talk to their partners about their feelings find that their relationships deepen.)

1. *Queasiness.* The most universal fear is of the birth process itself. The desire to participate does not reduce discomfort with the daunting prospect of seeing blood and other bodily fluids. Men may also worry about helping their partners without fainting or getting sick.

2. *Increased responsibility.* Most men are concerned about the financial responsibilities of parenting. Some take on two jobs, work overtime, or change to better-paying jobs, even though the change may result in more stressful employment conditions. As economic pressure mounts, some men worry whether they will be able to spend as much time with their children as they would like. According to Betcher and Pollack (1993: 140), they begin to realize, as Senator Paul Tsongas once phrased it, that "no man on his death bed ever said 'I wish I had spent more time with my work'."

3. *Uncertain paternity.* More than half of the men in Shapiro's study had some nagging doubts about whether they were really the child's father. For most men, such fears are based on a general insecurity brought on by the enormous responsibility of creating a new life rather than any real concern that the wife has been unfaithful.

4. *Loss of spouse and/or child.* Many of us have heard stories about women who died in childbirth generations ago. Almost every expectant father mentions fear that something will happen to his wife during delivery or that the child will be unhealthy or abnormal in some way.

5. *Feeling vulnerable.* Today's expectant fathers are more likely than are those of previous generations to know divorce—either their parents' or their own—firsthand. Some be-

come concerned whether the marriage can survive the additional stress of a child. Others have affairs because they feel abandoned during the pregnancy, even when they recognize that getting caught could end the marriage.

Like mothers, some fathers worry about being good parents. And even when they feel anxious, many men feel that their task is to be calm, strong, and reassuring (another gender stereotype). Their tendency to keep their worries to themselves may increase the tension and distance between the partners. The couples who fare best are those who can listen sympathetically to each other without expecting immediate solutions (Cowan and Cowan, 1992).

Married couples are not the only people who become parents. Before we discuss other kinds of parents we need to consider some of the widespread societal changes that shape contemporary parenthood.

SOCIETAL CHANGES THAT AFFECT PARENTHOOD

As we discussed in Chapter 1, there have been many changes in U.S. society since the turn of the century. Two changes that have had a major impact on parenthood are the decline in the fertility rate and the rising numbers of women in the labor force.

Fertility Patterns in the United States

One of the measures that demographers use to gauge population growth is the **fertility rate,** or the number of births per year per 1000 women in their childbearing years (ages 15 to 44). In the United States, even with the baby boom, the overall fertility rate decreased from 118 in 1960 to 63 in 1992. As we will see shortly, there is considerable variation among fertility rates for subgroups within the population, such as Latinos and African Americans.

Much of the decrease in the overall fertility rate is attributed to macro-level societal changes. Beginning with the Industrial Revolution in the mid-1800s, entry into paid employment allowed women to postpone motherhood. Improvements in the technology of contraception and greater opportunities in higher education gave women

choices other than the traditional roles of wife and mother. Furthermore, advancements in medicine and hygiene decreased infant mortality rates. Families no longer had to have six children because three or four would die before their first birthday.

About 80 percent of the babies born in the United States in 1992 were white, but fertility rates (numbers of births per 1000 women) vary considerably by race and ethnicity. Within the Hispanic American population, which has the highest fertility rates across all age groups (see Figure 11.2), fertility rates range from a high of 107 for Mexican American women to a low of 50 for Cuban Americans (National Center for Health Statistics, 1991). Some of the reasons for

*Figure 11.2 **Racial, Ethnic, and Age Differences in Fertility Rates, 1992.** Latino women have the highest fertility rates at all ages, but in the prime childbearing years, from 15 to 29, African American women closely match them. Because black women between the ages of 30 and 44 have lower fertility rates than any other group, however, their overall rate is well below that of Latinas and not very different from rates for other groups* (Based on Bachu, 1993, Table A).

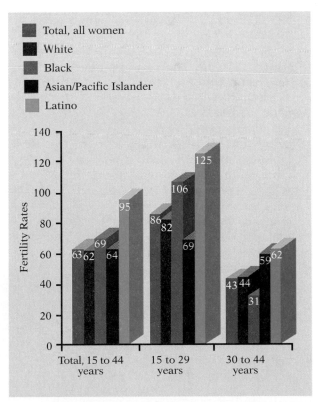

these variations among Spanish-speaking peoples reflect demographic and cultural differences. For example, most Mexican Americans have emigrated from rural areas that value large families. Children perform important economic functions, including contributing to the family income as migrant workers. In contrast, Cuban Americans are predominantly middle class, have low unemployment rates and higher education levels, and do not depend on children to augment family income.

You will recall from Chapter 7 that young African American men and women typically begin sexual activities earlier than do their white counterparts and have more partners. As we will discuss later in this chapter, some African American youth have babies purposely to fill emotional voids in their lives. Compared to white communities, black communities also tend to be more tolerant of out-of-wedlock births and less accepting of abortion. Among other things, the finding that fertility rates of college-educated black women are lower than those of college-educated white women has led some researchers to conclude that the most effective way to reduce teenage pregnancy is to improve teenagers' educational and earning opportunities. If teenage girls expect to work throughout their lives and find work worthwhile, it is argued, they will

delay childbearing (Plotnick, 1993; Robinson and Frank, 1994; Trent, 1994).

Work and Babies

The traditional family is changing to a family in which both parents are employed full time outside the home, creating a family type that has been referred to as **DEWKS, or dual-employed with kids** (Bachu, 1993). As Figure 11.3 shows, the proportion of DEWKS families in the United States has increased from 33 percent of all families in 1976 to almost 50 percent in 1992. In contrast, the proportion of dual-earner spouses with no children has remained fairly constant—about 13 percent since 1976.

In DEWKS families, spouses are likely to be 30 years or older, college graduates, and to hold managerial or professional positions (Bachu, 1993). In contrast, the partners in dual-employed families without children tend to be younger and to hold jobs that require less responsibility. It is likely that DEWKS families evolve when partners are employed by companies that provide child-care services (see also Chapter 12), when they have saved enough money to hire domestic help, or when their jobs provide health benefits that cover pregnancy.

Figure 11.3   The Decline of the Traditional Family.
Between 1976 and 1992, the proportion of DEWKS families increased while the proportion of traditional families decreased about equally. The numbers of childless working couples remained pretty much the same, but the numbers of childless couples in which only the male was employed decreased (Bachu, 1993, Figure 1).

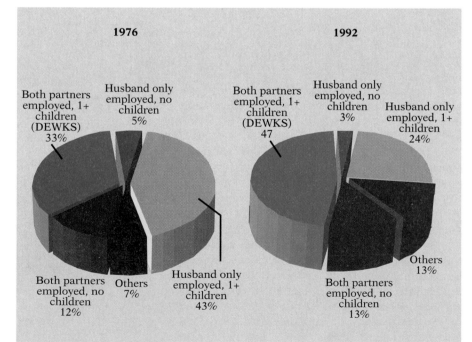

POSTPONING PARENTHOOD

Although it is still relatively uncommon for a woman to have her first child at age 30 or over, the numbers of first-time older mothers are rising. In the early 1970s, only 4 percent of American women having their first babies were 30 or older, but by 1992 the number had increased to 22 percent. Thus, women are beginning to postpone not only marriage (see Chapter 9) but parenthood as well.

Reasons for Postponing Parenthood

Both individual-level and macro-level factors affect the decision to postpone parenthood. As we discussed in Chapter 9, being single has many attractive features, including independence, the opportunity to develop a career, and having more time for fun. Women, especially, have been enjoying the chance to achieve a higher level of education rather than marry right after high school, and they have been choosing to pursue careers because they want to be financially independent. Moreover, the advances in reproductive technology that have made it possible for women to bear children successfully at older ages or to have children in other ways (see the section "Becoming a Parent Despite Infertility") have lessened women's concerns about biological clocks and finding mates.

On the macro level, disturbed by the current high rates of divorce (see Chapter 16), many young couples are apprehensive about their own chances of marital success and thus are postponing parenthood until they feel sure the marriage will work. In addition, economic recessions have encouraged many people to postpone parenthood. As we discussed in Chapter 10, more young adults are living with their parents or returning to the nest because of financial problems. Young couples living with their parents generally don't have the resources to start a family. They may also be reluctant to make already crowded living conditions even worse.

Characteristics of Older Parents

Older mothers tend to feel more self-assured, more ready for responsibility, and better prepared for parenthood than younger women; the latter sometimes feel trapped by having a baby at a young age (Langer, 1985). Compared to younger mothers, older mothers are more likely to be white, married, and highly educated. Moreover, they tend to work in professional occupations and to have high family incomes (Bachu, 1993).

There are some distinct drawbacks in deferred parenthood, however. The older people are, the more difficult it is to find the energy and patience required to care for children. Some women who have waited to have children find that it is too late to have as many children as they wished. Mature mothers, and especially those who have risen to powerful but demanding executive positions, may feel especially guilty about splitting their time between their families and their employers and "cheating" both.

Men who postpone parenthood usually enjoy more advantages and have fewer constraints than women. For one thing, most men do not face gender discrimination in the workplace, they earn higher salaries, and they have better health benefits. Thus, they are less likely to worry about not having the resources to raise children later in life. With fewer economic concerns, men remarry more often and sometimes, after a divorce, support children from two families. Older fathers may have less energy to play with their children. Because, however, their careers are more established, they may have more flexibility to spend their nonwork hours and weekends with their families.

INVOLUNTARY CHILDLESSNESS

Infertility is generally defined as the inability to conceive a baby after 12 months of unprotected sex. According to some estimates, infertility affects about 15 percent of all couples of reproductive age. The incidence of infertility increases, however, as childbearing is delayed. For example, the rate of infertility for couples between 30 and 34 years of age is more than 50 percent greater than the rate for those between 25 and 29 (Mosher and Pratt, 1991).

Infertility rates have remained fairly stable since the mid-1960s, but because more medical help is available, more couples are trying to circumvent this problem. Since 1968 the demand for treatment of infertility has more than tripled: Every year more than a million American couples seek medical assistance. As a result, combating infertility has become a multi-billion-dollar industry (Schwartz, 1993). Although some large employers offer medical benefits for the treatment of infertility, in most cases the couple must pay the costs (DeWitt, 1993).

Reasons for Infertility

Although infertility is attributable about equally to problems in males and females—each sex accounts for about 40 percent of cases and both together for about 20 percent—until recently, most research on infertility focused on women (Halpern, 1989). For years it was believed that the major reason for female infertility was aging. Although it is true that reproductive organs age faster than other parts of the human body, the notion that infertility is a predictable "career woman's curse" is simplistic at best and stereotypical at worst.

The two major causes of female infertility are failure to ovulate and blockage of the *fallopian tubes,* which each month carry the egg, whether or not it has been fertilized by male sperm, from the ovaries to the uterus. A woman's failure to *ovulate,* or to produce a viable egg each month, may have a number of causes, among them poor nutrition, chronic illness, and drug abuse. Rarely, the lack of ovulation may be attributed to psychological stress (Masters et al., 1992).

The fallopian tubes can be blocked by scarring caused by **pelvic inflammatory disease (PID),** an infection of the uterus that spreads to the tubes as well as to the ovaries and surrounding tissues. PID, in turn, is often caused by sexually transmitted diseases like chlamydia (see Chapter 7 and Appendix D for more information about sexually transmitted diseases). **Chlamydia,** a bacterial infection often referred to as "the silent epidemic" because it exhibits no symptoms in 75 percent of women and 33 percent of men, is a rapidly rising cause of PID today. According to some authorities, an average of 20 to 40 percent of all people tested for STDs at clinics are found to have chlamydial infections (Masters et al., 1992). Once diagnosed, this infection is easily cured with antibiotics.

Another leading cause of infertility in women over 25 years of age is **endometriosis,** in which the tissue that forms in the *endometrium* (the lining of the uterus) spreads outside the womb and attaches itself to other pelvic organs, such as the ovaries or the fallopian tubes. Endometriosis, caused by as yet unknown factors, can cause PID, uterine tumors, and blockage of the opening to the uterus. Table 11.1 summarizes the major reasons for infertility in women.

Table 11.1
Some Possible Causes of Female Infertility

Failure to ovulate, caused by poor nutrition, drug abuse, chronic illness, or, rarely, psychological stress

Blockage of the fallopian tubes, caused by pelvic inflammatory disease that results from infection with sexually transmitted bacteria or microorganisms

Endometriosis, which may cause infertility by blockage of the fallopian tubes by uterine tissue that migrates outside the uterus

Scarring, adhesions, and cysts around the ovaries and fallopian tubes that may be caused by sexually transmitted diseases (STDs) and pelvic inflammatory disease (PID)

Cervical mucus (from the *cervix,* the lower portion of the uterus) that is too thick for sperm to penetrate or that has an acid/alkaline balance harmful to sperm

Excessive exercise or rapid weight loss that may interfere with the production of reproductive hormones due to the loss of body fat

The regular use of douches and vaginal deodorants that may contain chemicals that either kill sperm or inhibit their movement

The rising incidence of infertility reflects not only the problems we have discussed with regard to women but the fact that since the 1930s male infertility, whose primary cause is a low sperm count, has become increasingly common. In fact, recent research has revealed that since 1938, sperm counts of men in the United States and 20 other countries have plunged by an average of 50 percent (Begley and Glick, 1994).

Chemical pollutants are believed to play a major role in male infertility. Because for years men have been more likely than women to work in environments in which they come in contact with toxic chemicals or in which they are exposed to other environmentally hazardous conditions, their risks of infertility from these sources are high. Some substances and conditions that either have been found to affect male reproductive capacity or that are suspected of doing so are described in Table 11.2.

Other causes of low sperm counts include the following: injury to the testicles, or scrotum; infections such as mumps in postchildhood years; testicular varicose veins; undescended testes (the testes in the male fetus normally descend from the abdominal cavity into the scrotum in about the eighth month of prenatal development); endocrine disorders; and excessive consumption of alcohol, tobacco, marijuana,

Table 11.2 _____

Some Chemical and Environmental Factors in Male Infertility

RISK FACTORS	EFFECTS
Lead used in making storage batteries and paints	Fewer sperm, sperm that move more slowly than normal, and more abnormally shaped sperm
Ionizing and non-ionizing radiation: former found in nuclear plants and medical facilities; latter in high-voltage switchyards and communications facilities	Possible damage to sperm cells and lowered fertility
Anesthetic gases	Unexposed female partners may have higher than normal number of miscarriages
Vinyl chloride used in plastic manufacturing	Unexposed female partners may have more miscarriages and stillbirths
Pesticides like kepone, and the carbon disulfide used in the manufacture of viscose rayon and as a fumigant	Possible loss of sex drive, impotence, abnormal sperm, lowered sperm count
Heat stress found in foundries, smelters, bakeries, and farm work	Lowered sperm counts and sterility
Estrogen used in manufacture of oral contraceptives	Possible loss of sex drive, abnormal sperm, lowered sperm counts
Methylene chloride used as a solvent in paint strippers	Possible very low sperm counts and shrunken testicles
EDB (ethylene dibromide) used as an ingredient in leaded gasoline and as a fumigant of tropical fruit for export	Possible lower sperm count and decreased fertility in wives of workers

SOURCE: Based on Kenen, 1993: 40-41.

narcotic drugs, or even some prescription medications. There is some evidence that long-distance bicycle riding or tight-fitting underwear can lower sperm counts, and prolonged and frequent use of saunas, hot tubs, and steam baths may also have a negative effect because sperm production is sensitive to temperature (Masters et al., 1992). Male infertility can also result from such problems as an inability to ejaculate, ejaculation only outside the vagina, or inability to achieve or maintain an erection (see Chapter 7).

Finally, approximately 20 percent of infertile couples are diagnosed as having *idiopathic infertility*. In plain language, this means that doctors simply do not know what is wrong.

Reactions to Infertility

People respond to their infertility in a number of ways. Many women, concerned that people will see them in a new and damaging light, engage in some sort of "information management." They may avoid the topic whenever possible, or they may attribute the problem to a disease like diabetes or kidney trouble, taking the focus off specific reproductive disorders. On the other hand, because male infertility may be considered a defect in one's masculinity, women will often accept the responsibility for infertility themselves:

When I tell them we can't have children, I generally try to leave the impression that it's me. I may mutter "tubes you know" or "faulty plumbing." I think it's easier for me to go with that than to deal with the idea that maybe my husband "can't get it up" (Miall, 1986: 36).

Still other women reveal their infertility because they fear they will be considered self-centered for not having children:

I know at one point I overheard someone saying, "Oh, they're too selfish, they're too interested in going on fancy holidays. Material things, that's why they're not having children." It was so untrue and it hurt (Miall, 1986: 37).

Some infertile couples enjoy vicarious parenthood through contact with the children of relatives and friends. Others become increasingly involved in work-related activities, and in some cases even begin to regard their childlessness as advantageous. Some couples accept infertility as a fact of life and remain childless. A much larger group, however, try to adopt a baby or turn to the many new reproduction technologies.

BECOMING A PARENT DESPITE INFERTILITY

The traditional solution to infertility was adoption. Increasingly, however, as many unwed mothers have begun to keep their babies, there has been a decrease in the number of normal, healthy infants available for adoption. Alternatively, many infertile couples are now exploring the various solutions that modern reproduction technology offers—artificial insemination, in vitro fertilization, embryo transplants, and surrogacy. We look first at the adoption alternative and then at some of the high-tech solutions.

Adoption–The Traditional Solution to Infertility

Adoption was typically the solution for childless couples; 80 percent of U.S. babies born out of wedlock were once given up for adoption. Today, however, this rate has dropped to about 2 or 3 percent (*U.S. News and World Report*, 1994). As we have seen, being a single, unmarried parent no longer bears the stigma it used to, and many unwed mothers are deciding to keep their babies. Although there are still tens of thousands of children available for adoption, there is a catch. According to estimates by the National Committee for Adoption, a minimum of 40,000 children who need homes every year are hard to place because they are perceived as "unsuitable"—they are sick, physically handicapped, emotionally disturbed, nonwhite, or "too old." And, as we will see shortly, advances in high-tech reproduction methods have encouraged many couples to try to have a baby on their own.

Emerging Controversial Issues When adoptions do take place today, they sometimes raise new issues. One such issue that has gained recent prominence is the nature and extent of the *rights of biological fathers*. For years, fathers of out-of-wedlock children were rarely involved in adoptions. In 1993, however, in a highly publicized case, a child given up for adoption by her biological mother was returned to her mother and her biological father when the Iowa courts ruled favorably on a custody suit brought by the father. Three years earlier, "Baby Jessica's" mother had agreed to let a couple in Michigan adopt her, but when the mother told her ex-boyfriend, the child's biological father, about the adoption, he decided to go to court and won on the grounds that under Iowa law, a father must consent to an adoption. The media showed "a crying toddler, strapped in a car seat en route to the biological parents she had never known" (LoLordo, 1993: 12A), but six months later, Jessica (renamed Anna) seemed happy with her newly married biological parents (Ingrassia and Springen, 1994).

In a somewhat similar case in 1994, the Illinois Supreme Court ruled that a three-year-old boy known as "Baby Richard" be returned to his biological parents. In this case, the biological father had been told by his former fiancée that the baby had died when he was on a trip to his native country. When he learned that the baby was alive and had been placed for adoption, however, the father began legal action to stop the proceeding and married the baby's biological mother (Walsh, 1994). In 1995 the U.S. Supreme Court refused to hear the "Baby Richard" case but gave no reason for its decision (Denniston, 1995).

Both of these cases expanded the rights of biological fathers in contested adoptions. They also raised concern among advocates of adoption that such rulings may undermine the legitimacy of the adoption system (Ingrassia and Springen, 1993). As a result, many groups have argued that to prevent such battles, uniform adoption laws should be implemented in all 50 states.

Another controversial issue is *transracial adoptions*. Advocates for transracial adoption claim that many African-American or biracial children—especially those with emotional or physical handicaps—would remain in foster homes until age 18 if they were not adopted by white families. And there is some evidence that when white adoptive families encourage children's participation in multicultural and multiracial activities, children in transracial adoptions have done well (Bagley, 1993; Hayes, 1993). If anything, Simon (1993) says, some black adoptees complain that their white parents tried too hard to educate them about their heritage, turning dinner conversations into lectures on black history.

On the other hand, the National Association of Black Social Workers has strongly opposed transracial adoptions:

When children are removed from their ethnic environment, they tend to associate with their ethnicity negatively, because they are alienated from their culture of origin. Positive role models and orientations about the child's ethnicity may help, but they do not adequately address the loss of being dislodged from the ethnic community (Kissman and Allen, 1993: 93).

A third controversial issue is open adoption. **Open adoption** refers to the practice of sharing information and contact between biological and adoptive parents both during the adoption process and during the child's life. The open adoption movement began in the 1960s when adoptees sought to abolish the secrecy surrounding their sealed adoption records. Since then, the movement has been supported by numerous television shows (such as "Unsolved Mysteries" and almost all of the talk shows) that revel in reuniting adopted children with their biological parents.

The general public has mixed feelings, however. For example, in a telephone survey of 640 randomly selected adults, Rompf (1993) found that only 52 percent either strongly or somewhat approved of open adoptions. And in a survey of 1268 adoptive parents in California, Berry (1993) found "considerable variation" in adoptive parents' willingness to be contacted by biological parents. The most guarded were adoptive parents of children who either were very young or who came from abusive backgrounds. Although open adoptions may become standard practice in the future, some practitioners recommend proceeding cautiously to safeguard the rights of adoptive parents and those of their children (see Etter, 1993).

International Adoptions Because the waiting period required to adopt a child from overseas is only one or two years, as opposed to the seven to ten years required in the United States, Ameri-

cans have increasingly turned to international adoptions. In 1993, over 7000 children were adopted from abroad compared to about 1200 children adopted in North America. Most children adopted from overseas have come from developing countries in Asia, South America, and Central America. Two countries that have provided many adoptees are Mexico and South Korea, and adoptions by U.S. citizens in Russia and Ukraine rose from 402 in 1992 to over 1000 in 1993 (Brink, 1994; Tinsley, 1993). Because there are no international adoption standards, however, prospective parents face many obstacles in the adoption process (see the box "The Politics of International Adoptions").

Benefits and Limitations of Adoption National data show that, compared to children raised by never-married mothers, adopted children are economically advantaged (Bachrach et al., 1990). In addition, adopted children in single-parent homes typically experience fewer emotional and behavioral problems than those in two-parent homes, and single-parent families are more likely than two-parent families to have a positive evaluation of the adoption (Groze and Rosenthal, 1991). Most single parents are women

The frustrations and risks of adopting a child, whether from one's own country or from abroad, can be great, but the gratification, especially for those who cannot conceive and bear their own children, can be even greater.

The Politics of International Adoptions

There are several risks in adopting a baby from a foreign country. Among these are the possibility that the child was obtained illegally by the agency handling the adoption; the presence in the child of illnesses that may range from mild to life-threatening; and the necessity to wade through endless bureaucratic red tape to complete the adoption process.

Mexican organizations estimate that a number of children destined for adoption by U.S. parents come from among the 500 to 20,000 children of lower socioeconomic classes that are kidnapped every year (Scott, 1994). South Korea was the source of 62 percent of the children Americans adopted from overseas in 1986, but in 1992 this percentage dropped to 27 because of media criticism that South Koreans were exporting their children. Seoul now tries harder to place children internally (Tinsley, 1993). When CBS's "60 Minutes" aired a segment on Romania's black-market babies in April 1991, Romania promptly closed its doors to overseas adoptions (Campbell, 1993).

In some countries, such as Russia, agencies will say that a child's health is fine, but American parents often find that their adopted child has one of a wide range of illnesses. These include hepatitis B, tuberculosis, intestinal parasites, congenital heart defects, brain damage, and "mysterious maladies" that U.S. physicians find difficult to diagnose (Brink, 1994).

Even though there are thousands of orphans in Eastern Europe, they are not easy to adopt. Some couples describe a "nightmarish journey through the minefield of international adoption" that includes endless bureaucratic obstacles and legal systems that are hostile to intercountry adoptions. Agencies may "forget" about a promised adoption because of a last-minute higher offer from a flourishing black-market baby industry. In addition, in some cases prospective parents have arrived in some East European countries only to find that adoption and immigration policies have been changed while they were en route. Prospective parents may have to pay exorbitant bribes, called "contributions," to private agencies, religious groups, and government offices, both in the United States and abroad, that profit from adoptions. In some cases, attorneys or adoption agencies in the United States have collected up to $20,000 from parents, promising them, for example, a healthy baby from Eastern Europe but have never delivered (Bogert, 1994; Tousignant, 1994; Borgman, 1995).

who tend to adopt girls or older, nonwhite, or mentally retarded children. Because only two states, Florida and New Hampshire, have laws expressly barring homosexuals from adopting children, gay men and lesbians are increasingly adopting babies and older children (Selby, 1995).

Some of the deterrents to adoption include societal beliefs that love and bonding in adoption are second-best, that adoptive parents are simply not "real parents," and that adopted children are second-rate because of their unknown genetic past. In addition, adoptive parents sometimes worry that a teenage girl who has not had medical care during the pregnancy and who may have poor nutritional habits may deliver a baby who may later have physical problems (Miall, 1987).

Assisted Reproductive Techniques

With the growth of genetic research, our ability to alter the course of nature has expanded greatly. The infertile couple now has many more options for having a child than before, although we will see that many assisted reproductive techniques are risky and success rates are not high. In this section we will also see that these new technologies have generated some difficult questions. Some are medical, involving the health of mother and baby. Some are legal, involving issues of custody and inheritance. And some are ethical, concerning such issues as parents' and scientists' right to "manufacture" babies, parents' right to reject imperfect fetuses, and the rights of both parents and embryos. For example, suppose both parents of a fertilized egg that has been frozen and held for future use die. Who is responsible for the frozen embryo? Should it be destroyed because the parents are dead? Given to relatives? Placed for adoption? Turned over to doctors for medical research?

As you consider each of the techniques and technologies described, ask yourself such questions as the following: Might the new science lead to the creation of a master race of children with only the most desirable traits? If so, is this something we want? Is it ethical to create our children by science rather than by nature? On the other hand, is it ethical to have a child who will be little more than a vegetable because it is born without a brain, for example? (For discussions of the ethics of reproductive technology, see, for example, Corea, 1985, and Robertson, 1994).

Artificial Insemination Artificial insemination is a medical procedure in which semen is introduced artificially into the vagina or uterus about the time of ovulation. The semen, taken from the woman's husband or from a donor, may be fresh or it may have been frozen. Artificial insemination was first performed successfully in the 1790s and was followed by a normal pregnancy and birth (Matanoski, 1994). In 1989 artificial insemination produced 65,000 births in the United States alone (Halpern, 1989). Some estimates suggest that 1.5 million Americans will be born through artificial insemination by the year 2000 (Bagne, 1983).

Artificial insemination is the most common treatment for male infertility, but it has also been used in cases where husbands feared transmitting a genetic disease. The procedure can be used to avoid such inherited disorders as diabetes, cystic fibrosis, and muscular dystrophy in one's children. In addition, artificial insemination has been used to preserve the sperm of young men who are likely to be exposed to chemical and radioactive mutagens in the environment and the workplace so that they will still be able to father a child in the future (Bagne, 1983).

For single women, artificial insemination offers a means of having children without waiting for Mr. Right. It offers lesbians a way of conceiving a child without having to be sexually intimate with a man. And for men going off to war, it offers an unusual kind of insurance: When the Persian Gulf War began in 1991, a sperm bank in California received over 300 calls from servicemen and their wives or girlfriends. According to one physician, men who decided to bank their sperm had a sense of some control: "They've managed to kind of defy their own mortality by leaving something of themselves behind that will live" (Ames et al., 1991). Some couples prefer artificial insemination to adoption because the mothers want to experience a pregnancy and birth or one or both parents want to contribute to the child's biological/genetic makeup (Daniels, 1994).

Artificial insemination has its drawbacks as well. Because the identity of the donor is almost always concealed and one donor may be used for as many as 15 pregnancies, inadvertent inbreeding may result. That is, two people might meet and mate not knowing that they share the same genetic father. Although such cases may be rare, a few years ago a prominent geneticist in the Washington, D.C., area used his own sperm to impregnate women who went to him for treatment of fertility problems. This man fathered at least 70 children without the mothers' knowledge or consent (Howe, 1991). Moreover, sperm banks that freeze sperm for later use can make mistakes. In 1990, for example, a Manhattan sperm bank was sued after a white couple gave birth to a black baby.

There are also emotional problems associated with artificial insemination. For example, if a couple divorce, the father may distance himself from a child he never considered his own, threaten disclosure, or withhold child-support payments (Baran and Pannor, 1989). Furthermore, although many lesbians purposely distance themselves from information about the donor-fathers of their children, the children themselves may eventually seek information about their biological fathers.

Disclosure issues will probably increase in the future. For example, a young woman, age 19, who was conceived by donor insemination feels frustrated because she has no idea of her father's biological roots:

With no records available, half my heritage is erased. I'll never know whose eyes I have inherited. I've searched family photo albums to no avail. . . . So, to couples seeking babies this way, I propose that you find out who your donors are, keep records and let your children know where they came from. And to a possibly brown-haired man who attended University of Tennessee Medical School in 1974 and made a donation on my mother's behalf, I thank you for the gift of life. I think I have your eyes, your jaw and your personality. I just wish I could find out for sure (Brown, 1994:12).

In Vitro Fertilization In vitro fertilization (IVF) involves surgically removing eggs from a woman's ovaries, fertilizing them in a petri dish (a specially shaped glass container) with sperm from her husband or another donor, and then reimplanting the fertilized eggs in her uterus. Louise

Brown, the first in vitro baby (*in vitro* is Latin for "in glass") was born in England in 1978. Since then more than 300 clinics have opened in the United States, and thousands of children worldwide owe their births to this procedure. More than one egg is usually implanted to increase the chances of success, and nearly half of all women using in vitro procedures have multiple births. Multiple birth babies are ten times more likely than single babies to be born prematurely and at low birth weight with poorly developed organs. This subjects them to medical risks that range from lung disease and brain damage to infant death (Brownlee et al., 1994; Bor, 1995).

There have been two recent variations in this procedure. To increase the chances that the fertilized egg will implant in the uterine wall, many doctors are now inserting both egg and sperm into the fallopian tube, a procedure known as **gamete intrafallopian transfer (GIFT).** Fertilization then takes place in the fallopian tube and the egg moves into the uterus. A woman must have at least one normal fallopian tube to be a candidate for GIFT, and the procedure has a somewhat higher success rate than does IVF.

In another variation, called **zygote intrafallopian transfer (ZIFT)**, the wife's eggs are fertilized by her husband's sperm in vitro and are then transferred to the fallopian tube. In other words, ZIFT combines IVF with GIFT. The advantage is that the physician can be certain that fertilization has occurred. If it has not, the couple can then decide if they want to try donor insemination.

Although IVF is a miracle come true for many couples, it has some drawbacks. It is expensive and time-consuming, and it can be emotionally exhausting. Halpern (1989: 148) describes women as "hostages" to the process:

She will have her blood drawn on selected days until the twelfth day of the treatment cycle. She will be injected at least once—and often twice—a day with powerful hormones, before and after she ovulates, to stimulate egg production and help support early pregnancy. She will be subject to regular ultrasound examinations. She will probably lose time from work, even if her physician is near her workplace. If she chooses to venture farther afield, to one of the nationally known programs, she will have to live out of a suitcase, away from friends, workmates, and, often, family, until the sixteenth day of the cycle, when the fertilized eggs are transferred to the uterus.

Furthermore, success rates vary widely across clinics. Some clinics have never had a successful pregnancy resulting in a live birth. Others report rates of live deliveries ranging from 3 to 15 percent (after six consecutive attempts in the latter case). Some experts believe that eventually about half of couples will be successful within the first four attempts. Because repeated attempts are necessary, however, and each treatment can cost up to $15,000, in vitro fertilization is an expensive proposition (Brownlee et al., 1994).

Embryo Transplants For about $10,000 for each attempt, a fertilized egg from a woman donor can be implanted into an infertile woman. The donor is paid an average of $2000 each time her eggs are removed. This technology is called **embryo transplant** (*embryo* is the term for the developing organism up to the eighth week of pregnancy). Donating eggs is much more difficult than donating sperm. A woman donor must undergo weeks of daily drug injections before the invasive medical procedure to extract the eggs. Donors must have a high degree of commitment and must be willing to undergo considerable risk to their own health. Moreover, the donation of eggs is far less successful than sperm donation; embryo transplant leads to the birth of a child in only about 30 percent of cases.

Despite these difficulties and the expense, egg donation is a growing enterprise that is practiced at nearly 50 clinics nationwide (Squires, 1991). Computer programs match the donors and recipients in terms of race, blood type, and hair and eye color. Recently, even women who have gone through menopause have become pregnant using younger women's donated eggs that are fertilized with sperm from the older women's husbands or from other donors (see the box "Motherhood after Menopause?"). This is possible because although a woman's ovaries shrivel up after menopause, her other reproductive organs remain viable.

Embryo transplants raise some sticky questions: The resulting children are genetically unrelated to the mothers who bear them. Suppose the birth mother later decides that she does not want the child. Is the biological mother then responsible for it? Further, although the risk is less than in artificial insemination, embryo transplant does carry the possibility that genetically related children might one day marry each other.

CHANGES

Motherhood After Menopause?

The Census Bureau and the National Center for Health Statistics define the childbearing years as between 15 and 44, but in the last few years, several women have had children after menopause:

❑ In 1992, a 53-year-old woman in California gave birth to a son after five embryos from younger women were fertilized and implanted.

❑ In 1994, a 59-year-old British woman who was artificially impregnated at a clinic in Italy gave birth to twins.

❑ In 1994, a 62-year-old Italian woman gave birth to a healthy boy after being implanted with a donated egg fertilized with her husband's sperm.

Public reaction to these events was mixed. Some people were delighted that older women have more options; others felt childbearing at such late ages is selfish because both parents might die while the child is very young (Capron, 1994). In 1994, the French government passed a law barring postmenopausal women from artificial impregnation because it is "both immoral and dangerous for older women to be implanted with test-tube embryos" (*Newsweek*, 1994). (Note that no government has required men over age 50 to have vasectomies.) In 1995 Italy's national association of physicians voted to deny artificial insemination to lesbians, single women, and women over 50. They also banned surrogate motherhood and the use of frozen sperm of dead donors for artificial insemination and prohibited married couples from seeking "designer babies" by choosing sperm based on a donor's physical attributes or social status.

Crass as it may sound, there is also a question of ownership of the embryos. In 1989, a Tennessee couple that was divorcing went through a heated custody battle over seven frozen embryos that had been produced through IVF. The judge awarded the embryos to the woman. A few years later, however, the Tennessee Supreme Court ruled that the husband could prevent his ex-wife from using the embryos because he has the right to avoid procreation.

Surrogacy Surrogacy has a long history. In the Book of Genesis, Abraham's barren wife, Sarah, sends her husband to "lie with" the slave girl Hagar, hoping to "found a family." Jacob's wife, Rachel, makes a similar arrangement with her slave girl, Billah, "so that she may bear sons to be laid upon my knees" (Institute for Philosophy and Public Policy, 1989: 1). Today surrogacy is becoming quite common; by 1990 2000 births each year were attributed to surrogacy (Kantrowitz et al., 1990).

In **surrogacy,** a woman who is capable of carrying a pregnancy to term serves as a surrogate mother for a woman who cannot bear children. Commonly, the surrogate is artificially inseminated with the sperm of the infertile woman's husband, and if she conceives, she carries the child to term. In some cases, the infertile couple's egg and sperm are brought together in vitro; and the resulting embryo is implanted in a surrogate who carries the child for them. Although the typical surrogate mother is 25 years old, married, and a high school graduate who agrees to surrogacy for a fee, some surrogates are family members. In 1991, for example, a 42-year-old woman in South Dakota served as a surrogate for her 22-year-old daughter who was born without a uterus. Eggs were removed from the daughter's ovaries, fertilized with her husband's sperm, and implanted in the mother's womb. When the mother gave birth to healthy twins she became the first grandmother to give birth to her own grandchildren. And in 1992 a woman in Buffalo, New York, underwent four implants of fertilized eggs from her son and daughter-in-law, ultimately giving birth to her grandson. As you can see, surrogacy raises complicated questions about kinship.

One of the risks associated with surrogacy is that a surrogate mother might refuse to give up the baby she bears. In 1987, Mary Beth Whitehead delivered "Baby M," whom she bore after being impregnated through artificial insemination by William Stern. Stern and his wife, who could not bear a child, had hired Whitehead as a surrogate. Whitehead, however, refused to give up the baby girl after birth. In the court battles that followed she lost custody but was later granted visitation rights. In 1990, a surrogate mother in Garden Grove, California, also refused to give up custody of a baby boy who had been conceived in a petri dish using the biological parents' sperm and egg. Even though she was not genetically related to the baby, the surrogate mother said she had become emotionally attached to the fetus by the third month of pregnancy. A superior court judge denied her both custody and visitation rights (Walker, 1990).

Many people who object to surrogacy argue that it exploits poor women in that rich couples can "rent a womb." According to some, Mary Beth Whitehead's contract with William Stern was extremely disadvantageous to her. She was obliged to assume all risks, including death and postpartum complications, and was offered no compensation in case of miscarriage and only $1000 if Stern demanded an abortion (Whitehead and Schwartz-Nobel, 1989). The typical surrogate mother is paid about $10,000 for her services. If we assume a month for the prepregnancy medical treatment and nine months for the pregnancy, a woman is paid about $1.40 per hour. The surrogate also risks pain, disease, surgery, and even death. Furthermore, the natural father is not contractually obligated to accept custody of a "defective" baby (Chesler, 1988).

Genetic Engineering: Its Benefits and Risks

Genetic research and biotechnology have been a blessing for many couples, but some wonder if scientists are going too far (see the box "So What's Next? Pregnant Men?"). Although many people in the United States and other countries support in vitro fertilization, they also worry that genetic manipulation for a presumably good purpose could lead to interfering with nature in other ways that would be unethical and detrimental to society (Macer, 1994).

Consider the implications of prenatal testing designed to detect genetic disorders and biochemical abnormalities in the fetus. Two procedures that have become fairly common are amniocentesis and chorionic villus sampling. In **amniocentesis,** performed during the twentieth week of pregnancy, a needle is inserted through

---

CHANGES

So What's Next? Pregnant Men?

In the movie *Junior,* a scientist (played by Arnold Schwarzenegger) loses funding for his research and implants a fertilized egg in his own body to test a wonder drug that ensures healthy pregnancies. According to Dick Teresi (1994: 54–55), we have all the technology we need right now to make a man pregnant.

Of course, there are some minor problems. Men don't produce the appropriate hormones. Men don't have ovaries and thus don't produce eggs. Men don't have wombs. However, hormones can be supplied by injection. In the first "test-tube" pregnancy, an egg was extracted from the mother and fertilized with the father's sperm

in vitro, or in a laboratory dish, inserted back into the mother, and carried to term. And as for wombs, they may not be totally necessary. Abdominal pregnancies—outside the womb—are rare, but they do happen about once in every 10,000 pregnancies.

An abdominal pregnancy may occur when the placenta, which is produced partly by the fetus, attaches to something other than the womb. In August 1979, for example, George Poretta attempted to perform an appendectomy on a Michigan woman suffering from stomach cramps. "I opened her up expecting to find an appendix," Poretta said, "and there was this tiny foot." The baby, Joseph Thomas Cwik, weighed 3 pounds 5 ounces.

Both male and female abdomens offer a similar environment, including a membrane called the *omentum* that encloses abdominal organs and in which, theoretically, a fertilized egg could implant. Thus, Teresi suggests, a male pregnancy could be produced by fertilizing an egg in vitro and inserting the developing embryo through a small incision in the abdominal cavity. Luck would be required for the fertilized egg to implant in the omentum (a little bit of luck is needed even in normal pregnancies), but if it did and the placenta partly developed from the embryo, pregnancy could be under way. An endocrinologist could administer hormones to keep gestation going. Finally, the baby would be delivered via laparotomy, not unlike a cesarean section. A sci-fi dream? We'll have to wait and see!

the abdomen into the amniotic sac, and the fluid withdrawn is analyzed for such abnormalities as Down syndrome and spina bifida (an abnormal opening along the spine). The same information can be produced at ten weeks by **chorionic villi sampling (CV)**, in which a catheter inserted through the vagina is used to remove some of the villi, or protrusions from the chorion that surrounds the amniotic sac. The chief advantage of detecting abnormalities earlier is that if parents decide on an abortion, a simpler technique can be utilized. Both these tests have risks such as spontaneous abortions and possible deformities, however (Boodman, 1992). Through a newer procedure, called *BABI (blastomere analysis before implantation)*, some couples have chosen to conceive several embryos in test tubes, keeping only the embryo that has no known defects.

Both the advent of BABI and the 1993 decision of Congress to lift the ban on embryo development research (studying embryos outside of the womb to learn more about various diseases) have engendered controversy. Both technologies risk the destruction of embryos, an act that some people regard as abortion (which we discuss later in this chapter) and that some critics find unethical (Cowley et al., 1993; Zapler, 1995).

The option to choose a child's sex also raises ethical questions. If it is possible, as some reproductive physiologists claim, to influence the sex of a fetus by inseminating the mother with the father's Y chromosome (which determines the boy's sex) or the father's X chromosome (which determines the girl's sex), it is also possible that the population of males will increase because most societies devalue females (Busch, 1993; see also Chapter 4).

Finally, a recent advance has made it theoretically possible to help infertile women to conceive by using eggs or ovarian tissue from aborted fetuses or cadavers. British scientists who have successfully transplanted ovaries in mice and sheep believe the procedure could be carried out in humans. Thus, egg-bearing ovarian tissue from aborted fetuses might be transplanted into infertile women, or eggs or ovaries from women who have died suddenly could also be transplanted. Many infertile couples applaud such technological progress, but others condemn such research as bizarre or even ghoulish. As Robinson (1994) points out, some complicated interpersonal relationships might ensue from such activity. For example, how would you ex-plain to your child that his or her biological mother had never even been born or had died before she could ever conceive?

HAVING CHILDREN OUTSIDE OF MARRIAGE

Although having children out of wedlock is not a recent phenomenon (see Chapter 3), the percentages of such births have increased dramatically (see Data Digest). By 1993, over a third of all children under 18 were living with a never-married parent, a more than sevenfold increase since 1960 (see Chapter 3).

Why have out-of-wedlock births increased? First, as we said earlier, such births have become more acceptable. And, although early sexual activity is becoming more widespread, the age at which people settle down to jobs and marriage has risen. Thus, during the period of 5, 10, or even 15 years between the beginning of sexual activity and marriage, more out-of-wedlock births occur (Taylor, 1991a). In addition, the increasing numbers of women who are postponing marriage because of better educational and employment opportunities (Chapter 9) are not necessarily postponing motherhood.

Although out-of-wedlock births are increasing in all racial-ethnic groups, there are some significant differences (see Figure 11.4). In 1992, among women of childbearing age, 67 percent of African

Drawing by Modell. © 1994 The New Yorker Magazine, Inc.

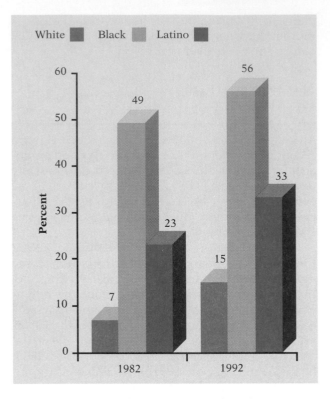

Figure 11.4 Childbirth Outside of Marriage (Based on Bachu, 1993, Table J).

American women gave birth outside of marriage compared to 27 percent of Latino women and 17 percent of white women. There is considerable variation within racial-ethnic groups as well. For example, among Latino women, 58 percent of all births to unmarried mothers were to Puerto Rican women, compared to 20 percent to Cuban women. Similarly, among Asian women, the highest out-of-wedlock births were to Hawaiian women (45 percent) and the lowest (5 percent) to Chinese women (U.S. Bureau of the Census, 1994).

Contrary to popular belief, unmarried teenagers have lower out-of-wedlock rates than older women. In 1992, 5 percent of teenagers had an out-of-wedlock child compared to over one-third of women in their thirties (Bachu, 1993). Nevertheless, the rate of out-of-wedlock birth is rising among teens.

Teenage Parenthood

The number of births to unmarried teenage women between the ages of 15 and 19 increased from 191,000 in 1970 to 408,000 in 1992 (U.S. Bureau of the Census, 1994). A major factor is

that more teenagers are having sex at increasingly younger ages (see Chapter 7). Another reason, as you will see shortly, is that many teenage girls and their partners do not practice contraception.

The increase in teenage out-of-wedlock births has serious, long-term consequences. The Children's Defense Fund (1989) has estimated that of all female adolescents who have had a first birth between the ages of 15 and 19, 43 percent will have a second birth within three years, and 73 percent of those who have had a premarital first birth will go on welfare within four years of giving birth. This suggests that teenage mothers have bleak educational and employment futures and a high likelihood of living in poverty.

Characteristics of Teenage Parenting Teenage marriages are highly unstable and often result in divorce (Trent and Harlan, 1990). Because teenage mothers are typically unskilled and untrained and have low educational levels, their ability to support themselves and their children is severely limited (Blackwell, 1991). As a result, only a small percentage head their own households. The majority live with others and are often supported by family and relatives.

Teenagers are often shocked at becoming fathers but, contrary to what many think, they are generally loving and spend time with their babies. Unfortunately, because jobs are hard to get, teen dads can rarely help support their children.

Many teenage mothers are as nurturant and caring as more mature mothers, but in general adolescent mothers tend to be less expressive and less likely to play or interact with their children and to have fewer positive attitudes toward their infants. Teenage mothers often have less realistic expectations of their children's development and are less empathic in meeting a child's needs. They are also more likely to feel sad, tense, and edgy, to worry about money, to lose control of their feelings, and to see infants as difficult to handle (Baranowski et al., 1990; Miller and Moore, 1990).

Although teenage fathers, especially those who are unmarried, are unlikely to provide economic support, many are more concerned about their babies than is generally thought. A number are "hit-and-run" victimizers who impregnate a girl and disappear. But there are also a number of teenage fathers who may be victims of a mythology that, according to Robinson (1988), has grown up from "insufficient data, a handful of anecdotal cases, historical stigma, and the media." As Table 11.3 suggests, many teenage fathers "are naive, scared young men [for whom] the historical link between fatherhood and breadwinning has been broken" (Griswold, 1993: 242).

Individual Reasons for Teenage Pregnancy

The reasons for the high rate of teenage parenthood are complex; both individual, or micro-level, and structural, or macro-level, reasons interact. We will start with the micro-level factors.

Most youths view teenage parenthood negatively. For example, in a recent national survey, four out of five youths age 18 to 22 said that becoming a teen parent is one of the worst things that could happen to a 16-year-old girl or boy. Only 15 percent of the births to girls age 17 and younger are wanted (Moore and Snyder, 1994). Why, then, is unmarried teenage pregnancy so common?

Some unmarried teenagers become pregnant because they do not understand the connection between sex and pregnancy. They may believe such myths as "I didn't think she'd get pregnant because she had such little breasts"; "She didn't look like the type [to get pregnant]"; "We only had sex once a week"; or "I didn't think you could get pregnant the first time." Younger teenagers, especially, are governed by the "personal fable": They think that death, automobile accidents, AIDS, and unwanted pregnancies will never happen to them (Robinson, 1988).

Table 11.3

Myths about Teenage Fathers

MYTH	REALITY
Super Stud	
Worldly-wise; knows more about sexuality than most teenage boys.	Teen fathers are usually no better informed about sexuality than other teens. Fewer than half understand the timing of conception, and many believe they can't get someone pregnant.
Don Juan	
Sexually exploits unsuspecting and helpless teenage girls by taking advantage of them.	Most teen fathers come from the same backgrounds and are within three years of their partners' ages. The two are usually involved in a long-term relationship.
Macho Man	
Feels psychologically inadequate, has no inner control and, unlike other boys his age, has a psychological need to prove his masculinity	Adolescent fathers actually are psychologically and intellectually similar to their peers who are not fathers.
Mr. Cool	
Usually has a fleeting, casual relationship with the young mother and has few emotional feelings about the pregnancy.	Teenage fathers typically have close ties with their partners, whom they've often known for a year and whom they are often considering marrying.
Phantom Father	
Absent and rarely involved in the support and rearing of his children, he leaves his partner and offspring to fend for themselves.	Many young fathers say they'll provide financial support but because they are often unable to get a job this rarely happens. Teen fathers are often actively involved in the pregnancy and maintain contact with the mother and baby after the birth.

Source: Based on Robinson, 1988: 22–32.

Even after conception, some teenagers know little about the anatomy and physiology of human reproduction. According to Jennifer, a student in one of my human sexuality courses, when a 19-year-old pregnant coworker saw the course textbook, she began asking Jennifer questions about pregnancy. According to Jennifer:

A coworker's pregnancy had left her baffled about her own reproductive organs. I was shocked by the lack of basic knowledge she had towards her body.

Some of her questions were so basic—such as where does implantation take place, and does the baby grow inside the uterus or in the fallopian tubes?

Some teenagers intentionally have a baby to satisfy emotional or status needs. "Babies may become a sought-after symbol of status, of passage to adulthood, of being a 'grown' woman" (Joan Anderson, 1990: 127; see also Sander, 1991). One teenage father who was also a drug dealer wanted a child to help him straighten out: "I felt like if I had a kid, it would settle me down" (Waldman, 1994: 36).

Because many young men do not have jobs—the American mark of manhood—sexual prowess often replaces work as an affirmation of masculinity, and a baby provides the evidence. In some cases, a young girl may offer sex as a gift to hold a young man, hoping that getting pregnant will nudge the boy toward marriage and give her the life she wants. In other cases, intercourse is an attempt to compensate for unsatisfactory intimate relationships with family members or friends with temporary closeness (Vobejda, 1995).

Another reason for high out-of-wedlock birth rates is that teenage mothers may reject abortion. Some feel that if they get pregnant, it is God's will and there is nothing they can do about it. Older black women are more likely than their white counterparts or younger black women to discourage abortion because of religious beliefs or the view that family planning is a form of black genocide (see Lynxwiler and Gay, 1994). Moreover, because many black communities place a high value on having children, they are often less disparaging of the out-of-wedlock child than are white communities (Taborn, 1987). Some observers also note that Latino teenagers are reluctant to seek information about contraception because of the Catholic Church's adamant opposition to contraception and abortion (Shapiro, 1993).

One of the primary reasons for teenage pregnancy is the failure of teenagers to use contraceptives: Nearly 25 percent of teenage women never use contraceptives (Forrest and Singh, 1990). There are a variety of reasons: procrastination ("I just didn't get around to it"); fear that the family might find out; and not knowing where to get birth control help (Zabin and Hayward, 1993). According to Furstenberg (1991), for the most part, our society keeps information about birth control in "a plain brown wrapper" instead of making it accessible to teenagers.

Many teenage pregnancies are the result of misinformation about contraception. Teenagers in lower socioeconomic classes, especially, are against taking the Pill, claiming that it causes cancer, obesity, ulcers, and a variety of other ailments. (Appendix C describes the most common contraceptives, including their usage, effectiveness, and possible problems.) The diaphragm is often scorned as a "middle-class method" that interferes with sexual spontaneity (Williams and Kornblum, 1985). The most common reason for the irregular use of contraceptives is that the male is either unprepared or unwilling. On the one hand, many teenage males believe that contraception is the female's responsibility. On the other hand, female adolescents often rely on males to use condoms or withdrawal (Sonenstein, 1986). This presents a serious problem because boys know even less than girls do about contraception and pregnancy risks (Children's Defense Fund, 1989).

Many teenagers rarely plan ahead, and they often feel that carrying around condoms or a diaphragm gives potential "public notice of one's sexuality." In contrast, spontaneous sex seems more innocent, not premeditated, and thus less promiscuous (Robinson, 1988). Even teenage girls who have sexually transmitted diseases may not insist on using condoms because fewer than 4 percent believe that they are likely to contract AIDS (McNally and Mosher, 1991).

Macro-Level Reasons for Teenage Pregnancy

Wanting a baby, as some teens do, can be a reaction to limited educational and economic opportunities. In general, teenagers who are socially and economically disadvantaged are more likely to become parents and to live in poverty: "They are less likely to complete their education, to be employed, to earn high wages, and to be happily married; and they are more likely to have larger families and to receive welfare" (Hayes, 1987: 138). In fact, women's education is one of the most effective contraceptives. Educated women usually have more job opportunities, more awareness of family planning, and more decision-making power. They are also more likely to marry late, to postpone the first pregnancy, to leave more time between births, and to have fewer children (UNICEF, 1994).

Leon Dash, a *Washington Post* reporter, lived for a year in one of Washington, D.C.'s, poorest, most run-down, and most isolated black neighborhoods, and studied the causes of high teenage pregnancy and childbearing. Although he observed only six families, Dash did not find "a single instance in which procreation had been accidental on the part of both sexual partners" (1989:15). The desire for a child was most acute among adolescents who were doing poorly in school and did not expect to graduate. These teenagers used a baby as a tangible achievement in an otherwise "dreary and empty future."

Although economically and socially disadvantaged teenagers are three to four times more likely to bear children out of wedlock than are more advantaged teenagers, not all disadvantaged teenagers become pregnant. For example, in a study of poor black teenagers who ranged in age from 13 to 17, Freeman and Rickels (1993) found that those who successfully avoided childbearing had educational goals beyond high school and families that supported their goals and actively discouraged early childbearing.

However unintentionally, the media often encourage teenage sex and pregnancy. As you saw in Chapter 6, even preteenagers are bombarded with advertising, music, movies, magazines, and TV sitcoms and MTV, all professing that sex is great. The media rarely deal with the real-life consequences of spontaneous and irresponsible sexual behavior. Instead, the daily message is that teenage sex, pregnancy, and out-of-wedlock birth are normal.

Social, economic, and political structures also affect teen birth rates. In the United States, for example, unwed fathers often aren't named on birth certificates. Because more than two-thirds of all teenage mothers are impregnated by men over age 20, even men who have jobs can impregnate teenage girls without being held responsible for child support (Males, 1994). In addition, there is a "marriage penalty" for poverty-level teens: If the young mother marries or lives with the father of her child, she can become ineligible for welfare, even if the father is unemployed (Waldman, 1994).

Family planning services are now less available to many teenagers, especially those in inner cities, than they were a decade ago. Between 1980 and 1992, total public expenditures for contraceptive services declined by 27 percent. Consequently, both family planning clinic personnel and state administrators report that, in response to reduction in funding for family planning during the past decade, they have charged higher fees, laid off staff, cut salaries, reduced hours, closed clinics, eliminated some services, and re-

duced education and outreach efforts (Moore and Snyder, 1994).

Although disproportionately more black than white teenagers become pregnant, out-of-wedlock birth rates are not solely an African-American problem. In fact, white American teenagers have more babies than teenagers in any West European country. A team of researchers who studied 37 countries found important structural differences to account for the difference between the high number of out-of-wedlock births to teens in the United States (for all racial groups) and the low number of such births reported in other countries. For example, in the United States highly vocal fundamentalist religious groups have been effective in blocking access to contraceptive and abortion services. Extensive private financing for political purposes in the United States enables pressure groups to mount effective campaigns that may not be representative of many people (Jones et al., 1986).

Furthermore, because the United States is so large and culturally diverse, direct communication between people is limited. In contrast, in countries like Sweden and the Netherlands, doctors tend to know one another, and people can communicate more effectively on issues like reproductive responsibility. European countries also have a centralized authority that facilitates quick and consistent decision making. In contrast, U.S. bureaucratic structures and practices make it difficult even to find out what decisions have been made (Jones et al., 1986).

Many people claim that the availability of public assistance encourages out-of-wedlock births (see Chapter 19). However, Jones et al. (1986) found that welfare support was much higher in all other Western countries. The countries surveyed provided extensive benefits for childbearing, food supplements, housing, and family allowances, as well as higher amounts than the average payments from Aid to Families with Dependent Children (AFDC) in the United States. Nonetheless, they still had lower teenage birth rates.

Single Parents

In the movie *Baby Boom*, Diane Keaton plays a successful marketing executive who suddenly finds herself the guardian of a baby girl. Frustrated by the problems of a high-pressure job and caring for a child, she moves to the country, buys an old farmhouse, and struggles to maintain her sanity. By the end of the movie, however, she starts her own successful business, meets a terrific guy, and lives happily ever after. Does this sound like a typical scenario to you? You're right—it's not.

Single parenthood is becoming more common, especially among the more affluent. Between 1982 and 1992, the percentage of educated, professional single-parent mothers increased from 3 to 8 percent (Ingrassia et al., 1993). Although the traditional—and still the most common—causes of single parenthood are out-of-wedlock births, separation, divorce, and widowhood, today some single parents choose this role voluntarily. Women who can afford to raise a child alone may feel that marriage is no longer necessary. In fact, nearly 33 percent of all women in a national poll said that if they were single and nearing the end of their childbearing years, they would consider having a child without getting married (Roper Organization, 1990). This willingness reflects an expectation that single parents can be effective family heads.

A majority of single-parent families are formed unintentionally, however. Although such families exhibit great diversity, emotional and economic problems are not uncommon. For example, approximately 67 percent of unwed mothers who eventually marry later divorce. Many out-of-wedlock children suffer family instability and poverty; indeed, an estimated 70 to 90 percent of all children born out of wedlock wind up on welfare at some point in their lives. In addition, such children are much more likely to stay on welfare for longer periods than are children of married parents who divorce (see Taylor, 1991a).

Some single parents are lesbians who were married and had children but sought divorce when they accepted their sexual orientation. Not uncommonly, these women maintain custody of their children, and their role as mother may take precedence over their sexual preference. For example, lesbian mothers may sever relationships with lovers who are reluctant to help with child-care responsibilities. They may keep their sexual orientation secret if this seems necessary to foster relationships with their children's grandparents. They may also agree to see former husbands to maximize their children's contact with the fathers (Lewin, 1994).

Whether heterosexual or homosexual, single parents must accomplish the same developmental tasks as two-parent families. The former face the same problems but must often deal alone with both instrumental and expressive tasks (see Chapter 4). Single parents are often tempted to place too much responsibility too early on children. If there has been a divorce, there may also be financial problems, and the children may feel guilty if they believe they are the cause of the divorce. As you will see in Chapter 16, the single parent may also have to deal with an uncooperative or difficult ex-spouse who may use the children as "spies" to report on the other parent's activities and lovers.

The problems of single parenting are magnified by socioeconomic forces. Low socioeconomic status limits a person's options, and continuous economic instability can decrease people's coping resources. Long-term single parenting under these conditions can produce chronic stress, and single mothers are especially vulnerable. It is the social isolation, and not simply the absence of a husband, that places a mother at risk. Gaining another adult family member eases financial pressures, helps with child-rearing responsibilities, and provides emotional support. For this reason, support systems made up of friends, relatives, and neighbors are important in combating feelings of loneliness and in providing needed psychological support.

DECIDING TO BE CHILDFREE

Just as some single parents make a conscious decision to have a child, some couples decide *not* to have children. The desire to have children is not universal. According to a 1990 nationwide survey, 4 percent of respondents said that they did not have children, did not want them, or were glad they had none (Gallup and Newport, 1990b). Although by 1992 the proportion of couples who planned not to have children had reached 7 percent, childless families are still very much a minority group (Bachu, 1993).

Who Are the Childless? Are They Happy?

Women who expect to remain childless are more likely to be white, in their 30s, college educated, and career oriented. They are more likely to be ambitious women who are determined to surmount obstacles such as gender discrimination in the workplace. They tend to have greater aspirations for upward mobility than other women, to be less willing to accept the position of "homemaker," and to plan to marry at a later age than other women (Kenkel, 1985).

The major reason that couples remain child-free is the freedom to do what they want:

Non-parents never have to budget for diapers or college educations. They can make decisions about where to live without worrying about the quality of local schools or which pediatricians offer week-end hours. They can even experience parenthood vicariously through nieces, nephews, and friends' children—but only if they choose to (Crispell, 1993: 23–24).

This freedom may well be one of the reasons childless couples say they are very happy. Women report enjoying stimulating discussions with their husbands, sharing projects and out-side interests, and a more egalitarian division of household labor (Houseknecht, 1982; Somers, 1993). There is also less pressure to share do-mestic chores because without children there is less work to be done.

Today the general public is much more ac-cepting of childless couples. For example, whereas a 1977 *Better Homes and Gardens* survey found that only 40 percent of the respondents approved of married couples who decided not to have children, ten years later, this number had increased to 76 percent (*Better Homes and Gardens*, 1978, 1988). Despite the shifts in societal attitudes toward the childless, some people are still suspicious of couples without children. Childless couples are often seen as self-indul-gent, less well adjusted emotionally, and less sensitive and loving, and have even been stereo-typed as "weirdos," "child haters," or "barren, career-crazed boomers" (Arenofsky, 1993).

Why should these stereotypes exist? Perhaps couples with children resent the childless be-cause the latter have (or seem to have) more freedom, time, money, and fun. As we will see in the next chapter, raising children is not an easy task, and parents sometimes feel unappreciated. A childless lifestyle can sometimes look very at-tractive.

Contraception

When a couple decides to remain childless, they must then decide how they will prevent child-birth. Among married couples abstinence from sexual intercourse is rarely a viable option, so the next most likely choice is to use some sort of contraceptive method or technology. In the next section we'll discuss abortion, which may be a couple's only option if pregnancy occurs despite their best efforts.

Contraception, which is the prevention of pregnancy by behavioral, mechanical, or chemi-cal means, means different things in different so-cial contexts. Besides its use in preventing spe-cific pregnancy, contraception is also used in controlling family size and the spacing of births, in decreasing overpopulation, and in discourag-ing out-of-wedlock or unwanted births that are costly to the community. (And, as we saw in Chapter 7, contraceptive methods are important in preventing the transmission of a number of serious infections and diseases, including HIV infection and AIDS.) In choosing the contracep-tive method that is right for them, a couple should review the wide variety of choices now available; Appendix C describes these methods and discusses the advantages and disadvantages of each.

In 1991 approximately 74 percent of all cou-ples in the United States reported using contra-ceptives, a figure that has remained virtually the same for almost 20 years (*Baltimore Sun*, 1991b). Sterilization and the Pill are the most common forms of contraception, and the latter is the most widely used by women age 15 to 44. Reports of possible health-related problems of using birth-control pills—including increased risks of heart attack, stroke, breast cancer, and blood clots—have not had a significant effect on the popular-ity of this method. The finding that birth-control pills may protect women against ovarian and uterine cancer may have supported their use de-spite the fact that neither of these diseases is nearly as common as breast cancer (Kolata, 1989a).

The only failproof contraceptive is absti-nence, of course, but as you might expect, it's not an acceptable option for most married cou-ples. Roughly 800,000 U.S. couples practice the rhythm method of periodic abstinence. About 19 percent of them will end up with a pregnancy within the first year (Herman, 1994). Barring total abstinence, no birth-control method is 100 percent effective—not even sterilization—and, as you can see from Table 11.4, some work better than others. Note that the effectiveness rates shown in the table are for so-called typical users, stable couples who use a particular method con-sistently. Effectiveness rates for never-married teens from economically disadvantaged families are often much lower because their usage is more sporadic (Jones and Forrest, 1992).

Table 11.4

Effectiveness Rates of Contraceptive Methods: United States*

Male sterilization	99.9%
Female sterilization	99.6
Implants (Norplant)	99.5
Injectable drugs (Depo-Provera)	99
Oral contraceptive (Pill)	94–97
Intrauterine device (IUD)	94
Cervical cap	73–92
Condom	86–88
Diaphragm	80–84
Withdrawal/Rhythm	76–80
Spermicide	70

*Effectiveness means the percentage of people who use a particular technique consistently, although not perfectly, and who successfully avoid pregnancy for at least one year.

SOURCES: Stein, 1993; Allan Guttmacher Institute data cited in Herman, 1994.

The Double Standard in Contraceptive Practices Of all the available methods, only sterilization (vasectomy) and condoms are designed for men. *Vasectomy*, in which the tube that carries sperm into the seminal fluid is tied off, is almost 100 percent effective and can be reversed in 98 percent of cases; yet only 490,000 men a year seek vasectomies. In contrast, every year more than 600,000 women seek sterilization by *tubal ligation*, a procedure in which the fallopian tubes are tied off. This procedure is not only riskier than vasectomy but far less capable of reversal.

Why do men shun vasectomy? Some experts feel that "men are notoriously skittish about tinkering with their sexuality, and many cling to the misconception that vasectomies reduce sexual prowess and enjoyment" (Stein, 1993: 11). It is for similarly false beliefs that many men refuse to use condoms, even though, unlike many women's contraceptives, condoms do not require time-consuming visits to physicians' offices and have no side effects or physical risks.

New technologies have been slow in coming. Fear of liability and the need to comply with the Food and Drug Administration's (FDA) stringent testing requirements have made the birth-control business extremely risky. Of nine major U.S. drug companies involved in birth-control research in the early 1970s, only two—Johnson & Johnson's Ortho Pharmaceutical Corporation and Upjohn Company—remain active in the field today.

In 1990 the FDA approved Norplant, the first new birth-control method available to American women in 30 years. In this method, a fan-shaped arrangement of silicone rubber capsules—about the size and shape of small matchsticks—is inserted under the skin of a woman's upper arm, where they slowly release steroid hormones into the bloodstream. In some users Norplant causes such side effects as weight gain, headaches, and irregular bleedings. Proven 99 percent effective in preventing pregnancies for up to five years, Norplant can be removed any time a woman decides she wants to become pregnant. Another recently approved birth control option is Depo-Provera, a chemical contraceptive that is injected every three months and that blocks ovulation. Although nearly 10 million women in 90 countries currently use this method, it does appear to cause a slightly higher risk of breast cancer in young women and such side effects as prolonged bleeding, depression, weight gain, and loss of libido (Beck and Hager, 1992).

The focus on developing female rather than male contraceptive methods has long sent a message that birth control is a woman's problem. Today, however, some research effort is being directed toward birth-control methods for men. One method, expected to be more effective than the Pill, condoms, or IUDs and to have almost no side effects, involves weekly injections of testosterone that, after four to six months, suppress sperm production entirely. (Sperm production recovers fully six months after the injections are discontinued.) The drawback is the necessity for regular treatments: Of the 271 men who participated in a study to test the new contraceptive, 152 dropped out because they disliked the weekly schedule (*Baltimore Sun*, 1990a). The World Health Organization (WHO), which is coordinating the research, is currently testing doses that require only three or four injections a year. A team in England is also developing a male contraceptive pill.

Despite these efforts, new methods for females continue to appear. In 1992 the FDA approved the "female condom," a polyurethane, prelubricated sheath that is the same length as a male condom, only wider, and that at its closed end has a ring that fits, like a diaphragm, around the cervix. The device not only blocks the entrance to the cervix but lines the vagina and covers the labia area as well, providing protection from sperm and, theoretically at least, sexually transmitted diseases. Reality, the brand name under which the new device is marketed, is reportedly somewhat cumbersome to insert, and some women are bothered by the ring that hangs outside the vagina. Most important, like its male counterpart, the female condom is used only once and then discarded, but it costs three times as much: about $2.25 compared with about 70 cents for a regular condom.

Contraception in Other Countries Approximately 50 percent of couples throughout the world practice contraception. About 20 percent of the time one partner is sterilized, and about 80 percent of the time, it is the woman. (Remember that female sterilization is very difficult to reverse, although reversing male vasectomy has a high success rate.) Another 11 percent of couples use IUDs, and 7 percent use the Pill. Condoms, the rhythm method, and withdrawal are each employed by another 4 to 5 percent (*Baltimore Sun*, 1991b).

China, which is confronting overwhelming population growth, has instituted a government policy that permits each family to have only one child. Despite its enormous size, great internal diversity, and relatively less advanced level of technological sophistication, China has been extremely successful not only in providing contraceptive information and technology to its people but in persuading them to use it (see the box on "Contraceptive Policies in China"). In a country where despite economic deprivation many people still believe in the value of having large families, this success is impressive.

Japan's problem is the opposite of China's. Japan has the lowest fertility rates in the world; the average woman of childbearing age has only 1.57 children (compared to 1.87 for the United States), down from 4.54 in 1949. Demographers attribute the plunging rate to several factors. Although Japan has one of the strongest economies in the world and faces a labor shortage, almost half of the nation's salaried workers are dissatisfied with their quality of life. In particular, wives who live with their in-laws report great discontent (Kamo, 1990). Young couples

---

CROSS CULTURAL

Contraceptive Policies in China

China makes up nearly 20 percent of the world's population. Since 1979 its government has maintained a strict policy of one child per family in order to limit the country's rapid population growth. Indeed, the 1982 Chinese constitution made practicing birth control a civic duty. Some rural areas, however, are exempt from this regulation. The reinstitution of family farming under China's economic reforms encouraged farmers to have more children to help in the fields. Many affluent farmers are able to pay the fines imposed for having more than one child, and in many rural areas farmers whose first child is not a boy are allowed to try again.

Most families are not exempt from family restriction, and some of the most populous areas in central China have enacted new rules and fines for illegal pregnancies. Fines for pregnancy can run as high as 33 percent of the average peasant's annual income, and if the woman refuses an abortion, the couple faces an additional fine of 20 percent for each of the child's first seven years. Local officials have also imposed sizable fines on women who have one child and who are not using an IUD and on healthy men or women who have two children and have not undergone sterilization. Besides these punishments, the government offers many incentives for practicing birth control: monthly bonuses; private plots of land; free medical, educational, and kindergarten facilities for the single child; and priority for jobs in rural industries. These tough policies have enabled China to reduce its fertility rates from 6 births per woman in 1965 to 1.7 in 1994 (Cowell, 1994). In addition, an estimated 10 percent of couples of childbearing age, primarily those who are well educated and live in urban areas, are choosing not to have children (Zhou, 1994).

Some provinces in China are experimenting with policies designed to raise women's status, on the theory that if girls are seen as more desirable, couples with a daughter may stop trying for a son. For example, girls with no brothers attend the local school for free, while parents pay $7.50 a semester for boys. A girl's parents can enroll in a pension plan that will guarantee them nominal pensions in their old age. The parents also get preferential access to jobs in village enterprises. When the girls are old enough, they will get first access to the same jobs (Lawrence,

who have to live with parents are unwilling to have children "under one tiny roof." Even individual housing is cramped, and there is a scarcity of neighborhood parks and playgrounds. Moreover, raising a child is very expensive because of the high costs of sending children to special cram courses or to the right private school to ensure their entry into an elite university. Women—40 percent of whom are in the labor force—are increasingly unhappy with traditional female roles (Benjamin, 1990; Impoco, 1990). Finally, because of increasing educational and employment opportunities for women and the growing disenchantment with marriage, many women are postponing marriage or deciding to remain single (Klitsch, 1994).

Abortion

Abortion is the expulsion of the embryo or fetus from the uterus. It can occur naturally—as in a spontaneous abortion, or *miscarriage*—or it can be induced medically. Practiced by people in all societies, abortion was not forbidden by the Catholic Church until 1869 and was legal in the United States until the mid-nineteenth century. It became illegal not for moral or religious reasons but out of political, economic, and ideological considerations. According to Rothman (1989), physicians redefined abortion and childbirth as medical issues to eliminate competition from midwives and other nonmedical practitioners, most of whom were women. Furthermore, Mohr (1981) claims, when abortion became widespread among white, married, Protestant, American-born women in the middle and upper classes, concern that the country would be overpopulated by "inferior" new ethnic groups with higher birthrates led to the outlawing of this procedure during the late 1800s. Abortion laws remained unchallenged until the 1960s and remained illegal until 1973, when the *Roe* v. *Wade* decision made abortion legal. Since then, there have been a number of changes in abortion laws (see the box "Changes: The Battle over Abortion Rights").

The number of abortions performed in the United States dropped from 1.6 million in 1990 to 1.5 million in 1992. Some reasons for this decrease include the greater use of condoms because of the fear of AIDS; the decision by more single women to keep their babies; and the pressure exerted by anti-abortion activists on small hospitals to stop performing abortions (Seligmann, 1994). Nearly 33 percent of all pregnancies are terminated by abortion, and 91 percent of these within the first trimester. Abortion is most common among women who are young, white, and unmarried (see Figure 11.5), but income level is not a factor. About a third of abortion patients earn less than $11,000 a year, another third earn between $11,000 and $25,000, and a final third earn $25,000 or over (Hall, 1991).

Is Abortion Safe? Safety can be measured on two levels—physical and emotional. On the physical level, a legal abortion in the first trimester (up to 12 weeks) is safer than driving a car, using oral contraceptives, undergoing sterilization, or even continuing a pregnancy (see Table 11.5). As for emotional health, there is no evidence that

Figure 11.5 ***Who Has Abortions?*** (Based on U.S. Bureau of the Census, 1994, p. 85).

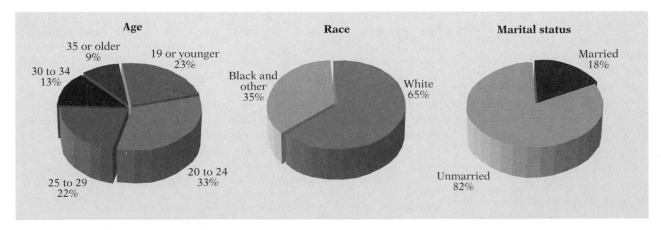

The Battle Over Abortion Rights

Norma McCorvey, the woman whose suit against the state of Texas culminated in the 1973 Supreme Court decision in *Roe* v. *Wade* that legalized abortion, is not a popular person. She has received death threats, she says, and shotgun blasts have been fired at her Dallas home (McCorvey and Meisler, 1994). Even her daily life is punctuated with hostility from antiabortion sympathizers:

Men come up to me in frozen foods and say, "You're responsible for babies being killed." Some people run into my basket with theirs. They're like children. Some have scooted their buggy up on the back of my heels. Grown people, old blue-haired, gray-haired ladies (Witchel, 1994: C1).

Although she has given some lectures on abortion rights and has done some volunteer work in abortion clinics, McCorvey spent only a short time in the limelight and currently works as a cleaning lady in Dallas.

The daughter of an alcoholic mother, McCorvey was arrested at age 10 for stealing and sent first to a convent school and later to a reform school. When she was 15 her mother sent Norma to board with a distant relative who raped her repeatedly. At 16 she married an itinerant steel worker who, she says, beat her. After giving up two babies for adoption, McCorvey, then 21, became pregnant again and this time decided on an abortion "in a clean clinic." At this point she met attorney Sarah Weddington, who was looking for a plaintiff to bring a suit that would overturn the Texas law against abortion. Weddington and co-attorney Linda Coffee won the Texas case for "Jane Roe" against Henry Wade, the Dallas district attorney and, two years later, successfully argued the case before the U.S. Supreme Court.

Since that landmark case, abortion opponents have made many inroads. For example, in 1991 the Supreme Court ruled, in *Rust* v. *Sullivan*, that federally funded family planning clinics (there are approximately 4000 across the United States) can't counsel women about the availability of abortion even if women ask for the information or if their own doctors believe abortion is medically necessary. *Prolife* advocates hailed the ruling as a major victory for taxpayers who do not want their dollars funding abortion, whereas *prochoice* activists worried that indigent women would have fewer choices about childbearing because most rely on community clinics for health information and treatment (Goldstein, 1991). Some states have cut or limited funds for clinics in low-income urban areas, and dozens of states have cut Medicaid funding for abortions. Teenagers in many states must now tell a parent, judge, or counselor before seeking an abortion. Because of pressure from pro-life activists, few doctors in rural areas perform abortions. It is estimated that in 83 percent of counties in the United States, not a single physician is willing to provide abortion services. In some states, like the Dakotas, for instance, in the entire state there is only one doctor who performs abortions, which means that women have to travel hundreds of miles for proper medical attention (Goodman, 1993; Banisky, 1994).

According to records compiled by the Bureau of Alcohol, Tobacco and Firearms, violence against women's health clinics since 1983 includes 123 cases of arson, 37 bombings in 33 states, and more than 1500 cases of stalking, assault, sabotage, and burglary (cited in Goodstein and Thomas, 1995). Death threats at abortion clinics jumped from 8 in 1992 to 78 in 1993; incidents of hate mail and harassing phone calls rose from 469 to 628; and bomb threats nearly doubled, from 12 to 22 (Beck et al., 1994). During 1993 and 1994, an abortion doctor in Wichita, Kansas, was shot and wounded as he was leaving his clinic, and two doctors who performed abortions and an escort were shot and killed in Pensacola, Florida. Some antiabortion activists, including some Catholic priests, described the killings as "justifiable homicide" (Rogers and Reiss, 1994). In 1994 the Supreme Court ruled unanimously that abortion clinics could sue antiabortion activists who, in picketing clinics, engage in criminal actions.

abortion has long-term, negative psychological consequences. In the mid-1980s C. Everett Koop, U.S. Surgeon General, outraged conservatives when he reported that the scientific research did not show that abortion has harmful effects. Several recent studies have drawn the same conclusions. In one study, women who underwent an abortion in the first trimester showed no later psychological distress (Raymond, 1990). A longitudinal study of unmarried black teenagers who were 17 years old or younger found that those who had abortions were more likely to graduate from high school and were less likely to become pregnant over the subsequent two years than were their counterparts who bore a child (Zabin et al., 1986). One study suggests that, without abortion, many young single mothers would have closely spaced children, which would increase economic stress and risk more child abuse and neglect (Russo et al., 1993).

This does not mean that women who have abortions never suffer from emotional problems. Anecdotal data suggest that some women experience feelings of guilt, sin, or remorse. And the insistence by increasing numbers of biological fathers that women should not have abortions without their knowledge further increases the potential for feelings of guilt in some women.

Attitudes About Abortion   In July 1989 the U.S. Supreme Court voted in a 5 to 4 decision to uphold the constitutionality of a Missouri law that sharply restricted the availability of publicly funded abortion services. The Missouri case, *Webster* v. *Reproductive Health Services*, was seen by both prochoice and prolife groups as narrowing the right to abortion that had been established 16 years earlier by *Roe* v. *Wade*. Several polls following the *Webster* decision found that most Americans opposed the Supreme Court ruling. A *Time*/CNN poll reported that 61 percent of the population disagreed with the ruling; a *Newsweek* poll found that 53 percent disapproved and 37 percent approved (*Baltimore Sun,* 1989a).

To many the basic conflict between abortion

Table 11.5
How Risky Is Abortion?

ACTIVITY	CHANCE OF DYING
Motorcycling	1 in 1000
Illegal abortion	1 in 3000
Driving a car	1 in 6000
Power boating	1 in 6000
Legal abortion after 15 weeks	1 in 8700
Continuing a pregnancy	1 in 14,300
Oral contraception use (smoker)	1 in 16,000
Legal abortion between 13 to 15 weeks	1 in 23,000
Playing football	1 in 25,000
Sexual intercourse (risk of pelvic infection)	1 in 50,000
Oral contraception use (nonsmoker)	1 in 63,000
Tubal ligation	1 in 67,000
Legal abortion between 9 and 12 weeks	1 in 67,000
Using IUD	1 in 100,000
Vasectomy	1 in 300,000
Tampons (risk of toxic shock syndrome), ages 15–44	1 in 350,000
Legal abortion before 9 weeks	1 in 500,000

SOURCE: Hatcher et al., 1990

proponents and opponents seems clear-cut. Prolifers insist that the embryo/fetus is not just a mass of cells but a human being from the time of conception and therefore has the right to live. On the other hand, many prochoice advocates believe that the organism at the moment of conception lacks a brain and other specifically and uniquely human attributes like consciousness and reasoning. Prochoice proponents also be-

These demonstrators were awaiting the Supreme Court's 1989 decision on Webster v. Reproductive Health Services. *In upholding the Missouri law (see text), the Court took the first of several steps that have put limits on its 1973 decision in* Roe v. Wade *to legalize abortion.*

lieve that a pregnant woman has a right to decide what will happen in and to her body. These very different perspectives have resulted in political clashes over the development of abortion-type drugs as the box "The Controversy over RU 486" illustrates.

Some believe that the volatility of the abortion issue is owing not so much to religious or philosophical definitions of life as to fears and anxieties about changing family structures and the possible collapse of traditional gender roles. For example, some prochoice Catholic leaders believe that the Catholic Church's decision to lead the opposition to universal abortion rights at the United Nations population conference in Cairo in 1994 was a symbol of a much larger issue: If women can control their own fertility they have more independence, and this challenges the Church's view of women as subservient to men (Roberts, 1994).

The Globalization of the Abortion Debate

Prolife organizations in the United States have accelerated efforts to support sympathizers abroad with money, literature, and organizational assistance. Prolife pressure has been

---

CRITICAL ISSUES

The Controversy over RU 486

RU 486, or mifepristone—called by some the "abortion pill"—is a synthetic steroid that blocks naturally produced hormones, causing the uterus to shed its lining in which a fertilized egg must implant. Etienne-Emile Baulieu, the French scientist who led the effort to create this drug, claims that its action should not be compared to abortion because rather than remove a growing embryo it prevents an egg's implantation in the uterus.

RU 486, which was first made available in France in 1988, is administered to a woman within seven weeks of conception. On the first day she is given three pills; a few days later she is given *prostaglandin*, a hormonelike substance, by either injection or suppository. In 96 percent of cases, this terminates the pregnancy. The side effects include minor symptoms—such as mild pain, cramps, and nausea—that are not uncommon during heavy menstruation. In 1 in 1000 cases, however, bleeding may be heavy enough to require a transfusion.

When the French company Roussel Uclaf began to market RU 486, the National Right to Life Committee quickly moved to prevent distribution. It lobbied in the United States and abroad and threatened to boycott all of Roussel's products as well as those of its corporate parent, Hoechst-AG, a German multinational company (Salholz et al., 1990). Under the Bush administration, the FDA refused to test RU 486 or to make it available in the United States on the grounds that it was too expensive to test, manufacture, and market. Proponents of RU 486 argued that conservatives were stalling, however, because they feared the wrath of prolife voters and because it would give women greater control over their bodies.

The Clinton administration lifted the ban against RU 486 and allowed San Francisco General Hospital to test the pill. If these clinical trials are successful, RU 486 may become available in 1996. Some antiabortion groups claim that the pill is a "human pesticide," but proponents argue that the issue of intentionally terminating a pregnancy will be less highly charged because it will be a more private matter between a woman and her physician.

The furor over the use of RU 486 for pregnancy termination has overshadowed its demonstrated promise as a treatment for diseases ranging from breast cancer to a rare disorder called Cushing's syndrome, caused by a tumor in the pituitary gland and characterized by obesity, hypertension, and diabetes (Wheeler, 1990). Medical research in some countries has also shown that RU 486 may reduce the number of cesarean deliveries because in making the uterus contract, the drug speeds the opening of the cervix (Lader, 1991). RU 486 is also believed to have potential for treating endometriosis (Glazer, 1991).

In the meantime, some physicians are adapting other drugs for abortions during the first eight weeks of pregnancy. For example, a gynecologist in New York uses methotrexate, a drug that inhibits tissue growth and has been used for decades to treat cancer tumors, arthritis, psoriasis, and ectopic pregnancies. Four days later, tablets of misoprostol—a drug approved for preventing stomach ulcers that has also been used in pregnant women to hasten labor—are inserted in the vagina. The woman goes home and usually expels the embryo within three days (Tierney, 1994).

---

growing in many industrialized countries. In Australia, for example, bills have been introduced to restrict government health payments for abortion. In Israel, where abortion is relatively accessible, religious political parties are exploring ways to limit abortion. In Germany, antiabortionists are campaigning to make it virtually impossible for a woman to have an abortion unless her physical health is endangered. In England, lobby groups have tried to impose a shortened time limit for abortion (Beyer, 1980).

One intriguing example of the abortion controversy comes from Korea. For generations Koreans have believed that women born in the Year of the Horse, the twelfth year in the Chinese lunar cycle, are smart and argumentative—in other words, bad wives. Years ago mothers expecting babies in this twelfth year tried to ensure they would give birth to boys by consuming special herbs. In 1990, the most recent Year of the Horse, some Koreans feared that tradition and modern medicine would cause an alarming rise in abortions of female fetuses. Prenatal tests that can tell the sex of a fetus were introduced in Korea in the early 1980s. Public concern over the issue forced the government to ban doctors from revealing fetal gender, although some will do so for a fee of up to $1500. In response, the government has cracked down on doctors who perform gender tests, including suspending their licenses. Although abortion is illegal in Korea, it is easily available; it is estimated that more than a million abortions are done each year (*Newsweek*, 1990a).

As you can see, deciding to remain childfree is not as simple as it sounds. If we survive criticisms of selfishness, our choices will be constrained by the availability of effective contraception and by highly vocal political groups who argue that pregnancy must result in birth.

CONCLUSION

If this chapter were summarized by an equation, it might be

changes + choices + constraints = contradictions.

We accept adults' postponing parenthood but are still somewhat suspicious of people who decide to remain childless. We recognize that most teenagers will encounter parenting problems, but reducing teenage pregnancy is still a low priority. We are developing reproductive technologies that help infertile couples become pregnant, but have many hazardous work environments that increase their chances of becoming infertile and of giving birth to infants with lifelong physical and mental disabilities. In addition, the high costs of reproductive technologies limit their availability to couples who are at the higher end of the socioeconomic scale. Even when the poor do not want babies, we cut off funds that provide information about contraception and restrict access to abortion services. Despite all these contradictions, most people look forward to raising children, which is the focus of the next chapter.

Taking Action

Planning and Creating Families

More changes, choices, constraints, and contradictions have contributed to a wealth of available information on family planning

• There has been a recent explosion of information about **adoptions** and transracial adoptions. Magazines include *New People—The Journal of the Human Race*, Box 47490, Oak Park, MI 48237; and *Interrace—America's #1 Magazine for Interracial Couples, Families, People*, Box 12048, Atlanta, GA 30355. Such organizations as Adoptive Families of America (612–535–4829) link adoptive parents for mutual support. The National Council for Adoption provides information on national and international adoptions.

Write to Dept. P., 1930 17th Street, N.W., Washington, D.C. 20009.

• There are several sources of information about **infertility.** The American Fertility Society is based in Birmingham, AL; 205–978–5000. RESOLVE is a national advocacy and support group for infertile couples based in Somerville, MA; 617–623–1156. RESOLVE has 57 chapters in 38 states and a nationwide membership of 14,000 families.

• **Postpartum depression** is common for most women following pregnancy and childbirth. For information, professional referrals, and local support group locations, contact Depression After Delivery, Box 1282, Morrisville, PA 19067; 215–295–3994.

• For information on **reproductive health and contraception,** contact the following: The Center for Population Options, 1025 Vermont Avenue, N.W., Suite 210, Washington, DC 20005 (202–347–5700); National Abortion Rights Action League, 1101 14th Street, N.W. (5th floor), Washington, DC 20005 (202–408–4600); Planned Parenthood Federation of America, 810 Seventh Avenue, New York, NY 10019 (212–541–7800). There are also planned parenthood clinics in most communities that provide information about contraception and family planning.

SUMMARY

1. Parenthood is an important rite of passage. Unlike other major turning points in our lives, becoming a parent is permanent and irreversible. People today have both more choices and more constraints in planning and having children than in the past.

2. There are both benefits and costs in having children. The benefits include emotional fulfillment and personal satisfaction. The costs include a decline in marital satisfaction, problems in finding adequate housing, and generally high expenditures.

3. Fertility rates in the United States have fluctuated in the past 70 years but are still low worldwide. Fertility rates are higher for Latino women than other women, but there are intragroup variations. For example, for several socioeconomic reasons, Mexican American women have much higher birth rates than do Cuban American women.

4. The postponement of parenthood is an important trend. On the one hand, remaining childless as long as possible has many attractive features, including independence and building a career. On the other hand, there are costs such as finding it impossible to have children later in life.

5. Approximately 15 percent of all couples are involuntarily childless. The reasons for infertility include physical and physiological difficulties, environmental hazards, and unhealthy lifestyles.

6. Couples have a variety of options if they are infertile, including adoption, artificial insemination, in vitro fertilization, embryo transplants, and surrogacy.

7. Some emerging issues in the area of adoption include the rights of the biological father, transracial adoption, and open adoption.

8. Reproductive technologies have allowed many people to become parents despite infertility. They have also generated a variety of legal, economic, social, and ethical concerns both in the United States and in other countries.

9. Contrary to popular belief, women in their 20s have higher rates of unwed childbearing than do teenagers, but the percentages of teenagers who are unmarried mothers have been increasing, especially among African Americans. There are both micro- and macro-level reasons for the surge of out-of-wedlock children.

10. Couples who decide not to have children are still a minority, but remaining childfree is becoming more acceptable. Improved contraceptive techniques and the availability of abortion have resulted in fewer unwanted births. The incidence of abortion has declined since 1990, but abortion continues to be a hotly debated issue in the United States and some other countries.

KEY TERMS

MARDY S. IRELAND, *Reconceiving Women: Separating Motherhood from Female Identity* (New York: Guilford, 1993). A psychological examination of childless women.

REGINA H. KENEN, *Reproductive Hazards in the Workplace: Mending Jobs, Managing Pregnancies* (New York: Haworth Press, 1993). Discusses how dangerous workplaces may affect fertility. Lists the major governmental regulatory agencies, state agencies, and nonprofit organizations that can be contacted for more information.

HELENA RAGONÉ, *Surrogate Motherhood: Conception in the Heart* (Boulder, CO: Westview Press, 1994). Examines such topics as surrogacy legislation and offers excerpts from interviews with surrogate mothers. For a more personal account on this issue, see also Mary Beth Whitehead with Loretta Schwartz-Nobel, *A Mother's Story: The Truth About the Baby M Case* (New York: St. Martin's Press, 1989).

JOHN A. ROBERTSON, *Children of Choice: Freedom and the New Reproductive Technologies* (Princeton, NJ: Princeton University Press, 1994). Robertson discusses a number of reproduction issues, including IVF, abortion, contraception, surrogacy, and the ethical issues surrounding these practices. For a discussion of reproductive choices directed at women specifically, see Jane Mattes, *Single Mothers by Choice: A Guidebook for Single Women Who are Considering or Have Chosen Motherhood* (New York: Random House, 1994).

JUDITH D. SCHWARTZ, *The Mother Puzzle: A New Generation Reckons with Motherhood* (New York: Simon & Schuster, 1993). An exploration of changes in the roles of women and mothers, particularly in regard to "career clocks" and societal pressures to parent.

RITA J. SIMON, *The Case for Transracial Adoption* (Washington, DC: American University Press, 1993). Reports on a longitudinal, 20-year study of 204 white families who adopted minority children. For more experiential accounts, see also Elizabeth Bartholet, *Family Bonds: Adoption and the Politics of Parenting* (Boston: Houghton Mifflin, 1993), and J. Douglas Bates, *Gift Children: A Story of Race, Family, and Adoption in a Divided America* (New York: Ticknor & Fields, 1993).

GALE A. SLOAN, *Postponing Parenthood: The Effect of Age on Reproductive Potential* (New York: Insight Books, 1993). The author, a health educator and nurse, offers readers the "information you need to decide how late you can wait."

12
Raising Children: Contemporary Prospects and Pitfalls

Data Digest

- In 1991, **20 percent of preschool children were cared for by their fathers** while their mothers worked outside the home, up from 15 percent since 1988. Nearly half of the nation's **kindergartners attend school all day,** up from about 31 percent in 1980.

- A 1994 national poll found that **67 percent of the respondents agreed that "a good, hard spanking"** is sometimes necessary to discipline a child, down from 84 percent in 1986. Views of spanking vary regionally: 67 percent of northeasterners support spanking compared to 86 percent of southerners. As of 1994, 23 states allowed corporal punishment in schools.

- According to a survey of more than 70,000 high school seniors, **nearly 75 percent worked for pay during their last year of high school.**

- In 1994, a Gallup survey asked for **working mothers' thoughts about life 20 years from now:** 91 percent said that even more women will work outside the home; 76 percent felt that most schools will offer before- and after-school programs for children; only 41 percent expected that fathers would take on half the child-care and household duties.

- Among **families with children under age 15** who pay for child-care services, in 1991 weekly costs amounted to $55 for one child, $67 for two, and $79 for three or more.

SOURCES: O'Connell, 1993; Banisky, 1994; Casper et al., 1994; Flynn, 1994; Rubenstein, 1994.

A Swahili proverb says that a child is both a precious stone and a heavy burden. Child rearing is both exhilarating and exhausting, a task that takes patience and sacrifice and a willingness to learn how to parent. There are many rewards but no guarantees.

LEARNING PARENTAL ROLES

Children affect adults long before they are born. Most parents invest emotionally and financially in planning for the arrival of a child. Some, like the infertile couples we discussed in Chapter 11, expend a great deal of time and money to become parents. Months before the baby is born, prospective parents begin to alter their lifestyles. The mother will probably eliminate such things as Big Macs from her diet and will increase her intake of dairy products and vegetables. The family will probably shop for baby clothing and nursery furniture and read books on how to raise children.

A Parent Is Born

Infants waste no time in teaching adults to meet their needs. Babies are not just passive recipients of care; they are active participants in their own development and socialization:

The infant modulates, tempers, regulates, and refines the caretaker's activities. . . . By such responses as fretting, sounds of impatience or satisfaction, by facial expressions of pleasure, contentment, or alertness he . . . "tells" the parents when he wants to eat, when he will sleep, when he wants to be played with, picked up, or have his position changed. . . . From his behavior they learn what he wants and what he will accept, what produces in him a state of well-being and good nature, and what will keep him from whining. The caretakers, then, adapt to him and he appears content; they find whatever they do for him satisfying, and thus are reinforced (Rheingold, 1969: 785–86).

Contrary to popular belief, parenting does *not* come naturally. Especially with the first child, most of us "muddle through" by trial and error or turn to "experts" for advice. Some of the advice can be invaluable, especially on such topics as the baby's physical care and the stages of social development (which we will discuss shortly). In some instances, however, even experts have promoted myths that have become

Baby Bonding: Fact or Fiction?

As you saw in Chapter 4, many people believe that parenting comes more "naturally" to mothers than to fathers because mothers "bond" with the infant. This is nonsense, claims developmental psychologist Diane Eyer (1992). Reports of research on bonding first appeared in 1972, when two pediatricians claimed that 28 mothers who had 16 hours of contact with their infants right after birth showed better mothering skills. The pediatricians toured hospitals around the country giving workshops on bonding. The mass media popularized the idea, and many hospitals provided special rooms for bonding.

By the early 1980s, research on the bonding of mothers and their newborns had been dismissed by much of the research community as unscientific, but the two pediatricians maintained that "there is strong evidence that at least thirty to sixty minutes of early contact [right after birth] . . . should be provided for every parent and infant to enhance the bonding experience" (cited in Eyer, 1992: 3). Even by the late 1980s, according to Eyer, T. Berry Brazelton, one of the foremost child-rearing experts in the United States, claimed that infants who had never bonded would be difficult in school, become delinquents, and eventually become terrorists.

Why, despite the lack of scientific evidence, has the bonding craze persisted? As larger numbers of women started to work outside the home, some psychologists and others worried that the traditional notion of motherhood was being undermined, and declared that mothers should bond with their newborns by staying at home for at least a year (Eyer, 1992). In addition, medical professionals (such as obstetricians, pediatricians, and nurses) used the requirement for bonding to enhance their authority over adults who did not visit or did not seem to want to care for their infants.

Eyer recommends discarding the word "bonding" entirely. She points out that it is not only mothers but fathers, brothers and sisters, grandparents, and friends who have an effect on children. People can nurture children intellectually, emotionally, through daily caretaking, through games, through music and art, through formal learning and even from long distances. Indeed, historically and in other cultures, children have been nurtured by many adults, not just mothers (Ambert, 1994).

After Eyer's book was published, she was "besieged by calls and letters from mothers who thanked her for releasing them from the guilt of not having bonded with their babies" (Wheeler, 1993: A6). Such reactions are understandable because there are millions of mothers who are unable to "bond" with their infants for various reasons—for example, either mother or baby may be ill immediately after the birth or a baby may have been adopted some time after its birth.

widely accepted. One of these myths is examined in the box "Baby Bonding: Fact or Fiction?"

How Infants Affect Parents

Many parents do not realize that *expecting* a baby is very different from *having* a baby. The first year of parenthood can be very demanding. To meet their child's survival needs, new parents must assume multiple roles. The working mother, especially, is torn between providing child care, being a wife, and accomplishing her work outside the home. Because caring for young children is a nonstop job, parents' workloads increase dramatically, especially that of the mothers. And both parents experience a loss of freedom, simply because they can no longer leave the house whenever they wish (Ambert, 1992).

An infant's fussy behavior may be another source of stress. Both mothers and fathers experience frustration when they cannot soothe a crying infant. Mothers, especially, may feel they are inadequate. Instead, parents must recognize that crying is the most powerful way a baby can summon attention. Babies cry during the first few months for a variety of reasons: They may be unable to digest cow's milk if they are bottle-fed; if they are breast-fed they may want to suckle even if they are not hungry; they may have ear or urinary tract infections; they may be allergic to juices; they may be wet; they may simply want some company (Kitzinger, 1989).

Parents' own activities are also altered. As the workload increases, parents have less time for each other. New parents may find themselves having sex very rarely or not at all for weeks or months at a time. Mothers, in particular, are often exhausted by child care. Some women experience considerable pain during intercourse if it is attempted too soon after childbirth. Mothers who are employed outside the home are tired and may temporarily lose interest in sex. It is not unusual for some women to view lovemaking differently after the baby's birth. According to one woman, "It has been hard to integrate the feelings of being a mother and being sexual. My breasts feel like they're the baby's for nursing and not for anyone else to touch" (Fishel, 1987: 76).

Although many couples experience strain, relationships can become richer. Some couples report being more in love than ever with their mate after the birth of a child. And as the baby starts sleeping through the night, and parents develop a schedule, life (including sex) gets back to normal. It just takes time.

Role Theory

Sociologists often use role theory to explain the interaction between family members. A role, you will recall, is a set of expected behavior patterns, obligations, and privileges. Theoretically, every role has both rights and responsibilities that are defined by a culture or group. In practice, however, role strain may occur as norms or role expectations change.

Despite the universality of parenthood, many mothers and fathers experience problems in these seemingly natural roles (LeMasters and DeFrain, 1989). Many of the difficulties stem from our unrealistic and one-sided expectations of parenting roles. To begin with, unlike other jobs, parenthood has no margin for error. Just as students accept the fact that some professors are better than others, most of us accept occasional mistakes from lawyers, ministers, social workers, and other professionals. Not every case can be won, not every parishioner will accept religious teachings, and not every child who is mistreated will be detected and moved to a safe environment. Parents, however, are expected to succeed with every child. Furthermore, because families today typically are smaller, parents feel especially guilty if each child does not turn out "as expected."

Another problem is that parents are faced with increasing responsibility but less authority. In recent court battles, parents have tried to fight state laws regarding such things as the right to educate their children at home, to con-

sent to a minor's abortion, or to take terminally ill children off life-support systems when there is no chance for recovery. Regardless of how we feel about these issues, parental authority has decreased.

A third difficulty is that being judged by professionals rather than by peers makes many parents feel insecure and guilty. If parents raised several children and one ran away from home, relatives and friends would feel that these "good" parents had had one "bad" child. In contrast, many psychiatrists, psychologists, academicians, lawyers, and social workers often automatically assume that "children do not run away from good homes." Therefore, they maintain, there must be something wrong with the parents.

Parental responsibility is a one-way street. Parents are expected to be responsible for their children, but children are not required to reciprocate. Children are not expected to pay off loans from their parents, to share bills during hard times, or even to help their parents in old age. Some of this lack of reciprocity continues into grandparenthood. When children grow up and have their own children, they may expect their parents to buy the grandchildren presents, to set up trust funds, and to baby-sit, yet they may not teach these grandchildren to write thank-you notes, to assist their elderly grandparents in household chores, or even to drop by and chat.

Finally, parents have no training for their difficult role, yet they must live up to high standards. We receive more training to get a driver's license than to become parents! And parents today are being judged by higher standards of parental performance. According to LeMasters and Defrain (1989), parents are expected to be informed about the latest medical technologies, to watch their children closely for early signs of physical or mental abnormalities, and to get their children to specialists immediately if they detect such things as problems in hearing or seeing or slowness in learning.

Parenthood changes both partners. As people make the transition to parenthood, they help each other learn the role of parent, deal with the ambiguity of what constitutes a "proper" parental role, and share in the care of their child (Stamp, 1994).

Motherhood—Ideal versus Realistic Roles

New mothers often face enormous pressures. The expectation that mothering comes naturally creates three problems. First, it assumes that a good mother will be perfect if she simply follows her in-

This four-year old girl seems as engrossed in filling her dump truck as she might be in dressing a doll. Do you think her mother hasn't spent enough time with her? Or that her father has had too much influence on her? Or that both her parents encourage her to try out different tasks and roles in a gender-neutral fashion?

stincts. Second, it assumes that there is something wrong with a mother who does not devote 100 percent of her life to child rearing. Third, it discourages the involvement of other adults, such as fathers or other caretakers.

Many mothers who work outside the home are torn between having to contribute to the family income and violating societal values about being a "real" mother. According to Spayd (1991a), although more than half of all employed mothers might prefer to be full-time homemakers, they cannot because of financial constraints. Despite the fact that more than 50 percent of mothers of children under six years of age are in the labor force, many Americans still feel that mothers should stay home with the children (see also Chapter 4).

Even mothers who are employed full time are expected to play active community roles, such as raising funds for Little League, organizing PTA activities, and providing a variety of services for religious organizations. This continuing emphasis on the mother-child relationship often leads researchers to "blame Mom" for adolescent problems, preschool misbehavior, and difficulties in school (see Denham et al., 1991; Moorehouse, 1991).

Because mothers still have the primary responsibility for parenting, they are more likely than their husbands to report conflict with chil-

dren, to absorb the guilt when things go wrong, and to feel more depressed in the parenting role (Webster-Stratton, cited in Jordan, 1990). The greater the participation by the father, the greater the mother's satisfaction with parenting and the marriage (Levy-Schiff, 1994).

Fathers' Increasing Role in Child Care One observer has complained that "the father in America has been toyed with and excluded, forgotten and banished, mocked and misinterpreted" and urges an "end to all discrimination against fathers" in the 1990s (Baber, 1992: 217). It is certainly true that mothers are still the primary caretakers of children, but fathers are playing a more active role in child care (see Data Digest). Among relatives, fathers are the single most important source of care for young children (see Figure 12.1).

Which fathers are child-care providers? Economic factors play a major role in fathers' assuming the role of primary child care while mothers work. Fathers are more likely to care for several children than just one (probably to eliminate high child-care costs); they are more likely to provide care if their wives work evening and weekend shifts; and they are more likely to provide child care if they are unemployed (O'Connell, 1993).

Some fathers may get very little opportunity

Figure 12.1 Primary Care Providers for Preschool Children While Mothers Work (Based on Casper et al., 1994: 27).

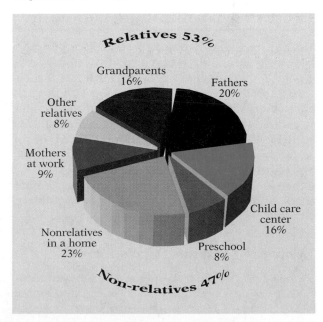

to learn the necessary parenting skills, especially during the first year of a baby's life:

An old joke for musicians goes like this: A young man asks an older musician, "How do I get to Carnegie Hall?" To which the older man answers, "Practice, my son, practice." You can say the same for fatherhood. It takes practice to know how to handle a crying baby in the middle of the night and to diaper a squiggly baby on a changing table. . . . But first-time fathers who work outside of the home . . . [are expected] to know how to be dads instantaneously, and this unrealistic expectation causes problems (Marzollo, 1993: 10).

In a historical analysis of fathering, Pleck (1990) describes the "new father" as one who is present at the birth, participates in day-to-day child care, and is involved with his daughters as much as his sons. Still, the father-as-breadwinner model continues to be dominant. Although in one survey 56 percent of male employees said they were interested in flexible work schedules that would allow them more family time, in reality fewer than 1 percent take advantage of the paternity leaves that some 30 percent of companies offer today. Most men still fear the career repercussions of taking paternity leaves (Sommer, 1994). In addition, many working-class and middle-class men feel that they show their commitment to parenthood by staying on their jobs (even jobs they hate) because doing so provides for their families (Cohen, 1993).

THE PARENT-CHILD RELATIONSHIP

Most parents play a major role in their children's lives until the children reach early adulthood. Although today children spend less time with their parents than in the past, parents are still the primary agents in a child's development and socialization. In this section we look at the ways parents influence their children's development. We begin with a brief overview of some of the major theories of human development and then explore the years of childhood, adolescence, and the "empty nest," as well as the dynamics of only-children families.

Theories of Human Development

Social scientists have proposed a number of theories of human development. Some, like George Herbert Mead, focus on the influence of social interactions on the developing human being. Others, like Jean Piaget, are interested in the child's cognitive development, the ability to think, reason, analyze, and apply information (see Chapter 4). And still others, like Erik Erikson, combine elements of psychological and sociological theories that encompass adulthood. Refer to Table 12.1 as we look briefly at some of the major developmental theories.

Mead's Theory of the Social Self George Herbert Mead (1863–1931) saw the *self* as the basis of humanity and proposed that the self develops not out of biological imperatives but out of social interactions. For Mead, the infant was a "blank slate" *(tabula rasa).* By that he meant that the baby has no predisposition to behave in any particular way. It is only as the infant interacts with other people in its environment, Mead said, that it begins to develop the attitudes, beliefs, and behaviors it needs to fit into society. According to Mead, the child learns first by imitating the behavior of specific individuals, such as parents, sisters, and brothers. As the child matures, he or she learns to identify with the generalized roles that these individuals and many others fulfill. When the child has learned the significance of roles, according to Mead, she or he has learned to respond to the expectations of society.

Piaget's Cognitive Development Theory Jean Piaget (1896–1980) was interested in the growing child's efforts to comprehend its world and to learn both how to adapt to that world and to develop its own independent identity. In his four major developmental stages, Piaget traced the child's acquisition of such abilities as differentiating itself from the external world and recognizing that objects in that world have an independent existence; learning to use symbols, such as language, to represent objects in the world; learning to take the perspective of another person; and learning to think and reason in abstract terms—as Piaget put it, to think "beyond the present and [to form] theories about everything" (Piaget, 1950: 48).

Erikson's Psychosocial Theory of Development Erik Erikson (1902–1994) is one of the few theorists whose developmental stages extend to middle age and the later years. In each of Erikson's eight stages of development, the growing person faces a specific challenge that presents both opportunity and danger. The outcome of these "crises" determines whether the person will move on successfully to the next stage. For example, the

Table 12.1
Some Theories of Development and Socialization

THEORY OF THE SOCIAL SELF (GEORGE HERBERT MEAD)

Preparatory stage (roughly birth to 1 year) The infant does not distinguish between the self and others. Gradually as it interacts with objects and people and begins to perceive others' reactions to itself, the infant builds the potential for a self.

Play stage (roughly 1½ to 5 years) As the child begins to use language and continues to interact with *significant others*—parents, siblings, teachers, schoolmates—it learns that it has a self distinct from that of others, that others behave in many different ways, and that others expect the child to behave in certain specific ways. In other words, the child learns social norms.

Game stage (roughly 6 years and beyond) As children grow older and interact with a wider range of people, they learn to respond to and to fulfill social roles. They learn to play different roles and to participate in organized activities.

COGNITIVE DEVELOPMENT THEORY (JEAN PIAGET)

Sensorimotor stage (birth to 1½ years) The child develops a physical understanding of its environment through touching, seeing, hearing, and moving around. It learns the concept of *object permanence*, the fact that objects continue to exist even when they are out of sight.

Preoperational stage (1½ to 7 years) Children learn to use symbols. For example, they learn to represent a car with a block, moving the block around. They learn to use language, putting words together to express increasingly complex ideas. But they have difficulty seeing things from the viewpoint of another.

Concrete operational stage (7 to 12 years) Children learn to discern cause and effect. They can anticipate possible causes of an action without having to try it out; they begin to understand the perceptions and views of others; they learn that quantities remain the same even when their shape or form changes (e.g., a fixed amount of liquid poured into a tall thin glass and into a short wide one is the same amount even though it looks different in the differently shaped containers).

Formal operational stage (12 years and beyond) Children can reason using abstract concepts. They can think in terms of future consequences and evaluate the probable outcomes of several alternatives. They can evaluate their own thoughts. They can think about major philosophical issues such as why pain and suffering exist.

PSYCHOSOCIAL THEORY OF HUMAN DEVELOPMENT (ERIK ERIKSON)

I. Trust versus mistrust (birth to 1 year) The mother-child relationship is the basis for the child's development of trust both in others and in itself (that is, in its ability to cope in its mother's absence). The danger is that a sense of abandonment may lead to mistrust.

II. Autonomy versus shame, doubt (1 to 3 years) The child's desire for independence leads it to explore new territories and to oppose parental restraints. The danger is that parental shaming to control the child's willfulness may lead to self-doubt.

III. Initiative versus guilt (3 to 6 years) A desire to learn and to master new tasks leads the child to pursue goals aggressively. The danger is a feeling of guilt for having attempted forbidden activities.

IV. Industry versus inferiority (6 to 12 years) The child's eagerness to learn intensifies as she or he begins to shift interest from play to productive work. The danger is failure or the fear of failure.

V. Identity versus identity confusion (12 to 20 years) Adolescents begin to sense their individuality and want to take their place in society. The danger is that the physiological changes of puberty and the need to make important decisions may lead to feelings of confusion or even to a feeling of being potentially bad or unworthy.

VI. Intimacy versus isolation (20 to 30 years) Young adults seek intimate relationships with friends, coworkers, and lovers and are ready to develop the strengths they need to fulfill commitments to others. The danger is isolation if the person is unable to take chances by sharing real intimacy.

VII. Generativity versus self-absorption (30 to 65 years) Adults want to establish and guide the next generation—their children—and/or to create and produce ideas and products. The danger is that not expressing this creative need may lead to stagnation.

VIII. Integrity versus despair (65 years and beyond) The older adult contemplates his or her life and feels satisfaction and dignity in what has been achieved. The danger is that disappointment and unrealized goals may bring about despair.

---

person may leave the first stage having learned to trust other people or being burdened by the inability to place confidence in anyone. For Erikson, resolving each of these "crises" is essentially the responsibility of the individual, but successful resolution also reflects the person's social relationships with family members, peers, and others.

The stages postulated by Erikson may occur in a different sequence or at different ages than those specified in Table 12.1. The important point is that we mature by learning to deal with continuing new challenges. The child who feels loved and secure has a good chance of developing into a reasonably happy and productive member of society.

Childhood

Most of us learn about child rearing from parents, friends, relatives, self-help books, and even television talk shows. Some of the advice is valuable, but other suggestions are more harmful than helpful. Some of the ideas parents have about child development are myths that reflect

These kindergartners seem very attentive to their teacher's instruction on how to use a computer. If they're loved and supported by their parents and families, they're more likely to meet this and other challenges successfully.

considerable misinformation about the child's early years (Segal, 1989).

- *Myth Number 1: You can tell in infancy how bright a child is likely to be later on.* On the contrary, a baby's early achievements, such as reaching, sitting, crawling, or talking, are not always good indicators of an infant's intelligence or predictors of later intellectual ability. For example, early agility in building with blocks or imitating words bears virtually no relationship to later performance in school.

- *Myth Number 2: The more stimulation a baby gets, the better.* Although it is true that a stimulating environment has a positive effect on babies' intellectual capacities (perhaps by influencing the brain's rate of growth), babies can be overstimulated, agitated, or even frightened into withdrawal by the relentless assault on their senses by the intrusive rattle, toy, or talking face.

- *Myth Number 3: If a baby cries every time the mother leaves, it is an early sign of emotional insecurity.* Not at all. It is normal for babies 8 to 15 months of age to become agitated, to cry, or to show anxiety when separated from their mother or other steady caretaker. Moreover, both babies reared at home by

their mothers and those who spend much of their early life at a day-care center are equally likely to show separation anxiety.

- *Myth Number 4: Special talents surface early or not at all.* This is totally inaccurate. Many gifted children do not recognize or develop their skills until adolescence or even later. Innate talents may never surface if there are no opportunities for their expression. For example, jazz musician Louis Armstrong was a neglected and abandoned child. It was only years later, when Armstrong was living in the New Orleans Colored Waifs Home for Boys, that he was taught to play an instrument, igniting his talent.

- *Myth Number 5: An only child is likely to have problems relating to others.* As you will see shortly, this myth that single children are maladjusted and self-centered loners has very little basis in reality. Although only children tend to be somewhat less eager for social intimacy, they are also bright, successful, self-confident, and resourceful.

- *Myth Number 6: Children who suffer early neglect and deprivation will not realize their normal potential.* Although early neglect and mistreatment often do have devastating effects on children, even those who have been severely deprived until the age of six or seven are capable of achieving normal functioning. Initial impairments are more likely to be linked to later problems in development only when combined with persistently poor environmental circumstances, such as chronic poverty, family instability, or parental illness. Although a highly unfavorable environment can be damaging, young children often prove to be resilient and capable of changing when circumstances change.

- *Myth Number 7: Parental conflicts do not affect very young children.* Wrong. Even infants and toddlers recognize expressions of suspicion, anger, or contempt. Children as young as 18 to 24 months become sufficiently upset to try to break up their parents' fights, and they may act more aggressively toward their peers.

Parenting is harder when adults believe these and other myths. Such fictions create unnecessary anxiety and guilt for many parents. The Additional Reading section at the end of this chapter suggests several books on parenting.

Adolescence

A good parent-child relationship may change suddenly during adolescence. As teenagers become more private and independent, parents may feel rejected. To find out what their children are doing, some parents are hiring detectives to conduct surveillance (see the box "Don't Trust Your Teens? Track 'Em!"). Teenagers, on the other hand, complain that parents treat them like babies. According to Minton (1994a), some of teenagers' "most unfavorite" lines from parents include the following:

"Have you done your homework?"
"Who's going to be at the party?"
"Turn down that stereo."
"Don't wait till the last minute."
"What did you do in school today?"
"Get a job!"
"But you went out last weekend."
"Remember to put the dishes away."

Major changes in social and economic circumstances have altered the relationships between many adolescents and parents in a variety of ways. Some changing circumstances include the structure of the family and the impact of gender and racial consciousness (see Coleman, 1993; Oskamp and Costanzo, 1993).

The Structure of the Family As you will see in Chapters 16 and 17, one in three teenagers will have experienced their parents' divorce by the age of 16, and even larger numbers will have stepparents. In addition, many adolescents are raised by single parents (see Chapter 11). In a national study of parents of children age 15 to 18, Thomson et al. (1992) found that both male and female single parents set less restrictive rules for their children than married parents about such things as watching television and letting them know where they were going. Compared to biological parents, stepparents engaged less frequently in activities with children such as shared meals, leisure activities away from home (such as going to the movies), working at home on projects or playing together, and having private talks.

Gender and Racial-Ethnic Changes In general, adolescent girls find the transition to puberty more difficult than boys do. Girls' self-esteem fluctuates more, and they tend to be more critical of their physical appearance and attractiveness (Jacklin and Baker, 1993). This is not surprising in light of the enormous cultural pressure on girls to be beautiful and popular. Whereas the magazines targeted at adolescent boys emphasize cars, sports, and hobbies, girls' magazines are full of advertisements and articles on looking gorgeous and having boyfriends.

As children enter the seventh and eighth grades, their relationships with their parents become more complex and their emotional experiences more mixed. Conflict over such issues as relationships, money, and access to the outside world often increase during puberty.

The most difficult part of parenting adolescents, according to some mothers, is dealing with adolescents' changing moods and behavior:

One day around when she turned 12, she told you in no uncertain terms she didn't like the dress you were wearing. You were surprised but thought: Maybe she's right. Soon she didn't like dinners you made. She said . . . there was something wrong

CHANGES

Don't Trust Your Teens? Track 'Em!

Many teens complain that their parents don't trust them (Minton, 1994a). Some of them may be right. Instead of sitting home and worrying or nagging, some parents are hiring detectives for $50 an hour (plus mileage) to conduct weekend surveillance, run background checks on friends, and otherwise "shadow" their teenagers. Although the number of parents who are tracking their children in this way is small, the manager of the National Association of Investigative Specialists in Texas reports that, nationwide, there has been a 25 percent increase since 1992 in the number of parents hiring detectives to follow their children. To blend in with the college population, some agencies use recent graduates to go undercover for routine surveillance: "For about $700, the parents get pictures or videos and a written play-by-play of their child's activities for 24 hours" (Hiaasen, 1994: 1A).

with everything you did. . . . By 14 she didn't hang around the kitchen after school anymore and tell you everything that happened. She endlessly told her friends on the phone instead. [Now] if you try to broach personal subjects, she leaves the room. She calls you names. She slams the door to her room and stays there. . . . She used to chatter incessantly on car rides; now . . . "What's new in school today?" you ask. "Nothing," she answers. Now she's 15 and 16, and a boy comes over. They go up to her room and close the door. You start to worry: If you set limits on them, won't they just find somewhere else to go (Patner, 1990: C5)?

Because mothers spend more time monitoring their teens' lives, they are more likely than fathers to be on the "front line" over many issues. Also, because girls typically have stronger ties with their mother than boys do, both positive and negative feelings toward mothers may be more intense (Larson and Richards, 1994).

Parents differ in their relationships with their children. Some children get along better with their mother, some with their father, and others report no difference. Fathers typically have a stronger influence on adolescent self-esteem than do mothers. This may be because the father's greater power and authority in family relations make his behavior more important for the child's self-concept. Because fathers are less likely than mothers to yield their authority as adolescents get older, they play an important leadership role, even though they are less likely to understand their teenagers (Larson and Richards, 1994).

Both teenagers and their parents report that most arguments are over minor issues like clothes and helping around the house. In a study of white, African American, and Latino families, Barber (1994) found that all three groups reported daily conflict over such everyday matters as chores, family relations (such as getting along with family members), dress, and school, but that parents and

---

The dinner-hour myth in which family members relax with each other and share their days' experiences is often exploded—if it hasn't been long before—when adolescents and parents meet head on over such things as where and with whom teenagers have been, when they're going to clean up their rooms, or why they took the family car out without permission.

adolescents simply didn't discuss such crucial issues as sex and drug use. Finding also that white parents reported more conflict with their children than either African American or Hispanic parents, Barber suggests that white parents may be more child-centered or authoritative than minority parents; that is, they may tolerate more argumentativeness in teenagers. He also suggests that minority parents may be more guarded when questioned by white researchers and thus report lower rates of conflict among family members.

As racial and ethnic numbers have increased, adolescents in both white and minority groups have had to deal with prejudice, discrimination, and a diversity of cultural values. These changes have affected parent-child relationships both within the family and across peer groups. In immigrant families, adolescents must often shift between adherence to traditional family values and conformity to the values of peer groups. For example, when they are at home, teenagers in recent immigrant Chinese, Filipino, and Vietnamese families maintain formal relationships with their parents and suppress the expressions of individuality expected by their European-American peers (Cooper and Cooper, 1992).

Only Children

Being an only child is no longer unusual; 20 percent of children today are "onlies." The general public's attitude toward only children hasn't changed much, however. In 1950, 71 percent of Americans said that being an only child was a disadvantage; 70 percent still said so in 1990 (Gallup and Newport, 1990b). Although, as we will see, there is no hard evidence to support this view, many people believe that only children are spoiled, selfish, and self-centered. Indeed, the founder of the national "Only Child Association" in Riverside, California, has noted: "It's incredible. Even our members are sometimes embarrassed to say they have only one child" (cited in Harding et al., 1993, 1K).

Only children do sometimes wish they had had siblings. One grandmother remembers:

Even though I loved being an only child, there was always this moment of loneliness when I walked home from school with my best friend and her sister. At the last corner they walked down one street to their house, and I had to walk down the other alone. I always wished I had a sibling to walk the rest of the way (McCoy, 1986: 119).

Only children may also feel that "it's easier for two kids to argue against parents." They report feeling overprotected and think that routine family problems are sometimes magnified because they are always the center of attention or because parents have unrealistically high expectations. Parents of only children also see disadvantages. They feel that only children do not learn important lessons in sharing, caring, and getting along, that they can't handle teasing from peers, and that they don't learn how to fight for themselves (McCoy, 1986).

On the other hand, several studies have found that, for the most part, "onlies" are not very different from children who grow up with siblings. They are no more selfish or maladjusted and are as likely to be successful in college and careers, to have happy marriages, and to be good parents (Falbo, 1984). If anything, onlies are often more successful. They do well in school, have higher IQs, and tend to be more self-confident and popular among their peers. They are more likely to have better verbal skills and to finish high school and go to college (Blake, 1989). In a review of 141 studies, Polit and Falbo (1987) concluded that the major difference between only children and children with siblings is that only children tend to have higher achievement motivation. Table 12.2 lists some famous onlies who have excelled in various fields.

Why should only children be more successful

Table 12.2
Famous Onlies

Edward Albee, playwright	William Randolph Hearst, publisher
Hans Christian Andersen, writer	Charles Evans Hughes, chief justice
Lauren Bacall, actress	Charles Lindbergh, aviator
Burt Bacharach, composer	Elvis Presley, singer
Frank Borman, astronaut	Franklin Delano Roosevelt, president
Sir Kenneth Clark, art historian	Jean-Paul Sartre, philosopher-writer
Van Cliburn, pianist	Upton Sinclair, writer
Leonardo da Vinci, artist-scientist	Roger Staubach, football player
Albert Einstein, scientist	Renata Tebaldi, opera singer
Edsel Ford, industrialist	Margaret Truman, writer
Clark Gable, actor	John Updike, writer
John Kenneth Galbraith, economist	
Indira Gandhi, prime minister	

than children with siblings? This difference may be due to financial resources. Several national studies have shown that when parental resources are diluted because they must be divided among a larger number of siblings, children have lower levels of educational attainment and achievement (Alwin and Thornton, 1984; Blake, 1985). In addition, parents of only children tend to be more flexible about their children's occupational aspirations and gender roles, particularly with girls who do not act in stereotypically feminine ways (Katz and Boswell, 1984).

Only children in single-parent families also seem to fare well. One study found that divorced women with one child had fewer financial problems than women who had several children, that the mothers entered the labor force more quickly after a divorce, and that their children were described as independent and highly mature for their age (Polit, 1984). It may be that only children in these families grow up faster because they are expected to pitch in and to depend only on themselves.

Parenting in the Crowded "Empty Nest"

During the economic depression of the 1930s, it was not unusual for young adults 18 to 29 years of age to live with their parents. The numbers plunged by the 1960s, however. During the 1960s and 1970s sociologists almost always included the "empty-nest" stage in describing the family life cycle—the stage when parents, typically in their 40s, watch their flock leave the nest (see Burr et al., 1979). These descriptions were primarily confined to white middle-class women, however. African American and Latino women rarely experienced the empty-nest syndrome because they were in the labor force or involved in extended-kin networks (see Chapters 1 and 3).

The pendulum, however, is swinging back, especially for some middle-class white families. More young adults are living at home longer, and there is a new group of young adults—called the **boomerang generation** by some—who move back with their parents after living independently for a while.

The Kids Are Back, with Their Kids   Although most young adults leave the parental nest by age 23, the proportion of adults age 25 to 34 who are living with parents increased from 9 percent in 1960 to nearly 13 percent in 1993. Twice as many

men as women in this age group are living at home (Thornton et al., 1993; Rawlings, 1994).

Among the middle classes, some boomerangers, especially men, are not moving out or are returning home because they are delaying marriage or because they enjoy the comforts of the parental nest: "They might even get maid service from mothers" (Quinn, 1993: 68). In general, however, it is structural, or macro-level, factors that are causing a larger number of young adults to stay or move home. First, many young adults have found it difficult to find employment (or well-paid employment) during the recent recessions. Second, marital dissolution and unmarried motherhood have increased in the past decade. Third, substantial growth in college enrollment after 1960, especially among women, has discouraged moving out. Because community colleges are near their parents' homes, and many students work part time, living with parents is both economical and convenient. Finally, changing norms regarding sexual relations outside of marriage have reduced the urgency to marry early.

In many cases, young adults and their children move in with relatives. In 1991, 9 percent of all children lived in extended families with a relative and at least one parent. African American and Latino children were well over twice as likely as white children to be living in such households (see Figure 12.2). Most of these children are in one-parent families, and they are

Figure 12.2   ***Children Living in Extended Families, 1991*** (Based on Furukawa, 1994: 7).

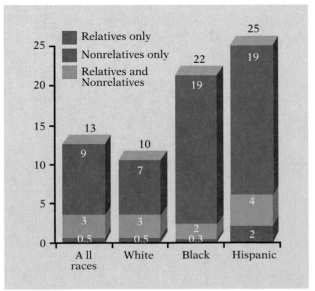

more likely to move in with grandparents than with any other relatives (Furukawa, 1994).

Relations Between Parents and Adult Children How do adult children and parents get along? Some parents report that they are tolerant of but unhappy with the return of their children. There is often conflict about clothes, helping out, the use of the family car, and the adult child's lifestyle (Clemens and Axelson, 1985). Pillemer and Suitor (1991) found that parents whose adult children suffer from mental, physical, or stress-related problems or who were unemployed or unwilling to help out with household expenses experience greater depression than do parents whose children do not have these problems. The biggest problems arose if the adult children were unemployed or if grandchildren lived in the home. Highly educated fathers reported especially high hostility. This may be due in part to the fathers' higher expectations for their children's success (Aquilino and Supple, 1991). Single mothers with young children were more unhappy than those with adolescent children because grandparents are more likely to interfere with the mother's child-rearing practices when the children are young (Stolba and Amato, 1993).

Other studies show that co-residence brings mutual benefits. For example, a national longitudinal study found that adult children who live with parents who are younger than 75 are likely to be the primary beneficiaries of the relationships in terms of such things as shared income and child care. The situation reverses, however, when the adult child reaches age 45; the child then provides assistance to the parent, cooking, for example, and doing housework (Speare and Avery, 1993). In a national study of parents whose children (age 19 to 34) were living with them, most reported being very satisfied. They shared leisure time with their adult children and reported few conflicts (Aquilino and Supple, 1991). Much of the conflict can be avoided if both sides agree to set up and follow such ground rules as not engaging in activities parents don't approve of (such as bringing in sexual partners) and respecting each side's privacy (Estess, 1994).

PARENTING STYLES AND DISCIPLINE

Parents differ greatly in the way they approach parenting. These differences probably reflect social class, racial or ethnic heritage, religious be-liefs, attitudes toward gender, and the parents' own childhood experiences.

Social Class and Parenting Approaches

Parents use a variety of child-rearing techniques. Diana Baumrind (1968, 1989) has identified three broad approaches in interacting with and disciplining children (see Table 12.3).

Parents who use the **authoritarian approach** are highly demanding, controlling, and punitive. They expect absolute obedience from their children and often use forceful measures to control behavior. Authoritarian parents, who tend to be working class, teach their children to respect authority, work, order, and traditional structure. Verbal give-and-take is not encouraged because the child is expected to accept parental authority without question. Authoritarian parents are typically not responsive to their children and project little warmth and supportiveness.

In the **permissive approach** parents are warm, responsive, and nondemanding. They value a child's freedom of expression and autonomy. Permissive households are characterized by a lack of rules or regulations, and the parents, who are usually middle class, make few demands on their children for orderly behavior or performing household tasks. They use reason rather than overt power to accomplish their ends. The boundaries that permissive parents set are often subtle, but these parents can also be manipulative (see Table 12.3). Although permissive parents do not bully or tyrannize their children, their inculcation of moral and social responsibility does not give the children total freedom of choice.

Parents who use the **authoritative approach** are demanding and controlling but also responsive and supportive. These parents encourage autonomy and self-reliance, and they

Table 12.3 _____

Three Approaches to Parenting

Authoritarian: Highly demanding, controlling, and punitive: "You can't have the car on Saturday because I said so."

Permissive: Highly responsive and warm, not demanding, but sometimes manipulative: "You can't borrow the car next Saturday because Uncle Charlie said he'd drop by and you haven't seen him in a while."

Authoritative: Highly demanding, controlling, supportive, and responsive: "You can borrow the car after you've picked your brother up from soccer practice. And remember to be home by curfew."

tend to use positive reinforcement and to avoid punitive, repressive discipline. They encourage verbal give-and-take and believe that the child has rights. Although they expect disciplined conformity, they do not hem the child in with heavy-handed restrictions. Instead, they are open to discussing and changing rules in particular situations when the need arises.

Although there are exceptions, a number of studies show that healthy child development is most likely to occur in authoritative family settings, where parents combine nurturance and discipline (Starrels, 1994). Children from authoritative households have better psychosocial development, higher school grades, greater self-reliance, and lower levels of delinquent behavior than children raised in authoritarian or permissive homes (National Research Council, 1993).

Parents' experiences outside the family, at work, and within the community doubtless shape their child-rearing attitudes, values, and practices. Working-class parents, for example, usually find themselves in situations where they have to obey bosses and follow the rules to succeed. In contrast, middle-class parents are more likely to be in managerial or professional jobs that require self-direction, autonomy, and creativity. Be careful about facile generalizations, however. For example, Grimm-Thomas and Perry-Jenkins (1994) found that working-class fathers whose jobs have high autonomy, clarity, innovation, supervisor support, peer cohesion, and physical comfort also have high self-esteem. According to the researchers, these fathers reported greater acceptance of their children and were less likely to try to control them psychologically than working-class fathers with less autonomy on the job and lower self-esteem.

Eight Parenting Styles

Parenting styles vary across families and may change over time. Moreover, they usually overlap; a particular family may use two or more styles at one time or another. Permissive and authoritarian methods of parenting are usually directed at the child, but other methods—typically those that are authoritative—often attempt to control the child's environment and relations with peers.

Influencing the Child Directly   Parental roles that shape the child directly include the martyr, the pal, the police officer, the teacher, and the booster (LeMasters and DeFrain, 1989; Larson and Richards, 1994):

1. *The parent as martyr.* The parent as martyr sacrifices everything for the children, lets them do whatever they want, buys them everything they want, waits on them hand and foot, and tries to fulfill their every whim and wish. If children do not revolt against the martyr model, they run the risk of being emotionally crippled because they may never become self-sufficient.

2. *The parent as pal or buddy.* To overcome the generation gap, parents often let their children set their own rules because they want to be liked by their children and to be their pals. Parents, however, are responsible for rearing and guiding their children. If there is disagreement, a parent who is a pal will have little authority. And, as someone once said, "What child needs a 40-year-old for a buddy?"

3. *The parent as police officer or drill sergeant.* The parent who acts as a police officer or drill sergeant is authoritarian and punitive. Even minor offenses are punished. Although children may be submissive during the early years, they often rebel against this type of authority in adolescence and may demand more independence, socializing with peers from less restrictive households.

4. *The parent as teacher.* Fathers, especially, relish playing the role of teacher. They get enjoyment from helping children with their homework and are especially pleased when children ask for their advice or opinion.

5. *The parent as booster and promoter.* Both mothers and fathers enjoy their children's accomplishments. They may be especially proud when their children do well in school, in sports, or other activities. There may be conflict, however, if the children don't live up to the parents' expectations.

Shaping the Child's Environment   Other parenting strategies include "managing" children's social development by influencing their social environments and their interactions with peers. These approaches include the parent as designer, mediator, or supervisor (Ladd et al., 1993):

1. *The parent as designer.* Parents act as designers when they try to influence the child's social environment, including the neighborhood, preschool, or child care. These social contexts may have an important impact on

the nature of children's early peer experiences and, ultimately, the types of social skills that children develop during this period.

2. *The parent as mediator.* As mediators, parents try to influence the child's play opportunities and relationships with specific peers. For instance, parents might help young children find playmates and initiate and arrange play groups. Participation in play groups may provide children with the skills they need to function well in larger peer environments (such as the classroom or playground).

3. *The parent as supervisor.* A parent may be an observer or facilitator of the child's activities.

For example, the parent might discourage or redirect objectionable behaviors or resolve conflicts between children. Or the parent might play a more active role by maintaining children's interest in peers or play or rewarding specific behaviors.

Some people believe that parenting in the United States is difficult because our cultural values (such as competition, independence, and success) encourage individuality rather than conformity. In contrast, the box "Parenting in Japan" shows how societal expectations mold parental values and child-rearing styles.

*C*ROSS CULTURAL

Parenting in Japan

Japan's approach to parenting is radically different from that of the United States. Most Americans value individualism, independence, and initiative and raise their children to be self-reliant. From the Japanese viewpoint, these kinds of attitudes and behaviors are too narrowly goal-oriented. The Japanese value loyalty and "proper" behavior over personal success. Respect for authority and obedience are taught early in the home, and they are reinforced in nursery school (Downs, 1994).

Japanese child rearing is based on a concept called *amae*, which is a sense of complete dependence based on the desire for love and caring. *Amae* is instilled in Japanese children by their mothers, who give them twenty-four-hour love. Many Japanese mothers typically spend every waking hour with their babies. They often take them into their beds at night, pick them up whenever they cry, and cater to their every whim. Most American parents think this kind of behavior will spoil a child and discourage independence and self-reliance. In contrast, the

Japanese feel that keeping children happy will motivate them to be cooperative later in life. *Amae*-based care and guidance is continued in the school system, where children are rewarded for cooperative behavior and teamwork. In the business world, Japanese drive and team spirit are the foundations of success, and the climb up the corporate ladder is based on how well employees have helped promote the good of the company overall rather than on how well they have performed individually (Shorto, 1991).

Although gender roles are changing in Japan, many families still socialize their children into traditional gender roles. Japanese mothers frequently emphasize the importance of boys being "diligent" and "responsible" workers and girls being "happy homemakers" (Ishii-Kuntz, 1993). In addition, although Japanese fathers are often absent from home, the father's authority is frequently reinforced in daily mother-child interaction:

"Since my husband is gone most of the time, my son really needs a role model to be a strong and responsible man. That's why I remind him

constantly of what a diligent, dedicated, responsible, and great father he has. I also tell my daughter that it is important for her to find a hard-working man like her father who earns a comfortable living for the family." This is from a homemaker-mother whose 9-year-old daughter and 6-year-old son see their father on the average of 4 minutes a day (Ishii-Kuntz, 1993: 59).

Since provider and father roles are synonymous, Japanese men who might choose to reduce work hours to be at home with their children may be criticized by coworkers or family members.

Some Americans feel that emulating Japanese parenting styles would create greater cooperation between children and less conflict between parents and adolescents. Others feel that loyalty to a company and unquestioned obedience stifle individual self-fulfillment and creativity. What do you think? Is one parenting model preferable to the other? What are the benefits and drawbacks for families in both societies?

Discipline

In 1994 a woman was shopping in a grocery store in Woodstock, Georgia, when her nine-year-old son, who reportedly was picking on his sister, talked back to his mother. The mother slapped him. Fifteen minutes later, in the parking lot, a police officer summoned by a store employee arrested the mother and charged her with cruelty to children, a felony that carries a jail sentence of 1 to 20 years. Many parents were outraged by the arrest. Why should the police intrude in a private family matter? And what's wrong with slapping or spanking kids? The incident fueled a national debate over how Americans should discipline their children.

All children must learn discipline because self-control is not innate. Parents spend many years teaching their children discipline, and this often includes spanking. However, many researchers and practitioners argue that physical punishment is an ineffective disciplinary method (see the box "Is Spanking Effective or Harmful?"). Increasingly, child experts recommend nonphysical methods of punishment that have better long-term results, such as removing temptation for misbehavior, making rules simple, being consistent, setting a good example, praising good behavior, and disciplining with love instead of anger (Gibson, 1991). Some authorities believe that corporal punishment is often damaging and increases a child's risk of developing problems because it is frequently administered inconsistently and is accompanied by parental disregard or disinterest in the child in general (Simons et al., 1994).

CHOICES

Is Spanking Effective or Harmful?

Five countries—Sweden, Finland, Denmark, Norway and Austria—have made it illegal for parents to spank their children. Germany may pass a similar law. In contrast, many parents in the United States support spanking (see Data Digest). A survey by the National Committee to Prevent Child Abuse found that 49 percent of Americans had spanked or hit their children in the preceding year (Banisky, 1994). Boys are twice as likely as girls to be punished physically (Straus, 1994).

Some pediatricians feel that a "mild" spanking (one or two spanks on the buttocks) is acceptable when all other discipline fails, but even they find slapping a child's face unacceptable. Others argue that spanking and all other types of physical punishment are unacceptable based on findings that children who are spanked regularly, from as early as one year old, face a higher risk of developing low self-esteem, depression, alcoholism, and aggressive and violent behavior, as well as of physically abusing their own children (Rebecca Socolar and Ruth Stein, reported in Squires, 1995). Several researchers (Hunt, 1991; Segal 1991) have offered a variety of reasons for not spanking or hitting children:

Children learn best by modeling their parents. Physical punishment sends the message that hitting is an appropriate way to express one's feelings and to solve problems.

Physical punishment gives the message that it is okay to hurt someone who is smaller and less powerful. Children also get the message that it is appropriate to mistreat younger or smaller children, and when they become adults, they feel little compassion for those less fortunate or powerful than they are.

No human being feels loving toward someone who deliberately hurts her or him. A strong relationship is based on loving feelings and through many examples of kindness and cooperation. Punishment, even when it appears to work, may produce only temporary and superficially "good" behavior based on fear.

Unexpressed anger is stored inside and may explode later. Anger that has accumulated for many years may explode during adolescence and adulthood, when the individual feels strong enough to show this rage. The "good" behavior punishment produced in the early years may disappear overnight.

Spanking can be physically damaging. It can injure the spinal column and nerves and even cause paralysis. Some children have died after relatively mild paddlings due to other undiagnosed medical problems.

Physical punishment deprives the child of opportunities for learning effective problem solving. Physical punishment teaches a child nothing about how to handle similar situations in the future. Loving support is the only way to learn true moral behavior based on strong inner values.

Children need three types of "inner resources" if they are to become responsible adults: (1) good feelings about themselves and others, (2) an understanding of right and wrong, and (3) alternatives for solving problems. Table 12.4 lists 12 building blocks that parents can use to establish these inner resources in their children.

It is important not to discipline too early. Many parents do not pick up crying babies because they are afraid of "spoiling" them. No one knows why this bad advice is so widespread, but it is a fallacy. Several studies have shown that it is almost impossible to spoil a child who is less than 1 year old. Crying is the only way a baby can "tell" its parents that it has a problem, such as hunger, discomfort, pain, or illness. Thus parents should pick up their baby as much as they want and not worry about discipline at such a young age (Kohn, 1991). Ignoring a newborn's cries sets off a vicious cycle that leads to more crying, which further discourages the parents from responding, which makes the baby even more irritable, and so on. Parents who worry about spoiling their baby are the least likely to provide a warm, caring, and emotionally supportive environment.

Finally, effective discipline involves more than rewards and punishments. The most powerful parenting approaches include such activities as joint decision making, whenever possible, between parents and children (especially adolescents), consistent parenting, and creating special times together (such as celebrating holidays or special events). Whether a parent is single or married, monitoring children is crucial in discouraging young children and adolescents from associating with objectionable peer groups or using drugs, and in encouraging them to do well in school (National Research Council, 1993; Olson and Haynes, 1993).

WHAT DO PARENTS AND CHILDREN WANT FROM EACH OTHER?

The generation gap between parents and children is not a new phenomenon. A 4000-year-old tablet discovered on the site of the biblical city of Ur was inscribed with the following: "Our civilization is doomed if the unheard-of actions of our younger generations are allowed to continue" (Lauer, 1973). One reason for the apparently age-old generation gap is that parents and children often have different expectations.

Table 12.4

Some Building Blocks of Discipline

1. **Show your love.** You can express your love not only through a warm facial expression, a kind tone, and a hug but also through doing things with your children, such as playing, working on a craft together, letting them help with grocery shopping, and reading their favorite books. When children feel loved, they want to please their parents and are less likely to engage in undesirable behavior.

2. **Be consistent.** Predictable parents are just as important as routines and schedules. A child who is allowed to do something one day and not the next can become confused and start testing the rules.

3. **Communicate clearly.** Ask children about their interests and feelings. Whenever possible, encourage them. Constant nagging, reminding, criticizing, threatening, lecturing, questioning, advising, evaluating, telling, and demanding make a child feel dumb or bad.

4. **Understand problem behavior.** Observe a problem behavior for several days and look for a pattern that may disclose its cause; for example, a child may become unusually cranky when tired or hungry.

5. **Be positive.** Sometimes children act up because they want us to notice them. Because children usually repeat attention-getting behavior, approval encourages them to repeat the positive behavior.

6. **Set up a safe environment.** Children are doers and explorers. Removing hazards shortens the lists of "no's," and changing play locations relieves boredom and prevents destructive behavior.

7. **Have realistic rules.** Set few rules, state them simply, and supervise closely. (Rules can become more extensive and abstract as toddlers become preschoolers.) Don't expect more than your child can handle; for instance, don't expect a toddler to sit quietly during long meetings.

8. **Defuse explosions.** Try to avert temper tantrums and highly charged confrontations (for example, guide feuding preschoolers into other activities).

9. **Teach good problem-solving skills.** Children under four years of age need very specific guidance in solving a problem and reinforcement for following suggestions.

10. **Give children reasonable choices.** Don't force them to do things that even you wouldn't want to do (such as sharing a favorite toy). Removing children from the play area when they misbehave and giving them a choice of other activities is often more effective than scolding or punishing.

11. **Seek professional help when needed.** Although most children grow out of common behavioral problems, some may need professional guidance, particularly if the parents themselves are experiencing a stressful time, such as divorce.

12. **Be patient with your child and yourself.** Parents may not always have enough control over their lives to be patient, but patience, love, and understanding are important for handling problems of all sizes (Harms, 1989; Goddard, 1994).

What Parents Expect from Their Children

In terms of values, some parental expectations have not changed very much over the years. For example, since the 1950s, parents have said that the most important quality they value in their children is the ability to think for themselves. Other important traits include obedience to established rules, hard work, and helping others (Alwin, 1988).

Parents are sometimes accused of expecting their children to be "superkids." Some middle-class parents push their kids toward competition and excellence instead of cooperation and normal play:

A girl who was involved in four different out-of-school activities (ballet, horseback riding, Brownies, and music lessons) developed severe facial ticks at age 8. A woman told me that her 7-year-old grandson ran away from home (and all the after-school lessons) and came to her house, where he could have milk and cookies and play with the dog. One mother asked me if I could cure her 6-year-old son of his nail biting by hypnosis or by teaching him relaxation. When I suggested that a less demanding extracurricular program might help, she replied, "Oh no, we can't do that" (Elkind, 1987: 60).

Some feel that parents have unrealistically high expectations of their children. Because many parents believe that a teenager who holds

"Oh, yes, indeed. We all keep a sharp eye out for those little clues that seem to whisper 'law' or 'medicine.'"

Drawing by D. Reilly. ©1994 The New Yorker Magazine, Inc.

down a job learns important lessons about responsibility (and should pay for such extras as designer jeans and car insurance), the typical parent encourages a teenager to work part time. The result is that three out of four high school juniors and seniors work after school and on weekends, and up to 30 percent of teenagers in high school work more than 30 hours a week (Stepp, 1993).

The problem is that many youths spend more time flipping hamburgers than doing homework. These students have poorer grades, fewer extracurricular activities, a higher rate of drug use and other delinquent behavior, and often fall asleep during classes (Saltzman, 1993; see also Data Digest). In addition, between 1980 and 1992, the number of child labor violations reported by the U.S. Labor Department more than doubled, to almost 20,000. In Massachusetts, the Department of Public Health found that 28 of every 100 workers under the age of 19 is injured on the job, compared to only 8 out of 100 adult workers, and several hundred of these "child workers" are killed each year in the United States (Amott, 1993).

What Children Want from Their Parents

In 1993, a middle-class couple in suburban Illinois left their daughters, age nine and four, home alone while they vacationed for nine days in Acapulco, Mexico. Upon their return, the couple was arrested and charged with child abandonment and cruelty to children. Although such behavior is not typical of most parents, the incident provoked national dialogue about parental responsibility.

Many children lack fathers: 40 percent of children who live in fatherless homes have not seen their fathers in at least a year, and more than half of all children who don't live with their fathers have never been in their fathers' homes (Gardner, 1994). Even when fathers are present, children are often "left to fend for themselves in a world of hostile strangers, dangerous sexual enticements and mysterious economic forces that even adults find unsettling" (Adler, 1994: 44). Many children express fears about family insecurity and their own physical safety. For example, more than half of the children in a recent poll said they were afraid of violent crime against them or a family member (Adler, 1994). In another poll of youths age 9 through 17, 61 percent worried about being able to find a good job in the future, 49 percent were anxious about their families' not having enough money, and 23 percent were concerned that their parents might lose their jobs (*Newsweek*, 1994). Such worries suggest that many children feel that parents can no longer protect them from social or economic problems.

Adolescence, especially, is a difficult period. Young people are torn between depending on their parents and wanting independence. Often, adolescents express this normal and healthy struggle for autonomy by challenging parental expectations and expressing disdain for parental authority and superiority. As Mark Twain observed: "When I was a boy of 14, my father was so ignorant I could hardly stand to have the old man around. But when I got to be 21, I was astonished at how much the old man had learned in 7 years." Consequently, some adolescents assert their individuality by taking on religious or political attitudes that are diametrically opposed to those of their parents. For example, if the parents are liberal, their children may espouse conservative stances. If the parents are religious, their children may belittle the importance of religion (Maushard and Thomas, 1989).

Not surprisingly, adolescents often have contradictory expectations about their parents. On the one hand, adolescents want more freedom (such as choosing their friends) and less responsibility (such as fewer household tasks). They also want their parents to nag them less about their behavior (Alwin, 1988). On the other hand, a recent *Times*/CBS News poll found that 40 percent of the 13- to 17-year-old teenagers they interviewed complained that their parents were sometimes or often unavailable to them (*Baltimore Sun*, 1994e).

Another important issue is communication. Several studies have found that many adolescents see the lack of communication with their parents as a severe problem that can lead to other problems, such as difficulty in school, drug abuse, and peer pressure. By late childhood, children start withholding private thoughts and feelings from their parents because they fear rejection. Parents should be careful not to react to their children's ideas with sarcasm, putdowns, or scorn. Communication and respect should be reciprocal, however. The "bill of rights" for parents and children shown in Table 12.5 makes it clear that both have many of the same rights. The biggest difference is that parental rights also

Table 12.5
Kids' and Parents' Rights

KIDS HAVE THE RIGHT . . .	PARENTS HAVE THE RIGHT . . .
1. To be treated with respect	1. To be treated with respect
2. To say yes or no	2. To say no and not feel guilty
3. To be alone sometimes	3. To know where their children are, who their friends are, and who they are with at any time
4. To make mistakes	4. To make mistakes and/or change their minds
5. To ask questions	5. To ask questions and expect answers about all things that may affect their children
6. To be cared for when they're sick and well	6. To monitor all school-related activities: academic, behavioral, and social
7. To be safe from physical and sexual hurt from grown-ups and other kids	7. To know and consult with adults who influence their children's lives (such as coaches, employers, teachers, youth-group leaders, ministers, and counselors)
8. To be safe and protected	8. To know what is happening within their own homes, to set "house rules," and to know the identity of guests who come into their homes
9. To want and get attention and affection	9. To promote time together as a family, which may include meals, outings, study time, and other planned activities
10. To choose what they like and don't like	10. To be authoritative when logical explanation and reason have failed

SOURCES: Based on material from the Tri-City Substance Abuse Coalition, cited in McMahon, 1993; and from Project Charlie, cited in Shoop and Edwards, 1994.

include adult responsibilities that some parents ignore. Spending more time together can also encourage more open communication by giving children and parents the opportunity to get to know each other better.

PARENTAL TIME WITH CHILDREN

The Reverend Jesse Jackson reportedly said, "Your children need your presence more than your presents." In 1993, a 15-year-old British boy went to court in an effort to force his mother to spend more time with him. Although such drastic measures are still relatively rare, many parents are spending little time with their children. Much of the evidence comes from the research on absentee fathers, latchkey kids, and child care.

Absentee Fathers

A February 1995 cover of *U.S. News & World Report* showed a father cuddling a baby. The headline read "Why Fathers Count" and the articles discussed the "crisis of 2 of every 5 children in America who do not live with their fathers." As you saw earlier, fathers play a critical role in nurturing babies and providing guidance for adolescents. We discuss the effects on children who do not see their fathers after a divorce or separation in Chapters 16 and 19. There are, however, millions of children born outside of marriage who also don't see their fathers.

Among unmarried fathers, 13 percent never see their children and another 21 percent see them only a few times a year (Jacobsen and Edmondson, 1994). Absentee fathers can have a tremendous negative impact on their children, from birth to young adulthood. Compared to children living with both biological parents, children with an absentee father are twice as likely to drop out of high school, more likely to spend time in juvenile correctional facilities, 20 to 42 percent more likely to suffer health problems, and more likely to have lower earning in young adulthood. They are also more likely to be poor, and to have a higher probability themselves of experiencing a marital disruption or having a premarital birth, thereby repeating the cycle of single parenthood (Goulter and Minninger, 1993; Lino, 1994).

Latchkey Kids

Latchkey kids have become a growing concern. The phrase **latchkey kids** is generally used to describe children who return home after school and let themselves in, with their own keys, to an empty house or apartment, where they are alone and unsupervised until their parents or another adult comes home. A recent Census Bureau study found that almost 8 percent (1.6 million) of children between the ages of 5 and 14 are latchkey kids (Casper et al., 1994). Other estimates have put the total number of latchkey chil-

One of the younger "latchkey kids" who return from school to empty homes, this boy may be alone for two or three hours. If he's lucky, he'll have a snack in the refrigerator and a number to call in an emergency. If he's self-reliant, he may do his homework and chores before watching TV.

dren as high as 10 million, nearly a quarter of the nation's school population.

There are a considerable number of children who care for themselves or are in the care of a sibling under age 14 at other times, such as before school or late at night. In 1990 Bianchi estimated 333,000 such children. And all these estimates of the numbers of latchkey kids are probably low because (1) they do not include the children of women who are not in the labor force but who nevertheless spend some part of the day in unsupervised situations or (2) children who are left alone occasionally (Casper et al., 1994).

Who are the children who are home alone? As Figure 12.3 shows, the older children are, the more likely they are to be latchkey kids. For ex-

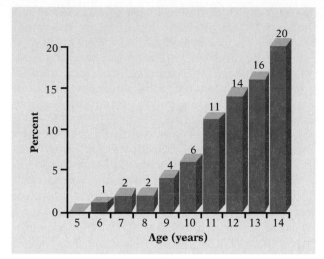

Figure 12.3   Home Alone in 1991: Percentages of Latchkey Kids Among Children Whose Mothers Were Employed (Bernstein, 1994).

ample, whereas in 1991 1 percent of all 6-year-old children whose mothers were employed were latchkey kids, 20 percent of 14-year-old children of working mothers were in this category.

Children of mothers who work full time are four times more likely to be latchkey kids than children whose mothers work part time. Suburban children arc about twice as likely to be home alone as children living in either cities or rural areas. This may be because suburban parents feel that their neighborhoods are safe or because their neighbors have agreed to be called on in emergencies. Socioeconomic status does not appear to affect a family's decision to leave children to care for themselves (Casper et al., 1994). This may be due to the scarcity of services: An estimated 10 million children need care before or after school, but there are places in child-care facilities for just 2 million to 3 million children (Creighton, 1993).

Although some children like the independence of being by themselves, others are afraid, lonely, bored, or resentful (Merrill, 1988). Moreover, some studies have found that the more hours children take care of themselves after school, the greater their risk of becoming involved in substance abuse. For example, children who take care of themselves for 11 or more hours a week are nearly twice as likely to drink alcohol, smoke cigarettes, or use marijuana as are children who are under adult supervision (Richardson, 1989).

Child Care

An estimated 80 percent of families will include two working parents by the end of the century. As the number of divorces and working single parents increases, parents are being forced to seek, and businesses are beginning to provide, more options for child care. For example, about 10 percent of the time businesspeople who must travel take their children with them because most major hotels arrange for baby sitters or daycare (Conn, 1990).

As the proportion of working mothers of young children has increased, the location of care has changed. In 1958, when 18 percent of mothers with a child under age six worked full time, over 80 percent of the children were cared for in their own home or in another family's home, and less than 5 percent were in day-care centers. By 1991, when more than half of mothers of children under age six worked full time, 23 percent were in day-care centers or nursery/preschool programs. Although in 1965 relatives provided 75 percent of all care to preschool-age children whose mothers worked, by 1991 this number had dropped to 53 percent, in large part because more women are working and thus are no longer available to help out (Casper et al., 1994). Because of all these problems in finding someone to care for their children—whether the children's fathers, other relatives, or commercial centers—mothers who work unusual hours or on weekends must often stitch together multiple arrangements (Folk and Yi, 1994; see also Chapter 14).

Who Has Access to Child Care?   Day care, even purely custodial daycare that does not provide educationally enriching programs, is not cheap. In 1991 families paid an average of $63 per week for child care (see Data Digest). Poor women (see also Chapter 14) paid an average of $60 per week, not significantly different from women in households above the poverty level. Because child-care facilities are in such short supply, the fees are highly competitive and few offer discounts or a sliding scale to accommodate lower-income families. Not surprisingly, poor families spend a considerably higher proportion of their monthly income on child care: 27 percent compared to 7 percent in families that are not poor (Casper et al., 1994).

Only those with child-care arrangements can find work or continue to work. In some states, poor women who depend on subsidized child care are on waiting lists an average of eight months before being offered a slot (Bowen and Neenan, 1992). Women in low-income families are more likely to have gaps in employment because they can't find adequate child-care arrangements (Veum and Gleason, 1991). Thus, many poor and low-income mothers often experience a vicious cycle. They have more erratic work histories because their low salaries do not pay for child care, so they leave the labor force temporarily to take care of their children and look for better work. Leaving the workplace results in lower seniority and lower wages. Then, when they again find work, their erratic work histories often force them to accept low-income or part-time work or both.

Effects of Child Care on Children When Jennifer Ireland was 16, she had a baby by a high school classmate whom she never married. At 19, she received a full scholarship from the University of Maryland, found a place to live and a licensed day-care center for their three-year-old daughter. When she sued the father for child support, he sued her for custody of the child and won. Although the father was a part-time student at a community college with only a part-time job mowing lawns, the judge ruled that the child would have better care with the father because the father's mother, a full-time homemaker, promised to care for her grandchild. According to syndicated columnist Ellen Goodman (1994: 9A), "Jennifer Ireland was guilty of committing child care." (Ms. Ireland's attorney filed an appeal, and the case was still pending in mid-1995.)

Thus, daycare is still a controversial issue. Revelations of sexual abuse by caregivers during the early 1990s made many parents fearful and suspicious. Yet a number of studies show that a well-run day-care center has positive effects on children's social and intellectual development. In high-quality daycare, even children from low-income families outscore more advantaged children on IQ tests by the time they enter kindergarten (Burchinal, cited in Moss, 1987; see also Posner and Vandell, 1994). Several studies have found that children attending child-care centers score higher on cognitive and independence tests than do children who are at home with baby sitters or in child-care facilities operated by private individuals in their own homes (see Vobejda, 1995c). A Gallup survey of 1000 working mothers with children under 18 found that many felt that child care offers young children many advantages: 77 percent said their children gained social skills and learned how to get along with other children, 72 percent said their children acquired better language skills, and 68 percent felt the children would be better prepared for school (Rubenstein, 1994).

Those day-care centers with the best results are small and have high adult-to-child ratios (see the box "How Can I Find a Good Day-Care Program?"). Good child-care providers often quit, however, because they earn among the lowest wages. According to Census Bureau figures, a typical child-care worker earns $154 a week compared to $191 a week for a cleaning person and $219 a week for a cashier. Few receive health insurance, and almost none receives retirement benefits (Baker, 1994). Consequently, 40 percent of day-care workers leave their jobs in less than a year (Ames, 1992). Top-notch quality day-care service that includes competent staff, high adult-to-child ratios, and staff stability is very expensive—at least $200 a week. Because this is more than many families can afford, quality day care remains a serious problem.

Unlike the United States, many Western countries offer high-quality child-care programs. Sweden has numerous government-financed day-care centers for the young children of working parents. Comprehensive day-care systems have characterized many European countries for years. For example, in France, Germany, and Italy most preschool children are in free full-day public programs. Many European countries routinely allow parents to leave work to care for sick children. Thus, there has been greater progress in meeting child-care needs in many European countries than in the United States, where "family values" are often celebrated (see Benokraitis and Feagin, 1995).

GAY AND LESBIAN PARENTS

It is estimated that in the United States there are 3 to 5 million gay and lesbian parents, raising 8 to 10 million children (Miller, 1991). In most respects, lesbian and gay families are like heterosexual families: The parents must make a living, and parents and children have the usual disagreements.

Gay and lesbian parents face the added burden of raising children who will often experience

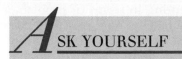
How Can I Find a Good Day Care Program?

Here are some questions that will help you evaluate the day-care programs you visit. Some are questions to ask of the administrators, teachers, and other staff, as well as of parents. Others are questions to ask yourself, as you mull over the information you've gathered.

1. What is the staff-child ratio? The best programs have enough staff members on hand so that children get plenty of attention. Suggested staff-child ratios are 1 to 3 for infants, 1 to 10 for five- and six-year-olds, and 1 to 12 for children over six.

2. What is the staff turnover rate? If half of the staff leave every year it probably means that they are paid extremely low wages or feel that the program is not run well. Another warning signal is finding that parents remove their children at a high rate, apparently having arranged for care elsewhere.

3. How do the staff and children look when you visit? If the children seem unhappy, have runny noses, and seem passive, the center is probably ignoring such things as colds (which are easily spread) and is not providing meaningful activities for the children. If the staff seem distant or lackadaisical, they are probably not engaging kids in interesting projects.

4. How well equipped is the facility? There should be interesting indoor activities that give children a choice of projects, as well as ample playground space with swings, jungle gyms, and other exercise equipment. If there is no adjacent outdoor area, do the children go regularly to a park or playground where they can run, jump, climb, and swing? In addition, is the day-care facility clean and organized?

5. What are the safety regulations and hygienic practices? Are children always accounted for when they arrive and leave? Are staff trained in first-aid? Do they use latex gloves when they change diapers or attend to a sick or bleeding child? What are the policies about children who take medications (for allergies, for example)?

6. Is the director of the center willing to have you talk to other parents who utilize the child-care center? If a center is run well, the director will be more than happy for you to talk to other parents. Beware of an evasive director (Berezin, 1990; Skruck, 1994; see also Cadden 1995 for a state-by-state evaluation of child-care).

---

discrimination because of their parents' sexual orientation. It is for this reason and for fear of alienating their children that not all homosexual parents reveal their sexual preference to their children even though they may want to. One reason for this is internalized homophobia. One man who had had a male lover for seven years and whose former wife had custody of the four teenagers they had once raised together said, "I don't want to say I'm gay because I'm ashamed of it. And I shouldn't be after all this time, but if you want to come right down to it, I guess that's what it boils down to . . . I'm ashamed." Another reason is that former spouses might be vindictive: "One man reported to the author that he did not disclose to his daughter, [because] if his wife were to find out, he believed she might inform the board of education where he taught elementary school" (cited in Bozett, 1987: 225).

Disclosure to Children

Despite the fears of some homosexual parents, many children are generally accepting of gay or lesbian parents. In none of the reported research have children rejected their parents because of homosexuality. This may be because many children have been taught by their homosexual parents to accept social and personal differences in others. If there is a strong parent-child bond, disclosure rarely undermines this relationship. Furthermore, disclosure may help to relieve family tensions. For example, parents may have been fighting about a partner's sexual orientation or may divorce because of it. Children often assume that they are somehow at fault when parents fight, and this tendency may be even stronger in children who do not know that a parent's homosexuality is the source of the difficulty. Parents

CHAPTER 12   *Raising Children: Contemporary Prospects and Pitfalls*   **341** who are ashamed or confused about their homosexuality report negative reactions from their children, and children who are told the truth at an earlier age tend to have fewer problems with acceptance than do children who are told later on (Bozett, 1987).

Although most children are accepting, they may be ambivalent about disclosing that a parent is gay to their friends (Miller, 1992). Some try to hide the information from their friends or try to prevent them from seeing how their home life differs from that of their friends:

Throughout high school, I constructed my social life around the fact that my mother and her lover were asleep by ten o'clock, making sure I had no guests in our house, who might see them go to bed. Should anyone actually see them disappear behind the same closed door, I was quick to invent an explanation (Fomby, 1991: 39).

As long as I know there aren't any gay magazines, gay movies—anything that would cause somebody to suspect—around. I used to do a sweep before I would bring a friend home, but now my dad keeps them in his room (Minton, 1994b: 14).

How children cope with parental homosexuality may depend on the availability of support systems. A study of lesbian mothers found, for example, that the mothers who coped most successfully with a homophobic environment had developed social networks with heterosexual mothers in the general community and had friends they could talk to in lesbian networks (Levy, 1992).

There is little difference between heterosexual and homosexual parenting in terms of problem-solving abilities, financial concerns, or child rearing (Pies, 1990; Koepke et al., 1992). In fact, children raised by gay and lesbian parents may have some advantages. For example, teachers may see the children as more affectionate and responsive, and gay and lesbian parents tend to report fewer behavioral problems with their children than do parents of heterosexual children (Laird, 1993). Compared to their heterosexual counterparts, many homosexual parents are more likely to emphasize verbal communication with their children. They also tend to be more responsive to children's needs and more actively involved in their children's activities (Bigner and Bozett, 1990).

Sometimes gay and lesbian parents are more strict in setting limits on their children's behavior (Bigner and Jacobsen, 1989). This may reflect the additional pressures that homosexual parents experience as a result of their guilt over their sexuality or their fear that accusations of bad parenting can limit visitation or custody rights. Such fears are often justified. In some cases gay and lesbian parents have succeeded in getting visitation rights or have regained custody of their children only after appealing their cases to higher courts (see, for example, Fisher, 1994).

Parents with Gay and Lesbian Children

Anecdotal data suggest that many heterosexual parents have a problem accepting their children's homosexuality. The following reactions from heterosexual parents are probably fairly typical:

Dr. Helen Cooksey and Dr. Susan M. Love with their daughter, Katie Love Cooksey, and family pets Sugar and Brownie. In 1989, after having been artificially inseminated, Dr. Love, a surgeon and director of the UCLA Medical Center's breast cancer program, bore Katie, and in 1994 Love and Cooksey won a long legal battle allowing Dr. Cooksey to adopt Katie.

A male student had written to his parents announcing that he was homosexual and was living with his lover off campus. He immediately received a phone call in which his mother offered to pay the bill if he would go to a psychiatrist and get himself "cured." Another student went home and told her parents she had become a lesbian. The mother began to cry, and the father became furious. He told the daughter never to come home again, that she was not considered a member of the family any more (LeMasters and DeFrain, 1989: 286).

Many parental reactions are initially negative because parents think that their children could be heterosexual if they wanted. A child who once was familiar now appears to be a stranger. Parents may also be concerned about becoming stigmatized themselves. Negative feelings are frequently followed with strong feelings of guilt and personal failure in their parenting roles. A common question is "Where did we fail?" Early in the disclosure process, parents typically feel grief, anger, sadness, guilt, failure, and shame. Some parents may never move beyond rejection or denial. They may break off contact with their children, try to convince them to change their sexual preference, or ignore the issue. Others, however, realize that they can't change the situation and accept the child's homosexuality (Barret and Robinson, 1990). Organizations such as Parents and Friends of Lesbians and Gays (P-FLAG) have helped parents to confront their homophobia, to obtain information about homosexuality, and to alleviate the sense of alienation that many parents experience.

Even when they are accepted by their families, gay and lesbian teenagers face particular perils in the outside world. An estimated 30 percent of young people who commit suicide do so because of the isolation they feel as homosexuals. Many suffer from self-hatred and low self-esteem, and feel unloved (Winston, 1991). Because they can't talk about their sexual preference, they increasingly feel isolated and deviant.

CHILDREN'S WELL-BEING

In 1990, 71 presidents and prime ministers came together for the first World Summit for Children. Two principal sets of data dominated this meeting. The first described the "quiet catastrophe"—the 40,000 deaths of children each day from ordinary malnutrition and disease, the 150 million children who are in ill health and whose growth is stunted, and the 100 million 6- to 11-year-olds who are not in school. On an international level, children appear to be disposable: 8000 die every day because they have not been immunized against such disease as measles, tetanus, and whooping cough; nearly 7000 die daily from dehydration caused by diarrhea; and 6000 die daily from pneumonia.

The second set of facts at the summit showed that the means of ending this quiet catastrophe are both available and affordable (Grant, 1991). For example, penicillin and other antibiotics could save the lives of millions of children. Most governments could prevent a great deal of disease by improving children's diets, alleviating overcrowded living arrangements, and eliminating unsanitary conditions. Compared to other countries, the United States has a poor track record when it comes to children's health and well-being, as the box "A Day in the Life of American Children" illustrates.

Children and Poverty

In the 1960s both the number and the percentage of children under age 18 living in poverty declined substantially. Between 1960 and 1969 the number dropped from 18 million to 10 million, and the official poverty rate fell from 27 to 14 percent. The poverty rates then leveled off during the 1970s and began rising again in the 1980s. By 1992 over 21 percent of children lived in poverty, a 25 percent increase from the 1970s (Bianchi, 1990; U.S. Bureau of the Census, 1993).

As we will see when we discuss poverty in more detail in Chapters 13 and 14, poverty has widespread, cumulative, and long-term negative effects on the family. The majority of families experiencing hunger are the working poor, who spend 60 percent of their incomes on housing and have little money for food after they've paid the rent and other essential bills such as electricity. Undernourished children grow more slowly than children on healthy diets, both physically and mentally. They have no energy to learn and thus do not do well in school. Moreover, they are less resistant to illness and more likely to miss school (Rich, 1991).

Economic deprivation leads to lower achievement among offspring. Poor families have less money to invest in children's educational activities, which often means children

A Day in the Life of American Children

A number of studies have expressed alarm over the state of America's children. The Annie E. Casey Foundation (1994) concluded that nearly 4 million American children are growing up in severely distressed neighborhoods. This 1994 study used five indicators to measure distress: a poverty rate above 28 percent; more than 40 percent female-headed households; a high school dropout rate over 23 percent; more than 47 percent of males unemployed; and more than 17 percent of families on welfare. Using these indicators, the researchers concluded that nearly half of all children living in severely distressed neighborhoods were in just six states: California, Illinois, Michigan, New York, Ohio, and Texas. And although only about one-third of all U.S. children are minorities, about four out of five children in distressed neighborhoods are minorities. One in four African American children and one in ten Latino children live in distressed neighborhoods, compared with only 1 out of every 63 white children (O'Hare, 1994).

According to several sources (Ross, 1993; Children's Defense Fund, 1994), for many American children, a typical day is filled with experiences caused by poverty and violence. Every day of the year, these sources say:

3	children die from child abuse
9	children are murdered
13	children are shot dead
13	runaways die
27	children die from poverty-induced causes
30	children are wounded by guns
63	babies die before they are one month old
101	babies die before their first birthday
145	babies are born at very low birthweight (less than 3.25 pounds)
202	children are arrested for drug offenses
307	children are arrested for crimes of violence
340	children are arrested for drinking or drunken driving
480	teenagers contract syphilis or gonorrhea
636	babies are born to women who had late or no prenatal care
1,115	teenagers have abortions
1,234	children run away from home
1,340	teenagers have babies
2,255	teenagers drop out of school
2,350	children are in adult jails
2,781	teenagers become pregnant
2,860	children see their parents divorce
2,868	babies are born into poverty
3,325	babies are born to unmarried women
5,314	children are arrested for all offenses
5,703	teenagers are victims of violent crime
7,945	children are reported abused or neglected
8,400	teenagers become sexually active
100,000	children are homeless
1,200,000	latchkey kids come home to houses in which there is a gun

have to drop out of school and find a job to help care for younger siblings. As discussed in Chapter 11, unemployment and financial problems often lead to low self-esteem and a void that many teenagers try to fill by having children outside of marriage. Poverty also means that families have fewer resources for dealing with stress, health problems, and family conflict.

It would cost $53.8 billion to eliminate poverty for all Americans. This may sound like a lot of money, but it is equivalent to only 1 percent of our gross national product. As the Children's Defense Fund (1990: 18–19) points out: "If bankers can get $164 billion to bail out deregulated, imprudent savings and loan institutions, and if we can afford the $5 billion in tax breaks for inherited capital gains for the wealthy, then this nation can afford to lift its 12 million poor children out of poverty."

Foster Homes

The growth of poverty, child abuse (see Chapter 15), and parental neglect has resulted in a burgeoning of out-of-home placements for children, including foster homes, hospitalization, residential treatment facilities, group homes (which house a number of children under the auspices of a charitable organization), and shelters for runaways (Woolf, 1990). Some feel that several of these residential facilities, like group homes, are euphemisms for modern orphanages. The parents are alive but are so disengaged from child rearing or are suffering from such overwhelming problems that the children are abandoned (Creighton, 1990).

The most common out-of-home placement for children is the **foster home,** where a family raises children who are not its own for a period of time but does not formally adopt them. Nationally, the number of children in foster care reached an estimated 442,000 in 1992, a 68 percent increase from a decade earlier. The number of children in foster care as a result of parental abuse or neglect has increased from 75,000 in 1963 to more than 200,000 in the early 1990s. Children who lose parents to AIDS are expected to swell the ranks of children in foster care even more. Estimates of the number of children who will have lost a mother to AIDS by the year 2000 range from 80,000 to 125,000 (Children's Defense Fund, 1994). Practitioners fear that the number of children who need foster care will soon greatly surpass the number of foster homes (Chamberlain et al., 1994). Drugs, especially crack, have forced many children to be cared for by foster parents. Since more women now work outside the home, however, and others feel ill-equipped to deal with the problems of children from crack families, it's not clear who will care for many of these children.

Some foster parents pursue adoption if they become attached to the child. Others have a history of "informal adoption" by caring for children for many years without adopting them. Legal adoption sometimes offers few rewards. It may even be threatening because it changes the situation between the child and the foster parent, entails legal action, and introduces the possibility of losing financial assistance. There are also specialized foster-care services that require out-of-home, long-term care for children who are emotionally or behaviorally disturbed or developmentally or medically disabled (Weisman,

1994). Some pilot programs pay women on welfare $21,000 a year to care for disabled children or adults whose families are unable or unwilling to care for them (Aguilar, 1990).

Characteristics of Foster Homes In theory, foster homes are supposed to provide short-term care until the children can be adopted or returned to their biological parents. In reality, many children go through multiple placements and remain in foster care until late adolescence. Approximately 25 to 30 percent of the children returned to their biological parents are soon back in foster care. Children who are older or have behavioral or emotional problems are the most likely to experience multiple placements (Pardeck, 1984).

African American children are overrepresented in the placement population. One national survey found the following median time spent in foster care: Asian Americans, 14 months; whites, 20 months; Native Americans, 25 months; Hispanic Americans, 26 months; and African Americans, 32 months. Thus, there is a year's difference between the average time black and white children remain in foster care (Jenkins and Diamond, 1985). Placement that extended beyond five years was highest for African American children (32 percent), followed by Latino children (25 percent), and Native American children (22 percent).

Problems of Foster Homes Not all foster parents are successful. Sometimes foster parents are looked down on, and biological parents tend to be idealized (Levine, 1988). Meyer (1985) sees foster mothers as "inevitable victims." The typical foster mother is paid very little and cares for a child whom no one else is able to love or parent. The mother is supervised by a social worker who is probably overworked and often inaccessible, must deal with a variety of people like teachers, police, judges, or medical staff, and sometimes must face angry biological parents who deny that they are incompetent or abusive.

Poverty is no longer the major reason for placement in foster homes. Many children are taken from their biological parents because the parents have substance-abuse problems or have abused or neglected their children. Some of these children are never able to adjust to a foster home (Fanshel et al., 1989). In addition, some must deal with separations from their siblings. One study found that 93 percent of children in foster home placements had full, half-, or step-siblings but that 75 percent of these children were separated during placements in foster homes (Timberlake and Hamlin, 1982). The grief and loss experienced by children who lose access to these natural support groups can be severe.

Children and the Future

Ignoring children has turned into a nightmare, according to many observers. During the last decade or so, there has been an increase in violence, high school dropout rates, and substance abuse by children who are still in elementary school.

Demands for change are coming from many quarters. Benjamin Spock (1994), the well-known "baby doctor," concludes that "our present society is not working." Some of the solutions he offers are spending more time with children, building family values, and parents participating in school and the community. Several others take a more structural perspective. British child psychologist Penelope Leach (1994) advocates doing whatever it takes to make sure that no child grows up in poverty because it is the single biggest risk factor for a variety of other problems, including violence, and teen pregnancy. Among its dozens of proposals, the Children's Defense Fund (1994) advocates developing a federal welfare reform plan that reduces child poverty, increasing the minimum wage, expanding child-care assistance for low-income working families, and promoting after-school and summer programs for disadvantaged youth. Researchers Zill and Nord (1994) propose that government programs, schools, community organizations and parents could work together to overcome many child-rearing problems.

CONCLUSION

As this chapter shows, there have been many *changes* in raising children. Family sizes have decreased, and there are more single-parent families, parents in shift work, and a massive need for quality day care. Parents are faced with many *constraints* at both the micro and macro levels. The most severe problems are generated by political and economic conditions. Even though the United States is one of the wealthiest countries in the world, the number of American children who live in poverty and are deprived of basic health care and food has been increasing since 1980. Parental *choices* are also often limited. Gay and lesbian, minority, and working-class parents, especially, have to struggle to raise healthy children. Chapter 19 discusses some of the recent legislation for providing children with more financial support. In the next chapter we address the unique constraints and choices that racial-ethnic families confront.

Taking Action

Help Our Kids

In the face of the enormous problems children face today, what can we do? One way to help is to "start next door."

• There are probably **latchkey children in your neighborhood or college community.** Because many working parents can't "check in" when their kids get home, you can help out. Churches and senior centers could be encouraged to provide a "hotline" service—especially between senior citizens and kids coming home to an empty house—so children can call an adult and tell them whether everything is okay or if they feel sick or are having problems. High school, college, and university students could provide a similar service. Especially in disadvantaged neighborhoods, the friendly voice at the other end of the line would show children that teenagers and college students care about them and might also provide role models of caring adults.

• Some of the best **child-care centers** are those organized by parents and implemented with community-wide help. Here are some organizations that can help you get such a program off the ground:

The School-Age Child Care Project (SACC Project) offers assistance in school-age child-care programs. For more information, write to

SACC Project, Wellesley College Center for Research on Women, Wellesley, MA 02181.

The National Association for the Education of Young Children has a booklet that describes how you can get a program for the care of school-age children accredited. Call 1-800-424-2460. "How to Implement Child Care Program Options" takes you through the steps of developing an on-site center. This free guide is available from the Work and Family Clearinghouse, U.S. Department of Labor, Women's Bureau. To order, call 800-827-5335.

• Whether you're going to run or participate in a child-care program or are or expect to be a parent yourself, an excellent, matter-of-fact, and useful resource is H. Wallace Goddard's **Principles of Parenting.** It includes dozens of examples on how to communicate with children, what to expect at various developmental stages, and what parenting methods have worked for other parents. You can get a whole set of publications for only $1.50. Write Dr. H. Wallace Goddard, Department of Family and Child Development, 206 Spidle Hall, Auburn University, Auburn, AL 36948-5604, for more information and updates.

• There is a national support group run by and for the **children of homosexual parents.** For information, write to: COLAGE, 2300 Market Street, No. 165, Dept. P, San Francisco, CA 94114.

SUMMARY

1. Infants are not just passive recipients of care from their parents but play an active role in their own development and socialization. Parenting is not a "natural" process but a long-term, time-consuming task that parents must learn without any formal training and often with little help from others.

2. Some of the major theories of child development and socialization are Mead's theory of the social self, Piaget's theory of cognitive development, and Erikson's psychosocial theory of development over the life cycle.

3. Many parents experience problems in raising children because they have unrealistic expectations and believe many well-entrenched myths about child development and child rearing.

4. There is no evidence for the stereotypical view of only children as spoiled, selfish, and self-centered. Only children are just as successful—sometimes more successful—in life as children with siblings.

5. Largely for economic reasons, adult children are staying in the home longer and are returning to their parents' homes, sometimes with their own children. Unless the children are chronically unemployed or have other severe problems like substance abuse, several generations living under the same roof do not have major conflicts.

6. Three broad approaches to child rearing have been identified: authoritarian, permissive, and authoritative. In addition, parenting styles vary across families. Some styles focus on changing the child, whereas others try to affect a child's environment.

7. Corporal punishment is a controversial issue. Although some parents maintain that physical punishment is necessary, many authorities argue that expressing love toward one's children, rewarding good behavior rather than punishing bad, encouraging joint decision making, being consistent, and creating special times with children are more successful methods of instilling discipline than spanking, slapping, or verbal putdowns.

8. Parents and children often want different things from each other. Whereas parents want adolescents to be more self-disciplined, obedient, and industrious, many adolescents think their parents expect too much of them and feel that their parents are generally unavailable. Also, because both mothers and fathers work more hours to provide for their families today, there is less time for nurturing children. One result has been increased parenting by day-care centers.

9. In general, gay and lesbian parenting is not different from heterosexual parenting. Some gay and lesbian parents fear disclosure of their sexual preference and feel more pressure to be successful because they risk losing visitation or custody rights. Heterosexual parents sometimes have difficulty accepting homosexual children's sexual preferences and may blame themselves.

10. Today, many children in the United States live in poverty; foster homes are caring for more children; and increasing numbers of children must live with hunger, violence, and poor health. A number of organizations, researchers, and child experts see a crisis in parenting and have proposed solutions that include building working relationships among parents, government, schools, and communities.

KEY TERMS

ADDITIONAL READING

Books that provide a realistic look at what to expect from children during the early years and offer some useful parenting tips include the following:

MYRNA B. SHURE, with THERESA FOY DiGERONIMO, *Raise Thinking Children* (New York: Henry Holt and Co., 1994).

What to Expect: The Toddler Years (New York: Workman, Publishing, 1994).

BURTON L. WHITE, *The First Three Years of Life* (Englewood Cliffs, NJ: Prentice Hall, 1991).

Several recent books have examined myths about parenting:

MARY FRANCES BERRY, *The Politics of Parenthood: Child Care, Women's Rights, and the Myth of the Good Mother* (New York: Penguin, 1993). Includes a discussion of the influence of interested and nurturant fathers on such historical figures as John Adams, James Madison, and Aaron Burr.

ROBERT L. GRISWOLD, *Fatherhood in America: a History* (New York: Basic Books, 1993). Shows how fatherhood has evolved historically.

SHIRLEY M. H. HANSON, MARSHA L. HEIMS, DORIS J. JULIAN, and MARVIN B. SUSSMAN, eds., *Single Parent Families: Diversity, Myths and Realities* (New York: Haworth Press, 1994). Reviews the literature on single families in Western countries.

JANE SWIGART, *The Myth of the Bad Mother: The Emotional Realities of Mothering* (New York: Doubleday, 1991). Discusses the myths of both the bad mother and the bad father, the complexities of nurturing, and letting go of parenting when children grow up.

SHARI L. THURER, *The Myths of Motherhood: How Culture Reinvents the Good Mother* (Boston: Houghton Mifflin, 1994). Argues that motherhood is a cultural invention rather than an innate instinct.

There have been several books on raising children of color in a racist society. Some of these are the following:

JAMES P. COMER and ALVIN F. POUSSAINT, *Raising Black Children* (New York: Penguin, 1992). Psychiatrists Comer and Poussaint propose how to raise children from infancy to adolescence in a racist society .

DEREK HOPSON and DARLENE POWELL HOPSON, *Raising the Rainbow Generation: Teaching Your Children to Be Successful in a Multicultural Society* (New York: Simon & Schuster, 1993). Practicing husband-and-wife clinical psychologists discuss how parents can teach their children—from three years old through their teenage years—to respect and appreciate cultural, ethnic, and racial diversity. Included is a guide to multicultural books, audiotapes, videos, dolls, and games.

Two recent books have explored issues involved in parenting by gays and lesbians:

LAURA BENKOV, *Reinventing the Family: The Emerging Story of Lesbian and Gay Parents* (New York: Crown, 1994). A clinical psychologist examines such issues as coming out, custody fights, foster care and adoption, and homophobia.

APRIL MARTIN, *The Lesbian and Gay Parenting Handbook: Creating and Raising Our Families* (New York: HarperPerennial, 1993). A resources section provides an especially valuable list of organizations, lesbian and gay parenting groups, recommended readings and films, and legal information and resources.

13
Racial-Ethnic Families: Strengths, Stresses, and Stereotypes

Bee Dityo (James King), Suppertime

Data Digest

What do the following well-known people have in common: consumer advocate Ralph Nader, singer Paula Abdul, deejay Casey Kasem, heart surgeon Michael De Bakey, Heisman Trophy winner Doug Flutie, Secretary of Health Donna Shalala, and Senator George Mitchell? It may surprise you to know that they are all Americans of Arab origin (El-Badry, 1994). Each of these people has made a significant contribution to U.S. society, as have millions of other non-European Americans.

In Chapter 3, we discussed some of the history of immigrant white and nonwhite families. This chapter focuses on contemporary Latino, African, Asian, and Native American families. We examine their changes in family structure, social and economic constraints, and racial-ethnic strengths. We conclude the chapter with an exploration of the ways people cope and respond to discrimination and prejudice. Let's begin with an overview of the growing diversity of American families.

THE INCREASING DIVERSITY OF AMERICAN FAMILIES

As you saw in Chapter 1, U.S. households are becoming more diverse in terms of racial and ethnic composition. As the number and variety of immigrants increase, the ways we relate to each other become more complex. Whether native-born or immigrants, families of color are often treated differently because of their racial or ethnic characteristics.

The Influx of Immigrants

The United States is essentially a country of immigrants (as we pointed out in Chapter 3, only American Indian tribes can claim to be native to the country). Since the turn of the century, there has been a significant change in the numbers of immigrants coming from specific countries. Whereas in 1900 almost 85 percent of immigrants came from European countries (Figure 13.1), in 1990, Europeans made up only 22 percent of all immigrants. Between 1980 and 1990, nearly 70 percent of newcomers arrived from Latin American and Asian countries (U.S. Bureau of the Census, 1994b). In addition, racial-ethnic categories incorporate new groups. For example, "Asian" now includes Hmong and Laotians; "Latino" encompasses Colombians and Peruvians; and "African American" now includes the growing number of black immigrants from African nations and the Caribbean (Coughlin, 1993). As the box "Do Americans Fear Growing Cultural Diversity?" indicates, some U.S. groups have shown considerable ambivalence toward recent immigrants.

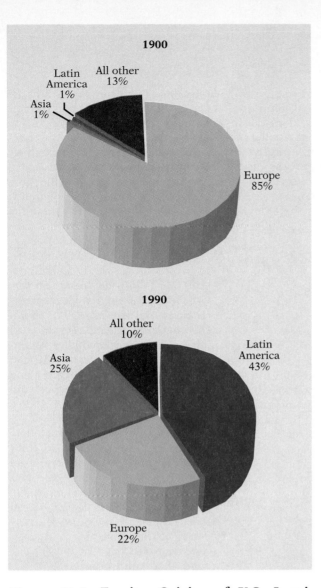

1900

Latin America 1%
Asia 1%
All other 13%
Europe 85%

1990

All other 10%
Asia 25%
Latin America 43%
Europe 22%

Figure 13.1 Foreign Origins of U.S. Immigrants: 1900 and 1990 (U.S. Department of Commerce, 1993).

Some Characteristics of Racial–Ethnic Families

Social scientists describe Latino, African, Asian, and Native American families as minority groups. The most important characteristic of a **minority group** is its domination by a more powerful group. Louis Wirth (1945) explicitly defined a minority group in terms of its subordinate position and went on to say that the people in such a group, "because of their physical or cultural characteristics, are singled out from others in the society in which they live for differential and unequal treatment." Numerically, a minority group can be larger than the majority, or dominant, group. Thus, the relative power or degree of dominance of a minority group is more significant than its numbers. For example, even though apartheid has been abolished in South Africa, that country's approximately 15 percent of whites still control most of the political and economic power as well as access to education and other services. Although Africa's black middle class is growing, many are concerned about the possibilities for career advancement and blacks' ability to move into jobs and neighborhoods once exclusively reserved for whites (James, 1994).

What kinds of "physical and cultural characteristics" single out minority groups from a dominant societal group? Two of the most important are race and ethnicity. Racial physical characteristics, such as skin color or eye shape, are easily observed and easily used to single out racial groups for unequal treatment. *Ethnicity*—an individual's or group's cultural or national identity—can also be a basis for unequal treatment. As we discussed in Chapter 3, many white European immigrants experienced considerable discrimination when they came to the United States. A group that has both distinctive racial and cultural characteristics is referred to as a **racial-ethnic group** (Eitzen and Baca Zinn, 1992). African Americans, Native Americans, Latinos, and Asian Americans are examples of racial-ethnic groups because both race and culture are central features of their heritage. We now turn to a closer examination of each of these four groups.

AFRICAN AMERICAN FAMILIES

African American families are heterogeneous. They vary in terms of kinship structure, values, lifestyles, and social class:

Contrary to what many people seem to think, there is no such thing as "the" African-American family. African-American families are as diverse as white, Hispanic, Asian, and other families in the United States today. Black families are not all headed by single women. . . . Far too many black families are certainly poor, but the majority of black families are not poor (McAdoo, 1990: 74).

E. Franklin Frazier (1937) was one of the first sociologists to point out that there are sev-

Do Americans Fear Greater Cultural Diversity?

In the 1994 elections, over 59 percent of Californians voted for Proposition 187, a proposed law that would bar illegal immigrants from receiving education, nonemergency health care, and most other public services that had been provided free by the state. Proposition 187 would also require service providers to report suspected illegal immigrants to the federal government. At this writing, federal courts have blocked enforcement of the new restrictions on the grounds that only the federal government can determine who may enter and remain in the United States, and that the loss of medical services for illegal aliens could result in greater health risks for the general population. California plans to appeal these rulings.

According to several recent polls, many Americans today are less welcoming of the tired, the poor, and the hungry. In a 1993 national survey, 59 percent said that immigration has been good for the United States in the past. But when respondents were asked whether they think immigration is a good thing for this country today, only 29 percent said yes; 60 percent said it was bad (*Public Perspective*, 1994). Similarly, when a Gallup poll asked, "In your view, does the increasing diversity that immigrants bring to this country mostly improve American culture or mostly threaten American culture?" the responses were largely negative (Moore, 1993: 4), as the following table shows:

	TOTAL	WHITES	AFRICAN AMERICANS
Mostly improve	35%	33%	39%
Mostly threaten	55	57	49

Many Americans, both black and white, say that immigration from Latin America should be restricted. A recent *Newsweek* poll asked, "Are the numbers of immigrants entering the U.S. from each of the following areas too many, too few or about right?" (Miller and Elam, 1995: 64). The breakdown of percentages saying too many is as follows:

AREA	BLACKS	WHITES
Europe	36%	30%
Latin America	40	59
Africa	24	35
Asia	39	45

Reactions have been especially negative toward the most recent immigrants. For example, nearly 70 percent of respondents said Iranian immigrants created problems for the United States and well over 50 percent had the same opinion about Mexicans. Fewer than 20 percent of respondents, however, said the same thing about Polish or Irish immigrants (Moore, 1993). Why these differences? Economic reasons are probably most significant. For example, one factor in the Proposition 187 vote was the nearly $3 billion a year that California spends on services for its 1.6 million illegal aliens (Impoco and Tharp, 1994). Moreover, in California and elsewhere, as job opportunities dwindle, American citizens, especially African Americans, feel that they are being pushed out of many service and blue-collar jobs (Dunn, 1994; Lee and Sloan, 1994).

It has been estimated that Italy and Poland rank second and third among countries supplying illegal immigrants to New York State, and only three countries send more illegals to the United States overall than Canada (Krafft, 1994). Why don't we hear hostile remarks directed toward these and other white illegal immigrants?

---

eral types of black family structures: those with matriarchal patterns; traditional families similar to those of middle-class whites; and families, usually of mixed racial origins, that "have been relatively isolated from the main currents of Negro life." More recently, Billingsley (1992) has maintained that African American family structures have changed and adapted to the pressures of society as a whole. Thus, as more men become jobless, some nuclear families are being replaced by extended families and augmented families in which nonrelatives function as members of the household. Despite such variations, many myths surround the black family (see the box "The Ten Biggest Myths About the African American Family").

Family Structure and Economic Well-Being

We noted earlier that African American families have formed diverse households in response to societal changes. Some of these households, such as those involving stepparents and grandparents, will be examined in later chapters. We

The Ten Biggest Myths About the African American Family

There are many misconceptions about the African American family, most of which can be reduced to the following ten myths:

Myth 1. Most black families are poor and on welfare. Although many African American children live in poverty (see Chapter 12), 30 percent of black families have annual incomes of $35,000 and more (U.S. Bureau of the Census, 1994b).

Myth 2. The major problem of black families is loose morals. In reality, black America has always condemned unrestrained sexual expression and has insisted on stable mating patterns. Unlike white families, however, black families have incorporated out-of-wedlock children into the community.

Myth 3. Most black single-parent families are pathological. Compared to the obstacles they face, many single-parent families are remarkably resilient. They are raising children who graduate from school, who are highly motivated, and who become quite successful (Rhodes and Hoey, 1994). The perception of most black children as delinquents is perpetuated by the media. Although such films as *Boyz n the Hood* offer a realistic portrayal of some working-class black neighborhoods, these negative images should not be generalized to all black communities (Gaiter, 1994).

Myth 4. The bonds of the black family were destroyed during slavery. A number of historical studies have shown that most slaves lived in families headed by a father and a mother. Furthermore, large numbers of slave couples lived in long marriages, some for 30 years or more (Bennett, 1989).

Myth 5. The black family collapsed after emancipation. In 1865 the roads of the South were clogged with black men and women searching for long-lost wives, husbands, children, brothers, and sisters. Most freed slaves, some of them 80 to 90 years old, remained with their mates. Few renounced their slave vows, much less sought new partners (Bennett, 1989).

Myth 6. Black parents avoid work, fail to motivate their children, and teach them to rely on handouts. For most of this century, blacks have actually been *more* likely to work than whites. Although black and white women participated in the labor force at nearly identical rates in the mid-1990s, black mothers have historically worked outside the home in larger proportions(see Chapter 3). Despite high unemployment, black men are only slightly less like than white men to be in the work force—70 versus 76 percent (Thornton et al., 1992).

Myth 7. The African American family owes its survival to white generosity and government welfare. Most blacks survived because of the support of the extended family, house-rent parties, church suppers, and black schools and churches, not handouts or welfare. In fact, some observers note that the African American family has survived *in spite of* white paternalism and welfare. For example, welfare encourages families to break up, because the families of men who are unemployed or in low-paying jobs are ineligible for benefits.

Myth 8. The black family has always been a matriarchy characterized by domineering women and weak or absent men. According to Billingsley (1992), black America has produced a long line of extraordinary fathers, as well as many mothers and fathers working, loving, and living together.

Myth 9. Black men can't sustain stable relationships. Many unmarried African American fathers maintain ties with their children and the mothers of their children. Some of these relationships last ten years or longer (Jarrett, 1994). Middle-class black fathers are often more family oriented than middle-class white fathers (Staples, 1994).

Myth 10. Black families no longer face widespread job and housing discrimination. In a 1993 Gallup poll almost 75 percent of white respondents said that "blacks have as good a chance as white people in my community to get any kind of job for which they are qualified" (G. Wheeler, 1993). Nevertheless, as we will see, qualified blacks are still less likely to be hired than their white counterparts. Moreover, black applicants are twice as likely to be rejected for mortgages as whites with comparable economic assets (Thornton et al., 1992).

---

focus here on children living with one or both parents and on the impact of economic factors on family formation.

Households with Children African American children have a greater likelihood of growing up with only one parent than do children in other racial-ethnic families (see Data Digest). Although in 1991 almost 75 percent of all children lived in two-parent homes, more black children lived in mother-only families than in any other type of household (see Figure 13.2), and mother-only households tend to be poorer than two-parent households. In 1993, for example, the median

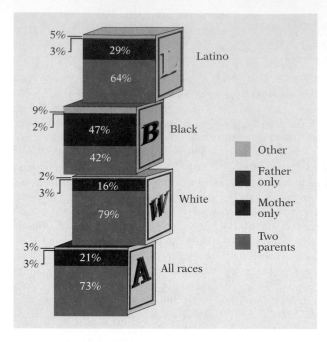

5%
3%
29%
64%
Latino

9%
2%
47%
42%
Black

2%
3%
16%
79%
White

3%
3%
21%
73%
All races

Other

Father only

Mother only

Two parents

Figure 13.2 **Where Children Live.** *Black and Latino children are less likely than their white counterparts to live in two parent families. In all racial-ethnic groups, children are much more likely to live in mother-only rather than father-only households. Note that people of Hispanic origin may be of any race* (Furukawa, 1994).

income of a mother-only household was $12,073 compared to $43,576 for a two-parent household (Saluter, 1994).

A *Newsweek* poll of single African American adults showed that 88 percent said that they wanted to get married (Ingrassia et al., 1993). As you saw in Chapters 9 and 10, however, black women are more likely to be single parents because they are also likely to postpone marriage or never to marry. As one black mother said, "I want to be married, but I also want to be married to somebody who is responsible" (Jarrett, 1994: 38).

Economic Factors Most African American men, including those in blue-collar or working classes, are "proud and moral figures whose personal behavior and work habits are exemplary" (Dyson, 1993: 209). They have nurtured their children, have had loving relationships with their wives, and have often served as role models in the community (Smith and Gelman, 1993).

Several economic factors have narrowed the pool of eligible African American men at all so-

cial class levels. Since the mid-1950s, changing industrial technology has brought about a sharp decline in stable blue-collar jobs. As the availability of such jobs decreased, many black men often ended up unemployed or underemployed. On the other hand, jobs in the service sector and in such professions as teaching and nursing expanded, making jobs for black women more plentiful. This produced more strain for families, as wives became the economic providers.

Black unemployment rates are twice as high as those of whites, and the median income of black families is about half that of whites (U.S. Bureau of the Census, 1994b). Joblessness has resulted in marital instability, high rates of out-of-wedlock births, and female-headed households. In addition, African Americans lucky enough to find work are disproportionately employed in low-wage jobs. Typically, they work in industries that are sensitive to recessions, such as manufacturing and construction, and often, because of their uneven job histories, they are not covered by benefit programs and seniority (Bowman, 1991). According to some writers, it is the high levels of poverty and unemployment among blacks that have led many black males to pursue illegal ways of making money.

Many young black men face very troubled futures: The leading cause of death of black males between the ages of 15 and 24 is homicide. A young black male has a 1 in 21 chance of being killed, and suicide rates among black males have tripled since 1960 (Dyson, 1993). Nationwide, black men represent 46 percent of state prison inmates but only 6 percent of the U.S. population. Nearly 25 percent of black men in their 20s are in prison or on probation or parole. Nearly 20 percent of all black males drop out of high school, and of those who finish, only 25 percent go to college (Bennett, 1989).

African American men who are married fare only slightly better. In 1991, for example, 7 percent of the black husbands in married-couple families were unemployed, compared to 4 percent of their white counterparts (U.S. Department of Labor, 1991). In 1991, 40 percent of black adult males were functionally illiterate (Duke, 1991a). All of these figures suggest that the number of black males, especially young black males, who are in a position to form lasting family relationships is decreasing. Remember, however, that these devastating statistics largely reflect the effects of social class. For example, middle-class blacks are similar to their white counterparts: They have high life expectancy rates and they earn college degrees (Koretz, 1994; Marshall, 1994; Walters, 1995).

Husbands and Wives

A long-standing controversy has revolved around the quality of the relationships between African American males and females, both within and outside the family. Throughout the 1970s a great deal of attention was focused on the alleged black matriarchy and the belief that black women had too much control and power in their families. In *Black Macho and the Myth of the Superwoman*, for example, Michele Wallace (1978) argued that there was a deterioration in the relationships between black men and women. In the late 1980s the movie *The Color Purple*, based on Alice Walker's novel, was criticized by many black men for depicting them as sadistic, exploitative, and brutal. In contrast, many black women felt the film realistically showed how black women supported one another and their families.

In 1991 Shahrazad Ali got enormous media attention with her book *The Blackman's Guide to Understanding the Blackwoman*. Among other things, Ali argued that the black woman's deficiencies included wanting her own way, failing to understand the black male, and having a smaller brain than the black man's. Ali also proposed that the black woman's disrespect for the black man is a direct cause of the destruction of the black family. Some of Ali's most provocative comments instructed black men to control black women:

Her unbridled tongue is a main reason she cannot get along with the Blackman. She often needs a reminder. This does not mean that she needs, or wants, to be battered or beaten to a bloody pulp. However, if she ignores the authority and superiority of the Blackman, there is a penalty. When she crosses this line and becomes viciously insulting it is time for the Blackman to soundly slap her in the mouth (Ali, 1990: 169).

For the most part, black and white scholars ignored Ali's book. It did, however, resurrect earlier concerns about the fragile nature of many African American families.

A critical flaw in polemics like Ali's is that many are based on the lives and experiences only of poor families. Relationships between husbands and wives are often tied to economic stability (Ball and Robbins, 1986). Ehrenreich (1986) points out that, because of the income inequalities of male breadwinners, it would take the earnings of four African American men working full time for a family to enter the middle-class mainstream, characterized by such things as owning one's own home.

Although the African American middle class is expanding, it is still small. Approximately 12 percent of black adults are college graduates (compared to 23 percent for whites), and 15 percent of black families earn $50,000 or more a year (compared to 36 percent for white families) (U.S. Bureau of the Census, 1994b). This often means not only that many wives work but that their husbands expect them to work to maintain financial security. Partly because of such expectations, African American husbands are more likely to share in the household chores than their white counterparts (Ross, 1987).

The division of domestic work is still not equal, however. Although black married couples are more egalitarian than are their white counterparts, black women are still more likely than men to do most of the traditional chores, such as cooking, cleaning, and laundry, and to be overworked. Some of the instability in black marriages has been a result of a conflict between the women's expectations that egalitarian domestic roles are a necessity and the assumption of many black men that their wives, like those of their white counterparts, should be doing more of the family tasks (Hatchett, 1991).

Parents and Children

There are many misconceptions about parenthood and child rearing in African American families. Although black families are stereotyped as matriarchal, the egalitarian family pattern—where both men and women share equal authority—is actually the most common authority pattern (see Connor, 1986). One reason African American husbands are involved in child rearing is that, historically, this practice allowed women to take advantage of work opportunities that were generally not open to men, such as domestic labor and jobs in sweatshops and service industries (Jones, 1985).

Like their white counterparts, blacks who are divorced or separated experience lower levels of satisfaction than do those who are married. Unlike white families, however, parental status increases, rather than decreases, marital happiness among blacks. Several studies have shown that intact, middle-class black families are very similar to their white counterparts in terms of parenting. If anything, the former are more flexible in family roles. Older children often help care for younger siblings. Black fathers also tend to be warm and loving toward their children and are involved in routine child-care activities, such as helping with homework and driving children to medical appointments: "The existing stereotype of the absent or otherwise deficient Black father is very much a product of research that focused in a very limited way on economically disadvantaged Black families, with the results often generalized to all Black fathers and their families" (McAdoo, 1988: 89).

Another misconception is that the African American father is usually absent. Even fathers who are not married to the mother are often involved in parenting their children. Their involvement may vary from living with the child to visiting daily or seeing the child three to six times per week. Many of the fathers play with the child during visits, and they often feed, diaper, and baby-sit young children (Rivara et al., 1985). Despite the popular notion that all lower-class black men are "studs" who try to avoid familial responsibility, many try to support their offspring as much as possible (Blackwell, 1991).

African American families are more likely than white or other racial-ethnic households to face violence or the threat of violence on an almost daily basis. In a recent Children's Defense Fund poll, 75 percent of the black adults surveyed reported being pessimistic about their children's future. While they were concerned about such problems as poor educational opportunities, drug abuse, and out-of-wedlock births to teenagers, three out of four black adults said they worried most that their children or other young people they know will become victims of violence (Fletcher, 1994).

The Extended Family

According to the Census Bureau, a child lives in an extended family "if at least one parent as well as someone beyond the nuclear family (related or unrelated to the child) also lives in the household" (Furukawa, 1994: 7). By this definition, in 1991 almost 13 percent of all children lived in extended families, and white children were half as likely to live in an extended family as were black and Latino children (see Figure 12.2 in Chapter 12). Variables that affect family formation include such economic factors as poverty, unemployment, and the shortage of affordable housing, as well as such cultural factors as a family's willingness to care for children who are not part of the nuclear family.

In some black households, and especially during emergencies, three generations often depend on one another for support. Mothers of black teenage parents are especially important in helping adolescent mothers achieve educational and economic goals (Hogan et al., 1990). Indeed, both black and white unwed mothers have a higher probability of living in an extended household than do their married counterparts (Furukawa, 1994).

What may appear to be a broken African American home to outsiders may be a strong extended family network in which the female head receives a significant amount of aid from both male (father, grandfather, brother, uncle, cousin) and female (mother, grandmother, sister, aunt, and cousin) members. African American family members visit and contact one another frequently and emphasize special family occasions and rituals (see Jackson, 1991). Such supportive family networks are most common in close-knit families, and they are prevalent in families of both low and high socioeconomic levels (Taylor et al., 1990; Hatchett and Jackson, 1993).

The Strengths of the African American Family

Much of the research on black families prior to the mid-1980s emphasized the problems these families face. Although the problems have not been solved, recent research and analysis have emphasized the diversity and strengths of the black family—strong kinship bonds, family members' ability to adapt their roles to outside pressures, a strong work orientation despite recessions and unemployment, a determination to succeed in education, and an unwavering spirituality that helps people cope with adversity (Hopson and Hopson, 1990; Taylor et al., 1990). Single-

Family reunions, like this birthday celebration for John Garrett (seated, wearing white cap), of New Jersey, not only bring extended families together but remind family members of their closeness and their shared history.

parent families headed by mothers, especially, show enormous fortitude and coping skills.

Even when resources are modest, one of the strengths of the African American family is to absorb other people into the family structure through informal adoption (Williams, 1992). Despite economic adversity, many African Americans see their families as cohesive, love their children whether they are born within or outside of marriage, and teach their children to be proud of their cultural heritage (Billingsley, 1992). Other strengths include teaching children self-respect, teaching them how to be happy, and stressing cooperation in the family (Hill et al., 1993). (For a good review of the literature on the strengths of black families, see Littlejohn-Blake and Darling, 1993.)

NATIVE AMERICAN FAMILIES

The 1990 U.S. Census recorded a population of nearly 2 million Native Americans, including Eskimos and Aleuts (Indians and Eskimos living in the western part of Alaska who speak Aleut). Although the percentage of Native Americans within the total population increased from 0.4 percent in 1970 to 0.8 percent in 1990, its small size may be the main reason why there is little information on the modern Native American family. What data we do have, however, show that the Native American family is struggling to overcome enormous economic and cultural handicaps.

Family Characteristics

The strategies that survived from their earliest culture have enabled Native Americans to maintain their families (Harrison et al., 1984). These strategies include a strong sense of tribalism and pride in their heritage. Native American families are still complex and diverse. They speak different languages, practice different religions and customs, and maintain different economies and political styles. Together, these practices create hundreds of separate tribal loyalties.

For example, many Navajos are still familiar with their native tongue and either live on or frequently return to the reservation. Even in the cities, Navajos confine most of their social contacts to other Navajos. They tend to marry within their own group and avoid contacts with either non-Navajo Native Americans or non–Native American organizations. Similarly, most Sioux, whether on the South Dakota reservations or in the cities, confine their social lives to contacts with other Sioux. Among the Pueblo people of the Southwest, tribal identities are especially strong, as are loyalties to traditional customs. The western Pueblos—Hopis, Hanos, Zunis, Acomas, and Lagunas—remain loyal to their matrilineal clan systems, native tongues, and religious ceremonies. The Hopis in Arizona rarely marry non-Hopis and are extraordinarily loyal to traditional values (Olson and Wilson, 1984).

Many Native Americans are assimilating, however. In fact, Native Americans have high exogamy rates compared to blacks and whites. Only 47 percent are married to other Native Americans, whereas 99 percent of whites and nearly 98 percent of blacks marry within their own racial-ethnic groups. Large numbers of Native Americans are marrying people with black, Asian, Latino, or white backgrounds. About half of those who intermarry have white spouses (Yellowbird and Snipp, 1994).

The living conditions on the 314 federally provided Indian reservations are so poor that only 22 percent of Native Americans live on these tracts of land (U.S. Department of Commerce, 1991). Many Native Americans have sought jobs in urban areas, and several tribes, including the Cherokee, Navajo, western Sioux, and most Apaches, have reported a massive loss of languages, customs, and values (Thomas, 1990).

Family Structure

The prevalence of traditional, couple-headed households with children is higher among Native American families than in black or white families (Sandefur and Sakamoto, 1988). In the past, the extended family was much closer, more organized, and more protective of other family members. Extended families are still important today, however, and are fairly common on Native American reservations. Among the Hopi and Navajo, for example, aunts and uncles are important family members. Sometimes the father's brothers are called "fathers," and uncles and aunts refer to nieces and nephews as "son" or "daughter." There is a strong sense of supportiveness among extended family members. For example, it was not unusual during the 1970s for Native American students to arrive at college laden with expensive items like rugs and jewelry given them by family members to be sold in case they needed money (Burgess, 1980).

Parents and Children

Although the extent of premarital pregnancy among Native Americans is not known, the limited evidence we have suggests that premarital pregnancy may be relatively common because no stigma is attached to having children outside of marriage. Both urban and reservation women disapprove of abortion as a response to economic hardship (for example, if the couple can't

afford another child), lack of desire for another child, or marital status (the woman is not married) (John, 1988).

Altough Native American families encourage their children to become self-reliant at an early age, they are very nurturant (John, 1988). Children are considered important units of the family. Parents spend considerable time and effort in making items for children to play with or to use in popular activities and ceremonies (such as costumes for special dances, looms for weaving, and tools for gardening, hunting, and fishing). Socialization in many tribes still continues to be the province of the clan, band, or tribe. Spiritual values are taught and emphasized in special rituals and ceremonies (Yellowbird and Snipp, 1994).

It is the custom among many tribes to teach children to show respect for authority figures by listening and not interrupting. As a result, European teachers have often misinterpreted the silence of a Native American student as apathy or a disinterest in learning (Yellowbird and Snipp, 1994). Failure to understand this and other values can also handicap white students who work with Native Americans. For example, in an internship program on the Oneida Indian Reservation in Wisconsin the most successful interns have been those who have learned to listen before beginning to map property ownership, examine legal papers, or write grant proposals to obtain help for youth centers. One intern was asked to leave soon after he arrived because he kept interrupting the tribal leaders despite a fellow student's warning, "You have two ears and one mouth for a reason" (Gose, 1994).

Many Native American families emphasize such values as cooperation, sharing, personal integrity, generosity, harmony with nature, and spirituality—values quite different from the individual achievement, competitiveness, and drive toward accumulation emphasized by the white community. Until the mid-1960s, when more militant, young Native Americans organized protests, older tribal leaders rejected combative tactics even when the federal government repeatedly violated treaties on fishing and land rights because confrontation was considered "undignified" and not "the Indian way" (see McLemore, 1991). As you will see later in this chapter, however, in order to survive economically some tribes have begun to adopt white business practices.

Some Native American parents feel they are

losing control over their children's behavior and development. Parents often complain that their children do not obey or listen to them and that the children are irresponsible and preoccupied with unproductive pastimes, such as hanging around with friends and drinking. Many parents feel at a disadvantage with regard to their children's school experience because they themselves do not read, write, or speak English and do not know how to support their children's education. Authoritarian and traditional methods of discipline no longer seem to work. Native American youth often complain that their parents do not understand them and are out of step with the times. Tribal elders believe that adolescents' destructive behaviors such as drug abuse and fast driving are an expression of alienation (U.S. House of Representatives, 1986).

Elders and Grandparents

Native American children are taught to respect their elders. Old age is a "badge of honor." To have grown old is to have done the right things and to have pleased your creator. Elders have traditionally occupied a central role in a family's decision making, and, because of the Indian emphasis on family unity and cooperation, they have expected family members and tribal officials to offer them assistance without their having to ask for it (John, 1988).

Grandparents play an important role in caring for the young and in passing down family traditions. Grandfathers are expected to take grandsons and nephews for long walks to talk about life, nature, and tribal values. The grandmother, especially, is often the center of family life and holds the family together. In the past, young, married college students, upon the birth of a child, would bring the grandmother to live with them so the child could learn tribal language and culture from the most respected teacher (Burgess, 1980). This activity was endorsed and expected by all members of the extended family.

Although many elders and grandparents are still primary providers of child care and link children with their tribal heritage, their influence and responsibilities have become more limited. Because of worsening economic conditions and a lack of resources, the elderly have become more vulnerable. Some fear that the status and authority they have enjoyed in the past may be

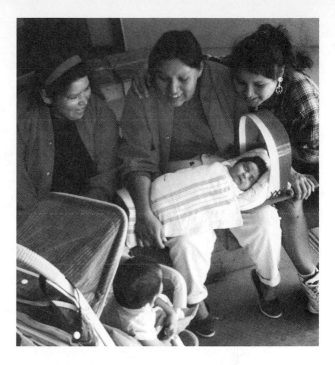

Among many Native American tribes, some people preserve traditional ways while others adopt the practices and products of the majority culture. These differences can be seen even within extended families.

undermined by deteriorating social and economic conditions that threaten the viability of the elders' roles in the extended family (Yellowbird and Snipp, 1994).

Health and Economic Well-Being

Two significant issues that tribal leaders have begun to address are mental health problems, such as depression and alienation, and the physical and sexual abuse of children. Suicide rates are high among Native Americans, especially among teenagers and men under the age of 40. Alcoholism is another problem that has been tackled by many Native Americans who live on reservations (see the box "You're in Indian Country—Switch to Schlitz").

Some of these problems reflect worsening economic conditions. Native Americans have higher unemployment rates than do other racial-ethnic families. On some reservations, unemployment rates have been as high as 90 percent (Harjo, 1993). Poverty rates are also very high; over 31 percent of all Native Americans live below the poverty level (U.S. Bureau of the Census, 1994a). One national study found that Native American

You're in Indian Country— Switch to Schlitz

Native Americans have forbidden the sale of alcohol on two thirds of all U.S. reservations, but alcohol consumption remains a serious problem. The rate of alcohol-related deaths is approximately three times higher among Native American than in the rest of the U.S. population. Native American deaths from alcohol-related diseases are four times the national average, and fetal alcohol syndrome is 33 times higher among Native Americans than among whites (McCarthy, 1992).

According to many tribal leaders, several major beer companies have specifically targeted Native Americans with their marketing strategies. The poorest reservations often accept sponsorship of annual tribal fairs and rodeos by major brewing companies. Such sponsor-

ship typically involves pushing their products: "As a loudspeaker on the truck blazed the strains of 'This Bud's for You,' two men dressed as Budweiser mascots Spuds MacKenzie and Bud Man tossed to excited children fistfuls of miniature rolls of Lifesavers-style candy packaged to look like tiny beer cans" (Haiken, 1992: 11).

Besides sponsoring more than 40 powwows, parades, and other Native American cultural and sports events each year, brewers use more direct methods, including roadside billboards with such slogans as "You're in Indian Country: Switch to Schlitz" accompanied by pictures of Indian rodeo riders and feather-bedecked chiefs. Coors has handed out free posters with slogans like "Coors Salutes the American Indian," as well as an annual calendar featuring photos of powwow dancers, musicians, and rodeo riders—plus the company's logo on

every page. Native Americans who attend national conferences often find that the events have been partly underwritten by beer companies, which also promote their brands with an open bar and free mementos. At a recent conference of the National Organization for Native American Women, participants were given tiny bottles of perfume with the Coors logo etched into the glass (Haiken, 1992).

Some Indian tribes, including the Cherokee Nation, have stopped accepting brewery money for cultural events. Major breweries maintain that their approach in targeting Native Americans is no different than their targeting any other segment of the population. But how many billboards advertising alcoholic beverages have you seen in middle-class or high-income communities?

---

couples with children constituted a larger proportion of the poor than did single mothers with children (Sandefur and Sakamoto, 1988). Among the Navajo of Arizona, New Mexico, and Utah, approximately 70 percent of households live in substandard houses that have no electricity, running water, or sewer facilities. As we will discuss later in this chapter, Native Americans have become increasingly aggressive in trying to solve some of the problems brought on by poverty and assimilation into the white society.

LATINO FAMILIES

There is a great deal of variation among Latino families. Some trace their roots to the Spanish and Mexican settlers who established homes and founded cities in the Southwest before the arrival of the Pilgrims. Others are immigrants or children of immigrants who arrived in large numbers by the beginning of the twentieth century (see Chapter 3). Latino families have

adapted differently to the surrounding white culture, depending on the economic and political realities they encountered.

The many different Spanish-speaking groups in the United States vary widely. Unfortunately, space limitations prevent us from exploring in depth family life in each of these groups, and thus we focus primarily on characteristics that these groups share. Where possible, we note inter-group variations. Keep in mind that people from Mexico, Ecuador, the Dominican Republic, or Spain are not all alike in their customs nor in their experiences in U.S. society.

Household Structure

In 1990 Latino households were on average larger (3.5 persons) than non-Latino households (2.6 persons), both because Latino families have more children and because more relatives live under the same roof (U.S. Bureau of the Census, 1991a). Look back again at Figure 12.2 in Chapter 12: as

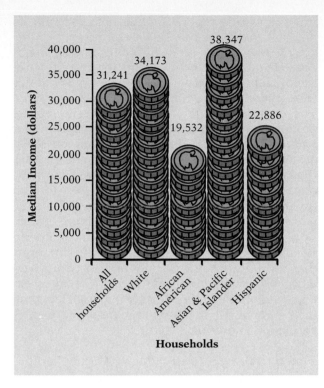

Figure 13.3 Median Incomes of White and Racial-Ethnic Households, 1994 (U.S. Department of Commerce, 1994).

you can see, in 1991 over 25 percent of children of Hispanic origin lived in extended families. Despite a general perception that Latino families are intact, only 64 percent of all children live in two-parent households (Furukawa, 1994). Like their white and African American counterparts, Latino children are more likely to be raised in mother-only households because of divorce, out-of-wedlock births, or separation.

Economic Well-Being and Poverty

Median incomes in Latino households are considerably lower than in white or Asian households and only slightly higher than in African American households (see Figure 13.3). Several factors are involved in these lower incomes: Both men and women often work in low-paying jobs; there has been a rise in the number of single mothers who have little education and cannot find jobs above the minimum-wage level; and Latinos often encounter job discrimination (which we discuss shortly).

Although more than half of all families living

in poverty are white, families of color are disproportionately poor. As Figure 13.4 shows, about one in three black families and one in four Latino families were living below the poverty level in 1993. And as Figure 13.5 shows, there can be considerable variation among subgroups. The proportion of Latino households earning more than $50,000 a year increased from 7 percent in 1972 to nearly 17 percent in 1993. Among the most economically successful are the Cubans in southern Florida. In 1993 nearly 28 percent of Cuban households earned more than $50,000 a year. In contrast, only 15 percent of Mexican American families earned this much (U.S. Bureau of the Census, 1994b).

Familism and Extended Families

Poor or affluent, Hispanic Americans have managed to preserve a strong family system despite discrimination and prejudice (Vega, 1990). Familism and the strength of the extended fam-

Figure 13.4 Families Living Below the Poverty Level, 1993 *Although nearly 65 percent of the 8.4 million families living in poverty in 1993 were white, families of color are disproportionately poor. For example, 31 percent of African American and Native American families are poor, compared to only 9 percent of white families* (Based on data from U.S. Bureau of the Census, 1995, p. xvii).

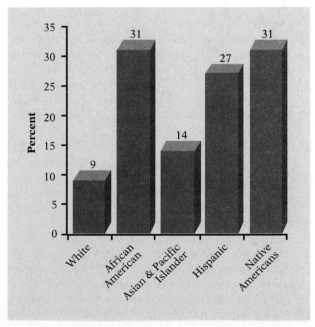

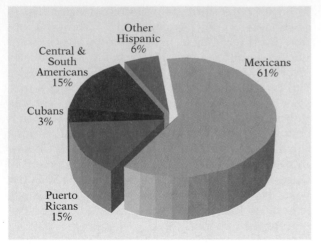

Figure 13.5 **Who Are the Hispanic Poor?** *About 1.4 million families, or 26 percent of all Hispanic-origin families, live below the poverty level. As you can see, the majority of Hispanic poor are Mexican. Note that people of Hispanic origin may be of any race* (Based on data from U.S. Bureau of the Census, 1994b: p. 51).

ily have provided emotional and economic support to Latino people. Much of the recent research on Latino families challenges the stereotypes introduced by earlier white and Latino investigators who saw the Latino family as rigid, cold, and unstable or as warm, nurturing, and cohesive, respectively (Mirande, 1977). Neither of these descriptions is entirely accurate.

Familism Familism, which we defined in Chapter 3 as the idea that the well-being of the family itself takes precedence over the concerns of individual family members, is often seen as a major characteristic of Latino families. The family is an important support system to which the individual may turn for emotional and economic help. Sharing and cooperation are key values (Markides et al., 1986). Some scholars argue that familism is often a response to historical conditions of economic deprivation, and that many Mexican American families survive only because they have the support of earlier immigrants (Baca Zinn, 1994).

Familism may vary by social class. For example, the high rates of visiting and exchange among Mexican American families may be most representative of poorer families, who must depend on large kinship networks for support and who have limited geographic mobility (Vega, 1990). In con-

trast, upwardly mobile middle-class families do not have to depend on family resources.

Even when the sense of familism is strong, it does not guarantee an idyllic life for a family. Like their white counterparts, Latino families suffer from divorce, desertion, and family instability. The degree of family disruption varies across groups, however. Divorce rates are much higher among Puerto Rican families than among Mexican American and Cuban American families (Vega, 1990). Puerto Rican women tend to have more children out of wedlock than do Mexican American or Cuban American women, and over 35 percent of all Puerto Rican households are headed by women. The high unemployment rate of Puerto Rican men may lead to stressful family situations that account for the high rates of divorce and separation (Carrasquillo, 1994). Because children become assimilated more quickly into a society than their parents, even a closely knit family can experience intergenerational conflict.

The Extended Family Many Latino families include aunts and uncles, grandparents, cousins, in-laws, godparents, and even close friends. The extended family exchanges a wide range of goods and services, including child care, temporary housing, personal advice, nursing, and emotional support (Muller and Espenshade, 1985). The family has been especially important in providing emotional and economic support during such major social transitions as migration to another country. For example, Mexicans have practiced a kind of "chain migration" in which those already in the United States find employment and housing for other kin who are leaving Mexico (Garcia, 1980; Ramirez and Arce, 1981). Especially among Mexican American families, two historical functions of the family have been to protect individuals from the hostilities of the dominant white society and to provide financial assistance. Some families have pooled their resources to buy a car or to provide higher education for their children.

Typically, Latino grandparents are welcome to live with the family. It is not unusual for older Puerto Rican women to relocate to the mainland to help their adult children raise their families (Sanchez-Ayendez, 1988). In many Mexican American families, the elderly often have *placitas*, or "talks" with their children or grandchildren and are often actively engaged in passing on religious beliefs to the younger members of their families (Paz, 1993). Grandmothers, especially, are seen not as a burden but as a blessing because they serve as role models and often take care of the children while the parents are working (Carrasquillo, 1991).

Again, there may be variations by residence and social class. In a study of Mexican families in Texas, Williams (1990: 137) concluded that "the extended family has been disappearing, and among economically advantaged Mexican Americans in urban centers, the extended family is not central to the routines of everyday life."According to Abalos (1993), in very poor communities where the family has been decimated by unemployment, drugs, or AIDS, social agencies and community-based organizations have sometimes become the new extended family, taking the place of grandparents and other family members.

One of the most distinctive features of the Cuban family in the United States is the widespread three-generation family. Cuban elderly may include parents and other relatives: "This phenomenon can be traced primarily to cultural norms and values regarding the care of the elderly. Many Cubans believe it is disgraceful to have a widowed parent living alone or in a nursing home" (Perez, 1994: 103). Moreover, many serve as caretakers for their grandchildren while their daughters or daughters-in-law work outside the home. In addition, some elderly make direct contributions to the family's income through gainful employment, or money obtained from Social Security or public assistance. Perez notes, however, that by this century's end, Cubans over 65 will nearly double in number. It is not clear if their children, most of whom were born in the United States, will adhere to the values that have maintained the three-generation family.

Machismo and Gender Roles

In Chapter 3 we defined *machismo* as a concept of masculinity that emphasizes such characteristics as dominance, assertiveness, pride, and sexual prowess. Unfortunately, the last of these qualities has gotten more press than the others, and although some Latino men (like non-Latino men) pursue extramarital sexual relations, *machismo* encompasses manliness in a broader sense. *Machismo* includes such elements as courage, honor, and respect for others, as well as the notion of providing for one's family and maintaining close ties with the extended family (Alvirez et al., 1981).

Some scholars claim that *machismo* has cre-

ated a "ludicrous stereotype" (Segura and Price, cited in Baca Zinn, 1994), that the concept has been misunderstood and misinterpreted in explaining Latino men and their conjugal relationships. For example, when the wife is employed and has a high school education, there is a greater likelihood that household chores and child care will be shared between the spouses, and conjugal roles are more egalitarian (Baca Zinn, 1994).

On the other hand, some writers feel that *machismo* is deeply internalized in many Latino families. Women, they say, are often viewed as submissive, naive, and somewhat childlike (Becerra, 1988). After interviewing 200 Latinas, Flores (1994: 51) concluded that "*machismo* is rampant within Latino marriages" and keeps women "in their place:"

From the day a Latina starts her role as a wife, she is subjugated by machismo. *She carries out her household chores without any assistance from her husband. She prepares his meals, does his laundry and manages his household. When her husband gets home from work, she's always there to greet him with dinner ready. If she's employed, she'll rush to take care of him. She is desperate for his approval.*

Machismo *gives a man a privileged position. In the Latino culture, the traditional wife must always be home waiting for her husband to get home from work. If she isn't he will demand to know why. He'll shout and rave at her as if she has committed a crime. Angrily, he'll remind her she is always to be there waiting for him (pp. 51–52).*

Other researchers have also found that even wives who work outside the home are often assigned a status subordinate to that of men. In many Puerto Rican families, for example, women are still responsible for the domestic realm, whereas men are seen as the main economic providers (Sanchez-Ayendez, 1988).

If a woman holds a high-status job, however, her husband may be less likely to exhibit the *machismo*, male-dominant stereotype. In her study of Mexican families, for example, Williams (1990) found that although neither working-class nor professional women had egalitarian relationships with their husbands, professional women had an advantage over their working-class counterparts in exerting more influence and power in specific decision-making areas such as the discipline of children and the purchase of major items like cars.

Bilingualism

Bilingual education—teaching in both the official language of a country and in the language of immigrant students—is a controversial issue in the United States. Nevertheless, the concept and practice of bilingual education are not new:

Between 1840 and 1917 schools in Cincinnati offered classes in German to German pupils who did not speak English. From time to time, New York City used Yiddish, German, Italian, or Chinese to educate new waves of immigrant children. It was around the First World War, when anti-German sentiment swept the country and speaking English became a kind of index of political loyalty, that the use of bilingual instruction was forbidden in the schools (Carrasquillo, 1991: 115).

Many Latino parents favor bilingual education for two reasons. First, it helps to maintain their children's cultural heritage. Second, they believe that, rather than plunge children into English, bilingual classes may be more effective in teaching children to function in American society. Others argue, however, that not knowing English reduces educational and career opportunities (Jacobson, 1994).

Several groups are pushing for a constitutional amendment to make English the official language of the United States. Two aggressive groups, English-Only and U.S. English, argue that bilingual education and bilingual voting rights threaten the country's unity. Other critics feel that bilingual education discourages assimilation into American society (Fukuyama, 1993). For example, a young woman who came to the United States as a child continued to receive good grades in Miami schools, where she was taught largely in Spanish, but she spoke English with a heavy accent and had poor comprehension and writing skills. An outstanding soccer player, she was offered several college scholarships but was afraid that if she left her Miami environment she would have difficulty keeping up with classwork. As a result, "she turned down all of her scholarship opportunities, deciding instead to attend a small college in Miami, where she will never have to put her English to the test" (Mujica, 1995: A19).

By 1988, voters in 17 states had endorsed referendums that proposed English as the official language of the United States (Carrasquillo, 1991). Supporters of bilingualism fear, however, that if English does achieve official status, Latino populations who are young and lack political clout will suffer. Some analysts predict that the aging white population will be reluctant to pay for bilingual education or for other family services (Acuna, 1988). Others think many Americans see "unilingualism " as a way of managing diversity and as the one bond that can override racial and ethnic differences (Crawford, 1992).

ASIAN AMERICAN FAMILIES

Asian American families, like Latino families, are far from homogeneous. "There are rich and poor Chinese, rich and poor Filipinos, rich and poor immigrants" (Gardner et al., 1985: 39). Not only is there no typical Asian American family, but all families of Asian origin are continually being pressured to change old ways and to adapt to American culture. Some of these changes are in family structure, socialization practices, parent-child relationships, and intergenerational interaction.

Family Structure

Many factors affect Asian American family structure—the family's origin, the time of their arrival, current immigration policies, whether or not the family came from a land ravaged by war, and the parents' original socioeconomic status. For example, there are at least four different Vietnamese family patterns in the United States: the *nuclear family*, made up of a husband, wife, and children; the *extended family*, composed of a nuclear family, grandparents, and other relatives living together; the *broken family*, in which the father or mother and some children are in the United States and the rest of the family live in Vietnam or died on their way to freedom; and the *one-person family*, which consists of the person who arrived in the United States alone and left a spouse, children, or parents in Vietnam (Tran, 1988).

Wong (1988) divides modern Chinese American families into two major types. The first type is the "ghetto or Chinatown Chinese." A dual-worker family, this type consists of the new immigrant Chinese family living in or near a Chinatown in one of the major metropolitan areas of the United States. Approximately half of these immigrants may be classified as working class, being employed as service workers, operatives, craftspeople, or laborers. The second type is the middle-class, white-collar, or professional family that has moved from Chinatown into the surrounding urban areas and suburbs. These immigrant or American-born Chinese are more modern and cosmopolitan in orientation and view themselves as more American than Chinese. In most cases one parent, if not both, has a college degree and is involved in a professional or white-collar occupation. Although grandparents may prefer to establish their own household, many live in the same building, block, or neighborhood as their children.

Many Asian American families see education as the single most important factor in getting ahead, and parents often help their children with homework.

Parents and Children

Major socialization values are very similar for most Asian American families. There is an emphasis on group cooperation, filial piety, and obedience, as well as responsibility and obligation to the family. As in the Latino emphasis on familism, the Asian American family is always more important than the individual. For example, the Vietnamese saying *mot giot mau dao hon ao nuoc la* ("one drop of blood is much more precious than a pond full of water") encourages the belief that family solidarity is always more important than outside relationships. A Vietnamese can always depend on family or relatives in time of need and considers it a moral obligation to support the family and relatives. The responsibilities of a Vietnamese to family are the same no matter how far away this person may live (Tran, 1988). Even when extended kin don't live together, they may cooperate in running a common family business, pool income, and share certain domestic functions, such as meal preparation (Glenn and Yap, 1994).

Encouraging children to get good grades in school, maintaining discipline, being concerned about what others think, and conformity (not standing out in a deviant way) are also important in most Asian American families (Kitano, 1988). Indeed, some Asian families avoid seeking available social services, such as counseling and legal assistance, because going to an outsider for help or allowing someone outside the family to become aware of family problems is perceived as shameful and "losing face " (Fong, 1994).

Independence and maturity are usually encouraged in Asian American children at a very young age. Aggressive behavior and sibling rivalry are not tolerated, and older children are expected to serve as role models for younger children. When parents are involved with their children, much of their time is spent in academic-related activities. For example, in a study of Vietnamese, Chinese-Vietnamese, and Lao families, Caplan et al. (1989, 1992) found that 45 percent of the parents read to their children and help them with their homework, even though they may not speak English well enough to supervise the content of the work.

Unlike American parents, Chinese parents are less likely to shield their children from family adversity. Thus, even if American parents suffer a major business or personal catastrophe, they are likely to tell their children "everything is going to be all right." Chinese parents are less likely to hide their problems, so that, very early in life, Chinese children "learn that reward and punishment are not necessarily consistent with the established rules of conduct and that justice and love do not always prevail" (Hsu, 1981: 91).

Many of these values are held by all generations. Some scholars explain the similarity of values as being grounded in cultural tradition and especially religion. Many Asian American groups follow Confucianism, which teaches harmonious social relations, mutual benevolence between parents and children, and children's obedience to and reverence for parents, other adults, and the elderly.

Socialization practices vary by social class and the degree of assimilation, however. For example, Korean American parents whose children were born and raised in Korea tend to be authoritarian. They use punishment more and are not likely to give monetary rewards for positive reinforcement as often as younger, middle-class Korean immigrants do. Immigrants with more education, especially those with American college or university degrees, have more liberal child-rearing practices. Like American middle-class parents, they tend to adopt more "democratic" methods of socialization in which both children's and adults' attitudes are given a hearing (Min, 1988). Lin and Liu (1993) also found a shift of emphasis in filial obligations among Chinese immigrant families in California. Although children were generous in providing resources for the well-being of their parents, they were reluctant to follow their parents' wishes in such areas as choosing marriage partners or general parental advice.

There is some evidence that gender-role socialization is still very traditional in many Asian American families. For example, Korean mothers who work outside the home expect girls but not boys, to help with cooking and dishwashing. In terms of extracurricular activities, boys are encouraged to take up sports, whereas girls take music and art lessons (Min, 1988). Again, however, some observers are noticing changes as families adapt to American culture: "A [Chinese] college student who immigrated with her parents as a young teenager reported that after immigration relations between her parents were much more equal. The father started helping with housework, and the mother had more say in decision-making" (Glenn and Yap, 1994: 131).

Husbands and Wives

In many Asian American families, males are valued more than females. Among Asian Indian families, for example, men are the heads of the household, the primary wage earners, the decision makers, and the disciplinarians. Women are typically subordinate to men and serve as caretakers (Segal, 1991). The role of the male as the authority figure may be slowly changing, however. Large numbers of Asian American mothers work outside the home because a double income is necessary for economic survival. In some cases, this has changed the traditional view that the husband should be the only or primary breadwinner. For example, many Vietnamese fathers who were rarely at home because of military service have had to adjust to being full-time

fathers and husbands in the United States. In some cases, a woman may work outside the home to support the family while the man undergoes educational or technical training for a skilled job (Kibria, 1994).

According to one Vietnamese husband, more Vietnamese American families are breaking up because of the stress that results when wives must work to make ends meet. When women work, they become independent and no longer tolerate indiscretions by their mates: "Over here they say the hell with you and they leave" (Seaberry, 1991: B9). Similarly, third-generation Japanese men and women have greater economic equality, which means that women have more choices in finding partners and are less dependent on marriage. Although the divorce rates among Japanese Americans are much lower than in the general population, this greater economic independence may help explain the rising incidence of divorce among Japanese women and men (Takagi, 1994).

In many cases, working outside the home has not decreased the wife's homemaker role. For example, in many Vietnamese families, although both husband and wife work full time, the wife is expected to cook, clean the house, and take care of the children:

Mrs. Nguyen is employed by a local sewing factory, where she works 40 hours per week and often works overtime. Her husband, Mr. Nguyen, is a machinist employed by a local factory. He also works 40 hours per week. The couple have four children who are all of school age. Every morning, Mrs. Nguyen gets up early to cook breakfast . . . and prepares lunches for the children, her husband, and herself. In the evening, Mrs. Nguyen hurries home to cook dinner. When she has to work overtime, her older daughter, a 16 year old, prepares dinner for the family. Mr. Nguyen never knows what is going on in the kitchen, but he would become angry if dinner were not ready at 7:00 P.M. Mrs. Nguyen takes care of all domestic affairs, including controlling and planning the family budget. During the weekend, Mr. Nguyen spends most of his time working with the Vietnamese Catholic community (attending meetings or other social activities) while his wife stays home and cleans the house or works in the garden (Tran, 1988: 292–93).

Unless a family immigrates together to the United States, it is typical for men to migrate first, followed by women and other family members. When the immigration cycle differs we sometimes find interesting changes. For example, in a study of Korean immigrants in Los Angeles, Min (1993) found that because of a shortage of potential Korean partners in the United States, Korean women who have immigrated to the country sometimes marry men in Korea who then join them in the States. Evidently it is not unusual for marriages of this sort to encounter problems because the women, already accustomed to U.S. ways, are unwilling to live up to the traditional gender-role expectations held by a man who has come directly from the home country.

Also important among some recent immigrant families is the expansion of women's roles beyond such traditional work as child care and housework. For example, Vietnamese refugee women must often deal with social institutions located outside the home, such as schools, hospitals, and welfare agencies. This "intermediary" role played by women is a potentially important source of power for wives in their relations with husbands (Kibria, 1994).

Generational Conflict

What often keeps many new immigrant families together is tradition, religion, and cultural bonds brought with them from their homeland. As children become more assimilated, however, their attitudes about marriage and family life tend to become dissimilar from those of their parents.

In some Asian American families, American-born children are rapidly outnumbering family members who were born outside the United States. For example, in 1979, 22 percent of Asian Indians living in the United States and between 14 and 24 years of age had migrated from India, but nine years later only 13 percent of this group were foreign-born (Segal, 1991). Thus, growing numbers of Asian Indian children are first-generation American citizens. This creates the potential for greater generational and cultural conflicts. Even families who have been in the United States a short time experience generational conflict. A social worker who worked with Vietnamese families noted that "the kids are completely American after 7 years in America. They want to date, they want to go out with their boyfriend, girlfriend. This idea never existed in Vietnam. So the older generation cannot stand this stuff. And the kids feel terribly upset when

mother says, "Hey—you have to stay home" (cited in Gold, 1993: 311).

Japanese Americans can be divided into five major groups: the *Issei* immigrants, who came to the United States between 1895 and 1942 and are over 70 years of age; the *Nisei*, their American-born children, age 30 and over, who grew up during the depression years of the 1930s and survived the wartime evacuation of 1942 to 1945; and the *Sansei*, the American-born children of the Nisei who are under age 30. The fourth generation of children of Japanese immigrants are called *Yonsei*, and the fifth generation *Gosei* (Kitano and Daniels, 1988). Sansei feel that there should be no parental interference with marriage and that they should have freedom of choice in marriage partners. This has resulted in high numbers of Japanese Americans marrying outside the group (Glenn and Yap, 1994; Takagi, 1994). A similar phenomenon has occurred among third-generation Chinese Americans. In other Asian American groups, such as Vietnamese Americans, adolescents and young adults do not see childbearing as the ultimate goal of marriage. They engage in more premarital sexual activities and have more freedom to choose marriage partners (Tran, 1988).

How quickly children assimilate may also reflect parental assimilation. A study of Vietnamese refugees in nine cities found that parents who worked with nonethnic employees assimilated more quickly than those working only with ethnic employees in terms of dress, speech, attitudes, and beliefs (Roberts and Starr, 1989). Some parents tolerate their children's Americanized behavior because they feel that it is necessary for adapting to American culture. A Cambodian father, for example, is unhappy that his eight-year-old daughter is more concerned about her friends than about her family and elders, but he feels that challenging authority has to be accepted because "she goes to school and has to learn to speak back" (Seaberry, 1991: B9).

Some recent refugee families face even more serious problems. Unlike some of the educated elite who fled Vietnam in the mid-1970s, the second and third waves are poor, lack education, and are finding it harder to assimilate. Many Southeast Asian teenagers, who often don't speak much English, are rejected by their American counterparts, and rebel against Old World values. They often deal with conflict and rejection by running away from home. For example, counselors in

Seattle estimate that a third of all Vietnamese, Cambodian, Laotian, and Hmong families in the area have had at least one child run away from home. Some are as young as 11 or 12. Some runaways become involved in crime or gangs; others stay in a network of "safe houses":

They sack out in "crash pads," small apartments or houses rented by large numbers of teens, that become hangouts for runaways. These "couch surfers" drift from house to house until they run out of places to stay. When they're caught—or bored—they go home, for a while (Ingrassia et al., 1994: 65).

Few parents call the police because they don't have the language skills to communicate, don't trust the authorities or feel they can't help, or simply don't know how to deal with the problem.

The most traditional families have experienced the greatest intergenerational conflict. In a study of Asian Indian families, for example, the major areas of conflict between parents and children centered on the relationship between the sexes (Segal et al., 1991). On the one hand, because American divorce rates are high and the number of available Asian Indian partners is small, parents endorse arranged marriages and do not allow dating. On the other hand, their adolescent children want to date, and they balk at arranged marriages.

Many Asian American children are bicultural; they have taken on some aspects of American life but have retained others from their own culture. And there are differences among siblings: One UCLA student daughter of a Nisei couple described herself as the most "Japanized" of her family. She did not wear such American fashions as designer jeans but "dressed in a Japanese *yukata* [cotton kimono] and *zori* [thong slippers] for the *obon* festival [a religious festival to honor ancestors]." According to this young woman, her siblings were less influenced than she by the Issei and Nisei ways of life (Taguma, quoted in Kitano, 1988: 271–72).

As a group, Asian American families have maintained most of their cultural identity and have remained cohesive despite assimilation and intergenerational differences. Ironically, their ability to succeed despite historical discrimination and exclusion has created other problems: Their reputation for being a "model minority" has both helped and hindered their progress.

The Model Minority—Fictions and Facts

In 1992 a report of the U.S. Commission on Civil Rights concluded that "Asian Americans are the victims of stereotypes that are widely held among the general public," and that the "model minority" stereotype "is perhaps the most damaging of these stereotypes" (p. 190). The notion that Asian Americans have overcome all barriers facing them obscures the real problems this group still encounters in American society

Perhaps the best publicized characteristic of Asian Americans is their exceptional performance in education, which most Americans view as the gateway to success. We often hear that Asian Americans are "whiz kids": They are disproportionately represented in many of the Westinghouse Science Talent Search competitions among high school students, they typically get the highest scores on the math sections of the Scholastic Aptitude Test, and they have high enrollments in such prestigious institutions as Stanford, Princeton, and the Massachusetts Institute of Technology. Although these statistics speak well for Asian Americans, much of the discussion about the model minority is both exaggerated and stereotypical.

Fictions About the Model Minority Although the median income of Asian American families compares favorably to that of other groups, such figures are misleading because many Asian American households are larger than average and include more workers (Takagi, 1994). Thus, higher median incomes represent more persons working per family, not necessarily higher salaries. Furthermore, about 60 percent of all Asian Americans live in the three states that have both higher incomes and higher costs of living— California, Hawaii, and New York (O'Hare et al., 1994). This means that family expenditures are also high.

Many Asians arrive in the United States with few skills and low educational levels. For example, the Vietnamese, especially the so-called boat people, are not a model minority but a disadvantaged minority. They are young (median age 21.5 years), not well educated, and often very poor (U.S. Bureau of the Census, 1994b). The Vietnamese girl who won the national spelling bee a few years ago is a success story, but she is not typical of most Vietnamese, Laotians, and Cambodians, who are among the poorest and least educated of all Asian American families (Daniels, 1990).

Some Asian American educators point out that lumping all Asians together and treating them as a "model minority" ignores many subgroups that are not doing well because of academic and economic difficulties. For example, only about 23 percent of the Hmong population, 36 of the Cambodians, and 38 percent of the Laotians have finished high school, compared with a rate of about 76 percent for all Asian Americans (U.S. Bureau of the Census, 1994b). In many colleges on the West Coast, there are more students enrolled in noncredit classes such as English as a Second Language (ESL) and vocational training than in academic courses for credit. Many students may have to wait as long as a year to get into the noncredit classes, and it typically takes them at least three years to complete the ESL sequence (Magner, 1993).

Income figures show that the most successful Asian Americans are those who speak English relatively well *and* have high educational levels (Hughey, 1990). Many recent immigrants who have top-notch credentials from their homeland often experience underemployment in the United States. That is, they work at much lower-level jobs than those for which they are qualified. Because they do not know English very well, or are not qualified to take state accreditation exams (because they have not received their degree from a U.S. institution or because their residence or citizenship status makes them ineligible), many former doctors, accountants, and engineers work as janitors, assembly-line laborers, or waiters. Some Korean doctors are forced to work as hospital orderlies and nurses' assistants because they can't support a family at the same time as they prepare for the English-language test and the medical exam in their field of specialization. Because of an oversupply in some medical professions in the United States, hundreds of Filipino pharmacists work as clerical, sales, and wage laborers. Even when Asian Americans are employed in professional jobs—such as architects, engineers, computer systems analysts, teachers, and pharmacists—they are not in the upper levels of management (Min and Jaret, 1985; Takaki, 1989).

Finally, many Asian American youths, especially the children of those who live in Chinatowns, do not see promising futures and turn to crime:

Many are alienated and angry. Facing an English-language barrier and prospects of low-wage work in restaurants and laundries, they turn to gangs, like the Ghost Shadows and Flying Dragons, and force Chinese shopkeepers to give them extortion money. "A lot of the owners pay," a Chinese businessman explained. "They are afraid the gang will break their window or set fire to the store." Asked why he became involved in crime, a gang member replied, "To keep from being a waiter all my life" (cited in Takaki, 1989: 431).

Facts About the Model Minority There are two major reasons why many Asian American families have become successful. One is that the United States has typically screened immigrants and allowed entry primarily to those who are the "cream of the crop" in their own country. The other is that some Asian values and traditions are particularly compatible with American capitalistic values.

In the first place, the immigrants from many Asian countries represent highly skilled and well-educated people. For example, nearly 66 percent of the recent Filipino immigrants have been professionals, usually nurses and other medical personnel, and nearly two thirds of all Asian Indian professionals in the United States have advanced degrees. Foreign-born professionals are willing to work the long hours demanded by public hospitals, and they are more likely than native-born medical personnel to work for lower salaries (Suro, 1994).

Second, many scholars argue, the mixture of Buddhist and Confucian values and traditions resembles traditional middle-class prerequisites for success in America. Both cultures emphasize such values as hard work, education, achievement, self-reliance, sacrifice, steadfast purpose, and long-term goals. Asian and American traditions do differ in at least one important way, however. Whereas American values stress individualism, competition, and independence, Buddhist and Confucian traditions emphasize interdependence, cooperation, and pooling of resources (Caplan et al., 1989). Thus, for example, many Korean immigrants have been able to secure capital to start a small business through *kae*, a credit-rotation system in which about a dozen families donate $1000 or more to help a shopkeeper set up a new business. Once established in business, Asian store owners lead anything but leisurely lives. A study of Korean business owners showed that more than 90 percent work harder and live more frugally in the United States than they did in Korea (Takaki, 1989). It is not unusual for small store owners who are husband-and-wife teams to work up to 137 hours a week. They try to keep their stores open as many hours as possible even when this puts them at risk of physical danger, for many of the stores are in slum areas and vulnerable to robberies (Bock, 1992).

Money pools like the *kae* are not limited to Koreans. According to Sun (1995), the rotating savings and credit organization is common to many ethnic groups in the Washington, D.C., area: Ethiopians call it an *ekub*, Bolivians call it *pasanaqu* (from the Indian word that means to "pass from hand to hand"), and Cambodians call it *tong-tine*. All operate on the same basic principles: Organize a group of close friends; agree on how much and how often to pay into the kitty; and determine how the money will be apportioned, whether by lottery or need. The winner can use the funds to start a business, pay for a wedding, put down a deposit for a home, or pay for a college tuition.

One of the most important catalysts in the success of the Asian American family has been its emphasis on education. During high school, many Indochinese students spend three hours per day on homework, two and a half hours in junior high, and an average of two hours in grade school. In contrast, many U.S. students study about one and a half hours per day at both the junior and senior high school levels (Caplan et al., 1992). Many affluent Asian Americans buy houses in suburban areas with good public schools. Others send their children to private schools, hire tutors to help their high school children study after school, and establish private institutions to provide Korean high school students with classes in English, mathematics, and preparation for the SATs (Min, 1988). Among young adults (age 16 to 24), Asian Americans are more likely than non-Hispanic whites to be in school and less likely to be in the labor force. In 1990, 66 percent of Asian Americans in this age group were in school, compared to just 54 percent of whites (O'Hare and Felt, 1991). Even the poorest Asian American families are determined to succeed. As the box, "Achievement as a Family Affair" shows, all of a family's energies are often directed toward education as a means of upward mobility. Despite the hard work and sacrifices, however, most racial-ethnic families still face obstacles due to discrimination.

PREJUDICE AND DISCRIMINATION: PERVASIVE PROBLEMS

- Wedowee, Alabama: In 1994 a high school principal announced that the school prom would be canceled because of interracial dating. He also told a girl who planned to attend the prom with a white male student that her parents (a white father and black mother) had made "a mistake" in having her.

- The Friars Club in New York City: At a private roast for movie star Whoopi Goldberg in 1993, Ted Danson, her (then) boyfriend, made up in blackface, told a string of dirty jokes laced with racial epithets.

- In 1994 Denny's restaurant chain reached an agreement with the Justice Department to pay $45 million in damages to individuals in Maryland and California who were alleged victims of racial discrimination by the chain. The class-action suit involved hundreds of complaints from African Americans that they had suffered discriminatory treatment, such as not being waited on or being required to pay for meals in advance.

- A book published in mid-1994 (Herrnstein and Murray, 1994) suggested that black Americans score lower than whites on IQ tests at least in part because of genetic differences.

Although education and employment opportunities have improved, African Americans and other racial-ethnic families have to deal, often on a daily basis, with prejudice and discrimination. **Prejudice** is a negative *attitude*. It is suspicion, intolerance, or hatred of individuals and groups (usually minority groups) who are different from oneself in such things as race, national origin, and religion. **Discrimination** is *behavior*. It encompasses all sorts of actions that treat people unfairly on the basis of their race, national origin, or other characteristics and ranges from social slights to the refusal of jobs or of decent salaries and the denial of housing applications. Both prejudice and discrimination have a serious impact on families, for, despite the evidence we have cited, many whites continue to believe that mem-

Achievement as a Family Affair

The Vietnamese are among the poorest and least educated of the Asian American groups. Many are struggling to be successful, however. The following excerpt comes from a Vietnamese American father who works two jobs and whose wife is also employed. Note the emphasis on cooperation, the respect for hard work and advancement, and the priority placed on education (Caplan et al., 1989: 117–27):

After school, my children always look for something to eat first. . . . My wife and I are not at home at that time, but my children have things to do at home. My oldest son cleans the living room and his bedroom and cooks the rice in the electric rice cooker. My third child, also a boy, has to help his brother. My second child, the oldest daughter, has to clean her room, too, with the help of her younger sister. They also have to do the laundry for the whole family and clean the kitchen. My wife gets home around 4:30 or 5:00 after work, with our youngest boy, a 4-year-old, from the child-care center. She has stopped to get the groceries on the way home.

When I get home, my children are studying at the dining table. . . . Usually, they do their schoolwork by themselves. My oldest daughter has to take care of her little brother. This boy is the laziest one I have

ever seen. He always forgets to take his homework home and tries to avoid doing anything, including chores.

Every evening my children study about 1 or 2 hours . . . then go take a bath and get ready for bed around 9:00 or 9:30. I don't let them watch [television] at night, but I know they turn it on in the afternoon right when they get home and watch it while doing their schoolwork and house chores. My wife likes to watch [television] and video, too, and the kids sneak out to join her if they finish their work. The kids . . . have to listen to their parents; that is the rule in my family.

About rewards for doing well in school or tasks around the house, I use different ways for each child. My oldest son is doing well in school; he gets straight A's, and I let him have the right to play the video keyboard game at home when he finishes his work. His brother is too lazy and doesn't do well in school. He always gets C's or D's and some F's and always forgets his home chores. He is not allowed to play the keyboard games or watch [television] but he always tries to sneak out and do it!

I also use money to reward them: a dollar for an A, for a B nothing. They have to save money, because when they get a C their savings must be debited a dollar, and if there is a D, a dollar plus a spank.

The other way to reward them is to take them out to McDonald's or Burger King. I always arrange a time to come to the PTA meetings and keep in touch with my children's teachers, especially the Vietnamese instructional assistant at school. They listen to this teacher and respect her well. They don't want to be reported on badly. . . .

Education is very important to everyone. It is the most important thing for us, the refugees. I myself want very much to go back to school, but I must work hard first to provide everything for my pretty big family with five children. I don't have a good education, and my English is too poor to get a good job. I talk to my children about the hard life without a good career and a high education. If I could finish school here, I would get a better job, better career, better position with better money.

I always remind them not to spend time playing and fooling around but to study because only a good education can help us to get out and get up higher and higher . . .

Our generation has to sacrifice for the next generation. We have our dreams, but we cannot make ours come true. We pass our dream to the next generation and ask them, push them, help them to make it.

bers of minority groups prefer to live on welfare and are lazy, prone to violence, and less intelligent and less patriotic than whites (Duke, 1991c).

The Department of Housing and Urban Development (HUD) conducted a nationwide study of the availability of housing for racial-ethnic families in 25 metropolitan areas. The study found that Hispanic Americans encountered bias

50 percent of the time when they tried to rent housing and 56 percent of the time when attempting to buy homes. African Americans faced bias more often—59 percent of the time when they tried to buy a house and 56 percent of the time when seeking rental housing (Mariano, 1991). Several studies done by the Federal Reserve Board have found that minority applicants

Migrant families at the lower socioeconomic level, like this family in Texas, not uncommonly rely on their children to help in the often backbreaking labor they perform on America's farmlands.

were 60 percent more likely to be denied home loans than white applicants, even if they had the same credit histories and incomes (Brenner and Spayd, 1993; Glater, 1994). Although poor black families are more segregated than ever, racial diversity has been increasing in some middle-class suburban developments, suggesting that African Americans and whites *can* live together in harmony (Marshall, 1994).

There is a large body of literature on the discriminatory experiences of racial-ethnic families in lower socioeconomic classes (the box "Are Migrant Families Taking Jobs Away from U.S. Workers?" focuses on a representative case in Maryland). Middle classes are not immune from discrimination, however. There are economic costs even in some everyday transactions where we would not expect inequality. In one study (Ayres, 1991), both white and black "testers" were sent to 90 Chicago car dealerships, wearing similar casual yuppie sportswear. All the testers were in their mid-20s, with three or four years of college education. They told the dealers they could finance the car themselves, and, if asked, gave an upper-class address in a Chicago neighborhood and a professional occupation, such as a systems analyst for First Chicago Bank.

As Table 13.1 illustrates, black females experienced the greatest discrimination, paying as much as $1000 more, or nearly triple the markup paid by white men in both the initial offers and final negotiated price of a car. Why are white males treated so differently than women and black men? Probably because dealers believe that white men know more about cars and about financial matters than do women and African Americans. Another reason may be that white men are more likely to shop around for a good deal and to test-drive a car. Finally, "forcing buyers to bargain—which most people in the U.S. aren't used to doing—lets car dealers target the customers who are least informed, least aggressive, and have the least free time. Then they charge them the most" (Mahony, 1991: 86–87).

In another recent study, the Urban Institute conducted "hiring audits" of white, black, and Latino job applicants in Washington, D.C., Chicago, and San Diego. The researchers matched male college students between the ages of 19 and 24 on such characteristics as height, weight, conventional dialect, conventional dress and hair, articulateness, and energy level, as well as their résumés. After a long training session, the students applied for entry-level jobs advertised in the newspaper. The studies found that, in general, African Americans were less likely than Hispanic Americans to be denied equal opportunity for advancement through the hiring process but more likely to be denied a job that was instead offered to a comparable white applicant. In 31 percent of the Hispanic-white employment audits, the white partner advanced farther through the hiring process, compared to 20 percent in the black-white audits (Turner et al., 1991).

Much discrimination is found in federally sponsored programs. For example, the terms of the Job Training Partnership Act encourage abuse of these programs that lowers the quality of their

Table 13.1
Discrimination in Car Buying

| | AVERAGE DEALER PROFIT | |
PURCHASER	IN INITIAL OFFER	IN FINAL, NEGOTIATED OFFER
White male	$818	$362
White female	829	504
Black male	1534	783
Black female	2169	1237

Source: Ayres, 1991. Copyright © 1991 by The Harvard Law Review Association.

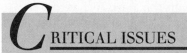
Are Migrant Families Really a Threat to U.S. Workers?

You saw earlier in this chapter that many Americans are ambivalent about the growing cultural diversity in their country because they feel that immigrants take away jobs from U.S. workers. As this excerpt shows, however, many immigrants work at jobs that Americans do not want and, even then, they are often exploited.

After a decade of peeling shrimp in a Mexican packing plant for as little as $5 a day, Gloria Osuna seized the chance to come to Maryland's Eastern Shore. Her employers offered her a job picking crab meat, which [they said] would net her $250 a week after food and lodging expenses. She says she was promised a bed in an air-conditioned house with a television and laundry room.

But when she arrived for work in the little town of Secretary, she found she would share a flea-ridden, one-bedroom house with a dozen Mexican workers. And she says the pay for her first 50-hour

week on the night shift–after the boss deducted money for food and rent–was only $15. "We had to work standing up. They wouldn't let us sit down because, they said, we wouldn't produce because we weren't North Americans."

The American Civil Liberties Union of Maryland filed suit against the packinghouse on behalf of Ms. Osuna and 14 other Mexican migrant workers. The owner said the 53-year-old family business had never hired foreign workers before but no longer could find enough American workers to get the job done.

The 15 migrant workers, all women from a coastal region of northwestern Mexico, had arrived in Secretary after a 4-day bus ride from Mexico. Many left low-paying jobs in Mexico, and some left children behind in the care of relatives. All said they came to Maryland to earn money for their poor families in Mexico. Teresa and Guadalupe Ruelas said eight members of their family shared a one-room shack in Mexico. The family was building a new, two-room house but ran out of

money before the roof was on. Now the rainy season has begun. "Our goal was to send $1,000 home between the two of us to put a roof on the house."

Once in Secretary, the women said, they were told the rules by [the foreman] Jamie Harrington. Another defendant [in the suit], Francisco Cabanillas, a bilingual Mexican, was interpreter and straw boss [assistant to the foreman who both works and supervises the work of others]. "Jamie and Francisco told us . . . not to talk with anybody because all Americans are very racist. Francisco said it was dangerous to go out because a girl had been raped around there. They told us nobody likes us. We don't speak English, and we were scared of people." If the workers broke the rules, the suit alleged, the employer threatened to tear up their work permits, turning them into illegal aliens, or to return them to the Mexican border "without money, food, or documentation" (Bock, 1991: D1, D3).

results. Local training programs are reimbursed for training minority applicants; the more applicants they train and place, the more money they get for future training. The General Accounting Office found that many of these programs were steering people into the areas that required the shortest training and had the best hope of finding work quickly; these were often the lowest-paying jobs. The GAO study also found that whereas white participants received classroom and on-the-job training, many black participants received only job-search assistance (Swoboda, 1991).

In a recent investigation of nine federal contracting companies, the Labor Department found that nine Fortune 500 companies had invisible barriers, sometimes called "glass ceilings," that blocked women and minorities from advancing in management positions. Only 17

percent of the 31,184 managers at the nine firms were women, and only 6 percent were minorities. Of the 4491 executive-level managers (defined as assistant vice president and higher), only 6.6 percent were women and 2.6 percent were minorities (Sugawara, 1991). Some managers (most of whom were white men) promoted people like themselves rather than select from a diversified pool of applicants and evaluated women and minorities on attitude and personality rather than job performance. In addition, there were few minority people in line positions, such as sales and production, from which promotions are generally made (Hawkins, 1991).

Drawing primarily on in-depth interviews with middle-class African American respondents, Feagin (1991) found that blacks are "put in their place" in everyday activities that white families do not have to even think about. According to a utility-company executive in an East Coast city:

I can remember one time my husband had picked up our son from camp and he'd stopped at a little store in the neighborhood near the camp. It was hot, and he was going to buy him a snowball. And the proprietor of the store—this was a very old, white neighborhood, and it was just a little sundry store—the proprietor said he had the little window where people could come up and order things. Well, my husband and son had gone into the store. And he told them, "Well, I can't give it to you here, but if you go outside the window, I'll give it to you." And there were other [white] people in the store who'd been served [inside]. So, they just left and didn't buy anything (Feagin, 1991: 106).

Such experiences are not isolated events. They happen daily, even to middle-class families.

Coping with Discrimination

Racial-ethnic parents are very aware of the discrimination their children will face throughout their lives. According to Ellis Cose (1993), even black professionals have to deal with "the dozen demons" that include a lack of respect, pigeon-holing, an inability to fit in, exclusion from social and community activities, and expectations that they will fail.

Psychiatrists James Comer and Alvin Poussaint (1992) show that besides being good parents, minority parents have the extra burden of teaching their children to survive and thrive in a racist society. Parents must begin promoting racial pride in a child's infancy and continue to build their children's self-esteem and resilience through adolescence and during college. People of color have learned to cope with racial slurs, stereotypes, prejudice, and discrimination through the support of their families, friends, and organizations (Feagin and Sikes, 1994).

The continued existence of prejudice and discrimination is due at least in part to the fact that white parents do not generally socialize *their* children to accept cultural diversity. Furthermore, adults who have the power and authority to discourage racism do not always take their responsibility seriously. For example, higher education has seen a number of racial incidents on campuses. One out of five African American students report some form of racial

harassment, and over the past five years racist episodes have been reported at more than 300 colleges and universities. For instance, after a reported rape on campus, ten black students at Yale University received anonymous "nigger" notes in their dormitory mailboxes, and racially offensive fraternity pranks have led to disciplinary action at such institutions as the University of Texas and George Mason University in Virginia (Morgenthau et al., 1991).

The Contradiction Between Success and Self-Help

Besides discrimination, racial-ethnic families face another dilemma. If they are poor, they are told to "pull themselves up by their bootstraps." If they succeed, they are accused of being uppity. In Washington, D.C., for example, Koreans hold nearly 33 percent of the city's 3000 vendor jobs. They have been described as pushy and are resented by other vendors of different racial-ethnic groups (as illustrated by the battles between Italian and Korean grocers in New York City) because much of their success is tied to the fact that their entire families work as a team and keep their stores open almost around the clock (Spayd, 1991b).

Contrary to widespread popular beliefs that most racial-ethnic families depend on welfare because they do not want to work, many have struggled in a variety of self-help activities. A number of scholars have documented the way racial-ethnic families have fought, historically against oppression and exclusion (Cornell, 1988; Takaki, 1989; Villareal and Hernandez, 1991; Jennings, 1994). Between 1965 and 1990 more than 200 political groups like the United Farm Workers, the League of United Latin American Citizens, and the Mexican-American Political Association have been working to improve educational and employment opportunities. And in 1990, the Puerto-Rican Association for Community Affairs began a program to encourage young Puerto Ricans to continue their education (Dinnerstein et al., 1990).

On college campuses, many racial-ethnic students are becoming more aggressive in demanding "true" diversity. At the University of Hawaii, for example, where three quarters of the university's students are nonwhite, students, staff, and some faculty have accused the university of applying mainland expectations to an institution that is 2600 miles from the continental United States and of not providing Hawaiian role models as professors and administrators. Among other things, they are pressuring for programs to combat stereotypes of native Hawaiians as lazy and inferior, providing more scholarships to Hawaiian students, and implementing curricula that incorporate Hawaiian history (Mercer, 1994).

The Latino Response to Oppression Latino efforts to seek legal redress for discrimination have been much less successful than have those of other groups, presumably because as yet Latinos have little political clout. The Equal Employment Opportunity Commission (EEOC) has dismissed Latino cases without remedy at a far higher rate than it has cases involving blacks or women. The Commission has also litigated on behalf of Hispanic Americans far less often. In 1990, for example, 72 percent of Latino cases were closed administratively without remedy, a higher percentage than for all other groups combined. Even when the EEOC took Latino cases to court, the awards the plaintiffs received were much smaller than were those of other groups. In 1988, for example, the average award in a case involving an Hispanic American was $6867 per single plaintiff suit, compared to $9270 in religious discrimination cases, $10,078 for black plaintiffs, $12,004 in gender discrimination cases, and $39,282 in age-bias cases (Duke, 1991b).

Although demands by university students have escalated, violent protests have not been common. At the University of California at Los Angeles, however, hundreds of Latino students occupied offices and smashed windows during their protest of the university's refusal to grant departmental status to its Chicano studies program. The demonstrators argued that departmental status would give the program more stature and financial support (McCurdy, 1993).

The Native American Response to Oppression Native Americans have a long history of resisting oppression. In 1969, a group of young Native Americans who called themselves Indians of All Tribes seized Alcatraz Island in San Francisco Bay, demanding that the abandoned federal high-security penitentiary be turned into an Indian cultural and educational center. In 1972, the Native-American Movement seized the Bureau of Indian Affairs headquarters building in

Washington, D.C., demanding a reinstatement of tribal sovereignty and enforcement of treaty rights (Prucha, 1985).

Soon after the release of the Academy Award-winning film *Dances with Wolves* in 1990, the Native-American College Fund started an aggressive fund-raising program for the 26 tribal colleges in the United States (McMillen, 1991). Most of these colleges face severe financial problems: Trailers often serve as classrooms, the libraries are poorly equipped, and the faculty members are poorly paid (Mooney, 1989).

Both men and women have participated in protest demonstrations and in programs to advance the cause of better education for Native Americans. Native American women have become politically active at both local and national levels, combining traditional family roles with political activism (LaFromboise et al., 1990).

Native Americans believe that one of the reasons for the high rate of alcoholism within their ethnic group, especially among the young, has been the gradual erosion of Indian culture. Urban Native American children have a particularly hard time maintaining their cultural identity and often feel like outsiders in both the Native American and white cultures. In response, hundreds of programs nationwide are fighting addiction by reinforcing Indian cultural practices and values:

Native-American adolescents considered at risk for serious substance abuse spend anywhere from 2 to 10 weeks participating in counseling, classes, and traditional healing activities. In addition to teepees and sweat houses, there are dormitories, a library, gym, and classrooms with computers. Participants sit inside a teepee or sweat house and express feelings and share whatever is on their heart at the time. Sweat-bath rituals, held in small canvas and willow-branch shelters built over fire pits, often include singing, chanting, and praying. In a process called smudging, wild herbs such as sage, sweet grass, and tobacco are burned in abalone shells or clay pots. It's believed that the smoke cleanses the mind and the soul. The program provides classes in traditional Indian arts, games, music, language, and dance, in addition to lessons about the effects of alcohol or cocaine in the body. Learning about the physical dangers of chemical addiction can help kids make wise decisions, but a main objective is developing pride, an essential tool for facing prejudice and negative stereotypes (Rauch, 1992: 10–11).

The increase in the number of Native Americans in undergraduate and doctoral programs has led to the emergence of a stronger voice on behalf of Indian scholarship. There has been a growing interest in publications on such issues as the resistance to colonialism, the biases in traditional ethnographies describing Indian life, the uses of oral histories, and the exploitation of Indians during America's colonial period (Raymond, 1992). The Native American Graves Protection and Repatriation Act of 1990 has given Native Americans the right to regain ownership of their ancestors' skeletal remains and artifacts that had been excavated from sacred burial grounds. In some cases, the skeletal remains have been reburied. A number of museums and universities have found that working with Native Americans on the repatriations has provided them with authentic information about tribal life (Coughlin, 1994).

Some tribes have become more "capitalistic" in attempting to eradicate poverty in their communities. The Mississippi band of Choctaw Indians has an industrial park with several businesses—one a greeting-card enterprise—that employ 1500 people, making the tribe the fifteenth largest employer in the state. Native Americans operate 124 gambling establishments in 24 states. A few, as in Connecticut and Wisconsin, are very lucrative and have created jobs, health clinics, new schools, sanitation systems, and services for the elderly (Holmstrom, 1994). Tribes in the Warm Springs confederation in central Oregon own a power plant that brings in more than $3 million a year in sales to Pacific Power & Light, manage the reservation's timber, run an upscale vacation resort, and operate an apparel company that has manufactured clothing for Nike. The White Mountain Apaches of northern Arizona operate nine enterprises that generate over $45 million in revenue, including a ski resort, timber operations, and a plant that produces insulation and other materials for McDonnell Douglas's Apache helicopter (Serwer, 1993).

The African American Response to Oppression Most of the progress in civil rights has been spearheaded and supported by blacks, not whites. Just a few examples of the numerous black self-help organizations include the National Association for the Advancement of Colored People (NAACP), the United Negro College Fund, the National Association for the Southern Poor (which helps low-income farmers obtain loans), the Minority Business Development Program, and Operation PUSH: People United to Serve Humanity (which helps to underwrite capitalization of black businesses).

Several innovative ventures have tried to enhance the educational experiences of young black boys. For example, Milwaukee opened two public schools, one elementary and one middle, geared to the needs of African American boys. Project 2000 is a program in which successful black men volunteer to act as teaching assistants

Gambling profits from the Mystic Lake Casino, owned and operated by the Shakopee Mdewakanton Sioux Indians in Minnesota, have enabled them to endow a program in Native American Studies at Augsburg College and to support Indian arts and the American Indian Dance Theatre. The casino also provides jobs for non-Indians, who make up more than half of its employees.

in four elementary schools in Washington, D.C., and Baltimore. The volunteers include retired professionals and college students who serve as role models for the students. Although the programs have been criticized by some, including blacks, as being sexist for ignoring the educational encouragement of girls, others have defended these efforts as attempts to reduce the decimation of young black men (see Ascher, 1991).

A number of higher education institutions have also implemented programs to recruit African American students and provide financial assistance. One of the outreach programs at the Center on the Family at Texas Southern University is the Black Male Initiative—an academic and personal support program that tries to inspire greater numbers of black males to go to college and pursue professional careers. Among other things, black business and community leaders speak at local high schools and provide internship programs for college students (Zook, 1994).

Similarly, there are hundreds of services in communities across the country that try to keep young people out of the drug culture and gangs. For example, in Atlanta, Georgia, a police lieutenant and a lawyer started Fathers Foundation, Inc., a group working to involve more black men in raising their children (Smith and Gelman, 1993). In Cleveland, a social worker set up the Institute for Responsible Fatherhood and Family Revitalization which has reconnected over 2000 inner-city absent fathers with their children (Shapiro et al., 1995).

The Asian American Response to Oppression

For many Asian Americans, the best revenge against discrimination has been educational and economic success. Like the other racial-ethnic groups, however, they have also been active since the turn of the century in protesting oppression and exploitation. For example, Japanese workers participated in at least 60 work stoppages in Hawaii and the mainland between 1870 and 1930 and were involved in numerous agricultural strikes on the West Coast (Feagin and Feagin, 1993).

The Japanese American Citizens League (JACL) has been instrumental in pressing for civil rights, getting compensation for losses sustained by Japanese who were sent to relocation centers during World War II, and helping to elect Japanese Americans to Congress. Many Asian American communities have successfully resisted pressure from local councils to make English the official language. They have organized voter registration campaigns, and students have helped to establish Asian American studies programs in colleges and universities and created journals that focus on discrimination issues (Kitano and Daniels, 1988).

As increasing numbers of Asian Americans move to the suburbs, some Asian entrepreneurs are providing services and products that compete with traditional businesses. One of the most successful is Yachan Plaza in the prosperous Chicago suburb of Arlington Heights. The mall draws consumers from several states. The supermarket provides authentic Asian food, imported items, spices, and a variety of fresh seafood for cooking or eating raw. The store sells more than a dozen types of tofu and eight varieties of fresh mushrooms, even in the middle of winter (Uehling, 1994). To counteract the stereotypical images of Asians in the mainstream press, Asian Americans have established more than 20 publications. One of the national magazines, *XO*, is targeted at men: "While mainstream America portrays Asian men as bespectacled nerds, industrious geniuses, and busy workers in factories, *XO's* . . . articles center on Asian men as being seductive, hot-blooded, and on the cutting edge" (Nguyen, 1994: D1).

When American businesses realized that Asian Americans offered new markets, they moved aggressively to woo these new groups. There have been some marketing snafus, however, when translators goofed:

- KFC (formerly, Kentucky Fried Chicken), which touts its chicken as "finger-lickin' good," tried to attract Asian customers, telling them "you will eat your fingers off."

- Pepsi, trying to expand the reach of its well-known slogan "Come alive, you're in the Pepsi generation," exhorted its Chinese customers to "come and wake up your dead ancestors" (Lam, 1992: C1, C21).

CONCLUSION

The racial and ethnic composition of American families is *changing*. There has been an influx of immigrants from many non-European countries, and the growth of African American, Native American, Asian American, and Latino families is expected to continue in the future. As this chapter has shown, there are many variations both between and among racial-ethnic families in terms of family structure, extended kinship networks, and parenting styles. This means that families have more *choices* outside of the traditional, white middle-class family model. These choices are often steeped in *constraints*, however. Even middle-class racial-ethnic families confront stereotypes and discrimination on a daily basis. Because many children are bicultural, they must live in two worlds. Whether or not they will succeed largely depends on the economic resources of their families, an issue we examine in the next chapter.

Taking Action

Fight Prejudice and Discrimination with Knowledge

One of the best ways to change the current patterns of prejudice and discrimination is to know where to find and use resources that refute the prevailing stereotypes and challenge legal, political, economic, and social racism.

• An invaluable and comprehensive resource is Charles A. Taylor, ed., *Guide to Multicultural Resources: 1993/1994* (Madison, WI: Praxis, 1993). This publication has chapters on specific **racial-ethnic groups,** each of which offers a list of resources, including names and locations, on racial-ethnic issues; arts/cultural organizations; racial-ethnic associations; civil rights/advocacy groups; colleges, universities, and educational organizations that feature racial-ethnic studies; fraternities and sororities; libraries and bookstores; publications that target racial-ethnic groups; museums and historical societies; religious organizations; and women's organizations.

• Some educators propose challenging racism by familiarizing children and young people with the **accomplishments of people who have fought for equality.** One of these recommended, annotated lists can be found in E. K. Laing's "Real-Life Stories Tell of Dignity and Diversity," *Christian Science Monitor*, February 5, 1993, p. 11.

• Some African Americans have given their children **names that more meaningfully reflect their African heritage.** Julia Stewart's *African Names* (New York: Citadel Press, 1993) presents a compilation of names from the African continent that includes their meaning in their original language as well as suggestions for converting your present name to an African variation.

• Another interesting resource on **African culture** is *African Homefront* magazine. It focuses on the African family and can be ordered at P.O. Box 2372, Grand Rapids, MI 49503 (616-365-0469). A recent issue included articles on African womanhood, images of childhood, quilting, the African economy, a description of a trip to Ghana by African Americans, and a "kids-front" section.

• For a useful guide to **videos on race, gender, and ethnicity,** see Barbara Abrash and Catherine Egan, eds., *Mediating History: The Map Guide to Independent Video by and About African American, Asian American, Latino, and Native American People* (New York: New York University Press, 1992).

• MUJER-L is a new e-mail list for those who share an interest in **Chicana and/or Latina issues.** Send your subscription message to LISTPROC@LMRINET.GSE.UCSB.EDU.

SUMMARY

1. U.S. households are becoming more diverse in terms of racial and ethnic composition. Demographers project that, if current migration, immigration, and birth rate trends continue, by 2050 almost half of the population in the United States will be nonwhite.

2. Latino, African, Asian, and Native Ameri-

can families are considered minority groups. One of the most important characteristics of a minority group is its lack of economic and political power.

3. Black families are very heterogeneous in terms of lifestyle. They also vary in kinship structure, values, and social class. Despite such variations, many myths surround the African American family.

4. One of the biggest differences between white and racial ethnic families is that the latter emphasize the importance of extended families.

5. Native American families are complex and diverse. Native Americans speak different languages, practice different religions and customs, and maintain different economies and political styles. Because of assimilation, however, a number of tribes have lost their language and customs during the last generation.

6. Latino families differ on a number of characteristics, including when they settled in the United States, where they came from, and how they adapted to economic and political problems.

7. Recent research has challenged many stereotypes about the Latino family. For example, family structure and dynamics vary greatly by social class and the degree of assimilation.

8. Asian American families are even more diverse than Native American and Latino families. Asian American family structures vary on the family's origin, when the immigrants arrived, whether or not their homeland was ravaged by war, and the socioeconomic status of the parents.

9. Prejudice and discrimination continue to be pervasive problems that affect all racial-ethnic families in such areas as housing, employment, and education.

10. Despite widespread beliefs that minority families are passive and dependent on welfare, data show that racial-ethnic families have resisted oppression, organized many self-help groups, and achieved economic and political success.

KEY TERMS

minority group   351
racial-ethnic group   352

bilingual education   364
prejudice   370

discrimination   370

ADDITIONAL READING

KARIN AGUILAR-SAN JUAN, ed., *The State of Asian America: Activism and Resistance in the 1990s* (Boston: South End Press, 1994). A compilation of articles about Asian American protests against racism and discrimination.

YEN LE ESPIRITU, *Asian American Panethnicity: Bridging Institutions and Identities* (Philadelphia: Temple University Press, 1992). An examination of the way different Asian nationality groups in the United States have united to achieve common goals.

CHRIS RAYMOND, "Growth of Scholarship on American Indians Brings New Insights About Native Cultures," *Chronicle of Higher Education*, January 15, 1992, pp. A8, A10. Includes a good reading list of some of the recently published books on Native American history and culture.

EARL SHORRIS, *Latinos: A Biography of the People* (New York: Norton, 1992). Shows how Cubans, Puerto Ricans, Mexicans, and other Spanish-speaking people vary in their attitudes toward education, money, and values.

ROBERT STAPLES and LEANOR BOULIN JOHNSON, *Black Families at the Crossroads: Challenges and Prospects* (San Francisco: Jossey-Bass, 1993). A very readable examination of such issues as work and money, sexual intimacy, gender roles, parenting, and kinship.

EARLE H. WAUGH, SHARON MCIRVIN ABU-LABAN, and REGULA BURCHKHARDT QURESHI, eds., *Muslim Families in North America* (Edmonton: University of Alberta Press, 1991). Although most of the articles focus on marriage strategies, this anthology shows the diversity of Muslim families in socialization and gender roles.

Following are a few of the books that have taken a more personal perspective, focusing on the conflict between pride and ambivalence about one's racial-ethnic identity:

BETTINA FLORES, *Chiquita's Cocoon* (New York: Villard, 1994).

NATHAN MCCALL, *Makes Me Wanna Holler: A Young Black Man in America* (New York: Random House, 1994).

RICHARD RODRIGUEZ, *Days of Obligation: An Argument with My Mexican Father* (New York: Viking, 1992).

Books that show racism to be a persistent problem even for minority middle classes and professionals include the following:

ELLIS COSE, *The Rage of a Privileged Class* (New York: HarperCollins, 1993).

JOE R. FEAGIN and MELVIN P. SIKES, *Living with Racism: The Black Middle-Class Experience* (Boston: Beacon Press, 1994).

JUDY SCALES-TRENT, *Notes of a White Black Woman* (University Park: Pennsylvania State University Press, 1995).

GREGORY H. WILLIAMS, *Life on the Color Line: The True Story of a White Boy Who Discovered He Was Black* (New York: Dutton, 1995).

14

Families and Work: Facing the Economic Squeeze

Diego Rivera, Sugar Cane

Data Digest

- The share of U.S. family income controlled by the **top 5 percent of households** increased from 16.6 percent in 1989 to 20 percent in 1993.

- At the same time, the **median family** income decreased by nearly $2000—from $38,710 to $36,956—between 1989 and 1993.

- In 1994, **pay raises averaged 4 percent,** barely above the inflation rate.

- The proportion of **families that might be termed traditional**—those in which the father worked year-round, full time and the mother was a full-time homemaker—declined from four out of ten families in 1970 to two out of ten in 1992.

- In 1991, **42 percent of families could not afford a modestly priced house** (defined by the Department of Labor as a house priced 25 percent below all homes in the surrounding area).

- In 1993, **26 percent of all children under age six were poor,** and 64 percent of children under six living with single-parent mothers were poor, compared to 13 percent of children in married-couple families.

- In 1992, **African American children represented 35 percent of all poor children under age six** but only 16 percent of all U.S. children in this age category.

- In 1992, **54 percent of women with newborn infants were in the labor force,** up from 44 percent in 1982 and 31 percent in 1976.

- Year-round, full-time **women workers earned 72 percent of what men earned** in 1993, up slightly from 69 percent in 1989.

SOURCES: Bachu, 1993; Hayghe and Bianchi, 1994; U.S. Bureau of the Census, 1994b; 1995; U.S. Department of Labor, 1994a.

One of the biggest problems many families face today is making ends meet in a changing economy:

Cleveland cabbie Tom Ventura, 49, wishes he could see more of his three teenage sons, but to make up for slowing business he now drives 12 to 14 hours a day, six days a week. Some nights he arrives home at 11:30 and is back in the taxi by 5 A.M. His wife cannot take up much of the slack at home because she works 10 hours a day as a courier. . . . As a result, the Ventura boys get themselves off to school and often take care of supper on their own. "We can't afford the time to do the things we used to do," Ventura laments. "I'll send them to a ballgame instead of going with them. You can't do it as a family" (Boroughs et al., 1992: 60).

Tom Ventura's experience is not unique. Macroeconomic conditions shape family composition, family roles, and even family dynamics. We begin this chapter with an overview of the economic health of the family.

THE ECONOMIC HEALTH OF THE FAMILY

A November 1994 cover of *U.S. News & World Report* practically shouted the question, "Why Are You So Angry?" The answer, according to the articles, was that many people were so irate about the economic situation that they were ready to vote political incumbents out of office. (And that is exactly what they did on election day, the following week.) According to a poll by the magazine, 57 percent of respondents said the economy was stagnating or declining and more than two thirds feared their children will not live as well as they do (Roberts et al., 1994). Many families felt that they were working harder and earning less. As several researchers noted, "Families seem to be in a situation where they have to run as fast as they can just to remain in the same place" (Zill and Nord, 1994: 11). Because of an increase in income inequality, poverty, and homelessness during the last 25 years, some families fell out of the race no matter how fast they ran while a growing number of families have watched the race from their penthouses.

Income Inequality

The Census Bureau uses several methods to measure income inequality. One of these methods is the share of combined household income where households are ranked from lowest to highest on the basis of income and then divided into fifths. As you can see from Figure 14.1, typically the data are presented in terms of the lowest fifth, or 20 percent, the highest 20 percent, and a middle group of 60 percent that includes the three middle fifths. (The Gini index, another way of measuring income concentration, is described in U.S. Bureau of the Census, 1995.) Census Bureau data on combined household incomes as well as other studies on income show that the rich are getting richer, the middle class is shrinking, and the working class is barely surviving.

The Rich Are Getting Richer According to a Federal Reserve study, the wealthiest 5 percent of Americans, or about 450,000 families, enjoyed about a 76 percent growth in net worth from 1982 to 1989—from an estimated $2.5 trillion to $4.4 trillion (Dentzer, 1992). As Figure 14.1 shows, the proportion of families both in the highest 20 percent and, within that group, in the top 5 percent has increased since 1968. The richest 20 percent of American households now make nearly half of the nation's total family income (U.S. Bureau of the Census, 1994a).

The Middle Class Is Shrinking Whereas the incomes of families in the highest 20 percent have increased, the incomes of families in the middle 60 percent have decreased by five percentage points between 1968 and 1993 (see Figure 14.1). In this sense, the middle class may be said to be shrinking.

The middle class is not easy to define because it encompasses a wide range of people—from professional workers at one end of the continuum to white-collar workers at the other—who may differ quite a bit on such variables as occupation, prestige, power, and lifestyle. For example, a new elementary school teacher may earn $23,000 a year while a chemical engineer may have an entry salary of about $55,000 a year. Both are defined as middle class because they have college degrees and hold professional jobs. However, the difference in salaries means considerably less access to more expensive housing, recreation, and other goods and services for the lower-paid worker. In addition, working-class families, many of whom are African American, Latino, or of other racial-ethnic groups, often maintain "middle-class" values, aspirations, and expectations for their children even when they are laid off, cannot find well-paying jobs, or are forced to accept subsistence wages (Boyd-Franklin, 1993).

The middle class has been shrinking primar-

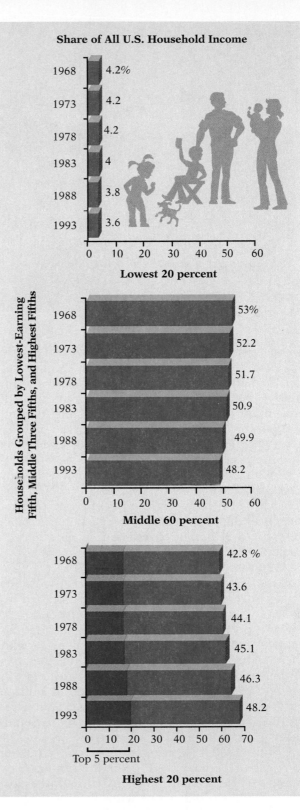

Figure 14.1 *Distribution of Household Income, 1968–1993* (U.S. Bureau of the Census, 1995, p. xii).

These unemployed executives meet to share ideas and experiences as well as leads to possible new positions.

ily because jobs have been eliminated and people have had to take positions that offer lower wages and benefits. During the 1990–91 recession, almost 400,000 jobs were permanently eliminated, and many workers have been unable to find comparable positions since that time (Hage et al., 1993). Even people at the higher end of the middle-class continuum are nervous because another 300,000 professional and managerial jobs have disappeared since the early 1990s. Thus, "corporate restructuring can sweep away . . . paychecks at any time; technology is changing markets so fast that no livelihood is guaranteed" (Spiers, 1993: 80).

With the dismantling of the Soviet Union and the end of the Cold War in 1991, thousands of scientists and engineers in defense-related industries were laid off permanently. In addition, the prospect of health-care reform led pharmaceutical and biotech firms to downsize and merge, shedding thousands of jobs for chemists and biologists (Begley and Shackelford, 1994). In many areas, the only jobs that recent college graduates have found are those that do not require a college degree, such as those in retail, sales, and lower-level management.

Since 1980, real income (or income adjusted for inflation) has been declining rapidly for many middle-class workers. In 1979, for example, a 30-year-old man with a high school diploma earned the equivalent of $27,074 in 1992 dollars; in 1992, that same person would have earned about $20,000 in actual money

(Roberts et al., 1994). Middle-class wage earners pay the highest taxes largely because of continuous payroll-tax increases since the 1970s. Measured in 1991 dollars, for instance, the tax rate for a $30,000 earner increased from 20 percent in 1985 to over 30 percent in 1994. In contrast, the tax rate for someone earning $200,000 a year (also in 1991 dollars) *declined* from 50 percent in 1965 to 43 percent in 1994 (Kudlow, 1994).

Homeownership rates, once a sure indicator of middle-class status, have declined precipitously for people under 35. Although the median value of a home increased 47 percent between 1970 and 1990, household income increased only 10 percent during this period. As a result, 92 percent of families whose head of household was between 25 and 34 years of age could not afford to buy a median-priced house of $79,100, and nearly half of all American families were unable to buy their own homes (Wilson, 1993; see also Data Digest). The major reasons for not being able to buy a median-priced house include having too much debt to qualify for a mortgage, not having enough cash for a down payment and for the costs of closing (costs associated with signing a mortgage agreement), and not having enough income to afford the monthly mortgage payments (Savage and Fronczek, 1993).

The Working Class Is Barely Surviving While many middle-class households have to forgo luxuries, numerous working-class families teeter on the brink of poverty:

When Howard Hagen took early retirement from a steel mill 10 years ago, he was making $23 an hour. Today, his daughter, Nancy, makes $5.25 an hour selling advertising. On that, she supports her four children. . . . Her ex-husband, a plumber, works only sporadically and hasn't kept up his child support payments. Even with public help—Medicaid for the children, subsidies for her heating bills—her budget, like an old car, is constantly breaking down. . . . She buys clothes at thrift shops, and even a simple purchase like new tennis shoes requires a juggling act. "Every Friday night we went out for dinner," she remembers. "Now, when I take the kids to McDonald's, it's a big deal!" (S.V. Roberts, 1994: 32).

Most of the reasons for the dire financial predicament of working-class families—whose members range from skilled blue-collar workers to those who barely make a minimum wage—are macro-level. First, technological changes have replaced many manual workers with machines. The so-called smokestack industries and assembly lines that employed many production workers have dwindled in number or have upgraded jobs that use robots or computerization.

Second, the entire industrial structure of the economy has changed. Many of the high-paying, goods-producing industries have been replaced by service industries that pay only a minimum wage. Between 1981 and 1989 the minimum wage of $3.35 an hour remained unchanged. The minimum wage—paid to 3 million Americans, over 60 percent of whom are adults—was raised to $3.80 an hour in 1990 and to $4.25 in 1991 (Ropers, 1991). Social scientists have pointed out that increases of these levels will not raise millions of low-wage workers above the poverty line. Moreover, between 1970 and 1990 the minimum wage lost almost 40 percent of its real value (Levine, 1994).

Third, the numbers of single-parent households, young workers with low salaries, and elderly women with small fixed incomes have increased. Finally, many American corporations have been exporting white-collar and blue-collar jobs overseas or to third-world countries (see Chapter 13). In 1994, for example, Motorola moved much of its software production to India. Multinational corporations, the majority of which are United States–based, relocate to poor countries because of their low wages and weak environmental laws, which lower corporations' operating costs. Faced with the threat of such relocation, many U.S. unions and workers succumb to pay cuts and a loss of health benefits. The box "Wanted: Workers for Low-Paying Jobs and Long Hours" looks at this issue more closely.

CONSTRAINTS

Wanted: Workers for Low-Paying Jobs and Long Hours

Bitter but resigned, factory workers at London Fog Corporation approved a contract that would keep a scaled-down Baltimore plant operating but would close two other plants in Maryland. London Fog was already producing half of its coats in foreign markets for $10 per coat instead of the $18 per coat production cost in the United States. The terms of the two-year contract signed by the Amalgamated Clothing and Textile Workers Union included laying off almost 400 of the 609 Baltimore employees, cutting the base hourly rate from $7.90 to $6.90, and requiring workers to meet hourly quotas to cut the 18-day production schedule per cost to 10 days. The state of Maryland agreed to provide funds to train workers and to give London Fog a "break" on its monthly rent (Hetrick, 1994).

Millions of U.S. workers are unemployed because large U.S. corporations have moved their production overseas. For example, virtually 100 percent of Nike's shoe assembly is performed in Asian countries. The company has a global payroll of over 8000 in management, sales, promotion, and advertising, but its actual production process is in the hands of about 75,000 Asian contractors.

Nike has opened up 35 new production sites in China, Indonesia, and Thailand, where wages are rock bottom. Nikes made in Indonesia cost $5.60 to produce, and sell for about $73 in North America and $135 in Europe. The Indonesian girls who sew the shoes may earn as little as 15 cents an hour. Overtime is often mandatory: "After an eleven-hour day that begins at 7:30 A.M. the girls return to the company barracks at 9:15 P.M. to collapse into bed, having earned as much as $2.00 if they are lucky" (Barnet and Cavanagh, 1994: 326).

Poverty

The **poverty line** is the minimal level of income that the federal government considers necessary for individuals' and families' basic subsistence. The poverty line is calculated by measuring such things as the annual cost of food that has the minimum nutrients and the cost of adequate housing. Poverty levels do not include the value of such noncash benefits as food stamps, medical services (such as Medicare and Medicaid), and public housing subsidies. The poverty line, which in 1993 was $14,763 for a family of four, changes every year to reflect changes in the *Consumer Price Index*, an index of prices that measures the change in the cost of basic goods and services in comparison to a fixed base period (U.S. Bureau of the Census, 1994).

Authorities disagree on the validity of official poverty statistics. Some point out that the amount of money needed for subsistence varies drastically by region. Others claim that the poverty level ignores the needs of single mothers who need affordable child care so that they can work, as well as transportation costs to child-care centers and jobs (Renwick and Bergmann, 1993; Bergmann, 1994). Nevertheless, according to Census Bureau data, in 1993 more than 39 million people—over 15 percent of the U.S. population—lived below the official government poverty line. This number was the highest since 1962, when 38.6 million were officially poor (see Figure 14.2). Nearly half of unemployed husbands in poor married-couple families are ill or disabled, and the remainder are unable to find work, are going to school, or are retired (U.S. Bureau of the Census, 1993). Disproportionately represented among the poor are children, the elderly, women, and racial-ethnic families.

Children and the Elderly In 1993 more than half of the nation's poor were either children or older people. Children make up only 25 percent of the total U.S. population but are over 40 percent of the poor. People 65 and over account for 12 percent of the total population and 10 percent of the poor (U.S. Bureau of the Census, 1995). Although government programs for the elderly have kept up with the rate of inflation, since 1980 many welfare programs for children have been reduced or eliminated. Currently, more than a quarter of all U.S. children under six years of age live in poverty, and it is estimated that by the year 2030 this proportion will rise to a third (Children's Defense Fund, 1989).

Slightly more than 50 percent of all African American children under age six are poor, compared to 45 percent of Latino children and 17 percent of white children in the same age group. Longitudinal studies have shown that black children who fare worst are those who face multiple risks, such as being born to young, never-married mothers who live in economically depressed areas and are on public assistance (Rexroat, 1994).

Women Single mothers and their children make up a large segment of the poor. Of children under age 6 living in families with a female householder, no spouse present, 64 percent were poor, compared to 13 percent of such young children in married-couple families. Researcher Diana Pearce (1978), who coined the term *the feminization of poverty*, to describe the likelihood that female heads of households will be poor, be-

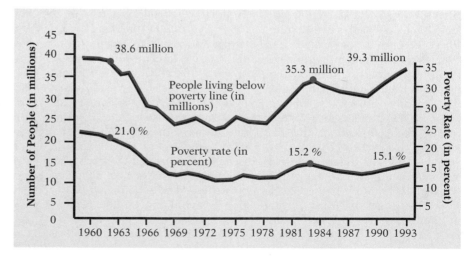

Figure 14.2 Poverty in the United States, 1959–1993 *The slight drop in the poverty rate, despite the sharp rise in the numbers of people living below the poverty line (see text for definition), reflects growth in the overall population* (U.S. Bureau of the Census, 1995, p. xv).

lieves that the official statistics tend to underestimate the number of poor women because many single mothers move in with relatives to save on housing costs. Two major reasons for the feminization of poverty are job and wage discrimination, which we touched on in Chapter 4 and will discuss further in this chapter.

Divorce also makes it more likely that women and mothers will be poor. Ex-husbands and absent fathers typically offer very little support to women and their families. The poorer the family is to begin with, the less likely it is that the father will provide support after a divorce (Amott, 1993). Gender-linked poverty is almost nonexistent in many other industrialized countries. In Sweden, for example, few single mothers arc poor because they have greater economic equality in the workplace. In the Netherlands, a generous welfare system provides benefits for all unemployed people, regardless of gender or marital status (Casper et al., 1994).

Racial-Ethnic Families   Although most poor people in the United States are white, most whites are not poor. In 1993, among people living below the poverty line, 12 percent were white, 33 percent were African American, and 31 percent were of Latino origin. However, among the general population, some 67 percent are white, but only 12 percent are black and 9 percent Latino (U.S. Bureau of the Census, 1995; see also the related discussion in Chapter 13 and especially Figure 13.5). Thus, people of color are disproportionately poor compared to their numbers in the general population.

Many Latino families are poor even though both parents work full time, year-round (Gomez, 1993). During economic recessions, African Americans and Latinos are particularly vulnerable to layoffs because they often fall victim to "last hired, first fired" policies.

The Working Poor   Although many people think that the poor are simply looking for handouts from the government, in 1992

- Nearly 10 percent of poor persons worked year-round, full-time.

- Among poor family householders, over 49 percent worked and over 15 percent worked year-round, full-time.

- In 69 percent of married-couple families at least one spouse worked, and both worked in 24 percent of these families.

- Almost 42 percent of poor female householders worked, and 9 percent worked year-round, full-time (U.S. Bureau of the Census, 1993: xv).

As these statistics indicate, the poor are not "a bunch of loafers and parasites," but working does not guarantee staying out of poverty. Almost one fifth of all full-time workers now fall into the category of the *working poor*, typically defined as people or families who work full time but are barely staying above the poverty line (Levine, 1994). The greatest hardships are faced by two-parent working-poor families in rural areas, where social services and benefits are less available than in urban areas (National Research Council, 1993).

Poverty in the Suburbs   Aging whites generally constitute the majority in poor suburbs, but these suburbs are beginning to house an increasing number of minorities and criminals. Some of the poorest suburbs, like Ford Heights, Illinois, have unemployment rates of nearly 60 percent. These areas often attract only those industries that other communities reject, such as landfills. They tend to have minimal social and recreational services and are often mismanaged because they can't afford to pay professional leaders. Without public transit systems, many of the poorest suburbanites are often isolated and unable to commute to suburban or city jobs (McCormick and McKillop, 1989).

Programs for Poor Families   What help is available for the poor? In general, state and federal government policies include three types of programs: cash support; direct provisions of necessities, such as food, shelter, and medical care; and social services, including birth-control assistance, child care, and compensatory and remedial education. There are also nonprofit organizations, such as community action groups, legal services, and community development agencies, that enable the poor to address social, legal, and economic issues at the local level.

None of these programs really helps families get off welfare, however. Although benefit payments vary across the country (according to Waldman et al., 1994, welfare payments per recipient range from $42 per month in Mississippi to $253 in Alaska), in most states, a single mother would need a full-time job paying nearly $6 an hour to match the value of the family welfare and food stamp grants alone. Many mothers stay on welfare because if they work they must relinquish some of their welfare payments and the result is often a lower income than from welfare alone. Even though many welfare recipients want to work, the longer they are on public assistance, the more their self-esteem declines and the less motivated they are to work (Popkin, 1990). We return to the issue of welfare in Chapter 19.

Why does the United States, one of the wealthiest countries in the world, have such high poverty rates? In a classic article on poverty sociologist Herbert Gans (1971) maintained that poverty and inequality have many functions, including the following: (1) They ensure that society's dirty work gets done; (2) the poor subsidize the middle and upper classes by working for low wages; (3) the poor buy goods and services that would otherwise be rejected (such as day-old bread, used cars, and the services of old, retired, or incompetent "professionals"); and (4) the poor, being politically powerless, can be forced to absorb the costs of change and growth in American society (such as providing the back-breaking work that built railroads and cities in the nineteenth century and being pushed out of their homes today by urban renewal and construction of expressways, parks, and stadiums). According to some observers, our political, social, and economic systems have pushed a large number of families into poverty (see Williams, 1994).

Homeless Families

One of the most devastating consequences of poverty is homelessness. Since 1980, it is estimated, the U.S. homeless population has doubled every year, and in early 1994 there were thought to be as many as 10 million homeless people in the country. Families have been the fastest growing group of homeless people (Stanford Center, 1991). According to the National Coalition for the Homeless, in 1990 single men made up 51 percent of the homeless population and families with children accounted for 34 percent.

More than half of the homeless are members of minority groups, but the homeless population in any one place reflects local and regional population trends. Major metropolitan areas on the East Coast have high proportions of homeless African Americans, whereas Minneapolis has many homeless Native Americans. In western cities like Los Angeles and Phoenix the homeless include many Latinos, and in the Northwest, some cities report that most of their homeless are white (Baum and Burnes, 1993).

Why do people lose their homes? In general, homelessness is caused by a combination of forces, some of which are beyond individuals' or families' control. Poverty, lack of education, lack of marketable skills, unemployment, domestic violence, substance abuse, the inability of relatives and friends to provide social and economic support during crises, and the absence of affordable housing are among the most common causes of homelessness (Van Ry, 1993; Winkleby and Boyce, 1994). Under the Reagan administration, federal housing assistance dropped drastically, from $29 billion in 1980 to less than $8 billion in 1986. In some places, this created waiting lists for public housing of up to 25 years. If a building burned down or was condemned or torn down, residents with low-paying jobs (such as waitresses, maids, dishwashers, or security guards) were unable to find new affordable housing and to meet other costs such as transportation and medical care (Sosin, 1989; Coughlin, 1991).

The 1970s also saw the loss of over a million *single-room occupancy* units (typically, single rooms in old hotels and rooming houses) that had housed many of the poor and the elderly as well as the chronically mentally ill—often single people without nearby relatives—who were released from mental institutions on the grounds that they would fare better reintegrated into their communities. They did not, for none of the requisite local community services was put in place to help them.

Some people attribute homelessness to "work aversion" (Lee et al., 1990). Although most people agree that the poor do not deserve their poverty, 42 percent believe that the poor are poor because they are lazy or because of other personal defects (Patterson and Kim, 1991). Although this may be true of some people, such perspectives ignore changing employment trends that have had a negative impact on many families. As we have already pointed out, many female heads of household cannot compete effectively in the job market. Young mothers with very young children are especially likely to become homeless (Rossi, 1994), and the homeless also include teenage runaways escaping from family violence or incest (see Chapter 12). In addition, men formerly employed in unskilled blue-collar jobs that have been eliminated may be unable to secure the training they need to move to new kinds of work.

FAMILIES' EFFORTS TO ADAPT TO CHANGING EMPLOYMENT TRENDS

Across the country, families are struggling to survive. In this effort, families have adopted a variety of techniques, including taking low-paying jobs, moonlighting, working shifts, doing part-time work, and working overtime. If and when these tactics fail, they join the ranks of the unemployed.

Low-Wage Jobs, Moonlighting, and Shift Work

Researcher Marc Levine (1994) has described the United States as "a nation of hamburger flippers" because of the economy's growing number of low-wage jobs. Levine notes that, measured in terms of buying power, hourly wages have actually declined 15 percent since 1973 and are now at levels reached in the mid-1960s.

Family members have reacted to this situation in several ways. To meet regular household expenses or to pay off debts, some are moonlighting. In 1993, more than 6 percent of all employed people held two or more jobs (Cohany et al., 1994). Most multiple jobholders are married and today nearly as many are women as men. Men are more likely than women to add a part-time job to a full-time one; women are more likely to hold two part-time jobs (Uchitelle, 1994). African American women and Latinas may be the most likely to moonlight to meet regular household expenses (Amott, 1993).

Parenting is especially difficult if parents have unconventional work schedules. More than 17 percent of working mothers with children under 14 and more than 20 percent of working fathers hold an evening or night job or work on a rotating shift. In addition, 17 percent of two-income couples with children under the age of six have work hours that do not overlap (McEnroe, 1991).

The increase in shift work reflects, in part, a changing economy. Businesses that provide services, such as restaurants and medical facilities, are in one of the fastest-growing employment sectors, and they require the most evening and weekend labor. The globalization of industries means that workers are needed almost around the clock because business is being conducted somewhere almost every hour of the day. In addition, because day care is so expensive, many two-income families are working split shifts so that parents can take turns at child-care tasks (McEnroe, 1991).

Shift work and evening shifts are almost twice as common among single parents who can't afford day care and must find relatives to baby-sit while they work. Married women are also more likely to work at night, when their husbands are available to take care of the children. Thus, the lack of affordable child care forces both single and married mothers to work part time and during the evenings (Casper et al., 1994).

Many husbands who work evening rotating shifts (six days on, three days off, for example) feel guilty and angry because the demands of their work limit their participation in family life. One father saw himself reliving a situation he had resented as a child: "I always remember my father as sleeping during the day. Never seeing him because he'd be in bed. Then I'd hear him get up and go to work at night. I didn't see much of my father. I missed that. Now I feel guilty if I can't have it with my family " (Hertz and Charlton, 1989: 501). If the mother also works, the couple may go to extra lengths to do whatever it takes to approximate a traditional family. Thus,

Dan Wasserman
Boston Globe

working wives often retain primary responsibility for the children and try to support their husbands' work demands and schedules.

Too Little Work or Too Much

Many families face an economic dilemma: On the one hand, an increasing proportion of available jobs are only part time. On the other hand, some employees are required to work unwanted overtime.

Part-Time Jobs In the United States, about 17 percent of all employed people work part time (defined as working less than 35 hours a week), and this group is likely to grow. In many Western industrialized countries, two thirds of all jobs are in the service sector in areas like health care, retail, travel, and telecommunications, and most of these positions are only part time, offering no health benefits or retirement programs. Most of these jobs are filled by new job entrants and to a great extent by women who are not highly educated or highly skilled. Women hold 85 percent of part-time jobs in Great Britain, 66 percent of all part-time positions in the United States, and 91 percent of part-time jobs in Germany (Knight, 1994).

Overtime Demands At the other extreme is the demand by some employers that experienced workers, especially those in production, work more overtime because this is cheaper than hiring and training new employees. According to the U.S. Department of Labor, weekly overtime for production workers has increased from about two hours in 1982 to almost five hours in 1994. Manufacturing workers in the United States already labor 360 more hours each year than their counterparts in France and 430 more hours than those in Germany. In 1994 thousands of assembly-line workers went on strike to protest General Motors' mandatory overtime that required employees to work more than nine hours a day, six days a week. They demanded that GM hire more workers, citing especially the company's billions of dollars in profits in the second quarter of 1994 (*U.S. News & World Report*, 1994).

Unemployment

The unemployed include such diverse groups as people who have been laid off or fired, have quit, or are about to begin a new job. Overall, more than 54 percent of the unemployed are people who have lost their jobs, and the average duration of unemployment is 18 weeks. Teenagers and African Americans are two to three times more likely to be unemployed than white workers (Cohany et al., 1994).

Families living under the threat of unemployment experience problems in communication and in problem solving, and relationships among spouses and children suffer (Larson et al., 1994). Unemployment is often associated with marital and familial dissatisfaction, as well as with separation and divorce. Unemployed workers argue more frequently with their spouses and experience less family cohesion. And the economic distress caused by unemployment has negative effects on children's physical health, psychological well-being, and behavior (Voydanoff, 1991).

A major new trend is unemployment among young and middle-aged men. Since 1970, the unemployment rate for men between the ages of 25 and 55 has tripled in Britain, France, and Germany and doubled in the United States (Knight, 1994). In the United States, the proportion of full-time, year-round male workers in this age group dropped from 80 percent in the 1970s to 70 percent in the late 1980s (Nasar, 1994).

One reason for this trend is that many out-of-work blue-collar male workers are unwilling to take what work is available after being laid off from fairly well-paying jobs in such smokestack industries as shipbuilding, coal mining, and steelmaking. Most new jobs for inexperienced people with less education are in areas traditionally "female," such as clerical work, sales, and personal service. "For men, whether black, Latino or white, there are strong cultural and social norms about what is appropriate work" (Nasar, 1994: D15).

Another reason for unemployment is the phenomenon of the **discouraged worker.** The discouraged worker wants a job and has looked for work during the preceding year but has not searched in the month prior to a survey because of the belief that job-hunting efforts are futile. Why do people give up? Usually for one of the following reasons: They've found no work available in their area of expertise; they lack necessary schooling, training, or experience; they believe employers have rejected them as too young or too old; or they have experienced other types of discrimination (Cohany et al., 1994). In 1993, 424,000 workers were classified as discouraged: 52 percent were men and 48 percent were women.

Finally, many experts feel that unemployment rates are misleading because they ignore the **underemployed worker.** The underemployed include workers who have part-time jobs but would rather be working full time, as well as those who accept jobs below their level of job experience and educational credentials (Ball, 1990). Women, particularly those with children, are more likely to suffer from underemployment than men because of problems in finding and being able to pay for good child care services.

VARIATIONS ON TRADITIONAL ECONOMIC ROLES WITHIN MARRIAGE

In Chapter 4 we examined the traditional male breadwinner–female homemaker roles. Although for many couples these traditional roles are evolving, if slowly, into more egalitarian arrangements, there are currently two variations on the traditional division of labor within marriage—the two-person single career and the househusband.

The Two-Person Single Career

In the **two-person single career,** one spouse, typically the wife, participates in the partner's career behind the scenes without pay or direct recognition (Papanek, 1979). The wives of many college and university professors, for example, support their husbands' careers by entertaining faculty and students, doing library research, helping to write and edit journal articles or books, and grading exams.

Probably the best example of the gratifying aspects of such unpaid work are presidential first ladies, who have often enjoyed considerable power and influence behind the scenes. Rosalynn Carter, Nancy Reagan, and Barbara Bush all played more or less quiet roles in their husbands' presidencies, but Hillary Rodham Clinton has been a very visible promoter of some of President Clinton's domestic policies. Many middle-class homemakers are proud of their husbands' accomplishments and experience a sense of fulfillment by helping them out, but some wives complain that a two-person career is very stressful and that they experience burnout as commonly as their high-powered husbands do.

Househusbands

In a reversal of traditional roles, some husbands relinquish the role of breadwinner to their wives. **Househusbands** are those rare men who stay home to care for the family and do the housework while their wives are the wage earners. In a 1983 study by Blumstein and Schwartz only 4 out of the 3632 husbands in the sample were full-time househusbands. In 1992, about 5 percent of fathers in two-parent families were not in the labor force, and the wives were the bread-

Another traditional form of work within a marriage is the husband-wife business, in which both partners work to support themselves and their family. The family as an economic unit has been on the wane, but as this Massachusetts couple demonstrate, it has not entirely disappeared.

winners (Hayghe, 1994). It is not clear, however, how many of these men were full-time house-husbands.

In addition, being a househusband is usually a temporary role. Some househusbands get the role by default—they are unemployed or are not working because of poor health or a disability. Sometimes graduate students who are supported by their wives take on a modified househusband role, doing household chores between classes or laboratory work and studying at the library.

In one of the few empirical studies of house-husbands, Lutwin and Siperstein (1985) found that people outside the family often questioned these men's motives, their sexual orientation, or their abilities. One father, for example, said that his child's pediatrician always prefaced his instructions with "Don't forget to tell your wife." Househusbands also complained of some things that many wives and mothers know only too well: a yearning to be with other adults and a distaste for the boring routines.

COMBINING FAMILY AND WORK ROLES: THE NEW "GOOD LIFE"?

Many young people today expect to combine both family and work roles and to live the good life. Some will, but more—especially women—will have to work very hard just to keep up with the rate of inflation.

Expectations About Work

Surveys of adolescents and college students suggest that many young people expect to "have it all." In a nationwide study of high school seniors, Crimmins et al. (1991) found that 80 percent of respondents expected to raise a family. Although nearly three quarters saw parenthood as a fulfilling role, there was a trend against stay-at-home mothers: Only 3 percent of high school females expected to be full-time homemakers, and only 20 percent thought that mothers of preschool children should stay at home. Whereas only 35 percent of the young men said that work would be a central part of their adult lives, over 60 percent said they want to make a lot of money. Many expect to own their own homes and a vacation home, have major labor-saving devices (such as dishwashers and rider

lawn mowers), quality stereos, stylish clothes, two or more cars, and recreational vehicles. Even "a lot of money" may not be sufficient to provide for child rearing *and* these material possessions, however.

College students have similar expectations. In 1994 nearly 74 percent of college freshmen surveyed by the Higher Education Research Institute at the University of California, Los Angeles, said that being very well off financially was very important or essential, and 71 percent felt the same way about raising a family. However, almost 31 percent of the men and 20 percent of the women said that "the activities of married women are best confined to the home and family" (data cited in *The Chronicle of Higher Education*, 1995).

Women's Increasing Participation in the Labor Force

The high proportions of both high school and college women who say they expect to marry, have children, and work are right on target, for many will have to work to support themselves and their families. In fact, the widespread employment of mothers is often cited as one of the most dramatic changes in family roles during the twentieth century. Except for a brief period after the end of World War II, the numbers of working women have been increasing steadily since the turn of the century (see Table 14.1).

Table 14.1

Participation of Women and Men in the Labor Force During the Twentieth Century

YEAR	PERCENT OF ALL MEN AND WOMEN IN THE LABOR FORCE		WOMEN AS A PERCENTAGE OF ALL WORKERS
	MEN	WOMEN	
1890	84	18	17
1900	86	20	18
1920	85	23	20
1930	82	24	22
1940	83	28	25
1945	88	36	29
1947	87	32	27
1950	87	34	29
1960	84	38	33
1970	80	43	37
1980	78	52	42
1993	76	58	45

SOURCE: U.S. Bureau of the Census, 1994b: 401.

Women's labor force rates are expected to grow more rapidly than men's in the near future. By the year 2005, for example, the Bureau of Labor Statistics predicts that about 65 percent of women will be in the labor force compared with 76 percent of men (Waldrop, 1994). One reason is that female baby boomers are far more likely than their predecessors to have gone to college and to have more and better-paying work opportunities (Waldrop, 1991).

An even more dramatic change has been the increase of mothers in the labor force who have a newborn child (see Data Digest). Historically, African American mothers with newborn babies were more likely than any other group to be employed, but the gap is narrowing. As Figure 14.3 shows, the majority of women with infants are going back to work within the child's first year of life, and the rates are nearly identical for white and black women. Education is now a more important factor than race. In 1992, among women workers with infants at home, 72 percent had college or professional degrees; only 30 percent had a high school education or less (Bachu, 1993).

What accounts for this difference by education level? As you saw in Chapter 11, many women, and especially those with college or pro-

Figure 14.3 Percentage of Women with Newborns in the Labor Force, 1992 (Based on Bachu, 1993, Table H).

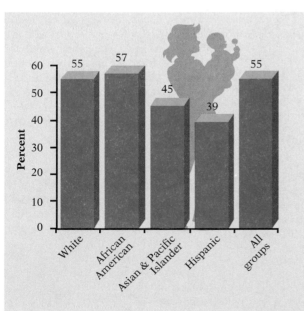

fessional degrees, have been postponing both marriage and childbearing. Because better-educated women are more likely to have had jobs to begin with and to have jobs with family leave benefits, they are more likely to have a job to return to after the birth of a baby. Educated mothers are also more likely to have had stable jobs and a greater job commitment. In addition, financial commitments play an important role in the timing of women's employment after childbirth. When families have higher incomes and higher tax rates, when they own their own homes and must make mortgage payments, wives are more likely to return to work within a few months of childbirth (Joesch, 1994). Finally, better-educated mothers are better able to pay for the child-care services that allow them to work (Yoon and Waite, 1994).

That most women are back on the job soon after childbirth challenges the old idea that women in their childbearing years should not be hired or promoted because they will quit as soon as they get pregnant. In addition, the evidence showing that women are just as committed to their jobs as men underlines the injustice of the existing gender-based wage gap.

Why Do Women Work?

There are two principal reasons why women work outside the home, and they are the same reasons that men work: individual fulfillment and supporting themselves and their dependents. The difference between men's and women's motivation reflects the social and economic changes of this century. It is only recently that most women have had the opportunity for fulfillment through work, and recent economic downturns have made it impossible for most families to survive on the earnings of one breadwinner.

Studies have generally reported positive effects of work for both men and women (see Rosenfield, 1989, for a review of this literature). Work usually adds meaning to life. The opportunity to succeed at tasks and to be rewarded for competence enhances self-esteem, which, in turn, increases overall well-being. This is especially true, of course, for people who enjoy their work or who are employed in stimulating, rewarding jobs.

Macroeconomic changes in recent years have altered not only the structure of the economy but the structure of the family itself. In the early 1980s many high-paying manufacturing jobs (which on the average paid nearly three times the minimum wage) began disappearing. Construction and production work accounted for 25 percent of all jobs in 1950 but made up only 13 percent of jobs in 1984. In 1981 state and local governments, once key sources of good service jobs, began reducing their labor forces by hundreds of thousands of workers across the country (Harrington and Levinson, 1985). As all these jobs disappeared, the dual-earner family began to evolve.

We have already noted the disastrous effects of recessions on the working class during the 1970s and early 1980s. And, as the Data Digest points out, the median U.S. income has declined since the mid-1980s. It is not surprising, then, that the proportion of women who work to support a family increased from 19 percent in 1980 to 31 percent in 1990. Although the need for a creative outlet motivates some women to work today, in most cases women are working because of economic necessity. The box "Variations in the Working Mother Role" examines motherhood and employment more closely.

Ernestina Galindo owns and operates a factory in Austin, Texas, that makes Mexican foods such as tortillas.

CHANGES

Variations in the Working Mother Role

Fewer women today have a choice between being full-time homemakers and working outside the home. Of Moen's (1992: 42–44) four categories of working mothers—captives, the conflicted, copers, and the committed—only members of the last group have fully chosen their roles.

❑ *Captives* would prefer to be full-time homemakers. These mothers may be single parents who are sole breadwinners, wives of blue-collar workers whose own incomes are insufficient to support the family, or middle-class wives who find two salaries necessary for a desired standard of living. Captives find their multiple responsibilities overwhelming and remain in the labor force reluctantly.

❑ *Conflicted* mothers feel their employment is harmful to their children. They are likely to leave the labor force while their children are young, and many quit work when they can afford to do so. Conflicted mothers include many Latinas whose husbands support their wives' employment as long as the mothers continue to fulfill all housework and child-care duties despite their outside work and who quit their jobs as soon as their husbands secure better-paying work (Segura, 1994).

❑ *Copers* are women with young children who choose jobs with enough flexibility to accommodate family needs. Some manage to reduce their daily or weekly working hours or leave the labor force for brief periods. As a result, they often must settle for minimally demanding jobs that offer lower wages and fewer benefits and, in the long run, forgo promotional opportunities, seniority advantages, and pay increases.

❑ *Committed* mothers have both high occupational aspirations and a strong commitment to marriage and family life. As the section on dual-earner families shows, however, mothers who can afford good child care and who are free to pursue career goals are still a minority.

DUAL-EARNER FAMILIES

After 61 years of being the traditional housewife and mother, the comic-strip character Blondie opened up a catering business and went to work for herself. Blondie's and Dagwood's shifts to dual-earner status reflect what has been happening in many U.S. families. In this section we look at several groups of dual-earner families like the Bumsteads—dual-career marriages, trailing spouses, commuter marriages, and marriages in which wives earn more than their husbands.

Dual-Earner and Dual-Career Families

Dual-earner couples are married partners both of whom are employed outside the home. Such couples are also referred to as *dual-income, two-earner,* or *dual-worker* couples. In seven out of ten of the 24.7 million two-parent families, both the mother and father worked at some time during 1992 (Hayghe and Bianchi, 1994). Despite their two incomes, these families are seldom affluent. Indeed, according to Waldrop (1991), only a small fraction of such households has a significant amount of **discretionary income** (income that remains after such basic necessities as food, rent, utilities, and transportation have been paid for and that is then available for other purposes) because many consist of middle-aged householders who are paying for children's college, caring for their aging parents, and saving for their own retirement.

Dual-career couples are marriage partners both of whom work in professional or managerial positions that require extensive training, a long-term commitment, and ongoing professional growth. Usually, but not always, dual-career partners earn incomes well above average. Only about 5 percent of dual-earner families are dual-career couples. Married women in such professions as law, medicine, high-level management, or college teaching remain a numerically small group among dual-earner couples as a whole. Because such women are less likely to have children, dual-career families with children make up an extremely small percentage of dual-earner families (Berardo et al., 1987).

In both dual-career and dual-earner marriages, couples must juggle multiple roles and multiple demands on their time. Men in both groups may be much less involved than their spouses are in household and parenting responsibilities (Gilbert, 1993). Women in both groups may interrupt their careers or jobs to have children, but they are also proud of their accomplishments and financial contributions to the family. Both dual-career and dual-earner families experience stress, but the causes may be different. A common source of stress for dual-earner families is the need to find affordable child care. Ironically, many dual-earner mothers work as child-care providers or baby sitters for dual-career mothers, who are better able to pay for such services.

The most common source of stress for dual-career couples is the pressure caused by work or role overload, especially when there are young children in the family. Both partners often feel the need to work intensely and competitively and feel an urgency to accomplish their job goals. As a result, they may feel guilty and frustrated when they neglect their spouses and children. In addition, the role overload caused by multiple work and family responsibilities can lead to increased health risks; decreased productivity; increased tardiness, absenteeism, and turnover; and poor morale at work (Duxbury et al., 1994).

Trailing Spouses

According to the Employee Relocation Council of Washington, D.C., about half of the major corporations have established programs or have recruited outside firms to provide employment assistance for the **trailing spouse**—the partner who gives up his or her work and searches for another position in the location where a spouse has taken a job (Maines, 1993). Male trailing spouses—only 10 to 15 percent of cases—fall into four categories: (1) those who have been unable to find suitable employment in their present location; (2) those who are confident that they can take their profession anywhere, such as photographers, computer programmers, or engineers; (3) those who take genuine pride in their wives' accomplishment and try to accommodate them; and (4) those who have blue-collar skills and are used to changing jobs and locations, such as construction workers (Brooks, 1987; Cohen, 1994).

Income, however, is usually the best predictor of who the trailing spouse will be. As a wife's income increases, both in absolute terms and relative to the income of her husband, she tends to have a greater influence on family mobility. Typically, however, the husband's job has the greater influence because his income is usually higher (Bielby and Bielby, 1992).

There are drawbacks to being the trailing spouse. Frame and Shehan (1994) found that moving was considerably harder on wives than husbands, who continued to perform similar tasks in new locations and maintained their contacts with colleagues through meetings and conferences. Wives, however, lost contact with friends; felt a lack of support from husbands who saw relocation as an important career step for them; were anxious about the children's adjustment to a new environment; and felt lonely and isolated. In addition, nearly 60 percent of the wives had been employed, and many felt anxiety over the loss of their jobs: "Having to get a new job in my profession . . . is very stressful for me, and the salary differential at each move is hard on my spouse. It's contributed greatly to our financial ups and downs" (Frame and Shehan, 1994: 202).

Commuter Marriages

In a **commuter marriage,** married partners live and work in different geographic areas and get together intermittently, such as over weekends. An estimated 1 million American couples have such long-distance marriages (Maines, 1993). Because most of the research has focused on dual-career rather than dual-earner families, information about commuter marriages is limited to highly educated couples with high-status jobs (Rindfuss and Stephen, 1990).

Benefits and Costs There are several reasons why a couple may develop a commuter marriage. If one partner (usually the wife) sees that relocation will have negative effects on her employment prospects, she may decide not to move. If the couple already has well-established careers in different cities, neither partner may be willing to make major sacrifices after marriage. In addition, a commuter marriage may create less stress on the family because it avoids uprooting teenage children or elderly parents.

There are several advantages in commuter marriages. Long-distance couples feel that they can devote more attention to their work during the week and that they learn to appreciate and make the most of the time they have together.

Each person is more independent and can take advantage of time alone to pursue hobbies or recreational interests that the other partner might not enjoy. Commuter marriages also force couples to reexamine the quality of their relationship and to make changes to improve it.

Commuter marriages also have several costs, one of which is the sheer expense involved. Telephone bills, airplane flights, the costs of maintaining two housing units with utilities—all these can be very high. The commuting partner may feel isolated from community and social relationships. And one of the partners may become involved in extramarital relationships. Friends and relatives sometimes hint that there must be something wrong with the marriage if the partners are willing to live apart. Employers may not like the fact that an employee refuses to work overtime or insists on taking three-day weekends. Furthermore, the stay-at-home parent may become resentful that the weekend parent is not shouldering his or her responsibility in raising the children. If the couple has no children, decision making as to whether and when to have children and where the children will live may prove stressful (Belkin, 1985).

Coping with Commuter–Marriage Stress The major dilemma for commuter couples is *role transition*. If a husband sees his family only every two weeks or so, for example, his wife and children may resent changing their lifestyles to suit his needs. Almost equally problematic is the *supersuccess syndrome*, in which partners feel guilty about their absences and seem driven to succeed at everything. If a couple wants happy and healthy children, a home with *House Beautiful* decor, luxurious garden and grounds, and gourmet cooking, managing the commuter marriage becomes extremely difficult. Commuting wives may try to prepare family meals for the week to come; fathers may try extra hard to "mother" their children in their wives' absence (Winfield, 1985; Anderson and Spruill, 1993).

Not surprisingly, physical exhaustion is a common problem in commuter marriages. Many commuting partners work 14- to 18-hour days during the week, live in hotel rooms or small apartments, and subsist on TV dinners or deli sandwiches. Their spouses, on the other hand, often work equally long hours and have the added burden of child care.

Why do they do it? The major motivation of commuter couples is not financial security. Partners in such marriages typically see their work as an integral part of their self-concept. For example, when Amy left her job to be with husband Paul in Los Alamos, she took a part-time job locally but soon felt as if she'd lost her "own separate sphere." When encouraged by her husband to go back to the work she'd left, Amy said, "When I did, I found myself in love again with working on a newspaper" (Winfield, 1985: 41).

When Wives Earn More Although, overall, U.S. women still make only about 72 cents for each dollar that men make, in nearly 27 percent of the 31 million marriages in which both spouses are earners, the wife earns more than her husband (U.S. Bureau of Labor Statistics, unpublished data, 1992). Wives who earn more than their husbands typically work full time, year-round as professionals or managers. The majority have no children at home, and many have attended college. Black women are more likely to outearn black men than are their white counterparts because they are more likely to have a college degree and to have more job experience (see Chapter 13). In some cases women's reported higher incomes may be short term. For example, a wife's income may be higher only for a year or so because her husband has been laid off or is on sick leave (see Roberts, 1994).

The few available studies of wives who earn more than their husbands suggest that these relationships often become troubled or disintegrate. For example, wives who have higher-status occupations tend to experience more psychological or physical abuse from their husbands (Hornung and McCullough, 1981). On the other hand, some anecdotal evidence suggests that a wife's higher earnings have a positive effect on the marriage when anticipated from the outset. For example, the husband may be relieved not to have to work late and is willing to take full responsibility for the children when the wife goes on business trips (Sandroff, 1994).

THE EFFECT OF WORK ON FAMILY DYNAMICS

Employment—whether in dual-earner families, dual-career marriages, or commuter marriages—affects the family in many ways. For better or worse, work roles influence the quality of a marriage, the performance of family work, and children's well-being.

Marital Quality and Spouse's Welfare

The impact of employment on marital and personal satisfaction depends largely on the couple's individual preferences. Wives tend to be happy when they want to work and are employed and most dissatisfied when they want to work and cannot (Mirowsky and Ross, 1986; Segura, 1994). Husbands are happiest when both agree that the wife should work and least happy when their wives work against their wishes. Men are especially likely to be opposed to their wives' employment if their own earnings are low; they fear others will see them as inadequate providers (Ulbrich, 1988).

Conditions in the family also affect job performance. There is a greater strain on the marriage if either partner has a job that carries high demands but little decision-making power or if a job has poor working conditions, little chance for promotion, low earnings, long hours, poor interpersonal relationships, the threat of job loss, or nonsupportive supervision (Hughes and

Although this working mother provides her daughter with a good role model, if her husband is unemployed or if he earns less than his wife does, there may be stress and conflict in the family.

Galinsky, 1994; Piotrkowski and Hughes, 1993). A study of working-class fathers in dual-earner families found that such positive work conditions as having autonomy, good peer relations, and supervisor support heightened the worker's self-esteem. Heightened self-esteem, in turn, increased the man's self-confidence and encouraged such positive parenting styles as having a positive attitude toward his children and of not using controlling behaviors such as nagging or guilt (Grimm-Thomas and Perry-Jenkins, 1994). In addition, and regardless of gender, job stress can be "buffered" by strong marital or parental ties (Barnett, 1994).

Family Work

Sociologist Joseph Pleck (1977) coined the term "family work" to describe the household chores and child-care tasks that must be performed by families to maintain the household and its members. As we've discussed, whether or not wives are employed outside the home, husbands' participation in household work is usually modest (Thompson and Walker, 1991; Manke et al., 1994). One survey found, for instance, that women do 77 percent of the cooking, 66 percent of the shopping, 75 percent of the cleaning, and 85 percent of the laundry (see Roberts, 1993). As in the United States, the numbers of mothers in the Canadian labor force have increased significantly. Using Canadian census data, Higgins et al. (1994) found that employed mothers spent more time on family work than did employed fathers across the child's life cycle. Thus, neither technology nor wives' increased participation in the labor force has brought much significant change in family work.

Working-class families, especially those where spouses are over 40, may experience even greater conflict over family work. Wives, worn out from working one shift at home and one at work, may feel entitled to their husbands' full participation in domestic labor: "Sure, he helps me out. . . . He'll give the kids a bath or help with the dishes. But when I ask him. He doesn't have to *ask* me to go to work every day, does he? Why should I have to ask him?" (Rubin, 1994: 87). Some men, on the other hand, feel that their wives' complaints are unreasonable, unjust, and oppressive:

The men, battered by economic uncertainty and by the escalating demands of their wives, feel embat-tled and victimized on two fronts—one outside the home, the other inside. Consequently, when their wives seem not to see the family work they do, when they don't acknowledge and credit it, when they fail to appreciate them, the men feel violated and betrayed. "You come home and you want to be appreciated a little. But it doesn't work that way, leastwise not here anymore," complains [a twenty-nine-year-old drill press operator] (Rubin, 1994: 87–88).

The division of family work varies not only by social class but also by occupational level and racial and national origin. According to Perry-Jenkins and Folk (1994), the more resources a wife has, such as job status and income, the more likely it is that family work will be divided more equitably between marriage partners. In addition, as you saw in Chapter 13, African American men are more likely than men of other races to cook, clean, and care for children. Rubin (1994: 92) suggests that this reflects the historical exclusion of African American men from many jobs:

"My mother worked six days a week cleaning other people's houses, and my father was an ordinary laborer, when he could find work, which wasn't very often," explains thirty-two-year-old Troy Payne, a black waiter and father of two children. "So he was home a lot more than she was, and he'd do what he had to do around the house. The kids all had to do their share, too. It seemed only fair, I guess."

In contrast, Rubin notes, Asian and Latino men tend to operate more often on the "old male model," feeling that their responsibility stops at bringing home the paycheck. One Latino man stated flatly that "taking care of the house and kids is my wife's job, that's all." And a dual-earner Chinese mother remarked, "A Chinese man mopping a floor? I've never seen it yet" (p. 91). Rubin observes, however, that the Asian and Latino men who are least likely to share in family work are those who live in ethnic neighborhoods where there is strong support for traditional gender roles even when the wife works outside the home.

Children's Well-Being

Managing family relationships in the dual-earner family can be very stressful:

[In] an all too familiar scenario, Mother comes home exhausted, wanting support from Father; Father comes home irritable and . . . wanting to be left alone; neither can give the other the support he or she needs, and their interactions are tense and brief. Meanwhile, the children are demanding attention—the little one needs diapering, while the older one is watching television instead of doing his homework. . . . [And] dinner still needs to be prepared (Piotrkowski and Hughes, 1993: 198).

Time and energy are precious commodities in many dual-earner families. Young families, especially, spend many years accommodating their child-rearing tasks to the demands of the workplace.

Mothers' employment can have benefits for children, including increased financial resources and more egalitarian sex-role models (see Chapter 4), but many women still feel guilty about returning to work after childbirth and consequently spend time with their children at the expense of their own sleep and leisure (Hoffman, 1989). Recently, researchers have suggested that the important question is not how a mother's employment per se affects children but how the *quality of child care*—whether parental or nonparental—affects children's development. Whether employed or not, parents who are unsupportive, unresponsive, and inconsistent can have more damaging effects on a child than can nonparental child care that is sensitive, responsive, and supportive (Belsky, 1991). In addition, just as important in children's well-being as a mother's employment is the father's role in dual-earner families. The interaction patterns between the spouses and between parents are important factors in shaping child development (Moorehouse, 1993).

Perhaps the greatest stressors for the dual-earner family are those created by work-related tensions. For example, when parents experience job stress, work-family role strain, and role conflict, they are more restrictive, they withdraw more, and they are less positive when interacting with their children. Parental job stress may also be associated with a child's poor academic achievement or behavioral problems in school, and it can also lead to child abuse (Piotrkowski and Hughes, 1993). The box "Juggling Competing Demands in Dual-Earner Families" offers solutions to some of the problems that many of these families encounter.

DISCRIMINATION IN THE WORKPLACE

The issues we've discussed that confront dual-earner families are often compounded by workplace problems that are specifically gender-related. Employed women are often romanticized by the media today, who present images of perfectly groomed women, briefcases in hand, chairing important meetings or flying across the country, airphone in hand and laptop in action. In fact, the majority of working women have much less exciting jobs. But regardless of their occupations, many women face similar problems, including lack of promotion, wage discrimination, and sexual harassment. Although men are more likely to be the discriminators than the discriminated, they, too, may suffer wage discrimination and harassment.

Gender-Related Discrimination

The structure of work is a major barrier to women's occupational mobility (Sokoloff, 1992). For years, many jobs have been informally categorized as either "women's work" or "men's work." For example, most word processors, receptionists, nurses, and seamstresses are women; most auto mechanics, financial advisers, and business entrepreneurs are men. So-called women's jobs often require little long-term commitment or specialized on-the-job training and have little occupational mobility. A woman on an assembly line, for example, may eventually supervise other women workers but typically can expect to go no further. A secretary in a corporation may become an executive secretary to a more powerful manager, but she is typically not in line for a managerial position, regardless of her knowledge of the business. A gender stereotype that women are not good managers or will not fit in a predominantly male-dominated culture continues to limit many women's opportunities for promotion.

In addition, most women are still largely excluded from such traditionally male occupations as construction and fire fighting. Even when they are hired, women are typically relegated to lower-status, lower-paying positions. For example, researchers have found that among pharmacists men are more likely to be found in management positions in retail pharmacies, whereas women usually work under them or in hospital

Juggling Competing Demands in Dual–Earner Families

The strains in juggling work and family life are bound to affect a marriage sooner or later. Here are several strategies that some practitioners (Beck, 1988; Crosby, 1991) suggest for maintaining one's sanity and the well-being of all family members:

❑ *Emphasize the positive.* Concentrate on the benefits you get from having a job: personal fulfillment, an increased standard of living, an ability to provide more cultural and educational opportunities for your children, and greater equality between you and your spouse.

❑ *Set priorities.* Because conflicts between family and job demands are inevitable, you need some guiding principles for resolving clashes. For example, parents might take turns meeting such emergencies as staying at home with sick children.

❑ *Be ready to compromise.* Keep in mind that it is unrealistic to strive for perfection in both family and job responsibilities. Instead, aim for the best possible balance among your various activities, making compromises when necessary. For example, you may have to spend a little less time with your children than you would like, or you may have to sacrifice an opportunity for advancement at work.

❑ *Separate your family and work roles.* Try to separate your roles. Many mothers, especially, feel guilty while at work because they are not with their children, and when they are, they feel guilty about not working on assignments they've brought home from the office. If you must work at home, set time limits for that work and spend the rest of the time fully with your family.

❑ *Be realistic about your standards.* Some people believe that their homes should be just as immaculate after they have children as before or when both spouses work instead of just one. You may need to adjust your standards and to accept some disorder.

❑ *Organize domestic duties.* Domestic overload can sometimes be resolved by dividing family work more equitably among spouses and children. Many families find it useful to prepare a weekly or monthly job chart, in which everyone's assignments are clearly written down. It's also useful to rotate assignments, so that everyone gets to do both the "better" and the "worse" jobs.

❑ *Cultivate a sharing attitude with your spouse.* Sit down with your spouse periodically and discuss what you can do to help each other in your respective jobs both at home and at work. Home problems deserve as much respect and attention as do work problems. Many husbands and wives are relieved when their partners offer a sounding board or give advice or encouragement.

❑ *Try to maintain a balance between responsibilities and recreation.* Remember that if you are both working to improve your standard of living, you should use some of your extra income to relish life. If you spend all your psychological resources on job and home responsibilities, you will have little energy to do the things that will make your life more enjoyable.

---

settings (Reskin and Roos, 1990). In 1995 the Central Intelligence Agency (CIA) agreed to a settlement of $990,000 in payments to 300 women who sued for discrimination. The CIA also agreed to change discriminatory hiring and promotion practices (Stanglin, 1995). Finally, because some men feel threatened by the entry of women into blue-collar craft jobs, they may react with verbal putdowns, sexual innuendo, and sabotage and may be unwilling to teach women the skills they would ordinarily teach a new male coworker (see England, 1992, for a summary of some of this literature).

The Mommy Track and the Daddy Penalty

In 1989 Felice Schwartz, the president of Catalyst, a women's business research group, proposed differentiating women managers in business into two groups following two different tracks—the career-primary track, and the career-and-family track. According to Schwartz, *career-primary* women, who sacrifice family and children for upward mobility, should be identified early and groomed for top-level positions alongside ambitious men. In contrast, she suggested, *career-and-family* women, who are also valuable assets to a company, should be allowed to work part time and to spend more time at home. The latter option, quickly dubbed the **mommy track** by the media, was clearly defined as a slower or even a side track for women who wished to combine career with child rearing.

Some employers agreed with Schwartz's thesis, but many feminists argued that the mommy track concept gave employers reasons not to hire or promote talented women to high-level positions and that it perpetuated gender-role stereotypes. Critics also pointed out that the concept could well legitimize the actions of employers who were not yielding to pressures for paid parental leave, flextime, and child care (Ehrenreich and English, 1989; Kantrowitz, 1989).

These concerns were probably justified. Although women make up 45 percent of the work force (see Table 14.1), men still hold more than 95 percent of the top management jobs in the country's largest corporations. Only 7 percent of the 1315 board members at America's 100 biggest companies are women, and only about 3 percent of the 6502 corporate officers employed by the Fortune 500 companies are women. In 1994, only two women were chief executives of Fortune 1000 companies (Wood, 1995). Of the highest-paid officers and directors of the 799 public companies, virtually none—fewer than 0.5 percent—are women. And only 27 women, fewer than 12 percent, hold leadership positions in the country's 25 biggest unions (Rudavsky, 1992).

Furthermore, in what some see as a backhanded attempt to keep women out of the workplace, some corporations are apparently penalizing the husbands of women who work outside the home, a phenomenon that the media called the **daddy penalty.** In 1994, two studies presented at the annual Academy of Management meetings showed that fathers who are managers and professionals in dual-career families are paid lower salaries than their counterparts in traditional families where wives are full-time homemakers. The *New York Times* propelled these findings into the national arena and gave the phenomenon its name (Lewin, 1994).

In one study, Reitman and Schneer found that, after controlling for the number of hours that the men worked, their degree of experience, their fields of employment, and any interruptions to their careers, men whose wives stayed at home earned 25 percent more than those with

working wives. In another study, Stroh and Brett found that male managers at 20 Fortune 500 companies whose wives stayed home to care for the children received raises that were on average 20 percent larger than those given colleagues married to women who worked outside the home. All the researchers suggested that there is a corporate prejudice in favor of traditional families, and one described this prejudice as a "double whammy": "The dual-career wife earns less than she would if she were her husband, and her husband earns less than he would if she were not working" (quoted and reported in Harris, 1995: 27).

The Gender Gap in Wages

Women who worked full-time, year-round in 1992 had a median income of $22,167 compared to $31,012 for men (U.S. Bureau of the Census, 1994). In some cases, a woman's income is lower than a man's *even when the man doesn't work,* because many men who don't work still have income from unemployment, disability, pensions, and investments (Krafft, 1994).

According to a number of studies, gender still explains much of the earnings differential between women and men (see, for example, Menaghan and Parcel, 1991; Voydanoff, 1991). Some of the reasons for the income gap are fairly straightforward. Even at the same occupational levels, women still earn less than men. As Table 14.2 shows, men earn more than do women in almost every occupational category, especially at the higher-paying managerial and professional levels. Moreover, as you can see from Table 14.3, the mere 2 percent of male secretaries and 14 percent of male elementary school teachers are earning more than the women who far outnumber them in these areas! Since all of these occupations have been traditionally "female" for decades, it can't be argued that men earn more because of seniority or greater work experience.

Women employees are exploited in many different areas of work and in many different parts of the world. For example, even though almost half of all sales jobs in U.S.-based firms are now held by women, it's been suggested that employers are offering more sales incentives to men than women. A survey of salespeople at such incentive-oriented and multinational companies like Equi-

Table 14.2

Median Earnings of Year-Round, Full-Time Workers, 15 Years Old and Over by Gender Racial-Ethnic Identity, 1993

OCCUPATIONAL CATEGORY	MEN			WOMEN		
	WHITE	BLACK	LATINO	WHITE	BLACK	LATINO
Managerial and professional	$45,155	$35,581	$34,515	$30,726	$30,351	$26,295
Technical, sales, and administrative support	31,711	26,807	22,799	20,948	20,094	19,142
Precision production, craft, and repair	28,327	22,507	21,474	21,490	21,888	17,286
Operators, fabricators, and laborers	24,003	19,435	17,435	15,773	14,845	13,493
Service	21,608	19,599	15,146	12,841	13,540	11,381
Farming, forestry, and fishing	15,994	9,927	13,421	10,461	11,450	13,169

SOURCE: Based on data from U.S. Bureau of the Census, 1994.

table Life Assurance, Philip Morris's Kraft General Foods, and PepsiCo found that incentive programs that awarded travel to interesting places and shopping sprees were offered to 72 percent of male sales representatives but to only 37 percent of women reps (Losee, 1992). In addition, as the box "Women as Cheap Labor Around the World" shows, the United States is not the only nation that exploits women in the workplace.

To redress wage discrimination policies, some women workers have turned to the courts. One of the most successful cases involved Lucky Stores, Inc., a grocery store chain with 180 branches throughout northern California. In 1984 one employee filed a complaint with the U.S. Equal Employment Opportunity Commission (EEOC) after being a checker for more than a dozen years even though she had applied for a more responsible and better-paying position. The complaint brought her to the attention of a law firm that persuaded two dissatisfied women from other Lucky Stores to agree to a *class action suit,* or a legal proceeding brought by one or more persons but representing the interests of a larger group. Although Lucky's attorneys argued that women were not promoted because they were not interested in senior-level jobs, the plaintiffs' attorneys had evidence that store managers did not post openings for management-track jobs, did not offer women training for higher-level positions, and expressed prejudicial ideas about women in training sessions.

In 1992 a U.S. district court judge ruled that the company was guilty of sex discrimination. Lucky agreed to a $108 million settlement, which included payouts to the plaintiffs and their lawyers, affirmative action programs for women, $5000 each for the 14,000 eligible employees, and promises to post job openings, set up training programs for women, and keep track of employee job requests. The results have been dramatic. By late 1993, women accounted for 9 percent of store managers, 19 percent of assistant managers, 21 percent of third-rank managers, and 35 percent of fourth-rank managers—levels that are more than double those in 1988 (Swisher, 1994).

Table 14.3

Men's and Women's Weekly Earnings in Selected Occupations, 1993

	NUMBER OF WORKERS (IN THOUSANDS)	MEN		WOMEN	
		PERCENTAGE OF TOTAL WORKERS	MEDIAN WEEKLY EARNINGS	PERCENTAGE OF TOTAL WORKERS	MEDIAN WEEKLY EARNINGS
Registered nurses	1334	7%	$678	93%	$688
Elementary school teachers	1489	14	666	86	588
Social workers	524	33	573	67	496
Secretaries, stenographers, typists	3295	2	399	98	385
Maids, housecleaners	438	21	274	79	239
Waiters, waitresses	589	25	272	75	220
Cashiers	982	26	252	74	221

SOURCE: U.S. Department of Labor, 1994a.

Women As Cheap Labor Around the World

A growing body of research shows that occupational sex segregation and wage disparities between men and women are the norm in many countries. Some of this discrimination is practiced by national governments and businesses themselves, but some is practiced by U.S. corporations that locate plants in third-world and other countries where labor in general is cheap.

Studying female-male earnings ratios in 33 countries, Terrell (1992) found one of the highest earnings disparities in Chile. Data on manufacturing workers showed that women earned only 47 percent as much as men who did the same jobs. One of the lowest income differences was in Paraguay, where, in nonagricultural jobs, women earned 97 percent as much as men. In most other countries earning disparities fell in the 60 to 80 percent range. According to Terrell, two important factors contributing to these disparities were the limits placed on girls' education by parents and teachers and employers' discriminatory practices.

Even countries that promote women's rights in many areas still lag in the workplace. In Norway, for example, where women have considerable political clout, even though the prime minister is a woman who supports equal rights, and though women hold almost half the seats in the cabinet and parliament, "Norwegian women remain second-class citizens in the job market. They are hired last, fired first, denied equal pay for the same work as men and held back from promotions to top executive jobs" (Coleman, 1994: 58).

Although Maoist political slogans proclaimed that "women hold up half the sky" and the constitution of the People's Republic of China grants women a high status, Chinese women apparently are still steered into traditional women's occupations, which are usually the least skilled and pay the least. A delegate to the local National People's Congress who has spoken out against bias toward women noted that "women are always in the low-paying, dead-end jobs, like nurses, grade school teachers, nursery school teachers and street sweepers" (*Baltimore Sun*, A Great Leap . . . 1993a: A24).

In 1993 the U.S. Department of Labor raided a San Francisco garment factory that worked on contract for Esprit. The owners paid its female workers the minimum wage and owed them $127,000 in back wages. The women worked 12-hour days with no days off and no break except for lunch. Other shops that were raided for similar exploitation included the Banana Republic, The Gap, Jessica McClintock, Macy's, and Ralph Lauren (Udesky, 1994).

Undocumented or illegal Latina immigrants make up another large group of abused U.S. workers. In a 1990 survey by the Coalition for Immigration and Refugee Rights and Services, nearly half of a group of 400 undocumented women workers in the San Francisco area reported that employers abused them emotionally, physically, or sexually, paid them less than their documented coworkers, or failed to pay them at all. Most of those surveyed worked as domestic servants or in stores, restaurants, or factories (Amott, 1993). The program director for the coalition said that "I have clients who work seven days a week, doing child care from 6 A.M. to 10 P.M. for $200 a month" (Chang, 1994: 260).

Multinational corporations that move their production units into countries with abundant and cheap labor may not always be the exemplary employers they appear to be. For example, although in 1994 the U.S. Council on Economic Priorities praised Levi Strauss, a U.S. company, for its "unprecedented commitment to non-exploitative work practices in developing countries," the company's jeans plant in Juarez, Mexico, which employed mostly women, was found guilty of many exploitative work conditions (Udesky, 1994). For example, rain that poured through a leaking roof caused sewing machine operators to get electric shocks. To sop up the water, managers would throw dirty toilet tissues and used sanitary napkins on the floor. "It smelled really bad, and there were no windows," one worker said. The U.S. owner that subcontracted with Levi Strauss and that abandoned the plant when these and other conditions were made public owed workers $400,000 in back wages.

Comparable Worth: A Remedy for the Gender Wage Gap?

Comparable worth is a concept that calls for equal pay for both males and females doing work that requires comparable skill, effort, and responsibility and is performed under similar working conditions. Proponents argue that jobs can be measured in terms of such variables as required education, skills, experience, mental demands, and working conditions, and that the inherent worth of a job, for example in terms of its importance to the society, can also be assessed. Assigning point values within these and other categories, several communities found that women were receiving much lower salaries than men even though their jobs had high points. For example, a legal secretary was paid $375 a month less than a carpenter, but both received the same number of job evaluation points (U.S. Commission on Civil Rights, 1984).

Since 1984, a few states (for example, Minnesota, South Dakota, New Mexico, and Iowa) have raised women's wages after conducting comparable worth studies. Although conservatives argue that these kinds of adjustments would be too costly to implement, proponents point out that the cost of implementing pay equity in Minnesota came to less than 4 percent of the state's payroll budget. A mid-1990s study found that the Minnesota law had improved women's wages in government by more than 10 percent, and a half dozen states now have similar pay-equity laws (Kleiman, 1993).

Sexual Harassment

In Chapter 4 we defined *sexual harassment* as any unwelcome sexual advance, request for sexual favors, or other conduct of a sexual nature that makes a person uncomfortable and interferes with her or his work. Sexual harassment is not only behavior that is unwelcome to its target. As we pointed out, it was held illegal by the Supreme Court in 1986 (*Meritor Savings Bank* v. *Vinson*). It was designated an illegal form of sex discrimination as early as 1964, in Title VII of the Civil Rights Act of 1964, and in the 1980 EEOC guidelines.

Sexual harassment behavior can take verbal, nonverbal, or physical forms (see Table 14.4), and it may occur in almost any situation, although it is generally documented in workplace or educational settings. Because harassing someone in the workplace, whether sexually or nonsexually, is a display of power, sexual harassment is usually perpetrated by a boss on a subordinate. Because men dominate positions of power in business and industry, it is far more likely that a harasser will be a man than a woman. The superior-subordinate relationship of perpetrator and victim also accounts for the fact that women often fail to report incidents of harassment. One study found, for example, that 60 percent of the women who experienced sexual harassment never reported it because they felt nothing would be done and they

Table 14.4
Sexual Harassment Can Take Many Forms

VERBAL SEXUAL HARASSMENT

Sexually offensive or suggestive comments, jokes, or teasing

Whistles or catcalls

Sexual remarks about a person's body or clothing

Use of crude or offensive language or of derogatory terms for the opposite sex

Pressure for dates even after the victim has said no

Demands for sexual favors in return for hiring, promotion, or tenure

Sexually oriented verbal abuse

Threats or insults

NONVERBAL SEXUAL HARASSMENT

Staring, leering, or ogling

Using indecent gestures such as winks or licking one's lips

Displaying posters, photos, or drawings of a sexual nature

Sabotaging the victim's work

PHYSICAL SEXUAL HARASSMENT

Patting, pinching, or grabbing

Brushing up against the victim's body

Touching, hugging, or kissing

Cornering or trapping

Physical assault or threat of physical assault

Threat of rape, attempted rape, or rape

SOURCES: Paludi and Barickman, 1991; Shoop, 1992.

feared they would lose their jobs if they complained (Pollack, 1990).

Some people argue that there is a fine line between sexual harassment and flirting or simply giving a compliment. Wrong. If someone says "stop it" and the perpetrator does not stop, it is sexual harassment. Most people know—instinctively and because of the other person's reaction—when sexual attentions are unwelcome or threatening. Take the quiz in the box "Do You Recognize Sexual Harassment?" It may help you discover how attuned you are to what sexual harassment really is.

The Prevalence of Sexual Harassment
In the film *Disclosure*, a male executive is the target of sexual harassment by a woman who is his former lover and new boss. As one commentator observed, "Too bad it's based on a scenario that hardly reflects reality" (Schuyler, 1995: 12).

Although men can be targets of sexual harassment, the overwhelming number of victims are women. According to the EEOC, only about 9 percent of the almost 12,000 sexual harass-

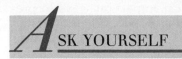

Do You Recognize Sexual Harassment?

Indicate for each statement whether you think the behavior it describes is acceptable or unacceptable. The answers are at the end of the box.

BEHAVIOR	ACCEPTABLE	UNACCEPTABLE
1. "Hey, great legs!"	☐	☐
2. Buying and enjoying pornographic books, tapes, etc., at home.	☐	☐
3. Making eye contact while speaking; giving someone a friendly pat on the shoulder.	☐	☐
4. Continuing to ask someone for dates despite the person's repeated refusals.	☐	☐
5. Telling bawdy jokes to friends who enjoy them in social, nonworkplace settings.	☐	☐
6. Asking a colleague with whom you're on good terms to accompany you to a company-sponsored social event.	☐	☐
7. Telling off-color or sexual jokes that you know will make some people uncomfortable.	☐	☐
8. Staring up and down someone's body.	☐	☐
9. Putting pornographic material on company bulletin boards or in lockers; accompanying such displays with sexual comments about coworkers.	☐	☐
10. "You look very nice today."	☐	☐
11. Patting a person on the behind.	☐	☐
12. Making frequent comments to coworkers on sexually oriented material in the media (films, television, magazines).	☐	☐

Answers: 2, 3, 5, 6, and 10 are acceptable; 1, 4, 7, 8, 9, 11, and 12 are sexual harassment.

SOURCES: Based on Bravo and Cassedy, 1992; Langelan, 1993.

ment cases in 1994 were filed by men (Schuyler, 1995). Men are probably more likely to be harassed when they are young, and especially if they are gay. In a survey of students in grades 8 through 11, 76 percent of boys and 85 percent of girls said they had experienced sexual harassment by being targets of obscene jokes, the subjects of graffiti on rest-room walls, or by being openly called gay (*U.S. News & World Report,* 1993). Yet only 7 percent of these students reported the incidents. Most victims don't report them because they fear reprisals, feel that no one will believe them, or expect ridicule from their peers.

One researcher has claimed that as many as half of all women will be harassed at some point during their academic or working lives (Fitzgerald, 1993). Other studies have reported claims of harassment ranging from 21 to 42 percent of women and 14 percent of men. In one study 42 percent of women said they knew someone who had been harassed (Kantrowitz et al., 1991). On an annual basis, 15 percent of women in Fortune 500 companies experienced sexual harassment,

and according to a 1993 survey, as many as 59 percent of women executives may have been harassed at some time in their careers (Walsh, 1995). In the highest estimate of the incidence of sexual harassment, the Government Accounting Office, the investigative arm of Congress, found that 97 *percent* of the female students at the nation's military academies have experienced sexual harassment (*Baltimore Sun,* 1994f).

Among the perpetrators of sexual harassment who escape prosecution are some of our best known public servants. For example, although Republican Senator Robert Packwood of Oregon has been accused of sexual harassment by more than two dozen women, as yet there have been no political or legal sanctions for his actions. In fact, corporate officials, prominent politicians, and labor groups have contributed generously to a fund to hire the most prestigious law firms in Washington, D.C., to defend Packwood (St. George, 1993).

Sexual harassment takes place throughout the world. Studying 23 industrialized countries, Husbands (1992) found that sexual harassment in the

In what is probably the most widely reported case of sexual harassment, members of the Tailhook Association were accused by women midshipmen of both verbal and physical sexual assault during a drunken convention. In the wake of the negative publicity and lawsuits that followed this event, Admiral Frank Kelso resigned his post as Chief of Naval Operations a few months earlier than scheduled.

workplace was widespread, although the perception of what constitutes sexual harassment varied greatly. In one survey by a French magazine, for example, 48 percent of women respondents said they did not consider it sexual harassment if a woman seeking a promotion was asked by her supervisor to go away with him for the weekend.

Sexual harassment can be very costly, both emotionally and financially, to victims, perpetrators, employers, corporations, and indeed, to all of us. As the box "Who Pays for Sexual Harassment? *You* Do!" shows, in the long run it's the taxpayer who pays for sexual harassment.

Dealing with Sexual Harassment Many companies have instituted grievance procedures for victims of sexual harassment. Victims can also file civil or criminal charges against an of-

fender. One of the most important ways to prepare a case is to keep a "paper trail" that documents the offenses. Here are some suggestions for preparing such evidence:

Document each incident of harassment. Include memos that record the dates, times, and specific details of offensive actions. Note the names of any witnesses.

Confront the harasser. There are several ways to do this. You can

- Write a letter to the harasser (a) describing the offensive behavior and when and where it occurred, (b) explaining why you object to the behavior, and (c) stating what you want to happen next; for example, "I am willing to forget what happened if our relationship is a purely professional one from this point on."

- Confront the person who is harassing you, either in person or by telephone. Neither of these approaches provides you with written documentation, however. Both are more likely to elicit an emotional response than other tactics.

- Have an attorney write the harasser for you, telling him or her immediately to stop such behavior or to run the risk of a lawsuit. Such a letter lets a harasser know you mean business.

File a grievance. File a formal complaint with the appropriate person, such as a union officer, an affirmative action officer, a personnel director, or an academic dean.

Seek help from sympathetic coworkers. If confronting the offender and filing a grievance do not work, check with coworkers. You may discover that others have been victims of the same harasser. Consider forming a group to discuss and deal with this issue.

File a formal complaint. If the forgoing steps do not get results, you can file a complaint with the Equal Employment Opportunity Commission or take the offender to court.

IS THE WORKPLACE FAMILY-FRIENDLY?

The mommy track, the daddy penalty, gender-related wage gaps, and sexual harassment can be devastating to workers and, consequently, to

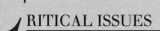

Who Pays for Sexual Harassment? You Do!

Sexual harassment is costly for victims and their families, organizations, and society at large. On the **individual level,** victims of sexual harassment experience many emotional and behavioral problems, including depression; dissatisfaction with work or study; a sense of powerlessness, helplessness, and vulnerability; changes in attitude toward sexual relationships or in sexual behaviors; irritability with family, friends, or coworkers; a general sense of anger, fear, or anxiety; and/or alcohol and drug dependency (Koss, 1990; Rabinowitz, 1990).

Many problems also manifest themselves at the **organizational level.** For example, sexual harassment victims may have high absenteeism, low productivity, and high turnover rates. One study found that sexual harassment had cost 160 major U.S. companies almost $7 million per year in such expenses (Husbands, 1992). Another study found that harassment of women in government jobs led to workplace problems that cost the government approximately $100 million per year in productivity costs (Fitzgerald, 1993).

Employers incur another cost for sexual harassment in terms of the management time that must be devoted to investigating and defending claims of harassment, to say nothing of the legal expenses and settlements associated with such cases. In one case a San Francisco jury awarded a secretary $7.1 million in punitive damages after finding that her former employer, Baker & McKenzie, one of the nation's biggest law firms, failed to stop a partner from harassing her (Solomon and Miller, 1994).

On the **societal level,** all of us pay for sexual harassment both directly and indirectly. As taxpayers, we all paid for the female employee who was awarded more than $210,000 in a lawsuit against the United Nations' Undersecretary-General Luis Maria Gomez, an Argentine diplomat, who harassed the employee and tried to fire her after she rejected his advances. We also paid for the $25.2 million that the EEOC paid out in 1993 in sexual harassment claims (Nayyar and Miller, 1994). And, of course, we all pay for the costs of maintaining the EEOC and other similar watchdog agencies throughout the United States.

Perhaps the most significant costs we pay are the nonmonetary ones: the loss of creative people and their valuable talents. Sexual harassment produces insecurity and destroys self-confidence. These reactions discourage the creative thinking that can produce scientific breakthroughs, entrepreneurial innovations, and artistic contributions.

---

their families. Is there anything in the workplace that supports the family? Absolutely. Pregnancy discrimination laws now give considerable protection to pregnant workers and their jobs, and family leave policies have made it easier to care for newborns and ill family members. On the other hand, provisions for child care and elder care still leave a great deal to be desired.

Pregnancy Discrimination Laws

The federal Pregnancy Discrimination Act of 1978 makes it illegal for employers with more than 15 workers to fire, demote, or penalize a pregnant employee. Some state laws extend this protection to companies with as few as four employees. In addition, many pregnant workers are now entitled up to 12 weeks of unpaid, job-protected parental leave under the new Family and Medical Leave Act, which we will discuss shortly.

Despite all these protections, the EEOC reports that charges of pregnancy discrimination are increasing. Charges reached a six-year high in 1993, when nearly 3600 women filed complaints alleging that they were fired, demoted, or had some of their responsibilities taken away when their employers learned they were pregnant. According to the National Association of Working Women, this is just the tip of the iceberg. The EEOC figures don't reflect the complaints filed with state human rights commissions or lawsuits settled out of court. Further, only a fraction of the women who suffer pregnancy-related job discrimination ever take action because many do not know what their rights are (Gilbert, 1994).

Why are pregnancy discrimination reports increasing? For one thing, more women are becoming aware of their rights and are willing to fight for them. For another, according to an equal rights attorney, pregnant workers are more vulnerable when a company downsizes. Pregnant women become "highly visible targets" because they are perceived as expensive employees, using more medical benefits than others and needing replacement with a temporary worker while on leave (Gilbert, 1994). Table 14.5 offers some advice on safeguarding your job during a pregnancy.

Family and Medical Leave Policies: Benefits and Limitations

One of the most important pieces of legislation for many families is the Family and Medical Leave Act (FMLA), which was first introduced into Congress in 1985 and finally signed into law by President Clinton in 1993. This law allows eligible workers of employers with 50 or more employees to take up to 12 weeks of unpaid, job-protected annual leave—with continuation of health benefits—following the birth or adoption of a child, to care for a seriously ill family member, or to recover from their own serious illnesses. The box "A Tour Through the Family and

Medical Leave Act" provides a closer look at the rights for which an estimated 2 million employees are now eligible.

The most obvious benefit of family leave policies is that many employees will no longer lose their jobs because of sickness, childbirth, or parental leave. Further, most employees, except for the top 10 percent, are guaranteed their jobs or equivalent jobs when they return. The FMLA defines an "equivalent" position as one with the same pay, benefits, and working conditions, as well as "substantially similar" duties and responsibilities. Most important, because the act is law, employees don't have to depend on the supervisor's goodwill. One observer has noted that the FMLA "dramatically alters the way corporate America must deal with family and work issues, blending the two in an unprecedented manner" (Kleiman, 1993: H2).

Unfortunately, the FMLA and other leave policies have several weaknesses. The biggest problem is that the 60 percent of U.S. employees who work in companies with fewer than 50 employees are not covered by the FMLA. Small companies are much less likely than companies with 50 or more employees to provide such employee benefits as health insurance, paid sick leave, and sickness insurance (U.S. Department of Labor, 1994a). Thus, millions of employees who already have limited benefits are ignored by the FMLA. In addition, because many women work in part-time, temporary positions, they are excluded from family leave policies (Trzcinski, 1994). Most important, and as we discussed at the beginning of this chapter, because low-paid, service jobs are expanding while higher paid jobs are shrinking, how many employees can afford to take unpaid leave?

Many employees are still not aware of the FMLA. An informal survey by 9 to 5, a national association of working women, found that only 46 percent of the employees responding to the survey said that their workplaces had posted information about the law, as required (Mendels, 1994).

Employees and employers may disagree about what constitutes an "equivalent" job or "substantially similar" responsibilities. For example, some women who returned after maternity leaves found that they were reassigned to positions with more clerical duties, fewer people to supervise, and less prestigious assignments (Saltzman, 1993a). Does a secretary have an "equivalent" job if it involves driving an extra 30

Table 14.5

Protect Your Job During Pregnancy

Before announcing your pregnancy

Don't broadcast your plans to become pregnant. One tactic some employers have used is to give an employee poor evaluation reviews, creating a record to protect themselves if you sue after being fired.

If you get good performance evaluations, confirm, in writing, any promises that are made (such as merit increases, bonuses, or promotions).

Find out as much as possible about your company's pregnancy and leave policies from both the personnel department and your supervisor. If you don't want your supervisor to know you are pregnant because you feel your job may be jeopardized, make this clear to the personnel department official.

When you give your supervisor the news, present the benefits information and discuss your leave in a businesslike manner, not as though you're asking for a special favor.

When announcing your pregnancy

Be prepared to suggest specific dates for your departure and return.

Take notes during all discussions. Confirm the agreements you reach, and write a memo detailing each. This is especially important if you negotiate changes in your schedule or duties.

If your supervisor is evasive, unresponsive, or vague about your departure and return dates, remind him or her of the leave policies that your company offers.

SOURCE: Based on Gilbert, 1994: 34–35.

A Tour Through the Family and Medical Leave Act

Employees who know their rights under the Family and Medical Leave Act (FMLA) are more likely to take advantage of its benefits. Here is some basic information:

WHO IS COVERED?

Any employee is eligible who has worked at least 1250 hours during a 12-month period—roughly the equivalent of 25 hours a week—at a company or work site employing at least 50 people. Note, however, that although the highest-paid 10 percent of employees must be granted a leave like all others, this group is not guaranteed a job on return. If their absences cause "substantial and grievous economic injury" to their employers, they may be denied reinstatement. These well-paid employees must be notified when they request family leave that they may be out of a job when they return.

FOR WHAT PURPOSES IS FAMILY AND MEDICAL LEAVE INTENDED?

An employee may take family or medical leave for the birth or adoption of a child and to care for a newborn; to care for a spouse, child, or parent with a serious illness; and to recuperate from a serious illness that prevents an employee from working.

WHO PAYS FOR THE LEAVE?

The employee pays for the leave. A company may require, or allow, employees to apply paid vacation and sick leave to the 12 weeks of family leave but does not have to pay workers who take leave. Employees must be given the same health benefits on return that they received before going on leave.

WHEN SHOULD THE EMPLOYER BE NOTIFIED?

In foreseeable cases, such as a birth, adoption, or planned medical treatment, 30 days oral or written notice is required. When that's impossible (for example, if a baby is born early), the employer must be notified as soon as possible, generally within one or two business days. Employers may ask for medical proof that a leave is needed.

MUST THE LEAVE BE TAKEN ALL AT ONCE?

Leave need not be taken all at once. For example, it can be used to shorten the workweek, when an employee wants to cut back following the birth of a child. Medical leave can also be taken piecemeal, for example, to accommodate weekly appointments for chemotherapy treatments.

WHAT IF YOU FEEL YOUR RIGHTS HAVE BEEN VIOLATED?

Any local or regional office of the U.S. Department of Labor's Wage and Hour Division, Employment Standards Administration, will accept complaints, which must be filed within two years of the alleged violation. Private lawsuits must also be filed within two years of the violation.

---

minutes to work to an unfamiliar office and a less desirable location?

Finally, our society neither encourages nor rewards fathers who take advantage of paternity leaves. Not only may organizations penalize men who share home duties with working wives and thus put in somewhat less overtime on the job with lower salaries—the daddy penalty that we discussed earlier—they may also see men who use flextime or paternity leave as not fully dedicated to their jobs or careers (Bailyn, 1993). And, with downsizing, "few [male] employees want to send a signal that they are less than 100 percent devoted to their jobs" (Saltzman, 1993: 66). In response, many men refuse paternity leave and instead use vacation days, sick days, or compensatory time off to spend time with their wives and newborns (Pleck, 1993).

Like American men, Swedish men fear being penalized by lowered salaries and fewer promotions. Thus, despite the very generous paternity leaves offered by the Swedish government, most men rarely take advantage of such leaves (Haas, 1992). One of the most innovative solutions to the problem of negative male stereotyping with regard to paternity leave comes from Norway. Norwegian women now get 52 weeks of paid maternity leave—but *only if their husbands take off the first month, too*. If they don't, the wives' paid leave is cut in half: "The idea is to encourage fathers to help with a baby from the beginning, in the belief that once they start, they will stay engaged in child rearing" (Coleman, 1994: 58). Interesting idea, isn't it?

Day Care for Dependents

One of the most serious problems facing families today is inadequate day care for young children, and increasingly families are confronting the need for day-care services for elderly parents as well. The absence of quality care for dependents creates many difficulties for working parents and keeps many mother-only households in poverty. In this section we focus particularly on what industry, business, and government are doing currently to help the family in this regard. In Chapter 19 we'll return to this topic to look at future prospects.

Child Care According to Piotrowski and Hughes (1993: 193), "The search for quality nonparental care for young children is daunting at best and can reach crisis proportions at worst, because our nation currently lacks a policy that ensures reliable, affordable, developmentally appropriate care for all children who need it." As we saw in Chapter 12, high costs, poor quality, and long waiting lists are just some of the obstacles that confront working parents who seek safe and reliable care for their children.

Several national studies have shown that child-care problems keep many women out of the work force and many working parents in poverty. Many unemployed young mothers, particularly those without a high school education or marketable skills, report that their inability to pay for child care is the major reason they are unable to enter the labor force. Poor women who work for minimum wages at unskilled jobs can rarely pay for child care let alone education and thus are often thrown back on welfare.

The government and most employers are not dealing with these problems. Only a few companies have recognized that offering family benefits is good for business and now provide some form of child-care assistance such as a company-run, on-site child-care center, access to a reputable child-care center near the company's facilities, and summer camps. One of the most popular issues of *Working Mother* magazine is its annual ranking of the 100 companies that offer the best working conditions and benefits for working mothers. Major criteria in these rankings include competitive wage levels, opportunities for advancement, support for child care, and such family-friendly benefits as leave for childbirth, flextime, and job sharing. Table 14.6 lists *Working Mothers'* top ten companies for 1994.

Even some of the top 100 companies in *Working Mothers'* list are not as family-friendly as they seem. For example, although described as permitting employees to work at home through telecommuting, John Hancock has no formal telecommuting policy and does not encourage such

Table 14.6

1994's Ten Best Companies for Working Mothers

NAME OF COMPANY	YEARS RANKED IN TOP 10	DESCRIPTION OF BUSINESS
AT&T	2	U.S. giant in long-distance telephone and other telecommunications services
Barnett Banks	2	The seventeenth largest bank in the United States
Fel-Pro	6	U.S. manufacturer of gaskets, sealants, and lubricants for cars
Glaxo	2	One of the largest pharmaceutical companies in the United States and the world, specializing in prescription drugs
IBM	7	One of the United States' and the world's largest computer manufacturers
John Hancock	1	One of the largest insurers in the United States
Johnson and Johnson	3	A U.S. and worldwide giant in the manufacture and sale of health care products and supplies
Lancaster Laboratories	1	U.S. provider of laboratory services to clients in the food, drug, and environmental fields
Nations Bank	2	The fifth-largest banking company in the United States
Xerox	3	A U.S. and world leader in document processing

SOURCE: Based on Moskowitz and Townsend, 1994: 21–68.

arrangements. Only a few workers at the company have telecommuted on an informal basis (Saltzman, 1993). Although a company may herald flextime, only a few supervisors may be sympathetic. Instead of supporting employees who want to work from 8 A.M. to 3 P.M. (so they can be home when their children get out of school), such supervisors may schedule important meetings late in the afternoon. Moreover, the lower employees are on the organizational chart, the less likely they are to be included in family-friendly programs. In one U.S. Department of Labor study, over 22 percent of managers and professional workers but only 8 percent of blue-collar workers were found to have been approved for flexible schedules (Saltzman, 1993). Working at home, or telecommuting, is one of the newest modes of more flexible work styles but, as the box "Working at Home: Still Not a Paradise" shows, it is still not an answer to a working parent's dreams.

Some companies that tout child-care assistance actually do little more than provide a list of potential child-care providers in the area. In addition, companies sometimes implement (and are applauded for) services that aren't useful. For example, many elderly family members don't live near their children and may be too frail to use company day-care services. Moreover, many companies charge for day-care services, and many blue-collar workers are unable to pay even these reduced costs.

Elder Care   Elder-care services are rarely provided or even subsidized by business as yet, but some companies are now providing employee seminars on a variety of elder-care topics, such as how to choose a nursing home or helping elderly family members with financial matters. A Canadian company, Microchip Human Services in suburban Toronto, maintains a 24-hour computerized database service that employees from client companies can call toll free for detailed information on elder-care services anywhere in the country (Mergenbagen, 1994). Thus, combining family and work is not impossible with a little help from enlightened businesses and the computer industry.

CONCLUSION

Because many families lack sufficient economic resources, they have very few *choices* in the workplace. Macro-level economic *changes* have created numerous *constraints* that often put the family in a catch-22 situation. Incomes are not keeping up with the rate of inflation, so more household members have to work. This cuts into family time and creates stress that can contribute to illness, absenteeism, and layoffs. The more successful men are, the more difficult it is for them to find time for family activities. But if

Sales representatives, like this Philadelphia father, can often work out of home offices successfully, which enables them to interact with their children.

Working at Home: Still Not a Paradise

Personal computers, many experts predicted, would help decrease the conflict between work and family roles by enabling people to work at home, or telecommute—that is, work from home through computer hookups to a company office. Absenteeism and tardiness due to family emergencies should decrease. Workers could vary their work hours to accommodate family needs, and badly needed workers who could not leave home due to family responsibilities or their own disabilities could still have jobs (Nguyen, 1989).

By the early 1990s about 17 percent of men and women were working from home. In addition, 60 percent of those who worked at home full time were self-employed, and among women, fewer than half had

children. Apparently work and family role conflict is still not a strong incentive for telecommuting (Presser and Bamberger, 1993).

Where companies have actually put telecommuting into practice, this new work style has had mixed results. On the positive side, a telecommuting pilot project by the Canadian government revealed that public servants who telecommuted had a 73 percent increase in productivity (*Toronto Star*, November 15, 1994, "Working at Home and Saving Money," Edupage, LIST-SERV@UMDD, November 16, 1994). On the negative side, several women's organizations have opposed electronic home work because it shifts overhead costs to employees. For example, employees may be required to rent their computers, they may be switched from hourly to piece rates, forced to pay a greater share of the costs of

health and life insurance, Social Security, and retirement income, and more readily laid off than in-house workers. The Blue Cross Cottage Keying Program in Washington, D.C., pays its home workers 16 cents per completed insurance claim but offers them no benefits, contributes nothing on their behalf to Social Security, and charges them over $200 rent per month for their computer terminals. And some companies have pressured professional as well as clerical home workers to work long hours without pay (Applebaum, 1987). In addition, working conditions in the home can be dangerous. In semiconductor manufacturing work at home, for instance, workers are exposed to hazardous substances that can also contaminate residential sewage systems (Amott, 1993).

men are not successful, they and their families have fewer choices in maintaining a decent standard of living. Many parents, and especially single mothers, can't afford child care because it is too expensive, but without child care, they can't get the training for jobs that will pull them out of

poverty. Many of the same economic and political structures also have an impact on whether interpersonal relationships within the family are healthy or destructive, something we look at in the next chapter.

Taking Action

Combine Family and Work More Effectively

Here are several things you can do to improve your own working conditions and family life. You can also join a dialogue on issues that affect families and work.

• Here are several good sources of information on **pregnancy discrimination and family leave policies:** Women's Bureau Clearinghouse,

U.S. Department of Labor (800-827-5335); and 9 to 5, National Association of Working Women (800-522-0925). One especially useful publication from the Women's Bureau is *A Working Woman's Guide to Her Job Rights*. Another is *In Case of Sexual Harassment . . . A Guide for Women Students*, $4, from Center for Women Policy Studies, 2000 P Street N.W., Suite 508, Washington, DC 20036 (202-872-1770).

SUMMARY

1. Social class and economic resources play a major role in what happens to families. A small proportion of affluent families is getting richer, an increasing number of middle-class families is experiencing more employment instability, unemployment or underemployment, and the numbers of poor families are growing.

2. On the one hand, some scholars feel that poverty rates are exaggerated because they have been based on figures that overstate inflation and because they ignore noncash benefits from the government, such as food stamps, housing subsidies, and medical services. On the other hand, many feel that the proportion of the poor is underestimated because the amount of money needed for subsistence varies drastically by region and because many of the poor are undercounted by the U.S. Census Bureau.

3. The major programs for poor families include cash support; direct provision of necessities for food, shelter, and medical care; social services; and several community services. None of these programs has been very effective in helping families who want to get off welfare, however.

4. The country's homeless population has doubled every year since 1980. Although there are no exact figures, the estimates range from 3 million to 10 million homeless people. An esti-

mated 34 percent of the homeless population includes families with children.

5. Many adolescents and college students say that they expect to combine both work and family. They feel that work is not a top priority but also expect to have a house, several cars, state-of-the-art recreational equipment, and other amenities. Furthermore, more young men than young women expect the wife to stay home with the children instead of seeking a career. Thus, the expectations of many young people may be unrealistic and contradictory.

6. Economic recessions have resulted in more dual-earner families. There is a great deal of variation in dual-earner families, however, in terms of social class and willingness to relocate or to have a commuter marriage.

7. Employment affects the family in many ways. Whether the results are positive or negative, work roles influence the duration and quality of a marriage, household labor, and children's well-being.

8. Employed women are frequently romanticized. In reality, and regardless of the occupation, most women face problems in sex-segregated workplaces, wage and pregnancy discrimination, and sexual harassment.

9. A landmark piece of legislation is the Family and Medical Leave Act. Although the law pro-

tects an employee's job during illness as well as maternity and paternity leave, the bill provides little or limited coverage to many families.

10. Due to economic changes and the increasing number of mothers with young children who must work, many families face serious problems in terms of child-care services and facilities. Furthermore, there is some evidence that such innovative employment options as working at home are not as effective as many people had predicted.

KEY TERMS

poverty line   386
discouraged worker   390
underemployed worker   391
two-person single career   391
househusband   391

dual-earner couple   395
discretionary income   395
dual-career couple   395
trailing spouse   395

commuter marriage   396
mommy track   401
daddy penalty   401
comparable worth   403

ADDITIONAL READING

FAYE J. CROSBY, *Juggling: The Unexpected Advantages of Balancing Career and Home for Women and Their Families* (New York: Free Press, 1991). As the title suggests, Crosby feels that women can manage both employment and family responsibilities. Some of the topics include the costs and benefits of trying to "have it all," the impact on children, and the role of men.

GERTRUDE SCHAFFNER GOLDBERG and ELEANOR KREMEN, eds., *The Feminization of Poverty: Only in America?* (New York: Praeger, 1990). There have been many studies on this topic. In this book the contributors examine the feminization of poverty in Canada, Japan, France, Sweden, and Eastern Europe.

MORLEY GUNDERSON, *Comparable Worth and Gender Discrimination: An International Perspective* (Albany, NY: International Labor Office, 1994). The author analyzes comparable worth programs in the United States and Canada.

DOUGLAS S. MASSEY and NANCY A. DENTON, *American Apartheid: Segregation and the Making of the Underclass* (Cambridge, MA: Harvard University Press, 1993). The authors argue that residential segregation is the principal structural feature of American society that is responsible for urban poverty and racial inequality.

ESTER REITER, *Making Fast Food: From the Frying Pan into the Fryer* (Montreal: McGill-Queen's University Press, 1991). Reiter examines the impact the fast-food industry has had on the organization of work and family life.

LILLIAN B. RUBIN, *Families on the Fault Line: America's Working Class Speaks About the Family, the Econ-* omy, Race, and Ethnicity (New York: HarperCollins, 1994). Much of the material, based on interviews, is presented in the respondents' own words.

CHRISTINE L. WILLIAMS, ed., *Doing "Women's Work": Men in Nontraditional Occupations* (Newbury Park, CA: Sage, 1993). Among other topics, the contributors examine comparable worth for men, and men's employment in such traditionally female jobs as secretaries, elementary school teachers, strippers, and elder caregivers.

Two books that give the reader an insight into the world of domestic work are the following:

BONNIE THORNTON DILL, *Across the Boundaries of Race and Class: An Exploration of Work and Family Among Black Female Domestic Servants* (New York: Garland, 1994); and Mary Romero, *Maid in the U.S.A.* (New York: Routledge, 1992).

There are a number of studies on homelessness. Several that are especially pertinent to family life include the following:

ALICE S. BAUM and DONALD W. BURNES, *A Nation in Denial: The Truth About Homelessness* (Boulder, CO: Westview Press, 1993); Elliot Liebow, *Tell Them Who I Am: The Lives of Homeless Women* (New York: Free Press, 1993); and Mary E. Walsh, *"Moving to Nowhere": Children's Stories of Homelessness* (Westport, CT: Greenwood Press, 1992).

15
Family Violence and Other Crisis-Related Issues

Paul Cézanne, Strangled Woman

Data Digest

- In 1994, an estimated 3.1 million children under age 18 were reported to child protective agencies for maltreatment. Nationwide, between 1989 and 1994, **the rate of reported child abuse or neglect increased 24 percent,** from 38 per 1,000 children to 47 per 1,000.

- In 1994, an estimated **1,271 children died from abuse or neglect.** Among the 3,140,000 children under 18 whose abuse or neglect was reported to authorities, 45 percent were neglected, 26 percent were physically abused, 11 percent were sexually abused, 3 percent suffered emotional abuse, and 15 percent were maltreated in other ways, sometimes by parents who were substance abusers.

- It has been estimated that as many as **3000 women are killed by their husbands or boyfriends** each year.

- Every year, an estimated **2 to 6 million battering incidents** occur in the United States, male and female. A widely cited statistic is that **a woman is beaten every 15 seconds.**

- An estimated 1.2 million American **women have been raped by their husbands** one or more times.

- It is estimated that between 4 and 17 percent of **women suffer from violent acts during pregnancy.**

- Domestic violence incurs **medical expenses of at least $3 billion** annually. Businesses lose another $100 million in sick leave, absenteeism, and nonproductivity.

- In the United States, the average prison sentence for a woman who kills her husband is **15 to 20 years;** for a man who kills his wife, the average sentence is **2 to 6 years.**

- Estimates of the extent of elder abuse vary, ranging from 500,000 to 2 million cases per year. Researchers report that about **5 percent of those over age 65 are abused** every year.

SOURCES: Bachman, 1994b; Cose, 1994; Lapchick, 1994; Laumann et al., 1994; U.S. Department of Justice, 1994c, Wiese and Daro, 1995.

In 1994, Susan Smith, a white woman, accused a black man of a carjack with her two young sons, ages 3 years and 14 months, still in their safety seats. A ten-day hunt ensued while Smith and her estranged husband pleaded on television for their sons' safe return. The mother begged, tearfully, for the boys' lives: "I have prayed to the Lord every day." Shortly thereafter, Susan Smith confessed that she had drowned her sons by driving her car into a lake, because her boyfriend did not want a ready-made family. (The boyfriend denied having said this.) The people in the small town of Union, South Carolina, were shocked by the murders, especially because they had seen Smith as a friendly person and a good mother who seemed devoted to her young children.

Families can be warm, loving, and nurturing, but they can also be cruel and abusive. As the Data Digest and the Smith story show, family members are more likely than outsiders to assault or kill other family members. In addition, researchers have traced the origins of many other destructive and self-destructive behaviors to stresses in family relationships.

We begin by examining the different forms of violence among family members. Next we explore several explanations for family violence and show why intervention and prevention have been largely ineffective. We then turn to such other crisis-related problems in the family as the abuse of drugs and steroids, teenage depression and suicide, eating disorders, and the early death of a family member.

MARITAL VIOLENCE

For years people have speculated as to the reason why the subject of Leonardo da Vinci's famous portrait known as the Mona Lisa smiles. According to a Maryland art expert and dentist, what Mona Lisa may have been hiding was a broken jaw! According to this expert, she could have been a battered woman because signs of scar tissue around her mouth suggest that she was missing teeth: "She isn't smiling. Her expression is typical of people who have lost their front teeth" (Cerio and Howard, 1993: 10).

Marital violence may be physical or emotional. *Physical violence* includes such behaviors as throwing objects, pushing, grabbing, shoving, slapping, kicking, biting, hitting, beating, choking, threatening with a knife or gun, or using a knife or gun. *Emotional abuse,* which may be equally damaging in the long run, is more insidious. Scorn, criticism, ridicule, or neglect by loved ones can be emotionally crippling. Listen to a 33-year-old mother of two children: "He rarely says a kind word to me. He is always critical. The food is too cold or . . . too hot. The kids are too noisy. . . . I am too fat or too skinny. No matter what I do he says it isn't any good. He tells me I am lucky he married me 'cause no one else would have me" (Gelles and Straus, 1988: 68).

It is difficult to measure marital violence. Violence is usually carried out in private, and, out of shame or fear of reprisal, victims are reluctant to report it. Nevertheless, more women are injured by their intimate partners' battering than by rapes, auto accidents, and muggings combined (Rovner, 1991). Moreover, as you can see from Figure 15.1, women are far more likely than men to be the victims of violent acts by an intimate partner.

Women can also be abusive (see Data Digest). As we will see, however, when women are violent they are more likely to be defending themselves than to be initiating violence, and they are far less likely than men to use lethal weapons like knives and guns. Moreover, in any physical fight women are more likely to sustain serious physical injuries because they are usually smaller than their partners or because they are attacked when pregnant and thus physically especially vulnerable (Gelles, 1988).

Characteristics of the Violent Household

A number of characteristics that are common to abusive marital partners are listed in Table 15.1. Some reflect macro-level influences, such as unemployment and poverty. Others reflect more micro-level factors, such as drug abuse. In most cases

Figure 15.1 *Victim-Offender Relationships in Violent Crimes, 1987–1991.*
Note that the percentages in this figure are based on total victimizations during the five-year period cited; they do not represent annual averages (Bachman, 1994b, p. 6).

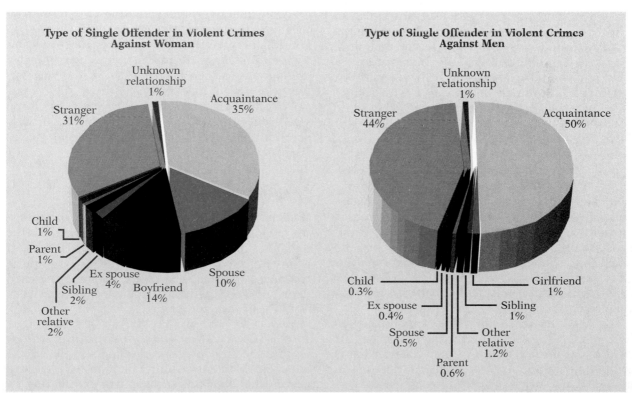

Table 15.1

Risk Factors Associated with Family Violence

The husband is sadistic, aggressive, or obsessively jealous.

He has threatened, injured, or killed a family pet.

He grew up seeing his father hit his mother.

Either husband or wife is violent and abusive with the children.

One or both spouses are divorced and remarried or their current marriage is common-law.

The husband is a blue-collar worker.

The wife does not have a college degree.

The husband is unemployed or a high school dropout.

Total family income is below the poverty line.

The husband is under the age of 30.

Either or both spouses abuse alcohol and other drugs.

Either spouse has been drunk five or more times in the past year.

The husband uses alcohol as an excuse for aggression.

The husband has assaulted someone outside the family or has committed some other violent crime.

The family is socially isolated from neighbors, relatives, and the community.

SOURCES: Flanzer, 1993; Leonard and Senchak, 1993; Straus, 1993; Bachman, 1994; Gelles, 1995.

several of these factors are involved, and the more risk factors there are, the more likely the violence. In addition, there are often complex relationships in abusive situations. For example, the combination of men in blue-collar status, heavy or excessive drinking, and an approving attitude toward violence against women is associated with a high rate of wife abuse (Kantor and Straus, 1987).

Contrary to common wisdom, family violence does not occur only in lower socioeconomic families but cuts across racial, ethnic, religious, and social class lines. Middle-class family violence is less visible, however, because such families are less likely to live in crowded housing where the neighbors call the police during fights. Moreover, their private family physicians are often reluctant to report injuries to the police or to social service agencies. Among affluent white families, Newberger (1985) found that hospitals reported only about half of cases involving spousal abuse.

In 1994, the American public was shocked by the arrest of O. J. Simpson for the murder of his ex-wife and a male friend of hers. Hall of Fame football player and a "national legend," Simpson had generally been described by the media as

handsome, bright, articulate, polite, charming, likable, and a widely respected celebrity . . . always willing to accommodate autograph-seekers (Glauber, 1994; Kurtz, 1994).

As an athlete, [Simpson] earned fame, fortune and enduring stature. He was a respected sports announcer and corporate spokesman. As an actor, he could make people laugh. Among friends and business acquaintances, he was nothing if not a nice guy (Vobejda, 1994: A18).

Whatever may be the outcome of the trial that began in early 1995, in which evidence was introduced to indicate that Simpson had battered his wife more than once in the past, the case put the spotlight on the issue of battered women.

What motivates batterers? And why do they so often look and act like "normal" men? The attorney-husband of a 50-year-old Colorado woman appeared to be a pillar of the community. According to his wife of 28 years, however, he hit her, threw her down the stairs, and tried to run her over. "One night in Vail," she said, "when he had one of his insane fits, the police came and put him in handcuffs. . . . My arms were still red from where he'd trapped them in the car window, but somehow, he talked his way out of it" (Ingrassia and Beck, 1994: 29).

One characteristic common to batterers is the need to control. As you read in Chapter 8, controllers often suffer from low self-esteem and a continuing need to prove themselves. Abusive men have also been described as feeling helpless, powerless, and inadequate in both their marriages and their jobs. And if their wives are more intelligent or more successful, the husbands may assert their superiority by beating their wives (Babcock et al., 1993).

The Cycle of Domestic Violence

Walker (1978) proposed a "cycle theory of battering incidents" that is often used to explain the dynamics of marital abuse. According to Walker, a three-phase cycle begins with a tension-building phase that leads to the acute battering incident and ends with a period of calm that lasts until the cycle starts again.

Phase One: The Tension-Building Phase

During the first phase of Walker's cycle, minor battering incidents occur, and the wife tries to prevent her husband's anger from escalating by catering to him or staying out of his way. At the same time, the battered wife often feels that her husband's abuse is justified: "When he throws the dinner she prepared for him across the kitchen floor she reasons that maybe she did overcook it, accidentally. As she cleans up his mess, she may think that he was a bit extreme in his reaction, but she is usually so grateful that it was a relatively minor incident that she resolves not to be angry with him" (Walker, 1978: 147). Although the wife hopes the situation will change, the tension typically escalates, the husband becomes more brutal, and the wife less able to defend herself.

Phase Two: The Acute Battering Incident In the second phase Mr. Hyde emerges, exploding in rage and beating and otherwise abusing his wife. Some women who have lived with abuse for a long time actually anticipate this phase and trigger the violent incident to get it over with. They often deny the severity of their injuries and refuse to seek medical treatment. One woman who wanted to go to a family party with her husband and sensed that an acute battering incident was about to occur deliberately provoked it during the week so that by the weekend her husband would be pleasant for the party.

Phase Three: Calm Mr. Hyde becomes the kindly Dr. Jekyll in the third phase, begging his wife's forgiveness and promising that he will never beat her again: "He manages to convince all concerned that this time he means it; he will give up drinking, dating other women, visiting his mother, or whatever else affects his internal anxiety state. His sincerity is believable" (Walker, 1978: 152). If his wife has been hospitalized because of her physical injuries, the husband often deluges her with flowers, candy, cards, and gifts. He may also get his mother, father, sisters, brothers, and other relatives to plead his case to his wife. They all build up her guilt by telling her that her husband would be destroyed if she left him and that a father should not be separated from his children. And because most battered women hold traditional values about love and marriage, the wife convinces herself that *this* time he will *really* change. Because he is now loving and kind, she identifies this "good man" as the one she loves. After a while, though, the calm, loving behavior gives way to battering incidents, and the cycle starts all over again.

Marital Rape

In 1991, England passed a law that made marital rape a criminal act. **Marital rape** (sometimes also referred to as "spousal rape" or "wife rape") is an act of violence in which a man forces his nonconsenting wife to engage in sexual intercourse. In the United States, raping one's wife is a crime in only about half of the states. Some states grant a *marital-rape exemption*. That is, they do not prosecute a rape case if the man is actually living with the woman, married or not. Some states permit prosecution of a husband-rapist only if the rape occurred after one spouse filed papers in court to end the marriage or if the parties were not living together at the time of the rape (Russell, 1990). Even in those states where a husband can be charged for marital rape, a wife may have difficulty proving rape if she shows no visible signs of having been forced, such as bruises or broken bones.

One reason marital rape is so common is that it is still accepted by many people as a legitimate act. Although a study by a House of Representatives committee estimated that 15 percent of married women are raped by their spouses, very few of these crimes are reported. A traditional wife, believing that she has no choice but to perform her "wifely duty," may accept the situation as normal, especially if her husband does not use a weapon or threaten her with physical harm (Michael et al., 1994).

In a study in the San Francisco area, one out of every seven women said they had been raped by their husbands. About a third of the respondents reported single incidents of rape, but another third reported they had been raped 2 to 20 times, and a final third said they had been raped more than 20 times (Russell, 1990). Why didn't they speak up? Many women remain silent because they assume that no one will believe them.

Why Do Women Stay?

Although battered wives have often been described as dependent women who suffer from low esteem and feelings of inadequacy and helplessness, we don't know whether these characteristics reflect personality tendencies and traits battered women possessed before they met their abusers, whether they are the result of the abuse, or a combination of both (Gelles and Cornell, 1990).

Thus the obvious question: Why do these

women stay? Despite the common tendency to think of abused women as passive punching bags, in their national survey of family violence Gelles and Straus (1988) found that 70 percent of abused women did seek help. Some women, like one of my students, find the courage to leave only when they suddenly realize that the abusive relationship is harming their children:

John never laid a finger on his daughter but struck me in front of her. . . . I cringe to remember but at the time I chose to believe that what Sheri saw wasn't affecting her. One afternoon when I heard Sheri banging and yelling, I rushed to [her] room. . . . Sheri was hitting her doll and screaming four-letter words she often heard her father yell at me. She was just starting to talk, and that was what she was learning. That moment changed our lives forever. . . . I left John that night [and] . . . never went back (Author's files).

Why is it that some victims never try to leave an abusive relationship? Among the several factors we discuss next, none is likely to be the sole reason. There are often multiple explanations for a victim's decision to stay with an abusive partner.

1. ***Negative self-concept and low self-esteem.*** Many battered women feel they have nothing to offer another person. Many batterers convince their partners that they are worthless, stupid, and disgusting: "Behind a closed door, a man calls a woman a 'slut' and a 'whore.' He tells her that she is too fat or too sexy or too frumpy, that she is 'a poor excuse for a mother,' a worthless piece of dirt" (Goode et al., 1994: 24). Such tyranny is effective because, in many cultures, a woman's self-worth still hinges on having a man. Women are often willing to pay any price to hold on to the relationship because they believe no one else could love them.

2. ***Belief that the abuser will change.*** One woman with a cheek still raw from her husband's beating said, "I'm still in love with him, and I know he's going to change as soon as he gets past these things that are troubling him." As we've said, our society has long nurtured the myth that women are responsible for changing men into kind and loving beings. Consider, for example, the message in the popular Walt Disney film *Beauty and the Beast.* The Beast turns into a

Hedda Nussbaum was the live-in lover of criminal attorney Joel Steinberg when he "adopted" infant Lisa (left). Six years later, battered beyond recognition by her "lover," (right) Hedda witnessed his arraignment for the murder of Lisa, whom he had begun to abuse as well. Doctors, teachers, and neighbors had noticed Lisa's bruises but did nothing. Late in 1987 Steinberg hit Lisa and left her lying on the floor, comatose; she died three days later. Steinberg was convicted and jailed. Nussbaum, judged incapable of either harming or helping Lisa, began slowly to rebuild her life.

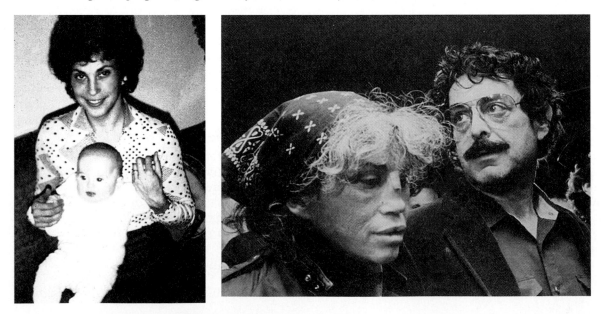

prince only after Beauty stays with him and says she loves him despite his cruelty, threats, and breaking furniture—in a word, acting like a beast.

3. *Economic hardship and homelessness.* Because many abused women do not work outside the home and have few marketable skills, they see no way to survive alone economically. Many batterers keep their wives in economic chains; nothing is in the woman's name—not checking or savings account, automobile, or home. Many abusers keep their victims isolated from friends and relatives, and as a result the women have no one to turn to. Moreover, those who might provide battered women a place to stay fear endangering their own families. Without resources, some abused women who do leave become homeless (Browne, 1993).

4. *Need for child support.* If leaving a husband or filing charges against him results in impairing his earning capacity, both the wife and children may lose his economic support. Many women believe that even an abusive husband (and father) is better than none. As one of my students, a former abused wife, once said in class, "This man brings in most of the family's income. Without him, you can't pay the rent, buy the groceries, or pay the electric bills. If he goes to jail, he'll probably lose his job. And then what will you and the kids do?"

5. *Fear of surviving alone in a hostile world.* Many women believe that if the people they love abuse them, so will everyone else. Strong cultural factors may also keep a woman from moving out of an abusive relationship. As the box "Out-of-Town Brides and Wife Abuse" shows, there is strong pressure among some Asian American communities not to bring shame or disgrace to the family by exposing such things as domestic violence.

6. *Shame, guilt, and sin.* Shame is common among battered wives because they know that many other women are not abused (Barnett and LaViolette, 1993). They often feel that somehow they have brought the violence on themselves. This is particularly likely if they have seen their mothers or grandmothers suffer similar treatment: "One woman whose bruises from her husband's beatings were clearly visible was told by her grandmother, 'You have to stop provoking him. You have two children, and the bottom line is you have nowhere to go. If he tells you to shut up, shut up'" (Goode et al., 1994: 27).

Thus a tradition is passed on. Women feel they are responsible for preventing male violence, and if they don't succeed, they accept the consequences (Jones, 1993). Moreover, because some priests, ministers, and rabbis will remind a woman that she is married "for better or for worse," religious women may feel guilty and sinful for believing that they have rights as human beings (see Table 15.2) and for wanting to end the abusive relationships.

7. *Fear of the husband.* Fear is a major reason why women stay in abusive marriages. Husbands have threatened to kill their wives, their wives' relatives, and even the children if the wives try to run away. Indeed, as I was told by directors of shelters for battered women when I was doing research on domestic violence a few years ago, it is not unusual for husbands to track down their families from as far away as 1000 miles and threaten violence to get them to return. And even when women go to court to protect themselves, they may find that a judge does not take domestic violence seriously. Consider this courtroom experience:

[The judge] took a few minutes to decide on the matter. . . . He said, "I don't believe anything that you're saying . . . because I don't believe that anything like this could happen to me. If I was you and someone had threatened me with a gun, there is no way that I would continue to stay with them. . . . Therefore, since I would not

---

Table 15.2
The Rights of a Battered Woman

I have the right to be angry over emotional or physical abuse.

I have the right to be free from fear or humiliation.

I have the right to have friends.

I have the right to privacy.

I have the right to express my thoughts and feelings.

I have the right to develop my talents and abilities.

I have the right to provide my children with a peaceful home.

I have the right to seek help.

I have the right to leave an abuser.

I have the right to prosecute an abuser.

I have the right to be happy.

SOURCE: Based on Fedders, 1990; Jones, 1994.

Out-of-Town Brides and Wife Abuse

Although Asian American families are generally close-knit, loving, and hardworking (see Chapter 13), they are not immune to abusive relationships. Among the Chinese American community, it is the "out-of-town bride" who is the most likely to suffer abuse and the least likely to leave an abusive situation (Chin, 1994).

Because they want traditional wives who are family-oriented, self-sacrificing, and obedient, many Chinese American men send for brides from China. Typically, these men feel that they are "saving" these women from the poor living conditions in China and from its oppressive government, and they feel their spouses should be grateful and live to serve them rather than to achieve anything on their own. The view of women as inferior to men is thus often transferred to the United States from China and other countries through such marriages (Heise et al., 1994).

Despite their belief that they are coming to the "Mountain of Gold" in America and that they will live in a spacious home, travel freely around the country, and make a lot of money to send home to relatives, these women usually find that the men they've married are much older than they are, unattractive, and far less successful than they had thought. Disappointed though they may be, the women are still bound by such traditional beliefs that if they divorce they will never again marry because a Chinese man will marry only a virgin (Rubien, 1989). Thus they try to make their marriages work, often seeking employment to supplement the usually low incomes of their husbands. Both partners are often handicapped by language difficulties and insufficient skills and are trapped in low-paying jobs with inadequate benefits and rare promotions. The wives often have the additional burden of being expected to have children as soon as possible, to care for elderly in-laws, and they feel obligated to send money to their families in China. Many are socially isolated, in touch only with their husbands' families, who may be totally unsympathetic to their problems.

Because of their different attitudes, beliefs, and expectations, husbands often resort to psychological and physical abuse to control their wives. Typically, the men try to keep their wives from engaging in any activities beyond homemaking and paid outside work, and if the women resist, violent behavior may be the result.

---

let that happen to me, I can't believe that it happened to you." When I left the courtroom that day, I felt very defeated, very defenseless, and very powerless and very hopeless (Maryland Special Joint Committee, 1989: 3).

8. **The home becomes a prison.** Both emotional and physical abuse literally trap the battered woman in her home, which becomes a prison rather than a refuge, with little chance of escape. For a comparison of prison life and life in an abusive home, see the box "The Battered Wife As Prisoner."

The battered woman's inability to leave her abusive spouse has serious consequences not only for her own welfare but for the welfare of her children. We will return to this issue later.

Women Who Abuse Men

In 1994, a highly publicized legal case brought attention to women's abuse of men. Lorena Bobbitt cut off her husband's penis with a kitchen knife, fled their apartment, and tossed the penis from her car window (doctors reattached the organ). Lorena Bobbitt claimed that she had acted impulsively after her husband had raped her and that he had repeatedly abused her during their five-year marriage. A jury of seven women and five men found her not guilty by reason of temporary insanity. When Lorena then charged John with marital rape, the jury acquitted him. A year later, however, John Bobbitt, who had begun appearing in pornographic films, was convicted of two domestic battery charges against a former fiancée and was ordered to serve 30 days in jail by a judge who called him a "bully."

In 1978, Steinmetz published several reports asserting that women hit men as often as men hit women and claiming that husband abuse was the most underreported form of marital violence. Steinmetz suggested three reasons why men do not protect themselves:

Chivalry According to Steinmetz many men believe that only a bully would hit a woman.

CONSTRAINTS

The Battered Wife as Prisoner

In a study of Israeli women at a shelter for battered women, Avni (1991b) has suggested some interesting parallels between Goffman's (1961) classic study of the life of the prisoner and the life of an abused woman (Cottle, 1994, also discusses battered women as prisoners in their homes):

	PRISON	ABUSIVE HOME
House rules	Inmates are punished until they submit to rules. Inmates' mobility is minimal.	Wife is punished if she questions husband's authority or "talks back." Wife's activities are limited.
Loss of autonomy	Inmates' daily lives are planned for them; they must ask permission for any activity.	The battered woman has no control over her own body, time, space, or social connections. One woman's husband sealed the door with plaster when he left for work to prevent his wife from going out.
Limited contact	Staff control all access to the outside world. Inmates feel inferior, weak, and detached from the real world.	By isolating wife from family, friends, and neighbors, the abusive husband controls her access to the outside world, including resources that could help her.
Distrust and suspicion	Inmates are watched constantly and treated with suspicion at all times.	Abusive husbands often accuse their wives of unfaithfulness and may follow or have them followed to be sure they are not cheating.
Denial of privacy and integrity of self	Inmates may be stripped naked and searched for drugs or weapons. Their belongings may be confiscated at will. They may be abused sexually by other inmates or guards.	Abused wives have little or no privacy. Husbands may screen their telephone calls and prevent them from reaching friends, relatives, or other helpers. They may force them to perform unwanted sexual acts or may rape them.

Self-restraint As we've noted, a man's greater physical strength enables him to inflict more severe physical injury. One man noted that when he hit his wife and "she went flying across the room," he realized how badly he could hurt her and so continued to take her abuse of him.

Punishment Many husbands felt they could punish their wives by showing them the injuries they had inflicted and making them feel guilty.

In 1991, women reported an average of 572,032 incidents of abuse by their male partners; men reported an average of 48,983 (Bachman, 1994). According to advocates for abused men, many men fail to report spousal assaults because "society simply doesn't take the issue seriously . . . [and] men who claim such abuse are deemed wimps and laughed at" (Hastings, 1994:1D; see also Brooks, 1994). In any case, battered men are less physically injured than battered women, less trapped than women because of greater economic independence, and more able to walk out of an abusive situation if they feel less responsible for the children.

VIOLENCE AGAINST CHILDREN

In 1990, police in San Bernardino, California, followed up on a telephone call from a neighbor and discovered a 12-year-old girl whose parents had kept her imprisoned in closets since the age of 2. The 4-foot-by-5-foot closet the girl was found in was littered with human waste and fast-food wrappers. The girl was barefoot and wore an oversized jogging suit that was soaked in urine. She was bruised from beatings allegedly administered by her father. Police said the girl's physical development appeared to have been so stunted by her decade-long ordeal that she looked about seven years old.

The abuse—physical and psychological—of children is not a recent phenomenon. Among the Puritans, women were instructed to protect the children "if a man is dangerously cruel with his children in that he would harm either body or spirit" (Andelin, 1974: 52). And men were not the only offenders: In 1638, Dorothy Talbie "was hanged at Boston for murdering her own daughter, a child of 3 years old" (Demos, 1986: 79). In 1946, John Caffey's observations of unexplained fractures in children he had seen earlier led this pediatric radiologist to suggest the possibility that these children had been abused. And in what may have been the first formal paper on the subject, physician C. Henry Kempe and his colleagues published an article on the battered-child syndrome in 1962 in the *Journal of the American Medical Association*. Nevertheless, it is only in recent years that child abuse has become a major public issue.

Defining Child Abuse

Although we will use the older and more familiar term *child abuse* frequently throughout this section, we will also employ a newer term, *child maltreatment,* which is beginning to be used interchangeably with the former. As you will see, the definitions of both terms are similar, but the newer term puts more emphasis on emotional abuse and the failure of caretakers to provide a child with proper care.

Child abuse, as defined by the National Center on Child Abuse and Neglect and codified in Public Law 93-237, is "the physical or mental injury, sexual abuse, negligent treatment, or maltreatment of a child under the age of 18 by a person who is responsible for the child's welfare under circumstances that indicate that the child's health or welfare is harmed or threatened thereby." **Child maltreatment** is characterized by a broad range of behaviors that place the child at serious risk, subsuming physical abuse, sexual abuse, neglect, and emotional maltreatment:

Physical abuse, which refers to an ongoing pattern of physically injurious actions, includes beating with hands or an object, scalding, severe physical punishments of various sorts, and a rare form of abuse called *Munchausen by proxy,* wherein an adult (usually the mother) will feign or induce illness in a child to attract medical attention and support for both her and her child. *Sexual abuse* includes making a child watch sexual acts, fondling a child's genitals, forcing a child to engage in sexual acts for photographic or filmed pornography, and incest. This category also includes sexual assault on a child by a relative or a stranger. *Child neglect* is the failure to provide basic caretaking obligations. Neglectful caretakers are usually the child's parents, but this term may be applied as well to personnel in residential centers for children or foster care homes. Child neglect includes educational, supervisory, medical, physical, and emotional neglect, as well as abandonment.

Finally, *emotional maltreatment,* a recently recognized form of child victimization, includes such acts as belittlement, verbal abuse, terrorizing a child by threatening physical harm, and a caretaker's failure to nurture the child and to be there emotionally for the child (National Research Council, 1993). Verbal abusers devalue and reject their children with constant criticism, put-downs, and sarcasm, making him or her feel inferior or unacceptable (Briere, 1992). Other forms of emotional maltreatment include neglect by parents who focus on their own problems and ignore those of their children; who use guilt and other manipulations to control children's lives; who subject children to unpredictable mood swings due to alcoholism and other drug abuse; and who frequently demand that children assume adult caretaking responsibilities (Forward, 1990).

Rates of Child Abuse

Estimates of the incidence of child abuse vary because of different data-collection procedures. For example, some states count only investigated reports of child abuse and neglect; others count reported cases (see Mash and Wolfe, 1991, for a discussion of definitional amd methodological variations). Child abuse is widespread and growing, however (see Data Digest). In a recent national study, for example, 13 percent of adult Americans reported that they had been punched, kicked, or choked by a parent or adult guardian, and 5 percent had suffered even more severe physical abuse (Moore, 1994b). About 3.1 million cases were reported to child protective agencies in 1994, but as many as 9 million children in the United States may suffer some form of neglect or abuse annually (Daro and McCurdy, 1991; Wiese and Daro, 1995).

The maltreatment of children may lead to an even more serious crime: murder. In 1993, an estimated 1300 children were killed by their parents or close relatives (Ingrassia and McCormick, 1994). As Figure 15.2 shows, in 21 percent of all murders committed within the family, children are the victims. Homicide, usually due to beating, is the leading cause of death among children under the age of one. When the child is under two, the mother is most likely to be the murderer, but an estimated one quarter to one third of child murders are committed by single mothers' boyfriends (McCormick, 1994).

Figure 15.2 Murder Victims in the Family. *In a study of 8,063 family homicides in the 75 largest U.S. urban areas, spouses were found to be the most frequent victims of family violence, and children made up the second largest group of victims. Among white spouse victims, 53 percent were wives, 47 percent husbands; among black spouse victims these percentages were 63 and 38, respectively. Note that numbers may not add up to 100 because of rounding* (Adapted from U.S. Department of Justice, 1994c).

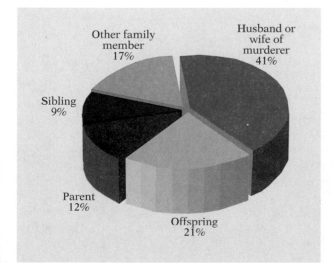

What Causes Child Abuse?

A number of problems contribute to child maltreatment. The biggest problem is parental substance abuse (Wiese and Daro, 1995). Other factors include the child's age and sex, the family's economic situation, the parents' marital status, and spousal abuse. One national study found that the older children were, the more likely they were to be abused, and that children from larger families (with four or more children) experienced more abuse and neglect than did children from smaller families. The study also showed that female children experienced more abuse than males—13 out of every 1000 girls as opposed to 8 of every 1000 boys (U.S. Department of Health and Human Services, 1988). These differences reflect girls' greater vulnerability to sexual abuse, which we will discuss shortly.

Economic stress and poverty characterize most abusive homes. Children from families with low incomes (under $15,000 a year) experience the greatest overall abuse—more physical, sexual, and emotional abuse, as well as all forms of neglect—and they suffer the most fatalities (Gelles and Cornell, 1990). Although increasing numbers of women work outside the home, many are in low-paying jobs, are single parents, or face serious child-care problems. Their frustration or lack of parenting skills may explode into the abuse of a child. In addition, children whose fathers are unemployed or who work part time are more likely to be abused than are children of fathers with full-time jobs (Wiese and Daro, 1995).

Child maltreatment is also highly likely in homes where the wife is abused. Noting that 70 percent of wife beaters also physically abuse their children, Kurz (1993) posits that family violence, including child maltreatment, is a direct outcome of men's attempts to maintain control over the powerless members of the family—women and children.

Baumrind (1994) has suggested that the early postdivorce period may make child maltreatment more likely because of increasing parental conflict and family stress. For example, the custodial parents may be changing residences, working longer hours, and experiencing more turmoil. Parents who are already stressed may react abusively to infants who, also affected by the parents' emotional state, become more irritable and harder to soothe.

Sexual Abuse and Incest

According to some estimates, between 6 and 62 percent of all females and between 3 and 31 percent of all males have been the victims of child sexual abuse at one time or another (Peters et al., 1986). In the most conservative "guesstimates" for 1994 (those based on reports to child protective agencies), among all reported cases of child abuse and neglect, 11 percent, or about 346,000 children, involved specifically sexual abuse (see Data Digest). Although this percentage has declined from 16 percent in 1986 (Wiese and Daro, 1995), it is not clear whether sexual abuse has actually declined over the years or whether it is simply less likely to be reported to agencies.

Most cases of reported incest are between fathers and daughters or stepfathers and stepdaughters. The rarest forms of sexual abuse, estimated to account for 1 percent of all cases, are between sons and fathers and sons and mothers (see Masters et al., 1992).

As we saw in Chapter 1 the *incest taboo*, which forbids sexual intercourse between close blood relatives, is a cultural norm in almost all known societies. In the United States, **incest** is defined by the law as sexual intercourse and/or marriage between members of the nuclear family, as well as between uncles and nieces, aunts and nephews, grandparents and grandchildren, and, often, first cousins and half-siblings. Moreover, there are strong social sanctions against sexual activity of any kind between such relatives.

Nevertheless, it has been estimated that as many as 17 percent of Americans have been involved in an incestuous relationship (Thornton, 1984). And in one national survey, 15 percent of adults said they had been victims of unwanted sexual touching and intercourse as children (75 percent of those who had been sexually abused were women), and nearly 50 percent said they had never told anyone about the experience (Patterson and Kim, 1991). One reason for the underreporting is that many people refuse to believe that incest is a serious problem (see the box "Myths and Facts About Incest").

One of the biggest misconceptions about rape is that this crime is perpetrated only on adult women. According to the U.S. Department of Justice (1994b), family members and relatives are often the assailants, especially in attacks on young girls, and fathers commit 20 percent of rapes of daughters under age 12. As you can see from Figure 15.3, although among older victims the perpetrators of rape are less likely to be family members, among children under 12 almost half of the offenders are relatives.

Figure 15.3 **Victim-Offender Relationships in Rape, 1992.** *Note that although the percentages of rapes committed by a stranger are higher at older ages, over two-thirds of victims age 18 or older are assaulted by people they know* (Based on data from U.S. Department of Justice, 1994a).

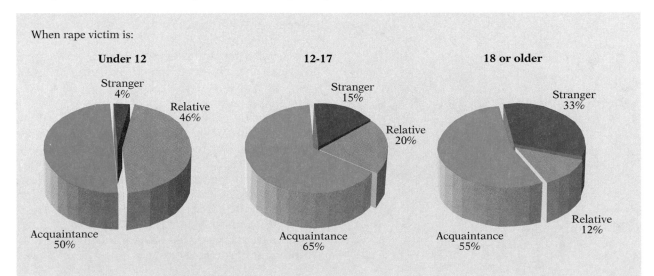

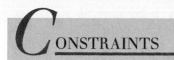

CONSTRAINTS

Myths and Facts About Incest

Forcing, coercing, or cajoling a child into incest or other sexual activities is probably one of the most devastating things an adult can do to a child. Although physical injury may not be severe or permanent, the psychological scars often last a lifetime. Yet even when family members are aware of incestuous behavior within the family, most neither report nor try to stop it. Why? Because they believe in myths like the following:

Myth: Children lie about incest.
Fact: Children rarely lie about incest. Most are too young to know about the sexually explicit acts they describe.

Myth: Children fantasize about incest. Every daughter fantasizes a romantic relationship with her father; every son imagines a romantic relationship with his mother.
Fact: A child wants and needs love and caring, not incest.

Myth: If the child is not coerced, it is not incest.
Fact: Whether a child has been verbally seduced or violently raped, the act of intercourse between blood relatives is incest and, in most states, a punishable crime.

Myth: If the child experiences pleasurable feelings during the encounter, the incest is not harmful.
Fact: A child's physiological excitement as an automatic response to sexual manipulation is one of the most damaging effects of incest. It can cause confusion and feelings of guilt or complicity, and it can make it difficult, later in life, for the person to separate satisfying sexual experiences from the original incestuous one.

Myth: The younger the victim, the less traumatic the incest.
Fact: Incest is traumatic at any age. People who are asked to recall incestuous experiences vividly describe feelings of pain and humiliation.

Myth: Incest happens only in poor, disorganized, or unstable families.
Fact: Incest is more likely to be *discovered* in poor, disorganized, or unstable families because these families often come to the attention of social services. Incest occurs in many seemingly "normal" middle-class families.

Myth: Fathers turn to their daughters for warmth and nurturance denied them by their wives.
Fact: The majority of men who are guilty of incest have gotten plenty of nurturance from their mothers, wives, and other women.

Myth: Incest is usually punished by incarceration.
Fact: Perpetrators are rarely charged or imprisoned, largely because a child's testimony is seldom accepted as evidence of incest. In addition, solid physical evidence is rarely available because the event is not reported and investigated quickly enough.

Myth: A daughter takes part in incest out of hatred for her mother.
Fact: A daughter is either forced or seduced into incest by her attacker. It is true, however, that the daughter sometimes blames her mother for not protecting her.

Myth: A child can be seductive and thus is often responsible for the adult's sexual arousal.
Fact: Children are *never* responsible for either adults' sexual arousal or for their physical advances.

Sources: Tamarack, 1986; Faller, 1990; Adams et al., 1994.

What Contributes to Sexual Abuse Within the Family?

Although people who commit incest vary greatly in personality characteristics, studies have found some common factors. Sexual offenders often have low self-esteem and lack self-control. Moreover, a disproportionate percentage were given minimal sex information by their parents. Typically, a man who abuses his child or children starts when a child is between 8 and 12 years of age, although in some cases, the child is still in diapers. The father may select only one child (usually the oldest daughter) as his victim, but it is common for several siblings to be victimized, either sequentially or simultaneously over the years (Masters et al., 1986). In addition, Abel et al. (1988) found that 49 percent of incestuous fathers and stepfathers referred for outpatient treatment had also abused children outside the family, and 18 percent had been raping adult women at the same time that they were sexually abusing their own children.

Some researchers have suggested that as long as children are nurtured almost exclusively by women, some men are going to continue to see their children—especially daughters—as sexual objects rather than as their flesh and blood

More than 35 years after she was crowned Miss America, Marilyn Van Derbur disclosed that as a child she was sexually abused by her father.

to be cared for and nurtured (Erickson, 1993). Incest offenders have been described as "narcissistic, uninhibited men who believe that their own sexual impulses must be fulfilled" (Hanson et al., 1994: 197–198). They often threaten physical retaliation against the victim and other family members if the victim doesn't keep the incestuous activity a secret, and that they will be arrested or the family will break up if the activity is revealed. Children remain silent out of fear.

According to Finkelhor (1984), stepfathers were the most likely men to abuse their (step)children. A female child, this researcher claimed, is far more likely to be sexually abused by a stepfather than by her biological father (1 out of 6 children vs. 1 out of 40). Undoubtedly the absence of blood relationship loosens normal constraints: "Incest offenders frequently viewed their sexually abusive behavior as a type of affair, particularly when the victim was a step-

daughter rather than a biological daughter" (Hanson et al., 1994: 197–198). On the other hand, Gelles and Harrop (1991) found very little difference in the abuse rates between genetic parents and nongenetic caretakers, such as stepparents and adoptive and foster parents.

Is Incest the Mother's Fault? Many people blame mothers for the incest that occurs between fathers and daughters: "Why didn't her mother do something about it? She must have known that something was going on" or "She probably wasn't giving her husband enough sex." Let's look first at a typology of mothers in incestuous families and then consider what factors may prevent a mother from protecting her child.

According to Jacobs (1990), the *mother as colluder* is selfish, irresponsible, or dysfunctional and sacrifices her daughter either intentionally or inadvertently. The mother may be a *voyeur*, someone who gets pleasure from watching other people involved in sexual activity. Whether she literally watches the behavior or fantasizes about it, she derives unconscious pleasure from it. Or a mother may lose interest in sex, withdraw from her husband, and ignore the incestuous relationship that may develop between the husband and the daughter.

The *mother as dependent* is seen as a helpless person who is suffering from a disabling condition like depression or a physical infirmity. She may have extremely low self-esteem and few problem-solving skills, and she may be psychologically maladjusted and have difficulty communicating with her daughter (Reis and Heppner, 1993). Rather than try to deal with the marital problem, or when efforts to deal with it fail, the husband may distance himself from his wife and turn to his daughter for emotional and sexual gratification. The daughter may then become a surrogate wife to her father and assume the mother's responsibilities in both homemaking and sex. Finally, the *mother as victim* fails to intervene in the father-daughter relationship because of her own victimization when she was a child. According to Jacobs (1990), this mother simply is accustomed to a situation in which the dominant male does whatever he wants.

But still, you may ask, how can a mother fail to protect her child from her own husband's sexual attacks? According to Elbow and Mayfield (1991), the general public has not been taught to recognize the symptoms of incest. Consequently, some mothers may not realize that incest is occurring. If a child shows increased interest in sexual matters, acts out, or withdraws, a mother may interpret this as part of a developmental stage. She may blame the onset of adolescence or a response to other difficulties, such as school problems or peer interactions. One mother, for example, interpreted her four-year-old daughter's resistance to her going to work as resentment rather than as fear of being left alone with her sexually abusive father (Elbow and Mayfield, 1991).

Some mothers may not try to protect their daughters for the same reasons they themselves fear to leave an abusive home (see earlier sections of this chapter). And many women lack the resources that may be required to protect their children. In 1989, a highly publicized case of alleged incest involved two physicians who were divorcing and their then five-year-old daughter. When a District of Columbia court ordered unsupervised visitation for the father, the mother accused her husband of molesting the child sexually and sent her daughter into hiding. The mother then spent 25 months in jail because she refused to reveal her daughter's whereabouts. For almost three years, the daughter traveled around the world with her maternal grandparents, both retired psychologists. Subsequently, the grandparents, mother, and child settled in New Zealand where the courts awarded custody to the mother but denied her the freedom to leave the country without permission. If the mother returns to the United States, she could be charged with contempt of court for hiding her daughter (Blumenfeld, 1994).

Abuse in Adolescence: The Runaway

According to Libertoff (1981), running away has been a response to serious family problems for hundreds of years, but it is only fairly recently that abusive behavior at home has been identified as a major cause of this behavior. During the seventeenth century, runaway children were among the earliest immigrants to the United States. Some ran away to seek adventure and excitement. Most, however, were poor children from English, Scottish, Irish, Dutch, or Portuguese families, who ran away from dreary, miserable, and often oppressive work conditions. The strict Puritan moral codes and child-rearing practices also motivated young boys—especially indentured servants and apprentices—to run away.

Today, we find that a large proportion of adolescent runaways have been abused. The numbers vary, from 5 percent in a national sample of runaway youths to as high as 75 percent in reports of local community runaway shelters. Another 10 to 20 percent leave home because they are "castaways" or "throwaways"—children put out of their homes by one or both parents (Garbarino, 1989). A recent survey of 170 shelters for runaways found that 38 percent had been in foster care at some time during the previous year, and 67 percent had been physically or sexually abused by a parent. Approximately 25 percent came from homes where at least one parent abused drugs. Thus, many children today are running away from dysfunctional families (Toth, 1992).

The Impact of Violence on Children

At worst, the physically violent abuse of a child may lead to death. A child abused by a much bigger and stronger person often cannot withstand the blows, punches, kicks, and other forms of torture inflicted by an adult. Even children who survive severe violence are often left with brain injuries; infants who are shaken violently may suffer intracranial (within the brain) bleeding; abused infants may have feeding and sleeping disorders, fail to thrive or demonstrate persistent lethargy, hyperactivity, or irritability; and children who are neglected may have poor physical growth, including underdevelopment of the brain and consequent problems in intellectual and speech development.

Whether abuse is physical, emotional, or sexual, children often suffer from a variety of physiological, social, and emotional problems, including headaches, bed-wetting, chronic constipation, difficulty in communicating, learning disabilities, and poor performance in school. Children from violent families are often more aggressive and more difficult to handle than children from nonviolent families, and they also are more likely to be arrested for delinquency, adult criminality, or violent criminal behavior (Holden and Ritchie, 1991; Beitchman et al., 1991, 1992). Adolescents who experience maltreatment are more likely than their nonabused counterparts to engage in early sexual activity, have unintended pregnancies, suffer emotional and eating disorders, abuse alcohol and other drugs, engage in delinquent behavior, and attempt suicide (Council on Scientific Affairs, 1993).

Incestuous relationships in childhood often lead to lack of trust, fear of intimacy, and sexual dysfunctions in adulthood. Often it is the abused child's unusual apprehension about what would be for most children a routine situation that betrays the sexual abuse. For example, a four-year-old girl responded to a picture of a father putting a child to bed by saying, "That's daddy getting me. He sees me asleep with a doll. He wants me to wake up and do things. Daddy is mean. I don't love him" (Gordon et al., 1990).

Sexually abused children have shown such symptoms as frequent and overt self-stimulation, inappropriate sexual overtures toward other children and adults, and excessive play and fantasy with sexual content. They are also more likely than nonabused children to have such symptoms as nightmares, withdrawn behavior, drug and alcohol use, and antisocial behavior, and they are more likely to exhibit general behavioral problems or to run away (Kendall-Tackett et al., 1993; Miller et al., 1993). Table 15.3 summarizes some of the physical and behavioral signs that a child is being abused and needs protection.

HIDDEN VICTIMS: SIBLINGS AND THE ELDERLY

Violence between siblings and the abuse of elderly family members may be less common than the forms of domestic abuse we've discussed, but they are equally devastating. They are also less

Table 15.3
Signs of Child Abuse

	PHYSICAL SIGNS	BEHAVIORAL SIGNS
Physical abuse	• Unexplained bruises (in various stages of healing), welts, human bite marks, bald spots • Unexplained burns, especially cigarette burns or immersion burns (glovelike) • Unexplained fractures, lacerations, or abrasions	• Self-destructive acts • Withdrawn and aggressive—behavioral extremes • Uncomfortable with physical contact • Arrives at school early or stays late as if afraid to be at home • Chronic runaway (adolescents) • Complains of soreness or moves uncomfortably • Wears inappropriate clothing to cover bruises
Physical neglect	• Abandonment • Unattended medical needs • Lack of parental supervision • Consistent hunger, inappropriate dress, poor hygiene • Lice, distended stomach, emaciated	• Fatigue, listlessness, falling asleep • Steals food, begs from classmates • Reports that no caretaker is at home • Frequently absent or tardy • School dropout (adolescents)
Sexual abuse	• Torn, stained, or bloody underclothing • Pain or itching in genital area • Difficulty walking or sitting • Bruises or bleeding in external genitalia • Venereal disease • Frequent urinary or yeast infections	• Withdrawal, chronic depression • Excessive seductiveness • Role reversal, overly concerned for siblings • Lack of self-esteem • Massive weight change • Hysteria, lack of emotional control • Sudden school difficulties • Sex play; premature understanding of sex • Threatened by closeness, problems with peers • Promiscuity • Suicide attempts (especially adolescents)
Emotional maltreatment	• Speech disorders • Delayed physical development • Substance abuse • Ulcers, asthma, severe allergies	• Habit disorders (sucking, rocking) • Antisocial, destructive acts • Neurotic traits (sleep disorders, inhibition of play) • Swings between passive and aggressive behaviors • Delinquent behavior (especially adolescents) • Developmental delay

SOURCE: American Humane Association brochure.

visible, largely because the authorities are rarely notified.

Sibling Abuse

Siblings' abuse of each other is so common it is almost normative. Although there are few recent empirical studies of sibling abuse, the available data show that physical, emotional, and sexual abuse is widespread.

Physical and Emotional Abuse Almost all young children hit a sibling occasionally. More than 80 percent of parents in one survey said that their children had engaged in at least one incident of sibling violence (such as kicking or punching) in the preceding year (Gelles and Straus, 1988). Furthermore, whereas only 0.3 percent of siblings used a knife or gun in the late 1970s, by the late 1980s this number had increased to 3 percent. Thus every year in the United States more than 100,000 children may face brothers or sisters with lethal weapons (Gelles and Straus, 1988). Although most sibling abuse does not involve weapons, it is highly traumatic nonetheless. Wiehe and Herring (1991) describe various forms of sibling abuse:

- **Name-calling and ridicule** Name-calling is the most common form of emotional abuse among siblings, and ridicule is closely linked to it. Victims still remember being belittled about things like their height, weight, looks, intelligence, or athletic ability. One woman is still bitter because her brothers called her "fatso" and "roly-poly" during most of her childhood. Another woman wrote: "My sister would get her friends to sing songs about how ugly I was" (p. 29).

- **Degradation** Degrading people, or depriving them of a sense of dignity and value, can take many forms: "The worst kind of emotional abuse I experienced was if I walked into a room, my brother would pretend he was throwing up at the sight of me. As I got older, he most often would pretend I wasn't there and would speak as if I didn't exist, even in front of my father and my mother" (p. 35).

- **Promoting fear** Siblings may often use fear to control or terrorize their brothers or sisters. A woman in her 40s said that her siblings would take her sister and her "out into the field to pick berries. When we would

hear dogs barking, they would tell us they were wild dogs, and then they'd run away and make us find our own way home. We were only five or six, and we didn't know our way home" (p. 37).

- **Torturing or killing a pet** The emotional impact on the child who loves, and is loved by, an animal that a sibling tortures or destroys can last for many years: "My second-oldest brother shot my little dog that I loved dearly. It loved me—only me. I cried by its grave for several days. Twenty years passed before I could care for another dog" (p. 39).

- **Destroying personal possessions** Childhood treasures, such as favorite toys, can become instruments of emotional abuse: "My brother would cut out the eyes, ears, mouth, and fingers of my dolls and hand them to me" (p. 38).

Besides experiencing sibling abuse, many children report that parents rarely take physical or emotional abuse seriously: "You must have done something to deserve it," parents might say. My parents seemed to think it was cute when [my brother] ridiculed me. Everything was always a joke to them. They laughed [at me]. Usually their reply was for me to quit complaining—"You'll get over it" (Wiehe and Herring, 1991: 22, 73).

Sexual Abuse A number of researchers believe that incest and other sexual abuse are common among brothers and sisters, but this type of behavior is rarely reported. Greenwald and Leitenberg (1989) found that 17 percent of the college students they surveyed had had a sexual experience with a sibling before age 13. Moreover, 2 percent of the incidents involved force and approximately 6 percent threatened force.

According to Wiehe and Herring (1991), many respondents said they were sexually abused by brothers who were baby-sitting. Some used trickery: "About age ten my brother approached me to engage in 'research' with him. He told me he was studying breast-feeding in school and needed to see mine. He proceeded to undress me and fondle my breasts" (p. 52). Others threatened violence: "I was about twelve years old. My brother told me if I didn't take my clothes off, he would take his baseball bat and hit me in the head and I would die. I knew he would do it because he had already put me in the hospital. Then he raped me" (p. 55).

Most children say nothing about sexual abuse, either because they are afraid of reprisal or because they think their parents won't believe them.

It is not coincidental, by the way, that many of the examples illustrating sibling abuse involve boys as the perpetrators. Although girls and sisters are also abusive, our society is more likely to condone violence by boys as normal or masculine (Miedzian, 1991; see also Chapter 4). Consequently, much of the research focuses on boys.

Elder Abuse

Although some older people are able to relax in their later years, others have a much less idyllic existence. They are abused by their spouses or younger members of their families. **Elder abuse** encompasses physical abuse (such as hitting or slapping), negligence (such as inadequate care), financial exploitation (such as borrowing money and not repaying it), psychological abuse (such as swearing at or blaming the elderly for one's problems), deprivation of such basic necessities as food and heat, isolation from friends and family, and failing to administer needed medications (Decalmer and Glendenning, 1993).

The lack of recent national data makes it difficult to determine the incidence of physical violence against older people. What information we do have suggests that an estimated 5 percent of the elderly are mistreated by their loved ones every year (see Data Digest). It is likely that this rate will increase as the older portion of the population continues to grow. Baby boomers, now in their mid-30s to early 50s, are often referred to as the **sandwich generation** because they care not only for their own children but for their aging parents as well. However, the percentage of young workers who can support the elderly is expected to shrink considerably. There is increasing pressure on these children of aging parents who are living longer but who are in frail health and who often have minimal financial resources (Zal, 1992). Most people in the sandwich generation are remarkably adept at meeting the needs of both the young and the old, but those who are not may abuse their children, their elderly parents and relatives, or both.

Characteristics of the Abused In a random survey of the over-65 population in the metropolitan Boston area, Pillemer and Finkelhor (1988) found that approximately equal percentages of men and women reported physical abuse but that women reported being more severely injured than men. The researchers also found that, for all forms of abuse, 58 percent reported that the abuser was their spouse. Later in life, according to Garbarino (1989), the likeliest victims are middle to lower-middle class white women between 75 and 85 years of age who have suffered some form of physical or mental impairment. Moreover, if either or both the caretaker and the elderly person abuse alcohol or other drugs or if they have had a poor relationship, the likelihood of abuse increases (Decalmer and Glendenning, 1993).

Why might older women be more likely, overall, to be victims of abuse? Some suggest that because women live longer than men, they are more likely to suffer from disabilities and chronic illnesses and thus to depend on caretakers who may be abusive (see Vinton, 1991). Others maintain that elderly men are at greater risk of mistreatment than elderly women because the former are more likely to be married or remarried and thus to be more dependent on family members who may be abusive. In contrast, older women are more likely to live independently and less likely to be targets of abuse (Douglass, 1992).

Disability may increase the likelihood that an elderly person will be abused by those who care for him or her.

Who Are the Abusers? Why Do They Do it?

Both men and women may abuse their elderly parents or other relatives, and both are equally likely to exploit them financially. Women caretakers are more likely to use psychological abuse or neglect, whereas men are more likely to employ physical force. We've suggested some of the macro-level stresses to which caregivers may be subjected; now we explore some micro-level reasons.

1. ***Impairment of the caregiver*** A 70-year-old "child" who cares for a 90-year-old parent—not an uncommon phenomenon today—may be frail, ill, or mentally disabled and thus unaware that he or she is being abusive or neglectful (Harris, 1990). In some cases caretakers are drug abusers who lack the resources to live elsewhere and tyrannize their elderly parents. One 65-year-old chronic alcoholic woman whose 90-year-old mother had taken her in because the daughter could not cope alone burned her mother's house down. While her mother was in hospital for a mastectomy, she threw cigarette ashes into a wastebasket and stumbled into bed. On a later occasion, the daughter nearly killed her mother by driving through a stop sign and colliding with another car. And, as her mother moved on into her 90s, the daughter continued to revile and abuse her for being confused and slow (Author's files). For more examples of the dependence of caregivers on those they abuse, see the box "Why the Elderly Tolerate Abuse."

2. ***Impairment of the care recipient*** Several studies have found that caregivers who are violent respond to the violence of those in their care. Elderly people with dementias may pinch, shove, bite, kick, or strike their caregivers. Caregivers, especially spouses, are more likely to hit back during such assaults (Coyne et al., 1993; Pillemer and Suitor, 1993).

3. ***Dependency in the older person*** Economic independence is often related to a sense of power and competence as well as self-esteem. Elderly people who are impaired by incontinence, serious illness, or mental disability become physically as well as economically dependent on their caretakers. If the elderly are demanding or tyrannical, caregivers may feel angry or resentful.

4. ***Medical costs*** Among middle-class families particularly, having to pay medical costs for an elderly relative may trigger abuse. Unlike working-class people, members of the middle class are not eligible for admission to public institutions, yet few can afford the in-home nursing care and service that upper-class families can provide. As a result, cramped quarters and high expenses increase the stress of caretakers.

EXPLAINING FAMILY VIOLENCE

Why are families violent? Why is violence among family members so widespread? Several theories have been proposed to explain the origins of family violence, why most violence is perpetrated by men on women and children, and why this victimization of women and children has long been ignored. As we look at the explanations offered by patriarchy/male-dominance theory, social learning theory, resource theory, conflict theory, and exchange theory, we will also see how societal institutions—religion, the law, government, and politics—support male violence in the family.

Patriarchy/Male-Dominance Theory

Family violence is found in societies around the world. According to a recent study by the World Bank, data from 35 countries showed that a quarter to more than half of the women surveyed reported having been physically abused by a present or former partner (Heise et al., 1994). The *patriarchy/male-dominance theory* suggests that in societies in which authority is held by men (see Chapter 1) and in which women and children are defined as the property of men, violence by men against women and children, particularly female children, will be more common. In such a society, men hold power, resources, and privilege and feel free to use women and children as sexual objects and as targets of physical abuse. Neither women nor children are likely to challenge them (see Ollenburger and Moore, 1992, for a discussion of patriarchy, capitalism, and gender):

Kate was involved in an incestuous relationship until she was 16. When she was 9, her father crept into her bedroom one night and "began fondling my genitals. I woke up because it was uncomfortable. I told him it hurt, so he stopped and ex-

Why the Elderly Tolerate Abuse

According to Pillemer (1985: 146–58), the elderly often tolerate abuse from younger caretakers because they care for their children, because they see no viable alternatives, because they are lonely, because they are afraid of depriving their grandchildren or of being deprived of contact with them or other family members, or because they have decided (unconsciously) to exchange submissiveness and passivity for the care they need (see Chapter 2 on exchange theory). Here are some representative comments by elderly people who live with abusive children:

"I'm her mother and there isn't anybody else to do these things for her."

"You can't throw your children out."

"We take him back because he don't have no other place to go."

"I can't put her out. Where can I put her? I haven't got the heart. She couldn't support herself."

"He's all I've got in the world."

"Having her live here helped because I'm afraid of crime. It's better not to get the reputation of living alone."

"I put up with her for my grandchil-

dren's sake. I didn't have the heart to say get out. . . . I'd miss the kids [and be] worried about [them]. . . . That's my main thing now, my grandchildren."

Finally, elderly parents, especially women, may tolerate abusive behavior in their old age because they have experienced violence all their lives. Women who suffered abusive parents may subsequently tolerate abuse from a spouse or partner and accept assaults from caregivers as normal (Simons et al., 1993).

plained my body to me. That was the first time anyone told me I had a vagina. My father was the household god—the absolute authority. All decisions went through him, and it didn't occur to me to question him" (Kinkead, 1977: 172).

In a society where women have little status, violence against them is often treated as a joke. For example, Ted Bundy, the handsome and charming law student who raped and murdered 38 women, escaped from Colorado prisons twice, and was finally tried and executed in Florida, became a folk hero in Aspen, Colorado, where he had lived:

T-shirts appeared reading: "Ted Bundy Is a One Night Stand." Radio KSNO programmed a Ted Bundy Request Hour, playing songs like "Ain't No Way to Treat a Lady." A local restaurant offered a "Bundyburger" consisting of nothing more than a plain roll, "Open it and see the meat has fled," explained a sign (Caputi, 1987: 51).

In American society, men may demonstrate their competence by acting "masculine," defined partly by showing contempt for anything feminine or for females in general. According to a number of authorities, as long as our culture encourages men to be controlling, dominant, callous, competitive, and aggressive rather than en-

couraging them to be nurturant, caring, and concerned for the welfare of others, they will continue to express their anger and frustration through violence and abuse against others (see, for example, Birns et al., 1994). And, as you can see from the box "Male Dominance and Violence Against Women," other cultures face similar problems.

In contemporary patriarchal societies the media—which are major contributors to the shaping of male and female images and role expectations—support male domination. Even when news, news analysis, and documentaries decry violence against women, their very focus on this phenomenon reinforces the belief in some that such violence is acceptable. Such American male authority figures as psychiatrists have actually told battered women to "take the good with the bad" (Barnett and LaViolette, 1993). In addition, male peer support groups often reinforce violence. For example, studies suggest that male peers often exchange the names of attorneys who are known for winning cases against battered wives and may agree themselves to testify falsely in support of a peer. As a way to "keep the upper hand" over women, they may justify battering or rape as "normal" when they are drinking (DeKeserdy and Schwartz, 1993).

Even religious dogma and institutions rein-

Male Dominance and Violence Against Women

In many areas of the developing world, both laws and custom work against women who are victims of violent attacks by men. In Pakistan, for example, for a rapist to be punished, four religious Muslim male adults must testify in court that they witnessed vaginal penetration. If a victim cannot prove that her rape occurred in this manner—the likelihood of such an event does not seem to be questioned—authorities often charge her with adultery (Okie, 1993). And as for marital rape, because Muslim law and religious practice make women the property of their husbands, there are no sanctions against forcible intercourse with one's wife.

Pakistan's Prime Minister Benazir Bhutto has begun to open all-women police departments across the country in an effort to protect the rights of women and stem the violence. Although many applaud her for trying to introduce such changes, critics feel that this and other endeavors may be only symbolic. Women are so poorly represented in governing circles—only 5 women sit among 304 members in the upper and lower houses of the government—it is unlikely that additional, more sweeping changes will be introduced, or even that Bhutto's innovations will be supported (Bokhari, 1994).

In Kenya and other countries of Africa, societal beliefs and customs hold that within a marriage a wife must always consent to sex. Thus most Africans do not accept the notion that a woman can be raped by her husband. Moreover, even outside of marriage, people do not see rape as a serious problem. In 1991, for example, 15 Kenyan schoolgirls were suffocated when they crowded into a tiny room in an effort to escape a gang of attacking male students. The school's headmistress said, "Oh, the boys did not mean the girls any harm. They only wanted to rape them" (Okie, 1993: A24)

Even countries that profess democracy fail to censure, prevent, and punish violence against women. For example, despite a constitution that bans discrimination against women and requires Brazil to combat violence, only 11 percent of the 11,000 battered women's cases in the Rio de Janeiro area in 1992 made it to court, and the few men convicted of murdering women served an average of just four years in prison. Further, many men who kill their spouses immediately check themselves into a psychiatric clinic to justify their claim of a disturbed mental state and thus serve no jail time at all. With a reported 337 assaults on women daily, Brazil has established more than 150 all-female police stations. Unfortunately, because there are only three women's shelters in the country, many victims are forced to return home, where the cycle of violence resumes (Robinson and Epstein, 1994). In addition, due to inadequate government funding, the women police officers "can't always get police cars that run, and they have to pool their money to buy paper or mail a letter" (Corral, 1993: 18).

In Thailand a predominantly Buddhist population espouses family harmony and compassion, but there is also a high level of wife abuse. According to Hoffman et al. (1994), for example, 20 percent of the Bangkok married women they surveyed reported battering. The fact that 93 percent of battering husbands were employed full time pretty much rules out the idea that unemployment or poverty underlay the violence and strongly suggests that in this culture, at least, male dominance is a factor in wife abuse.

force female submissiveness and male violence. For example, according to Islam's Qur'an, men are in charge of women because God (Allah) has made the one of them "to excel the other" (one translation says "stronger than the other") and because men support women financially. How should good Muslims deal with rebellious women? They should "admonish" them, refuse to share their beds, and, if necessary, beat them (Banales, 1990).

Studying abusive men in a treatment program, Brutz and Allen (1987) found that among Quakers the husbands who professed the greatest religious commitment were also the most likely to abuse their wives physically. Many of these men, as well as others from fundamentalist Christian sects, who headed blue-collar and middle-class families, cited the Bible and their "natural patriarchal rights" to beat their wives if they did not submit to the husbands' rules. And those who said they had been "saved" by Jesus Christ also said they felt no concern about beating their wives because Jesus Christ forgives all sins and weaknesses—thereby tacitly admitting that what they were doing was wrong.

Many wives of these men tolerated their husbands' abuse "because that's the way it's supposed to be." Others whose pastors often supported their husbands' behavior said that their relationship with God would make them strong enough to endure whatever their husbands might do (Shupe et al., 1987). Christian counseling centers may also reinforce wife battering by giving mixed messages:

We were members of a strict Protestant denomination. . . . We talked to the counselor about . . . everything except the violence. Finally, I told him I was afraid of my husband. The counselor told me in front of my husband to be a better wife and mother, to pray harder, to be more submissive. He told my husband that he shouldn't hit me. When we got home, my husband only remembered the part about how I should be more submissive (Barnett and LaViolette, 1993: 32).

Social Learning Theory

You will recall from Chapter 2 that, according to social learning theory, we learn by observing the behavior of others. For most people the family is the first school of behavior, so to speak. But this does not mean that all children who witness abuse or are themselves abused grow up to be violent themselves. Some people purposely seek to avoid the kind of violence to which they've been accustomed. However, studies indicate that continuous exposure to abuse and violence during childhood increases the likelihood that a person will be violent as an adult (McKay, 1994). Moreover, people learn and internalize social and moral justifications for abusive behavior. A child may interpret "it's for your own good" as legitimizing violent behavior (Gelles and Cornell, 1990).

So far, no one really knows whether, or how much, family violence is transmitted intergenerationally through modeling or imitation (see National Research Council, 1993, for a review of some of this literature). Modeling probably plays an important role in learning abusive behavior, but macro-level stressors such as unemployment exacerbate the probability of family violence. Furthermore, cultural values that demean, debase, and devalue women and children promote and reinforce abusive behavior. In a study of battered women and their children, Holden and Ritchie (1991) found that violent husbands were reported to be less involved in child rearing and

to use more physical punishment. As long as men continue to dominate and abuse their wives and children and as long as women continue to nurture and comfort others, girls and boys will grow up believing that male violence and female nurturing are "the way it's supposed to be."

Resource Theory

Applying resource theory (see Chapter 2) to the study of family violence, we start by suggesting that because in general men command greater financial, educational, personal, and social resources than women do, they have more power. Theoretically, power can be used for good or for ill, and in general it is those who lack these kinds of resources, and thus feel *powerless*, who resort to force and violence. For example, a husband who wants to play the dominant role in the family but who has little education, holds a job low in prestige and income, and lacks communication skills may use violence to maintain his dominant position (Babcock et al., 1993). Many women cannot assert themselves against men simply because their resources are even fewer than those of their partners.

Resource theory also helps explain premarital violence. As we discussed in Chapter 8, violence is not uncommon in dating relationships. If a woman feels she has few resources to offer she may be willing to date an abusive man just to have *someone*. Even worse, she may convince herself that she can reform the batterer. On the other hand, women who have more resources (such as money, a good job, or a college education) may be less willing to put up with the abuse.

Conflict Theory

Conflict theory, like resource theory, posits that groups with such resources as wealth, power, and prestige can impose their rules or their will over groups who lack these resources. Remember, though, that conflict theory is a macro theory. It examines the absence of resources through a wide-angle lens. Conflict theorists, therefore, argue that women and children are victimized in the family not only because they have few individual resources but because societal institutions such as the legal system, religious organizations, and medical personnel rarely take violence against women and children seriously. As we will explore shortly, conflict theorists often support their positions with evidence that there is little institution-wide commitment to preventing or treating such violence.

Exchange Theory

In the exchange theory framework, both victimizers and victims tolerate or engage in violent behavior because it offers them more benefits than costs. As we said earlier, victims may stay in an abusive relationship because of economic benefits. Rewards for perpetrators include the release of anger and frustration as well as the accumulation of power and control. Repeated acts of violence wear victims down to the point where they will say or do anything to please the batterer. For example, a 35-year-old teacher said that after two years of violence she would go to any length to please her husband:

I would . . . try to anticipate his moods, cook his favorite dish, dress the way he liked. I would have the kids washed and in bed when he got home from work so there wouldn't be any stress. . . . I gave up my first job so I could be at home, but then he got too worried about money, so I got another job as a teacher. I think I spent 24 hours a day either doing things to please him or thinking ahead to prevent his getting mad (Gelles and Straus, 1988: 32).

Being in control can give a person a false sense of self-worth. When an adult's self-esteem has been damaged or devalued by experiences outside the home—for example, losing a job or being humiliated by a boss or coworker—control at home becomes even more likely. If people can't assert themselves with adult associates, they may turn to weaker family members, like wives and children, who are more submissive and more easily controlled (Hodson and Skeen, 1987).

Violence also has costs, however. First, it's possible that the victim will hit back. Second, a violent assault could lead to arrest and/or imprisonment as well as to a loss of status among family and friends. Finally, an abuser may carry the violence too far, causing the dissolution of the family (Gelles and Cornell, 1990). Remember, however, that if a patriarchal society condones violence against women and children and defines violence as an important resource, the costs will be largely ineffective.

INTERVENING IN FAMILY VIOLENCE

Many clinicians, social workers, and health-care practitioners feel that families need help to prevent abuse before it starts. Until professionals and the public acknowledge that family violence is a serious problem, however, effective intervention programs—prevention, treatment, rehabilitation, and legal services—will not be developed (Flynn, 1990).

Prevention and Treatment Programs

One of the most effective intervention programs yet devised is the University of Rochester's effort to prevent child abuse by teenage mothers. In this program, nurses cultivate warm relationships with new mothers by visiting them regularly in their homes from the onset of pregnancy until their child's second birthday. The nurses not only show the new mothers how to care for their new babies but how to play with them and talk to them, and they also help mothers find jobs and obtain benefits. According to Levine (1991), only 4 percent of the low-income teenage mothers who received this help neglected or abused their children, compared to 19 percent of the young women who were not part of the program. The program has also been successful with parents who were themselves abused as children.

As we have seen, however, most abuse is perpetrated by men, and it is with these offenders that society has been least successful. First, we have the problem of the tendency to blame the victim rather that the abuser, particularly in cases of marital abuse. Although researchers have been successful in challenging many myths about family violence, many people still believe that a husband is justified in abusing a wife who "nags" him. And, as we've seen, many people also think that abused wives are masochistic and that fathers abuse their little daughters because the latter behave seductively. Since we are not going to eliminate sexism and the norms that legitimize violence overnight, our immediate concern must be to help victims of abuse recognize that they have rights.

Shelters are very important in providing a haven for abused wives and children where they can avoid further injury or even death. A shelter can't work miracles, however. To benefit from a shelter's help a woman must be willing or able to take control of her life. According to Kurz

(1993), a basic requirement for a woman to feel safe in beginning a new life is to ensure that legal restraining orders placed on her assailant are enforced. Many districts are training their police departments to take domestic violence restraining orders more seriously. And finally, women need support and encouragement in making the one decision that can stop the violence—that is, to leave the marriage or relationship permanently.

During the 1980s a number of police departments in Minnesota, Wisconsin, North Carolina, Florida, Colorado, and Georgia experimented with arresting abusers (with and without warrants) to reduce future assaults. The results were mixed. Arrest deters domestic violence primarily for white or Latino men who are married and employed. However, arrest escalated violence for African American, unemployed, unmarried suspects (Schmidt and Sherman, 1993). Because unemployment and poverty are increasing (see Chapter 14), some researchers suggest that there should be more effort in protecting victims from retaliation and ensuring their safety. For example, specialized domestic violence prosecution units would enhance the relationship of the prosecutor with the victim and enhance the expertise of those handling domestic violence cases. If prosecution cases proceeded quickly, victims would be more likely to testify against the assailant. Sentencing should be swift and probation should be replaced by incarceration. Finally, victims should be protected after the abuser gets out of prison or violates probation or parole conditions (Hart, 1993).

Barriers to Intervention

Many cases of domestic violence never come to the attention of protective service agencies. Even when they do, the penalties imposed on assailants are usually insignificant. In some large cities, fewer than 1 percent of those arrested for wife abuse spend any appreciable amount of time in jail (Hirschel and Hutchinson, 1992). According to reports produced at the beginning of O.J. Simpson's trial in mid 1994, Simpson's wife, Nicole, had called the police on eight separate occasions before he was finally arrested for the first time, in 1989, on charges of battery. On the latter occasion the judge fined Simpson $200 and ordered him to make a $500 donation to a battered women's shelter and to perform 120 hours of community service.

In a recent case in Baltimore, a husband returned home unexpectedly and found his wife in bed with another man. After drinking and arguing with his wife for several hours, the husband shot and killed her. The judge sentenced the husband to serve only 18 months, and remarked during the sentencing that "I seriously wonder how many married men . . . would have the strength to walk away without inflicting some corporal punishment" (Lyons and James, 1994:1A). Do you think that if the situation had been reversed—the wife had found her husband in bed with another woman—that the judge would have reacted in the same way?

Taking appropriate legal action in cases of incest is often hindered by mothers' tendency to see incest as an emotional or family matter rather than as a legal issue. Mothers often worry that numerous interviews and possible court appearances will retraumatize the abused child. Although this is an understandable and legitimate concern, the child has already been traumatized beyond anything the courts can do, and children generally realize that they are being helped. Many mothers, of course, have been intimidated by threats of violence or by actual physical abuse and thus are afraid for themselves as much as for the child. Such fear and isolation may preclude reporting and other attempts to limit the perpetrator's abuse of the child (Elbow and Mayfield, 1991). These concerns require macro-level remedies, including passing laws that protect victims rather than offenders, appropriating sufficient funds to investigate and prosecute abuse and neglect problems when they are reported, and providing quality child day-care and educational and employment opportunities equally to women and men.

Although states require that abuse and neglect of the elderly be reported, these laws are not always taken seriously either. Many health providers are reluctant to testify in court because of the long waits and delays, loss of time from their practice, and potential indignity of attacks on their credentials and judgment. Physicians may be reluctant to get involved because of malpractice suits: "You say 'court' to a physician and he'll shudder. . . . They'd rather be spending their spare time volunteering in a clinic than testifying" (Rovner, 1991: 7). Furthermore, it is difficult for health-care workers who suspect abuse to question a victim in the presence of a family member who has accompanied the person to the hospital and stays close at hand to monitor what is said. Laws and medical practices must be changed to support health-care providers who deal with family violence.

Legal Issues

In 1991, the governors of Maryland, Ohio, and Washington pardoned a group of women who had been imprisoned for killing or assaulting partners who had abused them physically. The women were pardoned based on the defense of the **battered-woman syndrome,** defined as a condition reached by a woman who has experienced many years of physical abuse and who feels incapable of leaving. In a desperate effort to defend themselves, such women sometimes kill their abusers. Some people were very sympathetic and applauded the governors' decisions. One observer noted that because more than 1 million women are battered every year by their husbands or boyfriends, it is amazing so *few* kill their aggressors. Others disagreed that all of the women should have been pardoned. Because some of the women had acted while their husbands slept or had hired hit men to do the job, some people felt the women had gotten away with premeditated murder.

It remains to be seen whether the battered-woman syndrome will become institutionalized as a valid defense for women who kill abusers and whether this new legal option will discourage wife abuse. Approximately 750 cases of battered-woman syndrome appear before the courts

every year, and in most instances, the murder is committed when the woman is threatened or attacked. Only about 25 percent of those accused of murdering an abusive partner are acquitted, however (Trafford, 1991).

OTHER CRISIS-RELATED HEALTH ISSUES

Although the crises precipitated by acts of abuse and violence are highly destructive to the well-being of the family and its members, other health-related problems can also take on crisis proportions. Moreover, when a family fails to deal with interpersonal issues that can affect physical health, it may confront such potentially long-term problems as drug abuse, teenage depression and suicide, eating disorders like anorexia and bulimia, and the excessive use of steroids. The family must also cope with the death—sometimes sudden and unexpected—of young family members.

Drug Abuse

An estimated 11 percent of all newborn babies have been exposed to drugs in the womb (Dart, 1991). Since 1989, children have been the fastest-growing segment of the $23 billion Supplemental Security Income program for the poor. Although exact figures are not available, experts expect that a number of the more than

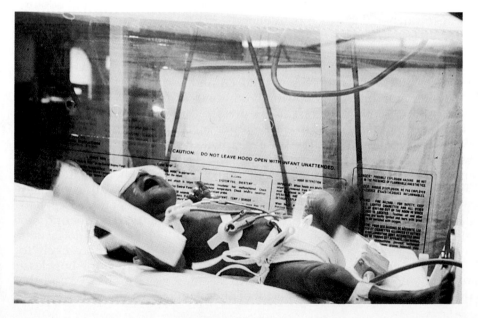

"Crack babies" start life with severe handicaps and may never function as successfully in life as children who have not been exposed prenatally to drugs.

635,000 receiving benefits were born prematurely or exposed to crack cocaine, alcohol, or the HIV virus while in the womb (Dixon, 1993). These children are considered disabled and are expected to need federal assistance for years to come.

In 1990, an estimated 158,000 babies were born to mothers who used cocaine or crack, the smokable form of the drug. These so-called crack babies are more likely to have shorter gestational periods and lower birth weights than infants who have not been exposed to cocaine, and they are more likely to be admitted to the intensive-care unit and to spend more time in the hospital. They also spend more time in hospitals waiting for placement in foster homes than do other non-drug-affected babies (Phibbs et al., 1991). Crack babies are hard to care for almost from the moment of birth because they may have brain damage or severe neurological problems. They often have poor sucking abilities that hamper feeding, and they may be either extremely irritable or very lethargic and have irregular sleep patterns. As they grow older, these children face severe developmental problems. They may be hyperactive and slow in learning to talk, and they may have trouble relating to others (Kantrowitz et al., 1990).

The first wave of babies born to mothers who used cocaine during pregnancy are now school age. Educators have been frustrated and bewildered by the behavior of these children. Sometimes withdrawn, these children may have trouble playing or even talking to other kids. Some experience tremors or periods when they seem to tune out the world; these phenomena could indicate a seizure disorder. It is not clear whether these kinds of problems are the result of prenatal exposure to cocaine and other drugs, maternal malnutrition, abuse and neglect, or a combination of these factors. Among grandparents who have custody of such children, many feel that a lot of the problems reflect neglect. Some caregivers described children who were bad sleepers because "his father used to keep him up all night," or "his Mom took him to those crack houses at all hours." Other grandmothers spoke of preschoolers who "used sex talk" and imitated sexual behaviors they had witnessed or had been subjected to as victims of molestation (Minkler and Roe, 1993).

Many states offer medical services and specialized foster-care homes for crack babies. In addition, 19 states now require that medical personnel and others report drug-exposed infants to child protective service agencies. Some pregnant drug addicts do not give birth in hospitals, thereby increasing the risk for permanent damage or death to the child (see Daro and McCurdy, 1991).

Drug use is not limited to adults. Although illicit drug use has declined in the general population since 1979, a recent University of Michigan survey found that one in four schoolchildren has used illegal drugs before reaching high school. According to the study, 35 percent of eighth-graders, almost 43 percent of tenth-graders and almost half of twelfth-graders have used illegal drugs; all these percentages have risen since 1991. In addition, half of twelfth-graders and one quarter of eighth-graders said they had had alcoholic drinks in the past 30 days (cited in *Washington Post*, 1994b).

A study by the Harvard School of Public Health examined "binge drinking" in college, defined as consuming five (for men) or four (for women) consecutive drinks. The study also reported the effects of heavy drinkers' behavior on students who do not drink. One in six had personal property damaged, one in four experienced an unwanted sexual advance, more than half had to take care of a drunken student, and two in three had their sleep or study interrupted (Castillo et al., 1994).

Teenage Depression and Suicide

Two major problems of adolescence are depression and suicide. Depressed children and adolescents frequently display the same symptoms that adults do, but young children may not be able to articulate their problems. The New York State Psychiatric Institute conducted a study of depressed children and adolescents and found the following commonly exhibited symptoms of depression: depressive mood, inability to feel pleasure, lack of interest, decreased concentration, irritability and anger, fatigue, negative self-image, insomnia, social withdrawal, suicidal ideas, excessive and inappropriate guilt, and anorexia. Children (whose average age was 10) were likely to exhibit such symptoms as a depressed appearance or agitation and complaints about poor sleep, phobias, and hallucinations. Adolescents (whose average age was 15) were more likely to exhibit such symptoms as feelings of hopelessness, excessive sleeping, weight change, and the use of alcohol and illicit drugs (Marbella, 1990).

Depression may lead to suicide, which is increasing as a major cause of teenage deaths. The suicide rate among adolescents between 15 and 19 years of age has increased to 11 per 100,000 population—triple the rate of the mid-1950s (U.S. Census Bureau, 1994). Teenagers often exhibit problematic behaviors during normal maturation, but experts feel that when some of these behaviors form a consistent pattern, parents, friends, teachers, and relatives should seriously consider the possibility that the adolescent is planning suicide and intervene in some systematic way. According to the Youth Suicide National Center, the most common suicide warning signs are the following:

- Withdrawal from family or friends
- Verbal expression of suicidal thoughts or threats, even as a joke
- Major personality change(s)
- Changes in sleeping or eating habits
- Drug or alcohol abuse or both
- Difficulty concentrating
- Violent or rebellious outbursts
- Running away
- Recent suicide of a relative or friend
- Rejection by a boyfriend or girlfriend
- Unexplained, sudden drop in quality of schoolwork or athletic endeavors
- Giving or throwing away prized possessions
- Showing a sudden lack of energy for one's friends or other activities
- Extreme and sudden neglect of appearance
- Anorexia

No one knows for sure why people, including teenagers, commit suicide. In more than 90 percent of cases of completed suicide, the person had shown evidence of mental disorder or addiction to alcohol, crack cocaine, or other drugs. According to a national survey of teenagers, drug and alcohol abuse headed the list of reasons for teen suicide (Bezilla, 1993). A family environment that includes violence in the form of physical or sexual abuse may also contribute to the risk of suicide. Especially among young people, there may be such triggering events as the sudden death of a friend or interpersonal rejection (Moscicki, 1994).

When Kurt Cobain, leader of the popular group Nirvana committed suicide in 1994, people were concerned that copycat teen suicides would follow. So, before signing off his Cobain special, MTV host Kurt Loder said to his viewers, "Don't do it." For the most part, however, teenagers who commit suicide have long-term and significant emotional problems. Sometimes if they are already depressed, they may exaggerate problems like being dumped by a boyfriend or girlfriend way out of proportion. In any event, teens are more likely to imitate the suicide of someone close to them than a rock star (Waters et al., 1994).

Anorexia and Bulimia

Although physicians have known about anorexia nervosa since the 1870s, the general public knew little about the disease until the 1970s. In 1983, the death of 32-year-old popular singer Karen Carpenter as a result of heart failure caused by prolonged starvation generated interest in the disease. In 1994, former gymnast Christy Henrich died of "multiple organ system failure" that resulted from a history of both anorexia nervosa and bulimia. She was 22 and weighed 60 pounds. Henrich, who missed making the 1988 U.S. Olympic team by .118 of a point, became concerned about her weight later that year when, at a meet in Hungary, she overheard a judge say that she was too fat to make the Olympic team. At that time, she was 4 feet 11 and weighed 93 pounds (Lonkhuyzen, 1994).

Anorexia nervosa is an often intractable and dangerous eating disorder characterized by fear of obesity coupled with a distorted body image and the conviction that one is "fat"; significant weight loss (in people over 18 at least 25 percent of original body weight); and an absolute refusal to maintain weight within the normal limits for one's age and height. **Bulimia** is also an eating disorder, characterized by a cyclical pattern of eating binges followed by self-induced vomiting, fasting, excessive exercise, or the use of diuretics or laxatives. The National Association of Anorexia Nervosa and Associated Disorders estimates that eating disorders affect some 7 million American women and 1 million men between age 10 and the early 20s.

Both disorders have physical complications that can result in death. Anorexia may cause a slowing of the heartbeat, a loss of normal blood pressure, cardiac arrest, dehydration, skin ab-

Christy Henrich performing on the balance beam in 1988, six years before her death from the effects of anorexia and bulimia.

normalities, hypothermia, lethargy, potassium deficiency, kidney malfunction, constipation, and the growth of fine silky body hair, termed *lanugo*, in an effort to conserve heat. Bulimia's binge-purge cycle can be devastating to health in many ways. It can cause fatigue, seizures, muscle cramps, irregular heartbeat, and decreased bone density, which can lead to osteoporosis. Repeated vomiting can damage the esophagus and stomach, cause the salivary glands to swell, make the gums recede, and erode tooth enamel.

Most anorexics and bulimics are young white women of relatively high socioeconomic status who often suffer from low self-esteem and a negative body image. These young women also tend to be highly motivated and perfectionistic.

Their family histories often include eating disorders in other family members and a higher than average incidence of the abuse of such substances as alcohol, marijuana, amphetamines, diet pills, or barbiturates. Girls who have experienced sexual abuse are also more likely to have severe eating disorder problems (DeGroot et al., 1992). Anorexic men include models, actors, gymnasts, and jockeys, as well as young men in nonprofessional sports training who are trying to keep their weight off during competitions (Seligmann and Rogers, 1994).

Anorexics and bulimics tend to equate body appearance with self-worth, and their preoccupation with body size and negative body image results in feelings of inadequacy (Kerr et al., 1991). Middle school girls who reach puberty early, by the sixth grade, *and* who begin to date at that time may be at an especially high risk for having negative body images and eating disorders (Smolak et al., 1993). Thompson (1994) suggests that eating disorders may also be a way of coping with racism: Some African American and Latina women with eating disorders have been taught that thinness is important for middle-class standing.

Because these illnesses are far less common in men than in women, more study has been devoted to their possible causes in women, which, according to Cantrell and Ellis (1991) are probably multifactorial. Although women are beginning to discard some of the worst stereotypical images associated with their traditional gender roles, dieting is still endemic because "a woman's appearance may be her most precious asset" (Rothblum, 1994: 54). In a study of nearly 500 girls, researchers at the University of California at San Francisco found that up to 50 percent of nine-year-olds and up to 80 percent of ten-year-olds had a fear of fatness, or were already dieting even though only 15 percent were actually overweight (reported in Pertig, 1994). Kilbourne (1994: 402) notes that women are conditioned to be terrified of fat: "Prejudice against fat people, especially against fat women, is one of the few remaining prejudices that are socially acceptable." Consequently, the most common explanation of anorexia and bulimia is that women are trying to live up to a cultural fixation that equates thinness with beauty and success:

If I'm thin, I'll be popular. If I'm thin, I'll turn people on. If I'm thin, I'll have great sex. If I'm thin, I'll be rich. If I'm thin, I'll be admired. If I'm thin, I'll be sexually free. If I'm thin, I'll be tall. If I'm thin, I'll have power. If I'm thin, I'll be loved. If I'm thin, I'll be envied (Munter, 1984: 230).

Several studies have suggested that anorexics and bulimics become obsessed with living up to an image of beauty promoted by the media and fashion industry. For example, a research team that studied the eating habits of 238 female students at Arizona State University found that women who spent a lot of time reading popular women's magazines and watching television were significantly more likely to display symptoms of eating disorders and to be dissatisfied with their physical appearance than those who did not (Vitousek and Manke, 1994).

Steroid Use

In 1988, one day after he set a world record in the 100-meter dash, Canadian sprinter Ben Johnson was stripped of his Olympic gold medal when it was discovered that he was using **steroids**—synthetic hormones, most often, testosterone. When taken orally or injected, steroids increase the size and strength of muscles in just a few months. An estimated 2 million to 3 million Americans, most of them men, "gobble up the drugs like candy" (Fultz, 1991), and an estimated 7 to 11 percent of adolescent males also take these drugs. In 1993, one percent of eighth-graders and an equal percentage of tenth-graders reported using steroids (U.S. Department of Justice, 1994a), mostly to improve their performance in sports, but often just to improve their appearance.

Steroids are dangerous. Many people who use them are unfamiliar with their side effects, which include a decrease in testosterone production, a possibly irreversible shrinkage of the testicles, disinterest in sex, acne, increased facial and body hair, early balding, strokes and heart attacks, reduced sperm counts, liver disorders, kidney disease, a sharp increase in aggression, and, with heavy usage, the possible development of psychosis. Teenagers run the particular risk of permanent damage to their reproductive and skeletal systems. Steroids may prevent one from reaching full height; for example, one 13-year-old who had taken steroids for two years stopped growing at five feet (Fultz, 1991).

There are more than 100 substances, referred to as "juicers," legal and illegal, that pre-

sumably boost physiques and enhance physical development. Illegal "juicers" are often available from gym owners or local "hard-core" gyms patronized by serious weightlifters. Drug-enforcement agents estimate, however, that 30 to 50 percent of the illegal muscle builders that teens buy are phony. One youth spent $3000 on what turned out to be a saline solution. In other cases, the pills are penicillin, deadly to anyone who happens to be allergic to this drug. Most parents are unaware of these dangers and so fail to protect their youngsters. According to the director of an Illinois sports medicine clinic, for example, up to a dozen parents a year call him to supply illegal performance enhancers to their children (Schrof, 1993).

Death and the Family

A death in the family always saddens and distresses family members, but the death of a child can be shattering. It often results in what Knapp (1987) calls *shadow grief*—a grief that is never totally resolved. Shadow grief involves depression, a dull ache that never goes away, ongoing sadness, and a mild sense of anxiety. Many parents who have lost a child say that they have never since feared their own death. They often become much less involved in worldly achievements, and much more concerned with cultivating and strengthening family relationships. Some fathers, for instance, become less interested in their jobs, less career motivated, less interested in simply making more money, and more involved in establishing better, more stable, and higher-quality relationships with other members of the family (Johnson, 1984–85). Although the death of a child can strengthen a conjugal bond, it can also result in separation or divorce when the grieving mother and father blame themselves or each other for not saving the child or when they cannot find solace through each other (Lang and Gottlieb, 1993).

Because of the AIDS epidemic, many parents today are outliving their children—even their grandchildren. Experts estimate that as many as 125,000 children will lose their mothers to AIDS by the year 2000 (Lee, 1994). In fact, today most of us are more likely to attend the funeral of a young adult who died from AIDS than of a young child who died from cancer, a car accident, or other cause. Even when AIDS is contracted through blood transfusions rather than sexual activity, death due to AIDS often elicits negative reactions rather than sympathy. Families are often torn between grieving for adult children they did not expect to die and facing the stigma of AIDS as the cause of death. As the box "How You Can Help Someone Grieve the Death of an Adult Child with AIDS" illustrates, however, the ways in which one can help such family members are not very different from the things one can do for parents whose children died due to other reasons.

The Right to Die

Have people and/or their family members the right to decide when a relative, especially one who has no chance of recovering from a vegetative state, can be allowed to die? The right to die issue goes back at least as far as the mid-1970s' case of Karen Ann Quinlan, a young adult who lapsed into a vegetative state after consuming alcohol and drugs. Because physicians said Karen would never recover, her parents fought to have her removed from life-sustaining machines. In

1976, the Supreme Court of New Jersey ruled that because Karen was not competent, her family, with the concurrence of a hospital ethics committee, could make this decision for her.

Cases like that of the Quinlans were fought on the state level until, in the late 1980s, the case of Nancy Beth Cruzan elicited national attention. Nancy's car overturned as she drove home from work one day in 1983. She was found face-down in a ditch, and paramedics restarted her heart. Because she had stopped breathing for nearly 15 minutes, however, she suffered severe brain damage. For nearly eight years, Nancy's body was rigid, and her feet and hands contracted and bent. She experienced occasional seizures and vomiting, and although her eyes sometimes opened and moved, she showed no sign of recognizing her family.

The Cruzan family spent years in courts trying to stop the life-support systems so that Nancy could die with dignity. When the case was first heard in 1988, the court weighed the testimony of friends and family, including the assertion that Nancy herself had said that she never wanted to be kept alive if she could not function

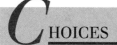

HOICES

How You Can Help Someone Grieve the Death of an Adult Child with AIDS

There are two significant differences between the way family members grieve the loss of an adult child with AIDS and the way they grieve the loss of a child due to other causes. First, because the debilitating effects of AIDS progress over several years and because the disease is, as yet, incurable, family members must accept the inevitability of what is to come and so often engage in "anticipatory mourning" (Dane, 1991). Second, religious beliefs and practices may deny to people who die of AIDS some of the rituals that are commonly performed for the dead and even memorial services or burial in hallowed grounds (Horn, 1993).

An important gesture of support for a family grieving a death due to AIDS is to write a caring condolence letter because "many people . . . reread letters of condolence again and again, days, months, and even years after the loss. Some even pass these letters down through the family" (Zunin and Zunin, 1991: 35). Such letters will be especially appreciated if the family has been stigmatized by others because of the family member's AIDS. According to Zunin and Zunin (pp. 43–44), there are four key components in writing a thoughtful note. You can change some of the wording if you didn't know the person who died:

1. Acknowledge the loss For example, "Our family was deeply saddened when we heard from Bill that your son died."

2. Express your sympathy "We are all thinking of you and send our heartfelt sympathy."

3. Note special qualities of the deceased or the bereaved, or recount a memory about the deceased "In the years we lived next door, your mother was the most wonderful neighbor! She was always warm, gracious, and ready to lend a hand. We feel fortunate to have known her."

4. Close with a thoughtful word or phrase "With affection and deepest condolences." Or, if you know the family is religious, you may want to offer a spiritual message.

normally, and then granted permission to remove the life-sustaining apparatus. The Missouri Supreme Court reversed the ruling four months later, however, arguing that "vague and unreliable" recollections were insufficient proof of Nancy's intent. The family then took the case to the U.S. Supreme Court, which ruled in 1990 that states have the right to prevent family members from taking a permanently unconscious patient off life-support systems if there is no "clear and convincing" proof that the patient wants to be removed. The Cruzan case was then returned to the Missouri courts, where, in 1991, the family finally won the right to remove the feeding tube. Nancy died 12 days later (R. Marcus, 1990; Smolowe, 1990).

During the early 1990s, Jack Kevorkian, a doctor who had built a "suicide machine" to help people who suffered from chronic pain or terminal illnesses to kill themselves, was arrested and went to jail briefly, but he was released because the state of Michigan is still struggling with suicide-assisted legislation. In 1994, Oregonians passed a suicide-assisted referendum that allows family members and physicians, rather than the courts, to decide when to "pull the plug." These issues are discussed in more detail in Chapter 18.

Some groups are strongly opposed to granting families the right to disconnect feeding tubes and let their members die. Consider the case of Jamie Butcher, a 17-year-old high school track star and straight-A student whose car skidded on some wet leaves and crashed into a tree in 1977. Jamie never regained consciousness even though his parents brought in medical experts, physical therapists, and chiropractors. When in 1994 the parents decided to disconnect Jamie's feeding tubes because they did not want him to remain in a vegetative state any longer, Nursing Home Action, a group representing disabled people, filed suit and asked to be appointed Jamie's legal guardian because his interests were not being represented by the family (Schmid, 1994). Unresolved at the time of this writing, this case indicates that some groups believe that decisions about death are not necessarily a family matter.

At the same time, all but a handful of states now have laws allowing people to make their wishes about medical treatment known *in advance* of illness. The American Hospital Association estimates that, based on such instructions, 70 percent of all hospital deaths are already negotiated in some way, with the concerned parties privately agreeing either not to start, or to withdraw, some form of life-support technology or treatment (Lewin, 1991). To avoid problems and protracted court litigation, however, many advocacy groups recommend drawing up a *living will* that specifies whether and when the person wants to be taken off life-support systems. Living wills are discussed in greater detail in Chapter 18.

CONCLUSION

Millions of U.S. families are experiencing many negative *changes*—for example, more domestic violence, more child abuse and neglect, more abuse of the elderly, and an increase in drug abuse among middle-school children. This does not mean that the situation is hopeless, however. As people become more informed about these and other problems, they have more *choices* in making use of community resources and legal intervention agencies. These choices, however, are sometimes eclipsed by a number of *constraints*. Laws are not always enforced, our society still condones male violence, and some groups feel that some issues, such as stopping life-support systems, should be made outside the family.

Taking Action

Family Violence: Prevention and Remedies

Despite the unhappy realities this chapter has highlighted, there are ways you can help the victims of violence, and there are things you can do to help prevent it.

• Call 800-777-1960 to get a copy of the **Community Action Kit.** This kit includes information on what to do if someone you know is being abused, gives contacts for organizations formed to **combat domestic violence** in every state, and provides inspiring accounts of community-based efforts to reduce and prevent domestic violence.

- **Victims of abuse who need shelter** should call police agencies and check phone directories. Other sources include Project Protect (800-380-4888); the National Organization for Victim Assistance (800-879-6682); the National Coalition Against Domestic Violence (303-839-1852); the National Resource Center on Domestic Violence (800-537-2238); the Child Help National Child Abuse Hotline (800-422–4453); and the National Resource Center on Child Sexual Abuse (800-KIDS-006).

- One way to support groups trying to protect abused children and adults is to **make monetary contributions.** If you do not know the names of specific agencies doing this work, earmark any contributions you make to umbrella charitable organizations like the United Way for such agencies. Another way is to order items from companies that use some of their profits to support victims of violence. The Company of Women (800-937-1193) will send you a catalog of merchandise from such companies, including T-shirts, coffee mugs, calendars, prints, and many other products that celebrate children, women, and the family.

- One way **to find a competent, reputable therapist** is to consult someone whose judgment you trust (a physician, counselor, friend, or relative) who has had a positive experience with therapy. You can also call the following national mental health organizations for the names of reputable therapists in your area: American Association for Marriage and Family Therapy (800-374-2638); National Alliance for the Mentally Ill (800-950-6264); National Institute of Mental Health (800-421-4211); and National Mental Health Association (800-969-6642).

- If your club is looking for campus speakers, consider inviting **someone who can address family violence issues.** Recently, for example, Congress passed the Violence Against Women Act that, among other things, will provide training for law enforcement officers and judges and funds for rape prevention efforts. Call or write one of your senators and ask him or her to explain to your group how the act will affect your state, city, or county. Or have a political leader address the progress of the Child Abuse Accountability Act, which would give victims who are awarded damages in court access to a child abuser's federal pension.

- The American Association of Retired Persons (AARP) provides numerous materials on **abused elders.** Its address is 601 E Street N.W., Washington, DC 20049. A short, informative brochure is *Domestic Mistreatment of the Elderly: Towards Prevention, Some Dos and Don'ts.*

- For information about **eating disorders,** contact the Eating Disorders Awareness and Prevention Group at 412-922-5922, or the National Association of Anorexia Nervosa and Associated Disorders at 708-831-3438.

- **INTVIO-L, Intimate Violence,** is a subscription list that deals with domestic and other forms of violence against women and men. To subscribe, write to LISTSERV@URIACC.URI.EDU.

SUMMARY

1. People are more likely to be killed or assaulted by family members than by outsiders.

2. Although either husbands or wives may be violent, wife beating generally results in much more serious physical and emotional damage than does husband abuse. Abusive men have been described as feeling helpless, powerless, and inadequate in both their marriages and their jobs.

3. Battered wives have often been described as dependent women who suffer from low esteem and feelings of inadequacy and helplessness,. We do not know whether these characteristics reflect basic personality traits or are the result of battering and abuse.

4. Several factors help explain why women do not end abusive relationships: poor self-concept, a belief that the men they love will reform, economic hardship, a need for child support, doubt that they can get along alone, fear, shame and guilt, and being imprisoned in their homes.

5. There are four major categories of child abuse: physical abuse, sexual abuse, neglect, and emotional maltreatment. Reports of child abuse

have soared since 1976. Factors that increase the likelihood that a child will be abused include being a female, being older (roughly 8 to 10), having a stepfather, having a single mother who brings home boyfriends, and being poor.

6. Whether or not the abuse is sexual, many studies have found that abused children suffer from a variety of physiological, social, and emotional problems, including difficulty communicating, increased aggression, learning disabilities, sleeping disorders, and poor performance in school. One of the major reasons for teenage runaways is family violence and abuse.

7. It is thought that much more physical and sexual abuse is perpetrated by siblings on each other and by family members on elderly relatives than is reported. Often the elderly are abused by adult children who are unable to take care of themselves because of drug abuse and other problems and whom their elderly parents feel constrained to live with.

8. The most significant theories proposed to explain the reasons for family violence and for female victimization are patriarchy/male-dominance theory, social learning theory, resource theory, conflict theory, and exchange theory.

9. One of the major reasons why effective programs have not been developed for the prevention and treatment of family violence is that professionals and the public still do not see this form of violence as a serious problem.

10. Besides violence, families must grapple with other health-related issues, such as drug abuse and the birth of children who are addicted to drugs or in other ways affected by parental drug abuse; increasing drug abuse among middle school and high school children; teenage depression and suicide; the disorders of anorexia and bulimia; the excessive and inappropriate use of steroids; and the issue of the right to die—how to ensure that family members die with dignity.

KEY TERMS

marital rape   419
child abuse   424
child maltreatment   424
incest   426

elder abuse   432
sandwich generation   432
battered-woman syndrome   439

anorexia nervosa   441
bulimia   441
steroids   443

ADDITIONAL READING

Family violence has begun to receive more scholarly attention, as evidenced by the appearance of several new journals: *Journal of Child Sexual Abuse, Journal of Interpersonal Violence, Journal of Family Violence, Child Abuse and Neglect, Violence and Victims, Elder Abuse,* and *Sexual Abuse.* Useful books on family violence include the following:

PAULINE B. BART and EILEEN GEIL MORAN, eds., *Violence Against Women: The Bloody Footprints* (Newbury Park, CA: Sage, 1993). Articles, originally published in the journal *Gender & Society,* on the different types of violence and on institutional responses to violence.

SUSAN BORDO, *Unbearable Weight: Feminism, Western Culture, and the Body* (Berkeley: University of California Press, 1993). An examination of cultural influences on our conceptions of the body. Several chapters are illustrated with ads from the media.

PATRICIA FALLON, MELANIE A. KATZMAN, and SUSAN C. WOOLEY, eds., *Feminist Perspectives on Eating Disorders* (New York: Guilford, 1994). The contributors discuss the causes and consequences of eating disorders from a feminist perspective.

RICHARD J. GELLES and DONILEEN R. LOSEKE, eds., *Current Controversies on Family Violence* (Newbury Park, CA: Sage, 1993). Articles on the conceptualization of family violence, its measurement, its causes, and social intervention in family violence.

MIC HUNTER, *Abused Boys: The Neglected Victims of Sexual Abuse* (Lexington, MA: Lexington Books, 1990). Emphasizes recovery and healing; presents 13 survival stories.

ANN JONES, *Next Time She'll Be Dead: Battering and How to Stop It* (Boston: Beacon Press, 1994). Jones examines why many women don't leave abusive husbands, the damage done by the criminal justice system, and some state and local programs that have been effective in decreasing wife battering.

CLAIRE M. RENZETTI, *Violent Betrayal: Partner Abuse in Lesbian Relationships* (Newbury Park, CA: Sage, 1992). Renzetti examines such correlates of abuse as dependency, jealousy, the balance of power, substance abuse, and how to get help.

WILLIAM A. STACEY, LONNIE R. HAZLEWOOD, and ANSON SHUPE, *The Violent Couple* (Westport, CT: Praeger, 1994). An empirical study of 86 couples—white, Hispanic, Asian, and African American—who have had violent relationships.

JACK C. WESTMAN, *Licensing Parents: Can We Prevent Child Abuse and Neglect?* (New York, Plenum Press, 1994). As the title suggests, Westman argues that one way to prevent child maltreatment is to license parents to have children only when they can prove that they will be competent.

16
Separation and Divorce

Edvard Munch, Separation

Data Digest

- The United States has the **highest divorce rate in the world.** About half of all American marriages are dissolved, compared to two out of five marriages in Britain, Denmark, and Sweden and one in ten in France and other European countries.

- China has one of the **lowest divorce rates in the world.** In 1992, for example, China registered nearly 10 million marriages and only 310,000 divorces.

- Half of all divorces in the United States occur during **the first seven years of marriage,** with the peak occurring about three years into the marriage.

- A 1993 survey found that **9 percent of whites, 11 percent of African Americans, and 7 percent of people of Latino origin** had been divorced.

- In 1993, 37 percent of children under age 18 were **living with one divorced parent,** up from 23 percent in 1960.

- The economic **costs of separation and divorce are higher for women** than for men in the United States. According to one study, median family income declined from $24,020 to $13,712 for white women but only from $26,500 to $22,000 for white men, and from $16,988 to $8971 for black women but only from $17,000 to $12,500 for black men. In Canada, women's family income dropped 50 percent, compared to 25 percent for men, during the first year of divorce.

- **Fathers with joint custody pay more child support** mandated by the courts (90 percent) than fathers who have visitation privileges (79 percent) or those without either joint custody or visitation rights (45 percent).

- By 1990, among all women between 15 and 65 years of age who remarried after a first divorce, over 3 million, or **29 percent, were redivorced.**

SOURCES: Norton and Miller, 1992; *The Economist*, 1993; Finnie, 1993; Smock, 1993; Saluter, 1994.

The early 1990s saw several highly publicized divorces: Nelson and Winnie Mandela, sex therapists Virginia Johnson and William Masters, televangelists Jim and Tammy Faye Bakker, and Joan and (Senator) Ted Kennedy. Most striking, perhaps, was the average length of each of these marriages: about 25 years up to the time of divorce. Benjamin Spock, the influential "baby expert," divorced his first wife after *48* years of marriage.

When I was in college, during the mid-1960s, divorce was rare. The few friends whose parents were divorced were often described, in hushed tones, as "unfortunate children" and "poor dears," and their parents were often criticized as being "shameful" and "selfish." As divorce rates climbed during the 1970s, however, marital dissolution became more commonplace. Statistically, nearly one out of every two students reading this chapter probably comes from a divorced home. Although during the 1960s it was not unusual for marriage-and-family textbooks to explore divorce as a form of deviant behavior, today divorce is discussed as a normal event in a person's life course. Thus, both divorce rates and our reactions to divorce have changed dramatically within just one generation.

Just as divorce rates have increased, so have the rates of remarriage and redivorce (see Chapter 17). This means that family structures and relationships are more complex today than they were in the past. As this chapter will show, whether these changes produce costs, benefits, or both, separation and divorce usually reflect long-term processes and consequences.

SEPARATION: PROCESS AND OUTCOME

Separation is not always followed by a divorce. A **separation** can mean several things. It may be a temporary "time-out" in a highly stressful marriage, in which the partners decide whether or not to continue their marriage. Usually one moves out of the home in such a separation but not always. Or partners may decide on a "trial separation" to see what living apart feels like. In this case, one partner may move in with parents or a friend or into a motel or other rental. Physical separation can also be a permanent arrangement when a partner's or couple's religious beliefs preclude divorce. Or partners may seek a "legal separation," that is, a temporary period of living apart that most states require before granting a divorce.

The Phases of Separation

Separation is usually a lengthy process that, for many people, involves four distinct phases—preseparation, early separation, midseparation, and late separation (Ahrons and Rodgers, 1987). Whether a particular separation takes a long or a short time and whether or not the partners go through all four phases, the important thing is that separation rarely happens overnight. It is typically a process during which people may agonize for months or years before they make a final break.

During the *preseparation* phase, partners may fantasize about what it would be like to live alone, to escape from family responsibilities, or to form new sexual liaisons:

[May] daydreamed about a high school sweetheart [whom] she had not seen since graduation. "We were at the twenty-fifth reunion and dancing to our favorite song. He invited me to go home with him that night."

[Don] imagined becoming an airline pilot. "I could travel to exotic places and make love . . . on the beach every night" (Everett and Everett, 1994: 38).

Although fantasies like these rarely become reality, they can make separation or divorce seem "sexy."

In the later stages of the preseparation phase, the couple splits up after a gradual, emotional alienation. The separation is initiated by one partner who feels that the marital dissatisfaction will increase. Even when couples are contemplating separation (or have already made the decision), they often maintain a public pretense that nothing is wrong. The couple may attend family and social functions together, and rituals like holding hands may continue right up until the actual separation. Despite such outward appearances of tranquillity, however, separation is usually traumatic, especially for the

person who is left. He or she may feel guilty for causing the separation and may also experience anxiety, fear of being alone, and panic about the future.

The *early separation* phase is beset with problems because our society does not have clear-cut rules for this process. Many questions—some serious, some trivial —plague the newly separated couple: Who should move out? What should the partners tell their family and friends? Should the child's teacher be told? Who gets the season tickets for the concert series? In addition, the partners may have very ambivalent feelings about the impending dissolution. They are confused and upset when their feelings vacillate—as they usually do—between love and hate, anger and sadness, euphoria and depression, and relief and guilt. Partners also must confront economic issues such as paying bills, buying the children's clothing, and splitting the old and the new expenses. Particularly problematic may be the question of the wife's survival. Even when employed outside the home, she typically earns considerably less than her spouse. As a result she faces a lower standard of living. This is especially likely if the children live with her. Some partners get support from family and friends, but most must cope on their own.

In the *midseparation* phase, the harsh realities of everyday living set in. The pressures of maintaining two separate households and meeting the daily emotional and physical needs of the children mount, and stress intensifies. If family or friends don't or can't help, or if their help diminishes, the partners may feel overwhelmed, especially if there are additional stressors, such as illness, unexpected expenses, a dependent elderly parent, or difficulties at school or work.

Because of these problems, and especially when couples have been married at least ten years, people may experience "pseudo-reconciliation." That is, the earlier preseparation expectations or fantasies may be followed by a sense of loss when partners don't see their children, by guilt over abandoning the family, and by disapproval from parents, relatives, or friends. As a result, partners may move back in, but this sort of second honeymoon, when partners feel less loneliness, fear, and guilt, rarely lasts. Soon the underlying problems that led to the separation in the first place surface again, conflicts reemerge, and the partners separate once again (Everett and Everett, 1994).

During the *late separation* phase, partners

Divorced men, particularly if they've been married to traditional wives, often find it difficult to do mundane household chores.

must learn how to survive as singles again. This phase may be especially stressful for men who have been raised with traditional gender-role expectations. For example, many men report frustration and anger when they can't perform such routine tasks as ironing their shirts or preparing a favorite dish. Both partners must often deal with mutual friends who have a hard time with the separation. Some friends may avoid both partners because it threatens their perceptions of their own marriages. Others may take sides, which forces separating partners to develop new friends and relationships. Finally, and perhaps most important, partners must help their children deal with anxiety, anger, confusion, or sadness. We return to this topic later in the chapter.

Some Results of Marital Separation

Not all separations end in divorce. Many low-income couples experience long-term separations without divorce because they may be unable to pay the necessary legal fees (Morgan, 1988). Higher family income, on the other hand, typically increases the likelihood of divorce.

Living apart does not make the heart grow fonder. For example, in a national study, Rindfuss and Stephen (1990) found that when one partner was in military service or in prison, the couple was twice as likely to split up as were couples who were living together. In the wake of the Persian Gulf War, a number of articles and television programs discussed the frequency of marital splits, suggesting that some women who stayed at home had learned to enjoy their independence and/or that returning fathers and husbands had suffered stress that affected their marriages.

Racial-ethnic status also influences living apart. Several studies have found that African Americans are more likely to experience marital dissolution than whites as a result of military service or incarceration. First, the armed forces are disproportionately racial-ethnic, with the result that African Americans are three times as likely as whites to be separated from their spouses because of military service (Rindfuss and Stephen, 1990). Second, blacks are more likely than whites to be convicted of a crime and, when convicted, to be incarcerated. Third, as we discussed in Chapter 13, because African American men are more likely to be unemployed than whites, some leave their families in search of jobs in other states.

On the positive side, separating partners may experience what Nelson (1994) calls "growth-oriented coping." In a study of separated women in Ontario, Canada, Nelson found that many separating women became more autonomous, furthered their education, and experienced an increase in confidence and a greater feeling of self-control.

Divorce: How Common Is It?

Divorce—the legal and formal dissolution of a marriage—is not new. The Code of Hammurabi, written almost 4000 years ago in ancient Mesopotamia, allowed the termination of a marriage. Among the nobility, especially, divorce was apparently as easy for women as for men:

If a woman so hated her husband that she has declared, "You may not have me," her record shall be investigated at her city council; and if she was careful and was not at fault, even though her husband has been going out and disparaging her greatly, that woman, without incurring any blame at all, may take her dowry and go off to her father's house (J. Monk, cited in Esler, 1994).

Although divorce rates have increased in many countries, especially those in Europe, the United States has the highest divorce rate in the world (Goode, 1993). In the United States the divorce rate has risen gradually throughout the twentieth century (see Figure 16.1). The small peak around 1945, when World War II ended, has been attributed by historians to divorces among young people who married impulsively before the men left for war and, when the men returned, found they had nothing in common (Tuttle, 1993; see also Chapter 3). In the mid-1960s, divorce rates began a dramatic and consistent climb. Since 1980, however, the divorce rate has dropped slightly and plateaued. According to some observers, it's expected to drop further, going from 50 percent of all marriages in the 1980s to 40 percent in the 1990s (Norton and Miller, 1991).

During the early part of the twentieth century, a number of marriages ended by desertion, even though no legal divorce was ever obtained. Thus, the rising divorce rate reflects not only more dissolution of marriages but more *legal* dissolution. According to Brehm (1985), this change is an improvement: When a spouse deserted his or her mate the mate often had no idea whether her spouse (deserters were more often male than female) would return. Moreover, the deserting partner rarely left his spouse any money or sent money later, which often put the wife and children in serious financial straits.

As we will see, legal protections for divorcing

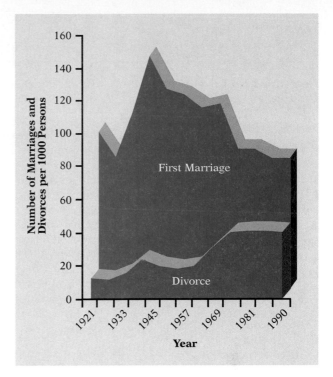

Figure 16.1 Rates of First Marriage and Divorce, 1921–1990. Each point on these curves represents a three-year average. These data represent women between the ages of 15 and 44 (Norton and Miller, 1992).

partners have improved economic conditions for many people. Do you think other conditions have also improved? Before you read further, take the brief quiz in the box "How Much Do I Know About Divorce?"

Divorce as a Transition

Few divorces are spontaneous, spur-of-the-moment acts. The divorce process is usually spread over a long period during which two people gradually redefine, reorganize, and sometimes rebuild their relationship and their expectations of one another. In navigating this transition, many people go through a number of stages; widely cited are Bohannon's (1971) six "stations" of divorce—emotional, legal, economic, coparental, community, and psychic.

The *emotional divorce* begins before any legal steps are taken. One or both partners may feel disillusioned, unhappy, or rejected. They may ir-

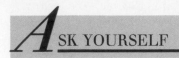
How Much Do I Know About Divorce?

For each statement check one box: "Reality," if you believe it's true; "Myth," if you believe it's false.

	Reality	Myth
1. People's problems end after they're divorced.	☐	☐
2. Once people are divorced, they find someone who makes them happy.	☐	☐
3. Most people have a friendly, civilized divorce with no hard feelings.	☐	☐
4. People generally remain friends despite the problems they experienced during their marriage.	☐	☐
5. Once you're divorced you need to look out for yourself and not worry about your ex-spouse.	☐	☐
6. "I'll never get married again. Marriage is for the birds, and my divorce proves it."	☐	☐

Answers and Scoring

All these statements are myths.

1. Myth. Divorcing partners may feel temporary relief but soon find themselves in the midst of such difficulties as finding another place to live, arranging for the children's custody, experiencing avoidance by friends and putdowns from relatives, suffering unexpected eruptions of guilt and remorse, having difficulties in establishing new relationships with the opposite sex, and, sometimes, facing a split with the lover for whom they left their spouse.

2. Myth. Although many divorced people expect this of new people they date, the reality is that no one can "make" another person happy. The best relationships are those in which the two partners are already happy as single persons but in which they hope to increase their happiness by being with a loved person, sharing hopes, adversities, and successes in a kind and loving way.

3. Myth. Truly friendly divorces are rare. Most people feel some hostility toward their ex-spouses. For example, people may feel angry because their spouses no longer love them. The facade of "we're still good friends" ordinarily cracks when people discuss financial issues, like spousal or child support, or when one has a new lover and the other becomes jealous. A divorcing couple can have friendly relationships eventually, but this may take years to materialize.

4. Myth. In most cases, if the relationship has been a poor one, former partners are no longer friends. Instead of striving for friendship, a former spouse can benefit by self-discipline and by being civil and cooperative.

5. Myth. When people focus only on their own needs and ignore an ex-spouse's concerns, the relationship can become increasingly antagonistic. Taking care of oneself is important, but selfishness, withholding, and unwillingness to compromise can have devastating effects, especially if children are involved.

6. Myth. Most people remarry within two or three years after a divorce (Belli and Krantzler, 1988: 56–67; Gold, 1992: 16–20).

Scoring: If you checked all items under "Reality," your perception of divorce is unrealistic. Thus, if you are contemplating divorce or have recently been divorced, make an effort to establish as healthy a relationship as you can with your spouse or ex-spouse.

---

ritate one another, but they remain in the marriage because they do not want to be alone, because they believe that divorce would hurt their children, or because they feel bound by their marriage vows of "for better or for worse." Partners may be aloof or polite, despite their anger, or they may engage in overtly hostile behavior, such as making sarcastic remarks or hurling accusations at each other.

In the *beginning phase* of the emotional divorce, partners feel disappointment in each other but hope that the marriage will improve (Kersten, 1990). During the *middle phase*, their feelings of hurt and anger increase as efforts to correct the situation seem unsuccessful. The partner who is more unhappy begins evaluating the rewards and costs of leaving the marriage. In the *end phase*, one of the partners stops caring and detaches emotionally from the other. Apathy and indifference replace loving, intimate feelings. Even when partners don't hate each other, it may be too late to rekindle the marriage:

I knew I was going to die if I didn't get out of this marriage. We couldn't talk. We buried our feelings until there was nothing between us except the shell of a life. I was depressed for a long time before I got the courage to leave. I think I must have been grieving for years. It was so sad. He is not a bad person (Gold, 1992: 45).

At this point, spouses may try counseling as a last resort, or they may seek legal advice to end the marriage.

The *legal divorce* is the formal dissolution of the marriage. During this stage, partners come to agreements on such issues as child custody and the division of property and other economic assets. In part because divorce is an adversarial process during which each partner's attorney tries to maintain the upper hand, the process is rarely trouble-free. For example, the partner who does not want the divorce may try to forestall the inevitable end of the marriage or to get revenge by making demands that the other spouse will find hard to accept. For example, she may demand that he sell his classical-jazz collection and split the proceeds, or he may insist on getting custody of the family dog.

Other issues may include **alimony**—monetary payments made by one ex-spouse to the other to support the latter's basic needs for survival—and **child support**—monetary payments by the noncustodial parent to the parent who has custody of the children to help pay child-rearing expenses. Partners often fail to agree on what is fair and equitable, however. They may use money to manipulate each other into making more concessions ("I'm willing to pay child support if you agree to sell the house and split the proceeds"). We'll look at alimony and child support in more detail later in the chapter.

Even after a divorce is legal, partners may experience ambivalence: "Did I really do the right thing in getting a divorce?" "Should I have been satisfied with what I had?" "What if my family rejects me now that I'm divorced?" Such doubts are normal, but some clinicians caution divorcing parents not to reveal their ambivalence to their children, who may become confused or anxious or deny the reality of divorce and fantasize about reconciliation (Everett and Everett, 1994).

During the *economic divorce*, the partners may argue about who should pay past debts, property taxes, and unforeseen expenses for the children (such as braces). Thus, discussions and conflict over economic issues may continue even after the legal issues have been settled. In addition, partners may try to change child support agreements or fail to make required payments.

The *coparental divorce* involves the agreements between mother and father regarding legal responsibility for financial support of the children, the day-to-day care of the children, and the rights of both the custodial and noncustodial parents in spending time with the children. The amount of conflict during this period may be short-lived or long-term, depending on how well the parents get along and whether or not the children are caught in the middle of parental hostility.

Partners also go through a *community divorce*, when they inform friends, family, teachers, and others that they are no longer married. Relationships between grandparents and grandchildren often continue, but in-laws may sever ties. The partners may also replace old friendships with new ones, and they typically start dating again.

Finally, the couple goes through a *psychic divorce*, in which the partners separate from each other emotionally. One or both partners may go through a process of mourning. Some people never complete this stage because they can't let go of the pain, anger, and resentment, even after they remarry.

Not all couples go through all six of Bohannon's stages. Also, some couples may experience several of the stages, such as emotional and economic divorce, simultaneously. The important point is that divorce is a *process* that involves many people and takes time to complete. Moreover, because people differ greatly, divorcing couples may respond to each other in varying ways, as the box "How You Relate Can Make All the Difference" illustrates.

WHY DO PEOPLE DIVORCE?

The reasons people divorce and the reasons for the rise in divorce rates have generated hundreds of articles and books. Researchers have collected an overwhelming amount of data that suggest that divorce itself, as well as the increase in divorce rates, can be explained on three major levels—macro, or societal; demographic; and interpersonal. As you read this section keep in mind,

How You Relate Can Make All the Difference

Because divorcing partners are often angry, hurt, or bitter, many divorces are unpleasant and painful. As the following discussion of five styles of relating to each other suggests, the more civility partners can maintain in their postdivorce relationship, the more productive their relationships with each other and with their children will be (Ahrons and Rodgers, 1987; Gold, 1992).

Perfect Pals Some partners remain friends even after they have decided to divorce. A small group of divorced spouses share decision making and child rearing much as they did in marriage, and many feel that they are better parents after the divorce. These former spouses may even spend holidays together and maintain relationships with each other's extended families.

Cooperative Colleagues Although a sizable number of divorced spouses do not consider themselves good friends, they are

able to cooperate. Working together often takes effort, but these people accept their responsibilities as parents and believe it is their duty to make responsible decisions about their children. Cooperative parents want to minimize the trauma of divorce to their children and try to protect the children from conflict. Such parents are willing to negotiate and compromise on some of their differences. They may also consult counselors and mediators to resolve impasses before going to court.

Angry Associates Anger is still an integral part of many relationships between divorced partners. These couples harbor bitter resentments about events in their past marriages as well as in the divorce process. Some have long and heated battles over such things as custody, visitation rights, and financial matters. These battles may continue years after the divorce.

Fiery Foes Some divorced spouses are completely unable to coparent. Such partners are unable to remember any good times in the

marriage, and each clings to the wrongs done by the other. Children are caught in the middle of the bitter conflict and are expected to side with one parent and regard the other as the enemy. One parent, usually the father, sees the children less and less frequently over the years, and both parents blame each other for this declining contact. The divorces tend to be highly litigious; legal battles sometimes continue for years after the divorce, and the power struggle pervades the entire family.

Dissolved Duos After the separation and/or divorce, the partners break off entirely with each other. Noncustodial parents may "kidnap" the children, and the other partner often leaves the geographic area where the family has lived. In some cases one partner, usually the man, actually disappears, leaving the other partner with the entire burden of reorganizing the family and the children with only memories and fantasies of the vanished parent.

---

as usual, that these varying types of factors often overlap. For example, comparing divorced and married people in a metropolitan area, Kitson and Holmes (1992) found that divorced people were more likely to come from different ethnic or religious groups than their ex-spouses or to have no religious affiliation at all (macro level); to have been divorced before, to have conceived a child out of wedlock, or to have no children (demographic level); and to complain of poor communication with their partners, frequent arguments, and the abuse of alcohol or physical abuse (interpersonal level).

Macro-Level Reasons for Divorce

There are many macro-level reasons for the increase in divorce rates (see White, 1991, for a summary of some of the research findings). We

will focus on four important sources of change: social institutions, social integration, gender roles, and cultural values.

Social Institutions Changes in legal, religious, and family institutions have affected divorce rates. The increasing number of people entering the legal profession and the growth of free legal clinics have made divorce more accessible and cheaper. Interestingly, 76 percent of the adolescents surveyed in a national study said they thought that divorce rates were high because divorce laws are too lax (Bezilla, 1993).

The question of whether the shift to **no-fault divorce**—the divorce process in which neither partner need establish the guilt or wrongdoing of the other—has led to a rise in the divorce rate continues to be debated. According to Balakrishnan and others (1987), although no-fault divorce

"What do you mean, you're getting cold feet? We've been married six years."
Drawing by Mankoff. © 1994 The New Yorker Magazine, Inc.

has increased the rate of marital dissolution in Canada and Australia, the United States has not experienced a similar change. Some authorities argue, however, that no-fault policies may have encouraged divorce in the long run by making alimony no longer a requirement and eliminating other former legal requirements for divorce. We return to these issues later in the chapter.

Even though many Americans see divorce as morally reprehensible, it is a thriving industry in the United States. Because domestic relations cases account for one third of all civil lawsuits, divorce cases provide jobs for many lawyers, judges, and other employees of the justice system. If a divorcing couple has had a long-term marriage, accountants may spend several years disentangling property rights, accumulated marital property, and the rights of children still living at home. "Forensic accountants" may be asked to track down hidden assets in a contested divorce, and attorneys may hire appraisers, who can charge up to $50,000 to determine the value of jewelry, cars, boats, antiques, and businesses. In child-custody dispute cases, attorneys may hire marriage counselors, psychologists, education specialists, medical personnel, clergy, social workers, and mediators (De Witt, 1994). Although not everyone who wants a divorce can afford all these services, their very availability may send the message that divorce is not only acceptable but that many professionals stand ready to help.

Religion plays a mixed role in divorce rates. On the one hand, people who claim that religion is very important in their lives are much less likely to divorce, regardless of their specific reli-

gious denomination (Colasanto and Shriver, 1989). Having the same religion is also highly associated with marital stability (Lehrer and Chiswick, 1993). In fact, spouses who follow the same religion or who convert to a spouse's religion at marriage are more likely to reconcile after a separation. Religious similarity may be important in marital stability because it increases the commonality between partners traditions, values, and sense of community (Wineberg, 1994).

On the other hand, many religious bodies are much more accepting of divorce today than in the past. For example, many Catholic parishes no longer excommunicate divorced people by refusing them the sacraments of the Church. In addition, the Catholic Church now allows divorce through annulments, approving some 90 percent of all petitions received. As a result, annulments have increased from 450 in 1968 to more than 50,000 in 1994 (Woodward et al., 1995).

Changes in the family as an institution have also had an effect on divorce. As we discussed in Chapter 1, the shift from a preindustrial to an industrial society altered some family functions. Family members became less dependent on one another for economic, recreational, and personal fulfillment because these and other needs could now be met by institutions outside the family. Nonetheless, as the box "Divorce in Other Countries" shows, even nonindustrial societies are experiencing increasing levels of marital disruption.

Social Integration Emile Durkheim argued, at the turn of the century, that people who are integrated into a community are less likely to divorce, to commit suicide, or to engage in other self-destructive behavior. A number of contemporary social scientists contend, similarly, that **social integration**—the social bonds that people have with others and with the community at large—discourages divorce. For example, researchers have found that communities in which people hold similar values about marital roles and in which people stay in the same neighborhoods for long periods tend to have high integration and low divorce rates (Glenn and Shelton, 1985; Shelton, 1987). Similarly, low divorce rates characterize religious groups, such as Orthodox Jews, in which members feel a strong commitment to the group (Brodbar-Nemzer, 1986). Social integration also helps explain the exceptionally high divorce rates in the United States: The

Divorce in Other Countries

Divorce rates in the United States are two to three times as high as rates in other industrialized countries, such as Sweden and the United Kingdom (Goode, 1993). Nevertheless, many Western countries share some common trends: Divorce is increasingly easy to obtain, men are less often required to provide their ex-wives with economic support, and the courts have instituted more stringent rules for the payment of child support and often encourage joint child custody (Fine and Fine, 1994).

Some developing countries are also experiencing increased rates of marital dissolution. In Iran, for example, the divorce rate has been rising despite traditional Islamic sanctions against divorce. Iranian women most likely to seek divorce are those who marry at older ages (19 and older), who are employed and economically independent, and who have few or no children (Aghajanian, 1986).

Divorce has become much simpler in China since the 1980 passage of a law that allowed couples who had fallen out of love to separate formally. The divorce rate has gone up most sharply in urban centers, such as Beijing, where it rose from 2 percent of marriages in 1981 to 18 per-

cent in 1992. According to Walker (1993), divorce nationwide reached 9 percent in 1992, and the rate continues to rise. Growing affluence appears to be loosening family bonds and men's sense of family responsibility. Other factors in the rising divorce rate in China, Walker claims, are Western television programs that depict extramarital sex; growing numbers, in urban areas, of well-educated women who are more likely to leave an unhappy marriage; and the growth of prostitution. As you can see in the tabulation that follows, an analysis of 1000 divorce cases in Shenyang by Ziaxiang and colleagues (1987; see also Linlin, 1993) revealed that the reasons for divorce are very similar to those given in the United States and other industrialized countries.

	PERCENT REPORTING
Hasty marriage: Picking a mate without much thought; falling in love at first sight; conceiving a child before marriage.	21

---

greater heterogeneity of American subcultures, languages, religious practices, and political organizations may decrease social integration.

Remember, by the way, that none of these studies is saying that all couples who stay married are happy. They are saying only that people who live in communities and societies that are more socially integrated are more likely to stay married.

Gender Roles Today, women in the United States are twice as likely as men to seek divorce. According to the National Center for Health Statistics, in 1991, 62 percent of divorces were initiated by wives and 33 percent by husbands; only about 6 percent were initiated jointly (London, 1991). Much of the research shows that changing gender roles, especially women's growing presence in the labor force, are associated with

an increase in divorce rates. As we discussed in Chapter 4, women are becoming more assertive of their needs and rights and expect their spouses to communicate with them and to share domestic tasks. If women are employed, they are more likely to leave unhappy relationships when these expectations are not met. Whether women work long hours for low wages or are paid well but are dissatisfied with their jobs, they may be at greater risk for divorce because fatigue and unpleasant work conditions can increase marital stress. In addition, according to Colasanto and Shriver (1989), women who are economically self-sufficient may be more likely to divorce husbands who engage in extramarital relationships. You'll recall from Chapter 7 that men engage in such relationships more frequently than women.

Some researchers suggest, however, that a woman's employment outside the home can

	PERCENT REPORTING		PERCENT REPORTING
Materialism: Being preoccupied with money and pleasure; breaking up a relationship as soon as demands are not met.	15	*Accommodation:* Breakup of a second marriage because of the interference of adult children.	7
Fickleness: Shifting one's affection; flirting with members of the opposite sex; having no spiritual ideals; seeking new relationships.	14	*Misconduct:* Chronic misbehavior leading to crime; rejection by the noncriminal spouse.	3
Extramarital affair: Alienation of affection; different personal interests; family tension created by extramarital affair.	11	*Physical problems:* Physiological defects; irritability of the disabled; unpleasant disposition.	3
Separation: Character flaws; old marital grudges; long separation; a couple in name only.	10		
Interference: Involvement of relatives and friends in marital trouble.	8		
Mistreatment of wives: Male chauvinism; irresponsible and brutal behavior toward wives.	8		

Taiwan's divorce rate, about 7 percent in 1992, is considerably lower than divorce rates in Western countries. According to Chang (1993), the rates are increasing, despite long-standing divorce laws that strongly favor men. For example, Taiwanese law states that custody belongs to the children's natural father, based on the tradition that children carry on the father's family name. Some women end up paying their husbands large sums of money in exchange for custody.

Although in 1992, 11 percent of divorce actions granted custody to the wives on the grounds of violence, domestic violence is hard to prove in Taiwan. Some husbands have learned how to beat their wives without leaving any visible marks, and even when there is evidence, many doctors refuse to provide medical statements lest a battered woman's husband takes revenge on them. In addition, friends, relatives, and neighbors are often reluctant to help a battered wife get a divorce, for this is tantamount to disrupting the harmony of another family, something many Chinese are loath to do. Also, although 95 percent of divorce suits are brought on the basis of the husband's adultery, only about 3 percent of divorces granted are based on this charge. A wife has to provide photographs of her husband and his mistress in bed together and, when the two are caught, a police officer must be called to the scene as an official witness (Chang, 1993).

have a stabilizing effect on a marriage. A wife's income increases the family's financial security, which makes remaining married a more attractive alternative for both partners than becoming single again. Furthermore, women with a strong career orientation may postpone marriage, and getting married at a later age also tends to decrease the risk of divorce (Greenstein, 1990).

Cultural Values American attitudes and beliefs about divorce have been changing. Some people feel that the expansion of the U.S. welfare system to provide more support for single mothers and their children has encouraged divorce. The women's movement during the late 1960s challenged traditional beliefs that women should stay in unhappy or abusive marriages. Throughout the 1970s and 1980s, many therapists and attorneys not only sent messages that "divorce is okay" but

flooded the market with self-help books on how to get a divorce, how to cope with loneliness and guilt after a divorce, how to deal with child-custody disputes, and other legal issues. Television programs like "Divorce Court" showed viewers that divorce is not an anomaly but an everyday occurrence. Although there is still some stigma attached to divorce, for the most part, American society now accepts it as normal.

Demographic Variables in Divorce

Many demographic factors help explain the divorce-prone couple. Among the factors that have elicited the greatest research attention are parental divorce, the presence of children, age at marriage, premarital childbearing, race and ethnicity, and education.

Parental Divorce   If the parents of one or both partners in a marriage were divorced when they were children, the partners themselves are more likely to divorce (McLanahan and Bumpass, 1988). One reason for this may be that children of divorced parents tend to have lower educational attainment and to marry at younger ages, as we will discuss shortly. Because children of divorced parents are less able to afford college, they are more likely to marry early, and the younger partners are when they marry, the more likely they are to divorce (Saluter, 1994).

The effect of parental divorce varies, depending on gender and social class. Using national data, Keith and Finlay (1988) found that daughters of divorced parents had a higher probability of being divorced in both middle and lower socioeconomic families. In contrast, sons of divorced parents run the same divorce risk *only if* they had lower social-class backgrounds. According to these researchers, when parents divorce, they may be less likely to encourage their daughters to continue their education after high school than their sons. They may also become more lax about checking on their daughters' dating partners. As a result, daughters may choose high-risk mates and at a young age. Sons from lower socioeconomic families may be unable to afford college. But because parents still tend to encourage higher education more often for sons than for daughters, many young men from middle class families continue to enjoy the parents' economic resources, which allow them to go to college and to postpone marriage.

Presence of Children   The relationship between the presence of children in a family and the likelihood that a couple will divorce varies according to the children's age and gender. Several studies have found that the presence of preschool children, especially firstborn children, increases marital stability. This may reflect the fact that some couples stay together "for the sake of the children." In addition, the presence of young children may make the divorce process more costly, both emotionally and financially.

Marital disruption is significantly more likely in families where children are 13 or older (Rankin and Maneker, 1985; Waite and Lillard, 1991). The risk of separation is relatively low when the youngest child is less than 3; it reaches a plateau as the youngest child passes through ages 7 to 12, peaks at the midteens, and drops sharply after age 17 (Heaton, 1990). Thus, whereas the presence of younger children appears to help hold marriages together, when children are older, couples may have fewer incentives to stay together. Or they may purposely postpone divorce until their children are older. In some cases, problems with adolescent children exacerbate already strained marital relationships and the marriage may fall apart.

An interesting finding by several researchers is that marital disruption seems less likely when children are male than when they are female (Katzev et al., 1994; Morgan et al., 1988). Discovering that women who had daughters were more likely to experience marital disruption than were those who had sons, some researchers have suggested that the fathers' role might be an important factor in divorce. Because fathers play a greater role in raising sons than daughters—such things as rule setting and discipline—they are more involved in the family that has sons and are less likely to seek a divorce when problems arise. The researchers also posit that because boys continue to be more valued in American society, mothers with sons may feel more satisfied in their marriages and less likely to consider separation from their spouses.

Age at Marriage   Several studies have found that early age at marriage increases the chance of divorce (Balakrishnan et al., 1987; Thornton and Rodgers, 1987; Kurdek, 1993). In fact, Martin and Bumpass (1989) found that early marriage is the strongest predictor of divorce in the first five years of marriage. Couples who marry under age 18 are especially prone to divorce.

Why do young spouses often divorce? Sometimes if young couples are experiencing problems, parents and relatives who disapproved of the marriage in the first place may encourage divorce. In most cases, however, young couples are poorly prepared for marital responsibilities (Booth and Edwards, 1985). They are more unhappy than older spouses about their partners in terms of love, affection, sex, wage earning, companionship, and faithfulness. They also complain that their spouses become angry easily, are jealous or moody, spend money foolishly, drink or use drugs, and get into trouble with the law. On the more positive side, some of these problems reflect an immaturity that may change over time. On the negative side, early marriage can stunt adolescent development so that the skills necessary to resolve personal and vocational crises are never learned and the difficulties may continue throughout adulthood (see Teti et al., 1987).

Premarital Childbearing Women who conceive or give birth to a child before marriage have higher divorce rates after the first marriage than women who conceive or have a child after marriage (Norton and Miller, 1992). Divorce is especially likely among adolescents, who generally lack the education or income to maintain a stable family life (Wineberg, 1988; Martin and Bumpass, 1989). The effects may be especially negative for young African American women. Teachman (1983) found that black women, marrying at age 16 or 17 after having had a child, had only a 38 percent chance of still being married 15 years later, compared to a 60 percent chance for white women under the same conditions. Other variables undoubtedly interact with early childbirth in this effect. For example, low educational attainment and high unemployment rates among young African American men and poverty among African Americans in general increase separation and divorce rates (see also Chapters 13 and 14).

Race and Ethnicity One of the most consistent research findings is that blacks are more likely to divorce than are whites. As Figure 16.2 shows, divorce rates among African Americans have been more than 75 percent higher than divorce rates among either whites or Latinos since 1960, and since 1980 they have been nearly twice as high. These differences persist at all income, age, educational, and occupational levels (Rank, 1987; White, 1991).

Being African American does not cause one, of course, to divorce. Other factors are at work and, indeed, marital instability among African Americans has been the subject of considerable discussion and speculation. One of the reasons for higher black marital dissolution rates is the higher rate of black teenage and premarital pregnancies. Women whose first birth is out of wedlock are more likely to separate than are those whose first birth occurred within marriage, and black women are more likely than white women to give birth outside of marriage. Thus, young black women face numerous obstacles to a lasting marriage. Compared to white women, they run a higher risk of teenage pregnancy, premarital pregnancy, early marriage, and separation or divorce (Garfinkel et al., 1994).

Another reason for the high divorce rate among blacks is poverty. According to some scholars, because African Americans are disproportionately poor, they are more likely to face the

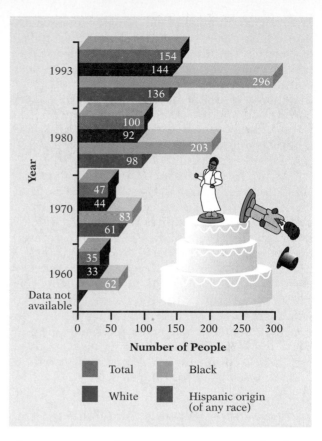

Figure 16.2 Divorce Among Racial-Ethnic Groups, 1960–1993. *Shown are the numbers of divorced people per 1,000 married people* (Based on Saluter, 1994).

many poverty-related stresses and strains that lead to divorce (Rank, 1987; Blackwell, 1991).

Finally, some researchers suggest that divorce may be more acceptable among African Americans. Divorce may be less strained because the community offers divorcing partners more social support. In addition, black mothers report less difficulty than white mothers in maintaining their parental authority. It may be that in preparing their children for the stresses of mainstream society—unemployment, poverty, racism, violence, crime—many African American mothers strengthen their authority as parents (McKenry and Fine, 1993).

Education and Income In general, low educational attainment and low income (especially the father's) increase the possibility of divorce (Kurdek, 1993). A national study of men and women 25 to 34 years of age found that people who had a bachelor's degree were less likely to divorce than those who had a high school education (Glick, 1984). Do people who have college degrees have more stable marriages because they are smarter? No. Rather, going to college postpones marriage for many couples, with the result that they are often more mature, more experienced, and more capable of dealing with personal crises when they marry. They also have better economic prospects, which decreases marital stress over financial problems.

As we've already seen, although the more education a man has the less likely he is to divorce, the effects of educational attainment on women's likelihood of divorce are more complex. Even when a wife's higher education decreases the probability of divorce early in a marriage, it may increase her risk of divorce later in the marriage (South and Spitze, 1986). This finding may reflect changes over the life course, including a wife's employment, her rising income, her increased dissatisfaction if her husband does not share domestic and child-rearing tasks, and her greater freedom from household responsibilities after children leave the home.

Interpersonal Reasons for Divorce

On the personal level, there are many possible reasons for divorce. Some feel that the divorce rate has increased because of the increased pressures on marriage itself. For example, because greater longevity means that a married couple may spend a significantly longer period of time together, there is a greater chance that over the years some partners may grate on each other's nerves. Because people have fewer children, they have more time to focus on their relationship as a couple, both while the children are living at home and after they move out. And because they have more time to focus on the marital relationships, there is a greater chance that some marital partners will become disillusioned. Partners may have higher expectations about marriage. They may expect to be comforted, to be told that they are loved, or to be shown in other ways that they are appreciated and valued. Or couples may compare themselves with unrealistic models as portrayed in films and on television and feel that they *should* have higher expectations about marriage.

Interestingly enough, surveys do not show that "falling out of love" is the major reason for divorce. In a national study, Patterson and Kim (1991) found communication problems to be the number one reason for divorce ("He doesn't understand who I am"; "She doesn't know me"). Infidelity ranked second, constant fighting third, emotional abuse fourth, and falling out of love fifth. In an earlier study (Colasanto and Shriver, 1989), basic personality differences, or incompatibility, were reported as the leading cause of marital breakup in 47 percent of divorces. Other interpersonal reasons included infidelity (17 percent); drug or alcohol problems (16 percent); disputes about money, family, or children (10 percent); and physical abuse (5 percent). Women were much more likely than men (24 percent versus 6 percent) to cite alcohol or drug problems and less likely to mention family disputes (6 percent versus 15 percent) as the principal cause of a divorce.

CONSEQUENCES OF DIVORCE

Marital dissolution is usually a painful process. Divorce has a significant impact in at least three areas of a couple's or family's life: both parents' and children's emotional and psychological well-being; economic and financial changes; and child-custody arrangements and the children's welfare.

Emotional and Psychological Effects

Despite today's greater acceptance of divorce, many separated and divorced people feel stigmatized by family, friends, and coworkers (Gasser and Taylor, 1990). Many respondents in a study by Gerstel (1987) said their friends often took sides, labeling one ex-spouse guilty and the other innocent. Many also felt that they were excluded from get-togethers with married couples. They felt others were afraid that their divorced status would "rub off on them," that their being sexually available again was perceived as a threat by married friends. Divorced couples themselves felt that being married was normal and being divorced abnormal. Many put off telling colleagues for fear of being treated differently. Many also avoided singles' organizations because they saw them as degrading or made up of misfits.

Children may also be stigmatized by their parents' divorces. People's negative and often unconscious perceptions of children from divorced families can result in self-fulfilling prophecies:

If teachers, school principals, counselors, psychologists, social workers, and parents expect children from divorced families to have more than their share of problems, they may treat these children in ways that exacerbate, or even generate, these very problems. For example, compared with other children, teachers may call on children of divorce less often, give them fewer opportunities to display their competence, reward them less often for good behavior, or punish them more often. The possibility of a self-fulfilling prophecy should be of concern to all people who deal with children from divorced families (Amato, 1991: 67).

Kitson and Morgan (1991) maintain that as divorce becomes more common, adjustment difficulties should decrease. This does not seem to be the case generally, however. In fact, in many instances, the stigma still attached to divorce increases stress both during and after the divorce process.

The psychic divorce that we described earlier may continue for many years. Even when both partners know their marriage cannot be salvaged, they are often ambivalent. They may fluctuate between a sense of loss and a feeling of emancipation; they may have periods of depression punctuated with spurts of euphoria. The box "Do You Know Someone with Divorce Hangover?" exam-

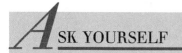

Although trashing wedding memorabilia may release some anger and hurt, it also suggests that the person has not come to terms with divorce and needs some physical sign to make it real.

ines some of the psychological adjustments the newly divorced face.

Economic and Financial Changes

Although both men and women undergo psychological adjustments after a divorce, gender has a dramatic effect on economic status. Income typically declines for both sexes, but a woman's income declines more drastically than a man's (see Data Digest). Most often this change reflects low educational attainment, which may restrict a woman to low-paying jobs in the service sector, or having a young child, which makes it difficult for a woman to find full-time employment and may limit her to part-time jobs that have more flexible hours (Smock, 1993). On the other hand, although many men are financially able to sup-

port their children and ex-wives, very few do so, especially if they disagree with the child-custody arrangements (Finkel and Roberts, 1994). In the early 1990s these fathers were referred to as "deadbeat dads." Posters of the most-wanted deadbeat dads (and some deadbeat moms) started appearing in newspapers and subways and on local community bulletin boards (Waldman, 1992).

Property Settlements and Alimony In the past the law assumed that one partner was responsible for a divorce and that the reason for the dissolution was a transgression, such as adultery, desertion, or cruelty. In 1970, California became the first state to abolish the requirement of fault as the basis for marital dissolution, and *no-fault divorce* has now been instituted in every state (see Appendix F). The intent of the no-fault divorce statute was to change the adversarial nature of divorce and to reduce the long court battles and emotional trauma associated with establishing fault as grounds for divorce.

According to some observers, no-fault divorce has done more harm than good to many women. Because both partners are now treated as equals, each, theoretically, at least, receives half of the family assets and the ex-wife is expected to support herself regardless of whether she has any job experience or work-related skills. According to Census Bureau data, in 1990, 32 percent of divorced women received property settlements (such as real estate, cars, and/or household furnishings), and the average total cash and property settlement was about $20,000 (Lester, 1991). Fathers without custody got 47 percent of the assets, whereas mothers with custody got only 28 percent (Quinn, 1993). Thus, in reality, no-fault divorce has not generated "equal" economic treatment.

Despite the institution of the no-fault divorce and evidence that very few women receive substantial cash payments in a divorce, many people still believe that many women profit through divorce by high alimony payments. Dubbing this the "alimony myth," Weitzman (1985) suggests several reasons for its persistence. First, many people are not aware that alimony payments have been awarded in only a minority of divorce cases. Second, Weitzman says, alimony is often confused with child support and perceived simply as "money that divorced men have to pay." Third, the few women who do receive significant alimony are highly visible because their spouses are celebrities. When wealthy men like Johnny Carson, Donald Trump, and Lee Iacocca were divorced, their alimony payments made headlines. Not all of the rich and famous receive or pay large alimony settlements, however, and often ex-wives must spend years in court and experience considerable emotional anguish. In a *Forbes* article on the biggest American divorce settlements, the author concluded that "divorce is one very tough way to make a buck" (Buchalter, 1991: 56).

In 1993, about 15 percent of divorced women were awarded alimony in their divorce settlements, but only 3 percent actually received any payments. Moreover, the average award in 1993 was only $7008 per year (personal communication, Bureau of the Census, February 1995). Thus, women who have been full-time housewives most of their lives and experience divorce in their 40s or 50s are especially likely to become poor. If they have low educational levels and few marketable skills, alimony payments will not keep them out of poverty.

Child Support   Nearly 50 percent of all men neither see nor support their children after a divorce (Hewlett, 1990). Many fathers have never provided any kind of help, including child-support payments and other forms of assistance like paying for clothes, buying presents, taking the children on vacations, paying for routine dental care or uninsured medical expenses, carrying medical insurance, helping the children with homework, and attending school events (Garfinkel et al., 1994). Two thirds of noncustodial fathers spend more on car payments than they do for child support (Kitson and Holmes, 1992).

According to the Bureau of the Census, about 77 percent of divorced mothers with children under 21 years of age were awarded child-support payments in 1990. Of these, about three quarters actually received payments that, on average, totaled $3300 a year. Although 44 percent of divorced mothers were awarded child support that included health-care benefits, only two thirds of fathers actually provided such benefits (Lester, 1991). Thus, many divorced mothers are the sole supporters of their children.

Why do parents—usually fathers—refuse to pay child support? According to Nuta (1986), nonpaying fathers fall into four major categories:

1. *The parent in pain* may feel shut out of the family and distance himself physically and/or emotionally from his children. He may even rationalize his distancing ("She turned them against me"). Other fathers are angry if they feel that visitation rights are unequal.

2. *The overextended parent* is overburdened with financial obligations. Anxious to get out of his marriage as soon as possible, he may agree to pay more support than he can actually afford. He may remarry and, unable to support two families, fail to provide for the children of his first marriage. Or he may become ill and unemployed and thus be unable to meet the child-support payments.

3. *The revengeful parent* uses child support as a form of control. He may use nonpayment to change a visitation agreement or to punish his wife for initiating the divorce.

4. *The irresponsible parent,* representing the greatest number of child-support dodgers, simply does not take his parental duties seriously. He may expect others to take care of his family ("Welfare will pay," or "Her family has more money than I do") or he may think that taking care of himself is more important than providing for his children.

In 1984, Congress passed Child Support Enforcement Amendments that require states to deduct delinquent support from fathers' paychecks and tax returns. The Family Support Act of 1988 authorizes judges to use their discretion when support agreements cannot be met, as, for example, when a father is unemployed and can't pay child support. This act also mandates periodic reviews of award levels to keep up with the rate of inflation. Because many divorced fathers rarely provide for their children through means other than child support, court-ordered awards are often the only monetary contributions that fathers make (Paasch and Teachman, 1991).

Court-ordered child support has several problems, however. Sometimes attorneys advise their clients to trade child-support payments for property settlements. For example, a mother may agree to minimal monthly child-support payments in exchange for ownership of the house. Before long the custodial parent may realize that the child support is inadequate because she is having difficulty meeting the monthly mortgage payments. Going back to court to increase payments or collect delinquent payments may be time-consuming and very expensive. Another problem arises from the discretionary nature of the judicial system: Custodial parents in similar economic circumstances may find themselves with very different support payments "depending on the disposition of the presiding judge or magistrate and the quality of the legal advice they receive" (Wong, 1993: 14; see Chisholm and Driedger, 1994, for a discussion of unpaid child-support payments in Canada).

States also vary a great deal in enforcing child-support laws. Fathers who have never married, who have less than a high school education, and who are black and poor are the least likely either to have support agreements or to meet them, and they are the most difficult divorced parents to locate and identify. In addition, so far the bureaucracy that tracks a noncustodial parent's payments is lumbering and tedious. If the noncustodial parent changes jobs often, it is very difficult for employers to implement income withholding and disburse the payments for child support (Williams, 1994). Thus, many divorced mothers are powerless to collect child-custody awards.

As might be expected, ex-spouses who have a good relationship with their former partners are more likely to receive court-ordered child-support awards than are those who do not. Good parental relationships appear critical in determining whether the children of divorced parents get economic and emotional assistance from their fathers (Garfinkel et al., 1994).

Some observers suggest that enforcing child-support payment laws will alleviate but not end poverty in single-mother homes. According to Amott (1993), for example, poverty in divorced-mother households will end only when women's earnings are comparable to those of men.

Family Income   In 1993, 86 percent of single parents were mothers, slightly fewer than the 90 percent who were mothers in 1970 and 1980 (Rawlings, 1994). Across all races, children in two-parent households are better off financially than are those in one-parent families. The most disadvantaged are children in mother-only homes. As Table 16.1 shows, 53 percent of all children living in mother-only households live below the poverty level. Among African American and Latino families, 66 and 64 percent live in poverty. Mothers—and especially young mothers—are less likely than are fathers to have

Table 16.1

Children Under Age 18, by Family Income, 1994

RACE AND LIVING ARRANGEMENT	MEDIAN INCOME	PERCENTAGE BELOW POVERTY LEVEL
All Families		
Living with both parents	$43,578	11
Living with mother only	12,073	53
Living with father only	23,305	24
White Families		
Living with both parents	44,371	10
Living with mother only	14,589	45
Living with father only	24,512	22
Black Families		
Living with both parents	35,676	17
Living with mother only	9,389	66
Living with father only	19,775	30
Latino Families		
Living with both parents	26,334	29
Living with mother only	10,857	64
Living with father only	14,701	46

SOURCE: Based on Saluter, 1994:36–55.

finished high school or to be employed, and even when they do work, their incomes are lower, due, in part, to wage discrimination.

Public benefits for single-mother families are meager. It is estimated that the two major programs—Aid to Families with Dependent Children and Survivors Insurance—account for only 15 and 25 percent of the income of both white and black mother-only families, respectively (McLanahan and Booth, 1991).

Custody Issues

Children are often caught in the middle of custody battles:

Mark, age eight: "I don't think either one of them should get me. All they ever do is fight and yell at each other. I'd rather live with my grandma."

David, age five: "Dad says he wants me there but every time we go over all he does is watch football and drink beer. I don't think he really wants us. I think he just says that to make Mommy mad."

Mary, age ten: "I hate going to my dad's because every time I come back I get the third degree from Mom about what we did and who was there and whether Dad did anything wrong or anything that made us mad. I feel like a snitch."

Robin, age seven: "Mom wants me to live with her and Dad wants me to live with him. But I want to live with both of them. Why do I have to choose? I just want us to be happy again" (Everett and Everett, 1994: 84–85).

Custody refers to a court-mandated ruling as to which parent will have the primary responsibility for the welfare and upbringing of a couple's children. Children live with a custodial parent, whereas they see the noncustodial parent according to specific visitation schedules worked out in the custody agreement. Approximately 90 percent of all divorces are not contested but are settled out of court through negotiations. In about 88 percent of cases, the mother gets custody of the children. According to a study of the Massachusetts courts, when men sue, they win either sole or joint custody more than 70 percent of the time (reported in Mansnerus, 1995). It is for this reason that divorce attorneys sometimes advise their male clients to wage an all-out battle for custody—even when they do not want it—simply as a bargaining chip in negotiations over child support. Mothers, afraid to lose custody, often agree to a modest alimony or child-support arrangement (Olson, 1988).

There are three types of custody. In **sole custody** (about 85 percent of cases), one parent has sole responsibility for raising the child; the other parent has specified visitation rights. Parents may negotiate informally over such things as schedules or holidays, but if an agreement can't be reached, the legal custodian has the right to make the final decisions. In **split custody** (about 5 percent of cases), the children are divided between the parents either by gender—the mother gets the daughter(s) and the father gets the son(s)—or by choice—the children are allowed to choose the parent with whom they want to live. In **joint custody** (about 10 percent of cases), the children divide their time between both parents, who share in the decisions about their upbringing (Teachman, 1991a). There are two types of joint custody: *joint legal custody,* which specifies that both parents are to share decision making on such issues as the child's education, health care, and religious training; and *joint physical custody,* which specifies how much time children will spend in each parent's home.

Joint custody is a controversial issue. Proponents advance several arguments. First, they maintain that men and women should have equal child-rearing responsibilities, both during marriage and after divorce. Second, many men say they want to care for their children and have formed such organizations as Fathers for Justice, Fathers United for Equal Justice, and Fathers Are Capable Too to lobby in almost every state for joint-custody laws. Third, much research indicates that the relationship between a noncustodial father and his children is critical in the children's development. Finally, a joint-custody arrangement lightens the responsibility of each parent and eases the economic burdens of parenting, particularly for mothers (Irving and Benjamin, 1991).

Opponents of joint custody, on the other hand, argue that it creates loyalty conflicts for children and exacerbates postdivorce conflicts between ex-spouses, who may disagree on child-rearing decisions (see Ferreiro, 1990, for a summary of the debates on whether or not joint custody should be mandated by state laws). As Maccoby and others (1991) point out, parents who argued a lot before they divorced are likely to continue to argue, and as a result, children may still have to deal with parental conflict. Critics of joint custody also say that this arrangement makes it possible for men who abused their wives or children before the divorce to continue the same behavior (Fineman, 1991). Finally, some argue that joint custody does more harm than good. School attendance may be disrupted as children are shuttled between two homes and a school. In addition, mothers who move out of state may lose custody of their children even when fathers don't show up for scheduled visits or totally ignore their children (Hoffman, 1995).

In general, joint custody works best when both parents want it. Fathers who seek joint (especially physical) custody are typically well educated and affluent (Pearson and Thoennes, 1990). They can enhance a child's social and intellectual growth: The father may take the child on trips, buy him or her expensive educational gifts like computers, and send the child to private schools and summer camps. A parent who is abusive, on the other hand, can make a joint-custody arrangement very traumatic for a child. If custody is awarded based on finances while ignoring domestic violence, fathers who have histories of abusive behavior toward family members can endanger the lives of both their children and their ex-wives (Johnston and Campbell, 1993; Saunders, 1994).

One of the most controversial issues during the mid-1990s has been whether divorced working mothers are being punished in custody cases. Some mothers claim that they must choose between their child and their job. In New York, for example, an appellate court ruled that an unemployed father, who repeatedly refused to pay child support, was better able to care for the child because he was at home while his employed wife was at the office. The decision reversed two lower court rulings in the mother's favor.

In Mississippi, a flight attendant whose work took her away two nights a week had to let her daughter live with her ex-husband when a judge ruled that his job as a Federal Express courier gave him a more regular work schedule (Steinbach, 1995). Some observers say that such cases are a minority because, as we noted earlier, mothers get custody of children in many uncontested cases. When custody is contested, however, some feel that courts are applying a double standard: "Often, men are judged by the availability of other child care, from a second wife to a girlfriend, while women are evaluated based on their own, personal ability to be with a child, ignoring the presence of a grandmother or a babysitter" (Feldmann and Goodale, 1995: 18). We discuss child custody and working mothers, whether unmarried or divorced, in greater depth in Chapter 19.

HOW DOES DIVORCE AFFECT CHILDREN?

The consequences of divorce vary and depend on a variety of factors: the absence of one parent can have serious effects on a child; a lower family income as a result of divorce can affect a child's educational opportunities and success in school; a child's relationship with the custodial spouse can influence his or her reaction to the divorce; the child's age at the time of divorce influences his or her behavior; a child's gender seems to determine his or her reactions to some degree; and the behavior of outsiders, like teachers, may have an impact on children's behavior. One of the most important influences on children's reactions to their parents' divorce is the parents' behavior and the way they choose to

handle the divorce, as the box "Children of Divorce" demonstrates.

Absent Fathers

We could call this section "The Absent Parent," but the fact is that the postdivorce single-father household from which the mother has totally disappeared is extremely rare. In most sole-custody cases, it is the mothers who have custody and the fathers who get visitation rights. Many children of divorce rarely see their fathers, however. In a national study, Bianchi (1990) found that more than 60 percent of fathers either did not visit their children or did not visit them and had no telephone or mail contact with them over a one-year period. Even when fathers do see their children, they typically slack off or stop visiting after about two years (Loewen, 1988). One study found that even when the parents were separated but not yet divorced the average child had seen the father only six to eight days during the preceding month (Braver et al., 1991).

Why do many fathers fail to take visitation rights seriously? For one thing, traditional cultural expectations about child rearing and nurturing emphasize the importance of mothers, not fathers (see Chapter 4). For another, when ex-spouses are engaged in continuing battles, fathers may try to avoid further conflict by not seeing their children. A third reason, according to some fathers, is that visitation is emotionally difficult for them or seems artificial. Finally, when a man forms new relationships or remarries, he may feel less committed to his children from an earlier marriage (Teyber and Hoffman, 1987; Loewen, 1988).

How important is a noncustodial father's involvement to his children's well-being? The findings are mixed. There is some evidence that the father's payment of child-support benefits the children's educational achievement. For example, children supported by such payments are more likely to finish high school and to enter college (Graham et al., 1994; Knox and Bane, 1994). Regular payments may also increase children's academic well-being because mothers, feeling more financially secure, are able to deal better with school-related problems (McLanahan et al., 1994). And when child-support payments are voluntary, fathers may have good relationships with their children and ex-spouses. The lack of parental conflict, which is ordinarily distressing and distracting, may help children focus

Children of Divorce

The way a divorcing couple deals with divorce may have long-term effects on the children. Interviewing adult children of divorce (sometimes called "ACODs") about their memories of their parents' divorce and their current behaviors and lifestyles, Fassel (1991) proposed five types of divorce and subsequent effects on children:

The Disappearing Parent Suddenly, one parent leaves the home, and the children receive little explanation beyond, "Your mother and I have been divorced today." Adults who recalled this situation often grew up suspicious of people, fearing that they too would leave them. Some tried to be perfect parents to avoid hurting their children in the ways they had been hurt.

The Surprise Divorce In this situation, parents often seemed close and open with each other, but without any warning, one filed for divorce. Adults recalled feeling shock and then bewilderment and anger that the parent who left disrupted what they had thought was a happy family. As they grow up, children may erect walls to protect themselves, becoming distant from friends and avoiding intimate relationships because they expect a partner, like the parent who left, to be unpredictable or undependable.

The Violent Divorce Spouse and sometimes child abuse as well causes many divorces. Children in such a setting don't learn how to handle anger because their role models could not handle it. The children often repress conflict for fear of violence, or they grow up believing that fighting is a way to test intimacy and to get a partner's attention.

The Late Divorce When parents stay together "for the children's sake" they often create an environment of veiled criticism and threats, unspoken anger, and even hatred. Many children in such homes learn to deny feelings just to survive and some equate love with suffering in silence. Many are wary of commitment, which they equate with loss of freedom, and become cynical about the possibility of having a good relationship with anyone.

Protect-the-Kids Divorce Some well-intentioned parents may decide to protect their children by withholding information about the real reasons for their divorce. They don't accuse one another, they communicate well, and each listens respectfully as the other tells the children about the divorce. Sound good? Not necessarily. In one case, a couple told their children that their father felt the need to explore, to be free, to see the world. When, many years later, the children learned that their father was gay, they felt betrayed and angry.

How can divorcing couples avoid these negative outcomes for their children? Gold (1992) recommends "CPR" (a play on the abbreviation for cardiopulmonary resuscitation, an emergency procedure used to keep the heart and lungs going in an emergency like a heart attack):

Continuity Introduce all changes gradually, and try to maintain regular routines and child-rearing responsibilities as far as possible.

Protection Be civil with one another, and don't put your children in the middle of your conflicts. Preserve your children's relationships with both of you.

Reassurance Assure your children that you love them, that the divorce is not their fault, and that you will not abandon them. Tell your children about your plans for them to spend time with each of you, let them know about the possibility that they may have to move or change schools, and give them warning ahead of time of any impending economic or financial changes.

---

on academic pursuits (Baydar and Brooks-Gunn, 1994).

There is less evidence that visits from a non-custodial father have beneficial effects on the child's emotional and behavioral well-being. It is not clear whether this reflects abuse by fathers—in which case visits clearly do more harm than good—poor mother-father relationships, or other characteristics of the fathers (King, 1994). For example, some fathers may abuse alcohol, some may be too depressed after a divorce to maintain meaningful ties with their children, some may feel that they are losing control over their children, and some may have developed closer relationships with new partners and their children (Aseltine and Kessler, 1993; Umberson and Williams, 1993).

Family counselors argue, however, that it is important for children and fathers to maintain a close relationship after a divorce (Portes et al.,

One way for a divorced father to maintain closeness with his children is to help them learn new skills.

1992). Thus, Pruett (1987) has suggested some specific steps that fathers can take to ensure the continuity of their relationship with their children:

1. A father should be guided by his child's developmental needs. For example, because toddlers' sense of time is different from adults' and their memories are shorter, it's better for a father to make frequent brief visits than long visits at greater intervals. On the other hand, older children who enjoy successful social and school activities need more visitation flexibility.

2. A father should live close to his children if at all possible, especially when they are young. Furthermore, whether or not he and his former wife are friendly, he should not give up seeing his children. He should be with his children whenever he can, whether he is changing their diapers or helping them with their homework.

3. A father should pay child support regularly. Skipping payments not only deprives the child of material things but lowers the father's self-respect. At the same time, a father should not overindulge his children; children of *all* ages expect a parent to establish limits for them.

4. A father should not cross-examine his children or dwell on the divorce. His job is to fig-

ure out how he and the children can fit into one another's lives and then to make that happen.

Crisis need *not* spawn failure. Although divorce is often sad and difficult for both fathers and their children, the rewards are immeasurable when a father perseveres in maintaining a relationship with his children.

Educational Attainment

Children whose parents divorce are less likely to complete high school, less likely to attend college, and more likely to be neither employed nor in school. They initiate sex earlier, are more likely to become pregnant in their teens, and have a higher incidence of cohabitation but do not marry earlier (Furstenberg and Teitler, 1994). Divorced parents are less likely than married parents to help their children with homework or to help them plan their high school curricula. Children who do poorly in school or drop out have fewer occupational options and thus earn less as adults (Biblarz and Raftery, 1993).

Parents As Peers

Divorced parents sometimes make the mistake of treating their children like peers. Particularly if the children are bright and verbal, a parent may see them as more mature than they really are. Mothers, who usually have custody, often share their feelings on a wide range of personal issues. They may express bitterness toward their ex-husbands, anger at men in general, or frustration over financial concerns or social isolation. In response, children may console the parent and appear concerned and caring, but they may also feel anger, resentment, sadness, or guilt. They may manifest these feelings through psychosomatic problems such as stomach pains, through sleeping or eating problems, through sexual or aggressive acting out, or through a use of drugs. They may be truant from school, exhibit a decline in academic performance, or run away. They may appear overcompliant with parental requests or simply withdraw (Devall et al., 1986; Glenwick and Mowrey, 1986).

Age- and Gender-Related Problems

Contrary to popular wisdom, most children of divorced parents are not necessarily more mature nor do they grow up more quickly. Children of divorce often experience emotional problems, but these difficulties do not often make them more mature. Because they tend to live in rental properties, they have fewer outside chores, and because younger brothers and sisters are often in day care centers while the mother works, older children of divorce do not have more household or child-care responsibilities than other children (Devall et al., 1986).

A study by the National Institute of Mental Health showed that when children who were younger than seven when their parents divorced became adolescents, they were three times more likely to be receiving psychological counseling and five times more likely to have been suspended or expelled from school than were children of intact families (cited in Taylor, 1991b). And some adolescents react to divorce by becoming more socially isolated; they disappear into their rooms, spend hours watching television, and jump at the chance to get out of the house. Others may react by becoming addicted to drugs or alcohol or by overeating, undereating, shoplifting, or becoming promiscuous (Walther, 1991).

Some studies have shown that teacher evaluations, often in the form of grades, are lower for children from single-parent families (Demo and Acock, 1988; Bianchi, 1990). It's not clear, however, whether these evaluations reflect behav-

In TV's "Grace Under Fire," the tough but funny heroine is a divorced mother who is doing her best to raise her three children on blue-collar wages without help from her abusive and alcoholic former husband.

ioral problems due to parental divorce or, as we discussed earlier, to teachers' negative expectations of children from divorced families.

Divorce appears to affect sons and daughters differently. Boys, particularly those with absent fathers, tend to have lower levels of achievement in school, to have to repeat a grade in school, and to have difficulty getting along with peers and teachers (Bianchi, 1990). In general, young boys experience more behavioral and emotional problems, such as increased levels of aggression, heightened anxiety, dependency, and a tendency to withdraw or to be easily distracted. In what Wallerstein and Blakeslee (1989) call a "sleeper effect," girls' negative reactions to divorce may be delayed until adolescence or young adulthood. For example, Glenn and Kramer (1987) found that women who were younger than 16 when their parents separated or divorced were 59 percent more likely to end up separated or divorced themselves compared to 32 percent of males.

There are more similarities between the sexes than differences, however. For example, in a study of young people ages 18 to 23 in divorced or separated families, Furstenberg and Teitler (1994) found that divorce appeared to produce similar effects for boys and girls. Both had a higher likelihood than children from intact families to drop out of high school, to have sex before age 17, and to cohabit, and the girls were more likely to become pregnant before age 19.

Behavioral and Emotional Problems

Studying children of divorced parents, Fassel (1991) found that many preschool children fear abandonment; elementary school age children are likely to be apprehensive about economic insecurity; and many teenagers experience anxiety and feel they have more responsibility. When these three groups of children become adults, they tend to avoid intimacy because they fear abandonment.

Several national studies have shown that adult children of divorce report lower satisfaction in such areas as leisure activities, friendships, family life, and happiness (Glenn and Kramer, 1987; Glenn, 1991). For example, young people ages 18 to 21 may experience anger, a sense of loss, anxiety, loyalty conflicts, and difficulty with schoolwork. Those in their 20s report overwhelming anger and resentment, as well as caution in making commitments in their own personal relationships. Adult children in their 30s may question the stability of their own marriages, even when there are no apparent problems (Corey, 1990c).

In part because parents exercise less supervision and control over children in single-parent households, adolescents of both sexes are more likely to engage in such deviant behavior as truancy, burglary, and alcohol and drug use (Bianchi, 1990). Much of the research throughout the 1970s and 1980s found that marital dissolution also resulted in emotional problems for children. Boys, especially, had more severe and longer-lasting adjustment problems (see Demo and Acock, 1991, for a summary of many of these studies). These problems were often explained in terms of social learning theories. That is, whereas girls had same-sex role models in their mothers, who are typically the custodial parents, boys had a harder time adjusting to living without a same-sex parent.

More recently, however, some social scientists have argued that emotional problems, regardless of gender, are influenced not by family structure (divorced or intact) but by several other conditions, including parental discord, poor parent-child relationships, and economic problems (Demo and Acock, 1991). In addition, some of the long-term negative reactions of adult children of divorced parents may reflect the unpredictability of the divorce and a lack of communication during the divorce:

> [Mary], a 35-year-old Chicago nurse, has been married for 6 years and has a son, age 3. Mary's parents had been married 25 years when her father decided he had had enough. He woke Mary . . . in the middle of the night to tell her he was leaving her mother. He hadn't even informed his wife, and he made Mary promise to keep his secret. A few weeks later, he gave her mother a long letter detailing all the things he thought were wrong. As upsetting as the divorce itself, Mary says, was the fact that she never knew her parents' marriage was in trouble (Kantrowitz et al., 1992: 53).

Some researchers have questioned whether divorce creates new dilemmas or crystallizes long-standing family problems. In longitudinal studies of the effects of divorce on children between the ages of 11 and 16 in Great Britain and the United States, a team of researchers found that, especially for boys, the achievement and behavioral problems existed well before the separation and divorce occurred (Cherlin et al., 1991). In a study of American adolescents and young adults from divorced families, Furstenberg and Teitler (1994) concluded that some of the processes that eventuate in divorce begin long before marital disruption actually occurs. That is, partners who divorce are more likely to have poor parenting skills and high levels of marital conflict or to suffer from persistent economic stress.

Helping Children During Divorce

Time and again, studies have shown that it is not divorce itself that is damaging to children but the *parental conflict* that becomes manifest not only before but during and after the divorce (Gabardi and Rosen, 1992; Booth and Amato, 1994; Forehand et al., 1994). Children experience the greatest stress when they are put in the middle of their parents' struggle, as when parents try to get children to side with them, use the children to get information about the other parent, or denigrate a former spouse (Buehler and Trotter, 1990; Massey, 1992). According to researchers and clinicians, parents can lessen some of these negative effects:

1. Help prepare children for the actual physical separation by giving them some extra time beforehand and by being around to answer their questions. Explain what divorce is as clearly as you can to the children, including changes they can expect in their day-to-day experience, and be prepared to repeat this information several times for younger children.

2. Each parent should contribute to the explanation given the children, speaking for himself or herself, and the couple should agree ahead of time on what they will and will not say. Speak about yourself, your feelings, and your perspective without criticizing your spouse.

3. Reassure the children that you love them and that you will remain actively involved with them. Partners should emphasize that both parents will continue to love and care for the children and that the children will always be free to love both parents.

4. Don't be afraid to talk about your feelings. This can set the stage for open communication between parents and their children. You can discuss your unhappiness and even your anger, but if you blame the other parent you will force the children to take sides.

5. Modify what you say based on the children's ages. For example, younger children need more concrete examples to help them understand the nature of divorce.

6. Emphasize that the children are not responsible for problems between the parents. Point out that each of you is divorcing the other but not the children.

7. Give the children the news when they are together so that they can lean on one another for support, and encourage them to ask any questions that occur to them both then and later.

8. Make it clear that you have made the decision to divorce carefully, rationally, but sadly. Expressing your sadness encourages children to cry and mourn without having to hide their feelings of loss from you or from themselves.

9. Reassure your children that they will continue to see their grandparents on both sides of the family.

10. Recognize the cries of help in your children's behavior during and after your divorce. The younger the children are, the more likely they are to express their feelings and needs through specific behaviors, rather than through words. For example, when preschool children feel unloved, neglected, or insecure, they may regress to an earlier stage of their development and suck their thumbs or be afraid of the dark. They may lose their appetites and wake frequently during the night crying anxiously. Elementary school children may "tell" you they are sad and depressed over the divorce when they suddenly show a lack of interest in school or get poor grades in courses in which they previously excelled. Adolescents may "tell" you that you need to work constructively on your relationship with them if they suddenly begin to cut class frequently, become verbally abusive or sexually irresponsible, defy curfew rules, or start using alcohol, cocaine, or other drugs.

11. Recognize that your children's fundamental need for security has not changed. Your children need to feel, above all else, that Mom and Dad will always provide them with the emotional and physical security they need to develop into confident maturity. Their security does *not* depend on your income or where you live but on whether you and your ex-spouse demonstrate by your behavior that both of you are fully competent to weather the storms of change that divorce entails and to shelter them from these storms (Lansky, 1989; Greif, 1990).

12. It is critical for the noncustodial parent, usually the father, to maintain an ongoing relationship with the children. Noncustodial fathers who maintain stable, frequent visitation provide more advice to their children, and their adolescent children are more satisfied with the support of the absent parent and less likely to experience depression (Barber, 1994).

ARE THERE ANY POSITIVE OUTCOMES OF DIVORCE?

Much of this chapter has focused on the debilitating effects of divorce on adults and their children. Does divorce, then, have any *positive* effects?

According to Gottman (1994: 427), "We need to remember that not all couples should remain married, and that helping a couple to decide to divorce is a perfectly valid function of marital therapy." In many cases, Gottman notes, partners never move beyond negative and destructive behaviors. For example, they continually complain or criticize their partners and show contempt for them. They are defensive, refusing to take the blame for any of the couple's problems, giving excuses during disagreements, and "stonewalling," or simply refusing to respond during a discussion.

The major positive outcome of divorce is that it provides options to people in unsatisfactory marriages. And insofar as divorce does away with an unhappy, frustrating, and stressful situation, it may improve the mental and emotional health of both ex-spouses and their children. Divorced parents who take joint-custody arrangements seriously, who maintain good communication with their children and with each other, and who receive support from family, friends, and the larger community report being physically and mentally healthy (National Research Council, 1993). In addition, research shows that parental separation is better for children, at least in the long run, than remaining in an intact family where there is continued conflict (Demo and Acock, 1991). A divorce that causes minimal disruption to a child's life may offer fewer long-term risks than does a marriage that children perceive as unhappy. Divorce can offer both parents and children opportunities for personal growth, more gratifying relationships, and a more harmonious family situation (Hetherington et al., 1993).

Not surprisingly, adult children of divorce have less idealized views of marriage than do people who come from intact families. Although most adult children of divorce value marriage, they are more aware of its limitations and more accepting of alternatives to traditional family forms (Amato, 1988). Some social scientists suggest that children who grow up in father-absent homes may be less pressured to conform to traditional gender roles and may instead learn more androgynous roles that will help them be better parents in adulthood (Gately and Schwebel, 1992).

Gold (1992) and other clinicians have suggested that the positive effects of divorce can be increased if adults remember to be adults. For example, divorcing parents can make "divorce vows" that reinforce their commitment to their children:

> I vow to continue to provide for our children's financial and emotional welfare.
>
> I vow to place our children's emotional needs above my personal feelings about my former spouse.
>
> I vow to be fair and honest about the divorce settlement.
>
> I vow to support the children's relationships with my former spouse and never to do anything that might compromise that relationship.
>
> I vow to deal with the issues in this divorce as constructively as I know how, so that we can all go forward.

COUNSELING AND DIVORCE MEDIATION

Traditionally, marital counselors and therapists focused on preventing divorce. Contemporary "divorce busters," who believe that problems can be solved in other ways, actively discourage divorce (see, for example, Weiner-Davis, 1992). Increasingly, however, marital counseling means helping families get through the process of divorce. According to some authorities, in trying to keep couples together serious problems may be overlooked, such as abuse (Johnston and Campbell, 1993).

About 15 years ago divorce mediation emerged as an alternative to the usual divorce lawsuit, and it has become increasingly popular. **Divorce mediation** is a technique and practice, carried out by a person trained in the mediation of disputes, in which a divorcing couple is assisted in coming to an agreement. Some of the areas that are resolved include custody arrangements, child-support and future college expenses, the division of marital property (which might include a house, furniture, stocks, savings accounts, retirement accounts, pension plans, cars, and computers), other assets such as rental property and vacation homes, debts, medical expenses, and self-employment income. In Canada, most provinces and local jurisdictions have provisions allowing the courts to mandate mediation in custody disputes. Although most mediators are either attorneys or mental health professionals, accountants and others are seeking training in mediation to facilitate divorce agreements (De Witt, 1994).

According to Gold (1992), mediators "are a bit like traffic cops." Over several sessions they direct the flow of dialogue and try to forestall accusations, inflammatory remarks, and angry outbursts. They try to steer both partners toward a positive course by setting and enforcing ground rules, bringing structure to the discussions, and generally making it possible for people to talk to each other without letting emotional baggage get in the way.

According to Diane Neumann (1989), a divorce mediator, mediation will not eliminate the hurt caused by separation and divorce, but it can pave the way for the emotional healing and adjustment of both the couple and the children. First, mediation increases communication between spouses. It decreases the anger and does not force the children to choose sides in the divorce. Second, mediation reduces the conflict between spouses. When parents can resolve a dispute—whether it is over a weekend visitation schedule or the division of the proceeds of an employee stock plan—without screaming at each other or exchanging bitter looks, children benefit.

Third, mediation creates a cooperative attitude, sparing the child from being forced into the difficult role of a go-between. Fourth, mediation reduces the time required to negotiate the divorce settlement. A mediation settlement typically takes two to three months; a divorce obtained through a court proceeding may take two or three years. It is even more important for children than it is for adults to put the divorce behind them as quickly as possible. Fifth, mediation helps parents adopt a stable schedule of visitation and reduces the potential for disputes.

Sixth, mediation allows for changes as the children grow. As Jennifer or Sam changes from a Saturday morning ballet lesson, at age 8, to Wednesday night driving lessons, at age 15, parents can negotiate schedule changes without resorting to costly and time-consuming requests for changes in court-imposed arrangements. Finally, mediation prevents children from being pawns or trophies in a divorce contest. The mediator's approach is "What arrangements are best for you, your spouse, and your children?" There is no room for the adversarial stance, "Which of you will win the children?" Mediation assumes that divorcing parents can work together to benefit both parents and children.

Some clinicians describe mediation as a win-win situation:

The children win because their parents are working toward a plan that is in their best interest and their fate is not being decided by a judge who has never met them. The parents win because they are dealing with each other . . . And saving themselves the humiliating experience of attacking and demeaning one another in a courtroom battle. . . . The attorneys win because they can work with cooperative clients who can benefit from their legal resources. The judges and courts win because they are not forced to make Solomon-like decisions about children and because every successfully mediated case represents a reduction of their overburdened case calendar (Everett and Everett, 1994: 96–97).

Several studies have found that fathers prefer mediation to litigation because they are more likely to get a joint-custody agreement. Although settlements reached by mediation and litigation do not differ in terms of the amount of time parents are given to spend with their children, in mediation fathers feel they have a greater voice in child-custody decisions (Bay and Braver, 1990; Emery et al., 1991). Playing a more active role during the marital breakup can encourage fathers to live up to a divorce agreement.

CONCLUSION

The greater acceptability of divorce today has created *change* in family structures. Indeed, separation and divorce now seem to have become "an intrinsic feature of modern family life rather than a temporary aberration" (Martin and Bumpass, 1989: 49). As this chapter has shown, a large segment of the adult population flows in and out of marriage during the life course. This means that people have more *choices* in leaving an unhappy marriage. Often, however, parents fail to recognize that what are choices for them may be *constraints* for their children, who often feel at fault, guilty, and torn between warring parents. If parents handled divorces in more rational and civilized ways, many children would be spared the emotional pain and economic deprivation that they now must suffer. Although there is much happiness, some of the pain that both parents and children experience may become even greater after parents remarry, which is the topic of the next chapter.

Taking Action

SUMMARY

1. A separation can be temporary or permanent, or it can precede a divorce. In most cases, separation is a lengthy process involving four phases—preseparation, early separation, midseparation, and late separation.

2. Marital separation leads to one of three outcomes: divorce, long-term unresolved separation, or reconciliation. The outcomes of marital separation often vary by race and socioeconomic status.

3. Divorce rates increased rapidly during the 1970s, reached a plateau during the 1980s, and have decreased slightly during the 1990s. Whereas in the past many marriages ended because of death or desertion, today divorce is a more common cause of marital dissolution.

4. Many men and women who divorce for the first time are under age 30. Wives seek divorces nearly twice as often as husbands do, in part because women employed outside the home are more independent and thus less inclined to tolerate the stresses of juggling job and child rearing, and because women today are less willing to tolerate husbands' extramarital affairs or other unacceptable behavior.

5. Divorce is often a long, drawn-out process. In most divorces, people go through one or more of six stages: the emotional divorce, the legal divorce, the economic divorce, the coparental divorce, the community divorce, and the psychic divorce.

6. The many reasons for divorce include macro-level causes, such as changing gender roles; demographic variables, such as marriage at a young age; and such interpersonal factors as poor communication and infidelity.

7. Divorce has psychological, economic, and legal consequences. Although property settlements are common, few women receive alimony payments. Furthermore, because child-support awards are either rare or very low, many women and children plunge into poverty after a divorce.

8. There are several types of child custody—sole, split, and joint. Although most mothers receive sole custody, joint custody is becoming more common.

9. In the past, much research indicated that divorce had detrimental effects on children. More recently, however, researchers have suggested that some problems may actually have existed before the divorce, and that others may be attributed to the absence of one parent, usually the father.

10. Divorce mediation has emerged as an alternative to the traditional adversarial approach common to the legal process. Mediation is characterized by less bitterness, it is less protracted, and it can give each partner more input in child-custody decisions.

KEY TERMS

separation 450
divorce 453
alimony 455
child support 455

no-fault divorce 456
social integration 457
custody 467
sole custody 467

split custody 467
joint custody 467
divorce mediation 474

ADDITIONAL READING

Among the many self-help books that offer parents and children practical guidelines for dealing with divorce and its aftermath are the following:

CONSTANCE AHRONS, *The Good Divorce: Keeping Your Family Together When Your Marriage Comes Apart* (New York: HarperCollins, 1994).

NOELLE FINTUSHEL and NANCY HILLARED, *A Grief Out of Season: When Your Parents Divorce in Your Adult Years* (Boston: Little, Brown, 1991).

RICHARD A. GARDNER, *The Parents Book About Divorce* (New York: Bantam, 1991).

LOIS GOLD, *Between Love and Hate: A Guide to Civilized Divorce* (New York: Plenum Press, 1992).

JOHN GOTTMAN and NAN SILVER, *Why Marriages Succeed or Fail: What You Can Learn from the Breakthrough Research to Make Your Marriage Last* (New York: Simon & Schuster, 1994).

There is a growing emphasis on the role of fathers and their relationships with their children after a divorce. Three publications on this topic are the following:

JOYCE A. ARDITTI, "Noncustodial Fathers: An Overview of Policy and Resources," *Family Relations* 39

(October 1990): 460–65. Arditti includes suggested articles, popular books, and support groups for noncustodial fathers.

GEOFFREY L. GREIF, *The Daddy Track and the Single Father* (Lexington, MA: Lexington Books, 1990).

M. F. MYERS, *Men and Divorce* (New York: Guilford, 1989).

Here are some other useful books on divorce:

R. THOMAS BERNER, *Parents Whose Parents Were Divorced* (New York: Haworth Press, 1992). Based on a study of 300 adult children of divorce, this largely experiential account describes children's feelings during divorce, custody and visitation, their relationships with friends, and their adjustment to divorce during adulthood.

HELEN ROSE FUCHS EBAUGH, *Becoming an Ex: The Process of Role Exit* (Chicago: University of Chicago Press, 1988). Don't be put off by the publication date. Ebaugh offers an intriguing analysis of "role exits" like divorce, in which people relinquish social roles. Ebaugh discusses such major areas of adjustment as learning to deal with social reaction to an "ex" status, negotiating and establishing intimate relationships, and dealing with "role residual," or issues and problems that linger after one has left a marriage.

CRAIG A. EVERETT, ed., *Divorce and the Next Generation: Effects on Young Adults' Patterns of Intimacy and Expectations for Marriage* (New York: Haworth Press, 1992). The contributors examine the intergenerational effect of divorce, primarily as perceived by college students whose parents divorce.

WILLIAM J. GOODE, *World Changes in Divorce Patterns* (New Haven, CT: Yale University Press, 1993). Discusses changes in practices since the 1950s in many European countries and in other regions of the world.

17
Remarriage and Stepfamilies: Life After Divorce

Data Digest

- Of all U.S. families, **21 percent were step-families** in 1990, up from 16 percent in 1980.

- In 1991, **15 percent of all children** lived in stepfamilies, and among these children 11 percent lived with a half-sibling.

- Within three years of divorce, **75 percent of women and 83 percent of men remarry.** Over 50 percent of men and 33 percent of women remarry within one year.

- **Partners in remarriage** are most commonly people whose previous marriages ended in divorce. In about 11 percent of remarriages, one or both partners have been widowed.

- People marrying for the second time have **formal weddings only about 20 percent of the time,** and they spend less than half the amount, about $6000, typically spent on a first marriage ceremony.

- In 1991, in **more than 40 percent of marriages in the United States,** the partners had been married between one and four times before.

SOURCES: Norton and Miller, 1992; Ahrons, 1994; DeWitt, 1994; Furukawa, 1994; Waldrop, 1994.

In 1992, the media had a bonanza in the highly publicized love affair between film actor-director Woody Allen, 56, and Soon-Yi Previn, 21, the adopted daughter of actress Mia Farrow, Allen's companion. Farrow had 12 children: with André Previn, her former husband, she had three children; she and Previn adopted three, including Soon-Yi; Farrow later adopted three more children, on her own; she and Allen then adopted two children; and finally she and Allen had a biological son together. The relationship between Allen and Soon-Yi received national attention because many people considered it incestuous. Allen and Farrow had been together for 12 years, and the children described Allen as their father figure. Allen maintained that Soon-Yi was *not* part of his family, however, and that he was a father figure only to his biological son and his two adopted children: "Those are the only three in my will," he said (Adler et al., 1992: 55).

Although most postdivorce families are not as complicated as the Farrow-Allen household, new family relationships formed after divorce, cohabitation, adoption, or the birth of biological children can become intricate. And despite the dramatic rise in divorce rates that we discussed in Chapter 16, people do not seem to be disillusioned with marriage. Indeed, many divorced people remarry, and some more than once. Because not all remarried couples have children from previous marriages living with them, we'll discuss remarriage and stepfamilies separately; quite clearly, though, the two topics overlap.

REMARRIAGE

The U.S. rate of remarriage, the highest in the world, has been erratic. It peaked in the mid-1940s and in the 1950s and 1960s and has declined steadily since about 1967 (see Figure 17.1). The rate is still high, however. Over 40 percent of all marriages are remarriages for one or both partners (Coleman and Ganong, 1991). More than 50 percent of today's youth will be stepsons or stepdaughters by the year 2000. Many of these stepchildren will have half-siblings as well because 54 percent of women have children in their remarriages (Wineberg, 1990).

Who Remarries?

Many factors affect people's decision to remarry. They include age, sex, race, income, educational level, and the marital status of potential partners. As you will see in this section, these variables often interact to explain remarriage rates.

Age, Sex, and Race The average divorced woman who remarries is 35 years old, and the average divorced man is 39. Typically, both men and women have been divorced for about four years. In addition, remarriage rates decline with age for both men and women (DeWitt, 1994).

Men remarry more quickly and more often than women. Because divorced men rarely have custody of their children, they are usually freer to socialize and to date. As we saw in Chapter 8, they

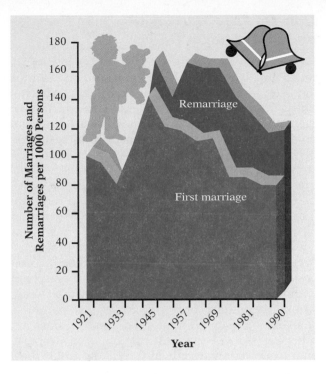

Figure 17.1 Rates of First Marriage and Remarriage, 1921–1990. These data are based on numbers of first marriages per 1000 single women between the ages of 15 and 44 and the numbers of remarriages per 1000 widowed or divorced women between the ages of 15 and 54 (Norton and Miller, 1992, p. 2).

also have a larger pool of eligible partners: Society deems it more acceptable for an older man to marry a younger woman than for an older woman to marry a younger man. Moreover, in the marriage market, men tend to be "worth more" than women of the same age because they are usually financially better off (Goode, 1993). In contrast, divorced women who are older, highly educated, and financially independent are less likely than men to remarry (Ganong and Coleman, 1994). In Canada, according to Wu (1994), the women most likely to remarry are those who married at a relatively young age, who have few marketable skills, and who want a family.

Whites are more likely to remarry than other racial-ethnic groups, and blacks are the least likely to remarry. As Figure 17.2 shows, for example, remarriage rates are higher for white women than for African American and Latino women in every age group, and especially between the ages of 30 to 49. Blacks are also more likely than other groups to separate without divorcing and to stay

single longer after a divorce (Ganong and Coleman, 1994). In particular, African American women with low socioeconomic status stand to gain little from marriage to the partners who are available to them (Smock, 1990).

Income and Education In general, the more money a divorced man has, the more likely he is to remarry. Divorced women, on the other hand,

*Figure 17.2 **Women Who Remarried After Divorce, 1990.** No percentages are given for African American or Latino women in the 20 to 24 age category because the sample was considered too small* (Based on Norton and Miller, 1992, p. 3).

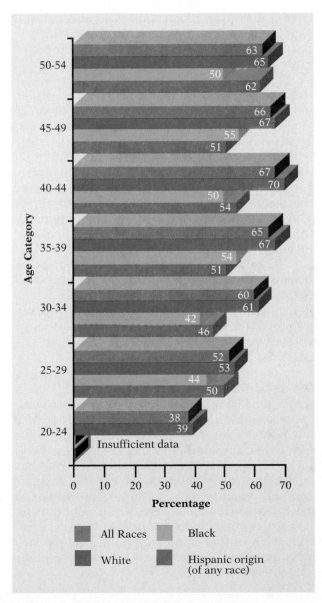

frequently have severe financial problems (see Chapter 16). It is not surprising, therefore, that women with low incomes and lower educational levels are more likely than other women to remarry. For many divorced women, the surest way to escape poverty is to remarry (Folk et al., 1992).

In his Canadian study, Wu (1994) found that men with high educational attainment were more likely to remarry than their female counterparts. Wu notes that although women with higher socioeconomic standing are more eligible remarriage candidates and are likely to attract more desirable marriage partners, they have less to gain from remarriage because they are often economically independent. Moreover, highly educated women have a smaller pool of eligible mates because they may be unwilling to marry someone from a lower socioeconomic level.

Marital Status   The majority of divorced men and women (61 percent) remarry other divorced people, 35 percent marry single men and women, and 4 percent marry widowed people (Wilson and Clarke, 1992). Widowers tend to remarry sooner than divorced men, probably because they have a more positive attitude toward married life. Conversely, widows are slower to remarry. This may reflect the strong emotional attachment many widows have to their deceased husbands. It may also reflect the fact that because widows are generally older than divorced women, they may be seen as less desirable by eligible men (Wu, 1994). Among middle-aged widows, blacks and those with dependent children at home are less likely to remarry than whites or women who have no children (Smith et al., 1991).

Other Variables   Other variables also affect remarriage decisions. For example, because the Catholic Church officially prohibits both divorce and remarriage, Catholics are less likely to remarry than Protestants (Wu, 1994). At the same time, the fact that the general divorce rate has been high for some time has created a large remarriage market for most people. Although some people take advantage of this pool of eligible partners and remarry quickly, others, especially men of higher socioeconomic status, may delay remarriage just because there are many available women.

How Do First Marriages and Remarriages Differ?

First marriages and remarriages differ in several important ways. The composition of the family tends to vary more in remarriages; role expectations in stepfamilies are less defined; family members in remarriages may be at different points in their life cycles; the combination of people from different original families produces strengths and weaknesses that are unique; the presence of children in remarriages creates certain kinds of problems; and people who remarry may look specifically for partners who offer more than their first partners did.

Remarriages often result in myriad new relationships and a dramatic change in *family composition*. Children may suddenly find themselves with **half siblings**—brothers or sisters with whom they share only one biological parent—stepsiblings, stepgrandparents, and a host of other relatives. As a result, the children's experiences may change radically. For example, they may have to share their biological parent's time with stepsiblings, as well as their physical space. Listen to one eight-year-old:

We feel like guests in Jim's house. We are careful of what we do. It is like we are the intruders. And I feel very bad that we took Tommy's room. They fixed up a room for him in the basement, with posters and all, but he's still mad at us for taking his room (Fishman and Hamel, 1981: 185).

The absence of normative *role expectations* for stepfamilies creates perplexing questions. For example, should stepparents have as much authority over children as the children's biological parents do? Should a noncustodial parent have the same decision-making rights regarding his or her children as a custodial parent does? Whether children are involved or not, should remarried partners maintain a friendly relationship with their ex-spouses? If they were married for a long time, should they help their ex-spouses economically or emotionally? Should a child born to a remarriage have more legal rights than the stepchildren of each partner in that marriage have? And finally, does the fact that few states have specific laws against marriage between stepchildren mean that such relationships are acceptable?

People who remarry sometimes find that they and their children are at different *stages of the family life cycle.* As a result their goals may conflict with those of other family members. For example, a man with young-adult children from his first marriage and who is planning for his retirement may marry a younger women who is looking forward to starting a family. Or his new wife may be an older woman who has already raised her family and now looks forward to a career:

Claire and Sydney had been married for 4 years. Sydney had two adult children, ages 25 and 27, who had never lived with the couple, and Claire had a daughter who was 18 and in college. Sydney was a computer expert who had risen from working in the field as a technician to heading the marketing department for a large and successful electronics firm. He now had a month's vacation each year and looked forward to retirement in 10 years. Sydney wished to purchase a vacation home on a lake, as he had spent a number of years "dreaming about retiring there and fishing to his heart's content."

Claire, on the other hand, had gone to work at the telephone company to support herself and her daughter after her divorce. Now that she and Sydney were married, she had been able to return to school and study to be a nurse. She was employed at a local hospital, loved her work, and hoped to become a supervisor before long. She worked various shifts and had little time off. Claire's favorite way to relax was to read or knit . . . [but she also] liked to go dancing or to the movies in the evenings. Claire and Sydney worked out many of the stresses of their relationship arising from the joining of their two family groups, but they began to argue over weekend plans and future arrangements (Visher and Visher, 1988: 161–62).

Remarriage creates a unique set of strengths and problems because it *combines people from at least two families.* Imagine the transition process involved when a custodial mother marries a custodial father and the couple then decide to have their own children. Each partner's children from the former marriage may fear that new children will be loved more or receive more attention because they belong to both partners rather than just to one or the other. For their part, the parents may worry about dividing their attention among three sets of children so that none feels left out. To complicate matters further, ex-spouses and ex-grandparents may want to have input to the new family system—input that may not be welcomed by the remarried spouses.

Finally, remarriage partners sometimes seek someone who is *more successful, more supportive, or more attractive* than the ex-spouse. The box "Trophy Wives, Trophy Husbands in Remarriages" examines this phenomenon at the higher socioeconomic levels of American society.

Courtship After Divorce

Despite the ending of the popular movie *War of the Roses,* most divorcing couples do not kill each other. They survive the divorce, and often the partners start dating again even before the divorce is legally final. To insulate themselves from the pain of divorce, many people rush into another relationship: "It's not unusual to see women and men frantically dating in the first year after their separation, trying to fill the void with an intense new love or even with just another warm body" (Ahrons, 1994: 65).

If the partners are young and have not been married very long, reentering the "dating scene" will not be very difficult. Dating and courtship may be more difficult for older men and women or for those who have been married a long time because they may feel insecure about new dating patterns. For example, one of my friends, a woman who divorced after 12 years of marriage, wanted to establish new relationships but was very anxious about dating: "Am I supposed to pay for myself when we go to dinner? Should I just meet him at the restaurant, or do men still pick women up? What if he wants to jump into bed after the first date?" Although all dating couples—whether or not they have been married previously—often express the same concerns, people who have not been dating for many years are usually much more anxious. Divorced people tend not only to feel that their dating skills are "rusty" but to be less self-confident in approaching new relationships because they believe they "failed" in their marriages. Both divorced men and women may avoid dating altogether or marry on the rebound, and some parents who date frequently may feel guilty about being unavailable to their children (Montgomery et al., 1992).

Custodial mothers may sometimes rush into a new marriage because they want their children to have a father figure and male model. Such women, however, may be seen as less attractive dating partners by men who do not want to become encumbered with parental responsibilities.

Trophy Wives, Trophy Husbands in Remarriages

Fortune magazine, in 1989, ran a cover story on the "trophy wives" for which, the story said, chief executive officers (CEOs) were trading in their loyal, self-sacrificing, matronly, child-rearing wives. The newer, younger, and flashier trophy wives were sexier and socially adept. They pampered their husbands and never criticized them, spent money on these men rather than hoarding it for "the children's education," and generally made the CEOs feel like kings of the castle.

According to the *Fortune* article, second wives were enticing for a number of reasons. They were younger and thinner than the first wife and bolstered the man's corporate image of being successful both professionally and sexually. Because many of these women were successful in their own right (many were well educated and had thriving small businesses of their own), they enhanced the man's status without overshadowing his success. The trophy wives also spent a lot of time on looking good. For example,

Nancy Brinker, 42, the third wife of Norman Brinker, 58, who founded the Steak and Ale and Bennigan's restaurant chains and who was the CEO of Chili's restaurant chain, said, "I work out one hour a day at aerobics, I diet rigorously, and I play polo with my husband. . . . Norman likes me to look good" (Connelly, 1989: 54).

Unlike the first wife, who is busy caring for the children, the trophy wife has the time and connections to improve her husband's reputation: "She totes him to small dinner parties, opera galas, museum benefits, and auctions for worthy causes, having secured the invitations by serving on various committees and getting her husband to cough up something suitable in the way of a donation" (p. 54).

Most important, the trophy wife has the advantage of being glamorous, independent, and available because she is not saddled with the husband's children: "The CEO now wants a playmate, someone who is free to travel with him and have fun" (p. 61). The husband can play father when he wants to, rather than when he must. His children

need not interfere in his or his trophy wife's economic or romantic life: "Having pots of money may ease the burden of not being there because the CEO can afford to fly the kids out to see him and go on exciting vacations with them" (p. 61).

More recently, Finke (1994) has suggested that a handful of successful women are now seeking trophy husbands in *their* second or third marriages: "The basic criterion is this: No matter how successful a woman is in her profession, he is at least her equal, and maybe her better. He has three or more of the five attributes that tend to accompany achievement: fame, prestige, power, brains, and money" (pp. 37, 39). For example, when news star Diane Sawyer married Academy Award–winning director Mike Nichols, the media circles claimed that "they hadn't so much wed as 'acquired' each other." Further, "Kennedy cousin Maria Shriver brought home perhaps the only thing she could find bigger than her famous family—Arnold Schwarzenegger" (p. 40).

Although some custodial parents believe that early dating will further disrupt their children's lives, some research suggests that delaying dating may increase rather than decrease future problems. In a longitudinal study of 57 remarried stepfather families with children ages 9 to 13, Montgomery et al. (1992) found that the more time children spent in a single-parent household, the more likely it was that a stepfather and his stepchildren would experience difficulties in their relationships.

Why is this the case? The researchers proposed several explanations. For one thing, daily family routines become more and more entrenched as time goes by, and changing accepted routines and rules may be especially stressful for

young adolescents. It may be less disruptive for children to move into a remarriage household relatively quickly after a divorce than to establish a stable single-parent household only to have that stability disrupted by another transition. In addition, divorced mothers often rely on their children, especially their daughters, for emotional support. The closer this dependency becomes, the more difficult it may be for a daughter to accept the loss of her role as her mother's confidante and supporter. And finally, a stepfather who provides emotional and financial support can be an important mainstay for the family.

Despite such constraints—or perhaps because of them—many divorced couples have very short dating and engagement periods (see Data Digest). Dating couples spend only half as much time dating and courting before remarriage—a median of seven months of dating and two months of engagement—as they do before a first marriage (O'Flaherty and Eells, 1988). Furthermore, divorced people rarely take steps to ensure a more successful remarriage. For example, in a study of men and women who were preparing for remarriage, Ganong and Coleman (1989) found that only about 50 percent discussed their children from a previous marriage, fewer than 25 percent said that they talked about financial matters, and 13 percent said they did not discuss any substantive issues at all.

Although these findings should not be generalized, they suggest that dating and courtship before a remarriage may be somewhat superficial. Wouldn't people be more careful "the second time around"? Not necessarily. Ganong and Coleman (1994) speculate that Americans are generally not oriented to preventing problems before they occur, and that couples considering remarriage are probably no exception. Some people may rush through the courtship process because they feel they are running out of time or are desperate for financial or child-rearing help. Others may feel that they do not need as much time to get to know each other because they have learned how to avoid past mistakes. As we will discuss later in this chapter, high redivorce rates show that such assumptions are often wrong.

Remarriage as a Process

Like divorce, remarriage is a process, but it is generally more complicated than divorce. For one thing, there are fewer social or legal guidelines for the remarried. If the husband's ailing mother wants to move in with her son, for example, should the second wife be willing to care for her? Or if the remarried couple didn't draw up a prenuptial agreement or a will and are killed in a car accident, should all of the children share in the estate, even though most of the estate came from one partner (Manners, 1993)? In addition, when problems arise that involve children from former marriages, should these issues be handled by the remarried couple? The children's biological parent or parents? Both biological and remarried partners?

According to Goetting (1982), the remarriage process may involve as many as six "stations," similar to Bohannon's six stations of divorce (see Chapter 16): emotional, psychic, community, parental, economic, and legal remarriage. Also like Bohannon's stages of divorce, the stages of remarriage aren't necessarily sequential, and not every couple goes through all of them or with the same intensity. If partners can deal successfully with each stage, they will emerge with a commitment to a new identity as a couple.

Emotional Remarriage The *emotional remarriage* is often a slow process in which a divorced person reestablishes a bond of attraction, commitment, and trust with a member of the opposite sex. Because many people feel inadequate after a divorce, this process often involves a fear that the new emotional investment will also lead to loss and rejection. These feelings may make the emotional remarriage a painful or volatile process.

Psychic Remarriage Through the process of *psychic remarriage* people change their identities from individuals to couples once more. Because for many men social status and personal identity are relatively independent of marital status, a shift in marital status does not represent an extreme change in personal identity. Because the marital scene has traditionally been seen as the woman's domain, however, the identify shift for a woman may be more difficult. For a traditional woman, the psychic remarriage represents the recovery of a valued identity as a wife. A nontraditional woman, however, for whom the role of wife is less important, may worry about the loss of her highly valued independence and freedom.

Community Remarriage In *community remarriage*, people must often make changes in their community of friends. This may be a turbulent process because unmarried friends, especially friends of the opposite sex, are typically lost and replaced by married or remarried couples. During the community remarriage stage, close personal ties that were established after a divorce may be severed. Thus, although the community divorce represents reentrance into the "normal" world of a married couple's common friends, it may also mean the loss of valuable friendships. It may be very painful to break off from friends who were there during personal crises.

Parental Remarriage The *parental remarriage* involves developing relationships between one partner and the children of the new spouse. If the children's other biological parent still plays an active role in their lives, the stepparent may have many hurdles to overcome. He or she cannot assume the role of either father or mother but must behave as a nonparent, deferring to the biological parent's rights. The stepparent and the biological parent generally share in making the residential, educational, financial, health, and moral decisions that affect the children. Because there are no guidelines for this formal cooperation, the parental remarriage stage can lead to confusion and frustration.

In some families, biological nonresidential fathers may step aside as stepfathers move in. In their national study of different family forms, for example, Acock and Demo (1994) found that children in divorced families averaged three weeks per year staying with their nonresidential father, compared to a little more than one week per year for children in stepfamilies.

Another difficulty in this stage is that remarried couples often fail to work out their expectations of each other as marital partners before they have to take on major responsibilities within marriage, such as child rearing. Particularly when one or both partners have children from previous marriages, there may be little time to develop workable and comfortable marital relationships and to establish a primary husband-wife bond before the arrival of children. Instead, both marital and parental roles must be assumed simultaneously, and this may encourage the inappropriate involvement of children in marital dissension. For example, the biological parent's prior relationship to his or her child can threaten the establishment of a primary husband-wife bond. This, in turn, may detract from the integration of the new family unit.

Economic Remarriage The *economic marriage* is the reestablishment of a marital household as an economically productive unit. The main problems in this stage stem from the existence of children from a former marriage. The economic behavior of the remarried couple and that of the ex-spouse(s) are often interrelated. For example, child-support payments may become sporadic once a custodial mother has remarried.

Filling the role of stepparent may be easier when stepchildren are grown than when they are very young.

Many stepfamilies can't predict how much money will be available from month to month because of the uncertainty of such payments.

Another source of economic instability is the unpredictable nature of the needs of the husband's children, who typically live with their biological mother. The possibility of unexpected expenses, such as dentists' and doctors fees, can cast a shadow over the remarriage. And there may be disagreements about the distribution of resources: If *his* daughter is taking ballet lessons, should he also pay for *her* son's tennis lessons? If the noncustodial parent is not honoring child-custody payments, should the stepparent provide the money for recreational, educational, and social expenses for the children?

Legal Remarriage   Current laws provide little guidance for remarried couples (see Ramsey, 1994). Remarriage does not mean that a person exchanges one family for another but, rather, that she or he takes on an additional family. Because legal responsibilities have not been defined, people are left to struggle with many problems on their own. For example, the *legal remarriage* raises such questions as which wife deserves a man's life and accident insurance, medical coverage, retirement benefits, pension rights, and property holdings. Do these legal rights belong to the former wife, who played a major role in building the estate, or to the current wife? Which children should a remarried father support—especially in such high-priced endeavors as providing a college education—his, hers, or theirs?

Goetting notes that each station of remarriage may be further complicated if one or both partners is still adjusting to his or her divorce. Some people begin the stages of remarriage without having completed the stages of divorce.

Remarriage and Marital Satisfaction

A popular song tells us that "love is better the second time around." But as we have seen, remarriages must often deal with more complicated issues than first marriages. Are second or third marriages more stable? Do remarried spouses cope more effectively with family problems? *Are* they happier the second time around?

Marital Stability   The results of studies comparing remarriages with first marriages are somewhat conflicting. A number of earlier stud-ies found that redivorce rates were slightly higher than divorce rates (see, for example, Martin and Bumpass, 1989; Norton and Miller, 1991). One of the most recent nationwide studies suggests, however, that when age is factored in, second marriages may be more stable than first marriages. Clarke and Wilson (1994) reported that among their nationwide sample, slightly fewer remarriages than first marriages ended in divorce. In addition, the most stable marriages were remarriages between people who were 45 years of age or older and in which *both* partners had been married before. The highest divorce rates were among couples, one of whom had been married before and both of whom were under 25 when they married. The researchers suggest that older couples may choose their second mates more carefully, have more resources to make the marriage work, and/or are reluctant to divorce again.

Why, in general, do remarried people divorce? There are several possible reasons. People who marry for the first time during their teenage years are more likely to divorce after a second marriage (Wilson and Clarke, 1992). This may reflect a lack of problem-solving skills or immaturity in dealing with marital conflict. Booth and Edwards (1992) described the people most likely to redivorce as "divorce prone." These couples saw divorce as a remedy for marital dissatisfaction, they married for the first time as teens, and they often felt estranged from their parents and their spouse's parents. These researchers also noted that the presence of stepchildren was related to high redivorce rates. Wineberg (1991) found that women who had a child between marriages were more likely to divorce than women who did not: Intermarital birth may force a newly married couple to cope with an infant rather than devote time to their marriage.

Marital Quality   For several reasons, the data on marital satisfaction in remarriage are mixed. First, much research in this area is fairly recent and is not based on national samples. Second, and perhaps more important, many researchers have changed their theoretical approaches. Initially, researchers took a problem-oriented perspective in which they compared remarriages to first marriages and found remarriages and step-families deviant or dysfunctional. By the mid-1980s, however, researchers had increasingly begun to abandon the problem-oriented perspective and had adopted a normative-adaptive perspective that described divorce and remarriage not as pathological but as normative lifestyle choices that are firmly established in society (Coleman and Ganong, 1991). Thus, current findings reflect both a limited body of knowledge and the gradual maturing and changing of theoretical and methodological paradigms. With these caveats in mind, we return to the initial question: How happy are remarried couples?

Vemer et al. (1989) examined past studies and concluded that, although people in first marriages reported greater satisfaction than did remarried spouses, the differences were minuscule and "certainly not substantial." Coleman and Ganong (1991), reviewing the remarriage literature, came up with the similar conclusion that there were very few differences between the two groups.

Besides family structure and composition, the internal dynamics of the remarried couple also affect marital satisfaction. According to Ihinger-Tallman and Pasley (1987), the instability of a remarriage may reflect failure in one of four main areas: commitment, cohesion, communication, and the maintenance of the family's boundaries.

People may fail to make a *commitment* to a remarriage because, having survived one divorce, they may feel that another divorce is a ready remedy for an unhappy marriage and they may thus make less effort to make the remarriage work. They may be unwilling to invest the time and energy necessary to try to resolve problems. Or one or both partners may have personal and/or emotional problems. For example, alcoholics, drug users, those who are physically violent, or those who are emotionally unstable are more likely to move in and out of marriage repeatedly.

Achieving *cohesion,* or developing bonds that hold the family together, requires time and effort. Merging two families is difficult because the members have no shared family history. To reduce conflict, family members may have to develop new rules (how many phone calls each member may make in an evening, or by what hour the children must be home) and redistribute resources (who may use the family car and when, or how much each child will receive as an allowance).

Communication is also important. Particularly if lack of communication was a problem in one or both partner's previous marriages, couples may have to break old habits and learn to interact with each other differently. Establishing effective communication may be especially diffi-

cult if children from a former marriage are part of the new family, in part because the couple has less time and privacy to cultivate new communication patterns.

Finally, remarried couples must deal with more *boundary-maintenance* issues than do people in first marriages. For example, people in remarriages often have to insulate themselves against undue interference from outside sources, such as ex-spouses and in-laws from the first marriage. Furthermore, as we have already noted, remarried couples have to spend more effort establishing boundaries with new family members and new relatives, especially if one of the partners is a custodial parent.

STEPFAMILIES

A **stepfamily** is a household in which there is an adult couple and at least one of the partners has a child from a previous marriage. Such terms as *blended family, reconstituted family,* and *binuclear family* are often used interchangeably with "stepfamily."

Stepfamilies Are Complex and Diverse

When a stepfamily is formed, new family networks emerge. Look at Figure 17.3. This genogram presents a picture of the possible family systems when two people who have been married before and have children from previous marriages marry each other. A **genogram** is simply a diagram showing the biological relationships among family members.

Stepfamilies can vary in terms of parent-child relationships. There are three most common types of stepfamily: In the **biological mother-stepfather family,** all the children are biological children of the mother and stepchildren of the father. In the **biological father-stepmother family,** all the children are biological children of the father and stepchildren of the mother. In the **joint biological-stepfamily,** at least one child is the biological child of both parents, at least one child is the biological child of only one parent and the stepchild of the other parent, and no other type of child is present.

Stepfamilies can get more complicated. The term *complex stepfamily* describes a family in which both adults have children from previous marriages. But there are even more complex relationships. For example, in joint step-adoptive fam-

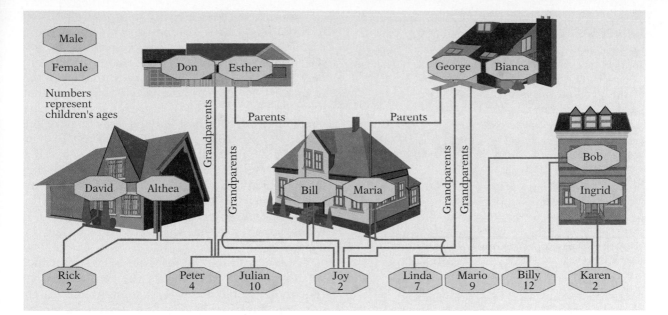

Figure 17.3 Stepfamily Networks. *Each set of parents of our target couple, Bill and Maria, are grandparents to at least two sets of children. For example, Maria's parents are the grandparents of her children with her former husband, Bob—Billy, Mario, and Linda—and of her child with Bill—Joy. Depending on the closeness of the relationship Bill maintains with his former wife, Althea, however, Maria's parents might play a grandparental role to Peter and Julian, Bill and Althea's boys, as well* (Based on Everett and Everett, 1994, p. 132).

ilies and joint biological-step-adoptive families, at least one child is a biological child of one parent and a stepchild of the other parent and at least one child has been adopted by one or both parents. Nor does "complex stepfamily" take account of relationships between cohabitants, one or both of whom have been married before and have children from earlier relationships, even though such cohabitants often consider themselves stepfamilies. The concept of stepfamily could also be expanded to include the increasingly common situation in which an unmarried mother and her child move in with a man who is not the child's biological father (Cherlin and Furstenberg, 1994). And some writers suggest that gay and lesbian stepfamilies should not be overlooked, although as yet there is practically no research in this area (Crosbie-Burnett and Helmbrecht, 1993).

A Demographic Profile of Stepfamilies

Children today live in a more diverse array of households than ever before. As Table 17.1 shows, in 1991 about 85 percent of U.S. children

were living with a biological mother and father. Nearly 10 percent lived in stepfamilies, and just over 1 percent lived with adoptive parents. Most children in stepfamilies live with a biological mother and a stepfather because it is still unusual for a father to retain custody of children under 18 years of age after a divorce (see Chapter 16). In 1991, only 830,000 children lived with a biological father and a stepmother, whereas 3.7 million lived with a biological mother and a stepfather (Furukawa, 1994).

Negative Images of the Stepfamily

The myth of the evil stepmother, perpetuated in Western culture by such classic tales as *Cinderella* and *Snow White*, is still so strong that Hallmark Cards' "Just How I Feel" line sells a card for a stepmother that tells her, "Whoever invented wicked stepmothers didn't know you" (Larson, 1992: 40). This myth, which presents stepmothers as cruel and unloving people who abuse or even try to get rid of their unwanted stepchildren, has had ripple effects over time so that many people have come

Table 17.1

Children's Living Arrangements, 1991

CHARACTERISTICS OF PARENTS	ALL RACES	WHITE	BLACK	HISPANIC ORIGIN[1]
Biological mother and father	85%	85%	81%	86%
Biological mother and stepfather	8	8	8	8
Biological father and stepmother	2	2	1	1
Adoptive mother and father[2]	1	1	2	1
Foster mother and father[3]	—	—	1	—
Other	4	4	7	4

[1]Persons of Hispanic origin may be of any race.

[2]Children living with one biological parent and one adoptive parent have been placed in a biological/stepparent category

[3]Foster relationships only include official placements by a government agency or representatives of a government agency.

SOURCE: Adapted from Furukawa, 1994, p.4.

to view the whole idea of the stepfamily with a jaundiced eye. In several survey studies, for example, college students offered more negative evaluations of stepparents than of biological, adoptive, or widowed parents (Bryan et al., 1986; Schwebel et al., 1991).

In contrast, the more recent "myth of instant love" maintains not only that remarriage creates an instant family but that stepmothers will automatically love their stepchildren because—according to another myth, discussed in Chapter 12—mothering comes easily and naturally to all women. Just why the stepmother has been more maligned than the stepfather or stepsiblings is a question that space won't allow us to explore here (see Quick et al., 1994, for a summary of the research). Whatever the answer, it is clear that the members of a newly constituted family who confront both of these myths may experience considerable stress as they try to adapt to new personalities, new lifestyles, and new schedules and routines (Dainton, 1993). And considering the unrealistic views that people hold of the intact nuclear family (see the section on Myths About Marriage and the Family in Chapter 1), it is not surprising that the stepfamily suffers by comparison.

One reason for the persistence of such widespread negative attitudes is the limited knowledge most people have about stepfamilies. An article on marriage-and-family textbooks noted that these texts generally based their accounts not on empirical data but on clinical work with people in distress or on popular, self-help source materials. The latter have implied, however subtly, that stepfamilies are rarely successful (Nolan et al., 1984). A more recent article (Coleman et al., 1994) saw some improvement in textbook coverage of remarriage and stepfamilies but noted that the texts still focus largely on problems rather than on the potential strengths of stepfamilies or on the positive outcomes of such family mergers.

The power of the myths and unsubstantiated

It is important in stepfamilies to make sure that all children receive love and attention, and that if signs of jealousy appear, both parents listen and try to understand.

beliefs can be seen in the fact that adults often enter relationships with stepchildren with unrealistic expectations. Many stepmothers, for example, usually have one of three common misconceptions about stepmothering: (1) the stepchildren will have little impact on the new marriage; (2) we will all be one big, happy family; (3) we will both love our stepchildren as though they were our own (Burns, 1985). Many men also have unrealistic expectations of their new families. According to Pill (1990), in 41 percent of stepfamilies in the study, one or both partners said that they had entered remarried life expecting that their stepfamily would become as close as a nuclear family. Many of the couples, however, reported disappointment and astonishment when the everyday realities of stepfamily life were fraught with problems.

When researchers ask people in a neutral situation to evaluate interactions between parents and children, their judgments as to whether biological parents or stepparents are effective parents do not differ significantly. For example, Dukes (1989) presented undergraduates with vignettes about stepparents that depicted good, average, or bad relationships with stepchildren. The vignette of a good relationship was the following:

Ten-year-old Tom was told by his stepmother, Sue, to do some chores around the house when he got home from school. Sue carefully explained the chores, and she asked Tom questions about them to make sure he understood what was expected. Sue dashed off to work, and Tom went to school. Upon returning home, Sue found out that Tom had completed all of the chores in a satisfactory manner. She [commended] Tom for his good work.

Dukes found that when the students were given information about specific situations, such as the one about Tom and Sue, their evaluations of effective and ineffective parenting in stepfamilies and biological families were very similar. This suggests that information dispels myths about stepfamilies.

Characteristics of Stepfamilies

Because they are composed of married adults and children living in the same household, stepfamilies may look like intact nuclear families but they differ from such families in several ways. According to Visher and Visher (1988), the first eight characteristics tend to remain somewhat

constant over time, but the last four change as a stepfamily develops and grows.

1. Stepfamilies have a complex structure. It bears repeating that stepfamilies create new roles: stepparents, stepsiblings, half-siblings. As Figure 17.4 shows, many children in stepfamilies are with one parent due to divorce, death, or desertion. Black children in stepfamilies are more likely to live in one-parent families (24 percent) than their counterparts. It is important to recognize that this structure does not make stepfamilies better or worse than nuclear families; they are simply *different*.

Stepfamilies offer the possibility for

Figure 17.4 *Children Living in Blended Families.* *Note that people of Hispanic origin may be of any race* (Furukawa, 1994, p. 6).

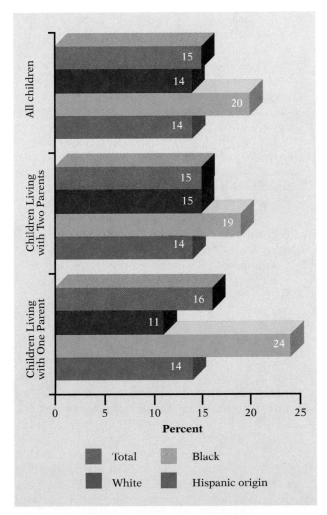

many different kinds of relationships, including relationships with uncles, aunts, and cousins. Ties between stepgrandparents and their stepgrandchildren range from no contact to close relationships, depending largely on the investment that stepgrandparents make (Cherlin and Furstenberg, 1994).

2. A stepfamily must fulfill different and unique tasks. Because of its more complex structure, a stepfamily must meet unique objectives. For example, the stepparent may struggle to overcome rejection because the children may still be grieving over the breakup of the biological family, or the stepparent may disagree with the biological parent about discipline and the enforcement of rules (Papernow, 1984).

    One of the most common tasks is redefining, and sometimes renegotiating, family boundaries. This may include making "visiting" children feel welcome, as well as working out "turf" problems:

    Consider the stepfamily in which the husband's three children rejoined the household every 3–4 days for a few days' time. The house was small, and the mother's three children who lived in the household had to shift where they slept, where they put their clothes, and where they could go to relax or to be alone in order to make the available space accommodate the extra family members. Bedrooms became dormitories, and the continual chaos created tension and instability for everyone (Visher and Visher, 1993: 241).

    The task of developing clear and consistent rules about "property rights" so that there is a stable place for each person is not an easy one.

3. Stepfamilies often have more stress than nuclear families. Much of the stress in stepfamilies is caused by ambiguity, complexity, and the "lack of fit" with cultural norms that, however unrealistically, define the "ideal" family. Ambiguity may decrease as family members adjust to new roles and lifestyles, and the sense that the family doesn't fit the ideal model may lose its intensity as family functioning improves.

    A major source of tension is the fact that family members must adjust to each other all at once rather than gradually, as the family grows. Stress may come from several

Sometimes a new baby causes stress in a stepfamily, but when the children from former marriages are adolescents or young adults, family members often adapt well to the new relationships.

sources: More people make more demands; parents may differ on how to discipline children; one partner may feel excluded from the relationship between her or his spouse and the spouse's biological children; or there may not be enough resources to meet the larger family's needs (Whitsett and Land, 1992).

4. Satisfactory stepfamily integration generally takes years, rather than months, to achieve. The age and sex of the children, as well as the type of stepfamily (stepmother, stepfather, children from both previous marriages) all can affect adjustment. As the box "The Stepfamily Cycle" suggests, it may take as long as seven years for a couple to consolidate their family and to work as a team. And if they have a new baby, or if there are unexpected problems such as unemployment or a death in the family, the process may take even longer.

5. Often, important relationships may be cut off or end abruptly. As we discussed in Chap-

The Stepfamily Cycle

Clinician Patricia Papernow (1993: 70–231) divides the process of becoming a stepfamily into three major stages. The early stage is characterized by fantasies, confusion, and slowly getting to know the others; in the middle stage the family begins to restructure; and in the late stage the family starts a solid identity.

THE EARLY STAGES: GETTING STARTED WITHOUT GETTING STUCK

Stage 1: Fantasy. Most remarrying couples start out not only with the fantasy that they will love the children of the person they love and be loved by them but that they will be welcomed into a ready-made family. They see themselves as filling empty spots for the children, for their spouses, and for themselves; and they believe they will be able to parent without the burdens and obligations of full-fledged biological parents.

Children in new stepfamilies, too, have fantasies, but they are a mixed collection of fear and hope. Most children fantasize that their biological parents will reunite. Thus they may fear losing or injuring one of their own parents if they come to love the stepparent of the same sex.

Stage 2: Immersion. This stage is often characterized by chaos and confusion. Familiarity and strangeness continually clash, but the problems are seen differently by biological parents, children, and stepparents. Stepparents may feel left out of the biological parent-child unit and may experience jealousy, resentment, and inadequacy. Feeling rejected is normal in this situation, but stepparents are often ashamed to tell anyone how they feel and may blame themselves for "their" failure to create a loving family.

The biological parent is often caught between the conflicting needs of the stepfamily members. Some exhaust themselves trying to meet everyone's needs and make it all work; others try to deny the difficulties. Particularly in the latter case, the children may feel lost and ignored. Some children respond with tears and angry outbursts; others withdraw.

Stage 3: Awareness. Members of the stepfamily get to know each other and "map the territory" of each family member. Stepparents can learn about the children's likes and dislikes, their friends, and their memories without trying to influence the children. Biological parents can articulate how much change his or her children can tolerate and to try to find the right balance between overprotecting children and asking too much of them. Biological parents should also recognize the feelings and needs of their partners. Children should be encouraged to see their noncustodial parents and grandparents on both sides. They should also be encouraged to look at the positive aspects of the stepfamily, such as the love both parents offer, or want to offer, them.

THE MIDDLE STAGES: RESTRUCTURING THE FAMILY

Stage 4: Mobilization. It is in this critical stage that many stepfamilies fall apart. The stepparent's task is to identify a few important changes that matter and make a sustained effort to communicate these to other family members while at the same time maintaining respect and empathy for the biological unit. The biological parent's task is to voice the needs of her or his children and ex-spouse while supporting and empathizing with the stepparent's needs for change. Children may voice their own needs especially loudly to ease the pressures of their conflicting loyalties.

Stage 5: Action. In this stage, the stepfamily can begin to make larger moves to reorganize its structure by making some truly joint decisions about how the family will operate. The stepparent begins to play a more active role in the family, and the biological parent doesn't feel the pressure to be all things to all people. Family members begin to invent new rules and rituals and both parents work together as a team in making decisions and carving time out for themselves.

THE LATER STAGES: SOLIDIFYING THE STEPFAMILY

Stage 6: Contact. In this stage, family members may not be crazy about each other, but they begin to interact more easily. Even when differences emerge, family members are more willing to discuss them. There is less withdrawal and more recognition of each other's efforts when things go right. The stepparent has become a firm insider in the adult couple relationship, and has begun to forge a more intimate, authentic relationship with at least some of the stepchildren. The biological parent can now step aside as the children and stepparent communicate with each other more fully and honestly.

Stage 7: Resolution. Relationships begin to feel comfortable. The stepparent role is now well defined and solid, as stepparents become mentors to some of their stepchildren. Other stepparent-stepchild relationships have reached a mutually suitable distance. The adult stepcouple has become a sanctuary, a place to turn for empathy, support, and cooperative problem solving. The stepfamily finally has a sense of character and its own clear identity.

ter 16, many fathers have no contact with their children after a divorce. Furthermore, siblings are sometimes split between parents and rarely see one another.

6. There may be continual transitions. In a stepfamily, the cast of characters living in a household can change continuously. The boundaries between who is a member of a stepfamily and who is not are not always clear: Is the new spouse of a child's noncustodial parent a part of the child's family? And who decides this question?

   Many families agree to "permeable boundaries" so that children can see both of their biological parents and can move easily between households, not only when they are still young but also when they are adults. If each adult child has parents who are divorced or remarried, there may be some difficulty in juggling individual needs, family traditions, and emotional ties among as many as four families.

7. Stepfamilies are less cohesive than nuclear or single-parent households. Stepchildren often feel closer to biological parents than to stepparents. As children grow up, they may also feel alienated because of differential economic support (for example, if some children are supported during college and others are not), unequal favors (at least as they perceive them) bestowed by grandparents, and inheritance inequities.

8. Stepfamilies vary greatly in terms of their patterns of everyday life. Varying custody and residential arrangements require different daily or weekly routines. Moreover, within the household, the "expected" ways a family operates may not apply. For example, when one stepfamily with children from two former families found it beneficial for the children to eat separately from the adults and for the adults to spend Saturdays doing something without the children, they were labeled a "bad" stepfamily. Creativity and flexibility provide family members with the time and space—both physical and psychological—that they need to develop and grow.

   The need for creativity and variety may decrease over time, but situations often arise (such as weddings, births, deaths, and holidays) that may require unusual solutions and arrangements. Should the noncustodial father (who rarely visits his children) pay for

"You're right, I should spend more time with the kids. Which ones are ours?"
Medical Economics/January 25, 1993.

his daughter's wedding, or should her stepfather pay for it? Or, if both the biological and stepfather are important in a young woman's life, who should walk down the aisle with her at her wedding? Both of them?

9. Stepfamily members need to rid themselves of unrealistic expectations. As we have already seen, stepfamilies often compare themselves to biological families and have expectations that are idealized or naive. There is no reason why members of the family—aside from the newly married adults—should automatically feel any sort of familial relation to one another. They need to accept that it is physically and emotionally impossible for a stepfamily to try to mirror a biological family; there are simply too many players and too many new relationships. As you saw in the box on "The Stepfamily Cycle," stepfamilies must forge their own rules and identities.

10. There is no shared family history. The new stepfamily is a group of individuals who must develop meaningful, shared experiences. To do this, they must learn one another's patterns of communication (verbal and nonverbal) and interaction. New stepfamily members often speak of "culture shock": Because their own behavioral patterns and those of others in the household are often different, they sometimes feel as if

they were in an alien environment. One way to ease some of the strangeness is to mesh rituals. In one remarried family, when a major holiday was approaching, family members were asked to suggest favorite foods. By preparing and serving these dishes the new family can honor the traditions of the previous families (Imber-Black and Roberts, 1993).

11. There are many loyalty conflicts. Although questions of loyalty arise in all families, loyalty conflicts in stepfamilies are intensified by the complex family structure. For example, suppose a child in the stepfamily feels closer to the noncustodial parent or to that parent's new spouse than to the biological and custodial parent or that parent's new spouse. Should these relationships be nurtured despite the resentment of the custodial parent or stepparent?

Furthermore, a newly remarried adult must make a sustained effort to maintain loyalty to a new spouse despite loyalty to biological children. For example, when Gwen, who had lived with her mother and stepfather for nine years and then lived on her own while attending college, came back home for a time, her mother felt conflicted:

Hugh [Gwen's stepfather] wants her to pay rent. I don't want her to. I feel that at this point in her life I would be a little more lenient than Hugh is. A lot of the difficulty is that she's been away for five years and now she's back in the fold. Hugh's a very rigid person—everything is preplanned and set up that way and that's the way you do it. I'm a little more loose (Beer, 1992: 133).

Gwen's mother's task was to find ways to help her daughter that did not infringe on her responsibilities to her husband. Had her husband been as "loose" as she was, adjustment might have been easier for this stepfamily.

12. Stepfamily roles are often ambiguous. On the one hand, a positive aspect of role ambiguity is that it provides freedom of choice: One may be able to choose among a variety of roles played with different children and adults. For example, a stepparent who is willing to be a friend to the children rather than a parent can serve as a mediator when there is conflict between the children and the biological, custodial parent. On the other hand, ambiguity creates problems because people do not know what is expected of them or what to expect from others. A partner may not want a mediator but a spouse who offers support when there are disagreements with the children.

The Dynamics of Merging Two Households

There are a number of tasks in merging two households after a remarriage. Four of the most common issues are a lack of institutional support, the distribution of resources, the integration of children into the family, and the couple's interpersonal relationship.

Institutional Support The English language has fairly clear terms for defining relationships in intact families, such as "father," "mother," "brother," and "daughter." There are no words at all for many stepfamily relationships, however. For example, "my spouse's ex-spouse's new spouse" or "my stepsister's stepbrother" require most people to stop and think for several minutes before they can understand what is meant (Beer, 1992).

Why is the lack of family terminology in stepfamilies a problem? Suppose, for example, that a new wife's own children want to call their stepfather "Dad," but the stepfather's biological children, their security threatened, refuse to permit this? Bad feelings may result all around. Moreover, according to Beer (1992: 11), "It may be difficult to think clearly about a relationship when the words to describe it are inaccurate or when there is no word at all. Being unable to think clearly may make it more difficult to decide how to behave."

The law is also inadequate to regulate or guide families after remarriage. For example, most states prohibit sexual relations between siblings and between parents and children in nuclear, biological families but have no restrictions about sexual relations between members of a stepfamily—either between stepchildren or between a stepparent and a stepchild. As we discussed in Chapter 15, there is considerable research evidence that some stepfathers and male cohabitants abuse children sexually. Although only 8 percent of all children live with a stepfather, 30 percent of all cases of adult-child sexual abuse involve a stepfather (Levine, 1990). Also, stepsiblings may drift into romantic relationships, which can lead to serious problems within the stepfamily. As the box on "Dealing with Sexual Boundaries in the Stepfamily" suggests, one way to cope with such sexual problems is to prevent them in the first place.

Resource Distribution Financial matters are more complicated in stepfamilies than in first marriages. Financial planners and marriage experts are nearly unanimous in urging people who are planning a second marriage to spell out their financial obligations to each other in a legally binding prenuptial agreement. The issues to be resolved include whether to share financial responsibility for children from previous marriages, how to divide up estates, whether to merge assets and liabilities, and how to divide property acquired before and after the marriage in case of divorce (Rowland, 1994).

The rules that control disposition of an estate vary from state to state, but almost everywhere, the spouse is entitled to a major share, from 25 to 50 percent. And no matter where you live, federal law says the spouse is the sole beneficiary of your company pension or profit-shar-

CRITICAL ISSUES

Dealing with Sexual Boundaries in the Stepfamily

Only some states prohibit romantic relationships between nonbiologically related members of a stepfamily. The weakened incest taboo within the stepfamily makes rules less clear (Bloomfield, 1993), but sexual liaisons can create confusion, anger, and a sense of betrayal. Practitioners Emily and John Visher (1982: 162–66) offer the following suggestions to remarried partners for dealing with sexuality in the stepfamily:

❏ Be affectionate and tender but not passionate with each other when the children are with you. Teenagers are particularly sensitive to open displays of affection because of their own emerging sexuality. Be aware of this sensitivity and forgo the stolen kisses and embraces in the kitchen.

❏ Don't be sexually provocative. Walking around in undershorts or a bra and panties are guaranteed not to keep sexuality under control in your household, even when there are only younger children around. Set a limit on teenagers' behaving in provocative ways. The first time a teenager parades around the house scantily or inappropriately clad, for example, he or she should be told firmly to go back to his or her room and to dress properly. Be firm in setting limits for appropriate dress and behavior.

❏ Avoid roughhousing with children after they are 10 or 11 years old. This kind of behavior may become a physical turn-on between stepsiblings or between children and stepparents.

❏ Relinquish some forms of intimate behavior with children after they turn 10 or 11 years of age. For example, sitting on a stepfather's lap and showering him with kisses is inappropriate behavior for a teenage stepdaughter.

❏ If a teenager develops a crush on a stepparent, talk to him or her openly. Discuss the nature of crushes. Point out that the teen's affections are misplaced (for example, you're older, you're married to his or her parent). Suggest alternatives, such as schoolmates. Finally, make it clear that there is a big difference between feelings and behavior, that just because people are attracted to others does not mean that they act on their impulses.

❏ When you and your partner are having an argument or there is some emotional distance between you, don't turn for emotional support to a younger person in the household. You may open the door to the expression of feelings of intimacy that ought not be encouraged. Instead, keep the lines of communication open between you and your partner.

❏ Rearrange the living space to cool off a sexual situation between stepsiblings. For example, avoid adjoining bedrooms and rearrange the bathroom sharing so that older children have both privacy and less temptation.

❏ Do not tolerate sexual involvement in your home. In one family, the adults asked the college-aged son to move out of the house because they were unwilling to accept his sexual relationship with his stepsister. Although stepparents can't control sexual attractions between stepsiblings, they can control what happens in their home.

ing plan, both of which may be the major portion of an estate. Unless there is a prenuptial agreement that allows a future spouse to waive his or her rights to a set share of an estate, children from a previous marriage may be practically disinherited even though this was not the intention of the parent (Spears, 1994).

Legal experts also advise setting up a trust fund to safeguard the biological children's or grandchildren's inheritance. Trusts allow parents to transmit gifts and inheritances to whomever they choose while they are alive or after their death. In addition, to minimize family friction, attorneys advise people to discuss their estate plans with those who are affected by them (Spears, 1994).

The partners must decide whether or not to pool their resources and how to do so. They may experience stress and resentment if there are financial obligations to a former family (such as custody awards, mortgage payments, or outstanding debts). There may also be conflict about whose children should be supported at college or how wills should be written (whether the common property should be divided equally between the two families or among the children). Disagreements may range from seemingly petty issues like how much should be spent for relatives' birthday and wedding presents to drastically different attitudes about whether money should be saved or spent. All of these issues should be discussed honestly and openly before a remarriage.

Because men typically have more economic resources than women do, stepfathers may have more decision-making power in the new family. Sometimes men use money to control the children's and spouse's behavior ("If you don't shape up, you can pay for your own car insurance next time"). This kind of manipulation creates hostility. The children of remarried fathers are typically at a financial disadvantage because the stepchildren may receive more support, such as loans, money gifts, and health coverage (White, 1992; see also Aquilino, 1994). The loss of economic support can impoverish biological children and produce hostility.

Resources such as time, space, and affection must also be allocated and distributed equitably so that all family members feel content with the new living arrangements. Mothers with live-in stepchildren sometimes are angry about spending much of their time and energy on stepchildren and feel that they receive few rewards in the process:

I'd rather not have my stepsons. Mind you, I care for them and I am attached to them but I never set out to have children, and having someone else's children is a burden. I often resent it. At the same time, I wish they didn't have their mother so that way I would benefit at least from being a mother. But in my situation I have all the problems a mother has since they live here and none of the advantages, maybe less so with the younger one because he was so little when I moved in (Ambert, 1986: 799).

When I was 28, I fell in love with a widower who was 38. He had four children. The youngest was 4 and the oldest was 12. Little did I know at the time that he was [only] looking for a mother for his children. . . . I have some advice for any woman who is considering marrying a man with children: Find a psychiatrist and get your head examined (from a Dear Abby *letter,* Baltimore Sun, *November 8, 1993, p. 2D).*

Relationships with Children   Several national studies have suggested that children from stepfamilies show only slightly less emotional, social, and familial adjustment than children from intact nuclear families (see Ganong and Coleman, 1994, for a summary and review of some of these studies). Hetherington (1993) found that 80 percent of the children of divorce and remarriage had no problems, compared to 90 percent of children in first-marriage families. Studying families of different structures, Hetherington and Clingempeel (1992) found that almost three times as many children in single-mother and remarried households as in nondivorced households were described by their mothers as having serious behavioral problems. On a positive note, however, young children recover from the debilitating effects of divorce or remarriage more quickly than do adolescent children.

Many factors affect the relationships among parents, stepparents, children, and stepchildren. For example, stepfathers are more likely than are stepmothers to have good relationships with their stepchildren, probably because the stepmother is more often the disciplinarian (Kurdek and Fine, 1993). If she is at home more of the time, she may be more involved in raising the stepchildren, and she is often expected to play a more active domestic role than is the father. Regardless of the parent's gender, relations between children and parents in both intact and remarried homes are more positive when the parents include the children in decision making and are supportive rather than always critical (Barber and Lyons, 1994; Crosbie-Burnett and Giles-Sims, 1994).

Parent-child relations are more distant when both adults bring children from previous marriages into the stepfamily (Clingempeel et al., 1994). The quality of the stepparent-stepchild relationship is also affected by whether the spouses are satisfied with the remarriage. Finally, stepfathers may have more positive and responsive attitudes toward children than do biological fathers. They may be less supportive, but they are also less punitive and controlling. In fact, a stepfather may resemble a sociable and polite stranger who wants to make a good impression (Hetherington, 1989).

Even though many stepfathers are more permissive than stepmothers, two of the biggest problems in stepfamilies concern discipline and authority, especially in relationships between a stepfather and adolescents. Teenagers complain, "He's not my father and I don't have to listen to him." Stepfathers resent not being obeyed both because they consider themselves authority figures and because they may be working hard to support the family. Mothers may feel caught in the middle. Although they love their husbands, they may feel guilty for having married someone whom the children do not like, or they may disagree with the stepfather's disciplinary measures (Giles-Sims and Crosbie-Burnett, 1989).

There may be other difficulties in merging children into one household. Whether they intend it or not, when parents find themselves forming strong relationships with the children of a new partner, they may feel that they are betraying their biological children. Similarly, children may feel guilty if they find themselves liking a stepparent better than a biological parent because the stepparent is more fun, more understanding, or easier to get along with (Papernow, 1993). Integrating a stepfamily that includes teenagers can be particularly difficult because adolescents begin to move away from their parents during puberty. If adolescent children have supportive relationships with friends, neighbors, and other relatives, their adjustment after a remarriage will be smoother (Quick et al., 1994). Finally, regardless of age, "visiting" children may feel awkward and uncomfortable, and if their visits are intermittent, they may not develop a sense of belonging or fitting in. As we noted earlier, however, ensuring that each family member

When a parent and stepparent must go to court over such things as support payments owed by a child's biological father, the pressures felt by the child may result in expressions of hostility toward the stepparent.

has stable physical space can lessen the alienation of "visitors."

As some data show that stepfamilies are faring better than we thought, how can we explain the persistence of the negative stereotypes we've described? One reason may be that some aspects of stepfamilies are more problematic than others and that these are the only ones we hear about. For example, several studies have found that stepdaughter-stepfather relationships are more negative than are those between stepsons and stepparents of either sex. Even when stepfathers make friendly overtures, stepdaughters may withdraw (Vuchinich et al., 1991). One explanation for this distancing behavior is that daughters, who once had a privileged status in the family because they shared much of the authority in helping to raise younger children, may resent being replaced with someone with more power in the family (Fischman, 1988). The stepdaughter-stepfather relationship may also be more distant because the stepfather has made sexual overtures or behaved in other inappropriate ways toward the stepdaughter (see Chapter 15).

Whatever the reasons for the problems experienced by girls in remarried families, they are serious enough to cause adolescent girls to leave stepfamily households at an earlier age than do girls in single-parent or intact homes. Stepdaughters also leave earlier to establish independent or cohabiting households (Goldscheider and Goldscheider, 1993). In a British study, 23-

year-olds were asked the main reason why they left their parental homes. Those who had lived in stepfamily households were substantially more likely than those who had lived in intact households to report that they left due to "friction at home" (Kiernan, 1992).

In many cases, the negative reactions of children (especially young children) are fairly short-lived. According to several national studies, stepmothers and stepchildren establish more positive relationships within a few years (Baydar, 1988; Hetherington and Clingempeel, 1992). Stepfathers, especially, caution new stepparents to be patient in establishing new relationships after a remarriage. In describing the gradual process of developing a relationship with the stepchild, one stepfather commented, "Brian is different now. At first he was reclusive and jealous and he saw me as infringing. It was a slow progression" (Santrock et al., 1988: 159). The box "The Ten Commandments of Stepparenting" provides some dos and don'ts for stepparents.

CHOICES

The Ten Commandments of Stepparenting

All families have to work at peaceful coexistence. Turnbull and Turnbull (1983: 227–30) offer the following advice to stepparents who want to increase family harmony.

1. *Provide neutral territory.* Most people have a strong sense of territoriality. Stepchildren may have an especially strong sense of ownership because some of their privacy may be invaded. If it is impossible to move to a new house where each child has a bedroom, provide a special, inviolate place that belongs to each child individually.

2. *Do not try to fit a preconceived role.* Be honest right from the start. Each parent has faults, peculiarities, and emotions, and the children will have to get used to these weaknesses. Children detect phoniness and will lose respect for any adult who is insincere or too willing to please.

3. *Set limits and enforce them.* One of the most difficult issues is discipline. Parents should work out the rules in advance and support each other in enforcing the rules. Rules can change as the children grow, but there should be agreement in the beginning on such issues as mealtimes, bedtimes, resolving disagreements, and household responsibilities.

4. *Allow an outlet for the children's feelings for the biological parent.* The stepparent should not feel rejected if a child wants to maintain a relationship with a noncustodial biological parent. Children's affections for their biological parents should be supported so that the children do not feel disloyal.

5. *Expect ambivalence.* Children's feelings can fluctuate between love and hate, sometimes within a few hours. Ambivalence is normal in all human relationships.

6. *Avoid mealtime misery.* Many families still idealize the family dinner hour as a time when family members have intelligent discussions and resolve problems. Although both parents should reinforce table manners, a less than blissful family mealtime should be ignored or sometimes avoided. Some suggested strategies include daily vitamins, getting rid of all junk foods, letting the children fix their own meals, eating out once in a while, and letting the father do some of the cooking.

7. *Do not expect instant love.* It takes time for emotional bonds to be forged; sometimes this never occurs. Most children under three years of age adapt with relative ease. Children over age five may have more difficulty. Some children are initially excited at having a "new" mother or father but later find that the words "I hate you" are potent weapons. This discovery frequently coincides with puberty. A thick skin helps in these hurtful times.

8. *Do not accept all the responsibility; the child has some, too.* Children, like adults, come in all types and sizes. Some are simply more lovable than others. Like it or not, the stepparent has to take what he or she gets. That does not mean assuming all the guilt for a less than perfect relationship, however.

9. *Be patient.* The words to remember here are "things take time." The first few months, and often years, are difficult. The support and encouragement of other parents who have had similar experiences can be invaluable.

10. *Maintain the primacy of the marital relationship.* The couple must remember that the marital relationship is primary in the family. The children need to see that the parents get along together, can settle disputes, and most of all, will not be divided by the children.

Intergenerational Relationships Ties across generations, especially with grandparents and stepgrandparents, can be healthy and meaningful or disruptive and intrusive. After a divorce or during a remarriage, grandparents can provide an important sense of continuity to children when many other things are changing. Although many children typically do not become as attached to their new stepgrandparents as to their biological grandparents, they can resent new grandparents who seem to neglect or reject them:

One twelve-year-old girl in our practice became angry and aggressive toward her two new and younger stepsiblings following their first Christmas holiday together, even though she had been very loving with them before that. Several weeks later she revealed to her father that she was hurt and disappointed because the stepsiblings received twice as many gifts from their grandparents as she received in total from everyone in the family (Everett and Everett, 1994: 140).

If parents notice big differences between the way grandparents treat different sets of children, they should discuss maintaining a sense of balance with the grandparents.

SUCCESSFUL REMARRIAGES AND STEPFAMILIES

What makes a remarried family successful? In a review of the literature, Visher and Visher (1993) suggest that six characteristics are common to remarried families in which children and adults experience warm interpersonal relationships and satisfaction with their lives. Don't worry if you have a feeling of déjà vu; some of these characteristics are in fact the opposite of the problems we've discussed earlier. The major point to remember is that these traits *can* be achieved. According to Crosbie-Burnett and Lewis (1993), moreover, white stepfamilies can learn something from African American family structures.

Characteristics of Successful Families

First, successful stepfamilies have developed *realistic expectations.* They have rejected the myth of instant love because they realize that trying to force a friendship or love simply doesn't work. In addition, they don't try to replicate the biological family because they accept the fact that the structure of the stepfamily is more complex. For example, teenagers who are beginning to rebel against authority generally are particularly sensitive to direction from adults. As one teenager in a stepfamily put it, "Two parents are more than enough. I don't need another one telling me what to do" (Visher and Visher, 1993: 245).

Second, adults in successful stepfamilies *let children mourn their losses.* These adults are sensitive to children's feelings of sadness and depression. They also support the children in their expression of fear and anger, neither punishing the children nor taking these reactions as personal rejection. According to Crosbie-Burnett and Lewis (1993), African American stepfamilies tend to focus more on nurturing and supporting a child than do white stepfamilies.

Third, the adults in well-functioning stepfamilies forge *a strong couple relationship.* This provides an atmosphere of stability because it reduces the children's anxiety about another parental breakup. It also provides children with a model of a couple who can work together effectively as a team and solve problems rationally.

Fourth, *the stepparenting role proceeds slowly.* A stepparent role is learned rather than acquired at a child's birth (see the discussion of achieved and ascribed status in Chapter 1). Except when there are young children present, the stepparent should take on disciplinary functions slowly. As one teenage girl stated, "My stepfather wasn't ever in my face, which was good, because I would have been mad if he had tried to discipline me" (Minton, 1995: 25). With teenagers, the biological parent should be the disciplinarian while the stepparent supports his or her behavior. In successful stepfamilies, adults realize that the relations between a stepparent and stepchildren can be quite varied—the stepparent may be a parent to some of the children, a companion to others, or just a good friend to all. And if there are no warm, interpersonal ties, it is enough that family members are tolerant and respectful of individual differences.

Here, again, white stepfamilies can learn from the experiences of many African American families. In black families, "living in two cultures simultaneously means that situations arise in which role expectations and definitions of self and family are ambiguous, or even in conflict" (Crosbie-Burnett and Lewis, 1993: 245). Thus, African American adults teach their children that there are several possible sets of behaviors, expectations, and roles.

Fifth, successful stepfamilies *develop their own rituals*. They recognize that there is more than one way to do the laundry, cook a turkey, or celebrate a birthday. It is not a matter of a right or a wrong way. Instead, successful remarried households may combine previous ways of sharing household tasks, develop new schedules of what to do together on the weekends, or try out several ways of sharing household tasks. The most important criteria are flexibility and a willingness to cooperate.

Finally, well-functioning stepfamilies *work out satisfactory arrangements between the children's households*. Adults don't have to like each other to be able to get along. In fact, it is useful for many adults to have a "business relationship" to work together during such family events as holidays, graduations, and weddings. Crosbie-Burnett and Lewis note that many African American families have flexible and permeable familial boundaries so that children feel welcome in several households regardless of biological "ownership." In addition, community members, including fictive kin (see Chapter 2), share material and emotional resources in raising children.

The Rewards of Remarriage and Stepparenting

Couples typically describe their remarriage as offering many more benefits than their first marriage. Many feel they learned valuable lessons in their first marriage and that they have matured as a result of the experience. They feel they know each other better than they knew their former spouses, talk more openly and more freely about issues that concern them, and are less likely to suppress their real feelings to avoid causing pain. Remarried couples say they try harder, are more tolerant of minor irritations, and tend to be more considerate of each other's feelings than they were in the first marriage. Finally, they report enjoying the new interests and new friends a remarriage brings (Westoff, 1977).

Reactions from stepparents are more mixed. For example, when Rosin (1987) asked stepfathers about the rewards they experienced, the responses ranged from one stepfather who felt that the rewards are "the same as the rewards of biological fathering" to another who said "none." In another study of 29 stepfamilies, nearly 33 percent of the couples said that living in a stepfamily required a continual and deliberate effort. One father wearily commented, "Stepfamily life is intense, and weekends feel like a workout!" Most were unprepared for the unrelenting nature of the demands placed on them (Pill, 1990: 190).

A child in a stepfamily may often be pulled between his biological father, with whom he spends time periodically, his mother, and his stepfather.

Despite the ups and downs, a stepfamily provides members with opportunities that may be missing in an unhappy, intact family. Because children see happy adults, they have positive models of marriage (Rutter, 1994). When remarried partners are happy, children benefit from being in a satisfying household. A well-functioning stepfamily increases the self-esteem and well-being of divorced parents and provides children who have lost touch with noncustodial parents with a caring and supportive adult (Pill, 1990). In addition, the children's economic situation is often improved after a parent, especially a mother, remarries (Cherlin, 1992). As you saw in Chapter 16, many mother-custody families are often plunged into poverty after a divorce.

One of the greatest benefits of remarriage and stepparenting is the opportunity to become more flexible and to learn patience. Family members learn to develop less rigid attitudes toward family issues and boundaries. Gender roles, for example, are less likely to be stereotypical because in well-functioning stepfamilies, both parents typically earn money, write checks, do housework, and take care of the children (Kelley, 1992).

In many stepfamilies, the children benefit by having a more objective sounding board to discuss problems, and they may be introduced to new ideas, different politics, and a new appreciation for art, music, literature, sports, or other leisure activities (Ihinger-Tallman and Pasley, 1987). Finally, if stepsiblings live together, they get more experience in interacting, cooperating, and learning to negotiate with peers.

In some cases, children don't recognize the contributions of stepparents until they themselves are adults. One of my students, who admitted to being very rebellious and "a real pain" after her mother remarried, is now grateful that her stepfather didn't give up:

The best solution to mine and my stepfather's problems was age. As I am getting older and supporting myself more and more, I realize just how much my stepfather has done for me. Even though he is not my "real" dad, he is the only father I have known. He has provided me with food, clothes, an education, and a home. Growing up, I thought I had it so rough. I now realize that he's my friend. It's funny, but now I actually enjoy watching TV or a movie with my stepfather (Author's files).

CONCLUSION

As this chapter shows, there *is* life after divorce. Of all the different marriage and family forms discussed in this textbook, stepfamilies are the most varied and complex. Thus, both children and adults must make many *changes* as the members adapt and work together. Despite high redivorce rates, remarriage and stepparenting give people more *choices* in establishing a well-functioning and satisfying family life. Although stepfamilies must deal with many *constraints* after a remarriage, there are also numerous rewards in establishing a new household.

Taking Action

Where to Get Professional Help

Seeking professional help may be helpful in dealing with remarriage and stepfamily problems.

• A useful resource is the **Stepfamily Association of America,** 215 Centennial Mall S, Suite 212, Lincoln, NE 68508 (402-477-STEP). Call for literature, resources, and videotapes on stepfamilies. This association has 70 chapters throughout the United States, holds annual conferences, and produces a quarterly publication.

• Biological parents and stepparents can play an important role in **encouraging state departments of education, school district administrators, school boards, and school-based professionals to support stepchildren and their families.** For example, state departments of education can sponsor educational workshops on stepfamilies for school personnel that describe children's experiences in stepfamilies. On a local level, counselors, psychologists, and therapists can facilitate discussion groups for parents that focus on school-related issues and student-focused problem solving (see Crosbie-Burnett, 1994: 211–15, for recom-

SUMMARY

1. The most dramatic changes in family structure and composition are due to remarriage and the formation of stepfamilies. Over 40 percent of marriages are remarriages for one or both partners.

2. Dating and courtship patterns vary by age and gender. Most divorced people marry within three or four years after a divorce.

3. Remarriage rates vary by sex, race, age, socioeconomic status, and marital status. Men remarry more quickly than do women; remarriage rates are much higher for white women than for African and Latino women; and women with low incomes and lower educational levels are the most likely to remarry.

4. Remarriage is a process that involves emotional, economic, psychic, community, parental, and legal aspects. Some of these phases occur independently of the existence of children, whereas others involve children.

5. There are several important differences between first marriages and remarriages. Some of these differences include the composition of the family, the children's experiences, stepfamily roles, life-cycle events, family goals and objectives, and family structure.

6. The research findings on remarriage and marital satisfaction are mixed, primarily because much of the research in this area is still recent and compares stepfamilies to first marriages.

7. Stepfamilies are very diverse in terms of parent-child relationships and their ties to biological families. Stepfamilies can have three "sets" of children under the same roof, which may result in strained living arrangements.

8. Stepfamilies still suffer from negative perceptions and stereotypes even though much of the research shows that stepfamilies are similar to biological families in fulfilling basic family functions.

9. Even though stepfamilies share many of the same functions as do intact nuclear families, there are a number of unique tasks in merging two households after a remarriage. Four of the most common issues are a lack of institutional support, the distribution of resources, the integration of children into the family, and intergenerational relationships.

10. Many couples who have remarried say they know each other better, communicate more openly, and are more considerate of each other's feelings than they were in their first marriage. Thus, although there are problems in remarriages, there are also many rewards.

KEY TERMS

half sibling   482
stepfamily   488

genogram   488
biological mother-stepfather family   488

biological father-stepmother family   488
joint biological-stepfamily   488

ADDITIONAL READING

HAROLD H. BLOOMFIELD with ROBERT B. KORY, *Making Peace in Your Stepfamily: Surviving and Thriving as Parents and Stepparents* (New York: Hyperion, 1993). This self-help book covers such topics as money matters, dealing with grandparents, and being proud of being part of a stepfamily. The bibliography includes 40 books for stepparents and 25 for stepchildren.

LAWRENCE H. GANONG and MARILYN COLEMAN, *Remarried Family Relationships* (Thousand Oaks, CA:

Sage, 1994). A good overview of much of the research on remarriage relationships, stepchild-stepparent relationships, and clinical and developmental perspectives.

CHRISTINA HUGHES, *Stepparents: Wicked or Wonderful?* (Brookfield USA: Avebury, 1991). As the title suggests, the author examines some of the myths about stepparenting.

N. B. MAGLIN and N. SCHNIEDEWIND, eds., *Women and Stepfamilies: Voices of Anger and Love* (Philadelphia: Temple University Press, 1989). Students who are interested in experiential discussions of stepfamilies may enjoy this collection of essays, letters, and poems written by stepmothers, stepdaughters, and stepgrandmothers.

GAY OCHILTREE, *Children in Stepfamilies* (Brookvalle, Australia: Prentice Hall, 1990). A good overview of the divorce and remarriage literature during the 1970s and 1980s; emphasizes both structure and process in stepfamilies.

PATRICIA L. PAPERNOW, *Becoming a Stepfamily: Patterns of Development in Remarried Families* (San Francisco: Jossey-Bass, 1993). Describes the stages involved in becoming a well-functioning stepfamily, with many experiential anecdotes.

KAY PASLEY and MARILYN IHINGER-TALLMAN, eds., *Stepparenting: Issues in Theory, Research, and Practice* (Westport, CT: Greenwood Press, 1994). The contributors discuss such issues as family relationships, marital adjustment, and the role of helping professions.

18

Aging and Family Life: Grandparents, the Widowed, and Caregivers

Data Digest

On a sweltering June weekend in Springfield, Massachusetts, more than 600 over-50-year-old athletes from 11 states competed in 20 events, ranging from basketball to the pole vault, in the 1994 U.S. National Senior Sports Classic. The 73-year-old woman who jumped 8 feet to win the gold medal in the long jump also won golds in the high jump, the shot put, and the hammer throw. Another contender, 84 years old in 1994, had collected 205 gold and 23 silver medals in such events as discus, shot put, javelin, and the 1500-meter run since the Senior Games began in 1992 (Rohde, 1994).

What's more, the contestants in the Senior Games are youngsters compared to many other active older people. Mieczyslaw Horszowski, the classical pianist, recorded a new album at age 99. At the same age, the twin sisters Kin Narita and Gin Kanie recorded a hit single in Japan and starred in a TV ad. At 97, Martin Miller of Indiana was working full time as a lobbyist for older citizens. At 92, Paul Spangler completed his fourteenth marathon, and at 91, Hulda Crooks climbed Mount Whitney, the highest mountain in the continental United States. Armand Hammer actively headed Occidental Petroleum at age 91 (Wallechinsky and Wallace, 1993). Comedian/actor George Burns, in his late 90s, is still performing at theaters and nightclubs as this book goes to press. Chef Julia Child tasted French food for the first time at the age of 37. She was in her 50s when she became famous for her expertise in French cuisine, her books, and her TV show, "Cooking with Julia Child"; in her 80s, in the spring of 1995, she embarked on a new show in which she played host to famous chefs from around the world. Although much younger than these other achievers, 65-year-old Connie Mason published her first novel at the age of 53 and continues to turn out at least two steamy romance novels (such as *Caress and Conquer* and *Wild Love*) per year, earning about $50,000 per title (Campbell, 1994).

Are these people unusual? Probably. But as we move into the twenty-first century, many older people will continue to be similarly active and productive. As the numbers of older people continue to grow (see Data Digest), the later years can become increasingly more interesting and fun. At the same time we must recognize that older family members must often deal with the death of loved ones, with their own health problems, and with both giving and receiving care. As this chapter shows, aging does result in changes for both older people and for their family and friends.

THE RISE OF MULTIGENERATIONAL FAMILIES

Despite the high incidence of illnesses like cancer and heart disease, people are continuing to live longer. More people are reaching age 65 than ever before, and American children born in 1990 have an average life expectancy of almost 76 years (Crispell, 1995). One of the fastest-growing groups are people over 85, a population that has increased more than 30 times (from 100,000 to 3 million) since the turn of the century. By 2030, this group is expected to constitute over 5 percent of the country's population (U.S. Senate Special Committee on Aging et al., 1991).

One of the most dramatic indicators of the aging of U.S. society is that the proportion of people age 65 and over is increasing while the proportion of young people is decreasing. A similar phenomenon is occurring in other societies (see the box "Protecting the Elderly in China"). As Figure 18.1 shows, by the year 2030 there will be more elderly people in the United States than young people. As a result, the years of parent-child relationships will be prolonged. Many adult children will need to care for frail and elderly parents, and many young children will have not only great-grandparents but great-great-grandparents as well.

Because many racial-ethnic groups in America have higher birth rates than whites, the numbers of elderly in these groups are expected to grow at an even greater rate. It has been estimated that between 1990 and 2030 the older white population will grow by 92 percent, but that the older African American and Hispanic American older populations will grow by 247 and 395 percent, respectively (U.S. Senate Special Committee on Aging et al., 1991). We discuss the implications of these burgeoning groups in Chapter 19.

AGING: CHANGES IN HEALTH AND SOCIAL STATUS

Gerontologists—scientists who study aging and the elderly—emphasize that the aging population should not be lumped into one group because

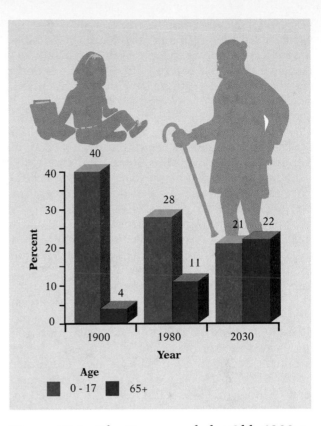

Figure 18.1 The Young and the Old: 1900 to 2030 (U.S. Special Committee on Aging et al., 1991: 9).

there is a great deal of diversity among **later-life families**—families that either are beyond the child-rearing years and have begun to launch their children or are childless but beginning to plan for retirement (Brubaker, 1991). Satisfaction with one's later life depends on a number of factors, including personality, attitude toward life, income, social status, and, perhaps most important, the quality of one's health. In this section we look first at the issue of health and then at the social status of the elderly and the societal stereotypes they must often confront.

Is Deterioration in Health Inevitable?

According to the 1990 census, 75 percent of those age 65 to 74 who were not living in institutions said they were in good health, and among those 75 and older, two thirds considered themselves healthy (cited in Vobejda, 1992). And even among those 85 and older, 63 percent have reported their health as good or excellent (National Center for Health Statistics, cited in Pol et al., 1992). Nevertheless, some physical decline across all three groups is normal and inevitable. As Table 18.1 shows, people over 85 typically experience the most severe failure of such biological functions as lung capacity and muscle strength.

Physical and Mental Health A gradual process of physical deterioration begins early in life and affects all body systems: Reflexes slow, hearing and eyesight dim, and stamina decreases. No matter how well tuned we keep our bodies, the parts eventually wear down. A healthy diet and regular exercise can help many older people preserve their good health, but other factors may explain why some older people fall prey to diabetes, heart trouble, stroke, cancer, and other life-threatening diseases.

People age differently, depending on such things as lifestyle, inherited predisposition, and attitude toward life. For those who take nutrition and exercise seriously, new businesses offer products designed to meet this new consumer need. Charles Harper of Healthy Choice and Alvin Binder of Thinny DeLites were inspired by health problems of their own to create new fat-free, cholesterol-free, sodium-free, and low-calo-

Table 18.1
Aging and Health

	AGE			
	25	45	65	85
Maximum heart rate	100%	94%	87%	81%
Lung capacity	100%	82%	62%	50%
Muscle strength	100%	90%	75%	55%
Kidney function	100%	88%	78%	69%
Cholesterol level	198	221	224	206

SOURCE: Begley et al., 1990: 44–48.

rie food items, and Entenmann's has offered a diet-conscious line of cakes and cookies for some years. On the other hand, even the knowledge that diet and exercise can delay illness or death does not prevent some people from overeating, drinking to excess, or engaging in other self-destructive behaviors (Stoller and Pollow, 1994).

Although inherited tendencies toward illness are difficult, if not impossible, to avoid, some measures can help those afflicted with diseases like arthritis, which makes many physical tasks difficult. For example, Oreck Floor Care Corporation introduced its XL line of vacuum cleaners with an orthopedic handle approved by the Arthritis Foundation because it does not require

CROSS CULTURAL

Protecting the Elderly in China

Zhao Chunlan, a 73-year-old widow, knows she can count on her son to look after her in her old age. It is not just the notion of filial piety that is putting this mother's mind at ease. Her 51-year-old son and her daughter-in-law have signed a formal support agreement to provide for her well-being. In this agreement, a new concept in China, the couple has promised to cook Chunlan special meals, to take her for regular medical checkups, to give her the largest room in their home, to put the family's color television in her room, and to "never make her angry." Chunlan acknowledges that her son took good care of her even before the agreement, but says that "now that

he's signed it, he will be conscious of his commitment" (Sun, 1990).

For thousands of years China prided itself on reverence for the aged. But today, with the rising incidence of elder abuse and neglect, the new support agreements—required by law in some localities—reflect the growing problem posed by the country's rapidly increasing elderly population. By the year 2040, almost 25 percent of China's population will be elderly—more than 370 million people, who will also constitute the largest elderly population on earth. Both a longer life expectancy and the implementation of a strict birth-control policy that permits families to have only one child have contributed to this rapid rise in China's over-60 population. According to an

official of China's National Committee on Aging, the trend of the future will be "the ratio of 4:2:1," meaning that one child will have to take care of two parents and four grandparents (Tefft, 1994).

In the countryside, where most of China's 1.1 billion people live, most rural workers have no retirement system, and the government expects sons and their spouses and children to provide financial support and all the necessary care for their aged parents. As a result, it is in rural localities that the new support agreements have become most popular. In fact, in some rural areas, up to 70 percent of families have signed such agreements (Tefft, 1994).

a strong grip. The Drackett Company, a division of Bristol-Myers that produces the O'Cedar line of products, has also made life easier for the elderly with its "Light and Thirsty" mop and "Easy Reach" tub-and-tile scrubber, both easy to hold and use (Ostroff, 1991).

In some illnesses, physical changes can lead to emotional and behavioral changes. Depression affects 15 percent of Americans age 65 or older. It is believed that depression is caused by changes in the body's biochemistry by such things as thyroid disease, heart disease, and kidney or liver dysfunction. **Depression** is characterized by pervasive sadness and other negative feelings like a sense of worthlessness. It is also often accompanied in the elderly by such physical symptoms as diarrhea, chest discomfort, nausea, or loss of appetite, for which no physical or physiological cause can be determined. Because family members tend to interpret the "down" mood they see in an older relative as a reaction to the death of loved ones or to the loss of a job or good health, they may not recognize the signs of depression. Of the nine symptoms of depression listed in Table 18.2, seven, including numbers 5 and 6 (depressed mood and loss of interest), must be present for at least a two-week period for a physician to diagnose major depression or depression that must be treated. Among the elderly, about 85 percent of those diagnosed

Table 18.2

Symptoms of Depression

1. Changes in appetite and weight
2. Disturbed sleep
3. Motor retardation or agitation
4. Fatigue and loss of energy
5. Depressed or irritable mood
6. Loss of interest or pleasure in usual activities
7. Difficulty thinking or concentrating
8. Feelings of worthlessness, self-reproach, excessive guilt
9. Suicidal thinking or attempts

SOURCES: Kaplan and Strawbridge, 1994; Henry, 1995.

can be treated successfully with antidepressants either alone or in combination with psychotherapy (Henry, 1995).

Alzheimer's Disease In an open letter to the nation in 1994, former President Ronald Reagan disclosed that he had symptoms of Alzheimer's disease and hoped his announcement would promote more awareness of this illness. Before you continue reading, take the quiz "What Do You Know About Alzheimer's Disease?"

Alzheimer's disease is a progressive, degenerative disorder that attacks the brain and impairs memory, thinking, and behavior. Medical researchers believe that Alzheimer's is caused by proteins that are toxic to nerve cells in the brain (Masur et al., 1994; Scinto et al., 1994). The dis-

Life in rural China has never been easy, and the government's current insistence that families support their elderly relatives has increased the burden for many people.

What Do You Know About Alzheimer's Disease?

Named for its discoverer, German neurologist Alois Alzheimer, this disease was first identified in 1906 (Cutler, 1987). Find out how much you know about the disorder by taking the following quiz; check the box under the answer you believe is correct.

	TRUE	FALSE	DON'T KNOW
1. Anyone who lives long enough will almost certainly get Alzheimer's disease.	☐	☐	☐
2. Alzheimer's disease is a form of insanity.	☐	☐	☐
3. At present there is no cure for Alzheimer's disease.	☐	☐	☐
4. A person with Alzheimer's experiences both mental and physical decline.	☐	☐	☐
5. The primary symptom of Alzheimer's disease is memory loss.	☐	☐	☐
6. If you are over 75, memory loss most likely indicates the beginning of Alzheimer's.	☐	☐	☐
7. Depression in an older person can sometimes look like Alzheimer's.	☐	☐	☐
8. Men are more likely to develop Alzheimer's than women.	☐	☐	☐
9. Alzheimer's disease is fatal.	☐	☐	☐
10. The majority of persons with Alzheimer's live in nursing homes.	☐	☐	☐
11. Aluminum is a significant cause of Alzheimer's disease.	☐	☐	☐
12. Alzheimer's disease can be diagnosed by a blood test.	☐	☐	☐
13. Alzheimer's patients become passive and withdrawn.	☐	☐	☐
14. Nursing home costs for Alzheimer's patients are covered by Medicare.	☐	☐	☐
15. Medicines taken for high blood pressure can cause symptoms that look like Alzheimer's disease.	☐	☐	☐

"And I'm telling you, Agnes, I'm not too old for a mid-life crisis."
© Charles Barsotti from The Cartoon Bank, Inc.

ease afflicts about 2 million to 4 million U.S. elderly—about 4 percent between 65 and 74, 10 percent between 75 and 84, and 17 percent over 85. Alzheimer's requires round-the-clock care, costing over $80 billion yearly measured in medical expenses, the time of unpaid caregivers, and the patients' earning losses (DiBacco, 1994; Ernst and Hay, 1994).

Social Status of the Elderly

We often hear that the elderly no longer have the respect and power that they enjoyed during "the good old days." Historians point out, however, that the elderly did not necessarily enjoy respect and deferential treatment in earlier days. Treatment of the elderly in colonial America, for example, depended very much on the person's wealth

1. **False.** Alzheimer's occurs most often in the elderly, but it is a disease and not the inevitable consequence of aging. Only about 3 percent of people over 65 suffer from this disease (DiBacco, 1994).

2. **False.** Alzheimer's is a disease of the brain, but it is not a form of insanity.

3. **True.** There is no known cure for Alzheimer's. Research suggests that some currently experimental drugs may be successful in slowing the disease (Scinto et al., 1994).

4. **True.** Memory and cognitive decline are characteristic of the earlier stages of Alzheimer's disease; physical decline follows in the later stages.

5. **True.** This is the earliest sign of Alzheimer's disease.

6. **False.** Although Alzheimer's does produce memory loss, memory loss can be caused by other factors.

7. **True.** Depression can cause disorientation that looks like Alzheimer's.

8. **False.** Both sexes are equally likely to get Alzheimer's.

9. **True.** Alzheimer's produces mental and physical decline that is eventually fatal, but the course of the disease may run from a few years to as many as 20. On average, death occurs within eight years (DiBacco, 1994).

10. **False.** The early and middle stages of the disease usually do not require institutional care. Only a small percentage of those with the disease live in nursing homes.

11. **False.** Although aluminum compounds have been found in the brain tissue of many Alzheimer's patients, these may simply be side effects of the disease. There is no evidence that using aluminum cooking utensils or foil causes Alzheimer's,

12. **False.** At present there is no blood test that can determine with certainty that a patient has Alzheimer's disease. Some recent studies do suggest that certain psychological tests may predict Alzheimer's disease among the healthy elderly (Masur et al., 1994).

13. **False.** Some Alzheimer's patients may become aggressive, physically violent, and combative with caretakers and others (Lyman, 1993).

14. **False.** Medicare generally pays only for short-term nursing home care after hospitalization, not for long-term care. Medicaid can pay for long-term nursing home care, but because it is a state-directed program for the medically indigent, coverage for Alzheimer's patients depends on state regulations and on the income of the patient and family.

15. **True.** Some antihypertensive medications can cause symptoms that resemble Alzheimer's.

and social class. For example, church fathers gave wealthy and successful men in their 30s seats in the front row, but poor men in their 70s occupied seats near the back (Demos, 1986). Elderly women were rarely treated with respect, primarily because many were poor and thus powerless.

It is probably true, however, that the status of the elderly has declined since the turn of the century. For one thing, the greater mobility of families today diminishes the influence the elderly have on their children and grandchildren. And because divorce and remarriage rates are high, familial ties in many cases have become loosened. For example, grandparents may have to compete with stepgrandparents at family get-togethers. Perhaps most important, whereas in many societies the elderly were once the source of all wisdom, contemporary advances in science, technology, and other areas have made some of the ideas of the elderly seem old-fashioned and outdated. Indeed, some widely read publications like *Parents* magazine have questioned the usefulness of "grandma" as a child-care provider. A recent article claimed that many professional caretakers have more training in child rearing than grandparents and that they take the job more seriously because it's work they're paid to do. The writer also asserted that regulation by a state's licensing system may be a more important factor in the quality of child care one provides than being related by blood (Ogintz, 1994). What do you think of these assertions?

In some cultures the elderly still maintain a position of some influence. Indeed, in the United States, Latino elderly are considered by some to be "the repositories of cultural wisdom [and to] give guidance in problem solving and child rearing" (Blea, 1992: 81). In general, societies that do not emphasize self-reliance and independence are more likely to give older people more power and privilege because the young depend on the old for approval and other rewards (Ishii-Kuntz and Lee, 1987). In addition, preindustrial societies that endorse *familism* and filial piety, characterized by absolute obedience to the elderly and a sacred duty to support one's parents in their old age, may be more likely to honor and respect the elderly (Cowgill, 1986). In these and many developing societies older women, for example, enjoy more leisure because they delegate most of the work of the family to daughters or daughters-in-law who defer to their knowledge and experience (Brown, 1992).

Dealing with Stereotypes

In our youth-oriented society many people dread growing old. Feminist writer Betty Friedan admits that her reaction to turning 60 was anything but jubilant: "When my friends threw a surprise [birthday] party . . . I could have killed them all. Their toasts seemed [to be] . . . pushing me out of life . . . out of the race. Professionally, politically, personally, sexually . . . I was depressed for weeks" (Friedan, 1993: 13).

As we discussed in Chapter 14, many midlife people with family responsibilities today feel economically vulnerable in a changing economy. They fear being laid off or forced out of the work force through early retirement plans as corporate America downsizes or moves much of its business overseas. As a result, younger and younger people are buying hair-coloring and other cosmetic products and turning to cosmetic surgeons for facelifts and other plastic surgery. According to the American Academy of Facial Plastic and Reconstructive Surgery, about 43 percent of patients are baby boomers (age 30 to 50 in 1995) who want to look youthful as long as possible, and men now account for one out of four cosmetic surgery patients (*Baltimore Sun*, 1995).

This emphasis on youth has made old people objects of fear to many, who see in them their own mortality. And fear can turn to loathing and contempt. Saporta (1991) maintains that our language is full of words and phrases that euphemize, malign, stereotype and generally disparage the old, including "senior citizen," "old bat," "old bag," "old fart," "old fogey," "fossil," "old goat,"
"old hag," "dead wood," "old maid," "dirty old man," "crotchety," and "over the hill." In contrast, how many negative words do we have insulting young people or youth?

In his classic book, *Why Survive? Being Old in America*, Butler (1975) coined the term **ageism** to refer to discrimination against people on the basis of age, particularly those who are old. Among other things, Butler pointed out the persistence of the "myth of senility"—the notion that if old people show forgetfulness, confusion, and inattention, they are senile. If a 16-year-old boy can't remember why he went to the refrigerator, we say he's "off in the clouds" somewhere or in love, but if his 79-year-old grandfather forgets why he went to the refrigerator, we're likely to call him senile (Slade, 1985). Although the data collected by gerontologists show otherwise, many people continue to believe that older Americans are less intelligent, less competent, and less active than younger people (see Levin, 1988). This view of the elderly is well illustrated by the experiment conducted by Patricia Moore, who wanted to know what it's like to be an older person in our society. As you can see from the box "Being Old in America," Moore found a strong and pervasive negative attitude toward the elderly.

Love, intimacy, and companionship are just as important to older adults as to younger people.

Being Old in America

With the help of a professional makeup artist, Patricia Moore, an industrial designer, put on latex wrinkles and a gray wig, wore splints under her clothes to stiffen her joints, and put plugs in her ears to dull her hearing. Putting baby oil in her eyes irritated them and blurred her vision. "The look was that of eyes with cataracts, as the baby oil would float on the surface of the eyeball" (Moore and Conn, 1985: 56). She used a special type of crayon, mixed with oil paint, to stain and discolor her teeth, and she gargled with salt to make her voice raspy (Ryan, 1993). Then she shuffled out into the world to find out what it's really like to be old in America.

Over a three-year period, Moore found dramatic differences between the way people reacted to "Young" and "Old" Pat Moore. For example, as Old Pat she went into a store to buy a typewriter ribbon. Ignoring her at first, the salesman finally approached her and was irritated when she was not sure what kind of ribbon she wanted and impatient when she fumbled with the clasp on her handbag. Wordlessly, he gave her her change and dropped the package on the counter instead of handing it to her. The next day, Young Pat, "sandy-blonde hair curled and falling on my shoulders, sunglasses and sandals," but wearing the same dress she had worn the day before, went to the same store to buy typewriter ribbon. This time the salesman smiled and immediately offered his assistance. When Pat pretended not to know what kind of ribbon she wanted, he was solicitous ("As long as you know it when you see it, you're all right"), and when she fumbled with

"Old Pat Moore."

Patricia Moore as herself.

the clasp of the purse, saying, "Darn thing always gives me trouble," he was amiable ("Well, better for it . . . to take a little longer to open than to make it easy for the muggers and the pickpockets"). He chatted as he counted out her change and opened the door because "it sticks sometimes."

What impressed Young Pat Moore, the researcher, almost as much as the negative attitudes and behavior she continued to encounter as Old Pat was the way she accepted and internalized those negative responses. For example, she found not only that when she appeared to be 85 people were more likely to push ahead of her in line but that she didn't protest this behavior: "It seemed somehow . . . that it was okay for them to do this to the Old Pat Moore, since they were undoubtedly busier than I was anyway. . . . After all, little old ladies have plenty of time, don't they?"

Moore found that clerks assumed she was hard of hearing, that she would be slow in paying for purchases, or that she would "somehow become confused about the transaction. What it all added up to was that people feared I would be trouble, so they tried to have as little to do with me as possible. And the amazing thing is that I began almost to believe it myself. . . . I became so intimidated by the attitudes of others, by the fear that they would become exasperated with me, that I absorbed some of their tacitly negative judgment about people of my age. It was as if, unconsciously, I was saying . . . 'You're right. I'm just a lot of trouble. I'm really not as valuable as all these other people, so I'll just get out of your way as soon as possible so you won't be angry with me. . . .' I think perhaps the worst thing about aging may be the overwhelming sense that everything around you is letting you know that you are not terribly important any more" (Moore and Conn, 1985: 75-76).

One of the most common stereotypes is that older people become ill-tempered as they age. In fact, most research shows that people's personality characteristics remain very stable over a lifetime (McCrea and Costa, cited in Belsky, 1988). Whether you're grumpy or pleasant at 75, the chances are you were either grumpy or pleasant at 15. Although work, marriage, and other life experiences do have effects on people, in general, those who are depressed, hostile, anxious, and poorly adjusted in their 20s are likely to be depressed, hostile, anxious, and poorly adjusted in old age.

Contrary to the popular notion that the elderly become stubborn, Tyler and Schuller (1991) found that older people actually are more flexible than many younger people. Older people have a larger repertoire of experiences, these researchers say, and they've developed ways of dealing with bureaucratic red tape and other daily problems. As a result, many older people realize that with a little patience they can often get what they want.

Some elderly people admit, however, that they have become less docile and subservient as they age. Thus, when older people "suddenly" seem stubborn and defiant, they may simply be shedding some long-term inhibitions:

One of the greatest thrills of being a woman of 70 is having the luxury to be open about what I really think. When I was younger, I was so afraid of hurting people or worried about what they would think of me that I . . . kept my mouth shut. Now when I don't like something, I speak up. It's gotten me into trouble with my daughter and sister, but I don't care. It's not that I try to be mean. . . . It's just that age has made me more truthful. And that's one of the reasons that I feel better about myself now than I have at any other time in life (Belsky, 1988: 65–66).

Many people age gracefully, with dignity, and maintain their sense of humor and values despite the ageism they encounter. When the centenarian Delany sisters, whom you met in Chapter 9, were in their 70s, they became interested in the new findings about nutrition and began eating healthier food. Now both Sadie and Bessie Delany also exercise regularly:

In the mornings, Monday through Friday, we do our yoga exercises. I started doing yoga exercises with Mama about forty years ago. Mama was starting to shrink up and get bent down, and I started exercising with her to straighten her up. . . . I kept doing my yoga exercises, even after Mama died. Well, when Bessie turned eighty she decided that I looked better than her. So she decided she would start doing yoga, too. We follow a yoga exercise program on TV. Sometimes, Bessie cheats. I'll be doing an exercise and look over at her, and she's just lying there! She's a naughty old gal (Delany et al., 1993: 202).

Retirement

Retirement is a recent phenomenon. Historians point out that many people who reached old age in colonial America worked well past the age of 65. Men in their 70s hauled grain, transported rugs, and tanned leather. One man still worked in the coal mines at the age of 102. Men over age 65 who were in government positions (such as governors and their assistants) or who were ministers typically retained their offices until death, and some women worked as midwives well into their 70s (Demos, 1986).

Because we have greater life expectancy today, we may well spend 20 percent of our adult life in retirement. Although we often hear that retirement is particularly difficult for men because the traditional male role calls for breadwinning and being "productive," researchers have found that health and financial security are the major determinants of retirees' satisfaction with life. When people are unhappy in retirement, it is more often because of health or income problems than because of the loss of the worker role (Gradman, 1994; Solomon and Szwabo, 1994). If pension benefits do not keep up with inflation, or if the retiree is not covered by a pension plan, poverty can be just a few years away.

Most African Americans retire because of poor health, and fewer African Americans are financially able to retire than whites (Gibson, 1993). Although the overall poverty rate for U.S. citizens age 65 and older dropped from 16 percent in 1980 to 12 percent in 1993, there are large differences by gender and race. As Figure 18.2 shows, older women are poorer than their male counterparts within each racial group, elderly African Americans are poorer than whites or Latinos, and African American older women are the most likely to be poor.

Retirement presents more financial problems to women than to men. **Social Security,** a

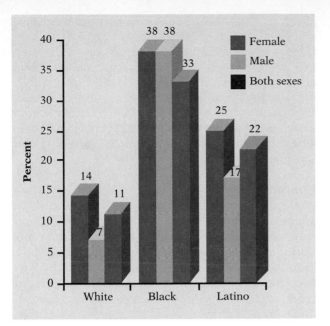

Figure 18.2 **People over 65 Living Below the Poverty Level, 1992** (Based on data in U.S. Bureau of the Census, 1993: Table 5).

public retirement pension system administered by the federal government, provides income support to over 90 percent of the elderly, but the benefits depend on how long people have been in the labor force and how much they have earned. Many women have had an uneven employment history because they have spent many years as homemakers and mothers or because they have periodically left jobs to raise children. Thus many women must continue to work at least part time after age 65 because their Social Security benefits are very low.

Another reason that women's benefits tend to be low is that even if women have worked full time they have often been confined to low-paying jobs. In 1990, for example, the average Social Security benefit was $530 a month for women and $713 for men. In the same year, only 27 percent of women over 65 received employer-provided pensions—even counting those who received such benefits as surviving spouses—and the benefit averaged $5478 a year. In contrast, 49 percent of older men received employer pensions, which averaged $9756 (Rich, 1992). In 1990, for men 65 and older the median total income from Social Security, pensions, and investments—excluding assets—was $14,183, but for women it was only $8044 (Noble, 1994). In addi-

tion, women who divorce after fewer than ten years of marriage are not entitled to any of their husbands' benefits (see Chapter 16). As a result, after retirement many women are at a high risk of becoming dependent on public agencies or on their families for support (Gonyea, 1994).

Retirement has an especially devastating impact on black women. Many African American women have worked in clerical or service positions that are low-paying and lack adequate pensions. If their husbands had low-paying jobs or a sporadic employment history because of recessions and discrimination, the husbands' benefits may also be inadequate. In one study, African American women over 65 said that work provided an alternative to welfare, and even highly educated African American women reported working as long as possible to maintain the economic security of their families (Coleman et al., 1987).

GRANDPARENTING

According to many gerontologists, grandparents are the cement, the glue, that keeps the family close. In many families, grandparents represent stability and the continuity of family rituals and values. They often help their adult children in parenting activities by providing emotional support, encouragement, help with day-to-day parental needs (such as baby-sitting), and help in times of emergency or crisis, including illness and divorce (Brubaker, 1991, offers a summary of the literature on later-life families). No matter how strict they were with their own children, many grandparents often serve as family mediators, advocates for their grandchildren's point of view, and shoulders to cry on.

In general, today's grandparents are more affluent than grandparents of just a decade ago. Between 1980 and 1990, the median income of families headed by people age 65 and older increased by 22 percent, compared to only a 6 percent gain for families overall. Thus many are able to buy their grandchildren frequent gifts that range from small toys and items of clothing to expensive computers, sporting goods, and financial investments like stocks, bonds, or trust funds. Over 25 percent of grandparents buy costly gifts for their grandchildren that average more than $500 each. In addition, many grandparents give their adult children, who can't afford such expensive items, cameras and camcorders to capture their grandchildren's growing years (Waldrop, 1993). With more money, more energy, and more leisure time than ever before, growing numbers of grandparents are also traveling with their grandchildren. Some travel agencies offer tour packages specifically for grandparents and grandchildren in the United States and overseas, but the trips are expensive, ranging from almost $2400 per person for a seven-day land-only tour of Washington, D.C., to $5800 per person for a 17-day tour of Australia, including air travel from Los Angeles (Marsh, 1993).

On these trips the two generations can enjoy an unforgettable time together. Some travel agencies include an escort to provide extra activities for the children when the energy levels of the young and old differ, and other grandparents may be available to look after a grandchild whose grandparent wants to sit out part of a trip (Beck et al., 1990). In Outdoor Vacations for Women over 40, the founder says that the "runaway best-seller" is a multigenerational trip where mothers, daughter, grandmothers, granddaughters, aunts, and nieces can hike, bike, beachcomb, or sightsee (Conover, 1993).

Styles of Grandparenting

Although many grandparents take great pleasure in their grandchildren and feel their new role gives their lives stability and provides them with new experiences, not all grandparents are the same. There are a number of different styles of grandparenting. In this section we look at five—the remote, companionate, involved, advisory, and surrogate styles.

Remote In the remote relationship, the grandparents and grandchildren live far apart and see each other infrequently, maintaining a largely ritualistic, symbolic relationship. For example, grandparents who are "distant figures" may see their grandchildren only on holidays or special occasions. Such relationships may be cordial and benevolent but are also uninvolved and fleeting (Thompson and Walker, 1991). Grandparents who both live far away and experience health problems are likely to be even less involved with their grandchildren (Field and Minkler, 1993).

Although they report feeling close to their great-grandchildren, great-grandparents may often have remote relationships, either because they are in frail health, live far away, or feel that grandparents play a more authoritative role. In other

cases, great-grandparents love their great-grandchildren but have difficulty adapting to new situations such as divorce and remarriage and often feel embarrassed, uncomfortable, or confused about great-grandchildren produced in cohabiting relationships. As one great-grandparent said, "I guess I have two or three great-grandchildren, depending on how you look at it. My grandson is living with someone and they have a child" (Doka and Mertz, 1988: 196).

Companionate The companionate style of grandparenting is the most common pattern. In a national survey, for example, the Roper organization found that 90 percent of the grandparents said they saw their grandchildren at least once a month, 66 percent talked to their grandchild by telephone at least once a month, 45 percent spent at least 100 hours a year taking care of their grandchildren, and 20 percent said they took their grandchildren on a trip, to see a movie or sports event, or to visit a museum once a month (reported in Waldrop, 1993).

Companionate grandparents often say that they love having their grandchildren with them and then remark, "And the best thing is that they go home!" According to satirist Erma Bombeck (1994: 8E), "Grandparenting is great. You can look at your grandchild with a diaper dragging on the floor and say to his mother, 'That kid is carrying a load! Change him!'" Companionate grandparents generally do not want to share parenting and tend to emphasize loving, playing, and having fun.

Involved In the involved grandparenting style, grandparents play an active role in raising their grandchildren. They may be spontaneous and playful, but they also exert substantial authority over their grandchildren, imposing definite—and sometimes tough—rules. Involved grandparents are often younger than other types of grandparents and, not infrequently, they have welcomed their daughter(s) and grandchildren back home after a divorce. In other cases, grandparents, usually the grandmother, care for the grandchildren while the mother works. Involved grandparents include those who step in, occasionally or daily, to help manage a family crisis because the parent, usually a single mother, is young, poor, immature, or irresponsible in caring for the children (Oysterman et al., 1993).

African American grandparents—especially those who live in inner cities—often see them-

Grandparents can often be excellent mentors to their grandchildren, encouraging and helping them with their studies.

selves as family protectors against separation, divorce, drugs, and crime (Poe, 1992). But it's not only when there are problems that African American grandparents are more involved with their grandchildren. For example, in a study of black and white grandfathers in a southeastern rural county, Kivett (1991) found that both groups provided warmth and affection. Black grandfathers, however, reported being closer to their grandchildren than their white counterparts. According to Kivett, black grandfathers are more likely to provide unconditional love because they see grandchildren as "holding the key to the future," whereas white grandfathers tend to emphasize the past and to see themselves as models for the younger generation.

Advisory In the fourth, *advisory*, type of grandparenting, the grandparent serves as an adviser, or what Neugarten and Weinstein (1964) call a "reservoir of family wisdom." In this relationship, the grandfather—who may be the family patriarch—may act also as a financial provider, and grandmothers often play crucial advisory roles in their grandchildren's lives. Especially when the mother is very young, a grandmother may be an "apprentice mother," helping her daughter make the transition to parenthood by supporting and mentoring her but not replacing her in the parenting role. The grandmother provides emotional, financial, and child-care support until the "apprentice" shows that she is responsive to and responsible for the baby (Apfel and Seitz, 1991).

Many teenage grandchildren begin to break

away from their families, including their grandparents. Sometimes the roles reverse at this stage, and teenage grandchildren may help their grandparents with errands or chores. Many adolescents, however, turn to their grandparents for advice or understanding. For example, a 17-year-old boy said: "With my grandpa we discuss usually technical problems. But sometimes some other problems, too. He told me how to refuse to drink alcohol with other boys." A 16-year-old girl said that she and her grandmother go for walks and added, "I can tell her about everything" (Tyszkowa, 1993: 136).

Surrogate An emerging grandparenting role is that of *surrogate*, in which the grandparent provides regular care or replaces the parents in raising the grandchildren. As Figure 18.3 shows, in 1993, 3.4 million grandchildren, or 5 percent of all children under 18 years old, lived in the homes of their grandparent(s), up slightly from 3 percent in 1970 (Saluter, 1994). Much of this change is due to continued high levels of divorce and the rise in out-of-wedlock childbearing (see Chapters 11 and 16). As both Figure 18.3 and the Data Digest show, however, African American children are much more likely than their white or Latino counterparts to be without their parents and to live with a grandparent.

According to Jendrek (1994), there are at least three categories of surrogate grandparents: custodial, living-with, and day-care grandparents. The *custodial* grandparents Jendrek interviewed had a legal relationship with their grandchildren through adoption, guardianship, or custody. Most did not view themselves as "taking the grandchild" away from the parent but believed they had taken legal action only when the situation became intolerable—for example, when the parent, usually the daughter, became an alcoholic or a drug addict and neglected or abandoned the grandchild.

Living-with grandparents, according to Jendrek, typically had the grandchild in their own home or, less commonly, lived in a home maintained by a grandchild's parent(s). Living-with grandparents took on these responsibilities either because their children had not yet moved out of the house or because the latter could not afford to live on their own with their young children. These grandparents felt that they could provide the grandchild with an economically stable and loving environment, and preferred that to allowing someone else to provide care.

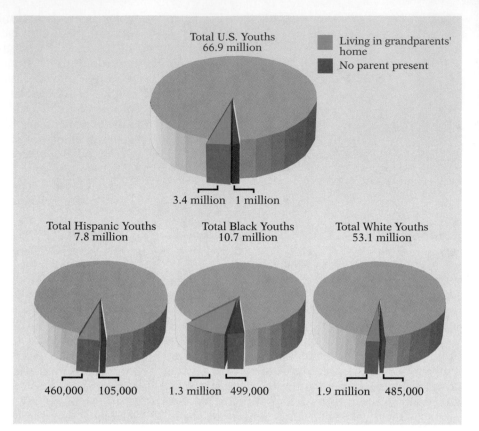

Total U.S. Youths
66.9 million

■ Living in grandparents' home
■ No parent present

3.4 million   1 million

Total Hispanic Youths
7.8 million

Total Black Youths
10.7 million

Total White Youths
53.1 million

460,000   105,000

1.3 million   499,000

1.9 million   485,000

Figure 18.3   Grandparents Rearing Children, 1993 (Saluter, 1994: xiv).

The *day-care* grandparents had assumed responsibility for the physical care of their grandchildren, usually their daughter's, until the parent(s) came home from work because of the high cost of quality day care and because of their own concerns about locating loving and reliable day-care providers. These grandparents were not casual baby-sitters, however. Some of the grandmothers even quit their part-time jobs to care for their grandchildren.

Some of the children in surrogate grandparent families are among the most needy and most emotionally damaged children in the United States. Many poor grandparents receive much less financial support to raise these children than foster parents get. The national average is $109 per child per month for grandparents who are sole caregivers, compared to $371 per child per month for foster parents (Creighton, 1991). The box "Grandparents as Silent Saviors" provides a closer look at the surrogate style of grandparenting.

On the other hand, grandparents who provide child care may sometimes prolong rather than improve a child's unsafe environment. For example, a New York family court judge criticized the city's kinship foster-care program because it does little to ensure that a child will be reunited with a biological parent. According to Sheindlin (1994), about 45 percent of New York City's children in foster care live with relatives, usually grandmothers or aunts, who are paid between $400 and $1100 a month per child, plus a clothing allowance and medical coverage. These are the same amounts paid to unrelated, foster parents. Sheindlin maintains that "the lure of tax-free dollars creates a disincentive to family reunification, because the monthly stipends are usually triple or quadruple those of public assistance" (p. A15).

According to Sheindlin, a grandmother caring for four grandchildren, two of whom are considered "special need" (for example, developmentally or learning disabled), can get as much as $3200 per month tax-free. She may continue to pay $138 a month in rent, and her drug-addicted daughter may come by for money from

Grandparents as Silent Saviors

Many grandparents have become the "silent saviors" of grandchildren whose parents have abandoned them because of poverty, drug abuse, or other problems. Creighton (1991: 85–86), describes one such family:

When the Richmond weather turns cold and bitter, 59-year-old May Toman and her two granddaughters pile blankets onto the worn living-room couch and chairs in their rundown row house. There, around an ancient gas burner, they sleep at night. The upstairs is without heat or electricity, and the leaky kitchen ceiling has already fallen in once. But May is afraid to complain for fear the landlord will raise her $110-a-month rent, a development that could leave them homeless. The girls–Shelly, 8, and Tabatha, 9–make do with thrift-shop clothing, and a steak dinner is a treat remembered for weeks.

Shelly's mother was only 17 when Shelly was born, and soon afterward she and Shelly's father began leaving the baby with friends or near friends, sometimes for long periods without contact. For May, the fi-nal straw came when Shelly was 2. May found her alone in the yard one evening. She took Shelly home and called the Richmond Department of Social Services. After an investigation, May got legal custody.

Several years later, May's son, Wayne, ran into marriage problems. When his wife left, he gave his daughter Tabatha, then 7, to his mother and his infant son to his mother-in-law. Tabatha's health had been neglected; her teeth were abscessed. May applied for custody and got it.

May, whom the girls call "Nanny" became their mother. May makes ends meet by taking in sewing and cutting corners. Up at 7, she walks the girls to school, then cleans house and grocery shops with food stamps. At 3, she meets the girls outside their brick school eight blocks away "so they know there's someone waiting."

One of Shelly's favorite pastimes is studying her baby album of herself and her mother smiling from behind plastic pages. The album ends abruptly when she is 2, and Shelly turns back to the first page to begin again. "I want to live with my mama in a big house," says Shelly, "but I don't really think I'll ever get that." Shelly's mother lives across town and sees Shelly fairly often. But she has another child now, a year old, and says she does not have plans to take Shelly back soon.

Tabatha says, "Well, my daddy lives in the neighborhood, but he can't take me right now. My mama used to call, which made me cry terribly, but she hasn't called now in a long time. She said she was going to send me a birthday card but she never did." Her father, Wayne, lives next door with two new children and their mother, and though in many ways he and Tabatha are close, he says, "I feel like Tabatha's better off with Nanny."

Although she loves her grandchildren, May is representative of many grandparents who had not anticipated raising their grandchildren. Even when a parent assumes some of the child-care responsibilities, many grandparents provide physical and emotional care but have little decision-making power. As one grandmother summed it up, "I've been feeling very hurt and self-pitying. . . . This is not what we had planned . . . and it's just not fair for this to happen to us" (Jendrek, 1993: 621)

time to time but has no incentive to change her life or that of her children. This situation is probably not typical, however. For example, Minkler et al. (1993) reviewed 124 programs in 25 large urban areas that provide community intervention and service programs for grandparents who are the sole or primary caregivers to children whose parents have been incarcerated, neglect their children because of drug use, or who have died of AIDS. The researchers found that many of the programs provide little direct help because they are unfunded or underfunded, cannot provide any child-care respite for the grandparents, and often rely on health and social service personnel, who are already overworked.

Grandparents and Their Children's Divorce

Divorce creates both opportunities and dilemmas for grandparents. Grandparents on the custodial side often deepen their relationships with children and grandchildren, especially when they provide financial assistance, a place to live, and help in child rearing, guidance, or advice. In contrast, grandparents on the noncustodial side typically have less access to the grandchildren. Many custodial parents move after the breakup, increasing the visiting distance. And troubled postdivorce relationships often result in a loss of contact between grandchildren and some of their grandparents. One longitudinal study found that only 11 percent of ex-spouses had good relationships with each other's parents (Ambert, 1988).

If a custodial parent remarries, the noncustodial parent may drop out of the children's lives, making it awkward for the noncustodial grandparent to arrange visits with the grandchildren. However, if the custodial parent tries to maintain a relationship with the noncustodial grandparents because he or she does not want the children to lose half of the family, and if the ex-spouses do not "bad-mouth" each other and the children have contact with the noncustodial father, children can have strong relationships with the noncustodial parent and grandparents even after the father's remarriage (Bray and Berger, 1990).

Many grandparent-grandchild relationships do become closer after the parents divorce and/or remarry (Thomas, 1994). For example, if the mother gets custody of the children but has little or no child support, she may move in with her parents. Baby sitting while the mother works and generally being in close physical proximity to the grandchildren can foster a close emotional relationship between grandparent and grandchild. And grandparents can provide a safe haven for grandchildren whose divorcing parents are often so emotionally distraught that they do not recognize the children's fears and worries about the breakdown of the parents' marriage:

Last night I was reading and Penny came out of the bedroom and she was crying a bit and I said "come sit on gramma's lap" and we cuddled. She was upset because she had wet her bed, so I changed her. Her father had gone away and she is afraid her mother will be going away, too. So I talked to her and reassured her that her mother wouldn't go away. Then I asked her if she'd like to get into bed with gramma and she said "yes" and then went to sleep (Gladstone, 1989: 71).

The close relationship between grandchildren and grandparents often continues into the grandchildren's young adulthood. For example, in a study of 704 college students who had at least one grandparent, the students from stepfamilies and single-parent families saw grandparents as playing a more active role in their families than did students from intact families. They reported that grandparents had important decision-making authority in the family, provided gifts or financial assistance, acted more like friends rather than respected elders, helped with communication between the grandchildren and the parents, and helped parents in child rearing (Kennedy, 1990).

A divorce can create unexpected financial burdens for the grandparents, however. If grandparents anticipate being cut off from their grandchildren after the divorce, they may have to petition for visitation rights, thus incurring legal expenses. (All 50 states authorize grandparent visitation under certain circumstances, most commonly following the death of a grandchild's parent and/or the dissolution of the marriage of the grandchild's parents; see Subcommittee on Human Services, 1992.) In other cases, parents may help children, especially daughters, to obtain a divorce. One father noted, for example, that "I'm at the age where a lot of my friends are retiring, and I'm spending all my retirement savings on attorneys" (Chion-Kenney, 1991: B5).

RELATIONSHIPS BETWEEN AGING PARENTS AND ADULT CHILDREN

When Mikhail Gorbachev was the leader of the former Soviet Union, his then 79-year-old mother, Maria, complained that he never wrote or called and that she never got to see him. When rumors spread that Mikhail was planning on moving her to Moscow, Maria reportedly said to a neighbor in Privolnoye, the small Russian village where she had lived most of her life, "I have already lived in Moscow. I don't see my son here and I wouldn't see him there. He leaves home at 6 A.M. and returns late in the evening" (Lee, 1990: D1). Ultimately, Maria Gorbachev did go to live near her famous son, but when she died in 1995 he flew her body back to Privolnoye, where she had asked to be buried.

In many cases, adult children and aging parents live close enough to stay in touch on a daily basis. Using Census Bureau data, Lin and Rogerson (1995) found that 60 percent of parents age 60 and older have at least one child within ten miles. The closest son lives a median of seven miles from his parents, the closest daughter a median of six miles, and it is the latter who are more likely to call and visit their parents. Geographic closeness is not the most critical factor that shapes intergenerational relationships, however. Divorced daughters with child custody have more contact than married daughters and often receive more help from parents. Sons, on the other hand, receive more baby-sitting help from their parents when they are married than in other situations (Spitze, 1994).

Reversing roles, adult daughters provide about the same amount of help to their parents whatever the parents' health, but sons tend to provide financial assistance only when parental health fails (Hamon, 1992). Another critical variable is the quality of family relationships. Regardless of their own marital status, both African American and white adults are more likely to provide emotional and instrumental support (such as providing transportation and health care when parents are ill) if early family relationships were caring and loving (Chatters and Taylor, 1993). These strong and helpful relationships continue into the parents' 70s and 80s (Johnson, 1993).

Elderly parents generally try to avoid moving in with their children, primarily because they don't want to give up control of their own lives and lifestyles. In addition, they don't want to cause or to endure crowding and are reluctant to do the increased housework in a crowded home. For many women, the "empty nest" is a relief. The late anthropologist Margaret Mead, who married several times and did some of her best work while she was in her 60s and 70s, maintained that "postmenopausal zest" or, as she called it, "PMZ," was a much more common occurrence than postmenopausal syndrome, a depressive state then thought to be common in older women (Rovner, 1990). Some older parents feel that there would be a clash over different lifestyles or child-rearing ideas, as well as increased household expenses (Mancini and Blieszner, 1991). Finally, both younger and older generations value independence, and aging parents want to be both financially and emotionally self-sufficient.

There are advantages, however, to multigenerational households. For one thing, multigenerational families exchange services and support on a regular basis. In a review of the literature, Mancini and Blieszner (1991) found that many reported the following behaviors in multigenerational households: caring for family members during illness; giving money; providing gifts; running errands; preparing meals; taking care of children; giving advice on home management; cleaning the house and making repairs; giving advice on jobs, business matters, and expensive purchases; helping with transportation; counseling about life problems; and giving emotional support and affection.

Rural elderly parents generally depend on their children for financial and emotional support more than do urban elderly parents. This is probably because the urban elderly typically have more resources and more access to resources, which makes them less dependent on their children. Even when formal support systems outside the family are available, however, the rural elderly still depend more on kinship networks. The older urban parents are, however, the more likely they are to rely on their children for assistance (Dorfman and Mertens, 1990).

Contrary to what many of us might expect, it is often the needs and circumstances of adult children rather than those of their elderly parents that trigger dependent relationships. For example, in a national study of parents and their adult children (age 22 and over), Ward et al. (1992) found that coresidency was most likely among adult children who were unmarried and whose parents were in good or excellent health and under age 69.

DEATH AND DYING

Woody Allen once said, "It's not that I'm afraid to die. I just don't want to be there when it happens." Although people who are very old and in poor health sometimes welcome death, most of us have difficulty facing it, no matter what our age and physical condition. In this section we look first at several theories of how people deal with imminent death. Then we examine the kind of care available to the dying. Finally, we explore the ways survivors deal with their own loss and grief and console each other.

Dealing with Death and Dying

The way we deal with death depends on whether we are the medical personnel treating the ill patient, the relatives and friends of the patient, or the patient. Physicians and other medical staff, although many try to be compassionate, must often be more concerned with patients' prognoses, that is, their realistic chances for survival. Patients and their loved ones, on the other hand, are generally concerned with getting the best possible treatment in the hope that the patients will survive.

Health-Care Professionals Physicians and other health-care professionals often use the term **dying trajectory** to describe the manner in which a very ill person is expected to die. In a *lingering trajectory*—for example, death from a terminal illness like cancer—medical staff do everything possible to treat the patient, but ultimately custodial care predominates. In contrast, the *quick trajectory* refers to the acute, crisis situation caused by a heart attack or a serious accident. Here staff typically work feverishly to preserve the patient's life and well-being—and sometimes they are successful.

When the patient is elderly and suffering from a terminal illness like cancer, health-care professionals and family members often perceive the course of dying and its treatment differently. For example, it is especially likely that overworked hospital staff who expect an elderly patient to have a lingering death will respond to the patient's requests more slowly, will place the patient in more remote wards, or even bathe and feed him or her less frequently. Family members, however, typically expect their elderly relatives to be treated as painstakingly as any other patient. Moreover, a patient's perceived social worth can influence care. For example, elderly patients in private hospitals or those with high socioeconomic status often receive better care than poor elderly patients or those in public hospitals (Hooyman and Kiyak, 1991).

Patients, Families, Friends Among the several perspectives of the dying process from the point of view of those most deeply concerned—patients and their loved ones—probably the most famous is that of Elizabeth Kübler-Ross (1969). Based on work with 200 primarily middle-aged cancer patients, Kübler-Ross proposed five stages of dying: denial, anger, bargaining, depression, and acceptance. Her theory has been criticized by many. Some claim that the stages are not experienced by everyone or in the same order. Others point out that the stages do not apply to the elderly. Many practitioners believe, however, that Kübler-Ross's conception offers some useful ideas in understanding the psychology of most patients and families, regardless of age or specific illness:

> *Denial stage* In an effort to cope with the dreaded news that a loved one will die, many people simply refuse to believe it. Patients and their families may ask for more tests, change

physicians, or try in other ways to stave off the inevitable.

> *Anger stage* When denial is no longer possible, people may become angry and sometimes project their anger onto medical staff or one another.

> *Bargaining stage* The dying person sometimes tries to forestall death by making a deal with God: "If I can just live until my daughter's college graduation, I'll make a large contribution to my church."

> *Depression stage* When the dying person recognizes that death is imminent, depression may set in. In *reactive depression*, patients experience sadness as a result of the various other losses that accompany illness and dying, such as the loss of hair during radiation therapy or the loss of functions such as the ability to walk unaided. *Preparatory depression* anticipates the loss of love objects; patients may give away prized belongings or spend extra time with family members.

> *Acceptance stage* When patients finally come to accept their approaching death, they may reflect on their lives and anticipate dying with quiet resignation.

In her model of dying among the elderly, Retsinas (1988) counters the Kübler-Ross theory on four primary counts, each of which is based on the notion of greater acceptance of the inevitability of illness and death. In the first place, Retsinas points out, whereas the middle-aged person facing death usually has one defined catastrophic illness, like heart disease or cancer, the illness and disabilities suffered by an elderly person may include such things as increasing visual and auditory problems, stroke, diabetes, and crippling arthritis. More used to the sick role, many elderly have had to confront the possibility of death for many years.

In addition, says Retsinas, the process of aging involves a series of role redefinitions. For example, even before the onset of illness, elderly people may have to give up such activities as driving, gardening, or climbing stairs. Unlike the middle-aged person, the dying elderly person does not suddenly confront the loss of an active social role and related worries like the effects on the family of the loss of a person's earning power.

Moreover, rather than deny death the elderly may actually welcome it. Many have seen their spouses and friends die over the years, and unlike middle-aged people, the elderly may have already outlived most of the people who mattered to them. Elderly patients often view death as a natural part of nature's cycle, and they may even await death as an end to pain, sorrow, social isolation, dependency, and loneliness. In sum, Retsinas suggests that the elderly may not experience Kübler-Ross's stages of denial, anger, bargaining, and depression because they have been experiencing a "social death" over many years.

Retsinas argues that, unlike Kübler-Ross's cancer patients, elderly people who suffer from painful, chronic, and often debilitating illnesses are not likely to deny the deterioration of their bodies, resent the loss of opportunity to experience life, or bargain for more time that will not bring the chance for accomplishing unrealized tasks. Although very old people may suffer from what seems to be depression, Retsinas claims, this may be a more natural "regression" from everyday activities as a result of pain, loneliness, or illness.

Which of these two approaches—Kübler-Ross's or Retsinas's—do you think is more applicable to aging people? Or are portions of each theory useful? If you have experienced the death of an older family member, try to recall how that person spoke, behaved, and seemed to feel.

Hospice Care for the Dying

The notion that dying, when it is inevitable, should be made as comfortable and painless as possible is a relatively new one. Specialized care for dying patients was first provided in 1967 at St. Christopher's Hospice near London, founded by Dr. Cicely Saunders. Taking the name of her facility from the medieval term that meant a place of shelter and rest for weary or sick travelers, Saunders began the modern use of the term **hospice**: a place for the care of the dying that stresses the control of pain, giving patients a sense of security and companionship and trying to make them comfortable. Hospice care is implemented in a variety of settings—in patients' homes, in hospitals, or in other freestanding inpatient facilities. There are nearly 1900 hospices in the United States, most of which provide in-home as well as inpatient services and which are open to all dying patients. In 1991, two out of three patients served were at least 65 years old and approximately 32 percent were adults (National Hospice Organization brochure and newsletter, 1991).

In the hospice approach, both professional and lay workers work as a team in assessing and meeting the physical, psychosocial, and spiritual needs of both the patient and family members and in providing dying people with full and accurate information about their condition. Another important function is to develop supportive environments in which people can talk about their lives with sympathetic listeners. Hospice staff members work directly with family and friends to help them deal with their feelings and relate compassionately to the dying patient. Although some people prefer to care for a dying person at home, some practitioners warn that the in-home approach can be stressful for both family and friends and may severely strain a family's resources.

Coping with Someone's Death

The state of having been robbed, or deprived, by death of a loved person is called **bereavement,** and those close to the dead person are known as the *bereaved.* Bereavement takes on different expressions in different people, but grief and mourning are among the most common reactions to the death of someone close.

The emotional response to loss, **grief** is seen by some as an entire process in which a variety of feelings—sadness, longing, bewilderment, anger, loneliness—combine. The grieving process may extend over a year or more after the death of a loved one. **Mourning** is the customary outward expression of grief that varies among different social and cultural groups. Mourning ranges from normal grief to pathological melancholy that may include such reactions as physical or mental illness.

There are clusters or phases of grief (Hooyman and Kiyak, 1991). People generally respond initially with shock, numbness, and disbelief, followed by an all-encompassing feeling of sorrow. Recently bereaved elderly report more illnesses and an increased use of new medications, and usually rate their overall health more poorly.

In the intermediate stage of grief people often idealize loved ones who have died and may even actively search for them. For example, a widow may see her husband's face in a crowd. New widows or widowers may also feel guilty, regretting every lapse: "Why wasn't I more understanding?" "Why did we argue that morn-

Family members in Chiba Prefecture, Japan, follow a Buddhist priest in a funeral procession. The daughter carries her father's photograph, the son his cremated remains.

ing?" Survivors may also become angry, blowing up at children and friends in a seemingly irrational way, and even the dead person may not escape their rage: "Why didn't he prepare me better for life on my own?" "Why didn't she take better care of her health?" When people are hurt, they tend to lash out and to try to find a source of blame. Some people may displace their anger onto doctors and medical science for having failed to preserve life even when they know that death in a particular case was inevitable (Belsky, 1988). When the grieving person finally accepts the loss and stops yearning for the deceased person, disorganization, anguish, and despair often follow. The person may feel aimless, without interest, purpose or motivation, incapable of making decisions, and lacking in self-confidence.

The final stage of recovery and reorganization may not occur for as much as several years after the death, although many people begin to readjust and to reorganize their lives after about six months. For the elderly, grieving may be more complex than it is for younger people. Over a relatively brief period, and at a time when their coping capacities and resources may be diminished, they often experience the deaths of many people who were important to them.

The intensity of a person's grief depends on a number of factors, including the quality of the lost relationship, the age of the deceased, and the suddenness of the death. For many people, no matter how private they may be in their grief, holidays are especially difficult because they are so connected to families and friends. People who are grieving may dread the normal festivities because everything—from cards and decorations to special meals and traditional music—may remind them of the loved one who has died. Counselors and therapists suggest that survivors not force themselves to participate in special family traditions if doing so is too painful (Thomas-Lester, 1994).

Consoling the Bereaved

Most of us feel awkward when we attempt to console a grieving friend or relative. We want to be helpful, but we don't know what will help. Typically, we resort to platitudes: "I know you must have many wonderful memories of so-and-so," or "Time will help ease your pain." Belsky (1988: 180–81) offers some suggestions for comforting an elderly family member or friend:

1. Often the best thing to do is say "I'm sorry" and then listen, giving the bereaved person a chance to talk if she or he wishes. Your goal is not to make things better, for nothing you say or do really can.

2. Even when you try your hardest to be sensitive, you may put your foot in your mouth. It does not matter. Even if you are rebuffed at times,

it is important that you continue to be there. In the long run, just your presence and caring will be a comfort to the bereaved person.

3. If you have special expertise, such as knowledge of estate law or taxes, and if the person seeks your advice, by all means offer it, but don't try to tell the person what to do: "You should be going out more," or "Why don't you sell your house?" Ask, instead, "What can I do to help?"

Adults sometimes don't realize that children may be confused or experience grief over a death. Parents may be so involved in their own loss that they overlook a child's attachment to the person who has died. Some *thanatologists*—social scientists who study death and grief—encourage parents and educators to talk about death with children openly and honestly (see the box "Helping Children Grieve"), and to teach children how to deal with loss, especially the loss of someone they love.

*C*HOICES

Helping Children Grieve

Because families are becoming increasingly complex and multi-generational, many children will experience the death not only of grandparents but also of great-grandparents, stepgrandparents, and other relatives. The following are some ways that Huntley (1991: 38–42) suggests for helping children grieve:

1. *Recognize that each child will grieve differently:* How children will grieve is influenced both by the responses of those close to them and by their relationship with the deceased. Moreover, children may have mixed emotions if the deceased was sometimes unloving or uncaring.

2. *Encourage questions:* When someone dies, children usually want to know what has happened and what will follow next. Tell them honestly what has occurred and explain what the word *dead* means. Don't be afraid to say "I don't know" when you don't know. If at any time you cannot deal with the children's questions (because you may be physically or emotionally exhausted, for example), tell

them why you can't explain now and specify when you will be able to talk with them about the death.

3. *Encourage the expression of feelings:* Encourage children to show their emotions. Don't say things like "Don't feel bad" because it suggests that children should bury their feelings (James and Cherry, 1988). Talk about other people's feelings as well. For example, if Grandma seems to be angry, explain that it is not because the children did anything wrong but because Grandma is upset that the doctors couldn't save Grandpa's life. Because children, like adults, vary in the degree to which they are comfortable expressing feelings, some may prefer to write down their thoughts, make an album of photos of the loved one, draw pictures or paint, or do some other kind of activity.

4. *Encourage participation in events following the death:* Tell the children about the events that will be taking place (wake, funeral, burial). Explain that these rituals provide us with a way to say good-bye to the deceased, but don't force children to participate in these events if they are uncomfortable or are fright-

ened by them. Instead, a child may prefer to commemorate the life of the deceased in his or her own way. For example, "If . . . Erin and her grandmother used to play under a particular tree at Grandma's house, then maybe Erin would like to plant a similar tree at home in her own backyard" (Huntley, 1991: 41).

5. *Try to maintain a sense of normalcy:* To restore some semblance of security, try to follow the children's normal routine as closely as possible. In the first few months following the death, try to avoid making any drastic changes, such as moving, unless it is absolutely necessary.

6. *Take advantage of available resources:* Schools, churches or local hospitals sometimes have children's support groups. When children get together with other bereaved children, they become aware that they are not alone in their grief. Books written for children can be helpful, whether read by an adult to children or by children themselves. When necessary, counselors who specialize in the area of grief and bereavement can help both you and your child.

BEING WIDOWED

The death of a spouse often means not just the loss of a life companion but the end of a whole way of life. Unfamiliar jobs—managing the finances, cooking meals, fixing the faucet—suddenly fall on the surviving spouse. Friendships may change or even end because many close relationships during marriage are based on being a couple. Other ties, such as relationships with in-laws, may weaken or erode.

Rates of Widowhood and Widowerhood

As Figure 18.4 shows, there are more widows than widowers in all age categories 65 and over for all races. At age 65 and over, 41 percent of women live alone, compared to only 16 percent of men (Saluter, 1994). The numbers of elderly people living alone are expected to increase from 9 percent in 1990 to over 15 percent in 2020. Most of them will be women. Why? First, the life expectancy of women at age 65 now exceeds that of men of the same age by almost seven years. Second, married men have death rates two to three times higher than those of married women

of the same age. Third, a wife is typically three or four years younger than her husband, which increases the likelihood that she will survive him. Fourth, widowers over age 65 are eight times as likely to remarry as are widows. As we discussed in Chapter 8, social norms encourage the marriage of older men to younger women but discourage marriage between older women and younger men. Given the large pool of eligible women (those who are younger, widowed, divorced, or never married) and the shortage of men, it is easier for older men to remarry.

Coping with Widowhood

Many recently widowed men and women exhibit such depressive symptoms as sadness, insomnia, appetite loss, weight loss, tearfulness, and self-dissatisfaction. Some longitudinal studies report that men and women experience similar physical and emotional difficulties initially and, with time, do not differ much in their ability to cope with the loss of a spouse (Brubaker, 1991). In a study of recent widows, however, George Zubenko and Wendy Nuss (cited in Herman, 1992) noted several risk factors that might iden-

Figure 18.4 The Widowed in the United States: 1993 (Saluter, 1994: 1-3).

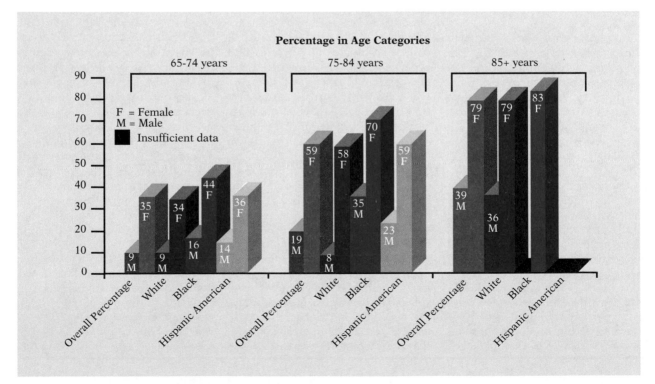

tify women likely to plunge into a protracted, major depression after the death of their husbands: never having worked outside the home having had earlier psychiatric disorders and believing that they had few friends and family to help them.

It is unclear whether, in the long run, widowhood is more difficult for women or men. Many researchers have found that adaptation to widowhood is related to income (see Brubaker, 1991, for a summary of the recent research on this topic). For both men and women, the financial situation is related to feelings of well-being. The emotional pain of losing a spouse coupled with the burden of the costs associated with a fatal illness can seem overwhelming.

Women who have been economically dependent on their husbands often find their incomes drastically reduced. If they are under 60 years of age and have never worked outside the home, they may experience the "widow's gap": Under present law, unless she is disabled, a widow is not eligible for Social Security benefits until she is 60. Moreover, some private pension plans provide no coverage for the spouse after the husband's death (Choi, 1992). Insurance benefits, when they exist, tend to be exhausted within two years of the husband's death. Financial hardships may be especially great for a woman who cared for a spouse during a long illness or who depleted their joint resources during the spouse's institutionalization. Furthermore, many older widows have few opportunities to increase their income through paid employment.

Widowers' financial problems vary according to their educational and occupational levels. Men with high educational levels and higher-status jobs often have generous Social Security benefits, pension plans that are supplemented by employers, and investments (such as stocks and bonds) that yield annual interest or can be sold. Not all widowers are so fortunate, however, and children are sometimes surprised that they must provide for fathers who have worked all their lives and, the children assume, have prepared for retirement (Burgess, 1988).

Social Isolation and Loneliness

Men more often complain of loneliness and seem to make slower emotional recoveries after the death of a spouse than do women. They may be less comfortable expressing such emotions as grief because they have been less intimately involved in family and friendship roles throughout life. Their limited homemaking skills and experience may also contribute to feelings of helplessness and isolation (Anderson, 1984).

Many men have depended on their wives not only for emotional support and household maintenance but for arranging a social life as well. Consequently, men appear to "need" remarriage more than women do in order to restructure their lives. Whereas widows often have fewer resources than married women, they often have more time and more freedom to help friends and relatives, such as preparing meals, taking care of children, or doing the laundry (Gallagher and Gerstel, 1993). Thus, their ties with family and friends may strengthen in widowhood.

Unlike women, many men have few confidants other than their wives. Thus, when their wives die, many men often find themselves alone in coping with their grief, without anyone to whom they can feel free to "bare their souls." In general, widowers tend to interact with others much less frequently than widows, and this pattern tends to become more noticeable over time (Burgess, 1988). Among African Americans, however, both widows and widowers may maintain contact with friends on an equally frequent basis (Taylor et al., 1993).

Generally, widowhood increases social isolation for both men and women. Community affiliations may be important in coping with loneliness. In their study of widowed men and women, Siegel and Kuykendall (1990) found that men were more depressed than women after a spouse's death, especially if they did not belong to any religious organization. Mental and physical impairments are higher for widowed persons of both sexes than they are for married persons of the same age. In addition, chronic illness, suicide, and death tend to be more common among widowed persons and particularly among men without additional support systems (Hooyman and Kiyak, 1991).

Many widows and most widowers begin to date again within a few years after losing a mate. Friendship is the most important reason for dating. Like younger people, older people enjoy having friends and companions to share interests and on whom they can call in emergencies. As we discussed in Chapter 8, dating also prevents loneliness and isolation. Having a confidant is especially important for men who grew up during an era when it was considered unmasculine to have intimate relationships with one's chil-

Dancing is not only a way to be with people and, sometimes, to meet possible companions or mates but also a healthy exercise. Square dancing and related forms of "country" dancing have become increasingly popular, especially among older adults.

dren, other men, or female friends. Lovers play a crucial role because love, intimacy, and sexual activity continue to be an important part of life for the older person. And finally, caregivers are important as providers of emotional and physical help in the event of accidents or illness.

FAMILY CAREGIVING IN LATER LIFE

We often hear that adult children today ignore their elderly parents and place them in institutions instead of caring for them themselves. In 1992, the media publicized the notion of "granny dumping"—abandoning an elderly person with Alzheimer's disease or some other form of mental disorder in a public place such as a shopping mall. However, such cases are the exception. Children today actually provide more care (and more difficult care) to more parents over much longer periods of time than they did in the so-called good old days. For example, fewer than 10 percent of family members who care for the frail elderly receive assistance from any formal services outside the home (Cox, 1993).

Who Provides Care?

You may have heard the expression "the sandwich generation." The **sandwich generation** is composed of midlife men and women who feel caught between meeting responsibilities to both

their own children and to their aging parents. According to Zal (1992: 1), "they find themselves tightly sandwiched between the needs and problems of their adolescent and young adult children, as they push toward independence, and their aging parents as they slowly slide into a more dependent role."

An estimated 20 to 30 percent of workers over age 30 are involved in caregiving, and these numbers are expected to grow well into the future (Field and Minkler, 1993). Midlife adults are not the only caregivers, however. Spouses are most likely to care for aging or infirm partners, and a third of the caregivers of the frail elderly are themselves over 65. As parents age, however, adult children provide more care, and daughters outnumber sons as caretakers by more than three to one (Cox, 1993).

Sometimes the need for caregiving arises abruptly. An aged mother suffers a stroke, and after a brief hospitalization, her grown children are told she is no longer acutely ill but will require constant care for the rest of her life. At other times the problem sets in gradually. An elderly man grows increasingly feeble and forgetful until his family reluctantly concludes he can no longer fend for himself. Either way, patient and family soon face a second issue: how to provide and pay for long-term care. **Medicare**—a federal hospital and medical insurance program for people age 65 and over—does not cover the costs of such custodial services. **Medicaid**—a health-care program financed jointly by state and federal government for low-income people of all ages—will pay for a nursing home, but only after the patient has depleted virtually all of his or her assets.

Family Support Systems

The family is an important caregiving unit for the elderly. The fact that only 5 percent of the elderly are institutionalized—typically in nursing homes—shows that families are the primary source of assistance for frail, elderly people. Some formal support services exist, but they are often expensive or limited to elderly people who are ambulatory, who can take care of their physical needs, and who do not suffer from mental illness.

Day Care for the Elderly
One formal support service that is catching on across the United States is the day-care center for the elderly. This type of program is in the vanguard of efforts to keep elderly people out of nursing homes and in their own homes and communities as long as possible. Most centers are run by nonprofit organizations, such as churches or government-funded senior centers. Increasingly, hospitals and nursing homes are also instituting day-care programs.

Many centers provide transportation, and some have medical personnel on staff. Most are open from early morning to midafternoon. Some even offer overnight and weekend services. These centers provide needed respite for family caregivers—allowing them to work, run errands, or spend time with their children. At an average cost to patients of $37 a day, the programs are inexpensive—less than the cost of one nursing visit to a patient's home. In comparison, most nursing homes charge more than $100 a day. For the aging participants, the centers offer structure, stimulation, social life, and a chance for renewed self-esteem.

The better centers offer a variety of programs, according to the level of care the older person needs. Clients may play bingo, volleyball, or other games, according to their physical capabilities. They attend picnics and lectures and sometimes join with preschoolers for activities like barbecues or finger painting. Most centers accept clients with mild to moderate mental difficulties. Some even offer "pet therapy," in which elderly patients, especially those who are withdrawn, often open up to the antics and affectionate behavior of pet dogs or cats, usually brought for visits by volunteers. Alzheimer's experts say the extra stimulation of a day-care center seems to help stave off some mental deterioration in these patients. Often the lighting, color schemes, furniture, and background music in the centers are chosen to have a calming effect, and many include fenced paths for patients who tend to wander. Some have exercise programs, showers, and beauty parlors run by local beauticians.

The day-care center's biggest problem is financial. More than half of existing programs are operating at a deficit. In some states, Medicaid will cover fees for elderly people who meet income requirements. The middle-income group is the one that can't afford to participate because attending five days a week can cost $700 or more a month—far more than the average Social Security check pays. Some long-term-care insurance providers are considering covering adult day-care expenses. Some for-profit groups, like ElderCare, Inc., feel there is a strong market for such a service. Members of such groups would be charged $40 a day, and the organization would serve up to 75 people (compared to about 20 for nonprofit groups) and have franchises (Beck et al., 1990).

Older people have more options today in finding appropriate living arrangements. As the box "Housing Options for Older People" indicates, the range of available amenities and services includes home health care, housekeeping, meals, property maintenance, recreational facilities, and transportation.

Caregiving Styles

Families care for their elderly members in different ways. According to Matthews and Rosner (1988), there are five primary types of family caregiving in later life.

The style that forms the backbone of the caregiving system is *routine* help. The adult child incorporates regular assistance to the elderly parent into his or her ongoing activities. For this system to work, a family member—generally one of the elderly person's children—is regularly available to do whatever needs to be done. Routine involvement may include a wide range of activities: household chores ("I do Mom's cleaning, dusting, vacuuming, and laundry"); checking to

Housing Options for Older People

You saw in Chapter 9 (see the box "Senior Communes") that some older people are pooling their resources and establishing communal living arrangements. Besides such traditional possibilities as apartments and mobile homes, there are many other options:

Accessory apartment: Completely private living unit created in surplus space inside a single-family residence and rented either to outside tenants or to relatives.

Assisted-living facility: Residential long-term care environment in which residents have rooms, meals, help with activities of daily living, and some protective supervision or 24-hour care.

Board-and-care home: Similar to assisted living except on a smaller scale; more personal-care services are included.

Congregate housing: Specially planned, designed, and managed multi-unit rented housing, typically with self-contained apartments. Supportive services include communal meals, housekeeping, transportation, and social and recreational activities.

Continuing-care retirement community: Housing development planned, designed, and operated to provide a full range of accommodations and services for older adults, including independent living, congregate housing, assisted-living, and nursing home care.

Cooperative housing: Facility occupied by tenants who own shares of stock in the complex (but not the individual unit) and share costs of maintaining it in exchange for the right to occupy the unit.

ECHO (elder cottage housing opportunity): Separate, self-contained removable living unit placed on same property as and adjacent to existing home as a residence for a relative or tenant.

Foster-care home: Single-family residence in which nonrelated older people live with a foster family that provides meals, housekeeping, and personal care. Many foster families care for frail or disabled elderly (see Gilman, 1994).

Retirement community: Large, self-sufficient, age-segregated residential development containing owned and/or rental units. Support services and recreational amenities are often available.

Retirement hotel: Remodeled hotel or apartment complex that has been converted to residential units designed for independent older people. Hotellike services, such as housekeeping and messages, are provided.

Townhouse/condominium: Collection of individual living units owned by residents; includes common areas that are shared. The complex of units usually includes parking, a swimming pool, and recreation rooms (*Modern Maturity*, 1993).

---

see the person is all right ("I call Dad twice a day"); providing outings ("Every Tuesday I take Mom shopping for the day"); running errands ("I've always done Mom's grocery shopping"); managing finances ("I pay all of Mom's bills"); and visiting ("Tuesday and Saturday afternoons I spend visiting Dad").

In a second style, relatives serve as *backups*. Although one person may provide routine care to an aging parent, a brother or sister may step in when needed. For example, one sister explained, "I do what my sisters instruct me to do." She responded to her sisters' requests but did not initiate involvement. Another sibling was described as the "favorite child" and was called in primarily when a parent needed to be "convinced" to do something that the routine caregivers thought was necessary.

The *circumscribed* style of participation is highly predictable but carefully bounded. For example, one respondent said of her brother, "He gives a routine, once-a-week call." This call was important to the parent. The brother was not expected to increase his participation in providing parental care, however. Siblings who adopt this style can be counted on to help, but there are clear limits to what they can be called on to do. For example, in one family, a son who was a physician was relied on for medical advice or assistance but was not expected to assume any other responsibility.

In contrast to the first three types of caregiving, the *sporadic* style describes adult children who provide services to parents at their own convenience. For example, one daughter said, "We invite Mom to go along when we take trips."

Another said, "My brother comes when he feels like it to take Mother out on Sunday, but it's not a scheduled thing." Some siblings don't mind this behavior but others resent brothers and sisters who avoid the most demanding tasks:

[My sister and I] were always very close, and we're not now. I don't think she comes down often enough. . . . She calls, big deal: that's very different from spending three to four hours a day. . . . She does not wheel my mother to the doctor, she does not carry her to the car, she does not oversee the help (Abel, 1991: 154).

The last style is *disassociation* from filial responsibility altogether. This behavior is quite predictable: Other siblings know that they cannot count at all on a sibling. In one family of three daughters, for example, the two younger sisters were routinely involved in helping their mother, whereas their older sister "is not included in our discussions or dealing with mother. . . . She doesn't do anything." Such children do not always disassociate themselves entirely from the family. In one case, the brother had broken off contact with his mother early in his life and consequently from parental care but not from contact with his siblings. His sister explained, "My brother has no interest at all and does not care about mother to any extent. The few times he comes into town, we deliberately don't discuss Mother with him" (Matthews and Rosner, 1988: 188–89).

The Joys and Stresses of Caregiving

Caregivers are not a homogeneous group. Some enjoy caregiving and believe that family relationships can be renewed or strengthened by helping elderly members. They see caregiving as a "labor of love" because of strong ties of affection that have always existed in the family. For others, caregiving provides a feeling of being useful and needed. As one daughter said, "For me, that's what life's all about!" (Guberman et al., 1992: 601). Caring for parents may be especially gratifying when the work does not conflict with employment and when the provider is not caring for a number of family members or relatives (Gerstel and Gallagher, 1993).

Often, however, caretaking can create stress and strain. Older people often need more support at a time when their children's lives are complicated with many varied responsibilities, and families are often unprepared for the problems involved in caring for an elderly person. In general, daily routines are disrupted, caregivers are confined to the home, and parent-child conflict may increase. Parents who are cognitively impaired, who can't accomplish basic daily tasks of self-care, and/or who engage in disruptive behavior are the most difficult to care for (Montgomery et al., 1985).

Financial burdens include not only the direct costs of medical care but also such indirect costs as lost income or missed promotions. Funds for services to reduce caregivers' strains are limited. Women are more likely than men to quit their jobs or to decrease their work hours to provide care (Abel, 1991). Those who interrupt employment to be parental caregivers generally receive fewer retirement benefits.

The emotional burdens of feeling alone, isolated, and without time for oneself appear to be the greatest costs of caregiving. Rates of depression increase, especially among female caregivers, and distress may be intensified by the lack of information about and access to potential helping services. Even when support is available, the caregiver of the disabled, frail, or mentally ill elderly frequently face many years of increasing dependence, decline, and demanding physical care tasks (see Wilson, 1990). Particularly when formal support services are unavailable or unknown, caregivers' feelings of isolation and stress may intensify. In some cases, stress may become severe enough to lead to family breakdown, neglect, or even abuse of the older person. In addition, an adult child may often have to forgo important social events and activities to meet caregiving needs. This may create additional strain and role conflict (Mui and Morrow-Howell, 1993).

Most often, it is a daughter or daughter-in-law who is responsible for organizing and providing care to an elderly family member. Although married female caretakers get more financial and emotional support from their spouses and children than do never-married, divorced, or remarried female caregivers, they often experience strain because of the competing demands from their spouses and children, on the one hand, and their elderly relative on the other (Brody et al., 1992). A troubled marital relationship may become more problematic with such added stress. Or, if female caretakers do not get support from their immediate family, they can fall into the "martyrdom trap" by making unreasonable demands on themselves (Couper and Sheehan, 1987).

For many women, caring for elderly relatives is not a single episode but continues throughout their life course, and dependence/independence issues may be replayed many times. The caregiving may be necessary for multiple elderly relatives and may be multilayered as a person's parents, in-laws, grandparents, and other elderly relatives require help sequentially or simultaneously. Given the discrepancy in life expectancy for men and women, it is inevitable that many of these women will also care for dependent husbands in the future.

CONCLUSION

As this chapter has shown, there are many similarities in later-life families. Women tend to live longer, and men are more likely to remarry after being widowed. On the one hand, because of an increased life expectancy, many of us will have more *choices* in later life as to how we will spend our "golden years" and how we will play grandparenting roles. On the other hand, we will also face *constraints,* the most serious of which is how we will care for aging family members, especially during economic recessions.

Another critical issue is how we will respond to the *changes* of an aging population that has diverse social, health, and financial needs. As we have discussed in earlier chapters, today's lifestyles vary greatly. Some people remain single, some marry but have no children, and some marry several times. These variations will probably continue as people age. Conner (1992: 203) notes that "perhaps the biggest challenge for the future is to successfully meet the needs of our increasingly diverse population of senior citizens." Meeting family needs in the future is the focus of the last chapter.

Taking Action_____

Check Out a Variety of Resources

Although many challenges are associated with aging, there are also a wealth of resources.

• For information about **housing for older people,** contact your local Area Agency on Aging or call the U.S. Administration on Aging's Eldercare Locator's toll-free number, 800–677–1116 (Monday–Friday, 9 A.M.–11 P.M.). You can also order *The Consumers' Directory of Continuing Care Retirement Communities,* which has profiles of more than 550 nonprofit communities across the country. Call the American Association of Homes and Services for the Aging, 800–508–9442 or 301–490–0677 ($24.95 plus $3.50 for shipment).

• Caregivers have access to a variety of resources. You can get a free copy of *a Checklist of Concerns/Resources for Caregivers* (D12895) and *A Path for Caregivers* (D12957) from the American Association of Retired Persons, AARP Fulfillment, EE0684, Dept. P., 601 E Street, N.W., Washington, DC 20049. You can also get free single copies of AARP's Women's Initiative Publication list, which covers such issues as **health, retirement, caregiving, and disability.** For $1.50 you can get a 15-page pamphlet, *Healthy Aging,* recommended by the Administration on Aging, that includes information about nutrition, exercise, mental health, and more. Send a self-addressed stamped envelope to ETNET, Box 7536, Dept. P, Wilton, CT 06897. A 34-page brochure, *Depression in Later Life: Recognition and Treatment,* from the Oregon State University Extension Service also costs $1.50; write OSU, #PNW347, Publication Orders, Dept. P, Agriculture Communications, Administration Services, Room A422, Corvallis, OR 97331–2119. In addition, you can get a free copy of the National Institute of Mental Health's booklet *If You're over 65 and Feeling Depressed* (call 800–421–4211 and specify that you're requesting publications for the elderly). For caregivers dealing with **Alzheimer's disease** or related problems, the Alzheimer's Association provides a wide range of services for people 50 or older. Consult your local chapter for information and assistance. Alzheimer's Family Care sponsors 24-hour telephone information, referral, and support services for caregivers (800–600–1600).

• Information and help to **grandparents** are available from a number of sources: *Grandparents Rights: A Resource Manual* (1992) can be obtained from the U.S. Government Printing Office, Washington, DC. Grandparents Reaching Out (GRO) offers support to grandparents who want to care for, or take custody of, their own grandchildren (141 Glensummer Road; Holbrook, NY 11741; 516–472 9728); the Brookdale Grandparent Information Project, Center on Aging, University of California, 140 Warren Hall, Berkeley, CA 94720 (510–643–6427), provides information on grandparents raising grandchildren and has a free mailing list.

• For information about **hospice care,** or for referral to a hospice program operating in your area, call the National Hospice Organization's Helpline at 800–658–8898. Or contact the group's offices at 1901 North Moore Street, Suite 901, Arlington, VA 22209 (703–243–5900).

• You can join **online discussions about aging-related topics** through GERINET (Geriatric Health Care Discussion Group), LISTSERV@UBVM.BITNET, or LISTSERV@UBVM.CC.BUFFALO.EDU. Aging women's issues are discussed in WMN-HLTH (LISTSERV@UWAVM.BITNET or LISTSERV@UWAVM.U.WASHINGTON.EDU).

SUMMARY

1. The aging of our society is occurring at an exceedingly rapid pace owing to several factors: a decrease in fertility rates, an increase in life expectancy, and a faster growth of the nonwhite and Hispanic American elderly populations.

2. Although there is great diversity in the aged population, people age 65 and over must confront such similar aging tasks as accepting changes in health, dealing with stereotypes, and coping with mandatory retirement.

3. One of the biggest changes during the last two or three decades has been the rapid growth of the multigenerational family. Because families now often span three or four generations, the importance of the grandparent role has increased.

4. There are at least five styles of grandparenting: remote, companionate, involved, advisory, and surrogate. The styles often reflect such factors as the grandparents' age, physical proximity, and relationships with their own children, especially their daughter.

5. Adult children's divorce creates both opportunities and dilemmas for grandparents. Sometimes their relationships with grandchildren are strengthened, but sometimes they increasingly lose touch.

6. All families must deal with the death of elderly parents. Physicians and other health-care professionals often view death in terms of the dying trajectory. Alternatively, the dying process can be understood from the point of view of the dying person and/or those who will survive the person.

7. Although many elderly parents and relatives die in hospitals and nursing homes, hospice care provides an alternative by making the patient more comfortable and by providing companionship, a sense of security, and control of pain.

8. On the average, women live nearly seven years longer than men. Although most women outlive their husbands, both widows' and widowers' coping strategies typically involve adapting to a change in income as well as dealing with loneliness and the emotional pain of losing a spouse.

9. Children today provide more care (and more difficult care) to more parents over much longer periods of time than ever before. As our population ages, more disabled and frail Americans will need long-term care.

10. Caregiving includes both family support systems and formal services such as day care for the elderly. There are several caregiving styles, and all involve love as well as some degree of stress. For the most part, the primary caregivers are women.

KEY TERMS

ADDITIONAL READING

Some of the periodicals devoted to aging issues are *Research on Aging, International Journal of Aging and Human Development, The Gerontologist,* and *The Journals of Gerontology.* The latter divides each issue into four sections: social, biological, medical, and psychological sciences.

RONALD P. ABELES, HELEN C. GIFT, and MARCIA G. ORY, eds., *Aging and Quality of Life* (New York: Springer, 1994). Includes articles on healthy aging, older people and the environment, race and the quality of life in aging, and health care policy.

SCOTT A. BASS and ROBERT MORRIS, eds., *International Perspectives on State and Family Support for the Elderly* (New York: Haworth Press, 1993). Contributors discuss caregiving and health-care policy in the United States, Canada, China, Hong Kong, the United Kingdom, Austria, Denmark, and Sweden.

MAGGIE CALLANAN and PATRICIA KELLEY, *Final Gifts: Understanding the Special Awareness, Needs and Communications of the Dying* (New York: Poseidon Press, 1992). Written by two hospice nurses, this book provides insights about dying patients and suggestions for coping with grief.

BETTY FRIEDAN, *The Fountain of Age* (New York: Simon & Schuster, 1993). Discusses the "age mystique," work and love, menopause, nursing homes, and dying.

EVA KAHANA, DAVID E. BIEGEL, and MAY L. WYKLE, eds., 1994. *Family Caregiving Across the Lifespan* (Thousand Oaks, CA: Sage). Contributors present theoretical and empirical studies on caregiving across the life cycle as well as on the relationships between formal care providers and caregiving families.

SHERWIN B. NULAND, *How We Die: Reflections on Life's Final Chapter* (New York: Knopf, 1994). A physician provides a compassionate, but very graphic, description of how people die.

LENORA MADISON POE, *Black Grandparents as Parents* (Berkeley, CA: L.M. Poe, 1992). Although based on only 14 interviews, Poe's study offers insightful comments on the role of black grandparents who become surrogate parents when their adult children start using drugs.

MICHAEL W. PRATT and JOAN E. NORRIS, *The Social Psychology of Aging: A Cognitive Perspective* (Cambridge, MA: Blackwell, 1994). Discusses such topics as theoretical perspectives on social cognition, thinking about self/others/relationships/society, decision-making, and communication.

EDWARD H. THOMPSON, JR., ed., *Older Men's Lives* (Thousand Oaks, CA: Sage, 1994). The contributors examine such issues as health, sexuality, marital and family roles, and retirement.

19
The Family in the Twenty-first Century

Data Digest

- By 2010, **couples with children under age 18** are expected to make up 38 percent of all married-couple households, dropping from 47 percent in 1990.

- The number of **households headed by single mothers under age 25** is expected to increase by 44 percent, from 831,000 in 1995 to 1.2 million in 2010.

- The number of single fathers could grow 44 percent between 1990 and 2010, to 1.7 million, but will remain less than 2 percent of all households.

- **One-person households,** 24 percent of all households in 1995, are expected to make up 27 percent of all households in 2010.

- Between 1995 and 2010, it is **middle-aged householders who are expected to increase most in number.** Householders age 45 to 54 are expected to go from 17 million to 25 million, a 45 percent increase; households headed by people between 55 and 64 are expected to rise from 12 million to 20 million, a 62 percent increase.

- The number of **elderly householders** will grow 5 percent between 1995 and 2000, from 21.7 million to 22.8 million. By 2010, this group is expected to increase another 14 percent in the following decade, to 26.1 million in 2010.

- Between 1985 and 1992, **federal and state spending on several major welfare programs increased:** Medicaid rose from $41 billion to $118 billion; Supplemental Security Income from $12 billion to $23 billion; Aid to Families with Dependent Children from $17 billion to $25 billion; and food stamps from $14 billion to $25 billion.

- **Social Security, Medicare, Medicaid, and federal retirement payments** amounted to about 30 percent of the U.S. budget in 1963. By 2003, these payments will be 72 percent of the federal budget.

- **Deadbeat parents** who don't pay child support are predominantly fathers (95 percent). In 1995, deadbeat parents owed $34 billion to 17 million children.

SOURCES: U.S. Bureau of the Census, 1994b; Miller, 1995; Simpson, 1995; Van Biema, 1995.

In 1992, in an unprecedented lawsuit, an 11-year-old Florida boy asked a judge to "divorce" him from his parents. To protect the boy and his two younger brothers from their abusive, alcoholic father and neglectful mother, the children had been placed in the care of social service agencies for nearly two and a half years. During that time, the 11-year-old had lived in three foster homes and a boys' home. He chose to stay with the last foster family, a couple with eight children, who wanted to adopt him. The boy's mother and father, who were separated, tried to regain custody of their son. The mother's attorney argued that parents have the constitutional right to control the custody of their children. The boy's foster father, also an attorney, maintained that children have a right to pursue happiness. The judge ruled that the boy could be adopted by his foster parents.

Some people would undoubtedly cite this case as another example of the American family in decline. Others might argue that the case illustrates the *strength* of the family because the boy was determined to be part of a loving household. The idea that the family is an important institution has been a major theme throughout this book. In this chapter we consider where the family is going in the future: how will the family of the next century differ from the family of today?

In considering the family of the twenty-first century, we will assume that the dynamic processes that have shaped the family in earlier times will continue to influence the family in the future. In this chapter we discuss some of the changes, choices, constraints, and critical issues that marriages and families are likely to encounter in the future. We will also consider the impact on families of **family policy**—the measures taken by governmental bodies to achieve specific objectives relating to the family's well-being. Remember, once again, that although this chapter has been organized into separate sections on changes, choices, and constraints, these dimensions overlap. For example, although changes may bring us more

In 1992 Gregory Kingsley won the right to "divorce" his biological mother and to stay with his foster parents, who planned to adopt him.

choices, our choices are often limited by a variety of constraints.

CHANGES IN THE FAMILY OF THE TWENTY-FIRST CENTURY

If we were suddenly transported to the year 2050, undoubtedly many of the families we would see would be very familiar. The greatest changes would probably be in four areas: racial and ethnic diversity, reproductive technologies, family structure, and children's rights.

Racial-Ethnic Diversity

One of the most striking changes in American society today, the growth of racially and ethnically diverse families, is expected to continue in the future. Factors such as immigration from abroad and higher fertility rates among African Americans and some Asian American and Hispanic American groups contribute to this change. People of color currently account for 24 percent of the U.S. population and are expected to account for 30 percent by 2020 (Population Reference Bureau, 1990). As minorities make up a larger share of the population and the labor force, they will have a greater impact on political, educational, and economic institutions.

In the next century we can expect to see continued growth and change among many racial-ethnic communities. For example, whereas the most recent Asian Indian, Cambodian, and South American immigrants often live and work in interethnic areas of many large cities, Filipino and Korean American families have been moving to the suburbs and establishing communities where they have their own houses of worship and programs to teach their native languages to their children. At the same time, interracial marriage has been increasing, particularly among African American men on the West Coast and second- and third-generation Asian Americans. Dating and marriage across ethnic and racial lines may create intergenerational conflict between children who are becoming more assimilated and their elders who try to maintain ethnic traditions, language, and rituals.

In 1992, the United Population Fund reported that the world population rate was increasing more rapidly than had been anticipated. For example, by 1998 the world's population is now expected to reach 6 billion rather than the 5 billion projected a few years ago. The fact that most of the growth will be in the poorest countries of Africa, southern Asia, and Latin America has several implications for the United States. Because many people in these areas still see the United States as a land of opportunity, many families from these countries will be immigrating to America. And because many Americans are unwilling to work for low wages that keep them in poverty, pressure will probably be brought on immigration authorities, leading to a more flexible policy that will allow entry to people who *are* willing to work at below minimum wage (see Chapter 13).

Reproductive Technologies

Many people are turning to what are often called "assisted" reproduction techniques because they are infertile or because they have waited until their 30s or later to start a family and have difficulty conceiving or because there are not many healthy babies available for adoption. As we discussed in Chapter 11, although the new technologies undeniably allow many people who could not otherwise have babies become parents, these technologies also create many dilemmas. One of the biggest problems is that because few sperm banks follow the American Fertility Society guidelines regarding donors and insemination, and because these banks are as yet unregulated, there is a high risk that semen used in artificial reproduction techniques may transmit such diseases as AIDS or other sexually transmitted diseases, cystic fibrosis, sickle-cell anemia, or Tay-Sachs, a neurological disorder (Squires, 1992).

Not all physicians who provide fertility services are ethical. In 1991, for example, a doctor in Vienna, Virginia, was arrested for illegal practices. Although he told his patients that he was impregnating them with sperm from a sperm bank, the physician had used his own sperm to father more than 70 children. Convicted on 52 counts of fraud and perjury, he was sentenced to five years in prison. He was also required to pay $116,805 in fines and restitution and to spend three years on probation after his release from prison. In 1992, doctors at Mount Sinai Hospital in New York City were accused of a similar crime. Illegal acts of this sort have serious implications. For example, it is possible that, in the future, half-siblings might unknowingly marry each other.

Some observers urge that laboratories like this one that freeze and store human sperm be regulated to screen out and dispose of samples that contain the genetic codes for diseases like AIDS or cystic fibrosis.

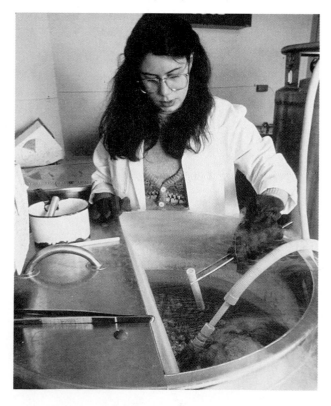

Given the variety of possibilities brought about by reproduction through artificial means, parenting may be quite different in the next century. For example, it will often be difficult to answer children when they ask, "Where did I come from, Mommy?" Many people may have minimal information about their genetic inheritance because many sperm donors are anonymous. There is little indication that laws protecting anonymity will change.

Family Structure

The traditional family structure has already experienced some fundamental changes. As we have seen in earlier chapters, diverse family forms are more acceptable today than ever before, as reflected in many television shows (see Table 19.1). At the same time, this lineup of shows is rarely realistic. For example, at least four shows feature single-father households, but only two portray single-mother households. The star of the one show that features an unwed mother—"Murphy Brown"—is white, upper middle class, and a successful professional. In some shows, such as "Home Improvement," the fathers are doofuses. And in other shows, such as "On Our Own," parents are unnecessary because they were killed before the series began (Rosenfeld, 1994).

In the future, it's likely that the varied family structures we have today will increase in numbers and forms. We will probably see more households that are multigenerational and comprising unrelated adults, as well as more stepfamilies with his, her, and their children. If society's attitude toward homosexuals becomes more positive and domestic partners acquire more legal rights, we may also see greater numbers of families headed by lesbian and gay parents.

Despite these changes, there is no evidence that marriage will be replaced. As we discussed in earlier chapters, although many people are cohabiting and remaining single longer, about 95 percent of Americans marry at least once. There may be small groups of people who practice "free love" or believe in group marriage or communes, but there is no evidence that such alternative structures will be prevalent. Although many family functions have changed since the turn of the century (see Chapter 1), the family is still the primary group that provides the nurturance, love, and emotional sustenance that peo-

Table 19.1

1990s Family Structure According to Television

FAMILY STRUCTURE	TELEVISION SHOW
Married couple with children; father as breadwinner	"Married . . . with Children," "The Simpsons," "The Mommies," "Dave's World"
Married couple with children; two earners	"The Cosby Show," "Roseanne," "Home Improvement"
Married couple with no children	"Mad About You"
Married couple with children and related adults	"Under One Roof," "All-American Girl"
Male householder with children and unrelated adults	"Full House"
Male householder with children and related adults from two generations	"Me and the Boys"
Male householder with children and grandchildren	"Thunder Alley"
Male householder with unmarried adult children	"Empty Nest"
Female householder with children	"Grace Under Fire"
Married couple with children from a previous marriage	"True Colors," "Major Dad"
Married couple with biological and stepchildren	"Fresh Prince of Bel Air"
Children, no adults present	"On Our Own," "Party of Five"
Unmarried mother	"Murphy Brown"
Related and unrelated adults	"Frasier"
Unrelated adults	"Living Single"
Single-person households	"Seinfeld," "Ellen"

ple need to be happy, healthy, and productive. Commuter marriages, increased work responsibilities, divorce, and other stressors aside, many Americans report that the family is one of the most important aspects of their lives (see Chapter 10).

The percentage of single-parent families has increased in recent years for many reasons, including divorce, the greater acceptance of out-of-wedlock births, and the increase in sexual activity among teenagers at earlier ages. Although 25 percent of all out-of-wedlock births are to two-parent, unmarried couples, most unmarried mothers become single parents. Over 6 million households with young children are headed by a single parent, and this number is expected to increase in the future (see Data Digest). As we dis-

cussed in earlier chapters, there is a strong association between socioeconomic status and both marital disruption and out-of-wedlock births. Many racial-ethnic families have been sinking more deeply into poverty (see Chapter 14). Unless there is a dramatic turnaround in the U.S. economy, there is no reason to believe that marriage will become a more attractive option for many young, poor Americans.

Children's Rights

A national study of American families concluded that the United States, the most prosperous nation on earth, is failing many of its children:

Although many children grow up healthy and happy in strong, stable families, far too many do not. They are children whose parents are too stressed and busy to provide caring attention and guidance. They are children who grow up without the material support and personal involvement of their mothers and fathers. They are children who are poor, whose families cannot adequately feed and clothe them and provide safe, secure homes. They are children who are victims of abuse and neglect at the hands of adults they love and trust, as well as those they do not even know. They are children who are born too early and too small, who face a lifetime of chronic illness and disability. They are children who enter school ill prepared for the rigors of learning, who fail to develop the skills and attitudes needed to get good jobs and become responsible members of adult society. They are children who lack hope for what their lives can become, who believe they have little to lose by dropping out of school, having a baby as an unmarried teenager, committing violent crimes, or taking their own lives (National Commission on Children, 1991: vii–viii).

As we discussed in Chapters 12 and 14, such conclusions are well founded. Much of the research has shown not only that the United States has abandoned many of its children, but that the situation has been deteriorating since 1980. Some scholars argue, moreover, that our children are being ignored because adults are investing more in themselves and their personal pursuits than in raising their children (Popenoe, 1993).

The Food Research and Action Center, a nonprofit organization working to alleviate hunger, reports that in the United States, more than 5 million children under 12 go hungry each month (cited in Greer, 1995). Scientific research indicates that hunger and undernutrition rob children of their potential. Biologists and neurologists have found that physical nourishment determines how many brain cells children develop. In addition, researchers also believe that stress activates hormones that can impair learning and memory and lead to intellectual and behavioral developmental problems (Roberts, 1994a).

One bright spot is the future of child support. The first federal legislation to enforce the payment of child support was enacted in 1950, and additional bills were passed in 1965 and 1967, but the 1975 Office of Child Support Enforcement law was the first really significant piece of legislation in this area. The new law not only requires all states to establish state offices of child-support enforcement but provides federal reimbursement for nearly 75 percent of each state's enforcement costs. The 1975 act thus created the bureaucracy to enforce the private child-support obligation. Enacted nine years later, the 1984 **Child Support Enforcement Amendments** require states to adopt formulas and guidelines that the courts can use to determine child-support obligations. These amendments also require the states to withhold moneys equal to child-support obligations from wages and other income of noncustodial parents who are delinquent in their payments (Garfinkel et al., 1994).

In 1988, the **Family Support Act** strengthened the 1984 guidelines, requiring that judges provide a written justification for review by a higher court if they wish to depart from the state guidelines in any way. The act also requires that states review and update the child-support awards handled by the Office of Child Support Enforcement at least every three years. In addition, the legislation requires that by 1994 the states withhold funds for child-support payment in all cases, not just those that are delinquent (Garfinkel, 1992). States have varied quite a bit in enforcing the latter legislation.

Some observers feel that the changes in the child-support system will lead to positive changes in father-child relations. One of the principal claims of fathers' rights organizations is that nonpayment of child support is a response to a mother's refusal to let the father spend time with his child. If this is true, it may be that mothers receiving regular support payments will be more accepting of fathers' visitation rights and wishes.

Moreover, assuming that fathers who have greater financial responsibility may have an incentive to become more involved in parenting, it is expected that child-support reforms will increase the number of fathers who request and obtain joint legal custody. In any case, it's expected that the fathers' rights movement will grow in the future. Proponents argue that caring fathers should get custody more often, have more access to their children, and play a major role in making decisions that affect their children's lives.

Others, however, see the reforms in a less positive light. Critics argue that strengthening the collection process will lead to greater parental conflicts, which, in turn, will have a negative impact on children. According to this view, divorced (or never-married) parents will not be able to cooperate in their coparenting activities without expressing the conflicts and hostilities that led them to separate in the first place (Garfinkel and McLanahan, 1990). Moreover, Bertola and Drakich's (1993) study of postdivorce fathers found that although many wanted equal access to their children and an equal share in decision making, they still were unwilling to share child-care and financial responsibility.

CHOICES OF THE FAMILY IN THE TWENTY-FIRST CENTURY

Some people may not be happy with all the projected changes we've discussed. But what are the alternatives? As Toffler (1980) pointed out, few people would be willing to go back to the "good old days" when there were no computers, no cable television, few educational opportunities for women and many minorities, and a less advanced medical technology. And these and other changes have provided people with more choices. Three areas in which choices have increased are divorce, remarriage, and aging.

Divorce

One of the most dramatic changes in marriages and families throughout the years has been the generally high divorce rate. As we discussed in Chapter 16, divorce rates climbed precipitously during the 1970s, reached a plateau during the 1980s, and declined slightly by the late 1980s. Just over 33 percent of first marriages remain intact for life (Population Reference Bureau, 1990).

It is difficult to predict the future rate of divorce. On the one hand, women who are employed or earn more than their husbands and are in unhappy or abusive marriages feel freer to divorce. In the future, even more women will have such options because the labor force participation of women is expected to increase during the next decade. Some people feel that women's increased educational attainment and employment have led to a rise in divorce rates. On the other hand, there is evidence that people who postpone marriage to pursue educational and career goals have a better chance of forming marriages that will not end in divorce (see Chapters 10 and 16). Still again, as we have seen, when both parents work they have less time to spend with each other and with their children, which also increases stress, guilt, and dissatisfaction with the relationship.

A major issue for the twenty-first century will probably be equitable child-care awards and responsibilities for both parents. Riley (1991: 187) has suggested that everyone might be better off if divorce decrees and child custody decisions were handled separately: "Let one court grant the divorce and another determine custody and financial arrangements. As long as custody of children and spousal support are tied to the divorce process . . . divorcing spouses [are encouraged] to use their children as weapons in their own battles." Separating the legal and social aspects of divorce might also lessen the likelihood that postdivorce children will be poor and might increase the numbers of fathers who maintain satisfying relationships with their children into old age (Cooney, 1993).

Regardless of whether divorce rates rise or remain stable, they will probably change the forms and dynamics of multigenerational families in the next century. As we discussed in Chapter 18, increased life expectancy has meant that many children have more than one grandparent well into their adulthood. Grandparents will probably play a more active role in the future in helping to raise grandchildren after a divorce or between the parents' remarriages.

Remarriage

Until the 1920s, nearly all people who remarried had been widowed. Today, nearly 90 percent of people who remarry have been divorced. The greater acceptance of divorce and remarriage

has given people the chance to create a happier family life the second (or third) time around. As we discussed in Chapter 17, stepfamilies—especially those with children—often face problems that are not present in a first marriage: Family boundaries become more complex and ambiguous, children often resent the "intrusion" of an "outsider," and marital partners may have difficulty providing economic resources and attention equally to biological children and stepchildren. Even when the parents in a stepfamily describe themselves as happy, their relationship with the children may be strained.

Despite these problems, there is no reason to expect remarriage rates to decline in the future. What will probably change are the characteristics of those who remarry. Today, for example, women who are divorced, over 30, and have children, are less likely to remarry (Bumpass et al., 1990). And, as we saw in Chapter 17, remarriage is less likely in general for African American and Hispanic American women. In the future, remarriage rates may be even lower for women who have good jobs and who are less economically dependent on men either for their own welfare or for that of their children.

Aging Issues

As we will discuss later, older people have been very effective in pushing through legislation that provides them with health-care benefits and Social Security benefits that keep up with inflation, as well as in securing tax exemptions for low-income elderly. Two areas in which older people will undoubtedly see changes in the near future are housing and decisions about death and dying.

Housing Changes Although many people 65 years and older are choosing to live in senior communes, retirement communities, and adult-only apartments and condominiums, 84 percent of those 55 and older prefer "aging in place," that is, remaining in their own homes as they grow older (Edelson, 1992). As the first group of baby boomers reaches age 65 in the year 2011, they will probably look for (and demand) houses and apartments that suit the special needs of the older person.

Architects have been designing and building houses and apartments specifically for the elderly for several decades. Examples of some of these structures can be seen in the annual exhibits of the American Institute of Architects and the American Association of Homes for the Aging. Many of these structures include bathrooms with handrails and shower stools to avoid accidents, emergency buttons that enable a resident to summon help, brightly lighted kitchens, cabinets whose drawers are low and easily reached, appliances with controls that are easy to reach, and wide doorways that accommodate wheelchairs or walkers. Other aids to the elderly are blinking lights that attract the attention of the hearing impaired, easy-to-operate faucets for those with arthritis, large-print cookbooks, and wheeled carts for transporting food from the oven to the table (Edelson, 1992). Figure 19.1 shows some of the simple modifications that can make a kitchen more "user-friendly" for an elderly person.

Figure 19.1 Age-Proofing the Kitchen.

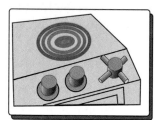

These controls, located in front of the burners, are safe to reach and easy to turn.

Drawer knobs can be replaced with loop handles you can slip your hand through.

Open space below a counter or sink lets you sit while working.

A rolling cart can be pulled out to reach stored items or to open leg space under the counter.

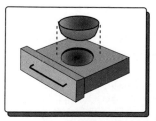

A drawer provides a low work surface that can be used as a cutting board or bowl holder.

A lazy susan brings items around to the front.

Unfortunately, the best-designed houses and apartments are currently available only to the middle and upper-middle classes. If the concept of elderly-oriented housing trickles down, however, by the turn of the century some of the same amenities may become standard for larger groups of elderly.

Death and Dying In 1994, Holland legalized physician-assisted suicide under certain conditions. The patient must have made voluntary, deliberate, and repeated requests to die; the patient must be suffering with no prospect of relief; and the doctor must consult with colleagues before acting. Government figures estimate that in 1991 about 2 percent of all deaths in the Netherlands were assisted suicides, and there is no evidence that Holland's liberal laws have led to an increased number of such suicides (Waxman, 1995).

In the United States, legal, religious, and medical groups have taken a strong stand against assisted suicide. In 1994, however, voters supported a referendum in Oregon to legalize assisted suicide. The provisions of the Oregon proposal were as follows:

- Right-to-die decisions were limited to competent adults who are terminally ill; children were not eligible.

- The patient was required to make at least three requests to the physician, two orally and one in writing over at least 15 days.

- A second physician had to make an independent diagnosis of both terminal illness and of emotional competence.

- If either physician felt the patient was not emotionally stable, the process was to be stopped and the patient was to be referred to a psychiatrist or clinical psychologist.

- The patient was to have the prescription filled and self-administer the drug. Patients not physically able to do this were not to be eligible for the "physician-aid-in-dying" process (Pridonoff, 1994).

Although the referendum passed, it is being appealed. Those opposed to the right-to-die movement argue, among other things, that the elderly may be pressured by caregivers to end their lives, that their acts may be due to feelings of guilt about being a burden, that they should be persuaded that much of their pain is treatable, and that physicians are responsible for extending rather than ending life (see Veatch, 1995).

As we discussed in Chapter 18, the elderly and their families are becoming more vocal about the elderly person's right to die in dignity, at home, and on his or her own terms. In 1992, one of the best-selling books was *Final Exit*, which describes how the elderly and terminally ill can commit suicide. Since then several authors have addressed the right-to-die issue (see, for example, Kramer, 1993; Quill, 1993).

In 1994, a Michigan jury acquitted Dr. Jack Kevorkian of charges that he violated the state's statute prohibiting assisted suicide. Since 1990, Dr. Kevorkian had aided twenty deaths, and five of these occurred after Michigan banned assisted suicide. Kevorkian was charged in four cases, but three were dismissed by judges who found the state law unconstitutional. A significant point made by Kevorkian's attorney in the 1994 jury trial was that the assisted suicide law permits medical procedures that are intended to alleviate pain and suffering—even if the side effects hasten death. Some of the jurors said they were sympathetic to Dr. Kevorkian's "patients" because they had also witnessed lengthy, painful deaths of loved ones. According to Quill (1993), Kevorkian is not alone; 3 to 37 percent of doctors may have helped a patient commit suicide.

Such organizations as Choice in Dying, the Hemlock Society, and Concern for Dying have reported widespread interest in information on living wills. A **living will** (see Figure 19.2) is a legal document in which people can specify what, if any, life support measures they wish to be provided with in the case of serious illness and if or when they wish to have such measures discontinued. Preparing such a document does not guarantee that its dictates will be followed, however. Physicians or hospitals may refuse to honor living wills if their policies support prolonging life at any cost, if family members contest the living will, or if there is any question about the patient's mental competence when the will was drawn up (see Veatch, 1995). For these reasons and because state laws and policies vary widely, people who want living wills to be enforced should consult attorneys to avoid legal problems in the future.

Such expressions of individual rights are bound to increase in the future. Because of their numbers, baby boomers will undoubtedly be instrumental in challenging or promoting euthanasia laws.

CONSTRAINTS ON THE FAMILY IN THE TWENTY-FIRST CENTURY

The family of the twenty-first century will face four major types of constraints. First, *health-related* constraints will be important. Second, families will be faced with increasing *economic concerns*, including poverty, unemployment, low wages, and gender inequality in the workplace. The third set of constraints includes such *work-related issues* as child-care services and parental leave policies. Finally, the *competition for scarce resources* between a graying America and a growing population of disadvantaged children may create tension and conflict for several generations.

Health-Related Issues

In some ways, many Americans are healthier than ever. Smoking and alcohol consumption have decreased. In 1974, for example, about half of those 12 to 17 years of age said they had tried cigarettes and alcohol. By 1992, only 34 percent of this age group had tried smoking, and only 39 percent had tried alcohol. And among older Americans, consumption of red meat and eggs—two foods purportedly associated with stroke and heart disease—decreased greatly between 1970 and 1992 (Holmes, 1994).

Although a number of Americans are adopting healthier lifestyles, three health-related issues will probably have considerable impact on marriages and families in the coming years: HIV and AIDS, the increasing concern about a national health-care system, and abortion rights.

HIV and AIDS Perhaps the single greatest factor affecting family life in the twenty-first century will be the spread of HIV and AIDS (see Chapter 7 and Appendix D). AIDS is increasingly being seen as a societal problem rather than one that affects only "high-risk" individuals. As we discussed in Chapter 7, most of the people who contract HIV today are heterosexual women. Despite this increase, some critics argue, scientists have failed to include women in AIDS research (Wheeler, 1995).

We might expect that people, knowing that

FLORIDA LIVING WILL

INSTRUCTIONS

PRINT THE DATE
PRINT YOUR
NAME

Declaration made this _____ day of _____, 19_____.

I, _____, willfully and voluntarily make known my desire that my dying not be artificially prolonged under the circumstances set forth below, and I do hereby declare:

If at any time I have a terminal condition and if my attending or treating physician and another consulting physician have determined that there is no medical probability of my recovery from such condition, I direct that life-prolonging procedures be withheld or withdrawn when the application of such procedures would serve only to prolong artificially the process of dying, and that I be permitted to die naturally with only the administration of medication or the performance of any medical procedure deemed necessary to provide me with comfort care or to alleviate pain.

It is my intention that this declaration be honored by my family and physician as the final expression of my legal right to refuse medical or surgical treatment and to accept the consequences for such refusal.

In the event that I have been determined to be unable to provide express and informed consent regarding the withholding, withdrawal, or continuation of life-prolonging procedures, I wish to designate, as my surrogate to carry out the provisions of this declaration:

PRINT THE NAME,
HOME ADDRESS
AND TELEPHONE
NUMBER OF YOUR
SURROGATE

Name: _____

Address: _____

_____ Zip Code: _____

Phone: _____

I wish to designate the following person as my alternate surrogate, to carry out the provisions of this declaration should my surrogate be unwilling or unable to act on my behalf:

PRINT NAME,
HOME ADDRESS
AND TELEPHONE
NUMBER OF YOUR
ALTERNATE
SURROGATE

Name: _____

Address: _____

_____ Zip Code: _____

Phone: _____

ADD PERSONAL
INSTRUCTIONS
(IF ANY)

Additional instructions (optional):

I understand the full import of this declaration, and I am emotionally and mentally competent to make this declaration.

SIGN THE
DOCUMENT
WITNESSING
PROCEDURE:
TWO WITNESSES
MUST SIGN AND
PRINT THEIR
ADDRESSES

Signed: _____

Witness 1: _____

  Signed: _____

  Address: _____

Witness 2: _____

  Signed: _____

  Address: _____

Figure 19.2 *This is an example of a Living Will for the state of Florida. For free information for your state, contact Choice in Dying at (800) 989–WILL.* Source: Choice in Dying, 200 Varick Street, New York, NY 10014.

there is no cure for AIDS, would engage in casual sexual intercourse less often and with fewer partners, and that they would use condoms. However, although some homosexuals have changed their patterns of sexual activity, there is little evidence that the threat of HIV-AIDS has changed sexual behavior among heterosexuals. Adolescent males and females are unlikely to protect themselves; and not even college students or other educated people who understand the risks of contracting AIDS are using condoms, even during casual sex (see Chapter 7).

HIV and AIDS will also affect multigenerational families. As the AIDS virus spreads, increasing numbers of children are being orphaned and will probably be cared for by grandparents or even great-grandparents (see Chapter 18). Moreover, in many cases, children are angry or confused at being separated from a dying parent because the parent is too ill to care for the children:

Ann, a 28-year-old woman who has been in the hospital 5 times in 2 years because of her [HIV] infection, says her 10-year-old and 2-year-old daughters have lived with a family friend for the last year because she is too weak to watch them. She lives in a rooming house and sees the children every day, but says they are confused about why they live apart. "They feel they're being punished for something because they can't have their mother there with them. They always ask me, 'When are we going to get a house?' When they lose me, they're going to be very angry" (Marcus, 1991: A12).

In 1995, researchers at the University of California at Los Angeles found that a 33-year-old mother diagnosed with HIV gave birth to a baby who tested HIV-positive shortly after birth but showed no sign of the infection five years later. Some researchers were optimistic because they felt that the human immune system may sometimes defeat the otherwise invincible AIDS virus. Most scientists, however, wondered whether the child had been actually infected and whether the blood tests were correct when the baby was tested for HIV shortly after birth (Lemonick, 1995).

National Health Care A major topic of debate in the presidential campaign of 1992 was national health insurance and its availability to all Americans. The United States is one of the world's few industrialized countries that does

Many Americans fear that healthcare plans being proposed would limit their right to choose their physicians, fill waiting rooms with even greater numbers of people, and provide care of lesser quality.

not have national health insurance or a system that makes health care a right of all citizens. Although health care is available to all people living in the United States, it is most accessible to those who have insurance or who can afford to pay for needed services. People who are unemployed or who are in jobs that do not provide health insurance do not have the same access to health-care services as those whose employers provide such coverage.

The Canadian system of health care has received considerable attention from the news media in the United States (see the box "An American in Canada's Health Care System"). This system is often applauded as a model that the United States should adopt. The Canadian health-care system is not without its problems, however. Some observers point out that socialized medicine, as practiced in Canada and England, is most effective when health problems are relatively minor and people are able to wait for services. Also, high-tech resources are often scarce in these countries.

During a recent flight I was conversing with a Canadian about Canada's health-care program. He whipped out his medical card and said, "See, this is all I need. No paperwork, no fuss. All I do is present this." A few minutes later, however, he said that he had flown an aging aunt to a medical center in New York because she needed immediate high-tech heart surgery that the Canadian hospitals couldn't provide.

Many Americans are ambivalent about national health-care coverage. About 88 percent,

An American in Canada's Health-Care System

Here is one American's experience of the Canadian health-care system (Klein, 1993):

My first job out of college was at a major daily newspaper. It was 1973, and by standards of the day I was paid well. However, the first time I had to visit a doctor I was given a bill for $100. Because my employer provided no health insurance, I had to pay the bill myself. I was very happy that the bill was for only $100. What would I have done if I had an illness that required expensive treatment?

Since then, all my jobs have provided health insurance. The type of coverage, the extent of coverage, and the forms that must be completed have varied, however. The simplest system was being a member of a Health Maintenance Organization (HMO), when I paid only a nominal fee per office visit; there were no other forms or expenses. I have never needed a high level of health care, but I always wondered how those who did not have health insurance managed when they were sick or needed to see a doctor.

Several years ago I moved from the United States to Canada, and a few months later I had my first experience with a nationalized health-care system. After making my appointment with a physician who had been recommended to me by friends, I waited only a brief time to see the doctor and when we were finished I asked the receptionist whether there was anything I needed to do—I expected to pay a bill or fill out some forms or sign something. The receptionist seemed puzzled by my question and when I explained she said that there was nothing for me to do and that I could leave.

In the Canadian health-care system, medical care is a right of all residents of the country. A person chooses his or her own doctor and receives whatever services are needed, all without cost or bureaucracy. In my experience, health-care services in Canada have always been available as quickly as they have been needed and have been of the same high quality as the care that I received in the United States.

---

who already have health insurance, worry that a national plan might erode some of their existing benefits. According to a recent Gallup poll, for example, 54 percent of respondents feared they could end up with worse coverage than they have at present, and 38 percent believed that national reform would hurt the middle class more than any other income group (Saad, 1994). Because many middle-class households are nervous about the economy (see Chapter 14), concern about helping the poor at the expense of middle and working classes may increase in the future.

Contraception and Abortion Issues A number of scientists are working on developing contraceptive vaccines designed to prevent pregnancies for six months to a year with a single dose. Such vaccines would induce a woman's immune system to attack sperm and therefore prevent conception (Wheeler, 1995; see also Appendix C).

Some researchers are developing drugs that might take the abortion controversy out of the public realm. For example, to perform abortions some gynecologists are beginning to use *methotrexate*, which works by attacking rapidly growing cells, in conjunction with *misoprostol*, which stim-

ulates uterine contractions and expels the embryo. Methotrexate, widely available as a generic drug, is inexpensive. One treatment, combining methotrexate and misoprostol, costs about $6; doctors' fees and clinic visits are extra. Because methotrexate is used for several diseases—including cancer, rheumatoid arthritis, and psoriasis—it is likely that a physician could prescribe it without becoming involved in the politics of RU 486 (see Chapter 11) or performing surgical abortions.

Economic Concerns

The vast majority of Americans' income comes from employment. However, the traditional assumption that holding a job will keep a person out of poverty or off welfare rolls is becoming increasingly shaky (see Chapters 13 and 14).

Poverty Early in 1995, 3000 nongovernmental organizations, thousands of delegates, and 130 heads of state gathered in Denmark for a United Nations summit meeting on how to alleviate world poverty, create jobs, and deal with unemployment. The summit, which could end up costing as much as $1 billion, was expected to result in a 125-page Action Plan to deal with poverty.

Some critics have complained that the United Nations was wasting money on such "bloated international conferences." What may be more telling is that three world leaders—U.S. President Bill Clinton, Russian President Boris Yeltsin, and British Prime Minister John Major—sent representatives to the meeting rather than attending themselves. Does the absence of these leaders send the message that poverty is a low priority? Or have we accepted poverty as a fact of life?

In the United States some research suggests that poverty, and especially child poverty, is not a compelling social issue. National reports have documented a high incidence of child poverty since 1909 (Jacobs and Davies, 1991). Moreover, the United States has higher child poverty rates than many other industrialized countries: 1 out of 5 U.S. children lives in poverty compared to 1 out of 10 in Canada and Australia, 1 out of 25 in France, 1 out of 50 in Germany, and 1 out of 100 in Sweden (Danziger and Danziger, 1993).

According to some researchers, one of the reasons that the United States has such high poverty rates is that it has never developed a *comprehensive* antipoverty agenda. Danziger and Danziger (1993), for example, suggest that an integrated set of policies would include many components: improved education and training, subsidies to working poor families (see Chapter 14), greater access to health care and child care, expanded support services for children and their parents (such as youth development programs and decent housing), elimination of labor market practices that discriminate against minorities and women, and provision of employment opportunities for those unable to find jobs.

Most important, child and family poverty could be alleviated if parents had jobs that paid enough (Lichter and Eggebeen, 1994). Today, for example, a householder would have to earn $7.15 an hour (well above the $4.25 hour minimum wage) and work full time, 52 weeks a year to have an annual gross salary (before taxes) of $14,872 to be above the $14,800 income level defined by the federal government as the poverty level for a family of four. How many full-time jobs pay $7.15 an hour to people with a high school education or less? Very few.

Welfare One of the biggest political issues in 1995 was what to do about welfare. A major campaign promise made by President Clinton

was to "end welfare as we know it," and the Republican "Contract with America" listed welfare reform as one of its ten key legislative priorities.

There are very few Americans who are not recipients, either directly or indirectly, of some form of **welfare**—government aid to those who can't support themselves, generally because they are poor or unemployed. The major programs that offer assistance to the poor are described in the box "Major Welfare Programs." However, there are many other programs, not called "welfare," that also help the middle classes and even the rich. For example, the middle class can take advantage of student loans, expensive farm subsidies that pay farmers not to raise crops, and loans to veterans. Corporate welfare is even greater. The federal government has directly subsidized the shipping industry, railroads, airlines, and exporters of iron, steel, textiles, paper, and other products. Since the late 1970s, the federal government has bailed out such companies as Chrysler Corporation, Penn Central, Lockheed, a number of petroleum companies, and hundreds of savings and loan banks when they declared bankruptcy because of fraud, bad investments, or widespread embezzlement (Eitzen and Baca Zinn, 1994).

Americans generally support the government's welfare system, but some think it needs reform. In a recent *Time*/CNN poll, 92 percent of respondents said they favored requiring able-bodied people on welfare to work or learn a job or skill, but 35 percent of the respondents in a CBS/*New York Times* poll said that people who really needed the help should get it (reported in Muzzio and Behn, 1995). A recent Gallup poll suggested that 68 percent of Americans believe most welfare recipients are just taking advantage of the present system, whereas 28 percent believe they genuinely need assistance (McAneny and Moore, 1994).

Many Americans are especially suspicious of two of the major programs—SSI and AFDC. Several observers have described Supplementary Security Income, or SSI, as the most generous welfare program in the nation, if not the world. The 7 million recipients include not only the aged, blind, and injured but alcoholics and drug addicts who allegedly support their habits with the cash, immigrants who can begin collecting $458 a month without having worked a day because they claim they are mentally disabled, and about 900,000 children who, their parents claim, have mental problems (Haner and O'Donnell, 1995; O'Donnell and Haner, 1995).

Major Welfare Programs

Four principal programs provide benefits to the poor: AFDC and Supplemental Security Income (SSI) provide cash benefits, whereas Medicaid and Food Stamps offer non-cash benefits.

Aid to Families with Dependent Children (AFDC).

Established by the Social Security Act of 1935, this federal-state program helps needy families care for their children rather than give them up to foster homes or other state facilities. Each state administers its own program and determines need and payment levels. In all states, eligible families are those with children under 18 in which one parent is absent due to death, desertion, divorce, incapacitation, or incarceration. Nearly half of the 50 states also provide aid to two-parent families when the father is out of work.

Supplemental Security Income (SSI).

Established by a 1972 amendment to the Social Security Act, this program provides monthly cash

A supermarket cashier counts a customer's food stamps.

payments to needy aged, blind, or disabled people to help bring their incomes above the poverty level. The payments are administered nationwide through local offices of the Social Security Administration.

Food Stamps.

Begun in the 1960s and currently operating under the Food Stamp Act of 1977, the food stamp program distributes coupons redeemable for food to individuals and families whose incomes are less than 130 percent of the poverty level. State welfare agencies are responsible for the day-to-day administration of the program within broad federal guidelines. In 1994, more than one-tenth of all Americans were receiving food coupons (Pear 1995).

Medicaid.

Under this program, established by 1965 amendments to the Social Security Act, the federal government provides open-ended matching payments to states to help cover the costs of medical services for AFDC families and for most people eligible for SSI payments. Within broad federal guidelines, each state designs and administers its own program, with considerable latitude to determine eligibility, benefits, and levels of payments to service providers.

Critics contend that much of the SSI program is open to fraud because there does not have to be any medical confirmation of disability; verbal reports alone of pain or behavioral difficulties can qualify applicants. In recent testimony before a commission appointed by the Clinton administration, a physician who oversees Social Security disability decisions said that many children and several school officials said that children are "coached" by their parents to misbehave and perform poorly in psychological and academic testing in order to get the monthly payment offered by the program (O'Donnell, 1995).

The other program that troubles many Americans is Aid to Families with Dependent Children, or AFDC. Although AFDC payments are earmarked for children, many people equate this program with welfare payments made to able-bodied adults who are not working, not in school, and not in job training programs. Nearly one in seven American children is receiving AFDC assistance, but, according to the U.S. General Accounting Office, only 11 percent of the almost 5 million parents on AFDC participate monthly in any of the education, training, or job search programs (Whitman et al., 1995).

Why are so few people in training programs? First, an estimated 16 percent of parents on AFDC assistance have substance-abuse problems, as many as 40 percent have learning disabilities, and about 35 percent have a partial disability or are caring for a disabled person at home (Whitman et al., 1995). Some experts estimate that 12 to 20 percent of the welfare population is hampered by an almost total lack of the skills needed to get a job, such as not being able to fill out a job application form, as well as by depression, serious health problems, and "generally chaotic lives" that discourage undertaking lengthy education and training efforts or a job search (Vobejda, 1995b). In some cases, women leave jobs because their boyfriends, threatened by the prospect of the woman's independence, assault them (DeParle, 1994). In other cases, women cannot hold on to jobs because they lack the social skills necessary for work. They resent the authority of supervisors, quarrel with coworkers or customers, fail to report to work on time, or don't take work-related rules seriously (DeParle, 1994; Whitman et al., 1995).

AFDC is alleged by some to encourage marital instability, illegitimate births, the establishment of independent households by unmarried mothers and to discourage marriage and remarriage (see, for example, Murray, 1994). Others contend, however, that blaming unwed mothers for poverty and welfare ignores the economic basis of such problems:

To say that unwed mothers cause poverty is like saying hungry people cause famine, or sick people cause disease. Out-of-wedlock births do not explain why [designer] Donna Karan has her clothes produced in Hong Kong, or why $100 sneakers are made by Malaysian women paid 16 cents an hour. Nor do the sex lives of the poor explain why corporations nationwide are laying off thousands of white-collar workers, or why one out of five college graduates is working at a job that requires no college degree (Pollitt, 1994: 740).

Although millions of people are dependent on welfare for survival, the median period of time over which a person receives welfare benefits throughout his or her lifetime is less than four years. About 30 percent of people are on welfare for less than a year, and 70 percent leave the system within two years. About 20 percent are welfare recipients for five or more years (Waldman et al., 1994). Furthermore, most children growing up in "welfare homes" do not themselves become dependent on welfare.

There is no reason to expect that welfare and poverty will decrease in the future. As the Data Digest points out, some major welfare costs have increased since 1985. And, if critics of the welfare system are successful in decreasing the aid to current welfare recipients without increasing jobs that provide a living, poverty levels will in all likelihood increase.

Child Care and Parental Leave

Very few U.S. families, and especially those on welfare, can afford quality child-care services (Offner, 1994). Moreover, because mothers are much more likely than fathers to take time off from work to care for their children, women workers, as a group, fall permanently behind male workers in terms of pay, benefits, and seniority. Women who are heads of households are even worse off. One national study found that nearly 23 percent of mothers between 21 and 29 years of age are out of the labor force because of child-care problems. Because many of these mothers lack high school diplomas, they have difficulty competing in the labor market (Cattan, 1991). And even for two employed parents, paying an average of $8540 per year per child for high-quality child care is more than most working-class or middle-class parents can afford (Gardner, 1995).

Middle-class families also have child-care problems, especially if the parents are divorced and the mother is working long hours. Recently, for example, Marcia Clark, the high-profile prosecutor in the O. J. Simpson case, filed for a divorce from her husband, Gordon Clark, before the Simpson murder trial began and has primary physical custody of their two boys, 3 and 5. The boys' father has frequent and regular visitation rights. Six months into the trial, Marcia Clark, who earns $97,000 a year (twice the salary of her computer engineer husband) and employs a housekeeper, asked the court to allot her more financial support because her 16-hour per day, 7-day workweeks had increased her child-care costs to more than $1000 a month. Her husband then petitioned for temporary custody, claiming that because he worked regular hours there was "absolutely no reason why the children shouldn't be with me instead of continually being with babysitters" (Hancock et al., 1995: 55).

The case generated angry reactions from other educated, hardworking, divorced mothers who claimed that they must often choose between a good job and living with their children. According to some mothers, judges still see "good mothers" as those who are home full time and may "punish" them if they are "career-oriented" (Holcomb, 1995). Divorced fathers, on the other hand, argue that courts often take fatherhood less seriously than motherhood by assuming that mothers are "naturally" better parents (see Chapter 4). According to a study in Massachusetts, however, when men sued for custody, they won sole or joint custody about 70 percent of the time (reported in Holcomb, 1995).

Some observers note that such battles would be unnecessary if we had high-quality day-care centers at workplaces and more reasonable work schedules for both mothers and fathers (see Chapter 14). Compared to those of other industrialized countries, the United States record of child-care provisions has been abysmal. Congresswoman Pat Schroeder of Colorado once remarked, "Under our tax laws, a businesswoman can deduct a new Persian rug for her office but can't deduct most of her costs for child care. The deduction for a thoroughbred horse is greater than that for children" (Gibbs et al., 1990: 42).

In contrast with the U.S. system, in Japan 60 percent of child care is provided by the government, and both government and most companies offer monthly subsidies to parents with children (Shimomura, 1990). France maintains a system of preschools, open to all children between 2 and 6 years of age and provides partially subsidized care for children under age 2 (Bloom and Steen, 1990). In Belgium, Italy, and Denmark, at least 75 percent of children ages 3 to 5 are in some form of state-funded preschool programs, and in Germany, parents may deduct the cost of child care from their taxes. In Sweden, parents receive the equivalent of $1,667 for each child in the form of a child-care subsidy, and local communities organize and maintain child-care centers to which parents pay about 10 percent of the actual cost (Herrstrom, 1990).

Even though the United States passed the Family and Medical Leave Act in 1993 (see Chapter 14), the results have been mixed. Within a year after its passage, the Labor Department received 80,000 phone queries about the act (Hermelin, 1994). Apparently, although some companies and employees have taken advantage of the unpaid leaves, many employees know nothing about the act, a number of employers have not informed their employees of their rights, and some companies have admitted outright that they are not complying with the provisions.

In contrast to the United States, a number of other developed nations provide generous parental leave benefits. For example, in France, all female employees are entitled to a maternity leave of six weeks before childbirth and at least ten weeks after, with a guarantee of returning to the same job at the same wage. Canada has a nationwide parental leave policy for all federal employees. Moreover, all but one of the provincial and territorial governments mandate unpaid maternity leave benefits for both public and private sector workers for 17 or 18 weeks, and some juris-

A child-care center in Denmark, where more than three-quarters of children between 3 and 5 are in state-funded programs.

dictions also mandate unpaid paternity leave. In the United Kingdom, the Employment Protection Act of 1975 mandates parental leave benefits for female employees. Women can receive maternity leave with pay equal to 90 percent of their salary for up to six weeks; for a maximum of an additional 29 they can receive unpaid leave. Women who work for employers with more than six employees are guaranteed reinstatement after maternity leave (Meisenheimer, 1989).

Sweden has the most comprehensive parental leave policy in the world. Either parent may take a 12-month leave upon the birth of a child, with a guarantee that the parent who is on leave can resume his or her old job. During the first nine months of this period the parent is paid 90 percent of his or her salary with a smaller benefit for the last three months. Parents have an 18-month job-protected leave, but if they want to be home only nine months at full compensation, they can work only six hours but be paid for eight for the remaining nine months. One parent has the legal right to work six-hour days (at proportionately lower compensation) until the child is eight years old. Parents are also entitled to 60 days of paid leave per year per child to care for sick children at home. In the first ten days after the birth of the child, both parents can stay home with the baby.

Because of the archaic parental leave policies in the United States, the lack of good child-care facilities, and the increased numbers of women entering the labor force or higher education institutions, battles over who should care for children will probably increase. According to some researchers, such conflicts will decrease only when family policies take children and working parents seriously (see Leach, 1994).

Competition for Scarce Resources

When the Social Security Act was passed in 1935, life expectancy in the United States was just below 62 years, compared to around 75 years today. By 2030, 20 percent of Americans will be age 65 or older, compared to approximately 12 percent in 1990, and the number of people age 85 or older is expected to triple by 2030. Nearly 50 percent of today's 20-year-olds can expect to reach age 80, compared to less than 25 percent in the 1930s (Population Reference Bureau, 1990). In the years ahead, the in-creasing numbers of older Americans will put a significant strain on the nation's health-care services and retirement-income programs.

According to Crenshaw (1992: 4), older people "are one of the largest and politically best organized groups in the nation." They vote in large numbers, follow issues carefully, and usually come well prepared to defend their positions during congressional hearings. The American Association of Retired Persons (AARP) is one of the most powerful advocates for the elderly. AARP has over 33 million members, more than $300 million in revenues, and "a ready force of more than 400,000 volunteers, which can be marshaled at any time" (Crenshaw, 1992: 5). Many other groups also lobby for older people: the American Association of Homes for the Aging; the AFL-CIO Department of Occupational Safety, Health, and Social Security; the American Federation of State, County, and Municipal Employees Retiree Program; the Gray Panthers; the National Association of Retired Federal Employees; the National Council of Senior Citizens; the National Council on the Aging; the Older Women's League; the United Auto Workers Retired Members Department; and the National Committee to Preserve Social Security and Medicare. It is not surprising that the elderly have been successful in winning numerous political battles.

Although the elderly once had the highest rates of poverty in America, they now have the lowest. Due in part to the growth of the Social Security system, in 1993 only 12 percent of the elderly had incomes below the poverty line, compared to more than a third in 1959 (Rich, 1995). Some observers have charged that in a time of fiscal austerity older people, seeking to ensure their access to federal funds to improve the quality of their lives, have benefited at the expense of others—primarily children, because AFDC support has been cut while programs for the elderly have maintained their funding. There is an increasing chasm between the young and the old that reflects racial and ethnic differences. For example, projections for 2030 indicate that 41 percent of the children but only 24 percent of the old will be minorities. Thus, it is suggested, the growing number of middle-aged minorities and parents with large numbers of children may resist increasing federal expenditures for the predominantly white elderly.

It should be remembered, however, that al-

This 70-year-old stone mason is laying the foundation for a fountain in a public park.

though today's older population is better off financially than previous generations, there are specific pockets of poverty. For example, poverty rates within the older population increase dramatically with age. In 1989, about 10 percent of people age 65 to 74 were living in poverty, but nearly 18 percent of those age 85 or older were poor. Furthermore, the number of elderly who will be 85 or older is expected to triple by the year 2030, and much of the elderly population will have chronic health conditions that will increase the need for long-term care (Light, 1988).

At the same time, the poverty rate for minority elderly is two to three times higher than for the white population: Whereas 9 percent of white elderly lived in poverty in 1989, 21 percent of Hispanic American elderly and 31 percent of African American elderly were poor. As we noted in Chapter 1, racial-ethnic minorities are expected to account for more than a third of the population by 2030. Moreover, because women tend to outlive men, marital status and living arrangements affect poverty status. Older widows and unmarried women who live alone are three to four times more likely than are their married peers to live in poverty. Continued increases in life expectancy, particularly for women, and changing marriage and divorce patterns put a substantial number of today's women at risk for spending some portion of their older years in poverty (Population Reference Bureau, 1990).

Some Possible Solutions

Some feel that the competition for scarce resources between the young and the old can be lessened. For example, the size of the elderly dependent population can be reduced by increasing the age of eligibility for old-age benefits from age 65 to age 70. Because, in general, people reaching age 65 now and in the future will be better educated and have more work-related skills than earlier cohorts, they are more likely to be productive employees. They may also offer an employer more skills than some young people, whose academic performance, as measured on standardized exams and college graduation, appears to have diminished.

Moreover, because the rates of adolescent criminal behavior, drug and alcohol use, out-of-wedlock births, and children living in poverty have increased, large numbers of retirees in the year 2010 will be depending on a relatively small group of people in the labor force to support their Social Security and health-care benefits. Thus, some observers suggest, redefining "old age" would be beneficial to both the young and the old. If old age and mandatory retirement were pushed up to age 70 or more, many productive older Americans could continue to work and contribute to Social Security. As a result, the burden of supporting an aging population would not fall wholly on younger workers.

Others recommend lifting the penalties now imposed on older people who want to continue to work. As it stands, people between ages 65 and 69 are often discouraged from working because they must give up $1 in Social Security benefits for every $3 they earn above $11,280. (This ceiling figure is recomputed on a yearly basis.) If these limitations were lifted, researchers estimate that at least 700,000 additional elderly retirees would enter the labor market. The nation's output of goods and services would increase by at least $15.4 billion a year; and government revenue would rise by $4 billion, outstripping increased Social Security payments by $140 million a year. Thus, there is controversy concerning the scope of government programs that benefit family dependents at both the beginning and end of life (Aldous and Dumon, 1991).

The *Quality Time* cartoon by Gail Machlis is reprinted by permission of Chronicle Features, San Francisco, California.

Other observers have suggested combining the needs of the elderly and those of children. For example, a few companies have built adjacent day-care facilities at workplaces for the young and the old, where both generations can visit, talk, and forge friendships. Such programs can help fulfill reciprocal needs for the elderly to help children and for children to understand an older generation. Some analysts also believe that if families took care of their children they would not be competing for benefits that have been allocated to older people.

DO WE REALLY LACK FAMILY VALUES?

Since the early 1990s, we've heard a lot, especially from politicians, about the decline of family values. Are American families really as chaotic as many politicians and journalists would have us believe? Consider a response by syndicated columnist Ellen Goodman, published just before Thanksgiving in 1994:

I reach for the phone . . . and hear the voice of a television producer. She wants to know whether I

might be available to comment on the decline and fall of the American family. A story for the season.

As I stand there, covered in batter, she rattles off the horrific list of stories that make her case. The South Carolina mother who drowned her children. The 19 toddlers found in a squalid Chicago apartment without food or clothes. The Pittsburgh couple who took off for two weeks without warning, abandoning three kids to teen-age babysitters.

I listen to this familiar litany with an equally familiar sense of gloom, and then I decline. I'm sorry, but this afternoon, I promised to visit my mother. Tomorrow, the cousins are coming from California. The next day is our wedding anniversary. Thursday, the young adults we call "the kids" are arriving. And there is a crisis in the care of an aged aunt (p. 17A).

Goodman's point is that *most* families are not dysfunctional, abnormal, or pathological. Quite to the contrary, most of us are occupied with maintaining, loving, and caring for our families.

CONCLUSION

The family in the twenty-first century will be much more diverse in terms of racial and ethnic characteristics. It is difficult to predict whether this *change* will lead to greater cooperation or to conflict. Because the United States is the only country in the world with such a heterogeneous mix of cultural groups, there are no models for comparison. Optimists argue that cultural diversity is healthy and will strengthen communities.

Another expected but unprecedented change is the growth of a relatively "old" population that will have to rely on a generally less educated young population for its resources and health care. Given the increased health-care and economic problems of recent years, the next century may see more multigenerational households and greater numbers of adult children providing care to their aging parents.

The family in the twenty-first century will probably incorporate a wide variety of work roles and family roles. Because women's participation in the labor force is expected to increase, work and family functions will continue to overlap. The *constraint* posed by the need to balance domestic and work responsibilities is not expected to diminish, however. Consequently, women (and some men) may become more vocal in demanding family policies that put a higher priority on children, parenting, and the family.

Overall, families in the twenty-first century will continue to have more *choices* than they did in the past. Because divorce and remarriages are no longer uncommon, these options will probably become even more widespread in the future. In addition, as the technology improves eyeglasses, hearing aids, electric wheelchairs, and biomedical devices to strengthen or replace legs, arms, toes, and fingers, many older Americans will be able to live independently instead of depending on care from others (Longino, 1994).

Taking Action

How You Can Make a Difference

Helping low-income and other disadvantaged people benefits both the giver and the receiver.

• Many communities have **soup kitchens and food pantries for the poor.** Volunteer two to three hours a week in an organization close to your home or campus. I have required students in my Social Problems classes to perform, describe, and evaluate community service experiences. Students who worked in soup kitchens said, for example: "It gave me a better idea of what the homeless confront," "It made me realize that I take many things for granted," "It was one of the most valuable experiences I've had in college."

• Offer to help eligible low-income people to fill out **applications for food stamps or jobs.** Many local groups train volunteers to do this.

• Join or help organize projects that cut food costs, such as **farmers' markets and community gardens** in low-income neighborhoods. If you belong to a campus organization, any of these projects would make a difference in your area. For more information, write to Food Research and Action Center, Dept. P, Suite 540, 1875 Connecticut Avenue N.W., Washington, DC 20009.

• Such organizations as the American Association of Retired Persons (AARP) have informed members who would be delighted to address one of your classes, student clubs, or community organizations on such topics as **Social Security, retirement, and pensions.** Contact AARP at 601 E Street N.W., Washington, DC 20049.

• LONGEVITY is a new e-mail subscription list that discusses factors that are important to **extending human life.** To subscribe to LONGEVITY, send an e-mail message to LISTSERV-@VM3090.EGE.EDU.TR.

SUMMARY

1. In the next century, some of the greatest changes will probably be in four areas: racial and ethnic diversity, technological changes in reproduction and fertility, family structure, and children's rights.

2. Demographers predict that racial-ethnic diversity will increase because of increased immigration, as well as higher fertility rates among blacks and some Asian American and Latino families. Family structures will continue to be diverse.

3. Today, children have few rights. Except for an increase in child-support payments, there is little evidence that the economic and emotional situation of children will improve very much in the future.

4. Three areas in which choices have increased are divorce, remarriage, and aging. Divorce rates may have stabilized, but remarriage rates are expected to increase as more people try to form a happier marriage and family life. Among the elderly, we can expect changes in housing arrangements and in attitudes and behaviors surrounding death and dying.

5. Health issues will probably be a major constraint on family life in the twenty-first century. Two of the dominant issues will be caring for HIV and AIDS patients and developing a national program that provides families with minimal health care.

6. There is little evidence that the economic problems of many families will decrease in the

future. In fact, because of the rise of single-parent households and of unemployment and underemployment, more families will probably face the prospect of poverty.

7. In the future, there will probably be increased competition between the young and the old in terms of resources. Because the elderly population is growing, is well organized, and has political clout, elderly issues will probably be a higher priority than children's issues.

8. There is little evidence that Americans lack family values. In fact, most of us spend much our time loving and caring for family members.

9. Overall, families in the twenty-first century will continue to have more choices than they did in the past, but there will also be many constraints.

KEY TERMS

family policy   536
Child Support Enforcement Amendments   540
Family Support Act   540

living will   543
welfare   547

ADDITIONAL READING

ELLEN BRAVO, *The Job/Family Challenge: Not for Women Only* (New York: John Wiley and Sons, 1995). Offers practical information on such issues as job discrimination and how to encourage companies to promote "family-friendly" policies.

IRWIN GARFINKEL, SARA S. MCLANAHAN, and PHILIP K. ROBINS, eds., *Child Support and Child Well-Being* (Washington, DC: Urban Institute Press, 1994). Contributors examine such issues as child support enforcement policies, the costs and benefits of child support, and the effects of child-support payments on children's well-being.

SHELDON R. GAWISER and G. EVANS WITT, *A Journalist's Guide to Public Opinion Polls* (Westport, CT: Praeger, 1994). Shows how an informed citizen can discriminate "between the reliable surveys of public opinion and the junk" in a number of polls on family issues.

LINDA HAAS, *Equal Parenthood and Social Policy: a Study of Parental Leave in Sweden* (Albany: State University of New York Press, 1992). Examines the effectiveness of Sweden's parental leave policies and discusses implementing similar programs in other industrial societies.

SHARON L. KAGAN and BERNICE WEISSBOURD, eds., *Putting Families First: America's Support Movement and the Challenge of Change* (San Francisco: Jossey-Bass, 1994). Contributors discuss how families can be strengthened through supportive policies in education, health-care systems, social services, and religious organizations.

LESTER A. KIRKENDALL and ARTHUR E. GRAVATT, eds., *Marriage and the Family in the Year 2020* (New York: Prometheus Books, 1984). Articles that describe the family as the authors envision it in the year 2020. Topics include mate selection, human reproduction, the evolution of sex roles, moral concepts, work, and government policy.

BARBARA H. SETTLES, ROMA S. HANKS, and MARVIN B. SUSSMAN, eds., *American Families and the Future: Analyses of Possible Destinies* (New York: Haworth Press, 1993). Includes such topics as international issues in long-term planning and the way macro-level variables will affect families in the future.

Appendix A
Sexual Anatomy

The better you understand your own body, the more comfortable you may become with your sexuality. Also, remember that the word *intercourse* means "communication"; sexual intercourse is an activity in which two people communicate with each other through mutual bodily stimulation. With greater knowledge, you may enhance your communication with your partner and, thus, your mutual pleasure as well.

FEMALE ANATOMY

Collectively known as the **vulva** (Latin for "covering"), the external female genitalia consist of the mons veneris, labia majora, labia minora, clitoris, and vaginal and urethral openings. Figure A.1 shows these structures as well as the internal female reproductive organs.

The **mons veneris** (Latin for "mount of Venus," referring to the Roman goddess of love) is the soft layer of fatty tissue overlaying the area where the pubic bones come together. Because of the many nerve endings in the mons area, most women find gentle stimulation of the mons pleasurable. Below the mons, are the **labia majora** (major, or larger, lips) and **labia minora** (minor, or smaller, lips), outer and inner elongated folds of skin that, in the sexually unstimulated state, cover and protect the *vaginal* and *urethral* open-

ings. The labia majora extend from the mons to the hairless bit of skin between the vaginal opening and anus, called the **perineum.** Located at the base of the labia minora are **Bartholin's glands,** which, during prolonged stimulation, secrete a few drops of an alkaline fluid that help neutralize the normal acidity of the outer vagina (male sperm cannot survive in an acidic environment).

Figure A.1 Side View of the Female Reproductive System (Adapted from Martini, 1995: 1078).

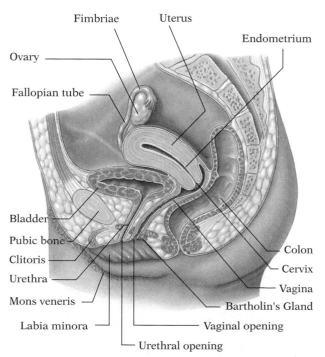

Appendix A is adapted from Bruce M. King, *Human Sexuality Today,* 2nd ed. (Englewood Cliffs, NJ: Prentice Hall, 1996), pp. 25–42. Copyright 1996. Adapted by permission of Prentice Hall, Englewood Cliffs, New Jersey.

The **clitoris** (Greek for "hill" or "slope") develops from the same embryonic tissue as the penis and is extremely sensitive to touch. In fact, it is the only structure in either females or males whose only known function is to focus sexual sensations. Sexual arousal results in engorgement and enlargement of the clitoris. Also highly sensitive are the labia minora, which meet at their upper end to form the **clitoral hood,** analogous to the male **foreskin** (or *prepuce*), hiding all but the tip, or **glans,** of the clitoris.

The area between the two labia minora is sometimes referred to as the **vestibular area** (Latin for "entrance hall") because it contains the entrance to the vagina. In sexually inexperienced females, or "virgins," a thin membrane called the **hymen** may partially cover the opening to the vagina. The urethral opening, also located in this area between the clitoris and the vaginal opening, is the outlet of the **urethra,** which carries urine from the bladder out of the body.

The internal female reproductive system consists of the vagina, uterus, Fallopian tubes, and ovaries. The **vagina** (Latin for "sheath") is an internal structure located behind the bladder and in front of the rectum. It serves not only to receive male sperm during sexual intercourse but as the passageway for a fully developed fetus at the time of birth.

The **uterus,** or womb, which holds and protects a developing fetus (see Appendix B), is connected to the vagina through its narrow end, called the **cervix.** The uterus has three layers: the innermost **endometrium,** in which a fertilized egg implants; a middle layer of muscles called the **myometrium,** which contract during labor; and an external cover called the **perimetrium.** Each month, after ovulation (see next paragraph), the endometrium thickens and becomes rich in blood vessels in preparation for the implantation of a fertilized egg. If fertilization does not occur, this tissue is sloughed off and discharged from the body as the menstrual flow. Uterus, cervix, and vagina are all capable of great expansion to accommodate a growing baby and its delivery.

Extending from each side of the uterus are the two Fallopian tubes. The *fimbriae,* fingerlike structures at the end of each tube, brush against the **ovary,** which is the female sex gland. The ovaries, or gonads, are supported by ligaments on each side of the uterus and have two functions: to produce eggs (*ova*) and female hormones (*estrogen* and *progesterone*). Each month,

in the process called *ovulation,* an egg is expelled from an ovary and picked up by the fimbriae, pulling it into one of the Fallopian tubes. Fertilization, if it occurs, usually happens within the tube.

MALE ANATOMY

The external male genitalia are the penis and the scrotum. (The external and internal male reproductive organs are shown in Figure A.2.) The **penis,** which has both reproductive and excretory functions, consists of three parts: the body or shaft, the glans, and the root. Only the first two parts are visible. The *shaft* contains three parallel cylinders of spongylike tissue: two *corpora cavernosa,* or cavernous bodies, on top; and a *corpus spongiosum,* or "spongy body," on the bottom. The **glans,** analogous to the glans of the female clitoris, is the smooth, rounded end of the penis. The raised rim between the shaft and glans is the **corona,** the most sensitive to touch of any part of the penis. The **urethra,** which serves as a passageway for both urine and sperm, runs through the corpus spongiosum, and the urethral opening (*meatus*) is normally located at the tip of the glans.

The root of the penis is surrounded by two

Figure A.2 Side View of the Male Reproductive System (Adapted from Martini, 1995: 1061).

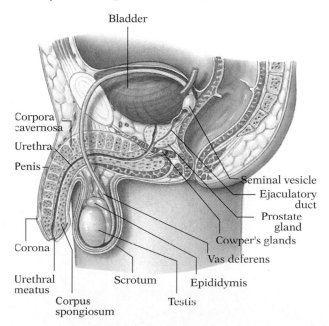

muscles (*bulbocavernous* and *ischiocavernosus*) that aid in both urination and ejaculation. (Other, *sphincter* muscles, which surround the urethra as it emerges from the bladder, contract during erection to prevent urine from mixing with semen.) The skin of the penis is very loose, to allow expansion during erection; unstimulated, the penis is about 3.75 inches long and 1.2 inches in diameter, but erect it is about 6 inches long and 1.5 inches in diameter. At birth, the skin is folded over, and many male babies undergo *circumcision,* a surgical procedure in which this *foreskin,* or *prepuce,* is cut away.

The sac located beneath the penis is called the **scrotum.** It holds the testicles outside of the body cavity to protect the sperm, which can be produced only at a temperature some 5° F lower than normal body temperature. For this reason the skin of the scrotum has many sweat glands that aid in temperature regulation.

The male internal reproductive system consists of the testicles, a duct system that transports sperm out of the body, the prostate gland, the seminal vesicles that produce the fluid in which the sperm are mixed, and Cowper's glands.

The **testes,** or testicles (the male gonads), develop from the same embryonic tissue as the ovaries (the female gonads) and like them have two functions: The testes produce sperm (properly called *spermatozoa*) and male hormones (*testosterone* and other *androgens*). Millions of new sperm are produced each day in several hundred *seminiferous tubules*. Each testis is suspended in the scrotum by the *spermatic cord* and is enclosed by a tight, fibrous sheath.

Once produced, sperm pass through a four-part duct system (*epididymus, vas deferens, ejaculatory duct,* and *urethra*) before being expelled from the penis during ejaculation. Although an average ejaculation of semen contains about 300 million sperm, most of the volume of the ejaculate is fluid from the prostate gland and seminal vesicles. Among other substances, the **seminal vesicles** secrete fructose, prostaglandins, and substances. The **prostate gland** also secretes these substances as well as a substance (fibrinogenase) that causes semen to coagulate temporarily after ejaculation, thus helping to keep it in the vagina.

Cowper's glands, or the bulbourethral glands, are two pea-sized structures located beneath the prostate. They secrete a few drops of alkaline fluid (a base) that may appear at the tip of the penis prior to orgasm. As Bartholin's glands in the female neutralize vaginal acidity, so Cowper's secretion serves to neutralize the normal acidity of the urethra, protecting sperm as they pass through the penis during ejaculation. It is important to note that Cowper's secretion often contains sperm, which is why withdrawal of the penis just before ejaculation is a very unreliable method of birth control (see Appendix C).

Appendix B
Conception, Pregnancy, and Childbirth

About midway through a woman's 28-day menstrual cycle, an *ovum*, or egg, is released into the abdominal cavity, where it is picked up by the *fimbriae* at the end of one of the Fallopian tubes. The ovum takes three to seven days to move through the Fallopian tube to the uterus, and it is only during the first 24 hours after the egg leaves an ovary that it can be fertilized.

CONCEPTION

At orgasm during sexual intercourse, a man ejaculates into a woman's vagina 200 million to 400 million sperm, all of which attempt to pass through the cervix and uterus into the Fallopian tubes. Only a few thousand live long enough, however, to complete the journey, and fewer than 50 reach the egg itself during its own journey through the tube. Because sperm can live for only 72 hours inside a woman's reproductive tract, the period during which conception can normally occur is extremely limited.

Conception takes place when one of the sperm penetrates the egg's surface. Within hours, spermatozoon (a single sperm cell) and ovum fuse to form a one-celled organism called a **zygote,** which contains the complete genetic code, or blueprint, for the new human life that has just begun. Shortly afterward, the zygote splits into two separate cells, then four, then eight, and so on.

Appendix B is adapted from Bruce M. King, *Human Sexuality Today* (Englewood Cliffs, NJ: Prentice Hall, 1996), Chapter 7. Copyright 1996. Adapted by permission of Prentice Hall, Englewood Cliffs, New Jersey.

While this cell division continues, the organism journeys through the tube toward the uterus—a trip that transforms it into a hollow ball of cells called a **blastocyst.** At about 11 to 12 days after conception, the blastocyst, whose inner cell mass will become an embryo and whose outer layers will form structures to nourish and protect the growing baby, burrows into the wall of the uterus in a process called **implantation.**

By about 14 days after conception, implantation is usually complete (see Figure B.1), and a series of connections between the mother and the **embryo**—the term for the developing organism after implantation—begins to form. The outer layers of the blastocyst begin to form the **placenta,** the organ that serves as a connection, or interface, between the infant's various systems and the mother's. One layer forms the **umbilical cord,** which connects the developing baby with the placenta. The **amnion,** a thick-skinned sac filled with fluid that surrounds and protects the baby from sudden movements and changes in temperature, and the **chorion,** which develops into the lining of the placenta, begin to form.

PREGNANCY

Pregnancy lasts an average of 260 to 270 days, or nine months. This time is divided into three-month periods called *trimesters.*

The First Trimester Women exhibit a varying number of symptoms during the first three months of pregnancy. Breasts may begin to en-

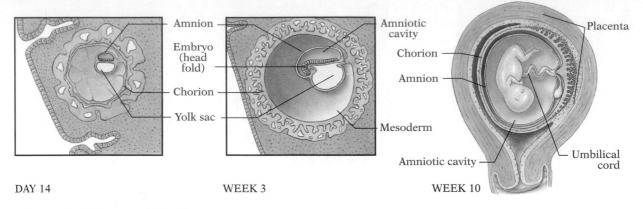

| DAY 14 | WEEK 3 | WEEK 10 |

Figure B.1 **Prenatal Development** (Adapted from Martini, 1995, Figure 29-4, p. 1114).

large and become tender. Veins may begin to show on the breasts, and the *areolas* (the darker rings surrounding the nipples) may turn dark. Nipples may also become larger. Urination may increase in frequency, and bowel movements may no longer be regular. Many women feel tired and run-down. One of the more common symptoms of pregnancy is nausea; although it is called "morning sickness," it can occur at any time of the day.

In the first trimester, the developing baby undergoes a great deal of change (see Figure B.1). After implantation, cell division continues, and portions of the organism begin to differentiate in an orderly fashion. Growth in the unborn child occurs from the head downward and from the center outward. In the embryo, three inner cell layers will form specific parts of the body. The **ectoderm** forms the nervous system, skin, and teeth. The **mesoderm** forms the muscles, skeleton, and blood vessels. The **endoderm** forms the internal organs (such as lungs, liver, and digestive system).

In the third week of pregnancy, a central structure—the *neural tube*—becomes a dominant feature. This will become the central nervous system. By the end of the fourth week, the umbilical cord, heart, and digestive system begin to form. By eight weeks, all organs have begun to develop. The heart is pumping, and the stomach has begun to produce some digestive juices. From eight weeks until birth, the developing organism is called a **fetus.**

The Second Trimester In the fourth or fifth month of pregnancy, the movements of the fetus can be felt by its mother. The first experience of

movement is called **quickening.** As her abdomen expands, red lines, or "stretch marks," may develop on the mother-to-be. The breasts begin to swell and may start to leak *colostrum*, a thick, sticky liquid that is produced before milk starts to flow. Water retention may cause swelling in the ankles, feet, and hands. Women may develop varicose veins and/or hemorrhoids. Morning sickness begins to diminish, which often brings an increase in appetite, and some women may experience heightened sexuality.

At this time, the fetus begins to make sucking motions with its mouth. In the fifth month, the fetus has a detectable heartbeat and will respond to sound. It also begins to show definite periods of sleep and wakefulness. In the sixth month, the fetus can open its eyes and will suck its thumb and respond to light. At the end of the second trimester, the fetus is almost a foot long and weighs well over a pound and a half.

The Third Trimester In the third trimester, walking, sitting, and rising become more difficult for the expectant mother, who may experience back pain as a result of the increasing burden she carries in her abdomen. The rapidly growing fetus puts pressure on the mother's bladder and stomach, often making urination more frequent. Indigestion, heartburn, gas, and constipation are also common complaints, and the active movements of the fetus may prevent restful sleep.

In the eighth month, the fetus's weight begins to increase dramatically. At the end of the eighth month, the fetus will weigh about 4 pounds and will be 16 to 17 inches long. From this point on, the fetus will gain about 0.5 pound per week. In the ninth month, the fetus will grow to about 20 inches in length and weigh 7 to 7.5 pounds, but these measurements vary considerably. Shortly before birth (weeks or even hours before birth), the fetus will rotate its position so that its head is downward. This is called **lightening** because once the fetus's head has lowered in the uterus, pressure on the mother's abdomen and diaphragm is greatly reduced.

COMPLICATIONS OF PREGNANCY

Teratogens are agents that can cross the placental barrier and harm a fetus, such as diseases, drugs, or environmental pollutants. Until recently the placenta was thought to be a perfect filter that kept out all harmful substances, but now we know that hundreds of teratogens can invade the fetus's small world. Three things determine the harm that can be caused by teratogens—the amount of the agent, the duration of time of exposure of the fetus, and the fetus's age. Each part of the fetus's body has a time, or *critical period*, when it is most susceptible to damage. Although teratogens should be avoided at all times, most body parts are maximally susceptible to damage during the first eight weeks of development.

Diseases Even the "weakened" disease organisms of certain vaccines can be harmful to a fetus if taken by the mother just before or during early pregnancy. Some strains of the flu, mumps, chicken pox, and other common diseases can also harm the fetus. One of the first teratogens to be discovered was the *rubella* virus, or "German measles." A fetus exposed to rubella may be born blind, deaf, and/or intellectually impaired. A woman can be safely inoculated against rubella any time up to three months before becoming pregnant. Most types of *sexually transmitted diseases* can also affect a fetus or newborn baby.

Toxemia of Pregnancy A pregnant woman can also have a disease called **toxemia of pregnancy,** referred to as *preeclampsia* in its early stages, whose symptoms include high blood pressure, excessive weight gain, swollen joints due to excessive water retention, and protein in the urine. In about 5 percent of cases, the disease advances to *eclampsia,* which is characterized by convulsions and coma. The cause of toxemia is unknown, but some researchers believe it is due to a parasitelike worm. A low-salt diet and bedrest are the usual treatments.

Rh Factor Most people's blood contains a protein called the **Rh factor.** If they do, they are "Rh positive"; if they don't, they are "Rh negative." The presence or absence of the Rh factor is determined genetically. In about 8 percent of pregnancies in the United States the mother is negative and her baby is positive. Although this is not usually a dangerous situation in a first birth, antibodies may build up in the mother's blood and attack a second fetus who is also Rh positive. In order to prevent this, an injection should be given an Rh negative mother immediately after her first delivery to prevent the buildup of antibodies.

Smoking Cigarette smoking is associated with an increased risk of miscarriage, complications of pregnancy and labor, preterm birth, lower birth weight, and higher rates of infant mortality. It has also been associated with an increased risk that the placenta will separate from the uterus too soon, as well as with malformation of fetal organs such as the heart.

Alcohol The mother's use of alcohol during pregnancy can lead to physical deformities and/or mental retardation in the infant, a condition known as **fetal alcohol syndrome,** or **FAS** (see also Chapter 11). Alcohol can also cause the umbilical cord to collapse temporarily, cutting off oxygen to the fetus and causing a condition known as **minimal brain damage,** which has been associated with hyperactivity and learning disabilities. Even if a woman consumes only moderate amounts of alcohol, her baby still may develop emotional problems or be unable to cope in school.

Other Drugs Many drugs—whether illegal, prescription, or over-the-counter—can cross the placental barrier. Women who are addicted to heroin (or methadone) while pregnant will give birth to infants who are addicted as well. These infants must go through withdrawal and typically show such symptoms as fevers, tremors, convulsions, and difficulty in breathing. Even moderate cocaine use by a mother can result in her baby's exhibiting low birth weight, and "crack babies" have a variety of sensorimotor and behavioral deficits, including irritability and disorientation. In addition, commonly used drugs like antihistamines and megadoses of certain vitamins have proven to have harmful effects; for example, over-the-counter aspirin products taken in the last trimester can affect fetal circulation and cause complications during delivery.

Environmental Pollutants Substances like heavy metals (lead and cadmium, for example) in drinking water can cause damage to the fetus. Physical deformities and mental retardation have been found in children whose mothers ate mercury-contaminated fish. Radiation and X-rays are also powerful teratogens, especially in the first trimester. Exposure to X-rays has been linked to increased risk of leukemia.

Detecting Problems in Pregnancy The safest technique of examining the fetus in the womb for possible abnormalities is *ultrasound*, a "noninvasive" method in which sound waves are bounced off the fetus and the uterus. This technique is useful primarily in detecting structural problems. Other, "invasive" techniques, those in which instruments are inserted into the womb or even the amniotic sac that holds the fetus, include *amniocentesis* and *chorionic villi sampling* (see Chapter 11), *celocentesis*, and *fetoscopy*. These methods can detect chromosomal problems, such as Down syndrome, and certain diseases.

CHILDBIRTH

Labor is divided into three stages (see Figure B.2). In the initial, start-up stage, the woman's body prepares to expel the fetus from the uterus and into the outside world. This stage usually lasts from 6 to 13 hours. At this time, uterine contractions begin to push the baby downward toward the cervix, which undergoes **dilation**—widening—and **effacement**—thinning out. At first, contractions are far apart (one every 10 to 20 minutes) and last no more than 15 to 20 seconds, but eventually they begin to come closer together (1 to 2 minutes) and last longer (45 to 60 seconds or longer).

During labor, the thick layer of mucus that has plugged the cervix during pregnancy (to protect the developing baby from infection) is dis-

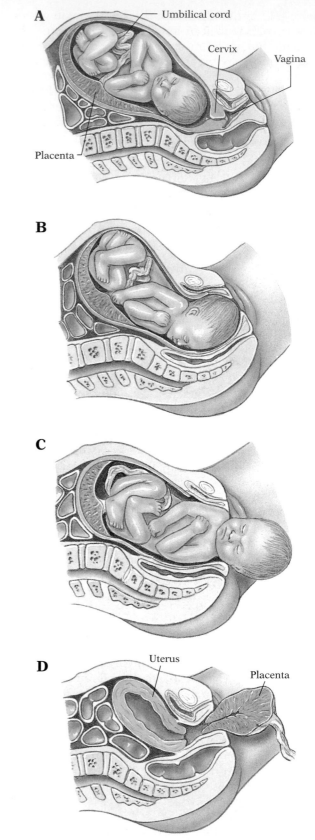

Figure B.2 The Stages of Labor. (A) The fetus is fully developed. (B) The first stage, dilation and effacement. (C) The second stage, expulsion. (D) The last stage, placental detachment (Adapted from Martini, 1995, Figure 29-12, p. 1130).

charged, either as a bloody plug that pops out like a cork or a little at a time. In 10 percent of cases, the amniotic sac will also break before labor begins, and the fluid gushes out (the "water breaks"). Labor usually begins within a day after this happens. If not, most physicians will induce labor with drugs in order to prevent contact with the outside world from causing infection in the fetus. Physicians sometimes break the amniotic sac on purpose to speed up labor.

The last part of the first stage of labor is called the *transition phase*. It takes place when the cervix is almost fully dilated (8 to 10 centimeters). Contractions are severe, and the woman may feel nauseous, chilled, and very uncomfortable. The transition phase usually lasts 40 minutes or less, and it marks the end of the initial stage of labor and the beginning of the next.

The second stage of labor, which concludes with the actual birth, begins when the cervix is fully dilated and the fetus begins moving through the birth canal. Contractions during this stage of labor are accompanied by an intense desire to push or "bear down," and they cause the opening of the vagina to expand. This stage lasts from 30 to 80 minutes, on average. Just before delivery, physicians often use a surgical procedure called an **episiotomy,** in which they make an incision from the lower portion of the vagina through the perineum to avoid tearing.

Crowning usually gives the first sight of the fetus. In most cases, the crown of its head appears at the opening of the vagina. In 2 to 4 percent of cases, a fetus will try to come through the birth canal feet or buttocks first, referred to as a *breech birth*. Sometimes it is possible to turn the fetus, but often this situation requires a cesarean section (see next section). The person delivering the baby will tell the mother when and how hard to push during contractions in order to get the newborn into the world. As the head is delivered, it is crucial to make sure the umbilical cord is not wrapped around the baby's neck. Suction is immediately applied to the baby's mouth and nose with a small rubber bulb to remove mucus so the baby can breathe more easily. The head then turns, and the shoulders and the rest of the body come out rather quickly. A newborn will usually cry at birth. If not, the baby's back will be rubbed to start the baby breathing. The umbilical cord is clamped and cut about 1.5 inches from the baby's body; this stub will fall off in a few days, leaving what we call a *navel*.

In the third stage of labor the placenta detaches from the uterus and leaves the mother's body (along with other matter). Called the **afterbirth,** this stage usually lasts only 10 to 12 minutes. If even small pieces of the placenta stay in the uterus, infection and bleeding can occur. In this case, physicians use a procedure called *dilation and curettage*, or *D and C*, in which the cervix is dilated to allow access to the uterus, which is scraped clean. After the third stage of labor, the uterus normally contracts, returning eventually to its usual size.

Cesarean Section A **cesarean section,** or *C-section*, involves the surgical delivery of a baby. In the past cesarean sections involved making a long vertical cut high on the abdomen, through which the baby was delivered. Abdominal muscles run horizontally, however, so after these muscles have been cut, they are too weak to withstand the stress of labor in future pregnancies. Now physicians typically use a new type of incision that is horizontal and low on the abdomen (the "bikini cut"), which makes it possible to have normal (vaginal) deliveries in later pregnancies.

Prepared Childbirth **Prepared childbirth** is the modern term for what was long called "natural childbirth"—techniques first used in the 1930s by a British physician, Grantly Dick-Read, and later expanded upon by the French physician Fernand Lamaze. On the theory that much of the pain and fear experienced by women during childbirth were the result of being in a strange environment, surrounded by strangers, and not knowing what was going to happen next, these and other medical professionals began to teach expectant mothers—and ultimately their partners as well—about pregnancy, labor, and birth. In addition, such physical methods as relaxation training and breathing techniques can help make labor easier.

Appendix C Contraceptive and Disease-Prevention Techniques

There are three primary questions to ask yourself when you choose a contraceptive, or birth-control, technique. First, do you wish to prevent both pregnancy and the transmission of diseases like AIDS and other sexually transmitted diseases? As you will see, the methods that are most effective in preventing pregnancy are not always those that are most effective in protecting against disease. If you are single and dating different people, your need to protect yourself against disease is very great. If you're married and certain of your and your spouse's faithfulness, your concern about pregnancy may take priority. Second, if you wish to prevent pregnancy, do you want only to postpone it or to rule it out permanently? The most effective method of contraception—other than abstinence—is sterilization by surgical means, and in most cases this is irreversible. Thus it is suitable only for those who are quite certain that they do not want (more) children. Third, do you need to take account of such factors as religious restrictions? For example, the Catholic Church forbids artificial means of contraception. Your answers to these questions will help you sort through the various alternatives we discuss.

PROTECTION AGAINST DISEASE

Although spermicides that contain nonoxynol-9 not only kill sperm but have been shown to be effective against the bacteria and viruses that cause some STDs, spermicides reduce the risk of disease by only about 50 percent. The safest method of protection against disease is the latex rubber male condom used with a nonoxynol-9 spermicide. The polyurethane female condom—one brand, the Reality Female condom, is currently available in the United States—should also be used with this type of spermicide; however, the effectiveness of the female condom in preventing against STDs has yet to be established.

PREVENTING PREGNANCY

The chart that follows provides information on the most common contraceptive methods, giving a general description as well as data on the effectiveness of each method, its particular advantages, and its possible side effects. Note that two figures are given for effectiveness. The first, labeled "With Perfect Use," is the rate at which pregnancy will occur if the method is used precisely as prescribed. The second, labeled "With Typical Use," allows for the fact that people often do *not* use these products as they are instructed to do; a woman may forget to take a pill, or a man may wait too late to put on a condom. In general, the chart moves from the most effective to the least effective methods; slight discrepancies in the progression of effectiveness rates reflect the desire to keep male and female methods (for example, male and female condoms) or related methods (the three different "fertility awareness" methods) together.

Appendix C is adapted from Bruce M. King, *Human Sexuality Today*, 2nd ed. (Englewood Cliffs, NJ: Prentice Hall, 1996), Chapter 6. Copyright 1996. Adapted by permission of Prentice Hall, Englewood Cliffs, New Jersey.

METHOD	PREGNANCIES PER 100 WOMEN IN FIRST YEAR OF CONTINUOUS USE		ADVANTAGES	PROBLEMS
	WITH PERFECT USE	WITH TYPICAL USE		
Voluntary Sterilization: A **vasectomy** is a male sterilization technique in which the vas deferens is tied off and cut, preventing passage of sperm through the male's reproductive tract. A **tubal ligation** is the procedure by which a woman's Fallopian tubes are tied off or, more often, cut and tied. The procedure prevents passage of the egg, which simply disintegrates and is discharged during menstruation. The procedure is performed by **laparoscopy,** in which a long, tubelike instrument that transmits television pictures is inserted through a small incision; once the tubes are located, they are cauterized. Some doctors approach the Fallopian tubes through the vagina (called a *culpotomy*).	0.1 for vasectomy; 0.2 for tubal ligation	0.2 for vasectomy; 0.4 for tubal ligation	Once done, many people report an increase in sexual desire because they no longer have to worry about pregnancy or contraceptive side effects; sexual relations can be completely spontaneous.	Surgical procedures always involve some risk, in part from the use of general anesthesia. Although it is sometimes possible to reverse vasectomy, and less often, a tubal ligation, sterilization should be considered permanent. Thus it should be used only by those who are quite sure they do not want any (more) children.
Norplant: Norplant is a hormonal implant that offers contraceptive protection for up to 5 years. Six flexible silicone rubber tubes (or two rods), each about the size of a match, are inserted under the skin of the inside of a woman's arm, in a fanlike pattern. The tubes or rods contain levonorgestrel, a synthetic form of progesterone that is slowly released over time and prevents pregnancy by inhibiting ovulation and thickening cervical mucus.	0.2	0.2	Believed by World Health Organization to be safer than the Pill because it contains no estrogen. Tubes can be removed at any time if woman wants to conceive.	Spotting or irregular bleeding, weight gain, and headaches; less often, nervousness, dizziness, nausea, breast tenderness, and acne. However, more than 2/3 of users are very satisfied with this method.
Depo-Provera: Known as "the Shot," this injectable drug contains progestin. **Depo-Provera** works by preventing ovulation and lasts for 3 months. After discontinuation of the injections, it may take a woman from several months to a year to regain her fertility.	0.3	0.3	Avoids problem of pregnancy resulting from missing a daily dose, as with the Pill.	Initially thought to increase risk of several cancers, the drug is now approved by the World Health Organization. Some side effects are menstrual irregularities, fatigue and weakness, dizziness, and/or headaches.
The Pill: The most popular **Pill** combines synthetic estrogen and progesterone (progestins). It works by preventing ovulation, by inhibiting the buildup of the uterine lining necessary for implantation, and by keeping the cervical mucus thick and thus impeding the passage of sperm. A *minipill,* containing only progestin, has only the second and third of these actions and is for women who are breastfeeding or who cannot tolerate the side effects of the Pill's estrogen. Some combination pills try to adjust the levels of progestins to mimic "natural" hormonal phases of the menstrual cycle, but manufacturers don't agree on what is "natural." The Pill is taken for 21 days and then discontinued for 7 to permit menstrual bleeding.	0.1 (Pill); 0.5 (minipill)	0.3	May reduce risk of cancer of endometrium, benign breast tumors, ovarian cysts, rheumatoid arthritis, and pelvic inflammatory disease. Alleviates premenstrual syndrome and menstrual pain and reduces menstrual bleeding.	Cardiovascular problems, particularly in women who smoke, are over 35, or have diseases like diabetes or hypertension. May be less effective if antibiotics, analgesics, or tranquilizers are used at same time. Backup methods must be used during first month and whenever a woman forgets to take a pill.

METHOD	PREGNANCIES PER 100 WOMEN IN FIRST YEAR OF CONTINUOUS USE		ADVANTAGES	PROBLEMS
	WITH PERFECT USE	WITH TYPICAL USE		
Intrauterine Device (IUD): The **intrauterine device,** or **IUD,** is a small, plastic, and/or metal device (of various shapes and sizes) that is placed within the uterus by a doctor. IUDs work primarily by impeding the transit of sperm, and a copper or progesterone coating further impairs this passage. The copper-coated IUD is effective for up to 10 years. Insertion of an IUD requires dilation of the cervical opening, which may be uncomfortable or painful. Doctors must be certain that a woman is not pregnant and does not have a sexually transmitted disease at the time of insertion, and they must use proper sterilization procedures to avoid infection.	0.8 (copper); 1.5 (progesterone)	1.0 (copper); 2.0 (progesterone)	97% of women who use the IUD have a favorable opinion of it. Progesterone coating decreases menstrual blood loss and pain. The IUD permits spontaneity in sexual relations.	Today's IUDS are generally regarded as safe, although they may cause spotting, bleeding, and infection and are sometimes expelled. Some earlier IUDs—the Dalkon Shield in particular—were associated with serious cases of pelvic inflammatory disease.
Male Condom: The best **condom** is a thin sheath made of latex rubber or polyurethane[a] that fits over the penis and thus traps sperm. It also prevents contact between the man's and woman's skin and membranes, thus preventing the spread of sexually transmitted diseases. The condom should be put on *as soon as the penis is erect.* If the condom does not have a nipple tip, the man should leave a little extra space at the tip of the penis to catch the ejaculate. He should also hold the base of the condom as he withdraws after intercourse. Condoms can be used only once and should not be stored for long periods of time in a warm place (such as a wallet) or where they are exposed to light. For greatest effectiveness, condoms should be used with a spermicide.	Less than 1.0 with spermicide; 3.0 without spermicide	12.0	**Highly effective in reducing the spread of sexually transmitted diseases, including AIDS.** Putting on a condom takes less time than inserting any female device, and spermicide application is less messy.	Some men will not use condoms because they say they are allergic to rubber or that condoms reduce their sensitivity. Others complain about lack of spontaneity. These detractions are far outweighed by the high rate of effectiveness of this method in preventing both conception and disease.
Diaphragm: A **diaphragm** is a shallow rubber cup with a flexible rim that fits snugly between the pubic bone and the back of the cervix, sealing the entrance to the uterus and preventing the passage of sperm. The diaphragm must be fitted by a doctor or health-care worker, and refitting may be needed after pregnancy or weight changes of 10 pounds or more. For maximum effectiveness, it must be used with a spermicide and inserted no more than 2 hours before intercourse (lest the spermicide dissipate). More spermicide should be added (with an applicator) if intercourse is repeated during lovemaking. Diaphragm should be left in for 6 to 8 hours after intercourse to make sure no live sperm remain.	2.8–5.0	15.0	Offers some protection against gonorrhea and chlamydia. Is inexpensive, lasting for several years (but should be checked regularly for defects). Is associated with very few serious risks to fertility or general health.	Possible infection if left in for a prolonged period of time. Some couples feel that insertion (if not done until sex play has begun) takes away from the spontaneity of sexual activity.
Female Condom: The **female condom** is a 7-inch-long polyurethane pouch that is closed at one end, which is surrounded by a flexible metal rim, and open at the other, which is surrounded by a similar ring. The inner ring fits over the cervix, like a diaphragm, thus closing the entrance to the uterus; the outer ring covers part of the vulva. At present, the Reality Female condom is the only one on the U.S. market.	5.0–6.0	15.0	Thinner than male condoms, feels softer than rubber, and transfers heat. Some feel that it simulates bare-skin intercourse.	Much more expensive than male condom and, like it, can be used only once.

METHOD	PREGNANCIES PER 100 WOMEN IN FIRST YEAR OF CONTINUOUS USE		ADVANTAGES	PROBLEMS
	WITH PERFECT USE	WITH TYPICAL USE		
Cervical Cap: The **cervical cap** is another barrier device designed to prevent passage of sperm from the vagina into the uterus. Made of latex rubber, it is smaller and more compact than a diaphragm and resembles a large rubber thimble. It should be used with spermicide, and it fits over the cervix by suction. It is especially useful for women whose vaginal muscles have been relaxed by childbearing. Insertion and removal of the cap are more difficult than for the diaphragm, but it is more comfortable and can be left in for 48 hours. Women should make sure after intercourse that the cap has not dislodged.	8.0–10.0[b]	18.0	May offer some protection against gonorrhea and chlamydia.	Possible infection with prolonged use due to long exposure to secretions trapped by the cap. Currently recommended only for women who have normal Pap smears lest it adversely affect cervical tissues.
Spermicides: Spermicides are chemicals that kill sperm (nonoxynol-9 or octoxinol-9). Used alone, spermicidal foams and suppositories are more effective than jellies and creams, but for maximum effectiveness any of these should be used with a physical barrier method (condom, diaphragm, etc.). Spermicides must be placed in the vagina shortly before intercourse begins; they lose their effectiveness over time, so new spermicide must be inserted before each time a woman has intercourse.	5.0	21.0	Spermicides reduce the risk of some STDs, including AIDS, by killing bacteria and viruses. They may also reduce the risk of cervical cancer.	Several studies have found that nonoxynol-9–containing spermicides increase the risk of urinary tract infection. Some complain that they irritate the vagina or penis, detract from oral-genital sex, and interfere with spontaneity.
Withdrawal: In **withdrawal,** or *coitus interruptus,* the male withdraws his penis just before reaching orgasm and ejaculates outside his partner's vagina. However, because sperm are found in the fluid secreted by the Cowper's glands just before a man ejaculates, this method is highly unreliable.	4.0	19.0	The withdrawal method is better than no method at all.	Highly ineffective compared to other methods. Also, withdrawal may not be very physically or emotionally satisfying for either partner.
Fertility Awareness: Fertility awareness (*natural planning* or *rhythm*) is based on predicting ovulation and identifying "safe days" in a woman's menstrual cycle. A woman can become pregnant only during the first 24 hours or so after ovulation; after that, the egg is overly ripe, and a sperm can't fertilize it. There are three variations of this method. The **calendar method** uses a formula to calculate the unsafe period based on the length of a woman's menstrual cycles. According to the **basal body temperature method,** or **BBT,** a couple should abstain from having sexual intercourse from the end of menstruation until 2 to 4 days after a temperature rise is noted (a woman's basal body temperature rises 24 to 72 hours after ovulation by a few tenths of a degree Fahrenheit). The **Billings method** attempts to pinpoint the time of ovulation by noting changes in the consistency of a woman's cervical mucus, which changes from white (or cloudy) and sticky to clear and slippery (like that of an egg white) 1 or 2 days before ovulation. The *symptothermal* method combines the BBT and Billings methods.	9.0 for calendar method; 2.0 for BBT; 3.0 for Billings	20.0+ for calendar method; 20.0+ for BBT; 16.0+ for Billings	Rhythm methods are usually considered to be safer than other contraception techniques and are acceptable to most religious groups.	All rhythm methods may be frustrating because they involve fairly long periods of abstinence from sex. However, chemical testing kits that will pinpoint the time of ovulation accurately enough to serve as contraceptives may soon be available for home use. To be effective, a method will have to predict ovulation at least 4 to 5 days in advance. Current products available, which predict 12 to 36 hours in advance, are useful only for couples who *want* to conceive.

[a]Do *not* buy condoms made of lamb intestine. These "skins" are porous, and HIV and other viruses and bacteria may easily penetrate through the tiny holes.

[b]In those who have not yet given birth.

Future Contraceptive Technology

Research into a *male pill* continues, but the difficulty is in finding a pill that inhibits sperm production without simultaneously lowering a man's sexual desire or his ability to achieve and maintain an erection. Now research is focusing on very specific aspects of spermatogenesis and, as we discuss next, the use of antibodies.

One of the most promising means of birth control in the future is *vaccination*. Believe it or not, it may be possible to prevent pregnancy the same way we prevent the flu. Researchers are working on a way to cause the body to produce antibodies to proteins contained in either the male or female germ cells. For example, if a woman could be inoculated with a vaccine that triggered production of antibodies to a protein found only in sperm, fertilization would be impossible. In India, scientists are testing a vaccine that creates antibodies to human chorionic gonadotropin, or HCG, a hormone necessary to maintain pregnancy.

The Reality Female condom will soon have some competitors. Under development are the *Woman's Choice Female Condomme*, which is inserted into the vagina with an applicator. And both men and women may soon be able to purchase the *unisex condom garment*, a polyurethane bikinilike item with an attached sheath that can be worn either over the penis or as a vaginal liner.

Appendix D
AIDS and Other Sexually Transmitted Diseases

Sexually transmitted diseases (once called *venereal diseases*, after the Roman goddess of love, Venus) are diseases that are spread either exclusively through sexual contact—like chlamydia, gonorrhea, herpes, and human papillomavirus infection (genital warts)—or primarily through sexual activity but by other means as well—like AIDS, hepatitis B, syphilis, and trichomoniasis. The chart on pages 570–571 gives information on the symptoms, causes, and means of transmission of the diseases we've just named, as well as current forms of treatment and the progress of these diseases if left untreated. (We also discuss STDs, with an emphasis on AIDS, in Chapter 7, pages 193–198.) Although there are probably more than 20 known STDs, these 8 have the highest incidence and the most serious effects.

In the United States, there have been major outbreaks of STDs from time to time. The present epidemic situation can probably be attributed to several factors. First, the discovery of penicillin and other antibiotics about the time of World War II may have given some people a false sense of confidence, leading them to engage in sexual intercourse when previously they might have feared to do so. Second, the fact that federal funding for STDs prevention efforts decreased considerably between 1945 and 1955 may have added to the public's tendency to overrate these new antibiotics. Third, the new feeling of sexual freedom given people by the arrival of the Pill and other reliable means of birth control may have lessened their attention to disease prevention. And fourth, because the condom, an effective means of disease prevention, was often replaced by the Pill, another preventive measure fell by the wayside.

Appendix D is adapted from Bruce M. King, *Human Sexuality Today*, 2nd ed., (Englewood Cliffs, NJ: Prentice Hall, 1996), Chapter 5. Adapted by permission of Prentice Hall, Englewood Cliffs, New Jersey.

DISEASE/SYMPTOMS	INCIDENCE[a]	CAUSE	HOW TRANSMITTED	PROGRESS OF DISEASE IF LEFT UNTREATED	CURRENT TREATMENTS
Acquired Immune Deficiency Syndrome: (AIDS): HIV may remain dormant for a time and then cause such flulike symptoms as diarrhea, fever, and other infections that linger on. In full-blown **AIDS,** diseases like lymphoma, Kaposi's sarcoma, and pneumocystis carinii pneumonia appear.	85,000+	*Human immuno-deficiency* virus, resident in semen, vaginal fluids, and blood.	Intimate sexual contact (anal or vaginal intercourse, occasionally oral sex); exposure to infected blood (sharing of needles among IV drug users); mother-to-fetus transmission through blood.	AIDS is terminal, but death can be postponed and quality of life improved with treatment.	Four *antiretroviral drugs* slow progression of HIV infection: zidovudine (AZT), didanosine (ddI), zalcitabine (ddC), and stavudine (d4T).
Chlamydia: In both men and women, irritation and burning of the urethra and a thin, clear discharge. However, many people have no symptoms in the initial stage.	4,000,000	*Chlyamydia trachomatis* bacterium.	Sexual activity; contact between mucous membranes of infected person and those of another person.	In men, infection of prostate and epididymis and possible sterility. In women, *pelvic inflammatory* disease leading to increased risk of tubal pregnancy and/or sterility. Babies born to infected women may have eye, nose, or throat infections.	Tetracycline, doxycycline, or an erythromycin. Some doctors are using newer drugs like azithromycin.
Gonorrhea: Inflammatation of urethra or vulva; discharge from penis or vagina; irritation during urination. Some men and many women show no initial symptoms	800,000	*Neisseria gonorrhoeae* bacterium (often referred to as *gonococcus*).	Almost exclusively through intimate sexual contact.	In men, inflammation of prostate, seminal vesicles, bladder, and epididymis; severe pain and fever; possible sterility. In females, pelvic inflammatory disease with severe abdominal pain and fever; possible sterility. Baby born to infected mother may become blind.	Ceftriaxone followed by tetracycline or an erythromycin.
Hepatitis B: Poor appetite, diarrhea, fever, vomiting, pain, fatigue, jaundiced or yellow tinge of skin and eyes; dark urine.	50,000–1,000,000	HBC virus.	By infected blood or body fluids such as saliva, semen, and vaginal secretions. About half of U.S. cases are contracted sexually (commonest through anal sex); also by sharing drug-use needles, by blood transfusions, and by blood exchange between mother and fetus.	Serious, sometimes fatal, liver disease.	Interferon is effective in about a third of patients. 90% of patients recover, but up to 10% remain infected and become carriers, infecting others.
Herpes: *Prodrome stage*—tingling, burning, itching of skin that contacted virus; *vesicle stage*—fluid-filled blisters, flulike symptoms,	200,000–500,000	Herpes simplex virus Types I and II. I is thought to cause oral herpes, II to cause genital herpes, but the	Direct contact between infected site on one person and skin of another. One can get genital herpes from contact with a blister on a	Herpes is leading cause of infectious blindness today. *Herpes encephalitis* is a rare disease of the brain that is often fatal. *Herpes meningitis* (inflammation of mem-	No cure. Once you have herpes, the potential for another attack is always there. Acyclovir relieves symptoms and

DISEASE/SYMPTOMS	INCIDENCE[a]	CAUSE	HOW TRANSMITTED	PROGRESS OF DISEASE IF LEFT UNTREATED	CURRENT TREATMENTS
painful urination; *crusting-over stage*—sores develop scales and form scabs.		symptoms and outcome of both types are the same.	partner's lip or oral herpes from a genital sore. People can spread their own herpes from one site to another (such as the eyes) by touch.	branes covering brain and spinal cord) is also possible. In women, risks cancer of cervix. A baby may be infected during childbirth, suffering neurological, eye, skin, and internal organ damage.	speeds healing during primary attack. Researchers are working on a herpes vaccine.
Human Papillomavirus Infection (also *genital warts*): Some people have symptoms that only a doctor can detect; others develop cauliflowerlike warts that cause itching, irritation, or bleeding. In males, warts usually apear on penis, scrotum, or anus and sometimes in the urethra; in females, on the cervix and vaginal wall, vulva, and anus.	200,000–500.000	Human papilloma virus causes nongenital warts and other skin conditions; two types of HPV cause genital warts.	By sexual intercourse or sometimes oral-genital sex; highly contagious, and most common STD caused by viruses in the United States.	In women, HPV infection increases risk of cervical cancer. Cancer of penis occurs but is rare. Recurrence of symptoms of HPV infection is common (see Current Treatments Column).	No cure. External treatment with podophyllin (brand name Codylox); large warts may be removed surgically, internal ones by laser surgery. Cervical HPV infection is treated with cryotherapy (freezing). Vaccine to prevent HPV infection may be developed in near future.
Syphilis: *Primary stage* begins with ulcerlike sore called *chancre*, usually on penis, cervix, lips, tongue, or anus, that is highly infectious but usually painless. Sore may disappear, but spirochete enters bloodstream and infection spreads throughout body. In *secondary stage*, itchless, painless rash spreads over body; sores appear in moist areas around the genitals; other flu- and cold-like symptoms.	113,000	*Treponema pallidum* bacterium (referred to as the *spirochete*).	Majority of cases are transmitted by sexual contact. Spirochete can also pass directly into the bloodstream through a cut or scrape; thus one can get syphilis by merely touching the sores of an infected person.	If initial chancre is ignored it will disappear, but person remains infected. In the third, *latent stage,* there are usually no symptoms although in about a third of victims large ulcers develop on skin and bones. In all cases bacteria continue their attack on the body's internal organs, particularly the heart, blood vessels, and brain and spinal cord. Deafness, paralysis, insanity, and death often result.	Spirochetes are easily eradicated with antibiotics; penicillin is still the most effective, although there are some indications that the bacterium may be becoming resistant to this agent.
Trichomoniasis: In women a heavy vaginal discharge with a foul odor accompanied by severe vaginal itching.	3,000,000+	One-celled protozoan, *Trichomonas vaginalis.*	Majority of cases are transmitted by sexual intercourse, but disease can be contracted from wet toilet seat or by sharing towels (protozoan survives in urine and tap water for hours to days).	Can lead to adhesions in the Fallopian tubes and sterility.	Metronidazole is the treatment of choice; however, this drug is under study as a possible carcinogen.

[a]Estimated new cases per year in the United States; based on 1995 data.

Appendix E
Nonmarital and Premarital Agreements

The following Premarital Agreement is only one of many examples of how such a contract may be drafted. It does not purport to be an all-encompassing "model" contract. The facts, parties, and state of Holmes are all fictitious.

Appendix E is based on Peter N. Swisher, H. Anthony Miller, and William I. Weston, *Family Law: Cases, Materials, and Problems* (New York: Matthew Bender,1990), pp. 107–12. Copyright © 1990 by Matthew Bender & Co., Inc. Reprinted by permission. All rights reserved.

PREMARITAL AGREEMENT
[OR ANTENUPTIAL CONTRACT]

This Premarital Agreement is made this ___ day of _____, 19__, between ELMER T. JONES of Centerville, Holmes (the prospective husband); and EUNICE L. GREEN of Wessex, Holmes (the prospective wife); who are also referred to as "the parties."

PREAMBLE

A. Elmer and Eunice plan to marry each other in the near future.

B. Elmer and Eunice both own substantial assets consisting of real and personal property that they wish to retain as separate property.

C. Elmer and Eunice wish to define their financial rights and obligations by this Agreement; and, except as herein stated, each wishes to retain and dispose of his or her separate property, free from any claim of the other by virtue of their contemplated marriage.

D. Elmer and Eunice now wish to fix by this Agreement the rights and claims that will accrue to each of them in the estate and property of the other by reason of this marriage, and to accept the provisions of this Agreement in lieu of, and in full settlement of, all such rights and claims.

[Optional: Both parties have been married previously, and have children by their previous marriages.]

NOW THEREFORE, IN CONSIDERATION of the mutual promises contained herein, and with the intent of being legally bound hereby, Elmer and Eunice agree as follows:

1. ***Full Disclosure.*** Each of the parties has made a full disclosure to the other of his or her financial situation, and the approximate worth of each party. A summary of Elmer's financial statement, prepared by _____, CPA, of Centerville, Holmes, is attached hereto as Schedule A. A summary of Eunice's financial statement, prepared by _____, CPA, of Wessex, Holmes, is attached hereto as Schedule B. [OR: The parties recognize that such schedules represent a reasonable approximation of the assets and liabilities, and were prepared informally without reference to documentation.] The parties further acknowledge that they have had an opportunity to review such summaries prior to the execution of this Agreement.

2. ***Property to Be Separately Owned.*** Each party, during his or her remaining lifetime, shall retain sole ownership of all of his or her respective separate property, and shall have the exclusive right to dispose of such separate property in a manner determined in the sole discretion of such owner thereof, by *inter vivos* or testamentary transfer, as if their forthcoming marriage had never taken place.

   [Note: In lieu of full disclosure, a fair provision may be made from one prospective spouse to the other. But caveat, this is a dangerous alternative, because a court may have to decide what is "fair." Under the Uniform Premarital Agreement Act, full disclosure may be waived by the parties.]

Any property, either real or personal, tangible or intangible, acquired by either party before, during, or after the marriage shall be the separate property of that party; and the other party shall make no claim or demand on that separate property.

(a) This separate property includes, but is not limited to, any property acquired by purchase, exchange, gift, or inheritance.

(b) For all purposes of this Agreement the term "separate property" shall mean, with respect to each party hereto, all of that party's right, title, and interest, legal or beneficial, in or to any property, real, personal, or mixed, wherever situated, and regardless of whether now owned or hereafter acquired.

3. *Release of Marital Rights by Elmer.*

(a) Except as specifically provided herein, Elmer waives and releases all rights to any of Eunice's separate property accruing to him, or in which he may be otherwise entitled as Eunice's husband, widower, heir-at-law, next of kin, or distributee; including but not limited to such rights as curtesy or its statutory equivalent; statutory or other allowances to the spouse of a decedent, intestacy distributions, and rights of election to take against Eunice's will.

(b) Also waived and released by Elmer are any property or support rights he may otherwise be entitled to as Eunice's husband based upon the termination of the forthcoming marriage by annulment, divorce, or dissolution of the marriage; except as specifically provided herein.

4. *Release of Marital Rights by Eunice.*

(a) Except as specifically provided herein, Eunice waives and releases all rights to any of Elmer's separate property accruing to her, or in which she may be otherwise entitled as Elmer's wife, widow, heir-in-law, next of kin, or distributee; including but not limited to such rights as dower or its statutory equivalent, statutory or other allowances to the spouse of a decedent, intestacy distributions, and rights of election to take against Elmer's will.

(b) Also waived and released by Eunice are any property or support rights she may otherwise be entitled to as Elmer's wife based upon the termination of the forthcoming marriage by annulment, divorce, or dissolution of the marriage; except as specifically provided herein.

[Note: A monetary award may be given for this release, or no monetary award may be provided, because the marriage itself can be consideration for this mutual release.]

5. *Gifts Not Prohibited.*

(a) No provision of this Agreement shall prohibit either Elmer or Eunice from making a voluntary gift in any amount to his or her respective spouse, and that gift shall become the sole property of the donee spouse.

(b) Such gifts may be lawfully conveyed or transferred during the lifetime of Elmer or Eunice, or by will or otherwise upon death, and neither Elmer nor Eunice intend by this Agreement to limit or restrict in any way the right or power of any party to receive such voluntary transfer or conveyance.

(c) Any such voluntary transfer or conveyance shall be deemed to be a voluntary gift, and shall not be deemed in any way a waiver or abandonment of this Agreement or any part hereof.

6. *Jointly Held Property.* Despite any other provisions of this Agreement to the contrary, the parties may, during marriage, acquire property, or interests in property, in both their names, with or without rights of survivorship. In such an event, the signatures of both parties shall be required to acquire, sell, transfer, convey, pledge, or encumber any such jointly held property. Entry into this arrangement shall not in any way be deemed a waiver of or abandonment of this Agreement or any part hereof. The parties may also establish and contribute to a joint checking account for household expenses on which either party can draw.

7. *Rights of Children.* The parties recognize the possibility that they might have children during the course of their forthcoming marriage, whether natural born or legally adopted. The parties hereby agree that the provisions of this Agreement are not intended to govern or affect the rights of any such children in or to the property of each party hereto; and the parties agree that such property or support for the children shall be governed by applicable law.

8. *Intent of the Parties in the Event of Dissolution, Divorce, or Legal Separation.* The parties contemplate a long and lasting marriage, terminated only by death; and it is the mutual intent of Elmer and Eunice to promote and encourage their marriage through this Agreement.

Nevertheless, the parties are cognizant of the fact that the ratio of marriages to divorces in America has reached a disturbing rate. Therefore, the parties mutually desire to agree upon: (a) the disposition of their property; and (b) the disposition of their support rights; in the event that their marriage, despite their best efforts to promote it, should fail. [Note: For further authority upholding divorce planning in antenuptial agreements, see also *Ivanhoe* v. *Ivanhoe*, 397 So. 2d 410 (Fla. 1981); *Osborne* v. *Os-*

borne, 428 N.E.2d 810 (Mass. 1981); and *Jackson* v. *Jackson,* 626 S.W.2d 630 (Ky. 1982). See also the Uniform Premarital Agreement Act, § 2.01[D] *supra.* Paragraphs 8, 9, and 10 however would not be valid in those jurisdictions that have not yet legally recognized divorce planning provisions in premarital agreements.]

9. ***Payments in Lieu of Spousal Support.*** In the event that the parties' marriage is terminated by dissolution, divorce, or legal separation—regardless of which party has initiated the action, and regardless of the jurisdiction or venue of such action—the parties hereby specifically agree as follows:

(a) Elmer shall not receive any spousal support from Eunice, periodic or lump sum, which otherwise might be available to him in accordance with applicable law.

(b) Eunice shall not receive any spousal support from Elmer, periodic or lump sum, which otherwise might be available to her in accordance with applicable law.

[OR: Limit any spousal support to a certain designated sum of money over a certain designated time period. Tax planning regarding spousal support may also be involved here.]

[OR: Spousal support may be designated in certain specified contingencies.]

(c) In connection with the provisions in this Paragraph 9, each party further acknowledges that he or she:

(i) has fully and fairly advised the other, and been advised by the other, of their respective financial situations;

(ii) has a fair understanding of the financial status of the other as set forth in annexed Schedules A and B, which are made a part of this Agreement;

(iii) considers the proposed payments in limitation of spousal support as fair under the current and probable future circumstances of each party; and

(iv) in sum, considers and believes after full and fair examination of the other's finances and after the advice of independent counsel that each has made a full disclosure to the other, each has a reasonable approximation of the financial situation of the other, and each considers the payments in limitation of spousal support and in lieu of all further obligation to be more than fair. [Alternately, this paragraph may be omitted.]

10. ***Property Division upon Dissolution, Divorce, or Legal Separation*** [Paragraphs in this paragraph, similar to Paragraph 9, may be made to extinguish or limit certain property rights on dissolution, divorce, or legal separation. Alternately, this paragraph may also be omitted.]

11. ***Binding Agreement.*** This Agreement shall be binding upon and inure to the benefit of the parties, their respective heirs, administrators, legal representatives, and assigns except as it affects Paragraph 7 above.

12. ***Further Assurances.*** The parties shall take all steps to make and deliver any documents or other assurances that are reasonably required to give full force to this Agreement.

13. ***Entire Agreement.*** This Agreement contains the entire understanding of the parties, and they shall not be bound by any understandings other than those expressly set forth in this Agreement.

14. ***Subsequent Modification.*** The parties may modify the terms of this Agreement, but any modification shall not be effective unless in writing, signed by both parties, with the same formality as this Agreement.

15. ***Governing Law.*** This Agreement shall be construed and governed according to the laws of the State of Holmes.

16. ***Interpretation.*** No provision in this Agreement is to be interpreted for or against any party because that party or that party's legal representative drafted the provision.

17. ***Paragraph Headings.*** Paragraph titles or headings contained herein are inserted as a matter of convenience only, and for reference, and in no way define or describe the scope of this Agreement or any provision hereof.

18. ***Counterparts.*** This Agreement may be executed in two or more counterparts, each of which shall be an original, but all of which shall constitute one and the same Agreement.

19. ***Sanctions and Penalties.*** Should any party retain legal counsel for the purpose of enforcing this Agreement or preventing the breach of any provision hereof, or for damages for any alleged breach of this Agreement, the prevailing party shall be entitled to be reimbursed by the losing party for all costs and expenses incurred thereby, including, but not limited to, reasonable attorneys' fees and costs for the services rendered to the prevailing party.

20. ***Severability of Provisions.*** If any provision or subprovision of this Agreement shall be deemed by a

court of competent jurisdiction to be invalid, the remainder of this Agreement shall nevertheless remain in full force and effect.

21. ***Advice of Counsel—Prospective Wife.*** Eunice Green hereby declares and acknowledges that she has read and fully understands everything set forth in this Agreement; that she has sought and obtained independent advice from legal counsel of her own selection, and has been fully informed of all legal rights and liabilities with respect hereto; that after such advice and knowledge, she believes this Agreement to be fair, just, and reasonable; and that she signs this Agreement freely and voluntarily.

22. ***Advice of Counsel—Prospective Husband.*** Elmer Jones hereby declares and acknowledges that he has read and fully understands everything set forth in this Agreement; that he has sought and obtained independent advice from legal counsel of his own selection, and has been fully informed of all legal rights and liabilities with respect hereto; that after such advice and knowledge, he believes this Agreement to be fair, just, and reasonable; and that he signs this Agreement freely and voluntarily.

IN WITNESS WHEREOF, the parties have set their hands and seals to this Agreement as of the date first above written.

(SEAL)
ELMER T. JONES
(SEAL)
EUNICE L. GREEN

STATE OF HOLMES
County of Brandeis, to-wit:
    This instrument was acknowledged before me this ____ day of ___, 19__ , by ELMER T. JONES.

    Notary Public

My commission expires:

STATE OF HOLMES
County of Brandeis, to-wit:
    This instrument was acknowledged before me this___ day of ___, 19__ , by EUNICE L. GREEN.

    Notary Public

My commission expires:

Appendix F
State-by-State Laws on Divorce, Child Custody, and Child Support

Table F.1 presents a state-by-state summary of divorce statutes in terms of residence requirements, grounds for action, alimony, and property. Tables F.2 and F.3 outline child custody and child support provisions.

In Table F.1, note that column 1 gives the time period for which one must have been an official resident of a state in order to initiate a divorce action. The remainder of the table indicates which of a number of rules regarding the grounds for divorce, determination and payment of alimony, and the apportionment of property owned by a couple are applicable in each state.

We cannot explore all the rules and regulations referred to in Table F.1 in detail. However, let's look at some of the major categories under each of the three main headings.

GROUNDS FOR DIVORCE

Breakdown Only In the case of irretrievable breakdown of the marriage or irreconcilable differences as the sole reason for divorce, a court may grant a divorce whether or not both parties join in the petition. Some of the states in which this rule applies also allow divorce on the grounds of mental illness or insanity.

Breakdown plus Findings In the states that apply this rule, irretrievable breakdown, irreconcilable differences, or incompatibility are the only bases for divorce if a petition is uncontested. If it is contested, a number of specific determinations must be made before the divorce can be granted.

Breakdown and Traditional Irretrievable breakdown or a similar reason has been added to traditional grounds for divorce in the states where this rule applies.

Living Separate and Apart Living separate and apart is either the sole basis for divorce in the jurisdictions where this rule applies, or has been added to the grounds of traditional fault or irretrievable breakdown. Where this ground for divorce action applies, the table lists both the time period during which a couple must live apart when a separation is voluntary and the period that applies if separation is involuntary.

No-Fault Divorce In a no-fault divorce, no formal proof is needed. Grounds for no-fault divorce may include breakdown of the marriage or living apart.

ALIMONY

Factors Set Out The phrase *factors set out* means that the statute lists specific factors that a court must consider when determining alimony. One of the factors most commonly cited is the homemaker contribution, or "the spouse's nonmonetary contribution to the family's well-being."

Fault Considered Fault, or "marital misconduct," is a consideration in some states in setting alimony payments.

Rehabilitative Alimony States in which this rule applies may limit alimony to a specifically stated period of time. Or they may allow a court

576

to set a time limit on an alimony award by specifying a period of time necessary to enable the party seeking alimony to acquire necessary training and appropriate employment.

Modifiable for Cohabitation   In a number of states, alimony may be modified or terminated if the person paying alimony can show that the recipient is openly cohabiting with a person of the opposite sex.

PROPERTY

Community Property   Some states have community property laws that distribute marital property equally, but there are many variations in these laws. For example, divisible property may include all property owned by both partners or only property acquired since the marriage began, and it may or may not include gifts and inheritances.

Fault Considered, Homemaker Contribution, Tax Consequences, Pensions Considered   Many state statutes contain specific guidelines for dividing property between the partners of a marriage in terms of (1) assessed fault on the part of either partner, (2) the contribution to the marriage of a homemaker, (3) the effects on taxes owed by the partners of the proposed apportionment, and (4) the existence of pension plans covering either partner.

CUSTODY AND CHILD SUPPORT

Statutory Guidelines   In both Tables F.2 and Table F.3, the first column indicates which states have statutes that provide courts with specific guidelines to follow when awarding custody and child support. As Table F.2 indicates, most states have statutes providing grandparent visitation, but they vary in terms of grandparent visitation after divorce or only on the death of a parent. Many states also consider the children's wishes in custody cases (Based on *Family Law Reporter*, 1989: 3)

Table F.1
State Divorce Statutes

State	Residence Requirement	Divorce Grounds	Breakdown Only	Breakdown Plus Findings	Breakdown and Traditional	Living Separate and Apart	No Fault Divorce	Factors Set Out (Alimony)	Homemaker Contribution (Alimony)	Fault Considered (Alimony)	Rehabilitative Alimony	Modifiable for Cohabitation	Community Property	Equitable Distribution	Fault Considered (Property)	Homemaker Contribution (Property)	Tax Consequences	Pensions Considered
Alabama	6 mos.				X		X	X				X		X	X			
Alaska	BFRes[1]				X		X							X				
Arizona	90 dy.		X					X			X		X					
Arkansas	60 dy.					3 yr.	X			X				X	X	X	X	
California	6 mo.	X						X		X	X		X					
Colorado	90 dy.	X						X			X			X		X		
Connecticut	1 yr.				X	18 mo.	X	X		X		X		X	X			
Delaware	6 mo.			X			X	X		X				X		X	X	
Dist. of Columbia	6 mo.					6 mo.–1yr.	X							X		X		
Florida	6 mo.	X					X	X	X	X	X		N					
Georgia	6 mo.				X		X	X	X	X		X	N					
Hawaii	6 mo.			X		2 yr.	X	X	X	X				X				
Idaho	6 wk.			X		5 yr.	X	X		X	X		X					X
Illinois	90 dy.			X	X	6 mo.–2 yr.	X	X		X				X		X	X	
Indiana	6 mo.				X		X			X				X		X	X	X
Iowa	1 yr.	X					X			X				X		X	X	X
Kansas	60 dy.		X				X			X				X				
Kentucky	180 dy.	X					X	X						X		X		
Louisiana	1 yr.					1 yr.	X	X		X	X	X	X					
Maine	6 mo.				X	1 yr.	X			X				X		X		
Maryland	1 yr.					2 yr.	X	X	X	X	X			X	X	X		X
Massachusetts	1 yr.				X		X	X	X	X				X		X		
Michigan	6 mo.	X					X							X				
Minnesota	6 mo.	X					X	X	X		X			X		X		X
Mississippi	6 mo.				X		X			X	X		N					
Missouri	90 dy.			X			X	X			X			X		X	X	
Montana	90 dy.			X			X	X						X		X		
Nebraska	1 yr.	X					X	X					X	X				
Nevada	6 wk.					1 yr.	X				X			X				X
New Hampshire	1 yr.				X		X							X				
New Jersey	1 yr.					18 mo.	X						X	X				
New Mexico	6 mo.				X		X				X	X		X				
New York	1 yr.					1 yr.	X	X	X	X				X		X		
North Carolina	6 mo.					1 yr.	X	X						X		X	X	X
North Dakota	6 mo.			X			X							X				X
Ohio	6 mo.			X		1 yr.	X	X	X			X	N					
Oklahoma	6 mo.			X			X				X			X				
Oregon	6 mo.	X					X	X		X	X	X		X		X	X	
Pennsylvania	6 mo.				X	3 yr.	X	X	X	X				X		X		
Rhode Island	1 yr.				X	3 yr.	X	X		X				X	X	X		X
South Carolina	1 yr.				X	1 yr.	X				X			X				
South Dakota	BFRes[1]			X						X	X	X		X				
Tennessee	6 mo.			X		3 yr.	X	X	X				X	X		X	X	
Texas	6 mo.			X		3 yr.	X					X		X				X
Utah	90 dy.					3 yr.	X				X			X				
Vermont	6 mo.					6 mo.	X			X				X		X		
Virginia	6 mo.					1 yr.–6 mo.	X	X	X	X			X	X	X	X	X	
Washington	BFRes[1]	X					X	X	X	X				X				X
West Virginia	1 yr.				X	1 yr.	X	X	X		X	X	X	X		X	X	
Wisconsin	6 mo.		X				X	X								X	X	
Wyoming	60 dy.	X					X							X				X

[1]Bona fide residence at time of institution of suit.

N = No statutory provisions for dividing marital property.

SOURCE: *Family Law Reporter—Reference File* (Washington, DC: The Bureau of National Affairs, Inc.) p. 4.

Table F.2
Custody

	STATUTORY CUSTODY GUIDELINES	CONSIDER CHILDREN'S WISHES	JOINT CUSTODY LAW	GRANDPARENT VISITATION
Alabama	X	X	X	
Alaska	X	X	X	X
Arizona	X	X	X	X
Arkansas	X			
California	X	X	X	X
Colorado	X	X	X	X
Connecticut	X		X	X
Delaware	X	X	X	X
Florida	X	X	X	X
Georgia	X		X	
Hawaii	X	X	X	X
Idaho	X	X	X	X
Illinois	X	X	X	X
Indiana	X	X	X	X
Iowa	X	X	X	X
Kansas	X	X	X	X
Kentucky	X	X	X	X
Louisiana	X	X	X	X
Maine	X	X	X	
Maryland	X			X
Massachusetts	X			X
Michigan	X	X	X	X
Minnesota	X	X	X	X
Mississippi	X	X		X
Missouri	X	X	X	X
Montana	X	X	X	X
Nebraska	X	X		
Nevada	X	X	X	X
New Hampshire	X		X	X
New Jersey	X		X	X
New Mexico	X	X	X	X
New York	X			
North Carolina	X			X
North Dakota	X	X	X	
Ohio		X	X	X
Oklahoma	X		X	X
Oregon	X	X		X
Pennsylvania	X			X
Rhode Island	X			
South Carolina	X			
South Dakota	X			X
Tennessee	X		X	X
Texas	X		X	X
Utah	X	X	X	X
Vermont	X	X		X
Virginia	X	X	X	
Washington	X	X	X	
West Virginia		X	X	
Wisconsin	X	X	X	X
Wyoming	X			X
Dist. of Columbia	X	X		

SOURCE: *Family Law Reporter–Reference File* (Washington DC, The Bureau of National Affairs, Inc.) p. 4; Timothy B. Walker, "Family Law in the Fifty States: An Overview," *Family Law Quarterly*, Vol. 25, No.4 (Winter, 1992): 473.

Enforcement of Child-Support Orders

	SPECIFIC SUPPORT STATUTES	DISCRETION TO HAVE DIRECT PAYMENTS TO COURT OFFICER	ALLOW WAGE ASSIGNMENTS OR INCOME DEDUCTIONS FOR SUPPORT
Alabama			X
Alaska	X	X	X
Arizona		X	X
Arkansas	X	X	X
California		X	X
Colorado	X	X	X
Connecticut		X	X
Delaware	X	X	X
Florida	X	X	X
Georgia		X	X
Hawaii		X	X
Idaho		X	X
Illinois	X	X	X
Indiana	X	X	X
Iowa		X	X
Kansas	X	X	X
Kentucky		X	X
Louisiana	X		X
Maine	X		X
Maryland	X	X	X
Massachusetts	X	X	X
Michigan		X	X
Minnesota		X	X
Mississippi	X		
Missouri	X	X	X
Montana		X	X
Nebraska			X
Nevada	X		X
New Hampshire		X	X
New Jersey			
New Mexico	X		X
New York	X		X
North Carolina	X	X	X
North Dakota		X	X
Ohio			X
Oklahoma	X		X
Oregon			X
Pennsylvania		X	X
Rhode Island			X
South Carolina	X	X	X
South Dakota	X	X	X
Tennessee	X	X	X
Texas	X	X	X
Utah	X	X	X
Vermont			X
Virginia	X	X	X
Washington		X	X
West Virginia			X
Wisconsin	X	X	X
Wyoming		X	X
Dist. of Columbia	X	X	X

SOURCE: Walker, 1992: 419–92.

Glossary

abortion The artificially induced or natural expulsion of an embryo or fetus from the uterus.

acquaintance rape Unwanted, forced sexual intercourse, often in a social context such as a party; the rapist may be a neighbor, friend of the family, coworker, or a person the victim has just met.

acquired immunodeficiency syndrome (AIDS) A degenerative disease caused by a virus that attacks the body's immune system and renders it susceptible to a number of diseases such as pneumonia and cancer.

afterbirth The placenta and other matter that detaches from the uterus and leaves the mother's body during the third stage of labor.

agape Love that is altruistic, self-sacrificing, and directed toward all humankind.

ageism Discrimination against people on the basis of age, particularly against those who are old.

alimony Monetary payments made by one ex-spouse to the other after a divorce to support the latter's basic needs for survival.

Alzheimer's disease A progressive, degenerative disorder that attacks the brain and impairs memory, thinking, and behavior.

amniocentesis A procedure performed in the twentieth week of pregnancy, in which a sample of the amniotic fluid is withdrawn by a needle inserted into the abdomen and fluid is analyzed for possible genetic disorders and biochemical abnormalities in the fetus.

amnion A thick-skinned sac filled with fluid that surrounds the developing fetus.

androgyny A blend of culturally defined male and female characteristics.

anorexia nervosa An often intractable and dangerous eating disorder characterized by fear of obesity coupled with a distorted body image and the conviction that one is "fat," significant weight loss, and an absolute refusal to maintain weight within the normal limits for one's age and height.

anorgasmia The inability to reach orgasm.

artificial insemination An assisted reproductive technique in which male semen is introduced artificially into the vagina or uterus about the time of ovulation.

attachment theory The notion that a warm, secure, and loving relationship is essential to human emotional growth and development.

authoritarian approach An approach to parenting that is demanding, controlling, and punitive; emphasizes respect for authority, work, order, and traditional family structure; often uses punitive, forceful measures to control behavior.

authoritative approach An approach to parenting that is demanding and controlling but supportive and responsive; encourages autonomy and self-reliance; and generally uses positive reinforcement instead of punitive, repressive discipline.

baby boomer A person born in the post–World War II generation between 1946 and 1964.

Bartholin's glands Glands located at the base of the labia minora in females that secrete a small amount of an alkaline fluid during sexual arousal.

basal body temperature method (BBT) A variation on the rhythm method of family planning, in which couples keep a record of the woman's body temperature in order to identify periods of fertility and infertility.

battered woman syndrome A condition in which women who have experienced many years of physical abuse come to feel incapable of making any satisfactory change in their way of life; recently used as a defense in cases in which such women have murdered their abusive husbands.

being-love Love that is giving, unselfish, and nonpossessive.

bereavement The state of having been robbed, or deprived, by death of the presence of a loved one.

bigamy The act of marrying one person while still legally married to another.

bilingual education Teaching in both the official language of a country and the native language of immigrant students.

Billings method A variation on the rhythm method of family planning, in which a woman monitors the condition of her vaginal mucus in order to identify periods of fertility and infertility.

biological father-stepmother family A family in which all the children are biological children of the father and stepchildren of the mother.

biological mother-stepfather family A family in which all the children are biological children of the mother and stepchildren of the father.

bisexual A person who is sexually attracted to members of both sexes.

blastocyst A hollow ball of cells, the inner cell mass of which will be transformed into an embryo and the outer layer the placenta.

boomerang generation Young adults who move back into their parents' homes after living independently for a while.

bulimia An eating disorder characterized by a cyclical pattern of eating binges followed by self-induced vomiting, fasting, excessive exercise, or the use of diuretics or laxatives.

bundling A custom in American colonial times in which a young man and woman, both fully dressed, spent the night in bed together, separated by a wooden board.

calendar method A variation on the rhythm method of family planning, in which a woman uses a formula to calculate periods of fertility and infertility based on the length of her menstrual cycles.

cervical cap A barrier contraceptive device made of latex rubber that fits over a woman's cervix and is used with a spermicide.

cervix The narrow end of the uterus that projects into the back of the vagina.

cesarean section The surgical delivery of a baby through incisions made in the mother's abdominal wall.

child abuse According to Public Law 93-237, the physical or mental injury, sexual abuse, negligent treatment, or maltreatment of a child under the age of 18 by a person responsible for the child's welfare under circumstances that indicate the child's health or welfare is harmed or threatened.

child maltreatment A wide range of behaviors that place the child at serious risk, including physical abuse, sexual abuse, neglect, and emotional maltreatment.

child support Monetary payments by the noncustodial parent to the parent who has custody of children to help pay the expenses of raising the children.

Child Support Enforcement Amendments Legislation enacted in 1984 that requires states to adopt formulas for determining child-support obligations and to withhold moneys to cover such support from wages and other income of delinquent noncustodial parents.

chlamydia A sexually transmitted bacterial infection that can contribute to infertility by triggering *pelvic inflammatory disease*. The symptoms of chlamydia often go unnoticed.

chorion A membrane that develops into the lining of the *placenta*.

chorionic villi sampling A procedure in which some of the villi, or protrusions, of the membrane that surrounds the amniotic sac are removed by a catheter through the vagina and analyzed for abnormalities in the fetus.

clinical research The study of individuals or small groups of people who seek help for physical and/or social problems from mental health professionals.

clitoral hood The part of the labia minora in females that covers the clitoris.

clitoris A small, elongated, erectile structure in females that develops from the same embryonic tissue as the male penis.

cognitive development theory A theory positing that children learn by interacting with their environment and, using the processes of thinking, understanding, and reasoning, by interpreting and applying the information they gather.

cohabitation A living arrangement in which two people who are not related and not married share living quarters and usually have a sexual relationship.

common-law marriage A nonceremonial form of marriage, established by cohabitation and/or evidence of consummation (sexual intercourse).

commuter marriage A marriage in which partners live and work in separate geographic areas and get together intermittently.

compadrazgo A Mexican-American family system rather like that of *fictive kin* in which close family friends are formally designated as godparents of a newborn, participate in the child's important rites of passage, and maintain continuing strong ties with their godchild.

comparable worth A concept that calls for equal pay for men and women who are doing work that entails comparable skill, effort, responsibility, and working conditions.

concept A word or set of words that expresses an abstract notion about some aspect of the world.

conception The fertilization of an egg by a spermatozoon.

condom The traditional condom for men is a thin sheath of latex rubber or polyurethane that is placed over the erect penis before intercourse to prevent ejaculated semen and sperm from entering the vagina. The condom also helps protect against HIV and other sexually transmitted diseases.

conflict-habituated marriage A marriage in which the partners fight both verbally and physically but do not believe that fighting is a reason for divorce.

conflict theory A macro-level sociological theory that examines the ways in which groups disagree and struggle over power and compete for scarce resources and that views conflict and its consequences as natural, inevitable, and often desirable.

conjugal family The family seen in terms of a marital rather than a blood relationship; considered synonymous with *nuclear family*.

consanguine family The family seen in terms of blood relationships; considered synonymous with *extended family*.

contraception The prevention of pregnancy by behavioral, mechanical, or chemical means.

contraceptive sponge A round sponge containing spermicide; works primarily by killing sperm and blocking the cervical opening.

corona The raised and rounded border of the glans of the penis.

courtship violence The physical abuse of a steady dating partner in the context of the dating relationship.

Cowper's glands In the male, two pea-shaped structures located beneath the prostate gland that secrete a small amount of an alkaline fluid prior to orgasm.

cross-sectional research Research that collects data on different people or groups at a single point in time.

cunnilingus Oral stimulation of a woman's genitals.

custody A court-mandated ruling as to which parent will have the primary responsibility for the welfare and upbringing of a child; the custodial parent cares for the child in her or his home, whereas the noncustodial parent may have specified visitation rights.

daddy penalty Paying men whose wives are employed outside the home lower salaries than their counterparts whose wives are full-time homemakers.

date rape Unwanted, forced sexual intercourse in the context of a dating situation; victim and perpetrator may be on a first date or in a long-term dating relationship.

dating The process of meeting people socially for possible mate selection.

deficiency-love Love that is selfish and seeks to fulfill only one partner's needs.

Depo-Provera Brand name of an injectable contraceptive drug preparation that contains progestin and that works by preventing ovulation.

depression A mental disorder characterized by pervasive sadness and other negative emotions and that often also finds expression in physical symptoms such as diarrhea, chest discomfort, nausea or loss of appetite for which no physical or physiological cause can be found.

developmental tasks Specific role expectations and responsibilities that must be fulfilled as people move through the family life cycle.

developmental theories Micro-level theories of marriage and the family that examine the ways in which family members accomplish *developmental tasks* as they move through the *family life cycle*.

devitalized marriage A marriage in which the partners are initially in love, spend time together, and have a satisfying sex life but in time find they are staying together out of duty; because they see no alternatives, they do not consider divorce.

DEWKS (dual-employed with kids) Term that describes a family in which both parents are employed full-time outside the home.

diaphragm A contraceptive device made of rubber and shaped like a shallow rubber cup with a flexible rim that fits between a woman's pubic bone and the back of her cervix, barring entry of sperm into the uterus. The diaphragm is used with a spermicide.

dilation The widening of the cervix during the birth process.

discouraged worker An unemployed person who wants to work but who has recently given up the search for a position because of the belief that the job hunt is futile.

discretionary income Income remaining after essentials, such as rent or mortgage, food, utilities, and transportation costs, have been paid and that people can then spend as they please.

discrimination Behavior, often based on prejudice, that subjects members of minority groups to unfair treatment, such as rejection of job applications and denial of housing opportunities.

divorce The legal and formal dissolution of a marriage.

divorce mediation The technique and practice in which a trained mediator helps a divorcing couple to come to an agreement and to resolve such issues as support, child custody, and the division of property.

dowry The money, goods, or property a woman in traditional societies brings to a marriage.

dual-career couple Marriage partners who both work in professional or managerial positions.

dual-earner couple Married partners both of whom work outside the home.

dying trajectory The manner in which a very ill person is expected to die; generally the distinction is made between lingering death and rapid or sudden, sometimes unexpected death.

dyspareunia Painful sexual intercourse.

ectoderm A cell layer in the embryo that forms the nervous system, skin, and teeth.

effacement The thinning out of the cervix during the birth process.

egalitarian pattern A familial relationship pattern in which authority is shared equally between the husband and wife.

elder abuse Physical abuse, negligence, financial exploitation, psychological abuse, deprivation of necessities like food and heat, isolation from friends and relatives, and failure to administer needed medications to people age 65 or older.

embryo The developing human organism after implantation up to the eighth week of the reproductive process.

embryo transplant A procedure by which an *embryo*, or a fertilized egg, is implanted in the uterus of an infertile woman.

endoderm A cell layer in the embryo that forms the internal organs.

endogamy A cultural rule requiring that people marry and/or have sexual relations only within their own particular group.

endometriosis A condition in which endometrial tissue spreads outside the womb and attaches itself to other pelvic organs, such as the ovaries or the Fallopian tubes.

endometrium In females, the innermost layer of the uterus.

engagement The formalization of a couple's decision to marry and the last step in the courtship process.

episiotomy A surgical process that involves making an incision from the lower portion of the vagina through the perineum to avoid tearing of the perineal tissue during childbirth.

equity theory A theoretical perspective that seeks to explain how people perceive injustice and how they will react when they find themselves in unjust relationships.

erectile dysfunction A man's inability to attain or maintain an erection; also called *impotence.*

eros Love based on love of beauty and physical attractiveness.

evaluation research Research that assesses the efficiency and effectiveness of social programs in both the public and private sectors.

excitement phase The first stage of human sexual response, in which blood pressure, pulse, and breathing rates accelerate and the external genitalia undergo such changes as swelling, erection, and lubrication.

exogamy A cultural rule requiring that people marry only outside of their particular group.

expressive role In structural-functional theory, the supportive and nurturing role of the wife or mother who must sustain and support the husband/father.

extended family A family in which two or more generations live together or in adjacent dwellings. Extended families may be based on both *consanguine and conjugal* relationships.

familism The notion that, within a given family, family relationships take precedence over the concerns of individual family members.

family Traditionally defined as a unit made up of two or more people who are related by blood, marriage, or adoption and who live together and form an economic unit. Defined in this book as any sexually expressive or parent-child rela-tionships in which (1) people live together with a commitment in an interpersonal relationship; (2) the members see their identity as importantly attached to the group; and (3) the group has an identity of its own.

Family and Medical Leave Act (FMLA) A law passed in 1993 that allows eligible employees to take up to 12 weeks of unpaid, job-protected annual leave following the birth or adoption of a child, to care for a seriously ill family member, or to recover from their own serious illnesses.

family life cycle A series of stages, each focusing on a different set of events, that the family goes through from the early days of a marriage to the death of one or both partners.

family of orientation The family into which a person is born.

family of procreation The family a person forms by marrying and having or adopting children.

family policy The measures taken by governmental bodies to achieve specific objectives relating to the family's well-being.

Family Support Act Legislation enacted in 1988 that strengthens the *Child Support Enforcement Amendments,* requiring that the courts justify in writing any departure from state guidelines, that states update child-support awards every three years, and that, by 1994, states withhold funds for support payments from all noncustodial parents' wages.

fellatio Oral stimulation of a man's penis.

female condom A seven-inch long polyurethane pouch that is closed at one end, which is surrounded by a flexible ring, and open at the other, surrounded by a similar ring. The inner ring fits over the cervix, like a diaphragm; the outer ring covers part of the vulva.

fertility awareness (natural planning, rhythm) Predicting when ovulation will occur in order to prevent or facilitate conception.

fertility rate The number of births per year per 1000 women of childbearing age (15 to 44).

fetal alcohol syndrome (FAS) Physical deformities and/or mental retardation in an infant caused by the mother's excessive use of alcohol during pregnancy.

fetus The developing human organism from eight weeks after conception up to birth.

fictive kin Nonrelatives who are accepted as part of a particular family.

filter theory The theory that people in

search of potential mates go through a process whereby they filter out eligible partners according to certain specific criteria and thus reduce the pool of eligibles to a relatively small number of candidates.

focus group In social science research, a group of people who engage in a guided discussion of a topic of interest to a researcher.

foreskin The loose skin of the penis that folds over the glans.

foster home A home in which a family raises a child or children who are not their own for a period of time but does not formally adopt them.

gamete intrafallopian transfer (GIFT) A variation of *in vitro fertilization* in which eggs and sperm are artificially inserted into a woman's Fallopian tube.

gender The socially learned attitudes and behaviors that characterize a person of one sex or the other; based on differing social and cultural expectations of the sexes.

gender identity An individual's emotional and intellectual awareness of being either male or female.

gender role stereotype The belief and expectation that women and men each display rigid, traditional gender-role characteristics.

gender roles Distinctive patterns of attitudes, behaviors, and activities that society prescribes for females and males.

gender schema theory The theory that children develop schema, or information-processing categories, that organize and guide their perceptions of cultural stimuli and use these schema to develop a gender identity.

general systems theory A micro-level theory that views the family as a functioning unit whose daily operations and survival depend on the interactions of its members with each other and with larger social groups.

genogram A diagram of the biological relationships among family members.

gerontologist One who studies aging and the elderly.

glans The smooth, rounded tip of the clitoris (in females) or the penis (in males).

grief The emotional response to loss.

half-sibling A brother or sister with whom one shares only one biological parent.

hermaphrodite A person born with both male and female (internal and/or external) sex organs.

heterosexual A person who is sexually attracted to members of the opposite sex.

homophobia Fear and hatred of homosexuality.

homosexual A person who is sexually attracted to persons of the same sex.

hormone A chemical substance secreted into the bloodstream by glands of the endocrine system.

hospice A place for the care of the dying that stresses the relief of pain, imparting a sense of security and companionship to dying patients, and making such patients comfortable.

household A group of related and/or unrelated people living together in the same dwelling.

househusband A man who stays home full time to care for his family and do the housework while his wife serves as family breadwinner.

human immunodeficiency virus (HIV) The virus that causes AIDS.

hymen The thin membrane that partially covers the vaginal opening in some sexually inexperienced females.

hypergamy Marrying or dating someone who is in a higher socioeconomic group than one's own.

identity bargaining A stage in the evolution of a marriage in which partners readjust their idealized expectations to the realities of their life together.

implantation The process in which the blastocyst burrows into the wall of the uterus, usually 11 to 12 days after conception.

impotence See *erectile dysfunction*.

incest Sexual intercourse between family members who are closely related. See also *incest taboo*.

incest taboo Cultural norms and laws that forbid sexual intercourse between close blood relatives, such as brother and sister, father and daughter, or mother and son.

infertility The inability to conceive a baby after 12 months of unprotected sex.

inhibited sexual desire (ISD) A low level of interest in sex that is a source of personal distress or of relationship problems.

instrumental role In structural-functional theory, the "breadwinner" role of the husband or father, who must be hardworking, tough, and competitive.

intrauterine device (IUD) A small plastic or metal birth-control device that is inserted into a woman's uterus to impede the passage of sperm through the reproductive tract.

intrinsic marriage A marriage that is inherently rewarding.

in vitro fertilization (IVF) An assisted reproduction technique in which eggs

are surgically removed from a woman's ovaries, fertilized with sperm from the woman's husband or a donor, and then reimplanted in the woman's uterus.

joint biological-stepfamily A family in which at least one child is a biological child of both parents, at least one child is the biological child of one parent and the stepchild of the other parent, and no other type of child is present.

joint custody A custody arrangement in which the children divide their time between both parents; in joint legal custody parents share decision making about the children's upbringing; in joint physical custody the children live alternately and for specified periods in each parent's home.

kinship system A network of people who are related by marriage, blood, or adoption.

labia majora In the female, two outer elongated folds of skin that extend from the mons to the perineum, covering the vaginal and urethral openings.

labia minora In the female, two inner elongated folds of skin located between the labia majora, that, like the latter, cover and protect the vaginal and urethral openings.

laparoscopy A surgical procedure, often used in a tubal ligation, in which very small incisions are made in the abdominal wall and surgery is carried out using instruments and cameras inserted through the incisions.

latchkey kids Children who return after school to an empty home and are alone and unsupervised until their parents or another adult arrives.

latent functions Functions that are not recognized or intended; present but not immediately visible.

later-life family A family that is beyond the years of child rearing and that has begun to launch the children into their own lives.

lightening The rotation of the fetus within the mother's womb so that its head is downward.

living will A legal document in which a person specifies what, if any, life support measures she or he wishes to be provided with in the case of serious illness and if or when such measures should be discontinued.

longitudinal research Research that collects data on people at different points in time.

ludus Love that is carefree and casual, "fun and games."

machismo A concept of masculinity that stresses such attributes as dominance, assertiveness, pride, and sexual prowess.

macro-level perspective A sociological perspective that focuses on large-scale patterns that characterize society as a whole.

male climacteric A "change of life" in men proposed by some as analogous to female menopause. More psychological than physiological, such a change affects only a small percentage of men and is not characterized by the cessation of reproductive capacity.

mania Love that is obsessive, jealous, and possessive.

manifest functions Functions that are recognized or intended; present in a clearly evident way.

marital burnout The gradual deterioration of love and, ultimately, the loss of an emotional attachment between marital partners.

marital rape A violent act in which a nonconsenting woman is forced by her husband to engage in sexual activity.

marriage A socially approved mating relationship.

marriage market Courtship seen as a process in which prospective spouses compare the assets and liabilities of eligible partners and choose the best available mate.

marriage squeeze The term for the oversupply of female *baby boomers*, born between 1945 and 1964, in relation to eligible males.

married singles Married partners who continue to live together, who may be good friends, and who may be sexually intimate but who, in many ways, have drifted apart.

masturbation Sexual self-pleasuring that involves some form of direct physical stimulation.

matriarchy A familial relationship in which the authority is held by the oldest female, usually the mother.

Medicaid A health-care program financed jointly by state and federal governments for low-income people of all ages.

Medicare A federal hospital and medical insurance program for people age 65 and over.

menopause The cessation of the menstrual cycle.

mesoderm A cell layer in the embryo that forms the muscles, skeleton, and blood vessels.

micro-level perspective A sociological perspective that focuses on small-scale patterns of social interaction in specific settings.

minimal brain damage A condition associated with hyperactivity and learning disabilities in an infant, caused by the collapse of the umbilical cord and the subsequent cutting off of oxygen to the fetus.

minority group A group of people who, because of their physical or cultural characteristics, are singled out from others in the society in which they live for differential and unequal treatment.

misogyny Hatred of women.

mommy track A slower or even side track in business along which women managers who wish to combine both career and child rearing are expected to move.

monogamy A marital or sexual relationship in which an individual is committed exclusively to one other individual.

mons veneris The soft layer of fatty tissue overlaying the area, in females, where the pubic bones meet.

mourning The customary outward expression of grief over the loss of a loved person that varies among different social and cultural groups.

myometrium The middle layer of uterine muscles that contract during labor.

no-fault divorce A divorce process in which neither partner need establish the guilt or wrongdoing of the other.

norm A culturally defined rule for behavior.

Norplant A contraceptive method for women that involves the implantation, just beneath the skin of the upper arm, of several silicon rubber rods that contain a synthetic form of progesterone, which is released slowly over a period of five years.

nuclear family A family made up of a wife, a husband, and their biological children.

observation A type of scientific investigation in which researchers collect data by systematically observing people in their natural surroundings.

open adoption An adoption process that encourages the sharing of information and contact between biological and adoptive parents during the adoption process and throughout the adopted child's life.

orgasm The third stage of human sexual response, in which sexual tension reaches its peak, or climax, and is suddenly discharged.

ovary The female gonad in which ova (eggs) and female hormones are produced.

palimony Financial settlements awarded to an unmarried live-in partner when the relationship ends.

part-time/limited cohabitation A type of *cohabitation*. into which people "drift" gradually.

passive-congenial marriage A marriage in which partners with minimal emotional investment and expectations of their union maintain independent spheres of interests and activities and derive satisfaction from relationships with others rather than each other.

patriarchy A familial relationship in which the authority is held by the oldest male, usually the father.

pelvic inflammatory disease (PID) An infection of the uterus that spreads to the Fallopian tubes, ovaries, and surrounding tissues and produces scarring that blocks the Fallopian tubes.

penis The external male reproductive organ that performs both a reproductive and an excretory function.

perimetrium The external layer, or cover, of the uterus.

perineum The hairless area of skin between the anus and the vaginal opening (in females) or scrotum (in males).

permissive approach An approach to parenting that is highly responsive and warm, not demanding, but sometimes manipulative; this approach encourages freedom of expression, autonomy, and internal control.

petting Physical contact between males and females that produces erotic arousal without necessarily leading to sexual intercourse.

Pill An oral contraceptive containing a combination of estrogen and progesterone (progestins) that is taken continuously by a woman over a 21-day period, between menstrual periods.

placenta An organ that connects the systems of a fetus and its mother.

plateau phase The second stage of human sexual response, in which such changes as swelling of the genitalia and heightened blood pressure and heart rate continue.

polygamy A form of marriage in which there are several spouses for one woman or one man.

population Any well-defined group of people or things that a researcher wants to study.

POSSLQs "Persons of the opposite sex sharing living quarters"; U.S. Census Bureau household category.

postpartum depression Depression experienced by some women soon after childbirth; thought to be at least partially caused by chemical imbalances.

poverty line The minimum income level determined by the federal government to be necessary for individuals' and families' basic subsistence.

power The ability to impose one's will on others.

pragma Love that is rational and based

on practical considerations, such as compatibility and perceived benefits.

prejudice A negative attitude toward individuals and groups (usually minority groups) who are different from oneself; based on suspicion, intolerance, and sometimes hatred.

premarital cohabitation Often a kind of trial marriage, a living arrangement in which a couple test their relationship before making a final commitment.

premature ejaculation An unintended ejaculation that occurs before or while the man is trying to enter his partner or soon after intercourse begins.

premenstrual syndrome (PMS) Physical and psychological symptoms reflecting a malfunction in the production of hormones during the menstrual cycle.

prepared childbirth (formerly called natural childbirth) A method of childbirth in which the expectant mother—and her partner—are educated about pregnancy, labor, birth, and birth procedures to reduce the pain and fear of childbirth.

propinquity Geographic closeness.

prostate gland In the male, a gland that surrounds the urethra and neck of the bladder and contributes several substances to the seminal fluid.

quickening The first movements of the fetus felt by the mother.

racial-ethnic group A group of people with distinctive racial and cultural characteristics.

refractory period A stage in the resolution phase of the sexual response cycle during which the male cannot become sexually aroused.

reliability The consistency with which a research instrument repeatedly produces the same results, whether it is administered to different individuals at one time or to the same individuals over time.

resolution phase The fourth, and final, stage of human sexual response, in which swelling of the genitalia subsides and heart rate, blood pressure, and breathing return to normal.

Rh factor A term for the inherited presence or absence in the blood of a particular protein. An Rh negative woman carrying an Rh positive fetus must be given specific injections immediately after delivery lest her blood build up antibodies to the negative factor and thus endanger the life of a second baby if it should also be Rh positive.

role Pattern of behavior attached to a particular status, or position, in society.

role conflict Frustration and uncertainty experienced by a person who is confronted with incompatible role requirements or expectations.

sample In social science research, a group of people or things that is smaller than but representative of the population under study.

sandwich generation Midlife men and women who feel caught between the need to care for both their own children and their aging parents.

scrotum The sac hanging beneath the penis that contains the testes, or testicles.

secondary analysis The analysis of data that have been collected by other researchers.

self-disclosure Open communication in which one person offers his or her honest thoughts and feelings to another person in the hope that truly open communication will follow.

seminal vesicles In the male, two structures that contribute several substances to the seminal fluid.

separation Separations are of several types: a temporary "time-out" while partners reassess their marriage; a "trial separation" during which a couple separate physically and evaluate the desirability of continuing their marriage; a permanent physical separation when one or both partners' religious faith precludes divorce; or a "legal separation," a temporary period of living apart required by most states before a divorce may be granted.

serial monogamy Marrying several people one at a time; that is, marrying, divorcing, remarrying, divorcing again, and so on.

sex The biological—chromosomal, anatomical, hormonal, and other physical and physiological—characteristics with which we are born and which determine whether we are male or female.

sexual aversion A persistent or intense feeling of anxiety or panic in sexual situations that often leads to avoidance of sexual contact.

sexual dysfunction A condition in which the ordinary physical responses of sexual function are impaired.

sexual harassment Any unwelcome sexual advance, request for sexual favors, or other conduct of a sexual nature that makes a person uncomfortable and interferes with her or his work.

sexually transmitted diseases (STDs) Diseases that are spread by contact with body parts or fluids that harbor what are usually bacterial or viral microorganisms. Most of the more than 20 currently prevalent STDs are spread exclusively by sexual contact, and most are curable or controllable. HIV-AIDS, however, is incurable.

sexual script A collection of norms that specifies what is acceptable and what is unacceptable sexual activity, identifies eligible sexual partners, and defines the boundaries of sexual behavior in time and place.

significant others People who play an important emotional role in an individual's socialization.

social exchange theory A micro-level theory that proposes that the interaction between two or more people is based on the efforts of each to maximize rewards and minimize costs.

social integration The social bonds that people have with others and the community at large.

socialization The process of acquiring the language, accumulated knowledge, attitudes, beliefs, and values of one's society and culture and learning the social and interpersonal skills needed to function effectively in society.

social learning theory The notion that people learn attitudes and behaviors through interaction with the environment; learning may occur through reward and punishment or through imitation or role modeling.

Social Security A public retirement pension system administered by the federal government.

sole custody A type of custody in which one parent has exclusive responsibility for raising a child and the other parent has specified visitation rights.

spermicide A substance containing chemicals, such as nonoxynol-9 or octoxinol-9, that kills male sperm.

split custody A custody arrangement in which children are divided between the parents, usually female children going to the mother, males to the father.

stepfamily A household in which there is an adult couple and at least one of the partners has a child from a previous marriage.

steroid A synthetic hormone, most often testosterone, that is taken to increase the size and strength of muscles.

storge Love that is slow-burning, peaceful, and affectionate.

structural-functional theory A macro-level theoretical perspective that examines the relationship between the family and the larger society as well as the internal relationships among family members.

substitute marriage A long-term commitment between two people without a legal marriage.

surrogacy An assisted reproduction technique in which a surrogate mother is artificially inseminated by the husband of a woman who cannot bear children or implanted with the woman's egg after it has been fertilized by the husband's sperm in vitro.

survey research A means of scientific investigation in which the researcher systematically collects data from respondents either by questionnaire or by interview.

symbolic interaction theory A micro-level theory that views everyday human interaction as governed by the symbolic communication of knowledge, ideas, beliefs, and attitudes.

teratogen A substance that can harm a fetus.

testes Also called testicles, the male gonads (produced from the same embryonic tissue as the female gonads, the ovaries) that produce sperm and male hormones.

theory A set of logically related statements formulated to explain why a phenomenon occurs.

total marriage A marriage in which the partners participate in each other's lives at all levels and have few areas of tension or unresolved hostility; more all-encompassing than the *vital marriage*.

toxemia of pregnancy A disease that can develop during pregnancy and includes such symptoms as high blood pressure, extreme weight gain due to water retention, and, if it advances far enough, convulsions and coma. It can be detected by the presence of excess protein in the urine.

trailing spouse A spouse who gives up her or his work and searches for another job in the location where her or his spouse has taken a position.

transsexual A person who feels that his or her gender identity is out of sync with his or her anatomical sexual characteristics.

true womanhood A nineteenth-century conception of womanliness that stressed piety, purity, submissiveness, and domesticity.

tubal ligation A form of sterilization in which a woman's Fallopian tubes are tied or, more often, cut and tied in order to prevent conception.

two-person single career An arrangement in which one spouse participates in the other's career behind the scenes without pay or direct recognition.

umbilical cord The link between the fetus and the placenta.

underemployed worker A worker who holds part-time jobs but would rather work full time or who accepts jobs below his or her level of expertise.

urethra In both males and females, the passageway from the bladder to the exterior of the body; in males also the passageway for semen during ejaculation.

uterus In females, the hollow, muscular organ in whose wall a fertilized egg normally implants and grows to a mature fetus.

utilitarian marriage A marriage based on convenience.

vagina In females, the passageway that extends from the vulva to the cervix and that receives the penis during intercourse and serves as the birth canal.

vaginismus A sexual disorder in which a woman experiences pain and persistent involuntary contractions of the muscles surrounding the outer third of the vagina when penile penetration is attempted.

validity The accuracy of a research instrument; an assessment of whether the instrument actually measures what it is supposed to measure.

variable A quality or quantity that changes over situations or time and that a researcher wishes to measure or evaluate.

vasectomy A form of sterilization in which a man's vas deferens is tied off and cut to prevent sperm from passing through the man's reproductive tract.

vestibular area In females, the area between the two labia minora.

vital marriage A marriage in which partners maintain a close relationship, resolve conflicts quickly through compromise, and often make sacrifices for each other.

vulva The external female genitalia.

welfare Government aid to those who can't support themselves, generally because they are poor or unemployed.

withdrawal (coitus interruptus) a highly unreliable method of contraception in which a man attempts to withdraw his penis from a woman's vagina just before he ejaculates.

zygote A one-celled organism that is formed by the sperm and the ovum and contains the complete genetic code for a human being.

zygote intrafallopian transfer (ZIFT) A variation of *in vitro fertilization* in which a woman's eggs are fertilized by her husband's or a donor's sperm in vitro and are then transferred to the Fallopian tube.

References

ABALOS, D. T. 1993. *The Latino family and the politics of transformation.* Westport, CT: Praeger.

ABEL, E. K. 1991. *Who cares for the elderly? Public policy and the experiences of adult daughters.* Philadelphia: Temple University Press.

ABEL, G. G., J. BECKER, J. CUNNINGHAM-RATHNER, M. MITTLEMAN, AND J. L. ROULEAU. 1988. Multiple paraphiliac diagnoses among sex offenders. *Bulletin of the American Academy of Psychiatry and the Law* 16, 153–68.

ABELES, R. P., H. C. GIFT, AND M. G. ORY, EDS. 1994. *Aging and quality of life.* New York: Springer.

ABELOVE, H., M. A. BARALE, AND D. M. HALPERIN, EDS. 1993. *The lesbian and gay studies reader.* New York: Routledge.

ABRAHAM, L., L. GREEN, M. KRANCE, J. ROSENBERG, J. SOMERVILLE, AND C. STONER, EDS. 1993. *Reinventing love: Six women talk about lust, sex, and romance.* New York: Plume.

ABRASH, B. AND C. EGAN, EDS. 1992. *Mediating history: The map guide to independent video by and about African American, Asian American, Latino, and Native American people.* New York: New York University Press.

ABURDENE, P., AND J. NAISBITT. 1992. *Megatrends for women.* New York: Villard.

ACKERMAN, D. 1994. *A natural history of love.* New York: Random House.

ACOCK, A. C., AND D. H. DEMO. 1994. *Family diversity and well-being.* Thousands Oaks, CA: Sage.

ACUNA, R. 1988. *Occupied America: A history of Chicanos,* 3rd ed. New York: Harper & Row.

ADAMS, B. 1980. *The family.* Chicago: Rand McNally.

ADAMS, B. N. 1988. Fifty years of family research: What does it mean? *Journal of Marriage and the Family* 50 (February): 5–17.

ADAMS, J. A., K. HARPER, S. KNUDSON,

AND J. REVILLA. 1994. Examination findings in legally confirmed child sexual abuse: It's normal to be normal. *Pediatrics* 94, no. 3 (September): 310–17.

ADAMS, V. 1980. Getting at the heart of jealous love. *Psychology Today,* May, 38, 41–44, 47, 102, 105–06.

ADLER, J. 1994. Kids growing up scared. *Newsweek,* January 10, 43–49.

ADLER, J., ET AL. 1992. Unhappily ever after. *Newsweek,* August 31, 52–59.

ADLER, J., WITH D. ROSENBERG. 1994. The endless binge. *Newsweek,* December 19, 72–73.

ADLER, J., WITH M. HAGER AND K. SPRINGEN. 1993. Clone hype, *Newsweek,* November 8, 60–62.

ADLER, P. A., AND P. ADLER. 1994. Observational techniques. In *Handbook of qualitative research,* ed. N. K. Denzin and Y. S. Lincoln, 377–92. Thousand Oaks, CA: Sage.

AGHAJANIAN, K. 1986. Some notes on divorce in Iran. *Journal of Marriage and the Family* 48 (November): 749–55.

AGUILAR, L. 1990. Helping their way off welfare. *Newsweek,* May 7, 70.

AGUILAR-SAN JUAN, K. 1994. *The State of Asian America: Activism and resistance in the 1990s.* Boston: South End Press.

AHRONS, C. 1994. *The good divorce: Keeping your family together when your marriage comes apart.* New York: HarperCollins.

AHRONS, C. R., AND R. H. RODGERS. 1987. *Divorced families: A multidisciplinary developmental view.* New York: Norton.

AHUVIA, A. C., AND M. B. ADELMAN. 1992. Formal intermediaries in the marriage market: A typology and review. *Journal of Marriage and the Family* 54 (May): 452–63.

AINSWORTH, M., ET AL. 1978. *Patterns of attachment: A psychological study of the strange situation.* Hillsdale, NJ: Lawrence Erlbaum Associates.

ALBA, R. D. 1990. *Ethnic identity: The transformation of white America.* New Haven, CT: Yale University Press.

ALBAS, D., AND C. ALBAS. 1987. The pulley alternative for the wheel theory of the development of love. *International Journal of Comparative Sociology* 28, nos. 3–4, 223–27.

ALCOCK, B., AND J. ROBSON. 1990. Cagney and Lacey revisited. *Feminist Review* 35 (Summer): 42–53.

ALDOUS, J., AND W. DUMON. 1991. Family policy in the 1980s: Controversy and consensus. In *Contemporary families: Looking forward, looking back,* ed. A. Booth, 466–81. Minneapolis, MN: National Council on Family Relations.

ALESCI, N. 1993. Can we talk? Bertice Berry begins national TV talk show. *ASA Footnotes* (December): 5.

ALI, S. 1990. *The blackman's guide to understanding the blackwoman.* Philadelphia: Civilized Publications.

ALIBHAI-BROWN, Y. 1993. Marriage of minds not hearts. *New Statesman & Society,* February 12, 28–29.

ALLEN, K. R., AND R. S. PICKETT. 1987. Forgotten streams in the family life course: Utilization of qualitative retrospective interviews in the analysis of lifelong single women's family careers. *Journal of Marriage and the Family* 49 (August): 517–26.

ALLEN, P., WITH S. HARMON. 1994. The fun of flirting. *Cosmopolitan,* March, 78, 82, 83, 84.

ALLGEIER, A. R. 1983. Sexuality and gender roles in the second half of life. In *Changing boundaries: Gender roles and sexual behavior,* ed. E. R. Allgeier and N. B. McCormick, 135–58. Mountain View, CA: Mayfield.

ALVARADO, D. 1991. Fathers' health and fetal harm. *Washington Post, Health Supplement,* August 20, 6.

ALVIREZ, D., F. D. BEAN, AND D. WILLIAMS. 1981. The Mexican American family. In *Ethnic families in America: Patterns and variations,* 2nd ed., ed. C. H. Mindel and R. W. Habenstein, 269–92. New York: Elsevier.

ALWIN, D. F. 1988. From obedience to autonomy: Changes in traits desired in children, 1924–1978. *Public Opinion Quarterly* 52: 33–52.

ALWIN, D. F., AND A. THORNTON. 1984. Family origins and the schooling process: Early versus late influence of parental characteristics. *American Sociological Review* 49: 784–802.

AMATO, P. R. 1988. Parental divorce and attitudes toward marriage and family life. *Journal of Marriage and the Family* 50 (May): 453–61.

AMATO, P. R. 1991. The "child of divorce" as a person prototype: Bias in the recall of information about children in divorced families. *Journal of Marriage and the Family* 53 (February): 59–69.

AMBERT, A.-M. 1986. Being a stepparent: Live-in and visiting stepchildren. *Journal of Marriage and the Family* 48: 795–804.

AMBERT, A.-M. 1992. *The effect of children on parents.* New York: Haworth.

AMBERT, A.-M. 1994. An international perspective on parenting: Social change and social constructs. *Journal of Marriage and the Family* 56, no. 3 (August): 529–43.

AMBERT, A.-M. 1988. Relationships with former in-laws after divorce: A research note. *Journal of Marriage and the Family* 50 (August): 679–86.

American Association of University Women Educational Foundation. 1992. *How schools shortchange girls.* Washington, DC.

American Demographics. 1993. The future of households. December, 27–40.

AMES, K. 1992. Who's minding our children? *Newsweek,* June 6, 51.

AMES, K., WITH J. GORDON AND M. MASON. 1991. Savings plan for a generation. *Newsweek,* February 18, 71.

AMOTT, T. 1993. *Caught in the crisis: Women and the U.S. economy today.* New York: Monthly Review Press.

ANDELIN, H. 1974. *Fascinating womanhood: A guide to a happy marriage.* Santa Barbara, CA: Pacific Press.

ANDERS, G. 1994. The search for love goes on. *Washington Post,* September 19, D5.

ANDERSEN, M. L. 1993. *Thinking about women,* 3rd ed. New York: Macmillan.

ANDERSON, E. 1990. *Streetwise: Race, class and change in an urban community.* Chicago: University of Chicago Press.

ANDERSON, E. A., AND J. W. SPRUILL. 1993. The dual-career commuter family: A lifestyle on the move. *Marriage & Family Review* 19, nos. 1–2: 121–47.

ANDERSON, J. 1990. *The single mother's book: A practical guide to managing your children, career, home, finances, and everything else.* Atlanta: Peachtree.

ANDERSON, P. B., AND R. AYMAMI. 1993. Reports of female initiation of sexual contact: Male and female differences. *Archives of Sexual Behavior* 23, no. 4 (August): 335–43.

ANDERSON, T. B. 1984. Widowhood as a life transition: Its impact on kinship ties. *Journal of Marriage and the Family* 46 (February): 105–14.

ANONYMOUS. 1994. Red flags that point to Mr. Wrong, Ms. Wrong. *Ebony,* February, 148, 10, 152.

ANSON, O. 1989. Marital status and women's health revisited: The importance of a proximate adult. *Journal of Marriage and the Family* 51, 185–94.

APFEL, N. H., AND V. SEITZ. 1991. Four models of adolescent mother-grandmother relationships in black inner-city families. *Family Relations* 40 (October): 421–29.

APPLEBAUM, E. 1987. Restructuring work: Temporary, part-time, and at-home employment. In *Computer chips and paper clips: Technology and women's employment,* ed. H. Hartmann, 268–310. Washington, DC: National Academy Press.

AQUILINO, W. S. 1994. Impact of childhood family disruption on young adults' relationships with parents. *Journal of Marriage and the Family* 56 (May): 295–313.

AQUILINO, W. S., AND K. R. SUPPLE. 1991. Parent-child relations and parents' satisfaction with living arrangements when adult children live at home. *Journal of Marriage and the Family* 53 (February): 13–27.

ARDITTI, J. A. 1990. Noncustodial fathers: An overview of policy and resources. *Family Relations* 39 (October): 460–65.

ARENOFSKY, J. 1993. Childless and proud of it. *Newsweek,* February 8, 12.

ARIES, P. 1962. *Centuries of childhood.* New York: Vintage.

ARLISS, L. P. 1991. *Gender communication.* Englewood Cliffs, NJ: Prentice Hall.

ARNOLD, M., AND S. L. PAUKER. 1987. *The first year of marriage: What to expect, what to accept, and what you can change.* New York: Warner.

ASCHER, C. 1991. School programs for African American males. *ERIC Clearinghouse on Urban Education Digest,* no. 72 (May): 3–4.

ASELTINE, R. H., JR., AND R. C. KESSLER. 1993. Marital disruption and depression in a community sample. *Journal of Health and Social Behavior* 34 (September): 237–51.

AUSTROM, D., AND K. HANEL. 1985. Psychological issues of single life in Canada: An exploratory study. *International Journal of Women's Studies* 8, 12–23.

AVIS, J. M. 1985. The politics of functional therapy: A feminist critique. *Journal of Marital and Family Therapy* 11, no. 2, 127–38.

AVNA, J., AND D. WALTZ. 1992. *Celibate wives: Breaking the silence.* Los Angeles: Lowell House.

AVNI, N. 1991a. Battered wives: Characteristics of their courtship days. *Journal of Interpersonal Violence* 6, no. 2 (June): 232–39.

AVNI, N. 1991b. Battered wives: The home as a total institution. *Violence and Victims* 6, no. 2, 137–49.

AXINN, W. G., AND A. THORNTON. 1993. Mothers, children, and cohabitation: The intergenerational effects of attitudes and behavior. *American Sociological Review* 58 (April): 233–46.

AYRES, I. 1991. Fair driving: Gender and race discrimination in retail car negotiations. *Harvard Law Review* 104, no. 4 (February): 817–72.

BABBIE, E. 1992. *The practice of social research,* 5th ed. Belmont, CA: Wadsworth.

BABCOCK, J. C., J. WALTZ, N. S. JACOBSON, AND J. M. GOTTMAN. 1993. Power and violence: The relation between communication patterns, power discrepancies, and domestic violence. *Journal of Consulting and Clinical Psychology* 61, no. 1, 40–50.

BABER, A. 1992. *Naked at gender gap: A man's view of the war between the sexes.* New York: Birch Lane.

BABER, K. M., AND K. R. ALLEN. 1992. *Women and families: Feminist reconstructions.* New York: Guilford.

BACA ZINN, M. 1994. Adaptation and continuity in Mexican-origin families. In *Minority families in the United States: A multicultural perspective,* ed. R. L. Taylor, 64–81. Englewood Cliffs, NJ: Prentice Hall.

BACA ZINN, M., AND B. T. DILL, EDS. 1994. *Women of color in U.S. society.* Philadelphia: Temple University Press.

BACHMAN, R. 1994. *Violence against women: A national crime victimization survey report.* U.S. Department of Justice, Office of Justice Programs, Bureau of Justice Statistics. Fall.

BACHRACH, C. A., P. F. ADAMS, S. SAMBRANO, AND K. A. LONDON. 1990. Adoption in the 1980's. *Vital Health Statistics*, no. 181, January 5, advance data. Hyattsville, MD: National Center for Health Statistics.

BACHU, A. 1993. *Fertility of American women: June 1992.* U.S. Bureau of the Census, Current Population Reports P20–470. Washington, DC: U.S. Government Printing Office.

BAGLEY, C. 1993. Transracial adoption in Britain: A follow-up study, with policy considerations. *Child Welfare* 72, no. 3 (May/June): 285–300.

BAGNE, P. 1983. High-tech breeding. *Mother Jones*, August, 23–29.

BAILEY, J. M., AND R. C. PILLARD. 1993. Heritable factors influence sexual orientation in women. *Archives of General Psychiatry* 50, no. 3 (March 1): 217–25.

BAILYN, L. 1993. *Breaking the mold: Women, men, and time in the new corporate world.* New York: Free Press.

BAKER, L. 1994. Day-care disgrace. *The Progressive* (June): 26–27.

BAKER, T. L. 1994. *Doing social research*, 2nd ed. New York: McGraw Hill.

BALAKRISHNAN, T. R., V. RAO, E. LAPIERRE-ADAMCYK, AND K. KROTKI. 1987. A hazard model analysis of the covariates of marriage dissolution in Canada. *Demography* 24, 395–406.

BALDWIN, J. D., AND J. I. BALDWIN. 1989. The socialization of homosexuality and heterosexuality in a non-Western society. *Archives of Sexual Behavior* 18, no. 1, 13–29.

BALL, K. 1990. Excluding "discouraged workers" said to mask extent of joblessness. *Baltimore Sun*, February 7, 3C.

BALL, R. E., AND L. ROBBINS. 1986. Marital status and life satisfaction among black Americans. *Journal of Marriage and the Family* 48 (May): 389–94.

Baltimore Sun. 1989a. Seek spouse in India? Take out an ad. June 7, F6.

Baltimore Sun. 1989b. Most Americans found to oppose court's abortion ruling. July 10, A6.

Baltimore Sun. 1989c. Working longer favored. September 14, A7.

Baltimore Sun. 1990a. Birth control shots for men called effective. October 21, 3A.

Baltimore Sun. 1990b. 55% of Americans flunk survey testing their knowledge of sex. September 6, 1A, 5A.

Baltimore Sun. 1990c. U.S. female troops shock men in Islamic country where women take back seat. August 16, 13A.

Baltimore Sun. 1991. U.N. studies world use of contraceptives. September 1, 15A.

Baltimore Sun. 1992. 20,000 total strangers wed in matches made by Moon. August 26, 2A.

Baltimore Sun. 1993a. A great leap back. March 31, A24.

Baltimore Sun. 1993b. Baby-book boom offers Spock options. February 10, 6C.

Baltimore Sun. 1993c. Murders cause 40 percent of deaths of women in workplace, survey says. October 2, 3A.

Baltimore Sun. 1994a. Bureau drafting major overhaul for 2000 census, May 16, 1A, 4A.

Baltimore Sun. 1994b. Drug firms' lack of interest imperils male birth control. September 2, 3A.

Baltimore Sun. 1994c. Human embryo research enters new era this week. September 25, 10A.

Baltimore Sun. 1994d. New parenting books focus on the big picture. October 13, D1.

Baltimore Sun. 1994e. Poll shows separate lives for teens. July 10, 21A.

Baltimore Sun. 1994f. Service academy sexism held rampant. February 4, 8A.

Baltimore Sun. 1994g. Survey: 5 percent of mothers-to-be used illegal drugs. September 13, 5D.

Baltimore Sun. 1994h. Teens' sex activity found less extensive than believed. June 7, 3A.

Baltimore Sun. 1994i. 30 AIDS viruses found to elude testing methods. August 9, 11A.

Baltimore Sun. 1994j. U.N. settles sex harassment case against ex-official, will pay women $210,000. December 25, 11A.

Baltimore Sun. 1994k. Women don't recognize risk of sexual diseases, survey finds. February 14, 2A.

Baltimore Sun. 1995a. Drawing the line. February 21, D1, D8.

Baltimore Sun. 1995b. Drug treatment offers abortion alternative. March 6, 3A.

Baltimore Sun. 1995c. U.N. summit on poverty opens today. March 6, 8A.

BANALES, J. 1990. Abuse among immigrants: As their numbers grow so does the need for services. *Washington Post*, October 16, 5E.

BANDURA, A., AND R. H. WALTERS. 1963. *Social learning and personality development.* New York: Holt, Rinehart & Winston.

BANISKY, S. 1994a. A matter of discipline. *Baltimore Sun*, July 10, J1, J8.

BANISKY, S. 1994b. Decline in abortions looks like a trend. *Baltimore Sun*, June 16, A1.

BANNER, L. W. 1984. *Women in modern America: A brief history*, 2nd ed. New York: Harcourt Brace Jovanovich.

BARAN, A., AND R. PANNOR. 1989. *Lethal secrets: The shocking consequences and unsolved problems of artificial insemination.* New York: Warner.

BARANOWSKI, M. D., G. L. SCHILMOELLER, AND B. S. HIGGINS. 1990. Parenting attitudes of adolescent and older mothers. *Adolescence* 25, no. 100 (Winter): 781–90.

BARBER, B. K. 1994. Cultural, family, and personal contexts of parent-adolescent conflict. *Journal of Marriage and the Family* 56 (May): 375–86.

BARBER, B. L. 1994. Support and advice from married and divorced fathers: Linkages to adolescent adjustment. *Family Relations* 43, no. 4 (October): 433–38.

BARBER, B. L., AND J. M. LYONS. 1994. Family processes and adolescent adjustment in intact and remarried families. *Journal of Youth and Adolescence* 23, no. 4 (August): 421–36.

BARLETT, D. L., AND J. B. STEELE. 1992. *America: What went wrong?* Kansas City, MO: Andrews and McMeel.

BARNET, R. J., AND J. CAVANAGH. 1994. *Global dreams: Imperial corporations and the new world order.* New York: Simon & Schuster.

BARNETT, O. W., AND A. D. LaVIOLETTE. 1993. *It could happen to anyone: Why battered women stay.* Newbury Park, CA: Sage.

BARNETT, R. C. 1994. Home-to-work spillover revisited: A study of full-time employed women in dual-earner couples. *Journal of Marriage and the Family* 56 (August): 647–56.

BARRECA, R. 1993. *Perfect husband (& other fairy tales): Demistifying marriage, men, and romance.* New York: Harmony.

BARRET, R. L., AND B. E. ROBINSON. 1990. *Gay fathers.* Lexington, MA: Lexington Books.

BARRETT, M. B. 1989. *Invisible lives:*

The truth about millions of women-loving women. New York: Morrow.

BARRET-DUCROCQ, F. 1991. *Love in the time of Victoria: Sexuality, class and gender in nineteenth-century London*. New York: Verso.

BART, P. B. 1971. Sexism and social science: From the gilded cage to the iron cage, or, the perils of Pauline. *Journal of Marriage and the Family* 33, no. 4 (November): 734–45.

BART, P. B., AND E. G. MORAN, EDS. 1993. *Violence against women: The bloody footprints*. Newbury Park, CA: Sage.

BARTHOLET, E. 1993. *Family bonds: Adoption and the politics of parenting*. Boston: Houghton Mifflin.

BARTHOLOMEW, K. 1993. *From childhood to adult relationships: Attachment theory and research*. In *Learning about relationships*, ed. S. Duck, 30–62. Newbury Park, CA: Sage.

BASS, S. A., AND R. MORRIS, EDS. 1993. *International perspectives on state and family support for the elderly*. New York: Haworth.

BASS, S. L. 1988. A lot of these affairs are never revealed. *New York Times*, December 19, C1.

BATES, D. 1993. *Gift children: A story of race, family, and adoption in a divided America*. New York: Ticknor & Fields.

BAUM, A. S., AND D. W. BURNES. 1993. *A nation in denial: The truth about homelessness*. Boulder, CO: Westview.

BAUMEISTER, R. F., AND S. R. WOTMAN. 1992. *Breaking hearts: The two sides of unrequited love*. New York: Guilford.

BAUMRIND, D. 1968. Authoritarian versus authoritative parental control. *Adolescence* 3, 255–72.

BAUMRIND, D. 1989. Rearing competent children. In *Child development today and tomorrow*, ed. W. Damon, 349–78. San Francisco: Jossey Bass.

BAUMRIND, D. 1994. The social context of child maltreatment. *Family Relations* 43, no. 4 (October): 360–68.

BAWER, B. 1993. *A place at the table: The gay individual in American society*. New York: Poseidon.

BAY, R. C., AND S. L. BRAVER. 1990. Perceived control of the divorce settlement process and interparental conflict. *Family Relations* 39 (October): 382–87.

BAYARD, T. 1991. *A medieval home companion: Housekeeping in the fourteenth century*. New York: HarperCollins.

BAYDAR, N. 1988. Effects of parental separation and reentry into union on the emotional well-being of children. *Journal of Marriage and the Family* 50 (November): 967–81.

BAYDAR, N., AND J. BROOKS-GUNN. 1994. The dynamics of child support and its consequences for children. In *Child support and child well-being*, ed. I. Garfinkel, S. S. McLanahan, and P. K. Robins, 257–84. Washington, DC: Urban Institute Press.

BA-YUNUS, I. 1991. *Muslims in North America: Mate selection as an indicator of change*. In *Muslim families in North America*, ed. E. H. Waugh, S. M. Abu-Laban, and R. B. Qureshi, 232–55. Edmonton: University of Alberta Press.

BECERRA, R. M. 1988. The Mexican American family. In *Ethnic families in America: Patterns and variations*, 3rd ed., ed. C. J. Mindel, R. W. Habenstein, and R. Wright., Jr., 141–59. New York: Elsevier.

BECK, A. T. 1988. *Love is never enough: How couples can overcome misunderstandings, resolve conflicts, and solve relationship problems through cognitive therapy*. New York: Harper & Row.

BECK, M., WITH J. GORDON AND R. DALLEN. 1990. Travels with grandpa. *Newsweek*, July 30, 48.

BECK, M., WITH M. HAGER. 1992. A new birth-control option? *Newsweek*, June 29, 70.

BECK, M., WITH P. KATEL AND P. ANNIN. 1994. Propaganda made me do it. *Newsweek*, February 28, 34.

BEER, W. R. 1992. *American stepfamilies*. New Brunswick, NJ: Transaction.

BEGLEY, S., WITH D. GLICK. 1994. The estrogen complex. *Newsweek*, March 21, 76–77.

BEGLEY, S., WITH L. SHACKELFORD. 1994, No Ph.D.s need apply. *Newsweek*, December 5, 62–63.

BEGLEY, S., WITH M. HAGER AND A. MUIR. 1990. The search for the fountain of youth. *Newsweek*, March 5, 44–48.

BEIGEL, H. G. 1951. Romantic love. *American Sociological Review* 16: 326–34.

BEITCHMAN, J. H., K. J. ZUCKER, J. E. HOOD, G. A. DaCOSTA, AND D. AKMAN. 1991. A review of the short-term effects of child sexual abuse. *Child Abuse and Neglect* 15, no. 4, 537–56.

BEITCHMAN, J. H., K. J. ZUCKER, J. E. HOOD, G. A. DaCOSTA, D. AKMAN AND E. CASSAVIA. 1992. A review of the long-term effects of child sexual abuse. *Child Abuse and Neglect* 16, no. 1 (January): 101–18.

BELCASTRO, P. A. 1985. Sexual behavior differences between black and white students. *Journal of Sex Research* 21, 56–57.

BELKIN, L. 1985. Affording a child: Parents worry as costs keep rising. *New York Times*, May 23, C1, C6.

BELKIN, L. 1986. The mail-order marriage business. *New York Times*, May 11, C28, C51, C55, C73, C76, C78.

BELL, A. P., AND M. S. WEINBERG. 1978. *Homosexualities*. New York: Simon & Schuster.

BELL, A. P., M. S. WEINBERG, AND S. HAMMERSMITH. 1981. *Sexual preference: Its development in men and women*. Bloomington: Indiana University Press.

BELL, R. R., AND K. COUGHEY. 1980. Premarital sexual experience among college females, 1958, 1968, and 1978. *Family Relations* 29, 353–57.

BELLI, M. M., SR., AND M. KRANTZLER. 1988. *Divorcing*. New York: St. Martin's Press.

BELSKY, J. 1991. Parental and nonparental child care and children's socioemotional development. In *Contemporary families: Looking forward, looking back*, ed. A. Booth, 122–40. Minneapolis, MN: National Council on Family Relations.

BELSKY, J. K. 1988. *Here tomorrow: Making the most of life after fifty*. Baltimore: Johns Hopkins University Press.

BEM, S. L. 1975. Androgyny vs. the tight little lives of fluffy women and chesty men. *Psychology Today*, September, 58–62.

BEM, S. L. 1983. Gender schema theory and its implications for child development: Raising gender-schematic children in a gender-schematic society. *Signs* 8: 598–616.

BEM, S. L. 1993. *The lenses on gender: Transforming the debate on sexual inequality*. New Haven: Yale University Press.

BEM, S. L. 1994. In a male-centered world, female differences are transformed into female disadvantages. *Chronicle of Higher Education*, August 17, B1–B3.

BENASSI, M. A. 1985. Effects of romantic love on perception of strangers' physical attractiveness. *Psychological Reports* 56 (April): 355–58.

BENJAMIN, R. 1990. Facing new baby boom, China steps up rural enforcement of one-child policy. *Baltimore Sun*, December 18, 2A.

BENKOV, L. 1994. *Reinventing the family: The emerging story of lesbian and gay parents*. New York: Crown.

BENNETT, L., JR. 1989. The 10 biggest myths about the black family. *Ebony*, November, 114–16.

BENNETT, N. G., A. K. BLANC, AND D. E. BLOOM. 1988. Commitment and the modern union: Assessing the link between premarital cohabitation and subsequent marital stability. *American Sociological Review* 53 (February): 127–38.

BENOKRAITIS, N. V., AND J. R. FEAGIN. 1995. *Modern sexism: Blatant, subtle, and covert discrimination*. Englewood Cliffs, NJ: Prentice Hall.

BENSON, J. R., AND M. JOHNSON. 1994. What a baby really costs. *Parents Magazine*, August, 90, 93, 95.

BERARDO, D. H., C. L. SHEHAN, AND G. R. LESLIE. 1987. A residue of tradition: Jobs, careers, and spouses' time in housework. *Journal of Marriage and the Family* 49, 381–90.

BERELSON, B. 1983. The value of children: A taxonomical essay. In *Current issues in marriage and the family*, 3rd ed., ed. G. J. Wells, 159–67. New York: Macmillan.

BEREZIN, J. 1990. *The complete guide to choosing child care*. New York: Random House.

BERGMAN, P. M. 1969. *The chronological history of the Negro in America*. New York: Harper & Row.

BERGMANN, B. 1994. The economic support of child-raising: Curing child poverty in the United States. *AEA Papers and Proceedings* 84, no. 2 (May): 76–80.

BERGSTROM-WALAN, M.-B., AND H. H. NIELSEN. 1990. Sexual expression among 60–80 year old men and women: A sample from Stockholm, Sweden. *Journal of Sex Research* 27, no. 2 (May): 289–95.

BERK, B. R. 1993. The dating game. *Good Housekeeping*, September, 192, 220–221.

BERNARD, J. 1973. *The future of marriage*. New York: Bantam.

BERNER, R. T. 1992. *Parents whose parents were divorced*. New York: Haworth.

BERNSTEIN, R. 1994. *Bureau of the Census, Statistical Brief*. April. U.S. Department of Commerce, Economics and Statistics Administration.

BERRY, B. 1994. My unexpected call to motherhood. *USA Weekend*, May 20–22, 8.

BERRY, M. 1993. Adoptive parents' perceptions of, and comfort with, open adoption. *Child Welfare* 72, no. 3 (May/June): 231–56.

BERRY, M. F. 1993. *The politics of parenthood: Child care, women's rights, and the myth of the good mother*. New York: Penguin.

BERSCHEID, E., K. DION, E. WALSTER, AND G. W. WALSTER. 1982. Physical attractiveness and dating choice: A test of the matching hypothesis. *Journal of Experimental Social Psychology 1*, 173–89.

BERTOLA, C., AND J. DRAKICH. 1993. The fathers' rights movement: Contradictions in rhetoric and practice. *Journal of Family Issues* 14, no. 4 (December): 592–615.

BESHAROV, D. J. 1993. Teen sex. *American Enterprise* 4, no. 1 (January): 52–59.

BETCHER, W., AND R. MACAULEY. 1990. *The seven basic quarrels of marriage: Recognize, defuse, negotiate, and resolve your conflicts*. New York: Villard.

BETCHER, W., AND W. POLLACK. 1993. *In a time of fallen heroes: The re-creation of masculinity*. New York: Atheneum.

Better Homes and Gardens. 1978. Report on the American family. Report from the Editors. Meredith Corporation.

Better Homes and Gardens. 1988. What's happening to American families? Report from the Editors. Meredith Corporation.

BEYER, L. 1980. The globalization of the abortion debate. *Time*, August 21, 42–43.

BEZILLA, R. ED. 1993. *America's youth in the 1990s*. Princeton, NJ: George H. Gallup International Institute.

BIANCHI, S. 1990. America's children: Mixed prospects. *Population Bulletin* 45, no. 1 (June): 3–41.

BIANCHI, S. M., AND D. SPAIN. 1986. *American women in transition*. New York: Russell Sage Foundation.

BIBLARZ, T. J., AND A. E. RAFTERY. 1993. The effects of family disruption on social mobility. *American Sociological Review* 58 (February): 97–109.

BIEBER, I., ET AL. 1962. *Homosexuality: A psychoanalytic study*. New York: Basic Books.

BIELBY, W. T., AND D. D. BIELBY. 1992. I will follow him: Family ties, gender-role beliefs, and reluctance to relocate for a better job. *American Journal of Sociology* 97, no. 5 (March): 1241–67.

BIERNAT, M., AND C. B. WORTMAN. 1991. Sharing of home responsibilities between professionally employed women and their husbands. *Journal of Personality and Social Psychology* 60, no. 6, 844–60.

BIGNER, J. J., AND F. W. BOZETT, 1990. Parenting by gay fathers. In *Homosexuality and family relations*, ed. F. W. Bozett and M. B. Sussman, 155–75. New York: Harrington Park Press.

BIGNER, J., AND R. B. JACOBSEN. 1989. Parenting behaviors of homosexual and heterosexual fathers. *Journal of Homosexuality* 18, 173–86.

BILLINGSLEY, A. 1968. *Black families in white America*. Englewood Cliffs, NJ: Prentice Hall.

BILLINGSLEY, A. 1992. *Climbing Jacob's ladder: The enduring legacy of African-American families*. New York: Simon & Schuster.

BILLY, J. O. G., K. TANFER, W. R. GRADY, AND D. H. KLEPINGER. 1993. The sexual behavior of men in the United States. *Family Planning Perspectives* 25, no. 2 (March): 52–60.

BIRNS, B., M. CASCARDI, AND S.-L. MEYER. 1994. Sex-role socialization: Developmental influences on wife abuse. *American Journal of Orthopsychiatry* 64, no. 1 (January): 50–59.

BLACKWELL, J. E. 1991. *The black community: Diversity and unity*, 3rd ed. New York: HarperCollins.

BLAIR, S. L. 1993. Employment, family, and perceptions of marital quality among husbands and wives. *Journal of Family Issues* 14, no. 2 (June): 189–212.

BLAKE, J. 1985. Number of siblings and educational mobility. *American Sociological Review* 50: 84–94.

BLAKE, J. 1989. *Family size and achievement*. Berkeley: University of California Press.

BLAKE, W. M., AND C. A. DARLING. 1994. The dilemmas of the African American male. *Journal of Black Studies* 24, no. 4 (June): 402–15.

BLANC, A. K.. 1987. The formation and dissolution of second unions: Marriage and cohabitation in Sweden and Norway. *Journal of Marriage and the Family* 49 (May): 391–400.

BLEA, I. I. 1992. *La chicana and the intersection of race, class, and gender*. Westport, CT: Greenwood.

BLOCK, J. 1994. *Family myths: Living our roles, betraying ourselves*. New York: Simon & Schuster.

BLOCKSON, C. L. 1977. *Black genealogy*. Englewood Cliffs, NJ: Prentice Hall.

BLOOM, D. E., AND T. P. STEEN. 1990. The labor force implications of expanding the child care industry. *Pop-*

ulation Research and Policy Review 9, no. 1 (January): 25–44.

BLOOMFIELD, H. M., WITH R. P. KORY. 1993. *Making peace in your stepfamily: Surviving and thriving as parents and stepparents.* New York: Hyperion.

BLOUNT, W. R., I. J. SILVERMAN, C. S. SELLERS, AND R. A. SEESE. 1994. Alcohol and drug use among abused women who kill, abused women who don't, and their abusers. *Journal of Drug Issues* 24, nos. 1/2 (Winter): 165–77.

BLUMENFELD, L. 1994. Prisoners in paradise. *Washington Post*, November 13, F1, F4–F5.

BLUMSTEIN, P. 1976. Identity bargaining and self-conception. *Social Forces* 53, no. 3, 476–85.

BLUMSTEIN, P. W., AND P. SCHWARTZ. 1977. Bisexuality: Some social psychological issues. *Journal of Social Issues* 33, no. 2 (Spring): 30–45.

BLUMSTEIN, P., AND P. SCHWARTZ. 1983. *American couples: Money, work, sex.* New York: Morrow.

BOCK, J. 1991. Migrant workers sue shore packinghouse. *Baltimore Sun*, July 12, D1, D3.

BOCK, J. 1992. Battle brews over plan for new city liquor license. *Baltimore Sun*, March 2, B1, B6.

BODNER, J. 1985. *The transplanted: A history of immigrants in urban America.* Bloomington: Indiana University Press.

BOERINGER, S. B., C. L. SHEHAN, AND R. L. AKERS. 1991. Social contests and social learning in sexual coercion and aggression: Assessing the contribution of fraternity membership. *Family Relations* 40 (January): 58–64.

BOGERT, C. 1994. Bringing back baby. *Newsweek*, November 21, 78–79.

BOHANNON, P. 1971. *Divorce and after.* New York: Doubleday.

BOKHARI, F. 1994. Violence against Pakistani women spurs Bhutto to act. *Christian Science Monitor*, June 28, 3.

BOLIG, R., P. J. STEIN, AND P. C. MC-KENRY. 1984. The self-advertisement approach to dating: Male-female differences. *Family Relations* 33 (October): 587–92.

BOMBECK, E. 1994. The art of grandmothering isn't lost. *Baltimore Sun*, February 24, 8E.

BOODMAN, S. G. 1992. Questions about a popular prenatal test. *Washington Post Health Supplement*, November 3, 10–13.

BOOTH, A., AND D. R. JOHNSON. 1994. Declining health and marital quality. *Journal of Marriage and the Family* 56 (February): 218–23.

BOOTH, A., AND J. N. EDWARDS. 1985. Age at marriage and marital instability. *Journal of Marriage and the Family* 47 (February): 67–75.

BOOTH, A., AND J. N. EDWARDS. 1992. Starting over: Why remarriages are more unstable. *Journal of Family Issues* 13, no. 2 (June): 179–94.

BOOTH, A., AND P. R. AMATO. 1994. Parental marital quality, parental divorce, and relations with parents. *Journal of Marriage and the Family* 56 (February): 21–34.

BOR, J. 1995. Rise in multiple births a concern to physicians. *Baltimore Sun*, February 1, 1A, 10A.

BORDO, S. 1993. *Unbearable weight: Feminism, Western culture, and the body.* Berkeley: University of California Press.

BORGMAN, A. 1995. Adoptions abroad mix highs, lows. *Washington Post*, January 8, B3.

BORLAND, D. M. 1975. An alternative model of the Wheel theory. *Family Coordinator* 24, no. 3 (July): 289–92.

BOROUGHS, D. L., WITH D. HAGE, R. F. BLACK, AND R. J. NEWMAN. 1992. Love & money. *U.S. News & World Report*, October 19, 54–60.

BOSSARD, J. 1932. Residential propinquity as a factor in marriage selection. *American Journal of Sociology* 38 (September): 219–44.

Boston Women's Health Book Collective. 1992. *The New Our Bodies, Ourselves: A book by and for women.* New York: Touchstone.

BOURIS, K. 1993. *The first time: Women speak out about losing their virginity.* Berkeley, CA: Conari Press.

BOUSTANY, N. 1994. Matchmaker, matchmaker, find me some wives. *Washington Post*, September 5, A14.

BOWEN, G. L., AND P. A. NEENAN. 1992. Child care as an economic incentive for the poor. *Families in Society: The Journal of Contemporary Human Society* 73, no. 5 (May): 295–303.

BOWLBY, J. 1969. *Attachment and loss.* Vol. 1. *Attachment.* New York: Basic Books.

BOWLING, A. 1987. Mortality after bereavement: A review of the literature on survival periods and factors affecting survival. *Social Science and Medicine* 24, no. 2, 117–24.

BOWMAN, P. J. 1991. Joblessness. In *Life in black America*, ed. J. S. Jackson, 156–78. Newbury Park, CA: Sage.

BOYD-FRANKLIN, N. 1993. Race, class and poverty. In *Normal family processes,* 2nd ed., ed. F. Walsh, 361–76. New York: Guilford.

BOZETT, F. W. 1987. *Gay and lesbian parents.* New York: Praeger.

BOZETT, F. W., AND M. B. SUSSMAN, EDS. 1990. *Homosexuality and family relations.* New York: Harrington Park Press.

BRADY, J. 1990. Why I [still] want a wife. *Ms.*, July/August, 17.

BRAVER, S. H., S. H. WOLCHIK, I. N. SANDLER, B. S. FOGAS, AND D. ZVETINA. 1991. Frequency of visitation by divorced fathers: Differences in reports by fathers and mothers. *American Journal of Orthopsychiatry* 6, no. 13 (July): 448–54.

BRAVO, E. 1995. *The job/family challenge: Not for women only.* New York: Wiley.

BRAVO, E. AND E. CASSEDY. 1992. *The 9 to 5 guide to combating sexual harassment.* New York: Wiley.

BRAY, J. H., AND S. H. BERGER. 1990. Noncustodial father and paternal grandparent relationships in stepfamilies. *Family Relations* 39 (October): 414–19.

BRAZELTON, T. B. 1991. Is TV harming my child? *Family Circle*, May 14, 35–56.

BRECHER, E. M. 1984. *Love, sex, and aging.* New York: Little, Brown.

BREHM, S. S. 1985. *Intimate relationships.* New York: Random House.

BREHM. S. S. 1992. *Intimate Relationships,* 2nd ed. New York: McGraw-Hill.

BRENNER, J. G., AND L. SPAYD. 1993. A pattern of bias in mortgage loans. *Washington Post*, June 6, A1, A24.

BRETSCHNEIDER, J. G., AND N. L. MCCOY. 1988. Sexual interest and behavior in healthy 80- to 102-year olds. *Archives of Sexual Behavior* 17, no. 2, 109–29.

BRIERE, J. N. 1992. *Child abuse trauma: Theory and treatment of the lasting effects.* Newbury Park, CA: Sage.

BRIGGS, J. L. 1970. *Never in anger.* Cambridge, MA: Harvard University Press.

BRINK, S. 1994. Too sick to be adopted? *U.S. News & World Report*, May 2, 66–69.

BROCK, L. J., AND G. H. JENNINGS. 1993. Sexuality education: What daughters in their 30s wish their mothers had told them. *Family Relations* 42 (January): 61–65.

BRODERICK, C. B. 1988. To arrive where we started: The field of family studies in the 1930s. *Journal of Marriage and the Family* 50 (August): 569–84.

BRODNAR-NEMZER, J. Y. 1986. Divorce and group commitment: The case of the Jews. *Journal of Marriage and the Family* 48 (May): 329–40.

BRODY, E. M., S. J. LITVIN, C. HOFFMAN, AND N. H. KLEBAN. 1992. Differential effects of daughters' marital status on their parent care experiences. *The Gerontologist* 32, no. 1, 58–67.

BRODY, J. E. 1994. New therapy for menopause reduces risks. *New York Times*, November 18, 1994, A1, A26.

BRONSTEIN, P. 1988. Father-child interaction: Implications for gender role socialization. In *Fatherhood today: Men's changing role in the family*, ed. P. Bronstein and C. P. Cowan, 107–26. New York: Wiley.

BROOKE, J. 1994. Women in Colombia move to job forefront, *New York Times*, July 15, A6.

BROOKS, A. 1987. Following a wife to a new job. *New York Times*, January 1, 8-2.

BROOKS, A. 1994. Sexism's bitterest trick. *New Scientist*, March 12, 48–49.

BROPHY, B. 1993. Epitaph: Devoted wife. *U.S. News & World Report*, July 5, 14.

BROWN, J. D., K. W. CHILDERS, AND C. S. WASZIK. 1990. Television and adolescent sexuality. *Journal of Adolescent Health Care* 11, no. 1, 62–70.

BROWN, J. K. 1992. Lives of middleaged women. In *In her prime: New views of middle-aged women*, 2nd ed., ed. V. Kerns and J. K. Brown, 17–30. Urbana: University of Illinois Press.

BROWN, L. M., AND C. GILLIGAN. 1992. *Meeting at the crossroads.* New York: Ballantine.

BROWN, M. R. 1994. Whose eyes are these, whose nose? *Newsweek*, March 7, 12.

BROWN, R. A. 1994. Romantic love and the spouse selection criteria of male and female Korean college students. *Journal of Social Psychology* 134, no. 2, 183–89.

BROWNE, A. 1993. Family violence and homelessness: The relevance of trauma histories in the lives of homeless women. *American Journal of Orthopsychiatry* 63, no. 3 (July): 370–84.

BROWNING, G. 1991. Modern women, modern ads. *Baltimore Sun*, February 2, 11C, 16C.

BROWNLEE, S. 1994. Hopeful hunt for an Alzheimer's cure. *U.S. News & World Report*, November 21, 89.

BROWNLEE, S., ET AL. 1994. The baby chase. *U.S. News & World Report*, December 5, 84–93.

BRUBAKER, T. H. 1991. Families in later life: A burgeoning research area. In *Contemporary families: Looking forward, looking back*, ed. A. Booth, 226–48. Minneapolis, MN: National Council on Family Relations.

BRUSH, L. D. 1993. Violent acts and injurious outcomes in married couples: Methodological issues in the national survey of families and households. In *Violence against women: The bloody footprints*, ed. P. B. Bart and E. G. Moran, 240–51. Newbury Park, CA: Sage.

BRUTZ, J. L., AND C. M. ALLEN. 1987. Religious commitment, peace activism, and marital violence in Quaker families. *Journal of Marriage and the Family* 48 (August): 491–502.

BRYAN, L. R., M. COLEMAN, AND L. H. GANONG. 1986. Person perception: Family structure as a cue for stereotyping. *Journal of Marriage and the Family* 48 (February): 169–74.

BUCHALTER, G. 1991. Splitsville. *Forbes*, October 21, 56–60.

BUEHLER, C., AND B. B. TROTTER. 1990. Nonresidential and residential parents' perceptions of the former spouse relationships and children's social competence following marital separation: Theory and programmed intervention. *Family Relations* 39 (October): 395–404.

BULCROFT, R. A., AND K. A. BULCROFT. 1993. Race differences in attitudinal and motivational factors in the decision to marry. *Journal of Marriage and the Family* 55 (May): 338–55.

BUMILLER, E. 1989. First comes marriage—then, maybe, love. In *Marriage and family in a changing society*, 3rd ed., ed. J. M. Henslin, 90–95. New York: Free Press.

BUMPASS, L. L., AND J. A. SWEET. 1989. National estimates of cohabitation. *Demography* 26, no. 4 (November): 615–25.

BUMPASS, L. L., J. A. SWEET, AND A. CHERLIN. 1991. The role of cohabitation in declining rates of marriage. *Journal of Marriage and the Family* 53 (November): 913–27.

BUMPASS, L., J. SWEET, AND T. C. MARTIN. 1990. Changing patterns of remarriage. *Journal of Marriage and the Family* 52, 747–56.

BURD, S. 1994. NIH issues rules requiring women and minorities in clinical trials. *Chronicle of Higher Education*, April 6, 50A.

BURGESS, B. J. 1980. Parenting in the Native-American community. In *Parenting in multicultural society*, ed. M. D. Fantini and R. Cardens. New York: Longman.

BURGESS, E. W., H. J. LOCKE, AND M. M. THOMES. 1963. *The family from institution to companionship.* New York: American Book.

BURGESS, J. K. 1988. Widowers. In *Variant family forms.* Families in trouble series, Vol. 5, ed. C. S. Chilman, E. W. Nunnally, and F. M. Cox, 150–64. Beverly Hills, CA: Sage.

BURNS, C. 1985. *Stepmotherhood: How to survive without feeling frustrated, left out, or wicked.* New York: Harper & Row.

BURR, W. R., R. HILL, F. I. NYE, AND I. L. REISS, EDS. 1979. *Contemporary theories about the family: Research-based theories*, Vol. 2. New York: Free Press.

BURTON, L. M., AND C. B. STACK. 1993. Conscripting kin: Reflections on family, generation, and culture. In *Family, self, and society: Toward a new agenda for family research*, eds. P. A. Cowan, D. Field, D. A. Hansen, A. Skolnick, and G. E. Swanson, 115–42. Hillsdale, NJ: Lawrence Erlbaum Associates.

BUSCH, L. 1993. Designer families, ethical knots. *U.S. News & World Report*, May 31, 73.

BUSH, B. 1994. *Barbara Bush: A memoir.* New York: Scribner's.

BUSS, D. M. 1994. *The evolution of desire: Strategies of human mating.* New York: Basic Books.

BUSS, D. M. AND M. BARNES. 1986. Preferences in human mate selection. *Journal of Personality and Social Psychology* 50, no 3: 559–70.

BUSSEY, K., AND A. BANDURA. 1992. Self-regulatory mechanisms governing gender development. *Child Development* 63, no. 5 (October): 1236–50.

BUTLER, R. N. 1975. *Why survive? Being old in America.* New York: Harper & Row.

BUTLER, R. N., AND M. I. LEWIS. 1986. *Love and sex after 40: A guide for men and women for their mid and later years.* New York: Harper & Row.

BUTLER, R. N., AND M. I. LEWIS. 1988. *Love and sex after 60.* New York: Harper & Row.

CADDEN, V. 1995. Child care: How does your state rate? *Working Mother* (March): 21–32.

CAGE, M. C. 1994. A course on homosexuality. *Chronicle of Higher Education*, December 14, A19–A20.

CALLANAN, M., AND P. KELLEY. 1992. *Final gifts: Understanding the special awareness, needs and communications of the dying.* New York: Poseidon.

CALLENDER, C., AND L. M. KOCHEMS. 1987. The North American berdache. *Current Anthropology* 24, no.4: 443–470.

CAMARILLO, A. 1979. *Chicanos in a changing society: From Mexican pueblos to American barrios in Santa Barbara and southern California, 1848–1930.* Cambridge, MA: Harvard University Press.

CAMPBELL, J. 1993. Seeking international standard for adoption. *U.S.A. Today,* May 29, 7A.

CAMPBELL, R. 1994. Grandma is full of exotic, steamy romance novels. *Baltimore Sun,* January 5, 6C.

CANCIAN, F. M. 1990. The feminization of love. In *Perspectives on the family: History, class, and feminism,* ed. C. Carlson, 171–85. Belmont, CA: Wadsworth.

CANTRELL, P. J., AND J. B. ELLIS. 1991. Gender role and risk patterns for eating disorders in men and women. *Journal of Clinical Psychology* 47, no. 1 (January): 53–56.

CAPLAN, N., M. H. CHOY AND J. K. WHITMORE. 1992. *Children of the boat people: A study of educational success.* Ann Arbor: University of Michigan Press.

CAPLAN, N., J. K. WHITMORE, AND M. H. CHOY. 1989. Culture values, family life, and opportunity. In *The boat people and achievement in America: A study of family life, hard work, and cultural values,* 94–127. Ann Arbor: University of Michigan Press.

CAPLOW, T., H. M. BAHR, B. A. CHADWICK, R. HILL, AND M. H. WILLIAMSON. 1982. *Middletown families: Fifty years of change and continuity.* New York: Bantam.

CAPRON, A. M. 1994. Grandma? No, I'm the mother! *Hastings Center Report* 24 (March/April): 24–25.

CAPUTI, J. 1987. *The age of sex crime.* Bowling Green, OH: Bowling Green State University Popular Press.

CARABILLO, T., J. MEULI, AND J. B. CSIDA. 1993. *Feminist chronicles 1953–1993.* Los Angeles: Women's Graphics.

CARGAN, L., ED. 1991. *Marriage and families: Coping with change,* 3rd ed. Englewood Cliffs, NJ: Prentice Hall.

CARGAN, L., AND M. MELKO. 1982. *Singles: Myths and realities.* Beverly Hills, CA: Sage.

CARLSON, L. H., AND G. A. COLBURN, EDS. 1972. *In their place: White America defines her minorities, 1850–1950.* New York: Wiley.

CARRASQUILLO, A. L. 1991. *Hispanic children and youth in the United States: A resource guide.* New York: Garland.

CARRASQUILLO, H. 1994. *The Puerto Rican family.* In *Minority families in the United States: A multicultural perspective,* ed. R. L. Taylor, 82–94. Englewood Cliffs, NJ: Prentice Hall.

CARTER, S., AND J. SOKOL. 1993. *He's scared, She's scared: Understanding the hidden fears that sabotage your relationships.* New York: Delacorte.

Annie E. Casey Foundation. 1994. *Kids count data book: State profiles of child well-being.* Greenwich, CT.

CASLER, L. 1974. *Is marriage necessary?* New York: Human Sciences Press.

CASPER, L. M., M. HAWKINS AND M. O'CONNELL. 1994. *Who's minding the kids? Child care arrangements.* Fall 1991. Bureau of the Census Current Population Reports. Washington, DC: Government Printing Office.

CASPER, L. M., S. S. MCLANAHAN, AND I. GARFINKEL. 1994. The gender-poverty gap: what we can learn from other countries. *American Sociological Review* 59 (August): 594–605.

CASSEDY, E., AND K. NUSSBAUM. 1983. *9 to 5: The working woman's guide to office survival.* New York: Penguin.

CASSELL, C. 1987. *Straight from the heart: How to talk to your teenagers about love and sex.* New York: Simon & Schuster.

CASSIDY, M. L., AND G. R. LEE. 1989. The study of polyandry: A critique and synthesis. *Journal of Comparative Family Studies* 20, no. 1 (Spring): 1–11.

CASSIDY, S. 1993. A single woman: The fabric of my life. In *Single Women: Affirming our spiritual journeys,* ed. M. O'Brien, and C. Christie, 35–48. Westport, CT: Bergin & Garvey.

CASTILLO, S., H. WECHSLER, AND G. DOWDALL. 1994. Health and behavioral consequences of binge drinking in college: A national survey of students at 140 campuses. *JAMA,* December 7, 1672.

CATALFO, P. 1994. Love at first link-up. *New Woman* 24, no. 3 (March): 56, 58.

CATANIA, J. A., ET AL. 1992. Prevalence of AIDS-related risk factors and condom use in the United States. *Science,* November 13, 1101–106.

CATE, R. M., AND S. A. LLOYD. 1992. *Courtship.* Newbury Park, CA: Sage.

CATTAN, P. 1991. Child-care problems: An obstacle to work. *Monthly Labor Review* 114 (October): 3–9.

CAVAN, R. S., AND K. H. RANCK. 1938. *The family and the depression: A study of one hundred Chicago families.* Chicago: University of Chicago Press.

CEJKA, M. A. 1993. A demon with no name: Prejudice against single women. In *Single women: Affirming our spiritual journeys,* ed. M. O'Brien and C. Christie, 3–11. Westport, CT: Bergin & Garvey.

Center for Women Policy Studies. 1994. *Midlife & older women & HIV/AIDS.* Washington, DC: American Association of Retired Persons.

Centers for Disease Control. 1992. Sexual behavior among high school students—United States, 1990. *Morbidity and Mortality Weekly Report* 40, 885–88.

Centers for Disease Control. 1994. *HIV/AIDS surveillance report* 5, 4.

Centers for Disease Control and Prevention. 1992, 1993. *Sexually transmitted disease surveillance report.*

CERIO, G., AND L. HOWARD. 1993. Mona Lisa: A toothless smile? *Newsweek,* November 22, 10.

CHAFE, W. H. 1972. *The American woman: Her changing social economic, and political roles, 1920–1970.* New York: Oxford University Press.

CHAFE, W. H., 1992. *The paradox of change: American women in the twentieth century.* New York: Oxford University Press.

CHAMBERLAIN, P., S. MORELAND, AND K. REID. 1992. Enhanced services and stipends for foster parents: Effects on retention rates and outcomes for children. *Child Welfare* 71, no. 5 (September-October): 387–402.

CHANCE, P. 1988. The trouble with love. *Psychology Today,* February, 22–23.

CHANG, G. 1994. Undocumented Latinas: The new "employable mothers." In *Mothering: Ideology, experience, and agency,* ed. E. Glenn, E. Nakano, G. Chang, and L. R. Forcey, 259–85. New York: Routledge.

CHANG, W. 1993. Unequal terms. *Free China Review* 43, no. 11 (November): 26–31.

CHAPMAN, A. B. 1994. *Entitled to good loving: Black men and women and the battle for love and power.* New York: Holt.

CHATTERS, L. M., AND R. J. TAYLOR. 1993. Intergenerational support: The provision of assistance to parents by adult children. In *Aging in Black*

America, ed. S. Jackson, L. M. Chatters, and R. J. Taylor, 60–83. Newbury Park, CA: Sage.

CHEAL, D. 1987. Showing them you love them: Gift giving and the dialectic of intimacy. *Sociological Review* 35 (February): 150–63.

CHERLIN, A. J. 1992. *Marriage, divorce, remarriage.* Cambridge, MA: Harvard University Press.

CHERLIN, A. J., AND F. F. FURSTENBERG, JR. 1994. Stepfamilies in the United States: A reconsideration. *Annual Review of Sociology* 20, 359–81.

CHERLIN, A. J., F. F. FURSTENBERG, JR., P. L. CHASE-LANSDALE, K. E. KIERNAN, P. K. ROBINS, D. R. MORRISON, AND J. O. TEITLER. 1991. Longitudinal studies of effects of divorce on children in Great Britain and the United States. *Science,* June 7, 1386–89.

CHESLER, P. 1988. *Sacred bond: The legacy of Baby M.* New York: Times Books.

Children's Defense Fund. 1989. *Preventing teen pregnancy: A special report.* Washington, DC.

Children's Defense Fund. 1990. *Children 1990: A report card, briefing book, and action primer.* Washington, DC.

Children's Defense Fund. 1994. *The state of America's children yearbook: 1994.* Washington, DC.

CHILMAN, C. S. 1991. Working poor families: Trends, causes, effects, and suggested policies. *Family Relations* 40, 191–98,

CHILMAN, C. S., E. W. NUNNALLY, AND F. M. COX, EDS. 1988. *Variant family forms.* Families in trouble series, Vol. 5. Beverly Hills, CA: Sage.

CHIN, K.-L. 1994. Out-of-town brides: International marriage and wife abuse among Chinese immigrants. *Journal of Comparative Family Studies* 25 (Spring): 53–69.

CHION-KENNEY, L. 1991. Parents of divorce. *Washington Post,* May 6, B5.

CHISHOLM, P., AND S. D. DRIEDGER. 1994. Paying for the children of divorce. *Maclean's,* January 10, 36–37.

CHOI, N. G. 1992. Correlates of the economic status of widowed and divorced elderly women. *Journal of Family Issues* 12, no. 1 (March): 38–54.

CHRISTOPHER, F. S., AND R. M. CATE. 1984. Factors involved in premarital sexual decision-making. *Journal of Sex Research* 20, 363–76.

Chronicle of Higher Education. 1991. Student with AIDS says professor discriminated. December 4, A4.

Chronicle of Higher Education. 1995. This year's freshmen: A statistical profile. January 13, A30–A31.

CLARKE, A. C. 1952. An examination of the operation of residential propinquity as a factor in mate selection. *American Sociological Review* 17: 17–22.

CLARKE, J. W. 1990. *On being mad or merely angry: John W. Hinckley, Jr., and other dangerous people.* Princeton, NJ: Princeton University Press.

CLARKE, S. C., AND B. F. WILSON. 1994. The relative stability of remarriages: A cohort approach using vital statistics. *Family Relations* 43, no. 3 (July): 305–10.

CLEMENS, A. W., AND L. J. AXELSON. 1985. The not-so-empty-nest: The return of the fledgling adult. *Family Relations* 34 (April): 259–64.

CLEMENTS, M. 1994. Sex in America today. *Parade Magazine,* August 7, 4–7.

CLINGEMPEEL, W. G., J. J. COLYAR, AND E. M. HETHERINGTON. 1994. Toward a cognitive dissonance conceptualization of stepchildren and biological children loyalty conflicts: A construct validity study. In *Stepparenting: Issues in theory, research, and practice,* ed. K. Pasley and M. Ihinger-Tallman, 151–73. Westport, CT: Greenwood.

CLUNIS, M. D., AND G. D. GREEN. 1988. *Lesbian couples.* Seattle: Seal Press.

COCKERHAM, W. C. 1991. *This aging society.* Englewood Cliffs, NJ: Prentice Hall.

COHANY, S. R., A. E. POLIVKA, AND J. M. ROTHGEB. 1994. *Revisions in the current population survey effective January 1994: Employment and earnings.* U.S. Department of Labor, Bureau of Labor Statistics, 42, no. 2 (February): 13–32.

COHEN, C. E. 1994. The trailing-spouse dilemma. *Working Woman* (March): 69–70.

COHEN, R. 1992. Schlafly's silence. *Washington Post,* September 24, A29.

COHEN, T. F. 1993. What do fathers provide? Reconsidering the economic and nurturant dimensions of men as parents. In *Men, work, and family,* ed. J. C. Hood, 1–22. Newbury Park, CA: Sage.

COHN, D. L. 1943. *Love in America: An informal study of manners and morals in American marriage.* New York: Simon & Schuster.

COLASANTO, D. 1989. Tolerance of homosexuality is on the rise among the public. *Gallup Report,* no. 289 (October): 11–15.

COLASANTO, D., AND J. SHRIVER. 1989. Middle-aged face marital crisis. *Gallup Report,* no. 284 (May): 34–38.

COLBURN, D. 1991. The way of the warrior. *Washington Post Health Supplement,* January 29, 10–12.

COLEMAN, B. C. 1994. Many gay teens know facts about AIDS but take risks anyway, surveys find. *Baltimore Sun,* August 8, 4D.

COLEMAN, F. 1994. Political power is only half the battle. *U.S. News & World Report,* June 13, 58.

COLEMAN, J. 1993. Adolescence in a changing world. In *Adolescence and its social worlds,* ed. J. S. Jackson and H. Rodrigues-Tomé, 251–68. East Sussex, UK: Lawrence Erlbaum Associates.

COLEMAN, L. M., T. C. ANTONUCCI, P. K. ADELMANN, AND S. E. CROHAN. 1987. Social roles in the lives of middle-aged and older black women. *Journal of Marriage and the Family* 49 (November): 761–71.

COLEMAN, M., AND L. H. GANONG. 1991. Remarriage and stepfamily research in the 1980s. In *Contemporary families: Looking forward, looking back,* ed. A. Booth, 192–207. Minneapolis, MN: National Council on Family Relations.

COLEMAN, M., L. H. GANONG, AND C. GOODWIN. 1994. The presentation of stepfamilies in marriage and family textbooks: A reexamination. *Family Relations* 43 (July): 289–297.

COLES, R., AND G. STOKES. 1985. *Sex and the American teenager.* New York: Rolling Stone Press.

COLLETTE, L. 1993. Creating a separate space: Celibacy and singlehood. In *Single women: Affirming our spiritual journeys,* ed. M. O'Brien and C. Christie, 59–84. Westport, CT: Bergin & Garvey.

COLLIER, J. 1947. *The Indians of the Americas.* New York: Norton.

COLLINS, G. 1986. 1,700 couples meet to improve marriages. *New York Times,* July 21, A14.

COLLINS, N. L., AND S. J. READ. 1990. Adult attachment, working models, and relationship quality in dating couples. *Journal of Personality and Social Psychology* 58, no. 4, 644–63.

COLLINS, P. H. 1990. *Black feminist thought: Knowledge, consciousness, and the politics of empowerment.* New York: Unwin Hyman.

COLLISON, M. N.-K. 1993. A sure-fire winner is to tell her you love her; women fall for it all the time. In *Women's studies: Thinking women,* ed. J. Wetzel, M. L. Espenlaub, M. A.

Hagen, A. B. McElhiney, C. B. Williams, 228–30. Dubuque, IA: Kendall/Hunt.

COLTRANE, S. 1989. Household labor and the routine production of gender. *Social Problems* 36, no. 5 (December): 473–90.

COLTRANE, S., AND M. ISHII-KUNTZ. 1992. Men's housework: A life course perspective. *Journal of Marriage and the Family* 54, 43–57.

COLTRANE, S., AND E. O. VALDEZ. 1993. Reluctant compliance: Work-family role allocation in dual-earner Chicano families. In *Men, work, and family*, ed. J. C. Hood, 151–75. Beverly Hills, CA: Sage.

COMER, J. P., AND A. F. POUSSAINT. 1992. *Raising black children*. New York: Penguin.

CONN, D. 1990. Taking along the children: Business travelers need different services. *Baltimore Sun. Maryland Business Weekly*, January 22, 18.

CONNELLY, J. 1989. The CEO's second wife. *Fortune*, August 28, 53–62.

CONNER, K. A. 1992. *Aging America: Issues facing an aging society*. Englewood Cliffs, NJ: Prentice Hall.

CONNOR, M. E. 1986. Some parenting attitudes of young black fathers. In *Men in families*, ed. R. A. Lewis and R. E. Salt, 141–58. Beverly Hills, CA: Sage.

CONOVER, K. A. 1993. Vacations bridge the generation gap. *Christian Science Monitor*, February 5, 13.

COOMBS, R. H. 1991. Marital status and personal well-being: A literature review. *Family Relations* 40 (January): 97–102.

COONEY, T. M. 1993. Recent demographic change: Implications for families planning for the future. *Marriage & Family Review* 18, nos. 3/4, 37–55.

COONTZ, S. 1992. *The way we never were: American families and the nostalgia trap*. New York: Basic Books.

COOPER, A. J. 1978. Actiology of homosexuality. In *Understanding homosexuality*, ed. J. A. Loriane. New York: Elsevier.

COOPER, C. R., AND R. G. COOPER, JR. 1992. Links between adolescents' relationships with their parents and peers: Models, evidence, and mechanisms. In *Family-peer relations: Modes of linkage*, ed. R. D. Parke and G. W. Ladd, 135–58. Hillsdale, NJ: Lawrence Erlbaum Associates.

COOTE, A. 1991. Anatomy of a penis. *Cosmopolitan*, May 1, 86, 88, 90, 92.

COPELAND, A. P. AND K. M. WHITE.

1991. *Studying families*. Newbury Park, CA: Sage Publications.

COREA, G. 1985. *The mother machine: Reproductive technology from artificial insemination to artificial wombs*. New York: Harper & Row.

COREY, M. 1990b. Move over, Barbie, now there's a mommy doll vying for the hearts—and arms—of little girls. *Baltimore Sun*, September 24, 1C.

COREY, M. 1990c. When a family falls apart: For adult children of divorce, the trauma can be long-lasting. *Baltimore Sun*, November 15, 1F, 2F.

COREY, M. 1993. Paying the price for love. *Baltimore Sun*, November 5, C1, C6.

CORNELL, S. 1988. *The return of the native: American Indian political resurgence*. New York: Oxford University Press.

CORNISH, E. 1987. Moonlight, violins, briefs, and bytes. *The Futurist* (January/February): 2, 58.

CORRAL, T. 1993. Brazil's women-run police stations fight the odds. *Ms.*, November, 18.

COSE, E. 1993. *The rage of a privileged class*. New York: HarperCollins.

COSE, E. 1994. Truths about spouse abuse. *Newsweek*, August 8, 49.

COTT, N. F. 1976. Eighteenth century family and social life revealed in Massachusetts divorce records. *Journal of Social History* 10 (Fall): 20–43.

COTT, N. F. 1977. *The bonds of womanhood*. New Haven, CT: Yale University Press.

COTT, N. F., AND E. H. PLECK, EDS. 1979. *A heritage of her own: Toward a new social history of American women*. New York: Simon & Schuster.

COTTLE, T. J. 1994. Women who kill. *North American Review* 279, no. 3 (May): 4–9.

COUGHLIN, E. K. 1991. Notes on research. *Chronicle of Higher Education*, November 27, A10.

COUGHLIN, E. K. 1993. Sociologists examine the complexities of racial and ethnic identity in America. *Chronicle of Higher Education*, March 24, A7–A8.

COUGHLIN, E. K. 1994. Mean streets are a scholar's lab. *Chronicle of Higher Education*, September 21, 8A, 9A, 14A.

Council on Scientific Affairs. 1993. Adolescents as victims of family violence. *JAMA*, October 20, 1850–56.

COUPER, D. P., AND N. W. SHEEHAN. 1987. Family dynamics for care-

givers: An educational model. *Family Relations* 36, 181–86.

COWAN, C. P., AND P. A. COWAN. 1992. *When partners become parents: The big life change for couples*. New York: HarperCollins.

COWAN, P. A., D. FIELD, D. A. HANSEN, A. SKOLNICK AND G. E. SWANSON, EDS. 1993. *Family, self, and society: Toward a new agenda for family research*. Hillsdale, NJ: Lawrence Erlbaum Associates.

COWELL, A. 1988. In Egypt, the in-laws still propose. *New York Times*, December 29, C1, C10.

COWELL, A. 1994. Cairo parley hits a new snag on migrants. *New York Times*, September 11, 10.

COWGILL, D. O. 1986. *Aging around the world*. Belmont, CA: Wadsworth.

COWHERD, K. 1994. State of the heart. *Baltimore Sun*, February 14, D1, D3.

COWLEY, G., WITH M. HAGER AND J. C. RAMO. 1993. The view from the womb. *Newsweek*, November 8, 64.

COX, C. 1993. *The frail elderly: Problems, needs and community responses*. Westport, CT: Auburn House.

COYNE, A. C., W. E. REICHMAN, AND L. J. BERBIG. 1993. The relationship between dementia and elder abuse. *American Journal of Psychiatry* 150, no. 4 (April): 643–46.

CRABB, P. B., AND D. BIELAWSKI. 1994. The social representation of material culture and gender in children's books. *Sex Roles* 30, nos. 1/2 69–79.

CRAIG, A. 1994. Quebec. *U.S. News & World Report*, September 12, 14.

CRAIG, S., ED. 1992. *Men, masculinity, and the media*. Newbury Park, CA: Sage.

CRANDALL, R. J. 1986. *Shaking your family tree: A basic guide to tracing your family's genealogy*. Dublin, NH: Yankee Publishers.

CRAWFORD, J. 1992. *Hold your tongue: Bilingualism and the politics of "English Only."* Reading, MA: Addison-Wesley.

CREIGHTON, L. L. 1990. The new orphanages. *U.S. News & World Report*, October 8, 37–41.

CREIGHTON, L. L. 1991. Silent saviors. *U.S. News & World Report*, December 16, 80–89.

CREIGHTON, L. L. 1993. Kids taking care of kids. *U.S. News & World Report*, December 20, 26–33.

CRENSHAW, A. B. 1992. Assessing the political power of seniors. *Washington Post Family and Retirement Supplement*, April 29, 4–7.

CRENSHAW, A. R. 1994. For many, tax

laws take the bliss out of wedded life. *Washington Post,* July 10, H1, H4.

CRIMMINS, E. M., R. A. EASTERLIN, AND Y. SAITO. 1991. What young adults want. *American Demographics* 13 (July): 24–33.

CRISPELL, D. 1992. Myths of the 1950s. *American Demographics,* August, 38–43.

CRISPELL, D. 1993. Planning no family, now or ever. *American Demographics,* October, 23–24.

CRISPELL, D. 1995. This is your life table. *American Demographics,* February, 4–6.

CRITELLI, J. W., E. J. MYERS, AND V. E. LOOS. 1988. The components of love: Romantic attraction and sex role orientation. *Journal of Personality* 54, no. 2 (June): 354–70.

CROSBIE-BURNETT, M. 1994. The interface between stepparent families and schools: Research, theory, policy, and practice. In *Stepparenting: Issues in theory, research, and practice,* ed. K. Pasley and M. Ihinger-Tallman, 199–216. Westport, CT: Greenwood.

CROSBIE-BURNETT, M., AND J. GILES-SIMS. 1994. Adolescent adjustment and stepparenting styles. *Family Relations* 43, no. 4 (October): 394–99.

CROSBIE-BURNETT, M., AND L. HELMBRECHT. 1993. A descriptive empirical study of gay male stepfamilies. *Family Relations* 42 (July): 256–62.

CROSBIE-BURNETT, M., AND E. A. LEWIS. 1993. Use of African-American family structures and functioning to address the challenges of European-American postdivorce families. *Family Relations* 42 (July): 243–48.

CROSBY, F. J. 1991. *Juggling: The unexpected advantages of balancing career and home for women and their families.* New York: Free Press.

CROSBY, J. F. 1991. *Illusion and disillusion: The self in love and marriage,* 5th ed. Belmont, CA: Wadsworth.

CROSSEN, C. 1994. *Tainted truth: The manipulation of fact in America.* New York: Simon & Schuster.

CROSSETTE, B. 1985. The politics of ruling and romance in Singapore. *New York Times,* April 11, 2.

CROSSMAN, R. K., S. M. STITH, AND M. M. BENDER. 1990. Sex role egalitarianism and marital violence. *Sex Roles* 22, nos. 5/6 (March): 293–304.

CUBER, J., AND P. HAROFF. 1965. *Sex and the significant Americans.* Baltimore: Penguin.

DAINTON, M. 1993. The myths and misconceptions of the stepmother identity: Descriptions and prescrip-

tions for identity management. *Family Relations* 42 (January): 93–98.

DALSIMER, M. 1981. Bible communists: Female socialization and family life in the Oneida community. In *Family life in America: 1620–2000,* ed. M. Albin and D. Cavallo, 30–46. New York: Revisionary Press.

DANE, B. O. 1991. Anticipatory mourning of middle-aged parents of adult children with AIDS. *Families in Society* 72, no. 2 (February): 108–15.

DANIELS, K. R. 1994. Adoption and donor insemination: Factors influencing couples' choices. *Child Welfare* 73, no. 1 (January/February): 5–14.

DANIELS, R. 1990. *Coming to America: A history of immigration and ethnicity in American life.* New York: HarperPerennial.

DANZIGER, S. K., AND S. DANZIGER. 1993. Child poverty and public policy: Toward a comprehensive antipoverty agenda. *Daedalus* 122, no. 1 (Winter): 57–84.

DARO, D., AND K. MCCURDY. 1991. Current trends in child abuse reporting and fatalities. The results of the 1990 annual fifty state survey. Mimeo. Washington, DC: National Center on Child Abuse Prevention Research.

DART, B. 1991. Adults turn to cocaine as teen-agers turn away. *Baltimore Sun,* December 20, 3A.

DASH, L. 1989. *When children want children: The urban crisis of teenage childbearing.* New York: Morrow.

DAVIS, F. J. 1991. *Who is black?* University Park: Pennsylvania State University Press.

DAVIS, K. 1985. Near and dear: Friendship and love compared. *Psychology Today,* February, 22–30.

DAVIS, S. 1990. Men as success objects and women as sex objects: A study of personal advertisements. *Sex Roles* 23, nos. 1/2, 43–50.

DEAN, C. R. 1991. Fighting for same sex marriage. *Partners, Newsletter for Gay and Lesbian Couples,* November/December.

DECALMER, P., AND F. GLENDENNING, EDS. 1993. *The mistreatment of elderly people.* Newbury Park, CA: Sage.

DEGLER, C. 1981. *At odds: Women and the family in America from the Revolution to the present.* New York: Oxford University Press.

DEGROOT, J. M., S. KENNEDY, G. RODIN, AND G. MCVEY. 1992. Correlates of sexual abuse in women with anorexia nervosa and bulimia ner-

vosa. *Canadian Journal of Psychiatry* 37 (7) (September): 516–18.

DEKESEREDY, W. S. 1990. Male peer support and woman abuse: The current state of knowledge. *Sociological Focus* 23, no. 2 (May): 129–39.

DEKESEREDY. W. S., AND M. D. SCHWARTZ. 1993. Male peer support and woman abuse: An expansion of DeKeseredy's model. *Sociological Spectrum* 13, no. 4, 393–413.

DELAMATER, J., AND P. MCCORQUODALE. 1979. *Premarital sexuality: Attitudes, relationships, behavior.* Madison: University of Wisconsin Press.

DELANY, S., AND A. E. DELANY WITH A. H. HEARTH. 1993. *Having our say: The Delany sisters' first 100 years.* New York: Kodansha International.

DEL CASTILLO, R. G. 1984. *La familia: Chicano families in the urban Southwest, 1848 to the present.* Notre Dame, IN: University of Notre Dame Press.

DEMARIS, A., AND W. MACDONALD. 1993. Premarital cohabitation and marital instability: A test of the unconventionality hypothesis. *Journal of Marriage and the Family* 55 (May): 399–407.

DEMO, D. H., AND A. C. ACOCK. 1988. The impact of divorce on children. *Journal of Marriage and the Family* 50 (August): 619–48.

DEMO, D. H., AND A. C. ACOCK. 1991. The impact of divorce on children. In *Contemporary families: Looking forward, looking back,* ed. A. Booth, 162–91. Minneapolis, MN: National Council on Family Relations.

DEMO, D. H., AND A. C. ACOCK. 1993. Family diversity and the division of domestic labor. *Family Relations* 42 (July): 323–31.

DE MOJA, C. A. 1986. Anxiety, self-confidence, jealousy, and romantic attitudes toward love in Italian undergraduates. *Psychological Reports* 58, no. 1 (February): 138.

DEMOS, J. 1970. *A little commonwealth: Family life in Plymouth colony.* New York: Oxford University Press.

DEMOS, J. 1986. *Past, present, and personal: The family and the life course in American history.* New York: Oxford University Press.

DENHAM, S. A., S. M. RENWICK, AND R. W. HOLT. 1991. Working and playing together: Prediction of preschool social-emotional competence from mother-child interaction. *Child Development* 62, no. 2 (April): 242–49.

DENNISTON, L. 1995. Adoptive parents

in Ill. lose bid for boy. *Baltimore Sun*, February 14, 1A, 6A.

DENSON, D. R., R. VOIGHT, AND R. EISENMAN. 1993. Factors that influence HIV/AIDS instruction in schools. *Adolescence*, 28, no. 110 (Summer): 309–13.

DENTZER, S. 1992. A wealth of difference. *U.S. News & World Report*, June 1, 45–47.

DEPARLE, J. 1994. Welfare mothers find jobs are easier to get than hold. *New York Times*, October 24, A1, A14.

DERLEGA, V. J., S. METTS, S. PETRONIO, AND S. T. MARGULIS. 1993. *Self-disclosure*. Newbury Park, CA: Sage.

DERN, D. P. 1994. *The internet guide for new users*. New York: McGraw-Hill.

DESTEFANO, L., AND D. COLASANTO. 1990. Unlike 1975, today most Americans think men have it better. *Gallup Poll Monthly* (February): 25–36.

DEUTSCH, C. H. 1986. Prenuptial decrees up, prenuptial trust down. *New York Times*, November 19, C1, C16.

DEUTSCHL, F. M., J. B. LUSSIER, AND L. J. SERVIS. 1993. Husbands at home: Predictors of paternal participation in childcare and housework. *Journal of Personality and Social Psychology* 65, no. 6, 1154–166.

DEVALL, E., Z. STONEMAN, AND G. BRODY. 1986. The impact of divorce and maternal employment on pre-adolescent children. *Family Relations* 35, no. 1 (January): 153–60.

DEW, R. F. 1994. *The family heart: A memoir of when our son came out*. Reading, MA: Addison-Wesley.

DEWITT, P. M. 1993. In pursuit of pregnancy. *American Demographics* (May): 48–54.

DE WITT, P. M. 1994a. Breaking up is hard to do. *American Demographics*, reprint package 8–12.

DE WITT, P. M. 1994b. The second time around. *American Demographics*, reprint package 14–16.

DIBACCO, T. V. 1994. Tracing the trail of Alzheimer's. *Washington Post Health Supplement*, November 29, 9.

DILL, B. T. 1994. *Across the boundaries of race and class: An exploration of work and family among black female domestic servants*. New York: Garland.

DILSWORTH-ANDERSON, P., L. M. BURTON AND W. L. TURNER. 1993. The importance of values in the study of culturally diverse families. *Family Relations* 42 (July): 238–42.

DINNERSTEIN, L., R. L. NICHOLS, AND D. M. REIMERS. 1990. *Natives and strangers: Blacks, Indians, and immigrants in America*, 2nd ed. New York: Oxford University Press.

DINNERSTEIN, M. 1992. *Women between two worlds: Midlife reflections on work and family*. Philadelphia: Temple University Press.

DION, K., E. BERSCHEID, AND E. WALSTER. 1972. What is beautiful is good. *Journal of Personality and Social Psychology* 24, 285–90.

DIXON, J. 1993. Children of cocaine, alcohol users swell list for federal disability benefits. *Baltimore Sun*, March 9, 6A.

DOANE, G., AND J. BELL. 1992. *Searching for your ancestors*, 6th ed. Minneapolis: University of Minnesota Press.

DOBSON, J. C. 1994. Pornography harms society. In *Taking sides: Clashing views on controversial issues in human sexuality*, 4th ed., ed. R. T. Francoeur, 80–86. Guilford, CT: Dushkin.

DOKA, K. J., AND M. E. MERTZ. 1988. The meaning and significance of great-grandparenthood. *The Gerontologist* 28, no. 2, 192–96.

DOLMETSCH, P., AND A. SHIH, EDS. 1985. *The kids' book about single-parent families: By kids for everyone*. Garden City, NY: Dolphin Books.

DORFMAN, L. T., AND C. E. MERTENS. 1990. Kinship relations in retired rural men and women. *Family Relations* 39, 166–73.

DORIUS, G. L., T. B. HEATON, AND P. STEFFEN. 1993. Adolescent life events and their association with the onset of sexual intercourse. *Youth and Society* 25, no. 1 (September): 3–23.

DORKENOO, E., AND S. ELWORTHY. 1992. *Female genital mutilation: Proposals for change*. London: Minority Rights Group.

DORTCH, S. 1994. What's good for the goose may gag the gander. *American Demographics* (May): 15–16.

DOUGLAS, J. D., AND F. C. ATWELL. 1988. *Love, intimacy and sex*. Beverly Hills, CA: Sage.

DOUGLASS, R. L. 1992. Domestic mistreatment of the elderly—towards prevention. Washington, DC: American Association of Retired Persons.

DOWELL, P. 1988. Sex makes a comeback. *Psychology Today*, September, 64–65.

DOWELL, W. 1990. Life in the slow lane. *Time*, November 26, 46.

DOWNS, L. 1994. In Japan where mom knows best. *Washington Post Education Review*, April 3, 16.

DOYLE, J. A. 1985. *Sex and gender: The human experience*. Dubuque, IA: Wm. C. Brown.

DRAKULIC, S. 1993. *How we survived communism and even laughed*. New York: HarperPerennial.

DU BOIS, W. E. B. 1990. *The souls of black folk*. New York: Vintage. (Originally published 1903.)

DUBROW, M., E. BARNES, V. BALFOUR, AND G. H. COLT. 1987. Sex and the presidency. *Life*, August, 70–75.

DUKE, L. 1991a. Conference studies plight of black males. *Washington Post*, May 23, A3.

DUKE, L. 1991b. Hispanic group criticizes EEOC record during Thomas era. *Washington Post*, July 16, A4.

DUKE, L. 1991c. Whites' racial stereotypes persist: Most retain negative beliefs about minorities, survey finds. *Washington Post*, January 1, A1, A4.

DUKES, R. L. 1989. The Cinderella myth: Negative evaluations of stepparents. *Sociology and Social Research* 73, no. 2 (January): 67–72.

DULLEA, G. 1987. Wives confront spouses' homosexuality. *New York Times*, April 27, B11.

DUNEIER, M. 1992. *Slim's table: Race, respectability, and masculinity*. Chicago: University of Chicago Press.

DUNN, A. 1994. In California, the numbers add up to anxiety. *New York Times*, October 30, 3.

DUVALL, E. M. 1957. *Family development*. Philadelphia: Lippincott.

DUXBURY, L., C. HIGGINS, AND C. LEE. 1994. Work-family conflict: A comparison by gender, family type, and perceived control. *Journal of Family Issues* 15, no. 3 (September): 449–66.

DWORKIN, A. 1974. *Woman hating*. New York: Dutton.

DWORKIN, A. 1989. *Pornography: Men possessing women*. New York: Penguin.

DYM, B., AND M. L. GLENN. 1993. *Couples: Exploring and understanding the cycles of intimate relationships*. New York: HarperCollins.

DYSON, M. E. 1993. *Reflecting black: African-American cultural criticism*. Minneapolis: University of Minnesota Press.

EARLE, A. M. 1899. *Child life in colonial days*. New York: Macmillan.

EBAUGH, H. R. F. 1988. *Becoming an ex: The process of role exit*. Chicago: University of Chicago Press.

Ebony. 1994. Black college students

tell what love means to them, February, 35, 38 ff.

ECCLES, J. S., J. E. JACOBS, AND R. D. HAROLD. 1990. Gender role stereotypes, expectancy effects, and parents' socialization of gender differences. *Journal of Social Issues* 40, no. 2: 183–201.

ECKLAND, B. K. 1968. Theories of mate selection. *Eugenics Quarterly* 15, no. 1: 71–84.

The Economist. 1993. Sexual strategies: Good for you. March 27, 86–87.

EDDINGS, J. 1994. Fighting the next battle. *U.S. News & World Report,* March 28, 53–54.

EDELMAN, M. 1987. *Families in peril: An agenda for social change.* Cambridge, MA: Harvard University Press.

EDELSON, H. 1992. Age-proofing the kitchen. *Washington Post Family and Retirement Supplement,* April 29, 9.

EHRENREICH, B. 1986. Two, three, many husbands. *Mother Jones,* July/August, 8.

EHRENREICH, B., AND D. ENGLISH. 1989. Blowing the whistle on the "mommy track." *Ms.,* July/August, 56–58.

EHRENREICH, B., E. HESS, AND G. JACOBS. 1986. *Re-making love: The feminization of sex.* Garden City, NY: Anchor.

EITZEN, D. S., AND M. BACA ZINN. 1992. *Social problems,* 5th ed. Boston: Allyn & Bacon.

EITZEN, D. S., AND M. BACA ZINN. 1994. *Social problems,* 6th ed. Boston: Allyn & Bacon.

EL-BADRY, S. 1994. The Arab-American market. *American Demographics* (January): 22–30.

ELBOW, M., AND J. MAYFIELD. 1991. Mothers of incest victims: Villains, victims, or protectors? *Families in Society* 72, no. 2 (February): 78–86.

ELDER, G. J., JR. 1984. Families, kin, and the life course: A sociological perspective. In *Review of child development research,* Vol. 7, *The family,* ed. R. D. Parke, 80–136. Chicago: University of Chicago Press.

ELKIND, D. 1987. Superkids and super problems. *Psychology Today,* May, 60–61.

ELLIS, L., AND M. A. AMES. 1987. Neurohormonal functioning and sexual orientation: A theory of homosexuality-heterosexuality. *Psychological Bulletin* 101, 233.

ELSHTAIN, J. B. 1988. What's the matter with sex today? *Tikkun: A Bimonthly Jewish Critique of Politics, Culture and Society* 3, no. 3, 42–43.

EMERY, R. E., S. G. MATTHEWS, AND M. M. WYER. 1991. Child custody mediation and litigation: Further evidence on the differing views of mothers and fathers. *Journal of Consulting and Clinical Psychology* 59, no. 3: 410–18.

ENGLAND, P. 1992. *Comparable worth.* New York: Aldine de Gruyter.

ENRICO, D. 1993. The male-order magazine. *Baltimore Sun,* May 13, 10E.

ENTWISLE, D. B., AND S. G. DOERING. 1981. *The first birth: A family turning point.* Baltimore: Johns Hopkins University Press.

EPSTEIN, A. 1990. Woman denied partnership for unfeminine style savors court win. *Baltimore Sun,* May 16, 1A, 12A.

ERICKSON, M. T. 1993. Rethinking Oedipus: An evolutionary perspective of incest avoidance. *American Journal of Psychiatry* 150, no. 3 (March): 411–16.

ERICKSON, R. J. 1993. Reconceptualizing family work: The effect of emotion work on perceptions of marital quality. *Journal of Marriage and the Family* 55 (November): 888–900.

ERNST, R. L., AND J. W. HAY. 1994. The US economic and social costs of Alzheimer's disease revisited. *American Journal of Public Health* 84, no. 8 (August): 1261–65.

ESLER, A. 1994. *The western world: Prehistory to the present,* 3rd ed. Englewood Cliffs, NJ: Prentice Hall.

ESPIRITU, Y. L. 1992. *Asian American panethnicity: Bridging institutions and identities.* Philadelphia: Temple University Press.

ESTESS, P. S. 1994. When kids don't leave. *Modern Maturity* (November-December): 56, 58, 90.

ETAUGH, C. E., AND M. B. LISS. 1992. Home, school, and playroom: Training grounds for adult gender roles. *Sex Roles* 26, nos. 3/4, 129–47.

ETTER, J. 1993. Levels of cooperation and satisfaction in 56 open adoptions. *Child Welfare* 72, no. 3 (May/June): 257–68.

EVANGELAUF, J. 1989. SAT called a "defective product" that is biased against women. *Chronicle of Higher Education,* May 3, A3.

EVANS, N. J., AND V. A. WALL. 1991. *Beyond tolerance: Gays, lesbians and bisexuals on campus.* Alexandria, VA: American Association for Counseling and Development.

EVATT, C. 1993. *Opposite sides of the bed.* Berkeley, CA: Conari Press.

EVERETT, C. ED. 1992. *Divorce and the next generation: Effects on young*

adults' patterns of intimacy and expectations for marriage. New York: Haworth.

EVERETT, C., AND S. V. EVERETT. 1994. *Healthy divorce.* San Francisco: Jossey-Bass.

EXTER, T. 1990. Entertaining singles. *American Demographics* (August): 6–7.

EYER, D. E. 1992. *Mother-infant bonding: A scientific fiction.* New Haven, CT: Yale University Press.

FADER, S. 1985. House power. *Working Woman,* December, 89–91.

FADERMAN, L. 1991. *Odd girls and twilight lovers: A history of lesbian life in twentieth-century America.* New York: Columbia University Press.

FALBO, T., ED. 1984. *The single-child family.* New York: Guilford Press.

FALLER, K. C. 1990. *Understanding child sexual maltreatment.* Beverly Hills, CA: Sage.

FALLON, P., M. A. KATZMAN, AND S. C. WOOLEY, EDS. 1994. *Feminist perspectives on eating disorders.* New York: Guilford Press.

Family Law Reporter—Reference File. 1989. Washington, DC: The Bureau of National Affairs, Inc., 4.

FANSHEL, D., S. J. FINCH, AND J. F. GRUNDY. 1989. Modes of exit from foster family care and adjustment at time of departure of children with unstable life histories. *Child Welfare* 68 (July/August). 391–402.

FARAGHER, J. M. 1986. *Sugar Creek: Life on the Illinois prairie.* New Haven, CT: Yale University Press.

FARAGHER, J. M., M. J. BUHLE, D. CZITRON, AND S. H. ARMITAGE. 1994. *Out of many—a history.* Englewood Cliffs, NJ: Prentice Hall.

FARBER, B. 1964. *Family: Organization and interaction.* San Francisco: Chandler.

FARBER, B. 1972. *Guardians of virtue: Salem families in 1800.* New York: Basic Books.

FARBER, B., C. H. MINDEL, AND B. LAZERWITZ. 1988. The Jewish American family. In *Ethnic families in America: Patterns and variations,* 3rd ed., ed. C. H. Mindel, R. W. Habenstein, and R. Wright, Jr., 400–437. New York: Elsevier.

FASSEL, D. 1991. *Growing up divorced: A road to healing for adult children of divorce.* New York: Pocket Books.

FAUSTO-STERLING, A. 1985. *Myths of gender.* New York: Basic Books.

FEAGIN, J. R. 1991. The continuing significance of race: Antiblack discrimination in public places. *American*

Sociological Review 56, no. 1 (February): 101–16.

FEAGIN, J. R., AND C. B. FEAGIN. 1993. *Racial and ethnic relations*, 4th ed. Englewood Cliffs, NJ: Prentice Hall.

FEAGIN, J. R., AND M. P. SIKES. 1994. *Living with racism: The black middle-class experience*. Boston: Beacon.

FEDDERS, C. 1990. In their own words. *Washington Post*, October 6, E5.

FEDDERS, C., AND L. ELLIOT. 1987. *Shattered dreams: The story of Charlotte Fedders*. New York: Harper & Row.

FEENEY, J. A., AND P. NOLLER. 1990. Attachment style as a predictor of adult romantic relationships. *Journal of Personality and Social Psychology* 58, no. 2, 281–91.

FEENEY, J. A., P. NOLLER AND J. PATTY. 1993. Adolescents' interactions with the opposite sex: Influence of attachment style and gender. *Journal of Adolescence* 16 (June): 169–86.

FEHR, B. 1993. How do I love thee? Let me consult my prototype. In *Individuals in relationships*, ed. S. Duck, 87–120. Newbury Park, CA: Sage.

FELDMAN, H. 1931. *Racial factors in American industry*. New York: Harper & Row.

FELDMANN, L., AND G. GOODALE. 1995. Custody cases test attitudes of judges. *Christian Science Monitor*, March 3, 1, 18.

FERREIRO, B. W. 1990. Presumption of joint custody: A family policy dilemma. *Family Relations* 39 (October): 420–25.

FIELD, D., AND M. MINKLER. 1993. The importance of family in advanced old age: The family is "forever." In *Family, self, and society: Toward a new agenda for family research*, ed. P. A. Cowan, D. Field, D. A. Hansen, A. Skolnick, and G. E. Swanson, 331–52. Hillsdale, NJ: Lawrence Erlbaum Associates.

FIESTER, L. 1993. Teen survey sparks concern. *Washington Post*, February 2, 1, 3.

FINCHAM, F. D., AND T. N. BRADBURY. 1987. The assessment of marital quality: A reevaluation. *Journal of Marriage and the Family* 49 (November): 797–809.

FINDLEN, B. 1987. Gay marriage: Lifting the bans. *Ms.*, February, 29.

FINE, M. A., AND D. A. FINE. 1994. An examination and evaluation of recent changes in divorce laws in five western countries: The critical role of values. *Journal of Marriage and the Family* 56 (May): 249–63.

FINE, R. 1985. *The meaning of love in human experience*. New York: Wiley.

FINEMAN, M. 1991. *The illusion of equality: The rhetoric and reality of divorce reform*. Chicago: University of Chicago Press.

FINK, D. 1992. *Agrarian women: Wives and mothers in rural Nebraska, 1880–1940*. Chapel Hill: University of North Carolina Press.

FINKE, N. 1994. Trophy husbands. *Working Woman* (April): 37, 39, 41, 88, 90–91.

FINKEL, J., AND P. ROBERTS. 1994. *The incomes of noncustodial fathers*. Washington, DC: Center for Law and Social Policy.

FINKELHOR, D. 1984. *Child sexual abuse*. New York: Free Press.

FINNIE, R. 1993. Women, men, and the economic consequences of divorce: Evidence from Canadian longitudinal data. *Canadian Review of Sociology and Anthropology* 30 (May): 205–41.

FINTUSHEL, N., AND N. HILLARED. 1991. *A grief out of season: When your parents divorce in your adult years*. Boston: Little, Brown.

FISCHMAN, J. 1988. Stepdaughter wars. *Psychology Today*, November, 38–41.

FISHEL, E. 1987. Baby makes three. *Parents*, September, 73–76, 78.

FISHER, H. 1992. *Anatomy of love: The natural history of monogamy, adultery, and divorce*. New York: Norton.

FISHER, H. E. 1993. After all, maybe it's . . . biology. *Psychology Today*, March/April, 40–45, 82.

FISHER, M. 1994. Court overturns limited visits to gay father. *Washington Post*, October 27, D1, D6.

FISHMAN, B., AND B. HAMEL. 1981. From nuclear to stepfamily ideology: A stressful change. *Alternative Lifestyles* 4, 181–204.

FITZGERALD, L. F. 1993. Sexual harassment: Violence against women in the workplace. *American Psychologist* 48, no. 10. (October): 1070–76.

FLANZER, J. P. 1993. Alcohol and other drugs are key causal agents of violence. In *Current controversies on family violence*, ed. R. J. Gelles and D. R. Loseke, 171–81. Newbury Park, CA: Sage.

FLETCHER, M. A. 1994. Blacks pessimistic about children's future, poll finds. *Baltimore Sun*, May 27, 13A.

FLORES, B. R. 1994. *Chiquita's cocoon*. New York: Villard.

FLYNN, C. P. 1990. Relationship violence by women: Issues and implica-

tions. *Family Relations* 39 (April), 194–97.

FLYNN, C. P. 1994. Regional differences in attitudes toward corporal punishment. *Journal of Marriage and the Family* 56 (May): 314–24.

FOLBRE, N. 1994. *Who pays for the kids? Gender and the structures of constraint*. New York: Routledge.

FOLK, K. F., J. W. GRAHAM AND A. H. BELLER. 1992. Child support and remarriage: Implications for the economic well-being of children. *Journal of Family Issues* 13, 142–57.

FOLK, K. F., AND Y. YI. 1994. Piecing together child care with multiple arrangements: Crazy quilt or preferred pattern for employed parents of preschool children? *Journal of Marriage and the Family* 56 (August): 669–80.

FOMBY, P. 1991. Why I'm glad I grew up in a gay family. *Mother Jones*, May, 39.

FONG, R. 1994. Family preservation: Making it work for Asians. *Child Welfare* 73, no. 4 (July/August): 331–41.

FOOTLICK, J. K. 1990. What happened to the family? *Newsweek* (special edition) (Winter/Spring): 14–20.

FORD, C., AND E. BEACH. 1972. *Patterns of sexual behavior*. New York: Harper & Row. (Originally published 1951.)

FOREHAND, R., B. NEIGHBORS, D. DEVINE, AND L. ARMISTEAD. 1994. Interparental conflict and parental divorce: The individual, relative, and interactive effects on adolescents across four years. *Family Relations* 43, no. 4 (October): 387–93.

FORREST, J., AND S. SINGH. 1990. The sexual and reproductive behavior of American women, 1982–1988. *Family Planning Perspectives* 22, no. 5 (September/October): 206–14.

FORREST, K. A., D. M. AUSTIN, M. I. VALDES, E. G. FUENTES, AND S. R. WILSON. 1993. Exploring norms and beliefs related to AIDS prevention among California hispanic men. *Family Planning Perspectives* 25, no. 3 (May/June): 111–17.

FORWARD, S. 1990. *Toxic parents: Overcoming their hurtful legacy and reclaiming your life*. New York: Bantam.

FOSSETT, M. A., AND K. J. KIECOLT. 1993. Mate availability and family structure among African Americans in U.S. metropolitan areas. *Journal of Marriage and the Family* 55 (May): 288–302.

FOX-GENOVESE, E. 1990. *Feminism without illusions: A critique of indi-*

vidualism. Chapel Hill: University of North Carolina Press.

FRAME, M. W., AND C. L. SHEHAN. 1994. Work and well-being in the two-person career: Relocation stress and coping among clergy husbands and wives. *Family Relations* 43, no. 2 (April): 196–205.

FRANKLIN II, C. W. 1988. *Men & society*. Chicago: Nelson-Hall.

FRAZER, J. M., AND T. C. FRAZER. 1993. "Father Knows Best" and "The Cosby Show": Nostalgia and the sitcom tradition. *Journal of Popular Culture* 27 (Winter): 163–72.

FRAZIER, E. F. 1937. The impact of urban civilization upon Negro family life. *American Sociological Review* 2, no. 5 (October): 609–18.

FRAZIER, E. F. 1939. *The Negro family in the United States*. Chicago: University of Chicago Press.

FREEDMAN, D. C. 1986. Wife, widow, woman: Roles of an anthropologist in a Transylvanian village. In *Women in the field: Anthropological experiences*, 2nd ed., ed. P. Golde, 333–58. Berkeley: University of California Press.

FREEMAN, E. W., AND K. RICKELS. 1993. *Early childbearing: Perspectives of black adolescents on pregnancy, abortion, and contraception*. Beverly Hills, CA: (Sage).

FREIFELD, K. 1994. Marriage really is taxing. *New Woman* (March): 133–34.

FRENKIEL, N. 1990. Shape up or ship out. *Baltimore Sun*, May 2, 1F, 8F.

FRIEDAN, B. 1993. *The fountain of age*. New York: Simon & Schuster.

FRIEDMAN, D. 1993. Eye on the '90s . . . delicate discussion. *U.S. News & World Report*, November 8, 23.

FRIEMAN, B. B., R. GARON, AND B. MANDELL. 1994. Parenting seminars for divorcing parents. *Social Work* 39, no. 5 (September): 607–10.

FROMM, E. 1956. *The art of loving*. New York: Bantam.

FUKUYAMA, F. 1993. Immigrants and family values. *Commentary* 95, no. 5 (May): 26–32.

FULLILOVE, R. E., W. BARKSDALE, AND M. T. FULLILOVE. 1994. Teens talk sex: Can we talk back? In *Sexual cultures and the construction of adolescent identities*, ed. J. M. Irvine, 31–32. Philadelphia: Temple University Press.

FULTZ, O. 1991. 'Roid rage. *American Health*, May, 60–64.

FUNDENBURG, L. 1994. *Black, white, other*. New York: Morrow.

FURSTENBERG, F. F. 1991. As the pendulum swings: Teenage childbearing and social concern. *Family Relations* 40 (April): 127–38.

FURSTENBERG, F. F., JR., AND J. O. TEITLER. 1994. Reconsidering the effects of marital disruption: What happens to children of divorce in early adulthood? *Journal of Family Issues* 15, no. 2 (June): 173–90.

FURUKAWA, S. 1994. *The diverse living arrangements of children: Summer 1991*. U.S. Bureau of the Census, Current Population Reports, Series P70, No. 38. Washington, DC: Government Printing Office.

GABARDI, L., AND L. A. ROSEN. 1992. Intimate relationships: College students from divorced and intact families. In *Divorce and the next generation: Effects on young adults' patterns of intimacy and expectations for marriage*, ed. C. Everett, 25–56. New York: Haworth.

GAGE, A. 1994. Marriage has its advantages, but taxes aren't one of them. *Washington Post*, March 13, H4.

GAINES, D. 1991. *Teenage wasteland: Suburbia's dead end kids*. New York: Pantheon.

GAINES-CARTER, P. 1990. Legal snag keeps gays from tying the knot: Couple denied marriage license sues D.C. *Washington Post*, December 6, C5.

GAITER, L. 1994. The revolt of the black bourgeoisie. *New York Times Magazine*, June 26, 42–43.

GALEENER-MOORE, L. 1987. *Collecting dead relatives: An irreverent romp through the field of genealogy*. Baltimore: Genealogical Publishing Co.

GALLAGHER, S. K., AND N. GERSTEL. 1993. Kinkeeping and friend keeping among older women: The effect of marriage. *The Gerontologist* 33, no. 5, 675–81.

GALLUP, G., JR., AND F. NEWPORT. 1990a. Time at a premium for many Americans. *Gallup Poll Monthly* (November): 43–49.

GALLUP, G., JR., AND F. NEWPORT. 1990b. Virtually all adults want children, but many of the reasons are intangible. *Gallup Poll Monthly* (June): 8–22.

GALLUP, G., JR., AND F. NEWPORT. 1991a. Baby-boomers seek more family time. *Gallup Poll Monthly* (April): 31–38.

GALLUP, G., JR., AND F. NEWPORT. 1991b. For first time, more Americans approve of interracial marriage than disapprove. *Gallup Poll Monthly* (August): 60–62.

GAMACHE, D. 1990. Domination and control: The social context of dating violence. In *Dating violence: Young women in danger*, ed. B. Levy, 69–118. Seattle: Seal Press.

GANONG, L. H., AND M. COLEMAN. 1987. Sex, sex roles, and familial love. *Journal of Genetic Psychology* 148, no. 1 (March): 45–52.

GANONG, L. H., AND M. COLEMAN. 1989. Preparing for remarriage: Anticipating the issues, seeking solutions. *Family Relations* 38 (January): 28–33.

GANONG, L. H., AND M. COLEMAN. 1992. Gender differences in self and future partner expectations. *Journal of Family Issues* 13, 55–64.

GANONG, L. H., AND M. COLEMAN. 1994. *Remarried family relationships*. Thousand Oaks, CA: Sage.

GANS, H. J. 1971. The uses of poverty: The poor pay all. *Social Policy* (July/August): 78–81.

GANS, H. J. 1979. *Deciding what's news: A study of CBS Evening News, NBC Nightly News, Newsweek and Time*. New York: Pantheon.

GARBARINO, J. 1989. The incidence and prevalence of child maltreatment. In *Family violence*, ed. L. Ohlin and M. Tonry, 219–61. Chicago: University of Chicago Press.

GARCIA, M. T. 1980. La familia: The Mexican immigrant family, 1900–1930. In *Work, family, sex roles, language*, ed. M. Barrera, A. Camarillo, and F. Hernandez, 117–40. Berkeley, CA: Tonatiua-Quinto Sol International.

GARDNER, M. 1994a. Good dad/bad dad: Modern-day images of fatherhood. *Christian Science Monitor*, June 16, 13.

GARDNER, M. 1994b. A hidden fact of life for teens: Dating violence. *Christian Science Monitor*, June 30, 12.

GARDNER, M. 1995. Who'll look after little Clara? *Christian Science Monitor*, March 27, 12.

GARDNER, R. A. 1991. *The parents' book about divorce*. New York: Bantam.

GARDNER, R. W., B. ROBEY, AND P. C. SMITH. 1985. Asian Americans: Growth, change and diversity. *Population Bulletin* 40, no. 4 (October): 1–43.

GARFINKEL, I. 1992. *Assuring child support: An extension of Social Security*. New York: Russell Sage Foundation.

GARFINKEL, I., AND S. MCLANAHAN. 1990. The effects of the child support provisions of the Family Support Act of 1988 on child well-being. *Population Research and Policy Review* 9, 205–34.

GARFINKEL, I., S. S. MCLANAHAN AND P. K. ROBINS, EDS. 1994. *Child support and child well-being*. Washington, DC: Urban Institute Press.

GASSER, R. D., AND C. M. TAYLOR. 1990. Role adjustment of single parent fathers with dependent children. *Family Relations* 40 (July): 397–400.

GATELY, D., AND A. I. SCHWEBEL. 1992. Favorable outcomes in children after parental divorce. In *Divorce and the next generation: Effects on young adults' patterns of intimacy and expectations for marriage*, ed. C. Everett, 57–78. New York: Haworth.

GATES, D., ET AL. 1993. White male paranoia. *Newsweek*, March 29, 47, 49–53.

GAULIN, S. J. C., AND J. S. BOSTER. 1990. Dowry as female competition. *American Anthropologist* 92 (December): 994–1005.

GAWISER, S. R., AND G. E. WITT. 1994. *A journalist's guide to public opinion polls*. Westport, CT: Praeger.

GAYLIN, W. 1992. *The male ego*. New York: Viking.

GECAS, V., AND M. A. SEFF. 1991. Families and adolescents: A review of the 1980s. In *Contemporary families: Looking forward, looking back*, ed. A. Booth, 208–25. Minneapolis, MN: National Council on Family Relations.

GELLES, R. J. 1988. Violence and pregnancy: Are pregnant women at greater risk of abuse? *Journal of Marriage and the Family* 50 (August): 841–47.

GELLES, R. J. 1993. Through a sociological lens: Social structure and family violence. In *Current controversies on family violence*, ed. R. J. Gelles and D. R. Loseke, 31–46. Newbury Park, CA: Sage.

GELLES, R. J. 1995. *Contemporary families: A sociological view*. Thousand Oaks, CA: Sage.

GELLES, R. J., AND C. P. CORNELL. 1990. *Intimate violence in families*, 2nd ed. Newbury Park, CA: Sage.

GELLES, R. J., AND J. W. HARROP. 1991. The risk of abusive violence among children with nongenetic caretakers. *Family Relations* 40, no. 1 (January): 78–83.

GELLES, R. J., AND D. R. LOSEKE, EDS. 1993. *Current controversies on family violence*. Newbury Park, CA: Sage.

GELLES, R. J., AND M. A. STRAUS. 1988. *Intimate violence*. New York: Simon & Schuster.

GELMAN, D., WITH K. SPRINGEN. 1993. How will the clone feel? *Newsweek*, November 8, 65–66.

GENOVESE, E. D. 1981. Husbands and fathers, wives and mothers, during slavery. In *Family life in America: 1620–2000*, ed. M. Albin and D. Cavallo, 237–51. St. James, NY: Revisionary Press.

GERBNER, G. 1993. Women and minorities on television. A report to the Screen Actors Guild and the American Federation of Radio and Television Artists. Mimeo. June.

GERSTEL, N. 1987. Divorce and stigma. *Social Problems* 34, no. 2 (April): 172–86.

GERSTEL, N., AND S. K. GALLAGHER. 1993. Kinkeeping and distress: Gender, recipients of care, and work-family conflict. *Journal of Marriage and the Family* 55 (August): 598–607.

GIBBS, N. 1991a. The clamor on campus. *Time*, June 3, 54–55.

GIBBS, N. 1991b. When is it rape? *Time*, June 3, 48–54.

GIBBS, N., J. JOHNSON, M. LUDTKE, AND M. RILEY. 1990. Shameful bequests to the next generation. *Time*, October 8, 42–46.

GIBSON, J. T. 1991. Disciplining toddlers. *Parents*, May, 190.

GIBSON, P. 1989. *Gay male and lesbian youth suicide*. U.S. Department of Health and Human Services Report to the Secretary's Task Force on Youth Suicide. Washington, DC.

GIBSON, R. C. 1993. The black American retirement experience. In *Aging in black America*, ed. J. S. Jackson, L. M. Chatters, and R. J. Taylor, 277–97. Newbury Park, CA: Sage.

GILBERT, E. 1994. Pregnancy discrimination alert. *Working Mother* (June): 34–35.

GILBERT, L. A. 1993. *Two careers/one family: The promise of gender equality*. Newbury Park: CA: Sage.

GILER, J. A., AND K. NEUMEYER. 1992. *Redefining Mr. Right: A career woman's guide to choosing a mate*. Oakland, CA: New Harbinger and Marin.

GILES, J., WITH R. SAWHILL. 1993. The Delany sisters tell all. *Newsweek*, November 1, 54.

GILES-SIMS, J., AND M. CROSBIE-BURNETT. 1989. Adolescent power in stepfather families: A test of normative-resource theory. *Journal of Marriage and the Family* 51 (November): 1065–78.

GILGUN, J. F., K. DALY AND G. MANDEL, EDS. 1992. *Qualitative methods in family research*. Newbury Park, CA: Sage.

GILMAN, E. 1994. Matching the elderly with foster families. *New York Times*, February 20, D8.

GILMARTIN, B. G. 1987. Peer group antecedents of severe love-shyness in males. *Journal of Personality* 55, no. 3 (September): 467–89.

GJERDINGEN, D. K., D. G. FROBERG, K. M. CHALONER, AND P. M. McGOVERN. 1993. Changes in women's physical health during the first postpartum year. *Archives of Family Medicine* 2, no. 3 (March): 277–83.

GLADSTONE, J. W. 1989. Perceived changes in grandmother-grandchild relations following a child's separation or divorce. *The Gerontologist* 28, no. 1, 66–72.

GLASWER, D., AND T. WOLF. 1994. Facing domestic partner issues. *Business & Health* 12, no. 2 (February): 53–54.

GLATER, J. D. 1994. Fed finds disparities in mortgage denials. *Washington Post*, October 27, B10, B15.

GLAUBER, B. 1994. O.J., the hero, doesn't fit the crime. *Baltimore Sun*, June 18, 1A, 4A.

GLAZER, N., AND D. P. MOYNIHAN. 1963. *Beyond the melting pot*. Cambridge, MA: MIT Press and Harvard University Press.

GLAZER, S. 1991. Controversy persists on French abortion pill. *Washington Post Health Supplement*, December 10, 7.

GLENN, E. N., G. CHANG, AND L. R. FORCEY, EDS. 1994. *Mothering: Ideology, experience, and agency*. New York: Routledge.

GLENN, E. N., WITH S. G. H. YAP. 1994. Chinese American families. In *Minority families in the United States: A multicultural perspective*, ed. R. L. Taylor, 115–45. Englewood Cliffs, NJ: Prentice Hall.

GLENN, N. 1992. What does family mean? *American Demographics* (June): 30–37.

GLENN, N. D. 1991. Quantitative research on marital quality in the 1980s. In *Contemporary families: Looking forward, looking back*, ed. A. Booth, 28–41. Minneapolis, MN: National Council on Family Relations.

GLENN, N. D., AND K. B. KRAMER. 1987. The marriages and divorces of the children of divorce. *Journal of Marriage and the Family* 49 (November): 811–25.

GLENN, N. D., AND B. A. SHELTON. 1985. Regional differences in divorce in the United States. *Journal of Marriage and the Family* 47: 641–52.

GLENN, N. D., AND C. N. WEAVER. 1988. The changing relationship of marital status to reported happiness. *Journal of Marriage and the Family* 50 (May): 317–24.

GLENWICK, D. S., AND J. D. MOWREY. 1986. When parent becomes peer: Loss of intergenerational boundaries in single parent families. *Family Relations* 35, no. 1 (January): 57–62.

GLICK, P. C. 1984. Marriage, divorce and living arrangements: Prospective changes. *Journal of Family Issues* 5, no. 1 (March): 7–26.

GODDARD, H. W. 1994. *Principles of parenting*. Auburn, AL: Auburn University, Department of Family and Child Development.

GODUKA, I. N. 1990. Ethics and politics of field research in South Africa. *Social Problems* 37, no. 3 (August): 329–40.

GOETTING, A. 1982. The six stations of remarriage: Developmental tasks of remarriage after divorce. *Family Relations* 31 (April): 231–22.

GOFFMAN, E. 1961. *Asylums*. New York: Anchor.

GOLD, L. 1992. *Between love and hate: A guide to civilized divorce*. New York: Plenum.

GOLD, S. J. 1993. Migration and family adjustment: Continuity and change among Vietnamese in the United States. In *Family ethnicity: Strength in diversity*, ed. H. P. McAdoo, 306–316. Newbury Park, CA: Sage.

GOLDBERG, G. S. AND E. KREMEN, EDS. 1990. *The feminization of poverty: Only in America?* New York: Praeger.

GOLDBERG, H. 1987. *The inner male: Overcoming roadblocks to intimacy*. New York: New American Library.

GOLDSCHEIDER, F. K., AND J. DaVANZO. 1989. Pathways to independent living in early adulthood: Marriage, semiautonomy, and premarital residential independence. *Demography* 26, no. 4 (November): 597–614.

GOLDSCHEIDER, F. K., AND C. GOLDSCHEIDER. 1993. *Leaving home before marriage: Ethnicity, familism, and generational relationships*. Madison: University of Wisconsin Press.

GOLDSCHEIDER, F. K., AND L. J. WAITE. 1986. Sex differences in the entry into marriage. *American Journal of Sociology* 92, no. 1 (July): 91–109.

GOLDSCHEIDER, F. K., AND L. J. WAITE. 1987. Nest-leaving patterns and the transition to marriage for young men and women. *Journal of Marriage and the Family* 49 (August): 507–16.

GOLDSTEIN, A. 1991. Ruling sows distrust, D.C. area clinics say. *Washington Post*, May 24, A, A14.

GOMEZ, M. 1993. Breaking the cycle. *Hispanic* (August): 12.

GONYEA, J. G. 1994. The paradox of the advantaged elder and the feminization of poverty. *Social Work* 39, no. 1 (January): 35–41.

GOODE, E. 1990. *Deviant behavior*, 3rd ed. Englewood Cliffs, NJ: Prentice Hall.

GOODE, E., ET AL. 1994. Till death do them part? *U.S. News & World Report*, July 4, 24–28.

GOODE, W. J. 1963. *World revolution and family patterns*. New York: Free Press.

GOODE, W. J. 1993. *World changes in divorce patterns*. New Haven, CT: Yale University Press.

GOODMAN, E. 1993. A pill to make abortions private. *Baltimore Sun*, March 2, 11A.

GOODMAN, E. 1994a. Role models for the new male: Beast or simpleton? *Baltimore Sun*, July 19, 11A.

GOODMAN, E. 1994b. Good luck, mother. *Baltimore Sun*, August 1, 9A.

GOODMAN, E. 1994c. It's the others, not we, who lack family values. *Baltimore Sun*, November 22, 17A.

GOODMAN, S. 1995. Quest to cut welfare has states knocking on dads' doors. *Christian Science Monitor*, March 10, 1, 5.

GOODSTEIN, L., AND P. THOMAS. 1995. Clinic killings follow years of antiabortion violence. *Washington Post*, January 17, A1, A8.

GORDON, B. N., C. S. SCHROEDER, AND M. ABRAMS. 1990. Children's knowledge of sexuality: A comparison of sexually abused and nonabused children. *American Journal of Orthopsychiatry* 60, no. 2 (April): 250–57.

GORDON, L. H. 1993. Intimacy: The art of working out your relationships. *Psychology Today*, September/October, 40–43, 79–82.

GORDON, M. 1981. Was Waller ever right? The rating and dating complex reconsidered. *Journal of Marriage and the Family* 43 (February): 67–76.

GORDON, M., AND R. L. MILLER. 1984. Going steady in the 1980s: Exclusive relationships in six Connecticut high schools. *Sociology and Social Research* 68 (July): 462–79.

GORDON, S. 1986. What kids need to know. *Psychology Today*, October, 22–26.

GORDON, T. 1994. *Single women: On the margins?* New York: New York University Press.

GOSE, B. 1994. Spending time on the reservation. *Chronicle of Higher Education*, August 10, A30–A31.

GOSLIN, D. A., ED. 1969. *Handbook of socialization theory and research*. Chicago: Rand McNally.

GOTTMAN, J. 1994. What makes marriage work? *Psychology Today*, March/April, 38–43, 68.

GOTTMAN, J., AND N. SILVER. 1994. *Why marriages succeed or fail: What you can learn from the breakthrough research to make your marriage last*. New York: Simon & Schuster.

GOTTMAN, J. M. 1994. *What predicts divorce? The relationships between marital processes and marital outcome*. Hillsdale, NJ: Lawrence Erlbaum Associates.

GOTTMAN, J. M., AND L. J. KROKOFF. 1989. Marital interaction and satisfaction: A longitudinal view. *Journal of Consulting and Clinical Psychology* 57, no. 1, 47–52.

GOULTER, B., AND J. MINNINGER. 1993. *The father-daughter dance: Insight, inspiration, and understanding for every woman and her father*. New York: Putnam's.

GOVE, W. R. 1984. Gender differences in mental and physical illness: The effects of fixed roles and nurturant roles. *Social Science and Medicine* 19, 77–84.

GRADMAN, T. J. 1994. Masculine identity from work to retirement. In *Older men's lives*, ed. E. H. Thompson, Jr., 104–21. Thousand Oaks, CA: Sage.

GRAHAM, J. W., A. H. BELLER, AND P. M. HERNANDEZ. 1994. The effects of child support on educational attainment. In *Child support and child well-being*, ed. I. Garfinkel, S. S. McLanahan, and P. K. Robins, 317–54. Washington, DC: Urban Institute Press.

GRANT, J. P. 1991. *The state of the world's children, 1991*. New York: Oxford University Press.

GRAY, L. A., AND M. SARACINO. 1991. College students' attitudes, beliefs, and behaviors about AIDS: Implications for family life educators. *Family Relations* 40: 258–63.

GRAY, P. 1993. What is love? *Time*, February 15, 47–49.

GREELEY, A. M. 1991. *Faithful attraction: Discovering intimacy, love, and fidelity in American marriage*. New York: Tom Doherty Associates.

GREENBERG, J., AND T. PYSZCZYNSKI. 1985. Proneness to romantic jealousy and responses to jealousy in others. *Journal of Personality* 53, no. 3 (September): 468–79.

GREENBLATT, C. S. 1983. The salience of sexuality in the early years of marriage. *Journal of Marriage and the Family* 45 (May): 289–99.

GREENSTEIN, T. N. 1990. Marital disruption and the employment of married women. *Journal of Marriage and the Family* 52 (August): 657–76.

GREENWALD, E., AND H. LEITENBERG. 1989. Long-term effects of sexual experiences with siblings and nonsiblings during childhood. *Archives of Sexual Behavior* 18, 389–400.

GREENWOOD, V. D. 1990. *The researcher's guide to American genealogy*. Baltimore: Genealogical Publishing Co.

GREER, C. 1995. Something is robbing our children of their future. *Parade*, (March 4), 4–5.

GREER, G. 1992. *The change: Women, aging and the menopause*. New York: Knopf.

GREIF, G. L. 1990. *The daddy track and the single father*. Lexington, MA: Lexington Books

GRIGSBY, J. S. 1992. Women change places. *American Demographics* 14 (November): 46–50.

GRIMM-THOMAS, K., AND M. PERRY-JENKINS. 1994. All in a day's work: Job experiences, self-esteem, and fathering in working-class families. *Family Relations* 43, no. 2 (April): 174–81.

GRISWOLD, R. L. 1993. *Fatherhood in America: A history*. New York: Basic Books.

GROSS, H. E. 1993. Open adoption: A research-based literature review and new data. *Child Welfare* 72, no. 3 (May/June): 269–84.

GROSS, J., WITH R. SMOTHERS. 1994. In prom dispute, a town's race divisions emerge. *New York Times*, August 15, A10.

GROVER, K. J., C. S. RUSSELL, W. R. SCHUMM, AND L. A. PAFF-BERGEN. 1985. Mate selection processes and marital satisfaction. *Family Relations* 34 (July): 383–86.

GROVES, E. R. 1928. *The marriage crisis*. New York: Longmans, Green.

GROZE, V. K., AND J. A. ROSENTHAL. 1991. Single parents and their adopted children: A psychosocial analysis. *Families in Society* 72, no. 2 (February): 67–77.

GRUSON, L. 1985. Jewish singles groups play matchmakers to preserve the future of Judaism. *New York Times*, April 1, B1, B2.

GUBERMAN, N., P. MAHEU, AND C. MAILLÉ. 1992. Women as family caregivers: Why do they care? *The Gerontologist* 32, no. 5, 607–17.

GUEST, J. 1988. *The mythic family*. Minneapolis, MN: Milkweed.

GUNDERSON, M. 1994. *Comparable worth and gender discrimination: An international perspective*. Washington, DC: International Labor Office.

GUPTA, G. R. 1979. Love, arranged marriage and the Indian social structure. In *Cross-cultural perspectives of mate-selection and marriage*, ed. G. Kurian, 169–79. Westport, CT: Greenwood.

GUTMAN, H. 1976. *The black family in slavery and freedom, 1750–1925*. New York: Pantheon.

GUTTMAN M., WITH D. McGRATH AND J. J. SIEDER. 1994. Separating the sisters. *U.S. News & World Report*, March 28, 49–50.

GWARTNEY-GIBBS, P. A. 1986. The institutionalization of premarital cohabitation: Estimates from marriage license applications, 1970 and 1980. *Journal of Marriage and the Family* 48 (May): 423–34.

GWARTNEY-GIBBS, P., AND J. STOCKER. 1989. Courtship aggression and mixed sex groups. In *Violence in dating relationships*, ed. M. Pirog-Good and J. Stets, 185–204. New York: Praeger.

HAAS, L. 1980. Role-sharing couples: A study of egalitarian marriages. *Family Relations* 29 (July): 289–96.

HAAS, L. 1992. *Equal parenthood and social policy: A study of parental leave in Sweden*. Albany: State University of New York Press.

HACKER, A. 1992. *Two nations: Black and white, separate, hostile, unequal*. New York: Ballantine.

HACKETT, G., WITH A. McDANIEL. 1989. Making a home in the White House. *Newsweek*, January 16, 32–33.

HAFFNER, D. W. 1993. Toward a new paradigm on adolescent sexual health. *Siecus Report* 21, no. 2, 26–30.

HAGE, D., L. GRANT, AND J. IMPOCO. 1993. White collar wasteland. *U.S. News & World Report*, June 28, 42–51.

HAHN, B. A. 1993. Marital status and women's health: The effect of economic marital acquisitions. *Journal of Marriage and the Family* 55 (May): 495–504.

HAIKEN, M. 1992. Liquor ads targeted at Indians dismay some tribal leaders. *Washington Post Health Supplement*, September 22, 11–12.

HALL, M. 1991. Foes successfully chip away at abortion rights. *USA Today*, June 3, 6A.

HALL, T. 1987. Infidelity and women: Shifting patterns. *New York Times*, June 1, B8.

HALPERN, S. 1989. Infertility: Playing the odds. *Ms.*, January/February, 147–51, 154–56.

HAMBURG, D. A. 1993. The American family transformed. *Society* 30, no. 2 (January): 60–69.

HAMER, D. H., S. HU, V. MAGNUSON, N. HU, AND A. M. L. PATTATUCCI. 1993. A linkage between DNA markers on the X chromosome and male sexual orientation. *Science*, July 16, 321–27.

HAMMER, J. A. 1992. Must blacks be buffoons? *Newsweek*, October 26, 70–71.

HAMON, R. R. 1992. Filial role enactment by adult children. *Family Relations* 41 (January): 91–96.

HANCOCK, L., ET AL. 1995. Putting working moms in custody. *Newsweek*, March 13, 54–57.

HANER, J., AND J. B. O'DONNELL. 1995. America's most wanted welfare plan. *Baltimore Sun*, January 24, A1, 8A.

HANSON, R. K., R. GIZZARELLI, AND H. SCOTT. 1994. The attitudes of incest offenders: Sexual entitlement and acceptance of sex with children. *Criminal Justice and Behavior* 21, no. 2 (June): 187–202.

HANSON, S. M. H., M. L. HEIMS, D. J. JULIAN, AND M. B. SUSSMAN. 1994. *Single parent families: Diversity, myths and realities*. New York: Haworth.

HARARI, S. E., AND M. A. VINOVSKIS. 1993. Adolescent sexuality, pregnancy, and childbearing in the past. In *The politics of pregnancy: Adolescent sexuality and public policy*, ed. A. Lawson and D. I. Rhode, 23–45. New Haven, CT: Yale University Press.

HARDIE, E. T. L., ED. 1994. *Internet: Mailing lists*. Englewood Cliffs, NJ: Prentice-Hall.

HARDING, W., AND A. VECIANA-SUAREZ. 1993. One & only. *Baltimore Sun*, December 5, K1, 8K.

HAREVEN, T. K. 1984. Themes in the historical development of the family. In *Review of child development research*, Vol. 7, *The family*, ed. R. D. Parke, 137–78. Chicago: University of Chicago Press.

HARJO, S. S. 1993. The American Indian experience. In *Family ethnicity: Strength in diversity*, ed. H. P. McAdoo, 199–207. Newbury Park, CA: Sage.

HARLOW, H., AND M. HARLOW. 1962.

Social deprivation in monkeys. *Scientific American* 206, 1–10.

HARMS, T. 1989. The 12 building blocks of discipline. *Parents,* August, 76–78, 81–82.

HARRINGTON, M., AND M. LEVINSON. 1985. The perils of a dual economy. *Dissent* 32: 417–26.

HARRIS, D. 1995. Salary survey: 1995. *Working Woman,* January, 25–34.

HARRIS, D. K. 1990. *Sociology of aging,* 2nd ed. New York: Harper & Row.

HARRIS, J. L. 1992. The portrayal of the black family in primetime network television: A look at stereotypic images and disorganization of family structure. *Journal of Intergroup Relations* 19, no 1 (Spring): 44–58.

HARRIS, M 1994. *Down from the pedestal: Moving beyond idealized images of womanhood.* New York: Doubleday.

HARRIS, R. 1994. Major's school for scandal. *Vanity Fair,* April, 134–40, 176.

HARRISON, A., F. SERAFICA, AND H. MCADOO. 1984. Ethnic families of color. In *Review of child development research,* Vol. 7, *The family,* ed. R. D. Parke, 329–71. Chicago: University of Chicago Press.

HARRY, J. 1983. Gay males and lesbian relationships. In *Contemporary families and alternative lifestyles: Handbook on research and theory,* ed. E. D. Macklin and R. H. Rubin, 216–34. Beverly Hills, CA: Sage.

HARRY, J. 1988. Some problems of gay/lesbian families. In *Variant family forms,* Families in Trouble series, vol. 5, ed. C. S. Chilman, E. W. Nunnally, and F. M. Cox, 96–113. Beverly Hills, CA: Sage.

HART, B. 1993. Battered women and the criminal justice system. *American Behavioral Scientist* 36, no. 5 (May): 624–38.

HARTMAN, A. 1993. Challenges for family policy. In *Normal family processes,* 2nd ed., ed. F. Walsh, 474–502. New York: Guilford.

HARTMAN, S. 1988. Arranged marriages live on. *New York Times,* August 10, C12.

HASS, A. 1979. *Teenage sexuality: A survey of teenage sexual behavior.* New York: Macmillan.

HASTINGS, D. 1994. Battered men continue to have no place to go. *Baltimore Sun,* August 1, 1D, 5D.

HATCHER, R. A., ET AL. 1990. *Contraceptive technology 1990–1992,* 15th ed. New York: Irvington.

HATCHETT, S. J. 1991. Women and men. In *Life in black America,* ed. J. S. Jackson, 84–104. Newbury Park, CA: Sage.

HATCHETT, S. J., AND J. S. JACKSON. 1993. African American extended kin systems: An assessment. In *Family ethnicity: Strength in diversity,* ed. H. P. McAdoo, 90–108. Newbury Park, CA: Sage.

HATFIELD, E. 1983. What do women and men want from love and sex? In *Changing boundaries: Gender roles and sexual behavior,* ed. E. R. Allgeier and N. B. McCormick, 106–34. Mountain View, CA: Mayfield.

HATFIELD, E., AND G. W. WALSTER. 1981. *A new look at love.* Reading, MA: Addison-Wesley.

HAWKE, D. F. 1988. *Everyday life in early America.* New York: Harper & Row.

HAWKINS, A. J., S. L. CHRISTIANSEN, K. P. SARGENT, AND E. J. HILL. 1993. Rethinking fathers' involvement in child care: A developmental perspective. *Journal of Family Issues* 14, no. 4 (December): 531–49.

HAWKINS, B. 1991. Glass ceiling low for minorities, women, U.S. says. *Baltimore Sun,* August 9, 1A, 3A.

HAYES, C. D. 1987. *Risking the future: Adolescent sexuality, pregnancy, and childbearing.* Washington, DC: National Academy Press.

HAYES, P. 1993. Transracial adoption: Politics and ideology. *Child Welfare* 72, no. 3 (May/June): 301–10.

HAYGHE, H. V. 1994. Are women leaving the labor force? *Monthly Labor Review* 117, no. 7 (July): 37–39.

HAYGHE, H. V., AND S. M. BIANCHI. 1994. Married mothers' work patterns: The job-family compromise. *Monthly Labor Review* (June): 24–30.

HAZAN, C., AND P. R. SHAVER. 1987. Conceptualizing romantic love as an attachment process. *Journal of Personality and Social Psychology* 52, 511–24.

HEATON, T. B. 1990. Marital stability throughout the child-rearing years. *Demography* 27, no. 1 (February): 55–63.

HEATON, T. B., D. T. LICHTER, AND A. AMOETENG. 1989. The timing of family formation: Rural-urban differentials in first intercourse, childbirth, and marriage. *Rural Sociology* 54, no. 1, 1–16.

HECHT, M. L., M. J. COLLIER AND S. A. RIBEAU. 1993. *African American communication: Ethnic identity and cultural interpretation.* Newbury Park, CA: Sage.

HECHT, M. L., P. J. MARSTON, AND L. K. LARKEY. 1994. Love ways and relationship quality in heterosexual relationships. *Journal of Social and Personal Relationships* 11, no. 1, 25–43.

HECHTMAN, S B., AND R. ROSENTHAL. 1991. Teacher gender and nonverbal behavior in the teaching of gender-stereotyped materials. *Journal of Applied Social Psychology* 21, no. 6, 446–59.

HEISE, L. L., WITH J. PITANGUY AND A. GERMAIN. 1994. *Violence against women: The hidden burden.* Washington, DC: World Bank.

HEISS, J. 1986. Family roles and behavior. In *Sex roles and social patterns,* ed. F. A. Boudreau, R. S. Sennott, and M. Wilson, 84–120. New York: Praeger.

HELLER, S. 1993. Scholars debunk the Marlboro man: Examining stereotypes of masculinity. *Chronicle of Higher Education,* February 3, A6, A7, A10.

HELM, L. 1993. Japanese prince finally gets a "yes." *Baltimore Sun,* January 7, 9A.

HENDIN, H. 1982. *Suicide in America.* New York: Norton.

HENDRICK, C., AND S. HENDRICK. 1992a. *Liking, loving and relating,* 2nd ed. Monterey, CA: Brooks/Cole.

HENDRICK, S. S., AND C. HENDRICK. 1992b. *Romantic love.* Newbury Park, CA: Sage.

HENDRICKSON, M. L. 1994. Couples should fight for a good marriage. *U.S. Catholic* 59, no. 4 (April): 20–25.

HENNEBERGER, M. 1994. Secrets of long life from 2 who ought to know. *New York Times,* Oct. 10, B1, B10.

HENRY, S. 1995. America's hidden disease. *Parade,* February 12, 4–6.

HENRY, W. A. III, AND L. WHITAKER. 1990. A muchness of maleness. *Time,* October 15, 90–92.

HENTON, J., R. CATE, S. LLOYD AND S. CHRISTOPHER. 1983. Romance and violence in dating relationships. *Journal of Family Issues* 4, 467–82.

HERBERT, C. 1989. *Talking of silence: The sexual harassment of schoolgirls.* New York: Falmer.

HERDT, G., AND A. BOXER. 1992. Introduction: Culture, history, and life course of gay men. In *Gay culture in America: Essays from the field,* ed. G. Herdt. Boston: Beacon.

HERMAN, D. L. 1989. The rape culture. In *Women: A feminist perspective,* 4th ed., ed. J. Freeman, 20–44. Mountain View, CA: Mayfield.

HERMAN, R. 1992. Depression in widows. *Washington Post Family and Retirement Supplement,* April 29, 10–11.

HERMAN, R. 1994. Whatever happened to the contraceptive revolution? *Washington Post Health Supplement,* December 13, 12–15.

HERMELIN, F. G. 1994. How well is family leave really working? *Working Woman* (September): 9.

HEROD, A. 1993. Gender issues in the use of interviewing as a research method. *The Professional Geographer* 45 (August): 305–17.

HEROLD, E. S., AND D.-M. K. MEWHINNEY. 1993. Gender differences in casual sex and AIDS prevention: A survey of dating bars. *Journal of Sex Research* 30, no. 1 (February): 36–42.

HERRNSTEIN, R. J., AND C. MURRAY. 1994. *The bell curve: Intelligence and class structure in American life.* New York: Free Press.

HERRSTROM, S. 1990. Sweden: Prochoice on child care. *New Perspectives Quarterly* 7, no. 1 (Winter): 27–30.

HERSHATTER, G. 1984. Making a friend: Changing patterns of courtship in urban China. *Pacific Affairs* 57 (Summer): 237–51.

HERTZ, R., AND J. CHARLTON. 1989. Making family under a shiftwork schedule: Air force security guards and their wives. *Social Problems* 36, no. 5 (December): 491–507.

HETHERINGTON, E. M. 1989. Coping with family transitions: Winners, losers, and survivors. *Child Development* 60, 1–18.

HETHERINGTON, E. M. 1993. An overview of the Virginia Longitudinal Study of divorce and remarriage with a focus on early adolescence. *Journal of Family Psychology* 7, no. 1 (June): 39–57.

HETHERINGTON, E. M., AND W. G. CLINGEMPEEL. 1992. Coping with marital transitions: A family systems perspective. *Monographs of the Society for Research in Child Development* 57, 2–3, serial no. 227.

HETHERINGTON, E. M., T. C. LAW, AND T. G. O'CONNOR. 1993. Divorce: Challenges, changes, and new chances. In *Normal Family Processes,* 2nd ed., ed. F. Walsh, 208–34. New York: Guilford.

HETRICK, R. 1994. London Fog workers swallow pride, cuts. *Baltimore Sun,* September 27, A1, A14.

HEWLETT, S. A. 1990. The feminization of the work force. *New Perspectives Quarterly* 7, no. 1 (Winter): 13–15.

HEYN, D. 1992. *The erotic silence of the American wife.* New York: Turtle Bay Books.

HIAASEN, R. 1994. Don't trust your teens? Try putting a tail on 'em. *Baltimore Sun,* January 5, 1A, 11A.

HIGGINS, C., L. DUXBURY, AND C. LEE. 1994. Impact of life-cycle stage and gender on the ability to balance work and family responsibilities. *Family Relations* 43, no. 2 (April): 144–50.

HILL, C. T., R. RUBIN, AND L. A. PEPLAU. 1976. Breakups before marriage: The end of one hundred three affairs. *Journal of Social Issues* 32, no. 1 (Winter): 147–68.

HILL, R. B., ET AL. 1993. *Research on the African-American family: A holistic perspective.* Westport, CT: Auburn House.

HINSCH, B. 1990. *Passions of the cut sleeve: The male homosexual tradition in China.* Berkeley: University of California Press.

HIRSCHEL, J. D., AND I. W. HUTCHISON, III. 1992. Female spouse abuse and the police response: The Charlotte, North Carolina, experiment. *Journal of Criminal Law & Criminology* 83, no. 1: 73–119.

HIRSH, J. 1988. Modern matchmaking: Money's allure in marketing mates and marriage. *New York Times,* September 19, B4.

HITE, S. 1981. *The Hite report on male sexuality.* New York: Knopf.

HITE, S. 1987. *Women and love: A cultural revolution in progress.* New York: Knopf.

HOBART, C. W. 1958. The incidence of romanticism during courtship. *Social Forces* 36 (May): 362–67.

HOCHSCHILD, A., WITH A. MACHUNG. 1989. *The second shift: Working parents and the revolution at home.* New York: Penguin.

HODSON, D., AND P. SKEEN. 1987. Child sexual abuse: A review of research and theory with implications for family life educators. *Family Relations* 36, 215–21.

HOFFMAN, J. 1995. Divorced fathers make gains in battles to increase rights. *New York Times,* April 26, B1, B5.

HOFFMAN, K. L., D. H. DEMO, AND J. N. EDWARDS. 1994. Physical wife abuse in a non-western society: An integrated theoretical approach. *Journal of Marriage and the Family* 56 (February): 131–46.

HOFFMAN, L. W. 1989. Effects of maternal employment in the two-parent family. *American Psychologist* 44, 283–92.

HOGAN, D. P., L.-X. HAO, AND W. L. PARISH. 1990. Race, kin networks, and assistance to mother-headed families. *Social Forces* 68, 797–812.

HOHN, C. 1987. The family life cycle: Needed extensions of the concept. In *Family demography: Methods and their application,* ed. J. Bongaarts, T. K. Burch, and K. W. Wachter, 65–80. Oxford: Clarendon.

HOLCOMB, B. 1995. Working mothers on trial. *Working Mother* (January): 29–31.

HOLDEN, G. W., AND K. L. RITCHIE. 1991. Linking extreme marital discord, child rearing, and child behavior problems: Evidence from battered women. *Child Development* 62, 311–27.

HOLLAND, D. C., AND M. A. EISENHART. 1990. *Educated in romance: Women, achievement, and college culture.* Chicago: University of Chicago Press.

HOLMAN, T. B., AND W. R. BURR. 1980. Beyond the beyond: The growth of family theories in the 1970s. *Journal of Marriage and the Family* 42, no. 4 (November): 729–41.

HOLMES, S. A. 1994. A generally healthy America emerges in a census report. *New York Times,* October 13, B13.

HOLMSTROM, D. 1994. Gambling ventures reverse poverty for only some Indians. *Christian Science Monitor,* July 8, 3.

HOLTZMAN, E. M. 1982. The pursuit of married love: Women's attitudes toward sexuality and marriage in Great Britain, 1918–1939. *Journal of Social History* 16 (Winter): 39–51.

HONEY, M. 1984. *Creating Rosie the Riveter: Class, gender, and propaganda.* Amherst: University of Massachusetts Press.

HONG, S.-M., AND S. FAEDDA. 1994. Ranking of romantic acts by an Australian sample. *Psychological Reports* 74, 471–74.

HOON, S. J. 1993. Farming for brides. *Far Eastern Economic Review,* March 4, 24.

HOOYMAN, N. R., AND H. A. KIYAK. 1991. *Social gerontology: A multidisciplinary perspective,* 2nd ed. Boston: Allyn & Bacon.

HOPSON, D., AND D. P. HOPSON. 1993. *Raising the rainbow generation: Teaching your children to be successful in a multicultural society.* New York: Fireside.

HOPSON, D. P., AND D. S. HOPSON. 1990. *Different and wonderful: Raising black children in a race-conscious society.* New York: Prentice Hall.

HORN, M. 1993. Grief re-examined.

U.S. News & World Report, June 14, 81–84.

HORNUNG, C. A., AND B. C. McCUL-LOUGH. 1981. Status relationships in dual-employment marriages: Consequences for psychological well-being. *Journal of Marriage and the Family* 43: 125–41.

HORTON, H. D., AND N. J. BURGESS. 1992. Where are the black men? Regional differences in the pool of marriageable black males in the United States. *National Journal of Sociology* 6, no. 1 (Summer): 3–19.

HOUSEKNECHT, S. K. 1982. Voluntary childlessness in the 1980s: A significant increase? In *Alternatives to traditional family living*, ed. H. Gross and M. B. Sussman, 51–69. New York: Haworth.

HOWARD, M., AND J. B. McCABE. 1990. Helping teenagers postpone sexual involvement. *Family Planning Perspectives* 22, no. 1 (January/February): 21–26.

HOWE, R. F. 1991. Fertility doctor accused of using his own sperm. *Washington Post*, November 20, A1, A38.

HSU, F. L. K. 1981. *Americans and Chinese: Passage to differences*, 3rd ed. Honolulu: University Press of Hawaii.

HUBBELL, L. J. 1993. Values under siege in Mexico: Strategies for sheltering traditional values from change. *Journal of Anthropological Research* 49, no. 1 (Spring): 1–16.

HUBER, J., AND B. E. SCHNEIDER, EDS. 1992. *The social context of AIDS*. Newbury Park, CA: Sage

HUDAK, M. A. 1993. Gender schema theory revisited: Men's stereotypes of American women. *Sex Roles* 28, nos. 5/6, 279–92.

HUDSON, J. W., AND L. F. HENZE. 1969. Campus values in mate selection: A replication. *Journal of Marriage and the Family* 31 (November): 772–75.

HUGHES, C. 1991. *Stepparents: Wicked or wonderful?* Brookfield, VT: Avebury.

HUGHES, D. L., AND E. GALINSKY. 1994. Gender, job and family conditions, and psychological symptoms. *Psychology of Women Quarterly* 18, 251–70.

HUGHEY, A. M. 1990. The incomes of recent female immigrants to the United States. *Social Science Quarterly* 71, no. 2 (June): 383–90.

HUNT, J. 1991. Ten reasons not to hit your kids. In *Breaking down the wall of silence: The liberating experience of facing painful trust*, ed. A. Miller, 168–71. Meridian, NY: Dutton.

HUNT, M. M. 1969. *The affair: A portrait of extra-marital love in contemporary America*. New York: World.

HUNT, M. M. 1974. *Sexual behavior in the 1970s*. Chicago: Playboy Press.

HUNTLEY, T., ED. 1991. *Helping children grieve: When someone they love dies*. Minneapolis, MN: Augsburg Press.

HUPKA, R. B., B. DUUNK, G. FALUS, A. FULGOSI, E. ORTEGA, R. SWAIN, AND N. V. TARABRINA. 1985. Romantic jealousy and romantic envy: A seven nation study. *Journal of Cross-Cultural Psychology* 16 (December): 423–46.

HUSBANDS, R. 1992. Sexual harassment law in employment: An international perspective. *International Labour Review* 131, no. 6, 535–59.

HUTTER, M. 1988. *The changing family: Comparative perspectives*, 2nd ed. New York: Macmillan.

HUTTER, M. 1991. *The family experience: A reader in cultural diversity*. New York: Macmillan.

HUZINGA, D., R. LOEBER, AND T. P. THORNBERRY. 1993. Longitudinal study of delinquency, drug use, sexual activity, and pregnancy among children and youth in three cities. *Public Health Reports* 108, supp. 1, 90–96.

HYER, M. 1988. Choice of black woman as bishop generates Episcopalian conflict. *Washington Post*, December 4, A3.

IDLE, T., E. WOOD, AND S. DESMARAIS, 1993. Gender role socialization in toy play situations: Mothers and fathers with their sons and daughters. *Sex Roles* 28 (November/December): 679–91.

IHINGER-TALLMAN, M., AND K. PASLEY. 1987. *Remarriage*. Beverly Hills, CA: Sage.

Illinois Coalition Against Sexual Assault. 1993. *Sexual violence: Facts and statistics*. Springfield.

IMBER-BLACK, E., AND J. ROBERTS. 1993. Family change: Don't cancel holidays! *Psychology Today*, March/April: 62, 64, 92–93.

IMPOCO, J. 1990. Motherhood and the future of Japan. *U.S. News & World Report*, December 24, 56–57.

IMPOCO, J., AND M. THARP. 1994. California tries to give back the tired and the poor. *U.S. News & World Report*, November 21, 42.

INGRASSIA, M., AND M. BECK. 1994. Patterns of abuse. *Newsweek*, July 4, 26–33.

INGRASSIA, M., AND J. McCORMICK.

1994. Why leave children with bad parents? *Newsweek*, April 25, 52–58.

INGRASSIA, M., WITH J. McCORMICK, K. SPRINGEN AND M. BRANT. 1993. Stalked to death? *Newsweek*, November 1, 1993, 27–28.

INGRASSIA, M., WITH T. PAYOR AND C. FRIDAY. 1993. Boy meets girl, boy beats girl. *Newsweek*, December 13, 66–68.

INGRASSIA, M., WITH M. ROSSI. 1994. The limits of tolerance? *Newsweek*, February 14, 47.

INGRASSIA, M., AND K. SPRINGEN. 1993. Living on Dracula time. *Newsweek*, July 12, 68 69.

INGRASSIA, M., AND K. SPRINGEN. 1994. She's not Baby Jessica anymore. *Newsweek*, March 21, 60–65.

INGRASSIA, M., AND K. SPRINGEN. 1993. Standing up for fathers. *Newsweek*, May 3, 52–53.

INGRASSIA, M., ET AL. 1993. Endangered family. *Newsweek*, August 30, 17–30.

INGRASSIA, M., ET AL. 1994. America's new wave of runaways. *Newsweek*, April 4, 64–65.

Institute for Philosophy and Public Policy. 1989. *Surrogate motherhood* 9, no. 1 (Winter): 1–5.

IRELAND, M. S. 1993. *Reconceiving women: Separating motherhood from female identity*. New York: Guilford.

IRVINE, J. M., ED. 1994. *Sexual cultures and the construction of adolescent identities*. Philadelphia, PA: Temple University Press.

IRVING, H. H., AND M. BENJAMIN. 1991. Shared and sole-custody parents: A comparative analysis. In *Joint custody and shared parenting*, 2nd ed., ed. J. Folberg, 114–31. New York: Guilford.

ISHII-KUNTZ, M. 1993. Japanese fathers: Work demands and family roles. In *Men, work and family*, ed. J. C. Hood, 45–67. Newbury Park, CA: Sage.

ISHII-KUNTZ, M., AND S. COLTRANE. 1992. Remarriage, stepparenting, and household labor. *Journal of Family Issues* 13, no. 2 (June): 215–33.

ISHII-KUNTZ, M., AND G. R. LEE. 1987. Status of the elderly: An extension of the theory. *Journal of Marriage and the Family* 49 (May): 413–20.

ISHWARAN, K., ED. 1989. *Family and marriage: Cross-cultural perspectives*. Toronto: Wall & Thompson.

IWAO, S. 1993. *The Japanese women: Traditional image and changing reality*. New York: Free Press.

JACKLIN, C. N., AND L. A. BAKER. 1993. Early gender development. In *Gender issues in contemporary society*, ed. S. Oskamp and M. Costanzo, 41–57. Newbury Park, CA: Sage.

JACKSON, D. 1992. *How to make the world a better place for women in five minutes a day*. New York: Hyperion.

JACKSON, J. S., ED. 1991. *Life in black America*. Newbury Park, CA: Sage.

JACOBS, F. H., AND M. W. DAVIES. 1991. Rhetoric or reality? Child and family policy in the United States. *Social Policy Report* 5, no. 4, 1–25.

JACOBS, J. L. 1990. Reassessing mother blame in incest. *Signs* 15, no. 3 (Spring): 500–14.

JACOBS, K. 1994. Robobabes: Why girls don't play video games. *International Design Magazine* 41, no. 3 (May/June): 38–45.

JACOBSEN, L., AND B. EDMONDSON. 1994. Father figures. *American Demographics, Parenting Reprint Package*, 31–37.

JACOBSON, A. R. 1994. Changing with the times. *Hispanic* (March): 20–30.

JACOBSON, N. S., AND M. E. ADDIS. 1993. Research on couples and couples therapy: What do we know? Where are we going? *Journal of Clinical and Consulting Psychology* 61, no. 1, 85–93.

JAIMES, M. A., WITH T. HALSEY. 1992. American Indian women: At the center of indigenous resistance in contemporary North America. In *The state of Native America: Genocide, colonization, and resistance*, ed. M. A. James, 311–44. Boston: South End Press.

JAMES, F. 1994. The black middle class. *Ebony*, August: 92–96.

JAMES, J. W., AND F. CHERRY. 1988. *The grief recovery handbook: A step-by-step program for moving beyond loss*. New York: Harper & Row.

JANKOWIAK, W. R., AND E. F. FISCHER. 1992. A cross-cultural perspective on romantic love. *Ethnology* 31, no. 2 (April) 149–55.

JARRETT, R. L. 1994. Living poor: Family life among single parent, African-American women. *Social Problems* 41, no. 1 (February): 30–49.

JARRETT, W. H. 1985. Caregiving within kinship systems: Is affection really necessary? *The Gerontologist* 25, no. 1, 5–10.

JAYAKODY, R., L. M. CHATTERS, AND R. J. TAYLOR. 1993. Family support to single and married African American mothers: The provision of financial, emotional, and child-care assistance.

Journal of Marriage and the Family 55 (May): 261–76.

JEMMOTT III, J. B., AND K. L. ASHBY. 1989. Romantic commitment and the perceived availability of opposite-sex persons: On loving the one you're with. *Journal of Applied Social Psychology* 19, no. 14, 1198–211.

JENDREK, M. P. 1993. Grandparents who parent their grandchildren: Effects on lifestyle. *Journal of Marriage and the Family* 55 (August): 609–621.

JENDREK, M. P. 1994. Grandparents who parent their grandchildren: Circumstances and decisions. *The Gerontologist* 34, no. 2, 206–16.

JENKINS, S., AND B. DIAMOND. 1985. Ethnicity and foster care: Census data as predictors of placement variables. *American Journal of Orthopsychiatry* 55, no. 2 (April): 267–76.

JENNINGS, J. ED. 1994. *Blacks, Latinos, and Asians in urban America: Status and prospects for politics and activism*. Westport, CT: Praeger.

JERROME, D. 1994. Time, change and continuity in family life. *Aging and Society* 14 (March): 1–27.

Jet. 1993a. Montel Williams blasts critics of his white wife. December 20, 54–55.

Jet. 1993b. White House cook sues after threats arise over his interracial marriage. July 12, 12–13.

JI, Y. 1993. China's new matchmakers. *Beijing Review*, May 24, 27–28.

JOESCH, J. M. 1994. Children and the timing of women's paid work after childbirth: A further specification of the relationship. *Journal of Marriage and the Family* 56 (May): 429–40.

JOHN, L. 1994. The travel and bridal industries find honeymoons most enjoyable. *Christian Science Monitor*, June 30, 8.

JOHN, R. 1988. The Native American family. In *Ethnic families in America: Patterns and variations*, 3rd ed., ed. C. H. Mindel, R. W. Habenstein, and R. Wright, Jr., 325–66. New York: Elsevier.

JOHNSON, C. 1992. *Lucky in love: The secrets of happy couples and how their marriages thrive*. New York: Penguin.

JOHNSON, C. L. 1985. The impact of illness on late-life marriages. *Journal of Marriage and the Family* 47 (February): 165–72.

JOHNSON, C. L. 1993. The prolongation of life and the extension of family relationships: The families of the oldest old. In *Family, self, and society: Toward a new agenda for family research*, ed. P. A. Cowan, D. Field, D.

A. Hansen, A. Skolnick, and G. E. Swanson, 317–30. Hillsdale, NJ: Lawrence Erlbaum Associates.

JOHNSON, D. 1989. Skeptical singles ask detectives to check their dates. *Baltimore Sun*, December 11, 1A, 11A.

JOHNSON, G. D., G. J. PALILEO, AND N. B. GRAY. 1992. Date rape on a southern campus: Reports from 1991. *Sociology and Social Research* 76, no. 2 (January): 37–41.

JOHNSON, R. 1985. Stirring the oatmeal. In *Challenge of the heart: Love, sex, and intimacy in changing times*, ed. J. Welwood. Boston: Shambhala.

JOHNSON, S. 1984–85. Sexual intimacy and replacement children after the death of a child. *Omega* 15, no. 2, 109–18.

JOHNSON, S., AND H. E. MARANO. 1994. Love: The immutable longing for contact. *Psychology Today*, March/April, 33–37, 64ff.

JOHNSON, W. R., AND D. M. WARREN, EDS. 1993. *Inside the mixed marriage: Accounts of changing attitudes, patterns, and perceptions of cross-cultural and interracial marriages*. Lanham, MD: University Press of America.

JOHNSTON, J. R., AND L. E. G. CAMPBELL. 1993. A clinical typology of interparental violence in disputed-custody divorces. *American Journal of Orthopsychiatry* 63 (April): 190–99.

JONES, A. 1994. *Next time, she'll be dead: Battering and how to stop it*. Boston: Beacon.

JONES, A., AND S. SCHECHTER. 1992. *When love goes wrong: What to do when you can't do anything right*. New York: HarperCollins.

JONES, C. 1994. Living single. *Essence*, May, 138–40.

JONES, E. F., AND J. D. FORREST. 1992. Contraceptive failure rates based on the 1988 National Survey of Family Growth. *Family Planning Perspectives*, January 1, 12.

JONES, E. F., J. D. FORREST, N. GOLDMAN, S. HENSHAW, R. LINCOLN, J. I. ROSOLL, C. F. WESTOFF, AND D. WULF. 1986. Teenage pregnancy in industrialized countries. New Haven, CT: Yale University Press.

JONES, J. 1985. *Labor of love, labor of sorrow: Black women, work and the family from slavery to the present*. New York: Basic Books.

JONES, R. K. 1993. Female victim perceptions of the causes of male spouse abuse. *Sociological Inquiry* 63, no. 3. (August): 351–61.

JORDAN, M. 1990. Area divorce rates dive in 10 years: Later marriages, more partnerships cited, but risk still high. *Washington Post*, August 9, A1, A10.

KAFFMAN. M. 1993. Kibbutz youth: Recent past and present. *Journal of Youth and Adolescence* 22, no. 6 (December): 573–604.

KAGAN, S. L., AND B. WEISSBOURD, EDS. 1994. *Putting families first: America's family support movement and the challenge of change*. San Francisco: Jossey-Bass.

KAHANA, E., D. E. BIEGEL, AND M. L. WYKLE, EDS. 1994. *Family caregiving across the lifespan*. Thousand Oaks, CA: Sage.

KAHNE, H. 1992. Progress or stalemate? A cross-national comparison of women's status and roles. In *Women's work and women's lives: The continuing struggle worldwide*, ed. H. Kahne and J. Z. Giele, 279–301. Boulder, CO: Westview.

KAIN, E. I., 1990. *The myth of family decline: Understanding families in a world of rapid social change*. New York: Lexington Books.

KALMIJN, M. 1993. Trends in black/white intermarriage. *Social Forces* 72, no. 1 (September): 119–146.

KAMO, Y. 1990. Husbands and wives living in nuclear and stem family households in Japan. *Sociological Perspectives* 33, no. 3, 397–417.

KANE, E. W., AND L. J. MACAULAY. 1993. Interviewer gender and gender attitudes. *Public Opinion Quarterly* 57, 1–28.

KANIN, E. G., K. R. DAVIDSON, AND S. R. SCHECK. 1970. A research note on male-female differentials in the experience of heterosexual love. *Journal of Sex Research* 6, no. 1 (February): 64–72.

KANIN, E. J. 1984. Date rape: Unofficial criminals and victims. *Victimology* 9, no. 1, 95–108.

KANTOR, G. K., AND M. A. STRAUS. 1987. The "drunken bum" theory of wife beating. *Social Problems* 34, no. 3 (June): 213–30.

KANTOR, R. M. 1970. Communes. *Psychology Today*, July, 53–57, 78.

KANTROWITZ, B. 1989. Trapped inside her own world. *Newsweek*, December 18, 56–58.

KANTROWITZ, B., WITH T. BARRETT, K. SPRINGEN, M. HAGER, L. WRIGHT, G. CARROLL, AND D. ROSENBERG. 1991. Striking a nerve. *Newsweek*, October 21, 34–40.

KANTROWITZ, B., WITH A. COHEN AND M. DISSLY. 1990. Whose baby will it be? *Newsweek*, August 27, 66.

KANTROWITZ, B., WITH D. ROSENBERG ET AL., 1994. Men, women & computers. *Newsweek*, May 16, 48–55.

KANTROWITZ, B., WITH K. SPRINGEN, L. DENWORTH, AND P. WINGERT. 1990. Can the boys be saved? *Newsweek*, October 15, 67.

KANTROWITZ, B., WITH P. WINGERT, N. DE LA PENA, J. GORDON, AND T. PADGETT. 1990. The crack children. *Newsweek*, February 12, 62–63.

KANTROWITZ, B., WITH P. WINGERT, D. ROSENBERG, V. QUADE, AND D. FOOTE. 1992. Breaking the divorce cycle. *Newsweek*, January 13, 48–53.

KAPLAN, D. A., WITH S. D. LEWIS AND J. HAMMER. 1993. Is it torture or tradition? *Newsweek*, December 20, 124.

KAPLAN, G. A., AND W. J. STRAWBRIDGE. 1994. Behavioral and social factors in healthy aging. In *Aging and quality of life*, ed. R. P. Abeles, H. C. Gift and M. G. Ory, 57–78. New York: Springer.

KAPLAN, N., J. K. WHITMORE, AND M. H. CHOY. 1989. *The boat people and achievement in America: A study of family life, hard work, and cultural values*. Ann Arbor: University of Michigan Press.

KAPRIO, J., M. KOSKENVUO, AND H. RITA. 1987. Mortality after bereavement: A prospective study of 95,647 widowed persons. *American Journal of Public Health* 77, 283–87.

KARANJA, W. W. 1987. "Outside wives" and "inside wives" in Nigeria: A study of changing perceptions of marriage. In *Transformations of African marriage*, ed. D. Parkin and D. Nyamwaya, 247–61. Manchester, England: Manchester University Press.

KATZ, P. A., AND S. L. BOSWELL. 1984. Sex-role development and the one-child family. In *The single-child family*, ed. T. Falbo, 63–116. New York: Guilford.

KATZEV, A. R., R. L. WARNER, AND A. C. ACOCK. 1994. Girls or boys? Relationship of child gender to marital instability. *Journal of Marriage and the Family* 56 (February): 89–100.

KAUFMAN, M. 1993. *Cracking the armour: Power, pain and the lives of men*. New York: Viking/Penguin.

KAUFMAN-ROSEN, L. 1994. The daddy differential. *Newsweek*, October 24, 44.

KAYSER, K. 1993. *When love dies: The process of marital disaffection*. New York: Guilford.

KEITH, V. M., AND B. FINLAY. 1988. The impact of parental divorce on children's educational attainment, marital timings, and likelihood of divorce. *Journal of Marriage and the Family* 50 (August): 797–809.

KELLEY, P. 1992. Healthy stepfamily functioning. *Families in Society: Journal of Contemporary Human Services* (December): 579–87.

KELLY, G. F. 1994. *Sexuality today: The human perspective*, 4th ed. Guilford, CT: Dushkin.

KEMPE, C. H., F. N. SILVERMAN, B. F. STEELE, W. DROEGMULLER, AND H. K. SILVER. 1962. The battered-child syndrome. *Journal of the American Medical Association* 181 (July): 17–24.

KENDALL-TACKETT, L., M. WILLIAMS, AND D. FINKELHOR. 1993. Impact of sexual abuse on children: A review of synthesis of recent empirical studies. *Psychological Bulletin* 113, no. 1 (January): 164–80.

KENEN, R. H. 1993. *Reproductive hazards in the workplace: Mending jobs, managing pregnancies*. New York: Haworth.

KENKEL, W. F. 1985. The desire for voluntary childlessness among low-income youth. *Journal of Marriage and the Family* 47 (May): 509–12.

KENNEDY, G. E. 1990. College students' expectations of grandparent and grandchild role behaviors. *The Gerontologist* 30, no. 1: 43–48.

KENNEDY, M., AND J. S. KING. 1994. *The single-parent family: Living happily in a changing world*. New York: Crown.

KENRICK, D. T., G. E. GROTH, M. R. TROST, AND E. K. SADALLA. 1993. Integrating evolutionary and social exchange perspectives on relationships: Effects of gender, self-appraisal, and involvement level on mate selection criteria. *Journal of Personality and Social Psychology* 64, no. 6, 951–69.

KEPHART, W. H. 1987. *Extraordinary groups: An examination of unconventional life-styles*, 3rd ed. New York: St. Martin's Press.

KEPHART, W. M., AND W. W. ZELLNER. 1991. *Extraordinary groups: An examination of unconventional life-styles*, 4th ed. New York: St. Martin's Press.

KERCKHOFF, A. C., AND K. E. DAVIS. 1962. Value consensus and need complementarity in mate selection. *American Sociological Review* 27, no. 3 (June): 295–303.

KERIG, P. K., P. A. COWAN, AND C. P. COWAN. 1993. Marital quality and gender differences in parent-child interaction. *Developmental Psychology* 29, no. 6, 931–39.

KERN, S. 1992. *The culture of love: Victorians to moderns.* Cambridge, MA: Harvard University Press.

KERR, J. K., R. L. SKOK, AND T. F. MCLAUGHLIN. 1991. Characteristics common to females who exhibit anorexic or bulimic behavior: A review of the current literature. *Journal of Clinical Psychology* 47 (November): 846–53.

KERSTEN, K. K. 1990. The process of marital disaffection: Interventions at various stages. *Family Relations* 39 (July): 257–65.

KHOO, S.-E. 1987. Living together as married: A profile of de facto couples in Australia. *Journal of Marriage and the Family* 49 (February): 185–91.

KIBRIA, N. 1994. Vietnamese families in the United States. In *Minority families in the United States: A multicultural perspective,* ed. R. L. Taylor, 164–76. Englewood Cliffs, NJ: Prentice Hall.

KIECOLT-GLASER, J. K., L. D. FISHER, P. OGROCKI, AND J. C. STOUT. 1987. Marital quality, marital disruption, and immune function. *Psychosomatic Medicine* 49, no. 1 (January-February): 13–34.

KIERNAN, K. E. 1992. The impact of family disruption in childhood on transitions made in young adult life. *Population Studies* 46, 213–34.

KILBOURNE, J. 1994. Still killing us softly: Advertising and the obsession with thinness. In *Feminist perspectives on eating disorders,* ed. P. Fallon, M. A. Katzman, and S. C. Wooley, 395–418. New York: Guilford.

KIMMEL, M. S. 1984. A window on wooing. *Psychology Today,* August, 12–13.

KIMMEL, M. S., AND M. A. MESSNER. 1995. *Men's lives,* 3rd ed. New York: Allyn & Bacon.

KING, B. M., C. J. CAMP, AND A. M. DOWNEY. 1991. *Human Sexuality Today.* Englewood Cliffs, NJ: Prentice Hall.

KING, F. 1993. Spinsterhood is powerful. *National Review,* July 19, 72.

KING, V. 1994. Nonresident father involvement and child well-being: Can dads make a difference? *Journal of Family Issues* 55, no. 1 (March): 78–96.

KINKEAD, G. 1977. The family secret. *Boston Magazine,* October, 100.

KINNAIRD, K. L., AND M. GERRARD. 1986. Premarital sexual behavior and attitudes toward marriage and divorce among young women as a function of their mothers' marital status. *Journal of Marriage and the Family* 48 (November): 757–65.

KINSEY, A. C., W. B. POMEROY, AND C. E. MARTIN. 1948. *Sexual behavior in the human male.* Philadelphia: Saunders.

KINSEY, A. C., W. B. POMEROY, C. E. MARTIN, AND P. H. GEBHARD. 1953. *Sexual behavior in the human female.* Philadelphia: Saunders.

KIRBY, D., ET AL. 1994. School-based programs to reduce sexual risk behaviors: A review of effectiveness. *Public Health Reports* 109 (May/June): 339–60.

KIRKENDALL, L. A., AND A. E. GRAVATT, EDS. 1984. *Marriage and the family in the year 2020.* New York: Prometheus Books.

KIRKPATRICK, L. A., AND K. E. DAVIS. 1994. Attachment style, gender, and relationship stability: A longitudinal analysis. *Journal of Personality and Social Psychology* 66, no. 3, 502–12.

KISSMAN, K., AND J. A. ALLEN. 1993. *Single-parent families.* Beverly Hills, CA: Sage.

KITANO, H. H. L. 1988. The Japanese American family. In *Ethnic families in America: Patterns and variations,* 3rd ed., ed. C. H. Mindel, R. W. Habenstein, and R. Wright, Jr., 258–75. New York: Elsevier.

KITANO, H. H. L., AND R. DANIELS. 1988. *Asian Americans: Emerging minorities.* Englewood Cliffs, NJ: Prentice Hall.

KITSON, G. C., AND L. A. MORGAN. 1991. The multiple consequences of divorce. In *Contemporary families: Looking forward, looking back,* ed. A. Booth, 150–61. Minneapolis, MN: National Council on Family Relations.

KITSON, G. C., WITH W. M. HOLMES. 1992. *Portrait of divorce: Adjustment to marital breakdown.* New York: Guilford.

KITZINGER, S. 1989. *The crying baby.* New York: Penguin.

KIVETT, V. R. 1991. Centrality of the grandfather role among older rural black and white men. *Journal of Gerontology: Social Sciences* 46, no. 5, S250–58.

KLAUS, M., AND J. KENNELL. 1976. *Maternal-infant bonding.* St. Louis, MO: Mosby.

KLEIMAN, C. 1993. Comparable pay could create jobs. *Orlando Sentinel,* October 13, C5.

KLEIMAN, C. 1994. Women who work from home don't fit the stereotype, a professor finds. *Washington Post,* April 17, H2.

KLEIN, R. 1993. Personal correspondence.

KLINKENBERG, D., AND S. ROSE. 1994. Dating scripts of gay men and lesbians. *Journal of Homosexuality* 26, no. 4, 23–35.

KLITSCH, M. 1994. Decline in fertility among Japanese women attributed not to contraceptive use but to late age at marriage. *Family Planning Perspectives* 26, no. 3 (May/June): 137–38.

KNAPP, M. L., AND J. A. HALL. 1992. *Nonverbal communication in human interaction,* 3rd ed. New York: Holt, Rinehart & Winston.

KNAPP, R. J. 1987. When a child dies. *Psychology Today,* July, 60–65.

KNICKERBOCKER, B. 1993. Gay rights may be social issue of 1990s. *Christian Science Monitor,* February 11, 1, 4.

KNIGHT, R. 1994. Gender, jobs and economic survival. *U.S. News & World Report,* September 19, 63.

KNOX, D. H., JR., AND M. J. SPORAKOWSKI. 1968. Attitudes of college students toward love. *Journal of Marriage and the Family* 30, no. 4 (November): 638–42.

KNOX, V. W., AND M. J. BANE. 1994. Child support and schooling. In *Child support and child well-being,* ed. I. Garfinkel, S. S. McLanahan, and P. K. Robins, 285–316. Washington, DC: Urban Institute Press.

KOEPKE, L., J. HARE, AND P. B. MORAN. 1992. Relationship quality in a sample of lesbian couples with children and child-free lesbian couples. *Family Relations* 41 (April): 224–49.

KOHLBERG, L. 1969. Stage and sequence: The cognitive-developmental approach to socialization. In *Handbook of socialization theory and research,* ed. D. A. Goslin, 347–480. Chicago: Rand McNally.

KOHN, A. 1991. The spoiled child. *Ladies Home Journal,* May, 78.

KOLATA, G. 1989a. Ambivalence over pill grows with risk data. *New York Times,* January 8, 23.

KOLATA, G. 1989b. Lesbian partners find the means to be parents. *New York Times,* January 30, A13.

KOMAROVSKY, M. 1950. Functional analysis of sex roles. *American Sociological Review* 15, 508–16.

KORETZ, G. 1994. U.S. death rates: Another social gap is widening. *Business Week,* June 27, 18.

KORTENHAUS, C. M., AND J. DEMAREST. 1993. Gender role stereotyping in children's literature: An update. *Sex Roles* 28, nos. 3/4, 219–32.

KOSS, M. 1990. Changed lives: The psychological impact of sexual harassment. In *Ivory power: Sexual harassment on campus*, ed. M. A. Paludi, 73–92. Albany: State University of New York Press.

KOURI, K. A., AND M. LASSWELL. 1993. Black-white marriages: Social change and intergenerational mobility. *Marriage and Family Review* 19, nos. 3/4, 241–55.

KOWALSKI, R. M. 1993. Inferring sexual interest from behavioral cues: Effects of gender and sexually relevant attitudes. *Sex Roles* 29, nos. 1/2 (July): 13–36.

KRAFFT, S. 1994. Why wives earn less than husbands. *American Demographics,* January, 16–17.

KRAFT, P. 1993. Sexual knowledge among Norwegian adolescents. *Journal of Adolescence* 16 (March): 3–21.

KRAMER, H. 1993. *Conversations at midnight: Coming to terms with dying and death.* New York: Morrow.

KRANCE, M. 1993. Conquest. In *Reinventing love: Six women talk about lust, sex, and romance*, ed. L. Abraham, L. Green, M. Krance, J. Rosenberg, J. Somerville, and C. Stoner, 159–61. New York: Plume.

KRICH, J. 1989. Here come the brides: The blossoming business of imported love. In *Men's lives*, ed. M. S. Kimmel and M. A. Messner, 382–92. New York: Macmillan.

KROKOFF, L. J. 1987. The correlates of negative affect in marriage: An exploratory study of gender differences. *Journal of Family Issues* 8, no. 1 (March): 111–35.

KROL, E. 1994. *The whole internet: User's guide & catalog.* Sebastopol, CA: O'Reilly & Associates.

KRUEGER, R. A. 1994. *Focus groups: A practical guide for applied research*, 2nd ed. Thousand Oaks, CA: Sage.

KÜBLER-ROSS, E. 1969. *On death and dying.* New York: Macmillan.

KUDLOW, L. 1994. Middle-class tax hike. *National Review*, June 13, 25–26.

KURDEK, L. A. 1993. Predicting marital dissolution: A 5-year prospective longitudinal study of newlywed couples. *Journal of Personality and Social Psychology* 64, no. 2, 221–42.

KURDEK, L. A. 1994. Areas of conflict for gay, lesbian, and heterosexual couples: What couples argue about influences relationship satisfaction. *Journal of Marriage and the Family* 56, no. 4 (November): 923–24.

KURDEK, L. A., AND M. A. FINE. 1993. The relation between family structure and young adolescents' appraisals of family climate and parenting behavior. *Journal of Family Issues* 14, 279–90.

KURDEK, L. A., AND J. P. SCHMITT. 1986. Early development of relationship quality in heterosexual married, heterosexual cohabiting, gay and lesbian couples. *Developmental Psychology* 22, 305–309.

KURTZ, H. 1994. Media largely ignored faults of football's "dream-come true." *Washington Post*, June 19, A18.

KURZ, D. 1993. Physical assaults by husbands: A major social problem. In *Current controversies on family violence*, ed. R. J. Gelles and D. R. Loseke, 88–103. Newbury Park, CA: Sage.

KURZWEIL, A. 1982. *From generation to generation: How to trace your Jewish genealogy and personal history.* New York: Schocken.

LADD, G. W., K. D. LE STEUR, AND S. M. PROFILET. 1993. *Direct parental influences on young children's peer relations.* In *Learning about relationships*, ed. S. Duck, 152–83. Newbury Park, CA: Sage.

LADER, L. 1991. *RU 486: The pill that could end the abortion wars and why American women don't have it.* Reading, MA: Addison-Wesley.

LaFROMBOISE, T. D., A. H. HEYLE, AND E. J. OZER. 1990. Changing and diverse roles of women in American Indian cultures. *Sex Roles* 22, nos. 7/8 (April): 455–76.

LAING, E. K. 1993. Real-life stories tell of dignity and diversity. *Christian Science Monitor*, February 5, 11.

LAIRD, J. 1993. Lesbian and gay families. In *Normal family processes*, 2nd ed., ed. F. Walsh, 282–330. New York: Guilford.

LAKOFF, R. T. 1990. *Talking power: The politics of language.* New York: Basic Books.

LAM, C. 1992. Ads target Asian Americans, and their growing wealth. *Baltimore Sun*, January 23, 1C, 21C.

LANDALE, N. S. 1989. Agricultural opportunity and marriage: The United States at the turn of the century. *Demography* 26, no. 2 (May): 203–18.

LANDALE, N. S., AND S. E. TOLNAY. 1991. Group differences in economic opportunity and the timing of marriage. *American Sociological Review* 56, no. 1 (February): 33–45.

LANER, M. R. 1989. Competitive vs. noncompetitive styles: Which is most valued in courtship? *Sex Roles* 20, nos. 3/4, 165–72.

LANG, A., AND L. GOTTLIEB. 1993. Parental grief reactions and marital intimacy following infant death. *Death Studies* 17 (May/June): 233–55.

LANGELAN, M. J. 1993. *Back off! How to confront and stop sexual harassment and harassers.* New York: Simon & Schuster.

LANGER, J. 1985. The new mature mothers. *American Demographics* 7, no. 7 (July): 29–31, 50.

LANSKY, V. 1989. *Vicki Lansky's divorce book for parents.* New York: New American Library.

LANTZ, H. R. 1976. *Marital incompatibility and social change in early America.* Beverly Hills, CA: Sage.

LAPCHIK, R. 1994. We can't overlook the ugliness any longer. *Sporting News*, July 4, 8.

LaQUEY, T. 1994. *The internet companion*, 2nd ed. Reading, MA: Addison-Wesley.

LARSON, J. 1992. Understanding stepfamilies. *American Demographics* (July): 36–40.

LARSON, J., AND B. EDMONDSON. 1991. Should unmarried partners get married benefits? *American Demographics* 13 (March): 47.

LARSON, J. H. 1988. The marriage quiz: College students' beliefs in selected myths about marriage. *Family Relations* 37, no. 1 (January): 3–11.

LARSON, J. H., S. M. WILSON, AND R. BELEY. 1994. The impact of job insecurity on marital and family relationships. *Family Relations* 43, no. 2 (April): 138–43.

LARSON, L. E., AND B. MUNRO. 1990. Religious intermarriage in Canada in the 1980's. *Journal of Comparative Family Studies* 21, no. 2 (Summer): 239–50.

LARSON, R., AND M. H. RICHARDS. 1994. *Divergent realities: The emotional lives of mothers, fathers, and adolescents.* New York: Basic Books.

LASCH, C. 1977. *Haven in a heartless world: The family besieged.* New York: Basic Books.

LASCH, C. 1978. *The culture of narcissism.* New York: Norton.

LASLETT, P. 1971. *The world we have lost*, 2nd ed. Reading, MA: Addison-Wesley.

LASSWELL, M. E., AND N. LOBSENTZ. 1980. *Styles of loving.* Garden City, NY: Doubleday.

LASSWELL, T. E., AND M. E. LASSWELL.

1976. I love you but I'm not in love with you. *Journal of Marriage and Family Counseling* 2, no. 3 (July): 211–24.

LAUER, J., AND R. LAUER. 1985. Marriages made to last. *Psychology Today*, June, 22–26.

LAUER, R. H. 1973. *Perspectives on social change*. Boston: Allyn & Bacon.

LAUMANN, E. O., J. H. GAGNON, R. T. MICHAEL, AND S. MICHAELS. 1994. *The social organization of sexuality: Sexual practices in the United States*. Chicago: University of Chicago Press.

LAVEE, Y., AND D. H. OLSON. 1993. Seven types of marriage: Empirical typology based on research. *Journal of Marital and Family Therapy* 19 (October): 325–40.

LAWRENCE, S. V. 1994. Family planning, at a price. *U.S. News & World Report*, September 19, 56–57.

LAWSON, A. 1988. *Adultery: An analysis of love and betrayal*. New York: Basic Books.

LAZARUS, A. A. 1985. *Marital myths*. San Luis Obispo, CA: Impact.

LEACH, P. 1994. *Children first: What our society must do—and is not doing—for our children today*. New York: Knopf.

LEATHERMAN, C. 1989. Nearly 1 in 10 female college students has had abortion, Gallup survey finds; polling officials surprised. *Chronicle of Higher Education*, May 31, A23.

LEDERMAN, D. 1995. Colleges report rise in violent crime. *Chronicle of Higher Education*, February 3, A31, A42.

LEE, B. A., S. H. JONES, AND D. W. LEWIS. 1990. Public beliefs about the causes of homelessness. *Social Forces* 69, no. 1 (September): 253–65.

LEE, C. S., AND L. SLOAN. 1994. It's our turn now. *Newsweek*, November 21, 57.

LEE, F. R. 1994. AIDS toll on elderly: Dying grandchildren. *New York Times*, November 21, B1, B6.

LEE, G. 1990. Gorbachev's mom: He's too busy to visit, she says. *Washington Post*, July 20, D1, D3.

LEE, J. A. 1973. *The colors of love*. Englewood Cliffs, NJ: Prentice Hall.

LEE, J. A. 1974. The styles of loving. *Psychology Today*, October, 46–51.

LEE, S. M., AND K. YAMANAKA. 1990. Patterns of Asian American intermarriage and marital assimilation. *Journal of Comparative Family Studies* 21, no. 2 (Summer): 287–305.

LEERHSEN, C., AND E. SCHAEFER. 1989.

Pregnancy + alcohol = problems. *Newsweek*, July 31, 57.

LEFF, L. 1990. Sexual practices law narrowed by Md. court: Ruling limits range of prohibited acts. *Washington Post*, October 10, B3.

LEFF, L. 1994. Becoming woman: At 15, Hispanic girls celebrate rite of passage. *Washington Post*, February 6, B1, B8.

LEHRER, E. L., AND C. U. CHISWICK. 1993. Religion as a determinant of marital stability. *Demography* 30, no. 3 (August): 385–404.

LEITENBERG, H., M. J. DETZER, AND D. SREBNIK. 1993. Gender differences in masturbation and the relation of masturbation experience in preadolescence and/or early adolescence to sexual behavior and sexual adjustment in young adulthood. *Journal of Social Behavior* 22 (April): 87–98.

LEJEUNE, C., AND V. FOLLETTE. 1994. Taking responsibility: Sex differences in reporting dating violence. *Journal of Interpersonal Violence* 9, no. 1 (March): 133–40.

LEMASTERS, E. E., AND J. DEFRAIN. 1989. *Parents in contemporary America: A sympathetic view*, 5th ed. Belmont, CA: Wadsworth.

LEMONICK, M. D. 1995. A tiny win against AIDS? *Time*, April 10, 62.

LEON, J. J., AND M. G. WEINSTEIN. 1991. The varieties of other Caucasian intramarriage in Hawaii: 1987. *Journal of Comparative Family Studies* 22, no. 1 (Spring): 75–83.

LEON, J. J., J. L. PHILBRICK, F. PARRA, E. ESCOBEDO, AND F. MALGESINI. 1994. Love-styles among university students in Mexico. *Psychological Reports* 74, 307–10.

LEONARD, K. E., AND M. SENCHAK. 1993. Alcohol and premarital aggression among newlywed couples. *Journal of Studies on Alcohol*, Supp. no. 11, 96–108.

LEPPARD, W., S. M. OGLETREE, AND E. WALLEN. 1993. Gender stereotyping in medical advertising: Much ado about something? *Sex Roles* 29, nos. 11/12, 829–37.

LESLIE, L. A., T. L. HUSTON, AND M. P. JOHNSON. 1986. Parental reactions to dating relationships: Do they make a difference? *Journal of Marriage and the Family* 48 (February): 57–66.

LESTER, D. 1985. Romantic attitudes toward love in men and women. *Psychological Reports* 56 (April): 662.

LESTER, G. H. 1991. U.S. Bureau of the Census, Current Population Reports, Series P-60, No. 173. *Child support*

and alimony: 1989. Washington, DC: Government Printing Office.

LEUNG, S. 1994. Sign of longing for Mrs. Right. *Baltimore Sun*, August 9, 1A, 7A.

LeVAY, S. 1993. The sexual brain. La Jolla, CA: MIP Press.

LEVER, J. 1978. Sex differences in the complexity of children's play and games. *American Sociological Review* 43, 471–83.

LEVESQUE, R. J. R. 1993. The romantic experience of adolescents in satisfying love relationships. *Journal of Youth and Adolescence* 11, no. 3, 219–50.

LEVIN, L., AND L. G. BELLOTTI. 1993. *You can't hurry love: An intimate look at first marriages after 40*. New York: Penguin.

LEVIN, W. C. 1988. Age stereotyping. *Research on Aging* 10 (March): 134–48.

LEVINE, A. 1990. The second time around: Realities of remarriage. *U.S. News & World Report*, January 29, 50–51.

LEVINE, A. 1991. The biological roots of good mothering. *U.S. News & World Report*, February 25, 61.

LEVINE, K. G. 1988. The placed child examines the quality of parental care. *Child Welfare* 67 (June/August): 301–10.

LEVINE, M. P., AND K. SIEGEL. 1992. Unprotected sex: Understanding gay men's participation. In *The social context of AIDS*, ed. J. Huber and B. E. Schneider, 47–71. Newbury Park, CA: Sage.

LEVINE, M. V. 1994. A nation of hamburger flippers? *Baltimore Sun*, July 31, 1E, 4E.

LEVINE, R. V. 1993. Is love a luxury? *American Demographics* (February): 27, 29.

LEVY, E. F. 1992. Strengthening the coping resources of lesbian families. *Families in Society: The Journal of Contemporary Human Services* (January): 23–31.

LEVY-SCHIFF, R. 1994. Individual and contextual correlates of marital change across the transition to parenthood. *Developmental Psychology* 30, no. 4, 591–601.

LEWIN, E. 1994. Negotiating lesbian motherhood: The dialectics of resistance and accommodation. In *Mothering: Ideology, experience, and agency*, ed. E. Glenn, E. Nakano, G. Chang, and L. R. Forcey, 333–53. New York: Routledge.

LEWIN, T. 1991. Right-to-die figure Nancy Cruzan dies: Parents won right to stop nourishment. *Baltimore Sun,* January 2, 1A, 3A.

LEWIN, T. 1994. Men whose wives work earn less, studies show. *New York Times,* October 12, A1, A21.

LEWIS, G. AND T. STAFFORD, EDS. 1986. *You call this a family?* Wheaton, IL: Tyndale House, CampusLife Books.

LEWIS, L., AND D. BRISSETT. 1967. Sex as work: A study of avocational counseling. *Social Problems* 15: 8–17.

LEWIS, P. H. 1994. Persistent E-mail: Electronic stalking or innocent courtship? *New York Times,* September 16, B18.

LI, G., AND S. P. BAKER. 1991. A comparison of injury death rates in China and the United States, 1986. *American Journal of Public Health* 81, no. 5 (May): 605–609.

LIBERTOFF, K. 1981. The runaway child in America: A social history. In *Family life in America: 1620–2000,* ed. M. Albin and D. Cavallo, 268–78. St. James, NY: Revisionary Press.

LICHTER, D. T., AND D. J. EGGEBEEN. 1994. The effect of parental employment on child poverty. *Journal of Marriage and the Family* 56 (August): 633–45.

LICHTER, S. R., L. S. LICHTER, AND S. ROTHMAN. 1991. *Watching America.* Englewood Cliffs, NJ: Prentice Hall.

LIEBOW, E. 1993. *Tell them who I am: The lives of homeless women.* New York: Free Press.

LIEF, L. 1994. An old oasis of tolerance runs dry. *U.S. News & World Report,* August 29/September 5, 39, 41.

LIGHT, P. C. 1988. *Baby boomers.* New York: Norton.

LIGHTFOOT-KLEIN, H. 1989. *Prisoners of ritual: An odyssey into female genital circumcision in Africa.* New York: Haworth.

LIN, C., AND W. T. LIU. 1993. Intergenerational relationships among Chinese immigrant families from Taiwan. In *Family ethnicity: Strength in diversity,* ed. H. P. McAdoo, 271–86. Newbury Park, CA: Sage.

LIN, G., AND P. A. ROGERSON. 1995. Elderly parents and the geographic availability of their adult children. *Research on Aging* 17, no. 3.

LINDSEY, L. 1994. *Gender roles: A sociological perspective,* 2nd ed. Englewood Cliffs, N.J.: Prentice Hall.

LINLIN, P. 1993. Divorce in the United States vs. in China. *Journal of Popular Culture* 27, no. 2 (Fall): 91–99.

LINLIN, P. 1993. Matchmaking via the personal advertisements in China versus in the United States. *Journal of Popular Culture* 27, no. 1 (Summer): 163–70.

LINO, M. 1994. Income and spending patterns of single-mother families. *Monthly Labor Review* (May): 29–37.

LIPS, H. M. 1991. *Women, men, and power.* Mountain View, CA: Mayfield.

LIPS, H. M. 1993. *Sex & gender: An introduction,* 2nd ed. Mountain View, CA: Mayfield.

LITTLEJOHN-BLAKE, S. M., AND C. A. DARLING. 1993. Understanding the strengths of African American families. *Journal of Black Studies* 23, no. 4 (June): 460–71.

LITWACK, E., AND P. MESSERI. 1989. Organizational theory, social supports, and mortality rates: A theoretical convergence. *American Sociological Review* 54, 49–66.

LLOYD, S. A. 1991. The dark side of courtship violence and sexual exploitation. *Family Relations* 40 (January): 14–20.

LOBSENZ, N. M. 1985. Helping love survive the first year of marriage. *Parade,* May 26, 14.

LOCK, M. 1993. *Encounters with aging: Mythologies of menopause in Japan and North America.* Berkeley, CA: University of California Press.

LOEWEN, J. W. 1988. Visitation fatherhood. In *Fatherhood today: Men's changing role in the family,* ed. P. Bronstein and C. P. Cowan, 195–213. New York: Wiley.

LoLORDO, A. 1993. Experts blame system's delay, state laws' diversity in Baby Jessica case. *Baltimore Sun,* August 6, 12A.

LONDON, K. A. 1991. *Cohabitation, marriage, marital dissolution, and remarriage: United States, 1988.* Vital Health Statistics. Hyattsville, MD: National Center for Health Statistics.

LONGINO, C. F., JR. 1994. Myths of an aging America. *American Demographics* (August): 36–42.

LONKHUYZEN, L. V. 1994. Female gymnasts prone to eating disorders. *Baltimore Sun,* July 29, C1, C3.

LOOMIS, L. S., AND N. S. LANDALE. 1994. Nonmarital cohabitation and childbearing among black and white American women. *Journal of Marriage and the Family* 56, no. 4 (November): 949–62.

LORBER, J. 1994. *Paradoxes of gender.* New Haven, CT: Yale University Press.

LOSEE, S. 1992. Gender gap in incentive pay. *Fortune,* November 2, 14–15.

LOTTES, I. L. 1993. Nontraditional gender roles and the sexual experiences of heterosexual college students. *Sex Roles* 29, nos. 9/10 (November) 645–69.

LOWRY, D. T., AND D. W. TOWLES. 1989. Soap opera portrayals of sex, contraception, and sexually transmitted diseases. *Journal of Communication* 39, no. 2 (Spring): 76–83.

LUEPNITZ, D. A. 1988. *Family therapy interpreted.* New York: Basic Books.

LUEPNITZ, D. A. 1991. A comparison of maternal, paternal, and joint custody: Understanding the varieties of post-divorce family life. In *Joint custody and shared parenting,* 2nd ed., ed. J. Folberg, 105–13. New York: Guilford.

LUSTER, T., AND S. A. SMALL. 1994. Factors associated with sexual risk-taking behaviors among adolescents. *Journal of Marriage and the Family* 56 (August): 622–32.

LUTWIN, D. R., AND G. N. SIPERSTEIN. 1985. Househusband fathers. In *Dimensions of fatherhood,* ed. S. M. H. Hanson and F. W. Bozett, 269–87. Beverly Hills, CA: Sage.

LYE, D. N., AND T. J. BIBLARZ. 1993. The effects of attitudes toward family life and gender roles on marital satisfaction. *Journal of Family Issues* 14, no. 2 (June): 157–88.

LYMAN, K. A. 1993. *Day in, day out with Alzheimer's: Stress in caregiving relationships.* Philadelphia: Temple University Press.

LYNCH, P. 1994. Lesbian retreat under fire, FBI launches investigation. *Baltimore Alternative,* February 3, 5.

LYNN, D. B. 1969. *Parental and sex role identification: A theoretical formulation.* Berkeley, CA: McCutchen.

LYNXWILER, J., AND D. GAY. 1994. Reconsidering race differences in abortion attitudes. *Social Science Quarterly* 75, no. 1 (March): 67–84.

LYONS, D. C. 1992. Dr. Comic. *Ebony,* April, 70, 72.

LYONS, S., AND M. JAMES. 1994. Man gets 18–month term for killing unfaithful wife. *Baltimore Sun,* October 18, 1A, 12A.

MACCOBY, E. E. 1990. Gender and relationships: A developmental account. *American Psychologist* 45, no. 4, 513–20

MACCOBY, E. E., C. E. DEPNER, AND R. H. MNOOKIN. 1991. Co-parenting in the second year after divorce. In *Joint custody and shared parenting,* 2nd ed., ed. J. Folberg, 132–52. New York: Guilford.

MACER, D. R. J. 1994. Perception of risks and benefits of in vitro fertilization, genetic engineering and biotechnology. *Social Science & Medicine* 38, no. 1 (January): 23–33.

MACFARQUHAR, E., ET AL. 1994. The war against women. *U.S. News & World Report,* March 28, 42–48.

MACIONIS, J. 1993. *Sociology,* 4th ed. Englewood Cliffs, NJ: Prentice Hall.

MACKEY, A. 1994. Domestic partner benefits are catching on . . . slowly. *Business and Health* 12, no. 4 (April): 73–78.

MACKLIN, E. 1974. Cohabitation in college: Going very steady. *Psychology Today,* November, 53–59.

MAGGIO, R. 1992. *The Beacon book of quotations by women.* Boston: Beacon.

MAGLIN, N. B., AND N. SCHNIEDEWIND, EDS. 1989. *Women and stepfamilies: Voices of anger and love.* Philadelphia: Temple University Press.

MAGNER, D. K. 1993. College's Asian enrollment defies stereotype. *Chronicle of Higher Education,* February 10, A34.

MAHONY, R. 1991. Car buying: Why women get a lemon deal. *Ms.,* January/February, 86–87.

MAINES, J. 1993. Long-distance romances. *American Demographics* (May): 47.

MAJORS, R. G., AND J. U. GORDON, EDS. 1994. *The American black male: His present status and his future.* Chicago: Nelson-Hall.

MALES, M. 1994. Why blame young girls? *New York Times,* July 29, A27.

MANCINI, J. A., AND R. BLIESZNER. 1991. Aging parents and adult children: Research themes in intergenerational relations. In *Contemporary families: Looking forward, looking back,* ed. A. Booth, 249–64. Minneapolis, MN: National Council on Family Relations.

MANKE, B., B. L. SEERY, A. C. CROUTER, AND S. M. MCHALE. 1994. The three corners of domestic labor: Mothers,' fathers,' and children's weekday and weekend housework. *Journal of Marriage and the Family* 56 (August): 657–68.

MANNERS, J. 1993. The perils of a second marriage. *Money,* January, 108–20.

MANNING, C. 1970. *The immigrant woman and her job.* New York: Ayer.

MANNING, W. D. 1993. Marriage and cohabitation following premarital conception. *Journal of Marriage and the Family* 55 (November): 839–50.

MANSNERUS, L. 1995. The divorce backlash. *Working Woman* (February): 38–45, 70.

MARBELLA, J. 1990. A chorus of opinions on what love's got to do with it. *Baltimore Sun,* February 14, 1F, 5F.

MARBELLA, J. 1994. Commercial message. *Baltimore Sun,* April 25, 1D, 5D.

MARCUS, E. 1990. Justice Department rape statistics called unrealistically low. *Washington Post,* September 30, A9.

MARCUS, E. 1990. Court rules "right to die" depends on patient's intent: Justices decide state may keep comatose Missouri woman alive. *Washington Post,* June 26, A1, A8.

MARCUS, E. 1991. AIDS creating a generation of orphans isolated by their anguish. *Washington Post,* September 9, A1, A12.

MARGOLIN, L. 1989. Gender and the prerogatives of dating and marriage: An experimental assessment of a sample of college students. *Sex Roles* 20, nos. 1/2: 91–102.

MARIANO, A. 1991. HUD study finds bias nationwide. *Washington Post,* August 30, G1, G4.

MARIN, B. V., J. M. TSCHANN, C. GOMEZ, AND S. M. KEGELES. 1993. Acculturation and gender differences in sexual attitudes and behaviors: Hispanic vs. non-Hispanic white unmarried adults. *American Journal of Public Health* 83 (December): 1758–1761.

MARIN, P. 1983. A revolution's broken promises. *Psychology Today,* July, 51–57.

MARIN, R., AND C. S. LEE. 1994. Too much sitcom, not enough Seoul. *Newsweek,* September 19, 70.

MARKIDES, K. S., J. S. BOLDT, AND L. A. RAY. 1986. Sources of helping and intergenerational solidarity: A three generation study of Mexican Americans. *Journal of Gerontology* 41, 506–11.

MARKIN, C. 1990. *Bad dates: Celebrities (and other talented types) reveal their worst nights out.* New York: Citadel.

MARKS, S. R. 1986. *Three corners: Exploring marriage and the self.* Lexington, MA: Heath.

MARKSTROM-ADAMS, C. 1991. Attitudes on dating, courtship, and marriage: Perspectives on in-group relationships by religious minority and majority adolescents. *Family Relations* 40 (January): 91–98.

MARSH, B. 1993. Grand adventures. *Endless Vacation* (May/June): 48–53.

MARSHALL, A. 1994. The quiet integration of suburbia. *American Demographics* (August): 9–11.

MARTIN, A. 1993. *The lesbian and gay parenting handbook: Creating and raising our families.* New York: HarperPerennial.

MARTIN, C. L. 1990. Attitudes and expectations about children with nontraditional and traditional gender roles. *Sex Roles* 22, nos. 3/4 (February): 151–65.

MARTIN, M. J., W. R. SCHUMM. M. A. BUGAIGHIS, A. P. JURICH, AND S. R. BOLLMAN. 1987. Family violence and adolescents' perceptions of outcomes of family conflict. *Journal of Marriage and the Family* 49 (February): 165–71.

MARTIN, P. Y., AND R. A. HUMMER. 1993. Fraternities and rape on campus. In *Violence against women.* ed. P. B. Bart and E. G. Moran, 114–31. Newbury Park, CA: Sage.

MARTIN, T. C., AND L. L. BUMPASS. 1989. Recent trends in marital disruption. *Demography* 26, no. 1 (February): 37–51.

MARTINI, F. H. 1995. *Fundamentals of Anatomy and Physiology,* 3rd ed. Englewood Cliffs, NJ: Prentice Hall.

Marvin v. *Marvin,* California Supreme Court; 18 Cal. 3d 660,134 Cal. Rptr. 815, 557 P.2d 106 (1976); Superior Court of the State of California for the County of Los Angeles, *Marvin* v. *Marvin,* Case # C23303, 5 Family Law Reporter 3079; *Marvin* v. *Marvin,* California Court of Appeal, 122 Cal. App. 3d 871, 176 Cal. Rptr. 555 (1981).

Maryland Special Joint Committee. 1989. *Gender bias in the courts.* Annapolis: Administrative Office of the Courts, May.

MARZOLLO, J. 1993. *Fathers & babies: How babies grow and what they need from you from birth to 18 months.* New York: HarperCollins.

MASH, E. J., AND D. A. WOLFE. 1991. Methodological issues in research on physical child abuse. *Criminal Justice and Behavior* 18, no. 1 (March): 8–29.

MASSEY, D. S., AND N. DENTON. 1993. *American apartheid: Segregation and the making of the underclass.* Cambridge, MA: Harvard University Press.

MASSEY, L. 1992. What is really the best interest of the child? *Legal Assistant Today* (November/December): 140–41.

MASTEKAASA, A. 1994. Marital status, distress, and well-being: An international comparison. *Journal of Comparative Family Studies* 25, no. 2 (Summer): 183–205.

MASTERS, W. H., AND V. E. JOHNSON. 1966. *Human sexual response.* Boston: Little, Brown.

MASTERS, W. H., V. E. JOHNSON, AND R. C. KOLODNY. 1986. *On sex and human loving.* Boston: Little, Brown.

MASTERS, W. H., V. E. JOHNSON, AND R. C. KOLODNY. 1992. *Human sexuality,* 4th ed. New York: HarperCollins.

MASTERS, W. H., V. E. JOHNSON, AND R. C. KOLODNY. 1994. *Heterosexuality.* New York: HarperCollins.

MASUR, D. M., M. SLIWINSKI, AND H. A. CRYSTAL. 1994. Neuropsychological prediction of dementia and the absence of dementia in healthy elderly persons. *Neurology* 44, no. 8 (August): 1427–433.

MATANOSKI, G. 1994. Different means of artificial insemination can give childless couples hope. *Baltimore Sun,* July 26, 3D.

MATE-KOLE, C., M. FRESCHI, AND A. ROBIN. 1990. A controlled study of psychological and social change after surgical gender reassignment in selected male transsexuals. *British Journal of Psychiatry* 157 (August): 261–64.

MATHES, V. S. 1981. A new look at the role of women in Indian society. In *The American Indian: Past and present,* 2nd ed., ed. R. L. Nichols, 27–33. New York: Wiley.

MATHIAS, B. 1992. Yes, Va. (MD & D.C.), there are happy marriages. *Washington Post,* September 22, B5.

MATTES, J. 1994. *Single mothers by choice: A guidebook for single women who are considering or have chosen motherhood.* New York: Random House.

MATTHAEI, J. A. 1982. *An economic history of women in America: Women's work, the sexual division of labor, and the development of capitalism.* New York: Schocken.

MATTHEWS, S. H., AND T. T. ROSNER. 1988. Shared filial responsibility: The family as the primary caregiver. *Journal of Marriage and the Family* 50 (February): 185–95.

MATTOX, W. 1994. The hottest valentines. *Washington Post,* February 13, C5.

MAUSHARD, M., AND K. THOMAS. 1989. Career first vs. family first. *Baltimore Sun,* March 15, B1, B16.

MAYNARD, M., AND J. PURVIS, EDS. 1994. *Researching women's lives from a feminist perspective.* Bristol, PA: Taylor & Francis.

MCADOO, H. P., ED. 1988. *Black families,* 2nd ed. Beverly Hills, CA: Sage.

MCADOO, H. P. 1990. A portrait of African American families in the United States. In *The American*

woman, 1990–91: A status report,* ed. S. E. Rix, 71–93. New York: Norton.

MCADOO, H. P., ED. 1993. *Family ethnicity: Strength in diversity.* Newbury Park, CA: Sage.

MCADOO, J. L. 1986. Black fathers' relationships with their preschool children and the children's development of ethnic identity. In *Men in families,* ed. R. A. Lewis and R. E. Salt, 159–68. Beverly Hills, CA: Sage.

MCANENY, L., AND D. W. MOORE. 1994. Public supports new programs to get people off welfare. *Gallup Poll Monthly* (May): 2–5.

MCCABE, M. P. 1984. Toward a theory of adolescent dating. *Adolescence* 19, no. 73 (Spring): 159–70.

MCCALL, N. 1994. *Makes me wanna holler: A young black man in America.* New York: Random House.

MCCARTHY, M. 1992. The myth of the drunken Indian. *Washington Post Health Supplement,* September 22, 10, 13–14.

MCCASLIN, R. 1993. An intergenerational family congruence model. In *Family, self, and society: Toward a new agenda for family research,* ed. P. A. Cowan, D. Field, D. A. Hansen, A. Skolnick, and G. E. Swanson, 295–316. Hillsdale, NJ: Lawrence Erlbaum Associates.

MCCORMICK, J. 1994. Why parents kill. *Newsweek,* November 14, 31–34.

MCCORMICK, J., AND P. MCKILLOP. 1989. The other suburbia: An ugly secret in America's suburbs: Poverty. *Newsweek,* June 26, 22–24.

MCCORVEY, N., WITH A. MEISLER. 1994. *I am Roe: My life, Roe v. Wade, and freedom of choice.* New York: HarperCollins.

MCCOY, E. 1986. Your one and only. *Parents,* October, 118–21, 236.

MCCURDY, J. 1993. UCLA's "no" on Chicano studies dept. brings violent protest. *Chronicle of Higher Education,* May 19, A16.

MCELROY, W., ED. 1991. *Freedom, feminism, and the state: An overview of individualist feminism.* New York: Holmes & Meier.

MCELVAINE, R. S. 1993. *The great depression: America, 1929–1941.* New York: Times Books.

MCENROE, J. 1991. Split-shift parenting. *American Demographics* 13, no. 2 (February): 50–52.

MCGILL, M. 1985. *The McGill report on male intimacy.* New York: Holt, Rinehart & Winston.

MCGINNIS, T. 1981. *More than just a friend: The joys and disappointments*

of extramarital affairs.* Englewood Cliffs, NJ: Prentice Hall.

MCGOLDRICK, M., M. HEIMAN, AND B. CARTER. 1993. The changing family life cycle: A perspective on normalcy. In *Normal family processes,* 2nd ed., ed. F. Walsh, 405–43. New York: Guilford.

MCILWEE, J. S., AND J. G. ROBINSON. 1992. *Women in engineering: Gender, power, and workplace culture.* Albany: State University of New York Press.

MCINTYRE, J. 1981. The structure-functional approach to family study. In *Emerging conceptual frameworks in family analysis,* ed. F. I. Nye and F. M. Berardo, 52–77. New York: Praeger.

MCKAY, M. M. 1994. The link between domestic violence and child abuse: Assessment and treatment considerations. *Child Welfare* 73, no. 1 (January–February): 29–39.

MCKENRY, P. C., AND M. A. FINE. 1993. Parenting following divorce: A comparison of black and white single mothers. *Journal of Comparative Family Studies* 24, no. 1 (Spring): 99–111.

MCLANAHAN, S., AND K. BOOTH. 1991. Mother-only families: Problems, prospects, and politics. In *Contemporary families: Looking forward, looking back,* ed. A. Booth, 405–28. Minneapolis, MN: National Council on Family Relations.

MCLANAHAN, S., AND L. BUMPASS. 1988. Intergenerational consequences of family disruption. *American Journal of Sociology* 94, no. 1 (July): 130–52.

MCLANAHAN, S. S., J. A. SELTZER, T. L. HANSON, AND E. THOMSON. 1994. Child support enforcement and child well-being: Greater security or greater conflict? In *Child support and child well-being,* ed. I. Garfinkel, S. S. McLanahan and P. K. Robins, 239–56. Washington, DC: Urban Institute Press.

MCLAUGHLIN, D. K., D. T. LICHTER, AND G. M. JOHNSTON. 1993. Some women marry young: Transitions to first marriage in metropolitan and nonmetropolitan areas. *Journal of Marriage and the Family* 55 (November): 827–38.

MCLEMORE, S. D. 1991. *Racial and ethnic relations in America.* 3rd ed. Boston: Allyn & Bacon.

MCMAHON, T. 1993. *It works for us! Proven child-care tips from experienced parents across the country.* New York: Pocket Books.

MCMILLEN, L. 1990. An anthropologist's disturbing picture of gang rape.

on campus. *Chronicle of Higher Education*, September 19, A3.

McMILLEN, L. 1991. American Indian college fund seeks recognition and $10 million for tribal institutions. *Chronicle of Higher Education*, May 1, A25.

McMILLEN, L. 1994. Same-sex rituals. *Chronicle of Higher Education*, June 29, A7, A11.

McNALLY, J. W., AND W. D. MOSHER. 1991. *AIDS-related knowledge and behavior among women 15–44 years of age: United States, 1986*. Hyattsville, MD: National Center for Health Statistics.

McPHARLIN, P. 1946. *Love and courtship in America*. New York: Hastings House.

MEAD, M. 1935. *Sex and temperament in three primitive societies*. New York: Morrow.

Mediawatch. 1994. Aging men's eternal fantasy, 1, no. 2 (Summer): 6.

MEDVED, M. 1994. *Hollywood vs. America: Popular culture and the war on traditional values*. New York: HarperCollins.

MEER, J. 1985a. Sex and the church. *Psychology Today*, May, 67.

MEER, J. 1985b. Videodating: A picture worth 1,000 words? *Psychology Today*, January, 71.

MEISENHEIMER, J. R. II. 1989. Employer provisions for parental leave. *Monthly Labor Review* 112, no. 10 (October): 20–24.

MELTZER, N., ED. 1964. *In their own words: A history of the American Negro, 1619–1865*. New York: Crowell.

MENAGHAN, E. G., AND T. L. PARCEL. 1991. Parental employment and family life. In *Contemporary families: Looking forward, looking back*, ed. A. Booth, 361–80. Minneapolis, MN: National Council on Family Relations.

MENDELS, P. 1994. A year later, leave act still in its infancy. *Baltimore Sun*, August 12, 6D.

MENDELSOHN, K. D., L. Z. NIEMAN, K. ISAACS, S. LEE, AND S. P. LEVISON. 1994. Sex and gender bias in anatomy and physical diagnosis text illustrations. *JAMA*, October 26, 1267–270.

MERCER, J. 1994. Native Hawaiians push to extend and deepen university's diversity. *Chronicle of Higher Education*, August 3, A28–A29.

MERGENBAGEN, P. 1994. Job benefits get personal. *American Demographics* (September): 30–38.

MERRILL, D. 1988. After-school or-

phans. In *Current issues in marriage and the family*, 4th ed., ed. G. J. Wells, 285–90. New York: Macmillan.

METHABANE, M., AND G. METHABANE. 1992. *Love in black and white: The triumph of love over prejudice and taboo*. New York: HarperCollins.

MEYER, C. H. 1985. A feminist perspective on foster family care: A redefinition of categories. *Child Welfare* 64 (May/June): 249–58.

MEYER, J. 1990. Guess who's coming to dinner this time? A study of gay intimate relationships and the support for those relationships. In *Homosexuality and family relations*, ed. F. W. Bozett and M. B. Sussman, 59–82. New York: Harrington Park Press.

MIALL, C. 1986. The stigma of involuntary childlessness. *Social Problems* 33, no. 4 (April): 268–82.

MIALL, C. E. 1987. The stigma of adoptive parent status: Perceptions of community attitudes toward adoption and the experience of informal social sanctioning. *Family Relations* 36 (January): 34–39.

MICHAEL, R. T., J. H. GAGNON, E. O. LAUMANN, AND G. KOLATA. 1994. *Sex in America: A definitive study*. Boston: Little, Brown.

MIEDZIAN, M. 1991. *Boys will be boys: Breaking the link between masculinity and violence*. New York: Anchor.

MILKMAN, R. 1976. Women's work and the economic crisis: Some lessons from the great depression. *Review of Radical Political Economics* 8, no. 1 (Spring): 73–97.

MILLER, A., ED. 1991. *Breaking down the wall of silence: The liberating experience of facing painful truth*. Meridian, NY: Dutton.

MILLER, A., C. FRIDAY, AND P. KING. 1992. Baby Makers, Inc. *Newsweek*, June 29, 38–39.

MILLER, B. 1995. Household futures. *American Demographics* (March): 4, 6.

MILLER, B. A., W. R. DOWNS, AND M. TESTA. 1993. Interrelationships between victimization experiences and women's alcohol use. *Journal of Studies on Alcohol*, Suppl. No. 11, 109–17.

MILLER, B. C. 1986. *Family research methods*. Beverly Hills, CA: Sage.

MILLER, B. C., AND K. A. MOORE. 1990. Adolescent sexual behavior, pregnancy, and parenting: Research through the 1980s. *Journal of Marriage and the Family* 52 (November): 1025–1044.

MILLER, L. F., AND J. E. MOORMAN. 1989. Married-couple families with children. In *Studies in marriage and the family*, Bureau of the Census, Current Population Reports, Series P-23, No. 162, 27–36. Washington, DC: Government Printing Office.

MILLER, S., G. BEALS, AND R. ELAM. 1995. What color is black? *Newsweek*, February 13, 63–65.

MILLER, W. L., AND B. F. CRABTREE. 1994. Clinical research. In *Handbook of qualitative research*, ed. N. K. Denzin and Y. S. Lincoln, 340–52. Thousand Oaks, CA: Sage.

MIN, P. G. 1988. The Korean American family. In *Ethnic families in America: Patterns and variations*, 3rd ed., ed. C. H. Mindel, R. W. Habenstein, and R. Wright, Jr., 199–229. New York: Elsevier.

MIN, P. G. 1993. Korean immigrants' marital patterns and marital adjustments. In *Family ethnicity: Strength in diversity*, ed. H. P. McAdoo, 287–99. Newbury Park, CA: Sage.

MIN, P. G., AND C. JARET. 1985. Ethnic business enterprises: The case of Korean small business in Atlanta. *Sociology and Social Research* 69, 412–35.

MINDEL, C. H., R. W. HABENSTEIN, AND R. WRIGHT, JR., EDS. 1988. *Ethnic families in America: Patterns and variations*, 3rd. ed. New York: Elsevier.

MINKLER, M., D. DRIVER, K. M. ROE, AND K. BEDEIAN. 1993. Community interventions to support grandparent caregivers. *The Gerontologist* 33, no. 6, 807–11.

MINKLER, M., AND K. M. ROE. 1993. *Grandmothers as caregivers: Raising children of the crack cocaine epidemic*. Newbury Park, CA: Sage.

MINTON, L. 1993. What kids say. *Parade*, August 1, 4–6.

MINTON, L. 1994a. Fresh voices. *Parade*, March 6, 10.

MINTON, L. 1994b. Fresh voices: When a parent is homosexual. *Parade*, September 11, 14.

MINTON, L. 1995. Stepfamilies. *Parade*, February 26, 24–25.

MINTZ, S., AND S. KELLOGG. 1988. *Domestic revolution: A social history of American family life*. New York: Free Press.

MIRANDE, A. 1977. The Chicano family: A reanalysis of conflicting views. *Journal of Marriage and the Family* (November): 747–56.

MIRANDE, A. 1985. *The Chicano experience: An alternative perspective*. Notre Dame, IN: University of Notre Dame Press.

MIROWSKY, J., AND C. E. ROSS. 1986. Social patterns of distress. *Annual Review of Sociology* 12, 23–45.

MIROWSKY, J., AND C. E. ROSS. 1987. Belief in innate sex roles: Sex stratification versus interpersonal influence in marriage. *Journal of Marriage and the Family* 49 (August): 527–40.

MITTELSTADT, M. 1994. Hispanics seek higher, more positive profile on television. *Baltimore Sun*, September 7, D1, D5.

Modern Maturity. 1993. Which living arrangement is for you? April/May, 32–33.

MOEN, P. 1992. *Women's two roles: A contemporary dilemma*. Westport, CT: Auburn House.

MOHR, J. 1981. The great upsurge of abortion, 1840–1880. In *Family life in America: 1620–2000*, ed. M. Albin and D. Cavallo, 119–30. St. James, NY: Revisionary Press.

MONEY, J. 1988. *Gay, straight and in-between: The sexology of erotic orientation*. New York: Oxford University Press.

MONTAGU, A. ED. 1953. *The meaning of love*. New York: Julian Press.

MONTAGU, A. 1974. *The natural superiority of women*. London: Collier Macmillan.

MONTEFIORE, S. S. 1993. Let the games begin: Sex and the *not*-thirtysomethings. *Psychology Today*, March/April, 66–69, 86, 90.

MONTGOMERY, M. J., E. R. ANDERSON, E. M. HETHERINGTON, AND W. G. CLINGEMPEEL. 1992. Patterns of courtship for remarriage: Implications for child adjustment and parent-child relationships. *Journal of Marriage and the Family* 54 (August): 686–98.

MONTGOMERY, R. J. V., J. G. GONYEA, AND N. R. HOOYMAN. 1985. Caregiving and the experience of subjective and objective burden. *Family Relations* 34: 19–26.

MOONEY, C. J. 1989. Colleges for American Indians said to need money and recognition. *Chronicle of Higher Education*, November 15, A20.

MOORE, D. M. 1993a. Americans feel threatened by new immigrants. *Gallup Poll Monthly*, July, 2–13.

MOORE, D. M. 1993b. Public polarized on gay issue. *Gallup Poll Monthly*, April, 30–32.

MOORE, D. W. 1994a. Approval of husband slapping wife continues to decline. *Gallup Poll Monthly*, February, 2.

MOORE, D. W. 1994b. One in seven Americans victim of child abuse. *Gallup Poll Monthly*, May, 18–22.

MOORE, J., AND H. PACHON. 1985. *Hispanics in the United States*. Englewood Cliffs, NJ: Prentice Hall.

MOORE, K. A. 1995. *Facts at a glance*, February. Brochure. Washington, DC: Child Trends, Inc.

MOORE, K. A., AND N. Q. SNYDER. 1994. *Facts at a glance*. Brochure. Washington, DC: Child Trends, Inc.

MOORE, P., WITH C. P. CONN. 1985. *Disguised*. Waco, TX: Word Books.

MOOREHOUSE, M. J. 1991. Linking maternal employment patterns to mother-child activities and children's school competence. *Developmental Psychology* 27, no. 2 (March): 295–303.

MOOREHOUSE, M. J. 1993. Work and family dynamics. In *Family, self, and society: Toward a new agenda for family research*, ed. P. A. Cowan, D. Field, D. A. Hansen, A. Skolnick, and G. E. Swanson, 265–86. Hillsdale, NJ: Lawrence Erlbaum Associates.

MORALES, E. S. 1990. Ethnic minority families and minority gays and lesbians. In *Homosexuality and family relations*, ed. F. W. Bozett and M. B. Sussman, 217–39. New York: Harrington Park Press.

MORALES, R., AND F. BONILLA, EDS. 1993. *Latinos in a changing U.S. economy*. Newbury Park, CA: Sage.

MORGAN, D. 1981. A contribution to the debate on homogamy, propinquity, and segregation. *Journal of Marriage and the Family* 43, 909–21.

MORGAN, D. I., ED. 1993. *Successful focus groups: Advancing the state of the art*. Newbury Park, CA: Sage.

MORGAN, L. A. 1988. Outcomes of marital separation: A longitudinal test of predictors. *Journal of Marriage and the Family* 50 (May): 493–98.

MORGAN, S. P., D. N. LYE, AND G. A. CONDRAN. 1988. Sons, daughters, and the risk of marital disruption. *American Journal of Sociology* 94, no. 1 (July): 110–29.

MORGAN, W. L. 1939. *The family meets the depression: A study of a group of highly selected families*. Westport, CT: Greenwood.

MORGENTHAU, T., WITH M. MABRY, L. GENAO, AND F. WASHINGTON. 1991. Race on campus: Failing the test? *Newsweek*, May 6, 26–27.

MORIN, R. 1994. How to lie with statistics: Adultery. *Washington Post*, March 6, C5.

MORSE, S. 1995. Why girls don't like computer games. *AAUW Outlook* 88, no. 4 (Winter): 14–17.

MOSCICKI, E. K. 1994. Gender differences in completed and attempted suicides. *Annals of Epidemiology* 4, no. 2 (March): 152–58.

MOSHER, W. D., AND W. F. PRATT. 1991. Fecundity and infertility in the United States: Incidence and trends. *Fertility and Sterility* 56, no. 2 (August): 192–93.

MOSHER, W. D., AND W. F. PRATT. 1993. *AIDS-related behavior among women 15–44 years of age: United States, 1988 and 1990*. U.S. Department of Health and Human Services, Centers for Disease Control and Prevention, December 22.

MOSKOWITZ, M., AND C. TOWNSEND. 1994. 100 best companies for working mothers. *Working Mother* (October): 21–68.

MOSS, R. J. 1987. Good grades for daycare. *Psychology Today*, February, 20.

MOSTAFA, J., T. NEWELL, AND R. TRENTHAM. 1994. *The easy internet handbook*. Castle Rock, CO: Hi Willow Research & Publishing.

MOTHERWELL, C. 1990. Epidemic of sexism has Canadian students, faculty members wondering how to stop it. *Chronicle of Higher Education*, November 21, A33, A35.

MOWRER, E. R. 1972. War and family solidarity and stability. In *The American family in World War II*, ed. R. A. Abrams, 100–106. New York: Arno Press and New York Times. (Originally published in *Annals of the American Academy of Political and Social Science* 229 [September 1943].)

MOYNIHAN, D. P., ED. 1970. *Toward a national urban policy*. New York: Basic Books.

MOYNIHAN, R. B., S. ARMITAGE, AND C. F. DICHAMP, EDS. 1990. *So much to be done: Women settlers on the mining and ranching farms*. Lincoln: University of Nebraska Press.

MUEHLENHARD, C. L., AND M. A. LINTON. 1987. Date rape and sexual aggression in dating situations: Incidence and risk factors. *Journal of Counseling Psychology* 34, no. 2, 186–96.

MUELLER, D. P., AND P. W. COOPER. 1986. Children of single parent families: How they fare as young adults. *Family Relations* 35, no. 1 (January): 169–76.

MUI, A. C., AND N. MORROW-HOWELL. 1993. Sources of emotional strain among the oldest caregivers: Differential experiences of siblings and spouses. *Research on Aging* 15, no. 1 (March): 50–69.

MUJICA, B. 1995. No comprendo. *New York Times*, January 3, A19.

MULLER, T., AND T. J. ESPENSHADE. 1985. *The fourth wave: California's newest immigrants*. Washington, DC: Urban Institute Press.

MUNCY, R. LEE. 1988. Sex and marriage in utopia. *Society* 25, no. 2 (January/February): 46–48.

MUNK, N. 1994. Easy nuptials. *Forbes*, April 25, 178–79.

MUNTER, C. 1984. Fat and the fantasy of perfection. In *Pleasure and danger: Exploring female sexuality*, ed. C. Vance, 225–31. Boston: Routledge & Kegan Paul.

MURRAY, C. 1994. Does welfare bring more babies? *American Enterprise* 5 (January/February): 52–59.

MURRAY, D. W. 1994. Every society is threatened by the disappearance of legitimate marriage. *Chronicle of Higher Education*, July 13, B5.

MURSTEIN, B. I. 1974. *Love, sex, and marriage through the ages*. New York: Springer.

MUZZIO, D., AND R. BEHN. 1995. Thinking about welfare: The view from New York. *Public Perspective* 6, no. 2 (February/March): 35–38.

MYDANS, S. 1988. How to marry up, and avoid the frogs and nerds. *New York Times*, July 11, A4.

MYERS, E. 1986. *When parents die: A guide for adults*. New York: Viking Penguin.

MYERS, M. F. 1989. *Men and divorce*. New York: Guilford.

MYLES, E. 1994. Gay rites: A wedding in Denmark, a ceremony in New York. *Village Voice*, June 28, 36.

MYRA, H. 1994. Love in black and white. *Christianity Today*, March 7, 18–19.

NANCE, J. 1975. *The gentle Tasaday*. New York: Harcourt Brace Jovanovich.

NANDA, S. 1990. *Neither man nor woman: The Hijras of India*. Belmont, CA: Wadsworth.

NASAR, S. 1994. More men in prime of life spend less time working. *New York Times*, December 1, D1, D15.

NASS, G. D., R. W. LIBBY, AND M. P. FISHER. 1981. *Sexual choices: An introduction to human sexuality*. Belmont, CA: Wadsworth.

National Academy of Sciences. 1988. *Homelessness, health, and human needs*. Washington, DC: National Academy Press.

National Center for Health Statistics. 1990. Advance report of final natality statistics, 1988. *Monthly Vital Statis-*

tics Report, 9, no. 4 (suppl.). Hyattsville, MD: Public Health Service.

National Center for Health Statistics. 1991. Advance report of final natality statistics, 1989. *Monthly Vital Statistics Report*, 40, no. 8 (suppl.). Hyattsville, MD: Public Health Service.

National Commission on Children. 1991. *Beyond rhetoric: A new agenda for children and families*. Washington, DC: Government Printing Office.

National Research Council. 1993a. *Losing generations: Adolescents in high-risk settings*. Washington, DC: National Academy Press.

National Research Council. 1993b. *Understanding child abuse and neglect*. Washington, DC: National Academy Press.

NAYYAR, S., AND S. MILLER. 1994. Making it easier to strike back. *Newsweek*, September 12, 50.

NELSON, G. 1994. Emotional well-being of separated and married women: Long-term follow-up study. *American Journal of Orthopsychiatry* 64 (January): 150–60.

NEUGARTEN, B. L., AND K. K. WEINSTEIN. 1964. The changing American grandparents. *Journal of Marriage and the Family* 26 (May): 199–204.

NEUMAN, W. L. 1994. *Social research methods: Qualitative and quantitative approaches*, 2nd ed. Boston: Allyn and Bacon.

NEUMANN, D. 1989. *Divorce mediation: How to cut the cost and stress of divorce*. New York: Holt.

NEWBERGER, E. H. 1985. The helping hand strikes again: Unintended consequences of child abuse reporting. In *Unhappy families: Clinical and research perspectives on family violence*, ed. E. H. Newberger and R. Bourne, 171–78. Littleton, MA: PSG.

NEWCOMER, S., AND J. R. UDRY. 1987. Parental marital status effects on adolescent sexual behavior. *Journal of Marriage and the Family* 49 (May): 235–40.

NEWMAN, B. S., AND P. G. MUZZONIGRO. 1993. The effects of traditional family values on the coming out process of gay male adolescents. *Adolescence* 28, no. 109 (Spring): 213–26.

NEWPORT, F. 1993. Americans now more likely to say: Women have it harder than men. *Gallup Poll Monthly*, October 11–16.

Newsweek. 1990a. Bad year for girls? April 16, 81.

Newsweek. 1990b. Murder America, July 9, 7.

Newsweek. 1990c. Teenage cruising takes a bruising. August 20, 45.

Newsweek. 1994a. What children fear. January 10, 50.

Newsweek. 1994b. Where the kids are. March 21, 65.

Newsweek. 1994c. Men, women and computers. May 16.

New York Times. 1987. Town in Montana endures as an outpost of polygamy. August 18, 18.

New York Times. 1994. Court lets landlord refuse unmarried couple. May 29, A3.

NGUYEN, L. 1989. More companies join growing trend. *Baltimore Sun*, July 3, B1, B8.

NGUYEN, L. 1994. XO magazine puts Asian-American men in a new light. *Baltimore Sun*, August 1, D1.

NICOLOSI, A., ET AL. 1994. The efficiency of male-to-female and female-to-male sexual transmission of the human immunodeficiency virus—a study of 730 stable couples. *Epidemiology* 5, no. 6 (November): 570–75.

NOBILE, P., AND E. NADLER. 1994. The Shadow Commission. In *Taking sides: Clashing views on controversial issues in human sexuality*, 4th ed., ed. R. T. Francoeur, 87–96. Guilford, CT: Dushkin.

NOBLE, B. P. 1994. Women's pensions, wilting fast. *New York Times*, May 29, 21.

NOBLE, R. C. 1991. There is no safe sex. *Newsweek*, April 1, 8.

NOLAN, J., M. COLEMAN, AND L. GANONG. 1984. The presentation of stepfamilies in marriage and family textbooks. *Family Relations* 33: 559–66.

NOLLER, P. 1984. *Nonverbal communication and marital interaction*. New York: Pergamon.

NORRIS, A. F., AND K. FORD. 1994. Condom beliefs in urban, low income, African American and Hispanic youth. *Health Education Quarterly* 21, no. 1 (Spring): 39–53.

NORRIS, J. E., AND J. A. TINDALE. 1993. *Among generations: The cycle of adult relationships*. New York: Freeman.

NORTON, A. J., AND L. F. MILLER. 1991. Marriage, divorce, and remarriage in the 1990s. Paper presented at the annual meeting of the American Public Health Association, Atlanta.

NORTON, A. J., AND L. F. MILLER. 1992. *Marriage, divorce, and remarriage in the 1990's*. U.S. Bureau of the Census, Current Population Reports, P23–180. Washington, DC: Government Printing Office.

NULAND, S. B. 1994. *How we die: Re-*

flections on life's final chapter. New York: Knopf.

NUTA, V. R. 1986. Emotional aspects of child support enforcement. *Family Relations* 35, no. 1 (January): 177–82.

NYE, F. I. 1988. Fifty years of family research, 1937–1987. *Journal of Marriage and the Family* 50 (May): 305–16.

NYE, F. I., AND F. M. BERARDO, EDS. 1981. *Emerging conceptual frameworks in family analysis.* New York: Praeger.

OCHILTREE, G. 1990. *Children in stepfamilies.* Brookvale, Australia: Prentice Hall.

O'CONNELL, M. 1993. *Where's papa? Fathers' role in child care.* Washington, DC: Population Reference Bureau.

O'DONNELL, J. B. 1995. "Coached" children wrongly get benefits. *Baltimore Sun*, March 11, A1, A10.

O'DONNELL, J. B., AND J. HANER. 1995. America's most wanted welfare plan. *Baltimore Sun*, January 22, 1A, 18A.

OFFNER, P. 1994. Day careless. *New Republic*, April 18, 18–19.

O'FLAHERTY, K. M., AND L. W. EELLS. 1988. Courtship behavior of the remarried. *Journal of Marriage and the Family* 50 (May): 499–506.

OGBURN, W. F. 1927. Eleven questions concerning American marriages. *Social Forces* 5, 5–12.

OGGINS, J., D. LEBER, AND J. VEROFF. 1993. Race and gender differences in black and white newlyweds' perceptions of sexual and marital relations. *Journal of Sex Research* 30, no. 2 (May): 152–60.

OGINTZ, E. 1994. Is Grandma always the best baby-sitter? *Parents*, September, 139.

O'HARE, S., AND A. S. KAHN. 1994. A computer bulletin board in women's studies courses. *Transformations* 5, no. 2 (Fall): 64–73.

O'HARE, W. P. 1994. 3.9 million U.S. children in distressed neighborhoods. *Population Today* 22, no. 9 (September): 4–5.

O'HARE, W. P., AND J. C. FELT. 1991. *Asian Americans: America's fastest growing minority group.* Washington, DC: Population Reference Bureau.

O'HARE, W. P., W. H. FREY, AND D. FOST. 1994. Asians in the suburbs. *American Demographics* 16, no. 5 (May): 32–38.

O'KELLY, C. 1986. The nature versus nurture debate. In *Sex roles and social patterns*, ed. F. A. Boudreau, R.

S. Sennott, and M. Wilson, 23–62. New York: Praeger.

O'KELLY, C. G., AND L. S. CARNEY. 1986. *Women and men in society: Cross-cultural perspectives on gender stratification*, 2nd ed. Belmont, CA: Wadsworth.

OKIE, S. 1993a. Where choosing a good mate is the "will of God." *Washington Post*, February 15, A33.

OKIE, S. 1993b. The boys "only wanted to rape them." *Washington Post*, February 17, A24.

OLDENBURG, D. 1994. The electronic gender gap. *Washington Post*, November 29, D5.

O'LEARY, K. D. 1993. Through a psychological lens: Personality traits, personality disorders, and levels of violence. In *Current controversies on family violence*, ed. R. J. Gelles, and D. R. Loseke, 7–30. Newbury Park, CA: Sage.

OLIVER, M. B., AND J. S. HYDE. 1993. Gender differences in sexuality: A meta-analysis. *Psychological Bulletin* 114, no. 1, 29–51.

OLIVER, M. B., AND C. SEDKIDES. 1992. Effects of sexual permissiveness on desirability of partner as a function of low and high commitment to relationship. *Social Psychology Quarterly* 55, no. 3, 321–33.

OLLENBURGER, J. C., AND H. A. MOORE. 1992. *A sociology of women: The intersection of patriarchy, capitalism and colonization.* Englewood Cliffs, NJ: Prentice Hall.

OLSON, E. 1988. Why more dads are getting the kids. *Business Week*, November 28, 118, 122.

OLSON, J. S., AND R. WILSON. 1984. *Native Americans in the twentieth century.* Provo, UT: Brigham Young University Press.

OLSON, M. R., AND J. A. HAYNES. 1993. Successful single parents. *Families in Society: The Journal of Contemporary Human Services* (May): 259–67.

ORENSTEIN, P. 1994. *Schoolgirls: Young women, self-esteem, and the confidence gap.* New York: Doubleday.

OROPESA, R. S., D. T. LICHTER, AND R. N. ANDERSON. 1994. Marriage markets and the paradox of Mexican American nuptiality. *Journal of Marriage and the Family* 56 (November): 889–907.

OSGOOD, N. J. 1985. *Suicide in the elderly.* Rockville, MD: Aspen Systems Corporation.

OSHERSON, S. 1992. *Wrestling with love: How men struggle with intimacy with women, children, parents and*

each other. New York: Fawcett Columbine.

OSKAMP, S., AND M. COSTANZO, EDS. 1993. *Gender issues in contemporary society.* Newbury Park, CA: Sage.

OSTROFF, J. 1991. Targeting the prime-life consumer. *American Demographics*, 13, no. 1 (January): 30–34, 52–53.

O'SULLIVAN, L. F., AND E. S. BYERS. 1993. Eroding stereotypes: College women's attempts to influence reluctant male sexual partners. *Journal of Sex Research* 30, no. 3 (August): 270–82.

OSWALT, R., AND K. MATSEN. 1993. Sex, AIDS, and the use of condoms: A survey of compliance in college students. *Psychological Reports* 72, 764–66.

OYSTERMAN, D., N. RADIN, AND R. BENN. 1993. Dynamics in a three-generational family: Teens, grandparents, and babies. *Developmental Psychology* 29, no. 3, 564–73.

PAASCH, K. M., AND J. D. TEACHMAN. 1991. Gender of children and receipt of assistance from absent fathers. *Journal of Family Issues* 12, no. 4 (December): 450–66.

PADILLA, E. R., AND K. E. O'GRADY. 1987. Sexuality among Mexican Americans: A case of sexual stereotyping. *Journal of Personality and Social Psychology* 52, no. 1, 5–10.

PALMER, S. A., M. J. LAMBERT, AND R. L. RICHARDS. 1991. The MMPI and premenstrual syndrome: Profile fluctuations between best and worst times during the menstrual cycle. *Journal of Clinical Psychology* 47, no. 2 (March): 215–21.

PALUDI, M. A., AND R. B. BARICKMAN. 1991. *Academic and workplace sexual harassment: A resource manual.* Albany: State University of New York Press.

PAPANEK, H. 1979. Family status production. *Signs* 4, 775–81.

PAPERNOW, P. L. 1984. The stepfamily cycle: An experiential model of stepfamily development. *Family Relations* 33, 355–63.

PAPERNOW, P. L. 1993. *Becoming a stepfamily: Patterns of development in remarried families.* San Francisco: Jossey-Bass.

PARDECK, J. T. 1984. Multiple placement of children in foster family care: An empirical analysis. *Social Welfare* 29 (November/December): 506–09.

PARSONS, T., AND R. F. BALES. 1955. *Family, socialization and interaction process.* Glencoe, IL: Free Press.

PASLEY, B. K., AND M. IHINGER-TALL-MAN. 1989. Boundary ambiguity in remarriage: Does ambiguity differentiate degree of marital adjustment and integration? *Family Relations* 38 (January): 46–52.

PASLEY, K., AND M. IHINGER-TALLMAN, EDS. 1994. *Stepparenting: Issues in theory, research, and practice.* Westport, CT: Greenwood.

PASLEY, K., AND E. SANDRAS. 1994. Marital quality and marital stability in remarriage and multiple remarriages: A test of Lewis and Spanier's hypothesis. In *Stepparenting: Issues in theory, research, and practice*, ed. K. Pasley and M. Ihinger-Tallman, 51–68. Westport, CT: Greenwood.

PASLEY, K., D. C. DOLLAHITE, AND M. IHINGER-TALLMAN. 1993. Bridging the gap: Clinical applications of research findings on the spouse and stepparent roles in remarriage. *Family Relations* 42 (July): 315–322.

PATER, R., AND P. MCCLELLAN. 1994. Violence is threatening workplace safety. *American City & County*, February, 57.

PATNER, M. M. 1990. Between mothers and daughters: Pain and difficulty go with the territory. *Washington Post*, November 8, C5.

PATTERSON, J., AND P. KIM. 1991. *The day America told the truth: What people really believe about everything that really matters.* Englewood Cliffs, NJ: Prentice Hall.

PAULY, I. B. 1974. Female transsexualism. Part 1. *Archives of Sexual Behavior* 3, 487–507.

PAZ, J. J. 1993. Support of Hispanic elderly. In *Family ethnicity: Strength in diversity*, ed. H. P. McAdoo, 177–83. Newbury Park, CA: Sage.

PEAR, R. 1995. Welfare and food stamp rolls end six years of increases. *New York Times*, March 14, A18.

PEARCE, D. 1978. The feminization of poverty: Women, work, and welfare. *Urban and Social Change Review* 11, 28–36.

PEARSON, J., AND N. THOENNES. 1990. Custody after divorce: Demographic and attitudinal patterns. *American Journal of Orthopsychiatry* 60, no. 2 (April): 233–48.

PEARSON, J. C. 1985. *Gender and communication.* Dubuque, IA: Wm. C. Brown.

PEAVY, L., AND U. SMITH. 1994. *Women in waiting in the westward movement: Life on the home frontier.* Norman: University of Oklahoma Press.

PEELE, S., WITH A. BRODSKY. 1976. *Love and addiction.* New York: New American Library.

PELTON, R. W. 1992. *Loony sex laws that you never knew you were breaking.* New York: Walker.

PENNEBAKER, R. 1994a. The perfect pregnant father. *Parents*, August, 55–56.

PENNEBAKER, R. 1994b. Winning the battle over chores. *Parents*, July, 111–15.

PEPE, M. V., D. W. SANDERS, AND C. W. SYMONS. 1993. Sexual behaviors of university freshmen and the implications for sexuality educators. *Journal of Sex Education and Therapy* 19, no. 1, 20–30.

PEREZ, L. 1994. Cuban families in the United States. In *Minority families in the United States: A multicultural perspective*, ed. R. L. Taylor, 95–112. Englewood Cliffs, NJ: Prentice Hall

PERRY-JENKINS, M., AND K. FOLK. 1994. Class, couples, and conflict: Effects of the division of labor on assessments of marriage in dual-earner families. *Journal of Marriage and the Family* 56 (February): 165–80.

PERTIG, J. 1994. A weighty problem. *American Health* (January/February): 82.

PERTMAN, A. 1994. Male, female jurors use differing scales of justice. *Baltimore Sun*, February 13, 8A.

PETERS, S. E., G. E. WYATT, AND D. FINKELHOR. 1986. Prevalence. In *Source on child sexual abuse*, ed. D. Finkelhor, 15–59. Beverly Hills, CA: Sage.

PETERSON, J. L., J. J. CARD, M. B. EISEN AND B. SHERMAN-WILLIAMS. 1994. Evaluating teenage pregnancy prevention and other social programs: Ten stages of program assessment. *Family Planning Perspectives* 26, no. 3 (May): 116–20, 131.

PETERSON, L. R. 1986. Interfaith marriage and religious commitment among Catholics. *Journal of Marriage and the Family* 48, 725–35.

PHIBBS, C. S., D. A. BATEMAN, AND R. M. SCHWARTZ. 1991. The neonatal costs of maternal cocaine use. *JAMA*, (September 18), 1521–1526.

PHILLIPS, D. 1992. Public policy, quality of child care, and children's development. In *New directions in child and family research: Shaping Head Start in the 90's*, ed. F. L. Parker, R. Robinson, S. Sambrano, C. S. Piotrowski, J. Hagen, S. Randolph, and A. Baker, 221–22. Washington, DC: Administration on Children, Youth and Families.

PIAGET, J. 1950. *The psychology of intelligence.* London: Routledge & Kegan Paul.

PIAGET, J. 1954. *The construction of reality in the child.* New York: Basic Books.

PIES, C. A. 1990. Lesbians and the choice to parent. In *Homosexuality and family relations*, ed. F. W. Bozett and M. B. Sussman, 137–54. New York: Harrington Park Press.

PILL, C. J. 1990. Stepfamilies: Redefining the family. *Family Relations* 39, 186–92.

PILLEMER, K. 1985. The dangers of dependency: New findings on domestic violence against the elderly. *Social Problems* 33, no. 2 (December): 146–58.

PILLEMER, K. A., AND D. FINKELHOR. 1988. The prevalence of elder abuse: A random sample survey. *The Gerontologist* 28, 51–57.

PILLEMER, K., AND J. J. SUITOR. 1991. "Will I ever escape my child's problems?" Effects of adult children's problems on elderly parents. *Journal of Marriage and the Family* 53 (August): 585–94.

PIÑA, D. L., AND V. L. BENGSTON. 1993. The division of household labor and wives' happiness: Ideology, employment, and perceptions of support. *Journal of Marriage and the Family* 55 (November): 901–12.

PIOTRKOWSKI, C. S., AND D. HUGHES. 1993. Dual-earner families in context: Managing family and work systems. In *Normal family processes*, 2nd ed., ed. F. Walsh, 185–207. New York: Guilford.

PITTMAN, F. 1989. *Private lives: Infidelity and the betrayal of intimacy.* New York: Norton.

PLECK, J. H. 1977. The work-family role system. *Social Problems* 24, 417–27.

PLECK, J. H. 1990. American fathering in historical perspective. In *Perspectives on the family: History, class, and feminism*, ed. C. Carlson, 377–89. Belmont, CA: Wadsworth.

PLECK, J. H. 1993. Are "family-supportive" employer policies relevant to men? In *Men, work, and family*, ed. J. C. Hood. Newbury Park, CA: Sage.

PLOTNICK, R. D. 1993. The effect of social policies on teenage pregnancy and childbearing. *Families in Society: The Journal of Contemporary Human Services* (June 1993): 324–28.

PLOTNIKOFF, D. 1994. Sexism and bias pollute cyberspace. *Baltimore Sun*, August 24, 6D.

POE, L. M. 1992. *Black grandparents as parents*. Berkeley, CA: L.M. Poe.

POL, L. G., M. G. MAY, AND F. R. HARTRANFT. 1992. Eight stages of aging. *American Demographics* (August): 54–57.

POLIT, D. 1984. The only child in single-parent families. In *The single-child family*, ed. T. Falbo, 178–210. New York: Guilford Press.

POLIT, D. F., AND T. FALBO. 1987. Only children and personality development: A quantitative review. *Journal of Marriage and the Family* 49 (May): 309–25.

POLK, N. 1988. Matchmaking as a retirement career. *New York Times*, October 23, 29.

POLLACK, W. 1990. Sexual harassment vs. legal definitions. *Harvard Women's Law Journal* 13 (Spring): 35–85.

POLLITT, K. 1994. Subject to debate. *The Nation*, May 30, 740.

POMERLAU, A., D. BOLDUC, G. MALCULT, AND L. COSSETTE. 1990. Pink or blue: Environmental gender stereotypes in the first two years of life. *Sex Roles* 22, nos. 5/6 (March): 359–67.

POPENOE, D. 1988. *Disturbing the nest: Family change and decline in modern societies*. New York: Aldine.

POPENOE, D. 1992. The controversial truth: Two-parent families are better. *New York Times*, December 26, 13.

POPENOE, D. 1993. American family decline, 1960–1990: A review and appraisal. *Journal of Marriage and the Family* 55 (August): 527–55.

POPKIN, S. J. 1990. Welfare: Views from the bottom. *Social Problems* 37 (February): 64–79.

Population Reference Bureau. 1988. *World population: Facts in focus*. Washington, DC.

Population Reference Bureau. 1990. *America in the 21st century: Social and economic support systems*. Washington, DC.

PORTES, P. R., S. C. HOWELL, J. H. BROWN, S. EICHENBERGER, AND C. A. MAS. 1992. Family functions and children's postdivorce adjustment. *American Journal of Orthopsychiatry* 62 (October): 613–17.

POSNER, J. K., AND D. L. VANDELL. 1994. Low-income children's after-school care: Are there beneficial effects of after-school programs? *Child Development* 65, no. 2 (April): 440–56.

POWELL, B. 1993. The reluctant princess. *Newsweek*, May 24, 28–29.

POWELL, E. 1991. *Talking back to sexual pressure*. Minneapolis, MN: CompCare.

POWELL, L. H., AND S. R. JORGENSEN. 1985. Evaluation of a church-based sexuality education program for adolescents. *Family Relations* 34 (October): 475–82.

PRATT, M. W. AND J. E. NORRIS. 1994. *The social psychology of aging: A cognitive perspective*. Cambridge, MA: Blackwell.

PRESSER, A. L. 1993. Palimony award for housework. *ABA Journal* (March): 32.

PRESSER, H. B., AND E. BAMBERGER. 1993. American women who work at home for pay: Distinctions and determinants. *Social Science Quarterly* 74, no. 4 (December): 815–27.

PRIDONOFF, J. A. 1994. Is the right-to-die movement a danger? *Washington Post Health Supplement*, October 18, 19.

PRIETO, Y. 1992. Cuban women in New Jersey: Gender relations and change. In *Seeking common ground: Multidisciplinary studies of immigrant women in the United States*, ed. D. Gabaccia, 185–201. Westport, CT: Greenwood.

PRUCHA, F. P. 1985. *The Indians in American society: From the Revolutionary War to the present*. Berkeley: University of California Press.

PRUETT, K. D. 1987. *The nurturing father: Journey toward the complete man*. New York: Warner.

Public Perspective. 1994a. *American Youth Culture: A Roper Center Review* 5, no. 4 (May/June): 21–24.

Public Perspective. 1994b. *Immigration* 5, no. 2 (January/February): 97.

Public Perspective. 1994c. *Women and the use of force* 5, no. 5 (July/August): 96.

PURCELL, P., AND L. STEWART. 1990. Dick and Jane in 1989. *Sex Roles* 22, nos. 3/4, 177–85.

PURVIS, A. 1990. The sins of the fathers. *Time*, November 26, 90–92.

PYKE, K. D. 1994. Women's employment as a gift or burden? Marital power across marriage, divorce, and remarriage. *Gender and Society* 8, no. 1 (March): 73–91.

QUEEN, S. A., R. W. HABENSTEIN, AND J. S. QUADAGNO. 1985. *The family in various cultures*, 5th ed. New York: Harper & Row.

QUICK, B. 1992. Tales from the self-help mill. *Newsweek*, August 31, 14.

QUICK, D. S., P. C. MCKENRY, AND B. M. NEWMAN. 1994. Stepmothers and their adolescent children: Adjustment to new family roles. In *Stepparenting: Issues in theory, research, and practice*, ed. K. Pasley and M. Ihinger-Tallman, 119–25. Westport, CT: Greenwood.

QUILL, T. E. 1993. *Death and dignity: Making choices and taking charge*. New York: Norton.

QUINN, J. B. 1993a. Sauce for the goose. *Newsweek*, January 25, 64.

QUINN, J. B. 1993b. What's for dinner, Mom? *Newsweek*, April 5, 1993, 68.

QURESHI, R. B. 1991. Marriage strategies among Muslims from South Asia. In *Muslim families in North America*, ed. E. H. Waugh, M. Abu-Laban, and R. B. Qureshi, 185–211. Edmonton: University of Alberta Press.

RABINOWITZ, F. E., AND S. V. COCHRAN. 1994. *Man alive: A primer of men's issues*. Pacific Grove, CA: Brooks/Cole.

RABINOWITZ, V. C. 1990. Coping with sexual harassment. In *Ivory power: Sexual harassment on campus*, ed. M. A. Paludi, 103–18. Albany: State University of New York Press.

RAGONÉ, H. 1994. *Surrogate motherhood: Conception in the heart*. Boulder, CO: Westview.

RAMIREZ, O., AND C. H. ARCE. 1981. The contemporary Chicano family: An empirically based review. In *Explorations in Chicano psychology*, ed. A. Baron, 3–28. New York: Praeger.

RAMSEY, S. H. 1994. Stepparents and the law: A nebulous status and a need for reform. In *Stepparenting: Issues in theory, research and practice*, ed. K. Pasley and M. Ihinger-Tallman, 217–37. Westport, CT: Greenwood.

RAMU, G. N. 1989. Patterns of mate selection. In *Family and marriage: Cross-cultural perspectives*, ed. K. Ishwaran, 165–78. Toronto: Wall & Thompson.

RANK, M. R. 1987. The formation and dissolution of marriages in the welfare population. *Journal of Marriage and the Family* 49 (February): 15–20.

RANKIN, R. P., AND J. S. MANEKER. 1985. The duration of marriage in a divorcing population: The impact of children. *Journal of Marriage and the Family* 47 (February): 43–52.

RAUCH, K. D. 1992. How Indian youths defeat addictions. *Washington Post Health Supplement*, March 10, 10–11.

RAWLINGS, S. W. 1994. *Household and Family Characteristics: March 1993*. U.S. Bureau of the Census, Current Population Reports, P20–477. Washington, DC: Government Printing Office.

RAYMOND, C. 1990. Studies of abortion's emotional effects renew controversial scholarly debate. *Chronicle of Higher Education*, February 2, A6, A7.

RAYMOND, C. 1992. Growth of scholarship on American Indians brings new insights about native cultures. *Chronicle of Higher Education*, January 15, A8, A10.

REID, J. 1993. Those fabulous '50s. *Utne Reader* 55 (January): 18–19.

REINHARZ, S. 1992. *Feminist methods in social research*. New York: Oxford University Press.

REINISCH, J. M., WITH R. BEASLEY. 1990. *The Kinsey Institute new report on sex: What you must know to be sexually literate*. New York: St. Martin's Press.

REIS, J., AND E. J. HERZ. 1989. An examination of young adolescents' knowledge of and attitude toward sexuality according to perceived contraceptive responsibility. *Journal of Applied Social Psychology* 19, no. 3, 231–50.

REIS, S. D., AND P. P. HEPPNER. 1993. Examination of coping resources and family adaptation in mothers and daughters of incestuous versus nonclinical families. *Journal of Counseling Psychology* 40, no. 1, 100–108.

REISMAN, J. A., AND E. W. EICHEL. 1990. *Kinsey, sex and fraud: The indoctrination of a people*. Lafayette, LA: Lochinvar-Huntington House.

REISS, I. 1960. Toward a sociology of the heterosexual love relationship. *Marriage and Family Living* 22, no. 2 (May): 139–45.

REISS, I. L., AND G. R. LEE. 1988. *Family systems in America*, 4th ed. New York: Holt, Rinehart & Winston.

REITER, E. 1991. *Making fast food: From the frying pan into the fryer*. Montreal: McGill-Queen's University Press.

RENN, J. A., AND S. L. CALVERT. 1993. The relation between gender schemas and adults' recall of stereotyped and counterstereotyped televised information. *Sex Roles* 28, nos. 7/8, 449–59.

RENWICK, T. J., AND B. R. BERGMANN. 1993. A budget-based definition of poverty: With an application to single-parent families. *Journal of Human Resources* 28, no. 1, (Winter): 1–24.

RENZETTI, C. M. 1992. *Violent betrayal: Partner abuse in lesbian relationships*. Newbury Park, CA: Sage.

RENZETTI, C. M., AND D. J. CURRAN.

1989. *Women, men, and society*. Boston: Allyn & Bacon.

RENZETTI, C. M., AND D. J. CURRAN. 1995. *Women, men, and society*, 3rd ed. Boston: Allyn & Bacon.

RESKIN, B. F., AND P. A. ROOS. 1990. *Job queues, gender queues: Explaining women's inroads into male occupations*. Philadelphia: Temple University Press.

RETSINAS, J. 1988. A theoretical reassessment of the applicability of Kübler-Ross's stages of dying. *Death Studies* 12, 207–16.

REXROAT, C. 1994. *The declining economic status of black children*. Washington, DC: Joint Center for Political and Economic Studies.

RHEINGOLD, H. L. 1969. The social and socializing infant. In *Handbook of socialization theory and research*, ed. D. A. Goslin, 779–90. Chicago: Rand McNally.

RHODES, W. A., AND K. HOEY. 1994. *Overcoming childhood misfortune: Children who beat the odds*. Westport, CT: Praeger.

RICH, S. 1988. Urban Institute study puts number of U.S. homeless at close to 600,000. *Washington Post*, November 4, A10.

RICH, S. 1990. U.S. isn't only place where modern family is being transformed: Similar marriage, birth trends seen in many developed nations. *Washington Post*, June 22, A25.

RICH, S. 1991. Hunger said to afflict 1 in 8 American children. *Washington Post*, March 27, A4.

RICH, S. 1992. Prosperity eludes many elderly women. *Washington Post*, September 14, A1, A80.

RICH, S. 1995. Delegates gather for aging conference as Social Security, Medicare face pressure. *Washington Post*, May 3, A6.

RICHARDS, T., M. J. WHITE, AND A. O. TSUI. 1987. Changing living arrangements: A hazard of transitions among household types. *Demography* 24, no. 1 (February): 77–97.

RICHARDSON, D. 1993. *Women, motherhood and childrearing*. New York: St. Martin's Press.

RICHARDSON, J. 1989. Substance use among eighth grade students who take care of themselves after school. *Pediatrics* 84, no. 3 (September 6): 556–66.

RICHARDSON, L. 1985. *The new other woman: Contemporary single women in affairs with married men*. New York: Free Press.

RICHARDSON, L. 1990. Lesbian couple

wed in district church: Ceremony moved to Westminster Presbyterian. *Washington Post*, June 2, B7.

RICHMOND-ABBOTT, M. 1992. *Masculine and feminine: Gender roles over the life cycle*, 2nd ed. New York: McGraw-Hill.

RILEY, G. 1991. *Divorce: An American tradition*. New York: Oxford University Press.

RINDFUSS, R. R., AND A. VANDENHEUVEL. 1990. Cohabitation: A precursor to marriage or an alternative to being single? *Population and Development Review* 16, 703–26.

RINDFUSS, R. R., AND E. H. STEPHEN. 1990. Marital noncohabitation: Absence does not make the heart grow fonder. *Journal of Marriage and the Family* 52 (February): 259–70.

RISMAN, B. J. 1986. Can men "mother"? Life as a single father. *Family Relations* 36, no. 1 (January): 95–102.

RIVARA, F. P., P. J. SWEENEY, AND B. F. HENDERSON. 1985. A study of lower socioeconomic status, black teenage fathers and their nonfather peers. *Pediatrics* 75, 648–56.

ROBB, D. 1995. Family values group urges NBC to omit lesbian kiss from "Serving in Silence." *Baltimore Sun*, January 2, 7D.

ROBERTS, A. E., AND P. D. STARR. 1989. Differential reference group assimilation among Vietnamese refugees. In *Refugees as immigrants: Cambodians, Laotians, and Vietnamese in America*, ed. D. W. Haines, 40–54. Totowa, NJ: Rowman & Littlefield.

ROBERTS, G. S. 1994. *Staying on the line: Blue-collar women in contemporary Japan*. Honolulu: University of Hawaii Press.

ROBERTS, L., AND L. J. KROKOFF. 1990. A time-series analysis of withdrawal, hostility, and displeasure in satisfied and dissatisfied marriages. *Journal of Marriage and the Family* 52 (February): 95–105.

ROBERTS, R. 1991. Love in bloom: Florists' rosy forecast. *Washington Post*, February 14, B1, B6.

ROBERTS, S. 1994. Hispanic population outnumbers blacks in four major cities as demographics shift. *New York Times*, October 9, 34.

ROBERTS, S. V. 1994a. Neglecting children—and parents. *U.S. News & World Report*, April 25, 10, 11.

ROBERTS, S. V. 1994b. The blue-collar blues. *U.S. News & World Report*, November 7, 32.

ROBERTS, S. V. 1994c. Unveiling the fact

of abortion politics. *U.S. News & World Report,* September 19, 10.

ROBERTS, S. V., K. HETTER, J. IMPOCO, AND S. MINERBROOK. 1994. Why are we so angry? *U.S. News & World Report,* November 7, 30–36.

ROBERTS, Y. 1993. We are becoming divorced from reality. *New Statesman & Society,* September 24, 16, 17, 19.

ROBERTSON, J. A. 1994. *Children of choice: Freedom and the new reproductive technologies.* Princeton, NJ: Princeton University Press.

ROBINSON, B. E. 1988. *Teenage fathers.* Lexington, MA: Lexington Books.

ROBINSON, E. 1994. Furor over fertility options. *Washington Post Health Supplement,* January 11, 6.

ROBINSON, I., K. ZISS, B. GANZA, AND S. KATZ. 1991. Twenty years of the sexual revolution, 1965–1985: An update. *Journal of Marriage and the Family* 53 (February): 216–20.

ROBINSON, J. P. 1988. Who's doing the housework? *American Demographics* 10, no. 12 (December): 24–28, 63.

ROBINSON, L., AND J. EPSTEIN. 1994. Battered by the myth of macho. *U.S. News & World Report,* April 4, 40–41.

ROBINSON, R. B., AND D. I. FRANK. 1994. The relation between self-esteem, sexual activity, and pregnancy. *Adolescence* 29, no. 113 (Spring): 27–35.

ROCHE, J. P., AND T. W. RAMSBEY. 1993. Premarital sexuality: A five-year follow-up study of attitudes and behavior by dating stage. *Adolescence* 28, no.109 (Spring): 67–80.

RODGERS, W. L., AND A. THORNTON. 1985. Changing patterns of first marriage in the United States. *Demography* 22, 265–79.

RODRIGUEZ, R. 1992. *Days of obligation: An argument with my Mexican father.* New York: Viking.

ROGERS, P., WITH S. REISS. 1994. Is murder "justifiable homicide"? *Newsweek,* August 8, 1994. 22.

ROHDE, D. 1994. Golden-aged athletes go for the gold. *Christian Science Monitor,* July 8, 10–11.

ROMERO, M. 1992. *Maid in the U.S.A.* New York: Routledge.

ROMPF, E. L. 1993. Open adoption: What does the "average person" think? *Child Welfare* 72, no. 3 (May/June): 219–30.

Roper Center for Public Opinion Research. 1994. Faith in America. *The Public Perspective* 5, no. 6 (September/December): 90–99.

Roper Organization. 1990. *The 1990 Virginia Slims opinion poll: A 20–year perspective of women's issues.* Storrs: University of Connecticut Press.

ROPERS, R. H. 1991. *Persistent poverty: The American dream turned nightmare.* New York: Plenum.

ROSCOE, B., M. S. DIANA, AND R. H. BROOKS II. 1987. Early, middle, and late adolescents' views on dating and factors influencing partner selection. *Adolescence* 22, no. 85 (Spring): 59–68.

ROSE, S., AND I. H. FRIEZE. 1993. Young singles' contemporary dating scripts. *Sex Roles,* 28, nos. 9/10 (May): 499–509.

ROSEN, B. C. 1982. *The industrial connection: Achievement and the family in developing societies.* New York: Aldine.

ROSEN, K. H., AND S. M. STITH. 1993. Intervention strategies for treating women in violent dating relationships. *Family Relations* 42 (October): 427–33.

ROSENBERG, J. 1993. Just the two of us. In *Reinventing love: Six women talk about lust, sex, and romance,* ed. L. Abraham, L. Green, M. Krance, J. Rosenberg, J. Somerville, and C. Stoner, 301–307. New York: Plume.

ROSENBLATT, P. C., AND R. A. PHILLIPS, JR. 1975. Family articles in popular magazines: Advice to writers, editors, and teachers of consumers. *Family Coordinator* 24 (July): 267–71.

ROSENBLATT, P. C. 1994. *Metaphors of family systems theory: Toward new constructions.* New York: Guilford Press.

ROSENFELD, M. 1994. Father knows squat. *Washington Post,* November 13, G1, G8.

ROSENFIELD, S. 1989. Sex differences in depression: Do women always have higher rates? *Journal of Health and Social Behavior* 30, 77–91.

ROSENTHAL, C. J. 1985. Kinkeeping in the familial division of labor. *Journal of Marriage and the Family* 47 (November): 965–74.

ROSENZWEIG, P. M. 1992. *Married and alone: The way back.* New York: Plenum.

ROSIN, M. B. 1987. *Stepfathering: Stepfathers' advice on creating a new family.* New York: Simon & Schuster.

ROSS, C. E. 1987. The division of labor at home. *Social Forces* 65, 816–33.

ROSS, C. E., J. MIROWSKY, AND K. GOLDSTEIN. 1991. The impact of the family on health: The decade in review. In *Contemporary families: Looking forward, looking back,* ed. A. Booth.

Minneapolis, MN: National Council on Family Relations.

ROSS, E. 1993. For runaway girls, a house that's a home. *Christian Science Monitor,* March 4, 14.

ROSSI, A. S., ED. 1994. *Sexuality across the life course.* Chicago: University of Chicago Press.

ROSSI, P. H. 1994. Troubling families: Family homelessness in America. *American Behavioral Scientist* 37 no. 3 (January): 342–95.

ROTHBLUM, E. D. 1994. I'll die for the revolution, but don't ask me not to diet: Feminism and the continuing stigmatization of obesity. In *Feminist perspectives on eating disorders,* ed. P. Fallon, M. A. Katzman, and S. C. Wooley, 53–76. New York: Guilford.

ROTHBLUM, E. D., AND K. A. BREHONY, EDS. 1993. *Boston marriages: Romantic but asexual relationships among contemporary lesbians.* Amherst: University of Massachusetts Press.

ROTHMAN, B. K. 1989. Women, health, and medicine. In *Women: A feminist perspective,* 4th ed., ed. J. Freeman, 76–86. Mountain View, CA: Mayfield.

ROTHMAN, E. K. 1983. Sex and self-control: Middle-class courtship in America, 1770–1870. In *The American family in social-historical perspective,* 3rd ed., ed. M. Gordon, 393–410. New York: St. Martin's Press.

ROTHMAN, S. M. 1978. *Women's proper place: A history of changing ideals and practices, 1870 to the present.* New York: Basic Books.

ROVNER, S. 1990. Debunking the "empty nest" myth. *Washington Post Health Supplement,* December 18, 14.

ROVNER, S. 1991. Battered wives: Centuries of silence. *Washington Post Health Supplement,* August 20, 7.

ROWE, G. P. 1981. The developmental conceptual framework to the study of the family. In *Emerging conceptual frameworks in family analysis,* ed. F. I. Nye and F. M. Berardo, 198–222. New York: Praeger.

ROWLAND, M. 1994. Love and money the second time around. *Working Woman* (August): 22, 24.

ROZEMA, H. J. 1986. Defensive communication climate as a barrier to sex education in the home. *Family Relations* 35 (October): 531–37.

RUBENSTEIN, C. 1994. The confident generation. *Working Mother* (May): 38–45.

RUBIEN, D. 1989. For Asians in U.S.,

hidden strife. *New York Times*, January 11, C1, C10.

RUBIN, L. B. 1976. *Worlds of pain: Life in the working-class family*. New York: Basic Books.

RUBIN, L. B. 1983. *Intimate strangers: Men and women together*. New York: Harper & Row.

RUBIN, L. B. 1994. *Families on the fault line: America's working class speaks about the family, the economy, race, and ethnicity*. New York: Harper-Collins.

RUBIN, R. 1994. A test to predict dementia. *U.S. News & World Report*, September 12, 91.

RUBY, R. 1990. Women's protest raises issue of Saudi traditions. *Baltimore Sun*, November 19, 1A, 3A.

RUDAVSKY, S. 1992. A status report on the glass ceiling. *Washington Post*, August 12, A19.

RUGGLES, S. 1994. The origins of African-American family structure. *Journal of Marriage and the Family* 59 (February): 136–51.

RUSSELL, C. 1994. No man shortage in the 1990s. *New Woman* (January): 113–14.

RUSSELL, C., AND T. G. EXTER. 1986. America at mid-decade. *American Demographics* 8, no. 1 (January): 22–29.

RUSSELL, D. 1984. *Sexual exploitation: Rape, child sexual abuse, and workplace harassment*. Beverly Hills, CA: Sage.

RUSSELL, D. E. H. 1990. *Rape in marriage*. Bloomington: Indiana University Press.

RUSSELL, D. E. H., ED. 1993. *Making violence sexy: Feminist views on pornography*. New York: Teachers College Press.

RUSSELL, K., M. WILSON, AND R. HALL. 1992. *The color complex: The politics of skin color among African Americans*. New York: Harcourt Brace Jovanovich.

RUSSO, N. F., J. D. HORN, AND S. TROMP. 1993. Childspacing intervals and abortion among blacks and whites: A brief report. *Women & Health* 20, no. 3, 43–51.

RUTTER, V. 1994. Lessons from stepfamilies. *Psychology Today*, May, 30–33, 60ff.

RYAN, M. P. 1983. *Womanhood in America: From colonial times to the present*, 3rd ed. New York: Franklin Watts.

RYAN, M. 1993. Undercover among the elderly. *Parade Magazine*, July 18, 8.

SAAD, LYDIA. 1994. Public has cold feet on health care reform. *Gallup Poll Monthly*, August, 2–5.

SADKER, M., AND D. SADKER. 1994. *Failing at fairness: How America's schools cheat girls*. New York: Scribner's.

SAFILIOS-ROTHSCHILD, C. 1977. *Love, sex, and sex roles*. Englewood Cliffs, NJ: Prentice Hall.

ST. GEORGE, D. 1993. Packwood's pals help with cash. *Baltimore Sun*, November 19, 1A, 19A.

SALHOLZ, E., WITH T. CLIFTON, N. JOSEPH, L. BEACHY, P. ROGERS, L. WILSON, D. GLICK, AND P. KING. 1990. The future of gay America. *Newsweek*, March 12, 20–25.

SALHOLZ, E., ET AL. 1993. For better or for worse. *Newsweek*, May 24, 69.

SALOVEY, P., AND J. RODIN. 1989. Envy and jealousy in close relationships. In *Close relationships*, ed. C. Hendrick, 221–46. Newbury Park, CA: Sage.

SALTZMAN, A. 1993a. Family friendliness. *U.S. News & World Report*, February 22, 59–66.

SALTZMAN, A. 1993b. Mom, Dad, I want a job. *U.S. News & World Report*, May 17, 68–72.

SALUTER, A. F. 1994. *Marital status and living arrangements: March 1993*. U.S. Bureau of the Census, Current Population Reports, Series P20–478. Washington, DC: Government Printing Office.

SAMET, N., AND E. W. KELLY, JR. 1987. The relationship of steady dating to self-esteem and sex role identity among adolescents. *Adolescence* 22, no. 85 (Spring): 231–45.

SANCHEZ-AYENDEZ, M. 1988. The Puerto Rican American family. In *Ethnic families in America: Patterns and variations*, 3rd ed., ed. C. J. Mindel, R. W. Habenstein, and R. Wright, Jr., 173–98. New York: Elsevier.

SANDAY, P. R. 1990. *Fraternity gang rape: Sex, brotherhood and privilege on campus*. New York: New York University Press.

SANDEFUR, G. D., AND A. SAKAMOTO. 1988. American Indian household structure and income. *Demography* 25, no. 1 (February): 71–80.

SANDER, J. 1991. *Before their time: Four generations of teenage mothers*. New York: Harcourt Brace Jovanovich.

SANDERS, G. F., AND R. L. MULLIS. 1988. Family influences on sexual attitudes and knowledge as reported by college students. *Adolescence* 92 (Winter): 837–46.

SANDROFF, R. 1994. When women make more than men. *Working Woman* (January): 39–41, 87–88.

SANTROCK, J. W., K. A. SITTERLE, AND R. A. WARSHAK. 1988. Parent-child relationships in stepfather families. In *Fatherhood today: Men's changing role in the family*, ed. P. Bronstein and C. P. Cowan, 144–65. New York: Wiley.

SAPORTA, S. 1991. Miscellany: Old maid and dirty old man: The language of ageism. *American Speech* 66, no. 3 (Fall): 333–34.

SARCH, A. 1993. Making the connection: Single women's use of the telephone in dating relationships with men. *Journal of Communications* 43, no. 2 (Spring): 128–44.

SARNOFF, I., AND S. SARNOFF. 1989. The dialectic of marriage. *Psychology Today*, October, 54–57.

SAUNDERS, D. G. 1994. Child custody decisions in families experiencing woman abuse. *Social Work* 39, no. 1 (January): 51–57.

SAVAGE, H., AND P. FRONCZEK. 1993. *Who can afford to buy a house in 1991?* U.S. Bureau of the Census, Housing and Household Economic Statistics Division. Washington, DC: Government Printing Office.

SAVIN-WILLIAMS, R., AND R. G. RODRIGUEZ. 1993. A developmental, clinical perspective on lesbian, gay male, and bisexual youths. In *Adolescent sexuality*, ed. T. P. Gullotta et al. Newbury Park, CA: Sage.

SCALES-TRENT, J. 1995. *Notes of a white black woman*. University Park: Pennsylvania State Press.

SCARF, M. 1987. *Intimate partners: Patterns in love and marriage*. New York: Random House.

SCHAIE, K. W. 1993. Ageist language in psychological research. *American Psychologist* 48, no. 1 (January): 49–51.

SCHILLINGER, L. 1994. Bride and seek. *New Republic*, June 27, 15–17.

SCIIMID, P. 1994. Parents seek right to let son die after 17–year coma. *Washington Post*, October 18, A4.

SCHMIDT, J. D., AND L. W. SHERMAN. 1993. Does arrest deter domestic violence? *American Behavioral Scientist* 36, no. 5 (May): 601–609.

SCHOEN, R., AND R. M. WEINICK. 1993. Partner choice in marriages and cohabitations. *Journal of Marriage and the Family* 55 (May): 408–14.

SCHOETTLER, C. 1994. Government study indicates breakdown in traditional family life in Britain. *Baltimore Sun*, (January 27): 6A.

SCHROF, J. M. 1993. Pumped up. *U.S. News & World Report*, June 1, 55–63.

SCHROF, J. M. 1994a. Different paths to success. *U.S. News & World Report*, September 26, 115–16.

SCHROF, J. M. 1994b. A lens on matrimony. *U.S. News & World Report*, February 21, 66–69.

SCHROF, J. M., WITH B. WAGNER. 1994. Sex in America. *U.S. News & World Report*, October 17, 75–81.

SCHUMM, W. R., AND M. A. BUGAIGHIS. 1986. Marital quality over the marital career: Alternative explanations. *Journal of Marriage and the Family* 48 (February): 165–68.

SCHUYLER, N. 1995. Indecent disclosure. *Working Woman* (January): 12.

SCHVANEVELDT, J. D. 1981. The interactional framework in the study of the family. In *Emerging conceptual frameworks in family analysis*, ed. F. I. Nye and F. M. Berardo, 97–129. New York: Praeger.

SCHWARTZ, F. N. 1989. Management women and the new facts of life. *Harvard Business Review* 89, no. 1 (January-February): 65–76.

SCHWARTZ, J. D. 1993. *The mother puzzle: A new generation reckons with motherhood.* New York: Simon & Schuster.

SCHWARTZ, P. 1994. *Peer marriage: How love between equals really works.* New York: Free Press.

SCHWEBEL, A. I., AND M. A. FINE. 1994. *Understanding and helping families: A cognitive-behavioral approach.* Hillsdale, NJ: Lawrence Erlbaum Associates.

SCHWEBEL, A. I., M. A. FINE, AND M. A. RENNER. 1991. A study of perceptions of the stepparent role. *Journal of Family Issues* 12, no. 1 (March): 43–57.

SCINTO, L., ET AL. 1994. A potential noninvasive neurobiological test for Alzheimer's disease. *Science*, November 11, 1051–1054.

SCOTT, C. S., L. SHIFMAN, L. ORR, R. G. OWEN, AND N. FAWCETT. 1988. Hispanic and black American adolescents' beliefs relating to sexuality and contraception. *Adolescence* 23, no. 91 (Fall): 667–88.

SCOTT, D., AND B. WISHY, EDS. 1982. *America's families: A documentary history.* New York: Harper & Row.

SCOTT, D. C. 1994. Child abductions: Mexico's hidden problems. *Christian Science Monitor*, June 30, 6.

SEABERRY, J. 1991. Household life's all in the family for Asians, Hispanics in D.C. area. *Washington Post*, September 8, B1, B9.

SECCOMBE, K. 1991. Assessing the costs and benefits of children: Gender comparisons among childfree husbands and wives. *Journal of Marriage and the Family* 53 (February): 191–202.

SEGAL, J. 1989. 10 myths about child development. *Parents*, July, 81–84, 87.

SEGAL, L., AND Z. SEGAL. 1991. Does spanking work? *Parents* (March), 188.

SEGAL, U. A. 1991. Cultural variables in Asian Indian families. *Families in Society* 72, no. 4 (April): 233–42.

SEGURA, D. A. 1994. Working at motherhood: Chicana and Mexican immigrant mothers and employments. In *Mothering: Ideology, experience, and agency*, ed. E. N. Glenn, G. Chang, and L. R. Forcey, 211–33. New York: Routledge.

SEITER, E. 1993. *Sold separately: Children and parents in consumer culture.* New Brunswick, NJ: Rutgers University Press.

SELBY, H. 1994. Is this a case of misinterpreted brotherly love? *Baltimore Sun*, July 28, D1, D7.

SELBY, H. 1995. Gay couples find joy as parents. *Baltimore Sun*, January 3, B1, B3.

SELIGMANN, J. 1994. On demand = less demand. *Newsweek*, June 27, 49.

SELIGMANN, J., AND P. ROGERS. 1994. The pressure to lose. *Newsweek*, May 2, 60–61.

SELIGMANN, J., ET AL. 1992. Is my baby all right? *Newsweek*, June 22, 62–63.

SELTZER, J. A. 1991. Legal custody arrangements and children's economic welfare. *American Journal of Sociology* 96, no. 4 (January): 895–929.

SERWER, A. E. 1993. American Indians discover money is power. *Fortune*, April 19, 136–42.

SETER, J. 1994. U.S. concerns: Bride burnings, infanticide. *U.S. News & World Report*, February 14, p.6.

SETTLES, B. H., R. S. HANKS, AND M. B. SUSSMAN, EDS. 1993. *American families and the future: Analyses of possible destinies.* New York: Haworth.

SHAMIR, B. 1986. Unemployment and household division of labor. *Journal of Marriage and the Family* 48 (February): 196–206.

SHAPIRO, J. L. 1987. The expectant father. *Psychology Today*, January, 36–39.

SHAPIRO, J. P., ET AL. 1993. Teenage sex: Just say "wait." *U.S. News & World Report*, July 26, 56–59.

SHAPIRO, J. P. 1994. Gray boomers. *U.S. News & World Report*, October 10, 14.

SHAPIRO, J. P., AND J. M. SCHROF WITH M. THARP AND D. FRIEDMAN. 1995. Honor thy children. *U.S. News & World Report*, February 27, 39–49.

SHAPIRO, L. 1990. Guns and dolls. *Newsweek*, May 28, 57–65.

SHAVER, P., C. HAZAN, AND D. BRADSHAW. 1988. Love as attachment. In *The psychology of love*, ed. R. J. Sternberg and M. L. Barnes, 68–99. New Haven, CT: Yale University Press.

SHEA, C. 1994. Queens College and a measure of diversity. *Chronicle of Higher Education*, May 11, A37–A39.

SHEA, J. A., AND G. R. ADAMS. 1984. Correlates of romantic attachment: A path analysis study. *Journal of Youth and Adolescence* 13, no. 1: 27–44.

SHEARER, L. 1990. Too much television = too much fat. *Parade*, May 27, 13.

SHEEHY, G. 1992. *The silent passage: Menopause.* New York: Random House.

SHEINDLIN, J. B. 1994. Paying grandmas to keep kids in limbo. *New York Times*, August 29, A15.

SHELTON, B. A. 1987. Variations in divorce rates by community size: A test of the social integration explanation. *Journal of Marriage and the Family* 49 (November): 827–32.

SHELTON, B. A., AND D. JOHN. 1993. Ethnicity, race, and difference: A comparison of white, black, and Hispanic men's household labor time. In *Men, work, and family*, ed. J. C. Hood, 131–50. Newbury Park, CA: Sage.

SHENON, P. 1994. A Chinese bias against girls creates surplus of bachelors. *New York Times*, August 16, A1, A8.

SHIMOMURA, M. 1990. Japan: Too much mommy-san. *New Perspectives Quarterly* 7, no. 1 (Winter): 24–27.

SHOOP, R. J. 1992. The reasonable woman in a hostile work environment. *Education Law Reporter*, April 23, 703–18.

SHOOP, R. J., AND D. L. EDWARDS. 1994. *How to stop sexual harassment in our schools: A handbook and curriculum guide for administrators and teachers.* Boston: Allyn & Bacon.

SHORR, J. L. 1985. Rock videos and values: A content analysis. Paper presented at the fifteenth annual Popular Culture Association meeting, Louisville, KY, April.

SHORRIS, E. 1992. *Latinos: A biography of the people.* New York: Norton.

SHORTER, E. 1975. *The making of the modern family.* New York: Basic Books.

SHORTO, R. 1991. Made-in-Japan parenting. *Health* (June): 54, 56–57.

SHOSTAK, A. 1987. Singlehood. In *Handbook of marriage and the family,* ed. M. B. Sussman and S. K. Steinmetz, 355–67. New York: Plenum.

SHOTLAND, R. L. 1989. A model of the causes of date rape in developing and close relationships. In *Close relationships,* ed. C. Hendrick, 247–70. Newbury Park, CA: Sage.

SHUPE, A., W. A. STACEY, AND L. R. HAZLEWOOD. 1987. *Violent men, violent couples.* Lexington, MA: Lexington Books.

SHURE, M. B., WITH T. F. DiGERONIMO. 1994. *Raising a thinking child: Helping your young child to resolve everyday conflicts and get along with others.* New York: Holt.

SIECUS. 1994. *Teens talk about sex: Adolescent sexuality in the 90's.* New York.

SIEGEL, J. M., AND D. H. KUYKENDALL. 1990. Loss, widowhood, and psychological distress among the elderly. *Journal of Consulting and Clinical Psychology* 58, no. 5, 519–24.

SIGNORIELLI, N., D. McLEOD, AND E. HEALY. 1994. Gender stereotypes in MTV commercials: The beat goes on. *Journal of Broadcasting & Electronic Media* (Winter): 91–101.

SIMENAUER, J., AND D. CARROLL. 1982. *Singles: The new Americans.* New York: Simon & Schuster.

SIMMONS, C. H., A. VON KOLKE, AND H. SHIMIZU. 1986. Attitudes toward romantic love among American, German, and Japanese students. *Journal of Social Psychology* 126, no. 3 (June): 327–36.

SIMON, R. J. 1993. *The case for transracial adoption.* Washington, DC: American University Press.

SIMONS, R. L., C. JOHNSON, J. BEAMAN, AND R. D. CONGER. 1993. Explaining women's double jeopardy: Factors that mediate the association between harsh treatment as a child and violence by a husband. *Journal of Marriage and the Family* 55 (August): 713–23.

SIMONS, R. L., C. JOHNSON, AND R. D. CONGER. 1994. Harsh corporal punishment versus quality of parental involvement as an explanation of adolescent maladjustment. *Journal of Marriage and the Family* 56, no. 4 (August): 591–67.

SIMPSON, A. 1995. The Social Security pie: Save a piece for the kids. *Christian Science Monitor,* March 10, 19.

SIMPSON, J. A. 1987. The dissolution of romantic relationships: Factors involved in relationship stability and emotional distress. *Journal of Personality and Social Psychology* 53, no. 4 (October): 683–92.

SINGER, J. L. 1980. Romantic fantasy in personality development. In *On love and loving,* ed. K. S. Pope, 172–94. San Francisco: Jossey-Bass.

SKOLNICK, A. 1991. *Embattled paradise: The American family in an age of uncertainty.* New York: Basic Books.

SKRUCK, K. 1994. 10 keys to quality. *Working Mother* (August): 40–42.

SLADE, M. 1985. Treating parents as children. *New York Times,* May 13, C5.

SLATER, S., AND J. MENCHER. 1991. The lesbian family life cycle: A contextual approach. *American Journal of Orthopsychiatrics* 6, no. 3 (July): 372–82.

SLOAN, G. A. 1993. *Postponing parenthood: The effect of age on reproductive potential.* New York: Insight Books.

SLOANE, L. 1987. Prenuptial agreements. *New York Times,* June 13, 34.

SMALL, S. A., AND D. KERNS. 1993. Unwanted sexual activity among peers during early and middle adolescence: Incidence and risk factors. *Journal of Marriage and the Family* 55 (November): 941–52.

SMALL, S. A., AND T. LUSTER. 1993. Adolescent sexual activity: An ecological, risk-factor approach. *Journal of Marriage and the Family* 56 (February): 181–92.

SMITH, K. R., C. D. ZICK, AND G. J. DUNCAN. 1991. Remarriage patterns among recent widows and widowers. *Demography* 28, no. 3 (August): 361–74.

SMITH, L. 1993. Perimenopause. *Baltimore Sun,* December 14, 1D, 5D.

SMITH, S., AND B. INGOLDSBY. 1992. Multicultural family studies: Educating students for diversity. *Family Relations* 41 (January): 25–30.

SMITH, T. 1990. The polls—a report: The sexual revolution? *Public Opinion Quarterly* 54 (Fall): 415–35.

SMITH, T. W. 1994. Can money buy you love? *The Public Perspective* 5, no. 2 (January/February): 33–34.

SMITH. T. W. 1994. Attitudes toward sexual permissiveness: Trends, correlates, and behavioral connections. In *Sexuality across the life course,* ed. A.

S. Rossi, 63–97. Chicago: University of Chicago Press.

SMITH, V. E., WITH D. GELMAN. 1993. Two dads and a dream—but no illusions. *Newsweek,* August 30, 21.

SMOCK, P. J. 1990. Remarriage patterns of black and white women: Reassessing the role of educational attainment. *Demography* 27, no. 3 (August): 467–73.

SMOCK, P. J. 1993. The economic costs of marital disruption for young women over the past two decades. *Demography* 30, no. 3 (August): 353–71.

SMOLAK, L., M. P. LEVINE, AND S. GRALEN. 1993. The impact of puberty and dating on eating problems among middle school girls. *Journal of Youth and Adolescence* 22, no. 4 (August): 355–68.

SMOLOWE, J. 1990. Bringing an end to limbo. *Time,* December 24, 64.

SMOLOWE, J. 1993. Intermarried . . . with children. *Time,* Fall, 64–65.

SNIPP, C. M. 1990. A portrait of American Indian women and the labor force experience. In *The American woman, 1990–91: A status report,* ed. S. E. Rix, 265–72. New York: Norton.

SOKOLOFF, N. J. 1992. *Black women and white women in the professions: Occupational segregation by race and gender, 1960–1980.* New York: Routledge.

SOLLIE, D. L., AND L. A. LESLIE. 1994. *Feminist research on families and relationships.* Newbury Park, CA: Sage.

SOLOMON, J., AND S. MILLER. 1994. "Hero" or "harasser"? *Newsweek,* September 12, 48–50.

SOLOMON, K., AND P. A. SZWABO. 1994. The work-oriented culture: Success and power in elderly men. In *Older men's lives,* ed. E. Thompson, Jr., 42–64. Thousand Oaks, CA: Sage.

SOMERS, M. D. 1993. A comparison of voluntarily childfree adults and parents. *Journal of Marriage and the Family* 55 (August): 643–50.

SOMERVILLE, F. P. L. 1994. Their faith offers better feminism. Muslim women say—rights with protection. *Baltimore Sun,* February 15, 4B.

SOMMER, M. 1994. Welcome cribside, Dad. *Christian Science Monitor,* June 28, 19.

SOMMERS, C. 1989. Philosophers against the family. In *Vice and virtue in everyday life: Introductory readings in ethics,* ed. C. Sommers and F. Sommers, 728–54. New York: Harcourt Brace Jovanovich.

SOMMERS-FLANAGAN, R., J. SOMMERS-FLANAGAN AND B. DAVIS. 1993.

What's happening on music television? A gender role content analysis. *Sex Roles* 28, nos. 11/12, 745–53.

SONENSTEIN, F. L. 1986. Risking paternity: Sex and contraception among adolescent males. In *Adolescent fatherhood*, ed. A. S. Elster and M. E. Lamb, 31–45. Hillsdale, NJ: Lawrence Erlbaum Associates.

SONENSTEIN, F. L., J. H. PLECK, AND L. C. KU. 1991. Levels of sexual activity among adolescent males in the United States. *Family Planning Perspectives* 23, 162–67.

SORENSON, T. 1981. A follow-up study of operated transsexual males. *Acta Psychiatrica Scandinavica* 63, 486–503.

SOSIN, M. R. 1989. Homelessness in Chicago. *Public Welfare* 47, no. 1 (Winter): 22–28.

SOUTH, S. J. 1993. Racial and ethnic differences in the desire to marry. *Journal of Marriage and the Family* 55 (May): 357–70.

SOUTH, S. J., AND G. SPITZE. 1986. Determinants of divorce over the marital life course. *American Sociological Review* 51 (August): 583–90.

SOUTHGATE, M. 1994. A funny thing happened on the way to prime time. *New York Times Magazine*, October 30, 52–55.

SOWELL, T. 1994. *Race and culture: A world view*. New York: Basic Books.

SPANIER, G. B. 1989. Bequeathing family continuity. *Journal of Marriage and the Family* 51 (February): 3–13.

SPAYD, L. 1991a. More women trading paychecks for payoffs of full-time parenting. *Washington Post*, July 8, A1, A4.

SPAYD, L. 1991b. On D.C. streets, vendors in struggle. *Washington Post*, October 29, A1, A7.

SPEARE, JR., A., AND R. AVERY. 1993. Who helps whom in older parent-child families? *Journal of Gerontology: Social Sciences* 48, no. 2, S64–S73.

SPEARS, G. 1994. Estate-planning musts for blended families. *Kiplinger's Personal Finance Magazine* 48, no. 12 (December): 91–96.

SPENCER, R. F., AND J. D. JENNINGS. 1977. *The Native Americans: Ethnology and backgrounds of the North American Indians*. New York: Harper & Row.

SPIERS, J. 1993. Upper-middle-class woes. *Fortune*, December 27, 80–84.

SPIGEL, L., AND D. MANN, EDS. 1992. *Private screenings: Television and the female consumer*. Minneapolis: University of Minnesota Press.

SPITZE, G. 1986. The division of task responsibility in U.S. households: Longitudinal adjustments to change. *Social Forces* 64, no. 3 (March): 689–701.

SPITZE, G. 1988. Women's employment and family relations: A review. *Journal of Marriage and the Family* 50 (August): 595–618.

SPITZE, G., J. R. LOGAN, G. DEANE, AND S. ZERGER. 1994. Adult children's divorce and intergenerational relationships. *Journal of Marriage and the Family* 56 (May): 279–93.

SPOCK, B. 1994. *A better world for our children: Rebuilding American family values*. New York: National Press Book.

SPRECHER, S., AND K. McKINNEY. 1993. *Sexuality*. Newbury Park, CA: Sage.

SPRECHER, S., K. McKINNEY, AND T. L. ORBUCH. 1991. The effect of current sexual behavior on friendship, dating, and marriage desirability. *Journal of Sex Research* 28, no. 3 (August): 367–408.

SPREY, J., ED. 1990. *Fashioning family theory*. Newbury Park, CA: Sage.

SQUIER, D. A., AND J. S. QUADAGNO. 1988. The Italian American family. In *Ethnic families in America: Patterns and variations*, 3rd ed., ed. C. J. Mindel, R. W. Habenstein, and R. Wright, Jr., 109–37. New York: Elsevier.

SQUIRES, S. 1991. The new motherhood. *Washington Post Health Supplement*, February 12, 12–15.

SQUIRES, S. 1992. Shopping for safe sperm. *Washington Post Health Supplement*, February 11, 11–12, 14.

SQUIRES, S. 1995. Should parents spank? *Washington Post Health Supplement*, February 14, 7.

SQUIRREL, G. 1989. Teachers and issues of sexual orientation. *Gender and Education*, 17–33.

STACEY, J. 1990. *Brave new families: Stories of domestic upheaval in late twentieth century America*. New York: Basic Books.

STACEY, W. A., L. R. HAZLEWOOD, AND A. SHUPE. 1994. *The violent couple*. Westport, CT: Praeger.

STACK, S. 1994. The effect of geographic mobility on premarital sex. *Journal of Marriage and the Family* 56 (February): 204–208.

STAMP, G. H. 1994. The appropriation of the parental role through communication during the transition to parenthood. *Communication Monographs* 61, no. 2 (June): 89–112.

STANFIELD II, J. M., ED. 1993. *A history of race relations research: First-generation recollections*. Newbury Park, CA: Sage.

Stanford Center for the Study of Families, Children and Youth. 1991. *The Stanford studies of homeless families, children and youth*. Stanford, CA: Stanford University.

STANGLIN, D. 1995. The angry women of the CIA. *U.S. News & World Report*, April 10, 47–49.

STANNARD, D. E. 1979. Changes in the American family: Fiction and reality. In *Changing images of the family*, ed. V. Tufte and B. Myerhoff, 83–98. New Haven, CT: Yale University Press.

STAPLES, R. 1981. *The world of black singles*. Westport, CT: Greenwood.

STAPLES, R. 1988. The black American family. In *Ethnic families in America: Patterns and variations*, 3rd ed., ed. C. H. Mindel, R. W. Habenstein, and R. Wright, Jr., 303–24. New York: Elsevier.

STAPLES, R. 1994. *The black family: Essays and studies*, 5th ed. Belmont, CA: Wadsworth.

STAPLES, R., AND L. B. JOHNSON. 1993. *Black families at the crossroads: Challenges and prospects*. San Francisco, Jossey-Bass.

STARK, E. 1993. A quickie guide to prenups for Trump, Gates—and you. *Money*, June, 17.

STARRELS, M. E. 1994. Gender differences in parent-child relations. *Journal of Family Issues* 15, no. 1 (March): 148–65.

STEIN, P. J., ED. 1981. *Single life: Unmarried adults in social context*. New York: St. Martin's Press.

STEIN, R. 1993. Why men avoid vasectomies. *Washington Post Health Supplement*, January 12, 11.

STEINBACH, A. 1995. Custody wars. *Baltimore Sun*, March 13, 1D-2D.

STEINBERG, L., AND S. B. SILVERBERG. 1987. Adolescent autonomy, parent-adolescent conflict, and parental well-being. *Journal of Youth and Adolescence* 16, 293–312.

STEINMETZ, S. 1978. The battered husband syndrome. *Victimology* 2, nos. 3/4, 499–509.

STEINMETZ, S. 1987. Elderly victims of domestic violence. In *The elderly: Victims and deviants*, eds. C. D. Chambers, J. H. Lindquist, O. Z. White, and M. T. Harter, 126–41. Athens: Ohio University Press.

STEPHENS, W. N. 1963. *The family in cross-cultural perspective*. New York: Holt, Rinehart & Winston.

STEPP, L. S. 1991. Presbyterians reject

new sex doctrine. *Washington Post,* June 11, A13.

STEPP, L. S. 1993. Teenagers at work. *Washington Post,* December 20, D5.

STEPP, L. S. 1994. On parenting. *Washington Post,* October 18, B5.

STERLING, A. J. 1992. *What really works with men.* New York: Warner.

STERNBERG, R. J. 1986. A triangular theory of love. *Psychological Review* 93, no. 2: 119–35.

STERNBERG, R. J. 1988. *The triangle of love.* New York: Basic Books.

STERRIT, D. 1993. A dysfunctional movie. *Christian Science Monitor,* March 1, 13.

STETS, J. E. 1993a. Control in dating relationships. *Journal of Marriage and the Family* 55 (August): 673–85.

STETS, J. E. 1993b. The link between past and present intimate relationships. *Journal of Family Issues* 14 (June): 236–60.

STETS, J. E., AND D. A. HENDERSON. 1991. Contextual factors surrounding conflict resolution while dating: Results from a national study. *Family Relations* 40 (January): 29–36.

STETS, J. E., AND M. A. PIROG-GOOD. 1987. Violence in dating relationships. *Social Psychology Quarterly* 50, no. 3 (September): 237–46.

STETS, J. E., AND M. A. PIROG-GOOD. 1990. Interpersonal control and courtship aggression. *Journal of Social and Personal Relationships* 7, 371–94.

STEWART, J. 1993. *African names: Names from the African continent for children and adults.* New York: Citadel.

STICE, E., E. SCHUPACK-NEUBERG, H. E. SHAW, AND R. I. STEIN. 1994. Relation of media exposure to eating disorder symptomatology: An examination of mediating mechanisms. *Journal of Abnormal Psychology* 103, no. 4 (November): 836–840.

STOCKEL, H. H. 1991. *Women of the Apache nation.* Reno: University of Nevada Press.

STODDART, T., AND E. TURIET. 1985. Housework: It isn't going to go away. *Philadelphia Inquirer,* September, 1, 11, 14.

STOLBA, A., AND P. R. AMATO. 1993. Extended single-parent households and children's behavior. *Sociological Quarterly* 34, no. 3: 543–49.

STOLLER, E. P., AND R. POLLOW. 1994. Factors affecting the frequency of health-enhancing behaviors by the elderly. *Public Health Reports* 109, no. 3 (May–June): 377–89.

STOLTENBERG, J. 1993. *The end of manhood: A book for men of conscience.* New York: Penguin.

STONE, A. 1993. Financial fitness for unmarried couples. *Business Week,* June 21, 162–63.

STRATTON, J. L. 1981. *Pioneer women: Voices from the Kansas frontier.* New York: Simon & Schuster.

STRAUS, M. A. 1993. Identifying offenders in criminal justice research on domestic assault. *American Behavioral Scientist* 36, no. 5 (May): 587–600.

STRAUS, M. A. 1994. Corporal punishment of children and depression and suicide in adulthood. In *Coercion and punishment in long-term perspective,* ed. J. McCord, 59–77. New York: Cambridge University Press.

STROMMEN, E. F. 1990. Hidden branches and growing pains: Homosexuality and the family tree. In *Homosexuality and family relations,* ed. F. W. Bozett and M. B. Sussman, 9–34. New York: Harrington Park Press.

STUDER, M. C., AND A. THORNTON. 1987. Adolescent religiosity and contraceptive usage. *Journal of Marriage and the Family* 49 (February): 117–28.

STUMBO, B. 1993. The state of hate. *Esquire,* September, 73–84.

Subcommittee on Human Services. Select Committee on Aging. 1992. *Grandparents rights: A resource manual.* House of Representatives. One Hundred Second Congress. Second Session. Washington, DC: Government Printing Office.

SUGAWARA, S. 1991. Study: Firms holding back women, minorities. *Washington Post,* August 9, B1, B3.

SUITOR, J. J., AND K. PILLEMER. 1993. Support and interpersonal stress in the social networks of married daughters caring for parents with dementia. *Journals of Gerontology* 48, no. 1 (January): S1–S8.

SULLIVAN, K. 1994. Blissful coexistence? *Washington Post,* May 24, A1, A10.

SULLIVAN, M. J. 1991. *Presidential passions: The love affairs of America's presidents—from Washington and Jefferson to Kennedy and Johnson.* New York: Shapolsky.

SUN, L. H. 1990. China seeks ways to protect elderly: Support agreements replacing traditional respect for the elderly. *Washington Post,* October 23, A1, A18.

SUN, L. H. 1995. Traditional money pools keep immigrants afloat. *Washington Post,* February 17, A1, A22.

SURO, R. 1994. Study of immigrants finds Asians at top in science and medicine. *Washington Post,* April 18, A6.

SWAIN, S. O. 1992. Men's friendships with women: Intimacy, sexual boundaries, and the informant role. In *Men's friendships,* ed. P. M. Nardi, 153–72. Newbury Park, CA: Sage.

SWEDLUND, A. C. 1993. Review of *Anatomy of love: The natural history of monogamy, adultery, and divorce* by H. E. Fisher (New York: W. W. Norton, 1992). *American Anthropologist* 95, 1053–1054.

SWIGART, J. 1991. *The myth of the bad mother: The emotional realities of mothering.* New York: Doubleday.

SWISHER, K. 1994. At the checkout counter, winning women's rights. *Washington Post,* June 12, H1, H6.

SWISHER, P. N., H. A. MILLER, AND W. I. WESTON. 1990. *Family law: Cases, materials and problems.* New York: Matthew Bender.

SWISS, D. J., AND J. P. WALKER. 1993. *Women and the work/family dilemma: How today's professional women are finding solutions.* New York: Wiley.

SWOBODA, F. 1991. GAO finds job training discrimination. *Washington Post,* July 17, A21.

SZAPOCZNIK, J., AND R. HERNANDEZ. 1988. The Cuban American family. In *Ethnic families in America: Patterns and variations,* 3rd ed., ed. C. J. Mindel, R. W. Habenstein, and R. Wright, Jr., 160–72. New York: Elsevier.

SZEGEDY-MASZAK, M. 1993. Dating passages. *New Woman* 23, no. 3 (March): 85–88.

SZYMANSKI, L. A., A. S. DEVLIN, J. C. CHRISLER, AND S. A. VYSE. 1993. Gender role and attitudes toward rape in male and female college students. *Sex Roles* 29, nos. 1/2, 37–57.

TABORN, J. M. 1987. The black adolescent mother: Selected, unique issues. In *The black adolescent parent,* ed. S. F. Battle, 1–13. New York: Haworth.

TAKAGI, D. Y. 1994. Japanese American families. In *Minority families in the United States: A multicultural perspective,* ed. R. L. Taylor, 146–63. Englewood Cliffs, NJ: Prentice Hall.

TAKAKI, R. 1989. *Strangers from a different shore: A history of Asian Americans.* Boston: Little, Brown.

TAKAKI, R. 1993. *A different mirror: A history of multicultural America.* Boston: Little, Brown.

TAKAYAMA, H. 1990. The main track at last. *Newsweek*, January 22, 50–51.

TAMARACK, L. I. 1986. Fifty myths and facts about incest. In *Sexual abuse of children in the 1980s: Ten essays and an annotated bibliography*, ed. B. Schlesinger. Buffalo, NY: University of Toronto Press.

TANAKA, Y. 1994. Tokyo's marriage bureau sifts many for elusive few. *Baltimore Sun*, February 24, 2A.

TANNEN, D. 1990. *You just don't understand: Women and men in conversation*. New York: Ballantine.

TANNEN, D. 1994. *Talking from 9 to 5*. New York: Morrow.

TANUR, J. M. 1994. The trustworthiness of survey research. *Chronicle of Higher Education*, May 25, B1–B3.

TAVRIS, C. 1992. *The mismeasure of woman*. New York: Simon & Schuster.

TAYLOR, C. A., ED. 1993. *Guide to multicultural resources: 1993/1994*. Madison, WI: Praxis.

TAYLOR, E. 1989. From the Nelsons to the Huxtables: Genre and family imagery in American network television. *Qualitative Sociology* 12, no. 1 (Spring): 13–28.

TAYLOR, J. 1992. *Paved with good intentions: The failure of race relations in contemporary America*. New York: Carroll & Graf.

TAYLOR, K., J. L. LESIAK, J. CARROLL, AND W. J. LESIAK. 1993. Kindergartners' responses to males in nontraditional roles: A replication of Styer (1975). *Psychological Reports* 72, 1179–1183.

TAYLOR, P. 1991a. Nonmarital births: As rates soar, theories abound: Levels once seen as aberration among blacks have become "norm for the entire culture." *Washington Post*, January 22, A3.

TAYLOR, P. 1991b. Therapists rethink attitudes on divorce: New movement to save marriages focuses on impact on children. *Washington Post*, January 29, A1, A6.

TAYLOR, R. J., L. M. CHATTERS, M. B. TUCKER, AND E. LEWIS. 1990. Developments in research on black families: A decade review. *Journal of Marriage and the Family* 52 (November): 993–1014.

TAYLOR, R. J., V. M. KEITH, AND M. B. TUCKER. 1993. Gender, marital, familial, and friendship roles. In *Aging in black America*, ed. J. S. Jackson, L. M. Chatters and R. J. Taylor, 49–68. Newbury Park, CA: Sage.

TAYLOR, R. L. 1994. Black American families. In *Minority families in the United States: A multicultural perspective*, ed. R. L. Taylor, 19–61. Englewood Cliffs, NJ: Prentice Hall.

TAYLOR, R. L., ED. 1994. *Minority families in the United States: A multicultural perspective*. Englewood Cliffs, NJ: Prentice Hall.

TEACHMAN, J. D. 1983. Marriage, premarital fertility, and marital dissolution: Results for blacks and whites. *Journal of Family Issues* 4, 105–28.

TEACHMAN, J. D. 1991a. Contributions to children by divorced fathers. *Social Problems* 38, no. 3 (August): 358–70.

TEACHMAN, J. D. 1991b. Who pays? Receipt of child support in the United States. *Journal of Marriage and the Family* 53 (August): 759–72.

TEACHMAN, J. D., AND K. A. POLONKO. 1988. Marriage, parenthood, and the college enrollment of men and women. *Social Forces* 67, no. 2 (December): 512–23.

TEACHMAN, J. D., AND K. A. POLONKO. 1990. Cohabitation and marital stability in the United States. *Social Forces* 69, no. 1 (September): 207–20.

TEACHMAN, J. D., J. THOMAS, AND K. PAASCH. 1991. Legal status and the stability of coresidential unions. *Demography* 26 (November): 571–86.

TEFFT, S. 1994. China's elderly face a care crisis. *Christian Science Monitor*, June 29, 12.

TENNESEN, M. 1993. Are there dating services for seniors? *Modern Maturity*, April–May, 84.

TEPPERMAN, L., AND S. J. WILSON, EDS. 1993. *Next of kin: An international reader on changing families*. Englewood Cliffs, NJ: Prentice Hall.

TERESI, D. 1994. How to get a man pregnant. *New York Times Magazine*, November 27, 54–55.

TERRELL, K. 1992. Female-male earnings differentials and occupational structure. *International Labour Review* 131, nos. 4–5, 387–403.

TESTA, R. J., B. N. KINDER, AND G. IRONSON. 1987. Heterosexual bias in the perception of loving relationships of gay males and lesbians. *Journal of Sex Research* 23, no. 2 (May): 163–72.

TETI, D. M., M. E. LAMB, AND A. B. ELSTER. 1987. Long-range socioeconomic and marital consequences of adolescent marriage in three cohorts of adult males. *Journal of Marriage and the Family* 49 (August): 499–506.

TEYBER, E., AND C. D. HOFFMAN. 1987. Missing fathers. *Psychology Today*, April, 36–69.

THOMAS, D. H., J. MILLER, R. WHITE, P. NABOKOV, AND P. J. DELORIA. 1993. *The Native Americans: An illustrated history*. Atlanta: Turner.

THOMAS, J. L. 1994. Older men as fathers and grandfathers. In *Older men's lives*, ed. E. H. Thompson, Jr., 197–217. Thousand Oaks, CA: Sage.

THOMAS, R. 1990. The vanishing Indian. *The Futurist* 24, no. 2 (March-April): 53–54.

THOMAS, W. I., AND F. ZNANIECKI. 1927. The Polish peasant in Europe and America, vol. 2. New York: Knopf. (Originally published 1918 by the University of Chicago Press.)

THOMAS-LESTER, A. 1994. Carrying on: A joyless time for the grieving. *Washington Post*, December 15, D5.

THOMPSON, A. P. 1983. Extramarital sex: A review of the research literature. *Journal of Sex Research* 19, no. 1 (February): 1–22.

THOMPSON, A. P. 1984. Emotional and sexual components of extramarital relations. *Journal of Marriage and the Family* 46 (February): 35–42.

THOMPSON, B. 1994. Food, bodies, and growing up female: Childhood lessons about culture, race, and class. In *Feminist perspectives on eating disorders*, ed. P. Fallon, M. A. Katzman, and S. C. Wooley, 355–78. New York: Guilford.

THOMPSON, E. H., JR. ED. 1994. *Older men's lives*. Thousand Oaks, CA: Sage.

THOMPSON, G. 1990. What makes a family? Gays must fight law. *Baltimore Sun*, Sept. 5, 1E, 4E.

THOMPSON, L. 1993. Conceptualizing gender in marriage: The case of marital care. *Journal of Marriage and the Family* 55 (August): 557–69.

THOMPSON, L., AND A. J. WALKER. 1991. Gender in families. In *Contemporary families: Looking forward, looking back*, ed. A. Booth, 76–102. Minneapolis, MN: National Council on Family Relations.

THOMPSON, T. 1990. 1973 navy discrimination suit languishes unresolved. *Washington Post*, November 5, D1, D7.

THOMSON, E., S. S. MCLANAHAN, AND R. B. CURTIN. 1992. Family structure, gender, and parental socialization. *Journal of Marriage and the Family* 54 (May): 368–78.

THORNE, B. 1993. *Gender play: Girls and boys in school*. New Brunswick, NJ: Rutgers University Press.

THORNE, B., WITH M. YALOM, EDS. 1992. *Rethinking the family: Some feminist questions*. Boston: Northeastern University Press.

THORNTON, A. 1988. Cohabitation and marriage in the 1980s. *Demography* 25, no. 4 (November): 497–508.

THORNTON, A. 1991. Influence of the marital history of parents on the marital and cohabitational experiences of children. *American Journal of Sociology* 96, no. 4 (January): 868–94.

THORNTON, A., AND D. CAMBURN. 1987. The influence of the family on premarital sexual attitudes and behavior. *Demography* 24 (August): 323–40.

THORNTON, A., AND W. RODGERS. 1987. The influence of individual and historical time on marital dissolution. *Demography* 24, no. 1 (February): 1–22.

THORNTON, A., L. YOUNG-DEMARCO, AND F. GOLDSCHEIDER. 1993. Leaving the parental nest: The experience of a young white cohort in the 1980s. *Journal of Marriage and the Family* 5 (February): 216–29.

THORNTON, E. 1994. Video dating in Japan. *Fortune*, January 24, 12.

THORNTON, J. 1984. Family violence emerges from the shadows. *U.S. News & World Report*, January 23, 66.

THORNTON, J., AND D. WHITMAN WITH D. FREEDMAN. 1992. Whites' myths about blacks. *U.S. News & World Report*, November 9, 41–44.

THURER, S. L. 1994. *The myths of motherhood: How culture reinvents the good mother*. Boston: Houghton Mifflin.

TICHY, A. M., AND M. L. TALASHEK. 1992. Older women: Sexually transmitted diseases and acquired immunodeficiency syndrome. *Nursing Clinics of North America* 27, no. 4, 937–50.

TIERNEY, J. 1994. A lone doctor adapts drugs for abortions. *New York Times*, October 10, B1, B2.

TIMBERLAKE, E. M., AND E. R. HAMLIN II. 1982. The sibling group: A neglected dimension of placement. *Child Welfare* 61 (November/December): 545–52.

TIMBERLAKE, E. M., AND S. S. CHIPUNGU. 1992. Grandmotherhood: Contemporary meaning among African American middle-class grandmothers. *Social Work* 37, no. 3 (May): 216–22.

TINSLEY, E. 1993. More countries restrict adoption. *USA Today*, May 29, 7A.

TOBIAS, S. 1978. *Overcoming math anxiety*. New York: Norton.

TOFFLER, A. 1980. *The third wave*. New York: Morrow.

TOTH, J. 1992. Study of runaways finds lives of abuse. *Baltimore Sun*, January 2, 3A.

TOUSIGNANT, M. 1994. Bogged down in Bucharest. *Washington Post*, October 26, B1, B5.

TOWNSEND, B., AND K. O'NEILL. 1990. American women get mad. *American Demographics* 12 (August): 26–29.

TRAFFORD, A. 1991. Why battered women kill: Self-defense, not revenge, is often the motive. *Washington Post Health Supplement*, February 26, 6.

TRAN, T. V. 1988. The Vietnamese American family. In *Ethnic families in America: Patterns and variations*, 3rd ed., ed. C. H. Mindel, R. W. Habenstein, and R. Wright, Jr., 276–302. New York: Elsevier.

TRENT, K. 1994. Family context and adolescents' expectations about marriage, fertility, and nonmarital childbearing. *Social Science Quarterly* 75, no. 2 (June): 319–39.

TRENT, K., AND S. L. HARLAN. 1990. Household structure among teenage mothers in the United States. *Social Science Quarterly* 71, no. 3 (September): 439–57.

TROTTER, R. J. 1986. Failing to find the father–infant bond. *Psychology Today*, February, 18.

TRZCINSKI. E. 1994. Family and medical leave, contingent employment, and flexibility: A feminist critique of the U.S. approach to work and family policy. *Journal of Applied Social Sciences* 18, no. 1 (Fall/Winter 1994): 71–87.

TUCKER, M. B., AND R. J. TAYLOR. 1989. Demographic correlates of relationship status among black Americans. *Journal of Marriage and the Family* 51 (August): 655–65.

TUCKER, M. B., R. J. TAYLOR, AND C. MITCHELL-KERNAN. 1993. Marriage and romantic involvement among aged African Americans. *Journal of Gerontology: Social Sciences* 48, no. 3 S128–S132.

TUCKER, R. K. 1992. Men's and women's ranking of thirteen acts of romance. *Psychological Reports* 71, 640–42.

TUCKER, S. K. 1989. Adolescent patterns of communication about sexually related topics. *Adolescence* 24, no. 94 (Summer): 269–78.

TULLER, D. 1994. Men, women respond differently to jealousy. *San Francisco Chronicle* June 24, A17.

TURNBULL, S. K., AND J. M. TURNBULL.

1983. To dream the impossible dream: An agenda for discussion with stepparents. *Family Relations* 32, 227–30.

TURNER, J. S., AND L. RUBINSON. 1993. *Contemporary human sexuality*. Englewood Cliffs, NJ: Prentice Hall.

TURNER, M. A., M. FIX, AND R. J. STRUYK. 1991. *Opportunities denied, opportunities diminished: Racial discrimination in hiring*. Washington, DC: Urban Institute.

TURQUE, B., ET AL. 1992. Gays under fire. *Newsweek*, September 14, 35–40.

TUTTLE, JR., W. M. 1993. *Daddy's gone to war: The Second World War in the lives of America's children*. New York: Oxford University Press.

TYLER, T. R., AND R. A. SCHULLER. 1991. Aging and attitude change. *Journal of Personality and Social Psychology* 61, no. 5: 689–97.

TYSON, A. S. 1994. Ethnic, economic divisions of U.S. growing. *Christian Science Monitor*, July 7, 3.

TYSZKOWA, M. 1993. Adolescents' relationships with grandparents: Characteristics and developmental transformations. In *Adolescence and its social worlds*, ed. S. Jackson and H. Rodriguez-Tomé, 121–43. East Sussex, UK: Lawrence Erlbaum Associates.

TZENG, O. C. S. 1993. *Measurement of love and intimate relations: Theories, scales, and applications for love development, maintenance, and dissolution*. Westport, CT: Praeger.

UCHITELLE, L. 1994. Moonlighting plus: 3-Job families on the rise. *New York Times*, August 16, D1, D18.

UDESKY, L. 1994. Sweatshops behind the labels. *The Nation*, May 16, 665–68.

UDRY, J. R. 1993. The politics of sex research. *Journal of Sex Research* 30, no. 2 (May): 103–10.

UEHLING, M. D. 1994. An Asian mall in the great Midwest. *American Demographics* 16, no. 5 (May): 36–37.

ULBRICH, P. M. 1988. The determinants of depression in two-income marriages. *Journal of Marriage and the Family* 50 (February): 121–31.

UMBERSON, D., AND C. L. WILLIAMS. 1993. Divorced fathers: Parental role strain and psychological distress. *Journal of Family Issues* 14, no. 3 (September): 378–400.

UNICEF. 1994. *The progress of nations*. New York.

United Nations Children's Fund. 1994. *The state of the world's children 1994*. New York: Oxford University Press.

U.S. Bureau of the Census. 1991a. *Mar-*

ital status and living arrangements: March 1990. Current Population Reports, Series P-20, no. 450. Washington DC: Government Printing Office.

U.S. Bureau of the Census. 1991b. *Poverty in the United States: 1990*. Current Population Reports, Series P-60, no. 175. Washington, DC: Government Printing Office.

U.S. Bureau of the Census. 1993. *Poverty in the United States: 1992*. Current Population Reports, Series P60–185. Washington, DC: Government Printing Office.

U.S. Bureau of the Census. 1994a. *Money income of households, families, and persons in the United States: 1988 and 1989*. Current Population Reports, Series P-60, No. 172. Washington, DC: Government Printing Office.

U.S. Bureau of the Census. 1994b. *Statistical abstract of the United States: 1994*, 114th ed. Washington, DC: Government Printing Office.

U.S. Bureau of the Census. 1995. *Income, poverty, and valuation of noncash benefits: 1993*. Current Population Reports, Series P-60–188. Washington, DC: Government Printing Office.

U.S. Commission on Civil Rights. 1984. *Comparable worth: Issue for the 80's*, vol. 1. Washington, DC: Government Printing Office.

U.S. Commission on Civil Rights. 1992. *Civil rights issues facing Asian Americans in the 1990s*. Washington, DC: Government Printing Office.

U.S. Department of Agriculture. 1994. *Expenditures on a child by families, 1993*. Agricultural Research Service, Family Economics Research Group.

U.S. Department of Commerce. 1991. *The black population in the United States: March 1990 and 1989*. Washington, DC: Government Printing Office.

U.S. Department of Commerce. 1993. *We the American foreign born*. Bureau of the Census. Washington DC: Government Printing Office.

U.S. Department of Commerce. 1994. Paper on poverty and health care coverage. October 6, mimeo.

U.S. Department of Health and Human Services. 1988. *Study findings: Study of national incidence and prevalence of child abuse and neglect: 1988*. Office of Human Development Services, Administration for Children, Youth and Families, Children's Bureau, National Center on Child Abuse and Neglect. Washington, DC: Government Printing Office.

U.S. Department of Justice. 1992. Immigration and Naturalization Service. *Statistical Yearbook of the Immigration and Naturalization Service*.

U.S. Department of Justice. 1994a. Bureau of Justice Statistics. Press release. Half of women raped during 1992 were younger than 18 years old. June 22.

U.S. Department of Justice. 1994b. *Fact sheet: Drug use trends*. Bureau of Justice Statistics. February.

U.S. Department of Justice. 1994c. Bureau of Justice Statistics. Press release. Wives are the most frequent victims in family, July 10.

U.S. Department of Justice. 1994. *Selected findings: Violent crime*. Office of Justice Programs, Bureau of Justice Statistics. April.

U.S. Department of Labor. 1991. *Employment and earnings*. Bureau of Labor Statistics. Washington, DC: Government Printing Office.

U.S. Department of Labor. 1994a. *Employee benefits in small private establishments, 1992*. Bureau of Labor Statistics. Washington, DC: Government Printing Office.

U.S. Department of Labor. 1994b. *Employment and Earnings*. Bureau of Labor Statistics. January. Washington, DC: Government Printing Office.

U.S. House of Representatives. 1986. *Native American children, youth, and families*. Pt. 3. Hearings before the Select Committee on Children, Youth, and Families. 99th Cong., 2nd sess. Washington, DC: Government Printing Office.

U.S. News & World Report. 1993. Americans: Anxious times. December 27, 40.

U.S. News & World Report. 1994. Outlook. June 6, 12.

U.S. News & World Report. 1994. Workers' new lament: Too much overtime. October 10, 12.

U.S. Senate Special Committee on Aging, American Association of Retired Persons, Federal Council on the Aging, and U.S. Administration on Aging. 1991. *Aging America: Trends and projections, 1991*. Washington, DC: Department of Health and Human Services.

URQUIZA, A. J., AND L. M. KEATING. 1990. The prevalence of sexual victimization of males. In *The sexually abused male*, ed. M. Hunter. Lexington, MA: Lexington Books.

VAN BIEMA, D. 1995. Dunning deadbeats. *Time*, April 3, 49.

VANCE, E. B., AND N. N. WAGNER. 1976. Written descriptions of orgasm: A study of sex differences. *Archives of Sexual Behavior* 5, 87–98.

VAN RY, M. 1993. *Homeless families: Causes, effects, and recommendations*. New York: Garland.

VEATCH, R. M. 1995. Death and dying. In *Ethics applied*, ed. M. L. Richardson and K. K. White, 215 43. New York: McGraw-Hill.

VEGA, W. A. 1990. Hispanic families in the 1980s: A decade of research. *Journal of Marriage and the Family* 52 (November): 1015–24.

VEMER, E., M. COLEMAN, L. H. GANONG, AND H. COOPER. 1989. Marital satisfaction in remarriage: A meta-analysis. *Journal of Marriage and the Family* 51 (August): 713–25.

VENTURA, J. N. 1987. The stresses of parenthood reexamined. *Family Relations* 36 (January): 26–29.

VERBRUGGE, L. 1979. Marital status and health. *Journal of Marriage and the Family* 41 (May): 267–85.

VEUM, J. R., AND P. M. GLEASON. 1991. Child care: Arrangements and costs. *Monthly Labor Review* 114 (October): 10–17.

VILLAREAL, R. E., AND N. G. HERNANDEZ, EDS. 1991. *Latinos and political coalitions: Political empowerment for the 1990s*. Westport, CT: Praeger.

VINTON, L. 1991. Abused older women: Battered women or abused elders? *Women and Aging* 3, no. 3, 5–20.

VISHER, E., AND J. VISHER. 1982. *How to win as a stepfamily*. New York: Dembner.

VISHER, E. B., AND J. S. VISHER. 1988. *Old loyalists, new ties: Therapeutic strategies with stepfamilies*. New York: Brunner/Mazel.

VISHER, E. B., AND J. S. VISHER. 1993. Remarriage families and stepparenting. In *Normal family processes*, 2nd ed., ed. F. Walsh, 235–53. New York: Guilford.

VITOUSEK, K., AND F. MANKE. 1994. Personality variables and disorders in anorexia nervosa and bulimia nervosa. *Journal of Abnormal Psychology* 103, no. 1 (February): 137–174.

VOBEJDA, B. 1991a. Average household shrinks as more in U.S. live alone. *Washington Post*, May 1, A1, A7.

VOBEJDA, B. 1991b. 25% of black women may never marry. *Washington Post*, November 11, 1A.

VOBEJDA, B. 1992. Census: Elderly population growth will lead to 4–generation families. *Washington Post*, November 10, A3.

VOBEJDA, B. 1994. Experts say allegations underscore familiar elements of spouse abuse. *Washington Post*, June 19, A18.

VOBEJDA, B. 1995a. Child-care centers get low ratings. *Washington Post*, February 6. A1, A8.

VOBEJDA, B. 1995b. Finding a way out proves no easy task. *Washington Post*, March 5, A1, A8.

VOBEJDA, B. 1995c. Welfare an afterthought, teen mothers say. *Washington Post*, February 14, A1.

VOGLER, C., AND J. PAHL. 1994. Money, power and inequality within marriage. *Sociological Review* 42 (May): 263–88.

VOYDANOFF, P. 1991. Economic distress and family relations. In *Contemporary families: Looking forward, looking back*, ed. A. Booth, 429–45. Minneapolis, MN: National Council on Family Relations.

VUCHINICH, S. 1987. Starting and stopping spontaneous family conflicts. *Journal of Marriage and the Family* 49 (August): 591–601.

VUCHINICH, S., E. M. HETHERINGTON, R. A. VUCHINICH, AND W. G. CLINGEMPEEL. 1991. Parent-child interaction and gender differences in early adolescents' adaptation to stepfamilies. *Developmental Psychology* 27, no. 4, 618–26.

WADE, C., AND S. CIRESE. 1991. *Human sexuality*, 2nd ed. New York: Harcourt Brace Jovanovich.

WAITE, L. J., AND L. A. LILLARD. 1991. Children and marital disruption. *American Journal of Sociology* 96, no. 4 (January): 930–53.

WALDMAN, S. 1992. Deadbeat dads. *Newsweek*, May 4, 46–50.

WALDMAN, S. W. 1994. Taking on the welfare dads. *Newsweek*, June 30, 34–38.

WALDMAN, S., ET AL. 1994. Welfare booby traps. *Newsweek*, December 12, 34–35.

WALDROP, J. 1991. The baby boom turns 45. *American Demographics* 13, no. 1 (January): 22–27.

WALDROP, J. 1993. The grandbaby boom. *American Demographics* (September): 4.

WALDROP, J. 1994a. Change is good, unless it happens. *American Demographics* (September): 12–13.

WALDROP, J. 1994b. What do working women want? *American Demographics* (September): 36–37.

WALKER, J. 1990. Genetic parents win custody of baby: California judge also denies surrogate mother visitation rights. *Washington Post*, October 23, A4.

WALKER, L. 1978. Treatment alternatives for battered women. In *The victimization of women*, ed. J. R. Chapman and M. Gates, 143–74. Beverly Hills, CA: Sage.

WALKER, T. 1993. Chinese men embrace divorce. *World Press Review* 40, no. 9 (October): 48.

WALKER, T. B. 1992. Family law in the fifty states: An overview. *Family Law Quarterly* 25 (A).

WALKER, W. D., R. C. ROWE, AND V. L. QUINSEY. 1993. Authoritarianism and sexual aggression. *Journal of Personality and Social Psychology* 65, no. 5, 1036–1045.

WALLACE, M. 1978. *Black macho and the myth of the superwoman*. New York: Routledge.

WALLECHINSKY, D., AND A. WALLACE. 1993. *The people's almanac presents the book of lists: The '90s*. New York: Little, Brown.

WALLER, W. 1937. The rating and dating complex. *American Sociological Review* 2 (October): 727–34.

WALLERSTEIN, J., AND S. BLAKESLEE. 1989. *Second chances: Men, women and children a decade after divorce*. New York: Ticknor & Fields.

WALSH, A. 1991. *The science of love: Understanding love and its effects on mind and body*. Buffalo, NY: Prometheus Books.

WALSH, E. 1994. Illinois court backs biological parents. *Washington Post*, July 14, A3.

WALSH, F., ED. 1993. *Normal family processes*, 2nd ed. New York: Guilford.

WALSH, K. T. 1994. A kinder, gentler Hollywood. *U.S. News & World Report*, May 9, 39–47

WALSH, M. E. 1992. *"Moving to nowhere": Children's stories of homelessness*. Westport, CT: Greenwood Press.

WALSH, S. 1995. Hushing up harassment? *Washington Post*, April 9, B1, B7.

WALSTER, E., E. BERSCHEID, AND G. W. WALSTER. 1973. New directions in equity research. *Journal of Personality and Social Psychology* 25, no. 2, 151–76.

WALTERS, J., AND N. STINNETT. 1971. Parent-child relationships: A decade review of research. In *A decade of family research and action, 1960–1969*, ed. C. B. Broderick, 99–140. Minneapolis, MN: National Council on Family Relations.

WALTERS, L. S. 1995. Minorities in higher education. *Christian Science Monitor*, March 13, 13.

WALTHER, A. N. 1991. *Divorce hangover*. New York: Pocket Books.

WANG, P. 1993. What every woman should know about stockbrokers. *Money*, June, 14–16

WARD, J. V., AND J. M. TAYLOR. 1994. Sexuality education for immigrant and minority students: Developing a culturally appropriate curriculum. In *Sexual cultures and the construction of adolescent identities*, ed. J. M. Irvine, 51–68. Philadelphia: Temple University Press.

WARD, R., J. LOGAN, AND G. SPITZE. 1992. The influence of parent and child needs on coresidence in middle and later life. *Journal of Marriage and the Family* 54 (February): 209–21.

WARD, S. K., K. CHAPMAN, E. COHN, S. WHITE, AND K. WILLIAMS. 1991. Acquaintance rape and the college social scene. *Family Relations* 40 (January): 65–71.

WARNER, D. 1992. *How to have a big wedding on a small budget: Cut your wedding costs in half—or more!* Cincinnati, OH: Writer's Digest Books.

WASHINGTON, J. R. 1993. *Marriage in black and white*. Lanham, MD: University Press of America.

Washington Post. 1994. Heterosexual AIDS spread? March 11, A8.

Washington Post. 1994. Use of drugs by teenagers "getting worse." December 13, A17.

WATERS, H. F. 1993. Black is bountiful. *Newsweek*, December 6, 59–61.

WATERS, H. F., ET AL. 1994. Teenage suicide: One act not to follow. *Newsweek*, April 18, 49.

WATKINS, T. H. 1993. *The great depression: America in the 1930s*. New York: Little, Brown.

WATLEY, M. H. 1994. Keeping adolescents in the picture: Construction of adolescent sexuality in textbook images and popular films. In *Sexual cultures and the construction of adolescent identities*, ed. J. M. Irvine, 183–205. Philadelphia: Temple University Press.

WATSON, P. 1993. Eastern Europe's silent revolution: Gender. *Sociology* 27, no. 3 (August): 471–87.

WATSON, R. E. L., AND P. W. DEMEO. 1987. Premarital cohabitation vs. traditional courtship and subsequent marital adjustment: A replication and follow-up. *Family Relations* 36 (April): 193–97.

WATSON, R. S., AND P. B. EBREY, EDS. 1991. *Marriage and inequality in Chi-*

nese society. Berkeley: University of California Press.

WAUGH, E. H., S. M. ABU-LABAN, AND R. B. QURESHI, EDS. 1991. *Muslim families in North America.* Edmonton: University of Alberta Press.

WAXMAN, S. 1995. The Dutch way of death. *Washington Post,* January 31, B1, B3.

WEATHERFORD, D. 1990. *American women and World War II.* New York: Facts on File.

WEIL, B. E. AND P. WINTER. 1993. *Adultery: The forgivable sin.* New York: Birch Lane Press.

WEINBERG, M. S., C. J. WILLIAMS, AND D. W. PRYOR. 1994. *Dual attraction: Understanding bisexuality.* New York: Oxford University Press.

WEINER-DAVIS, M. 1992. *Divorce busting: A revolutionary and rapid program for staying together.* New York: Summit.

WEISMAN, M.-L. 1994. When parents are not in the best interests of the child. *The Atlantic,* July, 42–59.

WEISS, C. H. 1972. *Evaluation research: Methods for assessing program effectiveness.* Englewood Cliffs, NJ: Prentice Hall.

WEISS, R.S. 1976. The emotional impact of marital separation. *Journal of Social Issues* 32, no. 1. 135–45.

WEITZMAN, L. J. 1985. *The divorce revolution: The unexpected social and economic consequences for women and children in America.* New York: Free Press.

WEITZMAN, L. J., D. EIFLER, E. HOKADA, AND C. ROSS. 1972. Sex-role socialization in picture books for preschool children. *American Journal of Sociology* 77 (May): 1125–150.

WELTER, B. 1966. The cult of true womanhood: 1820–1860. *American Quarterly* 18, no. 2, 151–74.

WESSEL, D. 1989. Counting the homeless will tax the ingenuity of 1990 census takers. *Wall Street Journal,* November 14, A1, A16.

WESTMAN, J. C. 1994. *Licensing parents: Can we prevent child abuse and neglect?* New York: Plenum.

WESTOFF, L. A. 1977. *The second time around: Remarriage in America.* New York: Viking.

WHATLEY, M. H., 1994. Keeping adolescents in the picture: Construction of adolescent sexuality in textbook images and popular films. In *Sexual cultures and the construction of adolescent identities,* ed. J. M. Irvine, 183–205. Philadelphia, PA: Temple University Press.

WHEELER, C. G. 1993. 30 years beyond

"I have a dream." *Gallup Poll Monthly,* October, 2–8.

WHEELER, D. L. 1990. Scientists criticize the FDA's restriction on import of French "abortion pill." *Chronicle of Higher Education,* November 28, A23, A29.

WHEELER, D. L. 1993. Psychologist deflates the modern craze of "baby bonding." *Chronicle of Higher Education,* March 10, A6, A7, A13.

WHEELER, D. L. 1995. Women and AIDS research. *Chronicle of Higher Education,* March 19, A7, A13.

WHEELER, D. L. 1995. A birth-control vaccine. *Chronicle of Higher Education,* April 7: A9, A15.

WHITBECK, L., D. R. HOYT, AND S. M. HUCK. 1994. Early family relationships, intergenerational solidarity, and support provided to parents by their adult children. *Journal of Gerontology* 49, no. 2, 585–94.

WHITE, B. L. 1991. *The first three years of life.* Englewood Cliffs, NJ: Prentice Hall.

WHITE, G. L., AND P. E. MULLEN. 1989. *Jealousy: Theory, research, and clinical strategies.* New York: Guilford.

WHITE, J. W., AND M. P. KOSS. 1991. Courtship violence: Incidence in a national sample of higher education students. *Violence and Victims* 6, no. 4, 247–56.

WHITE, L. K. 1991. Determinants of divorce. In *Contemporary families: Looking forward, looking back,* ed. A. Booth, 150–61. Minneapolis, MN: National Council on Family Relations.

WHITE, L. 1992. The effect of parental divorce and remarriage on parental support for adult children. *Journal of Family Issues* 13, no. 2 (June): 234–50.

WHITEHEAD, M. B., WITH L. SCHWARTZ-NOBEL. 1989. *A mother's story: The truth about the Baby M case.* New York: St. Martin's Press.

WHITLOCK, M. 1994. Marriage—and the price you pay. *Washington Post,* April 4, A20.

WHITMAN, D., ET AL. 1995. Welfare: The myth of reform. *U.S. News & World Report,* January 16, 30–39.

WHITSETT, D., AND H. LAND. 1992. The development of a role strain index for stepparents. *Families in Society: The Journal of Contemporary Human Services* (January): 14–22.

WHITTELSEY, F. C. 1993. *Why women pay more: How to avoid marketplace perils.* Washington, DC: Center for Study of Responsive Law.

WHYTE, M. K. 1990. *Dating, mating,*

and marriage. New York: Aldine de Gruyter.

WIEHE, V. R., WITH T. HERRING. 1991. *Perilous rivalry: When siblings become abusive.* Lexington, MA: Lexington Books.

WIESE, D., AND D. DARO. 1995. *Current trends in child abuse reporting and fatalities: The results of the 1994 annual fifty state survey.* Chicago: National Committee to Prevent Child Abuse.

WILCOX, M. D., 1994. Your retirement: How divorce affects women's social security. *Kiplinger's Personal Finance Magazine* 48, no. 10 (October): 132, 134.

WILLIAMS, A. M. 1992. The role of the African-American woman in preserving family unity and strength in the face of drugs and crime. In *A town meeting: African-American male: A need for family empowerment,* ed. S. A. Doherty, 27–38. Brentwood, TN: D.S.H.

WILLIAMS, B. L. 1994. Reflections on family poverty. *Families in Society: The Journal of Contemporary Human Services* (January): 47–50.

WILLIAMS, C. L. ED. 1993. *Doing women's work: Men in nontraditional occupations.* Newbury Park, CA: Sage.

WILLIAMS, G. H. 1995. *Life on the color line: The true story of a white boy who discovered he was black.* New York: Dutton.

WILLIAMS, J. A., J. VERNON, M. WILLIAMS, AND K. MALECHA. 1987. Sex role socialization in picture books: An update. *Social Science Quarterly* 68, no. 1, 148–56.

WILLIAMS, JR., J. A., L. K. WHITE, AND B. J. EKAIDEM. 1979. Romantic love as a basis for marriage. In *Love and attraction: An international conference,* ed. M. Cook and G. Wilson, 245–50. New York: Pergamon.

WILLIAMS, N. 1990. The *Mexican American family: Tradition and change.* New York: General Hall.

WILLIAMS, R. G. 1994. Implementation of the child support provisions of the Family Support Act: Child support guidelines, updating of awards, and routine income withholding. In *Child support and child well-being,* ed. I. Garfinkel, S. McLanahan and P. K. Robins, 93–132. Washington, DC: Urban Institute Press.

WILLIAMS, T., AND W. KORNBLUM. 1985. *Growing up poor.* Lexington, MA: Lexington Books.

WILLIAMSON, J. B., J. A. SHINDUL, AND L. EVANS. 1985. *Aging and public policy: Social control or social justice?* Springfield, IL: Charles C. Thomas.

WILLIE, C. V., ED. 1970. *The family life of black people.* Columbus, OH: Merrill.

WILSON, B. F., AND S. C. CLARKE. 1992. Remarriages: A demographic profile. *Journal of Family Issues* 13, no. 2 (June): 123–41.

WILSON, E. 1993. *First-time homeowners in 1989: A comparative perspective.* U.S. Bureau of the Census, Current Housing Reports, H121/93–1. Washington, DC: Government Printing Office.

WILSON, G. 1990. The consequences of elderly wives caring for disabled husbands: Implications for practice. *Social Work* 35, 417–21.

WILSON, J. B. 1993. *Human immunodeficiency virus antibody testing in women 15–44 years of age: United States, 1990.* Advance Data from Vital and Health Statistics, no. 238. Hyattsville, MD: National Center for Health Statistics.

WILSON, J. Q. 1993. The family-values debate. *Commentary*, April, 24–31.

WILSON, M. L. 1989. Child development in the context of the black extended family. *American Psychologist* 44, 380–85.

WILSON, S. M., AND N. P. MEDORA. 1990. Gender comparisons of college students' attitudes toward sexual behavior. *Adolescence* 25, no. 99 (Fall): 615–26.

WILSON, W. J. 1987. *The truly disadvantaged: The inner city, the underclass and public policy.* Chicago: University of Chicago Press.

WINEBERG, H. 1988. Duration between marriage and first birth and marital stability. *Social Biology* 35, 91–102.

WINEBERG, H. 1990. Childbearing after remarriage. *Journal of Marriage and the Family* 52 (February): 31–38.

WINEBERG, H. 1991. Intermarital fertility and dissolution of the second marriage. *Social Science Quarterly* 75, no. 2 (January): 62–65.

WINEBERG, H. 1994. Marital reconciliation in the United States: Which couples are successful? *Journal of Marriage and the Family* 56 (February): 80–88.

WINFIELD, F. E. 1985. *Commuter marriage: Living together, apart.* New York: Columbia University Press.

WINKLEBY, M. A., AND W. T. BOYCE. 1994. Health-related risk factors of homeless families and single adults. *Journal of Community Health* 19, no. 1 (February): 7–23.

WINSTON, D. 1991. Gay teen-agers face special perils, conference is told. *Baltimore Sun*, May 6, 4B

WINTON, C. A. 1995. *Frameworks for studying families.* Guilford, CT: Dushkin.

WIRTH, L. 1945. The problem of minority groups. In *The science of man in the world crisis*, ed. R. Linton, 347–72. New York: Columbia University Press.

WISENSALE, S. K., AND K. E. HECKART. 1993. Domestic partnerships: A concept paper and policy discussion. *Family Relations* 42 (April): 199–204.

WITCHEL, A. 1994. Of Roe, dreams and choices. *New York Times*, July 28, C1, C9.

WOLF, D. 1979. *The lesbian community.* Berkeley: University of California Press.

WOLFE, L. 1981. *The Cosmo report.* New York: Arbor House.

WOLFF, C. 1971. *Love between women.* New York: Harper & Row.

WOLL, S. B., AND P. YOUNG. 1989. Looking for Mr. or Ms. Right: Self-presentation in videodating. *Journal of Marriage and the Family* 51 (May): 483–88.

Women on Words and Images. 1975. *Dick and Jane as victims: Sex stereotypes in children's readers.* Princeton, NJ: Author.

Women's Initiative. 1993. *Abused elders or older battered women?* Washington, DC: American Association of Retired Persons.

WONG, M. G. 1988. The Chinese American family. In *Ethnic families in America: Patterns and variations*, 3rd ed., ed. C. H. Mindel, R. W. Habenstein, and R. Wright, 230–57. New York: Elsevier.

WONG, P. 1993. *Child support and welfare reform.* New York: Garland.

WOOD, D. B. 1995. States' bid to change workplace hire laws leaves women split. *Christian Science Monitor*, April 7, 1, 4.

WOOD, J. T. 1994. *Gendered lives: Communication, gender, and culture.* Palo Alto, CA: Mayfield.

WOODWARD, K. L. 1992. The elite, and how to avoid it. *Newsweek*, July 20, 55.

WOODWARD, K. L., AND K. SPRINGEN. 1992. Better than a gold watch. *Newsweek*, August 24, 71.

WOODWARD, K. L., V. QUADE, AND J. KANTROWITZ. 1995. Q. When is marriage not really a marriage? *Newsweek*, March 13, 58–59.

WOODWARD, K. L., WITH S. KEENE-OSBORN. 1994. The gospel of guyhood. *Newsweek*, August 29, 60.

WOOLF, G. D. 1990. An outlook for foster care in the United States. *Child Welfare* 69 (January/February): 75–81.

WORTHINGTON, R. 1994. Mixed-race Americans seek official identities. *Baltimore Sun*, July 5, 1A, 9A.

WRIGHT, D. W., AND S. J. PRICE. 1986. Court-ordered child support payment: The effect of the former-spouse relationship on compliance. *Journal of Marriage and the Family* 48 (November): 869–74.

WU, Z. 1994. Remarriage in Canada: A social exchange perspective. *Journal of Divorce & Remarriage* 21, nos. 3/4, 191–224.

YELLOWBIRD, M., AND C. M. SNIPP. 1994. Native American families. In *Minority families in the United States: A multicultural perspective*, ed. R. L. Taylor, 179–201. Englewood Cliffs, NJ: Prentice Hall.

YELSMA, P. 1986. Marriage vs. cohabitation: Couples' communication practices and satisfaction. *Journal of Communication* 36 (Autumn): 94–102.

YOON, Y.-H., AND L. J. WAITE. 1994. Converging employment patterns of black, white, and Hispanic women: Return to work after first birth. *Journal of Marriage and the Family* 56 (February): 209–17.

YORK, J., AND B. KRUEGER. 1993. *Beyond putting the toilet seat down: 433 real comments from men and women about their relationships.* Cincinnati, OH: Armchair Press.

YOUNGER, F. 1992. *Five hundred questions kids ask about sex and some of the answers.* Springfield, IL: Charles C. Thomas.

ZABIN, L. S., AND S. C. HAYWARD. 1993. *Adolescent sexual behavior and childbearing.* Newbury Park, CA: Sage.

ZABIN, L. S., M. B. HIRSH, E. A. SMITH, R. STREET, AND J. B. HARDY. 1986. Evaluation of a pregnancy prevention program for urban teenagers. *Family Planning Perspectives* 18, 119–26.

ZABLOCKI, B. 1980. *Alienation and charismas: A study of contemporary American communes.* New York: Free Press.

ZAL, H. M. 1992. *The sandwich generation: Caught between growing children and aging parents.* New York: Plenum.

ZAPLER, M. 1995. States may be next battleground for human-embryo research. *Chronicle of Higher Education*, January 20, A24.

ZHOU, B. 1994. New childless families in China. *Beijing Review*, January 31–February 6, 24–5.

ZIAXIANG, A., L. XINLIAN, AND G. ZHAHUA. 1987. The causes of divorce. In *New trends in Chinese marriage and the family,* ed. L. Jieqiong, 162–77. Beijing: China International Book Trading.

ZILL, N., AND C. W. NORD. 1994. *Running in place: How American families are faring in a changing economy and an individualistic society.* Washington, DC: Child Trends.

ZOGLIN, R. 1990. Home is where the venom is. *Time,* April 16, 85–86.

ZOOK, J. 1994. Recruiting black males. *Chronicle of Higher Education,* November 23, A34.

ZUNIN, L. M., AND H. S. ZUNIN. 1991. *The art of condolence: What to write, what to say, what to do at a time of loss.* New York: Harper-Collins.

ZURAWIK, D. 1994a. Prime time race. *Baltimore Sun,* July 24, 1H, 7H.

ZURAWIK, D. 1994b. Out of the shadows. *Baltimore Sun,* May 1, H1, H10.

Credits

CHAPTER OPENER ART

Chapter 1: Betty Patterson, *Pictorial Navajo Rug*, 1993. Courtesy of Cristofs Gallery, Santa Fe, New Mexico; photo: © Jerry Jacka. Patterson is among a number of contemporary Navajo weavers who use the pictorial style to depict aspects of Navajo and other Native American cultures.

Chapter 2: Diana Ong, *The Family*, 1993. Superstock. An experimental and prolific artist, Ong finds her creative challenge in combining different media in new ways.

Chapter 3: Anonymous, *The Quilting Party*, American, probably 1854-1875. Abby Aldrich Rockerfeller Folk Art Center, Williamsburg, Virginia. Rare period documentation for the traditional "quilting bee," this painting also catches a glimpse of nineteenth-century family life and courting behavior.

Chapter 4: Archibald J. Motley, Jr., *Cocktails*, c 1926. Courtesy of Michael Rosenfeld Gallery, New York. For Motley, art was a way of affirming the basic gaiety of everyday life. He painted ordinary people engaged in ordinary activities in urban settings of the 1920s.

Chapter 5: William Dyce (1806-1864), *Francesca de Rimini*. National Gallery of Scotland, Edinburgh. Bridgeman Art Library/Art Resource, New York. Strongly religious, a composer of church music, and an accomplished stained-glass designer in his native Scotland, Dyce painted in a style that was at once spiritual and open to the sensuous delight of nature.

Chapter 6: Miram Shapiro, *The Garden of Eden*, 1990. Courtesy of Steinbaum Krauss Gallery, New York; photo: Gamma One Conversions. Schapiro was born in Canada but has spent most of her creative years in the United States, where she is known as the leader of the Feminist Art Movement.

Chapter 7: Ben Shahn, *Spring*, 1947, tempera on masonite, 17" x 30." Albright-Knox Art Gallery, Buffalo, New York, Room of Contemporary Art Fund, 1948. As a young artist, Shahn produced many works that highlighted social problems. Later, this Lithuanian-born painter's style became increasingly personal.

Chapter 8: Anna Belle Lee Washington, *Courting over the Fence*, 1924. Superstock. After nearly forty years as an urban social worker, Washington began a second career as a painter. A primitivist, she told an interviewer that her works "make people smile."

Chapter 9: Diego Rivera, *Two Women*, 1914. The Arkansas Arts Center Foundation Collection; gift of Abby Rockefeller Mauze, New York, 1955 (55.10). Widely known as a muralist, Rivera celebrated indigenous Mexican culture in his murals.

Chapter 10: Lucille Corcos, *The Wedding*, 1947. Courtesy of Janet Marqusee Fine Arts and Babcock Galleries, New York. A reviewer has described Corcos's work as "a scene within a scene behind a scene." Presenting a clearly unified overall design, she also pays close attention to the minutest details.

Chapter 11: David Landis Fick, *Child in the Gold Forest*, 1983. Courtesy of Gremillion & Co. Fine Art, Houston, Texas. Fick, a native of Iowa, evokes images of tranquility through the sleeping infant, whose repose is seen as pure and untroubled.

Chapter 12: Oksana Bondar, *Peace*, c 1986. Courtesy of the Children's Art Exchange, Middlebury, Vermont; photo: Erik Borg. The young creator of this piece is a participant in the Children's Art Exchange, a program founded to promote U.S.–Russian relations through exchange visits of young artists and their works.

Chapter 13: B'ee Dityo (James King), *Suppertime*, 1987. Collection of Joe Tanner, Tanner's Indian Arts, Gallup, New Mexico; photo: © Jerry Jacka. B'ee Dityo is a Navajo artist who paints in the traditional European style but whose work reflects Indian life and thought.

Chapter 14: Diego Rivera, *Sugar Cane*, 1931. Philadelphia Museum of Art; gift of Mr. and Mrs. Herbert Cameron Morris. Rivera's murals expressed his Marxist–Communist political views as well as his fascination with technology as a means of benefiting the working class.

Chapter 15: Paul Cézanne, *Strangled Woman*, c 1870-1872. Musée d'Orsay, Paris, France. Giraudon/Art Resource, New York. Unlike most of Cézanne's works, this painting may reflect dark passions from the painter's allegedly troubled relationships with women.

Chapter 16: Edvard Munch, *Separation*, 1896. Munch Museum, Oslo, Norway. Scala/Art Resource, New York. According to a reviewer, the paintings of this Norwegian artist "take on the character of passionate interpretations of universal human suffering."

Chapter 17: Carmen Lomas Garza, *Empanadas*, 1991. Courtesy of the artist; photo: Judy Reed. Garza, born in Texas, was inspired by the chicano movement of the late 1960s "to depict the special and everyday events in the lives of Mexican Americans."

Chapter 18: Pablita Velarde, *Old Father Story Teller*, 1961. Courtesy of the artist. In this painting, taken from her 1960 book of tribal legends, Velarde illustrates a migration myth of her people, the Santa Clara Pueblos.

Chapter 19: Fernand Léger (1881-1955), *The Excursion*. Musée Fernand Léger, Biot, France. Erich Lessing/Art Resource, New York. © 1996 Artists Rights Society (ARS), N.Y./SPADEM, Paris. Constant themes for the French artist Léger were the socioeconomic realities of the world in which he worked and the creation of an art that reflected the life of the common man.

PHOTOGRAPHS

Name Index

Dunn, A., 351
Durkheim, E., 457
Duvall, E.M., 35
Duxbury, L.C., 395
Dworkin, A., 96, 155
Dyson, M.E., 354

E

Earle, A.M., 55
Eccles, J., 91
Eckland, B.K., 211
Eddings, J., 84
Edelman, M., 263
Edelson, H., 541, 542
Edmondson, B., 247, 338
Edwards, D.L., 337
Edwards, J.N., 460, 487
Eells, L.W., 485
Eggebeen, D.J., 547
Ehrenreich, B., 152, 401
Eichel, E.W., 47
Eisenhart, M.A., 126, 206, 236
Eitzen, D.S., 88, 352, 547
Elbow, M., 428–29, 438
Elder, G.J., Jr., 45
Elders, J., 145
Elkind, D., 336
Ellis, H., 143
Ellis, J.B., 442
Ellis, L., 162
Elshtain, J.B., 152
Elworthy, S., 157
Emery, R.E., 475
Encino, 351
England, P., 400
English, D., 401
Enrico, D., 213
Epstein, A., 101
Epstein, J., 435
Erickson, R.J., 271, 272
Erickson, M.T., 428
Erikson, E., 324–25
Ernst, R.L., 510
Esler, A., 453
Espenshade, T.J., 362
Estess, P.S., 331
Etaugh, C.E., 91
Etter, J., 297
Evangelauf, J., 94
Evans, N.J., 244
Evatt, C., 234
Everett, C., 451, 455, 463, 467, 475, 489, 500
Everett, S.V., 451, 455, 463, 467, 475, 489, 500
Exter, T., 23, 237
Eyer, D.E., 321

F

Fader, S., 267
Faedda, S., 124
Falbo, T., 329
Faller, K.C., 427
Fanshel, D., 345
Faragher, J.M., 11, 60
Farber, B., 56, 209, 211
Farrow, M., 480
Fassel, D., 469
Fausto-Sterling, A., 186
Feagin, C.B., 63, 70, 377
Feagin, J.R., 63, 70, 93, 95, 222, 223, 247, 340, 373–74, 377
Feeney, J.A., 115
Fehr, B., 123, 124
Feldman, H., 63
Feldmann, L., 468
Felt, J.C., 370
Ferreiro, B.W., 467
Field, D., 516, 528
Fiester, L., 47
Fincham, F.D., 268
Findlen, B., 247
Fine, D.A., 458
Fine, M.A., 458, 461, 497
Fine, R., 125
Fineman, M., 467
Fink, D., 70, 71
Finke, N., 484
Finkel, J., 464
Finkelhor, D., 428, 432
Finlay, B., 460
Finnie, R., 450
Fischer, E.F., 124
Fischman, J., 498
Fishel, E., 322
Fisher, H., 116
Fisher, H.E., 206
Fisher, M., 342
Fishman, B., 482
Fitzgerald, L.F., 405, 407
Fletcher, M.A., 356
Flores, B.R., 173, 363
Flynn, C.P., 320, 437
Folbre, N., 288
Folk, K., 267, 339, 398, 482
Follette, 222
Fomby, P., 342
Fong, R., 365
Footlick, J.K., 14
Ford, C., 139, 159
Ford, K., 165
Forehand, R.B., 472
Forrest, J., 306
Forrest, J.D., 309
Forrest, K.A., 196
Forward, S., 424
Fossett, M.A., 256
Fox-Genovese, E., 45

Frame, M.W., 396
Frank, D.I., 292
Franklin, C.W., II, 153
Frazer, J.M., 14
Frazer, T.C., 14
Frazier, E.F., 44, 62, 63, 352
Freedman, D.C., 42
Freeman, E.W., 307
Freifeld, K., 236
Frenkiel, N., 180
Freud, S., 81, 143
Friedan, B., 512
Friedman, D., 145
Frieze, I.H., 206
Fromm, E., 111, 112, 117
Fronczek, P., 9, 384
Fukuyama, F., 364
Fullilove, R.E., 166
Fultz, O., 443
Fundenburg, L., 264
Furstenberg, F.F., 306, 470, 472, 489, 492
Furukawa, S., 330, 331, 350, 354, 356, 361, 480, 489

G

Gabardi, L., 472
Gage, A., 236
Gaines-Carter, P., 213
Gaiter, L., 353
Galinsky, E., 398
Gallagher, S.K., 527, 531
Gallup, G., Jr., 14, 17, 264, 287, 308, 329
Gamache, D., 221
Ganong, L.H., 212, 480, 481, 485, 488, 497
Gans, H.J., 28, 388
Garbarino, J., 429, 432
Garcia, M.T., 64, 362
Gardner, M., 220, 222, 223, 336, 549
Gardner, R.W., 364
Garfinkel, E.M., 461, 466, 540
Gasser, R.D., 462
Gately, D., 474
Gates, D., 99
Gaulin, S.J.C., 216
Gay, D., 306
Gaylin, W., 85, 87, 111
Gecas, V., 140
Gelles, R.J., 134, 417, 418, 419, 420, 425, 428, 431, 436, 437
Gelman, D., 354, 377
Genovese, E.D., 62
Gerbner, G., 15, 97
Gerrard, M., 175
Gerstel, N., 462, 527, 531
Gibbs, N., 550

Klitsch, M., 312
Knapp, M.L., 91, 280
Knapp, R.J., 443
Knickerbocker, B., 246
Knight, R., 390
Knox, D.H., 127
Knox, V.W., 468
Kochems, M., 105
Koepke, L., 342
Kohlberg, L., 89–90
Kohn, A., 335
Kolata, G., 245, 246, 309
Komarovsky, M., 91–92
Koretz, G., 355
Kornblum, W., 306
Kortenhaus, C.M., 94
Koss, M., 407
Koss, M.P., 220
Kouri, K.A., 264
Krafft, S., 351, 401
Kraft, P., 178
Kramer, H., 543
Kramer, K.B., 471, 472
Krance, M., 182
Krauskopf, J.M., 575
Krich, J., 207
Krokoff, L.J., 274, 276, 279
Krueger, R.A., 28, 39
Kübler-Ross, E., 522–23
Kudlow, L., 384
Kurdek, L.A., 244, 460, 461, 497
Kurtz, H., 418
Kurz, D., 425, 437–38
Kuykendall, D.H., 527

L

Ladd, G.W., 332
Lader, L., 315
LaFromboise, T.D., 375
Laird, J., 35, 342
LaJeune, 222
Lakoff, R.T., 102
Lam, C., 377
Land, H., 492
Landale, N.S., 241, 255
Laner, M.R., 213
Lang, A., 443
Langelan, M.J., 405
Langer, J., 293
Lansky, V., 473
Lantz, H.R., 53
Lapchik, R., 416
Larson, J., 247, 489
Larson, L.E., 211
Larson, R., 265, 328, 332
Lasch, C., 12, 130
Laslett, P., 52
Lasswell, M., 264
Lasswell, M.E., 120, 121

Lasswell, T.E., 120, 121
Lauer, J., 271
Lauer, R., 271
Lauer, R.H., 335
Laumann, E.O., 138, 140, 145, 146, 148, 178, 190, 191, 416
Lavee, Y., 260, 261
LaViolette, A.D., 421, 434, 436
Lawrence, S.V., 311
Lawson, A., 183
Lazarus, A.A., 276
Leach, P., 346, 551
Leatherman, C., 140
Lee, B.A., 388
Lee, C.S., 15, 351
Lee, F.R., 443
Lee, G.R., 8, 117, 512
Lee, J.A., 119, 120
Leerhsen, C., 289
Leff, L., 190, 204
Lehrer, E.L., 457
Leitenberg, H., 147, 431
LeMasters, E.E., 265, 322, 332, 343
Lemonick, M.D., 545
Leon, J.J., 124, 264
Leonard, K.E., 418
LePlay, F., 37
Leppard, W., 96
Leslie, L.A., 44, 213
Lester, D., 127
Lester, G.H., 464
Leung, S., 201
LeVay, S., 162
Levesque, R.J.R., 121
Levin, W.C., 512
Levine, A., 496
Levine, K.G., 345
Levine, M.P., 197
Levine, M.V., 385, 387, 389
Levine, R.V., 111, 253
Levinson, M., 394
Levy, E.F., 342
Levy-Schiff, R., 323
Lewin, E., 28, 308
Lewin, T., 401, 445
Lewis, E.A., 500, 501
Lewis, G., 14
Lewis, L., 180
Lewis, M.I., 188
Lewis, P.H., 132
Li, G., 106
Libertoff, K., 429
Lichter, D.T., 547
Lichter, S.R., 97, 256
Lief, L., 105
Light, P.C., 552
Lightfoot-Klein, H., 157
Lillard, L.A., 460
Lin, C., 366
Lin, G., 520
Linlin, P., 218

Linton, M.A., 221
Lips, H.M., 96, 183, 274
Liss, M.B., 91
Littlejohn-Blake, S.M., 357
Litwack, E., 270
Liu, W.T., 366
Lloyd, S.A., 220, 221, 225
Lobsenz, N.M., 263
Lock, M., 186
Loewen, J.W., 468
LoLordo, A., 296
London, K.A., 458
Longino, L.F., 554
Lonkhuyzen, L.V., 441
Loomis, L.S., 241
Lorber, J., 20
Losee, S., 402
Lottes, I.L., 177
Lowry, D.T., 141
Luepnitz, D.A., 277
Lutwin, D.R., 392
Lye, D.N., 275
Lyman, K.A., 516
Lynch, P., 164
Lynn, D.B., 89
Lynxwiler, J., 306
Lyons, D.C., 22
Lyons, J.M., 498
Lyons, S., 438

M

Macaulay, L.J., 275, 276
Macauley, R., 40
Maccoby, E.E., 90, 467
MacDonald, W., 242
Macer, D.R.J., 302
MacFarquhar, E., 84
Machung, A., 100
Macionis, J., 5
Mackey, A., 257
Macklin, E., 240
Maggio, R., 131
Magner, D.K., 369
Mahony, R., 372
Maines, J., 395, 396
Males, M., 307
Mancini, J.A., 521
Maneker, J.S., 460
Manke, B., 398
Manke, F., 443
Mann, D., 13
Manners, J., 485
Manning, C., 68
Manning, W.D., 253
Mansnerus, L., 467
Marano, H.E., 113
Marbella, J., 247, 440
Marcus, E., 40, 445, 545
Margolin, L., 225

Z

Zabin, L.S., 263, 306, 314
Zablocki, B., 248
Zal, H.M., 432, 528
Zapler, M., 303

Zellner, W.W., 248
Zhou, B., 311
Ziaxiang, A., 458
Zill, N., 346, 382
Znaniecki, F., 69

Zoglin, R., 96
Zook, J., 377
Zunin, H.S., 444
Zunin, L.M., 444
Zurawik, D., 14, 164

Subject Index

Areolas, 560
Arranged marriages, 208, 216–18
Artificial insemination, 299
Artisan class, in colonial America, 56
Asexual homosexuals, 189
Asian American families, 9, 20, 233
   family structure, 364–65
   generational conflict, 367–68
   husbands and wives, 366–67
   as model minority, 368–70
   parents and children, 365–66
   response to oppression, 377
   wife abuse, 422
Assisted reproductive techniques, 298–303
Attachment theory:
   adults and, 115–16
   children and, 113, 115
Attractiveness, physical, 214
Australia, romantic love in, 124
Authoritarian parental approach, 331–32
Authoritative parental approach, 331–32
Authority patterns, familial, 8–9
Avoidant adults, 115

B

BABI (blastomere analysis before implantation), 303
Baby boomers, 17
Baby Jessica case (1993), 296
Baby M case (1987), 301–302
Baby Richard case (1994), 296
Bachelor party, 258
Backup family caregiving in later life, 530
Bargaining stage of dying, 522
Bartholin's glands, 556, 557
Basal body temperature method (BBT), 567
Battered-woman syndrome, 439
Battered women compared to prisoners, 423
Beginning date rapist, 222
Being-love, 117
Berdache, 105
Bereavement, 523–25
Beta-endorphins, 290
Better Homes and Gardens, 276, 309
Bigamy, 3
Bilineal descent pattern, 9
Bilingual education, 364
Billings method of contraception, 567
Binuclear family. *See* Stepfamilies
Biological changes, after 40, 186
Biological father-stepmother family, 488

Biological mother-stepfather family, 488
Biological theories of homosexuality, 162
Biological theories of love, 116
Biology, gender identity and, 82
Birth control pill, 152, 309, 565
Birthing rooms, 289
Bisexuality, 162–63
Blaming, 221, 279
Blastocyst, 559
Blended family, 245. *See also* Stepfamilies
Bonding, 321
Books, gender roles and, 94
Boomerang generation, 330–31
Boosters, parents as, 332
Boredom, sexual dysfunction and, 193
Boston Women's Health Book Collective, 81, 289
Boundary-maintenance issues in remarriage, 488
Brazil, violence against women in, 435
Breaking up, 225–26
Breech birth, 563
Bridal shower, 257–58
Brotherly love, 117
Bulbourethral glands, 557
Bulimia, 441–43
Bundling, 53

C

Calendar method of contraception, 567
Canada:
   child poverty rate, 12
   child support payments, 466
   cohabitation in, 20
   divorce mediation, 474–75
   endogamy and exogamy in, 5
   health care, 545, 546
   marital separation in, 452
   parental leave policy, 550–51
Career-and-family women, 401
Career-primary women, 401
Caregiving, 528–32
Case-study method, 41
Catholic Church:
   abortion, 315
   divorce, 3
   remarriage, 482
Celocentesis, 562
Centenarians, 506
Center for Women Policy Studies, 195
Centers for Disease Control and Prevention, 47, 171, 173, 194, 195, 196

Central Intelligence Agency (CIA), 400
Ceremonial marriage, 3
Cervical cap, 567
Cervix, 557
Cesarean section, 289, 563
Child abuse, 423–30
   in adolescence, 429
   causes, 425
   defining, 424
   rates, 424–25
   sexual abuse/incest, 426–29
   signs, 430
Childbirth, 562–63
Child care, 339–40. *See also* Day care
   fathers and, 323–24
Childhood, myths about, 325–26
Childless couples, 308–309
Child maltreatment, 424
Child neglect, 424
Child rearing, 320–46. *See also* Parenthood
   African American, 355–56
   Asian American, 365–66
   current crisis in, 343–46
   discipline, 334–35
   by gay/lesbian parents, 340–43
   learning parental roles, 320–24
   Native American, 358–59
   parental time with children, 337–40
   parent-child relationship, 324–31, 335–37
   parenting styles, 331–33
   suburban living and, 75
Children:
   African American, 355–56, 517
   AIDS and, 443–44, 545
   attachment theory, 113, 115
   in colonial America, 55
   of common-law partners, 3
   in companionate families, 69
   costs/benefits of having, 287–88
   death of, 443–44
   deciding not to have, 308–16
   effects of divorce on, 460, 462–63, 468–73
   in foster homes, 345
   in future, 346
   gay and lesbian, 342–43
   in Great Depression, 71
   grieving by, 525
   homeless, 21
   industrialization and, 66–67
   lack of emotional support for, 6, 113
   latchkey, 338–39
   marital conflict over, 275–76
   Mexican American, 64
   mother's employment and, 399
   Native American, 59, 358–59
   only, 329–30

Children (*cont.*)
out of wedlock, 303–8
postponing having, 293
poverty and, 2, 21, 343–44
presence of, divorce rates and, 460
raising. *See* Child rearing
rights, 536, 539–40
socialization, 6
in stepfamilies, 497–99
under 5, global death rates, 12
violence against, 423–30
Children's Defense Fund, 306, 344, 345, 346, 356, 386
Child support, 455, 465–66, 540, 577
Child Support Enforcement Amendments (1984), 465, 540
China:
contraceptive policies, 311
divorce rate, 450
families, 105–106
homosexuality, 159
mate selection, 218
protection of elderly, 508
Chinese American families, 364–65
wife abuse, 422
Chlamydia, 194, 294, 570
Chorion, 559
Chorionic villi sampling (CV), 303, 562
Christian Men's Movement, 103
Chronicle of Higher Education, 197
Circumcision, 557
female, 155
Circumscribed family caregiving in later life, 530
Civil Rights Act (1964), 404
Civil rights movement, 23
Class action suit, 402
Classified advertisements, personal, 207
Climacteric, 186, 187
Clinical research, 41, 45
Clitoral hood, 556
Clitoral orgasm, 150
Clitoris, 556
Clockspring alternative theory of love, 117–18
Close-coupled homosexuals, 189
Code of Hammurabi, divorce and, 453
Coercion/contempt, in marital conflict, 279–80
Cognitive development theory, 89–90, 324, 325
Cohabitation/cohabitants, 3, 19, 238–43
advantages and disadvantages, 241–43
communal households, 247–49
homosexual households, 243–47
in other countries, 243

types of, 240
Coitus interruptus, 567
College students, 140, 143, 147, 154, 164, 206, 221–25, 222–23, 490
Colonial family, 52–56
children's lives, 55
husbands and wives, 54–55
sexual relations, 53
social class and regional differences, 55–56
structure, 52–53
treatment of elderly, 511
Colostrum, 560
"Coming out," homosexuality and, 160
Coming-out parties, 204
Common-law marriage, 3
Communal households/communes, 247–49
Communication:
divorce and, 462
gender differences, 102–103
in marriage, 272, 274–80
barriers to, 279–80
conflict and, 274–77
effective patterns, 280
power struggle, 274
ways of improving, 277–78
parent to child, 91
in remarriage, 488
sexual dysfunction and, 192
Community divorce, 455
Community property, 577
Community remarriage, 485
Commuter marriages, 396–97
Compadrazgo, 64
Companionate family, 69
Companionate grandparenting style, 516
Comparable worth, 403–404
Complex stepfamily, 488–89
Compromise technique, in family conflict, 276
Computer-assisted
dating, 208–209
telephone interviewing (CATI), 39
Concept, defined, 37
Conception, 559
Concern for Dying, 543
Condoms:
female, 310, 564, 566, 568
male, 566
Conflict, marital, 274–77
Conflict-habituated marriage, 260
Conflict theory, 32
of family violence, 436–37
Conjugal family, 7
Consanguine family, 7
Consumer marketplace, gender roles in, 101–102
Consumer Price Index, 386
Consummation, 3

Contraception, 309–12
cross-cultural variations, 311–12
double standard, 310–11
effectiveness rates, 309–10
in future, 546, 568
techniques, 564–68
Contracts, premarital, 281–82
Control:
batterers and, 418
love and, 126, 131–34
power and, 220
Conversational dominance, 102–103
Coparental divorce, 455
Corona, 557
Council on Scientific Affairs, 430
Courtship, 214, 219, 226
after divorce, 483–85
Courtship violence, 220–25
Cowper's glands, 557
Crack babies, 440, 561
Critical period, fetal, 561
Cross-complaining, 279
Cross-cultural perspective, 24
Cross-cultural variation:
arranged marriages, 208
child care/parental leave policies, 549–51
cohabitation, 243
contraception, 311–12
divorce rates, 458
female genital mutilation, 155, 156–57
forms of marriage, 8
gender roles, 89, 105
homosexuality, 159
jealousy, 132
mate selection, 216–19
Native American women, 58
parenting in Japan, 333
protection of elderly in China, 508
race-ethnicity, 38
violence against women, 435
women as cheap labor, 403
Cross-sectional research, 38, 39
Crowning, 563
Cruising, 206
Cuban Americans, 291, 362, 363
Culpotomy, 565
Culture. *See* Popular culture
Cunnilingus, 147–48
Cushing's syndrome, 315
Custodial grandparents, 517
Custody issues, 455, 466–68, 577

D

Daddy penalty, 401
Date rape, 221–225
solutions for, 224–25
Dating. *See also* Mate selection
after divorce, 483–85

parental leave policy, 550
romantic love, 124
Fun, love and, 126–27
Functional homosexuals, 189
Functional myths, 9–10

G

Gamete intrafallopian transfer
(GIFT), 300
Gay rights movement, 23
Gays. *See also* Homosexuality
causation theories, 161–62
gender and, 161
identity formation, 160–161
prevalence, 158–59
societal reactions, 138, 163–65,
246–47
Gender, difference between sex
and, 80
Gender differences:
acceptance of date rape
responsibility, 222–23
in breaking up, 225–26
effects of divorce, 464–66, 471–72
expressing love, 127–29
language/communication,
102–103
masturbation rates, 146
premarital sex, 176–77
response to discovery of
extramarital affair, 185
sexual fantasies, 155–56, 158
sexual orientation, 161
singlehood option, 233–34
spending patterns of singles, 237
Gender gap in wages, 401–402
comparable worth as remedy for,
403–404
Gender identity, biology and, 82
Gender inequality in workplace,
399–406
Gender roles, 80–134
in adulthood, 98–102
consumer marketplace,
101–102
housework, 99–100, 266–68
workplace, 101
advertising and, 95–96
ambivalence about change in,
103–105
in colonial America, 54–55
conflict over, 275
controversial issues, 103–104
cross-cultural variations, 89,
105–107
defined, 80
divorce and, 458–59
effects of Great Depression,
71–72
hormones and, 81–82
importance, 80–81

machismo, 363–64
in marriage, 267–68
movies and, 98
nature-nurture debate, 81–85
and Persian Gulf War, 104
socialization agents, 90–98
socialization theories, 89–90
traditional, 85–89
Gender schema theory, 90
General systems theory, 35, 36
Generational conflict, Asian
Americans and, 367–68
Genetic engineering/research,
298–303
Genital mutilation, female, 155,
156–57
Genital warts, 571
Genogram, 488
Gerontologists, 507
Getting together, 205
Glans, 556, 557
Going dutch, 206
Going steady, 204
Goin' with, 205
Golden Fifties, 17, 73–75
Gonorrhea, 194, 570
Grandparenting, 515–20
children's divorce and, 519–20
Native American, 359
styles, 516–19
Great Depression (1929–1939), 69–72
Greenhorns, 67
Grief, 523, 525
Group marriage, 7, 8
G spot, 151
Guadalupe Hidalgo, Treaty of, 63
Guilt trip, 133–34
Gunnysacking, 278

H

Half-siblings, 482
Halo effect, 255
Hanging out, 204
Happiness, marital, 268, 271–72
social class and, 179–80
Health-related issues:
aging, 507–10
anorexia nervosa, 441–43
bulimia, 441–43
death of child, 443–44
drug abuse, 439–40
future of, 543–46
marriage, 270–71
pregnancy, 289
right to die, 444–45
steroid use, 443
teenage depression/suicide, 440
Hemlock Society, 543
Hepatitis B, 570
Hermaphrodites, 82
Herpes, 570–71

Heterosexuals, 157
HIV/AIDS and, 195
Higher Education Reauthorization
Act (1992), 225
Hijra, 105
His and her marriage, 269–70
Hispanics. *See* Latinos
HIV (human immunodeficiency
virus), 192, 194, 195, 214, 543,
545
Home, gender work roles in, 99–100
Homecoming parties, 206
Homelessness, 20–21, 388–89
Homophobia, 130, 131, 163–64
Homosexual households, 243–47
Homosexuality, 138, 157–62. *See
also* Lesbians, Gays
ambivalence about, 246
causation theories, 161–62
gender and, 161
identity formation, 160–61
in non-Western cultures, 159
parenting and, 340–43
prevalence, 158–59
social/demographic
characteristics, 159–60
societal reactions, 138, 163–65,
246–47
Homosexual marriages, 213–14, 257
Homosexual relationships, 189–90,
244–45
Honeymoon, 253, 259
Hormone replacement therapy,
186–87
Hormones, sex, 81–82
Hospice care, 523
Hot flashes, 186
Households:
changes in, 19
communal, 247–49
family and nonfamily, 19
homosexual, 243–47
unmarried-couple, 239
Househusbands, 391–92
Housework:
child care and, 267
roles, 99–100, 266–68
Housing:
discrimination, against racial-
ethnic families, 371–72
for elderly, 541–42
for immigrant families, 68–69
singles and, 238
Human development, theories of,
324–25
Human papilloma-virus infection,
571
Husbands:
African American, 62, 355
Asian American, 366–67
in colonial America, 54–55
Latino, 363–64
trophy, 484

in long-term relationships, 121–22
romantic, 122–25
same-sex, 128–29
of self, 111
sexual orientation differences, 128–29
stages, 117
test of knowledge about, 114
theories of, 113, 115–21
threats to, 131–34
Loving, styles of, 119–21
Loving refuge, myth of family as, 12–13
Loving v. Virginia, 264
Loyalty, marital conflict over, 275
Ludus, 119, 120, 121
Lust, love and, 127

M

Machismo, 65, 363–64
Macro-level perspective, 21–22, 24
reasons for divorce, 456–62
reasons for marriage, 255–56
reasons for teenage pregnancy, 306–307
Magazines, 30
gender roles and, 96
Mail-order brides, 207–208
Male anatomy, 557–58
Male condom, 566
Male contraceptive pill, 568
Male sexual dysfunctions, 190–91
Mania, 119, 120, 121
Manifest functions, 31
of dating, 202
Marianismo, 174
Marital burnout, 272, 273
Marital rape, 419
Marital-rape exemption, 419
Marital rituals and customs, 256–59
Marital sex, 178–80
frequency, 178–79
happiness and, 179–80
importance of, 180
Marital success, 268–72
Marital violence, 416–23
characteristics, 417–18
cycle, 418–19
marital rape, 419
Marriage. *See also* Cohabitation/cohabitants; Families
among slaves, 60–61
ceremonial, 3
changes in, during life cycle, 264–66
common-law, 3
communication in, 272, 274–80
contracts, 281–82

defining, 2–3
forms, 7–8
health and, 270–71
homosexual, 213–14
interracial, 264
myths about, 9–13
reasons for, 253–56
rituals, 256–59
study of. *See* Social science research
success/happiness, 268–72
teenage, 262–64
types, 260–62
work and. *See* Work, families and
Marriage bureaus, 208
Marriage market, 201
Marriage penalty, 236
Marriage squeeze, 234
Married singles, 261–62
Martyrs, parents as, 332
Marvin v. Marvin, 4
Mass society, 129, 130
Masturbation, 138, 144–47
Maternal love, 117
Mate selection. *See also* Dating
age and, 211
choices/constraints, 209–12
courtship, 214
cross-cultural variations, 216–19
methods, 207–209
classified advertisements, 207
computer-assisted, 208–209
mail-order brides, 207–208
marriage bureaus, 208
race/ethnicity and, 210–11
religion, 211
social class, 211
theories, 212–16
Matriarchy, 8
Matrilineal descent pattern, 9
Matrilocal residence pattern, 9
Media, influence of, 94–98, 222–23
Mediators, parents as, 333
Medicaid, 528–29, 548
Medicare, 528
"Me-first" individualism, 129, 130
Menopause, 186
Merchant class, in colonial America, 56
Meritor Savings Bank v. Vinson, 404
Mesoderm, 560
Methotrexate, 546
Mexican-American Political Association, 374
Mexican Americans, 57, 63–65, 291, 362
Mexico, romantic love in, 124
Micro-level perspective, 21
reasons for divorce, 462
reasons for marriage, 235–55
reasons for teenage pregnancy, 305–306
Middle-aged families, 266

Middle class:
decreasing size, 383–84
family violence, 418
Midlife crisis, 187
Minimal brain damage, 561
Minorities. *See also* Race and ethnicity; Racial-ethnic families
poverty rate, 552
research by, 44–46
Minority Business Development Program, 376
Minority group, defined, 351
Miscarriage, 312
Miscegenation laws, 3
Misogyny, 222
Misoprostol, 546
Mixers, 206
Model minority, Asian Americans as, 368–70
Modern Maturity, 530
Mojave Indians, 59, 105
Mommy track, 400–401
Money, marital conflict over, 275
Monogamy, 7
Mons veneris, 556
Moonlighting, 389
Mormon Church, polygamy and, 7, 248
Mothers:
African American, 62–63
effects of parenthood on, 290
ideal *vs.* realistic roles, 322–23
incest and, 428–29
lesbian, 245
single, 307–308
teenage, 305
unmarried, 2
working, 20, 399
Motivational support, 278
Mourning, 523
Movies:
family roles, 34, 307
gender roles, 98
sex/sexuality, 141
Multigenerational families, 507
Multiple orgasms, 150
Munchausen by proxy, 424
Mundugumor tribe, 82
Music, sexual attitudes/behavior and, 142
Music Television (MTV), 97, 142
Muslim societies, 105, 106, 217, 435
Mutual dependence stage, 117
Myths:
about African American families, 353
about childhood, 325–26
about past, 10
about what is natural, 10–11
affection myth, 133–34
Asian-Americans as model minority, 368–70

Performance anxiety, 275
Perimenopause, 186
Perimetrium, 557
Perineum, 556
Permanent availability model, 209
Permissive parental approach, 331
Personal classified advertisements, 207
  in China, 218
Personality need fulfillment stage, 117
Personality traits, love and, 131
Petting, 147
Phenylethylamine (PEA), love and, 116
Physical abuse, 134, 221, 424
Physical attractiveness, 214, 255
Physical sexual harassment, 404
Pill, the. *See* Birth control pill
Pioneer families, 11
Placenta, 559
Plateau phase of sexual response, 150
Play, gender roles and, 92–93
Police officers/drill sergeants, parents as, 332
Political issues, social science research and, 46–48
Polyandry, 7, 8
Polygamy, 8
Polygyny, 7–8
Poor families. *See* Poverty
Popular culture:
  divorce and, 459
  gender roles and, 94–98
  sex/sexuality and, 141–42
Population, in survey research, 39
Population Reference Bureau, 537, 540, 551
POSSLQs, 238–39
Postmenopausal syndrome, 521
Postmenopausal zest (PMZ), 521
Postpartum depression, 290
Poverty, 20–21
  among elderly, 386, 552
  children in, 343–44, 386
  growth of, 386
  programs, 387–88, 346–47
  racial-ethnic families, 387
  reasons for, 388
  in suburbs, 387
  women in, 386–87
  working poor and, 387
Poverty line, 386
Power, 272, 274
Pragma, 119, 120–21
Preeclampsia, 561
Pregnancy, 286–89, 559–61. *See also* Contraception
  complications, 561–62
  discrimination laws, 407–408
  first, married-couple reactions to, 286–87
  job protection during, 408

joys/fears in, 288–89
  trimesters, 559–61
Pregnancy Discrimination Act (1978), 407
Prejudice:
  against homosexuals, 246, 247
  against immigrants, 69, 70
  against racial-ethnic families, 370–77
Premarital childbearing, divorce and, 461. *See also* Teenage parenthood
Premarital cohabitation, 240
Premarital contracts, 281–82, 572–75
Premarital sex, 173–77
Premarital violence, 220–25
Premature ejaculation, 191
Premenstrual syndrome (PMS), 82
Preparatory depression, 522
Prepared childbirth, 563
Prepuce, 556, 557
Preschool programs, 6
Primary anorgasmia, 192
Principle of least interest, 220, 274
Privacy, marital conflict over, 275
Probability sample, 39
Procreation, 5–6
  family of, 7
Progesterone, 81, 557
Project 2000, 376–77
Proms, 206
Propinquity, 212–13
Proposition 187, 22, 351
Prostate gland, 557
Protect-the-kids divorce, 469
Psychic divorce, 455
Psychic remarriage, 485
Psychoanalytic theories of homosexuality, 161
Psychosocial theory of development, 324–25
Puberty, in Native American societies, 59
Public Perspective, The, 14, 253, 351
Pueblo cultures, 58
Puerto-Rican Association for Community Affairs, 363, 374
Puerto Ricans, 18, 304

Q

Quality of life, love and, 126
Questionnaires, 39
Quickening, 560
Quick trajectory of dying, 522
Quinceañera, 204

R

Race and ethnicity:
  dating, 210–11
  decision to marry, 256

divorce, 450, 461
  fertility rates, 291–92
  housework roles, 267
  mate selection, 210–11
  out-of-wedlock births, 303–304
  remarriage, 481
  separation, 452
  singlehood, 234–36
Racial-ethnic families. *See also* African American families; Asian American families; Latino families; Native American families
  characteristics, 351–52
  immigration, 350
  poverty, 387
  prejudice/discrimination against, 370–77
  in twenty-first century, 537
Racial-ethnic groups, 18, 38, 352
Random-digit dialing, 39
Rappites, 248
Rapport stage, 117
Reactive depression, 522
Reciprocity, in self-disclosure, 277
Reconstituted family. *See* Stepfamilies
Refractory period of sexual response, 151
Reindeer Chukchee of Siberia, 8
Relational date rapist, 222
Reliability, defined, 37
Religion:
  dating/mate selection and, 211
  divorce rates and, 457
  sex/sexuality and, 140–41
Remarriage, 19, 480–88. *See also* Stepfamilies
  age/sex/race, 480–81
  courtship before, 483–85
  first marriages compared with, 482–83
  future rates, 541
  income/education, 481–82
  intergeneration relations in, 500
  marital quality, 487–88
  marital satisfaction in, 487–88
  marital stability, 487
  marital status and, 482
  process, 485–87
  successful, 500–502
Remote grandparenting style, 516
Reproduction, 559–63
Reproductive technologies, 298–303, 537–38
Research, importance of, 28–29. *See also* Social science research
Residential patterns, 9
Resolution phase of sexual response, 151
Resource theory of power, 274
  family violence and, 436
Retarded ejaculation, 191
Retirement, 514–15
Retrograde ejaculation, 191